中国田野考古报告集
考古学专刊
丁种九十七号

龙口归城

胶东半岛地区青铜时代国家形成过程的考古学研究
（公元前1000～前500年）

（下）

中国社会科学院考古研究所
哥伦比亚大学东亚语言和文化系　编著
山东省文物考古研究院

李　峰　梁中合　主编

科学出版社
北　京

内 容 简 介

本书为山东龙口归城周代遗址中美联合考古调查和试掘的中英文双语考古科学报告，分为上下两编：上编共分为十章，集中总结归城周代城址2007年到2011年中美联合调查的收获，并就有关方面进行研究。下编包括五章，总结归城乃至龙口地区1896年至2006年之间已有的考古发现，主要是青铜器和玉器的发现。另包括附录三篇，报告归城遗址的碳十四数据和植物、动物标本分析结果。

本书可供从事文物考古、历史学及相关学科的研究者和大专院校相关专业师生阅读、参考，并可为中英考古文献翻译参考。

图书在版编目（CIP）数据

龙口归城：胶东半岛地区青铜时代国家形成过程的考古学研究：公元前1000～前500年 / 中国社会科学院考古研究所，哥伦比亚大学东亚语言和文化系，山东省文物考古研究院编著，李峰，梁中合主编.—北京：科学出版社，2018.8

ISBN 978-7-03-058396-3

Ⅰ.①龙… Ⅱ.①李…②梁… Ⅲ.①古城遗址（考古）-考古调查-龙口-青铜时代 Ⅳ.①K878.35

中国版本图书馆CIP数据核字（2018）第171163号

责任编辑：孙 莉 闫向东 / 责任校对：邹慧卿

责任印制：肖 兴 / 封面题字：徐天进

科学出版社 出版

北京东黄城根北街16号

邮政编码：100717

http：//www.sciencep.com

中国科学院印刷厂 印刷

科学出版社发行 各地新华书店经销

*

2018年8月第 一 版 开本：889×1194 1/16

2018年8月第一次印刷 印张：65 1/4 插页：72

字数：2 000 000

定价：980.00元（上、下册）

（如有印装质量问题，我社负责调换）

Guicheng

An Archaeological Study of the Formation of States on the Jiaodong Peninsula in Late Bronze-Age China, 1000-500 BCE

(II)

Li Feng Liang Zhonghe *Chief Editors*

Department of East Asian Languages and Cultures, Columbia University
The Institute of Archaeology, Chinese Academy of Social Sciences
Shandong Provincial Academy of Cultural Relics and Archaeology

Editors

Science Press

Beijing

主持单位

中国社会科学院考古研究所
哥伦比亚大学东亚语言和文化系
山东省文物考古研究院

合作单位

烟台市博物馆
龙口市博物馆

Sponsoring Institutions

Department of East Asian Languages and Cultures, Columbia University
The Institute of Archaeology, Chinese Academy of Social Sciences
Shandong Provincial Academy of Cultural Relics and Archaeology

Collaborating Institutions

Yantai Municipal Museum
Longkou Municipal Museum

下　编

Part Ⅱ

第一章　2002年归城内城北部和平村遗址的发掘

赵　娟　孙兆锋

第一节　引　　言

一、发掘的目的及其相关背景

2002年10月底，归城内城范围内的和平村（或称“东和平村”）遗址中部有遗迹暴露，且经雨水冲刷，破坏严重。为了保护这处青铜时代的重要遗址，烟台市博物馆和龙口市博物馆联合组成考古队对其进行了调查与抢救性发掘，获得一批重要的考古资料。归城遗址虽然在过去屡次出土青铜器等重要文物，但多数是本地村民们在农田生产中的偶然发现（见下编第二章）。这次发掘虽然规模较小，但它是归城历史上第一次主动进行的科学发掘，因此有其特殊意义。本章即对此次发掘的收获进行重点介绍。

二、发掘区的地理环境及位置

和平村遗址位于归城故城遗址内城范围内。发掘区在兰高镇和平村委大院之东约50米处一土台之上，原来是果园，台地北、西两侧均为断崖，东、南分别被民房所压（图Ⅰ.3.1）。这片台地是和平村内少有的一块空地，东西长40米、南北宽25米，现有面积约1000平方米。沿台地西侧小路向北，再折而向东，断崖逐渐变高；沿台地北沿小路东行可至和平村东边临河断崖。

三、发掘经过

2002年10月30日开始对和平村遗址进行正式发掘，至11月13日发掘结束。在发掘区布设探沟2条，编号分别为TG1（2002TG1）、TG2（2002TG2）。TG1位于台地南部边沿，TG2位于台地北沿（图Ⅱ.1.1）。TG1为正东西向，面积25×1平方米；TG2为正南北向，面积10×1平方米。

在台地北断崖暴露遗迹处布方2个，方向正北，因探方北壁为断崖，形状均非规则的方形，在西侧者编号为T1（2002T1），在东侧者编号为T2（2002T2），T1布方面积3×5平方米，T2布方面积约1.5 × 5平方米。

另外，我们还对台地断崖上暴露的遗迹及村东一处古井进行了抢救性清理，实际发掘总面积约为60平方米。

第二节 地层堆积

发掘区内TG1和TG2的地层堆积不同，现分别介绍如下。TG1的地层堆积情况以北壁剖面为例分述如下（图Ⅱ.1.2）：

第1层：耕土层，厚20 ~ 40厘米，土质松软，黄褐色。遍布整个探沟，包含现代瓷片、东周陶片等。该层下开口的遗迹有一现代坑。

第2层：扰乱层，分A、B两层。A层厚0 ~ 45厘米，为黄褐色花土，土质疏松。包含大量陶片。B层厚0 ~ 70厘米，为黑褐色花土，土质稍硬，与A层交错分布，包含大量陶片。

第3层：文化层，厚20 ~ 100厘米，为黑褐色土，夹杂白色小石粒、红烧土块、木炭等。土质坚硬。包含陶片、兽骨等。陶片以灰陶为主，有少量红陶。器形有罐、豆、鬲等，时代约为战国时期。该层下开口的遗迹有H9 ~ H13。

第3层下即为生土层。呈黄色，稍黏。

TG2的地层堆积情况以其南段西壁剖面为例分述如下（图Ⅱ.1.3）：

第1层：耕土层，厚20 ~ 40厘米。黄褐色土，较疏松。

第2层：扰乱层，厚2 ~ 20厘米。黄褐色土，土质较硬。出较多陶片。

第3层：文化层，厚10 ~ 50厘米。灰褐色土，土质坚硬，含料姜石、石块等。出土陶片。可辨器形有鬲、豆、绳纹罐、绳纹瓦等。时代约为战国时期。

第4层：文化层，厚0 ~ 50厘米。灰褐色土，土质较硬，料姜石含量更多，并夹杂大量草木灰、白色小石粒、木炭、红烧土块等。出土陶片、兽骨等，陶片以灰陶为主，有少量红陶。可辨器形有罐、鬲、豆、簋等。时代为西周晚期。有一灰坑开口于此层，因暴露范围太小，故未扩方发掘。

第4层下即为生土。

第三节 重要遗迹

此次发掘遗迹有房址、灰坑和井，共清理灰坑13个，均位于TG1内，依次编号为H1 ~ H13，其中H1 ~ H8为现代坑，不做介绍。房址发现11座，编号为F1 ~ F11，均暴露在遗址所处台地的西、北断崖上，其中F1 ~ F7破坏严重，未清理。井1座，编号为J1，位于村东鸦鹊河西岸断崖上（图Ⅱ.1.1）。

下面就发现的各类遗迹按顺序编号逐一描述如下：

一、房 址

房址共清理4座，编号为F8～F11，均位于北断崖上，从断面上可看到，都遭到不同程度的破坏。

F8：位于遗址的东北角，其东为TG2，北为村路，西、南为农田。F8 为圆角方形，半地穴式，东西长316、南北残宽66～134、深44～56厘米。四壁微内斜，中部有一直径60厘米的柱洞坑，其东有不规则的黑灰面，南为一呈圜底状坑，可能是用火处。房址内有一白灰面，东部薄，西部厚，厚1～10厘米。房址内的堆积分为两层，上层为夹砂较多的灰土，下层为较硬的灰褐土，夹有较多炭灰和红烧土粒，出土陶片，还有一定数量的兽骨。可辨器形有大沿簋、夹砂红褐陶鼎、罐、豆等。柱洞底不平，西部有一小坑，壁平直，深18厘米。洞内堆积为灰褐土，土质较硬，内含石块、碎陶片、红烧土块等。由于该房址的北半部已被破坏，房内详细结构不明确。根据出土陶片判断，其年代约在西周中晚期（图Ⅱ.1.4）。

F9：开口在3层下，打破4层及F11。其北半部被农民取土破坏，南、西部被一小坑打破，只余东壁一小段。坑内填土为灰褐色土，含较多细砂和烧土颗粒，上层堆积较松软一些。从出土陶片观察，其年代约为春秋早期。

F10：位于台地的北部断崖上，平面呈圆形，在东部有台阶（未清理）。房屋开口略宽于房底，敞口式。房址内有白灰、草木灰、墨绿色风化石、黄土等做成的白灰面。中间有中心柱；与柱子南北向相通有一矮墙，房子分为东西两部分。东部白灰面制作粗糙，有草木灰堆积，发现野猪头骨等兽骨，可能当时是灶的位置。西部生土面做得比较平整，撒上草木灰，再向上做有二层白灰面，白灰制作的较规整，可能是当时人们居住的地方。

房址堆积分两层，第一层属近现代层，第二层属房屋堆积，房屋堆积上部为黄褐土，土质结构紧密、坚硬，房屋底部是大量草木灰堆积。出土少量陶片，可辨器形有绳纹鬲、壶、罐、完整纺轮等。底部有一东西向的长方形土坑竖穴墓，由于棺椁的塌陷，造成房址内堆积向东倾斜。根据出土陶片判断，其年代约在春秋早期。房址北壁已被破坏，南壁压在住户垒的砖石墙下，故未清理。房址下墓葬也因此未清理，墓葬从断崖上测量长395厘米，在村民家里征集到此墓出土的1件车軎和1件车辖（编号采：7和采：6）（图Ⅱ.1.5）。

F11：开口在3层下，打破4层，被F9打破。因为F9的底面高于F11，故只破坏了F11东部的上层。从现存情况看，F11原为方形，半地穴式。底部为一夹杂墨绿色石粉面、白膏土面、炭灰、烧土粒及砂粒的硬面，颜色较杂。硬面东薄西厚，东边2厘米，西边约3厘米。房址西壁高73厘米，东壁残高40厘米（南壁的东端），南壁残长210厘米，西壁残长160厘米。底面至地表深190厘米。南壁正中有一缺口，外有圆形门道，门道直径54厘米。南壁外侧有一圆洞，直径6.5、深12厘米，可能是柱洞。填土为黑褐色，含黑色炭灰粒，出土马牙和一些陶片。从出土陶片观察，其年代约为西周中晚期（图Ⅱ.1.6）。

二、灰　坑

灰坑介绍5个，编号为H9～H13。由于发掘面积较小，除H9基本完整外，大多数未窥其全貌。但根据可见形制分析，以圆形居多。

H9：位于TG1距西壁8.9米处，开口于3层下。H9平面形状基本呈圆形，壁斜直，内收，底部较平整，坑口距地表深100、口径172、坑深80厘米。坑内堆积为黑色，土质较松软，包含大量陶片。底部有一小圆坑，直径62、深50厘米，壁直，圆筒形，底不平整。填土为黄褐色，稍黏。坑内包含物有石块、陶片、鹿角，鹿角经过切割，切去部分应是用作工具。根据出土陶片判断，其年代约在西周中晚期。

H10：位于TG1西部，开口于3层下，平面形状基本呈圆形，东侧为直边，西侧为弧形，口内收，坑底不平。坑口距地表深85、口径240、坑深60厘米。填土最上层为灰褐色土，厚约30厘米，含陶片较多。中间层为黑土，厚约15厘米。下层为灰土，厚约10～20厘米。根据出土陶片判断，其年代约在战国时期。

H11：位于TG1东部，开口于3层下，平面形状基本呈圆形，圆筒状，壁直，底平整。填土总体为灰褐色，夹杂大块绿石粉、红烧土块、木炭等，较疏松。出土有大量陶片。根据陶片判断，其年代约在春秋晚期。

H12：位于TG1中部，开口于3层下，不规则形，东壁较直，西壁弯曲，底不平，东深西高，坑口距地表深60、口径210、坑深约155厘米。填土为灰褐色，较松软，包含物有陶片、兽骨等。根据出土陶片判断，其年代约在西周晚期。

H13：位于TG1东部，开口于3层下，平面形状基本呈圆形，坑口距地表深95、口径220、坑深60厘米，填土为灰褐色，土质较硬，包含物有陶片、兽骨等。根据出土陶片判断，其年代约在西周晚期。

三、井

井1座，编号为J1，位于村东鸦鹊河东岸断崖上。“1969年董家村农民在村东南临近河岸的土台上整地，挖出铜器4件”（李步青，林仙庭 1991：915）。J1就处在这片台地东沿。平面形状接近长圆形，东边较直，西部已在烧窑取土时挖掉，长径180、深425厘米。井内堆积分为4层：

第①层为黄土，厚160厘米，又细又硬，没有任何包含物。第②层为杂土堆积，厚200厘米，以草木灰土堆积为主，有明显分层。靠底部为近黄白色的炉灰层。此层中兽骨、陶器都很多，可辨器形有豆、盆、纽绳肩的大罐，应是春秋时期。这些均为井废后的垃圾堆积。第③层为木灰浸染黏土形成的细土层，厚40厘米，淡灰色，较松软。本层出土陶片，能辨清器形的少，是井废后的第一次自然堆积，未做垃圾坑用。第④层为粗砂层，厚25厘米，灰绿色。紧贴井底，无其他包含物，应是水井使用时形成的沉淀。井底以下为生土。根据出土陶片判断，其年代约在春秋时期。

第四节　出土遗物

本次发掘出土遗物主要是陶器，另发现少量骨角器。陶器以泥质陶居多，陶色主要是黑、灰两种。夹砂陶以红褐为主，其中少量夹云母、滑石。器型可复原者不多，可辨器型主要有鼎、鬲、簋、豆、罐、盆等。其中以鼎、鬲、簋、豆、罐数量最多。陶器素面较多，纹饰有绳纹、凹弦纹、凸棱纹、磨光等。关于遗物的详尽介绍采用列表形式，另附于后文（图Ⅱ.1.7～Ⅱ.1.16；表Ⅱ.1.1～Ⅱ.1.14；图版69～71）。

第五节　结　　语

和平村遗址本次发掘出土大量陶器，给我们提供了第一手断代资料。遗址出土的瓮（TG1：9）与山东栖霞泊子村东周水井出土的瓮类似（烟台市文管会等 2006：35～41），出土的豆（J1：13）与山东蓬莱柳格庄春秋墓出土的豆类似（烟台市文管会 1990：805～810），根据出土陶器判断遗址的形成年代主要应为东周时期。

归城城址是胶东半岛最重要的先秦古城，是莱国都城。以前的考古发现有规模宏大的城墙，有出土贵重青铜器的墓葬，都是两周时期的重要遗迹。但城址中的平民居住遗迹，还从未做过考古工作。这次东和平遗址的试掘填补了这方面的空白，使我们对归城城址的内涵有了更全面的认识。

这次试掘虽然面积不大，但是严格按照《田野考古工作规程》（1984年）进行。出土遗物颇具时代特点和地域特色，对于研究胶东地区周代考古学大有裨益。受试掘面积所限，探沟内的遗迹现象不太完整，难以完整地提取信息。出土陶片不少，但可复原器物不多，限制了对器物本身及其提供考古讯息的准确把握。

参加发掘工作的人员主要有：烟台市博物馆林仙庭、王富强、闫勇、于晓丽、王金定、赵娟、龙口市博物馆陆元晨等。发掘负责人为林仙庭。摄影为林仙庭、赵娟，绘图为萧宇。后期整理有赵娟、肖靖、张文明等。

参考文献

李步青，林仙庭，1991：山东黄县归城遗址的调查与发掘. 考古，10：915.

烟台市文管会，栖霞市文管处，2006：山东栖霞市寨里镇泊子村东周和唐代水井清理简报. 考古，5：35-41.

烟台市文管会，1990：山东蓬莱县柳格庄墓群发掘简报. 考古，9：805-810.

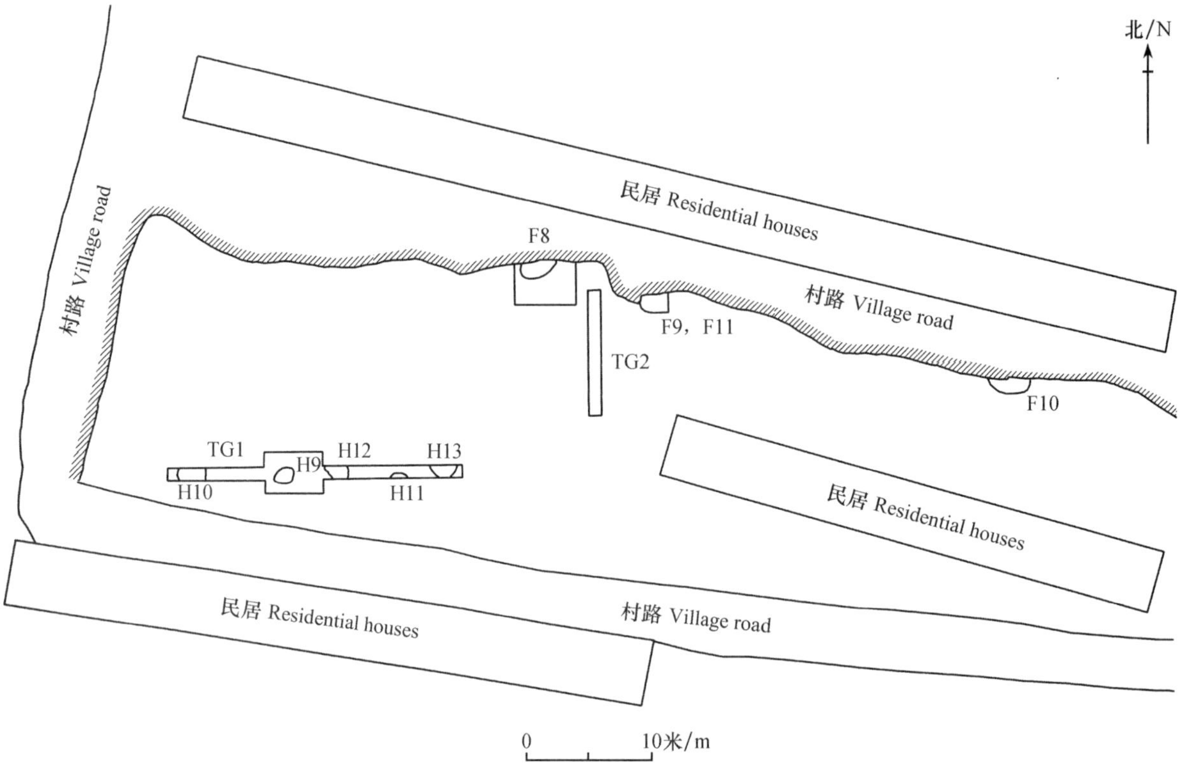

图Ⅱ.1.1　2002年和平村遗址探沟、探方位置平面图

Figure Ⅱ.1.1　Distribution of test trenches and test square at the Heping Village site, 2002.

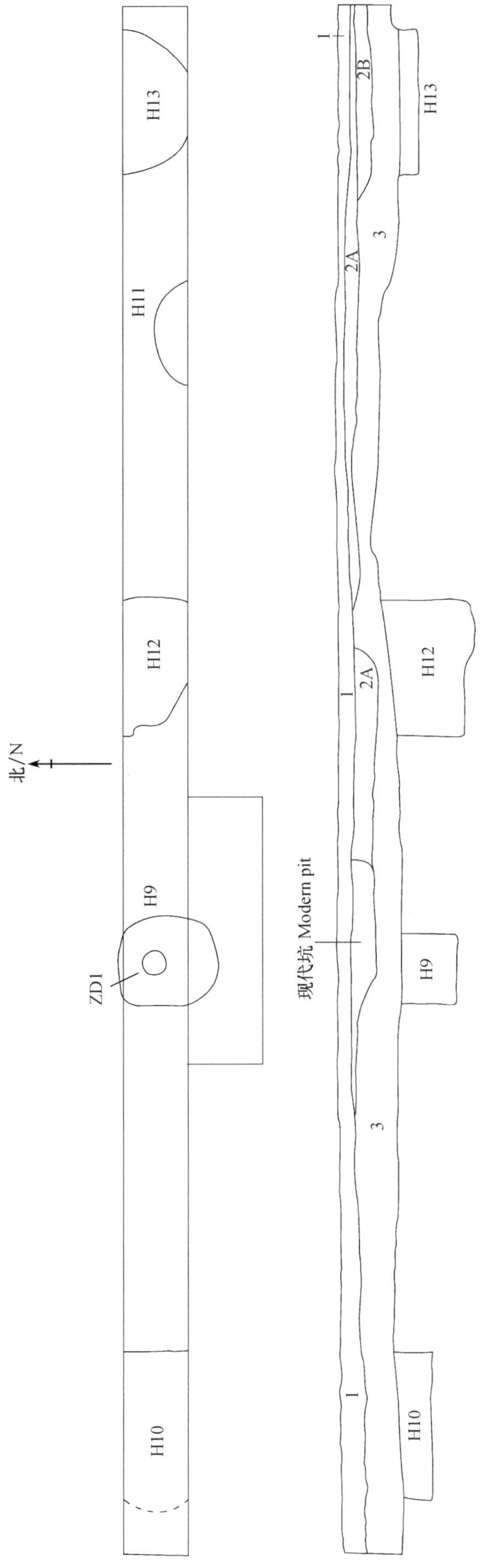

图Ⅱ.1.2　TG1的平面及其北壁地层剖面图

Figure Ⅱ.1.2　Plan of GT1 and add hyphen profile of its northern wall.

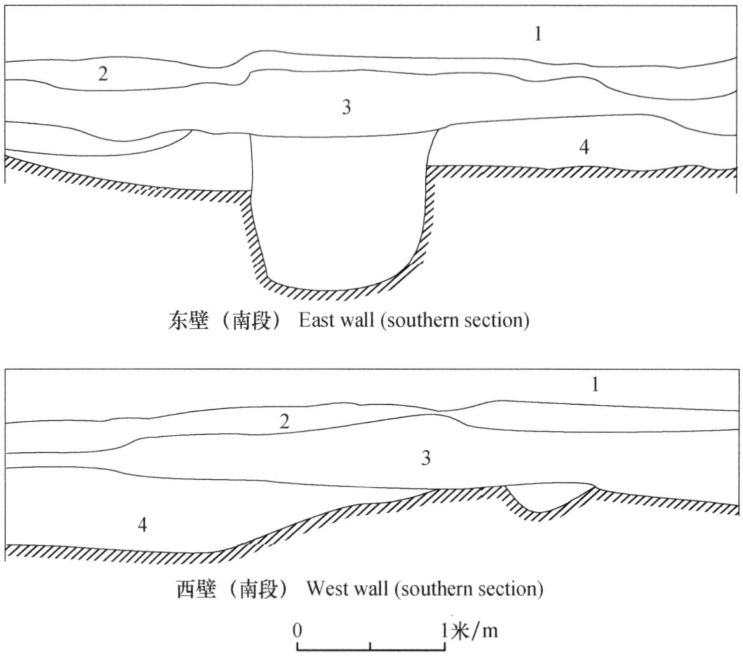

东壁（南段） East wall (southern section)

西壁（南段） West wall (southern section)

图Ⅱ.1.3　TG2南半部的地层剖面图

FigureⅡ.1.3　Cross-sections of TG2 (southern section).

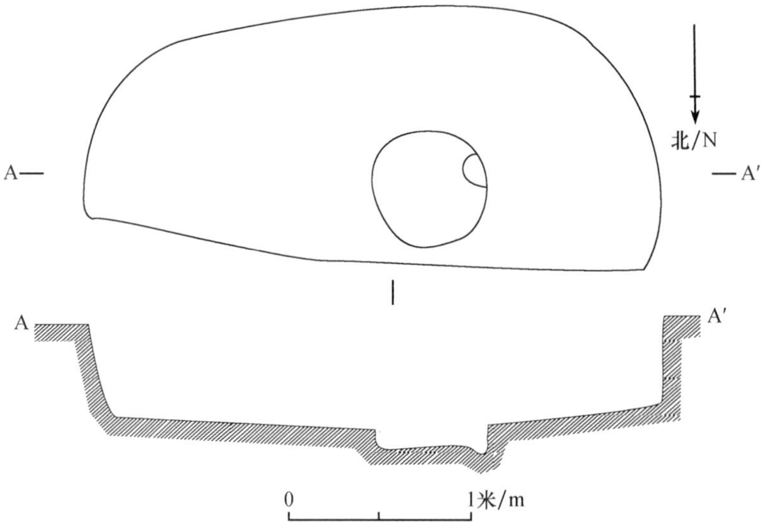

图Ⅱ.1.4　F8平、剖面图

FigureⅡ.1.4　Plan and cross-sectional profile of F8.

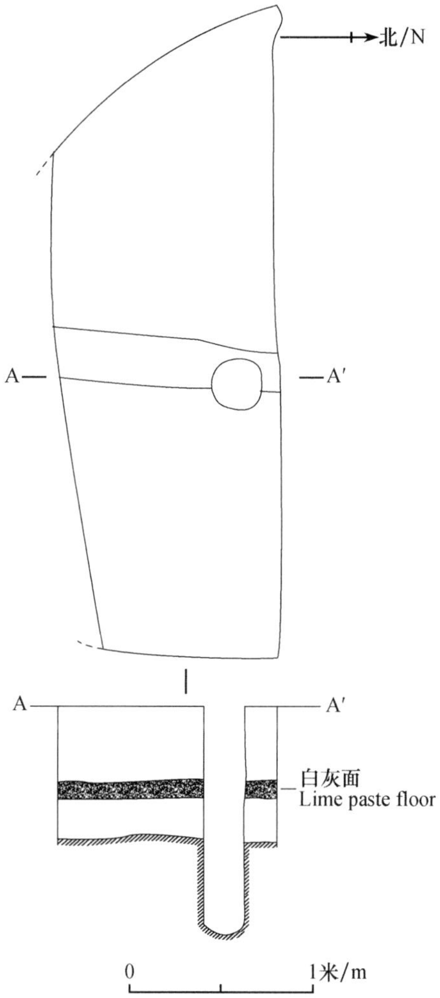

图Ⅱ.1.5　F10平、剖面图

Figure Ⅱ.1.5　Plan and cross-sectional profile of F10.

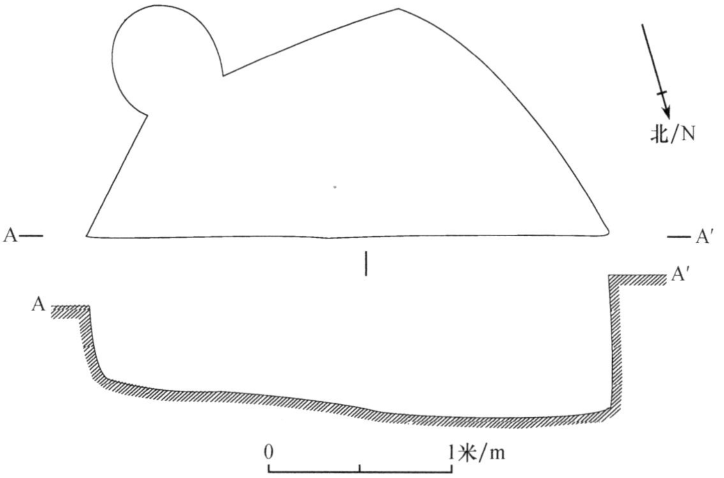

图Ⅱ.1.6　F11平、剖面图

Figure Ⅱ.1.6　Plan and cross-sectional profile of F11.

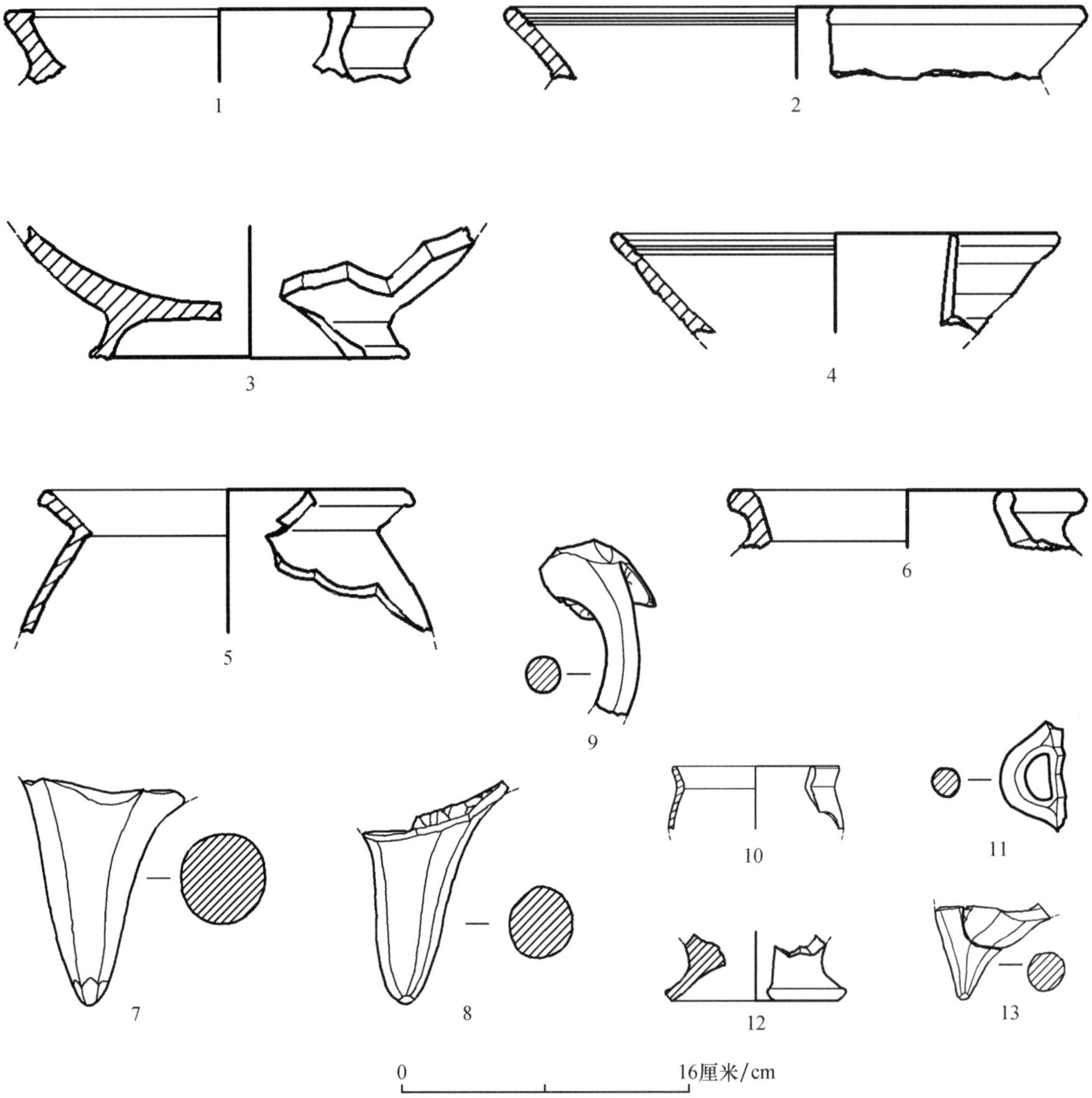

图Ⅱ.1.7　F8出土器物

Figure Ⅱ.1.7　Artifacts from F8.

表Ⅱ.1.1　F8出土器物登记表

Table Ⅱ.1.1　Artifacts from F8

图号 Number on Fig. Ⅱ.1.7	标本号 Excavation number	器物名称 Artifact name	出土时间 Excavation date	位置 Location	尺寸（厘米）Size (cm)	特点描述 Description of features
3	02SLDH F8：1	簋圈足残片 Fragment of circular foot of *gui* tureen	2002-11	F8	H: 7.2 B: 18	泥质灰陶，轮制磨光，弧腹，矮圈足。Grey fine clay; wheel-turned and burnished; arching belly; low, circular foot.
4	02SLDH F8：2	簋口沿残片 Fragment of rim of *gui* tureen	2002-11	F8	H: 5.4 M: 25	属宽沿簋，泥质黑皮陶，轮制磨光，圆唇，侈口，内部靠口沿处有两道凹弦纹，外部有三道刻划纹。Wide-rimmed *gui*-tureen; fine clay and black slip ceramic; wheel-turned and burnished; round lip; flared mouth; interior has two intaglio ring patterns near vessel rim; exterior has three bands of incised patterns.

续表

图号 Number on Fig. Ⅱ.1.7	标本号 Excavation number	器物名称 Artifact name	出土时间 Excavation date	位置 Location	尺寸 (厘米) Size (cm)	特点描述 Description of features
6	02SLDH F8：3	罐口沿残片 Fragment of rim of *guan* jar	2002-11	F8	H: 3.2 M: 20	夹砂灰陶，轮制磨光，双唇，卷沿，侈口，斜插肩。 Grey ceramic tempered with sand; wheel-turned and burnished; double lip; rolled rim; flared mouth; inclined, inset shoulders.
1	02SLDH F8：4	罐口沿残片 Fragment of rim of *guan* jar	2002-11	F8	H: 4 M: 24	泥质黄褐陶（心为灰陶），重唇，卷沿，口微敛。 Fine clay, yellowish-brown ceramic (body, grey ceramic); double lip; rolled rim; slightly constricted mouth.
12	02SLDH F8：5	簋圈足残片 Fragment of circular foot of *gui* tureen	2002-11	F8	H: 3.6 B: 10.2	泥质灰陶，轮制磨光，矮圈足。 Fine grey ceramic; wheel-turned and burnished; short, circular foot.
2	02SLDH F8：6	宽沿簋口沿残片 Fragment of rim of wide-rimmed *gui* tureen	2002-11	F8	H: 4 M: 32.6	泥质黑陶，轮制磨光，圆唇，侈口，内部靠口沿处有两道凹弦纹。 Fine black ceramic; wheel-turned and polished; round lip; flared mouth; interior has two lines of intaglio ring patterns near vessel rim.
9	02SLDH F8：7	罐提手 Handle of *guan* jar	2002-11	F8	H: 9.8	残，泥质灰陶，应当是横向安装在罐上，很罕见。 Damaged; fine grey ceramic; probably installed horizontally atop a *guan*-jar; rarely seen.
11	02SLDH F8：8	罐耳 Ear of *guan* jar	2002-11	F8	H: 6.1	泥质灰陶。 Fine grey ceramic.
7	02SLDH F8：9	鼎足 Foot of *ding* cauldron	2002-11	F8	H: 12.5	夹砂红褐陶，呈圆锥体，形体硕大，手制粗糙。 Reddish-brown ceramic tempered with sand; conical; massive; hand-formed and coarse.
8	02SLDH F8：10	鼎足 Foot of *ding* cauldron	2002-11	F8	H: 12.2	夹云母红褐陶，呈圆锥体，形体硕大，手制，做工粗糙。 Reddish-brown ceramic tempered with mica; conical; massive; shaped by hand; crudely formed.
13	02SLDH F8：11	鬲足 Foot of *li* tripod	2002-11	F8	H: 5.1	夹砂红褐陶，呈圆锥体，手制。 Reddish-brown ceramic tempered with sand; conical; shaped by hand.
5	02SLDH F8：12	鼎口沿残片 Fragment of rim of *ding* cauldron	2002-11	F8	H: 7.8 M: 23.2	夹砂红褐陶，手制，口沿轮修，方唇，卷沿，侈口，斜弧腹。 Reddish-brown ceramic tempered with sand; shaped by hand; vessel rim modified on potter's wheel; square lip; rolled rim; flared mouth; inclined, arching belly.
10	02SLDH F8：13	鬲口沿残片 Fragment of rim of *li* tripod	2002-11	F8	H: 6.8 M: 19	夹砂红褐陶，手制，圆唇，卷沿，侈口，斜弧腹。 Reddish-brown ceramic containing sand; shaped by hand; round lip; rolled rim; flared mouth; inclined, arching belly.

尺寸标志：L=长度；H=高度；W=宽度；D=直径；R=半径；M=口径；B=底径；T=厚度；d=深度；h=孔径。

Measurements: L=length; H=height; W=width; D=diameter; R=radius; M=mouth diameter; B=bottom diameter; T=thickness; d=depth; h=hole diameter.

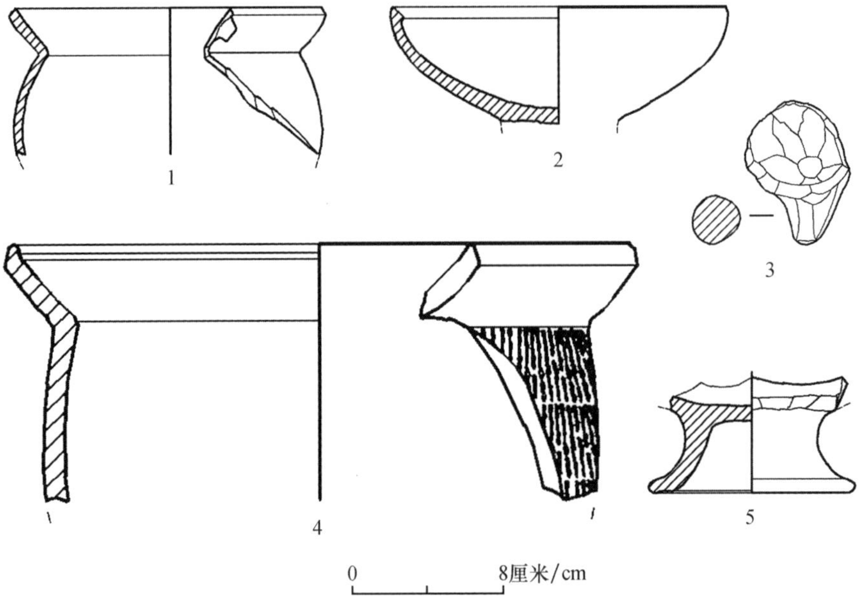

图Ⅱ.1.8　F9、F10、F11出土器物
Figure Ⅱ.1.8　Objects from F9, F10, and F11.

表Ⅱ.1.2　F9出土器物登记表
Table Ⅱ.1.2　Objects from F9

图号 Number on Fig. Ⅱ.1.8	标本号 Excavation number	器物名称 Artifact name	出土时间 Excavation date	位置 Location	尺寸（厘米）Size (cm)	特点描述 Description of features
3	02SLDH F9：1	鬲足 Foot of *li* tripod	2002-11	F9	H: 7.4	夹砂红陶，手制，呈羊角状，做工粗糙。Red ceramic; sand-tempered; shaped by hand; horn-shaped; crudely formed.

表Ⅱ.1.3　F10出土器物登记表
Table Ⅱ.1.3　Objects from F10

图号 Number on Fig. Ⅱ.1.8	标本号 Excavation number	器物名称 Artifact name	出土时间 Excavation date	位置 Location	尺寸（厘米）Size (cm)	特点描述 Description of features
1	02SLDH F10：1	鼎口沿残片 Fragment *ding* cauldron rim	2002-11	F10	H: 7.6 M: 17	夹云母黑皮陶，方唇，卷沿，口微敛，弧腹。Black-surfaced ceramic containing mica; square lip; rolled rim; slightly constricted mouth; arching belly.
2	02SLDH F10：2	豆盘 Plate of a *dou* pedestal dish	2002-11	F10	H: 6.1 M: 17.9	泥质灰陶，磨光，双唇，口内敛，折弧腹，深盘，钵形。Fine grey ceramic; polished; double lip; inwardly constricted mouth; angled, arching belly; deep dish; bowl-shaped.

表Ⅱ.1.4 F11出土器物登记表

Table Ⅱ.1.4 Objects from F11

图号 Number on Fig. Ⅱ.1.8	标本号 Excavation number	器物名称 Artifact name	出土时间 Excavation date	位置 Location	尺寸（厘米） Size (cm)	特点描述 Description of features
5	02SLDH F11：1	簋圈足 Circular foot of *gui* tureen	2002-11	F1	H: 6 B: 11	泥质灰陶，轮制，通体磨光，做工精细。 Fine grey ceramic; wheel-turned; completely polished; finely crafted.
4	02SLDH F11：2	罐口沿残片 Fragment *guan* jar rim	2002-11	F11	H: 13.4 M: 33.2	泥质黑陶，轮制，圆唇，卷沿，侈口，直弧腹，口沿内侧有一道凹弦纹，颈部以下施绳纹。 Fine black ceramic; wheel-turned; round lip; rolled rim; flared mouth; straight, arching belly; inside rim of vessel bears single intaglio line pattern; vessel has cord patterns from neck down.

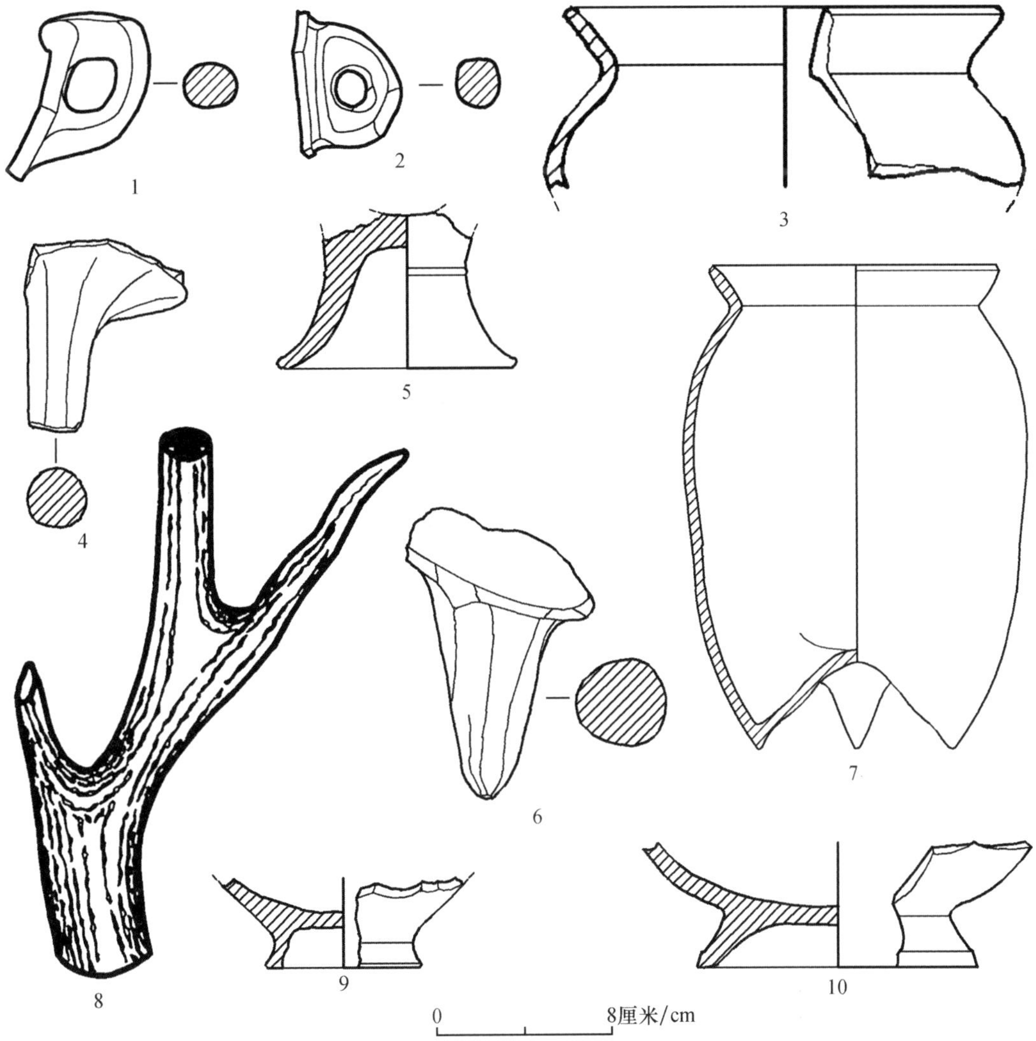

图Ⅱ.1.9 H1、H9出土的器物

Figure Ⅱ.1.9 Objects from H1 and H9.

表Ⅱ.1.5　H1出土器物登记表
Table Ⅱ.1.5　Objects from H1

图号 Number on Fig. Ⅱ.1.9	标本号 Excavation number	器物名称 Artifact name	出土时间 Excavation date	位置 Location	尺寸（厘米） Size (cm)	特点描述 Description of features
4	02SLDH H1：1	鼎足 Foot of *ding* cauldron	2002-11	H1	H: 8.5	夹砂红褐陶，呈圆柱形，手制，做工粗糙。 Reddish-brown ceramic; sand-tempered; cylindrical; shaped by hand; crudely formed.
5	02SLDH H1：2	簋圈足 Circular foot of *gui* tureen	2002-11	H1	H: 7 B: 11	泥质黑皮陶，轮制，中上部有一道凸棱纹，整体不规整。 Fine clay black-surfaced ceramic; wheel-turned; upper part of center has a ridge design; entire object irregularly shaped.
7	02SLDH H1：12	鬲 *Li* tripod	2002-11	H1	H: 43.4 D: 32	夹砂红褐陶，方唇，卷沿，斜肩，小弧腹，三乳状袋足，全手制。 Reddish-brown ceramic; sand-tempered; square lip; rolled rim; inclined shoulders; small, arching belly; three hollow, breast-shaped feet; entirely hand-formed.

表Ⅱ.1.6　H9出土器物登记表
Table Ⅱ.1.6　Objects from H9

图号 Number on Fig. Ⅱ.1.9	标本号 Excavation number	器物名称 Artifact name	出土时间 Excavation date	位置 Location	尺寸（厘米） Size (cm)	特点描述 Description of features
6	02SLDH H9：1	鼎足 Foot of *ding* cauldron	2002-11	H9	H: 13	夹砂红褐陶，圆锥状，手制，整体硕大规整。 Reddish-brown ceramic; sand-tempered; conical; shaped by hand; entire item massive and regularly shaped.
1	02SLDH H9：2	罐耳 Ear of *guan* jar	2002-11	H9	H: 6.5	夹砂灰陶，整体粘接。 Grey ceramic; sand-tempered; entire item glued on jar.
3	02SLDH H9：3	鼎口沿残片 Fragment of *ding* cauldron rim	2002-11	H9	H: 8 M: 20 D: 22	夹砂黑陶，轮制，方唇，卷沿，侈口，弧腹，做工粗糙。 Black ceramic; sand-tempered; wheel-turned; square lip; rolled rim; flared mouth; arching belly; crudely formed.
9	02SLDH H9：4	簋圈足残片 Fragment of circular foot of *gui* tureen	2002-11	H9	H: 4 B: 7	泥质黑皮陶，轮制磨光，圈足内侧由两道折弧构成。 Fine black-surfaced ceramic; wheel-turned and polished; interior of circular foot shaped with two arcs.
10	02SLDH H9：5	簋圈足残片 Fragment of circular foot of *gui* tureen	2002-11	H9	H: 5.6 B: 13 D: 18	泥质黑皮陶，轮制磨光，只有圈足尖部与地面接触，整体粗糙。 Fine black-surfaced ceramic; wheel-turned and polished; only tip of circular foot made contact with ground; entire item crudely shaped.
8	02SLDH H9：6	鹿角 Deer antler	2002-11	H9	H: 25	有人工切割痕迹。 Shows traces of cutting by hand.

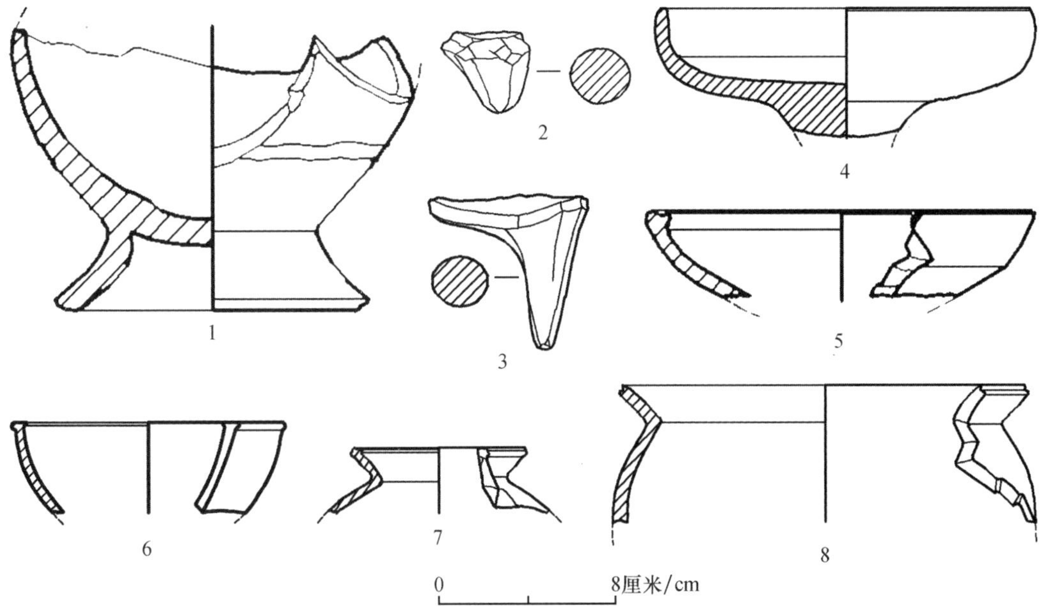

图Ⅱ.1.10　H11、H12出土器物

Figure Ⅱ.1.10　Objects from H11 and H12.

表Ⅱ.1.7　H11出土器物登记表

Table Ⅱ.1.7　Objects from H11

图号 Number on Fig. Ⅱ.1.10	标本号 Excavation number	器物名称 Artifact name	出土时间 Excavation date	位置 Location	尺寸（厘米）Size (cm)	特点描述 Description of features
1	02SLDH H11：1	簋残件 Fragment of *gui* tureen	2002-11	H11	H: 12.6 B: 14.4	泥质灰陶，轮制磨光，圆弧腹，腹中部偏下有两道不规则凹弦纹，整体器形不规则。Fine grey ceramic; wheel-turned and polished; round and arching belly; lower portion of center belly has two irregular, intaglio ring patterns; entire vessel irregularly shaped.
2	02SLDH H11：2	鬲足 Foot of *li* tripod	2002-11	H11	H: 3.6	夹砂红陶，手制，圆锥状，做工粗糙。Red ceramic; sand-tempered; shaped by hand; conical; crudely formed.
4	02SLDH H11：3	豆盘 Dish of a *dou* pedestal dish	2002-11	H11	H: 5.8 M: 17.6	泥质灰陶，轮制，外表磨光，方唇，直口，小弧底，浅盘，盘内有一道若有若无凸棱纹，豆柄已残缺，残处磨光再用，用途不明。Fine grey ceramic; wheel-turned; outer surface polished; square lip; straight mouth; small, arched bottom; shallow dish contains an indistinct ridge pattern; stem of *dou* pedestal dish missing; damaged locations were polished; manner of reuse unclear.

表Ⅱ.1.8　H12出土器物登记表
Table Ⅱ.1.8　Objects from H12

图号 Number on Fig. Ⅱ.1.10	标本号 Excavation number	器物名称 Artifact name	出土时间 Excavation date	位置 Location	尺寸（厘米） Size (cm)	特点描述 Description of features
3	02SLDH H12：1	鼎足 Foot of *ding* cauldron	2002-11	H12	H: 7	夹砂红褐陶，呈圆锥状，手制，做工细致。 Reddish-brown ceramic; sand-tempered; conical; shaped by hand; meticulously crafted.
5	02SLDH H12：2	豆盘残片 Fragment of plate of *dou* pedestal dish	2002-11	H12	H: 3.8 M: 18	泥质黑皮陶，轮制磨光，双唇，折斜弧腹，外表面有一道不明显折痕。 Fine black-surfaced ceramic; wheel-turned and polished; double lip; angled arching belly; outer surface bears an indistinct fold.
6	02SLDH H12：3	盆口沿残片 Fragment of rim of *pen* basin	2002-11	H12	H: 8 H: 25	泥质红陶，轮制磨光，双唇平顶，卷沿微内敛。 Fine red ceramic; wheel-turned and polished; double lip with flat top; rolled rim turned slightly inward.
7	02SLDH H12：4	罐口沿残片 Fragment of rim of *guan* jar	2002-11	H12	H: 5.8 H: 16 D: 20	泥质灰陶，轮制，双唇，卷沿外侈，折肩。 Fine grey ceramic; wheel-turned; double lip; rolled rim flared outward; angled shoulders.
8	02SLDH H12：5	罐口沿残片 Fragment of rim of *guan* jar	2002-11	H12	H: 12.2 M: 38 D: 39	夹砂红陶，手制，轮修口沿，双唇，卷沿，侈口，小斜肩。 Red ceramic; sand-tempered; shaped by hand; rim decorated on potter’s wheel; double lip; rolled rim; flared mouth; small, inclined shoulders.

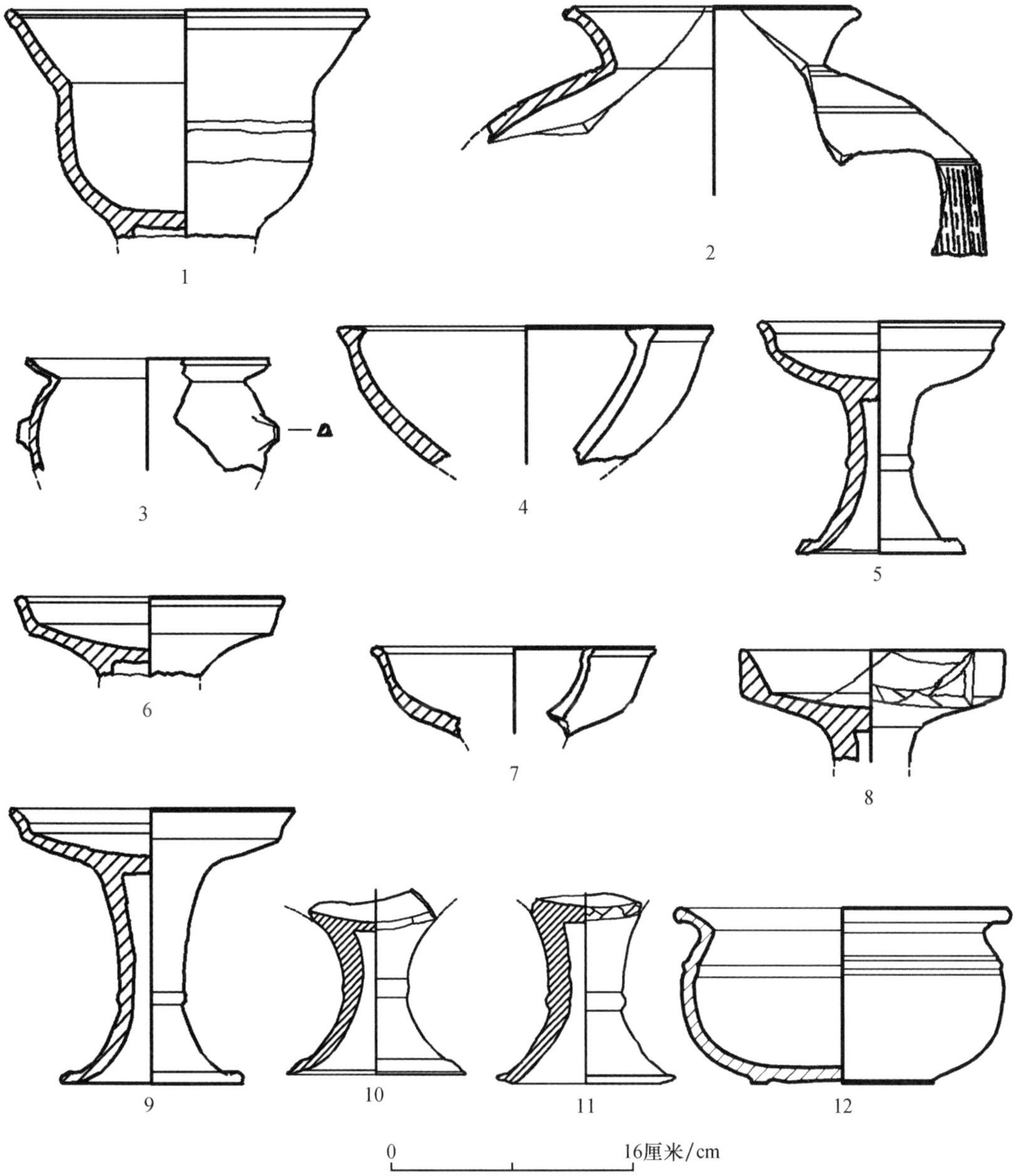

图Ⅱ.1.11　J1出土器物

Figure Ⅱ.1.11　Objects from J1.

表Ⅱ.1.9　J1出土器物登记表

Table Ⅱ.1.9　Objects from J1

图号 Number on Fig. Ⅱ.1.11	标本号 Excavation number	器物名称 Artifact name	出土时间 Excavation date	位置 Location	尺寸（厘米）Size (cm)	特点描述 Description of features
10	02SLDH J1：1	豆柄残件 Fragment of stem of a *dou* pedestal dish	2002-11	J1	H: 12 B: 11.9	泥质黑皮陶，轮制磨光，柄中部偏上有一道凸棱纹，底座呈二层台式，做工粗糙。Fine black-surfaced ceramic; wheel-turned and polished; upper middle of stem has single ridge; terraced base; crudely formed.

续表

图号 Number on Fig. Ⅱ.1.11	标本号 Excavation number	器物名称 Artifact name	出土时间 Excavation date	位置 Location	尺寸（厘米） Size (cm)	特点描述 Description of features
3	02SLDH J1：2	鼎口沿残片 Fragment of rim of *ding* cauldron	2002-11	J1	H: 7.2 M: 16 D: 17.4	夹砂红褐陶，手制，方唇，卷沿，侈口，圆弧腹，带长梯形乳钉纹。 Reddish-brown ceramic; sand-tempered; shaped by hand; square lip; rolled rim; flared mouth; round, arching belly; has trapezoidal studs.
1	02SLDH J1：3	簋 *Gui* tureen	2002-11	J1	H: 14.9 M: 24.4	泥质黑皮陶，圈足残，圆唇，侈口，直弧腹，内唇有一道凹弦纹，腹部三道凹弦纹，其中两道并列，做工粗糙。 Fine black-surfaced ceramic; circular foot damaged; round lip; flared mouth; straight, arching belly; inside of vessel lip has single intaglio ring pattern; belly has three intaglio ring patterns, two positioned close to each other; crudely formed.
12	02SLDH J1：4	盂 *Yu* basin	2002-11	J1	H: 11.6 B: 23	泥质灰陶，施红陶衣，圆唇，卷沿，口微敛，圆弧腹，肩部有两道凹弦纹和一道凸棱纹，假圈足，整体厚重稳健。 Fine grey ceramic; outer layer has red clothing; round lip; rolled rim; slightly constricted mouth; round, arching belly; shoulders have two intaglio line patterns and one ridge; false circular foot; entire vessel massive and sturdy.
2	02SLDH J1：5	绳纹罐 *Guan* jar with cord patterns	2002-11	J1	H: 16.2 M: 18.6	泥质黑皮陶，轮制，双唇，卷沿，侈口，斜肩，直腹，腹部绳纹，肩部有三对凹弦纹，位于两端和中间。 Fine black-surfaced ceramic; wheel-turned; double lip; rolled rim; flared mouth; inclined shoulders; straight belly; vessel belly has cord patterns; shoulders have three pairs of intaglio line patterns, positioned at both ends and center.
11	02SLDH J1：6	豆柄残件 Fragment of handle of a *dou* pedestal dish	2002-11	J1	H: 12.4 B: 11.9	泥质黑皮陶，轮制磨光，柄中部偏下有一道凸棱纹，底座上还有一圈凸棱纹，做工粗糙。 Fine black-surfaced ceramic; wheel-turned and polished; lower middle portion of handle has a single ridge; area above base also encircled by single ridge; crudely formed
6	02SLDH J1：7	豆盘 Dish of a *dou* pedestal dish	2002-11	J1	H: 5.2 D: 18	柄残，泥质黑皮陶，轮制，通体磨光，圆唇，微敞口，折腹，小弧底。 Stem missing; fine black-surfaced ceramic; wheel-turned; entire item polished; round lip; slightly open mouth; angled belly; small, arched base.
5	02SLDH J1：8	豆 *Dou* pedestal dish	2002-11	J1	H: 15.2 M: 16.6	泥质黑皮陶，轮制，圆唇，敞口，浅盘，折腹，小弧底，柄中部有一道凸棱纹，做工稍显粗糙。 Fine black-surfaced ceramic; wheel-turned; round lip; open mouth; shallow dish; angled belly; small, arched base; middle portion of stem has a single ridge pattern; workmanship somewhat crude.
7	02SLDH J1：9	豆盘残片 Fragment of plate of *dou* pedestal dish	2002-11	J1	H: 5.8 M: 19	泥质黑皮陶，轮制，圆唇，卷沿，侈口，斜弧腹。 Fine black-surfaced ceramic; wheel-turned; round lip; rolled rim; flared mouth; inclined, arching belly.

续表

图号 Number on Fig. Ⅱ.1.11	标本号 Excavation number	器物名称 Artifact name	出土时间 Excavation date	位置 Location	尺寸（厘米） Size (cm)	特点描述 Description of features
4	02SLDH J1：10	豆盘残片 Fragment of plate of a *dou* pedestal dish	2002-11	J1	H: 4.5 M: 25	泥质灰陶，轮制，通体磨光，双唇，卷沿，口内敛，斜弧腹较深。 Fine grey ceramic; wheel-turned; entire item polished; double lip; rolled rim; inwardly constricted mouth; relatively deep, inclined, arching belly.
	02SLDH J1：11	罐口沿残片 Fragment of *guan* jar rim	2002-11	J1	H: 5.3 M: 22	泥质红陶，施红陶衣，轮制，通体磨光，圆唇，卷沿，口外侈，斜插肩，做工精致。 Fine red ceramic; red slip; wheel-turned; entire item polished; round lip; rolled rim; outwardly flared mouth; inclined, inset shoulders; fine workmanship.
8	02SLDH J1：12	豆盘残件 Fragment of dish of a *dou* pedestal dish	2002-11	J1	H: 7.2 M: 18	泥质灰陶，轮制，方唇，折弧腹，浅盘。 Fine grey ceramic; wheel-turned; square lip; angled, arching belly; shallow dish.
9	02SLDH J1：13	豆 *Dou* pedestal dish	2002-11	J1	H: 18 M: 19	泥质灰陶，施黑陶衣，轮制磨光，圆唇，卷沿，侈口，折斜弧腹，浅盘，柄中下部有一道凸棱纹。 Fine grey ceramic; black slip; wheel-turned and polished; round lip; rolled rim; flared mouth; angled, inclined, arching belly; shallow platter; lower middle portion of stem has a single ridge.

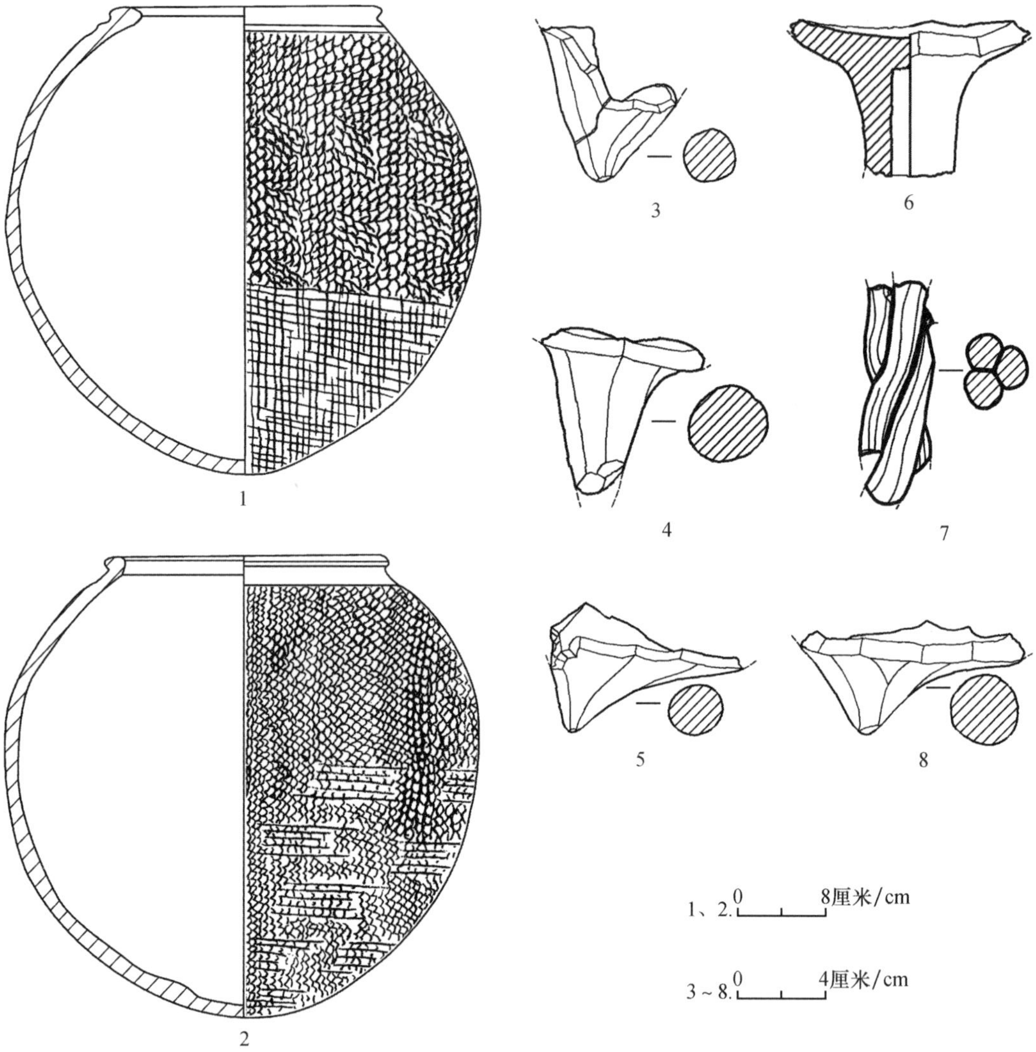

图Ⅱ.1.12　TG1出土器物（1）

Figure Ⅱ.1.12　Objects from TG1 (1).

表Ⅱ.1.10　TG1出土器物登记表（1）

Table Ⅱ.1.10　Objects from TG1 (1)

图号 Number on Fig. Ⅱ.1.12	标本号 Excavation number	器物名称 Artifact name	出土时间 Excavation date	位置 Location	尺寸（厘米）Size (cm)	特点描述 Description of features
2	02SLDH TG1②：10	罐 *Guan*-jar	2002-11	TG1②	H: 41 M: 25.6	夹砂灰陶，方唇，卷沿，口微敛，圆鼓腹，圜底，上半部饰纵向绳纹，下半部饰纵横交错的绳纹。Grey ceramic; sand-tempered; square lip; rolled rim; slightly constricted mouth; round, bulging belly; round bottom; upper half decorated with vertical cord impressions; lower half decorated with cross-hatched cord impressions.
7	02SLDH TG1③：5	罐把手 Handle of *guan*-jar	2002-11	TG1③	H: 10.1	泥质灰陶，由三股泥条拧成。Fine grey ceramic; formed from three strips of clay twisted together.

续表

图号 Number on Fig. Ⅱ.1.12	标本号 Excavation number	器物名称 Artifact name	出土时间 Excavation date	位置 Location	尺寸（厘米） Size (cm)	特点描述 Description of features
6	02SLDH TG1③：7	豆柄 Upper stem of *dou* pedestal dish	2002-11	TG1③	H: 7 D: 11	泥质灰陶，做工粗糙。 Fine grey ceramic; crudely formed.
1	02SLDH TG1③：9	罐 *Guan* jar	2002-11	TG1③	H: 41.6 M: 25.2	夹砂灰陶，圆唇，敛口，圆鼓腹，圜底，上半部饰纵向绳纹，下半部饰纵横交错的绳纹。 Grey ceramic; sand-tempered; round lip; constricted mouth; round, bulging belly; round bottom; upper half decorated with vertical cord impressions; lower half decorated with cross-hatched cord impressions.
4	02SLDH TG1③：16	鼎足 Foot of *ding* cauldron	2002-11	TG1③	H: 7.5	夹砂红褐陶，呈圆锥状，手制。 Reddish-brown ceramic; sand-tempered; conical; shaped by hand.
5	02SLDH TG1③：17	鬲足 Foot of *li* tripod	2002-11	TG1③	H: 5.8	夹砂灰陶，呈尖锥状，手制。 Grey ceramic; sand-tempered; forms a pointed cone; shaped by hand.
8	02SLDH TG1③：18	鬲足 Foot of *li* tripod	2002-11	TG1③	H: 5.1	夹砂红陶，呈圆锥状，手制，非常短小。 Red ceramic; sand-tempered; conical; shaped by hand; extremely short and small.
3	02SLDH TG1③：21	鬲足 Foot of *li* tripod	2002-11	TG1③	H: 7	夹砂红褐陶，呈乳状，手制，粗糙但形体精致。 Reddish-brown ceramic; sand-tempered; breast-shaped; shaped by hand; crude, but well-shaped.

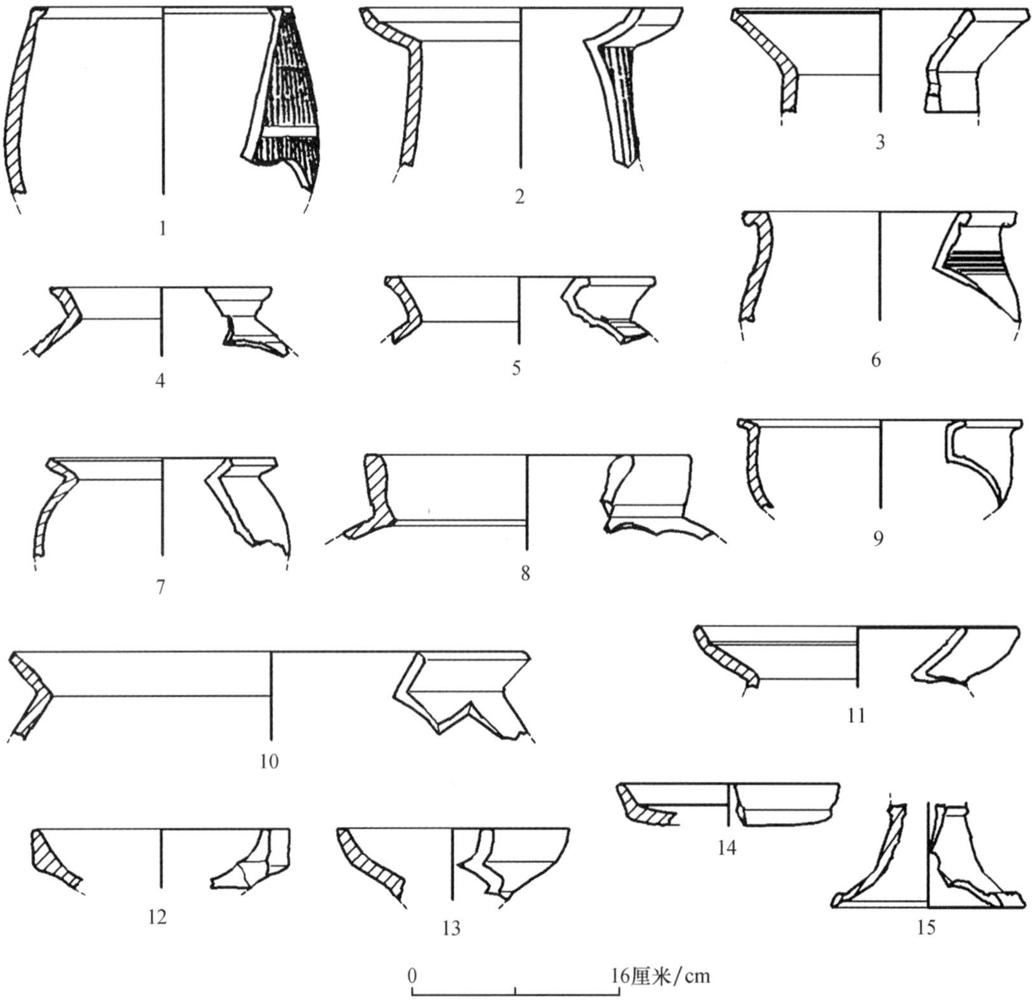

图Ⅱ.1.13　TG1出土器物（2）
Figure Ⅱ.1.13　Objects from TG1 (2).

表Ⅱ.1.11　TG1出土器物登记表（2）
Table Ⅱ.1.11　Objects from TG1 (2)

图号 Number on Fig. Ⅱ.1.13	标本号 Excavation number	器物名称 Artifact name	出土时间 Excavation date	位置 Location	尺寸（厘米）Size (cm)	特点描述 Description of features
10	02SLDH TG1③：1	鼎口沿残片 Fragment of *ding* cauldron rim	2002-11	TG1④	H: 6.6 M: 40.6	夹滑石红褐陶，手制，方唇，卷沿，侈口，弧腹。 Reddish-brown ceramic containing talc; shaped by hand; square lip; rolled rim; flared mouth; arching belly.
1	02SLDH TG1③：2	罐口沿残片 Fragment of *guan* jar rim	2002-11	TG1④	H: 14 M: 20	泥质灰褐陶，轮制，双唇，敛口，直弧腹，器形呈鼓状，比较特殊，通体绳纹。 Fine greyish-brown ceramic; wheel-turned; double lip; constricted mouth; straight, arching belly; vessel forms a drum shape; relatively unique; entire vessel has cord patterns.

续表

图号 Number on Fig. Ⅱ.1.13	标本号 Excavation number	器物名称 Artifact name	出土时间 Excavation date	位置 Location	尺寸（厘米） Size (cm)	特点描述 Description of features
2	02SLDH TG1③：3	罐口沿残片 Fragment of *guan* jar rim	2002-11	TG1④	H: 12 M: 25	泥质灰陶，轮制，圆唇，卷沿，口微敛，直弧腹，腹部绳纹。 Fine grey ceramic; wheel-turned; round lip; rolled rim; slightly constricted mouth; straight, arching belly; belly has cord patterns.
3	02SLDH TG1③：4	簋口沿残片 Fragment of *gui* tureen rim	2002-11	TG1④	H: 7.8 M: 23	泥质灰陶，轮制磨光，方唇，卷沿，侈口，沿口内部近沿口部位有一道凹弦纹。 Fine grey ceramic; wheel-turned and polished; square lip; rolled rim; flared mouth; interior of vessel has single intaglio ring pattern near rim.
15	02SLDH TG1③：6	豆柄残片 Fragment of stem of a *dou* pedestal dish	2002-11	TG1④	H: 7.8 B: 15	泥质灰陶，中部有一道凸棱纹，由于烧造原因，整体不规则。 Fine grey ceramic; middle portion has single ridge; entire body irregular due to firing.
4	02SLDH TG1③：8	罐口沿残片 Fragment of *guan* jar rim	2002-11	TG1④	H: 5.2 M: 17	泥质灰陶，轮制磨光，双唇，卷沿，侈口，肩部有一道宽条凹弦纹。 Fine grey ceramic; wheel-turned and polished; double lip; rolled rim; flared mouth; shoulder has single, broad intaglio ring pattern.
14	02SLDH TG1③：10	豆盘残片 Fragment of dish of a *dou* pedestal dish	2002-11	TG1④	H: 3.2 M: 17	泥质黑皮陶，轮制磨光，圆唇，侈口，浅盘，斜弧腹。 Fine black-surfaced ceramic; wheel-turned and polished; round lip; flared mouth; shallow dish; inclined, arching belly.
12	02SLDH TG1③：11	豆盘残片 Fragment of dish of a *dou* pedestal dish	2002-11	TG1④	H: 4.4 M: 20	泥质灰陶，轮制磨光，圆唇，侈口，深盘，斜弧腹。 Fine grey ceramic; wheel-turned and polished; round lip; flared mouth; deep dish; inclined, arching belly.
6	02SLDH TG1③：12	罐口沿残片 Fragment of *guan* jar rim	2002-11	TG1④	H: 8.2 M: 21	泥质灰陶，轮制磨光，圆唇，卷沿，口微侈，肩部有五道凹弦纹。 Fine grey ceramic; wheel-turned and polished; round lip; rolled rim; slightly flared mouth; shoulders have five intaglio ring patterns.
13	02SLDH TG1③：13	豆盘残片 Fragment of dish of a *dou* pedestal dish	2002-11	TG1④	H: 5.4 M: 18	泥质灰陶，轮制磨光，方唇，侈口，深盘，圆弧腹。 Fine grey ceramic; wheel-turned and polished; square lip; flared mouth; deep dish; round, arching belly.
5	02SLDH TG1③：14	罐口沿残片 Fragment of *guan* jar rim	2002-11	TG1④	H: 5 M: 21	泥质灰陶，轮制磨光，方唇，卷沿，侈口。 Fine grey ceramic; wheel-turned and polished; square lip; rolled rim; flared mouth.
	02SLDH TG1③：15	罐耳 Ear of *guan* jar	2002-11	TG1④	H: 7.5	泥质灰陶，耳直接安装在罐的口沿上，一部分折压过去包裹住口沿，耳上部较平。 Fine grey ceramic; ear attached directly to rim of jar; partly folded and pressed around rim; upper part of ear relatively flat.
7	02SLDH TG1③：19	鼎口沿残片 Fragment of *ding* cauldron rim	2002-11	TG1④	H: 7.4 M: 20	夹砂红褐陶，手制，方唇，卷沿，侈口，圆弧腹，做工粗糙，慢轮修口沿。 Reddish-brown ceramic; sand-tempered; shaped by hand; square lip; rolled rim; flared mouth; round, arching belly; crudely formed; vessel rim modified with slow potter's wheel.

续表

图号 Number on Fig. Ⅱ.1.13	标本号 Excavation number	器物名称 Artifact name	出土时间 Excavation date	位置 Location	尺寸（厘米） Size (cm)	特点描述 Description of features
11	02SLDH TG1③：20	簋口沿残片 Fragment of *gui* tureen rim	2002-11	TG1④	H: 4.6 M: 25	泥质黑皮陶，轮制磨光，圆唇，卷沿，口微敛。 Fine black-surfaced ceramic; wheel-turned and polished; round lip; rolled rim; slightly constricted mouth.
9	02SLDH TG1③：22	簋口沿残片 Fragment of *gui* tureen rim	2002-11	TG1④	H: 6.6 M: 22	泥质黑皮陶，轮制，方唇，卷沿，直弧腹。 Fine black-surfaced ceramic; wheel-turned; square lip; rolled rim; straight, arching belly.
8	02SLDH TG1③：23	罐口沿残片 Fragment of *guan* jar rim	2002-11	TG1④	H: 6.4 M: 25	泥质灰陶，轮制磨光，方唇，直领，口微侈，领根部有一道宽条凹弦纹，罐内肩领结合处有一道凸棱，制作别致。 Fine grey ceramic; wheel-turned and polished; square lip; straight neck; slightly flared mouth; base of neck has single, broad intaglio ring pattern; interior of jar has a single ridge at junction point between shoulder and neck; uniquely made.

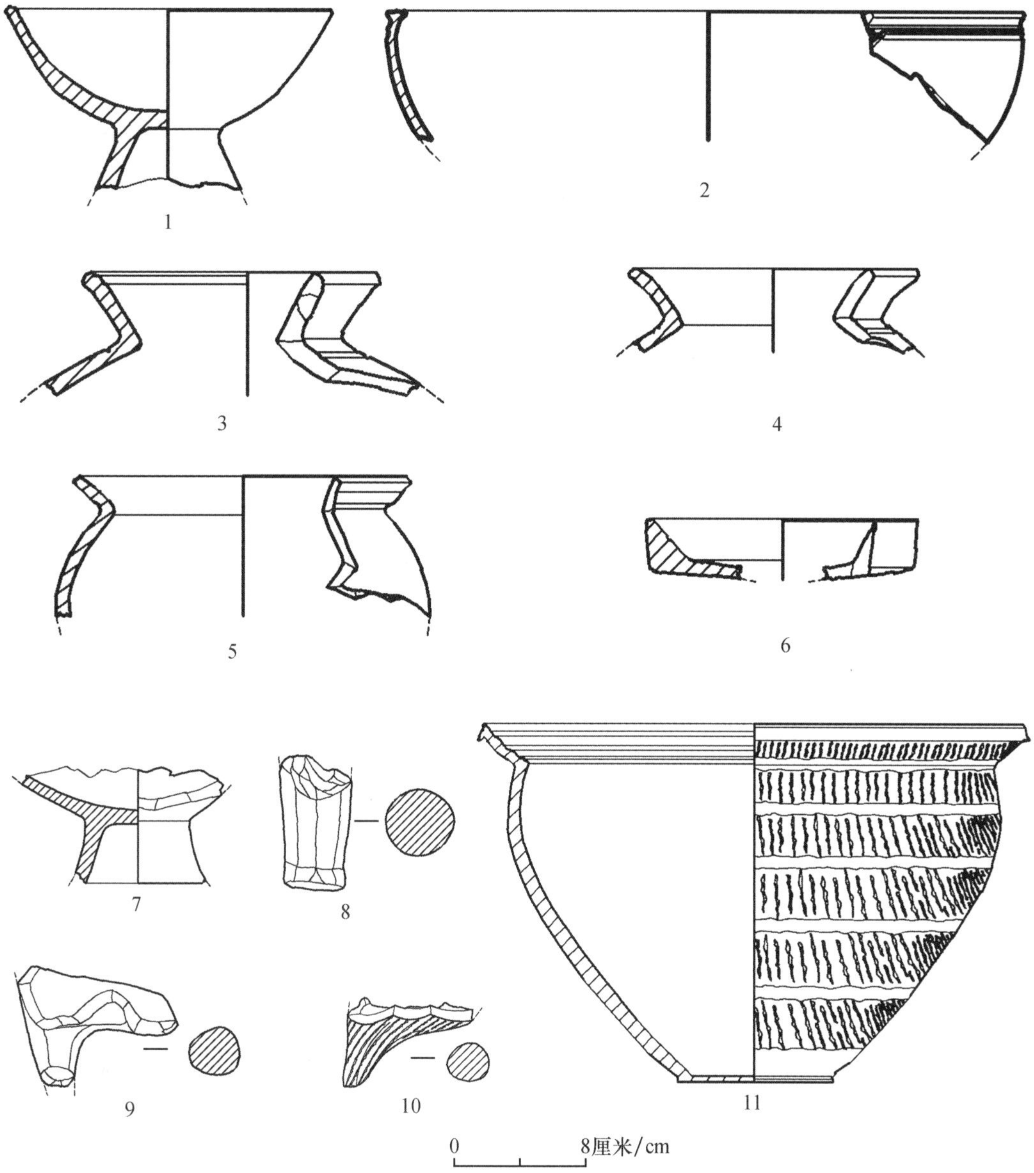

图Ⅱ.1.14　T1出土器物

Figure Ⅱ.1.14　Objects from T1.

表Ⅱ.1.12　T1出土器物登记表

Table Ⅱ.1.12　Objects from T1

图号 Number on Fig. Ⅱ.1.14	标本号 Excavation number	器物名称 Artifact name	出土时间 Excavation date	位置 Location	尺寸（厘米） Size (cm)	特点描述 Description of features
1	02SLDH T1②：5	簋 *Gui* tureen	2002-11	T1②	H: 10.8 M: 20	泥质黑皮陶，轮制，圈足残，方唇，圆弧腹，钵形。 Fine clay, black-surfaced ceramic; wheel-turned; circular foot damaged; square lip; round, arching belly; bowl-shaped.

续表

图号 Number on Fig. Ⅱ.1.14	标本号 Excavation number	器物名称 Artifact name	出土时间 Excavation date	位置 Location	尺寸（厘米） Size (cm)	特点描述 Description of features
11	02SLDH T1②：2	甗 *Yan* steamer	2002-11	T1②	H: 21.4 D: 34	夹砂黄褐陶，轮制，双唇，卷沿，口微敛，斜弧腹，底口微外卷，通体绳纹。 Yellowish-brown ceramic; sand-tempered; wheel-turned; double lip; rolled rim; slightly constricted mouth; inclined, arching belly; opening at base curled slightly outward; entire vessel has cord impressions.
2	02SLDH T1③：1	盆残片 Fragment of *pen* basin	2002-11	T1③	H: 7.8 M: 39.6	泥质黑陶，轮制磨光，双唇，口微敛，口沿下方有三道凹弦纹，弧腹。 Fine black ceramic; wheel-turned and polished; double lip; slightly constricted mouth; area below vessel rim has three intaglio ring patterns; arching belly.
3	02SLDH T1③：2	罐口沿残片 Fragment of *guan* jar rim	2002-11	T1③	H: 7.4 M: 25	泥质灰褐陶，轮制磨光，方唇，卷沿，侈口，口内侧顶端有两道凹弦纹，靠近领部有两道凹弦纹，陶质有点像夹心饼干，中间灰，两边灰褐。 Fine greyish-brown ceramic; wheel-turned and polished; square lip; rolled rim; flared mouth; top inside part of rim has two intaglio ring patterns; portion near neck has two intaglio ring patterns; consistency of ceramic somewhat like a layered cookie, grey in the middle with greyish-brown on both sides.
4	02SLDH T1③：3	罐口沿残片 Fragment of *guan* jar rim	2002-11	T1③	H: 5 M: 18	泥质灰褐陶，轮制磨光，圆唇，卷沿，侈口，肩头处有道凹弦纹，斜肩，陶质中间灰，两边灰褐。 Fine greyish-brown ceramic; wheel-turned and polished; round lip; rolled rim; flared mouth; top of shoulders has intaglio ring pattern; inclined shoulders; ceramic grey in the center with greyish-brown on both sides.
7	02SLDH T1③：4	簋残段 Fragmentary section of a *gui* tureen	2002-11	T1③	H: 7 B: 12.3	泥质灰陶，轮制磨光，小弧腹。 Fine grey ceramic; wheel-turned and polished; small, arching belly.
6	02SLDH T1③：5	豆盘残片 Fragment of dish of a *dou* pedestal dish	2002-11	T1③	H: 3.6 M: 17	泥质灰陶，轮制，圆唇，侈口，浅盘，斜折小弧腹。 Fine grey ceramic; wheel-turned; round lip; flared mouth; shallow dish; small, inclined, angled, arching belly.
8	02SLDH T1③：6	鼎足 Foot of a *ding* cauldron	2002-11	T1③	H: 8.1	残，夹砂黄褐陶，圆柱形，手制，底部像象脚，形体硕大。 Fragmentary; yellowish-brown ceramic; sand-tempered; cylindrical; shaped by hand; bottom portion resembles elephant's foot; massive.
10	02SLDH T1③：7	鬲足 Foot of a *li* tripod	2002-11	T1③	H: 5.4	夹砂灰陶，呈羊角状，通体绳纹。 Grey ceramic; sand-tempered; horn-shaped; entire vessel has cord patterns.
9	02SLDH T1③：8	鼎足 Foot of a *ding* cauldron	2002-11	T1③	H: 7.2	残，夹砂红陶，不规则圆锥体，手制，工艺粗糙。 Fragmentary; red ceramic; sand-tempered; forms an irregular cone shape; shaped by hand; crude workmanship.

续表

图号 Number on Fig. Ⅱ.1.14	标本号 Excavation number	器物名称 Artifact name	出土时间 Excavation date	位置 Location	尺寸（厘米） Size (cm)	特点描述 Description of features
5	02SLDH T1③：9	鼎口沿残片 Fragment of a *ding* cauldron rim	2002-11	T1③	H: 8.4 M: 20 D: 23	夹砂红褐陶，手制，慢轮修整口沿，方唇，卷沿，侈口，圆弧腹，领中偏下有一道凸棱纹，整体工艺粗糙。 Reddish-brown ceramic; sand-tempered; shaped by hand; vessel rim finished on slow potter's wheel; square lip; rolled rim; flared mouth; round, arching belly; lower middle portion of neck has single ridge pattern; entire item exhibits crude workmanship.

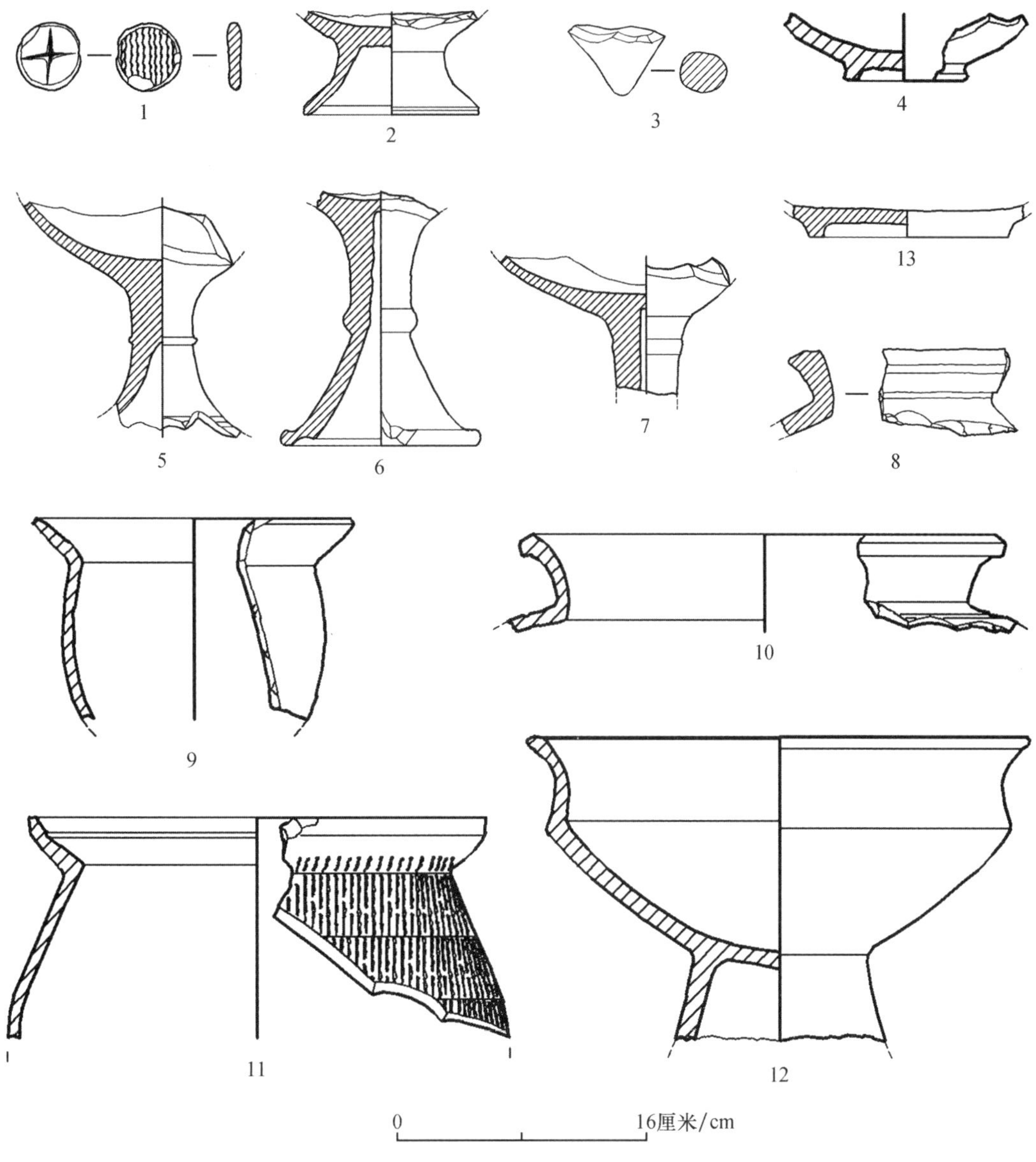

图Ⅱ.1.15　T2出土器物

Figure Ⅱ.1.15　Objects from T2.

表Ⅱ.1.13　T2出土器物登记表

Table Ⅱ.1.13　Objects from T2

图号 Number on Fig. Ⅱ.1.15	标本号 Excavation number	器物名称 Artifact name	出土时间 Excavation date	位置 Location	尺寸（厘米） Size (cm)	特点描述 Description of features
12	02SLDH T2②：1	簋 *Gui* tureen	2002-11	T2②	H: 19.2 M: 33	泥质黑皮陶，轮制，通体磨光，圈足残，圆唇，侈口，折斜弧腹，形体硕大。 Fine black-surfaced ceramic; wheel-turned; entire item polished; circular foot damaged; round lip; flared mouth; angled, inclined, arching belly; massive.
1	02SLDH T2②：2	绳纹罐残片 Fragment of a *guan* jar with cord impressions	2002-11	T2②	D: 4.3	夹砂黑皮陶，被加工成圆片，一面保留绳纹，一面有十字星形磨痕，用途不明。 Black-surfaced ceramic, sand-tempered; worked into a round disk shape; one surface has cord patterns; one surface has cross-shaped grinding mark; manner of use unclear.
3	02SLDH T2②：3	鬲足 Foot of a *li* tripod	2002-11	T2②	H: 4.4	夹砂红褐陶，不规则圆锥状。 Reddish-brown ceramic; sand-tempered; forms an irregular cone shape.
5	02SLDH T2②：4	豆残件 Fragment of a *dou* pedestal dish	2002-11	T2②	H: 15 B: 14.2	泥质黑皮陶，柄中部有一道凸棱纹，柄底部有三道凹弦纹，柄内是一圆锥形空心，做工粗糙。 Fine black-surfaced ceramic; middle portion of handle has single ridge; lower portion of handle has three intaglio ring patterns; interior of handle forms conical hollow; crudely formed.
6	02SLDH T2②：5	豆残件 Fragment of a *dou* pedestal dish	2002-11	T2②	H: 16.1 B: 13	泥质灰陶，柄中部有一道凸棱纹，非常粗壮，做工粗糙。 Fine grey ceramic; middle portion of stem has single ridge; extremely solid; crudely formed.
2	02SLDH T2②：6	簋圈足 Circular foot of a *gui* tureen	2002-11	T2②	H: 6.6 B: 11.4	泥质黑皮陶，轮制磨光，底口为双唇。 Fine black-surfaced ceramic; wheel-turned and polished; lower opening has paired lip.
4	02SLDH T2②：7	簋圈足残片 Fragment of circular foot of a *gui* tureen	2002-11	T2②	H: 4.2 B: 8	泥质灰陶，施红陶衣，轮制磨光，假圈足，制作精细，陶质硬朗。 Fine grey ceramic; red slip; wheel-turned and polished; false circular foot; finely made; robust ceramic.
9	02SLDH T2②：8	鼎口沿残片 Fragment of a *ding* cauldron rim	2002-11	T2②	H: 12.8 M: 21	夹砂红褐陶，方唇，卷沿，侈口，直弧腹。 Reddish-brown ceramic; sand-tempered; square lip; rolled rim; flared mouth; straight, arching belly.
10	02SLDH T2②：9	罐口沿残片 Fragment of a *guan* jar rim	2002-11	T2②	H: 6.2 M: 31.8	夹砂灰陶，轮制磨光，双唇，卷沿，侈口，插肩，肩靠颈部有两道凹弦纹。 Grey ceramic; sand-tempered; wheel-turned and polished; double lip; rolled rim; flared mouth; inset shoulders; portion of shoulders near neck has two intaglio ring patterns.
7	02SLDH T2②：10	豆残件 Fragment of a *dou* pedestal dish	2002-11	T2②	H: 8.8 B: 15	泥质灰陶，轮制磨光，柄上部有一道宽凸棱纹，柄内是一细圆空心。 Fine grey ceramic; wheel-turned and polished; upper portion of handle has single, wide ridge; inside of handle forms thin, round hollow.

续表

图号 Number on Fig. Ⅱ.1.15	标本号 Excavation number	器物名称 Artifact name	出土时间 Excavation date	位置 Location	尺寸（厘米） Size (cm)	特点描述 Description of features
11	02SLDH T2②：11	罐残片 Fragment of a *guan* jar	2002-11	T2②	H: 13 M: 29.6 D: 32.6	夹砂灰陶，轮制，方唇，卷沿，口微敛，小斜肩，口沿内侧有一道凹弦纹，从肩部开始布满绳纹，且绳纹间隔性改变方向。 Grey ceramic; sand-tempered; wheel-turned; square lip; rolled rim; slightly constricted mouth; small inclined shoulder; inside rim has a single intaglio ring pattern; covered in cord patterns from shoulders down; cord patterns change direction at intervals.
8	02SLDH T2③：1	罐口沿残片 Fragment of rim of a *guan* jar	2002-11	T2③	H: 5.4	夹砂灰陶，轮制，双唇，卷沿，侈口，斜肩。 Grey ceramic; sand-tempered; wheel-turned; double lip; rolled rim; flared mouth; inclined shoulder.
13	02SLDH T2③：2	簋圈足 Circular foot of a *gui* tureen	2002-11	T2③	H: 2 B: 13	泥质黑陶，轮制，通体磨光，系假圈足。 Fine black ceramic; wheel-turned; entire item polished; false circular foot attached.

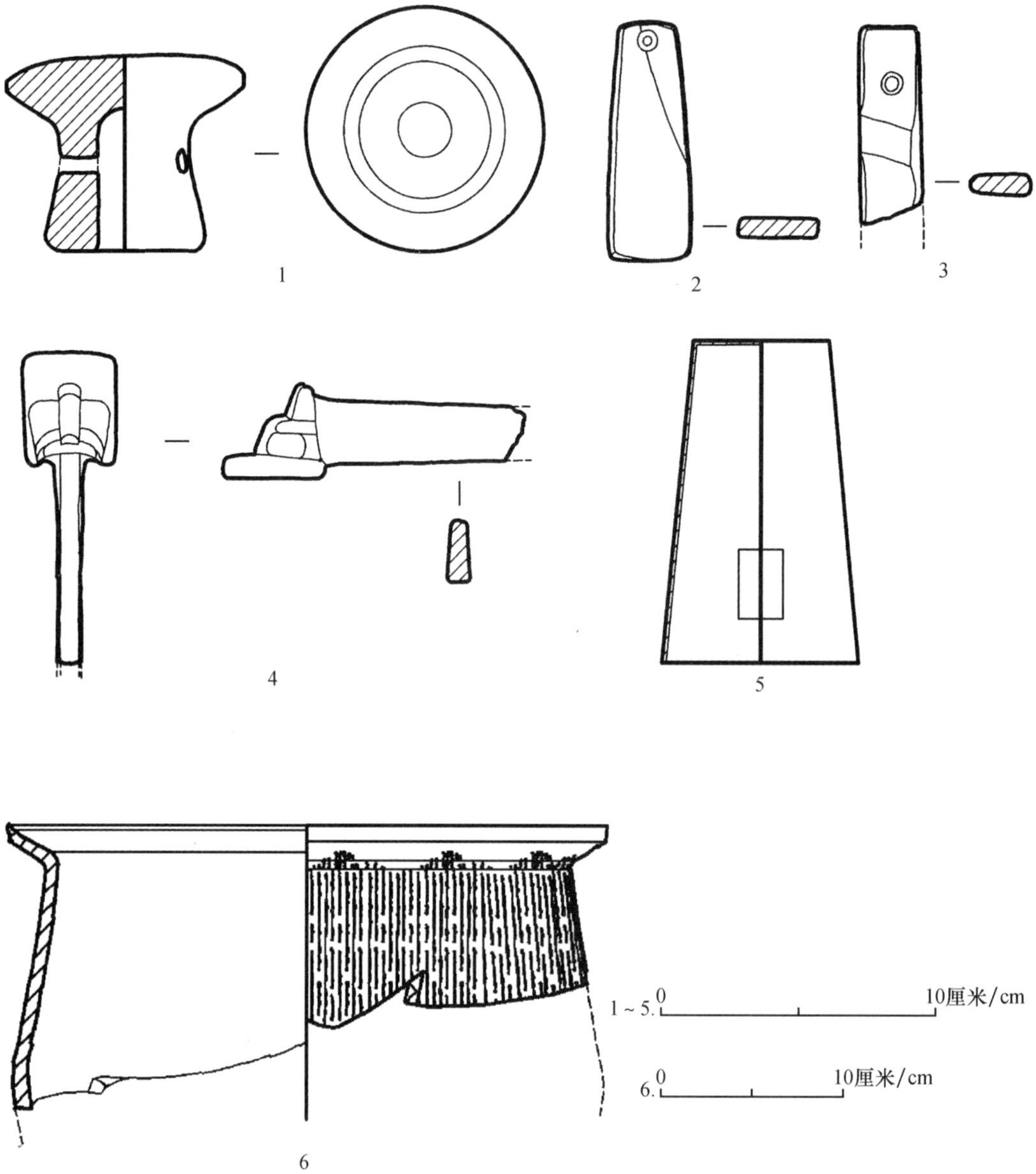

图Ⅱ.1.16　和平村遗址采集器物

Figure Ⅱ.1.16　Objects collected from the Heping Village site.

表Ⅱ.1.14　和平村遗址采集器物登记表

Table Ⅱ.1.14　Objects collected from the Heping Village site

图号 Number on Fig. Ⅱ.1.16	标本号 Excavation number	器物名称 Artifact name	出土时间 Excavation date	位置 Location	尺寸（厘米） Size (cm)	特点描述 Description of features
6	02SLDH 采：1 Coll.：1	绳纹环底罐 Round-bottomed *guan* jar with cord patterns	2002-11	采集 Collected	H: 15.6 M: 33.8	泥质黑皮陶，轮制，双唇，卷沿微内敛，无肩，直斜腹，细绳纹。 Fine black surfaced ceramic; wheel-turned; double lip; rolled rim constricted slightly inward; no shoulder; straight, inclined belly; fine cord impressions.

续表

图号 Number on Fig. Ⅱ.1.16	标本号 Excavation number	器物名称 Artifact name	出土时间 Excavation date	位置 Location	尺寸（厘米） Size (cm)	特点描述 Description of features
5	02SLDH 采：7 Coll.：7	车軎 Axle cap	2002-11	采集 Collected	T: 0.15 H: 11.6 D: 5-7.2	青铜，锈蚀严重。 Bronze; severely corroded.
4	02SLDH 采：6 Coll.：6	车辖 Linchpin	2002-11	采集 Collected	H: 11.2	青铜，锈蚀严重。 Bronze; severely corroded.
1	02SLDH 采：2	陶拍 Ceramic paddle	2002-11	采集 Collected	D: 8.8 H: 7.1	泥质灰陶，两串孔不对称，做工精细完美。 Fine clay grey ceramic; two asymmetrically placed holes; finely and perfectly crafted.
2	02SLDH 采：3	砺石 Grindstone	2002-11	采集 Collected	L: 8.6 W: 3.1 T: 0.7	页岩，青绿色，制作精美。 Shale; green in color; finely made.
3	02SLDH 采：4	砺石 Grindstone	2002-11	采集 Collected	L: 7.1 W: 2.3 T: 0.6	含云母黑色火山岩，已残。 Black volcanic rock containing mica; damaged.

尺寸标志：L=长度；H=高度；W=宽度；D=直径；R=半径；M=口径；B=底径；T=厚度；d=深度；h=孔径。

Measurements: L=length; H=height; W=width; D=diameter; R=radius; M=mouth diameter; B=bottom diameter; T=thickness; d=depth; h=hole diameter.

Chapter 1: The Excavation of the Ruins at Heping Village in the Northern Part of the Inner City of Guicheng in 2002

Zhao Juan   Sun Zhaofeng

Section 1: Introduction

1. Context and Objectives of the Excavation

In late October 2002, remains near the center of the Heping Village (a.k.a. "Dongheping Village"), within the inner city site of Guicheng, became exposed and were badly damaged by erosion from rainfall. In order to protect this important Bronze Age site, a joint archaeological team from the Yantai Municipal Museum and the Longkou Municipal Museum conducted a survey and rescue excavation. This excavation yielded a number of important archaeological materials. Although bronzes and other important relics had frequently been unearthed from the Guicheng city site in the past, most of these were random discoveries made by local villagers when conducting agricultural activities (see Part Ⅱ, Chapter 2 below). Although the scale of this excavation was relatively small, it was the first time that a scientific excavation was actively conducted in Guicheng, lending it special significance. This chapter offers an introduction to the key elements of the results of this excavation.

2. Location and Geographic Environment of the Excavation

The Heping Village site is located within the inner city of the Guicheng old city site. The excavation zone was located atop an earthen terrace approximately 50 m to the east of the open court of assembly of the Heping Village (Fig. Ⅰ.3.1), which belongs to Langao Township, in an area originally taken up by an orchard. The north and west sides of the terrace ended in steep cliffs, while the east and south sides butted up against private residential houses. The terrace constitutes a rare piece of empty space in Heping Village, with a current area of approximately 1,000 sq m and measuring 40 m from east to west and 25 m from north to south. A path runs northwards along the west side of the terrace and then angles to the east, running along a cliff of gradually increasing height; following this path eastwards will lead one to a cliff overlooking a river on the east side of Heping Village.

3. Excavation Process

Formal excavation of the Heping Village site began on October 30 and was completed on November 13, 2002. Two test trenches were dug in the excavation zone, designated "Test Trench 1" (2002TG1) and "Test Trench 2" (2002TG2). TG1 was located in the south portion of the terrace along the edge, while TG2 was located at the north edge (Fig. Ⅱ.1.1). TG1 ran in a precise east-west direction, covering an area of 25 by 1 m^2; TG2 ran in a precise north-south direction, covering an area of 10 by 1 m^2.

Two other test squares were placed in the area of exposed remains located on the northern cliff of the terrace. Since the northern cliff itself formed the north wall of the test squares, they formed irregular rectangles. The square on the west side was designated as "Test Square 1" (2002T1), while that on the east side was designated as "Test Square 2" (2002T2). T1 faced directly northwards and covered an area of 3 by 5 m^2; T2 also faced directly northwards and covered an area of 1.5 by 5 m^2.

In addition, we also conducted salvage excavations among the exposed ruins on the terrace cliff as well as of an old well to the east of the village. The total area excavated was approximately 60 m^2.

Section 2: Stratigraphy

The stratigraphy differed between Test Trenches 1 and 2, so they will be introduced separately. With a section of the northern wall as an example (Figure Ⅱ.1.2), the strata of TG1 can be described as follows:

Stratum 1: Tilled earth, 20-40 cm deep. Composed of loose soil, tan in color. This layer extends throughout the entire trench and contained sherds of modern porcelain, Eastern Zhou-period pottery sherds, etc. Remains opening beneath this layer included one modern pit.

Stratum 2: Disturbed earth, subdivided into two layers designated A and B. Layer A ranged from 0-45 cm thick and was composed of loose, multicolored earth with a tan color base. It contained large numbers of pottery sherds. Layer B ranged from 0-70 cm thick and was composed of slightly hard, multicolored earth with a brownish-black base. Its distribution was intercepted with that of layer A. Layer B also contains large numbers of pottery sherds.

Stratum 3: Cultural deposits, ranging from 20-100 cm thick; it was composed of hard, brownish-black earth interspersed with small white pebbles, chunks of red and burnt earth, and charcoal, etc. This layer contained pottery sherds, animal bones, and other materials. The pottery sherds were generally grey, with a small proportion of red specimens. Vessel types included *guan* jars, *dou* pedestal dishes, *li* tripods, etc., and date approximately to the Warring States period. Remains opening beneath this layer included refuse pits H9, H10, H11, H12, and H13.

Underneath Stratum 3 is virgin soil, yellow and slightly sticky.

With a section of the western wall as example, the stratigraphy of the southern section of trench TG2 is described as follows:

Stratum 1: Tilled soil, ranging from 20-40 cm deep. Consists of relatively loose, tan soil.

Stratum 2: Disturbed earth, 10-50 cm thick. Tan soil, relative firm, containing many pottery sherds.

Stratum 3: Cultural layer, 0-50 cm thick. Grey-brown earth, very hard, containing calcified loess chunks and stones; pottery sherds were found. Identifiable pottery types included *li* tripods, *dou* pedestal dishes, cord-marked *guan* jars, and cord-marked tiles. They date approximately to the Warring States period.

Stratum 4: Cultural layer, ranging from 0-50 cm thick. Greyish-brown earth, relatively firm, containing lots of calcified earth chunks, mixed with ash, white pebbles, charcoals, and chunks of red-burnt earth. Unearthed were pottery sherds and animal bones, etc.; pottery sherds are largely grey with some in red. Identifiable vessel types are *guan* jars, *li* tripods, *dou* pedestal dishes, and *gui* tureens, etc. They date to the late Western Zhou period. A refuse pit opens beneath this layer, but because only a small part of it was exposed, we did not enlarge the test trench in order to excavate it.

Underneath Stratum ④ is virgin soil.

Section 3: Important Remains

Units of remains discovered during this season of excavation included building foundations, refuse pits, and wells. A total of thirteen refuse pits were cleared, all located inside TG1, and were assigned the designations H1-H13. H1-H8 were modern pits and will not be introduced here. Eleven sets of building remains were discovered and were designated F1-F11. All of these were exposed on the cliffs along the west and north sides of the terrace atop which the ruins are located. Those designated F1-F7 were badly damaged and have yet to be cleared. One well, designated J1, was found atop a cliff forming the east bank of the Yaque River to the west of the village (Fig. Ⅱ.1.1).

Below, the features discovered are discussed individually in order of their numerical designations.

1. House Foundations

Four house foundations, assigned the numbers F8-F11, were excavated, all of which were located atop the northern cliff. From above the cliff face, one could see that all had suffered various degrees of damage.

F8: This foundation was located in the northeast corner of the site, with trench TG2 to its east, the village road to its north, and fields to its west and south. F8 was square shape with rounded corners, subterranean, measuring 316 cm long from east to west, with a remaining width ranging from 66-134 cm from north to south and a depth of 44-56 cm. The four walls sloped slightly inward. A post-hole pit measuring 60 cm in diameter was found in the middle. To the east of this was an irregular, greyish-black surface and to the south a round-bottomed pit, perhaps used as a hearth. The floor surface was hardened with limestone paste which was thinner on the east and thicker on the west, varying between 1 and 10 cm. Two distinct deposit strata were found inside the house. The upper stratum was composed of grey earth containing relatively large amounts of sand. The lower stratum was of relatively hard, greyish-brown soil containing large amounts of charcoal ash and grains of red burnt earth; this layer yielded a fairly large number of pottery sherds, as well as a certain number of animal bones. Discernible pottery vessel types included *gui* tureens with a wide-rim, *ding* cauldrons made of reddish-brown pottery tempered with sand, *guan* jars, *dou* pedestal dishes, etc. The bottom of the posthole was not level, containing a small pit in the western part, but the wall was smooth, measuring 18 cm deep. The deposit in the post-hole was composed of comparatively hard, greyish-brown soil containing stones, pottery fragments, chunks of red burnt earth, etc. Since the northern half of this house had been destroyed, the details of the internal structure of the building remain unclear. Based on the pottery sherds it yielded, this house can be dated to the mid to late Western Zhou period (Fig. Ⅱ.1.4).

F9: Opens beneath stratum 3 and broke into stratum 4 and F11. Its northern half had been destroyed by the reclamation of earth by farmers, and its southern and western portions were broken into by a small pit, such that only a small section of its eastern wall remained. The fill in the pit was composed of grayish-brown soil containing relatively large amounts of fine sand and granules of burnt earth; the upper level of the accumulation was relatively loose. Based on a survey of the pottery sherds recovered from it, the house foundation can be dated approximately to the early Spring and Autumn period.

F10: Located on the northern cliff of the terrace. Its surface formed a circular shape with steps on the east side (these were not excavated). The opening of the house foundation was slightly wider than the floor, creating an open chamber. The interior contained a whitish hardened floor made of lime paste mixed with vegetal ash, dark green metamorphic rock pieces, and loess. There was a pillar at the center of the chamber. Connecting with the pillar in both north and south directions was a short wall that divided the room into eastern and western sections. The whitish surface of the eastern portion was relatively coarse and contained accumulations of vegetal ash. A feral pig skull and other animal bones were discovered, indicating that this may have been a kitchen area. The western portion of the chamber was built in a relatively level fashion atop virgin soil. Vegetal ash was scattered on top, and a second layer surface composed of lime paste was laid out, fairly neatly applied. The people of the time may have used this area as a living space.

The strata in F10 consisted of ten separate layers. The first layer was modern, while the second layer and below belonged to the building remains. The upper portion of the strata of the building remains was composed of hard, tightly packed tan earth, while the accumulation at the bottom of the chamber consisted of large volumes of vegetal ash. This yielded a few pottery sherds, from which identifiable vessel types included *li* tripods with cord patterns, *hu* bottles, *guan* jars, intact spinning whorls, etc. The bottom contained a rectangular pit tomb with vertical shaft, oriented east-west. The collapse of the coffins in this tomb had caused the accumulation within the tomb chamber to tilt towards the east. Based on the pottery sherds recovered, this house foundation can be dated approximately to the early Spring and Autumn period. The northern wall of the remains had been destroyed, and its southern wall lay beneath a brick wall constructed by local residents and was therefore not excavated. The tomb beneath the house was left unexcavated for the same reason. As surveyed from the top of the cliff, the tomb measured 395 cm long. An axle cover and linchpin unearthed from this tomb were collected from a local household (designations: *cai*. 6 and *cai*. 7). (Fig. Ⅱ.1.5: F10 in cross-sectional view)

F11: Opened beneath stratum 3, broke into stratum 4, and was broken into by F9. Since the floor level of F9 was higher than F11, however, F9 damaged only the upper portion of the eastern wall of F11. Based on the state of the extant remains, F11 was originally a semi-subterranean square. The bottom portion consisted of a hard, multicolored surface mixing dark green stone powders, white-clay paste, charcoal ash, granules of burnt earth, and sand. This surface was thicker on the west, measuring 3 cm, than on the east, measuring 2 cm. The west wall of the house foundation measured 73 cm high, while the remaining portion of the east wall (and the east section of the south wall) was 40 cm high. The remaining portion of the south wall was 210 cm long; the remaining portion of the west wall was 160 cm long. The floor of the house lay 190 cm below ground level. There was a gap in the precise center of the south wall, with a round gateway on the outside measuring 54 cm in diameter. Outside the south wall was a round hole measuring 6.5 cm in diameter and 12 cm deep; this may have been a post-hole. The fill was composed of brownish-black soil containing granules of black charcoal. Horse teeth and a few pottery sherds were unearthed from the remains. Based on the latter, the house can be dated approximately to the mid to late Western Zhou period (Fig. Ⅱ.1.6).

2. Refuse Pits

Five refuse pits, numbered H9-H13, will be introduced here. Since the area excavated was relatively limited, most of the refuse pits were not seen in their entirety, with the exception of the relatively complete H9. Based on the visible portions, however, they were mostly round in shape.

H9: Located 8.9 m from the west wall of TG1 and opened beneath stratum 3. Its surface was basically round, and its straight walls sloped inward toward the relatively flat bottom. The opening of the pit lay 100 cm beneath ground level and measured 172 cm in diameter; the pit itself was 80 cm deep. The deposit in the pit was composed of relatively loose, black soil containing large numbers of pottery sherds. The floor of H9 in turn had a small, round pit, measuring 62 cm in diameter and 50 cm deep, which opened into the floor of H9; this pit was cylindrical, with straight walls and an uneven floor. The fill soil was yellowish-brown in color and slightly sticky. Items in pit H9 included stones, pottery sherds, and deer antlers. The latter had been cut; the portions cut away were likely used to make tools. Based on the pottery sherds unearthed there, this refuse pit can be dated approximately to the mid to late Western Zhou period.

H10: Located in the western part of TG1 and opened beneath stratum 3. Its surface was basically round. It had a straight side on the east and an arching side on the west; the mouth was constricted, and the floor was uneven. The opening of the pit was 85 cm below ground level and measured 240 cm in diameter; the pit itself was 60 cm deep. The upper layer of the fill was composed of grayish-brown earth measuring ca. 30 cm thick and containing a relatively large number of pottery sherds. The middle layer was composed of black earth measuring ca. 15 cm thick; the lower layer was composed of grey earth measuring ca. 10-20 cm thick. Based on the pottery sherds unearthed there, this refuse pit can be dated approximately to the Warring States period.

H11: Located in the eastern part of TG1 and opened beneath stratum 3. Its surface was basically round in shape. The pit itself was cylindrical, with straight walls and a level bottom. The deposit consisted entirely of greyish-brown earth containing large chunks of green stone powder, chunks of red burnt earth, and vegetal ash, etc. The soil of the fill was relatively loose and contained large numbers of pottery sherds. Judging from these, the pit can be dated approximately to the late Spring and Autumn period.

H12: Located in the middle section of TG1 and opened beneath stratum 3. It was irregular in shape, with a relatively straight east wall, a curved west wall, and an uneven floor that was higher on the west side and lower on the east side. The opening of the pit lay 60 cm below ground level and measured 210 cm in diameter, while the pit itself was approximately 155 cm deep. The fill was composed of comparatively loose, greyish-brown earth containing pottery sherds, animal bones, etc. Judging from the pottery sherds found there, this refuse pit can be dated approximately to the late Western Zhou period.

H13: Located in the eastern part of TG1 and opened beneath stratum 3. Its surface was basically round. The opening of the pit lay 95 cm below ground level and measured 220 cm in diameter, the pit itself was 60 cm deep. The fill was composed of relatively hard, greyish-brown earth containing pottery sherds, animal bones, etc. Judging from the pottery sherds unearthed there, this refuse pit can be dated approximately to the late Western Zhou period.

3. Well

The single well, designated J1, was located on a cliff along the east bank of the Yaque River, to the east of the village. "In 1969 villagers from Dongjiacun, while preparing fields atop an earthen terrace near the riverbank to the southeast of the village, unearthed four bronzes" (Li Buqing and Lin Xianting 1991, 910-918). J1 was located on the eastern edge of just this terrace. Its surface was nearly oval; the east side was relatively straight, while the western part had already been destroyed in the process of digging earth for firing in kilns. The well measured 180 cm long and 425 cm deep. The fill inside the well was divided into four strata.

Stratum ①, composed of yellow earth, was 160 cm thick; the soil of this layer was both fine and hard and contained no other materials. Stratum ②, a mixed layer, was 200 cm thick; it consisted chiefly of vegetal ash and contained obvious layers. Toward the bottom of this stratum was a layer of yellowish-white stove ash containing numerous animal bones and pottery sherds. Discernible vessel types included *dou* pedestal dishes, *pen* basins, and large *guan* jars with knot patterns on their shoulders, probably of Spring and Autumn date. This was a layer of refuse deposited after the well was abandoned. Stratum ③ was a sticky soil layer composed of fine clay measuring 40 cm thick infiltrated by vegetal ash; its relatively loose soil was light grey in color. The layer yielded pottery sherds, but relatively few of these could be identified with particular vessel types. This was the first layer of natural accumulation formed after the well was abandoned and before it began to be used as a refuse pit. Stratum ④ was a layer of coarse sand, greyish-green in color, measuring 25 cm thick. It was pressed closely against the floor of the well and contained no other materials. This was probably the layer of sediment formed while the well was in use.

Virgin soil was below the bottom of the well. Judging from the pottery sherds unearthed from the well, it can safely be dated to the Spring and Autumn period.

Section 4: Relics Unearthed

The relics unearthed during this excavation consisted mainly of pottery, with a few items of bone and horn. Most of the pottery vessels were made of fine clay, generally either grey or black in color. Ceramics tempered with sand were chiefly reddish-brown in color, a small number containing mica and/or talc. Few vessel shapes could be restored, but those that could be distinguished included *ding* cauldrons, *li* tripods, *gui* tureens, *dou* pedestal dishes, *guan* jars, *pen* basins, etc. Most numerous of these were *li* tripods, *gui* tureens, *dou* pedestal dishes, *guan* jars, and *ding* cauldrons. Most of the pottery was undecorated, but decorations observed included cord marks, intaglio ring patterns, raised flanges, polished surfaces, etc. A detailed introduction to the relics found appears in the tabulated lists before the chapter (Figs. Ⅱ.1.7- Ⅱ.1.16; Tables Ⅱ.1.1- Ⅱ.1.14; Pls. 69-71).

Section 5: Conclusion

This season of excavation at the Heping Village site yielded numerous ceramic vessels, providing us with first-hand materials for periodization. A *weng* urn unearthed from the Heping Village site (TG1 ∶ 9) was similar to examples recovered from a well of Eastern Zhou date at Pozicun, Qixia City, Shandong (Yantai shi wenguanhui 2006: 35-41), and a *dou* pedestal dish (J1 ∶ 13) resembled examples unearthed from a Spring and Autumn-period tomb at Liugezhuang, Penglai City, Shandong (Yantai shi wenguanhui 1990: 805-810). Judging from the pottery recovered, the site was mainly formed during the Eastern Zhou period.

The Guicheng city site, the former capital of the state of Lai, was the most important pre-Qin city on the Jiaodong Peninsula. Previous archaeological discoveries made there include a city wall of massive scale and tombs yielding precious bronzes, all-important relics of the Western and Eastern Zhou periods. However, the remains of commoners, dwellings within the site had not undergone archaeological work before. This test excavation of the Heping Village site filled that gap, providing us with a more comprehensive understanding of the nature of the Guicheng site.

Though the area covered by the test excavation was not large, the work was conducted in strict accordance with the *Work Regulations for Field Archaeology* (1984). The abundant relics uncovered from the site exhibit chronological and regional characteristics, and are of great benefit to the study of Zhou dynasty archaeology of the Jiaodong region. Due to the limited area of the excavation, the phenomena observed within the exploratory trenches were somewhat incomplete, making it difficult to draw comprehensive information from them. Numerous pottery sherds were unearthed, but few of the original vessel shapes could be restored, thus limiting the precise understanding of the vessels themselves, as of the archaeological information they convey.

The primary participants in the excavation included: Lin Xianting, Wang Fuqiang, Yan Yong, Yu Xiaoli, Wang Jinding, and Zhao Juan, from the Yantai Museum; Lu Yuanchen, from the Longkou

Municipal Museum; and others. Lin Xianting directed the excavation. Photography was done by Lin Xianting and Zhao Juan; drawings were provided by Xiao Yu. Later analysis of data was performed by Zhao Juan, Xiao Jing, Zhang Wenming, and others.

References

Li, Buqing 李步青 and Lin Xianding 林仙庭, 1991. "Shandong Huangxian Guicheng yizhi de diaocha yu fajue" 山东黄县归城遗址的调查与发掘 (Survey and excavation of the Guicheng site at Huang County, Shandong), *Kaogu* 考古, 10: 910-918.

Yantai shi wenguanhui and Qixia shi wenguanchu, 2006. "Shandong Qixia shi Zhailizhen Pozicun Dong Zhou he Tang dai shuijing qingli jianbao" 山东栖霞市寨里镇泊子村东周和唐代水井清理简报 (Preliminary Report on the Clearing of Wells of Eastern Zhou and Tang Date at Pozi Village, Zhaili Township, Qixia City, Shandong), *Kaogu* 5: 35-41.

Yantai shi wenguanhui, 1990. "Shandong Penglai xian Liugezhuang muqun fajue jianbao" 山东蓬莱县柳格庄墓群发掘简报 (A brief report of the excavation of the cemetery at Liugezhuang, Penglai County, Shandong), *Kaogu* 9: 805-810.

(Translated by Paul Nicholas Vogt)

第二章　归城及周边区域青铜器的考古发现与研究综述

王富强　闫旭东　刁　鹏

第一节　引　　言

归城遗址位于老黄县（今龙口市）南6千米，南依莱山，东、西为低丘环绕。鸦鹊河（又称莱阴河）于内城东侧自南向北穿过入海。归城遗址由内城和外城组成：内城坐落于归城姜家村（又称“归姜村”）和和平村（又称“东和平村”），面积为22.5万平方米；外城环绕于东、南、西、北的丘陵上，面积约8平方千米。它是目前胶东地区保留较完整的周代城址。自二十世纪初以来，归城内的各自然村便陆续出土了两周时期的遗物，多为村民生活和生产活动中意外发现。由于许多重要的考古信息并不完整，这给我们全面认识这些出土遗物带来了一定的困难。但缘于出土过一定数量的有铭青铜器，归城遗址曾引起了国内外学者的关注和研究。

众所周知，胶东地区进入周代以后呈现出十分复杂的历史演变态势：首先是西周时期周文化开始侵入胶东地区，在半岛的西部建立了若干个桥头堡，包括莱州的黑羊山遗址、莱阳前河前遗址、招远曲成遗址、黄县归城遗址和蓬莱村里集遗址等。这大约发生在西周中期左右。这些区域经历了周文化对地方文化的改造之后，周文化继续向东拓展，出现了以周文化为主、两种文化并存的考古现象。到了东周时期，在齐国称霸的背景下，胶东地区和齐文化融合的节奏进一步加快；特别是到了战国时期整个半岛基本被“齐文化化”。在这一历史进程中，各式各样的陶器当然是我们准确把握这一历史大势的主要依据。但是，那些华美的青铜器更是我们认识胶东地区遗址、墓葬的性质和等级的重要标尺。

二十世纪五六十年代，王献唐（王献唐 1983：1～159）等先生曾对归城出土的有铭文铜器进行了考据；到八十年代，齐文涛（齐文涛 1972：3～18）、李学勤（李学勤 1983：18～22）、王恩田（王恩田 1984：71～76）、王锡平（王锡平，孙敬明 1984：77～79）、孙敬明（孙敬明 1988：163～186）、李步青（李步青，王锡平 1992：64～84）、林仙庭（林仙庭 1992：267～275）等先生均对这些铜器进行了分析和论证。这些成果对归城乃至整个胶东地区周代文化内涵和古国古代史的研究起到了很大的推动作用。本章则在前人研究的基础上，以近年来烟台市博物馆考古调查和发掘的资料为依据，对历年来归城及其周边区域考古发现的墓地和青铜器进行全面梳理和总结。

第二节　归城及周边区域墓地的分布和青铜器出土情况

归城及周边区域发现青铜器的历史大约可追溯到清末光绪年间。其后，断断续续有村民在生产活动中发现铜器出土，特别是二十世纪五六十年代有较多青铜铭器出土，从而引起了学界的重视和讨论。但是，这些均应被视为采集所得遗物。对已经被发现的墓葬进行科学清理的则是七十至八十年代和二十一世纪初做的一些考古工作；而对归城遗址进行科学发掘的只有2002年在内城的清理和试掘（见下编第一章）。

作为胶东地区周代重要的中心聚落，许多青铜重器发现于归城城内和周边区域，且多为墓葬的随葬品。从考古调查和文物普查的资料看，内城大约有和平村和归姜村东北部，外城有归姜村、南埠村、董家村、曹家村、小刘家村、大于家村等处墓地，合计有8处（地图Ⅱ.2.1）。城外则有东韩家村、东营周家村、东营曹家村、集前赵家村、庄头村、鲁家沟村、单家庙村、东梧桐村、张郑村、小赵家村、海徐村、渤海姚家村、欧头于家村等，合计15处左右（地图Ⅱ.2.2）。这些墓地多为贵族墓地，其中和平、南埠、曹家、小刘家、大于家、东韩家、东营周家、庄头、集前赵家、鲁家沟、海徐等村庄均出土过带铭文的重要青铜器，它们现分藏于国家博物馆、山东省博物馆、烟台市博物馆和龙口市博物馆（表Ⅱ.4.1）。

从这个小区域来看，这些铜器的出土地点或墓地位于黄水河和界河（上游马南河）之间的滨海地带。北部的滨海平原是宜居之地，被誉为“胶东粮仓”。同时它又是富庶的胶东半岛北岸东西通联的要冲，而南部又有群山环抱，更具有易守难攻的战略地位。归城及其周边墓地主要分布在南部山前丘陵高地和山谷盆地，处于攻防兼备地带。而北部平原则是其稼穑的平畴沃野，可提供充足的食物资源。这大致反映了归城统治者的治国方略，由此也可看出以归城为中心的一个聚落群的基本形态。

第三节　归城及周边区域墓地和青铜器的重要发现

如前文所述，归城及周边区域墓地和青铜器的发现比较丰富，是胶东地区同时期最为集中的区域，对研究胶东地区周代文化的演变和古代国家的形成历史具有十分重要的学术价值。为此，我们将其重要发现分城内和城外两个区域介绍如下。

一、归城城内墓地和青铜器的重要发现

归城城内主要包括和平村、曹家村、南埠村、小刘家村和董家村等墓地，出土了较多有铭文的青铜重器，但多为群众生产活动挖出，三次经清理的墓葬也遭严重破坏。

1．和平村发现的墓葬和铜器

1973年烟台地区文管会在和平村中西部清理了一座墓葬和一个车马坑。墓葬编号为M2，为竖穴土坑墓。其西部遭轻微破坏，东西长约2.5米、南北宽1.77米、深2.27米，北、西、南三面有熟土二层台，宽度在7～15厘米。葬具为单棺，东西长 2 米、南北宽0.65米，棺东有头箱。墓向100°。人骨为仰身直肢，头向东，双臂合交于腹前，身高约1.55米。头箱内随葬8件陶器，分别为2件素面鬲、2件绳纹鬲、2件簋、1件甗、1件盔（图Ⅱ.2.1：1～5）（表Ⅱ.2.1），时代为西周中期。

车马坑位于M2的北部，靠近村民的房舍，被村民生产扰乱严重，整个车马坑形态不完整，从层位看晚于M2。坑内除马肋骨在原始位置外，马头骨、肢骨及青铜车马器等分布凌乱，马肋骨下可见一层朱红髹漆。出土车马器有马衔、马镳、车辖以及铜环、铜管等（图Ⅱ.2.1：6～12），时代为春秋时期。此坑应为一大墓的车马坑，因压在民房下未能清理（李步青，林仙庭 1991a：912～914）。

另外，烟台市博物馆历年从和平村村民手中征集来的重要青铜器有鼎、鬲、甗（鬲部）、壶、盒、钠、甬钟、车軎等（表Ⅱ.2.2；图版72～79），其他如剑、戈、镞（图Ⅱ.2.2）更有较多发现不一一列举。

2．曹家村发现的墓葬和铜器

曹家村发现的墓葬位于曹家村南300米的台地上，1965年修水库挖土筑坝时发现并破坏的。有文章将这批铜器定为归姜村，经调查核定为曹家村南。清理时，仅余墓之东部。墓底南北4.2米，东西残长1米。据调查，墓原长5米左右，深3米，墓向为东西向。墓底有一层朱彩，估计为棺椁的髹漆。墓西部曾出土众多陶器，大部分被破坏散失，仅余一陶罐（M1：9）。墓东部出土铜器8件（图Ⅱ.2.3：1～8；图版80～87）。还有一玉戈，应是棺内随葬品（表Ⅱ.2.3）。据出土的朽木和一些铜器外壁的人字形席纹看，该墓以苇席敛葬，规格较高。这批铜器器形、装饰风格都很典型，特别是壶、尊、卣的形态都非常有时代特点，只流行于西周中期偏早的一段时间。另外，共出的陶罐小口圆肩，形态也较早（李步青，林仙庭 1991：912～914）。因此，我们认为这群铜器和陶器的时代为西周中期早段。

3．董家村发现的铜器

1969年，董家村农民在村东南临近河岸的土台上整地，挖出铜器9件，甗2、盘1、鼎1、卮1、戈1、镞3（图Ⅱ.2.4：1～6；图版88～92）；其中甗、盘同出，这应是墓葬随葬品（表Ⅱ.2.4）。这几件铜器中，圆甗的形制在这一时期（西周晚期）少见。鼎上的回首夔龙纹按其在西周中心地区的流行时代应在西周中期。但是鼎的造型为半球形腹，马蹄足，盘的造型为圈足下有三小足，时代无疑在西周晚期甚或更晚。因此，我们定这组铜器的时代为西周晚期至春秋初年（李步青，林仙庭 1991：915）。

4．南埠村发现的铜器

1951年南埠村村民在村东平整土地时挖出铜器共十件，后收公。八件铜器分别为鼎1、鬲1、盨4、盘1、匜1（表Ⅱ.2.5）（图Ⅱ.2.5：1～6；图版93～95）；另外还有青岛博物馆藏的甗（甑部）和小壶，时代为春秋时期。王献唐先生在《黄县㠱器》一书中对其进行了详细分析和考据（王献唐 1960）。王恩田、孙敬明等先生也对其进行过讨论（王恩田 1984；孙敬明 1988）。这批铜器中盨铭："㠱白（伯）子庭父作其延（征）盨，其陰其陽，以延（征）以行。割（匄）瞏（眉）壽無疆，慶其以臧"（集成04442）；盘铭："㠱伯庭父媵姜無□般（盤）"（集成10081）；匜铭："㠱伯庭父媵姜無□匜"（集成10211）。由于这组铜器为"㠱伯（子）庭父"或"㠱伯庭父"所作，故过去王献唐先生曾以此为据，推测归城为㠱国都城，而莱国都城则另有他处（王献唐 1983：144）。实际上，盘、匜显然为㠱伯嫁女的媵器，而四件盨实为他继位前所作，和专门作的这套媵器一起陪嫁给了女儿。它们在归城的出土正说明归城不是㠱国都城，而是㠱与归城主人通婚的证据（李步青，林仙庭 1991：912～914）。

5．小刘庄村发现的铜器

1969年，小刘庄村民在生产活动中挖出一组铜器，有卣、尊、卣盖和觯四件铜器（图Ⅱ.2.6：1～4；图版96、97）。其中卣、尊、卣盖铸有铭文，这就是启尊、启卣组群（表Ⅱ.2.6）。时代为西周中期早段。齐文涛等先生进行过分析和研究（齐文涛 1972：5～7）。从铭文内容讲它们仍然是目前为止山东地区发现的最重要的一组青铜器。启卣铭："王出獸（狩）南山寇遭山谷，至于上侯滰川上。啓從征，堇（謹）不夒（擾），乍（作）且丁寶旅障（尊）彝，用匄魯福，用夙夜事。戉箙"（集成5410）。启尊铭："啓從王南征逌山谷，在洀水上。啓乍（作）且丁旅寶彝。戉箙"（集成5983）。两篇铭文记载的明显是同一次战役中的两个环节，在不同地点。所征伐的对象"遭山谷"或"逌山谷"虽写法不同，应为同人。

过去学者间关于启卣、启尊有一些误解。因为它们提到南征，遂有学者将它们与昭王南征联系起来，器的时代也就被定在昭王时期（唐兰 1995：277～278）。现在我们有关西周青铜器的年代研究已经细化，根据启卣、启尊的器形，它们无疑属于西周中期偏早时期铸造。而周王南征可有多次，并不一定都与昭王有关，这是我们首先要订正的。重要的是这里所讲的事件、地点也见于西周中心地区的其他铜器；因此它们虽然出土于胶东半岛，其铭文内容显然是和周王室有关的。

二、归城城外墓地和铜器的重要发现

1. 韩栾村的铜器发现

1964年在归城西南韩栾村村民挖出一件鼎：方唇，折沿，直口，立耳外撇；腹微鼓，分裆，三柱足。腹饰云雷地饕餮纹，足饰云纹。口径17.6、高21.2厘米。腹壁铸一行六字“句监作宝尊”（图Ⅱ.2.7；图版98）。时代为西周早期（李步青，林仙庭 1991b：84～85）。

2. 鲁家沟的铜器发现

据王道新《黄县志稿》〈金石目〉记载：“光绪二十二年春，城东南鲁家沟田中出古铜器有十”（王道新 1934，14：806），包括：钟3、鼎2（1碎）、壶1（碎）、盘1、甗1、盉1、觯1。鼎、甗、盉、觯四器有铭，此即学界所说的“莱（或郲）伯鼎”铜器组群。鼎铭曰：“莱白（伯）作旅鼎”；盉铭：“作宗尊，厥子孫永寳用”；觯铭：“公賞貝，朿用作父辛于彝”。甗上有较长铭文，这件甗现藏于日本京都的泉屋博古馆（住友吉左卫门 1918，1：12）（图Ⅱ.2.8；图版99）：

“隹（唯）六月既死霸丙寅，師雝（雍）父戍，才（在）古自（師），遹從。師雝（雍）父肩史遹事（使）于𧻚（胡）侯，侯蔑遹曆，易（賜）遹金。用乍（作）旅獻（甗）”（集成948）。

光绪二十二年春，与遹甗同出于鲁家沟的还有㝬鼎，现藏台北中央研究院历史语言研究所（图版100）。

1962年11月，烟台市博物馆由蓬莱县和黄县调拨一批铜器。因两县合并，多原存黄县，可能与归城有关，更可能是丁氏收藏之物。这批铜器包括“父丙”鬲、“父癸”鼎、“伯荀父”盨、“父癸”簋等。因出土地点不详或为赝品，不予描述。

另外，庄头、东营周家、集前赵家、东梧桐等出土铜器在另章有描述（见下编第三章）。

第四节　归城及周边区域墓地和青铜器的研究

归城及周边区域发现的铜器因多为采集遗物，所以已往讨论和研究最多的为金文的考据和古国史等方面的内容。以聚落为中心的区域考古调查过去虽然也做了一些工作，取得了一些基本认识，但工作仍显单薄。总体上看，目前的考古研究成果主要有以下几个方面。

1. 归城的内城外郭

早在1973年烟台地区文管会对归城城址进行了调查和勘探，基本摸清了内城外埠的形状、规模和走向。2007～2009年中国社会科学院考古研究所、哥伦比亚大学东亚语言与文化系、山东省文物考古研究所再次对归城城址进行了详细的区域调查和勘探，丰富了以往的考古收获，新发现了壕、道路、城门和建筑基址，并确定了内城东城墙的位置、走向和外城的形状、走向和规模等（中美联合归城考古队 2011：30～39）。可以说，对于归城的文化内涵、聚落形态和演变又有了新的收获和认识。这为进一步了解归城的文化内涵、聚落形态和演变打下了坚实的科学基础。

2．归城及周边区遗址和墓葬的时代

从上述发现来看，这些墓地（墓葬）和青铜器的时代主要是西周中期到春秋时期。无论是采集还是发掘清理出的遗物西周中期到春秋时期占大宗，战国时期也占有一定比例。从2002年的抢救性发掘的资料看（见下编第一章），内城战国时期的遗存仍十分丰富，因此归城在战国时期仍然沿用。至于西周早期的遗存，目前来看资料还比较单薄。尽管个别遗迹和遗物有早期的特点，均在西周中期左右，部分断代已在前文中予以更正。关于归城西周早期遗存是否存在是一个相当重要的问题，这有可能彻底改变我们以往对归城历史和归城的国别族属等的认识，我们必须慎重。如果在归城发现了西周早期或更早的地层和遗存，那我们对归城的认识必将是重大的突破。

3．国别族属

归城的主人是谁？其渊源在哪里？都有哪些古国古族曾与归城的统治者发生过关系？这是目前所有讨论和研究中最受关注的问题。国别族属主要从发现的青铜铭文和相关史学记录来展开论析的。目前在归城及周边区域发现的青铜铭器中，可确定的古国古族有㠱、己（纪）、莱或瓠、内（芮）、朐等。其中芮、句、己等似没有太大争议，应该是芮、朐、己（纪）等古国或古族的遗物，因嫁娶、馈赠、战争、迁徙等原因到了胶东地区。然而，己、㠱、莱等的认定却存在较大的分歧，但不外乎以下几点认识：

（1）“㠱非杞亦非纪”。王献唐先生从㠱、杞、纪等国的考古发现和史学记录等方面进行了详细的考据，提出了三个古国古族不同的渊源和演变。他并推测㠱国在山东潍坊东南、莒县北部的箕山一带（王献唐 1983：1～159）。这是归城出土铜器研究的一部重要著作。

（2）纪、㠱、莱为一国。王恩田先生曾两论“纪、㠱、莱为一国说”，并从纪、㠱、莱现存的遗址和铜器铭文及其族属渊源论析了三者为一国的依据和合理性。当然也有学者赞同㠱、纪为一国，莱为一国。

（3）㠱族的北迁和南下说。孙敬明先生依据考古发现，稽考古籍，以更广的视野考察了河南、北京、辽宁和山东等地发现的㠱器和㠱器组群。他认为㠱在商时封地位于商王畿服内的淇水流域；周初一支㠱族北迁至匽（燕）地及大凌河流域，西周中晚期又一支㠱族自匽地和大凌河流域南下至山东莱地，并在迁徙中与匽、孤竹、齐、莱、纪等发生不同的关系。尤其是㠱、孤竹、纪、莱等国，面对齐、匽等大国的侵迫，可能结成联盟，与之抗衡（孙敬明 1988：163～186）。

（4）归城的统治者。关于归城的主人目前主要有两种推测，一种认为是莱国的君主，一种认为是瓠（华）国的领主，所依据的均为鲁家沟出土的铭器“莱（瓠）伯鼎”，且以第一种观点占主流。至于其他铜器，如启尊、启卣等虽反映了一些重大历史事件，多有论述，但对探索归城的历史没有太大帮助，不再梳理。

综上，归城和周边区域发现的墓地（墓葬）及其出土的青铜器是我们认识其文化内涵和聚落形态的重要资料，更是研究山东古国史的科学依据。然而，面对周代胶东乃至中国纷然杂陈的古国关系，它们仍然是沧海一粟。如果我们从区域文化的共性来讲，单就淄博以东的考古发现而言，这个区域确实是珍珠门文化的分布范围，或者说是大“莱”文化区。从这个意义上讲，它们为同一个东方集团还是成立的。然则在这个大“莱”区内又有多少古国古族还要细思量。我们可以认为纪的一支东迁胶东，但我们又不能因同一墓葬出土有“己”、“曩”铭器而遽下结论其为一国或一族。同样，我们仅以“莱（瓠）伯鼎”来判定归城的主人，资料还显太单薄；为何归城内众多铭器中没有相同的发现呢？很显然，莱文化区内包括本地的、东迁的等许多古国古族，而且在时代的变迁中又有不同的演变形态。这都需要更多的资料加以推衍。特别是我们应该注意准确释读中原王朝或其他诸侯国对莱的称谓是泛指还是特称，也就是所谓的“大莱”和“小莱”。诸如此类，我还需要更多的考古发现给予科学的探索和论证。

参考文献

李步青，林仙庭，1991a：山东黄县归城遗址的调查与发掘. 考古，10：910-918.

李步青，林仙庭，1991b：山东省龙口市出土西周铜鼎. 文物，5：84-85.

李步青，王锡平，1992：建国以来烟台地区出土商周铭文铜器概述. 古文字研究，18：66-84.

李学勤，1983：试论山东新出土青铜器的意义. 文物，12：18-22.

林仙庭，1992：胶东青铜文化初探，纪念山东大学考古专业创建20周年文集. 济南：山东大学出版社. 267-275.

齐文涛，1972：概述近年来山东出土的商周青铜器. 文物，5：3-16.

孙敬明，1988：考古发现与曩史寻踪. 东夷古国史研究，10：163-186.

唐兰，1995：论周昭王时代的青铜器铭刻，唐兰先生金文论集. 北京：紫禁城出版社. 236-333.

王道新，1934：黄县志稿. 济南：山东省博物馆藏.

王恩田，1984：纪、曩、莱为一国说. 齐鲁学刊，1：71-76.

王锡平，孙敬明，1984：莱国彝铭试释及论有关问题. 东岳论丛，1：77-79.

王献唐，1960：黄县曩器. 济南：齐鲁书社.

王献唐，1983：山东古国考. 济南：齐鲁书社. 3-224.

中美联合归城考古队，2011：山东龙口市归城两周城址调查简报. 考古，3：30-39.

住友吉左卫门，滨田青陵，原田淑人，1918：泉屋清赏（第一集）. 东京：国华社.

简称：

集成：中国社会科学院考古研究所：殷周金文集成（18卷）. 北京：中华书局，1984-1994.

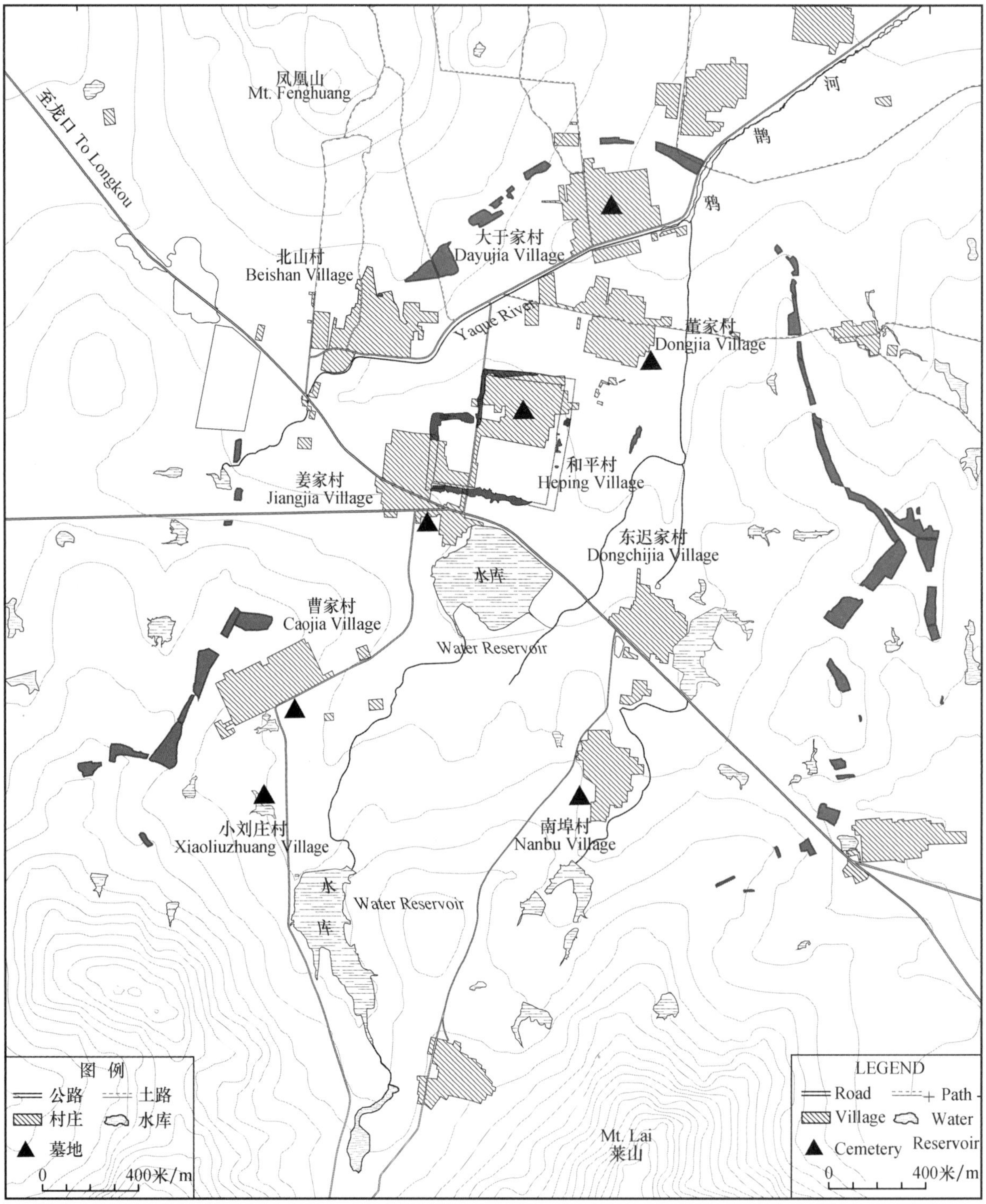

地图Ⅱ.2.1　归城内墓地分布图

Map Ⅱ.2.1　Distribution of cemeteries in Guicheng.

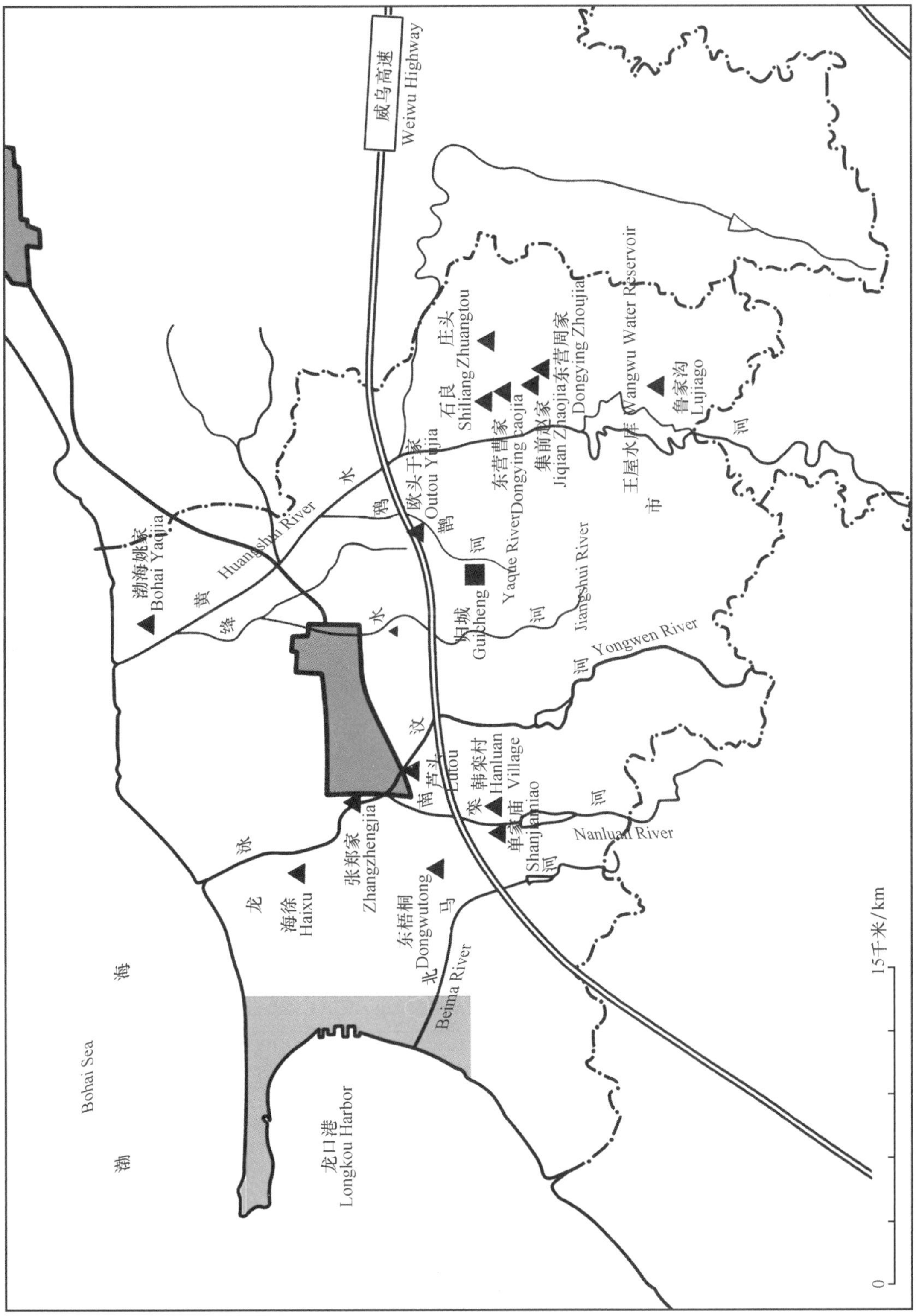

地图Ⅱ.2.2　归城及其附近地区墓地及其遗址分布图

Map Ⅱ.2.2　The distribution of cemeteries and sites in Guicheng and its surroundings.

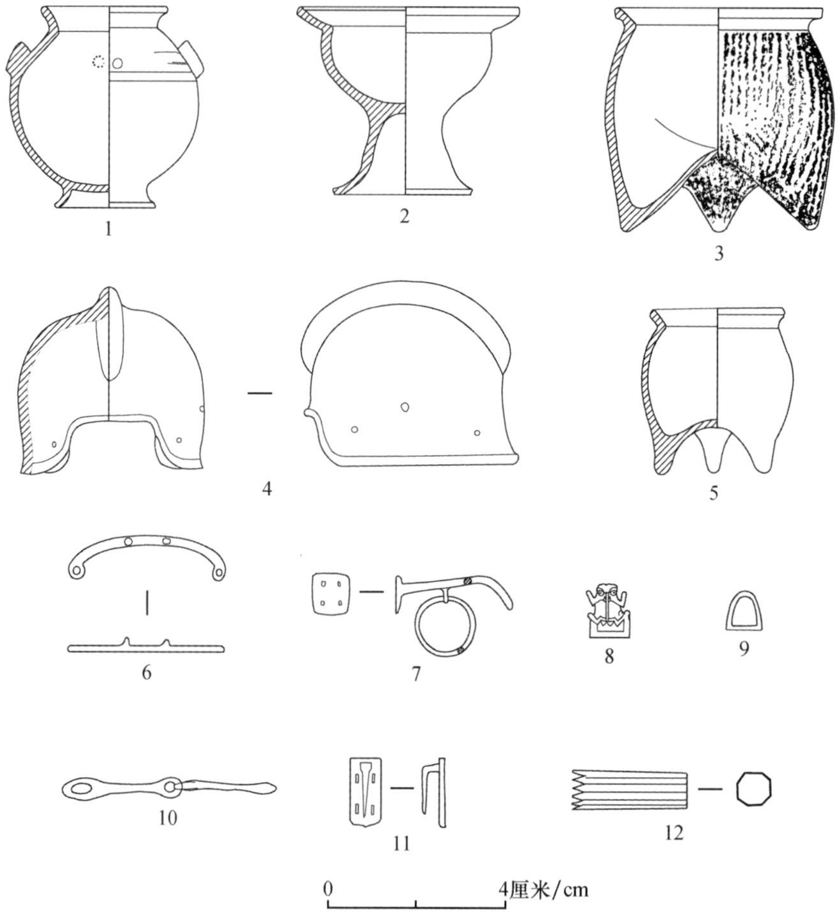

图Ⅱ.2.1　和平村M2出土随葬品
Figure Ⅱ.2.1　Burial artifacts from M2 at Heping Village.

表Ⅱ.2.1　和平村M2随葬品统计表（图Ⅱ.2.1.1～Ⅱ.2.12）

Table Ⅱ.2.1　Burial artifacts from M2 at Heping Village

图号 Number on Fig. Ⅱ.2.1	标本号 Excavation number	器物名称 Artifact name	尺寸（厘米）Size (cm)	特点描述 Description of features
1	M2：1	陶瓿 Pottery *bu* jar	M: 24 H: 20.5	夹砂灰陶，圆唇，侈口，折沿，圆鼓腹，圈足，素面，肩置两对称的菱状扳手，并饰两对对称的泥饼。Grey ceramic tempered with sand. Rounded lip, flaring mouth, angled rim, round bulging belly, and ring circular base. Plain surface. A pair of diamond-shaped handles and two pairs of cookie-shaped mud lumps attached to the shoulders.
2	M2：2	陶簋 Pottery *gui* tureen	M: 13.8 H: 22	泥质灰褐陶，方唇，侈口，宽折沿，鼓腹，粗圈足较高，素面，沿内有一周凹弦纹。Greyish-brown ceramic, fine clay. A square rim, flaring mouth, and wide angled rim. Round bulging belly, and a high and heavy ring foot. Plain. An intaglio ring pattern inside rim.
	M2：3	陶簋 Pottery *gui* tureen	同M2：2 Same as M2：2	同M2：2。Identical to M2：2.

续表

图号 Number on Fig. Ⅱ.2.1	标本号 Excavation number	器物名称 Artifact name	尺寸（厘米）Size (cm)	特点描述 Description of features
5	M2：4	陶鬲 Pottery *li* tripod	M: 14 H: 18	夹砂红陶，方唇，侈口，折沿，鼓腹，浅袋足，实足尖较高，素面。Red ceramic tempered with sand. Square lip, flaring mouth, angled rim. Bulging belly, three shallow hollow legs, supported by three high, solid foot-tips. Plain.
	M2：5	陶鬲 Pottery *li* tripod	同M2：4 Same as M2：4	同M2：4。Identical to M2：4。
3	M2：6	陶鬲 Pottery *li* tripod	M: 22.2 H: 24.5	夹砂灰陶，方唇，侈口，折沿，腹微鼓，高档稍瘪，饰绳纹。Grey ceramic tempered with sand. Square lip, flaring mouth, angled rim, slightly bulging belly. High and slightly sunken crotch. Impressed with cord patterns.
4	M2：7	陶盔 Pottery helmet	H: 19.2	泥质灰陶，底口椭圆，面口呈"凹"形，顶有凸粱，两侧护耳各置三孔。Grey pottery made of fine clay. The bottom is oval and the brow 凹-shaped, with an arched flange on the top and three holes above the ear guard on both sides.
	M2：8	陶鬲 Pottery *li* tripod	同M2：6 Same as M2：6	同M2：6。Identical to M2：6.
11	M2：8	铜车器 Bronze chariot fitting	L: 6 W: 2.5	长方形平板，有四穿孔。Rectangular tablet with four holes.
	K1：1	铜车辖 Bronze axle-cap	L: 8	1件。One.
6	K1：2	铜马镳 Bronze horse cheek pieces	L: 18	一副，弧形，中部有双孔。One pair. Curve with two holes at the center.
8	K1：4、5	铜方环 Bronze square ring	L: 4 W: 3.5	四件，方环一侧铸蛙形装饰。Four items. Square ring with frog ornament on the one side.
10	K1：6	铜马衔 Bronze horse bit	L: 26.5	半付。Half piece.
	K1：7	铜圆环 Bronze ring	L: 10.5	
	K1：8	铜圆环 Bronze ring	L: 8	
9	K1：9	铜半环 Bronze semi circle ring	L: 4.4	
12	K1：10	铜管形器 Bronze tubular object	L: 12.6	八棱筒形，口呈锯齿状。Octagonal tube with the edge in zigzag shape.
7	K1：11	铜车器 Bronze chariot part	L: 10.5	一铜杆连一铜环。One bronze stick connected to a bronze ring.

尺寸标志：L=长度；H=高度；W=宽度；D=直径；R=半径；M=口径；B=底径；T=厚度；d=深度；h=孔径。

Measurements: L=length; H=height; W=width; D=diameter; R=radius; M=mouth diameter; B=bottom diameter; T=thickness; d=depth; h= hole diameter.

图Ⅱ.2.2　和平村历年征集铜器

Figure Ⅱ.2.2　Bronze artifacts collected from Heping Village.

表Ⅱ.2.2　和平村历年征集铜器统计表

Table Ⅱ.2.2　Bronze artifacts collected from Heping Village

图号 Number on Fig Ⅱ.2.2	标本号 Excavation number	器物名称 Artifact name	尺寸（厘米）Size (cm)	特点描述 Description of features
2	01727	鼎 *Ding* cauldron	M: 17.3 H: 20.7	方唇，直口内敛，折沿，立耳，鼓腹偏下，三小兽蹄形足，圜底近平，沿下饰一周放大的云纹。Square lip, straight mouth converging, angled rim, two upright handles; belly bulging toward the bottom, three small hoof-shaped legs, and round bottom nearly flattened. One band of enlarged cloud patterns under the rim.
1	00266	鼎 *Ding* cauldron	M: 26.1 H: 22	方唇，直口，立耳外撇，折沿，鼓腹，圜底，三兽蹄足，沿下饰一周蟠虺纹。Square lip, straight mouth, two flaring upright handles, angled rim, bulging belly, round bottom, and three hoof-shaped legs. One band of coiled serpent pattern under the rim.
5	00272	甗（鬲部）*Yan* steamer (the tripod part)	M: 17.5 × 25 H: 26	长方口，口上有凹槽，双直耳，分裆，四肥足，足上饰简化的兽目。Square mouth with a groove in the rim, two upright handles, a separate crotch and four fat feet, decorated with degenerated animal eyes.
3-4	00259	鬲 *Li* tripod	M: 14.1 H: 10.5	圆唇，侈口，折沿，鼓腹，弧裆较平，矮足，腹部有三扉棱，口沿有一周铭文“己侯□□姜□□□子子孫孫永寶用”。Rounded lip, flaring mouth, and angled rim; bulging belly, flattened curve crotch, and three short feet. Three flanges attached to body. Inscriptions on the rim reads：“Jihou···Jiang···[May my] sons' sons and grandsons' grandsons eternally treasure and use it!”
6	01487	壶 *Hu* bottle	M: 14.5 × 19.5 H: 16.5	直口平沿，鼓腹偏下，圈足，颈有两贯耳，体扁圆。Upright mouth with flat rim, bulging belly towards bottom, ring foot. Two tubular ears attached to neck. The vessel body has a flattened globular shape.
7	00270	鉌 *He* oval container	M: 12.2 H: 8.4	圆唇，折沿，鼓腹，平底，上腹设两环耳。Rounded lip, angled rim, bulging belly, and flat bottom. Two ring ears attached to the upper belly.
	00269	鉌 *He* oval container	M: 14 H: 6.4	同7 Identical to 7.
8	01488	盒 Bronze-box	M: 23 H: 9	方唇，折沿，折肩，弧腹，平底，盖及腹设环纽和环耳，腹饰两周凸棱。Square lip, angled rim and angled shoulder; curved belly, and a flat bottom. Ring knobs and ring ears placed on the lid and belly; vessel decorated with two ridge patterns.
9	01512	甬钟 Stem-bells	H: 19.5	两件。一件钟口呈叶形，长枚，甬带挂钩，枚间饰乳钉和云雷纹，钲中有款识。另一件残断，形制相近。Two bells. One has a leaf-shaped mouth, high bosses, and *yong* stem with a hook. Spaces around the bosses decorated with nipple patterns and cloud patterns. Inscriptions were cast on the *zheng* panel. The other bell is similar in form and décor but was damaged.

图Ⅱ.2.3　曹家村墓葬出土器物

Figure Ⅱ.2.3　Artifacts unearthed from the tombs at Caojia Village.

表Ⅱ.2.3　曹家墓葬出土器物统计表

Table Ⅱ.2.3　Artifacts unearthed from the tombs at Caojia Village

图号 Number on Fig. Ⅱ.2.3	标本号 Excavation number	器物名称 Artifact name	尺寸（厘米） Size (cm)	特点描述 Description of features
1	M1：1	铜鼎 Bronze *ding* cauldron	M: 25.5 H: 26.8	方唇，直口，折沿，立耳。腹斜直，圜底近平，三柱足。口沿下纹带为火纹与四瓣目纹相间，雷纹地。 Square lip, straight mouth, angled rim, two upright handles. Belly straight and slanting, round bottom nearly flattened, and three solid cylindrical legs. The decorative band under the rim composed of fire patterns alternating with four-petal eye patterns; thunder spiral patterns as background.
2	M1：2	铜鼎 Bronze *ding* cauldron	M: 18.8 H: 21.7	形制同M1：1，沿下纹带为夔纹。 Form and décor identical to M1：1, but the decorative band under the rim consists of *kui* dragon patterns.
3	M1：3	铜甗 Bronze *yan* steamer	M: 28 H: 40.6	方唇，侈口，立耳，直腹，袋足，足较高。口沿下饰兽面纹，袋足饰高浮雕兽面。腹内有抹角三角形铜箅。 Square lip, flaring mouth, two upright handles, straight belly, and three tall hollow legs. Below the rim decorated with zoomorphic motifs; legs decorated with zoomorphic motifs in high relief. A rounded triangular bronze grate was placed in the belly.
4	M1：4	铜壶 Bronze *hu* bottle	M: 9 H: 46	器体瘦长，平沿，直口，鼓腹。高圈足，颈设贯耳；饰兽面纹。盖为内插口，喇叭形捉手；饰凤纹。 Tall, slender body, flat rim, upright mouth, bulging belly. High ring base, two tubular ears attached to the neck; decorated with zoomorphic motif. The lid's mouth tenon-shaped, to be capped by the vessel, trumpet-shaped handle; decorated with phoenix motif.
5	M1：5	铜尊 Bronze *zun* pitcher	M: 17.5 H: 18.5	圆唇，敞口，鼓腹，高圈足。腹饰兽面纹、凸弦纹。内底铭："作父辛宝彝"。 Rounded lip, flaring mouth, bulging belly, and high ring foot. Belly decorated with zoomorphic motifs and raised ring patterns. Inscription on the inner bottom reads："Make this treasured vessel for my deceased father Xin".
6	M1：6	铜卣 Bronze *you* jar	M: 15.4 H: 17.7	子母口，扁鼓腹，圈足，环形耳。腹饰兽纹，纹带中间兽首凸起。提梁两端作兽头状。盖有捉手，饰凤纹。盖内与卣内底对铭"作宝尊彝"。 Lid interlocks with the rim of the vessel, flattened bulging belly, ring foot, two ring ears. Belly decorated with zoomorphic motifs; animal heads in relief placed on the decorative band. An animal head placed at each end of the hoop handle. Lid has a handle decorated with phoenix patterns. Identical inscriptions on the interior of the lid and the vessel bottom read: "Make this treasured vessel".
	M1：7	铜爵 Bronze *jue* cup	H: 21.8	直腹，圜底。腹饰二道凸弦纹。 Straight belly and a round bottom. Two raised ring patterns decorate the belly.
7	M1：8	铜爵 Bronze *jue* cup	同M1：7 Same as M1：7	同M1：7。 Identical to M1：7.
9	M1：9	陶罐 Pottery *guan* jar	M: 10 H: 16.8	夹砂灰陶。圆唇，侈口，卷沿，矮领，溜肩，平底内凹底。饰细绳纹。 Grey ceramic tempered with sand. Flaring mouth with rounded lip and rolled rim; short neck, sloping shoulder and a concave vessel bottom. Decorated with fine cord patterns.
10	M1：10	玉戈 Jade *ge* dagger	L: 25.8 W: 6	黄白色，中起脊，偏锋，内端有孔。 Yellowish-white color, a raised ridge in the center tapers toward the point, uneven blades, a hole through the haft end of the dagger.
8	M1：11	残器底 Vessel bottom fragment		铸一行三字"作旅彝"。 Inscribed with three characters in one line："Make this sacrificial vessel".

1

2

3

4

5

6

图Ⅱ.2.4　董家村出土青铜器

FigureⅡ.2.4　Bronze artifacts from Dongjia Village.

表Ⅱ.2.4　董家村出土铜器统计表

Table Ⅱ.2.4　Bronze artifacts from Dongjia Village

图号 Number on Fig. Ⅱ.2.4	标本号 Excavation number	器物名称 Artifact name	尺寸（厘米） Size (cm)	特点描述 Description of features
1	HG250	盘 *Pan* basin	M: 44.5 H: 16.5	方唇，平折沿，直口，直腹，腹设二方形附耳。平底，圈足接三兽足，足饰兽头。 Square lip, flat angled rim, straight mouth, and straight belly with two rectangular appended ears. Flat bottom, and ring foot supported by three hoof-shaped feet, upper ends decorated with animal heads.
2	HG251	鼎 *Ding* cauldron	M: 29 H: 26	方唇，折沿，直口，立耳外撇。半球腹，大圜底，兽足。沿下饰夔纹，足根饰兽面。 Square lip, angled rim, straight mouth with two upright flaring handles. Hemispheric belly, big round bottom, and three hoof-shaped legs. Below the rim a band of *kui* dragon patterns; the upper ends of the legs decorated with animal masks.
3	HG252	甗 *Yan* steamer	M: 35 H: 56	方唇，直口，折沿，绳状附耳。腹微鼓，弧裆，实足较高，无箅。素面，腹有一道凸弦纹。 Square lip, straight mouth, angled rim, two cord-like appended ears. Slightly bulging belly, curved crotch, three high solid feet, and no grate found. Plain surface, belly decorated with one raised ring pattern.
4	00116	甗 *Yan* steamer	M: 33 H: 35.5	甑：方唇，折沿，侈口。腹微鼓，平底，沿下设双耳。腹饰蟠虺纹（漫漶不清）。鬲：方唇，圆肩，鼓腹，连裆，蹄足（残），肩置双附耳。素面。 Colander (upper)：Square lip, angled rim, flaring mouth. Slightly bulging belly, flat bottom, two ears placed under the rim. Belly decorated with coiled serpent patterns (indistinct). Tripod (lower)：Square lip, round shoulders, bulging belly, joint crotch, and three hoof-shaped feet (incomplete). Two appended ears placed on the neck. Plain surface.
5	00117	卮 *Zhi* cup	M: 6.5 × 6 H: 12	残。体扁圆，圆唇，微侈口，圆肩，椭圆鼓腹，平底。肩设二环纽，腹设一环纽。素面。 Incomplete. Flattened round body, rounded lip, slightly flaring mouth, round shoulders, oval and bulging belly, and flat bottom. Two rings attached to the shoulders, one ring on the belly. Plain surface.
6	00118	马衔 Horse-bit	L: 23.5	半副。 One of a pair.
	00119	镞 Arrow		三件，均残碎严重。 Three. All seriously damaged.
	C0263	戈 *Ge* dagger	L: 16	残损不全。 Damaged and incomplete.

1

2

3

4

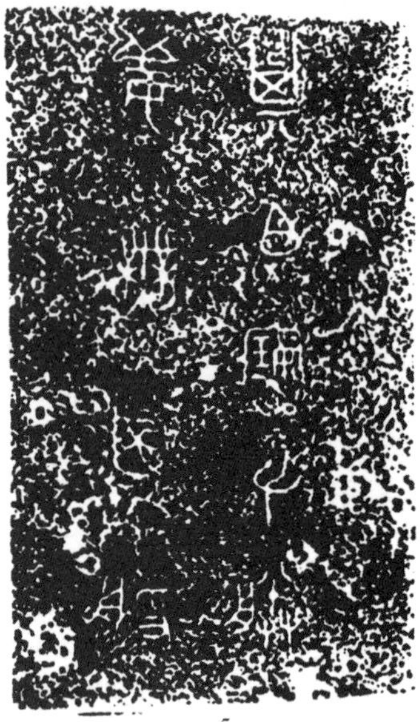

5

图Ⅱ.2.5　南埠村出土青铜器

FigureⅡ.2.5　Bronze artifacts from Nanbu Village.

表Ⅱ.2.5　南埠村出土铜器统计表

Table Ⅱ.2.5　Bronze artifacts from Nanbu Village

图号 Number on Fig. Ⅱ.2.5	标本号 Excavation number	器物名称 Artifact name	尺寸 （厘米） Size (cm)	特点描述 Description of features
1	178	盨 *Xu* square tureen	M: 20.8 × 16.4 W: 14.6 H: 15.3	四件同式，子母口，两附耳，腹微鼓，圈足。腹饰瓦纹。盖器同铭，各铸五行二十六字："㠱白（伯）子宐父作其延（征）盨，其陰其陽，以延（征）以行。割（匄）睂（眉）壽無疆，慶其以臧。" Four identical sets. Lid interlocks with the rim of the vessel, two appended ears, and slightly bulging belly. Decorated with deep and wide groove patterns. Identical text of 26 characters in five columns found on both lid and vessel: "Jibo's son Rengfu makes this campaign *xu* vessel. May it be used on sunny and gloomy days, as [he] carries it on campaigns and travels. May [he] enjoy boundless longevity, and celebrate good outcomes".
	179	甗 *Yan* steamer	H: 22.2	鬲部，子母口，附耳与器体相连。鼓腹，弧裆，兽足。腹饰龙纹。无铭。 Only the tripod part. Rim interlocks with the bottom of missing colander above, two side ears connected to the body. Bulging belly, arched crotch, and three hoof-shaped legs. Belly decorated with dragon patterns. No inscription.
2, 3	180	匜 *Yi* pouring vessel	H: 14.7	流口上翘，圜底，四方蹄足，兽首鋬。口部有一周夔纹，腹饰瓦纹。内底铸两行九字铭文："㠱伯宐父塍姜無□匜"。 Rising spout, round bottom, four square, hoof-shaped feet, and a single ear topped by an animal head. Rim decorated with a band of *kui* dragons, belly has groove patterns. Two-line inscription of nine characters cast in the bottom: "A dowry X *yi*-vessel [cast] by Jibo Rengfu for Jiang Wu".
4, 5	181	盘 *Pan* basin	M: 43.9 H: 9.3	方唇，直口，平折沿，两附耳。直腹，圜底，圈足。腹饰夔纹，圈足饰鳞纹。底铸两行九字铭文："㠱伯宐父塍姜無□般（盘）。" Square lip, straight mouth, flat and angled rim, and two side ears. Straight belly, round bottom, and ring foot. Belly decorated with *kui* dragon patterns and the ring foot with fish-scale patterns. Two-line inscription,of nine characters inscribed in the bottoM: "A dowry X *pan* basin [cast] by Jibo Rengfu for Jiang Wu".
	182	鼎 *Ding* cauldron		方唇，直口、平折沿，直立耳。腹微鼓，圜底，兽足。沿下饰夔纹，腹饰重鳞纹。无铭。 Square lip, straight mouth, flat and angled rim and two upright ears. Slightly bulging belly, round bottom, and three hoof-shaped legs. Under the rim a band of *kui* dragon patterns, belly with fish-scale patterns. No inscription.

1

2

3

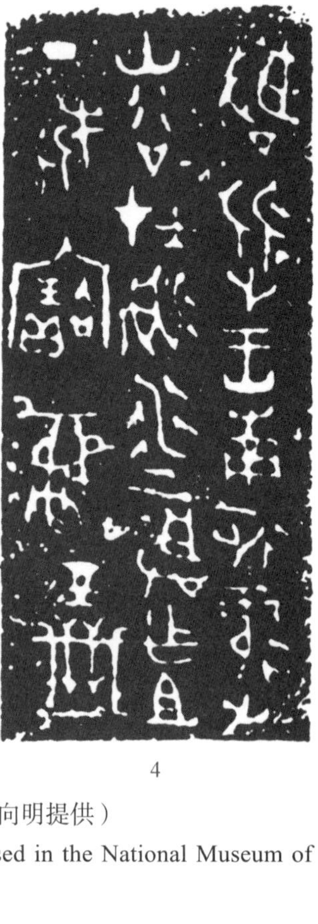

4

图Ⅱ.2.6　小刘庄出土铜器（3 卣 现藏国家博物馆，戴向明提供）

Figure Ⅱ.2.6　Bronze artifacts from Xiaoliu Zhuang Village (3 *you* currently housed in the National Museum of China, image provided by Dai Xiangming).

表Ⅱ.2.6　小刘庄出土铜器统计表

Table Ⅱ.2.6　Bronze artifacts from Xiaoliu Zhuang Village

图号 Number on Fig. Ⅱ.2.6	标本号 Excavation number	器物名称 Artifact name	特点描述 Description of features
1, 2		启卣 Qi *you* jar	子母口，鼓腹，圈足，环形耳。兽首提梁，盖有捉手。腹、盖饰屈身龙纹，腹纹带中间饰凸起兽面。器盖对铭，各铸五行37字："王出獸（狩）南山寇遭山谷，至于上侯滰川上。啓從征，堇（謹）不嬱（擾），乍（作）且丁竇旅隮（尊）彝，用匄鲁福，用夙夜事。戉箙"（集成5410）。 Lid interlocks with the rim of the vessel, bulging belly, ring foot, two ring ears. Handle with animal heads at both ends, lid has a knob. Belly and lid decorated with S-shaped dragon patterns, The band of decoration on the upper belly has an animal head at the center. Identical inscriptions, consisting of thirty-seven characters in five lines inscribed on both vessel and lid: "The king campaigned against the bandits of the southern mountains, Ceshangu, and arrived at the domain of Shanghou on the Jing River. Qi accompanied the king on the campaign. He was cautious and caused [the king] no worries. [He] makes for [his] Grandfather Ding this treasured travel and sacrificial vessel, with which [he] prays for felicitous good fortune, and which [he] uses day and night in service [to the King]. Wu-Fu (emblem)" (JC: 5410).
3, 4		启尊 Qi *zun* pitcher	方唇，敞口，颈较长。鼓腹下垂，圈足。颈、腹间铸两周凸弦纹，中间饰屈身龙纹，纹带中间兽首凸起。外底铸三行十九字："啓從王南征逴山谷，在洀水上。啓乍（作）且丁旅竇彝。戉箙"（集成5983）。 square lip, flaring mouth, and long neck. Pendulous bulging belly and ring foot. Between neck and belly decorated with two raised rings, and between them are S-shaped dragon patterns with an animal head in high relief at the center. Three-line inscription of nineteen characters, inscribed on the outside bottom: "Qi accompanied the king in campaigning to the south against Ceshangu. It was on the Zhou River. Qi makes for [his] Grandfather Ding this traveling, treasured vessel. Wu-Fu" (JC: 5983).
		卣盖 Lid of a *you* jar	子母口，有捉手，饰饕餮纹，盖内底铸一行三字"父辛"。 Knobbed lid interlocks with the vessel rim which is missing. Decorated with *taotie* masks. One-line inscription of three characters inscribed in the bottoM: " Father Xin".

尺寸标志：L=长度；H=高度；W=宽度；D=直径；R=半径；M=口径；B=底径；T=厚度；d=深度；h=孔径。

Measurements: L=length; H=height; W=width; D=diameter; R=radius; M=month diameter; B=bottom diameter; T=thickness; d=depth; h=hole diameter.

图Ⅱ.2.7　东韩家村出土铜鼎

FigureⅡ.2.7　Bronze *ding* cauldron from Donghanjia Village.

图Ⅱ.2.8　鲁家沟村出土铜甗（现藏于泉屋博古馆；见《泉屋清赏》，第12图；《彝器部解说》第18页；左图像由泉屋博古馆提供）

FigureⅡ.2.8　Bronze *yan* steamer from Lujiagou Village.

(Currently housed in Sen'oku Hakukokan; see *Sen'oku seisho*, no. 12; *Iki bu kaisetsu*, p. 18; image on the left courtesy of Sen'oku Hakukokan).

Chapter 2: An Overview of Archaeological Discoveries and Research on the Bronzes from Guicheng and Surroundings

Wang Fuqiang, Yan Xudong, and Diao Peng

Section 1: Introduction

The Guicheng city site, located 6 km south of the old Huangxian County (present-day Longkou City), is surround by Mt. Lai on the south and hills of moderate height on the east and the west. The Yaque River (or Laiyin River) runs from south to north along the east wall of the inner city of Guicheng and thereafter into the sea.

The entire Guicheng city site consisted of an inner city and an outer city. The inner city is located around Jiangjia Village (a.k.a, "Guijiang Village") and Heping Village (a.k.a. "Dongheping Village"), covering an area of 22,500 m^2. The outer city wall is situated atop hills to the east, south, west and north of the site, encircling an area of 8 km^2. It is one of the most well-preserved urban centers from the Zhou Dynasty in the eastern Shandong region. Since the early twentieth century, remains from the Zhou Dynasty have been unearthed in the villages in the Guicheng city site, most of them discovered by peasants during farm work. Due to the special circumstances of the discoveries that resulted in the loss of crucial information about their archaeological contexts, it is difficult for us to gain a full understanding of the cultural meaning of these unearthed artifacts. Still, the sheer number of inscribed bronze vessels from Guicheng attracted scholarly interest both in China and abroad.

It is well known that since the establishment of the Western Zhou Dynasty, the history of the Jiaodong Peninsula in eastern Shandong was characterized by very complicated changes. First, the Zhou culture started to infiltrate the Jiaodong Peninsula and established a number of bridgeheads in the western peninsula, including the Heiyangshan site in Laizhou, the Qianheqian site in Laiyang, the Qucheng site in Zhaoyuan, the Guicheng site in Huangxian County and the Penglai Cunliji site. These sites emerged roughly during the mid-Western Zhou period. Once the region's indigenous cultures had largely been modified by the Zhou culture, Zhou culture continued to expand eastward, resulting in the coexistence of the dominant Zhou culture with regional archaeological cultures. By the Eastern

Zhou period, the rising hegemony of the state of Qi accelerated the pace of cultural assimilation of the Jiaodong region with the Qi culture. Particularly during the Warring States period, the whole peninsula had basically become "Qi-acculturated." During this long process of historical development, the various types of pottery constitute our primary evidence to accurately understand the broad historical trend. However, it is also those exquisite bronzes which provide us with the criteria for determining the nature and ranks of settlements and cemeteries in the Jiaodong region.

During the 1950s to 1960s, Wang Xiantang and others studied the inscribed vessels discovered in the Guicheng city site (Wang Xiantang 1983: 1-159). In the 1980s, Qi Wentao (Qi Wentao 1972: 3-18), Li Xueqin (Li Xueqin 1983: 18-22), Wang Entian (Wang Entian 1984: 71-76), Wang Xiping (Wang Xiping and Sun Jingming 1984: 77-79), Sun Jingming (Sun Jingming 1988: 163-186), Li Buqing (Li Buqing and Wang Xiping 1992: 64-84), Lin Xianting (Lin Xianting 1992: 267-275) and others further examined and discussed the pertinent bronzes. These studies contributed significantly toward clarifying the contents of the Zhou Culture not only in Guicheng, but more broadly in the Jiaodong region, and are helpful in uncovering the history of the ancient states in Eastern Shandong.

Building on previous studies, and on the basis of the new data acquired through archaeological surveys and excavations conducted by the Yantai Municipal Museum in recent years, the present chapter offers a comprehensive review and analysis of the cemeteries and the bronzes which Guicheng and its surroundings have yielded in the past.

Section 2: The Location of Cemeteries and the Discoveries of Bronzes in Guicheng and Its Surroundings

The history of bronze discoveries in Guicheng and its surroundings dates back to the Guangxu Era in the late Qing Dynasty. Thereafter, there have been continuous discoveries of bronzes by peasants during farm work, and particularly in the 1950s and 1960s a considerably large number of inscribed bronze vessels was unearthed, provoking scholarly interest and debate. However, all of these vessels should be regarded as objects collected on the surface. It was only in the 1970s to the 1980s, and then in the early twenty-first century, that scientific archaeological methods were applied to excavating tombs that were discovered. As for the archaeological excavation of the Guicheng site, there was only one test excavation of the inner city of Guicheng, carried out in 2002 (see Part Ⅱ, Chapter 1).

As one of the most important regional centers in the Jiaodong region during the Zhou Dynasty, numerous bronze vessels have been discovered inside Guicheng and its surroundings. Most of them were mortuary objects. According to the data obtained from archaeological investigations and general cultural relic surveys, cemeteries were located in Heping Village and the northeast part of

Guijiang Village within the inner city. In the outer city, cemeteries were found at Guijiang, Nanbu, Dongjia, Caojia, Xiaoliujia, and Dayujia, eight cemeteries in total (Map Ⅱ.2.1). Beyond the outer city wall, cemeteries were found at Donghanjia, Dongying Zhoujia, Dongying Caojia, Jiqian Zhaojia, Zhuangtou, Lujiagou, Shanjiamiao, Dongwutong, Zhangzheng, Xiaozhaojia, Haixu, Bohai Yaojia, Outou Yujia etc., in all fifteen locations (Map Ⅱ.2.2). Most of these were aristocratic burial places. Among them, inscribed bronzes were found in the villages of Heping, Nanbu, Caojia, Xiaoliujia, Dayujia, Donghanjia, Dongyinzhoujia, Zhuangtao, Jiqianzhaojia, Lujiagou, and Haixu. These bronzes are currently housed in the National Museum of China, the Shandong Provincial Museum, the Yantai Museum and the Longkou Municipal Museum (Table Ⅱ.4.1).

Viewed from the perspective of regional geography, these cemeteries and locales where bronzes were discovered are located in the coastal region between the Huangshui River and the Jie River (whose upper stream is called Ma'nan River). As a coastal plain favorable for living, the northern part of this region is called the "Granary of Jiaodong." Strategically speaking, it is a pivot point on the east and west communication route in the populous Jiaodong Peninsula, and also a region that is well-protected by the mountains to the south. Cemeteries in Guicheng and its surroundings are mainly situated on the hilly lands and in the valleys or basins stretching from the mountains to the south. This topography offered both offensive and defensive advantages. Furthermore, the northern plain has fertile soil, which provided people with ample food resources. These factors probably reflect the state policy of Guicheng's rulers, and reveal the general outline of the settlement system centered on Guicheng.

Section 3: Major Discoveries of Bronzes and Cemeteries in Guicheng and its Surroundings

As noted above, the discoveries of bronzes and cemeteries were concentrated at Guicheng and its surroundings. Compared with other contemporaneous sites in the Jiaodong Region, Guicheng has proved to be the most important. It is particularly significant for the study of the evolution of the Zhou culture and the development of ancient states in this region. In view of this, here we review the major discoveries, divided between the inner city and in the outer city of Guicheng.

1. Cemeteries and Bronzes Discovered in the City

Cemeteries in the city included those in Heping Village, Caojia Village, Nanbu Village, Xiaoliujia Village and Dongjia Village, etc. A number of inscribed bronzes have been discovered there. Unfortunately, most of them were unearthed by farmers during agricultural work, and the only three scientifically recovered tombs had been badly damaged.

1) Bronzes and cemeteries in Heping Village

In 1973, a tomb and a chariot pit in the west-center of Heping Village were excavated by archaeologists from the Yantai Cultural Relics Management Commission. The tomb, a vertical shaft earth pit, was numbered M2. Its western part had been slightly damaged. It was 2.5 m long east to west, 1.77 m wide north to south, and 2.27 m deep. An artificial second-level platform (*ercengtai* 二层台), 15 cm wide, was located on the north, west, and south of the coffin. It measured 2 m east to west and 0.65 m north to south. A head box was placed on the east end of the coffin. The orientation of the tomb was 100°. The 1.55 m skeleton was laid supine in an extended posture head to the east, and with the arms crossed on the midsection. Eight pottery vessels were found in the head box, including 2 plain *li* tripods, 2 cord-impressed *li* tripods, 2 *gui* tureens, 1 *bu* jar, and 1 helmet (Fig. Ⅱ.2.1: 1-5; Table. Ⅱ.2.1). They can be dated to the mid-Western Zhou period.

The chariot pit was situated to the north of tomb M2, close to the residential area in the village. It had been badly disturbed by the villagers' activities and had become structurally incomplete. Stratigraphic evidence for it suggested a date later than M2. Inside the pit, only the ribs of the horse remained in their original location, while the skull and the limbs of the horse were scattered and mixed with the bronze fittings of the chariot. Underneath the ribs was a coating of red lacquer. The bronze chariot and harness fittings excavated from the pit included a horse-bit, cheek-pieces, an axle-cap, bronze rings, and a tube, etc. (Fig. Ⅱ.2.1: 6-12). They can be dated to the Spring and Autumn period. This chariot pit might belong to a large tomb lying under private residential houses which could not be excavated (Li Buqing and Lin Xianting, 1991a: 912-914).

In addition, over the years the Yantai Municipal Museum collected some important bronzes from the villagers of Heping Village. These included *ding* cauldrons, a *li* tripod, a *yan* steamer (the tripod part), a *hu* bottle, a bronze box, a *he* box, two stem bells, and axle-caps, etc. (Table Ⅱ.2.2; Pls. 72-79). There were also discoveries of bronze swords, daggers, and arrows, etc. (Fig. Ⅱ.2.2), which we will not enumerate here.

2) Bronzes and tombs discovered at Caojia Village

The tomb discovered at Caojia Village was located on a terrace 300 m south of the village. Peasants discovered the site, but also damaged it while removing earth for the construction of a water reservoir in 1965. Some reports placed the site at Guijiang Village, but our survey confirmed that it is situated south of Caojia Village. When scientifically excavated, only the eastern part of the tomb remained intact. The remaining tomb pit was 4.2 m north to south and 1 m east to west at the bottom.

The original tomb should have been about 5 m long and 3 m deep, oriented east to west. In the bottom of the tomb was a layer of red pigment, probably a remnant of the lacquer coating of the coffin. The western part of the tomb yielded a large number of pottery vessels; all but a pottery jar (M1: 9) were dispersed or destroyed. Eight bronzes were unearthed from the eastern part of the tomb (Fig. Ⅱ.2.3: 1-8; Pls. 80-87). There was still a jade dagger, which was probably among those funeral objects placed inside the coffin (Table Ⅱ.2.3). Judging from the traces of rotted wood and the zigzag pattern imprints left on the exterior of some of the bronzes, that tomb might have been curtained with a reed mat, a sign of high status. The forms and ornamentation of these bronzes, in particular that of the *hu* bottle, the *zun* pitcher and *you* jar, are typical of the early mid-Western Zhou period. Furthermore, the accompanying pottery jar had a small mouth and a rounded shoulder, both indicative of an early date (Li Buqing and Lin Xianting 1991: 921-914). Therefore, we concluded that these bronzes and the pottery can be dated to the early part of the mid-Western Zhou.

3) Bronzes from Dongjia Village

In 1969, nine bronzes were discovered near Dongjia Village when farmers were preparing the fields for planting on the terrace overlooking the riverbed southeast of the village. The excavated bronzes included 2 *yan* steamers, 1 *pan* basin, 1 *ding* cauldron, and 1 *zhi* cup, 1 *ge* dagger, and 3 arrows (Fig. Ⅱ.2.4: 1-6; Pls. 88-92). Based on the composition of the group that included *yan* steamers and *pan* basin, they must have been mortuary items from a tomb (Table Ⅱ.2.4). As for the date of these objects, the design of the round steamer is rarely seen in this period (late Western Zhou). Judging from the chronological sequence of bronze décor in the core area of the Zhou Dynasty, the S-shaped *kui* dragon pattern on the *ding* cauldron was popular during the mid-Western Zhou. However, the *ding* cauldron had a hemispherical shape supported by three hoof-shaped feet, and the *pan* basin had a ring foot supported by three small legs, all indicating that they are from the late Western Zhou period, if not later. Therefore, we concluded that these bronzes can be dated to the late Western Zhou through the early Spring and Autumn period (Li Buqing and Lin Xianting 1991: 915).

4) Bronzes from Nanbu Village

In 1951, ten bronzes were discovered to the east of Nanbu Village when farmers were leveling ground for cultivation, all confiscated by the government. Eight of them included 1 *ding* cauldron, 1 *li* tripod, 4 square *xu* tureens, 1 *pan* basin, and 1 *yi* vessel (Table Ⅱ.2.5) (Fig. Ⅱ.2.5: 1-6; Pls. 93-95). In addition, included in the group were a *yan* steamer (the tripod part) and a small *hu* bottle, currently housed in the Qingdao Museum. They are dated to the Spring and Autumn period. In his *Huangxian ji qi* ("Ji vessels from Huangxian"), Wang Xiantang examined these vessels in some detail (Wang

Xiantang 1960). Two other scholars, Wang Entian and Sun Jingming, also discussed the bronzes in their studies (Wang Entian 1984; Sun Jingming 1988). The inscription on the *xu* tureens reads: "Jibo's son Rengfu makes this campaign *xu* vessel. May it be used on sunny or gloomy days, as [he] carries it on campaigns and travels. May [he] enjoy boundless longevity, and celebrate good outcomes" (JC: 0442). The inscription on the *pan* basin reads: "Jibo Renfu [makes] a dowry X *pan* basin for Jiang Wu" (JC: 10081). The inscription on the *yi* vessel reads: "Jibo Renfu [makes] a dowry X *yi* vessel for Jiang Wu" (JC: 10211). Because the inscriptions were cast by "Jibo's son Renfu" or "Jibo Renfu," Wang Xiantang suggested that Guicheng was the capital of the Hu 瓠 State. By the same token, the capital of the state of Lai must have been located elsewhere (Wang Xiantang 1983: 144). In fact, the *pan* basin and *yi* vessel were dowries made by Jibo for his married daughter, and the four *xu* square tureens were cast before he became the ruler of the state of Ji, which were then given to his daughter in marriage together with the *pan* basin and the *yi* vessel. Therefore, their presence in Guicheng precisely suggested that Guicheng was not the capital of Ji. They testified to the marital relationships between the state of Ji and the ruler of Guicheng (Li Buqing and Lin Xianting 1991: 921-914).

5) Bronzes from Xiaoliuzhuang Village

In 1969, a group of bronzes was discovered by the peasants of Xiaoliuzhuang Village during farm work, including 1 *you* jar, 1 *zun* pitcher, the lid of a *you* jar, and 1 *zhi* cup (Fig. Ⅱ.2.6: 1-4; Pls. 96-97). Among them, the inscribed ones, the *you* jar, the *zun* pitcher, and the lid of a *you* jar formed the so-called Qi *zun* and Qi *you* set. They can be dated to the early part of the mid Western Zhou. Qi Wentao and others have analyzed the vessels (Qi Wentao 1972: 5-7). Insofar as the content of the inscriptions is concerned, they are still the most important group of bronzes ever discovered in the Shandong region.

The inscription on the Qi *you* reads: "The king campaigned against the bandits of the southern mountains, Ceshangu, and he arrived at the domain of Shanghou on the Jing River. Qi followed the king on the campaign and he was cautious and caused [the king] no worries. [He] makes for [his] Grandfather Ding this treasured travel and sacrificial vessel, with which [he] prays for felicitous good fortune, and which [he] uses day and night in service [to the King]. Wu-Fu (emblem)" (JC: 5410). The inscription on the Qi *zun* reads: "Qi followed the king in campaign to the south against Ceshangu, and was on the Zhou River. Qi makes for [his] Grandfather Ding this travel and treasured vessel. Wu-Fu" (JC: 5983). It is clear from the inscriptions that the two instances recorded took place at two different locations in two different stages during the same campaign. Although the target of the campaign was written differently in the two inscriptions, one as Ceshan'gu 遭山谷" and one as Nishan'gu 逕山谷, they must be the same person.

There have been some misunderstandings about the Qi *zun* and Qi *you* in the past. Because both inscriptions mention an expedition to the south, some scholars interpreted them in the context of King Zhao's southern campaigns and therefore dated them to King Zhao's reign (Tang Lan 1995: 277-278). However, research on the chronological sequence of Western Zhou bronzes is more advanced since then, and it is clear, based on the style of the Qi *zun* and the Qi *you*, that they must have been cast in the early phase of the mid-Western Zhou. Consequently, they are not necessarily related to King Zhao's southern campaigns, as other Zhou kings might have also conducted expeditions in the south. But the most important point is that although they were buried in the Shandong Peninsula, the event and the place names mentioned in the inscriptions also appear on vessels from the core region of the Zhou Dynasty. This suggests that the content of the inscriptions is closely related to events that happened at the Zhou central court.

2. Major Discoveries of Tombs and Bronzes outside of Guicheng

1) Bronzes from Hanluan Village

In 1964, a *ding* cauldron was discovered in Hanluan Village, southwest of Guicheng. The cauldron has a square lip, angled rim, straight mouth, and two flaring upright handles; a slightly bulging belly, divided crotch, and three solid feet. The belly is decorated with *taotie* motifs on a ground of spiral patterns, and the feet are decorated with cloud patterns. The diameter of the mouth is 17.6 cm, and the height is 21.1 cm. One line of inscription was cast on the interior wall of the vessel, reading: "Inspector of Gou makes this treasured vessel" (Fig. Ⅱ.2.7; Pl. 98). It can be dated to the early Western Zhou period (Li Buqing and Lin Xianting 1991b: 84-85).

2) The Discovery of Bronze in Lujiagou

The "Metal and Stone Section" of *Huangxian zhi gao* ("Draft Gazetteer of Huangxian"), compiled by Wang Daoxin, mentions: "In the spring of 1896 (the twenty-second year of the Guangxu reign period), ten ancient bronzes were excavated in the field of Lujiagou south of the county seat" (Wang Daoxin 1934, 14: 806). They included 3 bells, 2 *ding* cauldrons (one fragmented), 1 *hu* bottle (fragmented), 1 *pan* basin, 1 *yan* steamer, 1 *he* vessel, and 1 *zhi* cup. The cauldron, steamer, *he* vessel, and the cup bear inscriptions, the assemblage being referred to among scholars as the "Laibo Cauldron" group of bronzes. The inscription on the *ding* reads: "Laibo makes this travel vessel"; the *he* vessel: "[I] make this sacrificial [vessel] for the ancestral temple. [May my] son and grandson eternally treasure and use it"; and the *zhi* cup: "The duke awarded [him] cowries; Ci herewith makes this vessel for father Xin." The *yan* steamer has a longer inscription, and it is currently in the Sen'oku Hakukokan in Kyoto, Japan (Sumitomo Kichizaemon 1918, 1: 12) (Fig. Ⅱ.2.8; Pl. 99):

It was the sixth month, after the dying brightness, on *bingyin* day, Shi Yongfu was on campaign, and he was at the Gu Garrison; Yu followed [him]. Shi Yongfu's X-scribe Yu was dispatched to Huhou, and Huhou acknowledged by recording Yu's merits, and awarded Yu metal. [Yu] herewith makes [this] sacrificial *yan* steamer (JC: 948).

At the same Lujiagou, in 1896, another bronze, the Yu *ding*, was unearthed together with the Yu *yan*. It is currently housed in the Institute of History and Philology, Academia Sinica, in Taipei (Pl. 100).

In November, 1962, a group of bronzes was transferred from Penglai and Huangxian to the Yantai Municipal Museum. Since Penglai and Huangxian had previously been merged into one county, these bronzes were originally mainly housed in Huangxian. They might have been related to discoveries in Guicheng, or perhaps more likely, they belonged to the collection of the Ding family. The group included the "Fu Bing" *li* tripod, the "Fu Kui" *ding* cauldron, the "Bo Xunfu" *xu* square tureen, and the "Fu Kui" *gui* tureen, etc. But since they came with no known provenance, and some of them may even be fakes, we will not describe them here.

Note that bronzes discovered at Zhuangtou, Dongying Zhoujia, Jiqian Zhaojia, and Dongwutong will be described in the next chapter (see Part Ⅱ, Chapter 3).

Section 4: An Analysis of the Cemeteries and Bronzes Discovered in Guicheng and its Surroundings

Due to the fact that most of the bronzes discovered in Guicheng and its surroundings were collected, previous studies have mainly dealt with their inscriptions and related history of the ancient states. Even though there have also been some archaeological surveys that centered on the study of the settlement system, providing us with a basic understanding about this region, what we have gained from them is very limited. Generally speaking, the major contributions of the previous archaeological work in the region can be summarized as follows:

1) The inner and outer city walls of guicheng

As early as 1973, the Cultural Relics Management Commission of Yantai carried out surveys of the Guicheng city site and acquired a basic understanding of the location, scale, and orientation of the inner and outer city walls. In 2007-2009, the Department of East Asian Languages and Cultures of Columbia University, the Institute of Archaeology of the Chinese Academy of Social Sciences, and the Shandong Provincial Institute of Cultural Relics and Archaeology jointly conducted thorough surveys of the Guicheng city site and its surrounding region. This project led to the discovery of the moats, road system, city gates, and architectural foundations in Guicheng. It also identified the location and orientation of the eastern wall of the inner city, and the location, orientation, and the dimensions of the outer city of Guicheng. The project greatly enriched our knowledge about Guicheng (The Sino-American Joint Guicheng Archaeological Team 201 : 30-39). It can be said that we have achieved a new level of understanding of the cultural contents, the settlement pattern, and changes centering on Guicheng. The project laid a solid basis for further studies of the ancient cultures of Guicheng and the settlement system in the region.

2) The dates of the sites and cemeteries in Guicheng and its surroundings

As far as the aforementioned cemeteries (or tombs) and bronzes are concerned, their dates fall mainly between the mid-Western Zhou and the Spring and Autumn period. The majority of the artifacts, collected or scientifically excavated, can be dated to this period, although there are also remains of the Warring States period. From the data obtained from the salvage excavation conducted in 2002 (see Part Ⅱ, Chapter 1), the inner city of Guicheng yielded rich materials from the Warring States period, indicating that Guicheng was still under occupation then.

On the other hand, so far materials from the early Western Zhou period are scarce. Although some artifacts show early features, they were all from about the mid-Western Zhou period, and we have corrected the dates of some of the artifacts described above. Whether there are remains in Guicheng that can be dated to the early Western Zhou period is a crucial issue, and the answer to that question may change our previous view of the history of Guicheng and the identity of its state and people; but we have to be cautious about it. If a stratum or remains dating to the early Western Zhou period or even earlier are discovered in Guicheng, it will be a major breakthrough in our knowledge.

3) The state and its people

Who were the rulers of Guicheng? Where were they originally from? What other states or lineages were in contact with the rulers of Guicheng? These are hot topics in the current discussion and research on Guicheng, which have to be answered through analysis of the bronze inscriptions and the relevant historical records.

So far, the names of a number of states or lineages have been identified in the bronze inscriptions from Guicheng and its surroundings, including Ji 㠱, Ji 己（纪）, Lai 莱 or Piao 瓢, Rui 芮 and Gou 朐, etc. There is not much debate about the identities of Rui 芮, Gou 句, and Ji 己 in the inscriptions, the three states whose bronze vessels were brought to the Jiaodong region through marriage, or as gifts, or due to war or migration. However, the identification of Ji 己, Ji 㠱, and Lai 莱 has been a major controversy; the different views can be summarized as follows:

a) "Ji 曩 was neither Qi 杞 nor Ji 紀". Based on close examination of the archaeological findings and textual records about the relevant states, Wang Xiantang argued that they were three independent states or lineages, each having its own origin and history (Wang Xiantang 1983: 1-159). He also speculated that the state of Ji 曩 was located near Mt. Ji 箕, southeast of Weifang and the north of Juxian. This is one of the most important treatments of the excavated bronzes from Guicheng.

b) "Ji 紀, Ji 曩, and Lai 莱 were the same state." Wang Entian has proposed this theory on two separate occasions. He substantiated his theory with evidence from the archaeological sites, bronze inscriptions, and textual records of their ancestral origins. However, there are also scholars who think that Ji 紀 and Ji 曩 were the same state, but Lai 莱 was a different state.

c) The northward and southward migrations of the Ji 曩 lineage. Based on archaeological discoveries and transmitted classics, Sun Jingming examined from a broad perspective the Ji 曩 vessels that were discovered individually or in groups in Henan, Beijing, Liaoning, and Shandong. He suggested that the Ji 曩 lineage was originally based on the Qi River in the royal domain of Shang. In the early Western Zhou, one branch of the Ji lineage moved northward to Yan and the Daling River region. During the mid to late Western Zhou, another branch of the Ji lineage migrated from Yan and the Daling River region to the Lai region in Shandong. During their long migration, they had contacts of varying degrees with the states of Yan, Guzhu, Qi, Lai, and Ji 紀. In particular, in response to the pressures imposed on them by the dominant states of Yan and Qi, the state of Ji 曩 probably formed alliances with Guzhu, Ji 紀, and Lai in order to counterbalance the major powers (Sun Jingming 1988: 163-186) .

d) About the rulers of Guicheng. As for the question who were the rulers of Guicheng, there are two hypotheses. The first view holds that they were the rulers of the state of Lai; the second, the rulers of the state of Piao (Hua). Both views based their arguments on the inscription of the Lai (Piao)-bo *ding* cauldron, excavated in Lujiagou. Currently, the first view enjoys wider acceptance among scholars than the second. As for other bronzes such as the Qi *zun* and Qi *you*, although their inscriptions certainly mention some historical events, the contents are not relevant to the history of the Guicheng city site. Since these have been discussed before, we will not repeat the discussion here.

In sum, cemeteries (or tombs) and bronzes discovered in Guicheng and its surroundings are the primary sources for understanding its cultural contents and settlement patterns. They are the scientific bases for the study of the history of the ancient states in Shandong. However, faced with the complicated relationships between the ancient states in the Jiaodong region and more broadly in ancient China, the current data merely constitute the tip of the iceberg of information needed to understand them. Viewed from the perspective of the commonality of archaeological cultures to the east of Zibo City, this was the large region in which the Zhenzhumen culture was distributed, or perhaps this was the zone of the greater "Lai" culture. In this sense, it is perhaps reasonable to regard them as belonging to a single eastern cultural entity. But as for how many states or lineages might once have been included in this greater "Lai" cultural zone, this is still a question that needs further investigation. For instance, it may be right to accept that one branch of the Ji lineage had migrated eastward to the Jiaodong region, but we cannot jump to the conclusion that Ji 紀 and Ji 曩 were the same state simply because bronzes inscribed Ji 紀 and Ji 曩 were excavated from a single tomb. Similarly, it is too early to determine the identity of rulers of Guicheng solely based on the inscription of Lai 莱 (Hu 瓠)-bo *ding*. Given the sheer number of inscribed bronzes excavated in Guicheng, why was the same name not found on any of them? Apparently the Lai cultural zone was an amalgam of both indigenous states and lineages and those which had migrated into this region. Both underwent significant modifications over time. All of these issues require more information to serve as the basis for further research. Above all, we need to clarify whether the name "Lai," used by the Zhou court and other regional states, was a general term for the region or the name of a specific state. This, in other words, implies a distinction between the "Greater Lai" and the "Smaller Lai." Issues such as these require more archaeological data to form the basis for scientific studies.

References

Li, Buqing 李步青 and Lin Xianting 林仙庭, 1991a. "Shandong Huangxian Guicheng yizhi de diaocha yu fajue" 山东黄县归城遗址的调查与发掘 (Survey and trial excavations of the site at Guicheng, Huangxian County, Shandong), *Kaogu* 考古, 10: 910-918.

Li, Buqing 李步青 and Lin Xianting 林仙庭, 1991b. "Shandong sheng Longkou shi chutu Xizhou tong ding" 山东省龙口市出土西周铜鼎 (A Western Zhou bronze *ding* unearthed in Longkou, Shandong), *Wenwu* 文物, 5: 84-85.

Li, Buqing 李步青 and Wang Xiping 王锡平, 1992. "Jianguo yilai Yantai diqu chutu Shang Zhou mingwen tongqi gaishu" 建国以来烟台地区出土商周铭文铜器概述 (An overview of the inscribed bronze vessels of the Shang and Zhou periods discovered in the Yantai region since 1949), *Guwenzi yanjiu* 古文字研究 (Studies of paleography), 18: 66-84.

Li, Xueqin 李学勤, 1983. "Shilun Shandong xin chutu qingtongqi de yiyi" 试论山东新出土青铜器的意义 (Discussion of the implications of the newly excavated bronzes from Shandong), *Wenwu* 文物, 12: 18-22.

Lin, Xianting 林仙庭, 1992. "*Jiaodong qingtong wenhua chutan*" 胶东青铜文化初探 (A preliminary investigation into the Bronze-Age cultures in Jiaodong), in *Jinian shandongdaxue kaogu zhuanye chuangjian 20 zhounian wenji* 纪念山东大学考古专业创建20周年文集 (Collected essays commemorating the 20 anniversary of the inauguration of the discipline of archaeology at Shandong University). Ji'nan: Shandong University Press. 267-275.

Qi, Wentao 齐文涛, 1972. "Gaishu jinnian lai Shandong chutu de Shang Zhou qingtongqi" 概述近年来山东出土的商周青铜器 (General discussion of Shang and Zhou period bronzes discovered in Shandong in recent years), *Wenwu* 文物, 5: 3-16.

Sun, Jingming 孙敬明, 1988. "Kaogu faxian yu Ji shi xunzong" 考古发现与曩史寻踪 (Archaeological discovery and the search for Ji history), *Dongyi guguo shi yanjiu* 东夷古国史研究 (Studies on the history of the ancient state of the Eastern Yi), 10: 163-186.

Tan, Lan 唐兰, 1995. "Lun Zhou Zhaowang shidai de qingtongqi mingke" 论周昭王时代的青铜器铭刻 (On the bronze inscriptions from the reign of King Zhao of Zhou), *Tang Lan xiansheng jinwen lunji* 唐兰先生金文论集 (Collected works on bronze inscriptions by Tang Lan). Beijing: Zijincheng Press.

Wang, Daoxin 王道新, 1934. *Huangxian zhi gao* 黄县志稿 (Draft gazetteer of Huangxian). Preserved in Shandong Provincial Museum.

Wang, Entian 王恩田, 1984. "Ji, Ji, Lai wei yiguo shuo" 纪、曩、莱为一国说 (The hypothesis that Ji, Ji, and Lai were one state), *Qi Lu xuekan* 齐鲁学刊 (Qi Lu journal), 1: 71-76.

Wang, Xiping 王锡平, Sun Jingming 孙敬明, 1984. "Laiguo yi ming shishi ji lun youguan wenti" 莱国彝铭试释及论有关问题 (An interpretation of the inscribed vessel from Lai and related questions), *Dongyue luncong* 东岳论丛 (Dongyue papers), 1: 77-79.

Wang, Xiantang 王献唐, 1960. *Huangxian Ji qi* 黄县曩器 (The *Ji* bronzes from Huang County). Ji'nan: Qi Lu shushe.

Wang, Xiantang 王献唐, 1983. *Shandong guguo kao* 山东古国考 (A study of the ancient states in Shandong). Ji'nan: Qi Lu shushe.

Sino-American Joint Guicheng Archaeological Team 中美联合归城考古队, 2011. "Shandong Longkou shi Guicheng liang Zhou chengzhi diaocha jianbao" 山东龙口市归城两周城址调查简报 (A brief report on the survey of the Guicheng city site of the Western-Eastern Zhou periods in Longkou, Shandong Province), *Kaogu* 考古, 3: 30-39.

Sumitomo, Kichizaemon 住友吉左衞門, Hamada Seiryō 濱田青陵, and Harada Yoshito 原田淑人, 1918. *Sen'oku seishō* 泉屋清賞, vol. 1. Tokyo: Kokkasha 國華社.

Abbreviation:

JC: Institute of Archaeology, CASS *Yin Zhou jinwen jicheng* 殷周金文集成 (A comprehensive collection of bronze inscriptions from the Shang and Zhou period), 18 vols. Beijing: Zhonghua shuju, 1984-1994.

(Translated by Chin-hau Lei)

第三章　归城城址历年出土青铜器调查综述（1980～2010）

刘玉涛　马志敏

第一节　引　　言

胶东半岛的地理位置，居于中国古代文明的边缘地区，因此在浩如烟海的先秦古籍中，有关胶东古国的记载却寥寥无几。在有关记载中略有一点明确线索的只有莱国和纪国等。

当周王朝灭商而立，为屏藩周室而大兴封邦之时，封于山东地区的有两个主要国家。一个是当国首辅周公旦的儿子伯禽被封于鲁，另一个是位于山东北部的齐国，受封者正是灭商之役的头号功臣姜太公。据汉代司马迁《史记》记述姜太公至齐时，“莱侯来伐，与之争营丘”。这个意思是说西周初年莱国已经存在，且势力已经很大，能够与齐国争夺地盘。但是，这既涉及齐国早期的历史地位，又问题点很多，能否作为史实的记载尚待进一步研究。先秦古籍《禹贡》中提到“莱夷”和“嵎夷”。嵎夷应即指胶东滨海地区的部族；而莱夷即指以“莱”为名号的夷人。在胶东半岛，名号与莱有关的山川事物很多，而胶东半岛与西部内陆的分界线即名胶莱河，实际上由向南流入胶州湾的一条胶河和向北流入莱州湾的一条莱河构成。莱河应与古代的“莱夷”、“莱国”有密切关系。另一部先秦史书《左传》中对春秋时期齐国和莱国的几次大的战争则有明确记载，发生的地点大都在莱河流域。可见莱国是胶东地区的古国，这一点应该没有什么疑问。

胶东地区与“莱”有关的地标最有名的即是莱山，位于今龙口市（旧称黄县）兰高镇，海拔550米。它在渤海湾畔的冲积平原的南缘拔地而起，气势雄伟，是胶东半岛的名山，也是古人自然崇拜的对象。在莱山北侧山脚下即坐落着归城城址，历代史家多认为是春秋莱国的都城。在归城城址周围，特别是沿着归城以东黄水河的干道，分布着星罗棋布的遗址和墓地，而且级别甚高。这一地区自晚清以来不断有重要青铜器的发现，而陶器及其他种类文物则时有所出。20世纪80年代以前出土文物大多经过烟台市博物馆研究人员的调查和整理，并相继发表（见下编第一、二章）。龙口市博物馆于1985年成立后，即致力于对归城及其周边遗址进行就近保护并收集出土遗物。本文基于龙口市博物馆的馆藏资料，对80年代以来归城城址及其周边地区的重要发现作一系统介绍。

第二节　东庄头墓群考古清理发掘概况

东庄头（或简称庄头）西周墓群位于龙口市东南22.5千米石良镇庄头村东5米处之高台地上。庄头河沿墓群的南部向西流过，墓地东南不远有群山环抱。1980年9月12日，当时的庄头大队社员刘永新等人在1队牛棚东部取土时，发现一批铜器，有鼎、甗、壶等共16件，其中有铭文的6件（3件能清出铭文的拓片附于本章）。经烟台地区文管会鉴定为西周时期器物，并认为出土地点是一处墓葬（编号为M1）。从清理发掘情况看，残墓东西长3米，南北宽3米，土坑竖穴。墓内有熟土二层台，留有棺椁和箱室朽痕，墓主人的骨架和随葬陶器均被破坏。

1981年黄县文物普查小组对该墓进行了复查，认为此处是一处西周墓群。墓群由于盖牛棚及取土所破坏部分约有2500平方米。我们调查时在牛棚东的断崖上见有几座土坑竖穴墓被破坏，有的残部还挂在断崖上。墓地现存南北长约200米，东西宽约100米，总面积约20000平方米。这是归城地区非常重要的一处墓地。

由社员刘永新送来的16件铜器很多破碎很厉害，不能辨形。现将经过修复，比较完整的约有10件加以介绍，包括鼎、簋、方壶、卣、甗、爵、觯（图Ⅱ.3.1～Ⅱ.3.5；表Ⅱ.3.1；图版101～109）。另外还有盘、盂、戈、勺等。

这批铜器风格其实都很接近，铸作年代大约在西周中期偏早阶段。其中最重要的是189号和190号两件方座簋。两件簋通体所饰之大鸟纹仅仅流行于西周中期前段的穆王在位时期，有明显时代特征。两件簋各有铭文两行八字："内（芮）公叔乍（作）斮（祈）宫寳毁（簋）"（图Ⅱ.3.26：1～4）。这是西周中期位于陕西的芮国所作器。与之相同的一件方座簋今年出现于纽约私人藏家。第186号壶的铭文为"熊奚乍（作）寳壶"（图Ⅱ.3.26：5），是为数不多的熊姓贵族作器。另外，192号卣造型较独特，铭文为"小夫乍（作）父丁不寳旅彝"。这些有铭文铜器的发现，为我们了解归城地区的文化及人员交流提供了重要信息。

第三节　东营周家西周残墓

1985年秋～1986年春，山东省龙口市石良镇东营周家村群众在村南窑场取土时先后发现了两座墓葬（编号M1、M2）。1986年6月原黄县博物馆与烟台市博物馆联合进行了实地调查和清理，关于这两座墓葬的情况取得了一些重要信息。

东营周家村位于黄县城东南25千米处，其南距鲁家沟7千米，北距庄头村2千米，东与蓬莱村里集一山之隔，西北距归城城址约为10千米。这里东、南、西三面有众多山丘环抱，黄水河自东南向西北流经村东，村南为东营河自西注入黄水河。墓地位于东营河南岸的台地上，北距东营周家村约0.5千米。台地东接崮山，由东而西呈缓坡状，南北长约220米，东西宽约150

米。东营周家村在此建有窑场，经历年取土台地西部已变成了一条高约3～4米的南北向断崖，此次清理的M1与M2两座墓葬即暴露在断崖上。

M1位于台地西北部，方向东偏南（110°）。墓室大部已被破坏掉，仅余下北部一小部分，东西长5米，南北残宽2.8米。此墓为土坑竖穴，有熟土两层台。墓底有朽木灰痕，当为棺椁朽烂后的遗迹。骨架已被破坏，性别无法辨认。随葬品包括铜器和陶器：2件铜簋置于头部，陶豆、鬲、罐放置于熟土二层台内（表Ⅱ.3.1）。M1出土之两件铜簋均失盖，敛口，双耳有珥，圈足下加三小足，腹部饰瓦纹，口沿下饰窃曲纹，圈足上饰斜角云纹，是西周晚期所流行的形态。两件铜簋内腹底均有铭文，分三行，共十一字："乍（作）朕寳毁（簋），其萬年用寳用。單"（图Ⅱ.3.27：1～2；图版110）。这件铜器很可能来自陕西周王畿著名的单氏宗族。陶鬲、豆与陕西长安张家坡西周晚期墓所出的同类器相似。因此，我们可以断定此墓年代为西周晚期。

M2北距M1约10米，方向东偏南（105°）。东西残长3.5米，南北宽2.7米。墓底距地表深3.54米，有宽约0.5米，高约0.9米的熟土二层台，并有南北长1.9米，东西宽0.9米的头箱，箱内放置陶器。墓底中部有一个长方形腰坑，内有殉葬者的遗骨。此墓虽然没有发现青铜器，但却出土了二百余件陶器，主要有鼎、簋、鬲、豆、罐等（表Ⅱ.3.2）。随葬的陶器不仅数量多，种类齐全，而且地方特色十分明显。如陶鼎圆锥足，足根内聚，这种鼎在胶东其他地点发现过，但中原地区同时期未曾见到。素面的陶鬲和陶簋也是胶东沿海土著文化的风格。而绳纹鬲、绳纹罐、绳纹大罐等却具有典型的周人文化特色（图Ⅱ.3.7～Ⅱ.3.13；图版111～119）。这充分显现了胶东沿海土著文化与周人文化的交流和融合。我们推测M2的年代应该在西周中期。

东营周家村两座西周墓的出土，是继1980年庄头西周墓发现之后胶东地区考古工作的又一重要发现。迄今除已被破坏和清理的三座墓葬外，在断崖上还有两三座亦已暴露，由此推测这里当是一处西周时期的墓地。

另外，东营周家过去还曾出土过一件铜鼎。这件鼎折沿立耳，深腹寰底，下有三个断面为半环形的足。沿下装饰一周回首夔纹。通高22.25、口径21.25、腹深11.8、耳高4.27厘米（图Ⅱ.3.14；图版120）。这件铜鼎是西周中期的典型形态。但其具体的出土时间和地点已均不可考。谨附记于此。

第四节　集前赵家西周墓葬的发现

集前赵家墓地位于石良镇集前赵家村之西北侧。其西距黄水河主干道约1.6千米，并紧靠省道213公路，南距黄水河支流东营河道约100余米，河道上通东营水库。其东距东营周家亦不远，约1千米。墓地最初由建设施工时发现，为西周、汉代时期的墓地。墓地现存长约110米，宽约50米，面积约5500平方米，属于黄水河干道以西缓缓升起的二层台地。2004年4月10日，集前赵家村西砖瓦窑场在取土烧砖过程中挖出了一处古墓葬，该村村民赵恒强得知后随即通知村长赵恒海，赵恒海随即报告了龙口市文物主管部门。由于博物馆工作人员及时赶到现场，遂使大部分青铜器得到保存，但墓葬形制已经不清楚。该墓共出土西周时期青铜器14件，其中带铭文者6件。2件铜器出土时即完整，其余大部分得以修复。

这批铜器共包括鼎3（其中一件仅剩残片）、方座簋2、尊1、卣1（仅有残片）、铜盘1、甗1、壶1、觯1、爵1（残片）、泡1，另有一件钟（图Ⅱ.3.15～Ⅱ.3.19；表Ⅱ.3.3；图版121～128）。残铜片中的铜提梁卣残片，按器形和花纹与铜尊显然是一套。这批铜器的最大特点就是比较一致，组合也相对完整。成套鼎、簋加一尊两卣，另有盘和爵、觯，这是西周中期的常见组合。器形也表明了这个时代特征。如鼎、簋、尊，及卣（残片）都有明显的倾垂，觯的体态较高。大多数铜器为素面，只略加装饰。总之，墓中所出的铜器器形风格接近，基本都是西周中期早段的典型器形。盘的深腹形态也是西周中期盘的典型形态。同出的钟体小枝端尖，花纹粗略，也是钟自南方传入不久的形态，过去在其他西周中期墓中也有发现。

但是，如果仔细考察墓中所出的铭文材料，我们会发现这批铜器可能有不同来源。一件饰长尾鸟纹的鼎（348号）铭文有5字，为“里父乍（作）障（尊）彝”（铭文左侧似另有一“永”字，原字数可能更多）（见图Ⅱ.3.27：3）；另一件弦纹的鼎（357号）则简单名为“乍（作）鼎”，无法判定作器者。两件方座簋为同人所作，铭文同为：“白（伯）應父易（賜）叔索金，用乍（作）寶簋”（见图Ⅱ.3.27：5、6）。作器者为叔索，为我们以前不知，但“伯應父”和“叔索”都是典型的周人族称谓。另外，值得注意的是另一件铜鼎残片上有“曩侯”及另外两个残字，不能辨识。但这显然是一件來自曩国的器物。

尽管这些铜器的来源可能不一，但它们的时代风格很一致。因此，集前赵家墓葬铜器的发现可以说为我们提供了西周中期早段的一个典型器群，这对我们研究归城及其地区周代遗址的年代非常重要。

第五节　海徐家出土的国宝辛𨆌簋

中村镇海云寺徐家村位于龙口市以西的泳汶河河畔，北距渤海湾海岸约4千米。1983年4月，徐家村果林队负责人仲跻会带领人员在果园内挖葡萄树沟时，挖出两件青铜器。一个为铜鬲，另一件是辛𨆌簋。仲跻会拿着铜鬲到龙口市文物店出售，收购人员将铜鬲收下，按规定付了奖励费。仲跻会走出不远又折回来，对收购人员讲，家中还有一件大的青铜器，在家做鸡食盆用，问要不要，收购人员说要。翌日，仲跻会又将辛𨆌簋送来，经山东省文物鉴定专家组台立业、关天相等先生鉴定，定为国家一级文物，这一发现引起文物界的轰动。

1986年11月，烟台市文管会组织专业人员，前往徐家村出土地点进行现场勘探发掘，再未发现任何器物。但对仲跻会先生保护、上交文物的行动，龙口市博物馆给予了奖励。

辛𨆌簋器束领，侈口，鼓腹，双兽耳有珥，喇叭形圈足，腹上部饰有兽面纹（图Ⅱ.3.20：

1；表Ⅱ.3.4；图版129）。通高12.8厘米，口径20厘米，重量2750克。腹内底部铸有53字铭文。这篇铭文字体不标准，多有错误，但作器者明显为“辛䣄”（图Ⅱ3.26：6）。

唯王十又一月，王在阠。王子至于方，辛䨱（䣄）。賓叔，報考辛柲。乍（作）用剌。辛䨱（䣄）叚（？）。叔竽（？）畲（賜）金。辛晤至，□玗（于）宫，畁（見？）。子子孫，□攸（作）寶㕡（器）。

（李峰释文）

这篇铭文虽不能通识，但大概意思可以读通。铭文讲王（应是周王）于某年十一月到达某地，并派遣王子到达方地。辛䣄可能前往晋见王子，并且宾（馈赠）叔某人礼物。同时他自己也得到金之物赏赐，辛䣄用金作此铜簋，子子孙孙永为纪念。文中出现“王子”二字，这在我国西周青铜器铭文中尚不多见。由于辛䣄簋年代久远，文字又不规范，曾请教很多专家、学者，释读全部铭文很难。

这件辛䣄簋，制作精美，造型独特，纹饰别具一格。它的铭文比之以前在归城小刘家发现的启尊、启卣还要长，是龙口地区目前发现的最长的一篇铭文。它的字体虽然不标准，这可能正说明了它非来自周人中心地区，而可能是在胶东本地铸造的青铜器。因此，它在胶东文化史上有其特殊意义。它说明西周中期胶东地区可能已经开始铸造青铜器，并且铸造技术已经相当发达。辛䣄簋为龙口市博物馆的镇馆之宝。

同出的这件铜鬲为宽平折沿，分裆，通身饰细密的直楞纹（图Ⅱ.3.20：2；表Ⅱ.3.4；图版130）；通高7.32厘米，口径6.72厘米，重量589克。这实际上是模仿西周陶器上的绳纹。同类型的仿陶铜鬲在西周中心地区的西周中期墓葬中屡有发现。

第六节　泳汶河畔出土的西周陶器

在龙口人民的母亲河——黄水河流域，有关西周时期乃至更早时期古人居住的遗址已多有发现，但在流经龙口市的另一条主要河流——泳汶河畔，反映西周及以前时期人类居住生活的遗物过去却鲜有发现。2009年10月12日，张郑家附近一个制砖厂的取土中发现了一大批陶器。在制砖厂旁边居住的村民郑波对古代文物抱有兴趣。听说了制砖厂在挖土时挖出古墓的消息，他每天下午下班后都要去捡，前后竟捡了有200件。这些捡来的陶器大多有残缺或仅是一些残片；另据郑波的母亲刘美芸介绍，一些比较完整的可能都已被在此干活的民工捡去了。

陶器积累多了，郑波遂萌发了把这些捡来的陶器捐献给国家的想法，这一方面可以让更多的市民欣赏到，另一方面，可以供专家进行研究。于是，他主动与龙口市博物馆取得了联系，表达了捐献意向。经过正在龙口市进行考古工作的中国社会科学院考古研究所梁中合研究员鉴定，这批陶器总共分四类，分别是陶豆、陶簋、陶鬲、陶罐，属于西周中晚期人们使用的炊具和食器，也是死后的殉葬品。另外，在这些陶器内表发现了大量鱼刺、粮食碳化物、兽骨等。从如此大规模的陶器出土来分析，这里应该有一个墓群，墓的主人是比较有身份的平民。

这批陶器除了捐献给龙口市博物馆的36件之外，剩余的陶器由中美联合归城考古队收集起来，有关情况在本书第七章有详细说明。这里我们仅选择由龙口市博物馆收集的四类陶器中各一件进行报道（图Ⅱ.3.21；表Ⅱ.3.5）。

第七节　归城及周边地区零星收集之西周铜器和陶器

除了上述成批出土的遗物以外，龙口市博物馆历年来还在归城范围内零星收集了一些青铜器和陶器。这些器物虽属零星出土，它们的器形也能够丰富我们目前对本地区青铜器群和陶器群组成的认识，有一定的学术意义。因此，我们在这里选择重要的作一介绍（表Ⅱ.3.6；图Ⅱ.3.22～Ⅱ.3.25；图版131～137）。

第八节　东庄头墓群出土古代龙形玉器

上文已经介绍1980年9月庄头西周墓葬出土铜器的情况。1983年，当地村民又陆续在M1周围墓葬挖掘出土了多件玉器，并及时上交龙口市博物馆收藏。现藏龙口市博物馆来源于石良镇庄头村的玉器计20余件，包括龙形玉佩4件、玉璜5件、玉璧1件、玉片10件（图Ⅱ.3.28、Ⅱ.3.29）。

庄头墓群出土玉器均系随葬玉器。其中龙形玉佩、玉片又是墓主人生前心爱的装饰佩件；玉璜、玉璧虽为礼仪玉器，但也一同殉葬。出土的玉器质地均为青玉。青玉在中国应用已有3000年历史，它的成分主要以透闪石—阳起石为主。青玉细腻温润，不易破碎，手感润滑。色泽呈灰白至淡绿色，最大特点是具有油脂—蜡状光泽，滋润柔和。青玉以其恒久、高雅品质赢得人们的喜爱。庄头墓群出土玉器于1983年入馆收藏成为馆藏玉之珍品。

庄头墓群于1992年由山东省人民政府公布为省级重点文物保护单位。出土的实物对于研究西周时期莱国的历史及经济、文化状况、生活习俗提供了不可多得的资料，具有重要的考古价值及历史价值。

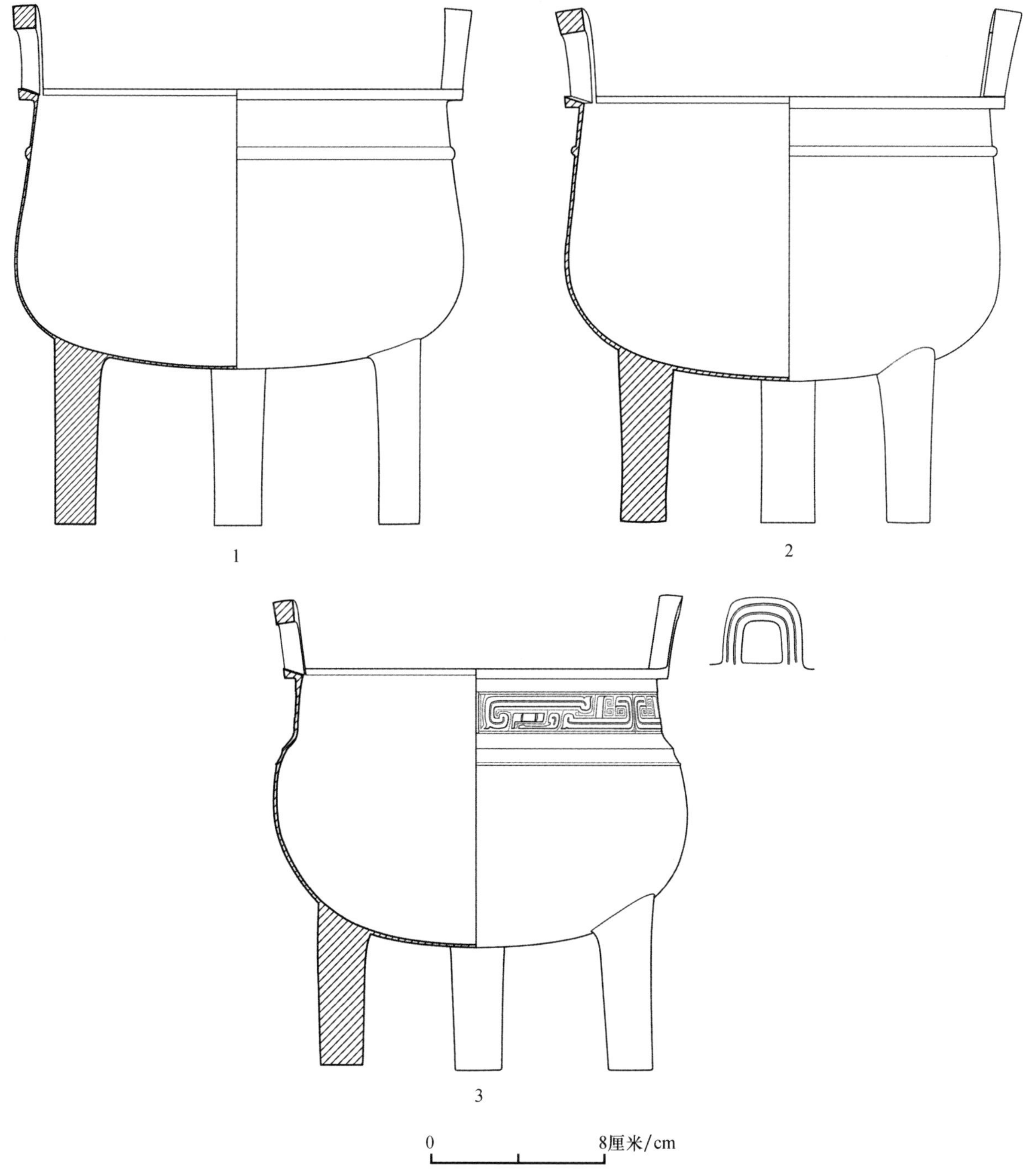

图 Ⅱ.3.1　庄头M1出土铜鼎

Figure Ⅱ.3.1　Bronze *ding* cauldrons from M1 at Zhuangtou.

1. #187　2. #194　3. #193

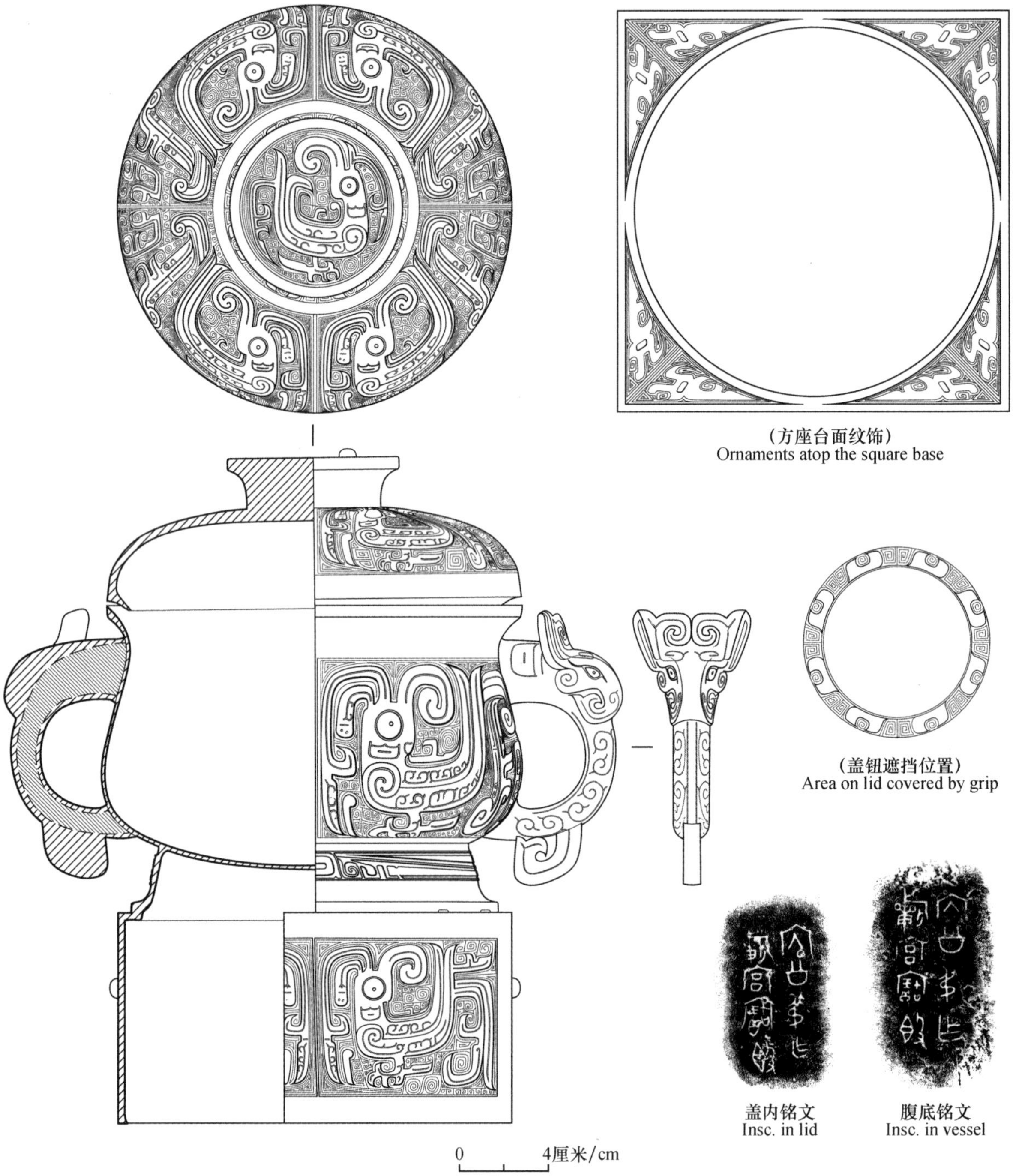

图Ⅱ.3.2　庄头M1出土189号方座铜簋

Figure Ⅱ.3.2　Square-based *gui* tureen (no. 189) from M1 at Zhuangtou.

图 Ⅱ.3.3　庄头M1出土190号方座铜簋器盖和器座纹饰细部

Figure Ⅱ.3.3　Detail of ornament on the lid and base of the square based *gui* tureen (no. 190) from M1 at Zhuangtou.

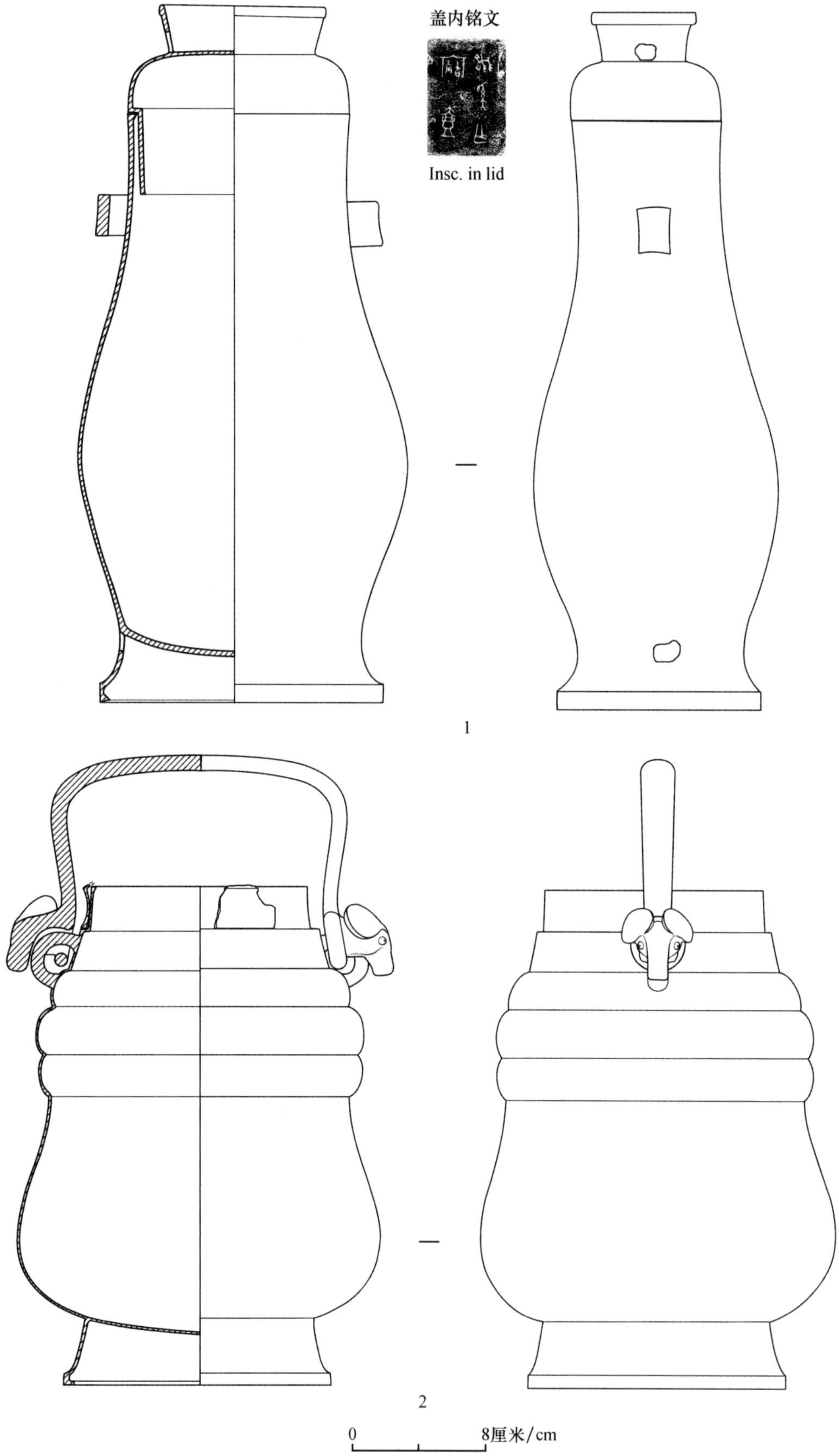

图Ⅱ.3.4　庄头M1出土铜器

1. 方壶（186号）　2. 卣（192号）

Figure Ⅱ.3.4　Bronzes from M1 at Zhuangtou.

1. Square *hu* (#186)　2. *You* jar (#192)

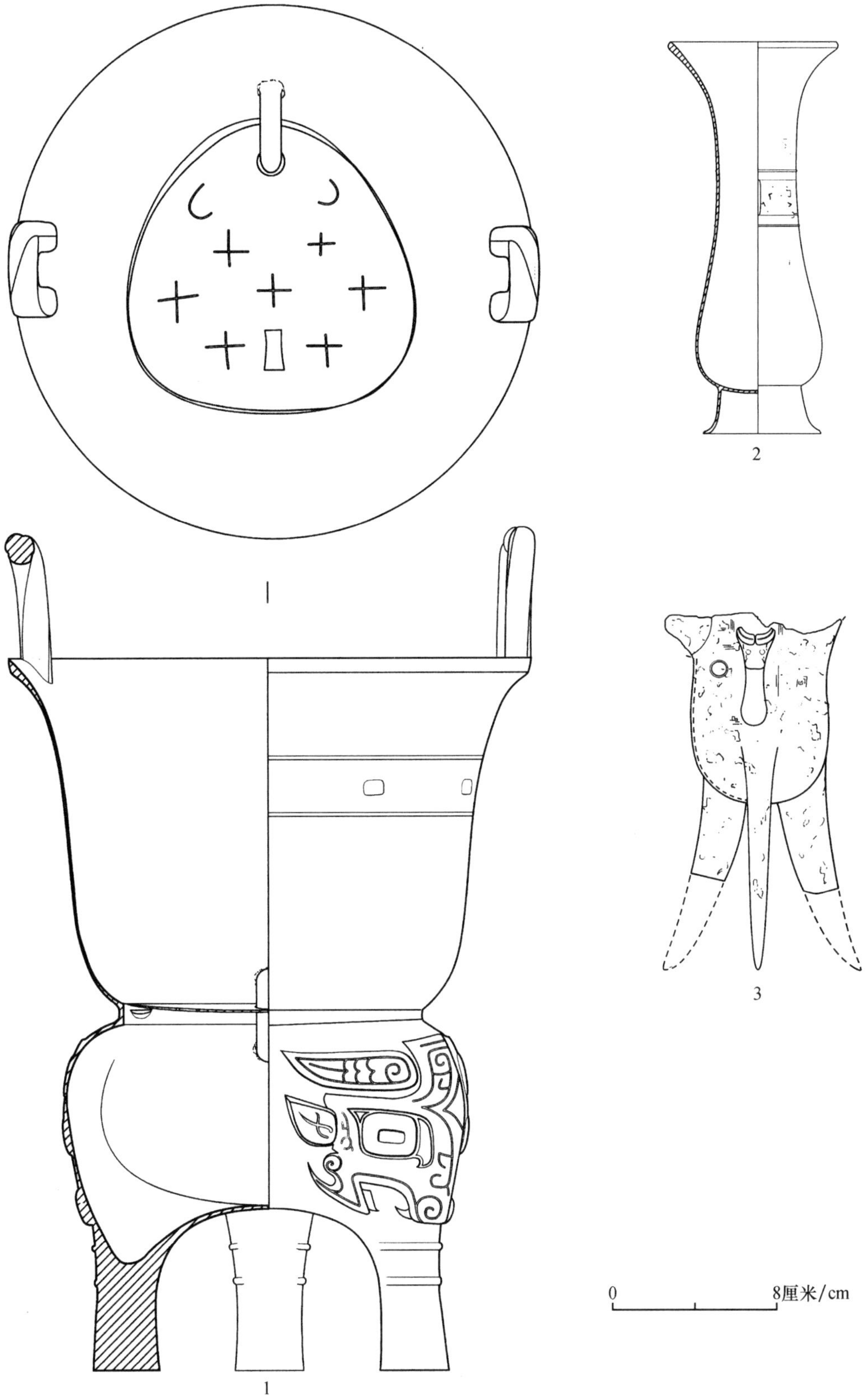

图Ⅱ.3.5 庄头M1出土铜器

1. 甗（200号） 2. 觯（201号） 3. 爵（188号）

Figure Ⅱ.3.5 Bronzes from M1 at Zhuangtou.

1. *Yan* steamer (#200) 2. *Zhi* goblet (#201) 3. *Jue* cup (#188)

表Ⅱ.3.1　庄头出土铜器登记表

Table Ⅱ.3.1　Bronzes unearthed at Zhuangtou

图号 Number on figures	龙口市博物馆编号 Longkou Museum number	器物名称 Artifact name	出土时间 Date discovered	尺寸（厘米）Size (cm)	特点描述 Characteristics	铭文 Inscription
Ⅱ.3.1：1	187 (KM.474)	鼎 *Ding* cauldron	1980.9	M: 20.35 D: 2.35 H: 23.25	方耳微外侈、平沿。腹部微下垂，素面，腹上部饰一道凸弦纹。圜底近平，下有三柱状足。 Square ears turn slightly outward; flat rim. Slightly sagging belly; plain surface; upper portion bears a single raised ring pattern. Round, but nearly flat bottom; three pillar-shaped legs.	
Ⅱ.3.1：2	194 (KM.481)	鼎 *Ding* cauldron	1980.9	M: 20.3 D: 12.5 H: 23	同上。 Same as above.	
Ⅱ.3.1：3	193 (KM.480)	鼎 *Ding* cauldron	1980.9	M: 17.56 D: 12.23 H: 21.53	方唇，立耳，束颈，圆腹圜底，三柱形足。束颈部饰解散的饕餮纹。 Square lip; upright ears; constricted neck; round belly with round bottom; three pillar-shaped legs. Neck decorated with deconstructed taotie pattern.	
Ⅱ.3.2	189 (KM.476)	簋 *Gui* tureen	1980.9	M: 18.68 W: 17.92 (base) H: 28.96	方座簋。深腹下鼓，腹侧兽首耳一对，耳下有珥。盖顶有圆环状纽，纽内实，顶有花纹。方座较矮。腹部、方座、盖上均饰典型大鸟纹。 *Gui* tureen with square base. Deep bulging and sagging belly; animal-head-shaped ear on each side of belly, with pedants. Crown of lid has a solid, circular grip; grip top ornamented. Low, square base. Vessel belly, base, and lid all decorated with typical large bird patterns.	盖、器同铭，各8字 Same inscription of 8 characters on lid and vessel.
Ⅱ.3.3	190 (KM.477)	簋 *Gui* tureen	1980.9	M: 18.68 W: 17.64 (base) H: 28.86	器型同上。盖纽顶饰环状大鸟纹，被盖上四个大鸟纹环绕。器座上亦饰大鸟纹。 Shape same as above. Large bird in circular formation atop grip, ringed by 4 large birds on the lid. Square base also decorated with large bird.	同上 Same as above.
Ⅱ.3.4：1	186 (KM.473)	方壶 Square *hu* bottle	1980.9	M: 13.35 ~ 8.95 D: 19.85 ~ 14.56 B: 16.95 ~ 12.1 H: 40.25 H: 34.1 (vessel) H: 10.9 (lid) W: 6.15 (top of lid) L: 9.95 (top of lid)	子母口，有盖，盖顶有方纽。深腹下部略鼓，体长方。二贯耳。方圈足。通体素面。 Interlocking rim with lid; crown of lid has square grip. Lower part of deep belly bulges slightly; vessel body is rectangular. Two tubular ears. Square ring foot. Plain surface on entire vessel.	内盖有铭文5字 Inscription of 5 characters inside lid.
Ⅱ.3.4：2	192 (KM.479)	卣 *You* jar	1980.9	M: 13 ~ 12.8 D: 21.8 B: 16 ~ 15.3 H: 36.45	子母口，鼓腹，圈足。体近于圆形。提梁两端有兽首。腹上部有三层重叠凸起。全身素面。 Interlocking rim; bulging belly; ring foot. Vessel body nearly round. Two ends of handle shaped as animal heads. Upper portion of belly has three bands of stippling. Plain surface on the entire body of the vessel.	盖器对铭，各8字 Identical inscriptions of 8 characters on vessel and lid.

续表

图号 Number on figures	龙口市博物馆编号 Longkou Museum number	器物名称 Artifact name	出土时间 Date discovered	尺寸（厘米）Size (cm)	特点描述 Characteristics	铭文 Inscription
Ⅱ.3.5：1	200 (KM.487)	甗 *Yan* steamer	1980.9	M: 25 H: 5.8 (ear) H: 7.5 (crotch) H: 39	敞口，索状立耳，腹底有心形箅子，上有七个十字形和两个弧形箅孔。鬲的部分弧形裆，直足。鬲肩部饰三兽面。腹上部饰两周弦纹，中间六个兽目。 Flaring mouth; rope-shaped ears stand upright; bottom of belly has heart-shaped grate with 7 cross-shaped and two curved holes. Tripod part has arching crotch and straight legs. Shoulders of tripod part decorated with 3 animal faces. Upper portion of belly has two raised ring patterns with six animal eyes between them.	
Ⅱ.3.5：3	188 (KM.475)	爵 *Jue* cup	1980.9	H: 16.5 W: 8.46	体饰雷纹，但损蚀严重。腹侧有錾，三足呈菱形刀状，足尖外撇。口沿和流部残。 Vessel body decorated with spirals, but badly worn. Handle on sides of belly; legs shaped like blades, and angled outward. Rim and spout portions damaged.	
Ⅱ.3.5：2	201 (KM.488)	觯 *Zhi* goblet	1980.9	M: 8.33 H: 18.15	深瘦腹，腹上部有一周凸棱，上边的纹饰已不清。下有圈足。 Deep, thin belly with raised ridge pattern on upper portion; upper margin of decoration unclear. Ring-shaped foot beneath.	

尺寸标志：L=长度；H=高度；W=宽度；D=直径；R=半径；M=口径；B=底径；T=厚度；d=深度；h=孔径。

Measurements: L=length; H=height; W=width; D=diameter; R=radius; M=mouth diameter; B=bottom diameter; T=thickness; d=depth; h=hole diameter.

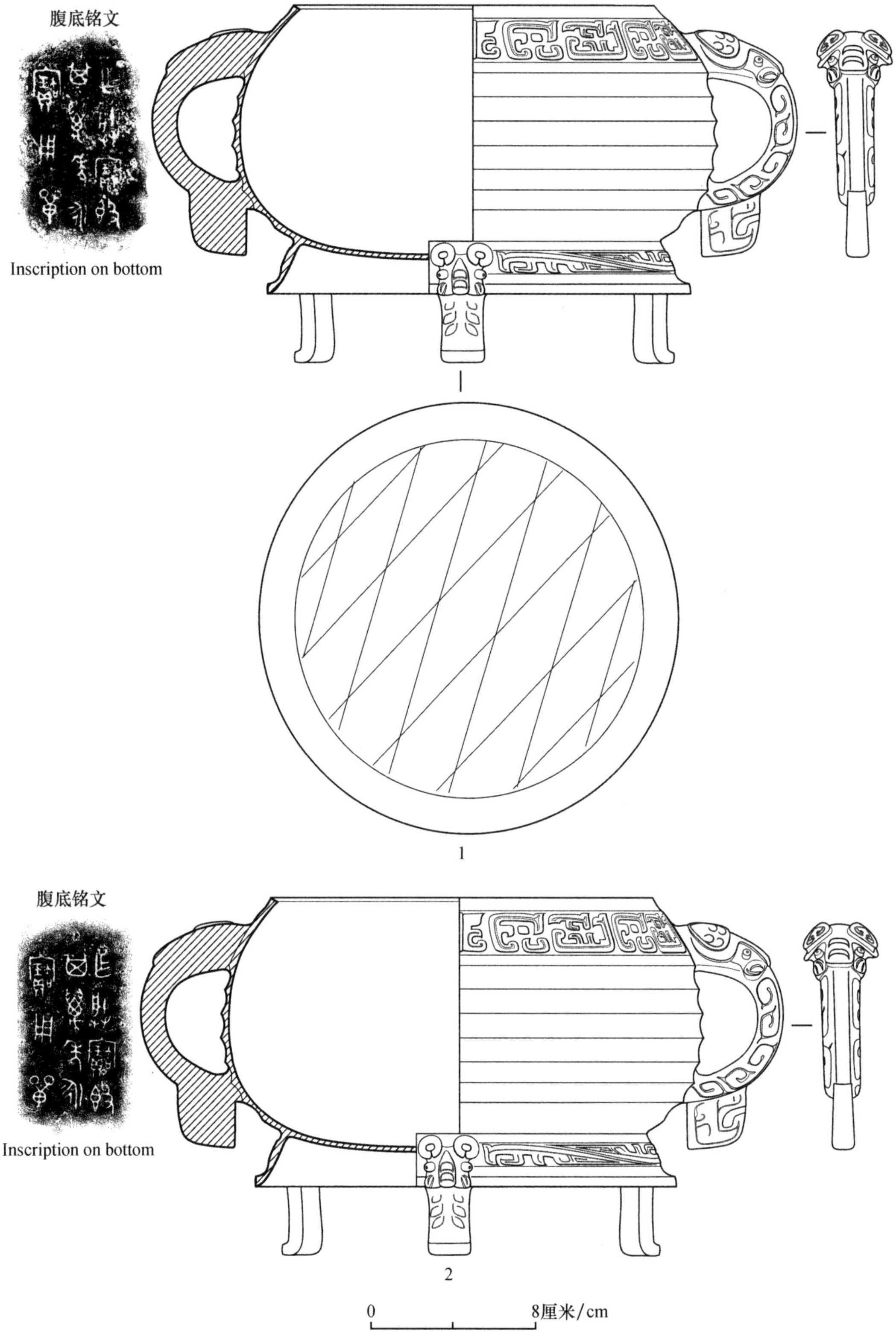

图Ⅱ.3.6　东营周家M1出土铜簋

1. M1：8（3号）　2. M1（4号）

Figure Ⅱ.3.6　Two *gui* tureens unearthed from M1 at Dongying Zhoujia.

1. M1：8 (#3)　2. M1 (#4)

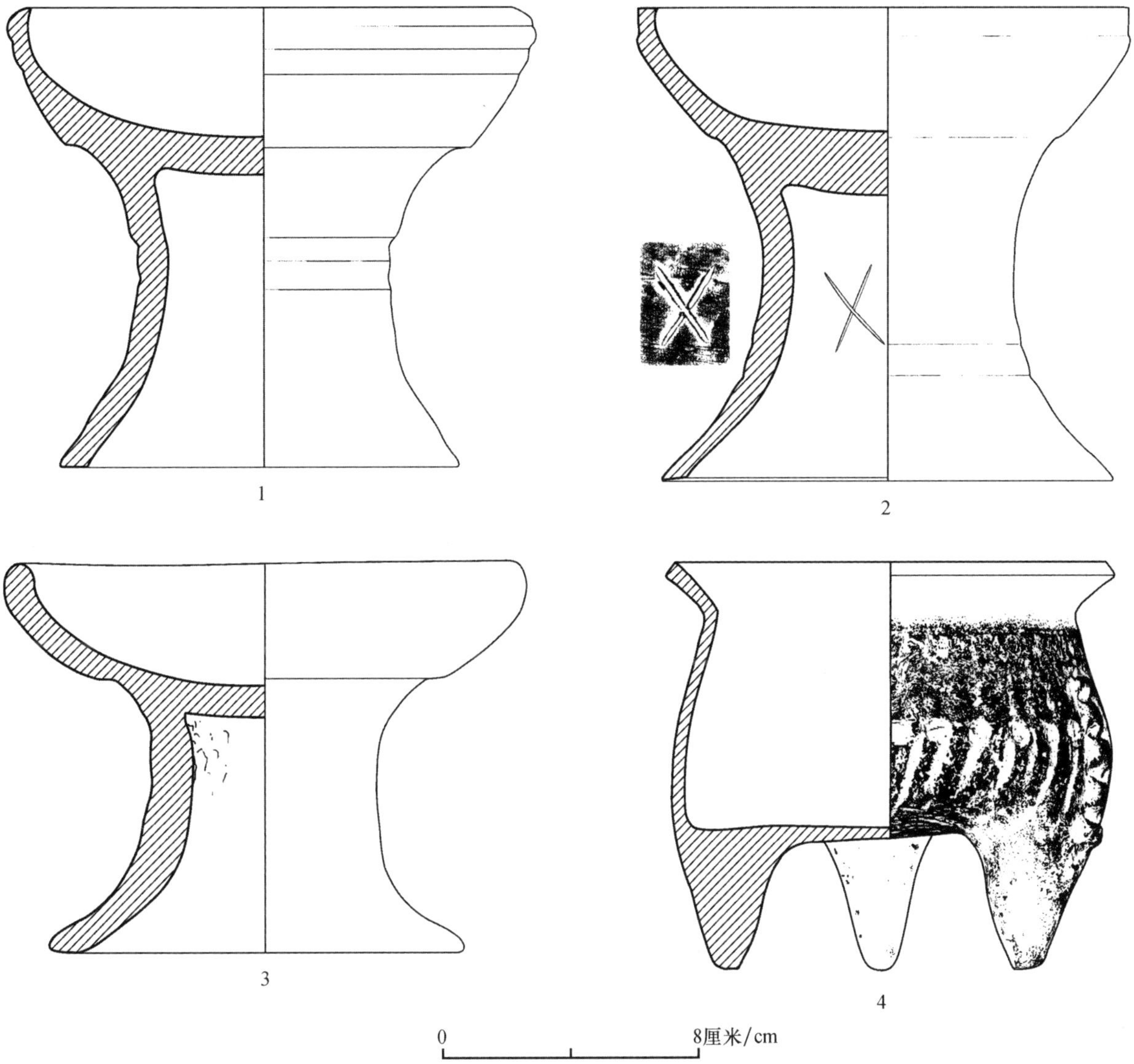

图Ⅱ.3.7　东营周家M1出土陶器

1. M1：6 豆（100号）　2. M1：12豆（103号）　3. M1：4豆（104号）　4. M1：14鬲（140号）

FigureⅡ.3.7　Pottery unearthed from M1 at Dongying Zhoujia.

1. *Dou* (M1：6, #100)　2. *Dou* (M1：12, #103)　3. *Dou* (M1：4, #104)　4. *Li* (M1：14, #140).

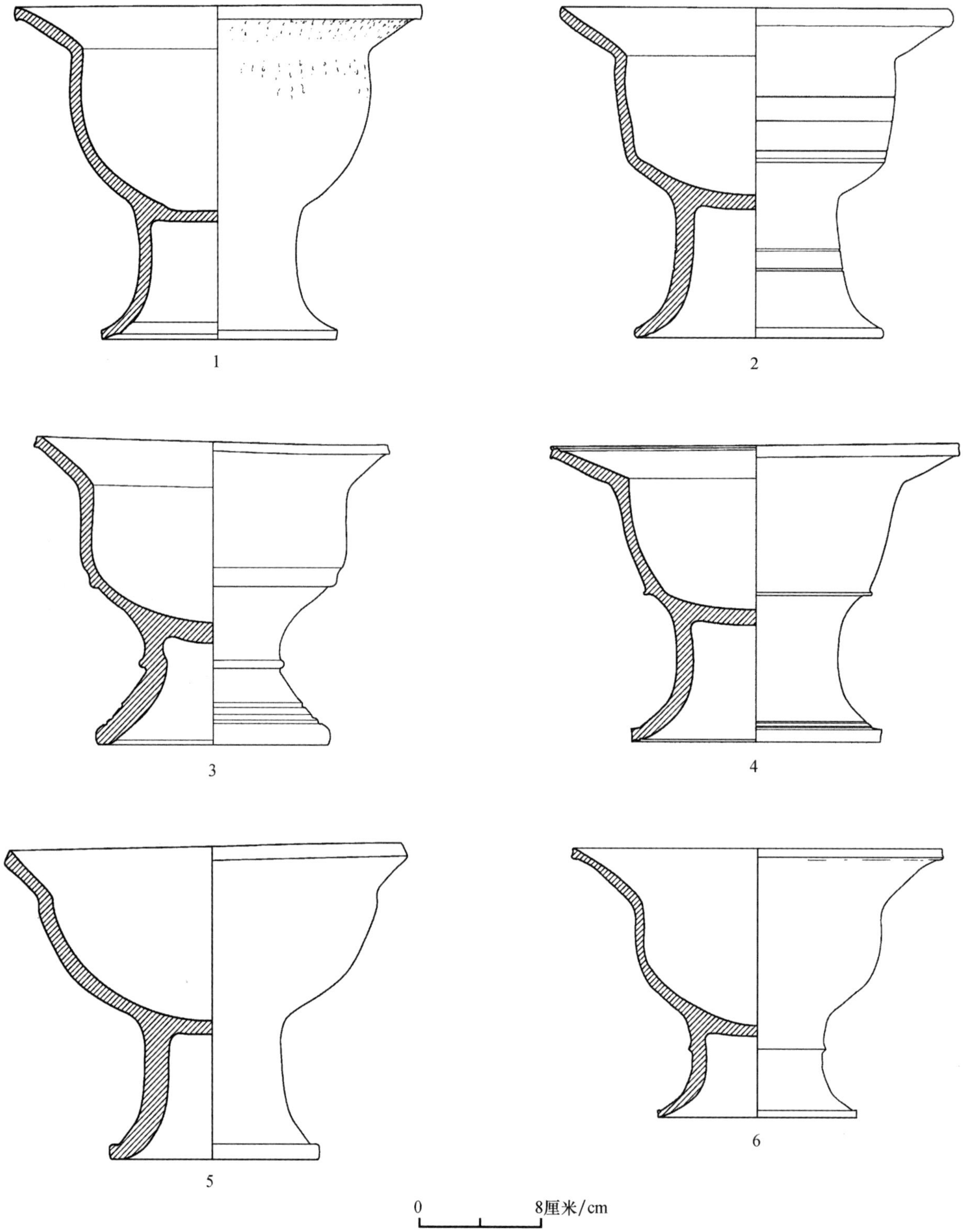

图Ⅱ.3.8　东营周家M2出土陶簋

Figure Ⅱ.3.8　Pottery *gui* vessels unearthed from M2 at Dongying Zhoujia.

1. M2：118 (#105)　2. M2：3 (#106)　3. M2：102 (#109)　4. M2：58 (#110)　5. M2：134 (#114)　6. M2：21 (#122)

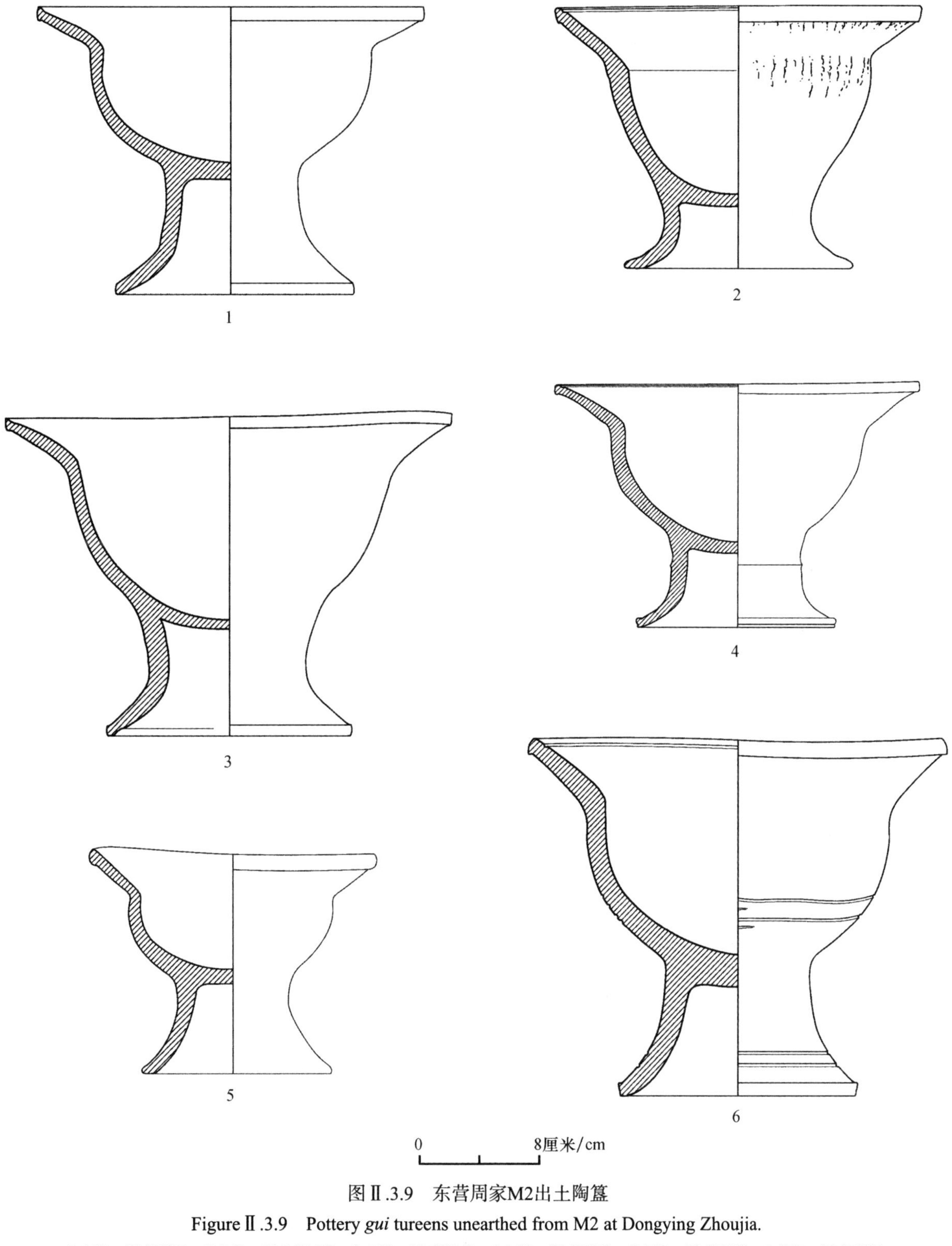

图Ⅱ.3.9　东营周家M2出土陶簋

Figure Ⅱ.3.9　Pottery *gui* tureens unearthed from M2 at Dongying Zhoujia.

1. M2：56 (#132)　2. M2：116 (#108)　3. M2：59 (#135)　4. M2：66 (#116)　5. M2：22 (#118)　6. M2：32 (#129)

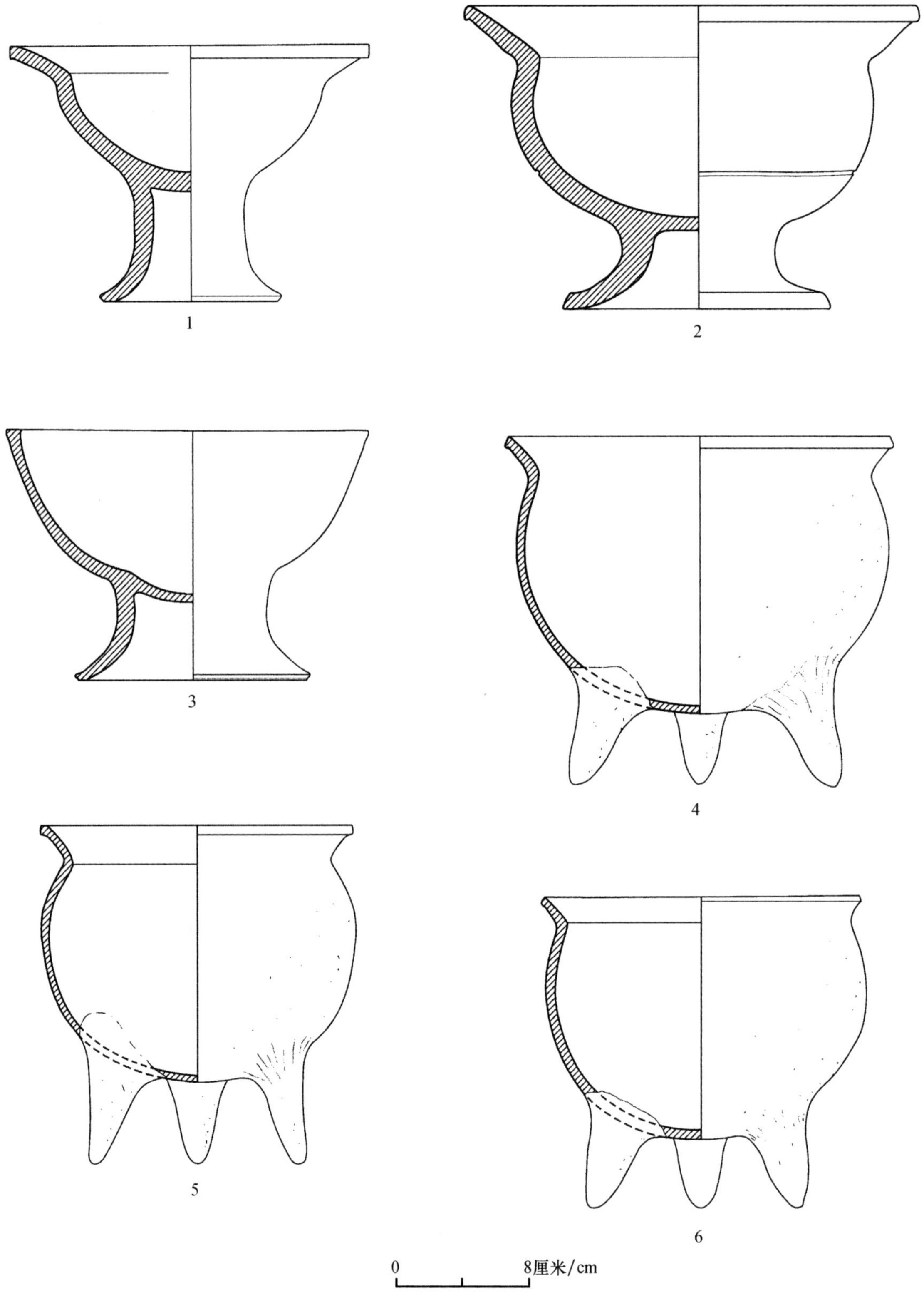

图Ⅱ.3.10　东营周家M2出土陶器

1. M2：25簋（117号）　2. M2：133簋（107号）　3. M2：24簋（136号）　4. M2：28鼎（141号）　5. M2：31鼎（142号）　6. M2：18鼎（143号）

Figure Ⅱ.3.10　Pottery unearthed from M2 at Dongying Zhoujia.

1. *Gui* (M2： 25, #117)　2. *Gui* (M2：133, #107)　3. *Gui* (M2：24, #136)　4. *Ding* (M2：28, #141)　5. *Ding* (M2：31, #142)　6. *Ding* (M2：18, #143)

图Ⅱ.3.11　东营周家M2出土陶豆

Figure Ⅱ.3.11　Pottery *dou* pedestal dishes unearthed from M2 at Dongying Zhoujia.

1. M2∶40 (#69)　2. M2∶65 (#18)　3. M2∶66 (#5)　4. M2∶31 (#15)　5. M2∶49 (#27)　6. M2∶126 (#75)　7. M2∶86 (#65)　8. M2∶15 (#9)　9. M2∶47 (#30)　10. M2∶76 (#95)　11. M2∶121 (#74)　12. M2∶27 (#96)

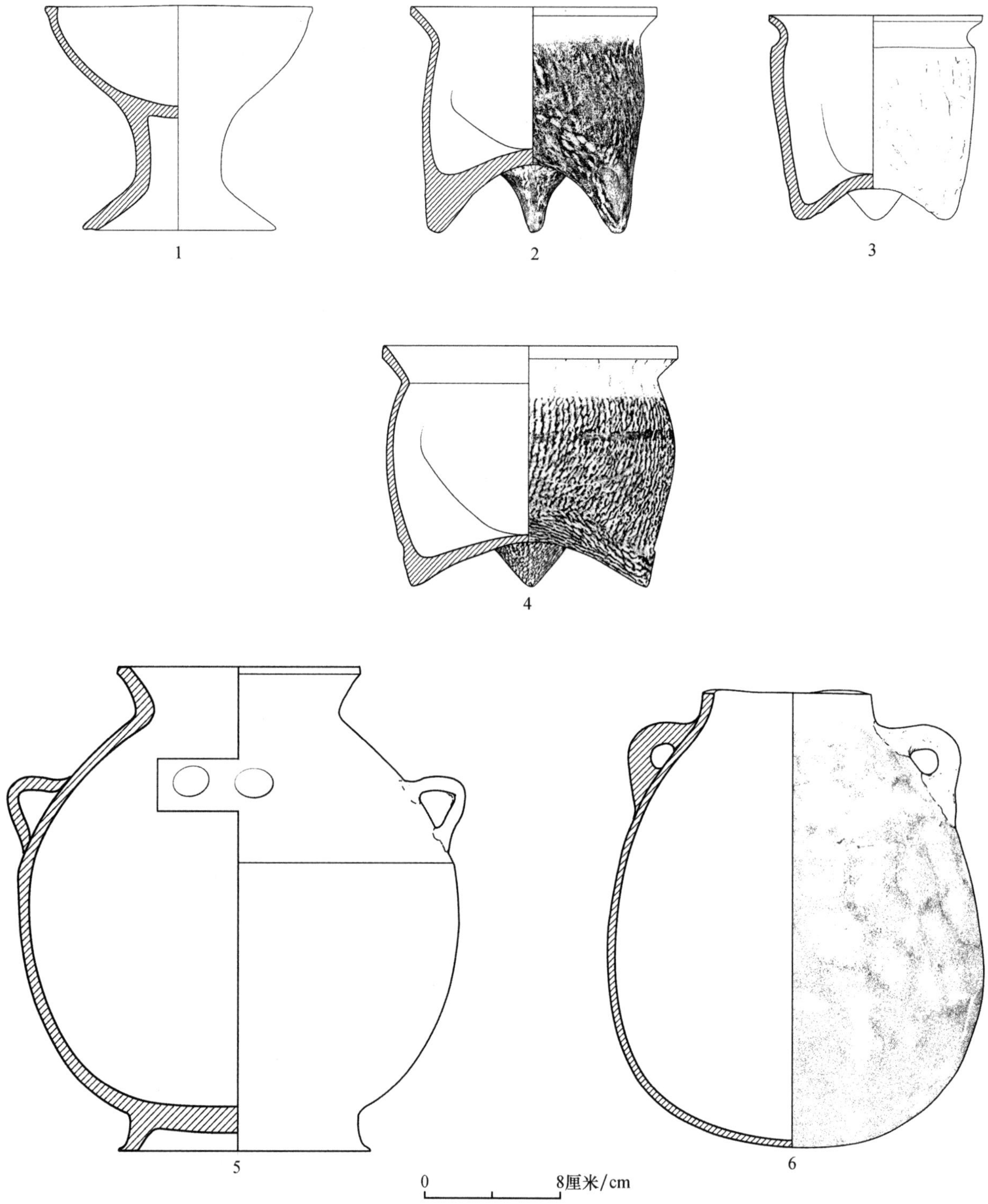

图Ⅱ.3.12　东营周家M2出土陶器

1. M2：105豆（49号）　2. M2：8鬲（137号）　3. M2：147鬲（139号）　4. M2：4鬲（138号）　5. M2：51瓿（152号）
6. M2：53壶（156号）

FigureⅡ.3.12　Pottery unearthed from M2 at Dongying Zhoujia.

1. *Dou* (M2：105, #49)　2. *Li* (M2：8, #137)　3. *Li* (M2：147, #139)　4. *Li* (M2：4, #138)　5. *Bu* (M2：51, #152)
6. *Hu* (M2：53, #156)

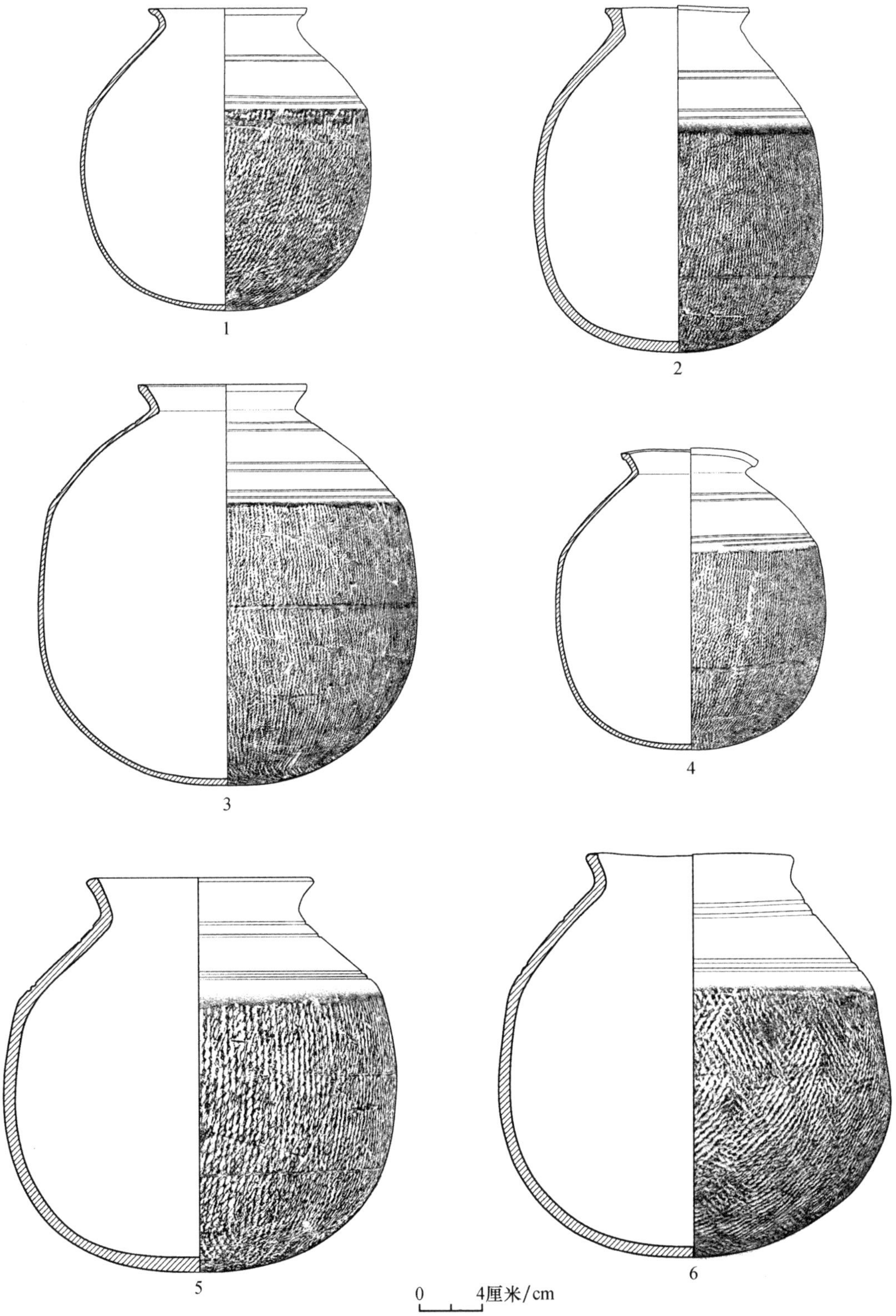

图Ⅱ.3.13　东营周家M2出土陶罐

Figure Ⅱ.3.13　Pottery *guan* jars unearthed from M2 at Dongying Zhoujia.

1. (#148)　2. M2：12 (#149)　3. M2：145 (#151)　4. M2：146 (#153)　5. (#154)　6. M2：52 (#155)

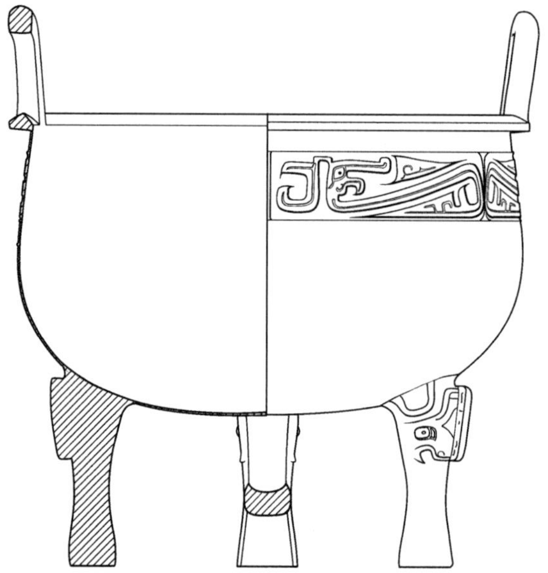

图Ⅱ.3.14　东营周家发现的铜鼎（5号）

Figure Ⅱ.3.14　*Ding*-caldrons from Dongying Zhoujia (#5).

表Ⅱ.3.2　东营周家M1、M2出土铜器、陶器登记表

Table Ⅱ.3.2　Bronzes and pottery vessels unearthed from M1 and M2 at Dongying Zhoujia

图号 Number on figure	发掘号 Excavation number	龙口市博物馆编号 Longkou Museum number	器物名称 Vessel type	出土时间 Date discovered	尺寸（厘米）Size (cm)	特点描述 Characteristics	铭文 Inscription
Ⅱ.3.6：1	M1：8	3 (KM.491)	铜簋 Bronze *gui* tureen	1986.6	H: 16.2 M: 18.6 D: 9.1	敛口鼓腹，兽首双耳有珥，圈足下附有兽足。腹部饰瓦纹，器颈饰变形兽面纹一周，圈足饰三角窃曲纹。 Constricted mouth and bulging belly; pair of ears shaped like animal heads, with pendants; ring foot with animal-shaped feet attached beneath. Vessel belly has wide groove patterns; neck has a circuit of modified animal face designs; foot has triangular curve patterns.	腹底有铭文11字。 Inscription in bottom: 11 characters.
Ⅱ.3.6：2	N/A	4 (KM.678)	铜簋 Bronze *gui* tureen	1986.6	H: 16.7 M: 18.2 D: 11.7	同上。 Same as above.	同上。 Same as above.
Ⅱ.3.7：1	M1：6	100 (KM.459)	陶豆 Pottery *dou* pedestal dish	1986.6	H: 14.02 M: 5.14 D: 3.9 H: 9.72 (handle)	浅盘，口微敛，尖唇，腹部弧收，盘底下部平。柄部较粗，稍有束腰，且位置偏上。柄下部微敞。束腰处有两周弦纹。 Shallow dish; mouth slightly constricted; pointed lip; round, gathered belly; bottom of dish flat. Stem thick with slight constriction in its upper portion. Lower portion of stem slightly flared. Waist has two ring patterns.	

续表

图号 Number on figure	发掘号 Excavation number	龙口市博物馆编号 Longkou Museum number	器物名称 Vessel type	出土时间 Date discovered	尺寸（厘米） Size (cm)	特点描述 Characteristics	铭文 Inscription
Ⅱ.3.7：2	M1：12	103 (KM.418)	陶豆 Pottery *dou* pedestal dish	1986.6	H: 14.39 D: 3.76 H: 10.3 (handle) M: 15.38	浅盘，子母口，平沿，腹部斜收，盘底平。盘、柄分界不明显。柄部较粗，束腰不明显，下部呈喇叭形。柄下部有两周弦纹。 Shallow dish; interlocking mouth; flat rim; angled, constricted belly; bottom of dish flat. Indistinct joint between dish and stem. Wide and sturdy stem; girdle unclear; lower portion trumpet-shaped. Lower portion of stem has two ring patterns.	柄内侧有刻划符号，为烧制前刻上。 Inner side of handle bears symbol carved before firing.
Ⅱ.3.7：3	M1：4	104 (KM.419)	陶豆 Pottery *dou* pedestal dish	1986.6	H: 11.87 D: 3.7 H: 8.24 (handle) M: 15.6	浅盘、敞口，圆唇，腹部内收，盘底平。盘底外侧有一道明显折棱。柄部较粗直，无明显束腰，下部外侈。 Shallow dish; wide mouth; rounded lip; constricted belly; bottom of dish flat. Outside of dish bottom bears a clear ridge. Stem relatively strong and straight, not clearly convergent; lower portion flared outward.	
Ⅱ.3.7：4	M1：14	140 (KM.455)	陶鬲 Pottery *li* tripod	1986.6	M: 13.5 H: 12.4 D: 8.1	泥质灰陶。斜沿，浅腹，平裆，三柱状实足较高，实足略内收。腹上有齿状扉棱，腹部饰粗绳纹，中部有一周指压凹坑。 Grey fine pottery. Angled rim; shallow belly; flat crotch; three relatively high, pillar-shaped solid legs constricted slightly inward. Tooth-shaped flange on vessel belly; belly has coarse cord patterns; middle portion has a circuit of dents.	
Ⅱ.3.8：1	M2：118	105 (KM.420)	陶簋 Pottery *gui* tureen	1986.6	H: 21.05 M: 26.5 D: 12.9 B: 15.5 H: 8.5 (foot)	大敞口，斜沿略卷，方唇。鼓腹，高圈足，较直。腹与沿部抹光但留有绳纹痕迹。泥质灰陶。 Large wide-open mouth; angled, slightly curled rim; square lip. Bulging belly; high, relatively straight ring foot. Belly and rim portions polished, but still show traces of cord patterns. Grey fine ceramic.	
Ⅱ.3.8：2	M2：3	106 (KM.421)	陶簋 Pottery *gui* tureen	1986.6	H: 21 M: 25.3 D: 11.8 B: 16 H: 8.9 (foot)	宽斜沿，直腹，高圈足。腹与沿部磨光，腹较直。腹与圈足饰数道凹弦纹。泥质灰陶。 Wide, angled rim; straight belly; high ring-foot. Belly and rim portions polished; belly relatively straight. Belly and ring-foot have several intaglio ring patterns. Grey fine ceramic.	
Ⅱ.3.8：3	M2：102	109 (KM.424)	陶簋 Pottery *gui* tureen	1986.6	H: 19.5 M: 23.15 D: 11.45 B: 15.4 H: 8.1 (foot)	宽斜沿，方唇，圈足高而外侈。腹和圈足顶部各饰一凸棱，圈足下部凹弦纹。泥质灰陶。 Wide, angled rim; square lip; ring-foot high and flared outward. Belly and crown of ring-foot each have a single raised flange; lower portion of ring-foot has intaglio ring pattern. Grey fine ceramic.	
Ⅱ.3.8：4	M2：58	110 (KM.425)	陶簋 Pottery *gui* tureen	1986.6	H: 18.7 M: 26.5 D: 10.3 B: 16.1 H: 8.2 (foot)	宽斜平沿，方唇。腹微浅，内收，近腹底部有一周凸棱。高圈足。泥质浅灰陶。 Wide, angled, flat rim; square lip. Slightly shallow belly constricted inward, with one protruding flange near bottom. High ring-foot. Light grey fine ceramic.	

续表

图号 Number on figure	发掘号 Excavation number	龙口市博物馆编号 Longkou Museum number	器物名称 Vessel type	出土时间 Date discovered	尺寸（厘米） Size (cm)	特点描述 Characteristics	铭文 Inscription
Ⅱ.3.8：5	M2：134	114 (KM.429)	陶簋 Pottery *gui* tureen	1986.6	H: 20 M: 26.3 D: 11 B: 13.85 H: 8.7 (foot)	敞口，浅腹呈半球形，圈足细高。泥质浅灰陶。 Wide mouth; shallow, hemispherical belly; slender, high ring-foot. Light grey fine ceramic.	
Ⅱ.3.8：6	M2：21	122 (KM.437)	陶簋 Pottery *gui* tureen	1986.6	H: 17 M: 24 D: 11.15 B: 12.9 H: 6.4 (foot)	大敞口，撇沿。颈部略收缩。高圈足圈足上有一周凸棱。泥质浅灰陶。 Very wide mouth, flaring rim. Slightly constricted neck. High ring-foot has a single flange. Light grey fine ceramic.	
Ⅱ.3.9：1	M2：56	132 (KM.447)	陶簋 Pottery *gui* tureen	1986.6	H: 18.5 M: 25.55 D: 10 B: 15.75 H: 8.4 (foot)	斜长沿微上卷，束颈明显，腹浅而鼓。高圈足。素面。泥质灰褐陶。 Long rim tilts slightly upward; obvious constricted neck; belly shallow and bulging. High ring-foot. Plain surface. Greyish-brown fine ceramic.	
Ⅱ.3.9：2	M2：116	108 (KM.423)	陶簋 Pottery *gui* tureen	1986.6	H: 17 M: 24.34 D: 12.1 B: 15.27 H: 4.6 (foot)	敞口，斜沿微折，圈足较矮。腹斜，略直；腹上部与口沿下有不甚清楚的绳纹。口沿上有一道凹弦纹。泥质灰陶。 Wide mouth; angled rim tilts slightly; short ring-foot. Slightly straight, oblique belly; blurred cord patterns appear on upper belly and below rim. Single intaglio ring pattern appears above rim. Grey fine ceramic.	
Ⅱ.3.9：3	M2：59	135 (KM.450)	陶簋 Pottery *gui* tureen	1986.6	H: 21 M: 29.5 D: 13 B: 16.3 H: 8.1 (foot)	敞口，斜沿微卷，圈足略高，足端外撇。腹斜直。素面。泥质深灰陶。 Wide mouth; oblique slightly curled rim; slightly high ring-foot; upper part of foot flared outward. Straight and oblique belly. Plain surface. Dark grey fine ceramic.	
Ⅱ.3.9：4	M2：66	116 (KM.431)	陶簋 Pottery *gui* tureen	1986.6	H: 15.63 M: 24.2 D: 10.12 B: 13.4 H: 6.1 (foot)	斜沿外撇，束颈，腹部较鼓。圈足较直，圈足上有一周凸弦纹。泥质浅灰陶。 Oblique rim flaring, constricted neck; relatively bulging belly. Relatively straight, ring-foot has a single raised ring pattern. Light grey fine ceramic.	
Ⅱ.3.9：5	M2：22	118 (KM.433)	陶簋 Pottery *gui* tureen	1986.6	H: 4.56 M: 18.75 D: 7.42 B: 12.53 H: 6.1 (foot)	形体较小。撇沿束颈，浅腹。高圈足。素面。泥质浅灰陶。 Relatively small. Flaring rim; constricted neck; shallow belly. High ring-foot. Plain surface. Light grey fine ceramic.	
Ⅱ.3.9：6	M2：32	129 (KM.444)	陶簋 Pottery *gui* tureen	1986.6	H: 22.95 M: 27.9 D: 13.7 B: 16 H: 8.6 (foot)	整体瘦高。撇沿，圆唇，沿上有凹弦纹。深腹，高圈足。腹下部和圈足下部各有两道弦纹。泥质浅灰陶。 Tall, narrow vessel body. Outwardly flaring rim; rounded lip; rim bears intaglio ring patterns. Deep belly; high ring-foot. Lower portions of belly and ring-foot each have two bands of ring patterns. Light grey fine ceramic.	

续表

图号 Number on figure	发掘号 Excavation number	龙口市博物馆编号 Longkou Museum number	器物名称 Vessel type	出土时间 Date discovered	尺寸（厘米） Size (cm)	特点描述 Characteristics	铭文 Inscription
Ⅱ.3.10：1	M2：25	117 (KM.432)	陶簋 Pottery *gui* tureen	1986.6	H: 14.8 M: 21.5 D: 7.3 B: 10.9 H: 7.3 (foot)	大敞口，平沿，盘极浅。圈足细高。泥质浅灰陶。 Large, flared mouth; flat rim; very shallow dish. Slender, tall ring-foot. Light grey fine ceramic.	
Ⅱ.3.10：2	M1：133	107 (KM.422)	陶簋 Pottery *gui* tureen	1986.6	H: 17.6 M: 27.05 D: 12.28 B: 15.88 H: 5 (foot)	宽斜沿，鼓腹如球状，束颈明显，矮圈足。素面，腹下部饰一道凹弦纹。泥质灰褐陶。 Wide, oblique rim; bulging and spherical belly; distinctly constricted neck; short ring-foot. Plain surface; lower portion of belly has intaglio ring patterns. Grey-brown fine ceramic.	
Ⅱ.3.10：3	M2：24	136 (KM.451)	陶簋 Pottery *gui* tureen	1986.6	H: 14.5 M: 21.8 D: 9.5 B: 14.1 H: 5.8 (foot)	敞口，半球形腹。矮圈足。素面。泥质深灰陶。 Wide mouth; hemispherical belly. Short ring-foot. Plain surface. Dark grey fine ceramic.	
Ⅱ.3.10：4	M2：28	141 (KM.456)	陶鼎 Pottery *ding* cauldron	1986.6	H: 20.1 M: 23 D: 16	斜折口沿。深腹，腹最大径接近束颈，三圆锥足较直外撇。素面，夹砂红褐陶。 Oblique folded rim. Deep belly; widest point of belly near constricted neck; three conical feet relatively straight and angled slightly outward. Plain surface; reddish-brown sandy ceramic.	
Ⅱ.3.10：5	M2：31	142 (KM.457)	陶鼎 Pottery *ding* cauldron	1986.6	H: 19.6 M: 18.7 D: 14.5	斜折沿较宽，方唇。鼓腹，圜底，有明显束颈。三圆锥足较直内聚。素面，夹砂红褐陶。 Relatively wide, oblique, folded rim; square lip. Bulging belly; round bottom; vessel has distinctly constricted neck. Relatively straight conical feet gathered inwards. Plain surface; reddish-brown, sandy ceramic.	
Ⅱ.3.10：6	M2：18	143 (KM.458)	陶鼎 Pottery *ding* cauldron	1986.6	H: 18 M: 19 D: 13.5	窄斜口沿，方唇，深腹，底近平，三圆锥足微外撇。最大腹径在腹上部。素面。夹砂红褐陶。 Narrow, oblique rim; square lip; deep belly; nearly flat bottom; three conical feet angled slightly outward. Vessel body widest at upper portion of belly. Plain surface. Reddish-brown, sandy ceramic.	
Ⅱ.3.11：1	M2：40	69 (KM.385)	陶豆 Pottery *dou* pedestal dish	1986.6	H: 12.75 M: 17.6 D: 4.22 H: 7.9 (handle) D: 5.0 (waist) B: 11.15	浅盘，敞口，沿面有一道凹槽，折腹，盘底呈圜底。盘、柄分界明显。柄部细，在中部束腰处有一周凸棱，下部呈喇叭形。通体素面，泥质深灰陶。豆柄与豆盘分制。 Shallow dish; wide mouth; groove on surface of rim; folded belly; round-bottomed dish. Clear joint between dish and stem. Slender stem; protruding ridge on middle section of handle; lower portion forms trumpet shape. Plain surface on entire body of vessel; dark grey fine ceramic. Stem and dish made separately.	

续表

图号 Number on figure	发掘号 Excavation number	龙口市博物馆编号 Longkou Museum number	器物名称 Vessel type	出土时间 Date discovered	尺寸（厘米）Size (cm)	特点描述 Characteristics	铭文 Inscription
Ⅱ.3.11：2	M2：65	18 (KM.334)	陶豆 Pottery *dou* pedestal dish	1986.6	H: 11.14 M: 14.58 D: 3.15 H: 7.4 (handle) D: 4.67 (waist) B: 10.65	不规整。浅盘，盘底不平。直口圆唇。细柄束腰明显，并有一周凸棱，下部呈喇叭形。泥质深灰。豆柄与豆盘分制后结合。柄上内侧有修整痕迹。Irregularly shaped. Shallow dish with uneven bottom. Straight mouth with rounded lip. Narrow stem, distinctly constricted waist with a single protruding ridge; lower portion forms trumpet shape. Grey fine material. Stem and dish made separately and assembled. Inner side of upper portion of stem has traces of finishing.	
Ⅱ.3.11：3	M2：66	5 (KM.321)	陶豆 Pottery *dou* pedestal dish	1986.6	H: 14.35 M: 15.13 D: 3.9 H: 9.88 (handle) D: 4.9 (waist) B: 11.4	浅盘，直口、尖圆唇，盘底呈圜底。柄部稍高，较细，下部呈喇叭形。柄略偏上部有一周凸棱。泥质浅灰陶。Shallow dish; straight mouth; round and pointed lip; round-bottomed dish. Stem portion somewhat high and relatively slender; lower portion forms trumpet shape. Stem has single ridge slightly above center. Light grey fine pottery.	
Ⅱ.3.11：4	M2：31	15 (KM.331)	陶豆 Pottery *dou* pedestal dish	1986.6	H: 12.75 M: 15 D: 3.8 H: 8.3 (handle) D: 4.87 (waist) B: 11	浅盘，直口微敛，圆唇，盘底平。柄部较细，束腰明显，位于柄中部，并有一周凸棱，下部呈喇叭形。泥质灰褐陶。Shallow dish; straight mouth, slightly constricted; rounded lip; flat-bottomed dish. Relatively slim stem; distinctly constricted waist has a single ridge; lower portion of handle forms trumpet shape. Grey-brown fine pottery.	
Ⅱ.3.11：5	M2：49	27 (KM.343)	陶豆 Pottery *dou* pedestal dish	1986.6	H: 11.12 D: 3.73 H: 7.12 (handle) M: 17.05 D: 5.46 (waist) B: 10.5	浅盘、平沿，腹部斜，盘底平。柄部较细，束腰位于中部，下部呈喇叭形。泥质灰褐陶。豆柄与豆盘分制结合。Shallow dish; flat rim; oblique belly; flat-bottomed dish. Relatively slim stem; constricted waist in middle section; lower portion forms trumpet shape. Greyish-brown fine pottery. Stem and dish made separately and assembled.	
Ⅱ.3.11：6	M2：126	75 (KM.391)	陶豆 Pottery *dou* pedestal dish	1986.6	H: 11.56 D: 4.1 H: 7.25 (handle) M: 16.15 D: 4.2 (waist) B: 10.65	深盘，大敞口，平沿，腹部微折，盘底近平。柄部细，中部束腰明显，下部呈喇叭形豆。柄与豆盘分制结合。泥质灰褐陶。Shallow dish; wide-open mouth; flat rim; slightly angled belly; bottom of dish nearly flat. Slender stem, middle portion distinct waist constriction; lower portion forms trumpet shape. Stem and dish made separately and assembled. Greyish-brown fine pottery.	
Ⅱ.3.11：7	M2：86	65 (KM.381)	陶豆 Pottery *dou* pedestal dish	1986.6	H: 9.75 M: 16.45 D: 3.27 H: 6.0 (handle) D: 5.13 (waist) B: 10.03	浅盘，平沿，腹部斜弧，盘底平。柄部细矮，束腰位置接近盘底并有一周不十分明显凸棱，柄下部呈喇叭形。豆柄与豆盘分制结合。泥质深灰陶。Shallow dish; flat rim; oblique belly; flat-bottomed dish. Short, thin stem; constricted waist near bottom of dish, with indistinct ridge; lower portion of stem forms trumpet shape. Stem and dish made separately and assembled. Dark grey fine pottery.	

续表

图号 Number on figure	发掘号 Excavation number	龙口市博物馆编号 Longkou Museum number	器物名称 Vessel type	出土时间 Date discovered	尺寸（厘米） Size (cm)	特点描述 Characteristics	铭文 Inscription
Ⅱ.3.11：8	M2：15	9 (KM.325)	陶豆 Pottery *dou* pedestal dish	1986.6	H: 11 M: 16.08 D: 3.27 H: 7.3 (handle) D: 4.85 (waist) B: 10.67	浅盘、敞口，平沿，弧腹。柄部较细高，最细处近盘底，下部呈大喇叭形。泥质浅灰。豆柄与豆盘分制结合。 Shallow dish; wide mouth; flat rim; curved belly bottom. Tall, relatively slim stem; narrowest point near bottom of dish; bottom portion forms large trumpet shape. Light grey fine material. Stem and dish made separately and assembled.	
Ⅱ.3.11：9	M2：47	30 (KM.346)	陶豆 Pottery *dou* pedestal dish	1986.6	H: 2.31 D: 4.1 H: 7.65 (handle) M: 14.77 D: 4.65 (waist) B: 11.28	浅盘，直口、平沿、腹部弧，盘底呈圜底。盘、柄分界明显。柄部细直，无束腰，下部外侈明显。泥质灰褐陶。豆柄与豆盘分制结合。 Shallow dish; straight mouth; flat rim; curved belly bottom; round-bottomed dish. Clear joint between dish and stem. Thin, straight stem without ridge; lower portion flared distinctly outward. Grey-brown fine pottery. Stem and dish made separately and assembled.	
Ⅱ.3.11：10	M2：76	95 (KM.411)	陶豆 Pottery *dou* pedestal dish	1986.6	H: 15.22 D: 3.45 H: 12.1 (handle) M: 16.15 D: 5.8 (waist) B: 11.17	浅盘、口微敛。平沿外侧稍有突脊。柄部高，无明显束腰，仅中部略细，有两周弦纹，中间为凸棱。柄下部呈外撇明显。泥质浅灰陶。豆柄与豆盘分制结合。柄上部内侧有明显修整痕迹。 Shallow dish; slightly constricted mouth. Outside of flat rim has slight ridge. Tall stem without distinct waist constriction, but with slightly narrow central portion and two ring patterns with a ridge between them. Lower portion of handle turns distinctly outward. Light grey fine pottery. Stem and dish made separately and assembled. Inner side of upper stem bears distinct traces of finishing.	
Ⅱ.3.11：11	M2：121	74 (KM.390)	陶豆 Pottery *dou* pedestal dish	1986.6	H: 11.13 M: 17.95 D: 2.4 H: 8.35 (handle) D: 5.48 (waist) B: 11.42	敞口，圆唇，浅盘，折腹，盘底平。柄部较细，无明显束腰，下部呈喇叭形。泥质浅灰陶。豆柄与豆盘分制结合。 Wide mouth; rounded lip; shallow dish; folded belly; flat-bottomed dish. Relatively slim stem without distinct waist constriction; lower portion forms trumpet shape. Light grey fine pottery. Stem and dish made separately and assembled.	
Ⅱ.3.11：12	M2：27	96 (KM.412)	陶豆 Pottery *dou* pedestal dish	1986.6	H: 11.77 D: 3.25 H: 8.0 (handle) M: 15.58 D: 6.65 (waist) B: 13	浅盘，直口，平沿。盘底较平。柄较粗，最细处位置偏上，下部呈喇叭形。通体素面，圈足中部有三个长方形镂孔。泥质浅灰陶。豆柄与豆盘分制结合。盘底部和柄上端内部有明显接痕。 Shallow dish; straight mouth; flat rim. Bottom of dish relatively flat. Relatively sturdy stem; thins slightly toward top; lower portion forms trumpet shape. Plain surface on entire vessel body; middle portion of stem has three rectangular holes. Light grey fine pottery. Stem and dish made separately and assembled. Bottom portion of dish and inner part of upper handle bear obvious traces of finishing.	

续表

图号 Number on figure	发掘号 Excavation number	龙口市博物馆编号 Longkou Museum number	器物名称 Vessel type	出土时间 Date discovered	尺寸（厘米）Size (cm)	特点描述 Characteristics	铭文 Inscription
Ⅱ.3.12：1	M2：105	49 (KM.365)	陶豆 Pottery *dou* pedestal dish	1986.6	H: 12.9 D: 5.8 H: 7.0 (handle) M: 15.83 D: 5.03 (waist) B: 11.4	敞口，平沿，沿外侧稍有凸起。深盘，弧腹斜收，盘底呈圜形。细柄下呈大喇叭形。泥质浅灰陶。豆柄与豆盘分制结合。 Wide mouth; flat rim; outside of rim has slight protrusion. Deep and hemispherical dish with lower part slightly constricted. Lower portion of narrow stem forms large trumpet shape. Light grey fine pottery. Stem and dish made separately and assembled.	
Ⅱ.3.12：2	M2：8	137 (KM.452)	陶鬲 Pottery *li* tripod	1986.6	M: 14.4 H: 13.2	卷沿，方唇。直腹，连裆，袋足下有实足根较高。腹下饰粗绳纹。夹砂灰陶。 Rolled rim; square lip. Straight belly; joined crotch; pocket-shaped legs with solid, relatively tall tips. Lower portion of belly has coarse cord patterns. Grey, sandy pottery.	
Ⅱ.3.12：3	M2：147	139 (KM.454)	陶鬲 Pottery *li* tripod	1986.6	M: 12 H: 12	卷沿，圆唇，束颈。直腹，袋足无足根。素面。夹砂灰陶。 Rolled rim; rounded lip; constricted neck. Straight belly; pocket-shaped legs without tips. Plain surface. Grey, sandy pottery.	
Ⅱ.3.12：4	M2：4	138 (KM.453)	陶鬲 Pottery *li* tripod	1986.6	M: 16.8 H: 13.8	斜折沿，方唇。腹微鼓，矮弧裆较低。沿下有抹去的绳纹痕迹，腹部饰竖绳纹，上部有一道抹断的痕迹。夹砂灰陶。 Folded oblique rim; square lip. Slightly bulging belly; short, arching, slightly low crotch. Traces of now-missing cord patterns appear below the rim; belly portion has vertical cord patterns; upper portion has a round of hand-smoothed rubbing. Grey, sandy pottery.	
Ⅱ.3.12：5	M2：51	152 (KM.468)	陶瓿 Pottery *pou* jar	1986.6	H: 27.8 M: 14.5 B: 15	小口，方唇。鼓腹，矮圈足微撇。肩饰有对称双耳和圆形泥饼，肩腹交接处有不显的突棱。泥质红褐陶。 Small mouth; square lip. Bulging belly; short, ring-foot flared slightly outward. Shoulder has paired, symmetrically placed ears and mud-cake button decorations; faint ridge appears at point of contact between shoulders and belly. Reddish-brown fine-clay pottery.	
Ⅱ.3.12：6	M2：53	156 (KM.472)	陶壶 Pottery *hu* bottle	1986.6	H: 26.15 M: 9.9 D: 22.1	小敛口，溜肩，肩上有双耳。深腹圜底。表面粗糙，素面。加砂红褐陶。 Small, constricted mouth; sloping shoulder with paired ears. Deep belly with large bottom. Plain, coarse surface. Sandy, reddish-brown pottery.	
Ⅱ.3.13：1	N/A	148 (KM.464)	陶罐 Pottery *guan* jar	1986.6	H: 36.8 M: 19.8 D: 36.32	大罐。小口，卷沿方唇。折肩上有两束各两道弦纹。深腹圜底，腹底饰绳纹，有交错。泥质浅灰陶。 Large jar. Small mouth; rolled rim with square lip. Two groups of double ring patterns on shoulders. Deep belly with round bottom; bottom has intertwining cord patterns. Light grey fine pottery.	

续表

图号 Number on figure	发掘号 Excavation number	龙口市博物馆编号 Longkou Museum number	器物名称 Vessel type	出土时间 Date discovered	尺寸（厘米） Size (cm)	特点描述 Characteristics	铭文 Inscription
Ⅱ.3.13：2	M2：12	149 (KM.465)	陶罐 Pottery *guan* jar	1986.6	H: 41.96 M: 18.22 D: 36.5	大罐。平沿，圆唇，斜肩，鼓腹圜底，腹最大径在中部。沿面有一周凹弦纹，肩饰数周凹弦纹。近颈部有抹去的绳纹痕迹。泥质深灰陶。 Large jar. Flat rim; rounded lip; oblique shoulders; bulging belly with round bottom, widest in middle portion. Surface of rim has a single intaglio ring pattern; shoulders have several intaglio ring patterns. Traces of erased cord patterns visible near neck portion of vessel. Dark grey fine pottery.	
Ⅱ.3.13：3	M2：145	151 (KM.467)	陶罐 Pottery *guan* jar	1986.6	H: 48.85 M: 21 D: 47.25	大罐。小口，平唇。折肩，肩上有三束各两道凹弦纹。圜底。腹部饰绳纹，分为上下两段。泥质红褐陶。 Large jar. Small mouth; flat lip. Folded shoulders with three groups of two intaglio ring patterns each. Round bottom. Vessel belly has cord patterns; divided into upper and lower portions. Reddish-brown fine pottery.	
Ⅱ.3.13：4	M：146	153 (KM.469)	陶罐 Pottery *guan* jar	1986.6	H: 36.75 M: 17.6 D: 34.5	大罐。小口，平唇。口部变形。折肩，肩上有两束弦纹。圜底。腹部饰绳纹，有抹断痕迹。泥质深灰陶。 Large jar. Small mouth; flat lip. Vessel mouth deformed. Folded shoulders have two groups of ring patterns. Round bottom. Vessel belly has cord patterns; traces of erasure present. Dark grey fine pottery.	
Ⅱ.3.13：5	N/A	154 (KM.470)	陶罐 Pottery *guan* jar	1986.6	H: 24.1 M: 14.2 D: 24.6	小罐。小口圆唇。窄折肩，肩上有两束各两道弦纹。鼓腹圜底，饰绳纹。泥质深灰陶。 Small jar. Small mouth and rounded lip. Narrow, folded shoulders with two groups of two ring patterns each. Bulging belly with round bottom, decorated with cord patterns. Dark grey fine pottery.	
Ⅱ.3.13：6	M2：52	155 (KM.471)	陶罐 Pottery *guan* jar	1986.6	H: 24.5 M: 13.2 D: 24.8	小罐。小口圆唇，平沿。溜肩明显，圆腹圜底。肩腹交接处折棱不太明显。肩部饰数周凹弦纹，腹底饰绳纹。泥质灰陶。 Small jar. Small mouth and rounded lip; flat rim. Distinct, sloping shoulders; round belly with circular bottom. Indistinct ridge at point of contact between shoulders and belly. Shoulders have several intaglio ring patterns; bottom of belly has cord patterns. Grey fine pottery.	
Ⅱ.3.14		5 (KM.611)	铜鼎 Bronze *ding* cauldron		H: 22.25 M: 21.25 D: 11.8 H: 4.27 (ears)	深腹圜底，立耳，三柱足，足根有兽首。沿下饰夔纹。 Deep belly with round bottom, upright ears; three solid pillar-shaped legs. *Kui* dragon pattern under rim.	

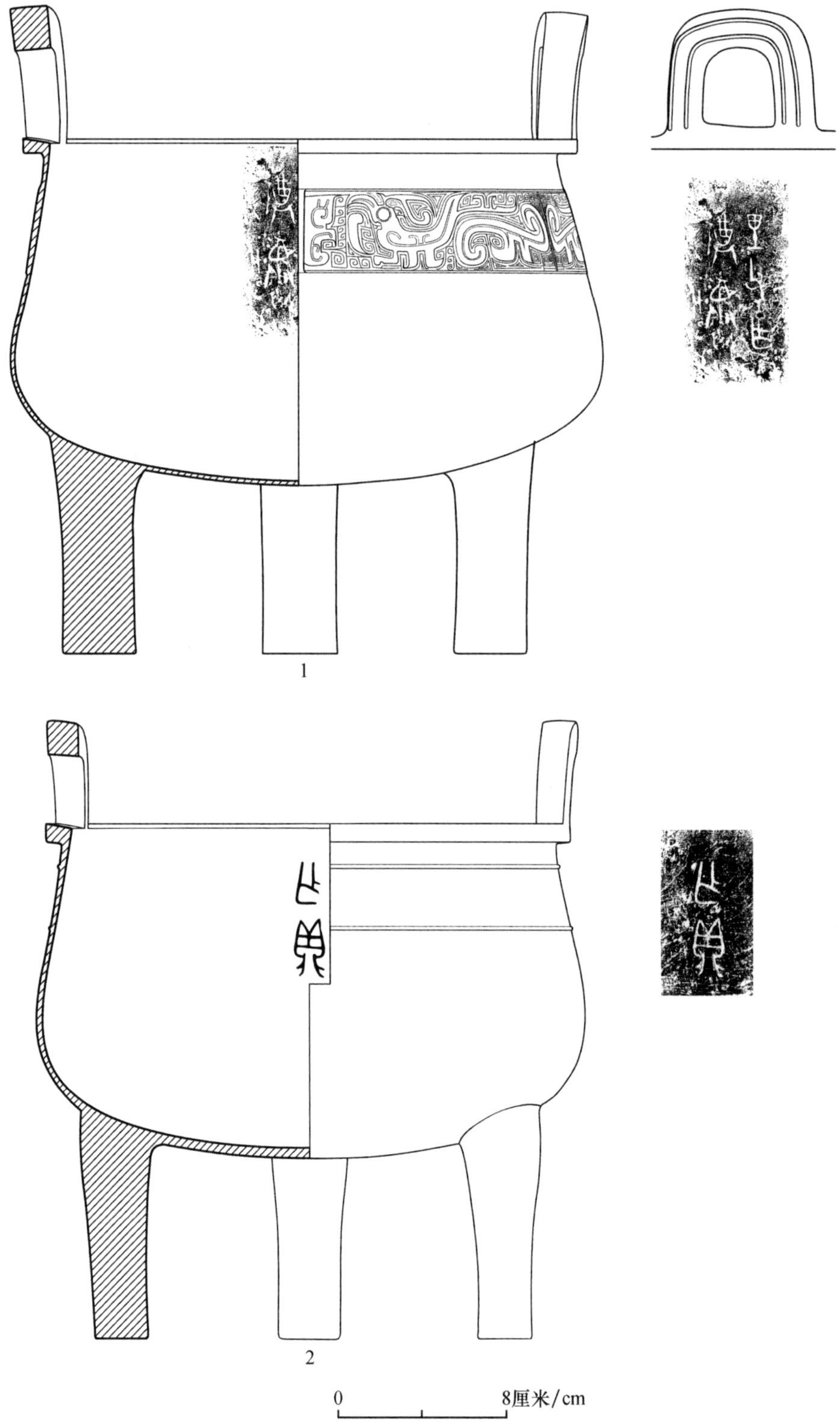

图Ⅱ.3.15　集前赵家出土铜鼎

FigureⅡ.3.15　*Ding* cauldrons from Jiqian Zhaojia.

1. #348　2. #357

腹底铭文

Inscription on bottom

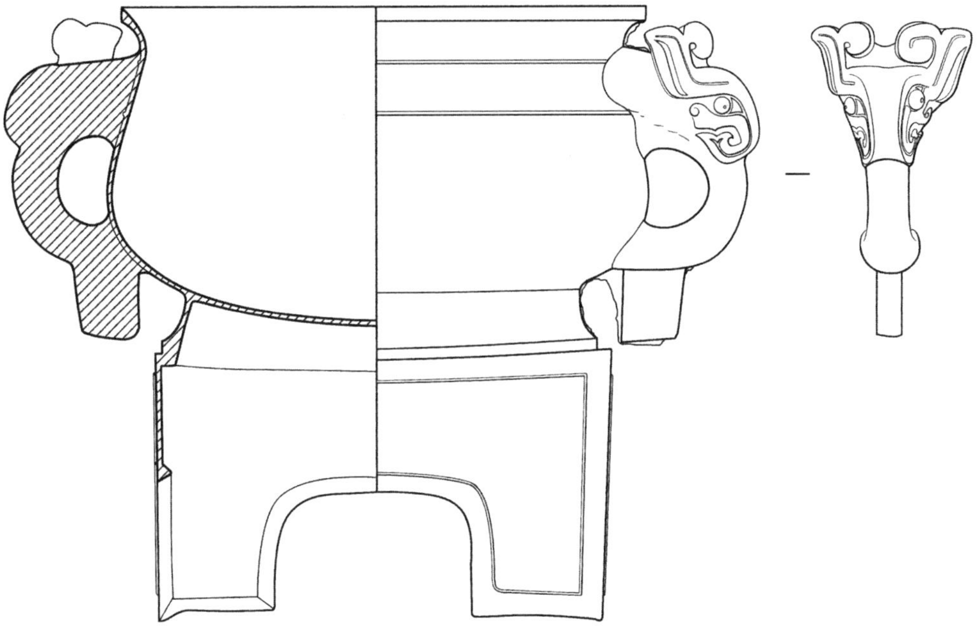

1

腹底铭文

Inscription on bottom

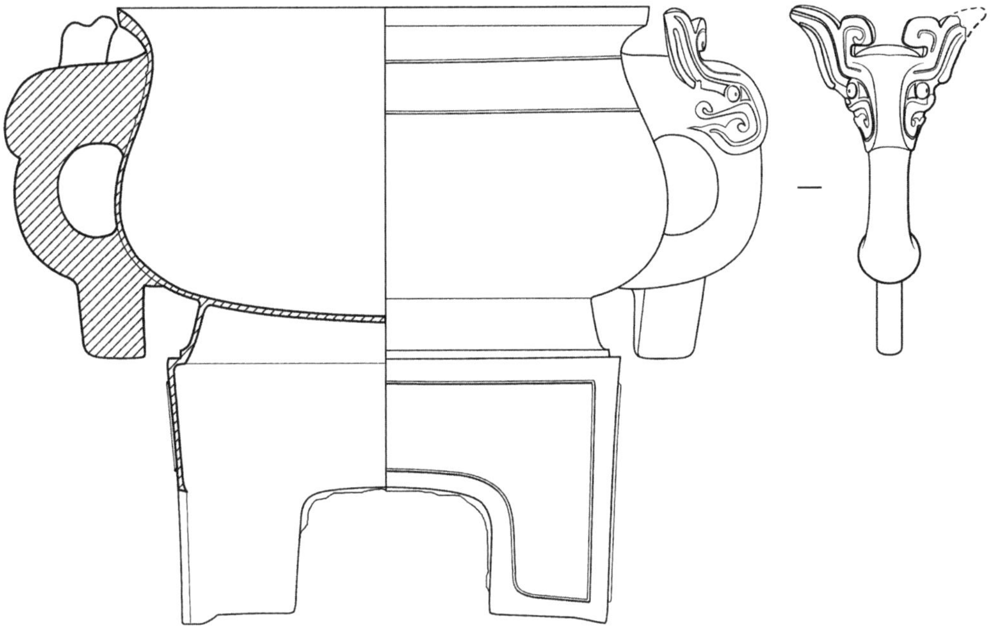

2

0　8厘米/cm

图Ⅱ.3.16　集前赵家出土铜簋

Figure Ⅱ.3.16　*Gui* tureens from Jiqian Zhaojia.

1. #350　2. #351

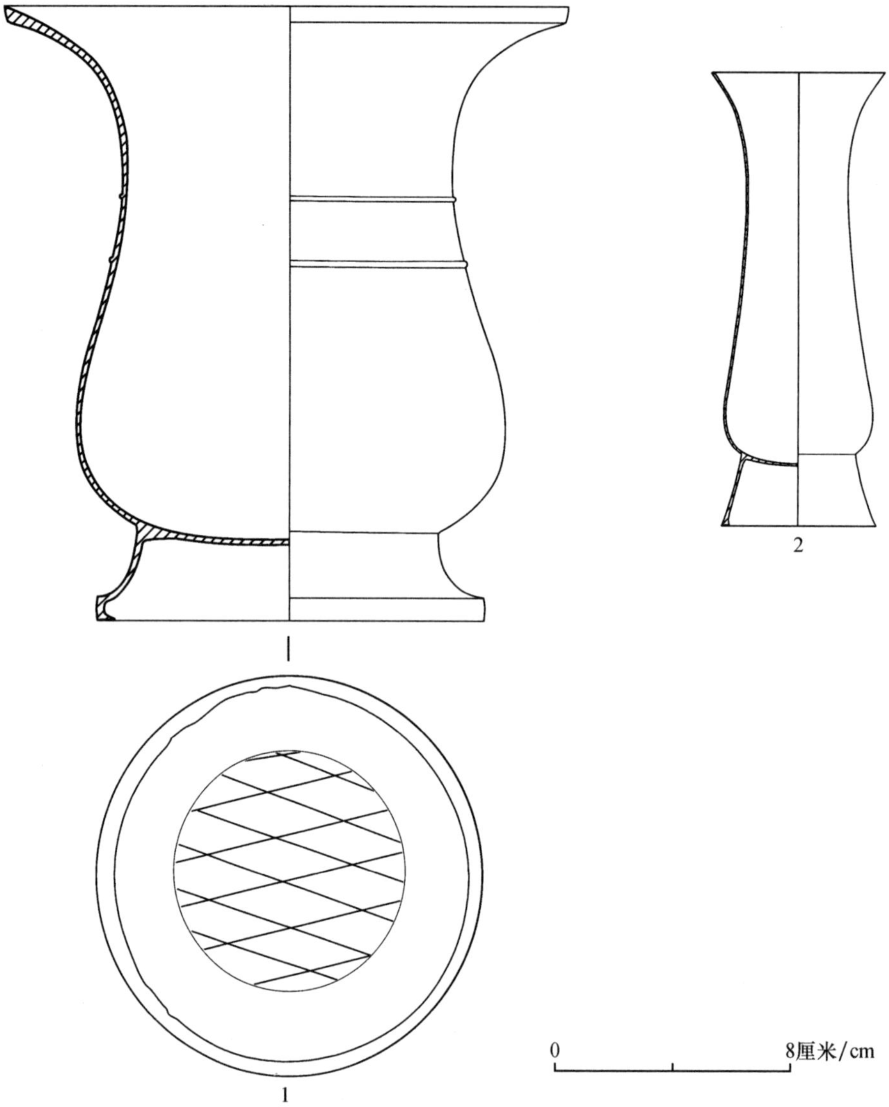

图Ⅱ.3.17　集前赵家出土铜器

1. 尊352号　2. 觯359号

Figure Ⅱ.3.17　Bronzes from Jiqian Zhaojia.

1. *Zun* [#352]　2. *Zhi* [#359]

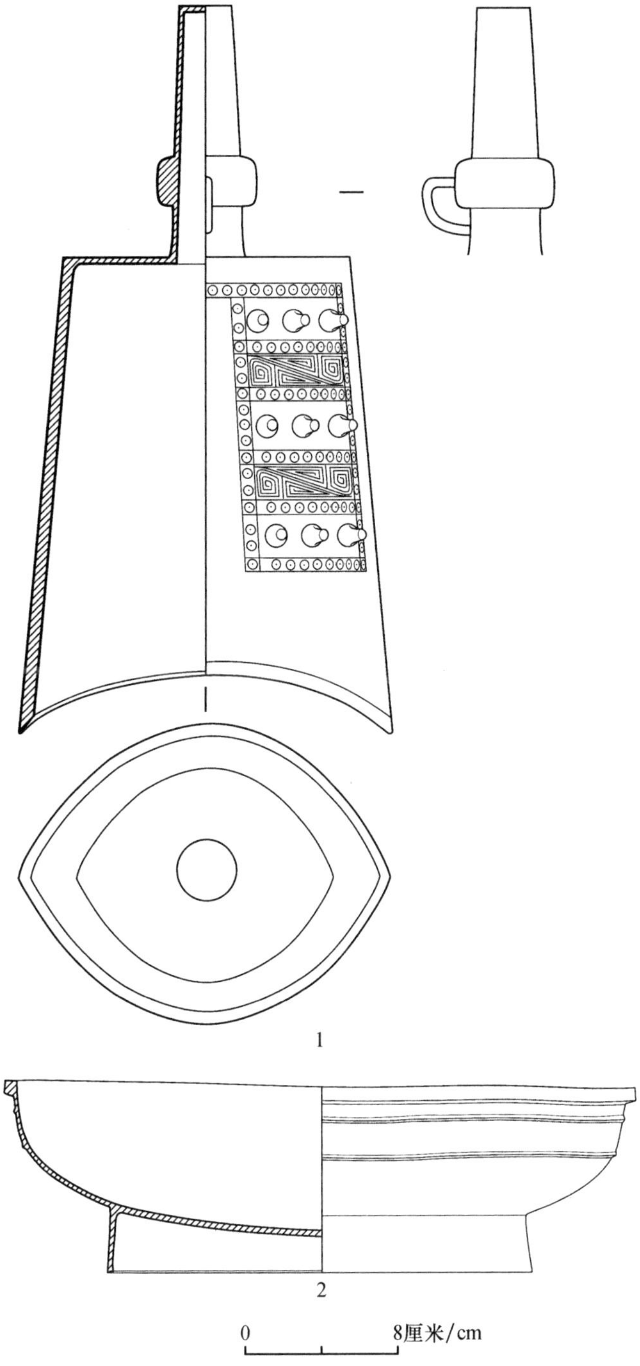

图Ⅱ.3.18　集前赵家出土铜器

1. 钟356号　2. 盘354号

Figure Ⅱ.3.18　Bronzes from Jiqian Zhaojia.

1. Bell [#356]　2. *Pan* [#354]

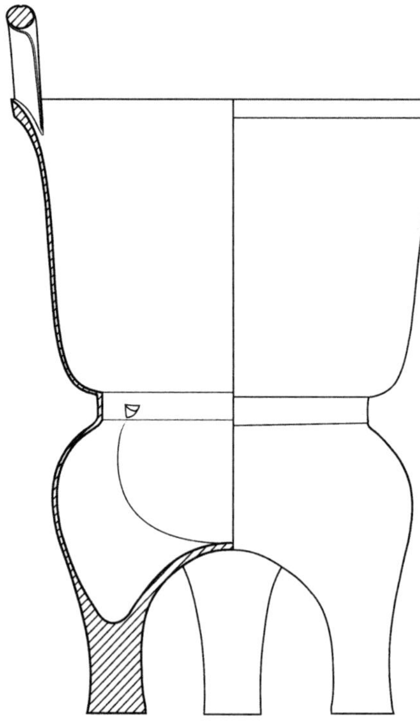

图Ⅱ.3.19　集前赵家出土铜甗（353号）

Figure Ⅱ.3.19　*Yan* steamer from Jiqian Zhaojia (#353).

表Ⅱ.3.3　集前赵家出土铜器登记表

Table Ⅱ.3.3　Bronzes previously unearthed at Jiqian Zhaojia

图号 Number on figure	龙口市博物馆编号 Longkou Museum number	器物名称 Artifact name	出土时间 Date discovered	尺寸（厘米） Size (cm)	特点描述 Characteristics	铭文 Inscription
Ⅱ.3.15：1	348	鼎 *Ding* cauldron	2004.4	H: 29.5 M: 26.2 D: 15.7 H: 5.95 (ears)	方唇、平沿、立耳。深腹下垂，寰底近平。三圆柱形足。口沿下饰细致的长尾鸟纹。 Square lip; flat rim; upright ears. Deep sagging belly; round but nearly flat bottom. Three cylindrical legs. Area below rim decorated with fine, long-tailed bird designs.	腹内有铭文5字或更多。 Inscription inside vessel belly; 5 characters or more
Ⅱ.3.15：2	357	鼎 *Ding* cauldron	2004.4	H: 28.3 M: 24.9 D: 14.85 H: 4.67 (ears)	器形同于348号鼎。但口沿下仅饰两道凸起的弦纹。 Same shape as *ding* cauldron no. 348, but area below rim has only two raised ring patterns.	腹内有铭文3字 Inscription inside vessel belly; 3 characters
Ⅱ.3.16：1	350	簋 *Gui* tureen	2004.4	H: 21.8 M: 19.1 D: 11.1 H: 9.7 (base) W: 16.7 (base)	方座簋。腹部略垂，双耳有珥。方座相对矮小，下部作桥形。全身素面，口沿下饰两道弦纹，方座沿周边亦饰一道弦纹。 *Gui* tureen with square base. Slightly sagging belly; paired ears with pendants. Relatively small square base; bridge-shaped lower portion. Plain surface on entire body of vessel; two ring patterns appear below vessel rim; along square base there is also a ring pattern.	腹内底铭11字 Inscription on inside bottom of vessel; 11 characters

续表

图号 Number on figure	龙口市博物馆编号 Longkou Museum number	器物名称 Artifact name	出土时间 Date discovered	尺寸（厘米） Size (cm)	特点描述 Characteristics	铭文 Inscription
Ⅱ.3.16：2	351	簋 *Gui* tureen	2004.4	H: 21.95 M: 19.4 D: 10.95 H: 9.45 (base) W: 16.6 (base)	同上 Same as above.	同上 Same as above
Ⅱ.3.17：1	352	尊 *Zun* decanter	2004.4	H: 20.35 M: 19.25 D: 17.6	大喇叭口外侈，深腹倾垂。下有圈足。素面，腹上部饰两道凸起弦纹。 Large, flaring trumpet-shaped mouth; deep, somewhat sagging belly. Ring-foot beneath. Plain surface; upper portion of belly has two raised ring patterns.	
Ⅱ.3.19	353	铜甗 Bronze *yan* steamer	2004.4	H: 27.8 M: 18.1 H: 3.7 (ears) H: 6.5 (crotch)	索状立耳，深腹近垂直，内箅情况不明。通体素面。 Rope-shaped upright ears; deep, nearly vertically hanging belly; placement of interior grate unclear. Plain surface over entire vessel.	
Ⅱ.3.18：2	354	盘 *Pan* platter	2004.4	H: 9.7 M: 32.9 D: 7.25 B: 22.2	小方唇，直口。深腹，直圈足。素面，仅在腹上部饰两道凸弦纹。 Small square lip; straight mouth. Deep belly; straight ring-foot. Plain surface, with only traces of two raised ring patterns on upper belly.	
	349	壶 *Hu* bottle	2004.4	M: 16 H: 30	体态低矮，鼓腹，口下两侧有贯耳，并有两道凸起弦纹。全身素面。 Low profile; bulging belly; tubular ears below vessel mouth, as well as two raised ring patterns. Plain surface over entire vessel.	
Ⅱ.3.17：2	359	觯 *Zhi* goblet	2004.4	H: 12.71 M: 5.9 B: 5.25	体态瘦直，下有圈足，素面。 Slim and straight profile; ring-foot beneath; plain surface.	
Ⅱ.3.18：1	356	钟 Bell	2004.4	H: 37.22 H: 24.24 (body) W: 15.15 (breadth of top surface) W: 19.48 (distance between two tips)	形体很小。外沿斜直，直至铣端。于呈弧形，较低。鼓部素面，钲和篆四周饰连珠纹。篆间饰斜角雷纹，枚短小。 Very small. Outer lines oblique and straight, running down to tips of aperture. Rim of aperture forms arc shape; relatively low. Plain on top surface of bell; four sides of central panel and side insets decorated with linked-pearl designs. Area between side insets decorated with diagonal spirals; short, small bosses.	
		鼎 *Ding* cauldron	2004.4		残片。 Fragment.	有两字铭文 2-character inscription
		卣 *You* jar	2004.4		残片。仅有附耳部分及一段提梁。 Fragment; only attached ears and a section of handle extant.	
		爵 *Jue* cup	2004.4		残片。 Fragment.	
		铜泡 Bronze button	2004.4			

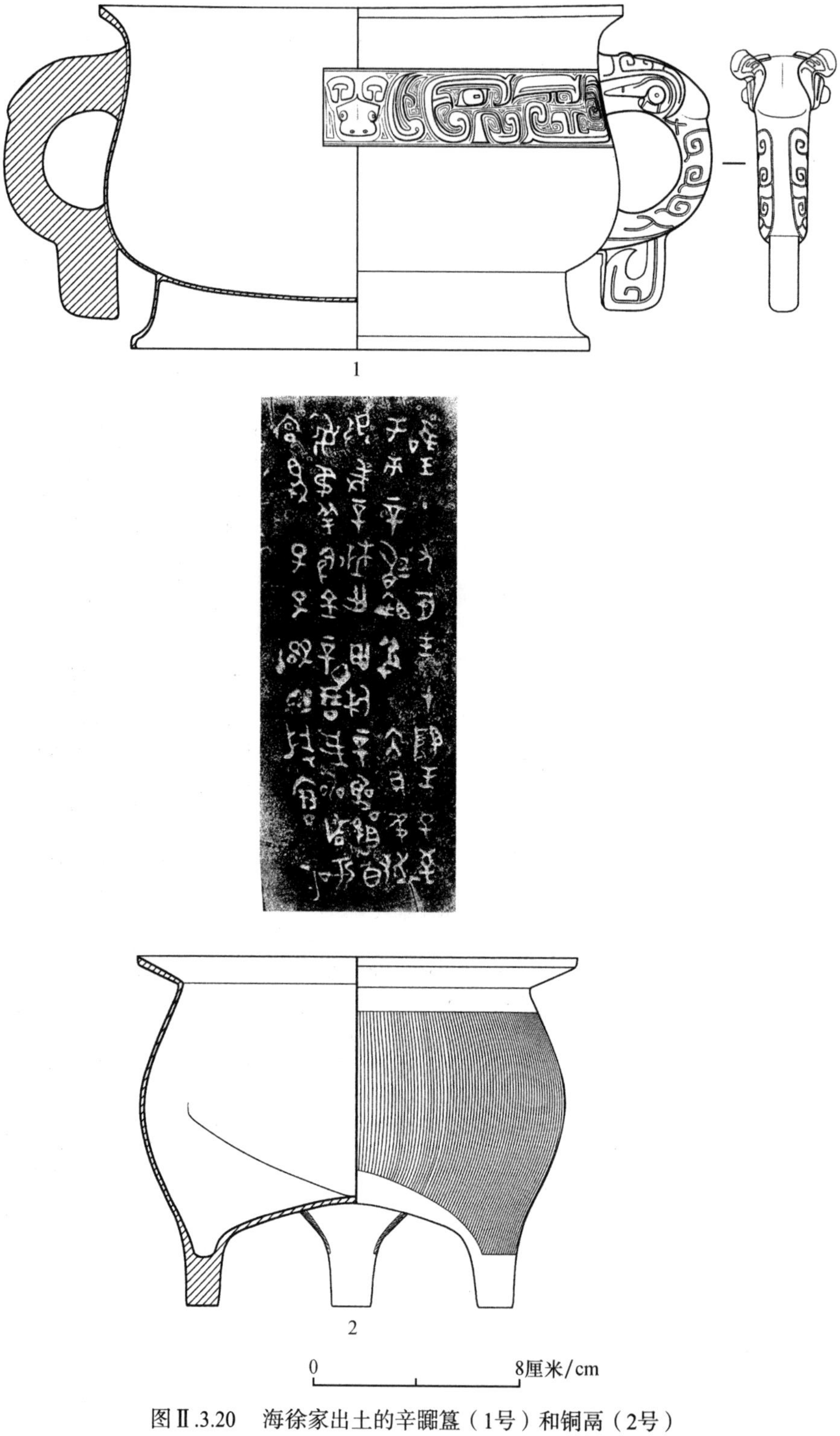

图Ⅱ.3.20　海徐家出土的辛䮆簋（1号）和铜鬲（2号）

Figure Ⅱ.3.20　The Xin Xiao *gui* (#1) and bronze *li* tripod (#2) from Haixujia.

表Ⅱ.3.4 海徐家出土铜器统计表

Table Ⅱ.3.4 Statistic table of bronzes from Haixujia

图号 Number on figures	龙口市博物馆编号 Longkou Museum number	器物名称 Artifact name	出土时间 Date discovered	尺寸（厘米） Size (cm)	特点描述 Characteristics	铭文 Inscription
Ⅱ.3.20：1	1 (KM.6)	簋 *Gui* tureen	1983.4	H: 12.8 M: 20	器束领，侈口，鼓腹，双兽耳有珥，喇叭形圈足，腹上部饰有兽面纹。 Constricted neck, flaring mouth, bulging belly; two animal-shaped ears have pendants; trumpet-shaped ring-foot. The upper portion of vessel body has animal-face patterns.	腹内底部铸有53字铭文。 Inscription of 53 characters at interior bottom.
Ⅱ.3.20：2	2 (KM.492)	鬲 *Li* tripod	1983.4	H: 7.32 M: 6.7	宽平折沿，分裆，通身饰细密的直楞纹。 Broad, folded flat rim, divided crotch; entire body covered with fine vertical ridge pattern.	

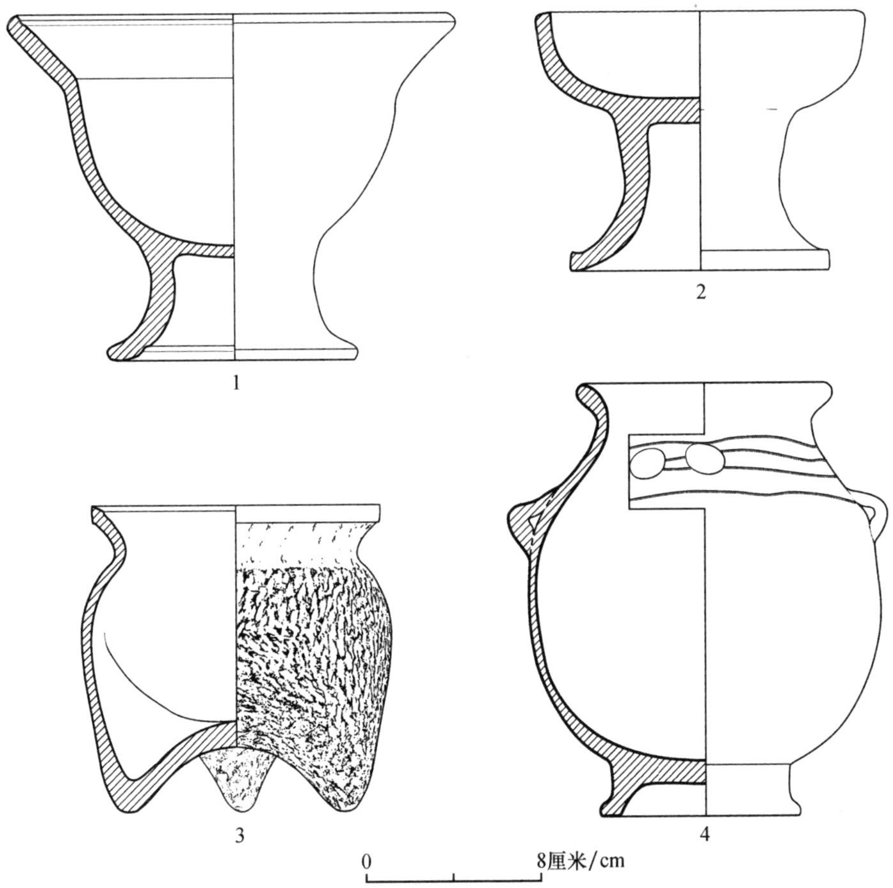

图Ⅱ.3.21 张郑家出土陶器

1. 簋（63号） 2. 豆（50号） 3. 鬲（53号） 4. 瓿（71号）

Figures Ⅱ.3.21 Ceramics recovered at Zhangzhengjia.

1. *Gui* (#63) 2. *Dou* (#50) 3. *Li* (#53) 4. *Bu* (#71)

表Ⅱ.3.5　张郑家出土陶器登记表

Table Ⅱ.3.5　Ceramics recovered at Zhangzhengjia

图号 Number on figure	龙口市博物馆编号 Longkou Museum number	器物名称 Vessel name	出土时间 Date discovered	尺寸（厘米） Size (cm)	特点描述 Characteristics
Ⅱ.3.23：1	张郑：63 Zhangzheng：63	陶簋 Pottery *gui* tureen	2009.10.12	H: 15.3 M: 20.34 B: 11.42	盆形腹，中高圈足。侈口，宽折沿，微上弧。个别器沿端上折，沿面有弦纹数周。腹部倾斜，个别器有小面积绳纹。 Basin-shaped belly; ring-foot of medium height. Flared mouth; wide folded rim; crotch arched slightly upward. Rim edge of some vessels angled upward; surface of rim has several ring patterns. Oblique belly; some vessels have small areas of cord patterns.
Ⅱ.3.23：2	张郑：50 Zhangzheng：50	陶豆 Pottery *dou* pedestal dish	2009.10.12	H: 11.58 M: 15.28	粗柄豆。柄粗矮，下端外撇，胎厚。 Sturdily stemmed *dou*-pedestal dish. Short, thick stem; lower portion angled outward; thick wall.
Ⅱ.3.23：3	张郑：53 Zhangzheng：53	陶鬲 Pottery *li* tripod	2009.10.12	H: 14 M: 13.29	卷沿小平唇，束颈有肩。弧形裆。饰粗绳纹。 Rolled rim with small flat lip; constricted neck with distinct shoulders. Arch-shaped crotch. Has coarse cord patterns.
Ⅱ.3.23：4	张郑：71 Zhangzheng：71	陶瓿 Pottery *bu* jar	2009.10.12	H: 19.42 M: 12	大口，肩部消失，小圈足。有两个侧耳。 Large mouth; shoulder disappearing; small ring-foot. Two ears on sides.

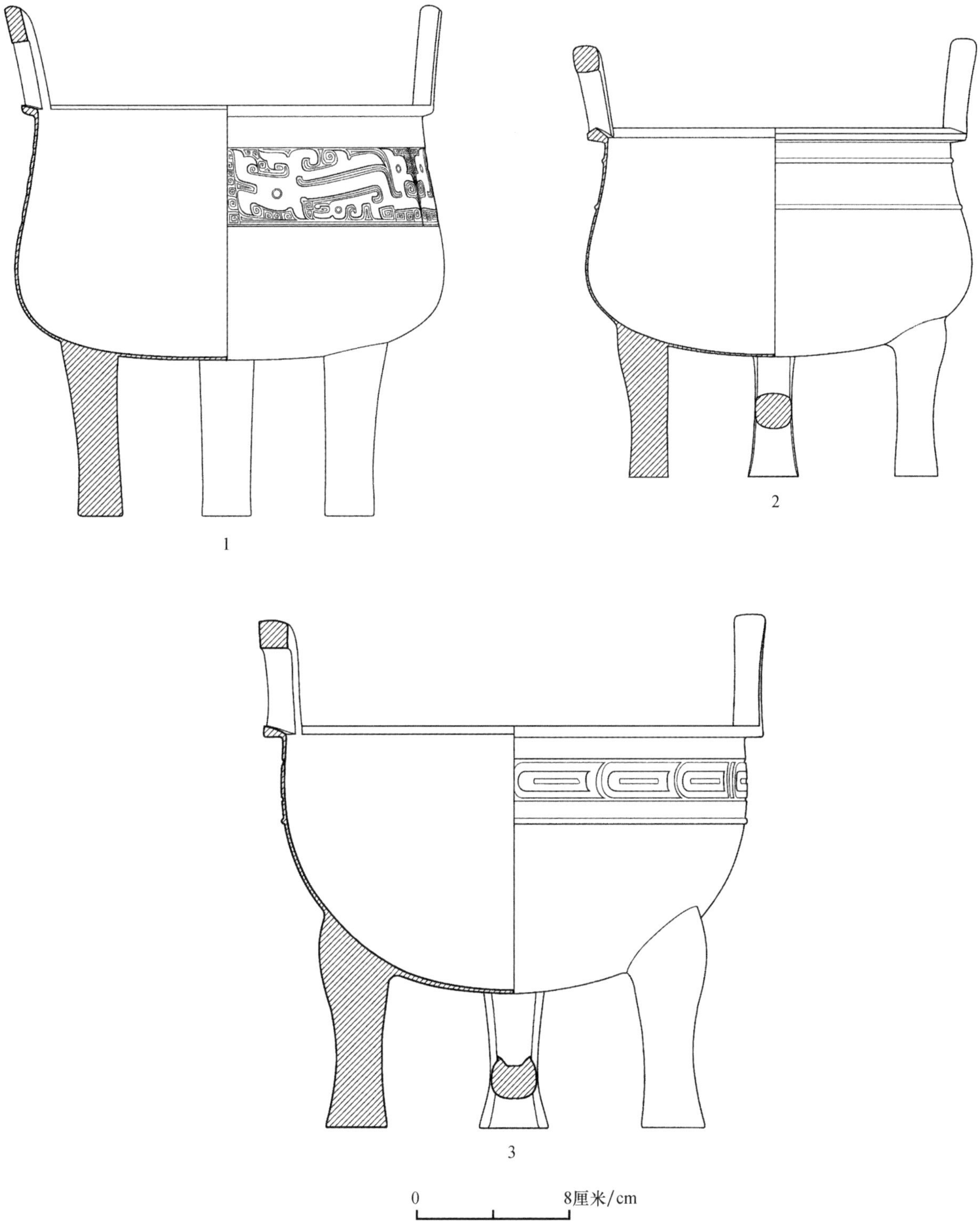

图Ⅱ.3.22　归城出土之西周铜鼎

1. 姜家7号　2. 姜家6号　3. 和平10号

FigureⅡ.3.22　Western Zhou bronzes unearthed in Guicheng.

1. Jiangjia：7　2. Jiangjia：6　3. Heping：10

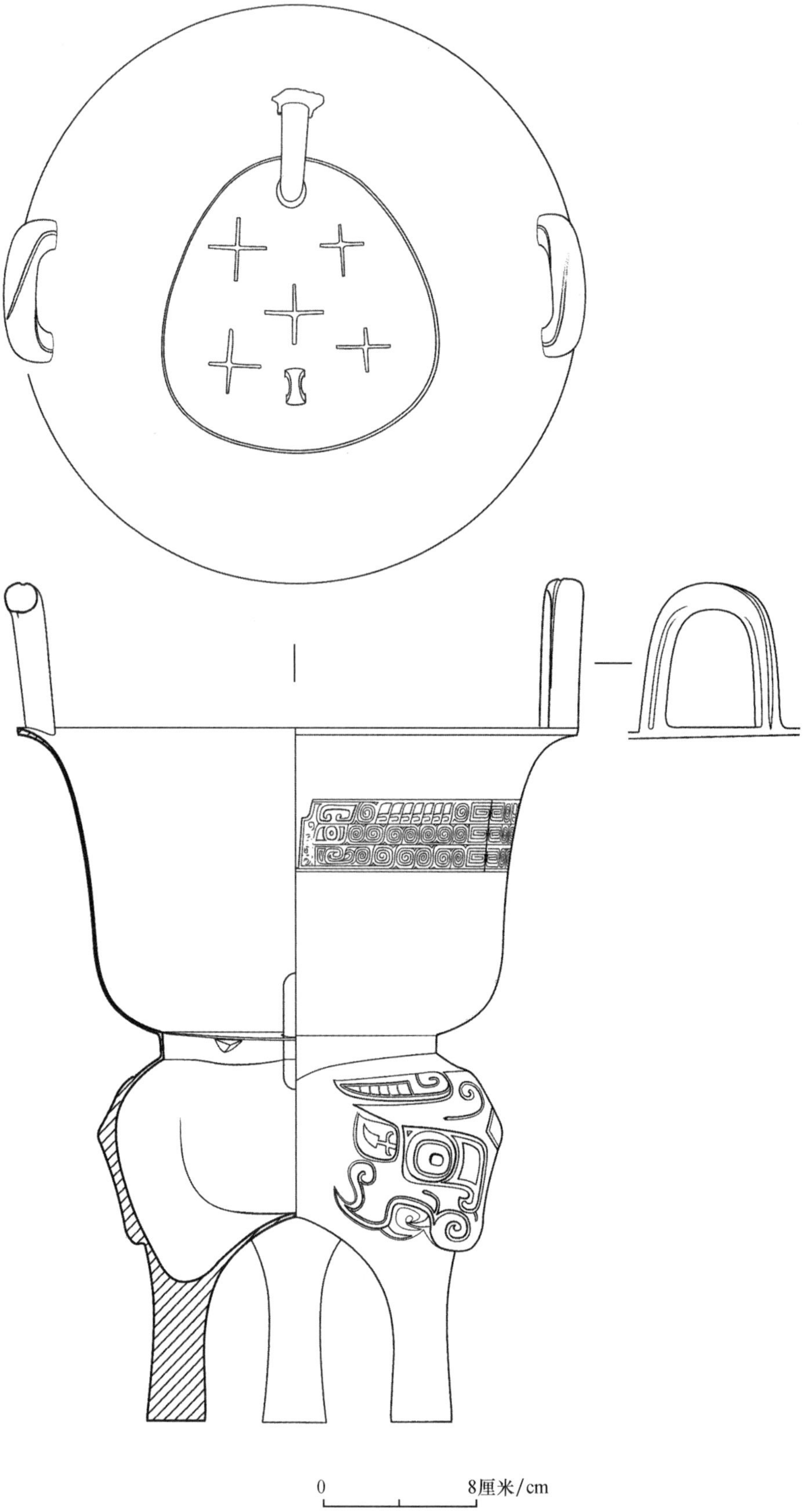

图Ⅱ.3.23　归城姜家村出土之西周铜甗鼎（姜家：75）

FigureⅡ.3.23　Western Zhou *yan* steamer unearthed at Jiangjiacun, Guicheng (Jiangjia：75).

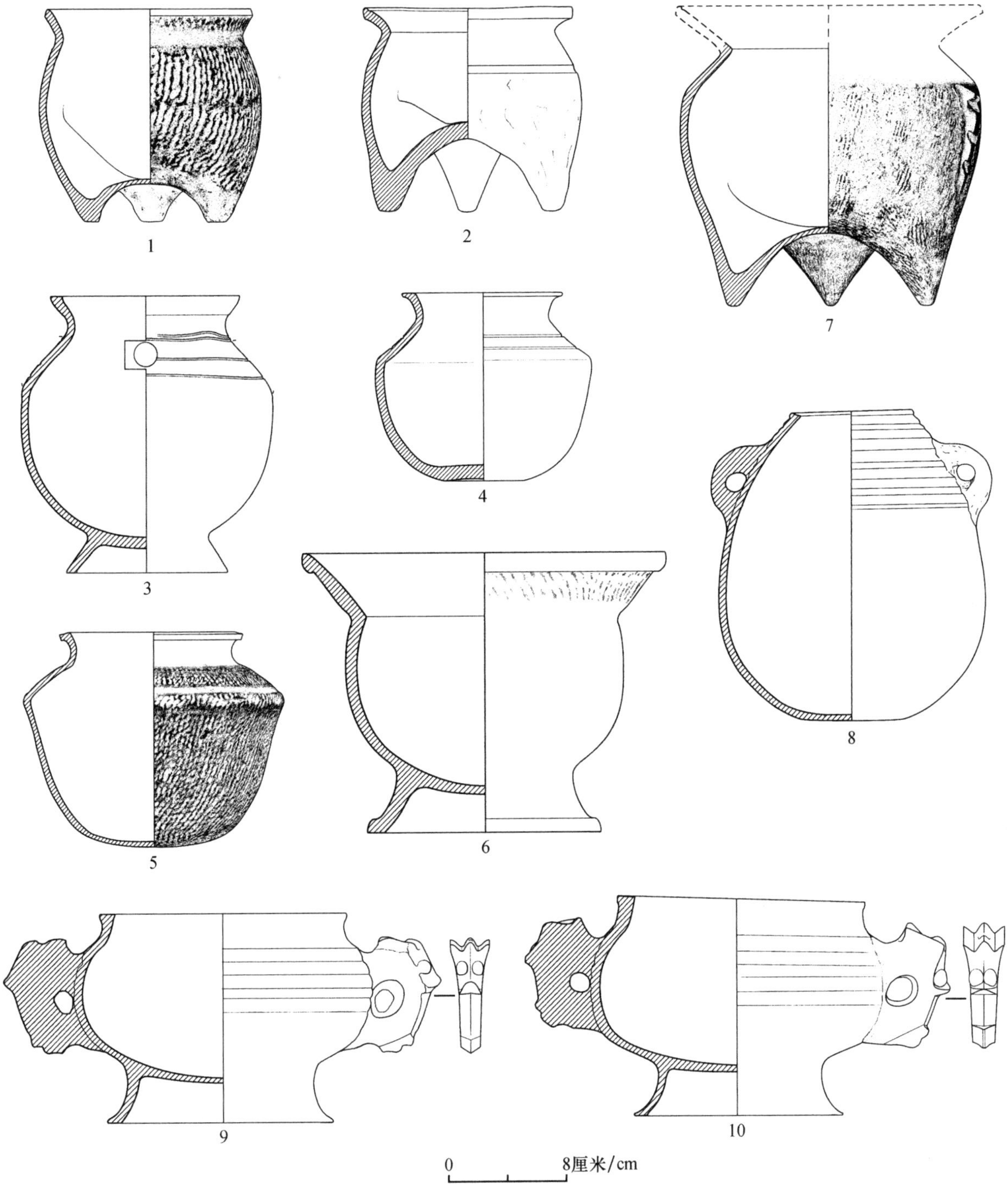

图Ⅱ.3.24 归城出土之西周陶器

1. 鬲（归城：1） 2. 鬲（东迟家：26） 3. 甂（归城：9） 4. 罐（和平：28） 5. 罐（归城：12） 6. 簋（归城：11） 7. 鬲（归城：10） 8. 壶（归城：8） 9. 簋（归城：23） 10. 簋（归城：5）

Figure Ⅱ.3.24 Pottery vessels unearthed in Guicheng.

1. *Li* (Guicheng：1) 2. *Li* (Dongchijia：26) 3. *Bu* (Guicheng：9) 4. *Guan* (Heping：28) 5. *Guan* (Guicheng：12) 6. *Gui* (Guicheng：11) 7. *Li* (Guicheng：10) 8. *Hu* (Guicheng：8) 9. *Gui* (Guicheng：23) 10. *Gui* (Guicheng：5)

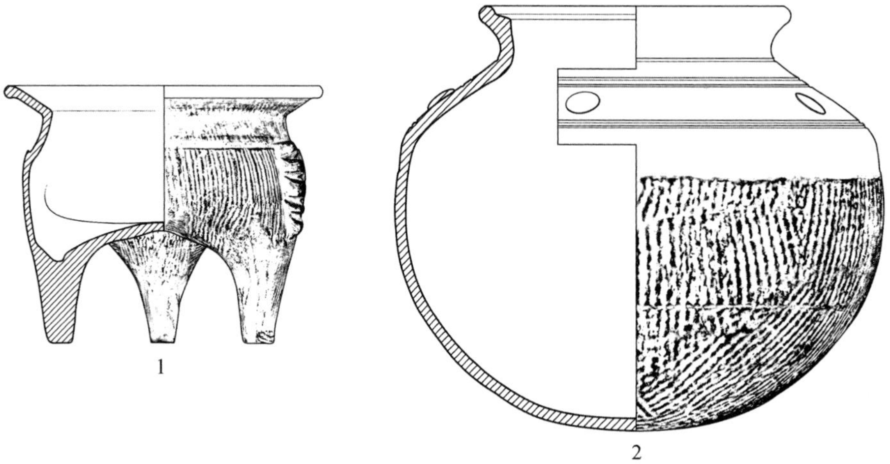

图Ⅱ.3.25　石良出土之西周陶器

1. 鬲（石良：1）　2. 罐（石良：2）

Figure Ⅱ.3.25　Pottery vessels unearthed in Shiliang.

1. *Li* (Shiliang：1)　2. *Guan* (Shiliang：2)

表Ⅱ.3.6　归城及周边地区零星出土的西周铜器和陶器

Table Ⅱ.3.6　Western Zhou bronzes and pottery sporadically collected at Guicheng and surrounding areas

图号 Number on figure	龙口市博物馆编号 Longkou number	器物名称 Vessel name	出土地点 Place discovered	出土时间 Date discovered	尺寸（厘米） Size (cm)	特点描述 Characteristics
Ⅱ.3.22：1	姜家：7 Jiangjia：7 (KM.28)	铜鼎 Bronze *ding* cauldron	归城姜家 Guicheng Jiangjia		H: 25.9 M: 21.5 D: 12.8 H: 5.1 (ears)	平沿立耳，腹倾垂。三柱足。腹饰夔纹。 Flat rim; upright ears; sagging belly. Three cylindrical legs. Belly has *kui* dragon patterns.
Ⅱ.3.22：2	姜家：6 Jiangjia：6 (KM.27)	铜鼎 Bronze *ding* cauldron	归城姜家 Guicheng: Jiangjia		H: 22.3 M: 20 D: 11.5 H: 4.57 (ears)	立耳，腹部倾垂，三柱足略外撇。腹上饰两道凸弦纹。 Upright ears, sagging belly; three cylindrical legs angled slightly outward. Belly has two raised ring patterns.
Ⅱ.3.22：3	和平：10 Heping：10 (KM.26)	铜鼎 Bronze *ding* cauldron	归城和平村 Guicheng: Hepingcun		H: 25.85 M: 26 D: 13.4 H: 5.4 (ears)	平沿立耳，半球形腹，三足呈马蹄形。腹上饰重环纹。 Flat rim; upright ears, hemispherical belly; three hoof-shaped feet. Belly has double-ring patterns.
Ⅱ.3.23	姜家：73 Jiangjia：73 (KM.30)	铜甗 Bronze *yan* steamer	归城姜家 Guicheng: Jiangjia		H: 43.71 M: 37.14 D: 15.71	索状立耳，敞口。心形箅有五个十字孔。鬲部饰兽面，柱足。腹上部饰细密饕餮纹。 Rope-shaped upright ears; wide mouth. Heart-shaped grate with five cross-shaped holes. Tripod portion has animal faces; cylindrical legs. Belly has fine *taotie* patterns.
Ⅱ.3.24：1	归城：1 Guicheng：1 (KM.45)	陶鬲 Pottery *li* tripod	归城 Guicheng		H: 14.5 M: 14.15	敞口束颈，弧裆内收。饰粗绳纹。泥质灰褐陶。 Wide mouth with constricted neck; arching crotch constricted inward. Has coarse cord patterns. Greyish-brown fine clay pottery.

续表

图号 Number on figure	龙口市博物馆编号 Longkou number	器物名称 Vessel name	出土地点 Place discovered	出土时间 Date discovered	尺寸（厘米） Size (cm)	特点描述 Characteristics
Ⅱ.3.24：2	东迟家：26 Dongchijia：26	陶鬲 Pottery *li* tripod	归城 东迟家 Guicheng Dongchijia		H: 13.6 M: 14.25	敞口，弧裆高，唇上钩。素面，腹上饰一道凹弦纹。泥质灰陶。 Wide mouth; high arching crotch; lip of rim tilts upward. Plain surface; single intaglio line pattern on upper belly. Grey fine ceramic.
Ⅱ.3.24：7	归城：10 Guicheng：10 (KM.20)	陶鬲 Pottery *li* tripod	归城 Guicheng		H: 17.4 D: 20.7	口部残。肩部突出，较宽。弧裆高。腹上有扉棱，绳纹较细。夹砂灰褐陶。 Mouth damaged. Prominent and relatively wide shoulders. High arching crotch. Flange on belly; relatively fine cord patterns. Sandy, greyish-brown pottery.
Ⅱ.3.24：3	归城：9 Guicheng：9 (KM.37)	陶瓿 Pottery *bu* jar	归城 Guicheng		H: 18.4 M: 12.9 D: 17.2	大口，平唇。肩部缓折，器体略瘦，小圈足。肩上有两泥饼饰。 Large mouth; flat lip. Gently angled shoulders; vessel body relatively slim; small, ring-foot. Shoulders have two mud-cake buttons.
Ⅱ.3.24：4	和平：28 Heping：28	小陶罐 Small pottery *guan* jar	归城 和平村 Guicheng Hepingcun		H: 12.5 M: 10.9 D: 14.7 B: 5.5	特小罐。敞口平沿，底微内凸。整体素面，肩上有两道弦纹。泥质深灰陶。 Especially small jar. Wide mouth with flat rim; slightly convex base. Plain surface over entire vessel; shoulders have two bands of ring patterns. Dark grey fine pottery.
Ⅱ.3.24：5	归城：12 Guicheng：12 (KM.38)	小陶罐 Small pottery *guan* jar	归城 Guicheng		H: 14.3 M: 12.5 D: 17.75	小罐。敞口小卷沿，肩部突出，圜底。整体饰绳纹。泥质深灰陶。 Small jar. Wide mouth with small rolled rim; prominent shoulders; round bottom. Entire vessel body has cord patterns. Dark grey fine pottery.
Ⅱ.3.24：6	归城：11 Guicheng：11 (KM.41)	陶簋 Pottery *gui* tureen	归城 Guicheng		H: 18.6 M: 24.7 B: 15.8	盆形簋。深腹略鼓、矮圈足。敞口，宽平折沿，外厚唇。口沿下及腹部局部饰绳纹，有抹光痕。泥质深灰陶。 Basin-shaped *gui* tureen. Deep, slightly bulging belly; low ring-foot. Wide mouth; wide and flat, folded rim; lip thicker toward outside. Area below rim and part of belly have cord patterns; traces of burnishing. Dark grey fine pottery.
Ⅱ.3.24.8	归城：8 Guicheng：8 (KM.36)	陶壶 Pottery *hu* bottle	归城 Guicheng		H: 20.6 M: 8.3 D: 18.4	形似鱼篓形。口内敛，上体部位有两耳。饰多道弦纹。泥质灰陶。 Vessel in shape of fish basket. Inwardly constricted mouth; upper portion of body has two ears. Decorated with several ring patterns. Grey fine pottery.
Ⅱ.3.24：9	归城：23 Guicheng：23 (KM.19)	陶簋 Pottery *gui* tureen	归城 Guicheng		H: 14 M: 16.8 B: 15.3 W: 29.7	仿铜陶簋。敛口圈足，腹饰瓦纹。泥质深灰陶。 Pottery *gui* tureen in imitation of bronze. Constricted mouth and ring-foot; belly has groove patterns. Dark-grey fine pottery.
Ⅱ.3.24：10	归城：5 Guicheng：5 (KM.18)	陶簋 Pottery *gui* tureen	归城 Guicheng		H: 14.63 M: 17 D: 11 B: 14.5 H: 3.4 (foot) W: 29	仿铜陶簋。敛口圈足，腹饰瓦纹。泥质深灰陶。 Pottery *gui* tureen in imitation of bronze. Constricted mouth and ring-foot; belly has groove patterns. Dark grey fine pottery.

续表

图号 Number on figure	龙口市博物馆编号 Longkou number	器物名称 Vessel name	出土地点 Place discovered	出土时间 Date discovered	尺寸（厘米） Size (cm)	特点描述 Characteristics
Ⅱ.3.25：1	石良：1 Shiliang：1 (KM.196)	陶鬲 Pottery *li* tripod	石良 Shiliang		H: 12.3 M: 15.7 H: 5.3 (crotch)	仿铜鬲。口沿宽平，腹浅，足细长，高裆。腹饰较细绳纹，印痕深而规整。夹砂深灰陶。 *Li* tripod in imitation of bronze. Broad, flat rim; shallow belly; slender legs; high crotch. Belly has relatively fine cord patterns; impressions deep and neat. Dark grey sand-tempered pottery.
Ⅱ.3.25：2	石良：2 Danliang：2 (KM.197)	陶罐 Pottery *guan* jar	石良 Shiliang		H: 20.15 M: 15.15 D: 23.8	圜底小罐。圆肩有乳钉，并饰成组弦纹。泥质灰陶。 Small, round-bottomed jar. Rounded shoulders with mud-cake buttons and decorated with groupings of ring patterns. Grey, fine pottery.

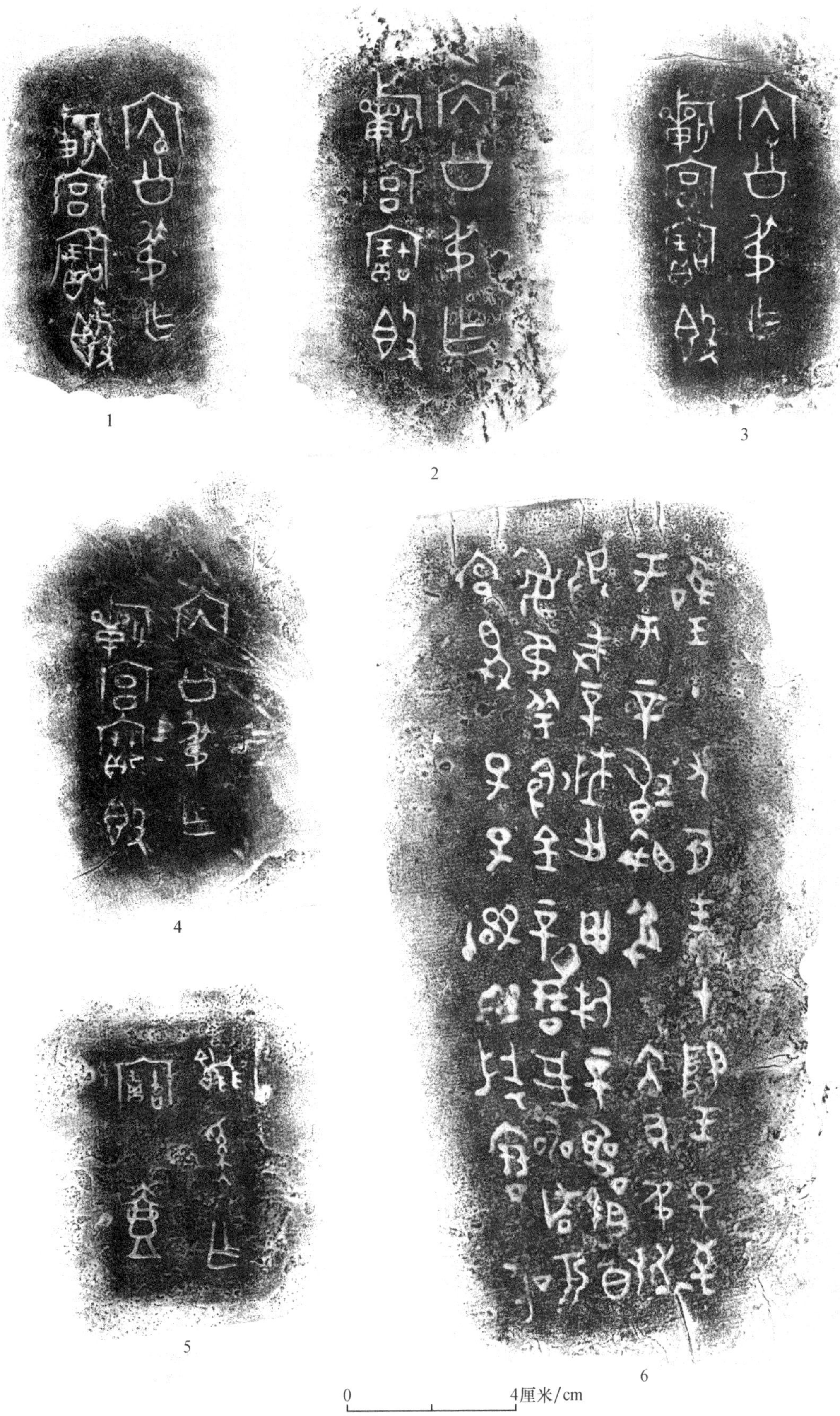

图 Ⅱ.3.26　庄头M1和海徐家出土青铜器铭文

1. 庄头M1：189簋盖　2. 庄头M1：189簋腹　3. 庄头M1：190簋盖　4. 庄头M1：190簋腹　5. 庄头M1：186方壶盖　6. 海徐家辛䣄簋

Figure Ⅱ.3.26　Inscriptions on bronzes from Zhuangtou M1 and Haixujia.

1. M1：189 *gui* (lid)　2. M1：189 *gui* (vessel)　3. M1：190 *gui* (lid)　4. M1：190 *gui* (vessel)　5. M1：186 square *hu* (lid) (above: all from Zhuangtou)　6. Xin Xiao *gui* from Haixujia

图 Ⅱ.3.27　东营周家和集前赵家出土青铜器铭文

1. 周家3号簋　2. 周家4号簋　3. 赵家348号鼎　4. 赵家357号鼎　5. 赵家350号簋　6. 赵家351号簋

Figure Ⅱ.3.27　Bronze inscriptions from Dongying Zhoujia and Jiqian Zhaojia.

1. *Gui* #3 from Zhoujia　2. *Gui* #4 from Zhoujia　3. *Ding* #348 from Zhaojia　4. *Ding* #357 from Zhaojia　5. *Gui* #350 from Zhaojia　6. *Gui* #351 from Zhaojia

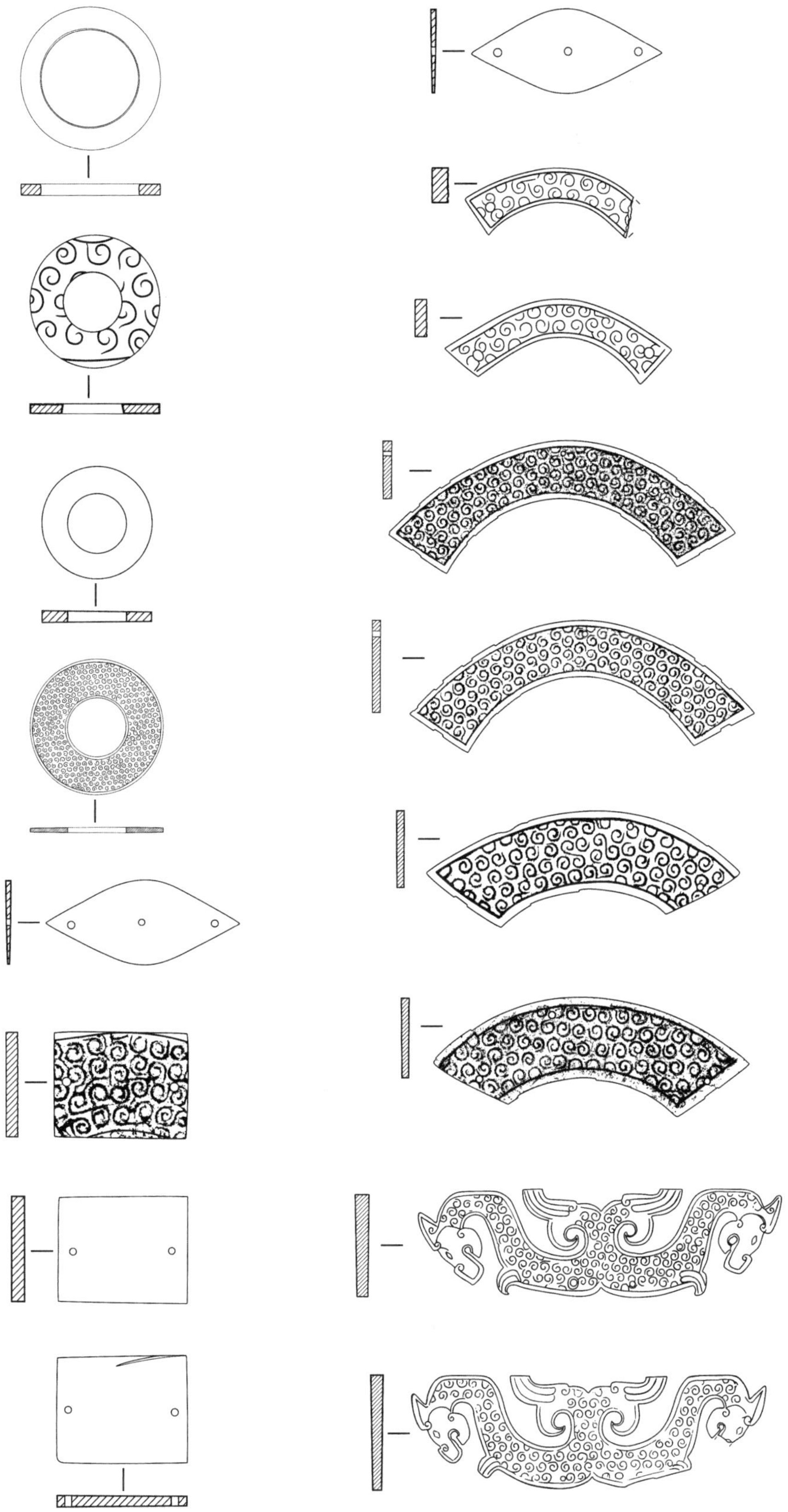

图Ⅱ.3.28　庄头村1983年出土玉器

FigureⅡ.3.28　Jades from Zhuangtou Village, 1983.

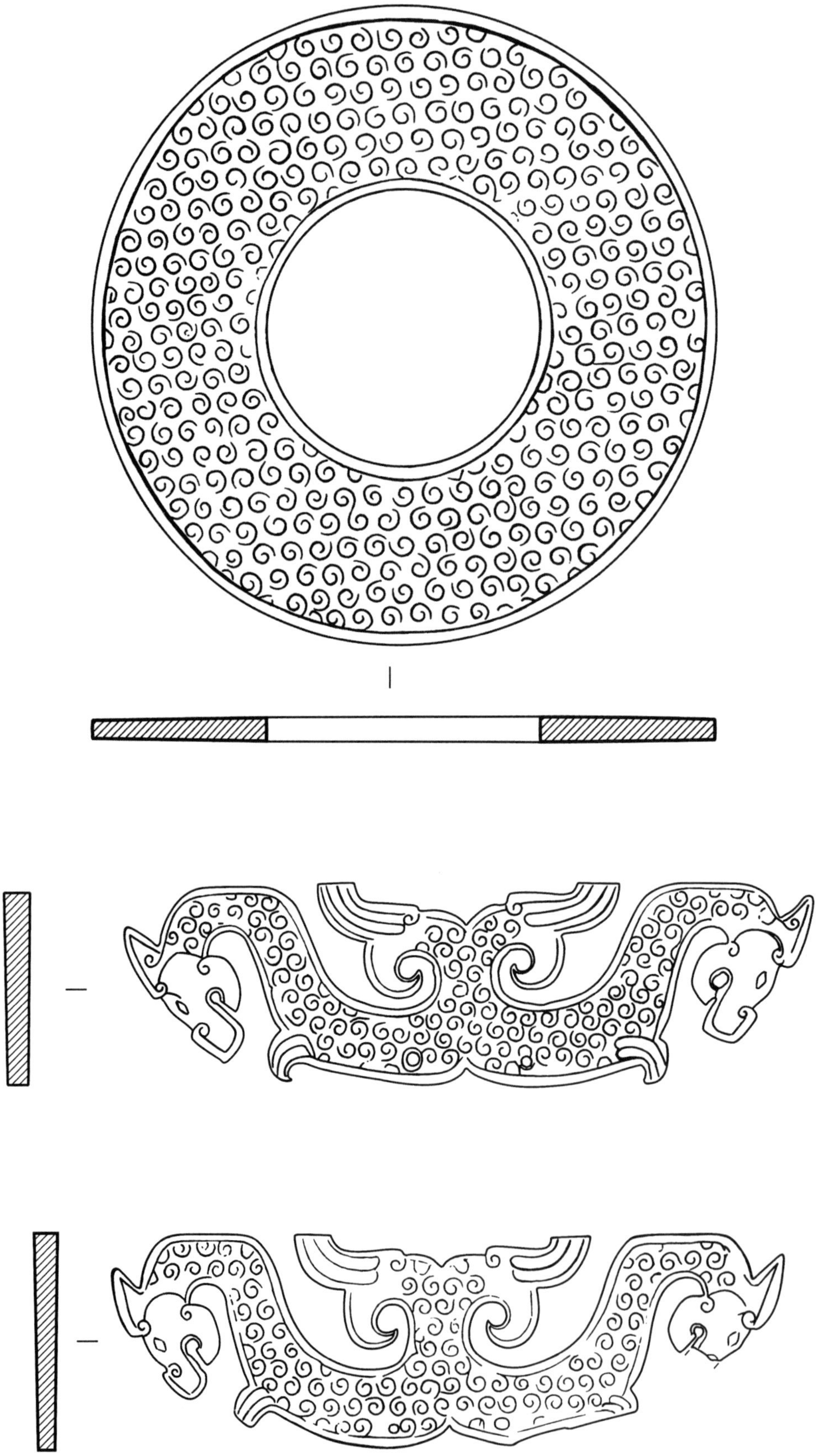

图Ⅱ.3.29　庄头村1983年出土玉器
FigureⅡ.3.29　Jades from Zhuangtou Village, 1983.

Chapter 3 : A Survey and Compendium of Bronzes Unearthed at the Guicheng City Ruins (1980-2010)

Liu Yutao   Ma Zhimin

Section 1: Introduction

Geographically speaking, the Jiaodong Peninsula lay on the fringes of ancient Chinese civilization. The ancient states of the Jiaodong area are therefore only rarely mentioned in the extensive body of pre-Qin records. Explicit clues exist in these records only concerning the states of Lai 莱 and Ji 纪, as well as a few others.

When the Zhou Dynasty conquered Shang and founded regional states to shield the Zhou royal house, two main states were installed in the Shandong area. One of these was the state of Lu 鲁, in which Bo Qin was established as ruler. Bo Qin was the son of the Duke of Zhou, Dan, the foremost aide to the Zhou king. The other was Qi 齐, located in the northern part of Shandong, where the Grand Duke Jiang, chief among the accomplished ministers who contributed to the conquest of Shang, was established. The Han dynasty text *Shiji* by Sima Qian (second century BCE) records that when Grand Duke Jiang reached Qi, "the ruler of Lai came and attacked, contending with him over Yingqiu." This account seems to suggest that the state of Lai already existed in the early years of the Western Zhou period, and further that it was already powerful enough to contend with the state of Qi for territory. However, since this assertion touches upon the early historical geography of Qi, concerning which many problematic points remain to be clarified, additional study is needed before it can be accepted as historical fact.

The pre-Qin text *Yu Gong* mentions the Laiyi and the Yuyi. The term "Yuyi" probably referred to tribes of the coastal area of the Jiaodong Peninsula, while "Laiyi" referred to Yi-people bearing the designation Lai. On the Jiaodong Peninsula, many mountains and rivers have names related to this term *lai*. The dividing line between the Jiaodong Peninsula and the western mainland is the Jiaolai River, formed in actuality by the Jiao River, which flows southward into the Jiaozhou Bay, and the Lai River, which flows northward into the Laizhou Bay. The Lai River was probably closely related to the ancient Laiyi and the ancient state of Lai. The *Zuozhuan*, another pre-Qin historical text, contains clear records of a few great battles between the states of Qi and Lai during the Spring and Autumn period, most of which occurred at locations within the Lai River valley. Clearly, Lai was an ancient state in the Jiaodong region; this much should be without question.

The most famous landmark in the Jiaodong region relating to Lai is Mount Lai, located in present Lan'gao Township, Longkou City (the latter formerly referred to as Huangxian), 550 m above sea level. Mount Lai rises from the southern margin of an alluvial plain along the edge of Bohai Bay. Imposing and majestic, it is one of the most famous mountains of the Jiaodong Peninsula, just as it was an object of natural worship for the ancients. At the northern foot of Mount Lai lies the Guicheng city site, which many past historians held to have been the capital of the state of Lai during the Spring and Autumn period. Elite ruins and cemeteries lie scattered about the environs of the Guicheng city site, particularly along the course of the Huangshui River to the east of Guicheng. Important bronzes have been continually discovered in this area since the late Qing dynasty, and pottery and other varieties of artifacts are occasionally found as well. Most artifacts unearthed before the 1980s were surveyed and collated by researchers from the Yantai Municipal Museum and subsequently published (see Part Ⅱ, Chapters 1 and 2). Since its establishment in 1985, the Longkou Municipal Museum has worked toward the careful preservation of the site of Guicheng and the surrounding area, as well as the relics unearthed there. Based on materials in the collection of the Longkou Municipal Museum, this chapter offers a systematic introduction to the important discoveries made at the Guicheng site and in the surrounding area since the 1980s.

Section 2: A Summary of the Archaeological Excavation of the Tombs at East Zhuangtou

The Western Zhou tombs at East Zhuangtou (or simply Zhuangtou) are located on a high terrace situated 5 m east of Zhuangtou Village in Shiliang Township, which itself lies 45 *li* southeast of Longkou City. The southern portion of the group of tombs lies on the bank of a river that flows toward the west, and not far to the southeast, the cemetery is bounded by a mountain. On September 12, 1980, a member of the Zhuangtou Brigade of that time, Liu Yongxin, and others were gathering soil from the eastern part of the cattle pen of Production Team 1 when they discovered a group of bronzes, sixteen in all, including *ding* cauldrons, *yan* steamers, *hu* bottles, etc. Six of these bronzes bore inscriptions (rubbings of three of these, from vessels which could be cleaned sufficiently to reveal the inscriptions, are included in this chapter). The Cultural Relics Management Commission of Yantai District identified these as belonging to the Western Zhou period and further assessed that the location where they were unearthed was a tomb (assigned the designation M1). Based on its clearing and excavation, this tomb was a vertical earthen pit, its remaining portions measuring 3 m long from east to west and 3 m wide from north to south. The tomb contained a second-level platform (*ercengtai*) of worked earth, as well as decayed traces of an inner and outer coffin and a containment chamber. The skeleton of the occupant, as well as the ceramic grave goods, had been destroyed.

In 1981, the Cultural Relics General Survey Team of Huangxian County reexamined this tomb and concluded that the location contained a group of Western Zhou tombs. An area of approximately 2,500 m^2 of this tomb group had been damaged by the cattle pen and the removal of earth. During our survey, we observed a few vertical earthen pit tombs that had been damaged, with their remaining portions still present on a cliff east of the cattle pen. The extant portion of the cemetery was approximately 200 m long from north to south and 100 m wide from east to west, making for a total area of approximately 20,000 m^2. This cemetery is of great significance in the context of the Guicheng area.

Many of the sixteen bronzes discovered by Liu Yongxin were so badly fragmented that their shapes could not be discerned. Below I introduce ten relatively complete restored specimens, including *ding* cauldrons, *gui* tureens, a square *hu* bottle, a *you* jar, a *yan* steamer, a *jue* cup, and a *zhi* goblet (Figs. Ⅱ.3.1- Ⅱ.3.5; Table Ⅱ.3.1; Pls. 101-109). Other items include *pan* basins, *yu* basins, *ge* daggers, and ladles, etc.

Stylistically, these bronzes are in fact all quite close; they were probably produced early in the mid-Western Zhou period. Most important among them are two square-based *gui* tureens designated nos. 189 and 190. The large bird patterns with which these *gui* tureens are completely covered were only popular during the reign of King Mu in the early phase of the mid-Western Zhou; thus the vessels are chronologically very characteristic. Each *gui* tureen bears an inscription of eight characters in two lines: "Ruigong's brother makes a treasured *gui* tureen for the Prayer Hall" (Fig. Ⅱ.3.26: 1-4). These bronzes were produced by the state of Rui in Shaanxi during the mid-Western Zhou. An identical square-based *gui* tureen has recently appeared in a private collection in New York. The no. 186 *hu* bottle inscribed "Xiong Xi makes a treasured *hu*" (Fig. Ⅱ.3.26: 5), is a rare vessel cast by an elite person surnamed Xiong. In addition, the no. 192 *you* jar is unique in body design and is inscribed: "Xiao Fu makes for Father Ding, Bu, this treasured traveling vessel." The local discovery of these artifacts provides us with important information about the cultural as well as interpersonal communications in the Guicheng region.

Section 3: The damaged Western Zhou tombs at Dongying Zhoujiacun

From the autumn of 1985 to the spring of 1986, the inhabitants of Dongying Zhoujiacun in Shiliang Township of Huangxian County, Shandong, discovered two tombs in succession (designated M1 and M2) while collecting earth from a brick kiln area south of the village. In June 1986, the former Huangxian County Museum and the Yantai Municipal Museum conducted a joint survey and clearing of the site that yielded some important information about these two tombs.

Dongying Zhoujia Village is located 25 km southeast of Huangxian County. Lujiagou lies 7 km to the south and Zhuangtou Village 2 km to the north. On the east, a mountain separates Dongying Zhoujia from Cunliji of Penglai County, while the Guicheng city site is approximately 10 km to the northwest. This area is enclosed on the east, south, and west sides by numerous hills. The Huangshui River flows past the east of the village, from northeast to southwest, while to the south of the village, the Dongying River empties into the Huangshui River from the west. The cemetery is located on a terrace on the south bank of the Dongying River, approximately 500 m south of Dongying Zhoujia Village. The terrace comes into contact with Mount Gu on its east side and slopes gradually from east to west; it is approximately 220 m long from north to south and approximately 150 m wide from east to west. Dongying Zhoujia Village set up brick kilns here, and years of collecting earth have cut the western portion of the terrace into a cliff approximately 3-4 m high, running from north to south. The two tombs cleared during this session of work, M1 and M2, lay exposed on the cliff.

M1 was located on the northwest portion of the terrace and oriented south of east (110° magnetic). Most of the tomb chamber had already been destroyed; only a small part of the northern section remained. The tomb measured 5 m long from east to west and 2.8 meters in remaining width from north to south. M1 was a vertical earthen pit tomb with a tomb terrace of worked earth. The bottom of the tomb contained traces of decayed wood, probably left behind when the inner and outer coffins rotted. The skeleton had already deteriorated, so that the sex of the occupant could not be determined. Grave goods included both bronzes and ceramics: two bronze *gui* tureens were placed near the head, while ceramic *dou* pedestal dishes, a *li* tripod, and *guan* jars were placed inside the worked earth secondary platform (Table Ⅱ.3.2). Both of the *gui* tureens unearthed from M1 had lost their lids. They have constricted mouths, pairs of ears have pendants below, and each has three small feet attached to a circular foot. The vessels bear wide and deep grooves on their bellies, stretched *qiequ* curve patterns below their rims, and diagonal cloud patterns on their circular feet, an overall pattern of designs popular in the late Western Zhou period. Each tureen bears an inscription of eleven characters in three lines on the inside bottom: "Makes his treasured *gui* tureen vessel. For ten thousand years may it long be treasured and used. Shan (family emblem)" (Fig. Ⅱ.3.27: 1-2; Pl. 110). These vessels may well have come from the famous Shan lineage of the royal domain in Shaanxi. The ceramic *li* tripods and *dou* pedestal dishes resemble specimens of the same types found in the late Western Zhou tombs of the Zhangjiapo cemetery in Chang'an, Shaanxi. We can thus conclude that this tomb was of late Western Zhou date.

M2 was located approximately 10 m south of M1 and oriented south of due east (105°). It measured 3.5 m in remaining length from east to west and 2.7 m in remaining width from north to south. The bottom of the tomb lay 3.54 m below ground level and had a secondary platform of worked earth approximately 0.5 m wide and 0.9 m high, as well as a head compartment, measuring 1.9 m long from north to south and 0.9 m wide from east to west, in which ceramic vessels had been placed. A rectangular waist-pit in the middle of the tomb floor contained the remains of a human victim. Although no bronzes were discovered in this tomb, it yielded more than 200 ceramic items, chiefly including *ding* cauldrons, *gui* tureens, *li* tripods, *dou* pedestal dishes, *guan* jars, etc. (Table Ⅱ.3.2). The ceramic vessels used as grave goods were not only numerous and comprehensive in terms of vessel type, but also showed very obvious regional characteristics. For example, the conical feet of the ceramic *ding* cauldrons were gathered inward at the ends. This sort of *ding* cauldron has been discovered before at other locations in the Jiaodong region, but has yet to be encountered at sites of the same period on the Central Plains. Plain-surfaced ceramic *li* tripods and some *gui* tureens are also in the style of the indigenous cultures of the coastal area of Jiaodong. Cord-impressed *li* tripods and cord-impressed *guan* jars of normal or large size, however, are all classically characteristic of the culture of the Zhou people (Fig. Ⅱ.3.7-13; Pls. 111-119). Their presence provides ample evidence of exchange and admixture between the aboriginal cultures of coastal Jiaodong and the Zhou culture. We surmise that tomb M2 can probably be dated to the mid-Western Zhou period.

The excavation of the two Western Zhou tombs at Dongying Zhoujia Village was another important discovery in Jiaodong archaeology, adding to that of the Western Zhou tombs at Zhuangtou. So far, besides the three tombs that were damaged and have been cleared, there are still two or three tombs on the cliff that have been exposed. One presumes that this area is a cemetery of Western Zhou date.

In addition, in the past Dongying Zhoujia had yielded a bronze *ding* vessel. This *ding* cauldron has an angled rim, upright ears, a deep belly, and round bottom, beneath which are three legs with a semicircular cross-section. A band of backward-facing *kui* dragon patterns appears below the vessel rim. The vessel is 22.25 cm in total height and 21.25 cm in diameter at the mouth; its belly is 11.8 cm deep, and its ears are 4.27 cm high (Fig. Ⅱ.3.14; Pl. 120). The form of this bronze *ding* is typical of the mid-Western Zhou. However, the specific time and place of its discovery can no longer be known. It is included here with caution.

Section 4: The Discovery of the Western Zhou Tombs at Jiqian Zhaojia

The Jiqian Zhaojia cemetery is located northwest of Jiqian Zhaojia Village in Shiliang Township. The main channel of the Huangshui River lies approximately 1.6 km to the west, and Provincial Highway 213 passes close by the site's west side. The Dongying River, a tributary of the Huangshui River, lies somewhat more than 100 m to the south, reaching up to the Dongying Reservoir. Dongying Zhoujia Village lies close to the east, about 1 km away. The cemetery was first discovered during a construction project; it was used during both the Western Zhou and Han periods. The extant area of the cemetery measures approximately 110 m long and approximately 50 m wide, with a total area of approximately 5,800 m^2. It forms a part of a terrace that rises gradually to the west of the main channel of the Huangshui River. In April 2004, in the process of collecting earth to make bricks, an ancient tomb was dug up. Upon learning of this, Zhao Hengqiang, a resident of Jiqian Zhaojia Village, informed the village ward, Zhao Henghai, who then reported the discovery to the Longkou Municipal office responsible for managing cultural relics. Since staff members of the Municipal Museum rushed to the scene, they were able to ensure that most of the bronze vessels were preserved; however, the structure of the tomb itself was already unclear. This tomb yielded a total of fourteen Western Zhou bronzes, six of which are inscribed. Two of these vessels were intact at the time of excavation, while the majority of the remainder were able to be restored.

This assemblage of bronzes included 3 *ding* cauldrons (one surviving only as a fragment), 2 square-based *gui* tureens, 1 *zun* pitcher, 1 *you* jar (surviving only as a fragment), 1 *pan* basin, 1 *yan* steamer, 1 *hu* bottle, 1 *zhi* goblet, 1 *jue* cup (fragmentary), and 1 bronze button, as well as a single bronze bell (Figs. Ⅱ.3.16-19; Table Ⅱ.3.3; Pls. 121-128). Based on the vessel shape and designs discernible from the fragment, the *you* jar with handle evidently formed a set with the *zun* pitcher. The most notable characteristic of this assemblage of bronzes is their relative similarity, as well as the fact that the grouping of vessels is comparatively complete. The *ding* cauldron and *gui* tureen pair, combined with the set of one *zun* pitcher and two *you* jars, and supplemented by a *pan* basin, a *jue* cup, and a *zhi* goblet, constitute an assemblage frequently seen from the mid-Western Zhou, and the vessel designs also show characteristics of this period. For instance, the *ding* cauldrons, *gui* tureens, *zun* pitcher, and fragmentary *you* jar all have clearly sagging bellies, and the *zhi* goblet is tall and thin. Most of the bronzes have plain surfaces, and are only rarely decorated. In all, the bronzes recovered from the tomb are close to each other in style; basically, they are all typical of the early phase of the mid-Western Zhou. Moreover, the deep belly of the *pan* basin is also typical for *pan* basins of mid-Western Zhou date. The bell unearthed along with these vessels has a small body with sharp bosses and crude decoration. This form of bell, dating to not long after bells were introduced from the south, has previously been discovered in other tombs of mid-Western Zhou date.

However, through careful examination of the inscriptions recovered from the tomb, we discovered that the vessels of this assemblage may have had different origins. One *ding* cauldron with long-tailed bird motifs (no. 348) carries an inscription in five characters that reads: "Lifu makes a sacrificial vessel" (the area to the left of the inscription seems also to bear the character *yong*, suggesting that there may be more) (Fig. Ⅱ.3.27: 3). Another *ding* cauldron with raised ring patterns (no. 357) bears the simple inscription "Makes a *ding* cauldron," providing no basis for identifying the vessel commissioner. The two *gui* tureens with square bases were made by the same person, as indicated by their inscriptions: "Bo Yingfu awarded Shu Suo metal; [Shu Suo] therewith makes a treasured *gui* tureen" (Fig. Ⅱ.3.27: 5-6). The commissioner of these vessels was Shu Suo, a figure previously unknown to us; however, "Bo Yingfu" and "Shu Suo" are both typical name styles for Zhou elites. In addition, it is worth noting that a fragment of a *ding* cauldron bears the inscribed characters *ji hou*, "The Ruler of Ji," as well as two other characters too damaged to recognize; but this vessel obviously came from the state of Ji.

Though the vessels of this assemblage may have different origins, they correspond closely to each other in style and dating. Thus, we can say that the bronzes discovered at Jiqian Zhaojia have provided us with a standard vessel assemblage from the early phase of the mid-Western Zhou period. This is of great importance for the study of the dating of Zhou dynasty remains at Guicheng and in the surrounding area.

Section 5: The Xin Xiao *Gui*, a National Treasure Unearthed at Haixujia

Xujia Village of Haiyunsi in Zhongcun Township is located beside the Yongwen River to the west of Longkou City and approximately 4 km south of the coast of Bohai Bay. In April 1983, Zhong Jihui, an orchard foreman from Xujia Village, unearthed two bronze vessels while leading the villagers in digging a furrow for grapevines. One of these vessels was a *li* tripod, and the other was the Xin Xiao *gui* tureen. Zhong Jihui took these items to the cultural relics shop of Longkou City for sale. The staff there accepted the bronze *li* tripod and paid out a reward in accordance with regulations. Before going far, Zhong returned to the shop and explained that he had another large bronze vessel at home, currently in use as a trough for chicken feed. Zhong asked if the shop would be interested, to which the staff replied in the affirmative. The next day, Zhong brought the Xin Xiao *gui* over as well. It was appraised by a group on experts on cultural relics from the Shandong Provincial authority, including

Tai Liye, Guan Tianxiang, and others, and was designated as a first-class national relic. This discovery attracted a great deal of attention among those concerned with cultural relics.

In November 1986, the Yantai Cultural Relics Management Commission organized a team of specialists to carry out an exploratory excavation at the site in Haixu Village where the bronzes were unearthed, but they discovered no further objects. However, the Longkou Municipal Museum issued a reward to Zhong Jihui in recognition of his contributions in preserving cultural relics and handing them over to the proper authorities.

The Xin Xiao *gui* is 12.8 cm in total height, measures 20 cm in diameter at the mouth, and weighs 2,750 grams. It has a constricted neck, a flaring mouth, a bulging belly, two animal-shaped ears with pendants, and a trumpet-shaped circular foot. The upper part of the vessel bears animal face patterns (Fig. Ⅱ.3.20: 1; Table Ⅱ.3.4; Pl. 129). An inscription of fifty-three characters is cast into the inside bottom of the vessel. The character forms are non-standard, and there are numerous errors, but the principal caster of the vessel was clearly a "Xin Xiao" (Fig. Ⅱ.3.26: 6):

> It was the king's eleventh month; the king was at Xian. The prince arrived at Fang. Xin Xiao X [He] presented Shu (a guest-gift of) X, and [Shu] recompensed for his deceased father Xin a wooden handle. (Thereupon he) made a stabbing weapon for use. Xin Xiao XX Shu Yu (?) awarded metal. Xin X arrived, X at the temple, and had an audience (?). [His] sons' sons and grandsons, X makes a treasured vessel.
>
> (Based on Li Feng's transcription)

Although this inscription cannot be fully deciphered, its general meaning is understandable. The inscription narrates that a king (presumably the Zhou king) arrived at a certain place during the eleventh month of a certain year and dispatched a prince to a place called Fang. Xin Xiao may have gone to have an audience with the prince and also presented a certain person bearing the seniority term "Shu" with a gift. He himself also received a reward of metal at the same time. Xin Xiao used the metal to make this bronze *gui* tureen, so as to eternally commemorate the event for his descendants. The word *wang zi*, "prince," appears in the inscription. So far this is still rarely seen in bronzes from the Western Zhou period. As the Xin Xiao *gui* is of a quite early date, and the characters of its inscription are non-standard, we have sought the opinion of many experts, but it is still difficult to decipher the inscription in its entirety.

The Xin Xiao *gui* is finely crafted, uniquely shaped, and distinctively decorated. Its inscription is longer than those of the Qi *zun* and the Qi *you* previously discovered at Xiaoliujia in Guicheng, making it the longest discovered in the Longkou region to date. Although its character forms are non-standard, this may mean that it did not come from the central zone of the Zhou population, but may instead have been cast locally in the Jiaodong region. It is therefore of special significance in the cultural history of that region. It shows that possibly the Jiaodong peninsula may already have begun producing bronze vessels by the middle of the Western Zhou period, and, moreover, that the casting techniques were already quite advanced. The Xin Xiao *gui* is a hallmark treasure of the Longkou Municipal Museum.

The bronze *li* tripod recovered at the same time is 7.32 cm high and 6.72 cm in diameter at the mouth, and weighs 589 grams. It has a broad, flat, angled rim, and a divided crotch, and its entire surface is covered with a pattern of fine vertical ridges (Fig. Ⅱ.3.20: 2; Table Ⅱ.3.4; Pl. 130); these are, in fact, in imitation of the cord patterns on Western Zhou pottery. Similar bronze *li* tripods made in imitation of pottery have been frequently discovered in mid-Western Zhou tombs from the central region of the Western Zhou state.

Section 6: Western Zhou Pottery Unearthed in the Yongwen River Area

In the valley of the Huangshui River – the "lifeblood" of the people of Longkou – many discoveries of ancient settlement remains from the Western Zhou period or earlier have been made. But in the plain of another important river flowing through Longkou, the Yongwen River, hardly any settlement remains of Western Zhou or earlier date have been discovered. On October 12, 2009, brick factory workers near Zhangzhengjia discovered a large group of pottery vessels while collecting soil. Zheng Bo, a villager living next to the brick factory, maintains an interest in ancient relics. Hearing the news that the brick factory had unearthed an ancient tomb, he tried to go there and collect items every day after work, eventually gathering a total of 200 items altogether. Most of these were substantially damaged or consisted only of fragments, according to Zheng Bo's mother, Liu Meiyi. A few of the relatively intact items may have been taken away by migrant workers employed at the location.

Once he had amassed a substantial store of pottery, Zheng Bo then conceived the idea to give these artifacts to the authorities, both to enable more city residents to appreciate them and to allow specialists to conduct research. He thus took the initiative to contact the Longkou Municipal Museum and expressed his wish to donate the vessels. According to an appraisal by Liang Zhonghe, Research Fellow of the Institute of Archaeology, Chinese Academy of Social Sciences, who was conducting archaeological work in Longkou at the time, this group of vessels can be divided into a total of four types: *dou* pedestal dish, *li* tripod, *gui* tureen, and *guan* jar. These were used by the people of the mid- to late Western Zhou period as cooking and eating utensils as well as for accompanying the dead in burials. In addition, numerous fish bones, carbon residue from foodstuffs, animal bones, etc., were discovered on the inside surfaces of the vessels. Judging from the finding of such a large quantity of pottery, this area probably contains a group of graves, the occupant or occupants of which were probably commoners of relatively high status.

Apart from the thirty-six items donated to the Longkou Municipal Museum, the remaining items in this group of pottery were collected by the Sino-American Joint Guicheng Archaeological Team. The circumstances are explained in detail in Chapter 7 of this book. Here we will introduce only a single example of each of the four types of vessels collected by the museum (Fig. Ⅱ.3.21; Table Ⅱ.3.5).

Section 7: Other Western Zhou Bronzes and Pottery Collected at Guicheng and in the Surrounding Region

Apart from the batches of relics discussed above, over the years the Longkou Municipal Museum has collected a few individual specimens of bronze vessels and pottery at Guicheng and the surrounding region. Although these items were sporadically unearthed, their morphology can enrich our understanding of the composition of the bronze and ceramic assemblages of the region, so they are certainly of academic significance. Therefore, we introduce a selection of important specimens here (Table Ⅱ.3.6) (Fig. Ⅱ.3.22- Ⅱ.3.25; Pls. 131-137).

Section 8: Dragon-shaped Jades of Ancient Date Unearthed from the Cemetery at Zhuangtou

The bronzes recovered from a Western Zhou tomb at Zhuangtou in September 1980 have already been discussed above. In 1983, villagers from the area successively unearthed a number of jade items from tombs in the vicinity of tomb M1 and submitted them in a timely manner to the museum collection. There are currently more than twenty jades from Zhuangtou Village in the collection of the Longkou Municipal Museum, including 4 dragon-shaped ornaments, 5 *huang* semi-circlets, 1 *bi* disk, and 10 flat jade pieces (Fig. Ⅱ.3.28, Ⅱ.3.29).

All of the jade items unearthed from the group of tombs at Zhuangtou are mortuary goods. Among these, the dragon-shaped jades and jade flat pieces might have been treasured by the tomb occupant in life as personal adornments. The *huang* semi-circlets and *bi* disk, though they were ceremonial jades, were also buried as grave goods. All are made of green jade, by then already used in China for 3,000 years, and are composed chiefly of tremolite and actinolite. Green jade is fine and soft, difficult to break, and smooth to the touch. Its color ranges from ashen to light green, but its greatest distinguishing characteristic is its oily-waxy luster, slick and silky. Green jade won the ancients' fondness for its qualities of durability and elegance. Upon their acquisition in 1983, the jades from the Zhuangtou cemetery became prized items in the museum's collection.

In 1992, the Zhuangtou cemetery was certified by the People's Government of Shandong Province as a Provincial Cultural Relics Protection Unit. The items unearthed there have provided rare information for the study of the history and economic and cultural life of the state of Lai. They are of significant archaeological and cultural value.

(Translated by Paul Nicholas Vogt)

第四章　归城遗址历年发现青铜器出土经过的调查综述

蒋惠民　唐锦琼

归城遗址及其附近地区，历年出土的文物十分丰富。其中出土的青铜器不但做工精美，而且具有浓厚的地域特色和时代特征，并且曾多次出土周代有铭文青铜器，被誉为“胶东青铜文化的摇篮”。据不完全统计，从清代光绪八年（1882年）起至今，历时130年，出土各种青铜器大约有400余件。大部分青铜器出土后即散失，未留下任何文字记录。有的出土是在兵荒马乱的战争年代，有的是“文化大革命”时期，有的是整地改土（1970～1980）的“战山河”期间。有的则是被发现者当作废旧物品，甚至砸碎卖给废旧物品收购部门。如县城绛水河畔的黄县废旧物品收购站、归姜村供销社、大脉村供销社等，都以收购废旧物品的名义，不同程度地收购了归城遗址出土的青铜器。还有的是非法盗掘，文物犯罪分子受利益驱使，私自挖掘，将盗掘的青铜器倒卖。而个别村民也有将在生产、生活中出土的青铜器隐匿不报，私自卖给文物贩子，从中牟取私利的。

归城遗址及其周边地区出土的青铜器，已经掌握的共有39批次（表Ⅱ.4.1）；其中有铭文的占14批次计41件。铭文最长的是海徐村出土的辛𨟻簋，同时也是胶东地区出土铭文最长的一件重器，腹底铸有铭文53字。凡是经烟台市博物馆和龙口市博物馆收藏的铜器，在本报告下编第二章和第三章中已有详细介绍。但是，对于它们复杂的出土背景过去则没有系统讨论，且有一部分青铜器的具体出土地点也有待进一步查证。2009年7月，中美联合归城考古队委派龙口市博物馆的副研究员蒋惠民和本队成员中国社会科学院的副研究员唐锦琼两人，共同对归城遗址历年出土的部分青铜器的发现背景和出土过程进行了详细调查。他们先后深入到归城曹家村、南埠村、东迟家村、小于家村，找当事人采访，并亲自到文物出土地点勘测数据，为归城地区青铜器及古代文化的研究提供了一批重要的背景资料。现将调查情况总结报告如下。

第一节　鲁家沟村出土的青铜器

鲁家沟村位于归城遗址的东南方向，现属石良镇管辖，距归城遗址15千米（图Ⅱ.2.1～2）。光绪二十二年（1896年），该村村民刘国亨到村东100米的高台地上取土，挖出青铜器10件，有钟3、鼎2（铭文2）、壶1、盘1、甗1（铭文）、盉1（铭文）、觯1（铭文），其中五件带有铭文。王道新先生编纂的《黄县志稿》金石目做了记述（王道新1934：806）。著名考古学家王献唐先生在《黄县𠙴器》一书中亦做过专门记载，认为这批青铜器属西周早期墓葬中器物（王献唐 1960：149）。收藏在日本京都的泉屋博古馆里，笔者对当年的出土情况进行了调查研究。

说来还有一段史话。石良镇鲁家沟村地处黄县东南部山区，村东田野有一片高台地，那里是村中盖房垫圈理想的取土处（图Ⅱ.4.1）。时间追溯到1896年的春天，村民刘国亨在高台地的自家田中取土，一下子挖出了10件青铜器，刘老汉虽然不懂考古，但却认为这东西能换一大笔钱来养家糊口。于是，他放下手中的活计，琢磨着如何将它们变成钱的事，就托人到黄县城打听。当他得知黄城丁家"泰来"（商号）的掌门人丁树桢（字干圃）热衷于古物收藏时，便择日从邻居家借了头小毛驴，驮着青铜器赶往黄县城。旧时鲁家沟到黄县城得走约25千米的山路，当他赶到"泰来"府上时，已近中午。丁树桢一见这批青铜器，爱不释手，深知其价值。转眼一看刘国亨的山里人打扮：脚上穿着三岔鞋，腰上系着根围脖，于是，就拉起了架子说不值钱，只给铜钱300吊。刘国亨心里也没底，究竟能卖多少钱也说不出，心想只要再加点钱就卖给他，只好说能不能再加点。刘国亨一听不能加，就嚷着嫌钱少不卖，要送到登州府去卖高价。

丁树桢一看到手的宝物要走，岂肯甘心，说什么也不能放过他，就动起了心计，言道："哎，急什么？大老远来的，买卖不成仁义在吗。天已经晌了，管家！让厨房备菜，我陪刘老哥喝两盅！今个咱是只喝酒吃饭不谈买卖。"刘国亨被半推半就地让到了酒席桌上。席间，丁树桢暗中吩咐管家，将铜钱撒到了府中厢房的地上。三杯酒过后，刘国亨已面红耳赤，就滔滔不绝地讲起挖铜器的经过。又三杯下肚，刘国亨已略有醉意，便自吹自擂地说起我老刘最讲仁义。丁树桢见时机已到，就说道："你算找对了，我丁百万家既仁义又有钱。"

随后，提出要领刘国亨去看看"泰来"家的钱库，让他一饱眼福，开开眼界。刘国亨好奇地跟随着丁树桢来到了厢房，进门一看惊呆了，只见满地都是铜钱。丁树桢趁机豪爽地言道："只要你把铜器留下，这库里的钱全归你！你看我老丁仁义不仁义。"刘国亨一个山区农民，从来未见到过这么多的钱就满口答应了。他把盛青铜器的袋子往外一倒，头也不抬一心只顾往里装钱。而后，双方立了字据，刘国亨高兴地哼着小曲赶着小毛驴回了鲁家沟。到家后，他把钱取出全部串起来，一数正好还是300吊。心中暗想咱乡下人就是斗不过城里人，因立有字据，这事只得作罢。

数年后，据说丁树桢将这批青铜器以3千吊的价格卖给了登州府，登州府又以6千吊的价格卖到了济南府，济南府则以8千吊的价格卖至京城。到了民国年间，这批青铜器流散于日本。这10件铜器中5件带有铭文，鼎铭为"莱白（伯）乍（作）旅鼎"5字；盉铭为"□乍（作）宗尊，厥子孙永宝用"10字；觯铭为"公赏贝，束用乍（作）父辛于彝"10字；遇甗通高40.6厘米，重5.2千克（图Ⅱ.2.10），腹内铸的铭文最长，共有37字，全文如下：

隹（唯）六月既死霸丙寅，師雝（雍）父戍，才（在）古𠂤（師），遹從。師雝（雍）父肩史遹事（使）于𢼸（胡）侯，侯蔑遹曆，易（賜）遹金，用乍（作）旅鬳（甗）。

铭文记载在某年六月丙寅日，师雍父率军驻扎在古師，遇跟随在一起。师雍父派遇出使胡侯国，胡侯对遇进行了“蔑历”的奖赏，并赐遇以青铜。遇因此作了这个旅甗，以示纪念。

第二节　南埠村出土的曩器

南埠村位于归城遗址的东南方向，现属兰高镇管辖，距归城遗址内城2千米。该村曾多次出土过青铜器，现分述如下。

一、著名的黄县曩器

在去南埠村采访时，8件曩器的出土当事人姜德科和李显安早已去世，因此我们采访了时年75岁的目击者姜培隆先生（图Ⅱ.4.2）。据姜培隆先生回忆，1951年系解放初期，中国广大农村还是实行单干的时代。那年他刚满17岁，听说村东北河边地里挖出青铜器的消息，他急忙跑过去观看。原来是村民姜德科和在村里扛活的李显安，在取土垫圈时，偶然挖出10件青铜器和一批陶器。两人将陶器砸碎丢弃，又怀疑铜器中含金，敲击验看，致使器身损伤。当时由南埠村分得一部分，李显安分得一部分，另有一件铜匜，归该村所属的黄县四区政府保管。铜器出土后，莱阳专区公署文物管理委员会黄县分会，派金经一、张敏生二人到南埠村调查，将其中8件青铜器收归国有。1952年移交给山东省文物管理委员会，1954年拨交山东省博物馆，现藏该馆。另有两件铜器（甗1、穿带壶1）被青岛市博物馆收藏。

在姜培隆先生的带领下，我们实地勘测了这批青铜器的出土地点。它位于东迟家村村南，在南北流向的一条小河的西岸旁。东经120°34′455″，北纬37°35′089″，海拔112米。

这10件青铜器中有盨4件，鼎、盘、匜、鬲、甗、穿带壶各1件。其中盨、盘和匜均有铭文。另外一起出土的还有玉佩和陶器等物，据此推测，这批器物应属墓葬中的随葬品。时代应为春秋时期。盨的作器者为“曩伯子㝬父”，为国家一级文物。该器高17.8厘米，口长21厘米，宽14.5厘米。口呈圆角长方形，子母口，口两侧有附耳，耳与器间有双梁连接。盖上有四个方纽，器下有方足。盖与器身均饰有瓦纹。器内底与盖对铭，各铸阴文5行26字（释文见下编第二章）。“曩”为古国名；从同出的盘铭文“曩伯㝬父媵姜無□般（盤）”（集成10081）判断，为姜姓。曩国的历史可上溯至商代，见于甲骨文。自武丁以来，曩就服务于商王朝。据研究，商代著名的贤臣箕子，就出自该曩族。周初，曩族向北、向东两个方向发展，其中一支便来到了山东境内。盘铭上的“㝬父”是曩伯（曩氏宗族长子）的字，而盨铭的“曩伯”则为“㝬父”之父的前代“曩伯”，器作于㝬父尚为世子之时。归城遗址发现的这组曩器，便是他们在春秋早期的遗存。也即曩伯㝬父嫁女姜氏到莱国归城时带来的一组铜器。1963

年，山东省图书馆馆长、著名考古学家王献唐先生，出版发行《黄县曩器》一书，专门论述了收藏在山东省博物馆的8件曩器（王献唐 1960：3～62）。

谈到媵器（陪嫁品），必然涉及莱国女儿出嫁的情况。1976年，古莒国的日照崮河崖发现两座春秋早期墓。一号墓出土有鼎、鬲、壶、盘、匜等14件青铜器。其中同形制鬲4件，口沿一周皆铸“釐（莱）白（伯）媵女子乍（作）寳鬲，子子孫孫永寳用”15字铭文。分析这四件铜鬲应为莱国王公所作，是莱国女子出嫁到莒国时所带的媵器。铜器现藏日照市博物馆。由以上两组铜器铭文可证，莱国和曩国、莒国均有姻亲关系，或可说结成联盟。

二、南埠村其他零散出土的青铜器

在南埠村采访时，我们遇到了一位转业军人，现任南埠村村委委员，名字叫郭兴礼。1952年生人，时年58岁（图Ⅱ.4.3）。据他反映，曾经听到村中老人们说过，1920年，在村东地里出土一件青铜壶，被村民拿到市场上卖掉了。1960年，郭兴礼在村东也挖出一件青铜贯耳壶，高约40厘米，因为残破，一直扔在家中后院里。夏季下大雨时，破铜壶堵住了院里的排水沟，他就将其砸碎扔掉了。1968年，他在该地又挖出过玉片，并向上级报告。是年，烟台市博物馆的李步青先生，带队前来考古调查。经其实地勘测，应为一座墓葬，地点位于村东河边地里，东经120°34′487″，北纬37°35′051″，海拔110米。

第三节　文基镇小刘庄出土的青铜器原委

小刘庄，位于归城遗址的正南方向，距归城遗址内城1千米，现该村已合并至归城曹家村，现属兰高镇管辖。

1969年8月，属“文化大革命”时期。正值末伏时节，小刘庄的30名村民，在时年26岁的第四生产队队长刘德清（图Ⅱ.4.4）的带领下，在村南将高低不平的小块土地，整平为大田。按照当地 “中伏萝卜，末伏菜”的俗语，以备种上大白菜。时近中午，由于天气炎热，准备提早收工时，社员刘志会一镢头刨出一个陶碗，大家十分惊奇，纷纷围拢过来。于是，队长下令，女社员全部回家做午饭，男社员留下来挖掘。他们共挖掘出青铜器20余件，整整装满了一大偏篓。其中有鼎1个，重约15千克，头盔1个、卣、尊、盉、觶、纽钟、矛等，另有毛发和骨头碎片，分析应为启的墓。

队长望着这批青铜器，从中挑选出4件完整的小件器物留下，有卣、尊、觶和卣盖，放到自家平房内，准备日后卖钱购买记工本用。其余的于是日下午，让曹金瑞骑自行车带到县城，送至绛水河东岸的废旧物品收购站卖掉。当到达废旧物品收购站时，收购站人员说，完整的不收，必须是废铜。曹金瑞等人又用大锤将青铜器砸碎，方才过秤。当时铜价每千克3.94元，重约50千克，卖了100余元钱，在场的社员每人分得2元，剩下的钱买了香烟、糖块分发，还买了一个小闹钟。

翌年春天，山东省博物馆来了三人，其中有一个大个子姓张，找到正在地里干活的刘德清，调查了解青铜器等文物出土情况，并将留在他家中的4件青铜器取走，写下一张收条。原来黄县（现龙口市）废旧物品收购站将收购的青铜碎块发往烟台，烟台发现后，将此事向省里做了汇报，省里委派山东省博物馆来人调查此事。

经我们实地勘测，该墓葬地点位于小刘家村南的水库旁边（图Ⅱ.4.5），东经120°33′392″，北纬37°34′916″，海拔135米，地质为砂岩。墓葬呈东北西南向，长2米，宽1米左右，深2米。

当然这批铜器中最重要的是启卣和启尊，按其形制属于西周中期偏早的器物。启卣现收藏在山东省博物馆，启尊于1989年调至中国历史博物馆，现藏中国国家博物馆。铜卣在商周青铜器中是比较常见的酒器，主要用来装盛以黑黍及一种草根所酿成的黑色酒，这种酒主要是在祭祀降神、祭享祖先之后才能饮用。启卣通高22.7厘米，椭圆形，子母口，圈足，扁圆形盖与纽，兽首提梁与环耳相连接。器中间突起一兽头，腹上部及盖均饰以云雷纹为地的波形带纹。器盖对铭，各铸铭文39字。启尊，高18厘米，大侈口，粗颈，腹下部鼓圆，矮圈足。颈部饰波带纹，中间突出一怒目圆睁的兽面（图Ⅱ.2.6）。器内底铸铭文3行19字，尾书符号2字，共计21字（释文见下编第二章）。它们记述了周王朝对南山寇遭山谷的一次征伐，而作器者启参加了这次战役。

启卣和启尊在归城范围的出土说明了归城遗址和周王朝紧密的政治关系。2011年5月12日，中央电视台国宝档案栏目对启尊和启卣的发现，制作了专题片进行播出。

第四节　和平村出土的己侯鬲和其他铜器

和平村（又称“东和平村”）位于归城遗址内城的东北，现属兰高镇管辖。20世纪50年代，该村村民在村南取土时，挖出30余件春秋早期青铜器，绝大部分被毁掉和卖掉，只剩下1件鬲，因作器者为己侯，故名己侯鬲。该器高10.5厘米，口径14.1厘米。宽沿斜折，弧裆近平，矮实足。通体素面，有扉棱。口沿上有一圈铭文，计14字，部分字体残蚀，铭文为：“己侯铸□姜□□子子孫孫永寳用”。1962年，烟台市文物店在黄县设点收购流散文物时，收得此鬲，是年转交烟台市博物馆收藏。1946年，村民王敬选在自家院中打井时，在井深达4米时，挖出编钟4件。翌年9月，国民党军占领黄县，他们下乡抢劫时，听说王敬选家中有宝物，便闯入其家中，硬是抢走两件编钟。建国初期，王敬选因家庭生活拮据，将剩余的两件编钟拿出一件，让其子去北京卖掉，换点钱贴补家用。结果被有关部门没收，付给其子15元的往返路费，这件编钟最后辗转收藏在烟台市博物馆。还剩一件仍存其家中。现在王敬选先生已经去世，最后一件编钟由其子王怀昌收藏。这件编钟高39.5厘米，柱状枚，饰云雷纹。钲部有徽识，为西周时期器物。

1964年，该村出土一批青铜器，有盒1、壶1、戈1、剑1，共4件，属春秋时期器物，现藏烟台市博物馆。

1965年5月，和平村村民在村东建房，挖出一鼎一矛，属西周晚期器物，现藏烟台市博物馆。

1969年，该村原党支部书记王敬强，在整地改土时，挖出一把青铜剑，当去废旧物品收购站出卖时，亦要求砸碎方才卖出。

1973年3月，烟台地区文物普查小组到归城故城遗址复查时，在和平村西果园断崖处发现暴露出四具骨架；且当地群众反映，前几年在这里用土时，曾发现陶罐、铜剑等物。为了不影响果树生长，烟台市博物馆于3月9日在断崖处组织人员开挖了一条探沟，探沟南北长2.6米，东西宽南头2.05米，北头1.61米，沟深1.07米。在沟的东部，发现一片涂有朱色的底面，上面压有一具较完整的马肋骨骨架。马是仰葬，头西尾东，为原葬形态，肋骨的上部有一个铜环。在沟西南底部发现一些马齿，杂有三件铜车饰和一个半圆形铜环。在沟的中部西边的底面，发现了一个盖弓帽，两个铜环和四个蛙形车饰。经过对探沟土层分析，该车马坑已经扰动，马骨、马齿位置凌乱，可见马头有两个，一个口中含有铜马衔半付，其余的铜马器、车器散布于坑内，分析这是一座春秋时期大墓的殉马坑。出土的铜器主要有马衔半副、马镳1副、车辖1、蛙饰方形环4、圆环1、半圆环1、车器2、铜管1，共计12件，现藏烟台市博物馆（李步青，林仙庭 1991：914～915）。

1989年，村民王怀忠在自家院中挖猪圈坑时，挖出一个车马坑，出土有马骨，青铜车軎、铜镞等，已移交龙口市博物馆收藏。

2002年11月，烟台文物考古队和龙口市博物馆一行10人对和平村先民居住遗址进行了抢救性发掘，发掘面积1500平方米，出土房屋遗址十余座。这次考古发现，填补了自20世纪50年代以来，归城故城居住遗址的空白（见下编第一章）。同时征集到往年出土的铜车軎一件，现藏烟台市博物馆。

第五节　海徐村出土的国宝辛𩡧簋

海徐村位于归城遗址的西北方向，属中村镇管辖，距归城遗址内城17.5千米。1983年4月，海徐村果林队负责人仲跻会先生带领村民徐士考、赵军强等人，在距村东300米处的果园内打葡萄沟时，挖出两件青铜器。一件为铜鬲，另一件是辛簋。仲跻会带着铜鬲到龙口市博物馆的文物商店出售，收购人员将铜鬲收下，按规定付了奖励费。仲济会走出不远又折回来，对收购人员讲，家中还有一件大的青铜器，在家做鸡食盆用，问要不要？收购人员说要。翌日，仲跻会又将辛𩡧簋送来，奖励其人民币20元。后经山东省文物鉴定专家组台立业、关天相等先生鉴定，确认为国家一级文物，这一发现引起文物界的轰动。1986年11月，烟台市文管会组织专业人员，前去海徐村出土地点进行现场勘探试掘，再未发现任何器物。对仲济会先生保护、上交文物的行动，召开群众大会，给予表彰，同时又奖励他人民币60元。这两件青铜器现藏龙口市博物馆。

辛𨇨簋通高12.8厘米，侈口，口径20厘米，束领，重量2750克，鼓腹，双兽耳有珥，喇叭形圈足，腹上部饰有兽面纹，腹内底部铸有5行53字铭文，为迄今胶东地区出土文字最多的一件重器，但其许多字在金文中不曾见过。因全文中“辛𨇨”两字出现数次，系作器者名字，故取名“辛𨇨簋”（释文见下编第三章）。铭文讲述：王某年十一月，王至古现，王子亦至，辛𨇨在叔某陪同下，晋见周王，并有所礼遇，得到金、贝之物赏赐，辛𨇨用金作此铜簋，子子孙孙永为纪念。

这件辛簋，制作精美，造型、纹饰都很有特点，属西周穆王时期青铜器。但是，这篇铭文文字不规范，许多字在金文中不曾见过，释读全部铭文难度较大。很明显是一件当地铸造的有铭文青铜器。它的发现证明归城地区历史悠久，同时也说明这里的冶炼技术在西周时期已相当发达。

第六节　集前赵家村出土的青铜器

集前赵家村位于归城遗址的东南方向，归属石良镇管辖，距归城遗址内城10千米。2004年4月10日，村西砖厂在劈泥烧砖时，开挖掘机的重庆民工一下子挖出了一批青铜器，民工们蜂拥而上，将青铜器私分藏匿。当接到报告时，已是第二天下午。我们会同公安部门赶到现场，查看了出土地点，当即将挖破的文物收回。由于大部分器物残损严重，经过清点，能辨认出器形的有14件，另有青铜残片一宗。其中青铜鼎3件，弦纹方座簋2件，提梁卣、甬钟、贯耳壶、甗、尊、盘、爵、觯、泡各1件（器物描述及尺寸见下编第三章图Ⅱ.3.16-20，表Ⅱ.3.3）。这14件器物中一件鼎和甬钟是完好无损的，余者均残损。另有碎陶片一宗，这里不排除有器物流失的可能。

墓葬已被挖至底部，从现场残留的痕迹上，我们对墓葬的范围进行清理测量。墓葬呈东西向，东西长4.75米，南北宽 3 米，距地表6.55米，现场只发现部分夹有红漆的炭灰，别无他物。我们对取回的器物进行清理，发现6件青铜器上带有铭文。

其中三件青铜鼎铭文情况如下：一件鼎仅有几块残片，在其中一小块残片上留有完整的“㠱候”二字，“候”字下似有一“史”字，“㠱”字左似有一“赐”字；另一鼎为凤鸟纹，腹内壁铭文处残损，铸3行阴文“里父乍（作）隩（尊）彝□□永□，”可能有10字，有四字因腐蚀严重难辨，下方因残是否缺字不明；再一件完整的鼎为弦纹，腹内壁铸阴文竖排“乍（作）鼎”2字。两件弦纹兽耳方座簋：耳下有珥，均铸2行阴文“白（伯）應父易（赐）叔索金，用乍（作）寶簋”11字，只是字的排列方法略微有点变化。贯耳壶腹内壁近沿处铸2行阴文“伊白（伯）賜應金乍（作）旅壶”8字。依据铭文，上述器物分别定名为：㠱候鼎、里父鼎、作鼎、叔索簋、應壶。从器物的形制特征和纹饰上看，此墓葬应属西周中期偏早，大约在周穆王时代早期。铭文中提到的“曩侯”“里父”“伊伯”“伯应父”“叔索”等人物名字，他们的关系似乎是上下级之间，值得进一步商榷。

关于墓的主人是谁？笔者作了初步分析探讨。从风格上看，“作鼎”“叔索簋”和盘、尊、卣、觯、甗等的造型、纹饰和工艺非常一致，器物颈部均饰有两道弦纹。组合为鼎1、簋2、盘1、尊1、卣1、觯1、爵1、甗1；其他器物的造型风格则与上述器物略有差异。从这点看，只有簋上的铭文可断定为墓的主人。因此，此墓应是“叔索墓”。在墓主人下葬时，又添配了风格略异的“曩候鼎”“里父鼎”和甬钟，还有“应”送给他的壶。形成的新组合是：鼎3、簋2、壶1、盘1、尊1、卣1、觯1、爵1、甗1、钟1。

2008年，这批器物中的12件已由国家博物馆的孙振翔组织人员进行修复，现在龙口市博物馆的《莱国春秋》中展出。

第七节　其他村庄出土的青铜器

一、石良村出土的青铜器

石良村位于归城遗址东南方向，距内城10千米，现为石良镇政府所在地。王道新先生编纂的《黄县志稿》金石目记载：光绪十六年秋，城东南石良村田中出土铜匜一件，有“鲁士商□（取？）乍（作）匜”6字铭文。器归丁彝斋收藏（王道新 1934：807）。

二、归姜村出土的青铜器

归姜村属兰高镇管辖。1949年之前归城曾出土带有“己侯乍（作）寳鐘”5字铭文的纽钟，为黄县丁氏家族丁树桢收藏，时代为春秋时期。现藏烟台市博物馆。

1974年是“大战山河”的年代，时任归姜村民兵连长的姜全开先生，在整地改土中，挖出一批青铜器，足足装了一小推车，大约有50件，送到废旧物品收购站。他只留下一件青铜环，准备做家中街门上的门铧用。

三、归城曹家出土的青铜器

归城曹家，位于归城遗址的正南方向，距归城遗址内城1千米。1965年5月，修筑归城姜家村水库大坝劈崖取土时，发现一处西周墓葬。墓在大坝西头山脚下，是一处河旁黄土台地。烟台市文管会会同黄县的文物工作者，立即对已遭破坏的墓葬进行发掘清理。该墓位于村南300米处，为长方形土坑竖穴墓。清理时，只剩墓之东部。墓底南北宽5.2米，东西残长1米，深3米，墓底有一层朱彩，分析为彩绘棺木。墓西部曾出土大量陶器，多数被破坏散失，仅余一陶罐。墓东部出土11件青铜器，有鼎2、甗1、壶1、尊1（铭文）、卣1（铭文）、爵2、觯1、凿1、器底1（铭文），其中3件腹内铸有铭文。铜器近旁有木板痕，器物上有席纹锈斑，说明曾用木匣装盛，并用草席包裹。另外还出土玉戈1件。器物现藏烟台市博物馆。

四、归城董家村出土的青铜器

归城董家村位于归城遗址的东北方向，现属兰高镇管辖，距归城遗址内城1.5千米。1969年，归城董家村窑厂取土时，挖出了9件青铜器，有素面弦纹甗1、雷纹兽足盘1、夔纹蹄足鼎1、戈1，经辨别系出土于两个不同时期的墓葬。其中甗和盘同时出土，9件均为西周时期器物，现藏烟台市博物馆。

五、东迟家村出土的青铜器

东迟家村位于归城遗址的正东方向，现属兰高镇管辖，距归城遗址内城0.5千米。这里过去曾有两批铜器出土：

（1）1984年，黄县农村实行分田到户，东迟家村的村民，时年38岁的迟元学，分得两行苹果树，位置在归姜村东水库的东岸上。由于地势呈南高北低，为了便于浇水，迟元学夫妇打算将这块土地整平，用小推车从地南头取土，推至地北头。在挖土时挖出了2件青铜器，有一件鼎和一件簋，送交龙口市博物馆，经过鉴定，为西周早期器物。迟元学于1996年去世，在其弟弟迟元强夫妇的带领下，我们进行了实地勘测。铜器出土地点位于水库东侧的高台地上（图Ⅱ.4.6），东经120°34′192″，北纬37°35′305″，海拔81米。

（2）2000年10月，东迟家村在村东修水库，挖掘机挖出一座墓葬，并出土一件青铜鼎。村党支部书记报告给龙口市博物馆后，我们立即组织人员对残墓进行了清理，又出土陶器4件，有豆2、盂1、鬲1，以及陶器碎片，经考证，此墓应为西周时期，出土器物收藏在龙口市博物馆。龙口市文物管理委员会向东迟家村颁发锦旗一面，奖励人民币800元。

六、大于家村出土的青铜器

大于家村位于归城遗址的东北方向，现属兰高镇管辖，距归城遗址内城1.5千米。这里出土的青铜器主要有以下两批：

（1）据《龙口市志》记载：光绪八年（1882年）秋，归城大于家出土古鉨一纽，文为“陈裕疾私鉨”。物藏丁树桢家，据考证为战国文物。“裕疾”，王献唐先生在《黄县䝨器》一书中解释为“去疾”（李继涛 1995：9）。

（2）1986年4月，风和日丽，南埠村的郭兴礼和弟弟郭兴智一起，到大于家村郭兴兰姐姐家，帮忙建设两栋房子。由于建筑规模较大，用土多，他们选中大于家村东南的泥场取土。

弟弟郭兴智是个拖拉机手，他一人开两辆拖拉机来回倒换拉土，开走一辆装土车，留下空车装土，回来时，再开下一辆。村南泥场4～5米高，向北突出的部位，土质坚硬，加上含有沙粒，村民很少有人使用。当他们刨土时，挖出了一批精美的青铜器，共计6件。有鼎、盘、匜、泡等。郭兴兰的丈夫时任村党支部书记，他立即打电话报告公社文书。经公社与县里文物部门联系，送交黄县文物店，由文物店的唐兆洛、梁桂英、张丽果三人收集，并奖励人民币80元。出土的这六件青铜器，现藏龙口市博物馆。经实地勘测，出土地点在村南偏东的一条东西向小河的南岸（图Ⅱ.4.7），东经120°34′484″，北纬37°36′105″，海拔39米。

七、东梧桐村出土的青铜器

东梧桐村位于归城遗址的正西方向，现属芦头镇管辖，距归城遗址内城10千米。这里也曾出土过两批青铜器。

（1）1995年4月4日下午，东梧桐村村北砖厂，窑工在放土采泥过程中，发现一座墓葬，出土了大量青铜器。接到村委报案后，我们马上与当地派出所联系保护好现场，并组织馆内业务人员立即前往该村。当我们赶到现场，看到一大堆青铜器被挖碎时，既感到惊讶又感到惋惜，仅有两个鼎、三个豆、五个圆盘和釜较完整。接着，我们对残墓进行了清理。此墓长3.8米，宽2.6米，深4.7米；墓上部为3.5米封土，下部为1.2米厚防盗用的河流子石填充，这在龙口尚属首次发现。内葬男尸一具，部分头骨和牙齿清晰可辨。我们清理出提链双耳方盘一件，盘上饰有精细的云雷纹；铜戈一件，腐蚀较严重；在男尸的头部发现玉片三枚，应为覆面玉器；另有陪葬狗一只。经考证，此墓应属战国时期贵族墓葬。三天的发掘结束后，奖给村委锦旗一面，人民币800元。

因出土的青铜器大部分被砖厂挖掘机挖碎，经过清点，可辨认出器形的青铜器有鼎4、壶2、豆4、圆盘5、方盘1、鎏金盆2、釜1、敦2、舟1、戈1，共23件。另有青铜镞、铁镞十多枚，青铜碎片一宗，玉器3件，陶罐4件，现藏龙口市博物馆。

（2）2007年4月，龙口市博物馆对南水北调工程沿线进行文物普查，在行至该村村北砖厂时，发现一处裸露的残墓。我们立即组织人员进行清理，出土鎏金铜带钩1、玉佩1、陶钵4，共计6件器物。经考证，该墓属战国时期，出土器物现藏龙口市博物馆。

八、东庄头村出土的青铜器

东庄头村位于归城遗址的正东方向，现属石良镇管辖，距归城遗址内城10千米。东庄头墓群是西周时代古墓群，位于村东高台地。该墓群南北长150米，东西宽119米，占地面积17850平方米。1987年，东庄头墓群被公布为烟台市文物保护单位，1992年又被公布为山东省文物保护单位。

1980年9月，村民刘永新等人在村东高台地取土时发现一批青铜器。烟台市文管会会同龙口市相关人员，前往取土地点进行清理发掘，确认为西周时期墓葬。出土的青铜器有鼎3、簋2（铭文）、壶1（铭文）、卣1（铭文）、甗1、爵2、盘1、觚1、勺1、觯1、盂1、戈1，共计16件，其中4件带有铭文。现藏龙口市博物馆。

九、东营周家村出土的青铜器

东营周家村位于归城遗址的正东方向，现属石良镇管辖，距归城遗址内城11千米。1986年6月，东营周家村南果园里有两座西周时期墓，已被破坏。龙口市博物馆接报后，立即组织人员前往进行抢救性发掘。墓为土坑竖穴墓，内有棺椁。一号墓清理出土带有铭文的青铜簋2件；二号墓出土陶器200余件，有鼎、豆、罐、壶、鬲、爵等，其中陶鼎很有地方特色，现均藏龙口市博物馆。

十、收购部门收购的青铜器

黄县废旧物品收购站、归姜村供销社、大脉村供销社等单位，都曾经以收购废旧物品的名义，不同程度地收购了归城遗址出土的青铜器。这些青铜器在被送到烟台废旧物品收购部门后，有的被文物部门捡出，有的被送往冶炼厂，未能存世。

参考文献

李步青，林仙庭，1991：山东黄县归城遗址的调查与发掘. 考古，10：910-918.

李继涛，1995：龙口市志. 济南：齐鲁书社.

王道新，1934：黄县志稿. 山东省博物馆藏，卷14.

王献唐，1960：黄县㠱器. 济南：山东人民出版社.

烟台市博物馆，2006：考古烟台. 济南：齐鲁书社.

烟台市文物管理委员会，烟台市博物馆，2004：胶东考古研究文集. 济南：齐鲁书社.

图Ⅱ.4.1　1896年鲁家沟铜器出土地点（2013年8月23日摄）
Figure Ⅱ.4.1　Location of the discovery of bronzes in Lujiagou, 1896 (photograph August 23, 2013).

图 Ⅱ.4.2　本文作者在南埠㠱器出土地采访见证人姜培隆（右）（2009年7月7日摄）
Figure Ⅱ.4.2　The author interviewing eyewitness Jiang Peilong (right) at the place where the Ji bronzes were excavated in Nanbu Village (photograph July 7, 2009).

图Ⅱ.4.3　在南埠村1960铜壶出土地点采访郭兴礼（左）（2009年7月7日摄）

Figure Ⅱ.4.3　Interviewing Guo Xingli (left) at the location where he excavated a bronze *hu* in 1960, Nanbu Village (photograph July 7, 2009).

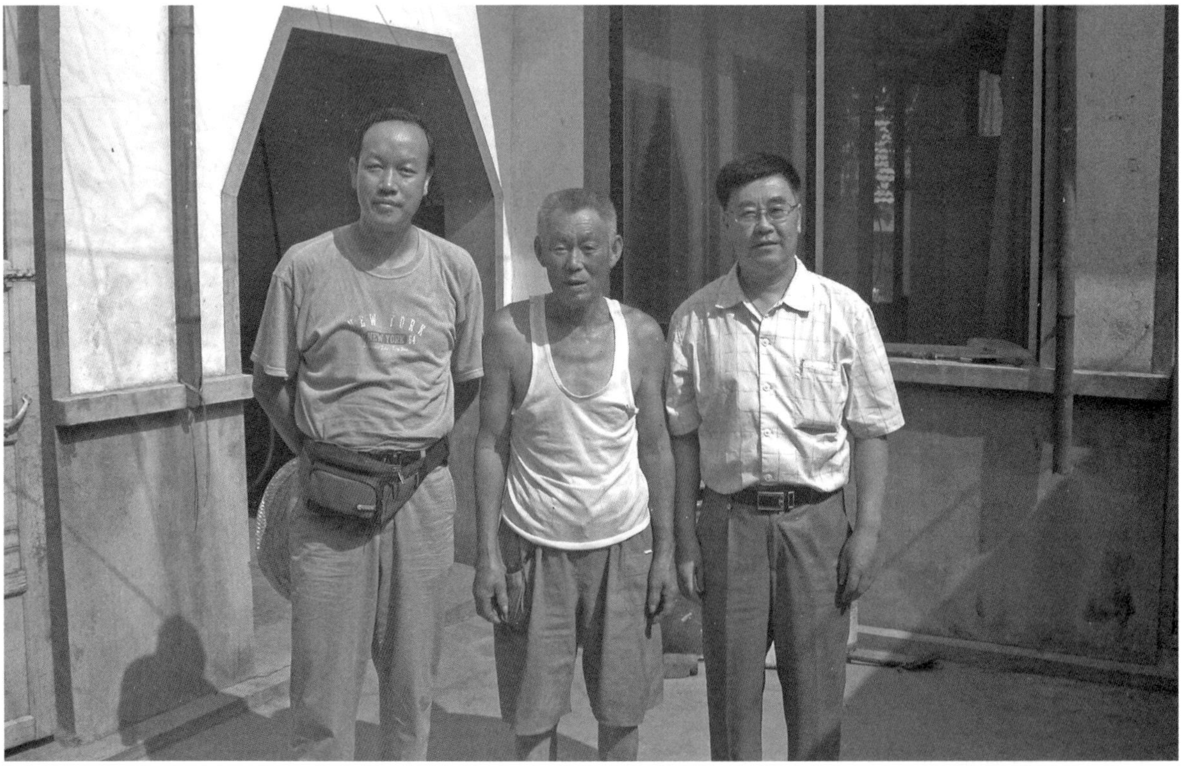

图Ⅱ.4.4　本文作者与启尊发掘人刘德清（中）李峰（左）于曹家村合影（2009年7月7日摄）

Figure Ⅱ.4.4　With Liu Deqing (center), excavator of the Qi *zun*, and Li Feng (left) in Caojia Village (photograph July 7, 2009).

图Ⅱ.4.5　本文作者蒋惠民（左）、唐锦琼（右）在小刘庄启尊出土地（2009年7月7日摄）

FigureⅡ.4.5　Authors Jiang Huimin (left) and Tang Jinqiong (right) at the location of the discovery of the Qi *zun* (photograph July 7, 2009).

图 Ⅱ.4.6　本文作者与迟元强（中）夫妇在东迟家村1984铜器出土地（2009年7月17日摄）

FigureⅡ.4.6　Author and Chi Yuanqiang (center) couple at the location of the discovery of bronzes in 1984, Dongchijia Village (photograph July 17, 2009).

图 Ⅱ.4.7　本文作者与郭兴礼（右）在大于家1986铜器出土地（2009年7月16日摄）

Figure Ⅱ.4.7　Author and Guo Xingli (right) at the location of the discovery of bronzes in 1986, Dayujia Village (July 16, 2009).

表Ⅱ.4.1 归城及周边地区历年发现铜器登记表（1882～2006年）

Table Ⅱ.4.1 Discoveries of Bronzes in Guicheng and Surroundings, 1882-2006

	出土地点 Provenance	出土时间 Time of Disc.	铜器 Bronzes	铭文 Inscription	年代 Date	发现者 Finder	现藏 Current Location	发表或信息来源 Publication or Source Infor.
1	和平村沟北 Heping Village, Ditch-North	ca. 1931	钟5 Bell 5				抗战时出售 Sold during WWII	《黄县㠱器》5页 *Huangxian Ji qi*, p. 5
2	和平村 Heping Village	1946	钟4 Bell 4	钟2 Bell2	春秋 SA	王敬选 Wang Jingxuan	烟台博物馆1；王怀昌家1；军队抢走2 Yantai Museum1; Wang Huaichang's home 1; taken by army 2	王敬强报告 Wang Jingqiang reports
3	和平村 Heping Village	1948	钟2 Bell 2		春秋 SA		烟台市博物馆 Yantai Museum	1984年由济南调烟台 Transferred from Ji'nan to Yantai, 1984
4	和平村 Heping Village	1958	剑1 Sword 1		春秋 SA		山东省博物馆 Shandong Museum	
5	和平村 Heping Village	1950s	己侯鬲，其余铜器约30失散 Jihou *li*; other 30 bronzes lost	己侯鬲 Jihou *li*	春秋 SA		烟台市博物馆 Yantai Museum	《胶东考古研究文集》344页 *Jiaodong kaogu yanjiu wenji*, p. 344
6	和平村 Heping Village	1962	鼎2、盨 1、簋1、鬲1、钟1 *Ding* cauldron 2, *xu* square tureen 1 *Gui* tureen 1, *li* tripod 1, *zhong* 1	鼎、盨、簋、鬲、钟 *Ding*, *xu*, *gui*, *li*, bell	西周中晚春秋、战国， M-LWZ, SA WS		烟台市博物馆 Yantai Museum	1962年由黄县和蓬莱县调拨 Transferred from Huangxian and Penglai to Yantai, 1962
7	和平村 Heping Village	1964	盒1、壶1、戈1、剑1 Box 1, *hu* bottle 1, *ge* dagger 1, sword 1		春秋 SA		烟台市博物馆 Yantai Museum	
8	和平村 Heping Village	1965	鼎1、矛1 *Ding* cauldron 1, spear 1		西周中 MWZ		烟台市博物馆 Yantai Museum	
9	和平村 Heping Village	1969	剑1 Sword 1			王敬强 Wang Jingqiang	卖于废品收购站 Sold to recycling station	

续表

	出土地点 Provenance	出土时间 Time of Disc.	铜器 Bronzes	铭文 Inscription	年代 Date	发现者 Finder	现藏 Current Location	发表或信息来源 Publication or Source Infor.
10	和平村 Heping Village	1973	车軎2、马衔半副、马镳1副、车辖1、蛙饰方环4、圆环1、半圆环1、铜管1 Chariot axle-cap 2, horse bit-half, horse cheek piece 1, chariot axle controller 1, frog-decorated square bronze ring 4, round ring 1, semi-circle ring 1, and bronze tube 1.		春秋 SA		烟台市博物馆 Yantai Museum	
11	和平村 Heping Village	1989	车軎1、铜镞1 Chariot axle-cap 1, arrow 1		春秋 SA	王怀忠 Wang Huaizhong	龙口市博物馆 Longkou Museum	
12	和平村 Heping Village	2002.10	车軎1 Chariot axle-cap 1		春秋 SA		烟台市博物馆 Yantai Museum	
13	归姜村 Guijiang Village	1974	鼎、环、剑等约50件 *Ding* cauldron, *huan* ring, sword etc., ca. 50			姜全开 Jiang Quankai	环在姜全开家，余卖废品收购站 *Huan* ring in Jiang Quankai's home, others sold to recycling station	
14	归城内城 Guicheng Inner City	1914	钟4 Bell 4				王曼生购得 Purchased by Wang Mansheng	《黄县㠱器》5页 *Huangxian Ji qi*, p. 5
15	归城内城 Guicheng Inner City	ca. 1914	方鼎等 Square *ding* cauldron, etc.				售于黄县达观阁古董铺 Sold to Daguange, antique dealer	《黄县㠱器》5页 *Huangxian Ji qi*, p. 5
16	归城内城 Guicheng Inner City	ca. 1949	己侯钟1 Jihou bell 1	己侯钟1 Jihou bell 1	春秋 SA		烟台市博物馆 Yantai Museum	《胶东考古研究文集》345页 *Jiaodong kaogu yanjiu wenji*, p. 345
17	曹家村 Caojia Village	1965	鼎2、尊1、卣1、爵2、甗1、壶1、觯1、凿1、器底1 *Ding* cauldron 2, *zun* pitcher 1, *you* jar 1, *jue* cup 2, *yan* streamer 1, *hu* bottle 1, *zhi* goblet 1, chisel 1, vessel bottom 1	尊、卣、器底 *Zun*, *you*, vessel bottom	西周中 MWZ		烟台市博物馆 Yantai Museum	
18	东迟家村 Dongchijia Village	1984	鼎1、簋1 *Ding* cauldron 1, *gui* tureen 1		西周早 EWZ	迟元学 Chi Yuanxue	龙口市博物馆 Longkou Museum	

续表

	出土地点 Provenance	出土时间 Time of Disc.	铜器 Bronzes	铭文 Inscription	年代 Date	发现者 Finder	现藏 Current Location	发表或信息来源 Publication or Source Infor.
19	东迟家村 Dongchijia Village	2000.10	鼎1 *Ding* cauldron 1		春秋 SA	水库工地农民 Farmers constructing the water-reservoir	龙口市博物馆 Longkou Museum	
20	南埠村 Nanbu Village	1920	壶1 *Hu* bottle 1				散失 Lost	郭兴礼 Guo Xingli
21	南埠村 Nanbu Village	1951.4	盨4、盘1、匜1、鼎1、甗（鬲部）1、甑1、壶1，共10件 *Xu* square tureen 4, *pan* basin 1, *yi* vessel 1, *ding* cauldron 1, *yan* steamer (lower) 1, *zeng* steamer 1, *hu* bottle 1, totaling 10	盨4、盘1 *Xu* square tureen 4, *pan* basin 1	春秋 SA	姜德科、李显安 Jiang Deke, Li Xian'an	山东省博物馆 8 青岛市博物馆2 Shandong Museum 8, Qingdao Museum 2	《黄县㠱器》3页；《考古烟台》129页 *HuangxianJi qi*, p. 3; *Yantai kaogu*, p. 129
22	南埠村 Nanbu Village	1960	贯耳壶1 *Hu*-bottle with tubular ears1			郭兴礼 Guo Xingli	砸碎扔掉 Broken and trashed	
23	董家村 Dongjia Village	1969	甗2、盘1、鼎1、戈1、卮1、镞3 *Yan* steamer 2, *pan* basin 1, *ding* cauldron 1, *ge* dagger 1, *zhi* goblet 1, and arrows 3		西周晚 LWZ		烟台市博物馆 Yantai Museum	
24	小刘家村 Xiaoliujia Village	1969	启尊1、启卣1、觯1、车軎2 *Zun* pitcher 1, *you* jar 1, *zhi* goblet 1 chariot-axle-cap 2	尊、卣铭作器者为“启” *Zun* and *you* inscribed by Qi	西周晚 LWZ		启尊藏国家博物馆，卣藏山东省博物馆 *Zun* in National Museum of China *you* in Shandong Museum	
25	大于家村 Dayujia Village	1882	鉨1 Seal 1	铭陈去疾作 Inscribed: “Cast” by Chen Quji	战国 WS			《黄县志稿》14卷807页；《龙口市志》9页 *Huangxian zhi gao*, 14, p. 807; *Longkou shi zhi*, p. 9
26	大于家村 Dayujia Village	1986.4	鼎、盘、匜、铜泡，共6件 *Ding* cauldron, *pan* basin, *yi*, button, totaling 6			郭兴礼 Guo Xingli	龙口市博物馆 Longkou Museum	
27	归城 Guicheng	Before 1911	钟11 Bell 11				山东省博物馆2 余散失 Shandong Museum 2; others lost	丁树桢旧藏 Previously owned by Ding Shuzhen

续表

	出土地点 Provenance	出土时间 Time of Disc.	铜器 Bronzes	铭文 Inscription	年代 Date	发现者 Finder	现藏 Current Location	发表或信息来源 Publication or Source Infor.
28	归城 Guicheng	1958	甗1 *Yan* steamer 1		西周早 EWZ		现藏蓬莱市文物保护管理委员会	《考古》1989年第3期 *Kaogu*, 1989. 3
29	归城 Guicheng		壶1 *Hu* bottle 1		商 Shang			《考古》1991年10期916页图8.2 *Kaogu* 1991.10, p. 916, fig. 8.2
30	归城 Guicheng		甗（鬲部）1 *Yan* steamer (the lower *li* part) 1		春秋 SA			《考古》1991年10期916页图8.5 *Kaogu* 1991.10, p. 916, fig. 8.5
31	韩栾村 Hanluan Village	1964	鼎1 *Ding* cauldron 1	铭“句監” Inscribed “Gou jian”	西周早 EWZ		烟台市博物馆 Yantai Museum	
32	东梧桐村 Dongwutong Village	1995.4	鼎4、壶2、豆4、盘5、方盘1、盆2、釜1、敦2、舟1、戈1、镞、玉器等共27件 *Ding* cauldron 4, *hu* bottle 2, *dou* pedestal dish 4, *pan* dish 5, square *pan* dish 1, *pen* basin 2, *fu* cooker 1, *dui* container 2, *zhou* cup 1, *ge* dagger 1, arrow, jades etc. totaling 27		战国 WS		龙口市博物馆 Longkou Museum	
33	东梧桐村 Dongwutong Village	2007	鎏金铜带钩1、玉佩1 Gilded belt-hook 1, jade ornament 1		战国 WS		龙口市博物馆 Longkou Museum	
34	海徐村 Haixu Village	1983	簋1鬲1 *Gui* tureen 1, *li* tripod 1	簋 *Gui*	西周中 MWZ	仲跻会等 Zhong Jihui et al	龙口市博物馆 Longkou Museum	
35	东营周家 Dongying Zhoujia	1986.6	簋2 *Gui* ureen 1	簋 *Gui*	西周晚 LWZ		龙口市博物馆 Longkou Museum	
36	集前赵家 Jiqian Zhaojia	2004.4	鼎3、簋2、甗1、壶1、尊1、盘1、钟1、卣1、爵1、觯1、泡1 *Ding* cauldron 3, *gui* tureen 2, *yan* steamer 1 *Hu* bottle 1, *zun* pitcher 1, *pan* basin1, bell 1, *you* jar 1, *jue* cup 1, *zhi* cup 1, button 1	鼎、簋、壶 *Ding, gui, hu*	西周中 MWZ		龙口市博物馆 Longkou Museum	
37	石良村 Shiliang Village	1890	匜1 *Yi* 1	匜1 *Yi* 1			丁彝斋家藏 *Ding* Yizhai’s home	《黄县志稿》14卷807页 *Huangxian zhi gao*, 14, p. 807

续表

	出土地点 Provenance	出土时间 Time of Disc.	铜器 Bronzes	铭文 Inscription	年代 Date	发现者 Finder	现藏 Current Location	发表或信息来源 Publication or Source Infor.
38	鲁家沟村 Lujiagou Village	1896	鼎2（铭文）、钟3、壶1、盘1、甗1（铭文）、盉1（铭文）、觯1（铭文），共10件 *Ding* cauldron 2, bell 3, *hu* bottle 1, *pan* basin 1, *yan* steamer 1, *he* vessel 1, *zhi* cup 1, totaling 10	鼎2、甗1、盉1、觯1 *Ding* 2, *yan* 1, *he* 1, *zhi* 1	西周早 EWZ	刘国亨 Liu Guoheng	日本京都泉屋博古馆 Senoku hakkokan Osaka, Japan	《黄县志稿》14卷806页 *Huangxian zhi gao*, 14, p. 806
39	庄头村 Zhuangtou Village	1980	鼎3、簋2、壶1、甗1、爵2、盘1、觚1、觯1、卣1、盂1、勺1、戈1 *Ding* cauldron 3, *gui* tureen 2, *hu* bottle 1, *yan* steamer 1, *jue* cup 2, *pan* basin 1, *gu* goblet 1 *zhi* goblet 1, *you* jar 1, *yu* basin 1, spoon 1, *ge* dagger 1	簋、壶、卣 *Gui*, *hu*, *you*	西周晚 LWZ	刘永新等 Liu Yongxin et al	龙口市博物馆 Longkou Museum	

Historical periods: EWZ=Early Western Zhou; MWZ=Mid Western Zhou; LWZ=Late Western Zhou; SA=Spring and Autumn; WS=Warring States.

Chapter 4: A Report on the Background Survey of Past Discoveries of Bronzes in the Guicheng City Site

Jiang Huimin　Tang Jinqiong

An abundance of ancient artifacts has been discovered in Guicheng and its surroundings over the years. Among them, the bronzes are not only a manifestation of high quality craftsmanship, but also display rich regional and temporal characteristics; moreover, there have been several cases in which inscribed bronzes from the Zhou Dynasty were unearthed. For this reason, Guicheng has been accredited the "Cradle of Bronzes in the Jiaodong Region." According to statistics, more than 400 bronze objects of various types have been discovered during the 130 years from 1882 (the eighth year of the Guangxu reign period) to the present. However, the majority of the bronzes were dispersed soon after discovery, without leaving behind any textual record. Some of this happened during the tumultuous years of war, while others took place during the Cultural Revolution, or in the process of "Battling the Mountains and Rivers" during the mass movement of land leveling (1970-1980). Some were regarded as rubbish by their finders, or were even intentionally smashed and sold to recycling stations. For instance, the recycling station of Huangxian located beside the Jiang River that flows through the county town, and the village shops of Guijiang and Damai, etc., have all purchased bronzes unearthed in Guicheng more or less in the name of waste recycling. Still others were illegally looted. Driven by hunger for profit, looters dug out bronzes and trafficked them into the antique market. There were also individual villagers who hid the bronzes that they had come across incidentally in their living or work without reporting to the authorities, and clandestinely sold them to antique dealers for a profit.

So far, thirty-nine cases of bronze discovery at Guicheng and its surroundings have been identified (Table Ⅱ. 4.1). Among them, inscribed bronzes appear in fourteen cases, totaling forty-one objects. Of special note is the Xin Xiao *gui* from Haixu Village which bears an inscription of fifty-three characters on the bottom, the longest inscription ever found in the Jiaodong region. Although we have presented detailed accounts of all bronzes housed in the Yantai Municipal Museum and the Longkou Municipal Museum in Part Ⅱ, Chapters 2 and 3, the often complicated circumstances surrounding the discoveries have not been systematically discussed, also leaving out some bronzes whose provenance needs to be further verified. Therefore, in July 2009, the Sino-American Guicheng Archaeological Team dispatched Jiang Huimin, Associate Researcher at the Longkou Municipal

Museum, and Tang Jinqiong, Associate Researcher at the Chinese Academy of Social Science and a member of the archaeological team, to conduct careful surveys of the background of the discoveries and the actual process of excavation of some of the bronzes from Guicheng. During the surveys, they interviewed eyewitnesses to the discoveries in Caojia Village, Nanbu Village, Dongchijia Village, and Xiaoyujia Village, respectively, and also reexamined in person the specific sites where the discoveries were made. They obtained crucial background information for the study of the bronzes and ancient cultures in the Guicheng region. We summarize the results of our surveys below.

Section 1: Bronzes from Lujiagou Village

The Lujiagou Village, administered by Shiliang Township, is located 15 km southeast of the Guicheng city site (Figs. Ⅱ.2.1-2). In 1896, the twenty-third year of the Guangxu reign, when Liu Guoheng, a resident of the village, was removing earth from a 100 m high terrace east of the village, he discovered a group of ten bronzes, including 3 *zhong* bells, 2 *ding* cauldrons (two with inscriptions), 1 *hu* bottle, 1 *pan* basin, 1 *yan* steamer (with inscription), 1 *he* vessel (with inscription), and 1 *zhi* goblet; five out of the ten bore inscriptions. This discovery was recorded in the "List of Metal and Stone Objects" section of the *Huangxian zhi gao* (Draft Huangxian Gazetteer), compiled by Wang Daoxin (Wang Daoxin 1934: 806). In his *Huangxian Ji qi* (The Ji vessels from Huangxian), the renowned archaeologist Wang Xiantang also made a special note about the discovery, and considered these bronzes to have been from an early Western Zhou tomb (Wang Xiantang 1960: 144-151). The bronzes are currently housed in the Sen-oku Hakukokan in Kyoto, Japan. We have investigated and analyzed the circumstances surrounding the excavation of these bronzes.

There is a fine tale about the discovery. Lujiaogou Village in Shiliang Township is a hilly area situated southeast of Huangxian. East of the village was a high terrace, which served as a perfect source of earth for constructing house foundations in the village (Fig. Ⅱ.4.1). It was in the spring of 1896 when a farmer, Liu Guoheng, was removing earth from his plot under that high terrace that he dug out ten bronze vessels. The old man knew nothing about archaeology, but he was convinced that these finds could earn him a fortune large enough to support his family. He immediately stopped working and, as he calculated about how to turn them into real profit, asked someone to look for opportunities in the county seat of Huangxian. News came back that Ding Shuzhen (whose cognomen is Ganpu), the owner of the Tailai Store of the famous Ding family in Huangxian, was passionate about acquiring antiques. So, he picked an auspicious day and rushed into the town with these treasures on the back of a donkey that he borrowed from a neighbor. The 50 *li* (25 km) journey on old rugged mountain road between Lujiago and Huangxian took him until noon to reach the Tailai Store. Ding

Shuzhen immediately fell in love with these bronzes; he well understood their high value. But seeing Liu's rustic dress – a pair of slippers on his feet and a scarf around his waist – he pretended to be indifferent and asserted that they were of little worth. He would only be willing to offer 300 strings of coins for the bronzes. On the other hand, Liu Guoheng had no idea about antiques, so he was himself unable to demand a high price. All he wanted was to ask just a little more and he would strike a deal. So he asked Ding if he would be able to pay more. When Ding refused, Liu complained about the price and said that he would rather take them to the Dengzhong Superior Prefecture for a better price.

Ding would never let the treasures escape his grasp. He would try every means to keep Liu from leaving, so he said: "Hey Liu, No hurry! You have come such a long way here. Although we failed to reach a deal, our friendship still counts! It's already late now. 'Housekeepers, ask the cooks to bring in some dishes.' I will have a couple of drinks with my old pal Liu. It's my treat, and no talk about business anymore!" Liu reluctantly agreed to come to the table. During the banquet, Ding secretly instructed his housekeepers to scatter coins on the floor of the wings of his mansion. Having emptied his glass thrice, Liu turned red. He started to reel off how he dug out those bronzes. After another round of toasting, Liu started to feel dizzy and boasted that he himself was a man who cherished friendship the most. Ding knew that the moment had come and said: "Yes, in front you is exactly the right man. I, Ding a millionaire, am not only wealthy but one who also cherishes friendship!"

As the story goes, Ding offered Liu a tour of the Tailai Store, which he thought would definitely open his eyes. Out of curiosity, Liu followed Ding to the wings of the house, where he was stunned by the sight of coins spread all over the floor. Ding took the opportunity to make a generous offer: "If you leave the bronzes here, you can take all this money! See, am I not, Old Ding, your generous friend?" Liu Guoheng, a farmer from the hills, had never in his life seen so much money. He was overwhelmed and immediately emptied the bronzes from his huge bag, which he then used to collect the money. The parties signed a contract and Liu left for his home in Lujiagou, joyfully humming songs while he rode his donkey back. As soon as he reached home, he strung all the coins that he brought back in his bag and counted them. To his surprise, they totaled exactly 300! He thought to himself, "we country folks can never be a match for townspeople." But since he had signed the contract, all he could do was resign himself.

Reportedly, years later Ding Shuzhen sold these bronzes to the Dengzhou Superior Prefecture for 3,000 strings of coins. Dengzhou Superior Prefecture then sold them to the Ji'nan Superior Prefecture for 6,000 strings. From Ji'nan, they were then sold to the capital for 8,000 strings. During the early Republican era, the bronzes were dispersed and transported to Japan. Five of the ten bronzes carry inscriptions. For example, the inscription of the *ding* cauldron reads: "Lai Bo makes this traveling *ding* cauldron." The one on the *he* vessel reads: "X makes this sacrificial [vessel] for the temple. May my grandsons and sons eternally treasure and use it." The one on the *zhi* goblet reads: "The Lord awarded [me] cowries. Shu used them to make for Father Xin this sacrificial vessel." The Yu *yan* steamer is

40.6 cm high, and weighs 5.2 kg (Fig. Ⅱ.2.10), and the inscription on the inside of its body wall has thirty-seven characters, the longest in the group. It reads:

> It was in the sixth month, after the dying brightness, on *bingyin* day, Shi Yongfu encamped at the Gu Garrison. Yu followed [him]. Shi Yongfu sent Yu as an envoy to the Ruler of Hu, and the ruler ceremonially recorded Yu's merits, and awarded Yu metal. Yu thereupon makes this traveling *yan* steamer.

The inscription records that on the *bingyin* day in the sixth month of an unknown year, Shi Yongfu led his troops to encamp at Gu. Yu attended the commander. Then Marshal Yongfu dispatched Yu to the state of the Ruler of Hu, where the state ruler performed the *mieli* ritual for Yu and awarded him metal. Yu then cast the *yan* steamer to commemorate the event.

Section 2: The Ji Vessels from Nanbu Village

Nanbu Village, currently administered by Lan'gao Township, is located 2 km southeast of the inner city of Guicheng. On a number of occasions bronzes were discovered in Nanbu Village, which we will discuss below.

1. The Famous Ji Vessels from Huangxian

Jiang Deke and Li Xian'an, the two people who discovered the eight Ji vessels, had long passed away when we visited Nanbu Village. So we interviewed the 75 year-old Jiang Peilong, a surviving witness to the discovery (Fig. Ⅱ. 4.3). Mr. Jiang related that it was in 1951, right after Liberation, when China's vast rural areas were still worked by individual households. He had just turned 17 years old at the time. One day, news reached him that bronzes had been dug up on the riverbank northeast of the village, so he at once rushed to the site. It turned out that Jiang Deke, a farmer of the village, and Li Xian'an, a porter working in the village, accidentally dug out ten bronzes and a group of ceramic wares when they were picking up soil which they would use to spread to dry an animal pen. They smashed the pottery wares and dumped them, but suspected that the bronzes might contain gold in them. They examined the bronzes by knocking on them, in the process damaging the vessel bodies. In the end, both Nanbu Village and Li Xian'an shared a portion of the discovery. The government of the Fourth District of Huangxian, to which the village belonged, also kept one *yi* vessel from the assemblage. After the news spread, the Huangxian branch of the Cultural Relics Management Commission of the Special

Administrative Office of Laiyang Region dispatched Jin Jingyi and Zhang Minsheng to investigate this incident at Nanbu Village, where they confiscated eight bronzes on behalf of the state. These bronzes were handed over to the Cultural Relics Management Commission of Shandong Province in 1952, which then assigned them to the Shandong Museum in 1954, where they are currently housed. Two other vessels (a *zeng* steamer and a *hu* bottle with tubular ears) were acquired by the Qingdao Municipal Museum.

Guided by Mr. Jiang Peilong, we surveyed the site where these bronzes were discovered. It is located south of Dongchijia Village, close to the west bank of a stream the flows from south to north. The geographic coordinates are N 37°35′089″, E120°34′455″, and 112 m above sea level.

The ten bronzes included 4 *xu* square tureens and 1 *ding* cauldron, 1 *pan* basin, 1 *yi* vessel, 1 *li* tripod, 1 *zeng* steamer, and 1 *hu* bottle with tubular ears. Among them, the *xu*, *pan* and *yi* carried inscriptions. Unearthed together with them were jade ornaments and ceramics, so that they were presumably funerary objects placed in a tomb dating to the Spring and Autumn period.

The commissioner of the *xu* is named "Renfu, a Son of Jibo." This vessel is rated as a first-class national cultural relic. It is 17.8 cm in height, and the mouth, a rounded rectangle in shape, is 21 cm long and 14.5 cm wide, capped by a lid. Two rectangular ears bending upright are attached under the rim in the shorter sides of the vessel. They are strengthened by two bridges connecting them to the vessel's body. Atop the lid are four square handles, and the vessel sits on a square ring foot. Wide horizontal grooves are applied to both the lid and the vessel body. Five columns of intaglio inscriptions, totaling twenty-six characters, are cast into the inside bottom of the vessel and the inner side of the lid, respectively (see Part Ⅱ, Chapter 2 for transcriptions).

Ji was the name of an ancient state, the surname of whose rulers was Jiang, as indicated by the inscription on a *pan* basin from the same group of bronzes. The inscription reads: "Jibo Renfu [makes this] dowry X *pan* basin for Jiang Wu" (JC: 10081). The history of the Ji State can be traced back to the Shang Dynasty since it appears on Shang oracle-bones. The Ji lineage had served the Shang court since the reign of King Wu Ding. Some studies indicate that the celebrated Shang statesman Ji Zi was a member of the Ji lineage. In early Western Zhou, the Ji lineage migrated both northward and eastward. One branch of the Ji came into Shandong. The name "Renfu" on the *pan* basin is the courtesy name of Jibo (the first-born son of the Ji lineage), but the Jibo on the *xu* is Renfu's father, the Jibo of the previous generation. This *xu* was cast when Renfu was still his heir. The group of Ji vessels discovered at Guicheng was what remained of the Ji lineage in the early Spring and Autumn period. They were the set of bronzes brought by Lady Jiang when her father, Jibo Renfu, married her into the state of Lai at Guicheng. In 1963, Wang Xiantang, the renowned archaeologist and then the Director of the Shandong Provincial Library, published his book, *Huangxian Ji qi* (Ji vessels from Huangxian), in which he focused his discussion on the eight Ji vessels housed in the Shandong Provincial Museum

(Wang Xiantang 1960: 3-62).

With regard to dowry vessels, it is relevant to mention another case in which the state of Lai married a daughter into another state. In 1976, two tombs dated to the early Spring and Autumn period were excavated at Rizhao Guheya, the capital of the ancient state of Ju. Bronzes from tomb M1 consisted of fourteen objects, including *ding* cauldron, *li* tripod, *hu* bottle, *pan* basin, and *yi* steamer, etc. Among them, the four *li* tripods of identical style each bears an inscription of fifteen characters on its circular rim, which reads: "Laibo makes this treasured *li* as a dowry for his daughter. [May her] sons' sons and grandsons' grandsons eternally treasure and use it." An analysis of these tripods revealed that they were probably made by the ruler of the state of Lai, who gave them as a dowry for his daughter who married into the state of Ju. These vessels are now in the Rizhao Municipal Museum. The two groups of bronzes attest to the marital connections between the state of Lai and the state of Ju as well as the state of Ji. The relationship could perhaps be interpreted as alliances.

2. Sporadic Discoveries of Bronzes from Nanbu Village

During our survey at Nanbu Village, we met Mr. Guo Xingli, a veteran of the army who has served as a member of the village committee of Nanbu. Guo was born in 1952 and is now fifty-eight years old (Fig. Ⅱ.4.3). He related a tradition that he had heard from the elders of the village about a bronze *hu* bottle uncovered from the eastern part of the village in 1920. The bottle ended up being sold in the market by the villagers. In 1960, Guo himself unearthed a bronze *hu* bottle in the eastern part of the village. The *hu* had tubular ears and was about 40 cm high. Since the bottle was already broken, he simply left it in his backyard. In a summer when it rained heavily, the sewage channel in his backyard got blocked by the broken bottle, prompting him to smash it and throw it away. In 1968, he dug out jades at the same spot. This time he reported the discovery to the authorities. That year, Mr. Li Buqing of the Yantai Municipal Museum led a team to survey this region archaeologically. Our survey revealed that there should be a tomb located in the field along the river east of the village. The geographic coordinates are N 37°35′051″, E120°34′487″, and the elevation is 110 m above sea level.

Section 3: A Full Account of the Discovery of Bronzes at Xiaoliuzhuang in Wenji Township

Xiaoliuzhuang, located due south to the Guicheng city site, is about 1 km from the inner city wall of Guicheng. It has now merged into Caojia Village of Guicheng and is under the jurisdiction of Lan'gao Township.

In August 1969, in the last phase of the Dog Days of that year during the Cultural Revolution, about thirty villagers from Xiaoliuzhuang were led by the twenty-six year-old Liu Deqing (Fig. Ⅱ.4.4), head of the Fourth Production Team, in an effort to level the rugged plots into a larger field south of the village. Following a local proverb, "Radish in the middle and vegetables in the last phase of the Dog Days," they were preparing the land for planting Chinese cabbages. It was almost noon and they were about to call it a day a little earlier due to the heat, when one Liu Zhihui suddenly dug out a pottery bowl with his pickaxe. Everyone gathered around the spot in surprise. In view of this, the head of the team ordered all the female villagers to go home and prepare lunch, leaving only male villagers to continue the digging. In the end, they unearthed more than twenty bronze vessels, filling up a large bamboo basket. What they found included 1 *ding* cauldron, weighing about 30 kg, 1 helmet, 1 *you* jar, 1 *zun* pitcher, 1 *he* vessel, 1 *zhi* goblet, bells, and 1 spearhead, etc. Hair and fragments of a skull were also found at the site, which may have been the tomb of a man whose name was later identified as Qi.

As he surveyed these bronzes, the head of the team picked up four smaller intact vessels for himself, including 1 *you* jar, 1 *zun* pitcher, 1 *zhi* goblet, and the lid of a jar, and took them to his house, planning to sell them later for money to buy work memo books. As for the rest of them, he asked Cao Jinrui to take them on a bicycle to the Recycling Station on the east side of the Jiang River in the county town that afternoon. When Cao reached the Recycling Station, workers there insisted that their policy was to recycle waste metals. To accept them, the bronzes must not be complete. So Cao Jinrui and others smashed those bronzes with a hammer; finally, the workers at the recycling station were willing to weigh and accept them. At the time, the price for copper was RMB 1.97 per 500 g. The bronzes totaled about 50 kg and worth more than RMB 100. As a result, each member of the Production Team who was present at the site received RMB 2, and the rest of the money was spent on cigarettes, candies and a small alarm clock.

The following spring, three people from the Shandong Provincial Museum came to the village. One of them, a tall fellow surnamed Zhang, found Liu Deqing while he was working in the field. Zhang investigated how the bronzes and other artifacts were discovered and confiscated the four bronzes in Liu's house, leaving him a receipt. It turned out that fragments of the smashed bronzes were sent by the Huangxian's (currently Longkou City) Recycling Station to Yantai City, where they were detected and reported to the Provincial government. The provincial government then ordered the Shandong Provincial Museum to investigate this incident.

Our survey revealed that the tomb was adjacent to a water reservoir located south of Xiaoliujia Village (Fig. Ⅱ. 4.5). The geographic coordinates are N 37°34′916″, E120°33′392″, and the elevation is 135 m above sea level. The geological makeup of the area consists mainly of sandstone. The orientation of the tomb was northeast to southwest, and it was 2 m long, about 1 m wide, and 2 m deep.

There is no doubt that the most important pieces of the assemblage are Qi *you* and the Qi *zun*.

Stylistically, they belonged to the early phase of the mid-Western Zhou. The Qi *you* is currently housed in the Shandong Provincial Museum, while the Qi *zun* was transferred to the Museum of Chinese History in 1989, and is now housed in the National Museum of China. Bronze *you* were one of the most commonly used wine vessels in the Shang and the Western Zhou period. The vessel was mainly used to hold a kind of black wine, brewed with millet and a particular grass root. The liquor was usually offered to the deities and ancestors before it was distributed to participants. The Qi *you* is 22.7 cm high, with an oblong body and a ring foot. The lid, topped by a knob, interlocked with the rim of the vessel. The handle is decorated with animal heads on both ends, which were locked into two loops on the vessel body. An animal band is placed at the center on each side of the vessel. The upper portion of the vessel and the lid are each decorated with a band of wave patterns meandering through a spiral background. The identical inscriptions cast on the vessel and lid each consisted of thirty-nine characters. The Qi *zun* is 19 cm high. It has a large flaring mouth, a wide neck, a bulging lower portion of the body, and a low ring foot. A band of wave patterns circles the neck, and an animal head is placed at its center (Fig. Ⅱ.2.6). The inscription of nineteen characters in three columns was cast into the inside bottom of the vessel in addition to which there are signs (family emblem), totaling 21 characters (translated in Part Ⅱ, Chapter 2). The inscription records a campaign that the Zhou court waged against an outlaw in the southern mountains, one Ce Shangu. Qi, the caster of these vessels, took part in this expedition.

The discovery of the Qi *you* and Qi *zun* in the Guicheng region testifies to the close political connections between Guicheng city and the Zhou central court. On May 12, 2013, CCTV's National Treasures Files released a special documentary about the discovery of the Qi *you* and Qi *zun*.

Section 4: The Jihou *Li* and Other Bronzes from Heping Village

Heping Village (a.k.a. "Dongheping Village") is located in the northeastern part of the inner city of Guicheng. It is under the administrative jurisdiction of Lan'gao Township. In the 1950s, more than thirty bronzes dated to the early Spring and Autumn period were excavated by the villagers while removing earth south of the village. Most of them were destroyed or sold off. Only one *li* tripod, the Jihou *li*, named after its caster Jihou, is extant. This vessel is 10.5 cm high, and 14.1 cm in diameter at mouth. It has a wide angled rim, an arching and nearly flat crotch, and three short, solid feet. The plain surface is without ornament except for three flanges. One circular inscription of fourteen characters was cast into the rim, but was partly damaged: "Jihou XX Jiang XX. (May his/her) sons' sons and grandsons' grandsons eternally preserve and use it." In 1962, this *li* tripod was acquired in Huangxian by the cultural relics store of Yantai City, and was later transferred to the Yantai Municipal Museum that same year.

In 1946, a villager, Wang Jingxuan, was digging a well in his yard. At a depth of 4 m he discovered four bronze bells. But in September 1947, the Kuomintang troops occupied Huangxian and raided the countryside. When they heard of the treasures in Wang Jingxuan's house, they broke into his home and took two of the bells by force. In the early years of the People's Republic of China, faced with a difficult living situation, Wang Jingxuan sent his son to take one of the surviving two bells to Beijing for sale in order to support his family. However, the bell was confiscated by officials and Wang's son was sent home with a RMB 15 train ticket. Afterwards the bell was transferred to the Yantai Municipal Museum. There is still one bell left in the Wang family, which was inherited by his son, Wang Huichang, after Wang Jingxuan's death. This bell is 39.5 cm high, with cylindrical bosses, and the body is decorated with geometric patterns. A family emblem was inscribed on the central panel of the bell. It is a Western Zhou object.

In 1964, the village yielded another group of bronzes including 1 *he* box, 1 *hu* bottle, 1 *ge* dagger, and 1 sword, in all four objects dated to the Spring and Autumn period. They are now housed in the Yantai Municipal Museum.

In May 1965, a *ding* and a spearhead were discovered in the eastern village by villagers building a house. These bronzes can be dated to the late Western Zhou period and are currently in the Yantai Municipal Museum.

In 1969, Wang Jingqiang, the former party secretary of the village branch of the CCP, uncovered a bronze sword when he was preparing a field for cultivation. When he took it to the Recycling Station, he was also asked to smash it in order to have it accepted as waste.

In March, 1973, when the Cultural Relics General Survey Team of the Yantai District was resurveying the Guicheng city site, the team discovered four skeletons exposed on a cliff in the orchard to the west of Heping Village. In addition, local people reported that they observed pottery and a bronze sword when taking soil from there a few years before. On March 9, to avoid disrupting the growth of trees in the orchard, the Yantai Municipal Museum decided to dig a test trench near the cliff. The test trench was 2.6 m north to south, 2.05 m east to west on the southern side, 1.61 m east to west on the northern side, and 1.07 m deep. What they found in the eastern portion of the trench was a layer of vermilion applied to the bottom surface, on which lay the relatively complete skeleton of a horse. The horse was buried in a lying posture, with its head facing west and tail pointing east, which should be the original burial position. A bronze ring was placed on the ribs. At the bottom of the southwest portion of the trench were some horse's teeth mixed with three bronze chariot fittings and a semi-circular bronze ring. In the middle of the western section of the trench were found one canopy controller for chariots, two bronze rings and four chariot fittings in the shape of frogs. Analysis of the stratigraphy of the test trench revealed that the chariot pit had already been disturbed, leaving the horse skeletons and teeth scattered. What could be identified were two horse skulls, one of which held half of a horse bit. The rest of the bronze horse and chariot fittings were scattered in the pit. It was concluded that this was a horse sacrificial pit for a large tomb from the Spring and Autumn period. The bronzes recovered from this pit included 1 half horse bit, 1 horse cheek-piece, 1 chariot axle-cap, 4 frog-shaped square rings, 1 round ring, 1 semi-circular ring, 2 chariot fittings, and 1 bronze tube, in all twelve objects. They are now in the Yantai Municipal Museum (Li Buqing and Lin Xianting 1991: 914-915).

In 1989, a villager, Wang Huizhong, found a horse and chariot pit when he was digging a pigpen in his backyard. The pit yielded horse skeletons, bronze chariot axle-caps, and bronze arrows, etc. They have been handed over to the Longkou Municipal Museum.

In November 2002, a salvage excavation was conducted in Heping Village by a team of ten people from both the Archaeological and Cultural Relics Team of Yantai and the Longkou Municipal Museum. The area excavated measured 1,500 m^2, and yielded more than ten house remains. The discovery filled a gap in Guicheng archaeology that had lacked residential sites ever since the 1950s (see Part Ⅱ, Chapter 1). At the same time, the team collected a bronze chariot axle-cap that had been unearthed in previous years and preserved it in the Yantai Municipal Museum.

Section 5: The Xin Xiao *Gui*: A National Treasure from Haixu Village

Haixu Village, administered by Zhongcun Township, is 17.5 km northwest of the inner city of Guicheng. In April 1983, two bronze vessels were discovered when Mr. Zhong Jihui, the orchard foreman of Haixu Village, led Xu Shikao, Zhao Junqiang, and other villagers dug vineyard furrows about 300 meters east of the village. One of the bronzes was a tripod, the other the Xin Xiao *gui*.

Zhong Jihui took the bronze *li* tripod to the cultural relics shop of Longkou Municipal Museum for sale. The staff there accepted the bronze *li* tripod and paid out a reward in accordance with regulations. Before going far, Zhong returned to the shop and explained that he had another large bronze vessel at home, currently in use as a trough for chicken feed. Zhong asked if the shop would be interested, to which the staff replied in the affirmative. The next day, Zhong brought the Xin Xiao *gui* over as well, and was awarded RMB 20. It was appraised by a group of experts of cultural relics from the Shandong Provincial authority including Tai Liye, Guan Tianxiang, and others, and was designated as a first-class national relic. This discovery attracted a great deal of attention among those concerned with cultural relics. In November 1986, a surface survey and trial excavation was conducted at the location where the Xin Xiao *gui* was found by a group of specialists from the Cultural Relics Management Commission of Yantai, but it failed to yield any new discoveries. As for Zhong Jihui, he was publicly recognized in a village meeting and awarded an additional RMB 60 for his contributions to protecting cultural relics and handing them over to the authorities. The two bronzes are currently housed in the Longkou Municipal Museum.

The Xin Xiao *gui* is 12.8 cm high, and weighs 2,750 g. It has a constricted neck, a flaring mouth 20 cm in diameter, and its bulging body sits atop a trumpet-shaped ring foot. A pair of ears with pendants are decorated with animal motifs. The upper body is decorated with animal masks, and five columns of inscriptions, totaling fifty-three characters, were cast into the bottom of the vessel. This is the vessel with the longest inscription ever discovered in the Jiaodong region. But some of the characters have not been seen before in the inventory of bronze inscriptions. Because the name "Xin Xiao" appears twice in the inscription and should be the name of its principal caster, it was called the "Xin Xiao *gui*" (see Part Ⅱ, Chapter 3 for translation). The inscription narrates the following event: In the eleventh month of an unknown year of a king's reign, the king and the prince visited the ancient Xi'an. Xin Xiao, presumably accompanied by an official, was given an audience with the king. He received a courteous reception and was awarded metal and cowries. Xin Xiao used the metal to make this *gui* vessel. He hoped that his descendants would commemorate this honor forever.

The Xin Xiao *gui* is not only exquisitely made, it is also characteristic in shape and ornament; it can be dated to the reign of King Mu of the Western Zhou. However, the fact that the inscription of the Xin Xiao *gui* included many irregular forms and some of its characters have never been seen in other inscriptions makes it difficult to fully transcribe. But, for the same reason it is clear that this inscribed bronze was produced in a local workshop. In this sense, its discovery testifies to the long history of Guicheng and that casting technique had already been highly advanced in this area during the Western Zhou period.

Section 6: Bronzes from Jiqian Zhaojia Village

Jiqian Zhaojia Village, under the jurisdiction of Shiliang Township, is 10 km southeast of the inner city of the Guicheng city site. On April 10, 2004, in the brickyard west of the village, a migrant worker from Chongqing who was operating a backhoe suddenly scooped out a batch of bronzes. The other migrant workers soon gathered around the site to divide up and subsequently hide the bronzes. It was not until the afternoon of the next day that a report reached the authorities. We rushed to the site together with officials from Public Security Bureau and, having examined the site, took back the damaged bronzes. Since most of them were seriously crushed, sorting through the fragments, we isolated fourteen vessels whose shapes could still be identified. There was still a pile of unrecognizable bronze pieces. Among the fourteen vessels, there were 3 *ding* cauldrons, 2 square-based *gui* tureens decorated with string lines, 1 *you* jar with a handle, 1 bell, 1 *hu* bottle with tubular ears, 1 *yan* steamer, 1 *zun* pitcher, 1 *pan* basin, 1 *jue* cup, 1 *zhi* goblet, and 1 bronze button (see Part Ⅱ, Chapter 3, Figs. Ⅱ.3.16-20 for detailed description of the vessels). Only one *ding* cauldron and a bell were intact. The rest all suffered damage. In addition, there was a pile of ceramic sherds. The possibility that some artifacts from the original group had been lost could not be ruled out.

Since the excavator had already reached the bottom, we carried out a clearing process based on traces that remained on the site to measure the full extent of the tomb. The tomb was oriented east-west, and was 4.75 m long, 3 m wide north to south, and 6.55 m deep. There was nothing left in the tomb except for some ashes mixed with red pigment. Having cleaned off the objects we brought back, we found that six bronzes were inscribed.

The inscriptions on the three cauldrons were as follows: one *ding* is represented by only a few remaining fragments, on the smaller of which are inscribed two characters: "Jihou," under the character *hou,* "Ruler," there may be the character *shi* (scribe), and to the left of *ji* there may be a *xi* (award). The second *ding* cauldron, decorated with a phoenix motif, was damaged in the area of its inscription on the belly wall, which is laid out in three columns and reads: "Lifu makes this sacrificial vessel (for) XX eternally X"; there should have been ten characters at least, four of which were damaged by serious corrosion. Whether below the ones seen there were additional characters is unclear due to damage. The third *ding* cauldron remained intact, and was decorated with string lines. Two characters were cast intaglio and in vertical alignment on the inner surface of the vessel body: "Made (this) *ding* cauldron".

The two *gui* tureens with square bases were decorated with raised string patterns. Their loop handles were rendered in animal shape, each having a pendent at the bottom. Both of them were inscribed with two columns of intaglio inscription in eleven characters: "Bo Yingfu awarded Shu Suo metal, with which (he) makes this treasured *gui* tureen." The arrangement of the inscription varied slightly between the two vessels. As for the *hu* bottle with tubular ears, there were two lines of inscription, eight characters in all, inscribed on the inner wall of the vessel just beneath the rim: "Yibo awarded Ying metal; (he) makes (this) traveling *hu* bottle." Based on the inscriptions, the bronzes are called, Jihou *ding*, Lifu *ding*, Zuo *ding*, Shu Suo *gui*, and Ying *hu,* respectively. Judging from the form and décor of the vessels in the tomb, this tomb can be dated to the early phase of the mid-Western Zhou period, roughly in the early years of King Mu. The relationship between those whose names appear in the inscriptions — "Jihou," "Lifu," "Yibo," "Bo Yingfu," and "Shu Suo"— is still an open question, but it may involve that of superior to subordinates.

As to who the person buried in the tomb was, I have done some preliminary analysis. In terms of the body design, ornament, and casting techniques, the Zuo *ding*, Shu Suo *gui*, and the *pan* basin, the *zun* pitcher, the *you* jar, the *zhi* goblet, and the *yan* steamer, are very similar to each other and are all decorated with two raised string patterns on their necks. They form a set of 1 cauldron, 2 tureens, 1 basin, 1 pitcher, 1 jar, 1 steamer, 1 goblet, and 1 cup; the other vessels are stylistically slightly different from these. In this regard, only the inscription on the tureens can be considered as having belonged to the occupant of the tomb. Therefore, the tomb should be the "tomb of Shu Suo." When Shu Suo was buried, the stylistically somewhat different Jihou *ding*, the Lifu *ding*, the bell, and the *hu* bottle given to him by Ying were added to his funerary set, thus forming the new bronze assemblage: 3 *ding*, 2 *gui*, 1 *hu*, 1 *pan*, 1 *zun*, 1 *you*, 1 *zhi*, 1 *jue*, 1 *yan*, and 1 *zhong*.

In 2008, twelve of these objects were restored by a conservation team led by Sun Zhengxiang at the National Museum of China. They are now included in the exhibition titled the "The History of the State of Lai" in the Longkou Municipal Museum.

Section 7: Bronzes from Other Villages

1. Bronzes from Shiliang Village

Shiliang Village, located 10 km southeast of the inner city of Guicheng, is where the government of Shiliang Township is located. According to the "List of Metal and Stone Objects" of the *Huangxian zhi gao* (Draft Gazetteer of Huangxian), edited by Wang Daoxin, in 1890 (the sixteenth year of the Guangxu Era), a bronze *yi* vessel was discovered in a field in Shiliang Village southeast of the county seat of Huangxian. On the bronze a six character inscription was inscribed: "Lu Shi Shang X (took?) makes this *yi* vessel." This bronze was collected by the Ding Yizhai (Wang Daoxin 1934: 807).

2. Bronzes from Guijiang Village

Guijiang Village is governed by Lan'gao Township. Before the establishment of New China, a bronze bell dating to the Spring and Autumn period and carrying a five-character inscription: "Jihou makes (this) treasured bell," was discovered in Guicheng. It was owned by Ding Shuzhen, a member of the Ding family in Huangxian, but is currently housed in the Yantai Municipal Museum.

The year 1974 was a special year in the era of "Battling Mountains and Rivers." Mr. Jiang Quankai, commander of the Guijiang Village militia at that time, dug out a batch of about fifty bronze vessels while leading villagers in leveling the field. He hauled those bronzes away to the recycling station on a fully loaded cart, keeping only one bronze ring that he hoped to use as a ring on a doorplate in front his building.

3. Bronzes from Caojia in Guicheng

The Caojia village in Guicheng is 1 km due south of the inner city of the Guicheng city site. In May 1965, a tomb dated to the Western Zhou period was found while people were removing earth from a cliff to construct the dam on the Jiangjia Village Water Reservoir in Guicheng. The tomb lay at the foot of a hill west of the dam, on a loess terrace beside the river. A clearing excavation of this already damaged tomb was immediately conducted by the Cultural Relics Management Commission of Yantai, in collaboration with the cultural relics management personnel of Huanxian. The burial was located 300 m south of the village. It was a rectangular, vertical pit tomb. When they carried out the clearing process, only the eastern part of it remained undamaged. The bottom of the tomb was 5.2 m north to south, 1 m (disturbed) east to west, and 3 m deep. A layer of red pigment was found covering the bottom, which, upon analysis, was found to be the imprint left by the painted coffin. A considerable number of ceramics were found in the western part of the tomb, but except for a jar they were all gone or in pieces. Eleven bronzes were found in the eastern part of the tomb, including 2 *ding* cauldrons, 1 *yan* steamer, 1 *hu* bottle, 1 *zun* pitcher (with inscription), 1 *you* jar (with inscription), 2 *jue* cups, 1 *zhi* goblet, 1 *zao*, and the bottom of a vessel (with inscription). Three of these bronzes carried inscriptions. Judging from traces of wooden boards found beside the bronzes, and the imprints of mats on the surface of the bronzes, it is likely that they were wrapped in a straw mat and originally stored in a wood casket. There was also a jade dagger from this tomb. Objects in this group are now housed in the Yantai Municipal Museum.

4. Bronzes from Dongjia Village in Guicheng

Dongjia Village, currently under the jurisdiction of Lan'gao Township, is located 1.5 km northeast of the inner city of the Guicheng city site. In 1969, four bronzes were unearthed when the kiln workers were removing earth at Dongjia Village in Guicheng. The unearthed bronzes included 1 *yan* steamer, whose surface was plain except for string lines, 1 animal foot *pan* basin, decorated with geometric patterns, 1 hoof-foot *ding* cauldron, decorated with *kui* dragon patterns, and 1 dagger. While all belonged to the Western Zhou period, their provenance was identified with two tombs of different dates. Among them, the steamer and the basin were unearthed together. They are now in the Yantai Municipal Museum.

5. Bronzes from Dongchijia Village

Dongchijia Village, currently under the jurisdiction of Lan'gao Township, is located 0.5

km due east of the inner city of the Guicheng city site. Two groups of bronzes were uncovered here:

(1) The policy of re-allocating lands to individual households was implemented in Huangxian in 1984, when Chi Yuanxue, a resident of Dongchijia Village, then thirty-eight years old, received two rows of apple trees on the east shore of the water reservoir east of Guijiang Village. As the topography there sloped from south to north, Chi Yuanxue and his wife planned to level this plot for better watering. When they were digging soil from the southern part of the plot and transporting it on a cart to the north, they dug up two bronze vessels, 1 *ding* cauldron and 1 *gui* tureen, both of which were sent to the Longkou Municipal Museum. Later examination dated the vessels to the early Western Zhou period. Since Chi Yuanxue died in 1996, we were guided by Chi Yuanqiang, his younger brother, to survey the actual site where the bronzes were unearthed. The site is on the terrace east of the water reservoir (Fig. Ⅱ. 4.6), and the geographic coordinates are N 37°35′305″, E120°34′192″. The elevation is 81 m above sea level.

(2) In October 2000, while constructing a water reservoir east of Dongchijia Village, a backhoe unearthed a bronze *ding* cauldron from a tomb. As soon as the Longkou Municipal Museum received the report from the party secretary of the village, we at once dispatched a team to clear out the damaged tomb. As a result, four ceramic vessels including 2 *dou* pedestal dishes, 1 *yu* basin, 1 *li* tripod, and ceramic sherds were unearthed. Later analysis of the artifacts shows that the tomb can be dated to the Western Zhou period. The artifacts from the tomb are now housed in the Longkou Municipal Museum. The Cultural Relics Management Commission of the Longkou City awarded Dongchijia Village an honor pennant together with a cash award of RMB 800.

6. Bronzes from Dayujia Village

Dayujia Village, currently under the jurisdiction of Lan'gao Township, is located 1.5 km northeast of the inner city of Guicheng. Two groups of bronzes were unearthed there:

(1) The *Longkou shi zhi* (Longkou City Gazetteer) records that in the fall of 1882 an ancient seal was unearthed at Dayujia Village in Guicheng. The inscription on it read “Chen Yuji's personal seal.” The seal was owned by Ding Shuzhen, and an analysis indicates that it was from the Warring States period. “Yuji,” the name on the seal, was interpreted as “Chuji” by Wang Xiantang in his monograph *Huangxian Ji qi* (Li Jitao 1995: 9).

(2) On a beautiful day in April 1986, Guo Xingli and his younger brother Guo Xingzhi, both residents of Nanbu Village, were helping their older sister, Guo Xinglan, build two buildings in Dayujia Village. Due to the scale of the construction, which required a large amount of earth, they chose a mound located southeast of Dayujia Village as the source of fill. Guo Xingzhi, the younger brother, was a tractor driver. He alternated between two tractors, one transporting the earth to the

construction site while the other was left at the earth source for reloading. The earth mound was 4-5 m high. A corner of the mound that protruded to the north contained sand and was harder, so the villagers rarely dug that part. When they did dig at that location, they pulled out a group of six delicately made bronzes including a *ding* cauldron, *pan* basin, *yi* vessel, and a bronze button, etc. Guo Xinglan's husband, who was the party secretary of the village, immediately phoned the secretary of the People's Commune. After the Commune secretary contacted the cultural relics office of Huangxian County, the bronzes were sent to the county cultural relics shop and received by Tang Zhaoluo, Liang Guiying, and Zhang Liguo, who then paid a reward of RMB 80. These six bronzes are now in the Longkou Municipal Museum.

Our onsite survey revealed that the site was situated on the south bank of an east-west flowing brook, southeast of the village (Fig. Ⅱ.4.7). The geographic coordinates are N 37°36′105″, E120°34′484″. The elevation is 39 m above sea level.

7. Bronzes from Dongwutong Village

Dongwutong Village, currently under the jurisdiction of Lutou Township, is located 10 km due west of Guicheng. Two discoveries of bronzes have been reported so far.

(1) On the afternoon of April 4, 1995, a tomb containing a large number of bronzes was discovered by workers in a brickyard north of Dongwutong Village. As soon as the news reached us from the village council, we notified the local police headquarters to protect the scene and dispatched a team from the Longkou Municipal Museum to the village. Once on the scene we were stunned and disappointed to see the bronzes already broken into fragments, leaving only 2 *ding* cauldrons, 3 *dou* pedestal dishes, 5 round *pan* basins, and 1 *fu* cooking wok relatively complete. Subsequently, we cleaned out the remaining tomb, which was 3.8 m long, 2.6 m wide, and 4.7 m deep. The grave mound was 3.5 m high, including in its lower part a 1.2 m layer of pebbles to protect the burial from tomb robbers. This was the first feature of this kind discovered in the Longkou region. A male corpse was buried in the tomb, part of whose skull and teeth were clearly visible. The artifacts we recovered from the pit included 1 square *pan* basin with a chain handle decorated with delicate geometric patterns, 1 *ge* dagger, seriously corroded, 3 pieces of jade near the head of the occupant, probably parts of his jade mask, and 1 sacrificed dog. This tomb belonged to an elite male of the Warring States period. After the three-day excavation was concluded, the village council was awarded an honor pennant and RMB 800.

Since most of the bronzes had been destroyed by the bulldozer, in a final count, the bronzes that could be identified by their shapes included: 4 *ding* cauldrons, 2 *hu* bottles, 4 *dou* pedestal dishes, 5 round *pan* basins, 1 square *pan* basin, 2 gilded *pen* basins, 1 cooking wok, 2 *dui* containers, 1 *zhou* cup, and 1 dagger, twenty-three objects in all. In addition, there were more than 10 bronze and iron arrowheads, 1 pile of bronze sherds, 3 jades, and 4 ceramic pots, etc. All are currently housed in the

Longkou Municipal Museum.

(2) In April 2007, the Longkou Municipal Museum was carrying out a general cultural relics survey in the areas affected by the ongoing "South-to-North Water Transfer Project". On reaching the brick lot north of the village, we discovered a tomb, already exposed and damaged. We immediately set our staff to clearing the site. In the end, six objects were unearthed, including 1 gilded belt-hook, 1 jade ornament, and 4 ceramic bowls, totaling 6 objects in all. Later analysis showed that they were from a Warring States period tomb. The excavated artifacts are now in the Longkou Municipal Museum.

8. Bronzes from Dongzhuangtou Village

Dongzhuangtou Village (or simply Zhuangtou), currently under the jurisdiction of Shiliang Township, is located 10 km east of the inner city of the Guicheng city site.

The Dongzhuangtou cemetery is located on a terrace east of the village and is dated to the Western Zhou period. The cemetery is 150 m from north to south, and 119 m from east to west, occupying an area of 17,850 m^2. In 1987, the Dongzhuangtou cemetery was designated as a cultural relics unit of the Yantai City, and in 1992 it was elevated to the status of provincial cultural relics unit of Shangdong.

In September 1980, a group of bronzes appeared when Liu Yongxin and others were removing earth on a terrace east of the village. The subsequent clearing excavation conducted by the members of the Cultural Relics Management Commission of Yantai together with associates from the Longkou City confirmed that this was a Western Zhou tomb. The bronzes unearthed from the tomb included 3 *ding* cauldrons, 2 *gui* tureens (with inscription), 1 *hu* bottle (with inscription), 1 *you* jar (with inscription), 1 *yan* steamer, 2 *jue* cups, 1 *pan* basin, 1 *gu* goblet, 1 *shao* spoon, 1 *zhi* goblet, 1 *yu* basin, and 1 *ge* dagger, totaling sixteen objects. Four among them were inscribed. All are currently housed in Yantai Municipal Museum.

9. Bronzes from Dongying Zhoujia Village

Dongying Zhoujia Village, currently under the jurisdiction of Shiliang Township, is located 11 km east of the inner city of the Guicheng city site. In June 1986, two tombs dated to the Western Zhou period were destroyed in the orchard located south of Zhoujia Village. As soon as the report reached the Longkou Municipal Museum, we dispatched a team to conduct a salvage excavation of the site. The tombs were vertical pits, both containing inner and outer coffins. After clearing, M1 yielded two inscribed bronze *gui* tureens, while M2 yielded more than two hundred ceramic vessels, including *ding, dou*, *guan*, *hu*, *li*, *jue* etc. Among them, the ceramic *ding* cauldrons exhibit distinctive local features. They are currently in the Longkou Municipal Museum.

10. Bronzes Collected through Purchase

The recycling station of Huangxian, the village shop of Guijiang, and the village shop of Damai have all acquired bronzes that originated in the Guicheng city site in the name of waste recycling. After being sent to the waste recycling base in Yantai, some of them were picked out by the cultural relics units, while many others were sent to a smelter and hence have vanished forever.

References

Li, Buqing 李步青 and Lin Xiantin 林仙庭, 1991. "Shandong Huangxian Guicheng yizhi de diaocha yu fajue" 山东黄县归城遗址的调查与发掘 (Survey and trial excavations of the site at Guicheng, Huangxian County, Shandong). *Kaogu* 考古, 11: 910-918.

Li, Jitao 李继涛, 1995. *Longkou shi zhi* 龙口市志 (Gazetteer of Longkou City). Ji'nan: Qi Lu shushe.

Wang, Daoxin 王道新, 1934. *Huangxian zhi gao* 黄县志稿 (Draft gazetteer of Huangxian). Preserved in Shandong Provincial Museum.

Wang Xiantang 王献唐, 1960. *Huangxian Ji qi* 黄县曩器 (The Ji bronzes from Huangxian). Ji' nan: Qi Lu shushe.

Yantai shi bowuguan 烟台市博物馆 ed., 2006. *Kaogu Yantai* 考古烟台 (Archaeology in Yantai). Ji'nan: Qi Lu shushe.

Yantai shi wenwu guanli weiyuanhui 烟台市文物管理委员会, and Yantai shi bowuguan 烟台市博物馆 ed., 2004. *Jiaodong kaogu yanjiu wenji* 胶东考古研究文集 (Studies in the archaeology of Jiaodong). Ji'nan: Qi Lu shushe.

(Translated by Chin-Hau Lei)

第五章　归城考古的收获和胶东半岛青铜器时代的社会变迁

李　峰

中美联合归城考古调查为期四年（2007～2010年）共五个季度，是归城目前为止规模最大，为期时间最长的一项考古工作。尽管这个考古项目仍处在调查阶段，但通过多方面的工作，我们目前已经掌握了比较丰富的资料。在田野工作的同时，我们也协同烟台市博物馆和龙口市博物馆的学者们对归城地区过去的考古资料进行了系统梳理。在比较全面掌握考古资料的基础上，再结合有关的金文和文献记载，我们可以对归城历史和文化上的一些关键性问题作进一步的探讨。对这些问题的探讨可以使我们对胶东半岛地区青铜时代的社会变迁取得一个初步的和具体的认识，并为今后的工作奠定一个基础。

第一节　地域聚落结构中的归城

在考古学上，胶东地区地处中国古代青铜器文化圈的边际，而我们对这个地区的文化和历史的认识还很薄弱。在周文化进入胶东半岛之前，这一地区曾经历了岳石文化的繁荣和衰落。岳石文化分布范围很广，从胶东半岛一直延伸到山东省西部，在胶东地区的则是岳石文化的一个地方类型——照格庄类型。在胶东地区，岳石文化延续的时间似乎更长，大约从公元前1900年前后一直到公元前1500年左右（见上编第一章），其末期黄河流域可能已经进入到商代的纪年（公元前1600～前1046年）。岳石文化虽然有发达的农业，但是其聚落大多为小型村落，而缺乏大型的中心性聚落遗址（表Ⅱ.5.1）。其中在胶东地区最大的照格庄遗址经测量大约也只有40000平方米（中国社会科学院考古研究所山东队 1986：448）。因此，一般认为岳石文化的社会可能尚处于前国家的发展阶段；而比之此前的龙山文化，岳石文化在人口密度和制陶工艺方面甚至处在一个衰落的阶段（方辉 2007：194～206；Liu and Chen 2012：275～276；Shelach-Lavi 2015：184，190）。而且有学者更进一步认为岳石文化的衰落是由于公元前4000年之后气候变得寒冷所导致的（方辉 2007：203）。在岳石文化以后兴起的是所谓的珍珠门文化，年代大约相当于黄河流域的商代到西周早期。虽说是“兴起”，但实际上能确定为珍珠门文化的遗址非常有限。珍珠门文化与岳石文化的区别主要是在陶器的形态上；在社会复杂化的程度上，它并未能超越岳石文化时期。在区域社会的集结化方面它甚至还不能达到岳石文化的水平。

周文化在胶东半岛的出现是沿渤海南岸由西向东突入的结果（图Ⅰ.10.5），时间大约在西周早期偏晚。种种迹象表明，胶东文化史上的这个大变局无疑与黄河流域西周国家的建立，特别是周人的诸侯国如齐、鲁、滕等在山东西部的建立有关。具体讲，它与西周金文中所记载的周王朝对山东半岛地区所谓东夷部族的频繁征伐关系十分密切（李峰 2007：349～356）。重要的是，周文化的入侵带来的是胶东地区社会发展史上的一次大断裂，而非继续或者渐变（见上编第十章）。这一变化在考古学上的一个主要表现是聚落等级分层化和大型聚落的出现。其社会历史背景则是"国家"的权力第一次在胶东半岛出现，随之而来的是人口的增加和区域社会的高度中心化。总之，周文化从西部的不断侵入是胶东地区青铜器时代晚期社会发展的主要动力。

由于我们对归城以外的绝大部分地区尚未进行系统的全覆盖式的地面调查，我们对胶东地区聚落分层化过程的细节的了解尚不足够。但是，基于我们这些年的初步调查并结合以往发表的资料，我们还是可以对胶东地区至少西周到春秋时期的聚落系统的宏观结构作一初步蠡测，从中我们也可以看到归城遗址的重要地位。现在可知，胶东地区青铜时代晚期有四个中心聚落，它们分别是招远东曲城、龙口归城、莱阳前河前和蓬莱的村里集古城。其中三处是有夯土城墙的大型聚落（图Ⅰ.0.1）。

东曲城遗址位于招远市东、西曲城村之南高起的台地上，有一条小河与村庄隔离。遗址东距招远市区约22千米，东北距归城约45千米。归城考古队于2009年7月21日调查了这处遗址。遗址南依陡然高起的山峦，西北翘望莱州湾，实际上位于胶东半岛山系到渤海湾过渡的一个三面环山的地带（图Ⅱ.5.1）。台地周围可见大量汉代砖瓦，断崖上亦可见城墙夯土，城址范围为东西950米、南北200米（190000平方米），但陶片分布远远超过了这个范围。这里曾是汉代曲城县的县址，但周代陶片的分布范围也很大，从台地之南山脚一带一直延续到小河之北村庄周围。1959年曾在小河北30米村庄边沿发现过一批铜器，共8件，包括鼎2、簋2，另有盘、盆、壶、甑等器（李步青，林仙庭，杨文玉 1994：377～378）。其中一件高三足的铜簋铭为"齊仲作寶簋"，时代应为西周中期之初；据发掘者推测，这批器物应出自墓葬，下葬年代可能在春秋时期。从我们采集的陶片看（图Ⅱ.5.2），东曲城遗址的居住活动可能在西周时期已经开始，在春秋早期可能已经形成了很大范围。

前河前村位于莱山南麓的莱阳市以南35千米，南距山东半岛南沿黄海海岸约30千米。遗址西北距曲城遗址87千米，北距归城遗址95千米。遗址南北长约300米，东西宽约250米，面积达75000平方米（图Ⅰ.7.24）。1974年曾在遗址范围内发现过一批八件铜器，包括鼎、壶、甗、盘、匜等，其中一件壶铭文为"己侯作鑄壺，事（使）小臣以汲，永寶用"（李步青 1983：7～8）。这批铜器下葬的时间应该在西周晚期。1975年春，山东省博物馆等单位又在附近发掘四座墓葬和一座车马坑，车后还发现殉人，规格较高。1981年春又在前河前遗址出土一件陶盉，按器形无疑是仿照西周中期略晚的铜盉。盉腹上有一周铭文，共18个字，仿效金文字体（图Ⅱ.5.3）。铭文内容尚有争议，但大致可识的字为："[illegible]巳父乙作[illegible]（盉）□□魚、鹿、黿。"从目前资料看，前河前遗址很可能和胶东半岛的另一个国家即己国有关（即和莱国、齐国一起随周王室军队南征淮夷的"曩"国；见下）。我们曾于2005年8月2日探查过此遗址，发现周围地势开阔平坦，东临流入黄海的五龙河，远处则有低山丘陵。地面陶片丰富，以周文化陶系为主，可辨器类有豆、簋、鬲、罐、盆等，并杂有胶东半岛本地文化陶片，其陶片群体与归城非常相似（图Ⅰ.7.25）。据说前河前遗址周围尚有城址，但今已不存。但是，前河前遗址无疑是胶东半岛南部青铜器时代晚期规模最大，规格最高的一处重要聚落。

村里集遗址和归城同在黄水河流域，但它在黄水河另一条支流流经的蓬莱境内。这条支流发源于艾山之阴，其上游基本与黄水河主干平行，隔有一列山脉；下游折而向西，在龙口市以东汇入主流（地图Ⅰ.7.1）。古城城址即坐落于村里集镇以西高起的台地上，其北垣尚保存有100多米，但其他三面均遭严重破坏。古城西界应在古城李家，东界在古城东村，南北约600米，东西约500米，估计面积为300000平方米（图Ⅰ.7.20）。据归城考古队2009年6月14日勘查，发现北墙夯层清晰可见（图Ⅱ.5.4），但城内陶片非常之少。但是，在古城址东沿黄水河支流两岸发现多处墓地，从南向北延续约10千米余。1976年曾在柳格庄和辛旺集两处发现十一座墓葬，并有车马坑，出土铜器多件，有几座并有殉葬人，年代大约多属东周时期（山东烟台地区文管组 1980：50～55）。1986年在之南的站马张家又发现一座较大型的木椁墓，出土铜钟，车马器和大量木器，年代可能为春秋晚期到战国时期（林仙庭 2006：134～136）。总体来看，村里集古城的居住活动的开始可能晚于归城，但是在一段时间内，两处古城可能是共存的。

上述三处（包括归城，共4处）中心聚落或城址的主要文化内涵是周文化，尽管在其中两处如归城和前河前遗址明显有本地文化与来自西方的周文化共存。它们共同形成了胶东半岛周文化分布区域的一个基本的空间结构，也是胶东地区社会活动的几个重要的集结点。它们在文化上有高度的相似性，特别是对青铜器的铭文研究告诉我们位于归城的古国曾和可能位于前河前的己国有重要的通婚关系（见下），这说明这些中心之间并非孤立，而是相互交流的。特别是北边的三个中心，东曲城、归城和村里集基本上是沿胶东半岛北海岸形成由西向东的一线排列，代表了周文化深入半岛东部一个路径。而前河前遗址则是莱山山系以南，周文化进入胶东半岛南部的一个重镇。在这几处遗址之中，归城遗址不论是从其规模，遗址文化内涵的丰富程度上，或是从遗迹现象的社会等级各方面看，均是一处超大型的城址，是中心中的中心，其重要地位是不言而喻的。同时，目前的材料也显示，归城是胶东地区西周文化出现最早，也是最集中的中心城址，它无疑是胶东地区自西周时期以来的文化中心。

在每一个中心聚落周围还应该分布着众多的不同规模的二级或三级遗址。由于几个地区都缺乏系统的调查，我们对其具体地域的遗址结构还不清楚。但是，至少在归城地区，过去的几次黄水河流域调查，特别是归城考古于2010年秋季和2011年夏季对其中的多数遗址的进一步调查，这使我们能够对归城邻近地区的聚落分布系统做出一个基本的复原（见上编第七章）（地图Ⅰ.7.1）。根据过去的调查，龙口地区约有20个地点出土过年代大致在西周或东周时期的遗物（不包括归城范围内的遗址点）（表Ⅰ.7.10）。这个聚落网主要是沿着黄水河流域，由莱山之北向莱山之东逐渐展开。归城西北方向的一处重要地点是张郑家，出土有大量的陶器，是一处与归城同时的规模不小的墓地。其南的台上李家到东周家一带可能是一处周代遗址。其北分布着唐家、徐乡和乾山三处遗址，我们在调查中均采集到周文化陶片。这些遗址形成一个半弧形，从西部延伸到归城之北黄水河主河道范围。黄水河下游东岸过去有赵刘家，程家，西张家等多处地点采集到周代遗物。而我们这两年的调查中则是重点调查了归城以东，黄水河主河道附近的庄头、集前赵家、东营周家和位于莱山之东的鲁家沟遗址。这些遗址基本上都是坐落于黄水河川道以东山前台地之上，分布有一定的规律性。而鲁家沟墓地则是已经深入到黄水河上游王屋水库东岸的台地上。这些遗址沿着黄水河河道由南向北一线展开，对归城形成了从东边的包围之势。特别是庄头和鲁家沟两处墓地过去都出土过重要的青铜器，被认为是在归城居住的贵族的墓地（王锡平 1991：62）。更重要的是，黄水河谷地提供了一条便捷的交通和交流的路线；控制了这条线，向南即可以到达莱阳、莱西所在的半岛中南部，向东则可以到达半岛东端的烟台地区。这使以归城为中心的黄水河流域成为向半岛东南进一步扩张的桥头堡。

归城的具体位置，则是在莱山北麓由黄水河支流鸦鹊河所形成的小盆地，也正坐落于莱山北部的地域性聚落系统的中心。它的东北通过鸦鹊河道，东南通过车格庄的缺口可以和黄水河主河道相通；西边则可以通达今龙口市一带的平地。这一地点既可以依托莱山进行防守，也可以有效控制进入半岛东部的交通主道，即黄水河及其支流。从归城的角度来看村里集古城及其周围遗址，我们就会看到它们实际上是以归城为中心的聚落体系，沿抓髻山之北黄水支流向半岛东部腹地进一步扩张的一个结果。只有通过对上述聚落体系的深入研究，我们才能真正理解支持和保障归城这样的大都会存在的地理政治结构。

第二节　金文和文献中所见之胶东半岛和莱国

在周代同时期的金文资料中，有一些是和山东东部的胶东半岛地区有联系的，其中有一篇甚至可能是与归城一带有密切联系的。北宋宣和五年（公元1123年），山东西部的青州临淄县民在齐国故城范围（今淄博市临淄区）掘得钟、镈一组多件，见于《博古》、《啸堂》和《历代》等书著录的共有全铭的一件镈（集成0285）和十三件钟（集成0272～0284），作器者为叔夷（薛尚功 1986，8：58～75；《博古图》：22.5～16）。根据陈梦家先生的推测，原初组合应有三套钟，共五十一器（或四十八），均与叔夷镈同铭，长达492字，无疑是周代钟铭中最长者（陈梦家 1998：8～9）。这套钟、镈后虽灭于兵火，但铭文流传下来，它记载齐灵公（公元前581～前554年）在淄水之滨对将军叔夷的一次册命，其体例颇似西周的册命金文。叔夷镈中最重要的一段讲道：

> 公曰：尸（夷），女（汝）敬共（龔）辝（台）命，女（汝）雁（膺）鬲公家，女（汝）巩（鞏）褮（勞）朕行師，女（汝）肇敏于戎攻。余易（賜）女（汝）釐（萊）都䏍劏，其縣三百。余命女（汝）辝（台）釐（萊）㔶（陶）或（鐵）徒四千，為女（汝）敵寮，……余易（賜）女（汝）馬車戎兵，釐（萊）僕三百又五十家。女（汝）台（以）戒戎㲋（作）。

铭文中的关键国名“釐”字读为“莱”，在古文字学家中是常识，先秦文献中也有不少通用的例子（陈槃 1969：388～389）。而叔夷镈更是明确记载莱国的都城称为“𩁹剸”，字尚不能释读。此器即作于公元前567年齐国灭莱之后；据郭沫若先生按历谱推定，应为灭莱之后的第二年，即公元前565年（郭沫若 1958：202）。铭文记载齐灵公将莱国国都及其辖下三百个所谓的“县”赏赐给叔夷，并令其统辖齐国驻扎在此地的四千“陶铁徒”，一般认为可能指某种特殊职业的工徒。这里莱国的“县”可能与春秋时期其他国家的“县”有所不同，应该指村落大小的单位。另外，叔夷自己并得到莱国奴仆三百五十家的赏赐，作此套钟、镈作为纪念。属于齐国的另一件铜器庚壶（集成9733），更是记明在伐莱之役中，崔子执鼓，庚首先攻入门中，之后将所得馘首献于齐公之所。这些长篇铭文的出现说明灭莱之役在春秋时期齐国历史上是一件大事，它使齐国的疆域从山东西部一直扩展到山东东部，从而形成了齐国独霸东方的局面。换言之，齐国正是通过牺牲莱这样的东方国家来完成它向“领土国家”的转变的。

在更早的西周同代的史料中我们看不到齐、莱相争的记载。相反地，位于山东东、西部的这两个地方性国家同为周人之与国，与西周国家保持着密切的关系。西周史料中有关莱国的可靠记载首先见于西周中期的史密簋，1986年发现于陕西安康县（张懋镕等 1989：64～71），其铭曰：

隹（唯）十又一月，王令（命）師俗、史密曰：“東征！𢼸南尸（夷）盧（盧）虎，會杞（杞）尸（夷）、舟尸（夷），雚（觀）不墜，廣伐東或（國）。齊𠂤（師）族土（徒）遂（馭）人，乃執啚（鄙）寬亞。”師俗率齊𠂤（師）遂（馭）□□伐長必；史密父率族人、釐白（伯）、僰、𡰥、周伐長必，獲百人。對䁈（揚）天子休，用乍（作）朕文考乙白（伯）障毁（簋），子子孫孫其永寶用。

这篇铭文无疑作于周王畿的陕西地区，其内容讲述周王派遣师俗和史密二人统帅军队，对南夷数个部族进行征伐。师俗在西周中期特别是恭王前后金文中又称“师俗夫”或“伯俗父”，他是西周中期共、懿时期的王畿地区重要的行政长官，见于师晨鼎、永盂等一批铜器铭文。史密又称为“密叔”，在虎簋等铭文中担任王室册命仪式中的右者（李峰 2010：134）。重要的是他们是周王派出，领导这次对南夷作战的将领。在史密麾下作战的则有釐伯，也就是莱伯，为莱国的国君。相似的记载还见于传世的明确属于西周晚期的師寰簋（集成4313）（图Ⅱ.5.5）：

王若曰：“師寰，𢦚，淮尸（夷）繇（舊）我負（賁）晦臣，今敢博乆（厥）眾叚，反乆（厥）工吏，弗速（迹）東郏（國）。今余肈（肇）令（命）女（汝）逹（率）齊帀（師），㠱、𠭯（釐）、僰、𡰥、左右虎臣，正（征）淮尸（夷），即𩠞（殘）乆（厥）邦嘼（酋），曰冉、曰𤼈、曰鈴、曰達。”師寰虔不㒸（墜），夙夜卹乆（厥）牆（將）旋（事），休既又（有）工（功），折首執訊，無諆徒馭，敺孚（俘）士女、羊牛，孚（俘）吉金。今余弗叚組（沮），余用乍（作）𣪘（朕）後男巤障毁（簋），其萬年子子孫孫永寶用亯（享）。

两篇铭文对读，我们可知史密簋“釐伯、僰、眉”指的就是師寰簋“巿（釐）、僰、尿”三国，它们和齐、己两国一同参加了征伐南夷或淮夷的战争，同属山东地区的小国。这里重要的是两器的时代：師寰簋因其与寰盘的同人关系（而寰盘和四十二年逨鼎有都讲到史減），它们无疑作于西周晚期宣王时期（李峰 2006：70～72）。也就是说它们和作于西周中期恭王前后的史密簋相隔约一百年。而两篇铭文“眉”字写作“尿”字的不同可能也反映了这种时代的变化。在这一百年里莱人可能一直是活跃在西周国家东部边缘的重要盟邦。更值得一提的是莱国所参加的战争很可能在南方淮水流域，而不是自己的近邻，这更说明莱国和周王朝的密切关系。

我们在西周金文中看到的莱国和周王朝的关系与后代文献中有关记载立场是有很大差异的。这其中《史记·齐太公世家》有太公初封，“营丘边莱”，莱侯与争营丘的著名说法，对后世影响很大。但是考虑到西周初年诸侯国的规模和地域特点及《史记》中资料的来源和记述形成的复杂过程，这个说法的可信度是有很大疑问的。首先，它并不了解古代国家作为“邑制国家”的基本特点（李峰 2010：296～302）。其次，它很可能将春秋时期齐、莱两国的敌对关系折射到西周初年的历史之上，但这种敌对是“邑制国家”向“领土国家”转变过程中的产物。尽管如此，《史记》的说法中所反映出来的莱国的东夷本土族源，在我们考虑西周国家与胶东半岛的国族的政治关系方面，就显得更为重要了。

文献中关于莱国地望的最早说法见《左传》杜预注云“莱国今东莱黄县”。《汉书·地理志》青州有东莱郡，治所为黄县，今龙口；初唐颜师古注称“故莱子国也”。这个说法为历代学者所遵循，即尽管并不能指出莱国都城的具体地点，但莱国应该就在黄县地界。进而，根据70年代对龙口归城城址的早期踏查，已有学者将莱国都城和归城遗址联系了起来（李步青，林仙庭1991：918；王锡平 1991：64）。但是，现代学者间也有另一说，认为莱国初在西边昌乐至临朐一带，后迁至黄县的说法（陈槃 1969：391～392）。这主要是由于拘泥于汉代文献的字面理解所致，推理的成分多但并无实据。特别是这种看法是受到上述《史记》所谓“营丘边莱”的误导，致使一些学者遂以莱国离齐国不远作为推测莱国都城位置的出发点。这实际上是不考虑史料的时代和价值而盲目进行使用的错误结果。

有关莱国早期地理的一个重要资料是一件可能由莱伯自己所作的䅘（釐/莱）伯鼎（集成2044）（图Ⅱ.5.6）；原器不存，只有铭文拓本传世，《殷周金文集成》据其字体定为西周中期。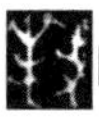的左侧按字体结构看似接近“華”字，因此过去曾有学者认为这个字从“華”，其音应该读瓠（王献唐 1983：142～145）。但是，我们看班簋（集成4341）上的（釐）字就知道，“釐”字的上半确实是可以这样写的，即下边两笔可以是直的。而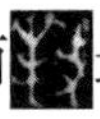最上两笔向左右撇折的样子也近似窅鼎（集成2755）上的（釐）或小克鼎（集成2796）上的（釐）字。因此，我们认为，把它释为“釐”，进而读为“莱”是可以接受的（“莱”是文献中写法）。而所谓“瓠”这个国家并不存在。这件铜器在柯昌济1916年前后编纂的《韡华阁集古录跋尾》中

即有著录（柯昌济 1935a：2.46），后在他1930年成书的《金文分域编》更指出器出自“黄县莱阴”（柯昌济 1935b：9.15）。按“莱阴”所指的范围应即莱山之北的归城范围（这里有莱阴河，是鸦鹊河的支流），但是柯氏同指出自“黄县莱阴”的还有光绪丙申年（1896年）实际上出自莱山之东鲁家沟墓地的遹鼎和遹甗［实为觳鼎（集成2721）和遇甗（集成948）］，可见柯昌济当时人在济南，他对黄县这些铜器的具体出土地点并不清楚。故又一种说法即认为䅘（莱）伯鼎即出自鲁家沟，离归城也不远（见下编第四章）；此说所据为1934年成书的民国黄县志（王道新 1934：14；林仙庭 2006：133）[1]。王道新为黄县本地学者，其所述较之济南的柯昌济氏可能更有所据。另一件重要的器物是旅鼎（集成2728）（图Ⅱ.5.8）；这件铜器柯昌济《韡华阁集古录跋尾》中亦有著录，但未讲出在何处（柯昌济 1935a：1.29）。1940年出版的《山东金文集存》则指出此器可能与觳鼎和与遇甗一起于1896年出自“黄县之莱阴”（曾毅公 1940：11～13）。旅鼎讲道“公太保来伐反夷年”，公太保即召公奭，器的年代自然不能晚于周康王前期。其“来伐反夷”的叙述法显然代表了山东地区国族的立场，说明器可能即作于本地。铭末旅的族徽为一个“丫”形，唐兰先生曾经释为“来”（唐兰 1995：242）。也有学者认为这个“丫”所指就是莱国（王锡平，孙敬明1984：77～79）。不过，此族徽尚未见于其他的铜器，它和莱国的关系尚需进一步证明。

上述是对西周时期莱国政治关系和地理方位的一个基本评估。关于莱国晚期的历史，先秦文献如《春秋》和《左传》中记载最为具体，其可信度也比之《史记》等汉代资料要高。根据这些信息我们可以把莱国于公元前567年灭亡之前约一百年的历史进行一个粗略的复原。据《春秋》，鲁宣公七年（前602年）齐、鲁两国国君曾会同攻伐莱国；据《左传》这次征伐主谋者为齐国。两年后的宣公九年（前600年），齐侯又单独伐莱，可见这段时间莱国是齐国的主要敌人。公元前573年（鲁成公18年），齐灵公诛灭齐国的权臣国氏，设计杀死国佐于朝，使清人杀国胜，国弱奔鲁，而国氏之党王湫奔莱国，成为莱国的重要谋臣，从而也进一步激化了齐国与莱国的矛盾。前572年，齐人又一次攻伐莱国，但莱人以马、牛各百匹买通了齐国的夙沙氏，导致齐军无功而还。齐国和莱国的关系也得到了暂时缓解。但是随后齐国招莱子与会，莱子不至，齐、莱两国又一次交恶。齐国于是又派出大将晏弱在东阳筑城，即今临朐县东，在战略上逼迫莱国，以使之屈服，直至公元前567年（鲁襄公6年）最终灭掉莱国。这是一场持续了七个月的大战役，《左传》中如此记载：

> 十一月，齊侯滅萊，萊恃謀也。於鄭子國之來聘也。四月，晏弱城東陽，而遂圍萊。甲寅，堙之環城，傅於堞，及杞桓公卒之月（春）。乙未，王湫帥師及正輿子，棠人，軍齊師，齊師大敗之。丁未，入萊，萊共公浮柔奔棠。正輿子王湫奔莒，莒人殺之。四月，陳無宇獻萊宗器于襄公，晏弱圍棠。十一月，丙辰，而滅之，遷萊于

1　王道新《黄县志稿》云：“文曰䅘伯作旅鼎。光绪二十二年春城东南乡卢家沟（应为鲁家沟）田中出土古铜器十。钟三、鼎二，一鼎破碎，钟无款识。尚有壶一、盘一，盘无款识，壶亦破碎。若甗，若盉，若觯，皆有铭，俱归丁幹圃。”《黄县志稿》的成书比《金文分域编》晚几年，两者的记述均在这批铜器出土三十余年之后，均不能被看作当时的现地纪录。

郳。高厚，崔杼，定其田。

这里值得注意的是《左传》讲道莱国的环城，应该是指环状的城，这与中原各国的方形或长方形城址都不相同[1]。可能由于莱国都城城墙很厚，齐军不能攻破，于是齐人积土至堞，攻入城内。这里讲的崔杼，正是上述庚壶（集成9733）铭文中讲的鼓噪入城的崔子。共公浮柔所奔的棠地在今平度县境，而莱人残余所迁的郳据考证应在鲁西滕县一带。可能正是因为郳地近鲁，公元前500年（鲁定公10年）齐、鲁两国“夹谷之会”时，齐国指使莱人劫持鲁定公，受到孔子的责斥。上述发展反映的实际上是齐国在形成“领土国家”的过程中向山东东部扩张，最终吞并莱国的一个自然历史进程。

关于莱国都城的位置，综合各方面信息，我们认为把它与归城联系起来应该是目前所能作出的最好的判断。其理由如下：首先，归城以前出土了己国的“曩伯庭父”所作的嫁女媵器（下编第二章），这说明归城即不是己（曩）国的都城；而莱国国君嫁女之器则出土于南方的日照，可能在莒国的范围内（见下）。因此归城当是与这两个国家有通婚关系的胶东半岛另一个主要国家的中心。其次，虽然上述关于赩（莱）伯鼎和旅鼎出土地点“鲁家沟”的指认是在它们出土三十余年以后，还有一些不确定因素，但是说它们发现于黄县范围以内，应该是没有问题的。第三，这一点和古代历史地理著作中莱国在黄县的最早说法相符。早期地理书特别是《汉书·地理志》中的资料值得重视，由于汉代的很多郡县名直接来自先秦的国族名。其资料的有效性在过去三十年间得到了考古发现的反复验证（李峰 2007：28）。第四，考虑到莱国在史密簋、師寰簋、叔夷钟和《春秋》及《左传》中的一系列记载，莱国无疑是胶东半岛上的一个强国，而归城遗址的超大型规模和其在胶东地区聚落结构中的中心地位正与此相符。就黄县（龙口）及周边地区而言再无发现另一处规模相当的城址，而第二大的村里集城址面积也只是归城的二十六分之一。我们必须考虑归城在胶东地区聚落体系中的这一特殊性，它与莱国的政治地位正向对应。最后，考古调查所知的归城的环形外城和宽厚的城墙与《左传》记述灭莱之役时莱都的细节也有相符之处。因此，虽然我们尚没有出自归城的铭文资料来作直接证明，我们认为以现有的证据为基础，归城至少在西周晚期到东周早期的一段时间内在所有可能的选项之中是莱国的都城的最好候选者。很可能归城就是叔夷镈中所讲的莱国都城“賫劆”。

第三节　从考古资料来探索归城遗址的年代和形成历史

那么，我们应该怎样看待归城的年代和形成历史？在考古学中，“遗址形成过程”（Site Formation Processes）是一个重要的专题或研究领域，也是所谓考古学中级理论的主干（Raab

1　“堙之環城，傅於堞”这一句的传统解法是“句谓环莱城之四周皆筑土山”（杨伯峻 1990：947）。但是，在“四周皆筑土山”高接城堞，这在战法上是很难理解的；因为攻城时一处突入全城皆破，实战中不可能有四周皆筑土山的费时费力的办法。很可能汉代以来的经学家并不知道莱都为环形，因此他们曲解了此句。

and Goodyear 1984：255 ~ 268；Schiffer 1983：675 ~ 706；1987）。也就是说对遗址形成过程的研究提供了将一般性的人类学理论和对文化遗物的具体考古学研究之间的一个有效连接。遗址形成研究中最重要的一点就是把所谓的文化过程（Cultural Process）和自然过程（Natural Process）相区别，从而试图对遗址形成、使用、废弃过程中人类行为因素和自然因素所起的作用进行探索，并进而从遗物的分类上探寻人类行为的方式。归城的研究目前尚处在调查阶段，有很多问题需要将来通过多学科的研究来回答。但是，基于我们目前调查和试掘中已经掌握的信息，通过试掘、调查、科学测定及其出土文字等各方面相互参照，我们可以对归城遗址居住活动及遗址形成和发展的过程进行一个初步的勾画。换句话说，本节我们要做的就是通过归城遗址的考古信息的分析来尝试建立它的考古性历史（Archaeological History）框架。

要探索归城的形成过程和历史，我们首先要找到可靠的年代依据（Chronological reference）。当然，最理想的办法是在胶东半岛本地文化的发展序列中确定归城遗址的遗迹、遗物的相对位置；但是由于目前这一本地文化传统的资料远不成系统，研究也很薄弱，这显然是不可能的。另一个方法是将归城出土属于周文化的器物类型与中原地区乃至渭水流域周人中心地区的陶器类型相比较，从而确定归城遗址的相对年代。由于周文化的来源本身就很复杂，在这个复杂体系中各地的陶器又都有其明显地域特点，而胶东半岛地处于周文化边缘地带，因此采用这种方法来推定归城的具体年代难免带来偏差和不确定性。但从另一方面讲，在黄河流域到山东半岛的广大地域内从西周到东周时期陶器演变的大趋势还是相当一致的，这为跨地域的比较提供了一个基础，并且过去已有学者结合山东地区的资料进行研究，可以作为很好的参考（崔乐泉 1992：73 ~ 97；王青 2002）。为了克服上述可能的偏差，我们在分析归城的陶器类型时确立了两个重点：第一是要抓住典型单位，全面地而非单件地来考察其文化现象；第二，我们要抓住与铜器共出的陶器形式并以之为标准，因为铜器在一个大的地理范围中的共性远远大于陶器。

在归城的发掘中我们掌握了两个典型单位，即H20和H3（见上编第五章）。H20位于TG2最下层，是发掘中所得最早的单位；H3位于TG1最上层，是发掘所得最晚的单位。两个单位陶片总体上差别是很明显的。H20陶片以细绳纹和中绳纹为主，且一般纹路比较规整，纹脊高而清晰。特别是H20下层，陶片纹路一般均细密，不见粗绳纹。相反，H3陶片中不仅出现了较多的粗绳纹，并且绳纹一般压印较浅，纹路散乱；另外还出现多量的呈麦粒状的麻点纹（图Ⅱ.5.7）。根据绳纹演变的一般规律我们可知，H20的陶片群体属于西周时期，H3则属于东周时期，但进一步断代则要靠典型器物。

从器形方面讲，H20：1的A1簋是典型的西周早期周文化陶簋（图Ⅰ.5.57），过去在山东地区的广饶五村及胶县西庵遗址也有出土（山东省文物考古研究所 1989：61 ~ 123；山东省昌潍地区文物组 1977：68），在胶东地区它无疑代表了这类簋中最早的形态。但是，H20这件簋已经发展出了长折沿，腹部变浅而敞，腹部除了上部一周外绳纹均已抹去，与西周早年承自商文化的深腹盆形簋相比已有了距离。因此这种簋在张家坡的新分期中是排在第二期的，如M385：5和M321：2（中国社会科学院考古研究所 1999：354），也就是西周早期的晚段到西周中期早段。H20：16的A1豆柄和H20：17的豆盘实际上是西周早期粗直柄豆和西周中期的粗柄节楞豆的过渡形态（图Ⅰ.5.52），这种豆在山东地区过去曾出土于昌乐宇家村M1和广饶五村M11；这两墓均有成套器物出土，年代属于西周中期偏早。在洛阳北窑墓地中它们也排在西周中期，如M702：1和M223：1~2。至于H20出土的三件A1袋足鬲，特别是H20：13和H20：15两件确实是比较典型的“乳状袋足”，在其他地区发现很少，而在关中地区一般多属于西周早期。总体来看，我们认为将H20的年代推定在西周早期偏晚阶段（见上编第十章）是有充分依据的。

H3①：17这件C3式浅盘、敞口的豆（图Ⅰ.5.11）在同一单位中还有几件。与这件豆类似者曾出土于栖霞县吕家埠M1和M2；这两座墓因为有成套的陶器和铜鼎及车马器随葬，年代比较明确地在春秋中期到晚期之交（M2较晚）（栖霞县文物管理所 1988：778~783）。H3①：1这件体型较大的D3鬲，显然是受了本地文化的影响，但是器形仍保持了周文化风格。它尽管没有绳纹，其外形比较接近曲阜鲁国故城所谓甲组墓M202：6，或者是章丘宁家埠M113：1或M30：1陶鬲；这些标本均被认为属于春秋中期（山东省考古研究所等 1982：95；王青 2002：44）。而类似H3②：4的器盖在鲁城M202中也出土。总体上来看H3的陶器中并没有太晚的器形，因此我们认为H3器群的大致年代应该在春秋中期范围。

上述形态学上的比较表明，H20和H3这两个单位之间的年代差别至少可能有约300年。以这两个单位为基点，我们将2009年试掘所得的单位分为三个阶段：第一阶段包括H20；第二阶段包括H18，H19；第三阶段包括H2，H3，H4，H8，H9（上编第十章）。进而，这个年代顺序可以用碳十四测定年代来做验证：H20=1090（61.1%）1000BC；H3=825（68.2%）795BC。但是，归城碳十四的测定年代普遍地比我们估计的历史年代要早（附录一），这是需要在今后的工作中进一步验证的。可能的一个解释是这些标本来自建筑物所用材料，如柱檐或屋顶的盖草，那么有关数据只能代表这些材料采摘的年代，而并不能代表所出灰坑埋葬的年代。

除了陶器和碳十四的分析以外，我们在研究归城遗址的形成历史时还有另外一个系列的信息可以作为参考，那就是归城范围及其周围出土的青铜器。这首先涉及启尊、启卣的年代问题；这两件著名的青铜器于1969年出土于归城范围内曹家村南小刘庄水库边上（下编第二章）（图Ⅱ.2.6）。过去唐兰先生将包括启尊、启卣在内的讲到“南征”的所有铜器都排在周昭王时期，这在青铜器研究上实际上有很大问题（唐兰 1995：236~333）。两器器型与2004年新出自集前赵家墓葬者基本一样，后者包括了多个器类，可以说是西周中期偏早的一个典型器群（图Ⅱ.3.15~Ⅱ.3.19）。1896年出土于鲁家沟的瘢鼎、遇甗讲到和淮夷的战争，属于所谓师雍父组（还包括稽卣，臤尊，彔尊，彔卣，伯雍父盘等），年代也在穆王时期，而器形与自集前赵家所出铜鼎完全一样。除了上述三宗铜器外，1965年曹家村出土的8件器中壶类似于传世的吕行壶（集成9689），属伯懋父组（还包括召尊、召卣、小臣謎簋等），年代在昭王到穆王早期；两件鼎的形制则更接近瘢鼎。因此曹家这批铜器的下葬时间也应该在西周中期偏早（图Ⅱ.2.3）。1980年庄头西周墓出土有“芮伯”铭的方座簋有穆王时期典型的大鸟纹（图Ⅱ.3.2），其他器形年代也基本一致（另见王锡平 1986：69~72）。另外值得一提的是，1983年出自归城之西海徐家的长铭文铜簋（图Ⅱ.3.20）也属于西周中期（马志敏 2004：79~80）。我们必须注意一个现象，那就是上述这几宗出自归城及附近的铜器群年代都十分接近，它们占据了本地出土铜器的绝大部分。这说明西周中期偏早阶段，也就是相当于周王室历史上的穆王时期，无疑是归城地区贵族活动最为频繁和集中的高峰时期。目前我们在归城地区看到的早于西周中期的铜器只有几个散出的单件。龙口市博物馆藏有一件铜簋，腹饰涡龙纹，两耳有珥，是典型的西周初年铜簋。1964年芦头镇韩栾村也曾出土一件分裆铜鼎，并有铭文，为“㾓监”所作（图Ⅱ.2.7），年代也在西周早期（李步青，林仙庭 1991b：84～85）。这件铜器和上文讲到的旅鼎（集成2728）器形花纹几乎完全一样（图Ⅱ.5.8），年代应不晚于康王前期。由于前两件铜器都属于散出，它们是否属于较晚器群中包含的早期之物，或者是代表了自身的埋葬时间，这一点还不能确定。但是，㾓监鼎和旅鼎的铭文既反映了“本地”的内容（特别是旅鼎讲“公大史來伐反夷年”），它们即应为本地所作，其铭文又反映了在西周早期晚阶段本地的国族已经和西周国家建立了密切的政治联系。归城地区比较晚的铜器主要有1969年出自董家村的一组铜器（图Ⅱ.2.4）和1951年出自南埠村的所谓黄县㠱器（图Ⅱ.2.5）。这两组铜器的年代分别在西周晚期和春秋初年。

综合上述各方面的信息进行分析，我们可以对归城遗址的形成过程和历史发展提出如下一个初步的描述。大约在西周早期偏晚一段，随着周文化侵入胶东地区，归城遗址的聚落中心开始形成。这个中心坐落在莱山北麓鸦鹊河两条支流之间形成的小台地上，东西两条支流外围有莱山余脉和北面凤凰山玉皇顶的保护，是一个理想的集聚之地。台地南高北低，周围的河流和小型湖泊提供了充足的水资源。即使在今天，台地西侧的这条支流虽已经干枯，但在归城外城范围以内仍然保留了面积大小不同的近十处湖泊。在公元前一千年内归城一带水资源的丰富更可想象而知。这处中心聚落的出现无疑与周文化向胶东半岛的挺进有密切关系，反映在同时代的铭文资料中则是西周国家对所谓东夷部族的一系列战争。由于发掘中所见最早的一个单位H20打破了归城内城墙基，我们可以知道归城内城的城墙可能即筑于这个时期。当然，我们在工作中发现这座城墙在以后的数百年中有数次被洪水冲坏和进行修补的痕迹。这些均需要今后的考古工作来阐明。

在内城城墙修筑之后，它很快迎来了归城历史上贵族活动最为频繁的一个时期，即西周中期。这一时期归城可能还是位于周文化的东部前沿上，但它显然已经成了半岛东部地区遗址和墓地所形成的网络的一个中心点。总的来说，遗址的规模并不是很大，主要仍在鸦鹊河两条支流之间，其内城的规模还小于北方周人封国燕国的都城。但是，根据西周时期陶片的分布范围推测，其遗址范围自然要大于内城范围，总面积应有4～5平方千米，主要在现在归城的西半部。我们在归城进行的系统地面调查中也发现，归城在东周时期有一个明显向外扩张的态势，很可能归城的外城即在这一时期修建。这条外城绵延8.15千米，沿山脊形成一个椭圆状，从东、西、北三面保护着归城，工程相当浩大。它一方面反映了归城人口的增加和经济实力的增强，另一方面也可能反映了胶东半岛地区日益激化的政治军事情势。特别应该提到的是，归城的南部并未筑墙，而是向莱山主峰张开，这样不仅完全保护了归城内丰富的水源，而且提供了广大的活动空间。我们在调查中发现归城南部陶片逐渐稀少，可见归城内居民的居住活动主要还是在北部，但是南部这个广阔的地带，特别是沿鸦鹊河上游两岸的山麓地带确可能为归城居民提供了理想的埋葬或休闲之地。

根据我们目前掌握的资料对归城遗址在整个东周时期的历史过程很难进行不待假设的讨论。在内城试掘中我们发现的最晚的单位H3大约在春秋中期，但是我们在地面采集中发现的一些器形明显要晚于这个时期（图Ⅱ.5.9）。它们与H3器群的差别是很明显的。譬如说，采自10-Y9附件的这件B2豆很接近蓬莱村里集附近柳格庄大墓所出土的陶豆，甚至可能还要更晚一些（烟台市文物管理委员会 1990：803～810）。而其他两件浅盘细直柄的B4豆，是黄河流域战国墓葬中普遍存在的器形；在山东地区最典型的例子则是出自长岛王沟墓群M10的多件豆，年代大约在战国早期（烟台市文物管理委员会 1993：62，83）。总之，这些器型大致代表了归城遗址从春秋晚期到战国时期的一个很长阶段。我们也发现这些晚期的器型主要集中在内城和其南的第九、十两个区域，在其他区的调查中极少见到这么晚的陶器。这似乎告诉我们归城遗址在这个时期已经式微，即归城沿外城墙的大部分地区已经废弃，其人类活动范围可能仅限于内城及邻近地段，比春秋中期以前范围小了很多。这一时期，黄水河另一个支流的蓬莱村里集古城可能已经形成。很有可能黄水河流域的文化和政治中心已经从归城转移到了村里集古城，并在周围留下了一大批春秋晚到战国时期的墓葬。

第四节　归城遗址的规模、内部结构及其所反映的古代国家形态

在公元前7世纪的春秋早期，归城应该是一个规模相当可观的大都市。它的外城跨越山顶，绵延8.15千米；东西两面城墙直接通向莱山山根，如果将其连接起来，周长将超过12千米。城内面积至少在8平方千米以上（上编第四章）。如果再算上归城南部深入莱山山地的一部分，由城墙和莱山山体所保护的总面积应该在10平方千米以上。这样的一个城市即使在中原地区也可称为一座大城。从表Ⅱ.5.1可以看出，归城的规模虽然比之战国时期的燕下都相差甚远，也小于齐、楚等春秋时期主要国家都城，但它大于蔡、薛等在西周已经立国的古国国都；其规模大约相当于曲阜的鲁国故城和洛阳的东周王城。在山东地区来讲，它无疑是首要的几座大城之一；在胶东地区则无疑是第一大城，是胶东半岛的政治和文化中心。

另一方面，我们在调查中发现归城城墙很厚，最厚处达100米以上，可能有与城墙有关的附属建筑设施；外城平均厚度大致也达到40米左右。这个数据与列国城墙数据相比，自然在很高的一端。《左传》讲到齐人灭莱时曾“堙之環城，傅於堞”，这很可能是因为莱国城墙过于厚实，冲墙不破，才积土上城堞攻入城中的。这是一个很有趣的现象。

基于我们已经掌握的资料，我们可以估算一下归城外城建筑所用的土方。城墙若以平均下宽40米计算，上宽若为30米，高为15米，其切面面积则为525平方米。那么，总长8.15千米的外城所需土方累计将达到4278750立方米。根据我们田野工作，特别是在南水北调有关考古工作中积累的经验，一个壮年劳力一天可以移动的最大土方不过2方，这尚不包括远距离转运。那么归城外城的建设所需的总劳力数即为2139375人/日。如果归城统治者每天可以组织10000

人的劳力专攻修建，则共需要213.93天，也就是说差不多7.13个月左右可以建成外城。这只是一个粗略的估计。我们在调查中发现，归城外城经过的山脊上基岩较高，原覆盖土层实际上很薄，因此我们在一些段落发现筑城所用的土质为淤土，其来源无疑是山下的支流河床地段（见上编第四章）。考虑到这样的土方搬运过程，归城外城的建筑所需要的人力可能大大超过我们上面估计的数据，这应该是一项相当浩大的工程。它在一定程度上反映了归城统治者的政治权力和组织能力。

关于一个城市或遗址的组织结构，我们实际上是说它可以分为不同使用功能的活动区域（Activity area），也就是说我们要从考古现象（包括遗物）的现在来考察人类相关城市或遗址的行为的过去（Carr 1984：106～107，125～126）。自2007年以来，通过对归城内城范围的全面钻探，使我们对其地下遗迹的分布和保存状况获得了具体的了解。钻探中我们在内城共发现地下夯土建筑基址17座（上编第三章）。另外在内外城之间还发现夯土基址两处，其功能我们将作单独考虑。尽管我们靠钻探是无法确定地下建筑的年代，而钻探所得的资料与将来正式发掘所可能揭露的情况也会有一定的出入，但是我们发现这些建筑基址的排列有一定的秩序，钻探中也未发现明显的相互叠压关系，因此我们可以初步判断它们应该是同一时代有布局规划的一系列建筑。当然这一个世代延续的时间会长一些，建筑之间仍可能有早晚的关系。以这个基本的认识为出发点，我们可以探讨归城内空间组织。当然，我们有关归城内部组织的初步认识要受到未来正式发掘的检验。

首先我们看到，归城内城实际上是分为两个大区的。这两个区之间有水系相隔，分界明显。据判断这条水系从内城南门西侧流入，连通城墙外之护城河。入城后向西成一弧形，然后向北直流到北城墙转弯处出城，与北墙外护城河相连。像这样的城内水系在燕下都和齐临淄城内都有发现；它们一方面提供了城内用水之便，另一方面也可供建筑物防火灾之用。因此，虽然我们尚没有直接证据表明这条水系一定是周代的，但是我们推测它应该是归城原来布局的一部分。水系之西的西区以南北长78米的九号基址为中心，形成了一个独立的空间。九号基址两侧有两座南北向建筑（八号和十号），与九号并行，并在东侧形成较宽阔的庭院。南侧另有两座较小的长方形基址。这组建筑位于内城西北角，相对封闭而又自成系统，我们推测它们应该是内宫一类的建筑，主要功能应该是供归城统治者及其家室起居生活之用。

内城东区相对开阔，以二号和三号基址为中心。其中三号建筑南北长56米，东西宽约21～33米，是东区现存规模最大的建筑。二号基址西距三号基址约60米，由于位置偏东，大部分已被历来侵入归城的洪水所破坏。但是二号基址无疑与三号基址形成了一个对称的布局，以10.5米宽的道路L1为中心，分置于其两翼。这条中心大道南北延长约56米，北端尚未探出，距离内城东、西城墙距离相等，显然是整个归城内城的中轴。它的存在说明东区建筑的分布有全局观念，而二号、三号基址组成的一组建筑显然是其核心。三号建筑北侧又有几座辅助性的小型基址，而其南有石块铺垫的平面，石块面周围又有广阔的踩踏面，共同形成一个开阔的广场，广场北端与中心大道相连。这些现象表明二号、三号这组对称的大型建筑的公共性质是显而易见的。我们推测，这组建筑代表了归城的行政和权力中心。至于这组中心建筑以东的部分，钻探得知地下遭洪水破毁范围较大；以北部分今压在和平村下，情况并不清楚。但是我们在村中道路和开阔之处进行了系统钻探，只在村中部断崖处发现一座小型夯土（十五号基址）。另外，和平村内过去曾发现车马坑和墓葬，在城南部中心建筑以东地区也发现较多墓葬，在中心建筑之南发掘的探沟中又发现了铸铜用的陶范，这说明这个大范围内古代活动的性质可能是复杂多样的。这个大范围内可能存在贵族甚至是一般平民的住宅，同时也有他们的墓地，另外还可能存在铸铜作坊一类的手工业作坊，甚至是池沼一类的遗迹。凡此种种功能究竟在空间上怎样划分，这要等将来的工作来揭示。

另外在内城和外城之间我们发现两处临河修建的基址。一处位于内城正北方，下临鸦鹊河并依台地筑起，现保存南北长约120米，东西宽30米，规模宏大，夯土层也厚。另一处在内城正东沿鸦鹊河支流高起的一条土岭上，我们在其周围发现很多铺地用的扁平石块。这些高规格的建筑，特别是内城北的大平台可能与礼仪活动有关。在内外城之间，特别是在内城之东有着较宽阔的空间；内城之南一直到莱山山脚，则有更广泛的空间。这个大范围内地形复杂，水流、池沼甚多，陶片分布广泛，有很多理想居住之地，根据过去的发现我们也知道有多处贵族墓地。特别是归城南部地势起伏，陶片分布减少，但过去有多宗重要青铜器的发现，这说明归城南部深入山地的部分可能是墓葬比较集中的地区。

关于归城的方向，内城整体走向约为17°，城内主要建筑和道路也都采取了北偏东的走向。这个方向与齐国的临淄及燕下都相仿，与商代主要城址和建筑的走向也大致相类。但是，它与洛阳的东周王城，甚至秦国的雍城的北偏西走向却不一致。近期的研究认为，古代城市或大型建筑物的走向与选用不同的星座来代表北极定向有关（Pankenier 2004：211～236；班大为2012：199～238）。从这一点讲，归城内城的走向或许可能是继承了东方的传统。但是，由于地势原因，我们认为归城应该是一座坐南朝北的城市，这与中原其他地区城市的坐北朝南是不同的。另外，归城外城依山势而建，呈不规则的椭圆形，也与中原地区常见的长方形城市很不同，这应该是当地文化因地制宜的特点。

总之，我们从归城的建筑遗迹可以看到，归城的社会是一个权力高度集中的社会。归城的政治领袖能够调动人力物力修筑其规模相当于洛阳东周王城和曲阜鲁国故城的中心城址，用于保护其中心都城的人口和财富，这说明他们至少拥有接近于鲁国的政治统治力量和人口资源。归城内城的建筑虽经破坏，但现存基址仍表现出有秩序的布局和对整体空间的考虑，这也能说明归城的统治机体已经有了相对高度的管理能力。比归城更大一些的其他同时期城址，如燕下都、齐临淄和郑韩故城，乃至南方楚国的纪南城都是战国时期领土国家中的大国都城。归城的政治实力当然不能与它们相比，但是说归城在其强盛时期具有了接近鲁国或者说宋国等次一级领土国家的实力，则应该并非言而过之。

第五节　胶东半岛的青铜文化及其地域性问题

本书上编第十章系统讨论了归城地区的陶器文化及其发展变化。胶东地区的陶器文化有着自新石器时代以来的自身发展系统。在岳石文化阶段，胶东地区已发展出了灰黑陶系（主要为泥质陶）和褐陶系（主要为夹砂）并存的局面，并以红褐和灰褐陶逐渐占上风。到了珍珠门文化时期（约公元前1400～前900年），红褐陶则成了占绝对主导地位的陶系。这些陶器一般烧制火候不是很高，胎质较松，表面色泽不均，且绝大多数陶器为素面，有不同程度的夹砂，云母（mica）、石英（quartz）和滑石（talc）。在强势的周文化从西部突然侵入之后，周文化在短时期内并很快成为本地区的陶器文化的主体，打断了本地文化的发展过程，形成胶东半岛古代文化的一个断裂现象。但是，本地文化的传统并没有因此而终结，而是继续存在，并在西周的某一个时期发展成为主要分布于半岛东南部的南黄庄文化。

胶东半岛地区这种独特的陶器制作传统在归城遗址有充分的表现，但是我们目前尚不能确定归城所常见的红褐或灰褐陶器是否可以被归入南黄庄文化范畴。这是在以后工作中要探索的问题之一。由于周文化的陶器以黑陶和灰陶系为主，因此以这两种文化传统的发展历史为背景，把它们区分开来并不困难。但是，随着时间的推移，一方面胶东地区的周文化逐渐发展出了不同于中心地区周文化的一些特点；另一方面，胶东地区本地文化的因素也在不断加强。其结果是出现了像H3这样的典型单位。其中，红褐陶系共占陶片总数的23.80%，而可以复原的主要器形均有周文化因素和本地文化因素混同的特点。这种混同反映了胶东地区西周晚期到春秋时期文化发展的大趋势。

我们在归城试掘工作中的一个重要发现是一块陶范，出土于灰坑H9中（图Ⅰ.5.28）。这件陶范的发现证明了本地青铜器铸造业的出现，也为西周晚期起山东半岛东部具有地方特点的青铜器文化的形成提供了证据。遗憾的是这件陶范接触器表的台面很小，因此无法判断所铸之器形。但是同一灰坑中出土了大量的陶片，我们可以据之判断H9的年代。H9位于探沟TG2南端，TG1北端，是一个圆形小坑。它开口于第3层以下，并打破早期的灰坑H20。H9有多数陶片上印有粗浅散乱的绳纹，有细柄的B2节楞豆，有浅盘的豆盘，有很低矮的鬲足（图Ⅱ.5.10）。总体判断，我们认为H9的年代应该不早于春秋早期，在年代上可能稍早于H3。这也为我们带来了一个问题：青铜器铸造技术究竟在什么时候引入到山东半岛东部并开始发展起来的？

大家知道，岳石文化中已经发展出了铸造小件青铜器的能力，在胶东的牟平照格庄遗址也有发现（中国社会科学院考古研究所山东队 1986：472）。上文已经讲道，西周中期早段应该是归城一带贵族活动的高峰期，有很多青铜容器的发现。但是，根据铭文的内容推测看，这些青铜器的拥有者与渭水流域的西周贵族有着紧密的联系（见下），铜器的造型和花纹风格也与中原地区常见的西周铜器不能区分，因此我们认为这时期归城地区铜器中至少有一部分是从中原或陕西地区带入的。但是，铭文中有“本地”内容的青铜器应该属于本地铸造。譬如，上文讲到的出自鲁家沟的旅鼎铭文讲“公大保來伐反夷年”，它就应该是胶东本地铸造。

另一个典型的例子是1983年龙口市西侧海徐家村出土的一件西周中期辛䣄簋（下编第三章）。这件铜簋束颈、垂腹，矮圈足，是比较标准的西周中期圈足簋的造型（图Ⅱ.5.11），与之同出的绳纹铜鬲在陕西一带西周墓中也有不少例子。这件铜簋的花纹也很符合西周中期的特点，是一种早期形态的窃曲纹，但是仔细比较我们会发现它的花纹实际上是比较简略，并略显松散的。其铭文目前尚不能完全释读：

> 唯王十又一月，王在阸。王子至于方，辛霸（郦）。賓叔，報考辛柲。乍（作）用剌。辛霸（郦）𠬝（？）。叔斧（？）𠭯（賜）金。辛𢍚至，□扜（于）宫，昇（見？）。子子孫，□𠓗（作）寶𡀚（器）。

这篇铭文遣词造句基本仿效一般西周金文，但它谬误甚多，字体正反相间。书写者可能并不一定识字，或者识字程度非常有限。但是，大致讲它记载王在限地，王子前至于方地，辛郦往拜见并受赏赐金，因而作器一事。这篇铭文的内容很可能与西周中期周王及其近臣在山东地区甚至可能是胶东地区的巡视活动有关，但器物的铸造者则可能是归城地区某地方国族的成员。笔者过去曾系统论述过，在西周国家周边地区往往有国族仿照西周青铜器铭文体例而铸造自己的青铜器，但其铭文往往违反常规，时有谬误，器物造型有时也不规范，最典型的例子就是眉敖簋（集成4213），鄂侯御方鼎（集成2810）和其他鄂国铜器（Li Feng 2002：210～242）。辛郦簋也明显属于这种情况。这些铜器反映了周边国族在与周文化接触过程中学习周人的青铜器铸造技术及其铭文文化的一个实际历史过程。海徐家这件铜簋的文化意义也正在于此。

无论如何，西周晚期到春秋时期胶东半岛地区青铜文化的主体仍然是继承了周文化的传统，但同时在这一时期也出现了一些具有地方造型特点的器物。这一时期我们可以据铭文确定属于莱国铸造的青铜器只有1976年出土于日照崮河崖一座西周晚期墓葬中的一套四件的𩰫（莱）伯鬲。其铭曰："𩰫（莱）伯□女子，乍（作）竇鬲，子孫永竇用"（杨深富1984：594～597）。按金文惯例，"𩰫伯"后一字即为"媵"字，器可能为莱国嫁女到日照一带国族的一套铜器，其夫家可能是莒国。这套铜鬲虽是比较典型的西周晚期鬲的风格，但与之共出的两件大壶（M1：1-2）则是山东本地的创造。其形小口、垂腹有四系，腹部饰窃曲纹与三角纹相间，其形可能仿自本地鱼篓一类的用器（图Ⅱ.5.12）。这种本地风格浓厚的三角纹也见于1969年烟台市上夼村的铜壶上（山东省烟台地区文物管理委员会 1983：289～292）。这种器形在本地的陶器中也有类似者，如归城地区的A1或A2壶即是这种形态。同墓所出尚有"㠱侯"和"己华父"所作之器，因此这是属于纪国的一套铜器。己侯（即㠱侯）所作的另外一件鬲于50年代发现于归城和平村南，铭文部分残损，共十二字："己侯鑄□姜□□子子孫孫永竇用"（李步青，林仙庭 1991a：915）。这件铜鬲很可能也是一件媵器，即己侯为嫁女到莱国所作之器。这件鬲虽有扉棱，具西周晚期常见铜鬲之外形，但其素面和尖足的形态则更接近本地素面陶鬲的风格，或者说二者兼有。

我们在西周国家周边地区常常看到一个有趣的文化现象：即在西周早中期周文化盛极一时的时候，很多国族接受了非常典型的西周青铜文化。但是随着时间的推移，本地的装饰风格和器形，往往是基于本地陶器的器形，逐渐开始回潮，形成本地青铜器文化的一个重要组成部分。我们在胶东地区看到的正是这样一个现象，而且这个现象和我们在陶器文化中所看到的本地文化因素的逐渐增加是相关联的，它们共同反映了胶东地区古代国家形成过程中的一个方面。不过，胶东半岛的国族，包括莱国和纪国等主要国家，似乎仅仅发展出了有限的几个器种，而其青铜器文化的主体仍然延续西周时代以来的传统。进而，这个发展过程很快就被由西边入侵的齐文化所打断了。

第六节　莱国的形成之蠡测和胶东半岛的国家化进程

通过分析归城地区的考古资料，并结合碳十四测定年代，我们可以对归城遗址的形成历史及其所表现出来的复杂文化发展过程有一个初步认识，也可以对占据归城的这个政治团体的权力和统治方式有一个基本的了解。另一方面，本地出土的青铜器铭文资料和文献中关于胶东地区古代国族，特别是莱国在西周中期以后到春秋时期的活动也有明确的记载（见上），它们可以帮助我们对考古学中所看到的文化现象建立一个深层次的有历史背景的解释。但是，要把这两方面的信息有效地结合起来，我们首先要对出土于本地的青铜器铭文资料进行一次系统梳理，分析其所反映的政治关系，进而作出比较客观的判断。

如上所述，目前可以确定为莱国所做的有铭文青铜器有两件：第一件是莍（釐/莱）伯鼎（集成2044），器已不存，但一定是莱伯所作，年代大约在西周中期。另一件是釐（莱）伯鬲，出自日照崮河崖一座西周晚期墓葬，可能是莱伯嫁女（可能到莒国）所作的媵器。

另外还有一件旅鼎（集成2728），铭末有一个“个”形的族徽，有学者认为即“莱”，但是这个族徽的意义待定。但是，铭文既然讲到“公太保来征反夷年”，说明它是胶东本地国族所作。上述莍伯鼎和旅鼎都可能与𣪘鼎（集成2721）、遹甗（集成948）一起出自归城东南约10千米的鲁家沟。如果这样，它们只能说明莱国（或族）和其他国族（包括㾡）在西周早期很可能已经在黄水河流域和龙口一带活动，但它们尚不能说明归城在此时已属于莱族或其他一族治下。

归城范围内时代属于这一时期的铜器最重要的当然是出土于曹家以南小刘庄的启尊（集成5983）和启卣（集成5410）。但是这篇铭文所涉及的史实背景比较复杂，讲到王由于出征南山寇遭山谷，遂至上侯之处，在滰川之上，启从王征伐，因此作器（图Ⅱ.2.8）。这里所提到的“上侯”另见于師艅尊（集成5995）和師艅鼎（集成2723），是周王外出所到之地，器传出陕西“京兆”。“上侯”另见于不栺鼎（集成2735），是周王暂居之所，而器出自扶风齐镇M3。他们均说明“上侯”应该是离宗周不远的一个地点，这对启尊和启卣的来历是一个很好的参考。我们认为这两件铜器有可能来自陕西或中原某地，而启所参加的这次战争应该发生在宗周以南。

属于这种情况的还有1980年出土于庄头墓葬的芮公叔所作一件方座簋，全身饰大鸟纹，高29.2厘米。这件簋与纽约范季融先生所藏的一件簋同形，同饰，只是后者为芮伯所作，高28.7厘米。两件铜器相似性极高（但庄头簋口沿下花纹省略），我们认为很可能是兄弟俩人同时所作的两件铜簋（图Ⅱ.5.13）。由于韩城梁带村近年来的发现，我们知道芮国无疑在陕西地区，由于某种原因，这件铜簋被带到了山东。同墓中还出土了由“熊奚”所作的一件壶。另外，出自东营周家的西周铜簋（龙口市博物馆藏号：KM491）铭：“作朕寶簋，其萬年永寶用。單。”铭文虽不记作器者名，但族徽为（單）。这个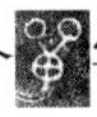字族名不应与商末周初屡见的族徽如（集成5195）相混。东营周家这件铜簋据其器形花纹，属西周晚期器。他们铭末的“單”所指应该是周人的单氏宗族，西周晚期活跃于陕西。它很可能是陕西眉县单氏宗族的器物，不知什么原因也被带到了胶东半岛。

2004年新出土于集前赵家墓葬的铭文资料显得更为复杂。这批铜器中四件有铭文，其中两件方座簋为“叔索”受“伯應父”赏赐金以后所做；另一件则为“里父”所作。虽然我们以前并不知道这些作器者，但是他们的名称都是典型的周人称法，铭文的书体和铜器器形与西周中心地区相比也基本相同。另一件值得关注的器物是上述有“痻监”所作铭文的分裆鼎，1964年出土于归城以西10千米的芦头镇韩栾村，年代在西周早期（图Ⅱ.5.8）。西周监国制度的实行金文中有明确证据，已知的例子有位于平顶山的应国的“應監”和位于南阳的南申国的“監伯”；而仲几父簋（集成3954）又有“诸侯诸监”的说法，说明周王朝在地方封国中派驻监官是常有的事（李峰 2010：248～249）。那么，痻监鼎在龙口地区的出现无疑说明这一带除了莱以外应该还有其他可能受西周国家控制的国族。我们推测史密簋中随周人、齐人和莱人一起作战的“眉”国，或是師寰簋“尸”国，可能和这个“痻”国有关；但字尚不可通，这只能是一个猜想。

我们应该指出，金文中所反映的归城地区与陕西周人中心地区的这种紧密人事联系在陶器上也有明显的反映。如上分析所示，西周早期晚段进入归城地区的应该是一种比较典型的周文化，它的源头似乎并不在与山东临近的河南和河北地区，而可能更直接的是陕西的周文化中心地区（上编第十章）。我们在归城地区往往能找到与陕西地区极其相似的陶器，比如说H20出土多件的低裆的袋足陶鬲（图Ⅰ.5.52），其相似程度甚至超过以洛阳器群为代表的中原地区陶器（受到商文化的深远影响）。这种跨越如此远距离的相似性所反映的更可能是一种人员的直接交流。虽然我们不能把考古中所看到的现象与政治历史直接挂钩，但是青铜器铭文中的信息（特别是关于人事关系和政治制度的信息）却可以为我们直接指示这种政治关系。归城遗址的文化现象和青铜器铭文中的信息确实反映了周文化对胶东半岛的入侵，而在其背后则是西周国家的强大的国家机器的驱动。特别是西周金文中屡屡记载的周人对所谓东夷的一系列战争可以提供对这种文化现象的一个很好解释。这个战争既可以在周人中心地区出土的很多青铜器铭文如小臣逨簋（集成4239）、明公簋（集成4029）中看到证明，也可以从胶东地区本地出土的青铜器铭文，如旅鼎的“公太保来征反夷年”中看到本地国族的记述。

综合考虑上述归城地区出土的考古资料和青铜器铭文信息，我们可以看到，与其说它们与莱国有关，不如说归城在其早期与周王室及渭水流域宗族贵族的活动关系更为密切。当然，将来正式发掘阶段归城范围内出土莱国铭文的可能性是有的，但目前我们尚不能把归城和西周早、中期的莱国联系起来。不管这些铜器是自陕西带来（至少有一部分应是外地带入），还是在本地铸造，它们反映的无疑是归城地区与西周国家周中心地区的频繁的人员交流和紧密的政治关系。即使可能在鲁家沟与莱国铜器共出的𩰬鼎、遹甗，它们所记载的也是遹本人参加周王朝在南方淮水流域对淮夷作战的事。同时我们也应该看到，我们在归城及附近看到的与周人有关的多国族铜器集中出土的现象在其他周边地区，如琉璃河燕国地区和平顶山应国地区，是不多见的，是一种特别的现象。总之，就目前资料看，并考虑到归城遗址的规模和重要性，我们认为最好把西周早期和中期早段归城看成是周人在胶东半岛活动的一个重要的集结地。

上述认识也为我们理解莱国的形成提供了重要的背景。莱国源出于东夷，它在早期很可能是接受了周文化并与周人有密切政治关系的本地部族中的一支。它在西周国家的政治体系影响之下逐渐形成了胶东地区的一个地方小国，并且在很长一段时间内和周人保持密切的政治联盟，如上引史密簋和師寰簋铭文中看到的那样参加了周人在山东以外地区组织的军事行动。这实际上反映了西周国家边缘地区特别是山东地区二次国家形成过程中的一种常态（Wu Minna 2013：18～23）。莱国后来能够入居归城，并以归城为中心发展壮大，这可能与西周国家在中期以后的逐渐萎缩有关系，这为莱国的发展提供了空间。上述我们在归城发掘中发现，早期文化层的陶片中周文化因素为主导，相反到了春秋时期的H3，以红褐陶为主的本地文化因素则有明显增加趋势，这可以从本地系统文化的发展壮大来解释。或者从狭义上讲，这可以从莱国自身的发展壮大，并逐渐摆脱周人影响的过程来解释。到了西周晚期特别是东周早期，莱国在胶东地区的活动在文献中留下了清晰的记录，而归城在这一时期也发展成了整个胶东地区独一无二的大城，把它与莱国都城联系起来问题是不大的。这个时期，莱国可能修筑了归城的外城，其规模接近曲阜的鲁国都城，这说明东周初期的莱国已经有了相当大的实力。莱国与其东南的己（纪）国和在山东半岛南部的日照某古国（可能是莒国）保持了密切的通婚关系，并与西方的强邻齐国相抗衡。而公元前567年莱国的最后灭亡实际上是中国古代国家进入“领土国家”阶段的必然结果。结合考古学，青铜器铭文和政治史的研究，我们可以对胶东半岛青铜时代晚期国家形成的背景和社会、历史发展过程做出一个比较丰富的解释。

参考文献

班大为（David Pankenier），2012. 再谈北极简史与“帝”字的起源. 当代西方汉学研究集萃・上古史卷. 上海：上海古籍出版社. 199-238.

博古图，1752. 亦政堂重修本.

Carr, Christopher, 1984. “The Nature of Organization of Intrasite Archaeological Records and Spatial Analytic Approaches to Their Investigation,” *Advances in Archaeological Method and Theory*, edited by M. B. Schiffer. Pp. 103-222. New York: Academic Press, Inc.

陈梦家，1998：叔尸钟镈考. 燕京学报，4：1-24.

陈槃，1969：春秋大事表列国爵姓及存灭表撰异. 台北：中央研究院历史语言研究所.

崔乐泉，1992：山东地区东周考古学的序列. 华夏考古，4：73-97.

方辉，2007：海岱地区青铜时代考古. 济南：山东大学出版社.

郭沫若，1958：两周金文辞大系图录考释. 北京：科学出版社.

柯昌济，1935a：韡华阁集古录跋尾.

柯昌济，1935b：金文分域编.

李步青，1983：山东莱阳县出土己国铜器. 文物，12：7-8，17.

李步青，林仙庭，1991a：山东黄县归城遗址的调查与发掘. 考古，10：910-918.

李步青，林仙庭，1991b：山东省龙口市出土西周铜鼎. 文物，5：84-85.

李步青，林仙庭，杨文玉，1994：山东招远出土西周青铜器. 考古，4：377-378.

Li Feng, 2002. "Literacy Crossing Cultural Borders: Evidence from the Bronze Inscriptions of the Western Zhou Period (1045-771 B.C.)," *Bulletin of the Museum of Far Eastern Antiquities* (Stockholm: Museum of Far Eastern Antiquities), 74: 210-242.

李峰，2006：西周金文中的郑地和郑国东迁。文物，9：70-78.

李峰，2007：西周的灭亡：中国早期国家的地理和政治危机. 上海：上海古籍出版社.

李峰，2010：西周的政体：中国早期的官僚制度和国家. 北京：生活・读书・新知三联书店.

林仙庭，2006：莱国与莱都，烟台考古，济南：齐鲁书社. 134-136.

Liu, Li, and Xingcan Chen, 2012. The Archaeology of China: From the Late Paleolithic to the Early Bronze Age. Cambridge UK: Cambridge University Press.

马志敏，2004：山东省龙口市出土西周铜簋. 文物，8：79-80.

Pankenier, David, 2004. "A Brief History of Beiji (Northern Culmen): with an Excursus on the Origins of the Character Di," *Journal of the American Oriental Society*, 124. 2: 211-36.

栖霞县文物管理所，1988：山东栖霞县松山乡吕家埠西周墓. 考古，9：778-783.

Raab, L. Mark, and Albert C. Goodyear, 1984. "Middle-Range Theory in Archaeology: A Critical Review of Origins and Applications," *American Antiquity,* 49. 2: 255-268.

Schiffer, Michael B., 1983. "Toward the identification of formation processes," *American Antiquity*, 48. 4: 675-706.

Schiffer, Michael B., 1987. *Formation Processes of the Archaeological Record.* Albuquerque: University of New Mexico Press.

山东省文物考古研究所，1989：广饶县五村遗址发掘报告. 海岱考古，1：61-123.

山东省文物考古研究所等，1982：曲阜鲁国故城. 济南：齐鲁书社.

山东省昌潍地区文物组，1977：胶县西庵遗址发掘简报，文物，4：68.

山东烟台地区文管组，1980：山东蓬莱县西周墓发掘简报，文物资料丛刊，3：50-55.

山东省烟台地区文物管理委员会，1983：烟台市上夼村出土㠱国铜器，考古，4：289-292.

Shelach-Lavi, Gideon, 2015. *The Archaeology of Early China: From Prehistory to the Han Dynasty*. New York: NY Cambridge University Press.

唐兰，1995：论周昭王时期的青铜器铭刻，唐兰先生金文论集. 北京：紫禁城出版社.

王道新，1934：黄县志稿. 山东省博物馆藏稿本.

王青，2002：海岱地区周代墓葬研究. 济南：山东大学出版社.

王锡平，1986：山东黄县庄头西周墓清理简报，文物，8：69-72.

王锡平，1991：对山东黄县庄头西周墓出土铜器铭文的初步研究. 烟台师范学院学报（哲学社会科学版），3：62.

王锡平，孙敬明，1984：莱国彝铭试释及论有关问题. 东岳论丛，1：77-79.

王献唐，1983：山东古国考. 济南：齐鲁书社.

Wu Minna, 2013: "On the Periphery of a Great 'Empire': Secondary Formation of States and Their Material Basis in the Shandong Peninsula during the Late Bronze Age, ca. 1000-500 B. C. E. " Ph. D. dissertation, Columbia University, New York.

薛尚功，1986：历代钟鼎彝器款识法帖（朱谋垔本）. 北京：中华书局.

烟台市文物管理委员会，1990：山东蓬莱县柳格庄墓群发掘简报. 考古，9：803-810.

烟台市文物管理委员会，1993：山东长岛王沟东周墓群. 考古学报，1：57-87.

杨伯峻，1990：春秋左传注. 北京：中华书局.

杨深富，1984：山东日照崮河崖出土一批青铜器. 考古，7：594-597.

曾毅公，1940：山东金文集存.

张懋镕，赵荣，邹东涛，1989：安康出土的史密簋及其意义. 文物，7：64-71.

中国社会科学院考古研究所山东队，1986：山东牟平照格庄遗址，考古学报，4：447-478.

中国社会科学院考古研究所山东队，烟台市文物管理委员会，1986：山东牟平照格庄遗址，考古学报，4：447-478.

中国社会科学院考古研究所，1999：张家坡西周墓地. 北京：中国大百科出版社.

表 Ⅱ.5.1　归城城址和东周各国都城规模比较

Table Ⅱ.5.1　Comparison of Guicheng city site with other state capitals of the Eastern Zhou period

国家 State	城市 City	面积（千米²） Area (km²)	形状 Shape	时代 Date
燕 Yan	下都 Xiadu	32	方形双城 Conjoined squares	战国 WS*
齐 Qi	临淄 Linzi	17+	长方 Rectangular	西周晚—战国晚 Late W. Zhou - Late WS
楚 Chu	纪南 Ji’nan	16	长方 Rectangular	春秋早战国晚 Early SA - Late WS
郑、韩 Zheng & Han	郑韩故城 City of Zheng & Han	16	大致长方+方形 Roughly square + Rectangle	春秋早—战国晚 Early SA - Late WS
宋 Song	宋故城 City of Song	10.2	长方 Rectangular	西周—春秋 W. Zhou - SA
秦 Qin	雍城 Yongcheng	10	大致方形 Roughly square	春秋早—战国晚 Early SA - Late WS
鲁 Lu	曲阜 Qufu	9	长方 Rectangular	西周晚—战国 Late W. Zhou - WS
周 Zhou	王城 Royal City	8.9	大致方形 Roughly square	春秋中—战国晚 Mid-SA - Late WS
莱 Lai	归城 Guicheng	8	椭圆 Oval	西周—春秋 W. Zhou - SA
薛 Xue	薛故城 City of Xue	7	大致长方 Roughly Rectangular	西周—春秋 W. Zhou - SA
蔡 Cai	蔡故城 City of Cai	6.7	大致长方 Roughly Rectangular	西周—春秋 W. Zhou - SA

Historical period: W. Zhou=Western Zhou; SA=Spring and Autumn; WS=Warring States.

图Ⅱ.5.1　招远东曲城遗址

Figure Ⅱ.5.1　The Dongqucheng site in Zhaoyuan.

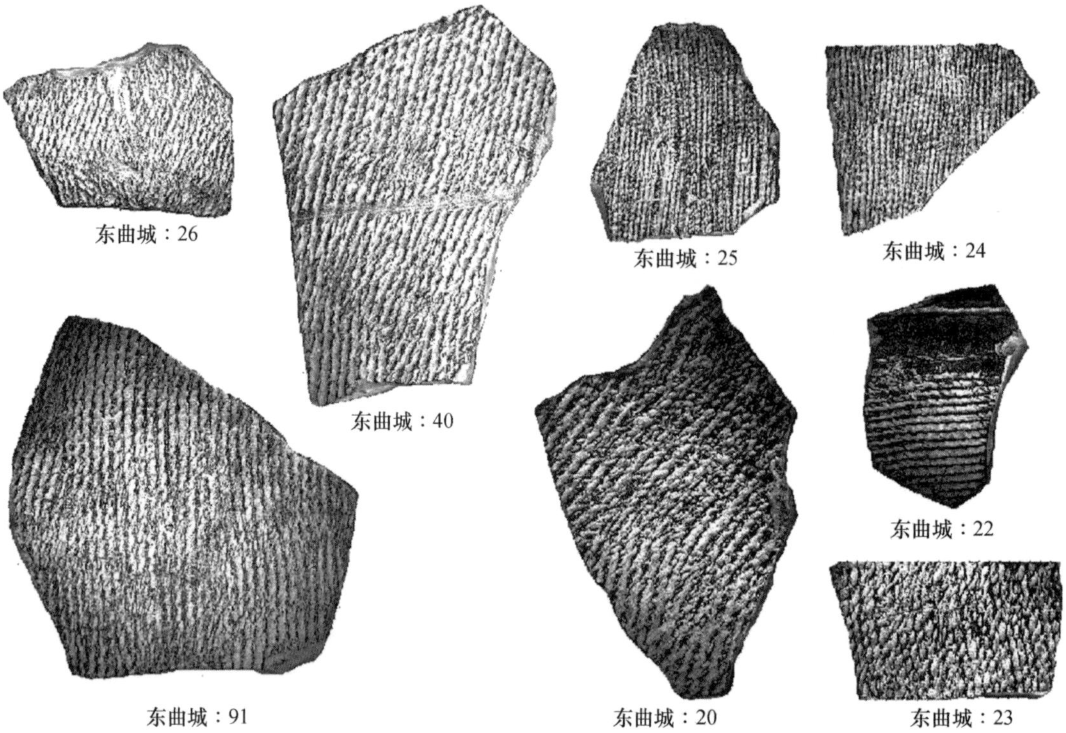

图Ⅱ.5.2　东曲城采集周代陶片

Figure Ⅱ.5.2　Zhou period pottery sherds collected at Dongqucheng.

图Ⅱ.5.3　前河前遗址出土周代陶盉

Figure Ⅱ.5.3　A Zhou period pottery *he* vessel unearthed at the Qianheqian site.

图Ⅱ.5.4　村里集古城北墙夯土

FigureⅡ.5.4　Rammed earth in the north wall of the Cunliji ancient city site.

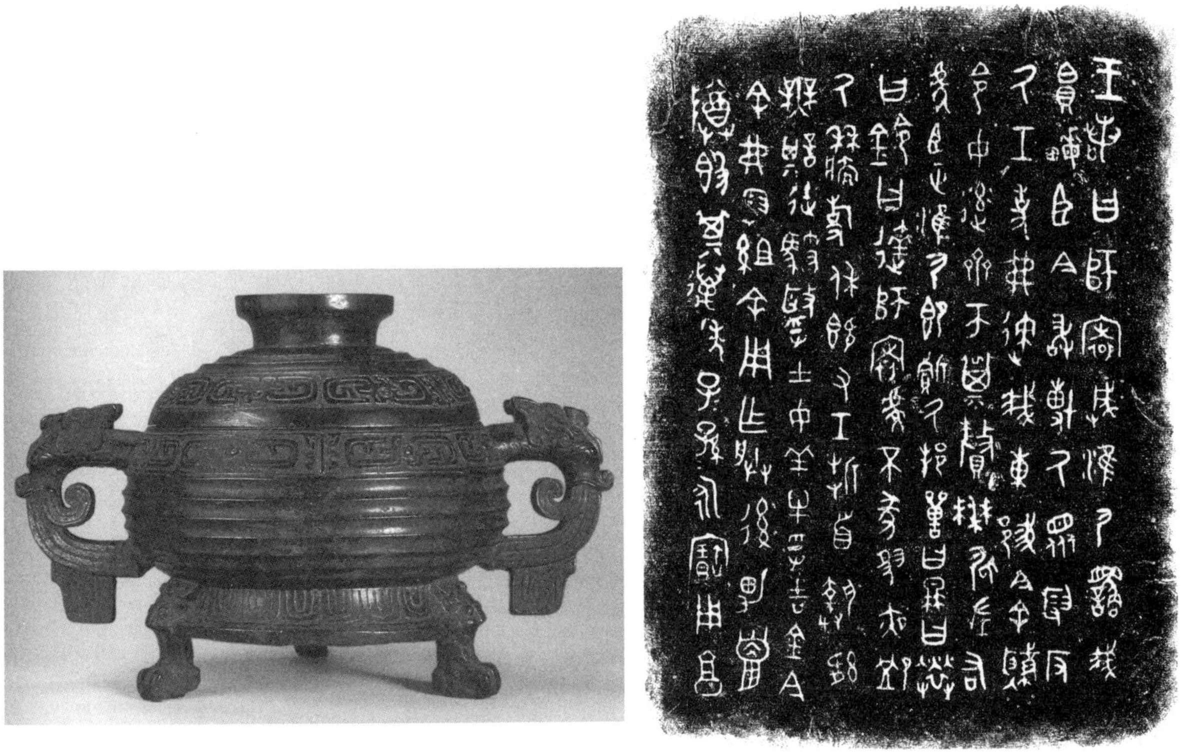

图Ⅱ.5.5　師寰簋及其铭文

FigureⅡ.5.5　The Shi Yuan *gui* and its inscription.

图Ⅱ.5.6　出土于“黄县莱阴”的莱伯鼎（集成2044）

FigureⅡ.5.6　The Laibo *ding* unearthed “north of Mt. Lai in Huangxian” (*Jicheng* 2044).

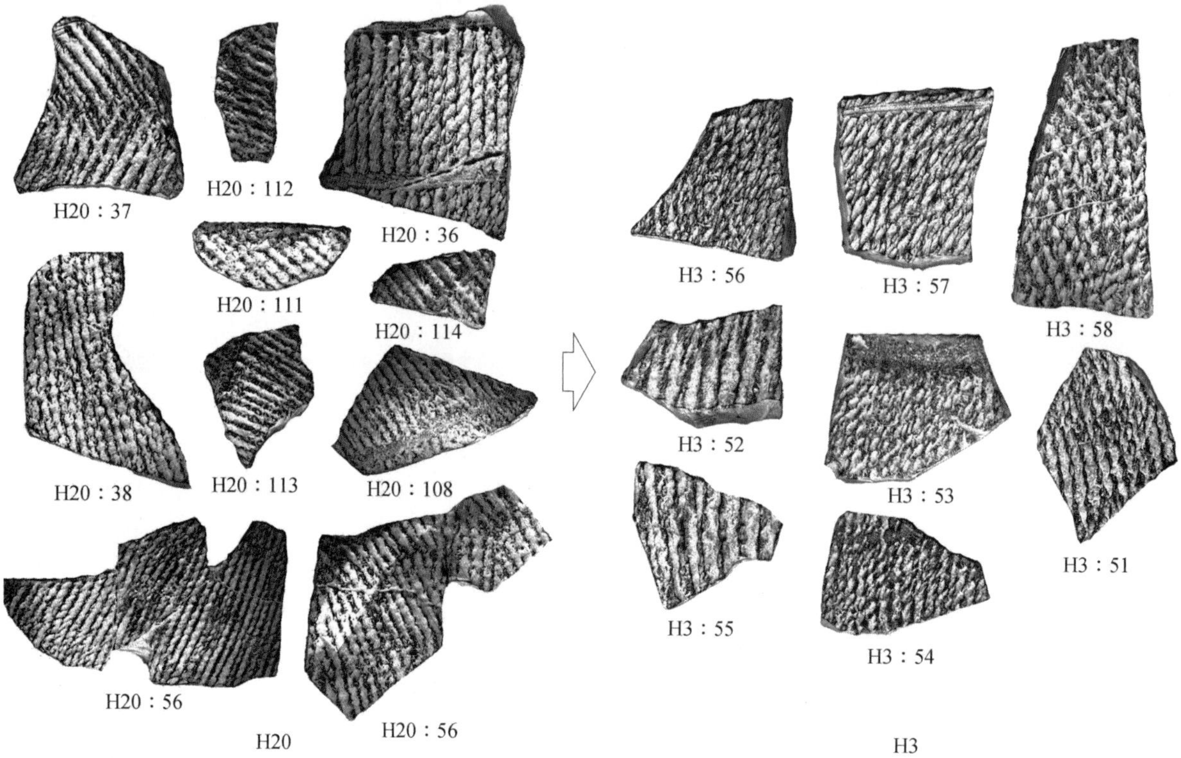

图Ⅱ.5.7　H20上层和H3出土陶片纹饰比较

FigureⅡ.5.7　Comparison of sherd decorations from H20’s upper stratum and H3.

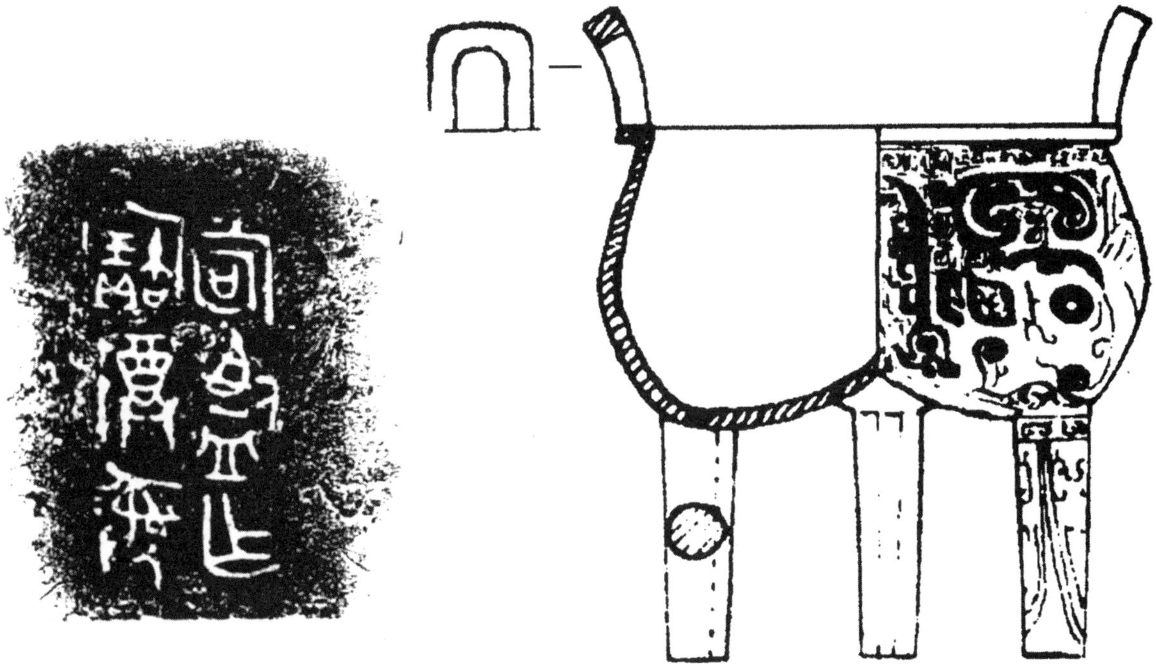

1

2

图Ⅱ.5.8　庿监鼎和旅鼎的比较

1. 庿监鼎　2. 旅鼎

Figure Ⅱ.5.8　Comparison of the X-Jian *ding* and Lü *ding*

1. X-Jian *ding*　2. Lü *ding*

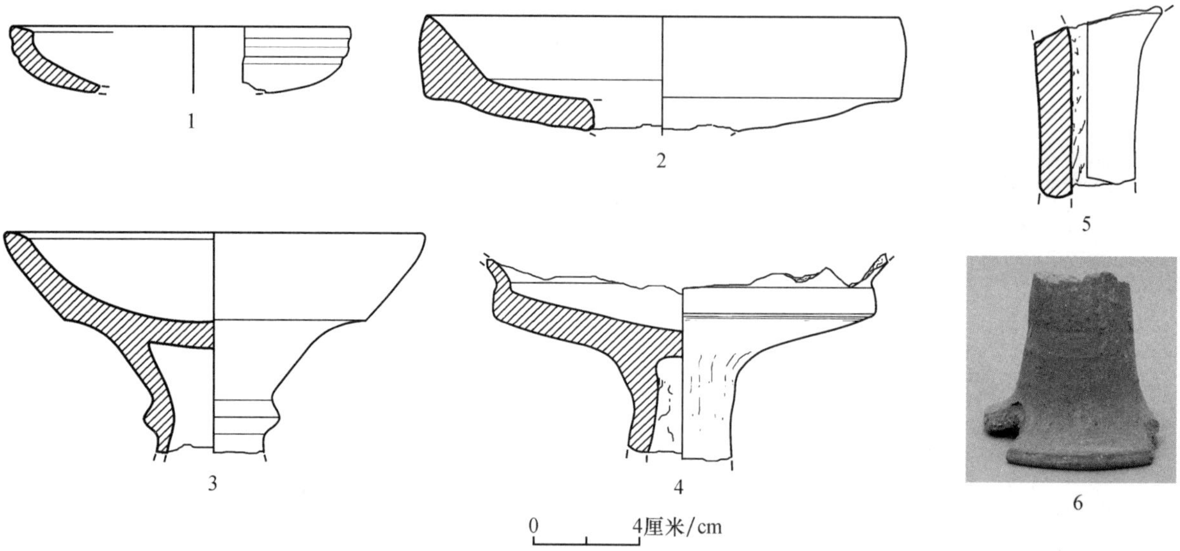

图Ⅱ.5.9　归城出土春秋晚期到战国时期陶豆

1. 9-r11：1　2. 和平村南采：6　3. 10-Y9（附近）：3　4. 10-Y9（附近）：4

5. 和平村南采：9　6.内城：38

Figure Ⅱ.5.9　Pottery *dou* of the late Spring and Autumn to Warring States period from Guicheng.

1. 9-r11：1　2. Heping-South：6　3. 10-Y9 (Near)：3　4. 10-Y9 (near)：4

5. Heping-South：9　6. Inner city：38

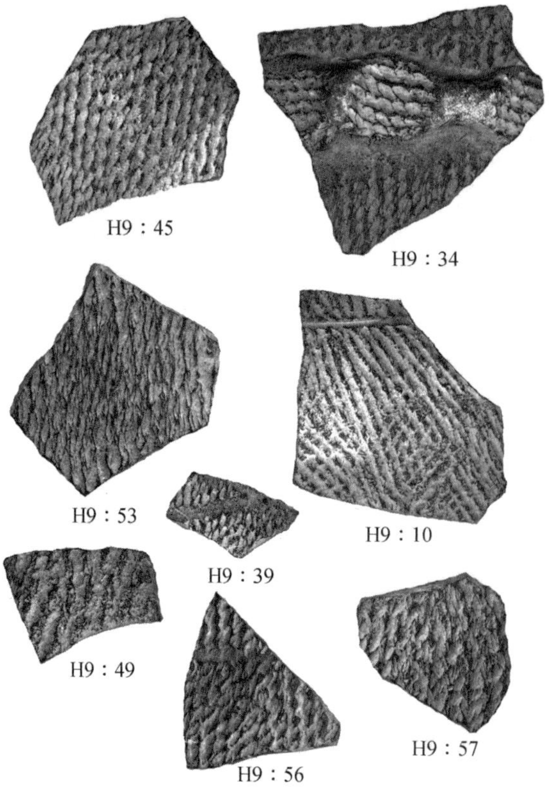

图Ⅱ.5.10　H9与陶范共出的陶片

Figure Ⅱ.5.10　Pottery sherds unearthed with the bronze casting mold from H9.

腹底铭文

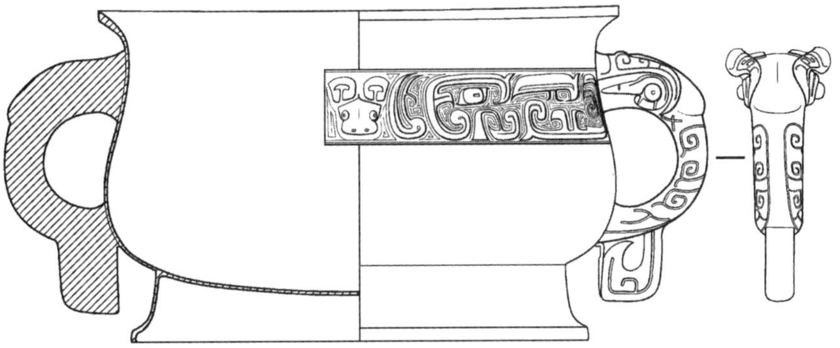

图Ⅱ.5.11　海云寺徐家村出土的辛䂂簋

Figure Ⅱ.5.11　The Xin Xiao *gui* unearthed at Xujia Village in Haiyunsi.

图Ⅱ.5.12　胶东半岛西周晚期铜器

1. 崮河崖M1（釐[莱]伯鬲）　2. 崮河崖　3. 上夼村　4. 归城和平村（己侯鬲）

Figure II.5.12　Late Western Zhou bronzes from the Jiaodong Peninsula.

1. Guheya M1 (Laibo *li*)　2. Guheya　3. Shangkuang Village

4. Heping Village, Guicheng (Jihou *li*)

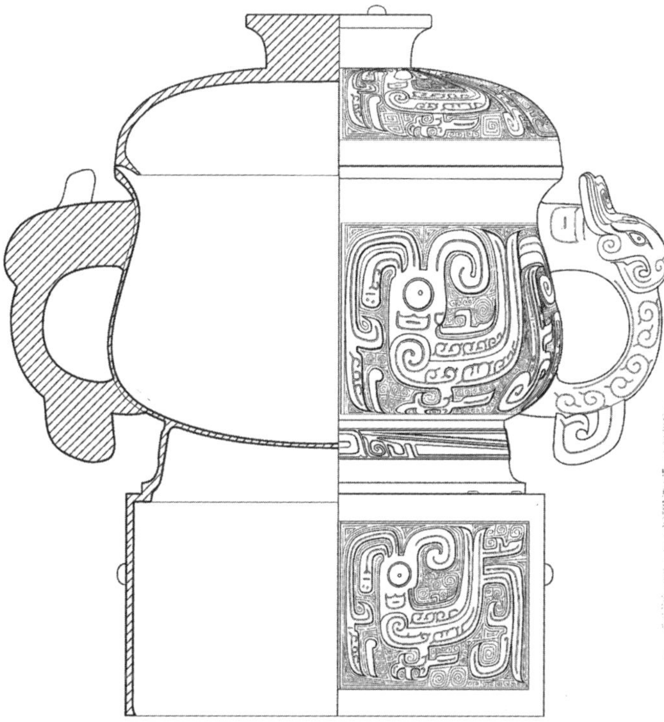

庄头墓葬出土铜簋

Bronze *gui* from the Zhuangtou tomb

纽约范季融藏簋

Bronze *gui* in the collection of George Fan.NY

图Ⅱ.5.13 芮公叔簋和芮伯簋

Figure Ⅱ.5.13 The Ruigong Shu *gui* and Ruibo *gui*.

Chapter 5: The Results of Guicheng Archaeology: Social Changes on the Jiaodong Peninsula during the Bronze Age

Li Feng

The Sino-American joint archaeological survey in Guicheng, which lasted for five field seasons over four years (2007–2010), was the largest and longest archaeological field project ever undertaken at Guicheng. Even though the archaeological project is presently still in the survey stage, based on the multifaceted survey we have already obtained a relatively rich pool of information. While the fieldwork was in progress, we also collaborated with scholars from the Yantai Municipal Museum and the Longkou Municipal Museum in an effort to systematically analyze archaeological materials discovered in Guicheng and the surrounding areas before the present survey. On the basis of a comprehensive analysis of the currently available archaeological data, and considering also relevant information from bronze inscriptions and transmitted historical texts, we can now discuss a few key questions in the history and culture of Guicheng. It is hoped that through the discussion we will reach a preliminary but specific understanding of the social changes that occurred in the Jiaodong region during the Bronze Age, laying the foundation for continuing work in this region in the future.

Section 1: Guicheng in the Regional Settlement System

Archaeologically, the Jiaodong region was located on the periphery of ancient bronze culture in China, and our knowledge of the culture and history of this region is still very limited. Before the coming of the Zhou culture, the region witnessed the rise and decline of the Yueshi culture. The sphere of distribution of the Yueshi culture was quite large, stretching from the Jiaodong Peninsula all the way to inland western Shandong; specifically, the Jiaodong region was home to the Zhaogezhuang type, a local branch of the broader Yueshi culture. It is also likely that the Yueshi culture lasted for even longer in the Jiaodong region than in the interior, roughly from 1900 to 1500 BCE (see Part Ⅰ, Chapter 1), and during its last phase the Shang Dynasty (1554–1046 BCE) had already arisen in the Yellow River basin. Although the Yueshi culture had developed advanced agriculture, Yueshi sites are all small villages, and there are no large central settlements. In the Jiaodong region, the largest identified Yueshi site, Zhaogezhuang, has an area of only 40,000 m^2 (Zhongguo shehui kexueyuan kaogu yanjiusuo Shandong dui 1986: 448). Therefore, the consensus among scholars is that Yueshi society was still in the pre-state stage of social development. Compared to the Longshan culture before it, the Yueshi culture was in a stage of decline both in terms of population density and of pottery-making technology (Fang Hu 2007: 194-206; Liu and Chen 2012: 275-276; Shelach-Lavi 2015: 184, 190). Furthermore, some scholars believe the decline of the Yueshi culture owed not a little to a major climate change that happened around 4000 BCE (Fang Hui 2007: 203).

The Zhenzhumen culture arose after the Yueshi culture, dating to a time roughly contemporaneous with the Shang Dynasty to the early Western Zhou in the Yellow River region. Although it "arose," in fact sites where Zhenzhumen cultural elements can be identified are very limited in number. The differences between the Yueshi culture and the Zhenzhumen culture are mainly in pottery typology; in terms of the level of social complexity, the Zhenzhumen culture did not surpass the Yueshi culture. In terms of regional social integration, the former had not even reached the level of the latter.

The appearance of the Zhou culture on the Jiaodong Peninsula was the result of a major incursion from the west to the east, dating approximately to the late phase of the early Western Zhou. Evidence suggests that this grand change in the cultural history of the Jiaodong region was doubtless related to the establishment of the powerful royal state of Western Zhou in the Yellow River region, and in particular to the founding of Zhou regional polities such as Qi, Lu, and Teng in western Shandong, granted by the royal court in Shaanxi. More specifically, this change was brought about through a series of military campaigns organized by the Zhou royal court aiming at the conquest of the Dongyi groups, as reflected in the bronze inscriptions of the Western Zhou period (Li Feng 2006b: 308-314). It is important to recognize that the incursion of the Zhou culture resulted in a major break in the social development of the Jiaodong region, and not a continuation with gradual changes taking place over time (see Part Ⅰ, Chapter 10). The most remarkable archaeological indication of this change was the appearance of large-scale settlements in this period, in a settlement system that was becoming increasingly stratified. The social background for this was that for the first time a "state" power emerged on the Jiaodong peninsula, along with an increase in population and the centralization of the regional society. In general, the incursion of the Zhou culture from the west provided a major driving force for social development in the Jiaodong region during the late Bronze Age.

Lacking a full-coverage systematic surface survey of areas beyond Guicheng, we know few details about the process of stratification of the settlement system in the Jiaodong region. However, based on surveys we have conducted in recent years, in combination with the archaeological data published previously, we can at least offer a preliminary assessment of the macro-structure of the settlement system in the Jiaodong region from the Western Zhou to the Spring and Autumn period, in which the important position of the Guicheng city site can be clearly seen. As far as we can tell at present, there were four central settlements in the Jiaodong region during the late Bronze Age: Dongqucheng in Zhaoyuan, Guicheng in Longkou, Qianheqian in Laiyang, and the Cunliji ancient city site in Penglai. Three of these were mega-settlements with rammed earth wall enclosures (Fig. Ⅰ.0.1).

The Dongqucheng site is located east of Zhaoyuan City, on a rising terrace south of Xiqucheng Village, and separated from the village by a small river. It is located about 22 km east of the districts of Zhaoyuan City, and 45 km northeast of Guicheng. On July 21, 2009, the Guicheng Archaeological Team surveyed this site. Located at the foot of mountain ranges that rise steeply to the south, and overlooking the Laizhou Bay to the northwest, the site is actually located on a transitional belt between the Bohai Sea and the mountain system of the Jiaodong Peninsula, which surrounds it on three sides (Fig. Ⅱ.5.1). The site's protected area measures 950 m from east to west and 200 m from north to south (190,000 m^2). Within this perimeter fragments of Han Dynasty bricks and tiles were found in large numbers along the edges of the terrace, on which the strata of a rammed earth wall are clearly visible. However, the distribution of pottery sherds goes far beyond this protected area. The site was the location of Qucheng County in the Han Dynasty, but the area of distribution of sherds from the preceding Zhou period is also large, stretching from the foot of the mountain to the edge of the village north of the small river. In 1959, a group of eight bronzes was discovered on the edge of the village about 30 m north of the river, including 2 *ding* cauldrons, 2 *gui* tureens, as well as 1 *pan* dish, 1 *pen* basin, 1 *hu* bottle, and 1 *zeng* steamer (Li Buqing, Lin Xianting, and Yang Wenyu 1994: 377-378). Among these, one of the bronze *gui* tureens with three high legs bore the inscription "Qizhong makes (this) treasured *gui* vessel," dating evidently to the early phase of the mid-Western Zhou period. The excavators concluded that the vessels likely came from a tomb of the Spring and Autumn period. However, judging from the pottery sherds we collected (Fig. Ⅱ.5.2), it is likely that the occupation of the site had already begun in the Western Zhou period and extended to the considerably larger area in the early Spring and Autumn period.

The Qianheqian site is located 35 km south of Laiyang City to the south of Mount Lai. Thirty kilometers farther south is the shore of the Yellow Sea. The site is 87 km southeast of Dongqucheng and 95 km south of Guicheng. The size is 300 m from north to south and 250 m from east to west, totaling 75,000 m^2 (Fig. Ⅰ.7.24). In 1974, a group of eight bronzes was excavated at the site, including types such as the *ding* cauldron, *hu* bottle, *yan* steamer, *pan* dish, and *yi* pourer. The *hu* bottle is inscribed: "Jihou makes and casts (this) *hu* vessel, and lets (his) Little Servant use (it) in drawing (water); eternally treasure and use (it)!" (Li Buqing 1983: 7-8). The date of the burial is probably the late Western Zhou period. Nearby, in 1975 the Shandong Provincial Museum excavated four tombs and one chariot-horse burial. A human sacrificial victim was found behind the chariot, indicating the high status of the tomb occupant. In 1981, again at the Qianheqian site, a pottery *he* vessel was unearthed, in a shape that doubtless imitates bronze *he* vessels of the late phase of the mid-Western Zhou period. The pottery *he* has an inscription of eighteen graphs under its rim, clearly in imitation of the calligraphy of bronze inscriptions (Fig. Ⅱ.5.3). The content of the inscription is still debated, but the graphs that can be recognized seem to say: "X Father Yi makes a *he* vessel ...... fish, deer, and turtle." Based on the evidence we have at present, the Qianheqian site on the Jiaodong Peninsula was likely associated with another state, Ji 己 (that is, the state of Ji 曩), which, together with Lai and Qi accompanied the Zhou royal army in campaigns against the Southern Huaiyi (see below). We surveyed this site on August 2, 2005 and found that the terrain in the surrounding area is rather flat with low hills dotting the landscape in the distance, and that the site borders on the Wulong River that flows into the Yellow Sea. The surface distribution of sherds on the site is dense. The sherds mainly belong to the Zhou pottery production tradition, including types such as the *dou* pedestal dish, *gui* tureen, *li* tripod, *guan* jar, and *pen* basin, mixed with sherds belonging to the local pottery tradition, thus yielding a sherd assemblage profile very similar to that of Guicheng (Fig. Ⅰ.7.25). It is said that the Qianheqian site was surrounded by a wall, which is no long present. By whatever measure, the Qianheqian site was the largest and highest ranking settlement in the southern part of the Jiaodong Peninsula during the late Bronze Age.

The Cunliji site is located in the same Huangshui River system as Guicheng, but it lies in the valley of a branch of the Huangshui River that flows through the area of Penglai City. This stream originates north of Mount Ai and its upper reaches run parallel to the main branch of the Huangshui River, separated from it by a mountain range. Its lower reaches then turn west and enter the Huangshui River (Map Ⅰ.7.1).

The Cunliji ancient city site is located on a terrace to the west of Cunliji Township; a 300 m long section of the northern wall of the city is still preserved, but the other three sides of the wall have all been destroyed. The ancient city lies about 600 m from present-day Gucheng Lijia in the west to Guchengdong Village in the east, and 500 m from north to south, totaling about 300,000 m^2 (Fig. Ⅰ.7.20). According to a survey conducted by the Guicheng Archaeological Team on June 14, 2009, rammed earth strata are clearly visible in the surviving section of the northern wall (Fig. Ⅱ.5.4), but very few pottery sherds were found in the city. However, along the two banks of the river that flows along the eastern edge of the city multiple burial grounds were located, stretching more than 5 km from south to north. In 1976, eleven tombs were excavated at Liugezhuang and Xinwangji, accompanying which were also chariot-horse burials dating to the Eastern Zhou period. The tombs yielded multiple bronzes together with two human sacrificial victims (Shandong Yantai diqu wenguanzu 1977: 50-55). In 1986, a large tomb with wooden chambers was excavated at Mazhangjia to the south, yielding bronze bells, chariot fittings and horse harnesses together with large numbers of wooden objects, dating possibly to the late Spring and Autumn to the Warring States period (Lin Xianting 2006: 134-136). Overall, the human occupation of the Cunliji city site might have begun later than that of Guicheng, but it is likely that the two ancient sites co-existed, at least for a period of time.

The cultural contents of the above three central settlements or city sites, as well as those of

Guicheng, by and large belong to the Zhou tradition, although in at least two of the centers, Guicheng and Qianheqian, the local tradition of pottery making evidently co-existed with the Zhou tradition from the west. These four centers together constituted the basic sphere of distribution of the Zhou culture on the Jiaodong Peninsula, and were important points of integration of Bronze Age society on the Jiaodong Peninsula. The centers display a high degree of similarity in terms of cultural profile, and the study of bronze inscriptions in particular suggests that the ancient state that was based at Guicheng might have had an intermarriage relationship with the state of Ji, based at Qianheqian (see below). This implies that the centers were not isolated, but were in close communication with one another. The three centers in the north, Dongqucheng, Guicheng, and Cunliji, being all situated on the north shore of the Jiaodong Peninsula, are in a linear formation from west to east, which shows the direction of movement of the Zhou culture deeper into the Jiaodong Peninsula. The Qianheqian site, on the other hand, located south of the Mount Lai range, represents a frontline base for further Zhou cultural penetration of the southeast corner of the peninsula. Among these centers, Guicheng, with its gigantic city size of 8,000,000 m^2, its superabundant cultural contents, and the social hierarchy evinced by its architectural foundations, deserves the label of a super-megacity site – the center among centers. At the same time, the present evidence also suggests that Guicheng was the central site at which the Zhou culture made its earliest and most concentrated appearance. It was doubtless the cultural center of the Jiaodong region beginning in the Western Zhou.

Numerous secondary or tertiary settlements were distributed around each of the central settlements. Due to the lack of systematic surveys in most of these areas, the particular sub-regional settlement system structure is not clear. However, at least in the Guicheng region, past surveys of the Huangshui River valleys, especially the survey by the Guicheng Archaeological Team in fall 2010 and summer 2011, have enabled us to offer a basic reconstruction of the settlement system in the areas surrounding Guicheng (see Part Ⅰ, Chapter 7) (Map Ⅰ.7.1). According to past surveys, about twenty locations in the Longkou region have yielded cultural remains from the Zhou period (excluding locations within Guicheng) (Table Ⅰ.7.10). This settlement network was deployed mainly along the river valleys running from north of Mount Lai to the east of the mountain. An important location to the north of Guicheng was Zhangzhengjia, where large quantities of pottery have been discovered in recent years, suggesting the existence of a cemetery of considerable scale contemporaneous with Guicheng. To the south of Guicheng, Taishang Lijia and Dongzhoujia were probably locations of a Zhou dynasty settlement. North of Guicheng are located three sites, Tangjia, Xuxiang, and Qianshan, where we have collected Zhou tradition sherds. The sites form a semicircle extending from the west to the main branch of the Huangshui River north of Guicheng. Across the river to the east are the sites of Zhaojiujia, Chengjia, Xizhangjia, and others, where Zhou Dynasty artifacts have been collected in the past. During the last two years of survey, we focused on sites located along the main branch of the Huangshui River, namely Zhuangtou, Jiqian Zhaojia, Dongying Zhoujia, and Lujiagou, which is located to the east of Mount Lai. Most of these sites are situated on terraces in the foothills east of the Huangshui River. The Lujiagou cemetery is located on the eastern bank of the Wangwu Reservoir in the upper reaches of the Huangshui River. These sites appear in a linear formation from south to north, and would have protected Guicheng from the east. Zhuangtou and Lujiagou are sites where important bronze vessels were discovered and have since come to be regarded as the cemeteries of the aristocratic residents of Guicheng (Wang Xiping 1991: 62). More importantly, the Huangshui River valley provides an important channel for transportation and communication. Control of this channel would have enabled the people from Guicheng to reach Laiyang and Laixi in the central and southern parts of the peninsula, or the Yantai region at the eastern tip of the peninsula. This makes the Huangshui River basin centered on Guicheng a frontline base for expansion into the southeastern part of the Jiaodong Peninsula.

More specifically, Guicheng is located in a small basin carved out by the Yaque River, a branch of the Huangshui River, which flows down from the northern foothills of Mount Lai. This location is at the center of the settlement system north of Mount Lai described above. Guicheng is connected to the main valley of the Huangshui River through the Yaque River valley to the northeast and the gap near Chegezhuang in the southeast. To the west, the way is relatively open to the plains around present-day Longkou City. This location can rely on Mount Lai for defense, and also provide Guicheng effective control of routes to the eastern peninsula through the valleys of the Huangshui River and its branches. Considering the Cunliji city site in light of Guicheng, it is not difficult to see that it resulted from further expansion of the Guicheng settlement system into the eastern lands of the peninsula through a branch of the Huangshui River that flows along the north side of Mount Zhuaji. Only after in-depth research into the regional settlement systems can we truly understand the geopolitical structure that supported and sustained the existence of the Guicheng metropolis.

Section 2: The Jiaodong Peninsula and the State of Lai in Bronze Inscriptions and Historical Texts

Among the contemporaneous bronze inscriptions of the Zhou Dynasty, there are quite a few that relate to the Jiaodong Peninsula in eastern Shandong, and the content of one of these might have even been closely connected to the Guicheng region. In the fifth year of the Xuanhe reign period (1123) of the Northern Song Dynasty, residents of Linzi County of Qingzhou Prefecture in western Shandong excavated multiple bronze bells at a locale within the ancient city of the state of Qi. These bronzes, cast by a person named Shu Yi, were subsequently recorded by Song scholars in catalogues such as the *Bogu tulu* (ca. 1110), *Xiaotang jigu lu* (ca. 1176), and *Lidai zhongding mingwen kuanzhi fatie* (1144).

They include a *bo* bell bearing a complete inscription, and thirteen *zhong* bells that each had a partial inscription (Xue Shanggong: 8.58-75; *Bogu tulu*: 22.5-16). According to an analysis by Chen Mengjia, the original set should have included three subsets of bells totaling fifty-one (or possibly forty-eight) objects that carried the same inscription as on the Shu Yi *bo* in 492 characters, doubtless ranking as the longest inscriptions on bells from the Zhou Dynasty (Chen Mengjia 1998: 8-9). Unfortunately, the bells were subsequently lost in wars, but their inscriptions were passed down. They record an appointment ceremony performed for the commander Shu Yi by Duke Ling of Qi (581-554 BCE), and are stylistically very similar to appointment inscriptions of the Western Zhou period. The most important part in the Shu Yi *bo* inscription says:

> The Duke said: "Yi! You respectfully upheld my order, you chest-carried (the mission) of the ducal house, you firmly put my armies in action, and you were nimble in military affairs. I award you the capital of Lai, XX, the counties of which are three hundred. I command you to take charge of my pottery and iron working labors in Lai, numbering four thousand, who will be your close subordinates……I award you horses, chariots, and weapons, and three hundred fifty households of Lai servants. You use (them) to assist you in military deeds.

The key state name in the inscription, Li 釐, is read Lai 莱, which is common knowledge among paleographers. Pre-Qin texts also have examples of the two being used interchangeably (Chen Pan 1969: 388-389). The Shu Yi inscription clearly gives 𨚕𠜱 as the name of the capital of the state of Lai, but the two characters cannot be deciphered at present. The bells were cast after Lai was conquered by the state of Qi in 567 BCE. Guo Moruo, based on a reconstruction of the calendar, has suggested that the bells were cast in the second year (565 BCE) after the conquest (Guo Moruo 1958: 202). The inscription records that Duke Ling of Qi awarded the state capital and three hundred counties previously under its control to Shu Yi, and ordered him to take charge of "pottery and iron-making labors" in Lai, usually understood to mean labor in certain types of production. The "counties" mentioned here in Lai were probably different from the counties in other states, and they were probably residential units similar in size to villages. On the other hand, Shu Yi was himself given slaves from Lai numbering 350 households, and he cast this set of bells to commemorate the awards. Another inscribed bronze from the state of Qi, the Geng *hu* (JC: 9733), mentions in a more specific way that during the conquest campaign against the capital of Lai, Geng first broke into the city while another official, Cuizi, was beating the drum. Afterwards, Geng offered the heads he cut off to the temple of the duke of Qi. These long inscriptions suggest that the conquest of Lai was a landmark event in the history of the state of Qi during the Spring and Autumn period. The conquest enabled Qi to expand its territory from western Shandong to eastern Shandong, and contributed to the rise of Qi hegemony in eastern China. In other words, Qi had transformed itself into a "territorial state" by victimizing eastern states like Lai.

Earlier in the contemporaneous Western Zhou sources we see no record of a contest between the state of Qi and the state of Lai. Instead, the two states, located in western and eastern Shandong respectively, were both allies of the Zhou, and maintained a close relationship with the Western Zhou state. The state of Lai is mentioned first in the inscription of a mid-Western Zhou bronze, the Shi Mi *gui*, discovered in Ankang County in Shaanxi in 1986 (Zhang Maoruo 1989, 64-71):

> It was the eleventh month, the king commanded Shi Su and Shi Mi: "Campaign to the east! It is the time when the Southern Yi, Luhu, together with the Jiyi, Zhouyi, are insurgent and incessant; they broadly attacked the eastern states. The Qi Army's lineage foot soldiers and charioteers captured (their) *kuan*-captains of Bi." Shi Su led the charioteers of the Qi Army … to attack Changbi; Shi Mifu led the lineage soldiers, Laibo, X 焚, X 屇, and Zhou to attack Changbi, capturing one hundred people. (Shi Mi) extols the beneficence of the Son of Heaven, herewith making for my cultured deceased father, Yibo, (this) sacrificial *gui* vessel; May (my) sons' sons and grandsons' grandsons eternally treasure and use it!

There seems little doubt that this bronze was cast in the Zhou royal domain in Shaanxi, and its inscription describes a campaign dispatched by the Zhou king against a number of groups of the Southern Yi and led by Shi Su and Shi Mi. Shi Su is elsewhere referred to as "Shi Sufu" or "Bo Sufu" in inscriptions such as the Shi Chen *ding* and Yong *yu*, cast around the time of King Gong, which suggests he was a prominent administrative official in the Zhou royal domain during the reigns of King Gong and King Yi in the mid-Western Zhou. Shi Mi is called "Mishu" in the inscription of the Hu *gui*, which describes his role as *guarantor* (a high official who guided the candidate into the courtyard and introduced him to the Zhou king) in the appointment ceremony taking place in the Zhou court (Li Feng 2008: 107-111, 128). The important thing to note is that they were commanders sent by the Zhou king to lead the campaign against the Southern Yi. Under the command of Shi Mi was a certain Libo, the same as Laibo, the ruler of the state of Lai. A very similar scenario involving the state of Lai is also mentioned in a late Western Zhou bronze, the Shi Yuan *gui* (JC: 4313) (Fig. Ⅱ.5.5):

> The king said as such: "Shi Yuan, Ho! The Huaiyi have long been our obscure tributary subjects. Now, they force their people in indolence (in matters of sending in tributes), rebel against their officials, and would not follow our eastern states. Now, I initiate by commanding you to lead the Qi Army, [that of] Ji, Lai, X 焚, X 屍, as well as the Tiger Servants to campaign against the Huaiyi. Quickly cut off the rebel chiefs of their polities—named Ran, X 莽, Ling, and Da!" Shi Yuan was cautious and did not fail [in his mission]; morning and night he was faithful to his military duty. It was good that he has had accomplishments, cutting off heads and taking

prisoners. [His] fearless foot-soldiers and charioteers wounded and captured men, women, sheep, and cows, [and they] captured auspicious metal. Now, I have no leisure to go there [again]. I herewith make [for] my son, Lie, [this] sacrificial *gui* vessel. May [my] sons' sons and grandsons' grandsons for ten thousand years eternally treasure and use [it] in offering!

Comparing the two inscriptions, we know that the "Laibo, X 焚, X 眉" in the Shi Mi *gui* are the same as the three states, "Lai, X 焚, X 尿 ," mentioned in the Shi Yuan *gui*. The three, all small states in Shandong, together with the other two states, Qi and Ji, participated in the campaigns against the Southern Yi and the Huaiyi. Here, the dates of the two vessels are important: because the Shi Yuan *gui* was cast by the same person who cast the Yun *pan* (which mentions a royal scribe named Shi Yu, also mentioned in the Forty-second Year Lai *ding*), there seems little doubt that they are from the reign of King Xuan during the late Western Zhou (Li Feng 2006a: 70-72). In other words, they were cast one hundred years after the Shi Mi *gui* was cast around the time of King Gong in the mid-Western Zhou. Furthermore, the difference between the two graphs, 眉 and 尿 , may well reflect the difference in date. It is thus very likely that over the course of one hundred or so years, the state of Lai continued to be active in the eastern periphery as an important ally of the Western Zhou. What is even more noteworthy is that the wars in which Lai took part were in the Huai River region in the south, and not against Lai's neighbors in eastern Shandong. This further suggests a close relationship between the state of Lai and the Western Zhou Dynasty.

This perspective that we gain from the bronze inscriptions about the relationship between the state of Lai and the Western Zhou Dynasty is in sharp contrast to that of the later texts. For instance, the "Genealogical Account of the Grand Duke of Qi" in the *Shiji* says that when the Grand Duke was first established in Qi, because "Yingqiu (Qi's capital) was a neighbor of Lai," therefore the ruler of Lai contested with him for the control of Yingqiu. This statement has had a major impact on later generations of scholars. However, considering the small scale and characteristics of the regional states in the early Western Zhou, together with the origin and the complex process through which the narrative in the *Shiji* was formed, the historicity of this statement is in serious doubt. First, the statement was made in ignorance of the essential features of the "settlement state" in ancient China (Li Feng 2008: 296-298). Second, the statement very likely projects the hostile relationship between Qi and Lai in the Spring and Autumn period back into early Western Zhou times, even though the animosity between the two states was a product of the transition from "settlement states" to the large "territorial states" that happened much later. Nevertheless, the view transmitted by the *Shiji* about Lai's indigenous origin among the Dongyi provides meaningful grounds for considering the political relationship between the states or groups of the Jiaodong Peninsula and the Western Zhou state.

The earliest statement in the texts concerning the geographical location of Lai was Du Yu's (222-285) commentary on the *Zuozhuan*, stating that the "State of Lai was in Huangxian (county) of

Donglai (Commandery)." The "Geography" chapter of the *Hanshu* also lists "Donglai Commendery," headquartered in Huangxian, which is present-day Longkou. The early Tang Dynasty scholar Yan Shigu (581-645) notes that this was the location of the ancient state of Lai. This view was followed by all pre-modern scholars. Although it does not identify the capital of Lai with a specific locale, there does not seem to be any doubt that Lai was in the territory of Huangxian. Based on a preliminary survey of the Guicheng city site in the 1970s, some scholars had already linked the capital of the state of Lai with Guicheng (Li Buqing and Lin Xianting 1991: 918; Wang Xiping 1991: 64). Some scholars also proposed that Lai was first located in an area between Changyi and Linqu in the west, and that Lai thereafter moved to Huangxian (Chen Pan 1969: 391-392). However, this view took the Han sources at face value, and was based mainly on inference and not on evidence. Moreover, this view was misled by the *Shiji* statement that "Yingqiu was a neighbor of Lai." This led scholars to think that Lai must have been located close to Qi, further inferring the geographic location of Lai based on this point. This mistake was a consequence of the indiscriminate use of sources without taking into consideration their dates and historical value.

An important source for the geography of early Lai is a *din*g cauldron, the Laibo *ding* 稜伯鼎 (JC: 2044), possibly cast by the ruler of the state of Lai (Fig. Ⅱ.5.6). The vessel has been lost, though rubbings of the inscription have been transmitted, on which basis the *Yin Zhou jinwen jicheng* dates it to the mid-Western Zhou. The structure of the left half of the character 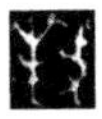 looks like the character *hua* 華, so in the past some scholars considered the character to have had a component *hua* 華, and to have been pronounced *hu* 瓠 (Wang Xiantang 1983: 142-145). We can observe that in the character  (*li* 釐) on the Ban *gui* 班簋 vessel (JC: 4341) the upper left part of the character *li* 釐 can indeed be written the same way, with two straight strokes. The two top strokes of  turning to two sides are similar to that of the character  (*li* 釐) on the Er *ding* 鼎 (JC: 2755), or the character  (*li* 釐) on the Xiao Ke *ding* 小克鼎 (JC: 2796). Therefore, we think that it is acceptable to read the character  as *li* 釐, which is indeed *lai* 萊, the latter being the name of the state in the transmitted texts. It follows then that there was no such state as Hu 瓠. The Laibo *ding* was first registered in the *Weihuage jigulu bawei*, compiled by Ke Changji in 1916 (Ke Changji 1935a: 2.46), and then appeared in *Jinwen fenyu bian*, compiled in 1930 by the same author, who noted that the bronze was unearthed in "Laiyin of Huangxian" (Ke Changji 1935b: 9.15). The term "Laiyin" refers to the area north of Mount Lai where Guicheng is located (there is also a Laiyin River, a tributary of the Yaque River). However, elsewhere Ke also attributed two other bronzes, the Yu 𩰫 *ding* 鼎 (JC: 2721) and Yu *yan* 遹甗 (JC: 948) (wrongly rendered by Ke as 遹鼎 and 遹甗), to "Laiyin of Huangxian," but we know that these bronzes were discovered in the Lujiagou cemetery to the east of Mount Lai in 1896. This suggests that Ke Changji, who resided in the provincial capital Ji'nan, did not really know the precise find places of the bronzes in Huangxian that he recorded. For the same reason, some scholars considered the Laibo *ding* to have been unearthed at Lujiagou, which is also not far from Guicheng (see Part Ⅱ, Chapter 4). The basis for this latter view is the record in the *Huangxian Gazetteer* compiled by Wang Daoxin in 1934 during the Republic period (Wang Daoxin 1934: 12; Lin Xianting 2006; 133).[1] Wang Daoxin was a native scholar of Huangxian, and his words should be more reliable than that of Ke Changji, who lived far away in Ji'nan. Another important bronze is the Lü *ding* 旅鼎 (JC: 2728) (Fig. Ⅱ.5.8), also registered in Ke Changji's *Weihuage jigulu bawei*, which does not indicate its provenance (Ke Changji 1935a: 1.29). However, the author of the *Shandong jinwen jicun* writes that the bronze was unearthed together with the Yu *ding* and Yu *yan* in "Laiyin of Huangxian" in 1896 (Zeng Yigong 1940: 11-13). The Lü *ding* mentions "The year the Duke Grand Protector came to attack the rebellious Yi people." We know that the Duke Grand Protector was the Duke of Shao, Shi, who lived no later than the early phase of King Kang's reign, to which the bronze may be dated. The statement, "came to attack the rebellious Yi people" apparently speaks from the standpoint of the local states or lineages in Shandong, indicating the bronze was likely produced locally. The  emblem at the end of the inscription used to be read as *lai* 來 by the paleographer Tang Lan (Tang Lan 1995: 242). Some other scholars have suggested therefore that  referred to the state of Lai 萊 (Wang Xiping 1984: 77-79). However, this mark does not appear on other bronzes, and its association with the state of Lai still awaits conclusive confirmation.

Presented above is a basic assessment of the political relationships surrounding the state of Lai and its geographical reconfiguration during the Western Zhou. With regard to the later history of Lai, pre-Qin texts, including the *Spring and Autumn Annals* and the *Zuozhuan*, offer much better contextualized records. The historical value of these records is doubtless higher than that of the *Shiji* and other Han Dynasty sources. They allow us to reconstruct at least a general outline of the history of Lai in the century before its conquest by Qi in 567 BCE. The *Spring and Autumn Annals* reports that in 602 BCE, the rulers of the states of Qi and Lu together led a campaign against Lai. The *Zuozhuan* further explains that this was planned by Qi. Two years later in 600 BCE, the ruler of Qi attacked Lai again, indicating that Lai was the main enemy of Qi. In 573 BCE, Duke Ling of Qi eliminated the prominent Guo lineage, plotting the assassination of the leader of the lineage, Guo Sheng, at court. Another leader of the lineage, Guo Ruo, escaped to the state of Lu, and Wang Jiao,

---

1 Wang Daoxin's *Huangxian zhi gao* says: "Its inscription reads: 'Laibo makes (this) traveling *ding* vessel.' Ten bronzes were unearthed in the fields of Lujiagou southeast of the county seat (of Huangxian) in the twenty-second year of the Guangxu Era (1896). Three bells, uninscribed, two *ding* cauldrons, one of which is broken. One *hu* bottle, broken, one *pan* basin which has no inscription. One *yan* steamer, one *he* vessel, and one *zhi* cup, all have inscriptions, and all entered the collection of Ding Gangfu (Ding Shuzhen)." The *Huangxian zhi gao* was compiled a few years later than the *Jinwen fenyu bian*. Records on the Lujiagou bronzes in the two books were produced more than thirty years after the discovery, so they cannot be treated as original on-site records.

a trusted subordinate of the lineage, fled to Lai and became an important advisor to its ruler. This further escalated the hostility between Qi and Lai. In 572 BCE, the Qi people launched another major attack on Lai, but Lai was able to bribe the Susha lineage in Qi with 100 horses and 100 cattle, thus leading the Qi army to withdraw without a victory. The relationship between Qi and Lai temporarily improved. However, when Qi summoned the Lai ruler to an interstate meeting, he refused to come, and the animosity between the two states was renewed. Therefore, the ruler of Qi dispatched the general Yan Ruo to construct a new city in Dongyang in present-day Linqu, in order to pose a strategic threat to Lai, in the hope that Lai would eventually be subjugated. After many years of effort, in 567 BCE Qi finally conquered Lai. This was a major battle that lasted for seven months, as narrated in the *Zuozhuan*:

> In the eleventh month, the Ruler of Qi vanquished Lai, which had relied on scheming. At this time, Zi Guo of Zheng officially visited [Lu]. In the fourth month, Yan Ruo constructed a city in Dongyang, and moved on from there to surround Lai. On day *jiayin*, (they) mounded earth up against the round city wall, reaching the battlements, until the month (in spring) when Duke Huan of Ji died. On day *yiwei*, Wang Jiao led the Lai Army, Zhengyuzi, and the people of Tang, to attack the Qi Army but was greatly defeated. On day *dingwei*, [the Qi Army] entered Lai, and Duke Gong of Lai, Furuo, fled to Tang. Zhengyuzi and Wang Jiao fled to Jü, but the people of Jü killed them. In the fourth month, Chen Wuyu offered the sacrificial vessels of Lai to Duke Xiang [of Qi], and Yan Ruo moved on to surround Tang. In the eleventh month, on day *bingchen*, [the Qi Army] conquered it and moved the remaining Lai people to Ni. Gao Hou and Cui Zhu settled the matter of their fields.

Noteworthy in the *Zuozhuan* is the mention of a "round city wall," which likely refers to a city with a circular layout,[1] in contrast with the square or rectangular city walls we normally see in the Central Plain. Possibly because the city wall of Lai's capital was too thick, the Qi Army was unable to break through it, so they massed earth to reach the parapets in order to enter the city. The officer Cui Zhu mentioned above is none other than the Cuizi mentioned in the Geng *hu* inscription discussed above, who beat the drum urging the soldiers to break into the city. Tang, the place to which Duke Gong of Lai, Furou, fled, was in present-day Pingdu county, and Ni, to which the remnants of the

---

1 The line "(they) mounded earth against the round city wall, reaching the battlements" was traditionally understood to be "talking about piling up earth mounds on the four sides of the Lai city" (Yang Bojun 1990: 947). However, the imagined method of mounting up earth on the four sides to reach the battlements hardly makes any sense from a tactical viewpoint. In actual battle, if the invading army could break through the enemy defenses on the wall at one point, the whole city would fall, so the method of piling earth on four sides is simply not feasible in terms of the time and labor it would demand. It is very likely that the Classicists of the Han Dynasty misinterpreted this line because they didn't know the capital city of Lai was "circular."

Lai people were relocated, is probably in the Tengxian area in western Shandong. In 500 BCE, Duke Ding of Lu was on his way to attend the interstate meeting between Qi and Lu in the company of Confucius, the so-called "Meeting of Jiagu." Perhaps, because Ni was close to Lu, the Lai people in Ni were dispatched by Qi to kidnap the Lu ruler, but they were berated by Confucius who forced them to give up. In fact, the above historical development reflects quite well the natural process of Qi's transformation into a "territorial state" through expansion into eastern Shandong and the eventual annexation of the state of Lai.

With regard to the location of Lai's capital, in full consideration of the information from various sources, we think that the best conclusion we can draw at present is to relate it to Guicheng, based on the following reasons: First, dowry bronzes cast by "Jibo Renfu" 曩伯庭父 of the state of Ji 己 (曩)have been found at Guicheng (Part Ⅱ, Chapter 2), suggesting that Guicheng is not the capital of Ji. Similarly, dowry vessels cast by the ruler of Lai were found in Rizhao to the south, possibly in the territory of the state of Jü (see below). For this reason, Guicheng should be the capital of another major state on the Jiaodong Peninsula that had a marriage relationship with the above two states. Second, although the provenance of the Laibo *ding* and Lü *ding* was only confirmed thirty years after their discovery, and there is still some uncertainty as to the specific location of the discovery, there can be no doubt that they were found in the territory of Huangxian. Third, this agrees with the information from ancient geographical works that the state of Lai was located in Huangxian. It should be noted that early geographical works, especially the "Geography" chapter of the *Hanshu,* offer verifiable information, particularly because the names of many commanderies and counties were derived directly from those of the pre-Qin states or lineages in the same region. The validity of this information in general has been well demonstrated by archaeological discoveries during the past thirty years (Li Feng 2006b: 20-22). Fourth, in view of the mentions of Lai in the Shi Mi *gui*, Shi Yuan *gui*, and the Shu Yi bells, as well as information about it in the *Spring and Autumn Annals* and the *Zuozhuan*, there can be no doubt that Lai was a powerful state on the Jiaodong Peninsula. The immense size of Guicheng and its central position in the settlement network of the Jiaodong region match this power well. In Huangxian (Longkou) and its surrounding regions, there is no other city site of comparable size and date. The second largest city in the region, the Cunliji city site, is only one twenty-sixth the size of Guicheng. The special status of Guicheng in the settlement system revealed by archaeological survey, corresponds well with the political status of the state of Lai. Lastly, some details of the conquest campaign against the capital of Lai in the *Zuozhuan* seem to match the physical features of Guicheng, which has a circular outer city wall that was remarkably thick. Therefore, although we still do not have direct proof, such as inscriptions excavated at Guicheng that speak about the state of Lai, based on current evidence, Guicheng is the best candidate for the Lai capital, at least among all the possible candidates from the late Western Zhou to the early Spring and Autumn period. It is also very likely the site of 䜌劇 mentioned in the Shu Yi bells.

Section 3: The Date and Formation History of Guicheng: Archaeological Approaches

How should we approach the study of the date and formation history of Guicheng? In archaeology, site formation processes have been an important area of specialized studies, which form what can be called middle-range theory in archaeology (Raab and Goodyear 1984: 255-268; Schiffer 1983: 675-706; 1987). The study of site formation processes provides an effective link between general anthropological theory and the analysis of specific cultural remains in archaeology. An important point in the study of site formation processes is a differentiation of cultural processes from natural processes, which offers a gateway to effective analysis of the impact of human behaviors vs. natural forces in the process of forming, using, and abandoning an archaeological site. It also enables the study of patterns of human behavior through the classification of archaeological remains. The Guicheng project is still in the survey stage, and there are many questions that await answers on the basis of multidisciplinary research in the future. However, based on the information we have obtained from current surveys and test excavation, and also taking into consideration the results of scientific laboratory analysis and information in inscriptions, at present we can construct an outline of the process of human occupation as well as the formation and development of the Guicheng city site. In other words, the purpose of this section is to construct a framework of the archaeological history of Guicheng through an analysis of the archaeological data.

In order to reconstruct the formation process and history of Guicheng, we first of all need a reliable chronological reference. Ideally, this reference is provided by a chronological sequence of the indigenous cultures of the Jiaodong Peninsula within which the remains and artifacts from Guicheng can be placed. Unfortunately, this is impossible at present due to a lack of systematic data representing the indigenous cultures and the weakness of relevant studies. Another method is to compare the vessel types associated with the Zhou tradition in Guicheng with pottery types at the centers of Zhou culture in the Central Plain or even in the Wei River valley, to establish the relative date of Guicheng through inference. However, this latter method involves a number of uncertainties and possible distortions due to the complex sources of the Zhou culture itself and the regional characteristics of pottery in this complex Zhou cultural system. Nevertheless, the main trends of changes in pottery from the Western Zhou to the Eastern Zhou in this wide cultural system from the Yellow River region to the Shandong Peninsula were in fact relatively consistent, and this provides a foundation for cross-regional comparisons. Furthermore, past scholars have already conducted some helpful analyses in this regard which can be put to good use (Cui Lequan 1992: 73-97; Wang Qing 2002). In order to preclude possible distortion, we suggest two base points in the analysis of pottery types from Guicheng: first, we should conduct focused analysis of representative stratigraphic units, examining the cultural feature of each unit as a whole but not of individual vessel types; second, we should conduct a focused analysis of pottery types that were unearthed together with bronze vessels to establish standards for dating, since the uniformity of bronzes across large regions was much higher than that of pottery.

In the test excavation at Guicheng, we identified two representative units, H20 and H3 (see Part Ⅰ, Chapter 5). H20 is located in the lowest stratum of Trench 2 and is the earliest stratigraphic unit found in the excavation; H3 is located in the uppermost stratum of Trench 1, and is the latest unit found. The difference between the sherd assemblages from the two units is very clear. Sherds from H20 are decorated with fine to medium cord impressions; the tracks of the cords are neat and the ridges between tracks are high and sharp. Particularly in the lower stratum of H20, the cord decorations are mostly very fine, and there is no appearance of coarse cord marks. In contrast, there are many sherds from H3 that have wide cord impressions; the impressions are shallow and the tracks are scattered. In addition, impressions that look like discontinuous tracks of wheat-grains are found on many sherds from H3 (Fig. Ⅱ.5.7). Based on this general trend in cord decorations, we can be confident that the assemblage from H20 belongs to the Western Zhou period, while that from H3 belongs to the Eastern Zhou period, but more specific dating must rely on pottery typology.

In terms of pottery typology, the A1 type *gui* tureen (e.g. H20：1) is typical of the *gui* in the Zhou culture during the early Western Zhou (Fig. Ⅰ.5.57). Similar pieces have been excavated at Wucun in Guangrao and Xi'an in Jiaoxian in the past (Shandong sheng wenwu kaogu yanjiusuo 1989: 61-123; Shandong sheng Changwei diqu wenwuzu 1977: 68), doubtless representing the earliest style of *gui* in the Jiaodong Region. However, the *gui* from H20 has already developed a long rim that turns sharply outwards, its belly has become shallow and open, and the cord impressions on the upper body have been erased, making it distinct from the deep-bellied *gui* that the Zhou inherited from the Shang culture at the beginning of the Western Zhou. This style of *gui* was placed in Period Ⅱ in the new chronology of the Zhangjiapo cemetery; for instance, objects M385：5 and M321：2 (Zhongguo shehui kexueyuan kaogu yanjiusuo 1999: 354), dated to the late phase of the early Western Zhou to the early phase of the mid-Western Zhou. The A1 *dou* pedestal dish from Guicheng (e.g. H20：16-17) is a transitional style between the strong and straight-based *dou* of the early Western Zhou and the strong-based *dou* with a ridge on its base that was popular during the mid-Western Zhou; for instance M702：1 and M223：1-2 from Zhangjiapo. In particular, the three pocket-footed A1 *li* tripods, especially H20：13 and H20：15, are typical of the so-called "breast-shaped pocket-foot *li*," which is rarely found in regions outside of Shaanxi, where it is dated to the early Western Zhou. Overall, these objects form a strong basis for dating the assemblage from H20 to the late phase of the early Western Zhou (see Part Ⅰ, Chapter 10).

In H3, there are a number of C3 style *dou* pedestal dishes (H3①：17) (Fig. Ⅰ.5.11) with shallow and open plates. Similar *dou* pedestal dishes were also found in tombs 1 and 2 at Lüjiabu in Qixia, which could be dated by the style of the pottery and bronzes to the middle to late Spring and Autumn period (M2 is slightly later than M1) (Qixia xian wenwu guanlisuo 1988: 778-783). The giant D3 type *li* tripod from Guicheng (H3① : 1) shows clear influences from the local pottery-making tradition, but overall it retains the features of *li* tripods in the Zhou culture. Although undecorated, its profile seems close to that of a *li* (M202 : 6) from tomb group A in the city site of Qufu in the state of Lu, or of a *li* (M113 : 1 or M30 : 1) from Ningjiabu in Zhangqiu. The latter specimens are considered to have belonged to the mid-Spring and Autumn period (Shandong sheng wenwu kaogu yanjiusuo et al 1982: 95; Wang Qing 2002; 44). The vessel lid (H3② : 4) is also similar to one found in tomb no. 202 in the city site of Lu. Overall, due to the lack of very late vessel types in H3, we believe that the assemblage from H3 can be dated to the mid-Spring and Autumn period.

The above typological analysis suggests that there is a gap of at least 300 years between the two units H20 and H3. Using the two units as points of reference, we divided the excavated units into three stages: Stage I includes H20; Stage Ⅱ includes H18 and H19; and Stage Ⅲ includes H3, H2, H4, H8, and H9 (see Part Ⅰ, Chapter 10). Furthermore, this chronological order is corroborated by ^{14}C dating: H20=1090 (61.1%) 1000 BCE; H3=825 (68.2%) 795 BCE. However, the ^{14}C data from Guicheng seem systematically earlier than the historical dates we suggested for the excavated units (Appendix 1), and the relevant figures still need further verification by future excavation. One possible explanation is that the carbon samples from Guicheng originated in construction materials, such as wooden pillars or grass on the roof. If so, the ^{14}C figures may only reflect the dates of their acquisition, but not the dates of their burial in the pits.

Besides pottery typology and ^{14}C dating, there is another pool of information that we can draw on in considering the formation history of Guicheng; that is, bronzes from Guicheng and its surroundings. In this regard, the first point we need to discuss is the date of the Qi *zun* and Qi *you* vessels, the two famous bronzes found on the shore of the water reservoir near Xiaoliuzhuang to the south of Caojia Village within Guicheng in 1969 (Part Ⅱ, Chapter 2) (Fig. Ⅱ.2.6). In the past, Tang Lan had dated all inscriptions that mention a "southern campaign" to the reign of King Zhao, resulting in some major problems in bronze studies (Tang Lan 1995: 236-333). Interestingly, the two bronzes are almost identical to two pieces from the tomb in Jiqian Zhaojia unearthed in 2004, which yielded more types and vessels typical of the early phase of the mid-Western Zhou period (Figs. Ⅱ.3.15-Ⅱ.3.19). The Yu *ding* and Yu *yan* from Lujiagou found in 1896 mention wars against the Huaiyi and belong to the Shi Yongfu group of bronzes (also including the Zi *you*, Jian *zun*, Lu *zun*, Lu *you*, Bo Yongfu *pan*, etc.), which are dated to the reign of King Mu. The Yu *ding* is identical to the *ding* from Jiqian Zhaojia. In addition, the *hu* vessels among the eight bronzes from Caojia Village found in 1965 are very similar to the transmitted Lüxing *hu* (JC: 9689). This vessel belongs to the Bo Maofu group of bronzes (which also includes the Shao *zun*, Shao *you*, and Xiaochen Lai *gui*, etc.), dated to the time from the reign of King Zhao to the early reign of King Mu. The two *ding* vessels from Caojia are also similar to the Yu *ding* discussed above. Therefore, it is evident that the bronzes from Caojia Village were buried in the early phase of the mid-Western Zhou (Fig. Ⅱ.2.3). The *gui* vessel with a square base found in a tomb in Zhuangtou in 1980 is inscribed "Ruibo" and bears the great-bird motif that is typical of King Mu's reign. Other bronzes from the same tomb are consistent with this period (Wang Xiping 1986: 69-72). It is also worth noting that the *gui* vessel with a long inscription from Haixujia Village to the west of Guicheng found in 1983 also belongs to the mid-Western Zhou period (Ma Zhimin 2004: 79-80).

It is noteworthy that the groups of bronzes from Guicheng and the surrounding regions are very close to each other in time, and altogether make up a large proportion of the locally discovered bronzes. This suggests that the early phase of the mid-Western Zhou, paralleling the reign of King Mu in Zhou royal history, was doubtless the climax of elite activity in the Guicheng region. At present, very few early Western Zhou bronzes have been found in the Guicheng region. A bronze *gui* in the collection of the Longkou Municipal Museum has coiled dragon patterns on its belly and is typical of early Western Zhou design. Another bronze *ding* with a divided crotch from Hanluan Village of Lutou Township found in 1964 is inscribed "Inspector of X" (Fig. Ⅱ.2.7), and also dates to the early Western Zhou (Li Buqing, Lin Xianting 1991b: 84-85). This bronze is almost the same as the Lü *ding* (JC: 2728) discussed above, and should not be dated later than the reign of King Kang. However, because these two bronzes were isolated finds, whether they were buried together with later bronzes or were buried in the period in which they were cast is not clear. Nevertheless, the inscriptions of the X-Jian (Inspector) *ding* and the Lü *ding* reflect "local" historical contexts (particularly as the Lü *ding* mentions: "In the year that the Duke Grand Protector came to attack the rebellious Yi"). Therefore, they were likely manufactured locally, and their inscriptions indicate that the local states or lineages had already established close political relations with the Western Zhou state during the late phase of the early Western Zhou. Later bronzes from the Guicheng region include a group of bronzes from Dongjia Village found in 1969 (Fig. Ⅱ.2.4) and an earlier a group of bronzes from Nanbu Village found in 1951, known as the "Ji bronzes from Huangxian" (Fig. Ⅱ.2.5). They can be dated to the late Western Zhou and the early Spring and Autumn period, respectively.

On the basis of a comprehensive analysis of the above information, we can now offer a sketch of the formation process as well as the occupational history of the Guicheng city site. In the late phase of the early Western Zhou, following the incursion into the Jiaodong region by the Zhou culture, the settlement core of Guicheng was formed. This core was located on a small terrace between the two tributaries of the Yaque River, flowing north from Mount Lai. This was an ideal location for settlement, protected not only by the rivers but also by the foothills of Mount Lai to the south and by the peaks of Mount Fenghuang to the north. The terrace is slightly higher in the south and lower in the north, with abundant water resources provided by the surrounding rivers and lakes. Today, even though the river to the west of the terrace is dry, there are still nearly ten such lakes or ponds of various sizes within the territory of Guicheng. One can only imagine the abundance of water in the Guicheng region in the first millennium BCE. The appearance of this central settlement was undoubtedly related to the expansion of the Zhou culture into the Jiaodong Peninsula, indicated by a series of wars recorded in the inscriptions conducted by the Western Zhou state against the so-called Dongyi people. Because the earliest unit that we excavated, H20, intrudes into the foundation of the inner city wall, we know that the construction of the inner city of Guicheng took place during this period of expansion of Guicheng. Our surveys also uncovered evidence of repairs, which indicates that in the hundreds of years after its initial construction, the inner city was flooded multiple times. This point needs clarification by future archaeological work.

Soon after the construction of the inner city wall in the mid-Western Zhou period, Guicheng entered a period of high intensity elite activity. In this period, Guicheng was possibly still situated on the eastern frontline of the Zhou culture, but obviously it had become the center of a network that connected the sites and cemeteries in the eastern Jiaodong Peninsula. On the whole, the area of the site was not very large, still being limited by the two tributaries of the Yaque River, and the area surrounded by the inner city wall was smaller than the capital city of the state of Yan established in the north by the Zhou court. However, based on the distribution of pottery sherds, the site certainly extended beyond the inner city, and the total area is estimated at 4-5 km^2, mainly located in the western half of the present extent of Guicheng. The results of our full-coverage surface survey suggest that Guicheng expanded eastwards during the Eastern Zhou period, and it is very likely that the outer wall of Guicheng was constructed during this period. The outer wall continues for more than 8.15 km, running along the mountain ridge to form an oval shape and protect Guicheng from the east, west, and north. The construction of this wall was a very large project. On the one hand, it reflects the increase in population and the growth of Guicheng's economic power; on the other hand, it reflects the intensification of political and military conflict on the Jiaodong Peninsula. It should also be noted that the south side of Guicheng was not surrounded by the wall but was open to the main peaks of Mount Lai, in order to ensure that enough water resources were available to Guicheng and that the city contained the largest possible space for activity. Our surface survey detected a clear scarcity of sherds in the southern part of Guicheng, indicating that human occupational activities were concentrated in the north, while the large space in the south, particularly the hill slopes along the upper reaches of the tributaries of the Yaque River, probably providing the residents of Guicheng with ideal locations for burial and for elite resort activities.

However, given our current data, we must still make certain key assumptions in order to discuss the historical development of Guicheng during the long Eastern Zhou period. Unit H3, the latest unit in our test excavation, can be dated to the mid-Spring and Autumn period, but during our surface survey we recovered sherds that are clearly later than this date (Fig. Ⅱ.5.9). They are apparently different from the sherds from H3. For instance, the B2 style *dou* pedestal dish collected near point 10-Y9 is very similar to *dou* pedestal dishes from the large tomb at Liugezhuang near Cunliji, or possibly even later vessels (Yantai shi wenwu guanli weiyuanhui 1990: 803-810). The other two B4 *dou* with shallow dishes and slender stems are of a style popular in Warring States period tombs in the Yellow River region. In Shandong, the most typical examples are some ten *dou* vessels excavated from the Wanggou cemetery in Changdao, dating to the early Warring States period (Yantai shi wenwu guanli weiyuanhui 1993: 62, 83). Generally speaking, the above types represent a long period from the late Spring and Autumn to the Warring States period at Guicheng. In addition, we have noticed that these late types are concentrated in the inner city and Areas 9 and 10 to its south, but rarely appear in other areas of Guicheng. This suggests that in this later period, the Guicheng city site had already declined, as areas along the outer wall were mostly abandoned and human activities were largely restricted to the inner city and adjacent lands, in a much smaller area than before the mid-Spring and Autumn period. In this period, the Cunliji city site, located near another tributary of the Huangshui River, had already formed. Very possibly, the cultural and political center of the Huangshui River region was transferred from Guicheng to the Cunliji city site, resulting in the burial of a large number of tombs near Cunliji dating to the late Spring and Autumn to the Warring States period.

Section 4: The Scale and Internal Organization of Guicheng: Reflections on the Ancient State

In the seventh century BCE, during the early Spring and Autumn period, Guicheng must have been an immense and magnificent metropolis. Its outer wall runs 8.15 km across mountain tops; the two ends of the outer wall run straight to Mount Lai. If the two ends of the wall had been connected, the whole wall enclosure would have had a perimeter of more than 12 km. The total area within the wall is 8 km^2 at least (see Part Ⅰ, Chapter 4). If we count the area that extends into the mountains to the south, the total area of Guicheng would be more than 10 km^2. A city of this size should be considered a great city even by Central Plain standards. Table Ⅱ.5.1 shows that although Guicheng was much smaller than the Yan capital Xiadu in the Warring States period, and it is also smaller than the capital cities of some major states of the Spring and Autumn period such as Qi and Chu, it is considerably larger than the capitals of Cai and Xue, ancient states that were founded in the Western Zhou period. The scale of Guicheng is roughly equal to that of the Qufu city site of the state of Lu, or to that to the Zhou royal capital in Luoyang. It was doubtless one of the most important cities in Shandong. In the Jiaodong region, it was the largest city and the political and cultural center of the peninsula.

On the other hand, our survey confirmed that the city wall of Guicheng is extremely thick, with the thickest sections reaching 100 m, including possible architectural structures that were attached to the wall body. The outer wall is 40 m wide on average. Compared to the cities of other states, this figure is at the upper end of the range. The *Zuozhuan* mentions that when the Qi army attacked Lai's capital, "(they) mounded earth against the round city wall, reaching the battlements on it." This was possibly because the city wall of the Lai capital city was too thick to be breached, and therefore the Qi army mounded earth to form ramps in order to enter the city, a very interesting phenomenon.

Based on current data, we can estimate the amount of earth used to construct the outer wall of Guicheng. Using the average of 40 m wide at the base, if the top of the wall was 30 m wide and the height was 15 m, the area of a trapezoidal section would be 525 m^2. To build such a wall of 8.15 km would have required a total of 4,278,750 m^3 of earth. Based on our fieldwork experience, and on the recent "South-to-North Water Transportation Project," in particular, the largest amount of earth a young laborer can move in a workday does not exceed 2 m^3, except if the earth has to be transported across a distance. By this count, a total of 2,139,375 person days would be needed to construct the outer wall of Guicheng. If the ruler at Guicheng could mobilize 10,000 people to work on the project, it would take 213.93 days, or about 7.13 months to complete the wall. But this is merely a rough estimate. During the survey, we found that the mountain ridges on which the outer wall of Guicheng runs often have bedrock near the surface and shallow deposits of surface soil, and in some sections the earth used to build the wall is sediment, doubtless coming from the riverbeds below the mountains (see Part Ⅰ, Chapter 4). Considering the process of earth transportation from such locations, the actual labor needed to build the outer wall of Guicheng must have far exceeded our estimate above. This must have been a gigantic construction project. This indicates the high degree of political power and the organizational capacity of the ruler of Guicheng.

With regards to the organization of a city or a site, we are actually talking about the potential division of the city (or site) into a number of functionally different activity zones. This division allows us to study past patterns of human behavior relevant to a city or site based on archaeological phenomena (including remains) (Carr 1984: 106-107, 125-126). The intensive coring we carried out in the inner city of Guicheng beginning in 2007 gave us specific knowledge about the distribution of subterranean structures as well as about their present condition of preservation. During the coring we discovered a total of seventeen rammed earth architectural foundations (see Part Ⅰ, Chapter 3). In addition, two architectural foundations were found in the area between the inner city and the outer wall of Guicheng. We will consider their functions separately. Although coring cannot help us determine the dates of the underground structures, and there will be discrepancies between what we know from the coring and what future excavation may tell us, we found that the layout of these building foundations exhibits clear regularities, and no evidence of overlap between them was confirmed by the coring. Therefore, we consider them to be a series of structures that were created according to a plan during roughly the same period of time. Of course, some of the buildings might have been used for a longer time than others and there may therefore be sequential relationships between them. On the basis of this understanding, we can discuss the spatial organization of Guicheng. Needless to say, whatever suggestions we can make here will need to be verified by formal archaeological excavation in the future.

The inner city of Guicheng was divided into two large zones, separated by a river running between them. We have determined that the river enters the inner city to the west of the south gate of Guicheng, where it connects with the moat that runs along the city wall. Once in the city, the river makes a large bend towards the west, and then it turns north and exits the inner city at the point of junction between the western section of the north wall and the northern section of the west wall, where it again connects to the moat that runs outside the north wall. Such intra-city water systems were also found in the Yan capital Xiadu and the Qi capital in Linzi. They both provided for the daily use of water in the city, and might be used to fight fires if they broke out in the city. Although we do not have definite proof that the river dates to the Zhou Dynasty, there are reasons to believe that it was part of the original plan of the inner city. To the west of the river system is the Western Zone, which is centered on Rammed Building Foundation 9, measuring 78 m long from south to north. To the two sides of Foundation 9 are Foundations 8 and 10, running in parallel, but leaving a relatively wide court in the east. To the south are two smaller square foundations. This architectural group is located near the northwest corner of the inner city, forming an independent unit that is relatively closed off from the larger area of the city. Therefore, we consider they might have functioned as the inner palaces for the ruler, providing for the living and daily life of the ruler and his family.

The Eastern Zone is relatively open, centering on Foundations 2 and 3. Foundation 3 measures 56 m from north to south, and 21-33 m from east to west, and is the largest architectural feature in the Eastern Zone. Foundation 2 is 60 m to the east of Foundation 3, and because it is the easternmost feature in the eastern group, a large part of the foundation has been damaged by floods that invaded the inner city in historical times. Nevertheless, it is clear that Foundations 2 and 3 have symmetrical locations, being located on the two sides of the 10.5 m-wide road L1. This central avenue continues for 56 m from south to north, and its northern end has yet to be located. It is equally distant from the western and eastern walls of the inner city and is ostensibly the axis of the inner city of Guicheng. The existence of this central avenue indicates that the layout of the architectural features in the eastern group was based on an overall plan, and the symmetry of Foundations 2 and 3 was centered on this central avenue. A number of other foundations are located north of Foundation 3. To its south is a large plain surface paved with stones. Around the stone surface were large areas of footpath surface, together forming a large square with its north end connected to the central avenue L1. This phenomenon strongly suggests the public function of the group of large architectural Foundations 2 and 3. We believe that this architectural group represents the political and administrative center of Guicheng. As for the large area to the east of this central group, coring suggested that large portions had been destroyed by the invading floods. The area to its north is under the residential houses of present-day Heping Village, so its subterranean deposits have not been explored. However, we also conducted coring along the roads in the village and in its open areas, which led to the discovery of a small rammed earth foundation located close to a cliff near the center of the village (Foundation 15). In addition, tombs and chariot and horse burials were found in the village in the past. We have also detected some tombs in areas east of the central architectural group, and we found a bronze-casting mold in the test-excavation trench located to the south of the group, suggesting that this large area might have accommodated diverse activities in ancient times. Within this large area east of the central group, there might have been elite or common residences, and there might also have been cemeteries, bronze-casting foundries and other craft production workshops, and even ponds and other natural features. Clarifying how these functions were differentiated in space will be the aim of future work.

In addition, we discovered two architectural foundations that overlook the rivers in the areas between the inner and outer city walls. One of these foundations is located just to the north of the inner city, constructed by ramming earth on the high natural terrace overlooking the Yaque River, which flows to its north. The preserved platform measures 120 m from north to south, and 30 m from east to west. It is a structure of gigantic dimensions and thick, rammed earth layers. The other foundation overlooking the rivers is located on a high ridge along the eastern bank of a tributary of the Yaque River to the east of the inner city. Around it, we found many worked stones with flat surfaces that were likely to have been used to pave building floors. These high-status buildings, particularly the huge platform to the north of the inner city, might have been related to ritual activities in the city. Furthermore, between the inner and outer city walls, particularly east of the inner city and southward to the foot of Mount Lai, there are even more expansive spaces. These were occupied by complex topographical features, in addition to numerous streams and lakes or ponds, and sherd distribution here is extensive. There are many ideal locations for residential activities, and there are also elite burials, according to past discoveries. Especially to the south, the land undulates dramatically, and the distribution of sherds is substantially sparser, but there have been multiple discoveries of important bronzes in the past in this area. This suggests that the area that extends into the mountains to the south of Guicheng has a concentration of burials.

As the overall orientation of Guicheng is 17° east of north, the main architectural features and roads in the city were also oriented east of north. This orientation is similar to that of Linzi, the capital of Qi, and the Yan capital at Xiadu, and is also consistent with the architecture in major Shang cities. Recent studies show that the orientation of major architectural features in ancient cities was related to the particular stars that were selected to represent the north-pole (Pankenier 2004: 211-36; Pankenier 2013: 83-117). Seen in this perspective, the orientation of the inner city of Guicheng might have reflected a tradition of eastern China. However, because of the topography of the region, Guicheng seems to be a city that faced north with its back to the south, which makes it different from almost all cities in the Central Plain, which conventionally face south. In addition, the outer wall of Guicheng runs along mountain ridges, forming an irregular oval. This also differs from the regular square or rectangular cities in the Central Plain, and reflects a tendency of the local culture to adapt to the situation of the land.

In all, the architectural remains at Guicheng show us a society marked by a high concentration of power. The political leaders at Guicheng were able to mobilize human labor and material resources to construct a gigantic central city that is comparable in dimension to both the capital city of Lu at Qufu and the Zhou royal capital at Luoyang. The city wall was constructed to protect both the population and the wealth of the capital, and this suggests that the state based at Guicheng must have exercised political power over a population that was close to that of the state of Lu. Although the architecture in the inner city of Guicheng has suffered heavy damage, the surviving rammed earth foundations still exhibit clear organization in relation to the overall layout of the city, and also suggest that the government at Guicheng was capable of management at a relatively high level. There were larger contemporaneous cities such as the Yan capital city at Xiadu, the Qi capital city at Linzi, the Zheng-Han capital city at Xinzheng in the Yellow River region, and even the Chu capital city of Ji'nancheng in the south. These were all capitals of major territorial states of the Warring States period, and the actual political power of Guicheng certainly could not match that of the above states. However, at its height, without exaggeration Guicheng had certainly come close to the level of political power once enjoyed by the secondary territorial states of China, such as Lu and Song.

Section 5: The Issue of the Regional Bronze Culture of the Jiaodong Peninsula

Chapter 10 of Part I of this book systematically discussed the ceramic cultures in the Guicheng region and their development over time. In the Yueshi culture period, the Jiaodong region had already developed a situation in which the greyish-black pottery tradition (mostly fine clay) co-existed with the brown pottery tradition (mostly tempered with sand), with the latter increasingly becoming dominant. During the Zhenzhumen cultural period (ca. 1400-900 BCE), reddish-brown pottery was established as the predominant pottery making tradition. Such pottery vessels were normally fired at a relatively low temperature, resulting in soft and loose body building and uneven surface color. Most vessels are undecorated and have inclusions of sand, mica, quartz, and talc. Because of the invasion of the powerful Zhou culture from the west, the line of development of the local cultural tradition was interrupted, and the Zhou culture became quickly established as the mainstream pottery making tradition in the Jiaodong region. However, the local pottery making tradition was not lost, but instead persisted and led to the emergence at some point during the Western Zhou period of the Nanhuangzhuang culture, distributed mainly in the southeastern part of the peninsula.

This unique Jiaodong tradition of pottery making is clearly represented at the Guicheng city site, though at present we are unable to determine whether the reddish-brown and greyish-brown pottery we frequently see at Guicheng all belonged to the Nanhuangzhuang culture. This is one of the subjects for research at Guicheng in the future. Because the Zhou tradition produced predominantly black and grey pottery, on the basis of a sound understanding of the developmental history of each, it is not difficult to differentiate the two pottery-making traditions. However, as time passed, the localized Zhou culture in the Jiaodong region gradually developed characteristics that were unknown to the Zhou central region; meanwhile, elements associated with the local pottery-making tradition increased steadily, leading to the appearance of pottery assemblages like that from H3. In this unit, reddish-brown sherds account for 23.80% of finds, and the pottery types that can be reconstructed all have a mixture of Zhou and indigenous cultural features. Such mixing reflects the general trend of the development of the Zhou culture in the Jiaodong region during the late Western Zhou and the Spring and Autumn period.

We discovered one bronze-casting mold in pit H9 during the test excavation at Guicheng (Fig. Ⅰ.5.28). This single mold testifies to the local manufacturing of bronzes in the Jiaodong region, which further explains the formation of a bronze culture with local characteristics in the eastern Shandong Peninsula during the late Western Zhou period. Unfortunately, the mold has a very small smooth surface that was in contact with the bronze, and therefore it is difficult to determine the type of bronze it was used to cast. Nonetheless, the relatively large number of sherds from the same pit enables us to determine the date of H9. The pit is located at the southern end of Trench TG2 and the northern end of Trench TG1. It is a small round pit, opening under stratum 3 and intruding into the earlier pit H20. Many sherds from H9 have scattered cord decorations. There are also B2 type of *dou* pedestal dishes with very slender stems, together with shallow *dou* dishes and *li* tripods with very low feet (Fig. Ⅱ.5.27). Considering the overall features of the sherd assemblage from H9, we think that it should be dated to no earlier than the early Spring and Autumn period, but it could be slightly earlier than H3. This raises a question: when was the bronze-casting technology that subsequently developed in the Shandong Peninsula introduced to the region?

It is well known that the Yueshi culture developed a capacity to cast small bronze objects. In the Jiaodong region, such an object was discovered in the Zhaogezhuang site of Muping (Zhongguo shehui kexueyuan kaogu yanjiusuo Shandong dui 1986: 472). As mentioned above, the early phase of the mid-Western Zhou period was the height of elite activity in the Guicheng region, as shown by the discovery of many bronze vessels. However, the contents of their inscriptions suggest that the owners of these bronzes were closely related to the Zhou elites residing in the Wei River valley of Shaanxi (see below), and the design and decoration of these bronzes are indistinguishable from Western Zhou bronzes from the Central Plain. Therefore, we believe that at least some of these bronzes discovered locally in the Guicheng region must have come from Shaanxi. However, bronzes inscribed with “local contents” were probably cast locally. For example, the Lü *ding* from Lujiagou mentioned above says:

"In the year when the Duke Grand Protector came to attack the rebellious Yi"; therefore, it was likely locally manufactured.

Another typical case is the Xin Xiao *gui* found in 1983 at Haixujia Village to the west of Longkou, dating to the mid-Western Zhou (Part Ⅱ, Chapter 3). The Xin Xiao *gui* has a constricted neck, a bulging belly, and a low circular foot, all typical of the designs of the mid-Western Zhou period (Fig. Ⅱ.5.11). In addition, the bronze *li* tripod found together with it is decorated with cord patterns, similar to many pieces from the Western Zhou tombs in Shaanxi. The *gui* is decorated with an early style of the *Qiequ* pattern, showing characteristics of the mid-Western Zhou period, but a careful examination reveals that the structure of the *Qiequ* pattern had already become relatively loose and simpler. The inscription cannot be completely deciphered at present, but it reads:

> It was the king's eleventh month; the king was at Xian. The prince arrived at Fang. Xin Xiao X. [He] presented Shu (a guest-gift of) X, and [Shu] recompensed for his deceased father Xin a wooden handle. (Thereupon he) makes a stabbing weapon for use. Xin Xiao XX. Shu Yu (?) awarded metal. Xin X arrived, X at the temple, and had audience (?). [His] sons' sons and grandsons, X makes a treasured vessel.

The text of this inscription follows the language convention of Western Zhou inscriptions but with many errors; its graphs contain some reversed forms. Possibly the scribe was illiterate or had a limited degree of literacy. The inscription mentions that the Zhou king was in a place called Xian, while the royal prince advanced to Fang, where he was greeted by Xin Xiao. Xin Xiao thereupon received the award of metal with which he made the bronze. Apparently, the contents of the inscription relate to tours of inspection by the Zhou king and his close attendants in the Shandong region or even the Jiaodong Peninsula, but the bronze was cast by a member of a local state or lineage in the Guicheng region. In the past, this author has systematically discussed the phenomenon of states or lineages in the periphery of the Western Zhou state casting inscribed bronzes that imitate the conventional Western Zhou inscriptions, as typified in the cases of the Mei'ao *gui* (JC: 4213), Ehou Yufang *ding* (JC: 2810), and other bronzes from the state of E in the south (Li Feng 2002: 210-242). The Xin Xiao *gui* clearly belongs to the same category. These bronzes reflect the historical process in which peripheral states or lineages gradually learned the technology of bronze casting and the culture of inscriptions of the Zhou people with whom they had come in contact. This is the true meaning of the inscribed *gui* from Haixujia Village,

In general, the bronze culture in the Jiaodong Peninsula during the late Western Zhou and the Spring and Autumn period inherited the tradition of the Zhou bronze culture, but during this period there emerged some types with marked local characteristics. The only bronzes from this period that can be determined to have been cast by the state of Lai include a set of four *li* tripods cast by Libo

(Laibo), found in a late Western Zhou tomb in Guheya in Rizhao in 1976. The inscription of the Laibo *li* says: "Laibo X his daughter; (he) makes this *li* vessel. May (her) son and grandson eternally treasure and use it!" (Yang Fushen 1984: 594-597). According to the conventions of bronze inscriptions, the character following Laibo must have been *ying* (send in company of a marrying daughter). The bronzes were likely cast by the ruler of Lai as dowry vessels for his daughter, who married into a state or lineage in the Rizhao region; her husband was possibly a personage of the state of Jü. Although this set of *li* was of standard late Western Zhou *li* design, the two large *hu* bottles that were found in the same tomb (M1 : 1-2) are identical and rich in local features. The mouth is small, its widest point near the bottom of the belly, and it is decorated with four small rings. The majority of the belly is decorated with *Quequ* pattern and a triangular pattern. The overall design of the *hu* is likely meant to imitate the fish baskets of the region (Fig. Ⅱ.5.12). A similar triangular pattern was also found on a bronze *hu* from Shangkuang Village in Yantai in 1969 (Shandong Yantai diqu wenwu guanli weiyuanhui 1983: 289-292). Examples of *hu* with similar designs are also found in pottery, for instance, the A1 and A2 style *hu* from Guicheng. In the case from Yantai, the same tomb yielded bronzes cast by Jihou and Ji Huafu, identifying the vessels with the state of Ji. Another bronze *li* tripod cast by Jihou was found to the south of Heping Village in Guicheng in the 1950s. This vessel had a damaged inscription of twelve characters: "Jihou casts X Jiang XX Sons' sons and grandsons' grandsons eternally treasure and use it" (Li Buqing and Lin Xianting 1991a: 915). This bronze *li* was possibly also a dowry vessel, that is, cast by the ruler of Ji for his daughter when she married into the state of Lai. This particular *li* has flanges and a body profile that is common in late Western Zhou bronze *li*, but its plain surface and sharp feet more closely resemble the local plain-surface pottery *li* tripods.

It is a common and interesting phenomenon that during the early and mid-Western Zhou period, when the Zhou culture was at its height of development, many states or polities in the periphery of the expanding Zhou world adopted the typical Zhou bronze culture. However, as time passed, designs and decorative patterns characteristic of local traditions, many originating in local pottery, gradually returned to popularity and became an important part of the local bronze culture. What we see in the Jiaodong Peninsula is typical of this phenomenon, which parallels the increase of local elements in the pottery assemblages of the region. Together they reflect an important aspect of the process of formation of ancient states in the Jiaodong region. However, the states or lineages on the Jiaodong Peninsula, including such major states as Lai and Ji, only developed a limited number of bronze types, and the local bronze culture by and large still continued the tradition that was inherited from the Western Zhou. Furthermore, this process of development was soon interrupted by the invasion of the Qi culture from the west.

Section 6: Assessment of the Formation of the State of Lai and the Process of State Formation on the Jiaodong Peninsula

Based on analyses of the archaeological data and the results of ^{14}C dating, we can reach a basic understanding of the complex cultural processes that underlay the formation history of the Guicheng city site. In addition, the locally discovered bronze inscriptions as well as the historical texts offer clues about the activity of the ancient states and lineages in the Jiaodong region, particularly the state of Lai, which can help us achieve a deeper interpretation of the archaeological phenomena in their historical contexts. However, in order to effectively utilize the two sets of information, we must first examine the inscribed bronzes that were locally excavated and analyze the political relations they reflect, in the hope of achieving objective understanding of the political situation in the region.

As mentioned above, at present there are only two inscribed bronzes that can be identified with the state of Lai: 1) the Laibo *ding* (JC: 2044) dating to the mid-Western Zhou period, which has been lost, but which must have been cast by the ruler of Lai; 2) the Laibo *li*, from a late Western Zhou tomb in Guheya in Rizhao, which was a dowry vessel cast by the ruler of Lai, who married his daughter into the local state (possibly Jü). In addition, another Lü *ding* (JC: 2728) has the emblem 丫 at the end of its inscription, considered by some to represent the state of Lai, though the meaning of this graph awaits further study. However, because its inscription mentions that "in the year when the Duke Grand Protector came to attack the rebellious Yi," there is good reason to assume that it was cast in a local state or lineage. It is probable that the Laibo *ding* and Lü *ding*, together with the Yu *ding* (JC: 2721) and Yu *yan* (JC: 948), were excavated in Lujiagou, about 10 km to the southeast of Guicheng. If this is the case, that would suggest that Lai and probably also other states or lineages (including [illegible]) were active in the Huangshui River valley and the Longkou area during the early Western Zhou, but they cannot prove that Guicheng was already under the control of Lai or any other particular polity in this period.

Within the territory of Guicheng, the most important inscribed bronzes are certainly the Qi *zun* (JC: 5983) and Qi *you* (JC: 5410) unearthed at Xiaoliuzhuang to the south of Caojia Village. The historical background of these inscriptions is rather complex, relating to the Zhou king's campaign against the bandit of the southern mountains named Ceshangu. The king arrived in the domain of Shanghou near the Jing River where Qi was in his company, and subsequently Qi cast these bronzes (Fig. Ⅱ.2.8). "Shanghou" also appears in inscriptions on the Shi Yu *zun* (JC: 5995) and Shi Yu *ding* (JC: 2723), referring to the place the Zhou king had reached, and the bronzes were found in Shaanxi. In addition, "Shanghou" is also mentioned in the Buzhi *ding* (JC: 2735), seemingly a place where the Zhou king took up temporary residence; it was found in tomb M3 at Qizhen in Shaanxi. These inscriptions suggest that "Shanghou" was a place located not very far from the Zhou capital, providing good reference for the origin of the Qi *zun* and Qi *you*. We believe that the two bronzes were brought to Guicheng from a location in Shaanxi or the Central Plain, and the campaign in which Qi participated took place to the south of the Zhou capital.

A similar situation surrounds the *gui* cast by Ruigong Shu. The *gui* sits on a square base and is decorated with "great-bird" patterns. It measures 29.2 cm high, and was excavated in a tomb at Zhuangtou in 1980. This *gui* is very similar to a *gui* with the same body design and ornamentation in the collection of Mr. George Fan in New York, the latter having been cast by Ruibo, and measuring 28.7 cm high. The two bronzes are nearly identical (the band of decoration under the rim was omitted on the Zhuangtou *gui*), and we think that they are bronzes cast by two brothers at about the same time (Fig. Ⅱ.5.13). Because of the discovery of the cemetery of the state of Rui at Liangdai Village in Hancheng, Shaanxi, we know for sure that the state of Rui was in Shaanxi, but for some reason, the Ruigong Shu *gui* tureen was brought to Shandong. A bronze *hu* bottle was also unearthed from the same tomb at Zhuangtou, cast by one "Xiong Xi". Moreover, a bronze *gui* from Dongying Zhoujia (Longkou Municipal Museum number: KM491) is inscribed: "Makes my treasured *gui* vessel; may (I) for ten thousand years eternally treasure and use it! Shan." Although the principal caster of the bronze was not named in the inscription, the emblem  (Shan) identifies the lineage. This  is not to be confused with the emblem  (JC: 5195) on late Shang and early Western Zhou bronzes. Based on examination of its design and ornamentation, the *gui* from Dongying must have been cast during the late Western Zhou. And the "Shan" at the end of its inscription must have referred to the Shan lineage in Shaanxi, active during the late Western Zhou period. Therefore, it is very likely that the vessel belonged the Shan lineage in Shaanxi, but for unknown reasons, it was brought to the Jiaodong Peninsula.

The situation surrounding the inscribed bronzes from Jiqian Zhaojia found in 2004 is more complicated. The group includes four inscribed bronzes, two of them cast by a certain "Shusuo" who received awards from "Bo Yingfu," and another cast by a certain "Lifu." Although we have not seen these names before, they are all typical Zhou style names. Furthermore, the calligraphic styles of the inscriptions as well as the design of the bronzes are all typical in the Zhou central region. Another noteworthy piece is the bronze *ding* cast by the "Inspector of X," found in 1964 at Hanluan Village of Lutou Township, 10 km west of Guicheng, which dates to the early Western Zhou (Fig. Ⅱ.5.8). Bronze inscriptions offer clear evidence for the institution of inspectors of the Western Zhou state, and known cases include the "Inspector of Ying" stationed by the Zhou court in the state of Ying, and the "Inspector Earl" stationed in the state of Southern Shen in the Nanyang basin in southern Henan. The inscription on the Zhong Jifu *gui* (JC: 3954) also mentions the "many rulers and many inspectors," suggesting that it was a common practice for the Zhou court to station royal inspectors in the regional states (Li Feng

2008: 251). Therefore, the occurrence of the bronze *ding* cast by the "Inspector of X" in the Longkou region strongly suggests that there were polities located in the Longkou region besides the state of Lai which were controlled by the Western Zhou state. We speculate that the 眉 mentioned in the Shi Mi *gui* and 原 mentioned in the Shi Yuan *gui*, the two polities that followed the people of Zhou, Qi, and Lai on campaigns, may be related to the state of 㡯, but the link between the graphs is unclear and this remains speculative.

It should be noted that the strong personnel links between the Guicheng region and the Zhou central region in the bronze inscriptions is also reflected in what we learn from pottery. As shown above, the pottery culture typical of the Zhou tradition entered the Guicheng region during the late phase of the early Western Zhou, but the origin of this invading culture does not seem to have been in the adjacent Henan and Hebei regions, but was in the Zhou central region in Shaanxi (Part Ⅰ, Chapter 10). In the Guicheng region, we can find types that are extremely similar to their counterparts in the Shaanxi region, for instance, the pocket-footed *li* tripods with very low crotches (Fig. Ⅰ.5.52), to a degree that is unmatched even by pottery assemblages from the Luoyang region (which was under strong influence from the Shang culture instead). This high degree of similarity across great distances very likely reflects a direct exchange of people. Although we cannot directly link phenomena seen in archaeology to political history, the locally unearthed bronze inscriptions indeed suggest such direct political connections (particularly personnel connections and the common background of political institutions). The information we have from Guicheng archaeology and the locally unearthed inscriptions definitely shows the invasion of the Jiaodong Peninsula by the Zhou culture, behind which the great state power of the Western Zhou was the driving force. In particular, a series of wars carried out by the Zhou people against the so-called "Dongyi" people, frequently recorded in the bronze inscriptions, can offer the best explanation for this cultural phenomenon seen in archaeology. We can see a record of these wars in both bronze inscriptions found in the Zhou central region, such as the Xiaochen Lai *gui* (JC: 4239) and the Minggong *gui* (JC: 4029), and the bronze inscriptions unearthed locally in the Jiaodong region, for instance, the Lü *ding* that says "in the year when the Duke Grand Protector came to attack the rebellious Yi."

Taking into consideration the archaeological data as well as information from the bronze inscriptions, it can be said that, rather than relating to the state of Lai, Guicheng in its early period was more closely related to the activities initiated by the Zhou court and the Wei River aristocracy in Shaanxi. Certainly there is the possibility of discovering inscribed bronzes of the state of Lai in Guicheng in future archaeological excavations, but at present we cannot connect Guicheng during the early and mid-Western Zhou period with the state of Lai. Whether the locally discovered bronzes were brought from Shaanxi (at least a part of them must have been from outside the region) or they were locally manufactured, they indicate a high frequency of exchange of people between Guicheng and the Zhou central region, and a close political relationship to the Western Zhou state. Even the Yu *ding* and Yu *yan*, unearthed together in Lujiagou with the Lai bronze, record campaigns organized by the Zhou court against groups in the Huai River region in which the caster of the bronzes took part. At the same time, the phenomenon we see in the Guicheng region in which there is a concentration of bronzes associated with multiple states or lineages is rather peculiar, and is a situation unseen in other peripheral areas like Liulihe in the state of Yan region, or Pingdingshan in the state of Ying. In all, given the information we presently have, it would be best to see Guicheng in the early Western Zhou and the early phase of the mid-Western Zhou as a focus of the activities of the Zhou people on the Jiaodong Peninsula.

The above understanding helps us reconfigure the background of the formation of the state of Lai. Originating among the Dongyi people, in its early history Lai must have been one of the local groups that accepted the Zhou culture and maintained a close political relationship with the Western Zhou state. Under the influence of the Western Zhou political system, Lai gradually grew into a small regional state in the Jiaodong Peninsula, and for a long time maintained its political alliance with the Western Zhou and participated in wars organized by the Zhou court outside the Shandong region, as indicated by inscriptions on the Shi Mi *gui* and the Shi Yuan *gui*. The case of Lai must have reflected the common path of secondary state formation on the periphery of the Western Zhou state (Minna Wu 2013: 18-23), particularly the Shandong region in the east. The later entry of Lai into Guicheng and Lai's development into a powerful state centered on Guicheng must have had to do with the decline of the Western Zhou state from the mid-Western Zhou on, which might have offered room for Lai's expansion. As mentioned above, the early pottery assemblage in Guicheng was dominated by the Zhou pottery tradition, but elements that represented the indigenous pottery-making tradition, marked by red and brown pottery, increased over time. This can be explained by a resurgence of the local culture. In a narrower perspective, this can also be explained by the growing power of the state of Lai itself, through a process in which Lai elites gradually rejected Zhou influence. During the late Western Zhou and early Eastern Zhou, the state of Lai left clear traces in the historical texts that record political developments on the Jiaodong Peninsula, and Guicheng during this period developed into the greatest metropolis in Jiaodong. It is certainly acceptable to relate Guicheng to Lai at this time. During this period, the state of Lai constructed the outer wall of Guicheng, which matches the scale of the capital of Lu in Qufu. This certainly also indicates that Lai during this period had amassed great political power. Lai enjoyed marriage relationships with the state of Ji to its southeast and with a certain state in the Rizhao region (possibly Ju) in southern Shandong, as they had a common interest in surviving the expansion of the superpower of the state of Qi in the west. The eventual fall of Lai in 567 BCE was the inevitable outcome of the transformation of ancient states in China into "territorial states." Through a comprehensive analysis of archaeological data, bronze inscriptions, and political history, we have achieved a richer understanding of the historical process as well as the social background of state formation on the Jiaodong Peninsula during the late Bronze Age.

References

Bogu tu 博古图, 1752. Recompiled edition of Yizhengtang 亦政堂.

Carr, Christopher, 1984. "The Nature of Organization of Intrasite Archaeological Records and Spatial Analytic Approaches to Their Investigation," in *Advances in Archaeological Method and Theory,* edited by M.B. Schiffer. Pp. 103-222. New York: Academic Press, Inc.

Chen, Mengjia 陈梦家, 1988. "Shuyi zhong bo kao" 叔尸钟镈考 (A study of the Shuyi *zhong* and *bo*), *Yanjing xuebao* 燕京学报, 4: 1-24.

Chen, Pan 陈槃, 1969. *Chunqiu dashi biao lieguo juexing ji cunmie biao zhuanyi* 春秋大事表列国爵姓及存灭表譔異 (An examination of differences in the "Table of major historical events of the Spring and Autumn period" and the "Table of ranks, surnames, and destructions of the many states"). Taipei: Institute of History and Philology, Academia Sinica.

Cui, Lequan 崔乐泉, 1992. "Shandong diqu Dongzhou kaoguxue de xulie" 山东地区东周考古学的序列 (The chronology of Eastern Zhou archaeology in the Shandong region), *Huaxia kaogu* 华夏考古, 4: 73-97.

Fang, Hui 方辉, 2007. *Haidai diqu qingtong shidai kaogu* 海岱地区青铜时代考古 (Bronze-Age archaeology of the Haidai region). Ji'nan: Shandong daxue chubanshe.

Guo, Moruo 郭沫若, 1958. *Liang Zhou jinwen ci daxi tulu kaoshi* 两周金文辞大系图录考释 (A catalog and an examination of bronze inscriptions from the Western and Eastern Zhou periods). Beijing: Kexue chubanshe.

Ke, Changji 柯昌济, 1935a. *Weihuage jigulu bawei* 韡华阁集古录跋尾 (Postscript to the collection of ancient inscriptions in Weihuage). Ji'nan.

Ke, Changji 柯昌济, 1935b. *Jinwen fenyu bian* 金文分域编 (A regionalized listing of bronze inscriptions). Ji'nan.

Li, Buqing 李步青, 1983. "Shandong Laiyang xian chutu Ji guo tongqi" 山东莱阳县出土己国铜器 (Bronzes of the state of Ji unearthed in Laiyang County, Shandong), *Wenwu* 文物, 12: 7-8, 17.

Li, Buqing 李步青, and Lin Xianting 林仙庭, 1991a. "Shandong Huangxian Guicheng yizhi de diaocha yu fajue" 山东黄县归城遗址的调查与发掘 (Survey and excavation of the Guicheng site in Huangxian County, Shandong). *Kaogu* 考古, 10: 910-918.

Li, Buqing 李步青, and Lin Xianting 林仙庭, 1991b. "Shandong sheng Longkou shi chutu Xi Zhou tong ding" 山东省龙口市出土西周铜鼎 (A Western Zhou bronze *ding* unearthed in Longkou City, Shandong), *Wenwu* 文物, 5: 84-85.

Li, Buqing 李步青, Lin Xianting 林仙庭, and Yang Wenyu 杨文玉, 1994. "Shandong Zhaoyuan chutu Xi Zhou qingtongqi" 山东招远出土西周青铜器 (Western Zhou bronzes unearthed in Zhaoyuan, Shandong), *Kaogu* 考古, 4: 377-378.

Li, Feng, 2002. "Literacy Crossing Cultural Borders: Evidence from the Bronze Inscriptions of the Western Zhou Period (1045-771 B.C.)," *Bulletin of the Museum of Far Eastern Antiquities* (Stockholm: Museum of Far Eastern Antiquities), 74: 210-242.

Li, Feng 李峰, 2006a. "Xi Zhou jinwen zhong de Zheng di he Zheng guo dongqian" 西周金文中的郑地和郑国东迁 (The place-name Zheng in Western Zhou bronze inscriptions and the move east of the state of Zheng), *Wenwu* 文物, 9: 70-78.

Li, Feng, 2006b. *Landscape and Power in Early China: The Crisis and Fall of the Western Zhou, 1045-771 BC*. Cambridge, UK: Cambridge University Press.

Li, Feng, 2008. *Bureaucracy and the State in Early China: Governing the Western Zhou, 1045-771 BC*. Cambridge, UK: Cambridge University Press.

Lin, Xianting 林仙庭, 2006. "Lai guo yu Lai du" 莱国与莱都 (The state of Lai and the Lai capital), in *Kaogu Yantai* 考古烟台 (Archaeology in Yantai), edited by Yantai shi bowuguan 烟台市博物馆. Pp. 134-136. Ji'nan: Qi Lu shushe.

Liu, Li, and Xingcan Chen, 2012. *The Archaeology of China: From the Late Paleolithic to the Early Bronze Age*. Cambridge UK: Cambridge University Press.

Ma, Zhimin 马志敏, 2004. "Shandong sheng Longkou shi chutu Xi Zhou tong gui" 山东省龙口市出土西周铜簋 (A bronze *gui* unearthed in Longkou City, Shandong Province), *Wenwu* 文物, 8: 79-80.

Pankenier, David, 2004. "A Brief History of Beiji (Northern Culmen): with an Excursus on the Origins of the Character Di," *Journal of the American Oriental Society,* 124.2: 211-236.

Pankenier, David, 2013. *Astrology and Cosmology in Early China: Conforming Heaven to Earth*. Cambridge, UK: Cambridge University Press.

Qixia xian wenwu guanlisuo 栖霞县文物管理所, 1988. "Shandong Qixia xian Songshan xiang Lüjiabu Xi Zhou mu" 山东栖霞县松山乡吕家埠西周墓 (A Western Zhou tomb at Lüjiabu, Songshan xiang, Qixia County, Shandong), *Kaogu* 考古, 9: 778-783.

Raab, L. Mark, and Albert C. Goodyear, 1984. "Middle-Range Theory in Archaeology: A Critical Review of Origins and Applications," *American Antiquity* 29.2: 255-268.

Schiffer, Michael B., 1983. "Toward the identification of formation processes," *American Antiquity,* 48.4: 675-706.

Schiffer, Michael B., 1987. *Formation Processes of the Archaeological Record.* Albuquerque: University of New Mexico Press.

Shandong sheng wenwu kaogu yanjiusuo 山东省文物考古研究所, 1989. "Guangrao xian Wucun yizhi fajue baogao" 广饶县五村遗址发掘报告 (A report on the excavation of the Wucun site in Guangrao County), *Haidai kaogu* 海岱考古, 1: 61-123.

Shandong sheng wenwu kaogu yanjiusuo 山东省文物考古研究所 et al., 1982. *Qufu Lu guo gucheng* 曲阜鲁国故城 (The ancient city of the state of Lu in Qufu). Ji'nan: Qilu shushe.

Shandong sheng Changwei diqu wenwu zu 山东省昌潍地区文物组, 1977. "Jiao xian Xi'an yizhi fajue jianbao" 胶县西庵遗址发掘简报 (A brief report on the excavation of the Xi'an site in Jiao County), *Wenwu* 文物, 4: 68.

Shandong Yantai diqu wenguan zu 山东烟台地区文管组, 1977. "Shandong Penglai xian Xi Zhou mu fajue jianbao" 山东蓬莱县西周墓发掘简报 (A brief report on the excavation of the Western Zhou tomb in Penglai County, Shandong), *Wenwu ziliao congkan* 文物资料丛刊, 3: 50-55.

Shandong Yantai diqu wenwu guanli weiyuanhui 山东省烟台地区文物管理委员会, 1983. "Yantai shi Shangkuangcun chutu Ji guo tongqi" 烟台市上夼村出土㠱国铜器 (Bronzes of the state of Ji unearthed at Shangkuang Village in Yantai City), *Kaogu* 考古, 4: 289-92.

Shelach-Lavi, Gideon, 2015. *The Archaeology of Early China: From Prehistory to the Han Dynasty*. New York: Cambridge

University Press.

Tan Lan 唐兰, 1995. "Lun Zhou Zhao wang shidai de qingtongqi mingke" 论周昭王时代的青铜器铭刻 (On the bronze inscriptions from the reign of King Zhao of Zhou), in *Tang Lan xiansheng jinwen lunji* 唐兰先生金文论集. Pp. 236-333. Beijing: Zijincheng chubanshe.

Wang, Daoxin 王道新, 1934. *Huangxian zhi gao* 黄县志稿 (Draft gazetteer of Huangxian). Preserved in Shandong Provincial Museum.

Wang, Qing 王青, 2002. *Haidai diqu Zhou dai muzang yanjiu* 海岱地区周代墓葬研究 (A study of the Zhou dynasty tombs in the Haidai region). Ji'nan: Shandong daxue chubanshe.

Wang, Xiping 王锡平, and Tang Luting 唐禄庭, 1986. "Shandong Huangxian Zhuangtou Xi Zhou mu qingli jianbao" 山东黄县庄头西周墓清理简报 (A brief report of the excavation of Western Zhou tombs at Zhuangtou in Huangxian, Shandong). *Wenwu* 文物, 8: 69-72.

Wang, Xiping 王锡平, 1991. "Dui Shandong Huangxian Zhuangtou Xi Zhou mu chutu tongqi mingwen de chubu yanjiu" 对山东黄县庄头西周墓出土铜器铭文的初步研究 (A preliminary study of the bronze inscriptions from the Western Zhou tomb at Zhuangtou in Huangxian, Shandong), *Yantai shifan xueyuan xuebao (zheshe ban)* 烟台师范学院学报（哲社版）, 3: 62.

Wang, Xiping 王锡平, and Sun Jingming 孙敬明, 1984. "Lai guo yi ming shishi ji lun youguan wenti" 莱国彝铭试释及论有关问题 (An interpretation of the inscribed vessel from Lai and related questions), *Dongyue luncong* 东岳论丛 (Dongyue papers), 1: 77-79.

Wang, Xiantang 王献唐, 1983. *Shandong guguo kao* 山东古国考 (A study of the ancient states in Shandong). Ji'nan: Qi Lu shushe.

Wu, Minna, 2013: "On the Periphery of a Great 'Empire': Secondary Formation of States and Their Material Basis in the Shandong Peninsula during the Late Bronze Age, ca. 1000-500 B.C.E." Ph.D. dissertation, Columbia University, New York.

Xue Shanggong 薛尚功, 1986. *Lidai zhong ding yiqi kuanzhi fatie* 历代钟鼎彝器款识法帖 (Copies of the inscriptions on bronze vessels of all dynasties). Zhu Mouyin edition. Beijing: Zhonghua shuju.

Yantai shi wenwu guanli weiyuanhui 烟台市文物管理委员会, 1990."Shandong Penglai xian Liugezhuang muqun fajue jianbao"山东蓬莱县柳格庄墓群发掘简报 (A brief report on the excavation of the cemetery at Liugezhuang in Penglai County, Shandong), *Kaogu* 考古, 9: 803-810.

Yantai shi wenwu guanli weiyuanhui 烟台市文物管理委员会, 1993. "Shandong Changdao Wanggou Dong Zhou muqun" 山东长岛王沟东周墓群 (The Eastern Zhou cemetery at Wanggou in Changdao, Shandong), *Kaogu xuebao* 考古学报, 1: 57-87.

Yang, Bojun 杨伯峻, 1990. *Chunqiu Zuozhuan zhu* 春秋左传注 (Commentary on the *Spring and Autumn Annals* and the *Zuozhuan*). Beijing: Zhonghua shuju.

Yang, Fushen 杨福深, 1984. "Shandong Rizhao Guheya chutu yipi qingtongqi "山东日照崮河崖出土一批青铜器 (A group of bronzes unearthed at Guheya in Rizhao, Shandong), *Kaogu* 考古, 7: 594-597.

Zeng, Yigong 曾毅公, 1940. *Shandong jinwen jicun* 山东金文集存 (Collection of bronze inscriptions from Shandong).

Ji’nan.

Zhang, Maorong 张懋镕, Zhao Rong 赵荣, and Zou Dongtao 邹东涛, 1989. “Ankang chutu de Shi Mi gui ji qi yiyi” 安康出土的史密簋及其意义 (The Shi Mi *gui* unearthed in Ankang and its significance), *Wenwu* 文物, 7: 64-71.

Zhongguo shehui kexueyuan kaogu yanjiusuo Shandong dui 中国社会科学院考古研究所山东队, and Yantai shi wenwu guanli weiyuanhui 烟台市文物管理委员会, 1986. “Shandong Muping Zhaogezhuang yizhi” 山东牟平照格庄遗址 (The Zhaogezhuang site in Muping, Shandong), *Kaogu xuebao* 考古学报, 4: 447-478.

Zhongguo shehui kexueyuan kaogu yanjiusuo 中国社会科学院考古研究所, 1999. *Zhangjiapo Xi Zhou mudi* 张家坡西周墓地 (The Western Zhou cemetery at Zhangjiapo). Beijing: Zhongguo dabaike chubanshe.

附 录

Appendices

附录一　山东龙口归城城址的碳十四测定

Appendix 1: ^{14}C Dating of the Guicheng City Site in Longkou, Shandong

张雪莲
Zhang Xuelian

实验室编号 Laboratory #	发掘编号 Excavation #	样品 Sample	碳十四年代 ^{14}C dates (BP-1950,5568)	误差 Error Range	树轮校正年代 Calibrated Dates (OxCai v3.10)
zk-3356	09SLGTG2H15②-5	碳土 Charcoal in earth	2919	29	1200 (68.2%) 1050 BCE
zk-3357	09SLGTG2③H9-5	碳样 Charcoal	2645	28	825 (68.2%) 795 BCE
zk-3358	09SLGTG2H12②-3	碳样 Charcoal	2594	30	805 (68.2%) 770 BCE
zk-3359	09SLGTG2③H20①-10	碳样 Charcoal	2872	26	1120 (7.1%) 1100 BCE 1090 (61.1%) 1000 BCE
zk-3361	09SLGTG1①H3-4	草木灰 Grass and wood ash	2619	26	810 (68.2%) 790 BCE
zk-3362	09SLGTG1③H8-4 (6.2m)	木炭 Wood charcoal	2604	26	810 (68.2%) 785 BCE

数据由中国社会科学院考古研究所科技考古中心张雪莲提供。样品前处理由中国社会科学院考古研究所科技考古中心碳十四实验室完成，样品制备与测定由西安加速器质谱中心完成。

Data provided by Zhang Xuelian, the Center for Scientific Archaeology, the Institute of Archaeology, Chinese Academy of Social Sciences. The sample-pretreating is completed by ^{14}C Laboratory of the Center for Scientific Archaeology, IA, CASS. The sample-preparing and dating are completed by Xi'an Accelerator Mass Spectrometry(AMS) Center.

附录二　山东烟台龙口归城城址浮选结果

赵志军

一、引　　言

归城遗址位于山东龙口，是一处西周中期至春秋时期的城址。2007～2009年，中国社会科学院考古研究所、美国哥伦比亚大学东亚语言与文化系和山东省文物考古研究所组成了联合考古队，对归城遗址进行了考古调查。基于对该遗址的全面调查，联合考古队于2009年7月选定在归城内城南部进行了小规模试掘（见上编第三章）。在试掘中，考古队采取了一些浮选土样，以期获得古代植物遗存，了解当时人们对植物的利用情况以及农业生产特点。

归城遗址浮选土样共有20份，均采自灰坑。每份浮选土样的土量约为8升，总计获取浮选土量158升。浮选工作是在发掘现场进行的，采用的是水波浮选仪（赵志军 2004：80～87）；使用的分样筛规格为80目（筛网孔径0.2毫米）。浮选进行的时间是2009年7月15～17日（图Ⅲ.2.1-Ⅲ.2.3）。

浮选结果在当地阴干后被运回中国社会科学院考古研究所植物考古实验室进行分类、植物种属鉴定和分析。

二、浮选结果

经过实验室的整理和鉴定，在归城遗址浮选样品中清理出的炭化植物遗存包括炭化木屑和植物种子两类。炭化木屑是指经过燃烧的木头的残存，其主要来源应该是未燃尽的燃料，或遭到焚烧的建筑木材以及其他用途的木料等。归城遗址浮选样品中清理出的炭化木屑十分细碎，需要送交专家进行树种的鉴定。

在归城遗址20份浮选样品中共发现了95粒炭化植物种子（表Ⅲ.2.1），从中鉴定出了粟（*Setaria italica*）、黍（*Panicum miliacium*）和小麦（*Triticum aestivum*）三种谷物遗存，合计85粒，占出土植物种子总数的89.5%。其他植物种子有禾本科（Poaceae）的狗尾草（*Setaria viridis*）和豆科（Leguminosae）的胡枝子（*Lespedeza bicolor*）（表Ⅲ.2.2）。

归城遗址浮选出土的植物种子以炭化粟粒的数量最多，共计47粒，占出土植物种子总数的

49.5%。这些炭化粟粒均呈圆球状，直径多在1.5毫米左右，粟粒的表面较光滑，胚部因烧烤而爆裂呈凹口状（图Ⅲ.2.4；图版138：1）。

炭化黍粒的出土数量很少，仅发现了1粒，呈长圆状，个体较大，粒长2.09毫米，粒宽1.89毫米，表面较粗糙，胚部因烧烤而爆裂呈簸箕状（图Ⅲ.2.5；图版138：2）。

小麦遗存是归城遗址浮选结果中最为重要的发现，共发现了37粒炭化小麦，占出土植物种子总数的38.9%，其中多数已经残破，完整的有14粒。这些出土炭化小麦粒的形态特征明显，呈圆柱状，背部隆起，腹部有腹沟（图Ⅲ.2.6；图版139）。通过对完整麦粒进行测量发现，归城遗址出土小麦粒的尺寸很小，粒长的平均值是3.27毫米，粒宽的平均值是2.20毫米，粒厚的平均值是1.94毫米（表Ⅲ.2.3）。现代小麦粒的粒长一般在7毫米上下，粒宽将近3毫米。农学家曾对甘肃东灰山遗址出土的炭化小麦粒作过形态学分析（李璠等 1989：60）。其中大粒型的平均粒长和粒宽分别是5.70毫米和3.75毫米，普通型的是4.90毫米和3.35毫米，小粒型的是4.05毫米和2.95毫米，由此推断大粒型和普通型属于普通小麦（*T. aestivum*），小粒型属于密穗小麦（*T. compactum*）。从我们的测量数据看，归城遗址出土炭化小麦粒的尺寸不仅小于普通小麦，而且还明显小于密穗小麦，即便考虑到植物籽粒炭化变形这一因素，归城遗址出土小麦粒的尺寸仍然异常，其究竟应该属于什么品种有待于今后的分析和判断。

在归城遗址浮选结果中发现了5粒狗尾草植物种子，呈扁椭圆形，背部略鼓，腹部扁平，尺寸较小。禾本科植物中有许多品种属于田间杂草，其中狗尾草就是现今十分常见的田间杂草类植物。

浮选出土的豆科植物种子被鉴定为胡枝子，共5粒，呈倒卵形，因都已经破碎，无法测量。豆科在植物界是一个大科，种类十分繁多，根据植株的形态可分为木本、藤本和草本三大类。胡枝子属于灌木，枝条易燃烧、火力旺、烟量小、热量大。是一种良好的薪炭植物品种。

三、分析和讨论

归城遗址浮选结果中的炭化植物遗存并不丰富，炭化木屑含量不高，炭化植物种子数量较少。但是经过鉴定发现，出土植物种子中的绝大多数属于农作物遗存，为探讨当时农业生产的特点提供了信息。

归城遗址浮选出土的农作物遗存包括粟、黍、小麦三种谷物。粟俗称谷子，黍称糜子，这两种谷物的籽粒非常细小，被统称为“小米”，是中国古代北方旱作农业的代表性谷物品种。小麦是优良的旱地作物，起源于西亚，后传入中国，逐步替代粟和黍两种小米成为中国北方旱作农业的主体谷物品种。这三种谷物的组合说明，在西周至春秋时期，归城遗址所处地区的农业生产特点应该属于典型的北方旱作农业。

在归城遗址浮选出土的三种农作物中，小麦遗存的出土数量值得关注，共发现了37粒炭化小麦粒，与炭化粟粒的出土数量相差不大。一般而言，考古遗址出土古代植物遗存的绝对数量是有误差的，由于在堆积过程、埋藏过程和提取过程中所存在的各种因素的影响，不同体积或不同质地的植物种子在量化统计上不具备绝对数值的可比性（赵志军 2003：78）。例如，考古遗址浮选出土的炭化小麦即便是破碎麦粒在体积上也比炭化粟粒大得多；因此，仅凭绝对数量的统计数据不足以说明小麦在当时农业生产中的重要性。

为此，我们又采用另外一种量化统计方法，即植物遗存的出土概率（ubiquity）对出土农作物进行了统计比较。植物遗存的出土概率是指在遗址中发现某种植物种类的可能性，是根据出土有该植物种类的样品在采集的样品总数中所占的比例计算得出的，这种统计方法的特点是不考虑每份浮选样品中所出土的各种植物遗存的绝对数量，而是仅以“有”和“无”二分法作为计量标准，因此在客观上减弱了埋藏机制和埋藏背景造成的误差对分析结果的影响。一般而言，考古遗址中所埋藏的植物遗存绝大多数应该属于文化堆积，即人类通过劳动主动地（如谷物）或被动地（如杂草）获得的、而后又被人类有意识地遗弃或无意识地遗漏在遗址中的植物的遗存。从逻辑上讲，与人类生活关系越为密切的植物种类被带回居住地的可能性越大、频率越高，因而被遗弃或遗漏在遗址中的概率就越高，散布在遗址中的范围就越广，由此出土的概率也就越高。据此，我们就可以根据不同植物遗存的出土概率推断出它们在人类生活中的地位，从而分析出当时农业经济的特征。

根据统计，归城遗址小麦的出土概率是55%，与粟的出土概率相同（表Ⅲ.2.2）。再结合绝对数量统计结果，可以推测，西周至春秋时期，归城遗址古代先民从事的旱作农业生产中，小麦与粟的地位同等重要。

小麦起源于西亚，后传入中国。近些年来通过开展浮选工作，在黄河中下游地区的一系列考古遗址中发现了属于龙山时代或二里头时期的小麦遗存，例如，河南的禹州瓦店遗址、博爱西金城遗址、登丰王城岗遗址、偃师二里头遗址，山东的日照两城镇遗址、日照六甲庄遗址、聊城校场铺遗址，安徽的蚌埠禹会村遗址等（赵志军 2011：29）。这说明，至迟在龙山时代至二里头文化时期小麦已经传入到黄河中下游地区。小麦在旱地农作物中是高产作物，传入黄河中下游地区后，势必对本土原有的产量较低的谷物品种造成冲击，促使当地农业生产逐步地由以种植粟和黍两种小米为主向以种植小麦为主的方向转化。归城遗址的浮选结果揭示，当发展到西周至春秋时期，小麦虽然仍然没有完全取代粟和黍这两种小米，但已经成为北方旱作农业的重要谷物品种。

参考文献

李璠等，1989. 甘肃省民乐县东灰山新石器遗址古农业遗存新发现，农业考古，1：56-69.

赵志军，2003. 考古出土植物遗存中存在的误差，文物科技研究（第一辑），北京：科学出版社，2003：78-84.

赵志军，2004. 植物考古学的田野工作方法 ~ 浮选法，考古，3：80-87.

赵志军，2011. 中华文明形成时期的农业经济发展特点. 国家博物馆馆刊，1：19-31.

表Ⅲ.2.1　山东龙口归城浮选结果

Table Ⅲ.2.1　Results from Guicheng flotation

浮选号 Flotation sample #	遗迹/层位 Feature/stratum	灰坑 Refuse pit	土量 Soil vol. (L)	炭化物 Charcoal (g)	粟 Foxtail millet	黍 Broom-corn millet	小麦整 Whole wheat	小麦碎 Partial wheat	狗尾草 Green foxtail	豆科 Legumes
1	G2③	H20②-13	8	0.012						
2	G2①	H18-4	7	0.075			1	1		
3	G2③	H20①-6	7	0.231			1	1		
4	G2③	H20①-7	9	0.117						2
5	G2③	H20②-12	8	0.015						
6	G2③	H9-3	8	0.045	3		6	3		
7	G2③	H20①-2	8	0.571					1	
8	G2	H17-1	9	0.034	1					
9	G2③	H9-4	7	0.125	7		2	3	1	
10	G2①	H18-3	8	0.073	3			2		
11	G2③	H20①-5	6	0.333	2					
12	G2③	H12②-6	9	0.181					1	
13	G2	H17-2	9	0	1				1	
14	G2③	H8-3	8	0.337	3		1	1	1	1
15	G2	H12D1-2-6	6	0				2		
16	G2③	H20①-3	9	0.656	10					1
17	G1③	H8-2	9	0.344		1		8		
18	G1③	H8-1	8.5	0.159	3		1	1		1
19	G2③	H20①-4	7	0.274	8		1			
20	G2	H19-5	8	0.49	6		1	1		

表Ⅲ.2.2　归城出土植物种子统计表

Table Ⅲ.2.2　Statistics of plant seeds from Guicheng

植物名称 Plant name	出土数量 Absolute number	出土概率 Ubiquity
粟 Foxtail millet (*Setaria italica*)	47	55%
黍 Broomcorn millet (*Panicum miliaceum*)	1	5%
小麦 Wheat (*Triticum aestivum*)	37	55%
狗尾草 Green foxtail (*Setaria viridis*)	5	25%
胡枝子 Shrubby bush clover (*Lespedeza bicolor*)	5	20%

表Ⅲ.2.3　归城出土小麦测量

Table Ⅲ.2.3　Measurements of wheat grains from Guicheng

粒长 Seed length	粒宽 Seed width	粒厚 Seed thickness
3.125	2.375	2.034
3.463	2.146	1.946
3.253	2.25	2.326
3.266	2.099	1.991
2.912	2.097	1.95
3.264	1.647	1.312
3.512	2.987	2.197
3.187	1.845	1.646
3.328	2.462	2.247
3.662	2.121	1.744
3.487	2.636	2.393
3.075	1.883	1.782
2.888	1.795	1.531
3.301	2.402	2.06

图Ⅲ.2.1　考古队员准备土样，进行浮选

FigureⅢ.2.1　Team members preparing soil samples for flotation.

图Ⅲ.2.2　考古队员进行浮选作业，2009年7月17日

FigureⅢ.2.2　Team members proceeding with flotation apparatus, July 17, 2009.

图Ⅲ.2.3　考古队员仔细冲洗细筛以备浮选下一包土样

Figure Ⅲ.2.3　Team member carefully washing the filter for use in flotation of the next soil sample.

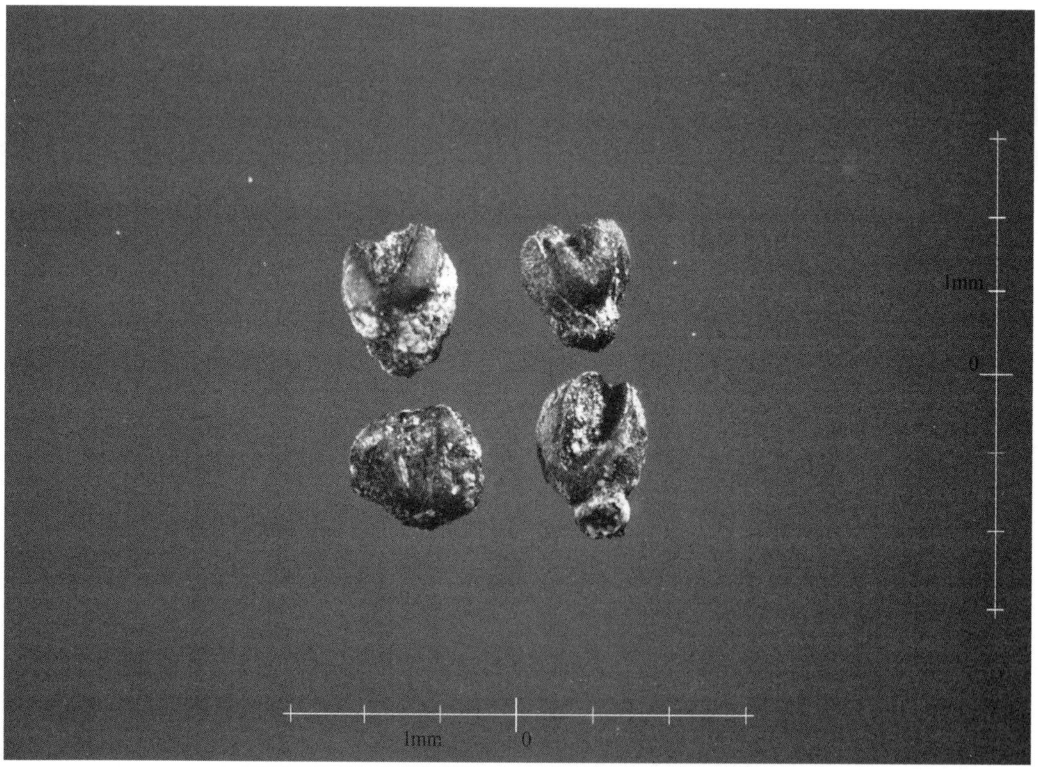

图Ⅲ.2.4　粟

Figure Ⅲ.2.4　Foxtail millet.

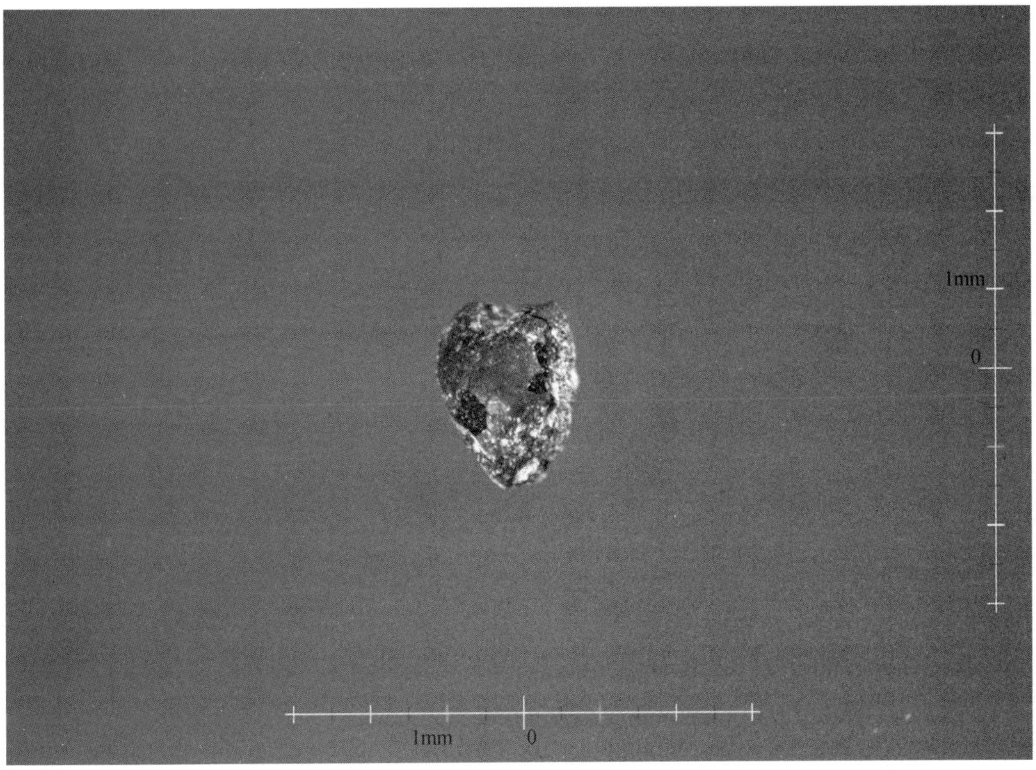

图Ⅲ.2.5　黍

FigureⅢ.2.5　Broomcorn millet.

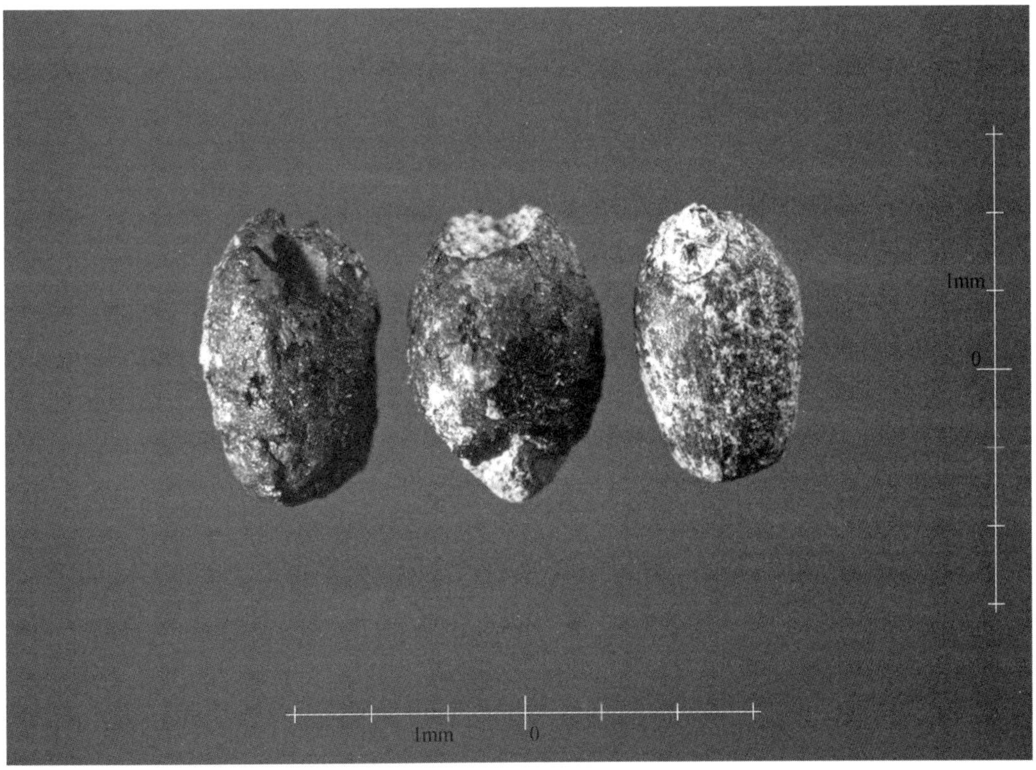

图Ⅲ.2.6　小麦

FigureⅢ.2.6　Wheat.

Appendix 2: Results of Flotation at the Guicheng City Site, Longkou, Yantai, Shandong

Zhao Zhijun

1. Introduction

The Guicheng site, located in Longkou County, Shandong Province, was an important city site that was occupied from the mid-Western Zhou period to the Spring and Autumn period. From 2007 to 2009, the Department of East Asian Languages and Cultures of Columbia University and the Institute of Archaeology of the Chinese Academy of Social Sciences (CASS) formed a joint archaeological team to conduct archaeological surveys at Guicheng. On the basis of a comprehensive survey of the site, in July 2009 the joint archaeological team chose to carry out a small-scale test excavation in the southern part of the inner city of Guicheng. During the test excavation, soil samples were collected for flotation in order to obtain plant remains that can help us understand the use of plants by the people who occupied Guicheng, and the characteristics of their agriculture.

A total of twenty flotation samples were collected at Guicheng, all from refuse pits. Each sample measured around eight liters, with a total of 158 liters of flotation material. The work of flotation was carried out at the excavation site, using a flotation apparatus (Zhao Zhijun 2004: 80-87) with a 0.2 mm-pore mesh sieve. The flotation took place on July 15-17, 2009 (Figs. Ⅲ.2.1-Ⅲ.2.3).

The plant samples collected in the flotation were dried and returned to the archaeobotanic laboratory of the Institute of Archaeology, CASS, to be sorted, identified, and analyzed.

2. Results of Flotation

According to the laboratory sorting and identification, the charred plant remains recovered from the Guicheng flotation samples consist of charcoals and plant seeds. Charcoals are most likely incompletely burned fuel or accidentally burned construction timber and lumber. The charcoals recovered from the Guicheng flotation sample are extremely fragmented, and they need to be examined by experts for identification of tree species.

In the twenty flotation sample bags from Guicheng, a total of ninety-five charred plant seeds were found (Table Ⅲ.2.1). Among these, three kinds of crops were identified: foxtail millet (*Setaria italica*), broomcorn millet (*Panicum miliacium*), and wheat (*Triticum aestivum*). These included eighty-five grains, accounting for 89.5% of the excavated seeds. Other seeds included green foxtail (*Setaria viridis*) from the Poaceae family, and shrubby bush clover (*Lespedeza bicolor*) from the Fabaceae family (Table Ⅲ.2.2).

Charred foxtail millet was the most abundant type of seed in the excavated sample, with a total of forty-seven grains accounting for 49.5% of the excavated seeds. The foxtail millet grains were typically spherical, with a maximum diameter of approximate 1.5 mm. The surface of the millet grains was relatively smooth, and the germs had a burst open shape with a notch as a result of being burned (Fig.Ⅲ.2.4; Pl, 138: 1).

The amount of excavated broomcorn millet was rather small, with only one grain recovered. It was round in shape and relatively large, 2.09 mm in diameter and 1.89 mm wide. Its surface was relatively coarse, with the germ assuming a dustpan shape as a result of being burned (Fig. Ⅲ.2.5; Pl, 138: 2).

The wheat remains were the most important discovery in the flotation results from Guicheng. There were thirty-seven wheat grains, accounting for 38.9% of plant seeds recovered. Most of the grains were fragmentary, with only fourteen complete specimens. The appearance of these charred wheat grains was distinctive, with a cylindrical shape, a bulging back, and a groove in the center (Fig. Ⅲ.2.6; Pl, 139). According to measurements of most specimens, the wheat grains discovered at Guicheng were very small, with an average length of 3.27 mm, an average width of 2.20 mm, and an average thickness of 1.94 mm (Table Ⅱ.2.3). Modern-day wheat grains are typically around 7 mm in length and 3 mm in width. Agronomists have analyzed charred wheat grains recovered from the Donghuishan site in Gansu Province (Li Fan et al 1989: 60) and found that the largest grains had a length and width of 5.70 and 3.75 mm respectively, regular-size grains were 4.90 by 3.36 mm, and small grains were 4.05 by 2.96. From this they concluded that the large and regular-grained wheat was common wheat (*T. aestivum*), and the small-grained wheat was club wheat (*T. compactum*). From our measurements, the dimensions of the wheat recovered at Guicheng are not only smaller than those of common wheat, but obviously also smaller than club wheat. Even accounting for the effects of burning on plant seeds, the dimensions of the wheat grains recovered at Guicheng are still remarkably small, and judgment as to their type will have to await further analysis and determination in the future.

In the Guicheng flotation sample, five seeds of green foxtail were also found. They had a flat oval shape, with a rounded back, a flat middle, and relatively small dimensions. There are many varieties of weeds in the Poaceae family, of which green foxtail are some of the most commonly seen today.

The legumes found in the Guicheng flotation sample have been determined to be of the *Lespedeza* genus. There were five leaf-shaped seeds found in total. Because they were all fragmentary, they could not be measured. Legumes form a large category in botany, including three sub-categories: woody plants, vines, and herbs, depending on their form. *Lespedeza* includes bushes whose branches are easily burned, create large flames, producing little smoke and much heat, making them a very suitable fuel wood.

3. Analysis and Discussion

The charred plant remains recovered in flotation at the Guicheng site are not very diverse. There are few charcoals, and the number of plant seeds is also relatively small. However, according to the results of our evaluation, the majority of the recovered seeds are crop remains, providing a basis for discussion of the agriculture of the period.

The recovered crop remains include foxtail millet, broomcorn millet, and wheat. Foxtail millet is conventionally called *gŭzi*, and broomcorn millet *méizi* in Chinese. The grains of the two types of cereals, collectively referred to as *xiăomĭ* 'millet', are quite small, and are representative examples of dryland agricultural crops of North China. Wheat is also a dryland crop, which originated in Western Asia and was later introduced to China, gradually displacing the millets to become the dominant crop in dryland agriculture in North China. The combined presence of these three crops together demonstrates that in the periods from the Western Zhou to the Spring and Autumn, the agricultural practices of Guicheng and its surrounding region were characterized by the typical dryland agriculture of North China.

Among the three crops recovered from the flotation results, it is important to note the quantity of wheat remains. There were thirty-seven charred wheat grains recovered, roughly the same amount as foxtail millet. Generally speaking, there can be some bias in determining the absolute amount of ancient plant remains from archaeological sites, and because of multiple factors during deposition, taphonomic, and recovery processes, seeds with different volumes or textures can be unsuitable for direct comparison with quantitative statistics (Zhao Zhijun 2003: 78). For example, the volume of charred wheat grains, even if they are fragmentary, is considerably greater than that of foxtail millet grains; therefore, relying on statistics based on absolute counts is not enough to clarify the importance of wheat in the agriculture of the time period.

For these reasons, we used a different quantitative statistical method, the *ubiquity* of the plant remains in the excavation, to conduct a statistical comparison of the excavated crops. The ubiquity of the plant remains refers to the likelihood of discovering a certain type of plant remains at the site, which is calculated according to the proportion of flotation samples that contained that type of plant. The advantage of this statistical method is that one does not need absolute counts of plant remains in any single sample, because it is only calculated based on presence or absence. Therefore, this method reduces the effect that deposition mechanisms might have had on the results of the analysis. Generally speaking, plant remains that are deposited at archaeological sites are cultural deposits, including plant remains that are obtained both actively (such as crop grains) and passively (such as weeds), and are later knowingly abandoned or unknowingly deposited at the site. Logically speaking, the bigger role a plant played in humans' lives, the more frequently it would have been taken back to residential areas, the more likely it was to be abandoned or dropped, the wider its distribution within the bounds of the site, and the higher its ubiquity score in the excavation. Therefore, based on the different frequencies of plant remains in the excavation, we can infer their importance in human life and can analyze the features of the economic system of the time.

The share of wheat in the Guicheng excavations was 55%, the same as foxtail millet (Table Ⅲ.2.2). If we look at the combined statistical results, we can surmise that from the Western Zhou to the Spring and Autumn periods, wheat and foxtail millet had equally important positions in the dryland agriculture practiced by the ancient residents of Guicheng.

Wheat originated in Western Asia and was later introduced into China. In recent years, with the development of flotation work, wheat remains have been discovered at a series of sites in the middle and lower reaches of the Yellow River region, dating to the Longshan Culture or Erlitou Culture period. For instance, there are the Wadian site in Yuzhou, the Xijincheng site in Bo'ai, the Wangchenggang site in Dengfeng, and the Erlitou site in Yanshi, all in Henan Province, the Liangchengzhen and Liujiazhuang sites in Rizhao, the Jiaochangpu site in Liaocheng, all in Shandong Province, and the Yuhuicun site in Bengbu, Anhui Province, among others (Zhao Zhijun 2011: 29). This demonstrates that during the timeframe from Longshan to the Erlitou Culture, wheat had already entered the middle and lower reaches of the Yellow River region. Wheat is a high-yield product in dryland agriculture, and after it entered this region, it was bound to threaten the relatively low-yield cereals previously cultivated there, the millets, and to bring about a shift from a system of agricultural production based on foxtail and broomcorn millet to one based on wheat. The results of the flotation at Guicheng show that during the development from the Western Zhou period to the Spring and Autumn period, though wheat had still not completely replaced millet, it had already become an important cereal crop in the dry-land agriculture of North China.

References

Li, Fan 李璠, *et al.*, 1989. "Gansu sheng Minle xian Donghuishan xin shiqi yizhi gu nongye yicun xin faxian" 甘肃省民乐县东灰山新石器遗址古农业遗存新发现 (New Discoveries of Ancient Agricultural Remains at the Neolithic Site of

Donghuishan, Minle County, Gansu Province), *Nongye kaogu* 农业考古, 1: 56-69.

Zhao, Zhijun 赵志军, 2003. "Kaogu chutu zhiwu yicun zhong cunzai de wucha" 考古出土植物遗存中存在的误差 (Bias in Excavated Archaeological Plant Remains), *Wenwu keji yanjiu* 文物科技研究 (Technical Research on Cultural Relics), vol. 1, pp. 78-84. Beijing: Kexue chubanshe.

Zhao, Zhijun 赵志军, 2004. "Zhiwu kaoguxue de tianye gongzuo fangfa: fuxuanfa" 植物考古学的田野工作方法——浮选法 (Fieldwork Methods of Paleoethnobotany: Floatation), *Kaogu* 考古, 3: 80-87.

Zhao, Zhijun 赵志军, 2011. "Zhonghua wenming xingcheng shiqi de nongye jingji fazhan tedian" 中华文明形成时期的农业经济发展特点, *Guojia bowuguan guankan* 国家博物馆馆刊 (National Museum Journal), 1: 19-31.

附录三　山东龙口市归城城址2009年试掘出土动物遗存研究

李志鹏　任乐乐　Tom A. Stidham

归城城址（120°34′E，37°35′40″N）位于山东省胶东半岛西部黄水河中下游的龙口市文基镇。它地理位置优越，背靠莱山，面朝黄水河，坐落在五陵盆地中（图Ⅰ.0.3）。归城故城分内、外两城，遗址总面积达800万平方米。其中内城南北长490米，东西宽525米；外城包含归城姜家、和平、男埠、北山、大于家、董家、东迟家、曹家村等8个自然村（中美联合归城考古队 2011：32～35）。2009年夏，中美联合考古工作队在内城南部试掘中清理了20个单位，出土了大量的陶器及部分动物骨骼遗存。2014年夏中国社会科学院考古研究所科技考古中心动物考古实验室受委托对这批动物遗存进行了鉴定和分析。

第一节　方法和材料

考古队在发掘过程中严格按照地层单位细致收集动物骨骼，便于整理鉴定过程中不同单位的对比统计分析。在整理过程中，按照种属、部位、方位（左右）、数量、痕迹记录、测量等顺序进行。测量内容主要参考《考古遗址出土动物骨骼测量指南》一书（安格拉·冯登德里施 2007），鉴定过程中主要比对中国社会科学院考古研究所科技考古中心动物考古实验室的现生对比标本，同时参考中外文的骨骼图谱及相关文章（伊丽莎白·施密德 1992；盛和林 1992；格罗莫娃 1960）。

这批动物骨骼主要来自归城城址2009年夏天试掘的H2、H3、H6、H8、H9、H11、H12、H15、H16、H17、H18、H19、H20等13个单位，共计345件标本，其中可鉴定标本为199件，另146件由于太过破碎，仅以大、中、小哺乳动物区分（图版140～141）。

第二节　鉴定结果

依照出土陶器形制，该遗址目前大致可分为三个阶段（见本书上编第10章），其中H20属于第一期，绝对年代为1000BC～920BC，骨骼标本数为70件；H18，H19属于第二期，绝对年代为860BC～750BC，骨骼标本数为128件；H2，H3，H8，H9属于第三期，绝对年代为750BC～500BC，骨骼标本数为6件。另外H6，H11，H12，H15，H16，H17，由于陶器出土数量太少无法分期，骨骼遗存也未分期。

一、第一阶段

1. 种属鉴定

软体动物门　Mollusca

　双壳纲　Bivalvia

　　帘蛤目　Veneroida

脊索动物门　Chordata

　鸟纲　Aves

　　鸡形目　Galliformes

　　　雉科　Phasianidae

　　　　雉属　*Phasianus*

　　　　　环颈雉　*Phasianus colchicus*

　哺乳纲　Mammalia

　　偶蹄目　Artiodactyla

　　　猪科　Suidae

　　　　猪属　*Sus*

　　　　　家猪　*Sus scrofa domesticus*

　　　鹿科　Cervidae

　　　　鹿属　*Cervus*

　　　　　梅花鹿　*Cervus nippon*

　　　　狍属　*Capreolus*

　　　　　狍　*Capreolus pygargus*

　　　牛科　Bovidae

　　　　牛属　*Bos*

　　　　　黄牛　*Bos taurus*

　　食肉目　Carnivora

　　　犬科　Canidae

　　　　犬属　*Canis*

　　　　　狗　*Canis familiaris*

2. 分类描述

帘蛤目　　Veneroida

标本与最小个体数：H8中有帘蛤目的贝壳碎片7片（图Ⅲ.3.1：1），由于保存状况不佳且缺乏对比标本，无法进行更为详细的种属鉴定。材料可代表的最小个体数为1。

雉科　　Phasianidae

　　环颈雉　　*Phasianus colchicus*

标本与最小个体数：H9中仅有一件愈合的左肱骨远端（图Ⅲ.3.1：2）。材料可代表的最小个体数为1。

猪科　　Suidae

　　家猪　　*Sus scrofa domestica*

标本与最小个体数：H8中枢椎一件，左桡骨近端一件，右股骨远端关节一件；H9中左下颌一件。材料可代表的最小个体数为1。

鹿科　　Cervidae

　　梅花鹿　　*Cervus nippon*

标本与最小个体数：H3中左掌骨近端一件，尺骨远端骨干一件，左桡骨远端一件；H9中右胫骨近端一件（图Ⅲ.3.1：3）。材料可代表的最小个体数为1。

鹿科　　Cervidae

　　狍　　*Capreolus pygargus*

标本与最小个体数：H3中左股骨远端一件（图Ⅲ.3.1：4）。材料可代表的最小个体数为1。

牛科　　Bovidae

　　黄牛　　*Bos taurus*

标本与最小个体数：H2中左上颌游离P2一件；H3中右中央跗骨一件，第四跗骨一件，Ⅱ趾一件（图Ⅲ.3.1：5）；H8中左下颌齿隙一件；H9中右跖骨远端一件。材料可代表的最小个体数为1。

犬科　　Canidae

　　狗　　*Canis familiaris*

标本与最小个体数：H3中右下颌一件（图Ⅲ.3.1：6），右肱骨近端一件，右尺骨近端，左股骨近端一件，肩胛骨远端一件，左胫骨近端一件，左胫骨远端一件，右盆骨一件；H8中左桡骨近端一件，左股骨远端一件；材料可代表的最小个体数为1。

二、第二阶段

1. 种属鉴定

哺乳纲　Mammalia

奇蹄目　Perissodactyla

马属　*Equus*

马　*Equus caballus*

偶蹄目　Artiodactyla

猪科　Suidae

猪属　*Sus*

家猪　*Sus scrofa domestica*

鹿科　Cervidae

鹿属　*Cervus*

梅花鹿　*Cervus nippon*

狍属　*Capreolus*

狍　*Capreolus pygargus*

牛科　Bovidae

牛属　*Bos*

黄牛　*Bos taurus*

食肉目　Carnivora

犬科　Canidae

犬属　*Canis*

狗　*Canis familiaris*

鼬科　Mustelidae

獾　*Meles sp.*

2. 分类描述

奇蹄目　Perissodactyla

马　*Equus caballus*

标本与最小个体数：H18中右盆骨一件，Ⅱ趾一件（图Ⅲ.3.1：7）。材料可代表的最小个体数为1。

猪科　Suidae

家猪　*Sus scrofa domestica*

标本与最小个体数：H18中右肩胛骨一件，左桡骨近端一件；H19中右上颌一件，右肩胛骨远端一件，右肱骨远端一件（图Ⅲ.3.1：8），右盆骨一件，左股骨远端一件，左胫骨远端一件，左第四跖骨一件。材料可代表的最小个体数为1。

鹿科　Cervidae

梅花鹿　*Cervus nippon*

标本与最小个体数：H18中左胫骨近端一件，右股骨远端骨干一件，腰椎一件；H19中有肱骨远端骨干一件，左桡骨远端骨干一件。材料可代表的最小个体数为1。

鹿科　Cervidae

狍　*Capreolus pygargus*

标本与最小个体数：H18中左胫骨远端一件（图Ⅲ.3.1：9）；H19中有肱骨远端骨干一件，左桡骨远端骨干一件。材料可代表的最小个体数为1。

牛科　Bovidae

黄牛　*Bos taurus*

标本与最小个体数：H18中左下颌髁突一件，左胫骨远端一件；H19中左下颌体一件，Ⅰ趾远端两件，Ⅱ趾两件，Ⅲ趾一件，左肱骨远端两件，右桡骨近端一件，左桡骨远端一件，右尺骨近端一件，右尺骨近端骨干一件，左尺骨近端一件，左股骨近端骨干一件，右股骨远端一件，右胫骨近端骨干两件，右胫骨近端关节一件，左胫骨远端一件，左胫骨近端两件，左距骨一件，右盆骨一件，左掌骨近端三件，左掌骨远端一件，右掌骨一件，左跖骨一件，跖骨远端两件，右跖骨远端一件，右中央跗骨一件，角心一件（图Ⅲ.3.1：11）。材料可代表的最小个体数为3。

犬科　Canidae

狗　*Canis familiaris*

标本与最小个体数：H19中左下颌一件，右股骨远端一件。材料可代表的最小个体数为1。

鼬科　Mustelidae

獾　*Meles sp.*

标本与最小个体数：H19中右胫骨一件（图Ⅲ.3.1：10）。材料可代表的最小个体数为1。

三、第三阶段

1. 种属鉴定

哺乳纲　Mammalia

偶蹄目　Artiodactyla

猪科　Suidae

猪属　Sus

家猪　*Sus scrofa domestica*

食肉目　Carnivora

犬科　Canidae

犬属　*Canis*

狗　*Canis familiaris*

2. 分类描述

猪科　Suidae

家猪　*Sus scrofa domestica*

标本与最小个体数：H20中右股骨近端骨干三件。材料可代表的最小个体数为1。

犬科　Canidae

狗　*Canis familiaris*

标本与最小个体数：H20中左上颌一件。材料可代表的最小个体数为1。

四、末分阶段

由于H6，H11，H12，H15，H16，H17没有具体的分期，本文仅统计各种属可鉴定标本数，其中狗为2件，环颈雉1件，黄牛20件，马1件，梅花鹿2件，羊2件（图Ⅲ.3.1：12，13），猪57件（图Ⅲ.3.1：14）。其中雉科鸟类标本经Tom Stidham鉴定可能为原鸡属（Gallus），但原鸡属的标本尺寸变化较大，目前的鉴定还不能十分肯定。不过，可以确定不是锦鸡属（Chyrsolophus）、角雉属（Tragopan）、长尾雉属（Syrmaticus）、雉属（Phasianus）。

第三节　讨　　论

一、数量统计及生业模式分析

由于发掘面积有限，出土的动物遗存数量相应较少，使我们后期分析的数据欠缺。归城遗址第一阶段属于西周早期，该时期遗址动物群中梅花鹿、狍子、黄牛、家猪、狗、环颈雉和帘蛤目的最小个体数均为1，各占遗址动物群动物最小个体数总数的14.29%；梅花鹿，狍子，黄牛，家猪，狗，环颈雉和帘蛤目可鉴定标本数分别为4、1、4、4、25、1、1，占遗址动物群动物遗存可鉴定标本数总数的10%、2.5%、10%、10%、62.5%、2.5%、2.5%。

归城遗址二期属于西周末到春秋早期，该时期遗址动物群中梅花鹿、狍子、獾、家猪、狗与马的最小个体数均为1，均占遗址动物群动物最小个体数总数的11%。黄牛的最小个体数为3，占动物群动物最小个体数的33%。可鉴定标本数分别占总体的8.06%，1.61%，1.61%，17.47%，3.23%，3.23%，64.52%；三期中只有家猪和狗，最小个体数和可鉴定标本数均为1，均占总数的50%（表Ⅲ.3.1）。

家养动物可鉴定标本数第一阶段中占动物总数的82.5%，第二阶段占90.32%，第三阶段占100%。家养动物最小个体数第一阶段中占动物总数的42.87%，第二阶段占66.66%，第三阶段占100%。由于骨骼数量较少，数量少的动物种属最小个体数比例比实际的肉食贡献大，因此我们以可鉴定标本数作为我们的参考标准，可以看出归城先民从西周早期到战国时期获取动物资源的方式皆以家畜饲养为主，包括黄牛、猪、马、狗。至于发掘区的动物遗存资料体现的渔猎经济在动物经济中的比重始终有限，东周时则纯粹为家畜饲养经济，但该时期发掘所获资料有限，难以确定渔猎经济在遗址中的实际比重。

二、骨骼表面痕迹与人类利用动物资源方式探讨

通过对归城城址动物骨骼表面痕迹进行观测分析，发现主要有人工改造痕迹和动物改造痕迹2种。其中动物改造痕迹主要为食肉类的（狗）啃咬痕迹（图Ⅲ.3.1：15），H19中居多且多数发生在黄牛骨骼上。狗啃咬痕迹的出现，表明当时人类可能畜养狗作为狩猎帮手抑或看家护院，反映归城先民已经畜养家畜狗，并能够提供一些骨骼（肉类）剩余物喂饲狗。人工改造痕迹主要有先民烤肉留下的烧痕，对动物肢体进行肢解、分割、剥皮、剔肉等多种肉食生产行为相关的砍痕（图Ⅲ.3.1：16），以及加工骨器或装饰品留下的磨光痕、孔痕（图Ⅲ.3.1：17，18）。

三、动物祭祀现象

用动物祭祀或随葬一直是考古发掘中常见的文化现象，在归城未归属到具体分期阶段的H12中，出土一具未成年猪的后半身骨骼。包括22件不完整肋骨，未愈合的胸椎5件，未愈合的腰椎5件，髋臼未愈合的较完整的髋骨1件，两端未愈合的左右股骨各1件，两端未愈合的左右胫骨各1件，左腓骨近端1件，右腓骨远端1件，未愈合的左右跟骨各1件，左距骨1件（图Ⅲ.3.1：19）。这些骨骼大多可关节相连，左右相对的同一骨骼尺寸基本相同，可见为同一个体，而且骨骼表面无任何人工痕迹，多数骨骼都应该是完整，不完整的骨骼都是在发掘时残断的，而这些骨骼本身不结实容易断，或是有些系骨骺未愈合的骨骼导致发掘中收集骨骼时骨骺缺失。由此推断，H12可能是一个祭祀坑，当时取一半幼猪进行祭祀也可能是一种风俗习惯。

虽然我们不清楚这些骨骼在出土时是否关节相连，但从上述骨骼表面无任何人工痕迹来判断，应该当时出土时是关节相连未被肢解的，否则会留下肢解的屠宰痕迹。上述猪骨中最早愈合的是髋骨的髋臼，愈合年龄为1岁（Silver 1989），因此该猪年龄在1岁以下。

第四节 小 结

通过对归城遗址出土的动物骨骼进行整理和分析，我们认为归城遗址先民借助其依山傍水的地理位置，既发展农耕经济，畜养猪、狗、黄牛、马，又以狩猎经济作为肉食资源的补充，捕获梅花鹿、狍子、獾、环颈雉等野生动物。但是，家养动物一直都是提供肉食资源的主体，偶尔捕获的野生动物只是作为必要的补充。

参考文献

安格拉・冯登德里施，2007. 考古遗址出土动物骨骼测量指南. 北京：科学出版社.

格罗莫娃，B，1960. 哺乳动物大型管状骨检索表，北京：科学出版社.

马萧林，2008. 灵宝西坡遗址的肉食消费模式——骨骼部位发现率、表面痕迹及破碎度. 华夏考古，4：73-87.

盛和林，1992. 中国鹿类动物. 上海：华东师范大学出版社.

Silver, I. A., 1989. “The Ageing of Domestic Animals,” in Brothwell, D. & Higgs, E. S. (eds.), *Science in Archaeology*, pp. 250-68. London: Thames and Hudson.

伊丽莎白・施密德，1992. 动物骨骼图谱. 武汉：中国地质大学出版社.

中美联合归城考古队，2011. 山东龙口市归城两周城址调查简报. 考古，3：30-39.

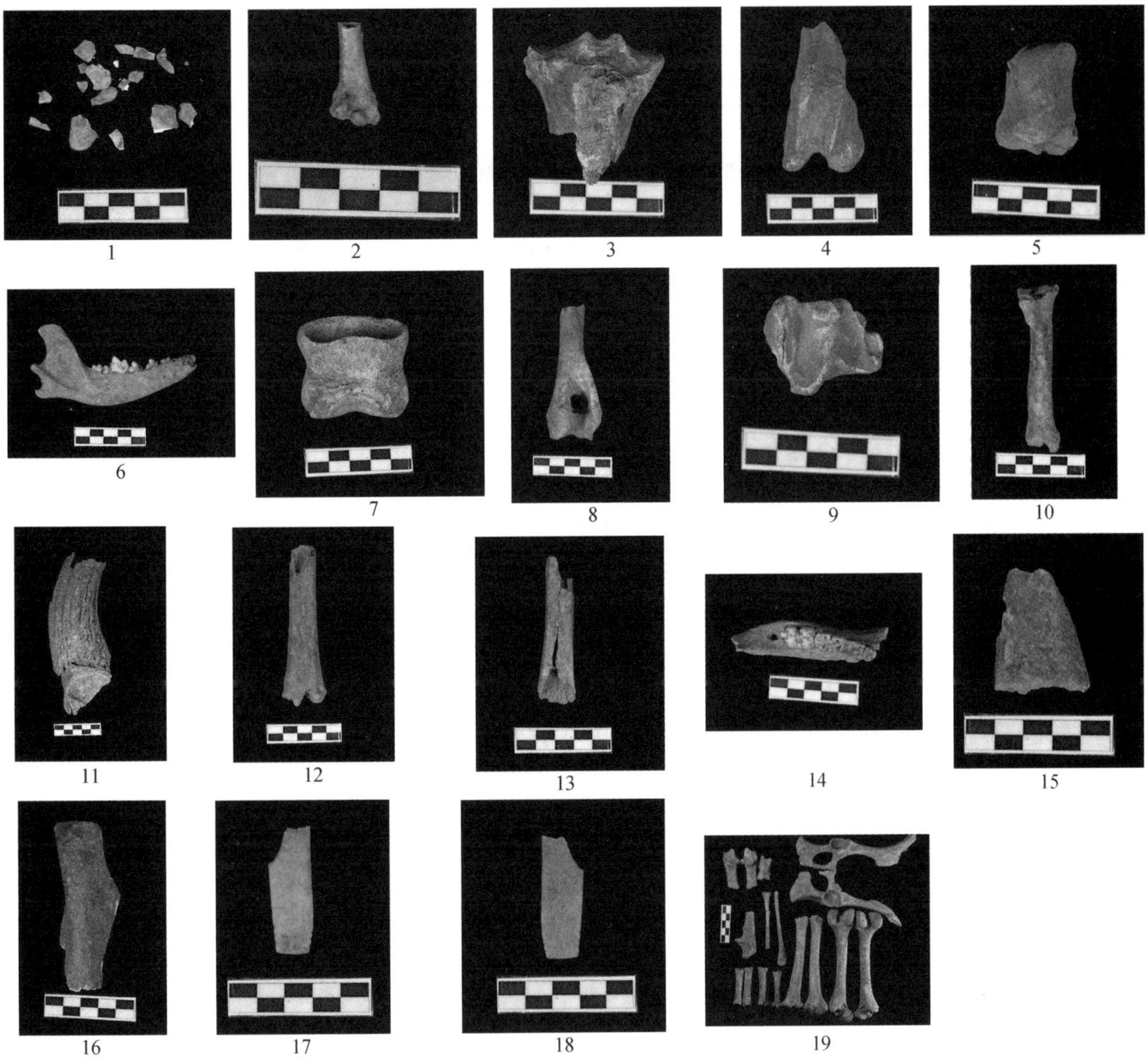

图Ⅲ.3.1　归城城址出土动物照片

1. 拟帘蛤目背侧（TG1③H8-5） 2. 环颈雉左肱骨腹侧（TG1③H9） 3.梅花鹿 右胫骨背侧（TG1③H9北隔梁） 4. 狍子左股骨背侧（TG1①H3③-10） 5. 黄牛Ⅱ趾背侧（TG1H3①） 6. 狗右下颌颊侧（TG1①H3③-10） 7. 马Ⅱ趾背面（TG2①H18-5） 8. 猪右肱骨背侧（TG2H19-3） 9. 狍子左胫骨远端（TG2①H18-5） 10. 獾右胫骨背侧（TG2H19-3） 11. 黄牛角心（TG2H19-3） 12. 羊右胫骨背侧（TG2H17-4） 13. 羊右掌骨腹侧（TG2③H11-1） 14. 猪右下颌嚼面（TG2H17-4） 15. 食肉动物（狗）咬痕中型哺乳动物肢骨碎块（TG2H2） 16. 砍痕黄牛右胫骨背侧（TG2H19-3） 17. 磨光与穿孔中型哺乳动物肋骨背侧（TG2H3②） 18. 磨光与穿孔中型哺乳动物肋骨腹侧（TG2H3②） 19. 幼年猪骨架2（TG2H12-4②）

Figure Ⅲ.3.1　Animal Remains Discovered in Guicheng.

1. Veneroida, dorsal（TG1③H8-5） 2. Common pheasant left humerus, ventral (TG1③H9) 3. Sika deer right tibia, dorsal (TG1③H9-separator of trenches) 4. Roe deer left femur, dorsal (TG1①H3③-10) 5. Cattle second phalange, dorsal (TG1H3①) 6. Dog lower right mandible, ventral (TG1①H3③-10) 7. Horse second phalange, dorsal (TG2①H18-5) 8. Pig right humerus, dorsal (TG2H19-3) 9. Roe deer distal left tibia (TG2①H18-5) 10. Badger right tibia, dorsal (TG2H19-3) 11. Cattle horn core (TG2H19-3) 12. Sheep/goat right tibia, dorsal (TG2H17-4) 13. Sheep/goat right metacarpal, ventral (TG2③H11-1) 14. Pig lower right mandible, chewing surface (TG2H17-4) 15. Carnivore (dog) bite marks on limb fragment of a medium size mammal (TG2H2) 16. Slash marks on cattle right tibia, dorsal (TG2H19-3) 17. Polishing and drilling marks on rib of medium-size mammal, dorsal (TG2H3②) 18. Polishing and drilling marks on rib of a medium-size mammal, ventral (TG2H3②) 19. Young pig skeleton 2 (TG2H12-4②).

表Ⅲ.3.1　归城城址出土动物最小个体数（MNI）和可鉴定标本数（NISP）及其百分比

Table Ⅲ.3.1　The percentage of bones found at Guicheng in terms of minimum number of individuals (MNI) and number of identified specimens (NISP)

动物种属	MNI			MNI%			NISP				NISP%			
	Ⅰ期	Ⅱ期	Ⅲ期	Ⅰ期	Ⅱ期	Ⅲ期	Ⅰ期	Ⅱ期	Ⅲ期	未分期	Ⅰ期	Ⅱ期	Ⅲ期	未分期
梅花鹿 *Cervus nippon*	1	1		14.29%	11.11%		4	5		2	10.00%	8.06%		2.35%
狍子 *Capreolus pygargus*	1	1		14.29%	11.11%		1	1			2.50%	1.61%		
獾 *Meles sp.*		1			11.11%			1		57		1.61%		67.06%
猪 *Sus domestica*	1	1	1	14.29%	11.11%	50%	4	11	1		10.00%	17.74%	50%	
黄牛 *Bos domestica*	1	3		14.29%	33.33%		4	40		20	10.00%	64.52%		23.53%
狗 *Canis familiaris*	1	1	1	14.29%	11.11%	50%	25	2	1	2	62.50%	3.23%	50%	2.35%
马 *Equus caballus*		1			11.11%			2		1		3.23%		1.18%
羊 *Ovis sp.*										2				2.35%
环颈雉 *Phasianus colchicus*	1			14.29%			1			1	2.50%			1.18%
帘蛤目 *Veneroida*	1			14.29%			1				2.50%			
总计	7	9	2	100%	100%	100%	40	62	2	85	100.00%	100.00%	100%	100.00%

Appendix 3: Animal Remains Discoveries during 2009 Test Excavations at the Guicheng City Site, Longkou, Shandong

Zhipeng Li, Lele Ren, and Tom A. Stidham

The Guicheng city site (120°34′E, 37°35′40″N) is located in Wenji Township of Longkou City, in the mid-lower reaches of the Huangshui River in the western Jiaodong Peninsula, Shandong Province. It has an excellent geographical position, situated in a basin surrounded by five hills, with its back to Mount Lai and facing on the Huangshui River (Fig. Ⅰ.0.3). The ancient city of Guicheng is about 8,000,000 m^2 in size and can be divided into inner and outer cities. The inner city is 490 m long from north to south and 525 m wide from east to west. The outer city wall now contains eight villages, including Jiangjia, Heping, Nanbu, Beishan, Da Yujia, Dongjia, Dongchijia, and Caojiacun (Sino-American Joint Guicheng Archaeological Team 2011: 32-35). In the summer of 2009, the Sino-American Joint Archaeological Team carried out a test excavation in the southern part of the inner city during which twenty stratigraphic units were cleaned yielding a large number of pottery sherds and animal bones. In the summer of 2014 the zooarchaeology laboratory of the Center for Scientific Archaeology of the Institute of Archaeology, CASS, was entrusted with identifying and analyzing these animal remains.

Section 1: Methods and Materials

While excavating, the archaeological team carefully collected animal bones in strict accordance with stratigraphic units, which made it straightforward for us to carry out comparative statistical analysis on the different units when sorting and identifying the remains. During the analysis, we recorded taxon, bone type, side (left or right), number, traces of marks, and measurements for all finds. For measurements, we followed Angela von den Driesch's *Guide to the measurement of animal bones from archaeological sites* (Von den Driesch 2007). For taxonomic identification, we mainly compared the remains with bones from the reference collection of the zooarchaeology laboratory of the Center for Scientific Archaeology of the Institute of Archaeology, but also consulted Chinese and foreign anatomical atlases and related articles (Schmid 1972; Sheng Helin 1992; Gromova 1960).

This collection of animal bones mainly came from the following thirteen stratigraphic units (pits) excavated at the Guicheng city site in the summer of 2009: H2, H3, H6, H8, H9, H11, H12, H15, H16, H17, H18, H19, and H20. There was a total of 345 specimens, 199 of which could be identified as to taxon and 146 too broken to distinguish beyond the categories of large, medium, and small mammals (Pls: 140-141).

Section 2: Results of Identification

The Guicheng site can be divided into three stages in accordance with the transition in pottery forms (see Part Ⅰ, Chapter 10). H20 belonged to the first stage, which was dated to 1000–920 BCE, and produced seventy bone specimens. H18 and H19 belonged to the second stage, dated to 860–750 BCE, and produced 128 bone specimens. H2, H3, H8, H9 belonged to the third stage, dated to 750–500 BCE, and produced six bone specimens. In addition, H6, H11, H12, H15, H16, H17 had too little pottery to distinguish their dates, so the bones from these pits were not divided into periods.

1. Stage Ⅰ

(1) Taxonomic identification

Mollusks　Mollusca
　Bivalves　Bivalvia
　　Veneroids　Veneroida
Chordates　Chordata
　Birds　Aves
　　Galliformes
　　　Pheasants and Allies　Phasianidae
　　　　Common (ring-necked) pheasant　*Phasianus colchicus*
　Mammals　Mammalia
　　Even-toed ungulates　Artiodactyla
　　　Pigs　Suidae
　　　　Pigs　*Sus*
　　　　　Domestic pig　*Sus scrofa domestica*

Deer Cervidae

Cervus *Cervus*

Sika deer *Cervus nippon*

Roe deer *Capreolus pygargus*

Bovids Bovidae

Cattle *Bos*

Domestic cattle *Bos taurus*

Carnivores Carnivora

Canids Canidae

Dogs *Canis*

Domestic dog *Canis familiaris*

(2) Description divided by type

Veneroida

Specimens and minimum number of individuals: H8 had seven clamshell fragments belonging to veneroida (Fig. Ⅲ.3.1: 1). Due to the poor state of preservation and the lack of reference specimens we cannot identify it to the species level. The minimum number of individuals (MNI) is one.

Pheasants and allies Phasianidae

Common pheasant *Phasianus colchicus*

Specimens and minimum number of individuals: H9 only had one distal left humerus (Fig. Ⅲ.3.1: 2). The minimum number of individuals is one.

Pigs Suidae

Domestic pigs *Sus scrofa domestica*

Specimens and minimum number of individuals: H8 had one axis, one left proximal radius, and a right distal femur ephiphysis; H9 had one left lower mandible. The minimum number of individuals is one.

Deer Cervidae

Sika deer *Cervus nippon*

Specimens and minimum number of individuals: H3 had one left proximal metacarpal, one shaft of distal ulna, and one left distal radius. In H9 there was one right proximal tibia (Fig. Ⅲ.3.1: 3). The minimum number of individuals is one.

Deer Cervidae

Roe deer *Capreolus pygargus*

Specimens and minimum number of individuals: H3 had one left distal femur (Fig. Ⅲ.3.1: 4). The minimum number of individuals is one.

Bovids Bovidae

Domestic cattle *Bos taurus*

Specimens and minimum number of individuals: H2 had one left second upper premolar; H3 had one right central tarsal bone, one fourth tarsal bone, and one second phalanx (Fig. Ⅲ.3.1: 5); H8 had a left lower mandible fragment with diastema; H9 had one right distal metatarsal. The minimum number of individuals is one.

Dogs Canidae

Domestic dog *Canis familiaris*

Specimens and minimum number of individuals: H3 had one right mandible (Fig. Ⅲ.3.1: 6), one right proximal humerus, one right proximal ulna, one left proximal femur, one distal scapula, one left proximal tibia, one left distal tibia and one right os coxae; H8 had one left proximal radius and one left distal femur. The minimum number of individuals is one.

2. Stage II

(1) Species identification

Mammals Mammalia

Odd-toed ungulates Perissodactyla

Equids *Equus*

Horse *Equus caballus*

Even-toed ungulates Artiodactyla

Pigs *Sus*

Pigs Suidae

Domestic pig *Sus scrofa domestica*

Deer Cervidae

Cervus *Cervus*

Sika deer *Cervus nippon*

Capreolus

Roe deer *Capreolus pygargus*

Bovids Bovidae

Cattle *Bos*

Domestic cattle *Bos taurus*

Carnivores Carnivora

Dogs Canidae

Dogs *Canis*

Domestic dog *Canis familiaris*

Weasels Mustelidae

Badger *Meles sp.*

(2) Description divided by type

Odd-toed ungulates Perissodactyla

Horse *Equus caballus*

Specimens and minimum number of individuals: H8 contained one right os coxae and one second phalanx (Fig. Ⅲ.3.1: 7). The minimum number of individuals is one.

Pigs Suidae

Domestic pigs *Sus scrofa domestica*

Specimens and minimum number of individuals: H18 had one right scapula and one left proximal radius; H19 had one right maxilla, one distal right scapula, one distal right humerus (Fig. Ⅲ.3.1: 8), one right os coxae, one distal left femur, one distal left tibia, and one left fourth metatarsal. The minimum number of individuals is one.

Deer Cervidae

Sika deer *Cervus nippon*

Specimens and minimum number of individuals: H18 had one left proximal tibia, one distal right femoral shaft, and one lumbar vertebra; H19 had one distal humerus shaft and one left distal radius shaft. The minimum number of individuals is one.

Deer Cervidae

Roe deer *Capreolus pygargus*

Specimens and minimum number of individuals: H18 had one left distal tibia (Fig. Ⅲ.3.1: 9); H19 had one distal humerus shaft and a left distal radius shaft. The minimum number of individuals is one.

Bovids Bovidae

Domestic cattle *Bos taurus*

Specimens and minimum number of individuals: H18 had one left mandibular condyle and one left distal tibia; H19 had one left mandibular body, the distal portions of two first phalanges, two second phalanges, one third phalanx, two distal left humeri, one right proximal radius, one left distal radius, one right proximal ulna, one right proximal ulnar shaft, one left proximal ulna, one left femoral shaft, one right distal femur, two proximal right tibial shafts, one right proximal tibia with articular surface, one left distal tibia, two proximal left tibiae, one left talus, one right os coxae, three left proximal metacarpals, one distal left metacarpal, one right metacarpal, one left metatarsal, two distal metatarsals, one right distal metatarsal, one right central tarsal and one fragment of a horn (Fig. Ⅲ.3.1: 11). The minimum number of individuals is three.

Dogs　Canidae

Domestic dog　*Canis familiaris*

Specimens and minimum number of individuals: H19 had one left mandible and one right distal femur. The minimum number of individuals is one.

Weasels　Mustelidae

Badger　*Meles sp.*

Specimens and minimum number of individuals: H19 had one right tibia (Fig.Ⅲ.3.1: 10). The minimum number of individuals is one.

3. Stage Ⅲ

(1) Species identification

Mammals　Mammalia

Odd-toed ungulates　Artiodactyla

Pigs　Suidae

Pigs　*Sus*

Domestic pig　*Sus scrofa domestica*

Carnivores　Carnivora

Dogs　Canidae

Dogs　*Canis*

Domestic dog　*Canis familiaris*

(2) Description divided by type

Pigs　Suidae

Domestic pigs　*Sus scrofa domestica*

Specimens and minimum number of individuals: H20 had three right proximal femoral shafts. The minimum number of individuals is one.

Dogs　Canidae

Domestic dog　*Canis familiaris*

Specimens and minimum number of individuals: H20 had one left maxilla. The minimum number of individuals is one.

4. Stage-unspecified Bones

Because H6, H11, H12, H15, H16, and H17 could not be divided into stages, we can only provide counts of taxa found. These include two dogs, one bird belonging to Phasianidae, twenty cattle, a horse, two deer, two sheep (Fig.Ⅲ.3.1: 12, 13) and fifty-seven pigs (Fig.Ⅲ.3.1: 14). The distal femur is a second species of Phasianidae (larger than Phasianus) according to the identification by Tom Stidham. It could be Gallus, but specimens of Gallus vary significantly in size, so we are not certain of its precise identification. However, we have eliminated many of the phasianid genera as possibilities for that femur (e.g. Chyrsolophus, Tragopan, Syrmaticus, Phasianus).

Section 3: Discussion

1. Statistics Analysis and Mode of Subsistence

Due to the limited excavation area, a relatively small number of animal remains was unearthed, so we lack data for further analysis. Stage I of the Guicheng city site dates to the early Western Zhou Dynasty, and includes sika deer (4 identified specimens, 10% of the total identifiable specimens), roe deer (1, 2.5%), cattle (4, 10%), pigs (4, 10%), dogs (25, 62.5%), common pheasant (1, 2.5%), and veneroida (1, 2.5%). The minimum number of individuals (MNI) of each species is one, so each constitutes 14.29% (1/7) of the minimum number of individuals for this period.

Guicheng Stage Ⅱ is dated to the late Western Zhou—early Spring and Autumn period. In terms of minimum number of individuals, there was one each of sika deer, roe deer, badger, pig, dog, and horse, each of which constitutes 11% of the total MNI. The minimum number of cattle was three, which constitutes 33% of the MNI of this period. In terms of the number of identified specimens, the percentages are sika deer 8.06%, roe deer 1.61%, badger 1.61%, pig 17.47%, dog 3.23%, horse 3.23% and cattle 64.52%. Stage III only contains one pig bone and one dog bone, each of which thus constitutes 50% of MNI and NISP (Table Ⅲ.3.1).

Domestic animal remains make up 82.5% of NISP (number of identified specimens) in Stage I, 90.32 % in Stage Ⅱ, and 100% in Stage Ⅲ, while the MNI of domesticated species was 42.87%, 66.66%, and 100% in the three stages. Since the number of bones is small, some species whose remains were found in small numbers occupy a higher proportion of MNI than their actual meat contribution would have been. Therefore, if we use the number of specimens as our reference standard, this would reveal that the people of Guicheng from the early Western Zhou to the Warring States period depended mostly on livestock for their animal resources, including cattle, pigs, horses and dogs. The remains excavated from the site show that hunting and fishing played a limited role in the economy of this period, and the Eastern Zhou period had only a livestock economy. But the Eastern Zhou era remains excavated from the site so far are limited, so it is difficult to determine the actual proportion of hunting and fishing in the economy of the time.

2. Discussion of Marks on the Bones and Human Uses of Animal Resources

After analyzing and observing the marks on the surfaces of the bones excavated from the Guicheng city site, we mainly discovered two types of marks on the bone: those caused by human action and those caused by animal action. Traces of animal activity on the bones are predominantly the result of gnawing by carnivores (dog) (Fig.Ⅲ.3.1: 15). In H19 the highest percentage and number of these occur on cattle bones. The discovery of dog bite marks suggests that humans kept dogs to help them in hunting or with guarding their houses, and reflects that the people of Guicheng bred domestic dogs and gave them leftover bones (meat). The main traces of human activity on the bones are burn marks from roasting meat and a variety of cut marks from meat processing, such as dismembering, dividing, skinning, and scraping (Fig.Ⅲ.3.1: 16). There were also bones processed to make ornaments and traces of polishing and drilling (Fig.Ⅲ.3.1: 17, 18).

3. The Phenomenon of Animal Sacrifice

Animal sacrifices or animals used as burial offerings have often been found in archaeological excavations. In Guicheng pit H12, which was not dated, the hindquarters of a juvenile pig were discovered. The remains included twenty-two incomplete ribs, five unfused thoracic vertebrae, five unfused lumbar vertebrae, one nearly complete ox coxae with an unfused acetabulum, one left and one right femur, each with both epiphyses unfused, one left and one right tibia, each with both epiphyses unfused, one left proximal fibula, one right distal fibula, one left and one right calcaneus, each with both proximal and distal ends unfused, and a left talus (Fig.Ⅲ.3.1: 19). Most of these can be articulated with each other, with the dimensions of the left and right being essentially the same, which shows that this is one individual. Moreover, there is no evidence of any of the bones having been modified by humans, and most elements are complete. Those which were not intact are relatively fragile elements and were mostly broken during excavation, or some bones may have had unfused epiphyses which were not collected during excavations. Therefore, we can infer that H12 may be a sacrificial pit, and that using half a young pig as a sacrifice may have been a social custom.

While we do not know whether these bones were articulated or not, from the condition described above in which the bones had no evidence of being modified by humans, it seems that the bones were probably articulated until they were excavated. If not, they should retain some evidence of being dismembered or slaughtered. In pigs, the acetabulum is the earliest part of the skeleton to fuse, at around one year (Silver 1989), so the pig's age was younger than one year.

Section 4: Conclusion

From our analysis of the animal bones excavated from Guicheng, we think that the people of ancient Guicheng, with the benefit of their favorable geographical location, developed an agricultural economy and raised livestock such as pigs, dogs, cattle, and horses. They also hunted sika deer, roe deer, badger, common pheasant, and other wild animals for meat as supplements to their diet. However, domestic animals always provided the main source of meat, and they caught wild animals only as a necessary supplement.

References

Gromova, V., 1960. *Opredelitel mlekopitayushikh SSSR po kostiam skeleta* (An index of mammals of the USSR by skeleton bones). Moscow: Akadmija nauk SSSR, 1950, 1960; Beijing: Kexue chubanshe, Chinese edition (trans. Liu Houyi et al.).

Ma, Xiaolin 马萧林, 2008. "Lingbao Xipo yizhi de roushi xiaofei moshi: guge buwei faxianlü, biaomian henji ji posuidu" 灵宝西坡遗址的肉食消费模式——骨骼部位发现率、表面痕迹及破碎度 (The mode of meat consumption at the Xipo site, Lingbao: Discovery rate of skeletal parts, surface marks, and the degree of fragmentation). *Huaxia kaogu* 华夏考古, 4: 73-87.

Schmid, Elisabeth, 1992. *Atlas of Animal Bones*. Amsterdam: Elsevier, 1972; Wuhan: Zhongguo dizhi daxue chubanshe, Chinese edition (trans. Li Tianyuan).

Sheng, Helin 盛和林, 1992. *Zhongguo lulei dongwu* 中国鹿类动物. Shanghai: Huadong shifan daxue chubanshe.

Silver, I. A, 1989. "The Ageing of Domestic Animals," in Brothwell, D. & Higgs, E. S. (eds.), *Science in Archaeology*, pp. 250-268. London: Thames and Hudson.

Sino-American Joint Guicheng Archaeological Team, 2011. "Shandong Longkou shi Guicheng liang Zhou chengzhi diaocha jianbao" 山东龙口市归城两周城址调查简报 (A brief report on the survey of the Guicheng city-site of the Western-Eastern Zhou period in Longkou, Shandong Province), *Kaogu* 考古, 3: 30-39.

Von den Driesch, Angela, 2007. *Guide to the Measurement of Animal Bones from Archaeological Sites*. Beijing: Kexue chubanshe, Chinese edition (trans. Ma Xiaolin and Hou Yanfeng).

(Translated by Brian Lander)

1. 莱山脚下的归城遗址
1. The Guicheng city site at the foothills of Mt. Lai.

2. 归城外城东城墙远眺
2. A view of the outer city wall of Guicheng, east.

图版 / Plate 2

1. 归城外城西城墙远眺
1. A view of the outer city wall of Guicheng, west.

2. 归城曹家村南侧水库
2. Water reservoir south of Caojia Village in Guicheng.

归城地区高清晰度卫星图像
High-resolution satellite image of the Guicheng region.

图版 / Plate 6

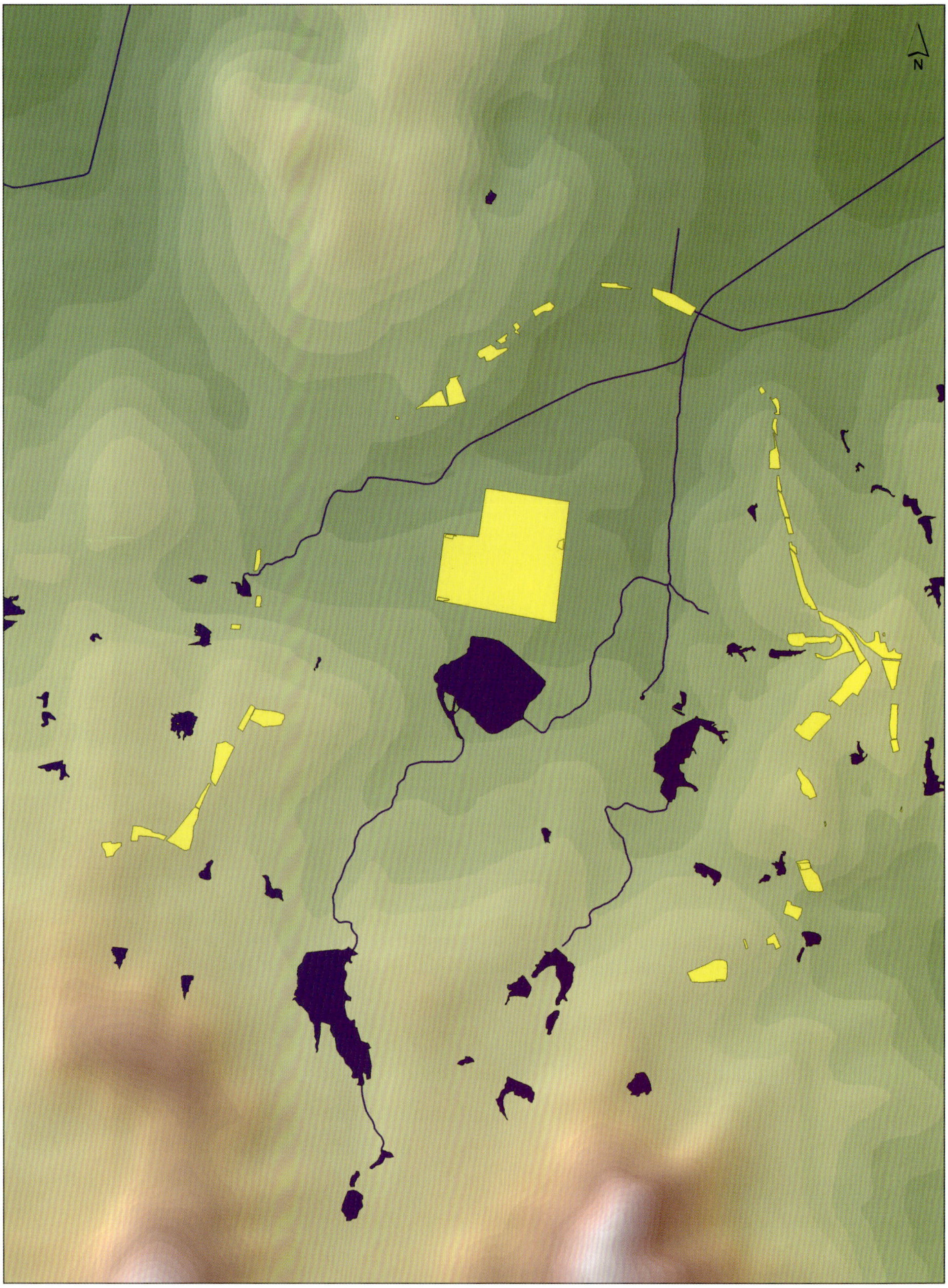

归城地区高程模型（黄色为城墙走向）

Elevation model of the Guicheng region (city walls in yellow).

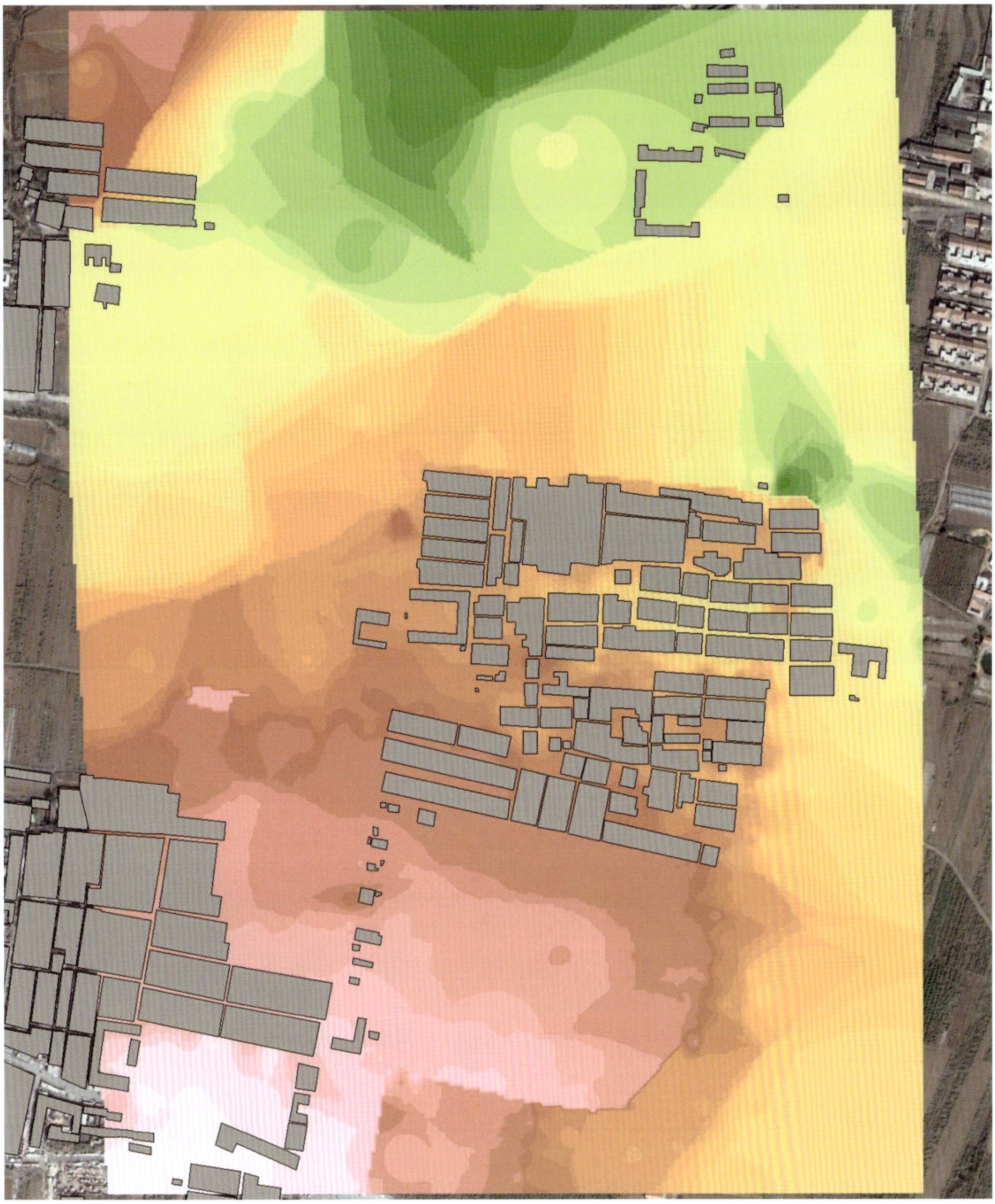

归城内城地表详细高程模型

Precise elevation model of the inner city ground surface of Guicheng.

1. 归姜村南地面保存内城城墙A
1. Above ground Wall Section A of the inner city, south of Guijiang.

2. 和平村东地面保留内城城墙C
2. Above ground Wall Section C of the inner city, east of Heping.

归姜村北、和平村西地面保存内城城墙B
Above ground Wall Section A of the inner city, north of Guijiang and west of Heping.

1. 南城墙剖面1夯土层（局部）
1. Rammed earth strata in Cross-section 1 on south wall (Partial).

2. 南城墙剖面2夯土层
2. Rammed earth strata in Cross-section 2 on south wall.

南城墙剖面3夯土层
Rammed earth strata on Cross-section 3 on south wall (Partial).

图版 / Plate 12

内城北城墙局部采集陶片（2009-7-14）

Pottery collection made on the north wall of inner city (July 14, 2009).

1. 瓿
1. *Bu* vase

2. 瓿
2. *Bu* vase

3. 豆
3. *Dou* pedestal dish

东迟家东迟家水库出土陶器
Pottery vessels from the Dongchijia Village reservoir.

1. 和平村西2组：1
1. Heping-West Group 2：1

2. 和平村西2组：2
2. Heping-West Group 2：2

3. 和平村西2组： 3
3. Heping-West Group 2：3

归城内城范围采集陶器
Pottery vessels collected in the inner city of Guicheng.

1. 石斧
1. Stone axe

2. 铜锛
2. Bronze chisel

归城内城范围采集器物
Artifacts collected in the inner city of Guicheng.

图版 / Plate 16

归城外城墙的钻探
The coring of the outer wall of Guicheng.

1. 清理剖面了解外城夯筑情况
1. Using cross-section to analyze the rammed earth strata.

2. 对钻探确定的城墙进行测量记录
2. Mapping outer walls determined by coring.

图版 / Plate 18

外城墙C、D及K段城墙
Outer wall of Guicheng, Rows C, D, and K.

归城外城G、H列城墙
Outer wall of Guicheng, Rows G and H.

1. 外城墙35上眺望莱山
1. Looking south to Mt. Lai on top of Wall Section 35.

2. 外城墙35附近地面发现的绳纹砖
2. Cord-impressed brick found on the surface near Wall Section 35.

1. 外城墙56、58所在台地
1. Outer Wall Sections 56 and 58 terrace.

2. 外城墙80
2. Outer Wall Section 80.

1. 外城墙88地面残存城墙及剖面B
1. Cross-section B on outer Wall Section 88.

2. 外城墙99断面掉落的夯土块
2. Rammed earth remnant from outer Wall Section 99.

外城墙83内侧
Outer Wall Section 83, inside facade.

1. 独立城墙77
1. The independent Wall Section 77.

2. 外城墙3剖面A
2. Cross-section A on outer Wall Section 3.

1. 外城墙13剖面
1. Cross-section on outer Wall Section 13.

2. 外城墙16剖面B
2. Cross-section B on outer Wall Section 16.

1. 外城墙35剖面A
1. Cross-section A on outer Wall Section 35.

2. 外城墙88剖面A
2. Cross-section A on outer Wall Section 88.

探沟一（TG1）表土之下遗迹现象（向南）
Test excavation Trench 1 (TG1) below topsoil (looking south).

1. TG1西北角剖面
1. Northwest corner of TG1.

2. TG1北壁
2. North wall of TG1.

1. TG1西壁北侧
1. West wall of TG1, northern section.

2. TG1东壁北侧
2. East wall of TG1, northern section.

1. TG2南壁
1. South wall of TG2

2. TG2西壁
2. West wall of TG2

夯土城墙边界
Boundary of rammed earth city wall.

1. 灰坑H3①内成堆陶片
1. Pottery sherds found in stratum ① of Pit H3

2. 灰坑H3②内狗骨
2. Remains of a dog in stratum ② of Pit H3

3. 灰坑H2
3. Pit H2

4. 灰坑H3全景
4. Complete view of Pit H3

1. 灰坑H6
1. Pit H6

2. 灰坑H6遗物
2. Object found in Pit H6

3. 灰坑H4
3. Pit H4

4. 灰坑H5
4. Pit H5

图版 / Plate 36

1. 灰坑H8
1. Pit H8

2. 灰坑H9
2. Pit H9

3. 灰坑H12D1剖面
3. A sectional view of hole D1 in Pit H12

4. 灰坑H12全景
4. Complete view of H12

1. 灰坑H15
1. Pit H15

2. 灰坑H16
2. Pit H16

3. 灰坑H17
3. Pit H17

4. 灰坑H18
4. Pit H18

1. H20
1. Pit H20

2. H20②内陶簋
2. Pottery *gui* tureen found in stratum ② of Pit H20.

1. 发掘工地远眺（北—南）
1. The excavation site seen from a distance (north to south).

2. 发掘场景（揭去表土）
2. The excavation scene (below the topsoil).

1. 完成探沟TG2灰坑H2的发掘
1. Completion of excavation of pit H2 in TG2.

2. 发掘接近尾声
2. Excavation close to the end.

1. 发掘结束时探沟T1和T2相连
1. Trenches 1 and 2 connected at the completion of the excavation.

2. 发掘结束时照相
2. Photographing at the end of the excavation.

图版 / Plate 42

1. 陶碗H2：1
1. Bowl H2：1

2. 器盖H3②：4
2. Vessel lid H3②：4

3. 陶豆H3②：5
3. *Dou* pedestal dish H3②：5

4. 器座H3②：19
4. Vessel base H3②：19

1. 陶簋H20②：1
1. *Gui* tureen H20②：1

2. 陶鬲H3①：1
2. *Li* tripod H3①：1

图版 / Plate 44

1. TG1③：3

2. TG1③：4

3. G1：1

4. G1：2

5. H3①：7

6. H3①：16

7. H3①：43

8. H3②：12

9. H3②：14

归城遗址发掘出土陶片
Pottery sherds from excavation in Guicheng.

1. H3①：3

2. H3②：15

3. H3②：22

4. H3②：23

5. H3③：33

6. H3③：34

7. H3③：36

8. H3③：49

9. H4：1

归城遗址发掘出土陶片和石镰（1. 石镰；余为陶片）

Pottery sherds and stone saw from excavation in Guicheng (1. Stone saw; rest, pottery sherds).

1. H4：6

2. H6：4

3. H6：13

4. H7：1

5. H8：1

6. H8：5

7. 骨锥（H9：2）

8. H9：12

9. H9：24

归城遗址发掘出土陶片和骨锥（7. 骨锥；余为陶片）
Pottery sherds and bone drill excavated in Guicheng (7. Bone drill; rest are pottery sherds).

1. H9：26

2. H9：38

3. H11：12

4. H11：17

5. H12①：5

6. H12①：16

7. H12②：1

8. H12②：19

9. H15①：7

归城遗址发掘出土陶片、陶范和角料（2. 陶范；7. 角料；余为陶片）

Pottery sherds, clay mold, and horn materials excavated in Guicheng (2. Mold; 7. Horn; rest are pottery sherds).

1. H16：9

2. H16：22

3. H16：32

4. H17：5

5. H7：15

6. H18：11

7. H18：15

8. H18：26

9. H19：1

归城遗址发掘出土陶片
Pottery sherds from the excavation in Guicheng.

1. H19：3

2. H19：9

3. H19：10

4. H19：11

5. H19：19

6. H19：23

7. H19：26

8. H19：55

9. H20①：3

归城遗址发掘出土陶片

Pottery sherds from the excavation in Guicheng.

图版 / Plate 50

1. H20①：14

2. H20①：12

3. H20①：16

4. H20①：17

5. H20①：19

6. H20①：24

7. H20①：34

8. H20①：36

9. H20①：102

归城遗址发掘出土陶片
Pottery sherds from the excavation in Guicheng.

1. H20①：107

2. H20①：140

3. H20②：3

4. H20②：6

5. H20②：7

6. H20②：21

7. H20②：149

8. H20②：157

归城遗址发掘出土陶片
Pottery sherds from the excavation in Guicheng.

灰坑H9出土铸铜用陶范（H9：38）
Clay mold (H9：38) for bronze casting from pit H9.

1. 学生调查组进入田野开始调查，第7区，2008年6月27日
1. A student group entering the field to begin survey, Area 7, June 27, 2008.

2. 第9区的调查，2009年6月25日
2. Survey in Area 9, June 25, 2009.

图版 / Plate 54

1. 完整采集单位CCUIII, 2009年7月13日

1. Complete Collection Unit CCIII, July 13, 2009.

2. 调查组成员在田埂上休息，2009年6月9日

2. Members of the survey team taking break at the edge of a field, June 9, 2009.

第10区的调查，2009年6月28日
Survey in Area 10, June 28, 2009.

图版 / Plate 56

调查组成员分析和记录所采集的陶片
Team members analyzing and recording the sherds collected during the survey.

1. Area 10-Y9

2. Area 10-Y9

3. Area 11-O50

4. Area 7-A21：3

地面调查中获得的陶器
Pottery obtained during the surface survey.

图版 / Plate 60

1. 10ZZJ采：9

2. 10ZZJ采：10

3. 10ZZJ采：11

4. 10ZZJ采：12

张郑家遗址出土陶器

Pottery from the Zhangzhengjia site.

1. 10ZZJ采：13

2. 10ZZJ采：14

3. 10ZZJ采：15

4. 10ZZJ采：16

张郑家遗址出土陶器

Pottery from the Zhangzhengjia site.

1. 10ZZJ采：17

2. 10ZZJ采：18

3. 10ZZJ采：19

4. 10ZZJ采：20

张郑家遗址出土陶器
Pottery from the Zhangzhengjia site.

1. 10ZZJ采：21

2. 10ZZJ采：22

3. 10ZZJ采：23

4. 10ZZJ采：24

张郑家遗址出土陶器
Pottery from the Zhangzhengjia site.

图版 / Plate 64

1. 10ZZJ采：25

2. 10ZZJ采：26

3. 10ZZJ采：27

4. 10ZZJ采：28

张郑家遗址出土陶器
Pottery from the Zhangzhengjia site.

1. 10ZZJ采：29

2. 10ZZJ采：30

张郑家遗址出土陶器
Pottery from the Zhangzhengjia site.

图版 / Plate 66

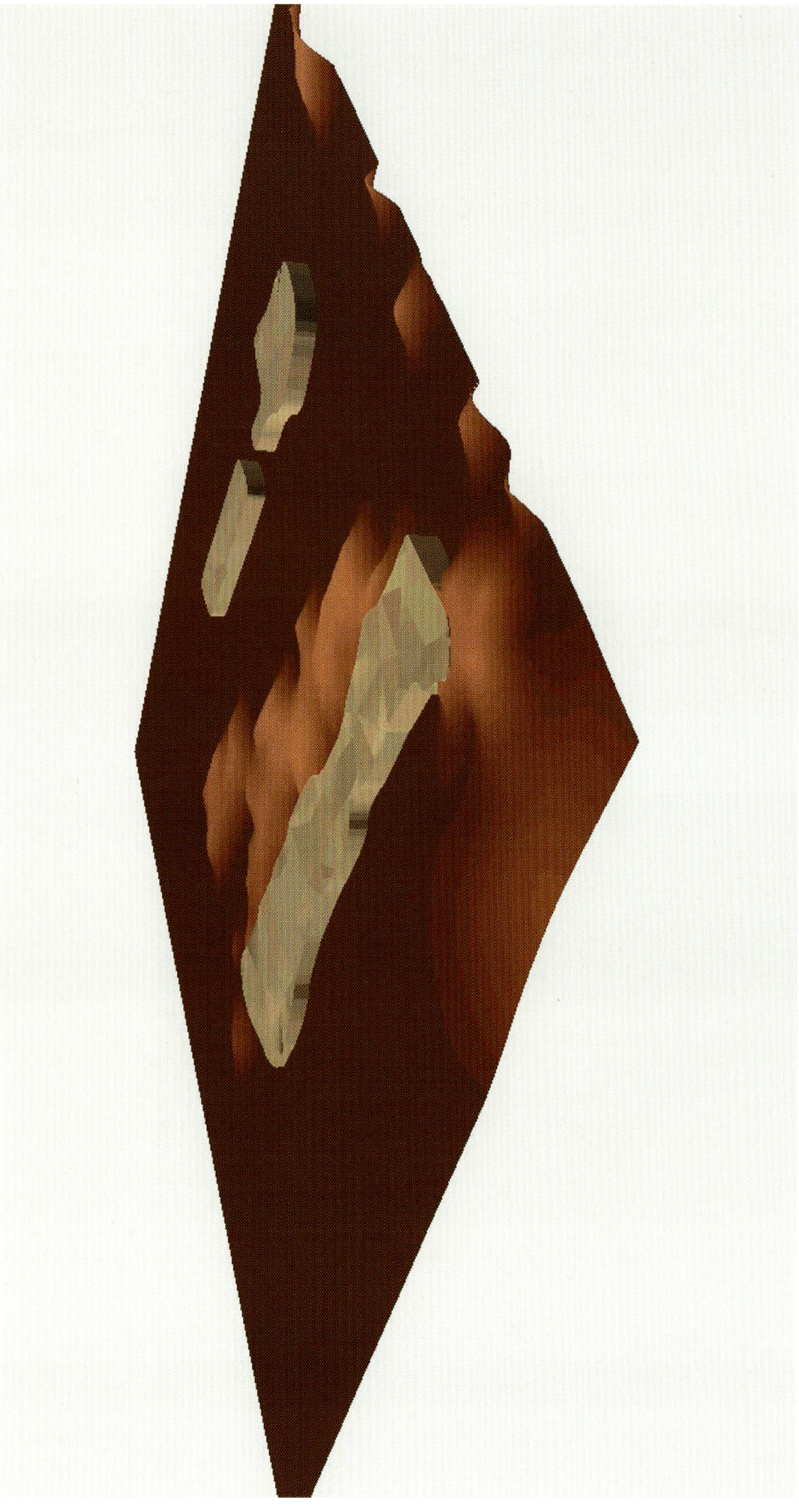

利用数据化的钻探资料进行视觉复原的地下夯土建筑基址（9、10和11号基址）

Visual reconstruction of underground Rammed Earth Building Foundations 9, 10, and 11 using digitized coring data.

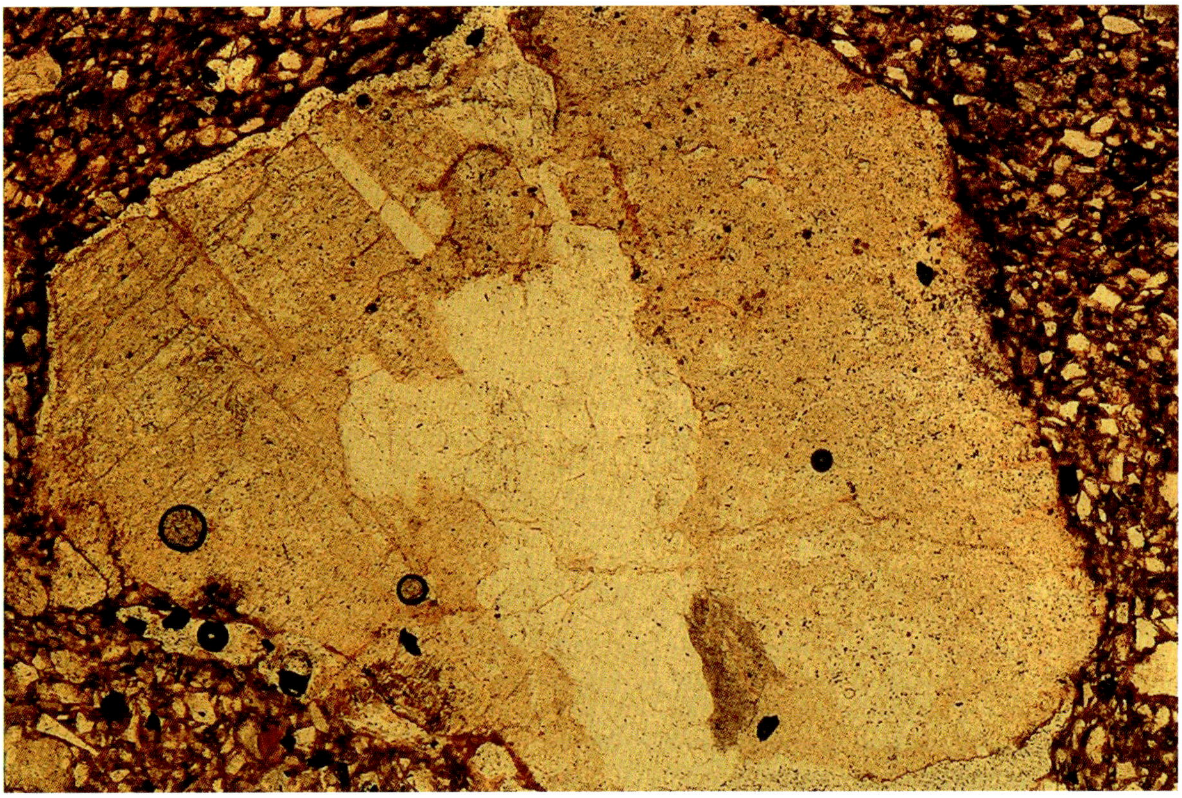

周文化传统鬲切片标本上所见两幅花岗岩夹砂图片
Two views of granite temper in thin section of Zhou tradition *li* tripod.

图版 / Plate 68

本土传统文化鼎切片标本上所见的两幅闪岩夹砂图片
Two views of amphibolite temper in thin section of indigenous *ding* cauldron.

1. F8：11

2. H1：12

3. J1：3

4. J1：4

归城和平村遗址2002年发掘出土陶器
Pottery excavated at Heping Village in Guicheng, 2002.

图版 / Plate 84

1965年曹家村墓葬出土铜尊（M1：5）
Bronze *zun* urn unearthed from tomb M1 at Caojia Village, 1965 (M1：5).

1965年曹家村墓葬出土铜卣（M1：6）
Bronze *you* jar unearthed from tomb M1 at Caojia Village, 1965 (M1：6).

1965年曹家村墓葬出土铜爵（M1：7）
Bronze *jue* cup unearthed from tomb M1 at Caojia Village, 1965 (M1：7).

1965年曹家村墓葬出土玉戈（M1：10）
Jade *ge* dagger unearthed from tomb M1 at Caojia Village, 1965 (M1： 10).

图版 / Plate 92

1. 卮（00117）
1. *Zhi* cup (00117)

2. 马衔（00118）
2. Horse bit (00118)

1969年董家村出土铜器
Bronze objects unearthed at Dongjiacun, 1969.

1951年南埠村出土铜盨（178号）
Bronze *xu* square tureen from Nanbu Village, 1951 (#178).

图版 / Plate 94

1951年南埠村出土铜匜（180号）
Bronze *yi* pouring vessel from Nanbu Village, 1951 (#180).

1951年南埠村出土铜盘（181号）
Bronze *pan* basin from Nanbu Village, 1951 (#181).

图版 / Plate 96

1969年小刘庄出土启尊（国家博物馆戴向明提供）

The bronze Qi *zun* urn unearthed at Xiaoliuzhuang Village, 1969 (image provided by Dai Xiangming, the National Museum of China).

1969年小刘庄出土启卣
The bronze Qi *you* jar unearthed at Xiaoliuzhuang Village, 1969.

1964年韩栾村发现的铜鼎

The bronze *ding* cauldron discovered at Hanluan Village, 1964.

1896年鲁家沟村出土遹甗（泉屋博古馆提供）
The bronze Yu *yan* steamer unearthed at Lujiagou Village, 1896 (image provided by Sen' oku Hakukokan).

图版 / Plate 102

1980年庄头墓M1出土铜鼎（193号）
Bronze *ding* cauldron from tomb M1 at Zhuangtou, 1980 (#193).

1980年庄头墓M1出土大鸟纹铜簋（189号）
Bronze *gui* tureen with large-bird patterns from tomb M1 at Zhuangtou, 1980 (#189).

图版 / Plate 106

1980年庄头墓M1出土铜壶（186号）
Bronze *hu* bottle from tomb M1 at Zhuangtou, 1980 (#186).

1980年庄头墓M1出土铜卣（192号）
Bronze *you* jar from tomb M1 at Zhuangtou, 1980 (#192).

图版 / Plate 108

1980年庄头墓M1出土铜甗（200号）
Bronze *yan* steamer from tomb M1 at Zhuangtou, 1980 (#200).

1. 觯（201号）
1. *Zhi*-cup (#201)

2. 爵（188号）
2. *Jue*-cup (#188)

1980年庄头墓M1出土铜器
Bronze vessels from tomb M1 at Zhuangtou, 1980.

1. 铜簋（4号）
1. Brone *gui* tureen (#4)

2. 陶豆M1：6（100号）
2. Pottery *dou* pedestal dish M1 ：6 (#100)

3. 陶豆M1：12（103号）
3. Pottery *dou* pedestal dish M1 ：12 (#103)

1985年东营周家M1出土器物
Bronze and pottery objects from tomb M1 at Dongying Zhoujia, 1985.

1. M2：118（#105）

2. M2：102（#109）

3. M2： 58（#110）

4. M2：21（#122）

1985年东营周家M2出土陶簋

Pottery *gui* vessels from tomb M2 at Dongying Zhoujia, 1985.

1. M2：56（#132）

2. M2：116（#108）

3. M2：59（#135）

4. M2：22（#118）

1985年东营周家M2出土陶簋
Pottery *gui* vessels from tomb M2 at Dongying Zhoujia, 1985.

1. M2：32（#129）

2. M2：25（#117）

3. M2： 133（#107）

4. M2：24（#136）

1985年东营周家M2出土陶簋
Pottery *gui* vessels from tomb M2 at Dongying Zhoujia, 1985.

图版 / Plate 116

1. M2：126（#75）

2. M2：86（#65）

3. M2：47（#30）

4. M2：121（#74）

5. M2：15（#9）

1985年东营周家M2出土陶豆

Pottery *dou* pedestal dishes from tomb M2 at Dongying Zhoujia, 1985.

1. M2：27（#96）

2. M2：105（#49）

3. M2：8（#137）

4. M2：147（#139）

1985年东营周家M2出土陶豆（1-2）和陶鬲（3-4）

Pottery *dou* pedestal dishes (1-2) and *li* tripods (3-4) from tomb M2 at Dongying Zhoujia, 1985.

图版 / Plate 124

2004年集前赵家出土铜簋（351号）
Gui tureen from Jiqian Zhaojia, 2004 (#351).

2004年集前赵家出土铜尊（352号）
Zun urn from Jiqian Zhaojia, 2004 (#352).

图版 / Plate 126

2004年集前赵家出土铜钟（356号）
Bronze stemmed bell from Jiqian Zhaojia, 2004 (#356).

2004年集前赵家出土铜盘（354号）
Bronze *pan* basin from Jiqian Zhaojia, 2004 (#354).

图版 / Plate 128

2004年集前赵家出土铜甗（353号）
Yan steamer from Jiqian Zhaojia, 2004 (#353).

1983年海徐家出土的辛䣕簋（KM. 6）
The bronze Xin Xiao *gui* tureen unearthed at Haixujia Village, 1983 (KM. 6).

1. 秦始皇离宫基址
1. Palace building foundation of the First Emperor of Qin.

2. 莱山山巅的月主祠2009年6月23日
2. Temple to the Moon God atop Mt. Lai, June 23, 2009.

1. 月主祠周围可见秦代砖瓦
1. Bricks and tiles found around the Temple to the Moon God.

2. 月主祠旁尚存的方形石基石
2. Square stone base found near the Temple to the Moon God.

内 容 简 介

本书为山东龙口归城周代遗址中美联合考古调查和试掘的中英文双语考古科学报告，分为上下两编：上编共分为十章，集中总结归城周代城址2007年到2011年中美联合调查的收获，并就有关方面进行研究。下编包括五章，总结归城乃至龙口地区1896年至2006年之间已有的考古发现，主要是青铜器和玉器的发现。另包括附录三篇，报告归城遗址的碳十四数据和植物、动物标本分析结果。

本书可供从事文物考古、历史学及相关学科的研究者和大专院校相关专业师生阅读、参考，并可为中英考古文献翻译参考。

图书在版编目（CIP）数据

龙口归城：胶东半岛地区青铜时代国家形成过程的考古学研究：公元前1000～前500年 / 中国社会科学院考古研究所，哥伦比亚大学东亚语言和文化系，山东省文物考古研究院编著，李峰，梁中合主编.—北京：科学出版社，2018.8

ISBN 978-7-03-058396-3

Ⅰ.①龙… Ⅱ.①李…②梁… Ⅲ.①古城遗址（考古）-考古调查-龙口-青铜时代 Ⅳ.①K878.35

中国版本图书馆CIP数据核字（2018）第171163号

责任编辑：孙 莉 闫向东 / 责任校对：邹慧卿

责任印制：肖 兴 / 封面题字：徐天进

科学出版社 出版

北京东黄城根北街16号

邮政编码：100717

http：//www.sciencep.com

中国科学院印刷厂 印刷

科学出版社发行 各地新华书店经销

*

2018年8月第 一 版 开本：889×1194 1/16

2018年8月第一次印刷 印张：65 1/4 插页：72

字数：2 000 000

定价：980.00元（上、下册）

（如有印装质量问题，我社负责调换）

Guicheng

An Archaeological Study of the Formation of States on the Jiaodong Peninsula in Late Bronze-Age China, 1000-500 BCE

(I)

Li Feng Liang Zhonghe *Chief Editors*

Department of East Asian Languages and Cultures, Columbia University
The Institute of Archaeology, Chinese Academy of Social Sciences
Shandong Provincial Academy of Cultural Relics and Archaeology

Editors

Science Press

Beijing

主持单位

中国社会科学院考古研究所
哥伦比亚大学东亚语言和文化系
山东省文物考古研究院

合作单位

烟台市博物馆
龙口市博物馆

Sponsoring Institutions

Department of East Asian Languages and Cultures, Columbia University
The Institute of Archaeology, Chinese Academy of Social Sciences
Shandong Provincial Academy of Cultural Relics and Archaeology

Collaborating Institutions

Yantai Municipal Museum
Longkou Municipal Museum

谢　　辞

山东龙口归城城址的中美联合考古调查、勘探项目自2006年确立以来，已经走过了十二个寒暑。在这十二年里我们得到了中、美两国很多机构和个人慷慨和热情的帮助，才使得这个项目能够顺利开展并取得重要收获。参加这个项目的全体同仁们也能不忘初心，不辱使命，认真完成自己承担的工作，最终写成这部考古报告。这是我们从内心感到欣慰，同时也是我们要深深表示感谢的！

该项目前期的田野工作经费主要由蒋经国基金会（美洲地区）和美国哥伦比亚大学东亚语言和文化系提供。后期得到哥伦比亚大学唐氏早期中国研究中心，东亚语言和文化系及哥伦比亚大学孔子学院提供的报告整理和编写方面的部分资助。我们首先对它们慷慨资助深表感谢。归城项目的确立和实施得到了国家文物局、山东省文化厅文物局的批准和支持，也谨在此表示我们真诚谢意。出版经费方面由中国社会科学院考古研究所、山东省文物考古研究院共同向国家文物局提出申请并得到资助，这也是我们需要特别提出并表示感谢的。

在学术研究机构方面，我们首先感谢归城项目的三个组织和主持单位，包括中国社会科学院考古研究所、哥伦比亚大学东亚语言和文化系、山东省文物考古研究院（前山东省文物考古研究所）。同时作为合作单位烟台市博物馆派人员参加了田野调查和资料整理及编写工作，为项目的开展给予很大帮助。另外，龙口市博物馆在我们田野工作期间、后期资料整理和编写报告过程中为我们提供了工作和生活上诸多的帮助和支持，这也是我们要特别感谢的。另外，吉林大学边疆考古研究中心在编者之一受吉林大学特聘任职期间允许以归城报告的编写工作立项，并给予支持，这也是我们要感谢的。

上述单位的学术领导和同事们也都给予我们及时的指导和支持，没有他们的热心帮助归城的田野考古工作目标将无法实现，当然也就不会有这本中英双语报告的整理和出版。他们包括中国社会科学院考古研究所所长王巍、陈星灿，山东省文物考古研究所所长李传荣、佟佩华、郑同修、王守功，烟台市博物馆馆长王锡平、高爱东、王富强，龙口博物馆馆长蒋惠民、马志敏、栾文弘等。特别是陈星灿所长多年来对归城项目给予关心和支持，为项目的实施乃至报告的编写做了大量的协调和组织工作，帮助我们解决困难，这是我们要特别表示感谢的。我们也感谢中国国家文物局宋新潮副局长对归城项目的关心和支持。在美国方面，哥伦比亚大学东亚语言和文化系前主任韩明士（Robert P. Hymes）教授指导了归城项目的设立，并在以后给予本项目以很强的支持。哥伦比亚大学人类学系的Terence N. D'Altroy教授帮助我们设计了在归城使用的地面调查方法，并在以后多予及时帮助。对他们我们表示真挚的谢意。我们也要感谢匹兹堡大学许倬云（Cho-yun Hsu）教授和哈佛大学王德威（David der-wei Wang）教授对这个项目的支持。

我们更要感谢参加归城田野调查和试掘的所有人员。他们有中国社会科学院考古研究所的唐锦琼、付群启、毕道传，山东省文物考古研究所韩辉，烟台市博物馆徐明江等。参加工作的美方研究生有哥伦比亚大学的何汉平（Han-Peng Ho）、吴敏娜、侯昱文（Paul Nicholas Vogt）、兰德（Brian Lander）、赵家华（Glenda Chao）、石蕙、关隐（Lee Crawford）、贝丽姿（Elizabeth Berger）、顾言（Jackson Cooper）和以色列耶路撒冷希伯来大学的哈克（Yitzchak Jaffe）等。器物照相、拓制工作由付群启担任。归城遗迹和地形图等由毕道全、唐锦琼绘制。器物绘图则全部由毕道传完成。GIS地理图像由哥伦比亚大学数据图书馆Jeremiah Trinidad-Christensen完成。由于哥伦比亚大学学期时间的限制，多年的田野工作（除2007年冬季外）只能选在每年的五月底到七月中旬来进行。盛夏时节，烈日炎炎，所有课题组的成员都能同甘共苦，恪尽职责，不怕困难，高质量地完成了田野考古调查、勘探等各项任务，从而确保了获取的归城考古调查资料的科学性、系统性和全面性。在此我们要对全体课题组成员的付出和辛勤的工作表达我们由衷的感谢！

作为国内第一本真正的双语考古报告，归城报告编写的工作量是要倍于一本同样规模的中文或英文报告的。我们参考了中、美两国近年出版的一些考古报告，创立了适合归城情况的一个双语考古报告编写体例。哥伦比亚大学和吉林大学的博士研究生们积极参与了报告中各章的英译或中译工作，而从保证我们能达到这个目标。我们感谢同学们对这本双语报告的贡献。他们包括哥伦比亚大学的侯昱文（Paul Nicholas Vogt）、赵家华（Glenda Chao）、兰德（Brian Lander）、贝丽姿（Elizabeth Berger）；吉林大学的刘晓霞、杨琳、周琪等同学。另在哥伦比亚大学习的台湾大学雷晋豪也参加了翻译。吉林大学刘晓霞同学还担任了报告中插图、表的编排和修改工作，勘定比例，对我们完成这部书稿做出了重要贡献，这是我们要特别感谢的。全部章节的翻译均经编者修改，校定，并纳入书中。另外，班大为（David W. Pankenier）教授担任了全书英文部分的统一校订工作，我们也要对他表示衷心的感谢。最后，我们感谢科学出版社赵越女士为编辑、出版好这本书所作的不懈努力。

李　峰　梁中合

2018年5月26日

Acknowledgments

Twelve years have passed since the establishment of the Guicheng Sino-American collaborative archaeological survey project in 2006. Throughout this long period, we have benefited from generous and often enthusiastic assistance by many institutions and individuals in the United States, and especially in China. Their assistance made possible the project's smooth progress and eventual achievement of significant results. All the participants in the project maintained their enthusiasm throughout, never flagging in attention to their responsibilities, carefully completing their assigned tasks, and duly contributing to the completion of this monographic report. We are genuinely pleased and deeply grateful for this successful outcome.

In its early phase, the Guicheng project fieldwork was awarded two grants from the Chiang Ching-kuo Foundation for International Scholarly Exchange (the American Region), and a start-up great from the Department of East Asian Languages and Cultures, Columbia University. In the later phases, the new Tang Center for Early China, the Department of East Asian Languages and Cultures, and the Confucius Institute at Columbia University each provided subsidies to underwrite the editing of the project's monograph. First and foremost, we are profoundly grateful for their generosity and support. The Guicheng project also garnered approvals and support from the National Bureau of Cultural Relics of China and the Bureau of Cultural Relics of the Provincial Council for Cultural Affairs of Shandong Province, to whom we would also like to express our sincere gratitude. To support the publication of this book, the Institute of Archaeology of the Chinese Academy of Social Sciences and the Shandong Provincial Academy of Cultural Relics and Archaeology jointly applied for and received funding from the National Bureau of Cultural Relics of China. We owe them special acknowledgement and thanks.

Among academic institutions, we would like first to thank the three primary sponsors of the Guicheng project: the Department of East Asian Languages and Cultures, Columbia University, the Institute of Archaeology of the Chinese Academy of Social Sciences, and the Shandong Provincial Academy of Cultural Relics and Archaeology (formerly Shandong Provincial Institute of Cultural Relics and Archaeology). Collaborating institutions included Yantai Municipal Museum, whose researchers participated in the fieldwork, data analysis, and the writing of this report, which greatly facilitated the fulfillment of the goals of the project; and Longkou Municipal Museum. The directors and colleagues of the latter tirelessly helped us in many ways to secure the logistics indispensable for the fieldwork after we returned to Longkou to analyze data to write this book. For this we owe them special heartfelt thanks. In addition, the Research Center for Chinese Frontier Archaeology, Jilin University, kindly allowed one of the editors of this book to make the preparation of the Guicheng report his target research project and provided support during his tenure as a "Specially-appointed Lecturing Professor" in the university. We acknowledge our thanks to them as well.

Academic leaders and colleagues at the above institutions have offered us timely advice and support on countless occasions. Without their enthusiastic assistance the objectives of the Guicheng fieldwork could never have been realized, let alone the publication of this Chinese-English bilingual monographic report. In the United States, Professor Robert P. Hymes, formerly Chair of the Department of East Asian Languages and Cultures, Columbia University, oversaw the establishment of the Guicheng project and lent his strong support from beginning to end. Professor Terence N. D'Altroy, Chair of Columbia's Anthropology Department helped us design the surface survey method used in Guicheng and subsequently offered timely assistance. We express our heartfelt thanks to both. We also thank Professor Cho-yun Hsu of the University of Pittsburgh and Professor David der-wei Wang of Harvard University for their support of this project. In China, we have a longer list of individuals to whom we owe debts of gratitude. Begging indulgence in advance for any omissions, we would like to thank in particular: Wang Wei and Chen Xingcan, Directors of the Institute of Archaeology (CASS); Li Chuanrong, Tong Peihua, Zheng Tongxiu, Wang Shougong, Directors of the Shandong Provincial Institute of Cultural Relics and Archaeology; Directors Wang Xiping, Gao Aidong, and Wang Fuqiang of the Yantai Municipal Museum; Jiang Huimin, Ma Zhimin, and Luan Wenhong, Directors of the Longkou Municipal Museum. Special thanks must be extended to Chen Xingcan, Director of the Institute of Archaeology (CASS), who has given the Guicheng project special attention and support, and has done much to coordinate and smooth the project's organization, helping us resolve difficult situations when they arose. We also thank Song Xinchao, Associate Director of the National Bureau of Cultural Relics of China for his attention to and support of the Guicheng project.

The colleagues and graduate students who actually took part in the Guocheng survey and test excavation all deserve our utmost thanks and respect. They include Tang Jinqiong, Fu Qunqi, and Bi Daochuan of the Institute of Archaeology (CASS), Han Hui of Shandong Provincial Academy of Cultural Relics and Archaeology, and Xu Mingjiang of the Yantai Municipal Museum. Graduate students who participated in the fieldwork include: Han-Peng Ho, Wu Minna, Paul Nicholas Vogt, Brian Lander, Glenda Chao, Shi Hui, Lee Crawford, Elizabeth Berger, and Jackson Cooper, all from Columbia University, and Yitzchak Jaffe from Hebrew University of Jerusalem, Israel. Photographing and ink-rubbing were performed by Fu Qunqi. Site and topographical maps were produced by Bi Daochuan and Tang Jinqiong. Drawings of objects were all completed by Bi Daochuan. GIS imaging was conducted by Jeremiah Trinidad-Christensen of the Digital Library of Columbia University. Due to the restrictions imposed by Columbia's semesters, the multiyear fieldwork (except in Winter 2007) all took place from late May to mid-July. During the hot summers, and despite multiple sunburns, all participants in the Guicheng fieldwork shared the joys and bitter hardships, took their duties seriously, and overcame tremendous difficulties in completing all segments of the fieldwork. Throughout they maintained the highest standards and thereby ensured the high scientific quality of the data we obtained. For their hard work and enormous contributions, we express our most heartfelt thanks!

As a true bilingual archaeological report, the editing of the Guicheng report doubled the editorial effort demanded by a monolingual monograph of equivalent magnitude, whether in Chinese or English. To accomplish this, we consulted recently published archaeological reports in both China and the United States, in order to create the style of bilingual report that suited our particular situation. Doctoral students from Columbia University and Jilin University performed the task of translating chapters from Chinese to English and vice versa, which enabled us to accomplish our goal. We thank these students for their contributions to the Guicheng report. They include Paul Nicholas Vogt, Glenda Chao, Brian Lander, Elizabeth Berger of Columbia University; Liu Xiaoxia, Yang Lin, and Zhou Qi of Jilin University. Lei Chin-hao, formerly a visiting PhD student at Columbia University from National Taiwan University, also translated two chapters. In addition, Liu Xiaoxia of Jilin University compiled the illustrations and tables, modifying the drawings and unifying the image scales when necessary, and made important contributions to the production of a well-organized manuscript. We would like to acknowledge our special thanks to her. All chapters in translation were collated by the editors before incorporation in the book. Professor David W. Pankenier copy-edited and proofread the English portions of the manuscript, and we would also like to express our thanks to him. Last but not least, we express our thanks to Ms. Zhao Yue, editor of Science Press, for her tireless effort to edit and publish a very satisfactory book.

Li Feng　Liang Zhonghe

May 26, 2018

作者介绍

姓名：（以首字音顺排列）	工作单位	学术职称
贝丽姿（Elizabeth Berger）	密歇根大学	博士后研究员
刁鹏	烟台市博物馆	馆员
韩辉	山东省文物考古研究院	馆员
侯昱文（Paul Nicholas Vogt）	印第安纳大学	助理教授
蒋惠民	龙口市博物馆	副研究馆员
李峰	哥伦比亚大学	教授
李志鹏	中国社会科学院考古研究所	副研究员
梁中合	中国社会科学院考古研究所	研究员
刘玉涛	龙口市博物馆	馆员
马志敏	龙口市博物馆	副研究馆员
任乐乐	兰州大学	博士研究生
Stidham, Tom A.	中国科学院古脊椎动物与古人类研究所	研究员
Stoltman, James B.	威斯康星大学	名誉教授
孙兆锋	烟台市博物馆	馆员
唐锦琼	中国社会科学院考古研究所	副研究员
Trinidad-Christensen, Jeremiah	哥伦比亚大学	地理空间服务馆员
王富强	烟台市博物馆	研究馆员
徐明江	烟台市博物馆	副研究馆员
闫旭东	烟台市博物馆	馆员
张雪莲	中国社会科学院考古研究所	研究员
赵娟	烟台市博物馆	副研究馆员
赵志军	中国社会科学院考古研究所	研究员

Contributors

Name *In alphabetical order*	Institution	Professional Title
Elizabeth Berger	University of Michigan	Postdoctoral Fellow
Diao Peng	Yantai Municipal Museum	Curator
Han Hui	Shandong Provincial Academy of Cultural Relics and Archaeology	Curator
Paul Nicholas Vogt	Indiana University	Assistant Professor
Jiang Huimin	Longkou Municipal Museum	Associate Research Curator
Li Feng	Columbia University	Professor
Li Zhipeng	Institute of Archaeology, CASS	Associate Research Fellow
Liang Zhonghe	Institute of Archaeology, CASS	Research Fellow
Liu Yutao	Longkou Municipal Museum	Curator
Ma Zhimin	Longkou Municipal Museum	Associate Research Curator
Ren Lele	Lanzhou University	Ph.D. Candidate
Stidham, Tom A	Institute of Vertebrate Paleontology and Paleoanthropology, CAS	Research Fellow
Stoltman, James B.	University of Wisconsin	Professor Emeritus
Sun Zhaofeng	Yantai Municipal Museum	Curator
Tang Jinqiong	Institute of Archaeology, CASS	Associate Research Fellow
Trinidad-Christensen, Jeremiah	Columbia University	Geospatial Services Coordinator
Wang Fuqiang	Yantai Municipal Museum	Research Curator
Xu Mingjiang	Yantai Municipal Museum	Associate Research Curator
Yan Xudong	Yantai Municipal Museum	Curator
Zhang Xuelian	Institute of Archaeology, CASS	Research Fellow
Zhao Juan	Yantai Municipal Museum	Associate Research Curator
Zhao Zhijun	Institute of Archaeology, CASS	Research Fellow

目　　录

上编

下编

附录

Contents

Appendices

绪　论

李　峰　梁中合

归城考古调查是一个研究山东半岛东部青铜时代晚期（约公元前1000～前500年）社会变化的国际田野合作项目。为了了解这个巨大的古代城市综合体的运作和它在区域聚落系统中的重要作用，并且为未来记录和保存相关信息，中美联合考古队于2007～2010年进行了这项多维度的田野研究工作。它也是曾经在山东半岛东部所实施的重点关注过去区域青铜时代的最大的考古学项目。在这篇前言中，我们将讨论这个项目的背景和当时的环境，它的组织和主要研究的问题。前言的最后我们将回顾这四年间田野工作的进展。

第一节　时代和地区社会文化背景

公元前568年，经过多年的准备，霸主国齐国的军队在大将晏弱的率领下大举入侵山东东部莱国的领土。为了支持这一战争，晏弱甚至率领齐国军队花费三年时间在边境建造了一座新的城市。文献记载中说，齐国军队在这一年的第四个月时到达莱国都城，并且可能由于莱国沿其城墙的严格防御，为了有效进攻，齐国军队不得不建造一条坡道以到达其顶部。公元前567年的第三个月，经过将近一年的艰苦抵抗，城内的莱国军队发起了一场反击，但被击败。在丁未这一天（应该是这个月的第二十七天；陈厚燿 1981：6.24），齐军最终破城而入，莱国君主浮柔（莱共公）逃至附近一个被称为棠的小地方，在那里他被抓获，并于年末被处决（左传30.1937）。

伐莱一事也被记录在同时期的青铜器铭文之中，显然是由参与此次历史事件的齐国官员所铸，它们证实了历史文献中令人印象深刻的一些细节。从政治意义上讲，吞并莱国有助于齐国上升为一个强大的以直接的官僚行政为基础的领土国家，其领土此后扩大到整个山东东部（地图Ⅰ.0.1）。在以后的世纪中，齐国将其著名的长城从现今济南附近的黄河岸边延伸至青岛海湾，几乎将山东半岛同中国的其他地区切断。但是将其放在社会和人类学的视角中，此次征伐决定性地打断了本地区——由新石器时代晚期的小族群向一些由国家力量所组织的大型社会（其中莱是最重要的）——的独立发展的漫长过程。对这一发展过程的外来刺激主要是由更大规模的王朝国家向东发展而带来的，比如商（公元前1554～前1046年），特别是以黄河中游为中心的西周（公元前1045～前771年）。因此，在并入齐国之前，山东东部的人类历史进程以两种宏大且相互联系的社会过程所呈现：即复杂社会的逐步发展和国家的崛起——类似于人类学家所描述的“二次国家的形成（Secondary state formation）”（Price 1978：161～224；Braswell and Prager et al. 2004：219～233；Shelach and Pines 2006：202～230）。这些都是本项目中要讨论的重要理论问题。

历史地理学的研究将莱国的中心定在现今一个叫“归城”的地方，在今天渤海南岸的龙口市（旧称黄县）东南约6.5千米处。区域内地貌主要由连绵起伏的丘陵、小湖泊以及在宽阔的山谷中和沿西北海岸分布的长短不一的带状平原所组成（图Ⅰ.0.1）。他们一起组成一个位于北部渤海和南部莱山之间的约600平方千米的大三角地带；莱山最高峰海拔550米，它把这个地带和半岛内陆地区隔离开来（龙口市的行政单位面积为893平方千米，包括山区）（图版1：2）。归城遗址在莱山脚下丘陵延伸地带，地处与东边黄水河河道相分隔的一个天然最易于防护的空间（地图Ⅰ.0.2；图版3～5）。遗址由两个城墙圈构成，并且据1973年烟台市博物馆组织的早期考古学调查所估计，原来外墙的总长度为10千米（李步青，林仙庭 1991：910）。其巨大的规模以及残存城墙的壮观程度与位于曲阜的鲁国故城相差无几（山东省文物考古研究所 1982：1～35）；在青铜时代晚期，归城城市综合体无疑是整个山东东部最大的城市中心。早在19世纪晚期，当地一系列带有铭文青铜器的发现表明了归城及其毗邻地区在考古学上中的显著地位。一些铭文明确提及了陕西周朝中心文武官员的活动，其中启尊和启卣记录了在南方由周王亲自领导的一场战争（齐文涛 1972：5～8）。这些发现使归城成为除周朝中心之外最重要的有铭文青铜器的集中发现地之一。

更多来自周朝中心地区的青铜器铭文中明确记载了以征服居住在山东地区，且通常被称之为“东夷”的当地人口为目标的军事活动。综合看这些铭文，它们表现了约公元前11世纪晚期以来周朝由黄河流域向山东地区进行军事扩张的一个大致过程（Li 2006：304～314），与归城本地及周边地区所发现的青铜器铭文联系起来，非常令人信服。这显示归城可能处在周朝扩张的前沿，甚至可能是一个边界基地，这使得其政治上极易变化，并且文化上被带有不同观念和风俗的不同人群所渗透。归城城市综合体和广泛遍及龙口地区的物质遗存显示了两个不同制陶传统的典型混合。一个明显与西部的制陶传统有关，另一个可能来自于东部山东半岛本地新石器时代文化，这似乎同样说明了这一边境环境的性质。

像归城这样具有丰富物质内容和复杂社会文化背景的重要遗址自然提供很多值得研究的问题：一方面是人类学考古学的问题，主要研究过去人类社会发展的动力和一般模式；另一方面是历史的问题，其关注点在于特定区域的政治根源和区域社会进程中人类的主体作用。我们认为这些问题并不互相排斥；相反地，对这些问题的答案可以相互支持。山东东部地区晚期青铜时代的特定历史和文化背景使我们不仅能够通过田野工作来探究这些问题，而且也可以从文字证据中得到帮助。

第二节　项目的确立

归城国际合作项目源起于2005年和2006年夏天我们对这一地区的两次考察，在此期间我们在龙口市博物馆馆长的引导下（蒋惠民 2005；马志敏 2006）查看了这座古城中最明显的古代地标（图Ⅰ.0.2）。特别是第一次参观适逢和平村自来水系统的安装，为此村民们挖掘了一条长的沟渠。沿着这条管道我们有一个难得的机会来直接观察地下堆积，并查看由挖掘而浮出地表的陶片。从归城出发，我们进而调查了位于黄水河主河道谷地中的一些同时代遗址，包括庄头和鲁家沟，这些地方都发现过重要的青铜器。这两次考察为我们评估遗址的保存状况提供了最初的机会，并为将来的田野考古工作打开了新的视角。基于其巨大的规模、丰富的物质内容和过去发现的历史，任何试图理解这一古城遗址的努力必须要通过有系统的计划来执行，并且一定要从全面的调查开始，这一点甚至在这个早期时段就已明确。之后，我们向所属的两个机构——中国社会科学院考古研究所和美国哥伦比亚大学反映了情况，并且向同行们征求了意见和建议，我们开始确立归城合作项目的构想方案。另外，在2006年夏天我们也确定了山东省文物考古研究所参与这一合作项目的意向。

在2006年年末至2007年年初，我们洽谈确定了这个合作项目的大多数条例，并最终产生了代表两方三个机构的正式合同。双方承诺共同组建“中美联合归城考古队”作为主要研究队伍，在最初阶段的三年内以归城古城遗址为中心进行系统调查。特别是哥伦比亚大学东亚语言与文化系（韩明士主任［Robert P. Hymes］）同意提供一笔用于2007年夏天第一季度田野调查的启动资金，同时我们将寻找支持后续工作的外部资金。2007年4月时任中国社会科学院考古研究所所长王巍的纽约之行为两个机构再次确认他们对此项目的承诺提供了一个合适的机会，并且签署了正式合同，这个合同之后也得到了当时山东省文物考古研究所所长的认可。合同中中方的两个单位随后协同行动，使归城合作项目的申请能够得到中华人民共和国国家文物局相关行政管理机构的批准。

中美联合归城考古队由三所机构的研究人员组成，由美国哥伦比亚大学李峰担任美方领队，中国社会科学院考古研究所王巍和山东省文物考古研究所佟佩华分别为中方领队和副领队。田野工作由李峰和中国社会科学院考古研究所梁中合领导实施。美方团队还包括哥伦比亚大学Terence N. D’Altroy，他在项目中发挥顾问的作用，特别是帮助设计了系统的地面调查方法（见下文）。此外在不同年份还有数目不等的研究生助理和本科学生，分别来自哥伦比亚大学和其他美国大学。中方的唐锦琼（中国社会科学院考古研究所）和韩辉（山东省文物考古研究所）连同两个机构每年提供的10～15名技术人员作为合同期内的固定成员。2008年夏，烟台市博物馆的徐明江也加入该团队，并继续参与了之后两年的田野工作。通常每期在田野的考古队员有25～30人。

第三节　学术目标

2007年6月13日，我们的中美联合国际合作考古队到达归城，开始了之后持续超过四年多的田野工作。这个项目是基于我们在田野工作中致力追求的几个长期学术目标来制定的。

我们第一个学术目标是探索归城内部社会和经济组织运转的动力；归城是位于商周文明边缘多元文化环境中的一个典型的大型城市中心。这样，我们希望把归城作为一个了解社会变化的基地，通过这个变化，山东东部地区的本土族群在一个政治上更具优势的文化的影响下，自我组织成为大型国家。这是人类历史上最常见的国家形成轨迹之一，并且我们希望归城的研究工作可以基于可靠的考古学证据来帮助我们具体描绘这一“二次国家形成（secondary formation of state）”过程。

其次，我们希望揭示青铜时代晚期龙口地区的聚落系统，并了解归城在这一系统中所扮演的角色。理想的话，我们希望使用在中国其他地区已经被实践的全覆盖调查方法（赤峰2003；Chifeng 2011；Underhill et al 1998：453 ~ 474；Underhill et al 2008：1 ~ 29）来确定区域聚落的等级，并解释归城是如何在较小的边远村落之上实现其政治统治的，及其这些聚落是如何反过来把归城作为国家权利的所在地而在经济上给予支持。为此，我们也希望未来的发掘可以揭示农业、渔猎水产业和贸易都可能在区域生业系统中发挥了重要作用。

第三，我们更为感兴趣的是文化间的关系和交流。归城遗址处在两个文化的接触地带（contact zone），周文化向山东东部的扩张为我们研究文化间相互应对的方式提供了一个理想的背景。然而，我们并没有预设当地族群在处理同先进周文化关系上的被动角色，而是我们希望展示当地或周边族群是如何积极主动地适应新环境，并最终成功地将这个环境变得对自己有利（Dietler 1998：288 ~ 314），或者如何产生一个为新文化的崛起提供土壤的中间立场（Gosden 2004：82 ~ 113）。地方政权莱国的崛起和一个可能的周人人口从归城的退出是这种区域自治趋势的一个好的证据。我们希望这样一个文化取向的研究将会为山东东部地区城市组织和聚落系统的研究增加新的维度。

遗憾的是，尽管有像归城这样重要的古城存在，山东东部地区的青铜时代在考古学上尚未得到较好的认识。特别是大致与位于西部的西周国家（公元前1045 ~ 前771年）同时的阶段基本上在先前的考古学研究中被漏掉，因为以前这个地区的考古学研究重点主要在新石器时代（公元前7000 ~ 前2000年）和东周—汉代期间（公元前770 ~ 公元220年）。因此，至少我们应该做到的是通过对归城和周边地区集中的田野考古工作来揭示本区域的物质文化序列，并为未来其他地区的研究建立时间标准。

上文所列的一些研究目标在短期内可以实现，其他则需要通过未来持续不断的努力来回答。但是我们希望至少可以开始探索这些问题，并为后人留下有益的研究途径。总之，我们希望归城项目能够帮助我们理解青铜时代晚期社会状况的变化，及其位于中心地区的国家和周边社会在中华文明形成这一共同过程中所共同扮演的角色。

第四节　研究空间的界定和田野工作的分隔

我们将归城考古视作一项长期的工作，依照两项指导原则来设计我们的田野工作：①作为一个可能需要几代研究者去实现的研究项目，田野工作必须运用适合于大遗址的作业方法，有系统的计划和执行。田野工作必须考虑到为未来的研究奠定基础，并且要为将来的遗址保护提供信息。基于归城作为一个“全国重点文物保护单位”的新地位，最后一点尤为重要。②由于目前的项目仅是一个田野调查项目（与系统的有计划的发掘不同），在未来系统发掘进行之前，必须确保采用的田野调查方法会使我们获得最大量的信息，以实现对遗址最充分和合理的了解。

根据以上两点，我们运用了1984年被谷歌地图所使用的世界测地系统（World Geodetic System［WGS84］）来界定整个研究空间，以其四个角的坐标永久地固定在：N37°34′15″～N37°36′39″；E120°32′49″～E120°35′13″。这确定了一个东西长3520米，南北长4480米的地面空间，而由城墙环绕的归城遗址即坐落在其中心附近的位置（地图Ⅰ.0.3）。这个大的空间随后被划分为16个900米×1120米的方块。这个系统被统一用来记录现在及其未来发现的建筑遗迹和遗存。在这个研究空间里，田野工作基本上被分为五个部分，每一部分都有其特定目标（中美联合归城考古队 2011：30～39）：①内城城墙系统钻探，这提供了关于内城城墙实际尺寸、方位和保存状态的可靠信息（见第二章）；②内城内部建筑遗迹的系统钻探，比如居住建筑、道路、露天广场以及供水系统，他们可以告诉我们内城的组织原则（见第三章）；③归城外墙的系统调查和记录（见第四章）；④内城南部的试掘，这为城市的居住历史和城墙建造的年代提供了直接的证据（见第五章）；⑤对整个归城城市综合体的密集型系统地面调查，这可以使我们确定在更大归城区域内地理景观之上的遗址集中点（见第六章）；⑥归城外围地区以沿黄水河流域为中心的聚落系统调查（见第七章）。

与田野工作并行，我们在哥伦比亚大学为归城项目建立两个重要的数据库，以此作为通过调查和钻探所获信息展示和分析的平台。这些工作在哥伦比亚大学电子数据服务部的地理资讯系统（GIS）专家Jeremiah Trinidad-Christensen的指导下进行。首先是一个可以对归城地下建筑进行计算机模拟的数据系统，向其中我们输入内城钻探所得的资料。其次是一个用来分析地面调查资料的数据系统，并由此产生调查结果的密度图及其三维图像（见第八章）。

第五节　田野工作进程

自2007年夏以来直到2010年末，我们花费总计六个季度的时间进行归城的田野考古工作。在这个绪论的最后部分中，我们将回顾过去四年的田野工作进程，并重点介绍我们在每个阶段所取得的重要发现。

2007年夏：6月13日～7月20日。此季度的大部分时间被用来制定识别土壤，包括夯土（夯土，通常指人造的建筑基址）的标准，界定研究区域，并选定一个可以在归城各处普遍应用的记录钻探孔位的系统。这个季度的主要目标是确定内城城墙的实际位置和范围，我们共花了30天的时间去完成这项工作。钻探开始于内城西南角姜家村高耸出地面上的一段城墙（图Ⅰ.0.3），由此处前进并找出归城内城墙的每一面。其中一个重要发现是此前未知的位于和平村东部的一个大的地面平台，并且钻探确认它即是东墙的一部分（1973年的调查认为东城墙已不存在；李步青，林仙庭 1991：912）。此一发现明确了归城内城的界限。钻探显示归城内城形成了一个反转的“L”形，覆盖了姜家村的大部分、和平村及其它们之间的空间，并且在很多地段城墙被外部的一条宽度不同的壕沟所保护。另一个重要发现是位于和平村之北的一个120米长的大块夯土台基，但是此建筑的功能尚未知。第一季度工作团队的研究人员包括李峰、梁中合及其韩辉，学生组有何汉平（Han-Peng Ho）、吴敏娜和侯昱文（Paul Nicholas Vogt）（图Ⅰ.0.4）。韩国檀国大学（Dankook University）的沈载勋（Jaehoon Shim）博士也参与了部分田野工作。

2007年冬：11月3～30日。在第二季度，钻探队移至内城内部，寻找重要的建筑遗迹和其他地下建筑。由内城的东南角开始钻探，到天气变得异常寒冷而不能进行户外工作时为止，考古队钻探了和平村南面南半部约3/4的露天区域，地面几乎完全被苹果树所占据。到季度结束时，除位于内城东部的两处大的宫殿基址外，我们还发现了宽阔的内城中央大道。归城外城墙的勘测于11月9日开始，到季度结束时我们发现了16段新的城墙遗址，从而确认了外城北部界限，并且用全站仪（full-station）在地图上标出（图Ⅰ.0.5）。冬季田野工作由李峰、梁中合、唐锦琼和韩辉四位研究人员领导，并且两所中方研究机构派遣的11名技工参与了此项工作。

2008年夏：6月7日～7月23日。一个扩大至28人的团队回到归城，实施更复杂的田野作业。钻探队覆盖了和平村南部剩余的空间，及其姜家村北部的一处宽阔区域，发现了总计10处建筑基址，并对这些基址进行了测量和绘图。对外城城墙的调查连续发现揭露了28段新城墙遗址。调查证实，归城外墙不像之前所认为的是一个完整的圈，而是形成了一个大的不完整的椭圆形，其南面朝向莱山深谷敞开。2008年6月13日，我们开始在归城内城和外城墙之间的空间进行系统的地面调查（图Ⅰ.0.6），主要由我们7个学生所组成的团队来承担这项工作，包括：何汉平（Han-Peng Ho），吴敏娜，侯昱文（Paul Nicholas Vogt），兰德（Brian Lander），赵家华（Glena Chao），贝丽姿（Elizabeth Berger）和Athena Hsieh。我们由内城边缘的7区开始，调查队随后穿过3区、2区、4区、8区和12区的一个狭长地带，进行系统的陶片采集。上一季度主持田野工作的研究人员全部返回归城参加工作。此外，烟台市博物馆的徐明江也参与了地面调查工作（图Ⅰ.0.7）。

2009年夏：6月5日～7月21日。一个新的学生团队到达归城继续进行系统的地面调查，主要有兰德（Brian Lander）、关隐（LeLand Crawford）、石蕙（Shi Hui）、顾岩（Jackson Cooper）和哈克（Yitzhack Jaffe）。此次小组继续了12区的调查，然后依次是5区、6区、9区、10区、11区和16区。另一方面，钻探队完成了姜家村和和平村之间整个空间的钻探，并且发现了另外5处建筑基址和城市河道系统。2009年夏，我们也对内城南部城址轴心线附近的区域进行了重要的试掘。此次挖掘使我们能够分析归城遗址的地下遗存，并为我们把归城内城城墙建造的年代定为西周时期提供了直接的地层学依据（图Ⅰ.0.8）。另外，利用归城田野工作的间隙，考古队也对山东东部其他两处重要的青铜时代遗址进行了初步调查，包括蓬莱的村里集和招远的东曲城。领导2009年夏季田野工作的研究人员有李峰、梁中合、唐锦琼、韩辉和徐明江（图Ⅰ.0.9）。

2010年夏：7月16日～8月30日。我们的考古队基地由归城转移至龙口，并在整个期间致力于对过去三年所获的材料进行分析和整理。对2009年试掘的每个地层单位出土遗物进行统计学的分析。此项工作包括去年参与田野工作的所有研究人员。

2010年冬：10月10日～11月6日。梁中合领队回到龙口，并领导了黄水河流域及沿渤海海岸地区十五处重要遗址的田野调查。

到2010年，我们认识到为了规划未来的研究，有必要暂停目前的田野工作，对过去几年里积累在手头的田野资料进行一个全面回顾和消化。这本书介绍了2007～2010年归城田野考古工作的细节以及我们对所获资料的初步分析结果。不过，本报告下编的若干章节对2007年以前在归城及其临近地区所做的考古工作及重要发现进行了回顾。本书大部分章节于2011～2012年完成，并在2013年7月27～28日于中国社会科学院考古研究所曲阜工作站所举行的工作会议上进行了发表和讨论（图Ⅰ.0.10）。我们希望通过把这些章节结合在一起，这本书能给我们一个新的基础，它至少能够让我们回答这个前言前面所提出的一部分问题。本书是一个对归城已知考古资料的总结，它将会作为我们未来继续研究的基础。

参考文献

Braswell, Geoffrey, Christian M. Prager, et al., 2004. "The Rise of Secondary States in the Southeastern Periphery of Maya World," *Ancient Mesoamerica*, 15: 219-233.

陈厚耀（1647～1722），1981：春秋长历（四库全书珍本）. 台北：商务印书馆.

赤峰中美联合考古研究项目，2003：内蒙古东部（赤峰）区域考古调查阶段性报告. 北京：科学出版社.

Chifeng International Collaborative Archaeological Research Project, 2011. *Settlement Patterns in the Chifeng Region*. Pittsburgh: Center for Comparative Archaeology, University of Pittsburgh.

Dietler, Michael, 1998. "Consumption, Agency, and Culture Entanglement: Theoretical Implications of a Mediterranean Colonial Encounter," in *Studies in Cultural Contact: Interaction, Cultural Change and Archaeology*, edited by James Cusick. Pp. 288-314. Carbondale: Southern Illinois University Press, Center for Archaeological Investigation.

Gosden, Chris, 2004. *Archaeology and Colonialism: Cultural Contact from 5000 BC to the Present*. Cambridge: Cambridge University Press.

李步青，林仙庭，1991：山东黄县归城遗址的调查与发掘. 考古，10：910-918.

Li, Feng, 2006. *Landscape and Power in Early China: The Crisis and Fall of the Western Zhou, 1045-771 BC*. Cambridge,

UK: Cambridge University Press.

Price, Barbara, 1978. “Secondary State Formation: An Explanatory Model,” in *Origin of the State: The Anthropology of Political Evolution*, edited by R. Cohen. Pp.161-224. Philadelphia: Institute for the Study of Human Issues.

齐文涛，1972：概述近年来山东出土的商周青铜器. 文物，5：3-16.

山东省文物考古研究所，1982：曲阜鲁国故城. 济南：齐鲁书社.

Shelach, Gideon, and Yuri Pines, 2006. “Secondary State Formation and the Development of Local Identity: Change and Continuity in the State of Qin (770–221 B.C.),” in *Archaeology of Asia*, edited by M. T. Stark. Pp. 202-230. Malden, MA: Blackwell.

Underhill, Anne P., G. M. Feinman, Linda Nicholas, G. Bennett, Fengshu Cai, Haiguang Yu, Fengshi Luan, Hui Fang, 1998. “Systematic, Regional Survey in SE Shandong Province, China,” *Journal of Field Archaeology*, 25.4: 453-474.

Underhill, Anne P., G. M. Feinman, L. M. Nicholas, G. Bennett, Hui Fang, Fengshi Luan, Haiguang Yu, and Fengshu Cai, 2002. “Regional Survey and the Development of Complex Societies in Southeastern Shandong, China,” *Antiquity*, 76.293: 745-755.

Underhill, Anne P., G. M. Feinman, L. M. Nicholas, Hui Fang, Fengshi Luan, Haiguang Yu, and Fengshu Cai, 2008. “Changes in Regional Settlement Patterns and the Development of Complex Societies in Southeastern Shandong, China,” *Journal of Anthropological Archaeology*, 27: 1-29.

中美联合归城考古队，2011：山东龙口市归城两周城址调查简报. 考古，3：30-39.

左传，1979：十三经注疏. 1697-2188. 北京：中华书局.

（翻译：刘晓霞）

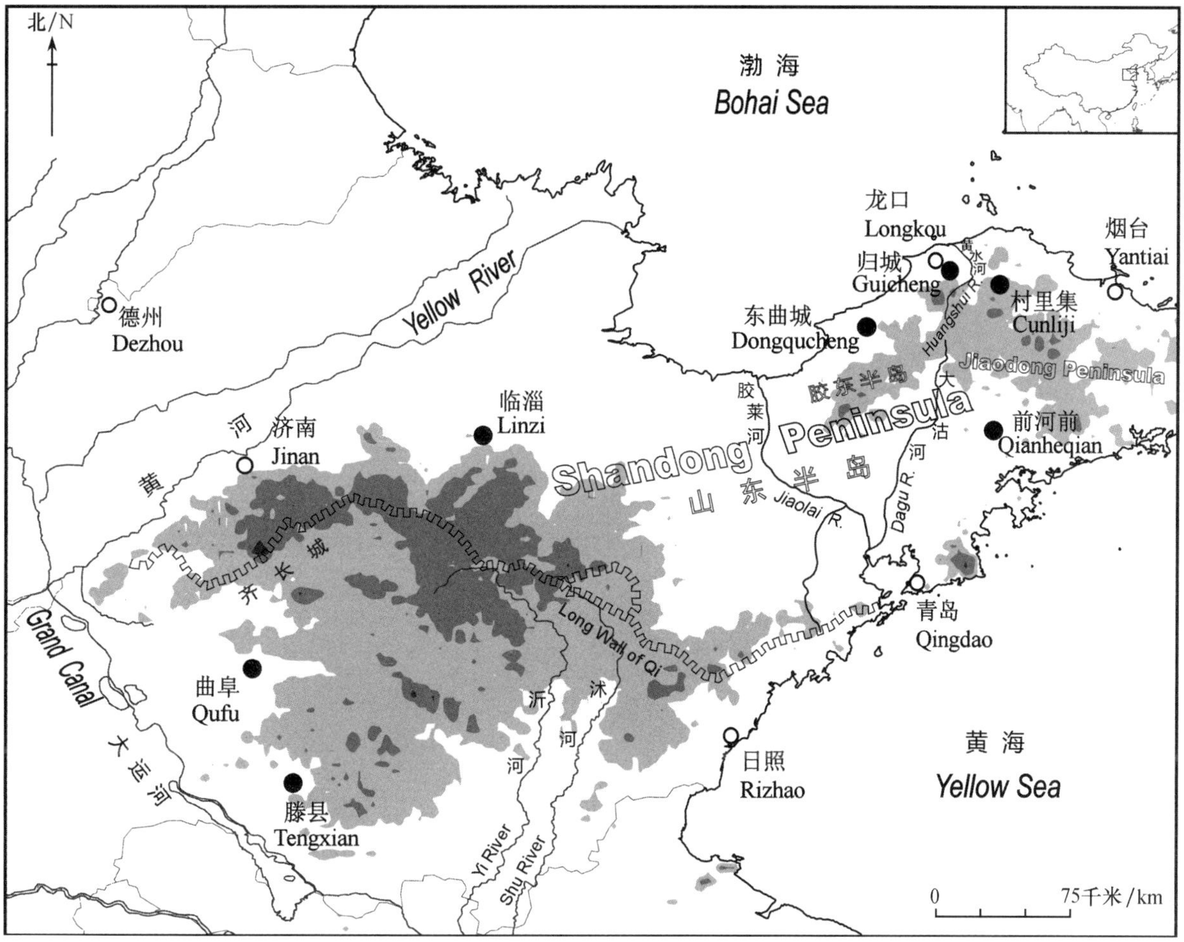

地图Ⅰ.0.1 归城在山东省东部的地理位置

Map Ⅰ.0.1 Location of Guicheng in eastern Shandong.

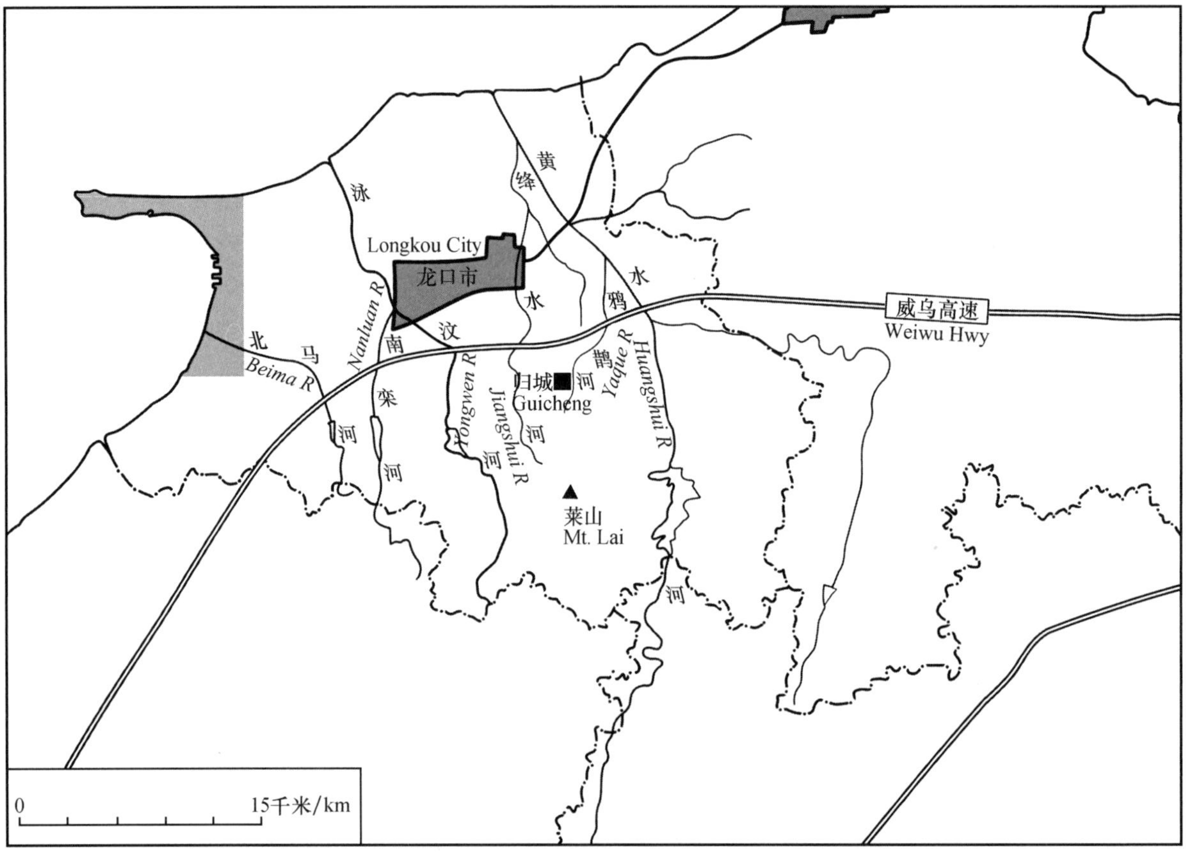

地图Ⅰ.0.2　归城遗址地理位置图

Map Ⅰ.0.2　The geographical location of the Guicheng site.

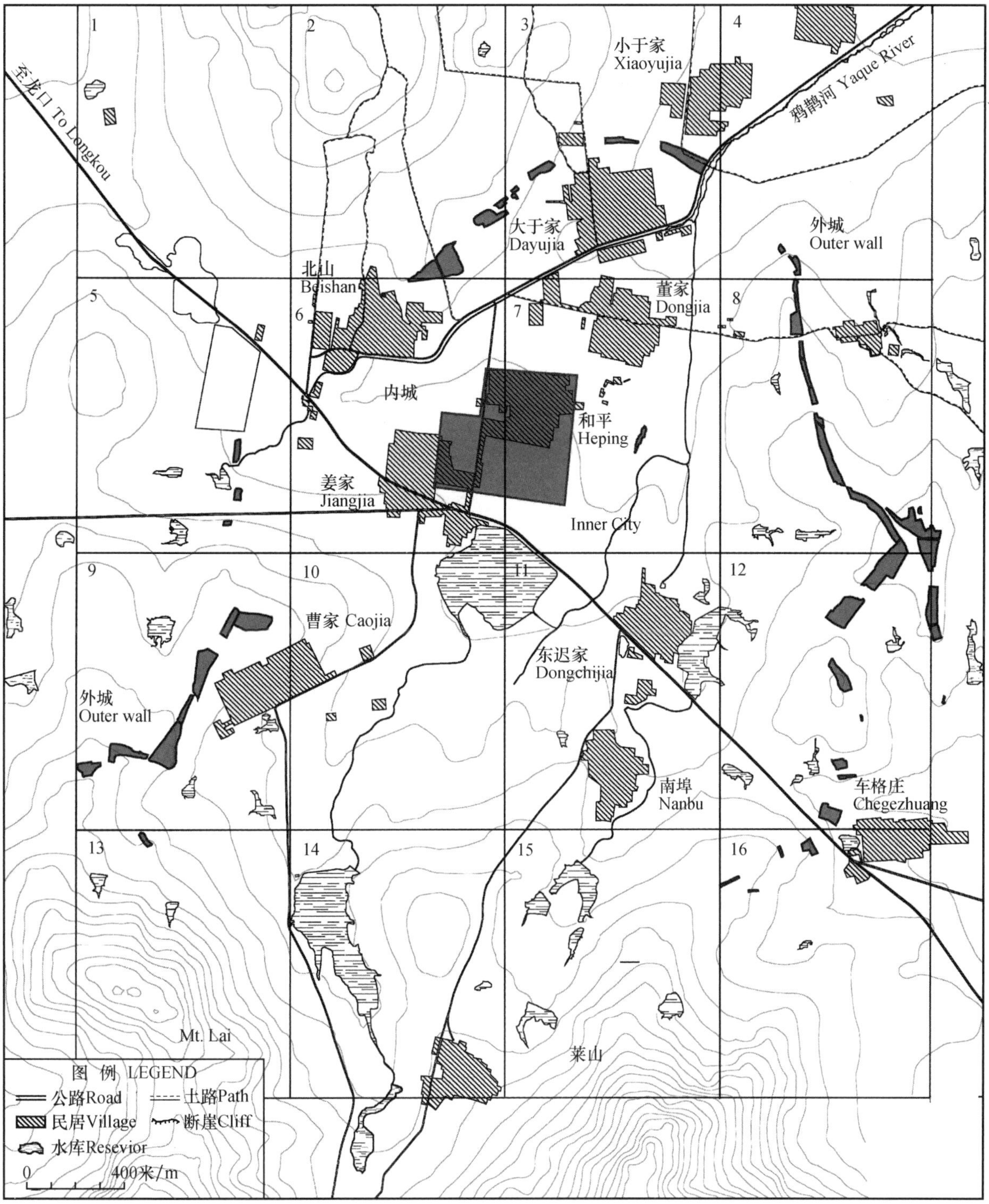

地图Ⅰ.0.3 归城工作区域的划分

Map Ⅰ.0.3 Division of work areas in Guicheng.

图Ⅰ.0.1　归城地区地貌

Figure Ⅰ.0.1　Landscape of the Guicheng region.

图Ⅰ.0.2　2006年对归城的第二次考察（左起：马志敏、罗泰、李峰、梁中合和闫勇）

Figure Ⅰ.0.2　Second visit to Guicheng in 2006 (from left: Ma Zhimin, Lothar von Falkenhausen, Li Feng, Liang Zhonghe, and Yan Yong).

图Ⅰ.0.3 2007年6月17日，钻探队员识别夯土开始田野工作，姜家村南地面站里的城墙

Figure Ⅰ.0.3 Fieldwork began with members of the coring team trying to identify the rammed earth (*hangtu*) section of the wall located south of Jiangjia Village, June 17, 2007.

图Ⅰ.0.4 2007年夏季参加工作队员

Figure Ⅰ.0.4 Team members in the summer of 2007.

图Ⅰ.0.5　2007年冬归城外城墙的调查
Figure Ⅰ.0.5　The search for the outer city wall of Guicheng, winter 2007.

图Ⅰ.0.6　2008年6月13日，考古队开始地面系统调查
Figure Ⅰ.0.6　The beginning of systematic surface survey, June 13, 2008.

图Ⅰ.0.7　2008年夏季考古队成员
Figure Ⅰ.0.7　Team members in the summer of 2008.

图Ⅰ.0.8　2009年7月4日，试掘开始
Figure Ⅰ.0.8　The beginning of test-excavation, July 4, 2009.

图Ⅰ.0.9　2009年夏季考古队成员
Figure Ⅰ.0.9　Team members in the summer of 2009.

图Ⅰ.0.10　2013年7月27日曲阜工作会议
Figure Ⅰ.0.10　The Qufu conference, July 27, 2013.

Introduction

Li Feng　Liang Zhonghe

The Guicheng archaeological survey was an international collaborative field project to study social changes in eastern Shandong peninsula during the late Bronze Age (ca. 1000-500 BCE). The fieldwork conducted by the Sino-American Joint Archaeological Team in 2007-2010 constituted a major multidimensional research effort to understand the operation of this immense ancient city-complex and its important role in the regional settlement system, and to document and preserve the relevant information for the future. It was also the largest archaeological project ever carried out in eastern Shandong peninsula with a chosen focus on the region's Bronze Age. In this Introduction, we discuss the background and temporal context of the project, its organization, and the main research questions. The last section of the Introduction reviews the progress of the fieldwork over the four years.

Section 1: The Period and the Regional Social-Cultural Context

In 568 BCE, after years of preparation, the army of the hegemonic state of Qi, commanded by general Yan Ruo, launched a full-scale invasion of the territory of the state of Lai in eastern Shandong. In order to support the campaign, Yan Ruo even led the Qi army in a three-year project of construction of a new city near the border. The historical record says that the Qi army reached the capital city of Lai in the fourth month of the year, and perhaps because of Lai's heavily defended city wall, the Qi army had to build ramps to reach the top in order to mount an effective attack. In the third month of 567 BCE, after nearly a year of stiff resistance, the impatient Lai military launched a counter-attack from the city but was decisively defeated. On day *dingwei*, (corresponding to the 27th day of the month; Chen Houyao, 1981: 6.24), the Qi army finally broke into the city and the Lai ruler, Furou (Duke Gong of Lai), fled to a small nearby settlement called Tang where he was captured for execution towards the end of the year (*Zuozhuan*, 1937: 30).

This conquest of Lai is also recorded in contemporaneous bronze inscriptions cast by Qi officials, who had apparently taken part in the historic event. These corroborate the transmitted historical record in some impressive details. In an immediate political sense, the annexation of Lai contributed critically to the rise of Qi as a powerful territorial state based on direct bureaucratic administration, whose sway thereafter extended over all of eastern Shandong (Map Ⅰ.0.1). During the century that followed, Qi expanded its famous Long Wall stretching from the Yellow River bank near present-day Ji'nan to the bay of Qingdao, virtually cutting off the Shandong peninsula from the rest of China. But viewing this in a social and anthropological perspective, the conquest decisively interrupted the long process of the region's independent development from small late Neolithic communities to a few large societies organized by the power of the state, of which Lai was the most prominent. The outside stimuli to this development were provided by the eastward advances of such more massive royal states as Shang (1554-1046 BCE), and particularly the Western Zhou (1045-771 BCE) based in the middle course of the Yellow River. Therefore, before its incorporation into the state of Qi, the human epic in eastern Shandong played out in two grand and interconnected social processes: the gradual development of complex society and the rise of states that resembled what anthropologists often describe as "secondary state formation" (Price 1978: 161-224; Braswell and Prager et al. 2004: 219-233; Shelach and Pines 2006: 202-230). These are important theoretical questions that we dealt with in this project.

Historical-geographical works locate the center of the state of Lai in a place now called "Guicheng," some 6.5 km to the southeast of present-day Longkou City (old name: Huangxian) on the south shore of the Bohai Sea). The landscape within the region consists mainly of undulating hills, swamps, and long or short strips of plains in the wide valleys and along the seacoast to the northwest (Fig. Ⅰ.0.1). Together they form a large triangular space of approximately 600 km^2 situated between the Bohai Sea in the north and Mt. Lai with its high peaks (elevation: 550 m) in the south. The latter segregate the area from the hinterlands of the peninsula (the administrative unit of Longkou City has an area of 893 km^2, including the areas taken up by the mountains) (Pl. 1-2). The site of Guicheng extends over the foothills of Mt. Lai and is situated in one of the best naturally protected sections, separated from the channel of the Huangshui River on the east (Map Ⅰ.0.2; Pl. 3-5). The site is marked by two concentric wall enclosures. An early archaeological survey conducted in 1973 by the Yantai Municipal Museum estimated that the original outer wall has a total length of 10 km (Li Buqing and Lin Xianting 1991, 910). Its immense size and the imposing magnitude of the remaining wall sections are comparable to the capital of the state of Lu in Qufu (Shandong sheng 1982: 1-35). During the late Bronze Age the Guicheng city complex must have been the greatest urban center in all of eastern Shandong. Since as early as the late nineteenth century, the high profile of Guicheng and its adjacent areas in the archaeological record was also indicated by a long series of discoveries of inscribed bronze vessels. Some of these inscriptions bear clear reference to the activities of civil or military officials in the Zhou central court in Shaanxi, including two, the Qi *zun* and Qi *you,* which record a military campaign in the south led personally by a Zhou king (Qi Wentao 1972: 5-8). These discoveries make the Guicheng region one of the most important concentrations of inscribed bronzes outside the Zhou centers.

More inscriptions from the Zhou central region unambiguously record military campaigns against the local population in the Shandong region customarily called “Dongyi” (Eastern Barbarians). When taken together, these inscriptions suggest a general process of Zhou military expansion from the Yellow River region to eastern Shandong, roughly from the late 11th century BCE onward (Li 2006: 304-314), that can be convincingly linked to information we also learn from inscriptions locally discovered in and around Guicheng. This suggests that Guicheng was possibly on the frontline of Zhou expansion and might have even served as a frontier base, susceptible to political changes and culturally permeable by different groups of people with different ideas and customs. Seemingly attesting to this character as a frontier environment, the material remains present in the Guicheng city complex, and across the Longkou region more broadly, show a typical mixing primarily of two distinctive ceramic production traditions, one evidently associated with the ceramic tradition in the west, and the other presumably originating in the indigenous Neolithic cultures of the eastern Shandong peninsula.

A prominent site like Guicheng, with its rich material content and complex socio-cultural context, naturally offers many questions for research, both anthropological-archaeological concerned with dynamics and common patterns of social development in the human past, and historical, focusing more on the political roots of specific regions and the role of human agents in regional social processes. We see these questions as not mutually exclusive; instead, their answers can be mutually supportive. The specific historical and cultural setting of the late Bronze Age in eastern Shandong allows us to investigate these questions, not only through fieldwork, but also with the help of written evidence.

Section 2: Establishment of the Project

The Guicheng international collaborative project has its origins in two trips we took together to the region in summer 2005 and summer 2006, during which we were guided by the directors of the Longkou Municipal Museum (Jiang Huimin in 2005 and Ma Zhimin in 2006), to look over most visible ancient traces of this city complex (Fig. Ⅰ.0.2). Incidentally, the first visit coincided with the installation of a communal water system in Heping Village for which a long ditch was excavated. Walking along this pipeline afforded us a rare chance to observe firsthand the subsurface deposits of the site and examine sherds surfaced by the dig. From Guicheng, we were further led on tours to a number of contemporary sites in the main valley of the Huangshui River, including Zhuangtou and Lujiagou, both known to have been places where important discoveries of bronze vessels were made in the past. These visits gave us two initial chances to evaluate the condition of the site and opened new perspectives for future archaeological fieldwork. It was clear even at this early stage that, given its immense size, rich material content, and the history of past discoveries, any serious effort to understand this city complex must be planned and executed systematically and it must begin with a full-scale survey. Reporting back to our two institutions, Columbia University in the United States and the Institute of Archaeology (CASS) in China, and after soliciting input and suggestions from colleagues, we began to conceive plans for a collaborative research initiative. Additionally, in the summer of 2006 we also confirmed the interest of the Shandong Provincial Institute of Archaeology in taking part in this joint effort.

Much of the negotiation about the terms of collaboration took place in late 2006 through early 2007, leading to the conclusion of the official contract between the three institutions as two parties. The two parties pledged to co-sponsor the "Sino-American Joint Guicheng Archaeological Team" as the main research body to conduct systematic surveys centering on the Guicheng city site for an initial period of three years. Columbia University's Department of East Asian Languages and Cultures (Chair, Robert P. Hymes) in particular, further agreed to provide a starting fund to cover the first field season in the summer of 2007, with the understanding that outside sources of continued funding would be sought soon. In April 2007 the visit to New York City of the director of the Institute of Archaeology (CASS), Wang Wei, served as a suitable occasion for the two institutions to reconfirm their commitments to the project and to sign the contract, which was later also ratified by the director of the Shandong Institute of Archaeology. The two institutes comprising the Chinese party to the contract soon afterwards coordinated to move the Guicheng project application through the administrative system of the government of the People's Republic of China.

The Sino-American Joint Guicheng Archaeologial Team was composed of researchers from all three institutions. Li Feng of Columbia University served as the American director of the team, and Wang Wei of the Institute of Archaeology (CASS) and Tong Peihua of the Shangdong Institution of Archaeology served as its Chinese director and associate Chinese director. Fieldwork was directed by Li Feng and Liang Zhonghe of the Institute of Archaeology (CASS). The American side of the team included also Terence N. D'Altroy of Columbia University who played an advisory role in the project and, in particular, helped design methods for the systematic surface survey (see below). Graduate research assistants and undergraduate students from Columbia and other US universities participated in the project in varying numbers in different years. The Chinese side included Tang Jinqiong (Institute of Archaeology of CASS) and Han Hui (Shandong Provincial Institute of Archaeology) as regular members of the team, together with 10-15 technicians supplied by the two institutes each year. In the summer of 2008, Xu Mingjiang from the Yantai Municipal Museum joined the team and continued to participate in the fieldwork over the next two years. Typically, the archaeological team comprised 25-30 people working in the field each season.

Section 3: Goals of the Research

The international collaborative team arrived in Guicheng on June 13, 2007 to begin the fieldwork that was to continue over the next four years. Underlying the project were a number of long-term research goals that we were committed to pursuing through the fieldwork. Our first goal was to discover the dynamics of the internal social and economic organization and operation of the Guicheng city complex, as a model urban center of prominent size located in the multicultural environment at the edge of the Shang and Zhou civilizations. In this way, we hoped to use Guicheng as a base for understanding social changes by which the indigenous eastern Shandong communities organized themselves into large states under the influence of a politically more advantageous culture. This was one of the most common trajectories of state formation in human history, and we hope that research work in Guicheng can help us delineate this process of "secondary state formation" with solid archaeological evidence.

Second, we hope to uncover the settlement system in the Longkou region during the late Bronze Age and to understand the role played by Guicheng in that system. Ideally, full-coverage survey methods that have already been used in other parts of China (Chifeng 2003; Chifeng 2011; Underhill et al. 1998: 453-474; Underhill et al 2008: 1-29) would be used to identify the regional settlement hierarchy and explain how Guicheng achieved political dominance over the outlying smaller villages as well as how these settlements in turn supported Guicheng economically as the locus of state power. To this end, we also hope that future excavations can shed light on the regional subsistence system in which agriculture, aquaculture, and trade might all have played an important part.

Third, we are genuinely interested in the relationship and communication between cultures. With respect to Zhou expansion to eastern Shandong, the specific location of the Guicheng site in the contact zone between the two cultures provides us with an ideal setting to study how cultures responded to each other. However, instead of assigning the local population a passive role in their relationship with the advanced Zhou culture, we hope to show how the local or peripheral communities took initiatives to adapt to the new environment and eventually succeeded in turning it to their advantage (Dietler 1998: 288-314), and furthermore, to show how a middle ground was formed which provided fertile soil for the rise of a new culture (Gosden 2004: 82-113). The rise of the local state of Lai and the withdrawal of a possible Zhou population from Guicheng is a good indication of this trend towards regional autonomy. We hope that such a cultural approach will add new dimensions to the study of urban organization and the settlement system in eastern Shandong.

Regrettably, despite the existence of a prominent city complex like Guicheng, the Bronze Age in eastern Shandong has been poorly understood in archaeology. In particular, the phase roughly contemporary with the Western Zhou state (1045-771 BCE) in the west has been largely omitted from the picture as previous archaeological researches in the region focused largely on the Neolithic (7000-2000 BCE) and Eastern Zhou-Han periods (770 BCE-220 CE). Therefore, at a fundamental level, we hope that intensive archaeological fieldwork in Guicheng and the surrounding areas will clarify the sequence of the regional material culture and establish chronological standards for future research elsewhere.

Some of the research goals laid out above can be accomplished in the short term, while others will require continuous efforts to accomplish in the future. But we hope that we can at least start to address them and open paths for future generations. On the whole, we hope that the Guicheng project will help us understand changes in the social conditions of the late Bronze Age and the joint roles played by the centrally located state and peripheral societies in the common process of the formation of Chinese civilization.

Section 4: Defining the Research Space and the Division of the Fieldwork

Recognizing the archaeological research in Guicheng to be a long-term effort, we designed our fieldwork in accordance with two guiding principles: 1) as a project with goals that may take a few generations of researchers to achieve, the fieldwork must be planned and executed systematically using methodologies appropriate to the study of prominent large-scale sites. The fieldwork must be done in a way that will lay the foundations for future studies and provide information to facilitate the planning of preservation of the site for the future. Given Guicheng's new status as a "National Heritage Site," the last point is especially important; 2) at the present stage, because of the nature of the project as a survey project (as distinguished from a systematically planned excavation), we must ensure that the field methods will enable us to obtain the greatest volume of information so as to achieve the fullest possible understanding of the site before systematic excavation is carried out in the future.

Guided by these two points, we used the World Geodetic System of 1984 [WGS84] which is used by Google Earth to define the entire research space with its four coordinates prominently fixed at: N37°34′15″-N37°36′39″; E120°32′49″-E120°35′13″. This designated a space on the ground of 3,520 m east to west and 4,480 m north to south, with the walled Guicheng site sitting in the center (Map Ⅰ.0.3). This large space was then divided up into sixteen blocks of 900×1120 m^2 each. At present, this system is universally used to record structures and remains and will likely continue to be used in the future. Within the research space, the fieldwork was largely divided into five parts, each having its specific objectives (Sino-American Joint Guicheng 2011: 30-39): 1) systematic coring of the inner city wall, to provide reliable information about its actual dimensions, orientation, and condition of preservation (see Chapter Two); 2) systematic coring of the interior structures, such as residential architecture, roads, open areas, and water systems, which should tell us about the organizational principles of the inner city (see Chapter Three); 3) systematic survey and recording of the outer wall of Guicheng (see Chapter Four); 4) test-excavation in the southern part of the inner city to yield direct evidence for the city's occupational history and the dating of the construction of the city wall (Chapter Five); 5) intensive systematic surface survey of the entire Guicheng city complex, to allow us to identify concentrations of sites across the larger landscape within the greater Guicheng region (see Chapter Six); 6) survey of the settlement system in the outlying region of Guicheng concentrated along the Huangshui River valley (see Chapter Seven).

In parallel with the fieldwork, on the Columbia University campus two major datasets have been constructed for the Guicheng project which served as platforms to display and analyze information obtained through the survey and the coring. These works have been supervised by Jeremiah Trinidad-Christensen, a GIS specialist at Columbia's Electronic Data Service. The first is a system into which the coring data from the inner city were entered for the purpose of computer simulation of the underground structures of the city. The second is a system designed to analyze the surface survey data, which can generate density maps as well as 3D images of the survey results (see Chapter Eight).

Section 5: The Progress of the Fieldwork

From the summer of 2007 until the end of 2010, we spent a total of six seasons conducting archaeological fieldwork in Guicheng. In this last section, we will review the progress of the fieldwork during the four years and highlight important discoveries made during each phase.

Summer 2007: June 13-July 20. A large part of the season was spent on developing standards for identifying soils, including rammed earth (*hangtu*, usually manmade architectural foundations), defining the research areas, and settling on a system for recording coring points that could be consistently applied throughout Guicheng. The main objective for the season was to determine the actual location and extent of the inner city wall, which took thirty days to complete. The coring began at the southwest corner of inner city around the section of wall that stands on high ground to the south of the Jiangjia Village (Fig. Ⅰ.0.3). Subsequently, coring moved to trace out each side of the inner wall enclosure. An important discovery was a large, previously unknown above ground platform east of Heping Village. The coring confirmed that this is a section of the east wall, which the 1973 survey presumed to no longer exist (Li Buqing and Lin Xianting 1991, 912). This discovery defined the limits of the inner city of Guicheng. The coring suggested that the inner city of Guicheng forms a reversed "L" shape, covering much of the Jiangjia and Heping Villages and the spaces between them. For the most part, the wall was protected by an external moat of varying width. Another important discovery was a large section of rammed earth 120 m long located to the north of Heping Village, but the function of this structure is unknown. The work team during the first season comprised Li Feng, Liang Zhonghe, and Han Hui as researchers, while the student group included Han-Peng Ho, Minna Wu, and Paul Nicholas Vogt (Fig. Ⅰ.0.4). Dr. Jaehoon Shim of Dankook University in Korea also participated in part of the fieldwork.

Winter 2007: November 3-30. In the second season, the coring team moved to the interior of the inner city in search of significant building remains and other subsurface structures. Starting at the southeast corner of the city, by the end of the season when the weather became too cold for outdoor work the team had covered about three-quarters of the southern half of the open area to the south of Heping, taken up almost entirely by apple trees. By the end of the season, we had discovered the broad central avenue of the city, in addition to two large palace foundations located to the east. The survey of the outer city wall of Guicheng began on November 9, and by the end of the season the remains of sixteen new sections demarcating the northern limit of the city had been identified and mapped out using a total-station (Fig Ⅰ.0.5). The winter fieldwork was led by four researchers, including Li Feng, Liang Zhonghe, Tang Jinqiong, and Han Hui, and eleven technicians supplied by the two Chinese institutes also participated in the work.

Summer 2008: June 7-July 23. An enlarged team of twenty-eight people returned to Guicheng where a more complex operation was carried out. The coring team covered the remaining space to the south of Heping and a wide strip of field north of Jiangjia, discovering a total of ten building foundations that were measured and recorded on the map. The search for the outer city wall continued by bringing to light twenty-eight new sections along the wall's circumference. The survey confirmed that, instead of being a complete circle as previously thought, the Guicheng outer wall actually forms a large incomplete oval whose south side is open to the deep valley of Mt. Lai. On June 13, 2008, we began to carry out a systematic surface survey in the space between the inner and outer city walls of Guicheng (Fig Ⅰ.0.6), conducted mainly by our student group of seven people, Han-Peng Ho, Minna Wu, Paul Nicholas Vogt, Brian Lander, Glenda Chao, Elizabeth Berger, and Athena Hsieh. Beginning at the edge of the inner city in Area 7, the survey team subsequently moved through Area 3, Area 2, Area 4, Area 8, and a strip of Area 12, making systematic collections of sherds. Researchers who led the fieldwork in the previous season all returned to Guicheng. In addition, Xu Mingjiang from the Yantai Municipal Museum also participated in the surface survey (Fig Ⅰ.0.7).

Summer 2009: June 5-July 21. A new student group arrived in Guicheng to continue the systematic surface survey, including Brian Lander, LeLand Crawford, Shi Hui, Jackson Cooper, and Yitzhack Jaffe. The group picked up the survey in Area 12 and then covered Areas 5-6, Areas 9-11, and Area 16, in that order. At the same time, the coring team covered the entire space between Jiangjia and Heping and discovered five more building foundations and the drainage system of the city. In the summer of 2009, we also conducted an important test excavation in the southern part the inner city close to the city's axis. The excavation enabled us to analyze the subsurface deposits of the site and provided direct stratigraphical evidence that dates the construction of the inner city wall of Guicheng to the Western Zhou period (Fig Ⅰ.0.8). During intervals of the fieldwork in Guicheng, the archaeological team also conducted preliminary surveys of two other important Bronze Age sites in eastern Shandong, Cunliji in Penglai and Dongqucheng in Zhaoyuan. Researchers who led the fieldwork in the summer of 2009 included Li Feng, Liang Zhonghe, Tang Jinqiong, Han Hui, and Xu Mingjiang (Fig Ⅰ.0.9).

Summer 2010: July 16-August 30. We transferred the base of the archaeological team from Guicheng to Longkou and devoted the entire period to analyzing materials acquired during the past three years. Statistical analysis was conducted for each subsurface unit test excavated in 2009. The work involved all researchers who took part in the previous year's fieldwork.

Winter 2010: October 10-November 6. Liang Zhonghe was back in Longkou and led a field survey of fifteen important sites in the Huangshui River valley and along the Bohai Sea coast.

By 2010, it had become clear that in order to plan future research, it was imperative that we pause the fieldwork for of a period of full review, to digest the information that had been accumulated. This volume presents the details of the archaeological fieldwork in Guicheng during 2007-2010 and the results of our preliminary analysis of the data. In addition, the report also includes portions that review significant early works and discoveries made in Guicheng and its surroundings before 2007. Most of the chapters of the book were written in 2011-2012 and were brought in for presentation and discussion at a working conference held in the workstation of the Institute of Archaeology in Qufu on July 27-28, 2013, during which their contents were finalized (Fig Ⅰ.0.10). We hope that by bringing these chapters together this volume will provide a basis to enable us to answer at least some of the questions posed earlier in this Introduction. This book is a synthesis of what is already known about Guicheng which can serve as the baseline for what we may continue to inquire about in the future.

References

Braswell, Geoffrey, Christian M. Prager, et al., 2004. "The Rise of Secondary States in the Southeastern Periphery of Maya World," *Ancient Mesoamerica*, 15: 219-233.

Chen, Houyao 陈厚燿 (1647-1722), 1981. *Chunqiu changli* 春秋长历 (The long calendar of the Spring and Autumn period), in Siku quanshu zhenben 四库全书珍本. Taipei: Shangwu yinshuguan.

Chifeng International Collaborative Archaeological Research Project 赤峰中美联合考古研究项目, 2003. *Regional Archeology in Eastern Inner Mongolia: a Methodological Exploration* 内蒙古东部（赤峰）区域考古调查阶段性报告. Beijing: Science Press.

Chifeng International Collaborative Archaeological Research Project, 2011. *Settlement Patterns in the Chifeng Region.*

Pittsburgh: Center for Comparative Archaeology, University of Pittsburgh.

Dietler, Michael, 1998. "Consumption, Agency, and Culture Entanglement: Theoretical Implications of a Mediterranean Colonial Encounter," in *Studies in Cultural Contact: Interaction, Cultural Change and Archaeology*, edited by James Cusick. Pp. 288-314. Carbondale: Southern Illinois University Press, Center for Archaeological Investigation.

Gosden, Chris, 2004. *Archaeology and Colonialism: Cultural Contact from 5000 BCE to the Present*. Cambridge: Cambridge University Press.

Li, Buqing 李步青 and Lin Xianting 林仙庭, 1991. "Shandong Huangxian Guicheng yizhi de diaocha yu fajue" 山东黄县归城遗址的调查与发掘 (Survey and excavation of the site at Guicheng, Huangxian County, Shandong). *Kaogu* 考古 (Archaeology), 10: 910-918.

Li, Feng 2006. *Landscape and Power in Early China: The Crisis and Fall of the Western Zhou, 1045-771 BCE*. Cambridge, UK: Cambridge University Press.

Price, Barbara, 1978. "Secondary State Formation: An Explanatory Model," in *Origin of the State: The Anthropology of Political Evolution*, edited by R. Cohen. Pp.161-224. Philadelphia: Institute for the Study of Human Issues.

Qi, Wentao 齐文涛, 1972. "Gaishu jinnian lai Shandong chutu de Shang Zhou qingtongqi" 概述近年来山东出土的商周青铜器 (General discussion of Shang and Zhou period bronzes discovered in Shandong in recent years). Wenwu 文物 (Cultural Relics), 5: 3-16.

Shandong sheng wenwu kaogu yanjiusuo 山东省文物考古研究所 et al., 1982. *Qufu Lu guo gucheng* 曲阜鲁国故城 (Qufu, the ancient capital of the state of Lu). Ji'nan: Qilu shushe.

Shelach, Gideon, and Yuri Pines, 2006. "Secondary State Formation and the Development of Local Identity: Change and Continuity in the State of Qin (770-221 B.C.)," in *Archaeology of Asia*, edited by M. T. Stark. Pp. 202-230. Malden, MA: Blackwell.

Sino-American Joint Guicheng Archaeological Team 中美联合归城考古队, 2011. "Shandong Longkou shi Guicheng liang Zhou chengzhi diaocha jianbao" 山东龙口市归城两周城址调查简报 (A brief report on the survey of the Guicheng city site of the Western-Eastern Zhou periods in Longkou, Shandong Province). *Kaogu* 考古, 3: 30-39.

Underhill, Anne P., G. M. Feinman, Linda Nicholas, G. Bennett, Fengshu Cai, Haiguang Yu, Fengshi Luan, Hui Fang, 1998. "Systematic, Regional Survey in SE Shandong Province, China," *Journal of Field Archaeology*, 25.4: 453-474.

Underhill, Anne P., G. M. Feinman, L.M. Nicholas, G. Bennett, Hui Fang, Fengshi Luan, Haiguang Yu & Fengshu Cai, 2002. "Regional survey and the development of complex societies in southeastern Shandong, China," *Antiquity*, 76 (293): 745-755.

Underhill, Anne P., G. M. Feinman, L.M. Nicholas, Hui Fang, Fengshi Luan, Haiguang Yu & Fengshu Cai, 2008. "Changes in regional settlement patterns and the development of complex societies in southeastern Shandong, China," *Journal of Anthropological Archaeology*, 27: 1-29.

Zuozhuan 左传, 1979. in *Shisanjing zhushu* 十三经注疏. Pp. 1697-2188. Beijing: Zhonghua shuju.

上　编

Part Ⅰ

第一章　自然地理环境和地域文化背景

梁中合

关注胶东半岛的自然地理环境和地域文化特征对于我们深入了解龙口归城城址的内涵与特征具有非常重要的意义，同时它也是探讨许多问题的基本起点。胶东半岛自然环境的特殊性和多样性造成了其文化的特殊性和多样性，而且这些特性往往在越早期的遗址或文化中表现越明显。根据我们观察，这一地理环境明显影响文化生态的现象可以一直延续到汉代（公元前206～公元220年）以前。当然上述现象也不是绝对的，而可被看作是一个发展和渐进的过程。

第一节　地理位置与地形特征

从宏观的地理单元来观察，龙口归城城址位于山东胶东半岛北部，而胶东半岛为我国最大的半岛，其主体向东伸入海洋，北临渤海，东和南临黄海。最东端的成山角是北黄海与南黄海分界线的端点。胶莱河、大沽河及二者间的废弃运河一线为其西界。胶东半岛所处的经纬度位置，从最西的胶莱河口到最东的成山角，经度由119°34′到122°39′；东西的跨度达到280千米。从最南的青岛市到最北的蓬莱市，纬度为36°03′到37°50′；南北跨度为230千米。半岛面积约39000平方千米，占山东全省面积的19%。

胶东半岛的行政范围包括烟台市及所属的招远、蓬莱、福山、栖霞、牟平、海阳、龙口、莱阳、莱州、长岛诸县市；威海市及所属的乳山、荣成、文登等市；青岛市及所属莱西、平度、即墨、诸城、胶州、胶南诸市（地图Ⅰ.1.1）。这些“县级市”进而下辖其周围的乡村地域。

在地质学上，胶东半岛地处华夏系第二隆起带，属中朝准地台胶辽台隆。它是完整的构造上升单元（杨怀仁 1987：42），与其两侧的坳陷区形成鲜明的对比。它的自然地理环境具有非常明显的地域特征，主要由花岗岩组成，太古代片麻岩和片岩等深变质结晶岩也有广泛分布。白垩纪末曾有广泛的火山岩喷发和酸性岩浆侵入活动。中新世以后，渤海总体大幅度下陷，成为华北—下辽河沉降带坳陷最深的大型新生代断裂－坳陷盆地。上新世末，特别是第四纪以来渤海海峡断裂下陷，山东半岛形成。全区被北北东—北东和北北西—北西两组断裂分割，形成大小不一的断块，经长期剥蚀分割，形成较破碎的低缓丘陵，丘陵海拔大多在200米左右。

少数山岭突出丘陵之上，包括数列东北—西南走向的山岭，海拔一般在500～1000米。半岛南部的崂山主峰崂顶海拔1133米，为半岛最高峰。中北部有牙山、昆嵛山、伟德山、罗山、大泽山、莱山等，多为近东北—西南走向。丘陵、低山占总面积的70%。山地丘陵间有桃村地堑盆地、莱阳断陷盆地和胶莱凹陷平原等。沿海有宽窄不等的带状平原，面积不足30%。以北部的蓬莱、黄县（今龙口）、掖县（今莱州）平原面积最大。

胶东半岛南岸多为砂坝—泻湖型和港湾型海岸，有的海湾两侧有小半岛或海岬相对峙，湾顶分叉向内地深入；底部呈浅湾溺谷状，底质为泥沙混杂。胶东半岛北岸的地质基础主要是岩质为大理岩和花岗岩的基岩，那里又处于迎风面，因此多形成宽阔的砂质海岸。而有的部位为开口较大的海湾，湾口有海岬或小半岛保护，经常受到波浪的冲击，继续保持着基岩海岸的特征。可见南北两岸的地质、地貌条件差别较大。

总之，胶东半岛海岸蜿蜒曲折，港湾岬角交错，岛屿罗列，是华北沿海良港集中地区。沿海岛屿除渤海海峡的庙岛群岛外，均分布于近陆地带，较大者有象岛、莫邪岛、杜家岛、田横岛、刘公岛、鸡鸣岛、崆峒岛、褚岛、苏山岛和南黄岛等。

第二节　自然环境特征

人类生存环境的自然因素很多，除地形、地貌外，还包括气候、水系、植被、土壤等。其中地形地貌和气候是环境中制约人类生存的条件的主要因素。

一、气　　候

胶东半岛处于华北东端，属暖温带大陆性季风气候。由于它濒临海洋，加上以低山丘陵为主的地势特点，因此气候特征虽在宏观上与华北地区一致，但又表现出降水量较丰沛、冬暖夏凉的海洋性气候色彩（侯学煜 1988：144）。

胶东半岛年平均降水量在600～900毫米。降水主要来自东南季风，年均降水总量的分布总体上呈东南向西北递减的趋势。由于胶东半岛南部海岸呈东北—西南向走向，半岛山地也是以东北—西南走向为主，与东南季风锋面近似垂直，有利于降水的形成。胶东半岛年均降水量一般在750毫米左右。北部沿岸处于东南季风的背风向，降水相对较少，一般在600毫米左右。如烟台为690毫米，蓬莱为626毫米。南部的崂山和昆嵛山则为两个多雨中心，年均降水量在800毫米以上。胶东半岛降水量的季节性变化显著，主要集中于夏季，且强度大，常出现暴雨，其降水量占全年降水总量的62.6%。春季（3～5月）、秋季（9～11月）也有一定的降水，分别占13.0%和19.4%；冬季降水量仅占5.0%左右。降水年均相对变率约20%。年均相对湿度在70%以上。

胶东半岛冬季受蒙古冷高压控制，盛行寒冷的偏北风。夏季主要受西太平洋副热带高压的影响，盛行暖湿的东南季风。季风的风向季节交替变化，不仅对这一区域的气温和降水产生深远影响，而且对海面风浪的形成也起到主要作用。受海陆轮廓和地形的影响，不同区域在不同季节盛行的风向和风速有较大差别。1月盛行风向除烟台为南西西（14%）、掖县（今莱州）为南南西（12%）以外，各地均为北、西北、北北西等风向。7月半岛盛行风向全部为偏南风，南风频率为15%～25%，偏南风频率达45%～60%。其年均风速一般在每秒4～6米，较内陆地区的3m/s略大。

胶东半岛北接东北温带，西南通过苏北与亚热带为邻，属暖温带湿润季风气候。1月均温-3～-1℃，8月（最热月）均温约25℃，极端最高温约38℃。10℃以上活动积温为3800～4100℃。半岛东侧南部沿海4～7月多海雾，年均雾日30～50天。

二、水　　系

胶东半岛的中部为低山和丘陵，河流多由此发源并向四周作散射状分布，形成众多的河流。其中北侧流入渤海、黄海主要河流有胶莱河、界河、黄水河、大沽夹河、沁河、辛安河等。南侧流入黄海的主要河流有大沽河、五龙河、母猪河、乳山河等。

由于半岛水系发源于中部山地，独流入海，河床比降较大。除胶莱河为平原型河流外，其他均属季节性的山溪性河流，其长度均在200千米以下（地图Ⅰ.1.2）。半岛的河川径流主要受降水补给，因此季节性变化十分明显，径流洪枯悬殊。其中汛期的流量占全年径流量的70%～80%。据大姑夹河、大沽河和五龙河的径流量年内分配资料统计，全年径流量的80%以上集中在汛期（6～9月），其中7～8月就集中了60%以上，枯水期的8个月内径流量只占年径流量的15%左右（韩洪暖 1991：43～46）。另外，河流的水位、流量过程线随降水变化而迅速涨落，但一般不至于形成灾害。如遇暴雨则山洪暴发，加之河口受海潮顶托，往往形成洪水危害；枯水季节河床暴露，甚至发生河水断流和枯涸现象。

河流入海泥沙量是海岸堆积地貌的主要物质基础。胶东半岛人类活动历史悠久，植被破坏严重，造成严重的水土流失，河流产沙量日益增加。胶东半岛年均输沙量在40万吨以上的河流有五龙河（84.0万吨）、大沽河（56.4万吨）、大姑夹河（56.4万吨）、老母猪河（42.21万吨）等，根据主要河流输沙量统计，胶东半岛年均输沙总量达255.12万吨。

三、植　　被

在中国植被分区中，胶东半岛地带性植被属暖温带落叶阔叶林区（中国植被编委会1980：788）。其中麻栎林是半岛最有代表性的地带性植被类型之一，是分布最广、面积最大的落叶栎林，多见于阳坡。其垂直分布可达1000米左右，林下有时出现常绿、半常绿植物，如山胡椒、扶芳藤、络石等。此外，栎林也较为常见，人工林仅分布在崂山和昆嵛山等山地的阴坡上部。

胶东半岛主要树种为栎类，包括麻栎、槲、枹等树，以麻栎最多，但常因放养柞蚕而伐去主干呈灌木状，构成山地丘陵特殊的“柞岚”景观。针叶树以日本赤松为代表。半岛的植物体系中还包括了亚热带的植物，如苦木、山胡椒、三椏乌药等。另外，还有东北区系成分，如蒙古栎、辽东栎、赤杨等。

除了落叶阔叶林外，半岛上还有针叶林、针叶落叶阔叶混交林、灌木丛及灌草丛、草甸沼泽与盐生沙生植被、农业植被等（周光裕 1963：62 ~ 74）。灌木丛的主要建群种有盐肤木、白檀、化香、刚竹等，灌草丛则以荆条、酸枣、黄背草群落为主。

现代植被不仅受气候、地形、土壤等自然地理条件及历史自然地理条件的制约，更深受人类经济活动的影响。人类长期活动的深刻影响，使胶东半岛的原始天然植被产生了巨大变化。山东半岛开发历史悠久，目前原生植物基本破坏殆尽。从植被的现状来看，自然植被以次生、混生的类型为主；人工植被则类型多样，分布广泛。

四、土　　壤

胶东半岛土壤主要是中生代花岗岩酸性岩类及喷发熔岩基性类，其母质有洪积冲积物、河流冲积物、河海相沉积物和现代残积物。土壤由东向西主要分布着棕壤土、潮土、砂浆黑土和盐土。棕壤土广泛分布，土体发育完整，呈微酸性反映，主要有林地壤土、棕壤性土、棕壤及潮棕壤等几种。胶东半岛的棕壤土为典型棕色森林土（俗称山东棕壤），一般分布在缓坡地和排水良好的平地，现多已辟为农田和果园，发育成熟化的耕作土。低山丘陵中上部残积、坡积物上的粗骨棕壤土层浅薄，质地较粗。潮棕壤主要分布在南北部部平原地区，属高产土壤类型。潮土主要分布在河流沿岸及近海平原，土层深厚，保水保肥。砂浆黑土类发育在浅海沼泽沉积物上，一般地势平坦，易发季节性碱渍化，不利于作物生长。盐土主要分布在河流入海处低洼平地，土壤含盐分高，地下水矿化度高，含盐约0.085% ~ 2.98%，仅生长碱蓬、芦苇等耐碱植物。

黄土在山东地区也有分布，它是最新的地质时期（距今约200万年的第四纪时期）形成的土状堆积物，所以其性质比较疏松、特殊。山东地区黄土开始堆积时期普遍较晚，目前已见的地质剖面中，以青州傅家庄剖面堆积厚度最大（30米以上）。山东地区黄土成因类型多样，物质来源广泛，其岩性特征与其他地区的黄土有明显的差别。这里的黄土粒度较粗，且普遍含有海相微体化石，其物质来源主要为末次冰期时期出露的渤海陆架物质；西北气流携带而来的内陆远源物质则占次要地位（徐树建 2010：1197 ~ 1201）。

五、现代农业和主要农作物

胶东半岛的生物资源种类多、数量大。地带性土壤的典型棕色森林土（俗称山东棕壤），一般分布在缓坡地和排水良好的平地，多已辟为农田和果园，发育成熟化的耕作土。低山丘陵中上部残积、坡积物上的粗骨棕壤土层浅薄，质地较粗，多种植花生、甘薯等作物。胶东半岛的果树栽培以苹果、梨、葡萄为主，著名者有烟台苹果、莱阳茌梨、平度大泽山葡萄。农作物可一年两熟，主产小麦、玉米、地瓜、大豆、谷子、高粱、棉花、花生、烤烟、麻类等，其中冬小麦、大豆、玉米等产量都很大，在全国占有重要地位。海洋资源更是得天独厚，近海海域占渤海和黄海总面积的37%，近海栖息和洄游的鱼虾类达260多种，主要经济鱼类有40多种，浅海贝类百种以上。其中，对虾、扇贝、鲍鱼、刺参、海胆等海珍品的产量均居全国首位。此外，沿海已建成多处大中型盐场，是全国四大海盐产地之一。

第三节　万年以来环境与海岸线演变

人类的生存与社会的发展，都是在特定环境背景下开展，自始至终离不开环境。在胶东半岛，海岸是海陆交互作用地带，是环境演变的敏感地区之一。气候演化、海岸变迁、海平面的升降对海岸带古代人类生存活动的空间范围、获取食物资源的类型、利用自然资源的方式等影响很大。因此，环境对古代人类社会的形成与发展起着非常重要的作用，它直接影响并制约着人类社会生产发展的进程。

一、环境的演变

众所周知，全新世气候总特点是温暖潮湿的。但在最近一万年以来气候发展是相当复杂的，经过若干冷暖和干湿气候轮回，冷暖差一般在5～6℃，最大变幅可达8～10℃。降水量则随着温度变化而相应地发生多次变化。在距今8500年前，胶东半岛气候变得温暖湿润。植物以木本含量占优势，阔叶树花粉显著增加，松属含量也较多。栎属花粉含量呈现最大值，其次是栗属。还有少量榆属、桦属、鹅耳枥属、柏科、榛属及个别枫香属、金合欢属、山毛榉属、胡桃属、枫杨属等北亚热带植物成分。草本以藜科、蒿属、香蒲属为主。蕨类属有水龙骨科和少量水蕨属。通过孢粉分析发现胶东半岛南部有一定数量现在只生长在江淮及江淮以南地区的植物，如水蕨，目前山东、华北地区已经绝迹。总之，当时的植被面貌大致相当于现在我国淮河平原地区，平均气温高出现在2.5℃左右。距今6500～5000年时，水热条件比前一阶段更好，植被以阔叶树种占优势，并含有少量亚热带成分，出现少量喜温暖湿的南方树种。这反映当时胶东半岛的气候温暖湿润，与现在的淮河流域北部相似，当时的气温高于现在2℃左右。

但是，自距今5600年前开始以松、冷杉、云杉为主的针叶林面积明显扩大，在全新世的大暖期中出现了短暂的降温事件。而从距今5000年以后，一些旱生、盐生的草本植物增多，反映气候趋向温和略干。在植物上，主要以松为主，阔叶树减少，草本植物自下而上增加。由此推断，这段时间古气候可与现代黄淮平原北部地区相当。年均气温当在14～15℃左右。比现代高2℃左右。年均降水量在800毫米以上，比现代多100～300毫米以上。

竺可桢先生过去曾经指出：在距今5000～3000年（大暖期后半段），黄河中下游的平均气温较今高出2℃，冬季温度则高出现在3～5℃（竺可桢 1972：15～38）。当时的亚热带北部区界，曾从北纬33°附近（现代淮河—南阳—汉中一线），向北推移至北纬34°30′～35°33′（徐州—郑州—西安或兖州—菏泽一带），位移2个纬度左右。位于此线以北的华北沿海区域，仍处于暖温带。距今4000多年前的龙山文化晚期阶段，总的气候趋势是向干凉方向发展，雨量减少，湖沼水域收缩。

二、海岸线的演变

在25000年前最后一个冰期的最冷时期，海平面比之现代海平面大约低120米。自15000年前冰期高潮开始退却，全球气温普遍升高，造成冰川溶化，海水涌上陆地，海平面最高时比现在要高4米以上（赵希涛等 1979：269～281）。因海平面升高而出现的沼泽地，可能是当时东部沿海地区常见的自然景观。伴随着全新世早期海平面升高，则是陆地水位上升和排水条件的恶化。大约距今一万年以来的六七千年间，胶东半岛地区海平面大体经历了两次升降过程，海岸线也经历了前移到后退的变化过程。

据海洋部门的资料，胶东半岛地区全新世初期，随着海面急剧上升，海岸线迅速向陆地推进。在胶东半岛北岸，海岸线到达莱州湾东岸的西由附近，距现在海岸线约6千米。这次海侵后，在距今8000年左右接着发生海退，在莱州湾东岸的西由附近，海岸线至少退至低于现代水深11米以外。距今7300～7000年海岸线推进到现代海岸线附近。到距今6000～5000年左右海岸线继续向陆地推进到最大范围，这一时期的海岸线比较清晰和明确，在莱州湾沿岸深入陆地30余千米。而在基岩港湾海岸大致与5米等高线相一致。海侵到达最大范围后，大约于距今4500年前海岸线开始后推。距今4000～3000年前海平面降到现代海平面以下，距今3000年以来，海平面在现代海平面上下小幅度浮动（何德亮 2004：24～38；中国社会科学院考古研究所 1999：183～185；韩有松，孟广兰 1984：1255～1258）。

第四节　新石器时代至秦汉时期胶东半岛古代文化的发展

胶东半岛是我国少数几个考古工作开展较早的地区之一。尽管我们目前对这一地区特别是青铜时代的了解还很粗略，但过去的考古工作已经廓清了胶东半岛新石器时代以来的古代文化发展的基本脉络，提供了一个大致年代框架和判定遗迹、遗物时代的基本标准。系统地回顾过去考古工作的成绩，对我们了解归城考古工作的文化和历史背景有着重要意义，对归城的田野考古更是有直接的参考价值。

一、研究历史

早在20世纪30年代，日本人曾在胶东地区发现了新石器时代的贝丘遗址。但是直到50年代初期，胶东半岛的新石器文化遗存还是仅限于一些零星的发现。1956年末1957年初，山东省组织文物大普查，在半岛地区发现了较多的新石器时代的遗址。当时由于资料和工作的限制，对半岛新石器文化的遗存还没有系统的认识，仅能将龙山文化遗存辨识出来。而学者们对早于或晚于龙山文化的遗存均不了解。这个时期，尽管人们对半岛新石器时代文化的发展脉络还不那么清楚，但当时的资料已经让人们看到它与内陆文化的区别（刘敦愿 1958：14～22）。

1961年，为进一步了解半岛地区新石器时代文化的面貌和特点，考古工作者对半岛地区八处遗址进行了重点调查。在调查的基础上，学者们第一次对半岛地区的新石器文化进行了较系统的论述。1963年10月山东省博物馆对蓬莱紫荆山遗址进行了试掘，第一次在胶东地区发现了早于龙山文化的地层堆积。之后，中国社会科学院考古研究又对平度岳石遗址进行发掘，发现了面貌独特、并晚于龙山文化的岳石文化。至此，胶东地区新石器时代至早期青铜时代文化发展的一个基本线索得以被揭示。

1973年，考古工作者在胶东地区进行了较大规模的文物普查和复查，发现一大批新的遗址。基于这次调查的成果，考古工作者将研究的重点放在了早于龙山文化的新石器早中期文化上，并提出了一些新的问题。为解决这些问题，山东省博物馆于1975年试掘了荣成河口遗址、烟台白石村遗址。1979年秋，北京大学考古专业、中国社会科学院考古研究所与烟台地区文管组又联合发掘了福山邱家庄和牟平照格庄遗址。这些考古工作首次较全面地揭示了半岛地区早于龙山时期文化遗存的面貌和特征，认识到它与山东内陆地区的大汶口文化有着较大的区别，并初步解决了其分期与年代问题。

80年代，胶东半岛新石器时代到早期青铜时代文化无论是在田野工作上还是在研究上都有了突破性的进展。在1980年至1985年进行的山东省的第二次文物大普查期间，仅新石器时代遗址就新发现了100余处，这基本上摸清了半岛地区新石器文化遗址分布的范围空间联系。在此新基础上，为真正建立胶东地区古代文化发展的谱系，北京大学、烟台地区文管会、中国社科院考古研究所山东队、山东省文物考古研究所等单位重点发掘或试掘了一批遗址，取得大量重要资料。

由于田野考古发掘材料的增多，对半岛新石器文化性质的认识和研究在这一时期有了长足的进展。较全面系统探讨胶东地区史前文化发展谱系、性质及与周围地区文化关系的研究文章有了显著的积累（严文明 1986：63～95；韩榕 1986：96～119；李步青，王锡平 1988：66～76）。而在1982年之后，随着田野发掘工作的不断深入，对胶东半岛一些重点遗址进行的专题研究或与周围地区文化的比较性专题研究等都有了很大的进展（佟伟华 1982；李权生 1985；王锡平，李步青 1987：89～95；何德亮，竞放 1985：75～82；宋承钧，史明 1984：84～87）。这些文章都从不同的角度对胶东半岛的新石器至青铜时代早期文化的年代、特征、经济、社会性质、文化渊源及其与周围地区的文化联系等方面进行了深入的探讨。

胶东半岛具有独特的地理位置和优越的自然条件，同时又是一个比较独立的地理单元。但更重要的是，胶东地区的古代文化发展自成体系，又和山东内陆地区的文化有很大不同。因此，大多数学者认为应将该地区在文化研究上独立划区，并应把它的文化从北辛—大汶口文化的内陆文化发展系统中分离出来，另外加以单独命名。

二、文化发展阶段

距今1万年以前，至今仍是胶东考古的空白。考古学者尽管已在蓬莱、长岛等地采集到一些打制石器，但没有发现与人类活动有关的遗址和遗迹。

新石器时代

距今7000～4000年，是胶东地区新石器文化繁荣时期。这一时期的胶东半岛考古学文化的发展大致经历了三个阶段：

早期阶段：距今7000～5700年，人类在半岛上已经定居，但活动范围很小。这种文化的来源目前尚不明确。现已发现的遗址都在沿海，人们主要采集海产为食，经济水平处于不很发达的状态。胶东半岛史前文化由贝丘遗址为主的采集、渔猎文化向农耕文化迈进。

代表性遗址有烟台白石村遗址（烟台市博物馆 1981：185～186；烟台市文物管理委员会 1992：577～578）、荣成河口等遗址（烟台市博物馆 2012：32）。其中属于白石村第一期的陶器群可以代表这一时期的主要文化特征。这时期的陶器以夹砂陶为主，泥质陶次之。在夹砂陶中，掺和云母和蚌壳的约占2%。器形多为侈口圜底器，最具特色的器物是钵形鼎、釜形鼎、盆形鼎、盂形鼎、筒形罐等。这些器形在之后白石村二期得到了保留，但在装饰方面则出现了较多的附加堆纹，为主要装饰形式。

在白石林遗址中亦发现大量的柱洞，草拌泥的红烧土块，说明当时存在着木骨泥墙的居住建筑。河口遗址面积约13.5万平方米。河口遗址中则发现大量的石器和骨器，包括有石斧、石锤、石球、砺石以及骨锥、骨针等。白石村一期测定的数据共三个，骨头标本（ZK—0952）距今为5840年±110年；蛤皮标本（ZK—1115）距今为5440年±110年，木炭（ZK—0954）距今5465年±110年。一般认为，这些测定的年代数据可能与实际年代有一定差距，应与用于测定年代的标本质量有关。尽管白石村遗址测定的年代均偏晚，但从文化特征上看，白石村一期文化是胶东半岛地区目前已知较早的新石器文化。与山东内陆的新石器早期的北辛类型相比，则有较大的差异。因此，它应该是胶东半岛地区具有地方特色的早期新石器时代文化。

中期阶段：距今5700～5000年，人类居住的遗址在胶东半岛已经很普遍，呈现空前繁荣的景象。但是遗址主要仍分布在半岛南北岸的近海附近，并主要以贝丘遗址的面貌出现。遗址的规模相对较小，呈现出一种分散式和缺乏中心型聚落的格局。该时期的遗址中堆积了大量海产贝类如蛤、螺、牡蛎等不易腐烂的遗骸，说明其生产方式主要以捕捞和采集为主。但是人们使用的石器、陶器从器类到器形都大量增加。

这一时期的典型遗址主要有福山邱家庄遗址（烟台市博物馆 1963：350）、长岛北庄遗址（北京大学考古实习队等 1987：385～394）、蓬莱紫荆山（山东省博物馆 1973：11～13）、乳山小管村（北京大学考古实习队，烟台市文物管理委员会 2000：200～243）等遗址。遗址主要分布于胶东半岛及部分岛屿。其中邱家庄遗址和北庄遗址面积都在3万平方米左右。在北庄遗址共发现房址16座，形状皆为圆角方形和长方形，细部结构略有差别。一般由居住面、墙基、灶、门道、柱洞等组成，居住面低于当时的地面，系用灰黄土铺垫而成，部分地方经火长期焙烧而形成红烧土硬面。房内设有所谓的“箕形灶”，门道开在南或东南面，呈斜坡状。这批房址布局合理，排列有序，为我们认识该时期聚落生活提供了重要资料。

另外，北庄遗址还发现了多数墓葬，皆为长方形土坑竖穴墓，除单人仰身直肢外，还有侧身、俯身和屈肢葬，存在拔除臼齿的习俗。北庄陶器方面，以夹砂红褐和红陶为主，夹砂灰、黑陶次之；另有少量泥质陶。纹饰主要有附加堆纹、弦纹、篮纹、刻划纹、镂孔等，彩陶较少。典型陶器有鼎、鬶、罐、觚形杯、筒形杯、豆等。邱家庄出土的陶器类型有鼎、筒形罐、钵、小口罐等。其中罐口上多有对称的蘑菇状或鸟首状器耳，这是胶东半岛地区的特点。邱家庄遗址上层年代经碳十四测定为距今5500年左右，下层的年代在距今5700年以前。

晚期阶段：距今5000～4000年。这一时期的遗址的分布范围明显扩大，不仅在半岛的沿海地区，同时还深入到半岛的内陆地区。该阶段的遗址不论在数量和面积有了明显的增加。这一时期的主要遗址有杨家圈（北京大学考古实习队，山东省文物考古研究所 2000a：151～206）、紫荆山（山东省博物馆 1973：11～13）、北城子（韩榕 1989：171）、大口（中国社会科学院考古研究所山东队 1985：1068～1083+1145）、于家店（北京大学考古实习队、山东省文物考古研究所 2000b：207～219）遗址等。在杨家圈和紫荆山遗址均发现早晚两个时期堆积，上层（杨家圈二、三层）为典型的龙山文化，下层（杨家圈四、五层）早于龙山文化，以彩陶为特征，其文化性质待定。总之，晚期阶段主要是龙山文化时期。这一时期房址均为地面建筑，平面近方形，建筑形式为四周挖基槽再密集立柱，然后垛泥起墙，门一般开在正南。这时已经具有比较发达的定居文化。墓葬以土坑竖穴为主，另有少量石棺墓。这一时期生业形态上也表现得更为多样性，食物种类丰富。捕捞和采集已经退居次要地位，种植业的比重明显上升。特别重要的是，杨家圈遗址灰坑中发现粟和水稻的皮壳，这是目前已知的新石器时期水稻种植中纬度最高的遗址。

另外，该遗址中还发现了铜器，证明出现了冶铜技术。陶器以杨家圈遗物为代表，主要为夹砂或泥质黑陶，陶器加工以轮制为主。纹饰主要有弦纹、划纹、附加堆纹、篮纹、竹节纹、雷纹等，弦纹数量最多。器类主要有罐形鼎、盆形鼎、袋足鬶、甗、罐、盆、杯、豆、盘、碗、蛋壳陶杯等。石器以磨制为主，主要有斧、锛、铲、凿、刀、镰、矛、镞等。其中石镞的数量较多。杨家圈遗址年代距今在4600～4000年。此时海岱地区的大部分地区已开始迈向了文明社会的进程。相形之下，胶东半岛却呈落伍之态。就陶器而言，其种类、数量和质量都远逊于西邻的内陆地区。

早期青铜时代

早期青铜时代，胶东半岛是远距中原政治中心的边陲之地，商文化尚未到达这里。山东地区这时期兴起的是一种具有地方特色的土著地方文化，即岳石文化，它大约相当于中原地区文献记载的夏代纪年。而胶东半岛则是它的地方类型——照格庄类型的分布区。

这一时期遗址非常丰富，几乎遍布半岛各地，但普遍缺乏大型的中心性聚落遗址。同时，相对于内陆地区岳石文化的整体衰落，半岛地区岳石文化表现出一种顽强存续的态势。该时期的遗址主要有牟平照格庄遗址（中国社会科学院考古研究所山东队 1986：447～478）、乳山小管庄遗址（北京大学考古实习队，烟台市文物管理委员会 2000：220～243）、烟台芝水遗址（北京大学考古实习队等 2000：96）、长岛大口遗址等（中国社会科学院考古研究所山东队 1985：1068～1083+1145）。这时农业已经非常发达，但是居住遗迹发现不多。在照格庄遗址清理灰坑40余个，有圆形、圆角方形和椭圆形。圆角方形的灰坑均为二连或三连坑，坑与坑之间有小土梁相隔，每个坑的面积大小不等，一般为3～4平方米，可能是房屋遗迹。该遗址发现青铜器。

在遗物方面芝水遗址更具有代表性。芝水一期文化（即岳石文化时期）陶器以夹砂为主，泥质陶较少。器表多素面，纹饰以凹弦纹为主，次为附加堆纹、刻划纹、乳钉纹等。那种坚硬、厚重的泥质灰陶和粗疏的夹砂褐陶是岳石文化的特点。器类有罐、碗、盆、钵、豆等。石器以磨制为主，有铲、斧、凿、刀、镞等。骨器有铲、锥、镞等。从生产工艺及技术方面观察，岳石文化时期制陶工艺已经相当成熟，但始终没有超越内陆地区。制石技术能够制造出多种类生产工具。从照格庄遗址测定的碳十四数据看，胶东半岛岳石文化遗存的年代上限为距今3900年前后，下限当不早于距今3500年。

商末到西周

这一时期，中原地区的商周文化开始影响胶东半岛地区。但胶东半岛兴起了一个有特色的珍珠门文化。这种文化主要分布在胶东半岛西北部沿海一带古代交通线上。代表遗址有长岛县珍珠门遗址（北京大学考古实习队等 1983：114～130）、龙口楼子庄遗址（烟台市文物管理委员会 2003：204～205）、乳山南黄庄遗址（北京大学考古系，烟台市文管会，乳山县文管所 1991：332～336）。珍珠门遗址位于长岛县北长山岛九丈崖公园内，1982～1983年由北京大学进行过正式发掘，时代大约相当于中原地区的商代中晚期到西周中期（公元前1400～前900年）。楼子庄遗址位于龙口市西南的楼子庄村，面积约 3 万平方米，东距离归城遗址约13千米。其年代与珍珠门遗址大体相当（烟台市文物管理委员会 2003：204～205）。南黄庄遗址则位于半岛东端的乳山县，遗迹主要包括21座墓葬，均为土坑竖穴石椁或石椁积石墓。此外，在墓区内还发现几处同期的居住遗址，遗址年代略早于墓葬。

珍珠门文化陶器中有大量的继承自岳石文化传统的素面褐色粗陶，又夹有少量商周文化传统的绳纹鬲，具有混合化的特点。但它主要是以红褐色的素陶器为主，器物主要有鬲、甗、簋、罐、碗等。这一时期总体上流行三足器和圈足器，平底器也占有一定比例，尤其是卷沿和圈足的风格特别突出。珍珠门文化陶器与中原系统的灰陶绳纹鬲、罐及豆等制陶风格迥然不同。无论是陶质、陶色，还是宽卷沿的制陶风格，以及罐、碗、豆等器物造型，珍珠门文化都是岳石文化的继承和发展。一般认为珍珠门文化代表了胶东半岛与商同时期的夷人文化。它主要分布在胶东半岛地区。在山东西北部的淄河、弥河流域则呈现出"插花地"式分布；即这一地区既有商、周文化遗址，又存在珍珠门文化遗址。西周早期晚段至西周中期珍珠门文化仅分布于长岛县和胶东半岛东南部的乳山市、海阳市和文登市。珍珠门文化是东夷文化的衰弱阶段，已退缩到半岛的最东端。

西周时期，强大的周文化如秋风扫落叶般涤荡胶东大地。从西周中期起，周文化逐渐成为胶东地区的主流文化，而归城正是这一强势文化的中心城址，它坐落在周文化向半岛东部推进的前沿。但这里的土著文化也在顽强生存。西周晚期至春秋中期，胶东半岛的国家则以莱国为主，之后又几乎全部纳入齐国版图。由于这一时期生产发展、人口兴旺，春秋晚期到战国时期中小墓群在胶东普遍发现。在齐文化的统治下，夷人文化的特色从此不复存在。

秦汉时期

秦帝国曾在胶东半岛地区设立胶东郡，治所即墨（非现在的即墨城址，而是在现平度市东南，莱西市西南方）。这是有记载的第一个以胶东命名的行政建置。当时胶东郡还包括了胶莱河西岸的部分地区，西至现潍坊城区、安丘、高密等地。

汉初分封诸王，胶东为胶东国，田市曾为胶东王，国都仍为即墨。后来这个胶东国被刘姓的胶东国代替，汉武帝即位前曾为胶东王。汉代实行的是郡国并行的制度，故在胶莱河以东地区还设东莱郡。而胶东东南沿海的现海阳、即墨、崂山等地划归琅琊郡。

东汉时期，全国重新划分郡、县，原归琅琊郡管理的胶东东南沿海地区等划归东莱郡。而胶东国则和北海郡合并为北海国。这时的北海国含胶东地区的即墨（平度市东南，莱西市西南方）和现平度市、即墨西等地。东莱郡治所迁至黄县（今龙口市），北海国治所迁至剧县（今昌乐西）。

总之，进入汉代胶东半岛进入鼎盛时期，这种情况完全被考古资料所证实。现已发现的汉代城址、遗址遥居历代之冠。在胶东，凡汉代设县的地点，大多数能找到城址和居住遗址，如烟台市开发区三十里堡牟平故城址、招远市曲成故城址、莱州市当利故城址等。两汉墓葬数量最多，在胶东约居古代墓葬总数的三分之二。这足以证明汉代人口众多、经济发达，是胶东地区古代社会发展的新高峰。

参考文献

北京大学考古实习队等，1983：山东长岛县史前遗址. 史前研究，创刊号：114-130.

北京大学考古实习队等，2000：烟台芝水遗址发掘报告. 胶东考古. 北京：文物出版社. 96.

北京大学考古实习队，山东省文物考古研究所，2000a：栖霞杨家圈遗址发掘报告. 胶东考古. 北京：文物出版社.

151-206.
北京大学考古实习队，山东省文物考古研究所，2000b：莱阳于家店的小发掘. 胶东考古. 北京：文物出版社. 207-219.
北京大学考古实习队，烟台市文物管理委员会，2000：乳山小管村的发掘. 胶东考古. 北京：文物出版社. 220-243.
北京大学考古实习队，烟台地区文管会，长岛县博物馆，1987：山东长岛北庄遗址发掘简报. 考古，5：385-394 .
北京大学考古系，烟台市文管会，乳山县文管所，1991：山东乳山县南黄庄西周石板墓发掘简报. 考古，4：332-336.
韩洪暖，1991：山东省胶东半岛地区水文特征. 水文，4：43-46.
韩榕，1986：胶东史前文化初探. 山东史前文化论文集. 济南：齐鲁书社. 96-119.
韩榕，1989：栖霞县北城子龙山文化及岳石文化遗址. 中国考古学年鉴. 北京：文物出版社. 171.
韩有松，孟广兰，1984：胶州湾地区全新世海侵及其海平面变化.科学通报，20：1255-1258.
何德亮，2004：山东新石器时代环境考古学研究. 东方博物，2：24-38.
何德亮，竞放，1985：试论杨家圈遗存的文化性质. 考古与文物，1：75-82.
侯学煜，1988：中国自然地理. 北京：科学出版社，1988.
李步青，王锡平，1988：胶东半岛新石器文化初论. 考古，1：66-76.
李权生，1985：胶东新石器文化序列及其与鲁中南的关系. 北京大学硕士学位论文，1985.
刘敦愿，1958：山东五莲县、即墨县两处龙山文化遗址. 考古，4：14-22.
山东省博物馆，1973：山东蓬莱紫荆山遗址试掘简报. 考古，1：11-15 .
宋承钧，史明，1984：胶东史前文化与莱夷的历史贡献. 东岳论丛，1：84-87.
佟伟华，1982：长岛北庄早期遗存提出的几个问题. 北京大学硕士学位论文，1982.
王锡平，李步青，1987：试论胶东半岛与辽东半岛史前文化的交流. 中国考古学会第六次年会. 沈阳. 89-95.
徐树建，2010：山东地区黄土沉积特征与环境意义及其与黄土高原的对比. 生态环境学报，19（5）：1197-1201.
严文明，1986：胶东原始文化初论. 山东史前文化论文集. 济南：齐鲁书社. 63-95.
杨怀仁，1987：第四纪地质. 北京：高等教育出版社.
烟台市博物馆，1963：山东烟台市丘家庄发现新石器时代遗存. 考古，7：350.
烟台市博物馆，1981：山东烟台市白石村遗址调查简报. 考古，2：185-186.
烟台市博物馆，2012：荣成市河口遗址发掘报告. 海岱考古（第五辑）. 北京：科学出版社. 32.
烟台市文物管理委员会，1992：山东烟台白石村新石器时代遗址发掘简报. 考古，7：577-588.
烟台市文物管理委员会，2003：龙口市楼子庄新石器及青铜时代遗址. 中国考古学年鉴. 北京：文物出版社. 204-205.
赵希涛等，1979：中国东部20000年来的海平面变化. 海洋学报，1（2）：269-281.
中国社会科学院考古研究所，1999：胶东半岛贝丘遗址环境考古. 北京：社会科学文献出版社.
中国社会科学院考古研究所山东队，1985：山东长岛县砣矶岛大口遗址. 考古，12：1068-1083，1145.
中国社会科学院考古研究所山东队，1986：山东牟平照格庄遗址. 考古学报，4：447-478.
中国植被编委会，1980：中国植被. 北京：科学出版社.
周光裕，1963：山东的植被分类和发展. 山东大学学报，1：62-74.
竺可桢，1972：中国近五千年来气候变迁的初步研究. 考古学报，1：16-38.

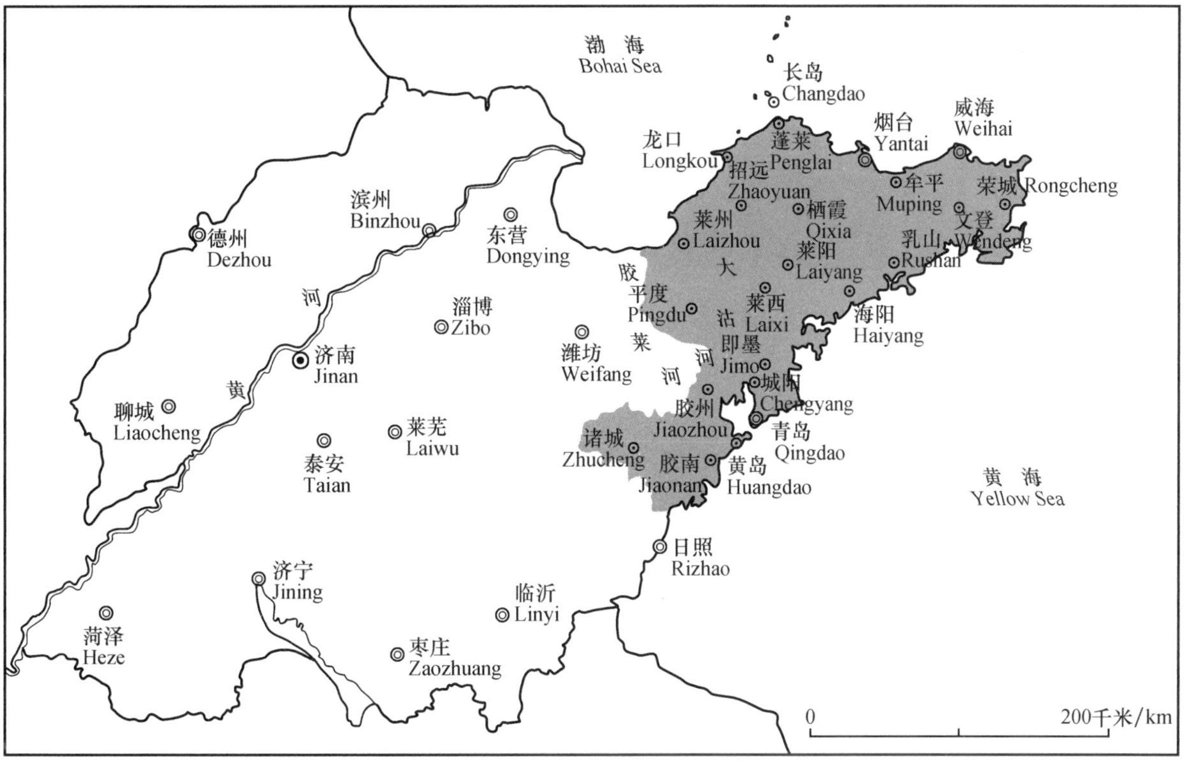

地图Ⅰ.1.1　胶东半岛在山东省的位置

Map Ⅰ.1.1　The location of Jiaodong Peninsula in Shandong Province.

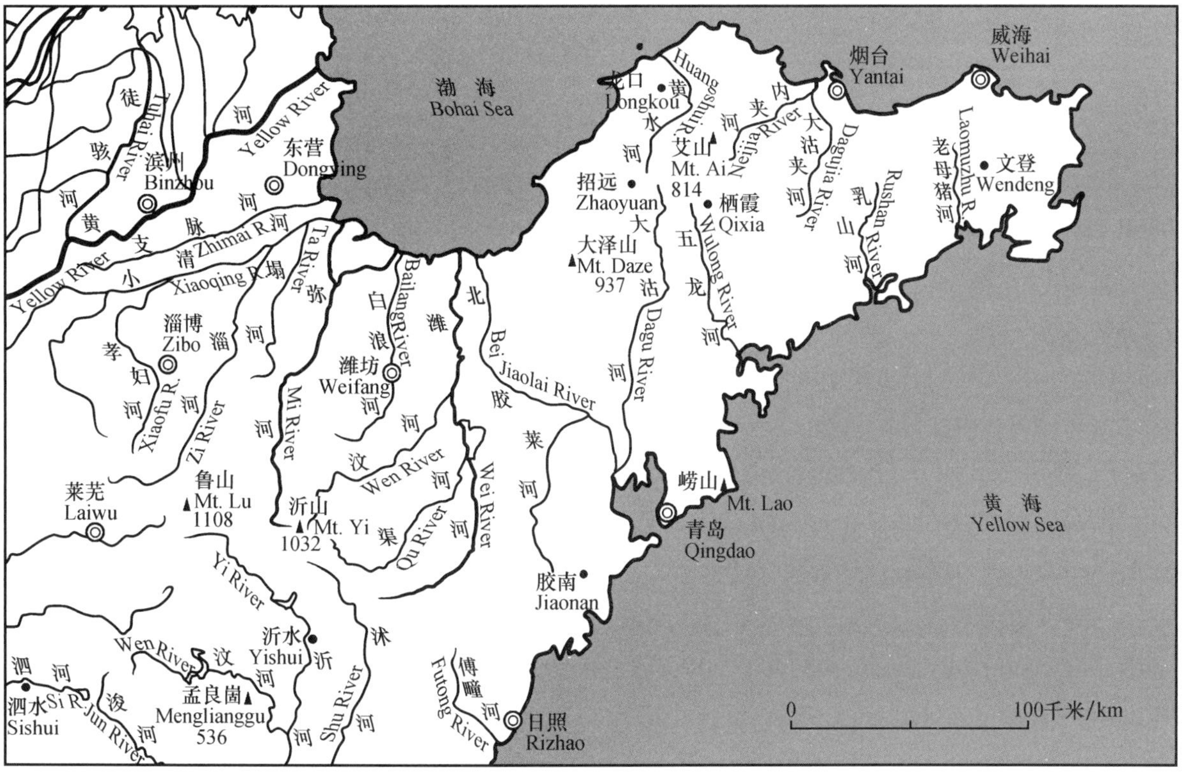

地图Ⅰ.1.2　胶东半岛主要水系分布图

Map Ⅰ.1.2　The main river systems in the Jiaodong Peninsula.

Chapter 1: Physical Geography, Environment, and Regional Cultural Background

Liang Zhonghe

In order to understand the Guicheng city site in Longkou, it is important to consider the physical geography, environment, and regional cultural characteristics of the Jiaodong Peninsula. These factors offer a starting point to consider an array of questions. The particularity and diversity of the peninsula's natural environment has resulted in the distinctiveness and variation of its archaeological culture, especially in the earlier periods. According to our observations, the geographical environment had a major impact on the region's cultural ecology until the Han Dynasty (206 BCE-CE 220). Certainly, such impact was not absolute, but can rather be seen as a developmental and gradual process.

Section 1: Location and Topographical Features of the Jiaodong Peninsula

From the perspective of macro-geography, the Guicheng city site is located in the north of the Jiaodong Peninsula, China's largest, which juts eastward into the sea. The Bohai Sea lies to the north and the Yellow Sea to the east and south. A small peninsula called Chengshanjiao, the eastern tip of the Jiaodong Peninsula, marks the division between the northern Yellow Sea and the southern Yellow Sea. The Jiaolai River, Dagu River and the abandoned canal that used to connect the two rivers form its western boundary. The longitude of the peninsula is 119°34′ at the mouth of the Jiaolai River and 122°39′ at the tip of the peninsula (Chengshanjiao) 280 km to the east. From the southern city of Qingdao at 36°03′ to the northernmost point, Penglai City, at 37°50′, the distance is 230 km. The area of the peninsula is about 39,000 km^2, which is about 19% of the area of Shandong Province.

Administratively, the Jiaodong Peninsula is divided into the jurisdictions of three major "cities" [1]: Yantai City, under which are the cities or countries of Zhaoyuan, Penglai, Fushan, Qixia, Muping, Haiyang, Longkou, Laiyang, Laizhou and Changdao; Weihai City, under which are Rushan,

1 The largest administrative units below the province are confusingly called "Cities," but in fact are large areas, not cities.

Rongcheng and Wendeng etc.; Qingdao City, under which are the cities of Laixi, Pingdu, Jimo, Zhucheng, Jiaozhou, and Jiaonan (Map I .1.1). These "county-level cities" then have under their control rural territories surrounding them.

In geological terms, the Jiaodong Peninsula is located in the Huaxia System Second Uplift Belt, belonging to the Jiaodong-Liaoning ridge of the Sino-Korean Paraplatform. As an integral high tectonic unit (Yang Huairen 1978: 42), it contrasts sharply with the low zones lying on its two sides. The natural geographical environment of the Jiaodong Peninsula exhibits clear regional characteristics featuring mainly granitic rock, but metamorphic rocks such as gneiss and schist formed during the Archaeozoic Era are also widely distributed. At the end of the Cretaceous Period, there were extensive volcanic eruptions that produced considerable deposits of acidic lava. Since the Miocene Epoch, the Bohai Sea region has sagged down, forming the deepest Miocene fault-basin in the North China-Liao River Subsidence Belt. At the end of the Pliocene, but particularly since the beginning of the Quaternary Epoch, the Bohai strait further disintegrated, thus the Shandong Peninsula was formed. The whole region was divided by a NNE-NE mountain system and a NNW-NW mountain system, leaving many land fragments, which after a long period of surface water erosion gave way to numerous low hills, most less than 200 m above sea-level.

A few mountain ranges rise above the surrounding hills, including some NE-SW oriented mountains, which average 500-1,000 m in elevation. The tallest mountain in the peninsula is Laoshan, which is 1,133 m above sea level. In the north-central area are Ya, Kunyu, Weide, Luo, Daze, Lai, and other mountains, which mostly follow a NE-SW direction. About 70% of the total area is taken up by hills and low mountains. Between the mountains and hills are located, for instance, the Taocun chasm basin, the Laiyang rift basin and the Jiaolai low plain. Along the seacoasts are coastal plains of various sizes, comprising less than 30% of the total area. The Penglai, Huangxian (now Longkou), and Ye County (now Laizhou) plains are the largest.

The south coast of the Jiaodong Peninsula is mostly sandbar type coastal lagoons and bays. Some of the bays cut deeply into the coast, forming small peninsulas or promontories, and the heads of the bays deeply divide the land. The bottoms of these bays form shallow flooded valleys in which the substrata are mixed clay and sand. The geological foundation of the northern coast of the peninsula is mainly marble and granite bedrock. On its windward shore it forms a broad sandy coast. However, some areas open onto large bays, their mouths protected by promontories or small peninsulas, often beaten by the waves. Here the shore continues to maintain the characteristics of the rocky coast. It is clear that the geology and geomorphology of the north and south vary greatly.

In general, the coast of the Jiaodong Peninsula is meandering, alternating between capes and bays, with nearby islands of various sizes. Concentrated here are North China's good harbors. In addition to the Miaodao group of coastal islands in the Bohai Strait, relatively large islands close to the mainland include Xiang, Moye, Dujia, Tianheng, Liugong, Jiming, Kongtong, Chu, Sushan, and Nanhuang Islands.

Section 2: Natural Environment

Many factors together form the environment in which humans live, including most notably topography and landscape, but also climate, hydrology, vegetation, and soil. Topography and climate are the major factors that define the conditions for human survival.

1. Climate

The Jiaodong Peninsula is situated at the eastern end of North China, which is characterized by a warm, temperate, continental, monsoon climate. Because of its proximity to the ocean and its predominately hilly terrain, the peninsula has cooler summers, warmer winters and somewhat higher precipitation than elsewhere in North China (Hou Xueyu 1988: 144).

The average annual precipitation of the Jiaodong Peninsula is 600-900 mm, much of which falls during the summer monsoons, which come from the southeast. Total annual rainfall is highest in the southeast and decreases to the northwest. As the southern coast of the Jiaodong Peninsula and its mountain ranges are mainly arrayed in a NE–SW direction, nearly perpendicular to the southeast monsoon fronts, they are conducive to the formation of precipitation, and receive about 750 mm on average. Behind the mountains, the north coastal region receives less precipitation, generally about 600 mm. For example, Yantai receives 690 mm and Penglai receives 626 mm. Mts. Lao and Kunyu in the south are centers of precipitation, with average annual rainfall of 800 mm or more. Of the total annual precipitation 62.6% falls in the summer, often in heavy rains. Spring (March to May) and autumn (September to November) also have some precipitation, accounting for 13% and 19.4%, respectively. Winter precipitation is only about 5.0%. The inter-annual variability of precipitation is about 20%. Average annual relative humidity is above 70%.

In the winter, the Jiaodong Peninsula is dominated by cold northerly winds pushed southwards by the Inner Asian high-pressure system. In summer it is mainly affected by the western Pacific subtropical high-pressure, which pushes warm monsoon winds in from the southeast. Seasonal changes of monsoon winds not only have a profound impact on the temperature and precipitation in the region, but also play a major role in the formation of waves on the sea. There are large variations in prevailing wind speed and direction in different places and seasons, which are affected by topography and the contours of the coast. The prevailing January wind direction in Yantai is W-SW (14%), in Ye County (now Laizhou) it is S-SW (12%), and in other parts of the peninsula it is N, NW, N-NW, etc. In July all prevailing winds are southerly, with a frequency of 15-25% and near-southern winds with a frequency of 45-60%. The average annual wind speed is generally 4-6 m/sec, slightly higher than the 3 m/sec of inland areas.

The north of the Jiaodong Peninsula is close to the Manchurian temperate zone, while the southwest is close to the subtropical belt in central Jiangsu, with a warm and humid temperate monsoon climate. The average temperature in January is between −3℃ and 1℃, while the average temperature in August, the warmest month, is about 25℃ with an extreme maximum temperature of about 38℃. The accumulated temperature above 10℃ is 3800-4100℃. From April to July the eastern side of the southern coast of the peninsula often has sea fog, and the annual average number of foggy days is 30-50 days.

2. River Systems

The central Jiaodong Peninsula has low mountains and hills. Many rivers originate in this region and radiate in four directions before eventually draining into the sea. The rivers in the north of the peninsula that flow into the Bohai Sea and Yellow Sea are the Jiaolai, Jie, Huangshui, Dagujia, Qin, and Xin'an Rivers. On the south side, the main rivers flowing into the Yellow Sea are the Dagu, Wulong, Muzhu and Rushan Rivers.

Because the rivers originating in the mountains of the central peninsula flow directly into the sea, their riverbeds have a fairly steep gradient. With the exception of the Jiaolai River, which flows through a plain, the others are all seasonal mountain streams under 200 km in length (Map Ⅰ.1.2). The peninsula's riverbeds are fed by rainfall with distinct seasonal variations, so they fluctuate between flood and dry. The rainy season accounts for 70-80% of annual runoff. According to the statistics from the Dagujia, Dagu and Wulong Rivers, more than 80% of the annual runoff is concentrated from June to September, with 60% in July and August. Only 15% of the annual runoff occurs in the eight-month dry season (Han Hongnuan 1991: 43-46). Water levels follow precipitation and can fluctuate rapidly. This rarely leads to disaster, but heavy rains can cause flash floods, which coupled with high tides in estuaries, can create a flood hazard. In the dry season, some rivers can dry up leaving riverbeds exposed.

Most of the accumulated sediments forming the coastal lowlands were deposited by rivers. The Jiaodong Peninsula has a long history of human activities and the vegetation is badly damaged, which causes serious soil erosion that increases river sediments. The rivers in the peninsula carrying over 400,000 tons of sediment per year include the Wulong (840,000 tons), Dagu (564,000 tons), Dagujia (564,000 tons) and Laomazhu (422,100 tons). According to the sediment load statistics of the main rivers, the total average annual sediment load of the entire peninsula is as high as 2,551,200 tons.

3. Vegetation

According to the division of China into natural vegetation zones, the Jiaodong Peninsula is classified as temperate deciduous broadleaf forest (China Vegetation Editorial Board, 1980: 788). Sawtooth oak (*Quercus acutissima*) forest is one of the vegetation types most representative of the peninsula, and is the largest and most widely distributed deciduous oak forest in the peninsula. These forests are more common on sunny slopes. They grow up to about 1,000 m above sea level. Below the canopy are some evergreen and semi-evergreen plants, such as mountain pepper (*Lindera glauca*), spindle (*Euonymus fortunei*) and star jasmine (*Trachelospermum jasminoides*). In addition, it is common to see forests of other kinds of oaks. The only timber plantations are distributed on the north-facing slopes at the higher levels of Mts. Lao and Kunyu.

The most common types of trees in the Jiaodong Peninsula are oaks like sawtooth oak, Daimyo oak (*Q. dentate*), and Serrata oak (*Q. serrata*), the former being the most common. However, the practice of cutting off the trunk in order to create more foliage to feed tussar silkworms creates a characteristic "tussar mist" landscape. Among conifers, Japanese red pine (*Pinus densiflora*) is the most representative. Subtropical plants that grow in the peninsula's temperate climate include bitterwood (*Picrasma quassioides*), mountain pepper (*Lindera obtusiloba*), etc. In addition, plants like Mongolian oak (*Q. mongolica*), Liaodong oak (*Q. liaotungensis*) and Japanese alder (*Alnus japonica*) are typical of Manchuria.

In addition to deciduous forest, there are coniferous forests, mixed coniferous and deciduous broadleaf forests, shrub-dominated landscapes, meadows, salt marshes, open sand, and, of course, agriculture (Zhou Guangyu 1963: 62-74). The dominant species in shrub-dominated environments are Chinese sumac (*Rhus chinensis*), *Symplocos paniculata, Platycarya strobilacea*, bamboo (*Phyllostachys sulphurea*), etc. Shrub grasslands are often dominated by chaste tree (*Vitex negundo*), Chinese date (*Ziziphus jujuba*) and red grass (*Themeda triandra*).

Modern vegetation is not only restricted by climate, topography, soil and other natural and historical-geographical conditions, but also by the impact of human economic activity. Human activity has drastically altered the vegetation of the Jiaodong Peninsula over the millennia. The long historical development of the peninsula resulted in the near total destruction of the original vegetation, and its replacement with secondary and mixed vegetation at the present time. Human-planted vegetation is diversified and widely distributed.

4. Soil

The soils of the Jiaodong Peninsula are mainly formed from Mesozoic granitic acidic rocks and erupted mafic lavas. Their base materials include floodwater deposits, river alluvium, ocean sediments, and modern deposits. From east to west the predominant soils are brown soil, wetland soil, black gravelly soil and saline soil. Brown soil is widely distributed; it is slightly acidic with a fully developed structure. Its main types are woodland soil, brown soil type, brown soil and moist brown soil, etc. The brown soil of the Jiaodong Peninsula (commonly known as "Shandong brown soil") is typical brown forest soil and is generally located on gentle slopes and well-drained ground. Areas with such soils have mostly been turned into farmland and orchards and now have mature cultivated soil. The rough-structure brown soils sometimes found on the top or middle of low hill slopes are thin with a coarse texture. Moist brown soil is mainly distributed in the northern and southern plains, and is a high-yield soil type. Moist soil is distributed along rivers and in coastal plains. It is deep and thick, conserving both moisture and nutrients. Black gravelly soil develops in the shallow coastal marsh sediments, generally in flat terrain that is prone to seasonal alkalinisation, and is not conducive to crop growth. Saline ground is mainly found in low-lying areas where rivers flow into the sea, the groundwater level is high, and the soil has a salinity of about 0.085-2.98%, so only seablite (*Suaeda glauca*), common reed (*Phragmites communis*) and other salt-tolerant plants grow there.

There is also loess in some areas. As a Quaternary deposit (beginning two million years ago), it is the most recent sediment in the region so it is quite loose. Shandong's loess began to form at a relatively late period. Of the loess sections uncovered to date, the thickest is the thirty-plus meter deposits at the site of Fujiazhuang, Qingzhou. The sources of Shandong's loess vary, since it contains materials of wide origin, and its geological characteristics are different from loess elsewhere. The particle size is relatively coarse. It contains marine microfossils and is largely composed of materials blown from the exposed Bohai Sea shelf when the sea level was much lower during the last glaciation. The next highest source of this loess is aeolian sediments from the northwest (Xu Shujian 2010: 1197-1201).

5. Modern Agriculture and Its Main Crops

The biological resources of the Jiaodong Peninsula are both diverse and plentiful. The typical brown forest soil (Shandong brown soil) is generally located on gentle slopes and well-drained ground. It has mostly been turned into farmland and orchards, becoming mature agricultural soil. The soils in the higher areas of the low mountains and hills derive from local weathering, while those accumulated on the slopes are thin, weakly-developed brown soils that are rather coarse. They are often used to grow peanuts, sweet potatoes and other such crops. The main fruit crops currently cultivated in the Jiaodong peninsula are apples, pears and grapes. The most famous are Yantai apples, Laiyang Chi pears and Pingdu Dazeshan grapes. Two crops can be grown in a year. The main crops are wheat, maize, sweet potatoes, soybeans, millet, sorghum, cotton, peanuts, tobacco and hemp. Of these, winter wheat, soybeans and maize are the major crops. The peninsula occupies an important position in the country in terms of agriculture. The region is also richly endowed with marine resources. Coastal waters comprise 37% of the total area of the Bohai Sea and the Yellow Sea. There are over 260 kinds of coastal fish and other edible creatures, including forty major species of economic fish and more than one hundred kinds of shallow-water shellfish. Among them, prawns, scallops, abalone, sea cucumber and sea urchins are valuable commodities, and the peninsula's output is among the highest in the country. In addition, many medium-sized coastal salt fields have been built so that the peninsula is one of the four main sea salt production areas in the country.

Section 3: Changes in the Environment and Coastline over the Past 10,000 Years

Human societies develop in particular environmental contexts, from which they are inseparable. As the interaction zone between land and sea, the coast is one of the most sensitive areas to environmental change in the Jiaodong Peninsula. Changing climate and coastlines and the rising and falling of the sea level affected the spatial extent of human activities, subsistence patterns, and methods used to exploit natural resources. Therefore, the environment played an important role in the formation and development of human society, placing limits on and creating possibilities for the development of productive forces in human society.

1. Environmental Change

As we all know, the Holocene is characterized by a relatively warm and humid climate. However, the climate over these 10,000 years has been quite complicated, alternating between a number of periods that were either cold and warm or dry and humid, with temperature fluctuations of 5-6℃. The largest temperature change has been between 8-10℃. The level of annual precipitation changed frequently along with the changing temperature.

Around 8,500 years ago the Jiaodong Peninsula became warm and humid. Woody plants came to dominate the pollen record and the percentage of broadleaf pollen increased, as did pine. Oak was the most common pollen type, followed by chestnut. Other pollen types include elm, birch, hornbeam (*Carpinus*), the cypress family, hazel, and occasional pollen of sweet gum (*Liquidambar*), acacia, beech, walnut, maple, and other temperate trees and shrubs. The most common herb (i.e., non-woody) pollen types are Chenopodiaceae, *Artemisia*, and *Typha*. There were also the spores of *Polypodium* and *Ceratopteris* ferns. The pollen record shows that the south of the Jiaodong Peninsula had plants that now only grow in the Jiang-Huai Region (roughly modern Jiangsu and Anhui) and further south, for example, *Ceratopteris* ferns, that are now extinct in Shandong and farther north. In short, given that the vegetation was roughly equivalent to that of the Huaihe Plain in modern times, the average temperature was probably around 2.5 ℃ higher than now. Between 6500 and 5000 BP, the region's climate became more favorable; broadleaf forests predominated, and there were a few sub-tropical plants, including those now only found in south China. This relatively warm and humid climate was similar to that of the northern part of the Huaihe River Basin at present, where the average annual temperature is about 2℃ higher.

However, beginning in 5600 BP, there was an increase in the pollen of conifers, most notably pine, fir and spruce. This indicates a temporary cooling in the Holocene warm period. After 5000 BP, there was an increase in herbs tolerant of aridity and salt, which reflects a drying trend. Pine pollen predominates, with a reduction of broadleaf pollen and an increase in herb pollen. By inference, the vegetation was similar to that of the northern Huang-Huai Plain at present, with an average annual temperature around 14-15℃, about 2℃ higher than now. The average annual rainfall was 800 mm or more, about 100-300 mm above present values.

As Zhu Kezhen argued, during the period between 5,000 and 3,000 years ago (the last half of the Holocene warm period) the average temperature of the Yellow River region was about 2℃ higher than at present, and winter temperatures were 3-5℃ higher (Zhu Kezhen 1972: 15-38). At that time the northern boundary of the subtropical zone extended along the Xuzhou–Zhengzhou–Xi'an or Yanzhou–Heze line (34°30′-35°33′N), about two degrees of latitude above its current position at the Huaihe–Nanyang–Hanzhong line (around 33° latitude). Thus it had moved about two degrees northward. North of this line, the coastal areas of North China were still part of the temperate zone. Around 4000 BP, the time of the Longshan culture, the climate began a cooling trend, precipitation declined and lakes contracted in size.

2. The Changes of the Coastlines

At the height of the last glaciation 25,000 years ago sea levels were about 120 m below present levels. Fifteen thousand years ago, after the end of the glaciation, global temperatures rose and caused the glaciers to melt. The sea rose and inundated the land so that sea level then reached up to four meters above the current level (Zhao Xitao 1979: 269-281). Sea level rise created wetlands, which may have been the natural environment of the eastern coastal regions at the time. Over the past 10,000 years the Jiaodong Peninsula has experienced the rising and falling of sea levels, which caused a retreat and then advance of coastlines.

According to marine data, there was rapid sea level rise in the Jiaodong Peninsula during the early Holocene; coastal areas were progressively inundated as the coastline moved inland. In the north, the coastline reached the present-day town of Xiyou on the east shore of Laizhou Bay, about six kilometers from the present shoreline. After this marine transgression there was a brief regression, as is shown by an 8,000 year-old shoreline 11 m below the current sea level in the same Xiyou area. About 7,300-7,000 years ago the sea had risen so the coastline was similar to the modern one. The greatest marine transgression of the Holocene occurred about 6,000-5,000 years ago. The maximum range is relatively clear and unambiguous. In Laizhou Bay the coastline reached 30 km inland of its current position. On the bedrock along the bay the shoreline of the ocean surface in that period was about 5 m above current sea level. After the maximum transgression, the ocean began to retreat around 4,500 years ago. Around 4,000-3,000 years ago the sea level dropped below its modern level. It rose to its current level around 3,000 years ago, since which time it has fluctuated only slightly (He Deliang 2004: 24-38; Zhongguo shehui kexueyuan kaogu yanjiusuo 1999: 183-185; Han Yousong & Meng Guanglan 1984: 1255-1258).

Section 4: Stages of Cultural Development from the Neolithic to the Qin-Han Period

The Jiaodong Peninsula is one of the first places in China to have been studied by archaeologists. Although our current understanding of the region's archaeology is still sketchy, especially during the Bronze Age, past archaeological work has already clarified the trajectory of cultural development in the Jiaodong Peninsula since the Neolithic, and has provided a general chronological framework and basic standards for dating sites and artifacts. A systematic review of past archaeological work is important, not only for our understanding of the cultural and historical background of the Guicheng site, but also because it can offer a direct reference for the archaeological fieldwork at the site.

1. History of Study

Early in the 1930s Japanese scholars discovered Neolithic shell mound sites in the Jiaodong region. But until the 1950s, after the establishment of the Peoples Republic of China, knowledge of the Neolithic cultures in the Jiaodong Peninsula was limited to some sporadic discoveries. In late 1956 and early 1957, archaeologists of Shandong Province carried out extensive cultural relics surveys and discovered quite a few Neolithic sites in the Jiaodong Peninsula. At that time, because very little fieldwork had been done, archaeologists did not yet have a systematic understanding of the Neolithic cultures in the region. They could only discern the existence of the Longshan culture, but not any earlier or later remains. Although scholars could not clearly see the developmental trajectory of the peninsula's Neolithic culture, they could already discern a difference between it and inland cultures (Liu Dunyuan 1958: 14-22).

In 1961, in order to further their understanding of the characteristics of the peninsular Neolithic culture, archaeologists selected eight sites as the focus of surveys. On the basis of these surveys, scholars for the first time offered systematic interpretations of the peninsula's Neolithic culture. In October 1963, The Shandong Provincial Museum carried out a test excavation at the Zijingshan site in Penglai. This was the first time that a pre-Longshan period cultural deposit was discovered in the peninsula. Afterwards, the Institute of Archaeology, CASS, excavated the Yueshi site in Pingdu and discovered the Yueshi culture, which has unique features and postdates the Longshan culture. Thus, a basic sequence of the cultural development of the peninsula down to the early Bronze Age was revealed.

In 1973, archaeologists carried out a large-scale survey and review of cultural remains on the peninsula and found a large number of new sites. Based on the survey results, they focused their research on the early and middle Neolithic period of the pre-Longshan cultures and posed some new research questions. To solve them, in 1975 the Shandong Provincial Museum carried out test excavations at the Hekou site in Rongcheng and the Baishicun sites in Yantai. In the fall of 1979, Beijing University, the Institute of Archaeology, CASS, and the Yantai Cultural Management Group jointly excavated the Qiujiazhuang site in Fushan and the Zhaogezhuang site in Muping. These excavations, for the first time, comprehensively revealed the features of the peninsula's pre-Longshan cultures. They made clear that they differed significantly from the Dawenkou culture of inland Shandong, and established a preliminary chronology of the region's archaeology.

In both fieldwork and research, the 1980s were a period that saw important breakthroughs in the study of the Neolithic to early Bronze Age period in the Jiaodong Peninsula. From 1980 to 1985, the second major cultural remains survey in Shandong Province was carried out, and over one hundred new Neolithic sites were found. This provided the basis for a clarification of the distribution and spatial relations among Neolithic sites on the peninsula. In order to obtain a genuine understanding of the cultural development on the peninsula, Beijing University, the Yantai Cultural Management Committee, the Shandong Team of the Institute of Archaeology, CASS, and the Shandong Provincial Institute of Cultural Relics and Archaeology carried out excavations or test excavations at a number of sites and obtained a lot of important information.

This fieldwork provided plenty of new material for study, and considerable progress was made during this period toward achieving a systematic understanding of the nature of the peninsula's Neolithic cultures. Many studies explored the peninsula's prehistoric archaeological cultures in terms of their genealogy, nature, and relationships with surrounding cultures (Yan Wenming 1986: 63-95;

Han Rong 1986: 96-116; Li Buqing & Wang Xiping, 1988: 66-76). After 1982, with the constant increase in fieldwork activity, there was also major progress in research that dealt with a number of key sites on the peninsula, or that specifically discussed the relationship between the peninsula's cultures and those of surrounding areas (Tong Weihua 1982; Li Quansheng 1985; Wang Xiping & Li Buqing 1987: 89-95; He Deliang & Jing Fang 1985: 75-82; Song Chengjun & Shi Ming 1984: 84-87). These articles approached the dating, features, economy, society, cultural origins, and connections with surrounding cultures of the region's Neolithic to early Bronze Age cultures from various angles.

The Jiaodong Peninsula has a unique geographical position and favorable natural conditions and is also a relatively independent geographical unit. More importantly, the ancient cultures of the peninsula developed on their own and are very different from those of inland Shandong. Therefore, most scholars believe that the region should be considered an independent culture zone for research purposes and its cultures should be treated separately from the inland Beixin-Dawenkou culture development series; they should be given their own names.

2. Stages of Cultural Development

The period before 10,000 years ago is still unknown in the archaeology of the Jiaodong Peninsula. Although archaeologists have collected chipped stone tools in Penglai, Changdao, and other places, they found no sites or other remains of human activity.

The Neolithic period

The period from 7,000 to 4,000 years ago was the time of Neolithic cultures on the Jiaodong Peninsula. The development of archaeological cultures in this period on the Jiaodong Peninsula passed through roughly three stages:

Early Phase: About 7,000-5,700 years ago, humans had settled on the peninsula, but the range of their activities was very small. The origins of this culture are still unknown. All sites found to date are on the coast, and their inhabitants mainly collected seafood for food, so the development level of the economy was low. The main prehistoric archaeological sites of the Jiaodong Peninsula are shell midden sites. These people depended on gathering, fishing, and hunting, and advanced gradually to farming culture.

Representative sites from this period include the Baishicun site in Yantai (Yantai shi bowuguan 1981: 185-186; Yantai shi wenwu guanli weiyuanhui, 1992: 577-578) and the Hekou site in Rongcheng (Yantai shi bowuguan, 2012: 32). Ceramics of Period Ⅰ of the Baishicun site can represent the main cultural features of this phase. The majority of pottery wares of this period are those tempered with sand, though some are fine clay pottery. About 2% of tempered pottery vessels contain mica and clam shells. Most vessels have wide flaring mouths and round bottoms. The most characteristic types are the bowl-shaped *ding* tripods, pot-shaped *ding* tripod, shallow basin-shaped *ding* tripod, deep bowl-shaped *ding* tripod, cylindrical jars, etc. These vessel types were still used in the subsequent Period Ⅱ of the Baishicun site, but there were more appliqué patterns, which became the main form of decoration.

A large number of postholes were found, along with burnt mud bricks mixed with grass, which indicates that there were residential buildings with mud walls with wooden posts. Many stone and bone tools were found at the approximately 135,000 m^2 Hekou site. These include axes, stone hammers, stone balls, grinding stones, and bone awls and needles. There are three ^{14}C dates from Baishicun. A bone specimen (ZK-0952) was dated to 5840 ± 110 BP; a clam-shell (ZK-1115) was dated to 5440 ± 110 BP, and a charcoal sample (ZK-0954) was dated to 5465 ± 110 BP. It is generally believed that these dates may differ from the actual dates, due to the quality of the specimens used to determine the age. Although the ^{14}C date of the Baishicun site is rather late, from the point of view of its cultural characteristics it is the earliest Neolithic culture on the peninsula. There are major differences between the Period Ⅰ Baishicun culture and the Beixin culture of inland Shandong. Therefore, it seems to be an early Neolithic culture of the Jiaodong Peninsula with local characteristics.

Middle Phase: About 5,700-5,000 years ago, humans already inhabited most areas of the Jiaodong Peninsula, giving the impression of unprecedented prosperity. But sites were still mainly distributed near the northern and southern shores of the peninsula, and were mostly composed of shell midden sites. These sites are relatively small, showing a scattered and decentralized settlement pattern. Large amounts of marine shellfish were accumulated at sites of this period, such as clams, oysters, and other non-perishable remains, indicating that the production mode of the period mainly comprised fishing and hunting. There was a great increase in the number of different types and styles of stone tools and pottery vessels in use during this period.

Typical sites of this period include Qiujiazhuang in Fushan (Yantai shi bowuguan 1963, 350), Beizhuang in Changdao (Beijing daxue kaogu shixidui 1987: 385-394), Zijinshan in Penglai (Shandong sheng bowuguan 1973: 11-13), and Xiaoguancun in Rushan (Beijing Daxue kaogu shixidui & Yantai shi wenwu guanli weiyuanhui 2000: 200-243). These are mainly distributed on the peninsula and on outlying islands. Of these sites, Qiujiazhuang and Beizhuang are about 30,000 m^2 in size. Sixteen house structures were found in the Beizhuang site, all of which were round-cornered square and rectangular shapes, though there were differences in the details of each structure. They generally consist of a living surface, wall base, hearth, doorway and postholes. The floors were situated below the surface level of the ground, and the bedding of the floor was composed of greyish-yellow earth, with some areas having turned into red burnt soil due to frequent fires on them. They included what are known as "dust-pan hearths." The doorways were slightly sloping and opened to the south or southeast.

The layout of these housing structures was rational, and they were arranged in order. They provide important information for our understanding of the life in settlements in this period. In addition, burials were discovered at the Beizhuang site, all of which were rectangular earthen pit burials. In addition to single corpses lying supine, some lay on their sides, some leaned over, and some were flexed. These people had the custom of removing molars.

Beizhuang pottery was mostly tempered reddish-brown or red. The next most common type was tempered grey and black pottery, and there was also a small number made of fine clay. The decorations mainly consist of appliqué patterns, rings, basket impressions, engraved lines, and openwork holes. There is very little painted pottery. Typical vessel types include *ding* tripods, *gui* tureens, jars, *gu* goblets, cylindrical cups, and *dou* pedestal dishes. Pottery unearthed at Qiujiazhuang includes *ding* tripods, cylindrical jars, bowls, and small-mouthed jars. Many jars have facing birds or mushroom-like handles on their rims, which are characteristic of the Jiaodong Peninsula. ^{14}C dating of the upper stratum of the Qiujiazhuang site yielded a date of 5500 BP, while the lower stratum dates to around 5700 BP.

Late Phase: The late Neolithic phase dates to 5000-4000 BP. The distribution of sites expanded significantly, not only in coastal areas but also deep inland. Both the number and area of the sites increased considerably. The main sites of this period are Yangjiaquan (Beijing daxue kaogu shixidui & Shandong sheng wenwu kaogu yanjiusuo 2000a: 151-206), Zijinshan (Shandong sheng bowuguan 1973: 11-13), Beichengzi (Han Rong 1989: 171), Dakou (Zhongguo shehui kexueyuan kaogu yanjiusuo Shandong dui 1985: 1068-1083, 1145), and Yujiadian (Beijing daxue kaogu shixidui & Shandong sheng wenwu kaogu yanjiusuo 2000b: 207-219). Both Yangjiaquan and Zijinshan sites have two deposit layers from occupation: upper and lower. The upper layer (Yangjiaquan strata 2 and 3) is typical of the Longshan culture, while the lower layer (Yangjiaquan strata 4 and 5) is earlier than the Longshan culture, characterized by painted pottery, but its cultural identification has not been determined. In short, the late phase mainly dates to the Longshan culture period. In this period, houses were all built from ground level up, were approximately square, and were built with a base trench dug on each side with a dense row of posts, which were then were covered with mud to form walls. The doors generally opened to the south. At this time we have a more developed sedentary culture. Most burials were earthen pit burials, while a small number had coffins. There was a diversity of subsistence methods in this period and a variety of food sources. Fishing and gathering were relegated to secondary status and farming became more important. It is particularly important that millet and rice husks were found in waste pits at Yangjiaquan, which is the northernmost evidence of rice cultivation in high latitudes during the Neolithic.

In addition, bronze was also found at the site, proof of smelting technology. Pottery from the late phase is represented by vessels from Yangjiaquan, which are mostly black, tempered or of fine clay, and were turned on wheels. The most common types of decoration were rings, engraved lines, appliqué patterns, basket impressions, bamboo patterns, and square spiral patterns. The most common vessel types are jar-shaped *ding* tripods, basin-shaped *ding* tripods, hollow-lobed *gui* tureens, steamers, jars, shallow basins, cups, *dou* pedestal dishes, plates, bowls, and eggshell pottery cups. As for stone tools, the majority are polished, including axes, adzes, shovels, chisels, knives, sickles, spearheads, arrowheads and so on. The most common were stone arrowheads. The date of the Yangjiaquan site is between 4600-4000 BP. At this point the cultures of the eastern coastal regions had begun to advance toward civilized society. In contrast, the Jiaodong Peninsula appears to have actually lagged behind. As far as pottery is concerned, in terms of the variety of types, quantity, and also quality, the peninsula seems to have lagged far behind the regions to the west.

The Early Bronze Age

In the early Bronze Age, the Jiaodong Peninsula was a remote border area far from the political centers in the Central Plain. The Shang culture had not yet arrived. At this time Shandong saw the rise of a culture with local characteristics, namely the Yueshi culture, which was roughly contemporaneous with the Xia Dynasty period in the textual record of the Central Plain. The Jiaodong Peninsula was the area of distribution of a local Yueshi culture type, the Zhaogezhuang type.

The sites of this period are very rich, and are found almost all over the peninsula, though there is a general lack of large central settlement sites. At the same time, in contrast to the overall decline of Yueshi culture in inland areas, they tenaciously survived on the peninsula. The main sites of this period are Zhaogezhuang in Muping (Zhongguo shehui kexueyuan kaogu yanjiusuo Shandong dui 1986: 447-478), Xiaoguanzhuang in Rushan (Beijing daxue kaogu shixidui & Yantai shi wenwu guanli weiyuanhui 2000: 220-243), Zhishui in Yantai (Beijing daxue kaogu shixidui et al. 2000: 96), Daokou in Changdao (Zhongguo shehui kexueyuan kaogu yanjiusuo Shandong dui 1985: 1068-1083, 1145). Agriculture was very well developed, but few residential structures have been discovered. At the Zhaogezhuang site more than forty waste pits were discovered, including round, square with rounded corners, and oval ones. The pits that are square with rounded corners are often two or three connected pits, with small earth partitions between them. The size of each pit varies; they are usually 3 to 4 m^2 and could potentially be the remains of houses. Bronze wares were also discovered at the site.

In terms of artefacts, the site of Zhishui is even more representative. The site's Period Ⅰ (i.e., the Yueshi period) pottery is mainly sand-tempered, with little fine clay pottery. Most vessels are plain, their decoration being mainly intaglio rings, but also including appliqué patterns, engraved lines, and nipples. The hard, thick, grey, fine clay pottery and crude, sand-tempered brown pottery are the most typical Yueshi features. Vessel types include jars, bowls, basins, cups, *dou* pedestal dishes and so on. Stone tools are mainly polished, including shovels, axes, chisels, knives, and arrowheads. Bone implements include shovels, awls and arrowheads. From the point of view of production processing and techniques, Yueshi period pottery technology was already quite mature, but had never expanded beyond the inland areas. The stone technology could produce various kinds of production tools. From radiocarbon dates taken from the Zhaogezhuang site, the upper time limit of the Jiaodong Peninsula's Yueshi culture is 1900 BC, while the lower limit is 1500 BC.

Late Shang to Western Zhou

In this period, and at the same time that the Shang-Zhou culture of the Central Plains region began to affect the Jiaodong Peninsula, a new culture known as the Zhenzhumen culture arose in the area. It was mainly distributed in the coastal travel route in the northwestern part of the peninsula. Representative sites include Zhenzhumen in ChangdaoCounty (Beijing daxue kaogu shixidui et al. 1983: 114-130), Louzizhuang in Longkou (Yantai shi wenwu guanli weiyuanhui 2003: 204-205), Nanhuangzhuang in Rushan (Beijing daxue kaoguxi & Yantai shi wenguanhui & Rushan xian wenguansuo 1991: 332-336). The Zhenzhumen site is located within Jiuzhangya Park on northern Changshan Island in Changdao County. In 1982-1983 Beijing University carried out official excavations there, and determined that its date is roughly contemporaneous with the mid to late Shang Dynasty to the mid Western Zhou period in the Central Plains (ca. 1400-900 BCE). The Louzizhuang site is located southwest of the village of that name southwest of Longkou City. The site area is about 30,000 m^2, and is about 13 km west of the Guicheng city site. It was occupied at roughly the same time as the Zhenzhumen site (Yantai shi wenwu guanli weiyuanhui 2003: 204-205). The Nanhuangzhuang site is located at the eastern end of the peninsula in Rushan County. Its main features were twenty-one burials, which were earthen pits with stone chambers or stone pile graves. In addition, several houses were found in the cemetery area dating to slightly earlier than the burials.

The Zhenzhumen cultural inventory included a large amount of plain brown tempered pottery, inherited from the local Yueshi tradition. It also included some cord-impressed *li* tripods of the Shang-Zhou cultural tradition, showing hybrid features. But the mainstream tradition was reddish-brown plain pottery, and the most important vessel types are *li* tripods, *yan* steamers, *gui* tureens, jars, and bowls. Most of these have either three legs or a round foot, though some have flat bottoms; especially notable features are the rolled rim and circular foot. There is a clear difference between the Zhenzhumen pottery and the grey cord-impressed *li* tripods, *guan* jars, and *dou* pedestal dishes of the Central Plains manufacturing tradition. Whether in terms of ceramic material, color, or such features as the wide rolled rims, or of the body design of the jars, bowls, and pedestal dishes, the Zhenzhumen culture was one that developed from the Yueshi tradition. Zhenzhumen is generally believed to have been the material culture of the Yi people who lived on the Jiaodong Peninsula contemporaneously with the Shang-Zhou period of the Central Plains. Yi remains are mainly found in the peninsula. There are also scattered sites in the Zi and Mi River drainages in northwest Shandong, where the Zhenzhumen culture sites are mixed with Shang-Zhou culture sites. From the late phase of the early Western Zhou to the mid-Western Zhou, the Zhenzhumen culture was mainly restricted to Changdao County, and the Rushan, Haiyang, and Wendeng cities in the southeastern part of Jiaodong Peninsula. The Zhenzhumen culture represents the material culture of the Eastern Yi people in their declining stage. By this period, the Yi had retreated to the eastern end of the peninsula.

In the Western Zhou period, the mighty Zhou culture cleansed the great land of the Jiaodong Peninsula like autumn wind blowing away fallen leaves. Beginning in the mid Western Zhou period, the Zhou culture gradually became the mainstream culture on the peninsula, and Guicheng was the central city site of this adventitious culture, being located on the frontline of the expansion of the Zhou culture into the eastern peninsula. But indigenous cultures survived tenaciously. From the late Western Zhou to the Spring and Autumn period, the state of Lai dominated the Jiaodong Peninsula. After that, almost the whole peninsula became the territory of the state of Qi. Because of the development of production and a population boom in this period, groups of small Spring and Autumn to Warring States period burials are common in the peninsula. However, under the rule of Qi, the cultural characteristics of the Yi people gradually disappeared.

The Qin and Han Period

The Qin Empire established the Jiaodong Commandery in the eastern peninsula, with its seat at Jimo (not the current Jimo city site, but at a site southeast of current Pingdu, southwest of Laixi). This is the first documented administrative unit established on the peninsula to have borne the name "Jiaodong," At that time, the Jiaodong Commandery also included parts of the west bank of the Jiaolai River and extended westward as far as the modern towns of Weifang, Anqiu, Gaomi and other places.

The early Han saw the establishment of many kings. The Jiaodong peninsula became the domain of the Jiaodong Kingdom ruled by King Tian Fu with its capital at Jimo. Later his family was replaced by the Liu family (the Han dynasty imperial family) and the Han Emperor Wu was its king before he became emperor. The Han Dynasty had a parallel Commandery and Kingdom administrative system, so the region east of the Donglai River was still Donglai Commandery, while the southeast coast of the peninsula, that is, modern Haiyang, Jimo, Laoshan and other places, was part of Langya Commandery.

In the Eastern Han the commanderies and counties of the empire were drastically reorganized. Areas on the southeast coast of the peninsula, formerly under Langya Commandery, were placed under Donglai Commandery. The Jiaodong Kingdom was merged with Beihai Commandery to become Beihai Kingdom. This Beihai Kingdom encompassed Jimo (the southeast of Pingdu and southwest of Laixi) and modern Pingdu City, Jimo-West, and other places. The seat of Donglai Commandery was moved to Huangxian (now Longkou City) The seat of Beihai Kingdom was at Juxian (now west of Changle).

In short, the heyday of the Jiaodong Peninsula was the Han Dynasty, and this is completely corroborated by archaeological data. There are more city sites and settlements dating to the Han Dynasty than to any other period. In Jiaodong, archaeologists have found town sites and residential settlements at almost all locations where the Han Dynasty once set up counties. Examples are the Muping city site in Sanshilibu in the Development Zone of Yantai City, the Qucheng city site in Zhaoyuan City, and the Dangli city site in Laizhou City. Han tombs are the largest in number, comprising about two-thirds of the ancient tombs in the Jiaodong Peninsula. This proves that the Han Dynasty population was the highest and the economy was developed, constituting a new peak in the region's ancient social development.

References

Beijing daxue kaogu shixidui 北京大学考古实习队 et al., 1983. "Shandong Changdao shiqian yizhi" 山东长岛史前遗址 (Prehistoric sites on Changdao in Shandong), *Shiqian yanjiu* 史前研究 (Research on Prehistory), 114-130.

Beijing daxue kaogu shixidui 北京大学考古实习队et al., 2000. "Yantai Zhishui yizhi fajue baogao" 烟台芝水遗址发掘报告 (Report on the excavation of the Zhishui site in Yantai), *Jiaodong kaogu* 胶东考古 (Jiaodong Archaeology), 96. Beijing: Wenwu chubanshe.

Beijing Daxue kaogu shixidui 北京大学考古实习队 and Shandong sheng wenwu kaogu yanjiusuo 山东省文物考古研究所, 2000a. "Qixia Yangjiayuan yizhi fajue baogao 栖霞杨家圈遗址发掘报告 (Report on the excavation of the Yangjiaquan site in Qixia County), *Jiaodong kaogu* 胶东考古, 151-206. Beijing: Wenwu chubanshe.

Beijing daxue kaogu shixidui 北京大学考古实习队 and Shandong sheng wenwu kaogu yanjiusuo 山东省文物考古研究所, 2000b. "Laiyang Yujiadian de xiao fajue" 莱阳于家店的小发掘 (Minor excavations at Yujiadian in Laiyang), *Jiaodong kaogu* 胶东考古, 207-219. Beijing: Wenwu chubanshe.

Beijing daxue kaogu shixi dui 北京大学考古实习队 and Yantai shi wenwu guanli weiyuanhui 烟台市文物管理委员会, 2000. "Rushan Xiaoguancun de fajue" 乳山小管村的发掘 (Excavations at Xiaoguancun in Rushan), *Jiaodong kaogu* 胶东考古, 220-243. Beijing: Wenwu chubanshe.

Beijing daxue kaogu shixidui 北京大学考古实习队, Yantai diqu wenguanhui 烟台地区文管会, and Changdao xian bowuguan 长岛县博物馆, 1987. "Shandong Changdao Beizhuang yizhi fajue jianbao" 山东长岛北庄遗址发掘简报 (A brief report on the excavation of the Beizhuang site on Changdao in Shandong), *Kaogu* 考古 (Archaeology), 5: 385-394.

Beijing daxue kaoguxi 北京大学考古系, Yantai shi wenguanhui 烟台市文管会, and Rushan xian wenguansuo 乳山县文管所, 1991. "Shandong Rushanxian Nanhuangzhuang Xizhou Shibanmu fajue jianbao" 山东乳山县南黄庄西周石板墓发掘简报 (A brief report on the excavation of the Western Zhou stone slab tomb at Nanhuangzhuang in Rushan County, Shandong), *Kaogu* 考古, 4: 332-336.

Han Hongnuan 韩洪暖, 1991. "Shandong sheng Jiaodong bandao diqu shuiwen tezheng" 山东省胶东半岛地区水文特征 (Hydrological characteristics of the Jiaodong Peninsula region of Shandong Province), *Shuiwen* 水文 (Hydrology),

4: 43-46.

Han Rong 韩榕, 1986. "Jiaodong shiqian wenhua chutan" 胶东史前文化初探 (Preliminary Study of the Prehistoric Cultures of Jiaodong), in *Shandong shiqian wenhua lunwenji* 山东史前文化论文集 (Collected Essays on the Prehistoric Cultures of Shandong), 96-119. Ji'nan: Qi Lu shushe.

Han Rong 韩榕, 1989. "Qixia xian Beichengzi Longshan wenhua ji Yueshi wenhua yizhi" 栖霞县北城子龙山文化及岳石文化遗址 (The Longshan and Yueshi Culture sites in Beichengzi, Qixia County), *Zhongguo kaoguxue nian jian* 中国考古学年鉴 (Archaeology in China Yearbook), 171. Beijing: Wenwu chubanshe.

Han Yousong 韩有松 and Meng Guanglan 孟广兰, 1984. "Jiaozhouwan diqu Quanxinshi haiqin ji qi hai pingmian bianhua" 胶州湾地区全新世海侵及其海平面变化 (Sea-level change and land encroachment at Quanxinshi in the Jiaozhou Bay area), *Kexue tongbao* 科学通报 (Science Bulletin), 20: 1255-1258.

He Deliang 何德亮, 2004. "Shandong xinshiqi shidai huanjing kaoguxue yanjiu" 山东新石器时代环境考古学研究 (Archaeological research on the Neolithic environment of Shandong), *Dongfang bowu* 东方博物 (Eastern Museum), 2: 24-38.

He Deliang 何德亮 and Jing Fang 竞放, 1985. "Shilun Yangjiaquan yicun de wenhua xingzhi" 试论杨家圈遗存的文化性质 (Discussion on the nature of the Yangjiaquan cultural remains), *Kaogu yu wenwu* 考古与文物 (Archaeology and Cultural Relics), 1: 75-82.

Hou Xueyu 侯学煜, 1988. *Zhongguo ziran dili* 中国自然地理 (Physical Geography of China). Beijing: Kexue chubanshe.

Li Buqing 李步青 and Wang Xiping 王锡平, 1988. "Jiaodong bandao xinshiqi wenhua chulun" 胶东半岛新石器文化初论 (Initial discussion of the Neolithic cultures of Jiaodong), *Kaogu* 考古, 1: 66-76.

Li Quansheng 李权生, 1985. "Jiaodong xinshiqi wenhua xulie ji qi yu Lu zhongnan de guanxi" 胶东新石器文化序列及其与鲁中南的关系 (Prehistoric Culture Series of Jiaodong and its Relation to the Lu Southeast). Beijing Daxue 北京大学, MA thesis.

Liu Dunyuan 刘敦愿, 1958. "Shandong Wulianxian ji Moxian liangchu Longshan wenhua yizhi" 山东五莲县及墨县两处龙山文化遗址 (Longshan Culture sites of Wulian and Mo Counties in Shandong), *Kaogu* 考古, 4: 14-22.

Shandong sheng bowuguan 山东省博物馆, 1973. "Shandong Penglai Zijingshan yizhi shijue jianbao" 山东蓬莱紫荆山遗址试掘简报 (A brief report on test excavations at the Zijingshan site in Penglai, Shandong), *Kaogu* 考古, 1: 11-15.

Song Chengjun 宋承钧 and Shi Ming 史明, 1984. "Jiaodong shiqian wenhua yu Lai Yi de lishi gongxian" 胶东史前文化与莱夷的历史贡献 (Historical contributions of the Jiaodong prehistoric cultures and the Lai Yi people), *Dongyue luncong* 东岳论丛 (Dongyue Collected Essays), 1: 84-87.

Tong Weihua 佟伟华, 1982. "Changdao Beizhuang zaoqi yicun tichu de jige wenti" 长岛北庄早期遗存提出的几个问题 (Some Questions Raised by the Early Remains at Beizhuang on Changdao), Beijing Daxue 北京大学, MA thesis.

Wang Xiping 王锡平 and Li Buqing 李步青, Wang Xiping 王锡平 and Li Buqing 李步青, 1987. "Shilun Jiaodong bandao yu Liaodong bandao shiqian wenhua de jiaoliu" 试论胶东半岛与辽东半岛史前文化的交流 (Initial discussion of communication between the prehistoric cultures of the Jiaodong and Liaodong Peninsulas) in *Zhongguo kaoguxuehui diliuci nianhui* 中国考古学会第六次年会 (Proceedings of the Sixth Annual Meeting of the Archaeological Association of China), Shenyang, 89-95.

Xu Shujian 徐树建, 2010. "Shandong diqu huangtu chenji tezheng yu huanjing yiyi ji qi yu huangtu gaoyuan de duibi" 山东地区黄土沉积特征与环境意义及其与黄土高原的对比 (Characteristics and environmental significance of loess strata in the Shandong region and a comparison with the Loess Plateau), *Shengtai huanjing xuebao* 生态环境学报 (Journal of Ecosystems), 19 (5): 1197-1201.

Yan Wenming 严文明, 1986. "Jiaodong yuanshi wenhua chulun" 胶东原始文化初论 (Initial discussion of the original cultures of Jiaodong) in *Shandong shiqian wenhua lunwenji* 山东史前文化论文集 (Collected Essays on the Prehistoric Cultures of Shandong), 63-95. Ji'nan: Qi Lu shushe.

Yang Huairen 杨怀仁, 1987. *Disiji dizhi* 第四纪地质 (Quaternary Geology). Beijing: Gaodeng jiaoyu chubanshe.

Yantai shi bowuguan 烟台市博物馆, 1963. "Shangdong Yantai shi Qiujiazhuang faxian xinshiqi shidai yicun" 山东烟台市丘家庄发现新石器时代遗存 (Prehistoric remains discovered at Qiujiazhuang, Yantai City), *Kaogu* 考古, 7: 350.

Yantai shi bowuguan 烟台市博物馆, 1981. "Shandong Yantaishi Baishicun yizhi diaocha jianbao" 山东烟台市白石村遗址调查简报 (A brief report on the investigation of the Baishi Village site in Yantai City, Shandong), *Kaogu* 考古, 2: 185-186.

Yantai shi bowuguan 烟台市博物馆, 2012. "Rongcheng shi Hekou yizhi fajue baogao" 荣成市河口遗址发掘报告 (Report on the excavation of the Hekou site in Rongcheng City), *Haidai kaogu* 海岱考古 (Haidai Archaeology), 5: 32.

Yantai shi wenwu guanli weiyuanhui 烟台市文物管理委员会, 1992. "Shangdong Yantai shi Baishicun xinshiqi shidai yizhi fajue jianbao" 山东烟台白石村新石器时代遗址发掘简报 (A brief report on the excavation of the Neolithic site at Baishi Village in Yantai City, Shandong), *Kaogu* 考古, 7: 577-588.

Yantai shi wenwu guanli weiyuanhui 烟台市文物管理委员会, 2003. "Longkou shi Louzizhuang xinshiqi ji qingtong shidai yizhi" 龙口市楼子庄新石器及青铜时代遗址 (Neolithic and Bronze Age Sites at Louzizhuang in Longkou City), *Zhongguo kaoguxue nianjian* 中国考古学年鉴 (Archaeology in China Yearbook), 204-205. Beijing: Wenwu chubanshe.

Zhao Xitao 赵希涛 et al., 1979. "Zhongguo dongbu 20,000 nian lai de haipingmian bianhua" 中国东部20000年来的海平面变化 (Sea-level changes in Eastern China during the past 20,000 years), *Haiyang xuebao* 海洋学报 (Journal of Oceanography), 1 (2): 269-281.

Zhongguo shehui kexueyuan kaogu yanjiusuo 中国社会科学院考古研究所, 1999. *Jiaodong bandao Beiqiu yizhi huanjing kaogu* 胶东半岛贝丘遗址环境考古 (Environmental archaeology of the Beiqiu site in Jiaodong Peninsula). Beijing: Shehui kexue wenxian chubanshe.

Zhongguo shehui kexueyuan kaogu yanjiusuo Shandong dui 中国社会科学院考古研究所山东队, 1985. "Shandong Changdaoxian Tuoji dao Dakou yizhi" 山东长岛县砣矶岛大口遗址 (Dakou site on Tuoji Island, Changdao County, Shandong), *Kaogu* 考古, 12: 1068-1083, 1145.

Zhongguo shehui kexueyuan kaogu yanjiusuo Shandong dui 中国社会科学院考古研究所山东队, 1986. "Shandong Mouping Zhaogezhuang yizhi" 山东牟平照格庄遗址 (Zhaogezhuang site in Mouping, Shandong), *Kaogu xuebao* 考古学报 (Acta Archaeologica Sinica), 4: 447-478.

Zhongguo zhibei bianweihui 中国植被编委会, 1980. *Zhongguo zhibei* 中国植被 (China's Flora). Beijing: Kexue chubanshe.

Zhou Guangyu 周光裕, 1963. "Shandong de zhibei fenlei he fazhan" 山东的植被分类和发展 (Types and development of vegetation in Shandong), *Shandong daxue xuebao* 山东大学学报 (Shandong University Journal), 1: 62-74.

Zhu Kezhen 竺可桢, 1972. "Zhongguo jin wuqian nian lai qihou bianqian de chubu yanjiu" 中国近五千年来气候变迁的初步研究 (Initial research into climatic change in China during the past 5,000 Years), *Kaogu xuebao* 考古学报, 1: 16-38.

(Translated by Brian Lander)

第二章　内城城墙的钻探

唐锦琼　韩　辉　李　峰

第一节　地 理 形 势

归城内城位于城址中部的一处高台地上。台地西北侧为鸦鹊河，东侧为鸦鹊河故道。两河在台地北侧交汇。台地北侧高出河道约5米。台地西南部与曹家村西侧山地相接。台地表面较为平整，由南向北略向下倾斜。台地边缘尤其北侧与两侧的河道有着明显的断崖。内城北部和西南角分别为和平村与姜家村（又称“归姜”）两村所占压。在两村之间有一条南北向的乡间公路穿城而过（地图Ⅰ.2.1；图版5～7）。

第二节　钻探经过和钻探方法

确定归城内城的范围是归城考古首先进行的工作。这项工作自2007年6月17日开始，至2007年7月16日结束，历时共计整30日。钻探工作从归姜村西南侧的城墙A（对这块城墙的介绍，详见下文）开始（图版8：1），首先确定地下保留城墙的外侧边界（南侧边界）及西端（即内城墙西南角）。由此向东一路追索南城墙之外侧边界及城外护城河的走向和具体范围，至6月24日到达南城墙东端夯土消失处。次日6月25日开始钻探南城墙北侧边界，到26日完成整个南城墙的钻探。6月27日钻探队开始由归姜村内向北追西城墙南段走向，并沿东西向街道确定其东西两侧边界（图Ⅰ.2.1）。至7月5日，越过西城墙南段北端的城墙B（对这块城墙的介绍，详见下文）（图版9），继续向东钻探北城墙西段。7月8日，转而向北钻探西城墙之北段，至7月10日到达归城内城城墙的西北角。7月11～12日钻探北城墙，确定了南北两侧边界，并于7月12日抽空粗探内城北方台地北端的夯土台基（见上编第三章第五节，六：“内城北部台地夯土基址”）。7月13日起开始钻探东城墙。首先钻探确认和平村东一块台地为夯土构筑，之后在其南侧杨树林中发现另外三小块夯土，从而确定它们均属于内城东墙的残留部分。至7月16日，内城城墙的钻探工作基本结束。

对于归城内城城墙的钻探，我们采用了与内城内部相同的钻探方法。即以普探和重点钻探相结合，将每个探孔位置在图上具体标明，并按照土样标准对每个探孔中所探知的层位及其他现象进行详细记录。最后在图上进行比对分析，确定下一步的钻探方向，直到完成整个内城城墙的钻探。这个方法，我们在内城内遗址的钻探中得到了更为系统和成熟的应用，因此我们将在本书上编第三章中对其进行详细说明。对钻探中各种土样，我们也进行了系统的分类，确立了土样标准，作为探孔中地层记录和比对的基础。关于归城土样分类的过程及其所依据的标准，在第三章中也有详细阐述（见上编第三章第三节："内城钻探工作方法"）。

第三节　内城城墙概况

1. 总体状况

内城城墙平面形状整体呈曲尺形，在西北侧内凹。以城墙中心计，内城南北长490米，东西宽525米。城墙西北处内凹部分南北长约180米，东西宽约180米。内城总面积约22.5万平方米。

北城墙沿和平村北断崖向西延伸，至和平村西的南北向乡间公路后折向南。南行约180米，城墙折向西，越过北侧水门，又西行约180米，在城墙B西侧约20米又折向南，经归姜村内南北向街道，至城墙A西侧约20米，折向东。再经由城墙A，通过归姜村南果园向东延伸，越过公路沿和平村南的高约2.5米断崖东行，至东端断崖结束处。内城的东南角为后期洪水冲刷破坏而大部无存。南城墙也有被洪水毁坏并进行二次修复的痕迹。东城墙已破坏殆尽，除城墙C外（图版8：2），仅发现前述埋藏较深的三小段。通过钻探，我们确定北墙东段残长约235米，西墙北段长约180米，北墙西段长约180米，西墙南段长约310米，南墙残长约435米（均按城墙中心计算，下同）。根据保存较好的西城墙走向判断，城墙走向约17°。

关于城墙宽度，由于钻探所得范围可能有墙体坍塌的夯土堆积，因此不易判断。但是较为规整的西城墙北段宽约20米，北城墙西段宽约35米，大致反映了城墙的原有宽度。

通过对局部断崖的清理，发现城墙的修建采取的是分段板筑的方式。在清理的城墙剖面上可见夯层为水平夯筑，夯层厚度不是十分统一，厚6～20厘米，其平均厚度在10厘米左右。夯土以较为纯净的黄褐色夯土为主，也有不少为灰土夯打而成，并夹杂有陶片。钻探中，未发现有基槽痕迹。内城城墙有修补和重筑的现象。

在南墙、北墙以及西墙北段外侧发现有城壕，走向与城墙一致，但宽度不一，在6～32米。城壕最深处约4.8米，其下层堆积为砂层和淤土，上部堆积多为灰土。在南墙内侧的部分地点也发现有内城壕，宽约7米，最深处距地表超过2米。内外城壕的存在表明城墙的修建可能在部分地段采取的两侧取土的方式。

在城墙上发现有两处城门。在南墙偏西处为水陆城门，北墙西段与西墙北段之间为水城门所在。在南侧城门发现有道路和入水口，北侧城门为城内水系的出水口。两端城门之间有城内南北向水系（G1）沟通。

2. 城墙保存状况

内城城墙由于自然侵蚀、后期破坏等，大部已湮没在地下，在地面已基本了无痕迹。仅在城内三处地点发现有地面残存的城墙，分别位于南城墙西端（编号为地面城墙A）、北城墙西端（编号为地面城墙B）和东城墙中部（编号为地面城墙C）。其中地面城墙A和地面城墙B在烟台文管会20世纪70年代的调查中发现，地面城墙C是此次调查中新发现并确认的。

地面城墙A：位于归姜村东南，为南墙的西端，距离西城墙拐角约20米。城墙东西残长约50米，残宽约13米，残高约8米。这段残存的城墙巍然屹立于归姜村的南沿。据钻探得知其墙基原有宽度在30米以上，北侧的城墙边界现已被压在民居之下，难以确认其具体宽度。为了防止村民对墙体的破坏，龙口市博物馆于20世纪90年代在城墙根基部四周筑起石头围墙，加以保护。2008年又在城墙上搭建遮雨棚来防止风蚀雨淋对城墙的进一步破坏。这段城墙已然成为归城遗址的地标（图Ⅰ.2.2；图版8：1）。

地面城墙B：位于归姜村北，为北墙的西段，距城墙西北角约20米。城墙呈刀把形台状，东侧被破坏，仅存长长的一条。城墙表面较为平整，周边被块石围砌，加以保护。城墙东西残长约65米，残宽2～16米，残高2.5米，偏东处有一宽约10米的缺口，是后期破坏所致。此段城墙与地面城墙A遥遥相对，大致确定了内城西墙南段的走向和位置（图Ⅰ.2.3；图版9）。

地面城墙C：为本次调查发现。其位于和平村东，距内城东北角约170米，残存形状不甚规整，为一南北长约35米，东西宽约27米，残高约3.5米的夯土台。这段城墙在2005～2006年的初步踏查中被认为是一个独立的台基。2007年归城田野工作开始，即对台基进行钻探，确定其为夯土筑成。随后在其南侧又发现三小段地下残存城墙，与之南北呼应。由此确定这个夯土台基实际上同为归城内城东墙的一段（图Ⅰ.2.4；图版8：2）。

这三段城墙构建了内城的大体框架，为进一步寻找和确认地下留存的城墙部分提供了线索和依据。

第四节　内城城墙分段介绍

归城内城的城墙大部湮没在地表之下。通过系统的钻探，确认地下残存城墙及内外侧城壕的分布状况。内城城墙呈曲尺形，特别是北墙和西墙呈“┌”形，南侧城墙被南侧城门分为东西两部分。为方便叙述，将各段城墙分为北墙东段、西墙北段、北墙西段、西墙南段，南墙西段、南墙东段和东墙等分别加以叙述。

1. 北墙东段

北墙东段位于和平村北。和平村北为一处高约3米的断崖，断崖处即为城墙所在。城墙东侧至鸦鹊河故道，西侧至南北向公路，残长约235米。

城墙的大部已被和平村最北一排现代民居所叠压。其北侧墙基外沿延伸到断崖下方，与断崖平行分布，距断崖约3米。断崖西部较矮，东部近鸦鹊河故道处由于地势变低，断崖逐渐变高，高约5米。城墙南侧为民居叠压，仅通过数处街道内的追踪钻探了解城墙宽约23～25米。断崖上部城墙夯土距地表约1米左右，或为村庄后期垫高所致。夯土较厚，一般厚度在1米以上。断崖下部的夯土在0.03米厚的表土层下即出露，深度在2米左右。城墙整体略呈东略偏南走向，方向为100°（图Ⅰ.2.5）。

在城墙外侧有城壕与其平行分布。城壕长度大体与城墙相当，宽约7.7～23.5米，基本宽度在20米左右。其中在近东侧处最窄，有明显的内收。值得注意。城壕最深处距地表在2米以上。城壕内填土以灰土为主，并有部分淤土分布。城壕以东钻探出大量砂土层，应为鸦鹊河故道，城壕与城墙一样东端为鸦鹊河冲毁。

城墙与城壕之间无明显的间隔，或是因为上部夯土坍塌到岸边，钻探过程中难以将坍塌夯土和原生夯土区分所致。

2. 西墙北段

西墙北段位于和平村西的南北向公路下，北侧与城墙西北角相接，南侧隔一缺口与北墙西段相望。这段城墙南北总长约180米。

城墙总体叠压在公路下，西侧边缘较为平直，或为城墙原有的边界。城墙方向若以此计约17°。城墙宽约11.5～20.5米。城墙南端呈舌状突出，长约10.5米，宽约4米。此段凸起的位置较西侧的北墙西段向南突出，结合在西侧紧挨着发现的水门遗迹，其或许为约束河道，保护城墙不被水流冲坏而专门设置的。

城墙的夯土一般距地表深约0.4～1米开口，多为在1米左右开口。夯土厚度不一，部分地点深度在2米以上，有些地点厚度仅有0.4米上下。

在城墙外侧（西侧）发现有外城壕分布。城壕与城墙总体平行，南侧约略拐向西南与北墙西段外的城壕及穿过北城墙的水门相通。城壕宽约8～24米，北侧较宽，略呈喇叭口状。沟最深处距地表2米以上。壕内填土不一，以灰土、砂土及淤土为主，反映了沟的不同淤积和填充过程。

3. 北墙西段

北墙西段位于归姜村北，和平村西。城墙总体呈东西走向，长约180米。其西北侧即为地面城墙B，城墙B略向西20米处城墙南拐，与西墙南段相接。城墙东侧隔一宽约15米的缺口与西墙北段相望。

城墙现存地貌为农田，在东侧为一矮断崖。城墙宽约23～35米，东西两侧略宽，中间较窄。城墙走向为南略偏东，约100°。

城墙夯土多开口在0.3米厚的表土层下，厚度不一，约在1米至1.5米之间，最深约在2米以上。

城墙外侧（北侧）有城壕，与城墙平行分布。城壕东侧呈弧形与西墙北段外的城壕相接。城壕宽约15米左右。沟周边多直接打破生土。城壕内填土以淤土为主。

4. 西墙南段

西墙南段位于归姜村北和村内。城墙整体呈南北走向，长约310米。其北侧与北墙西段相接，南侧在地面城墙A西侧约20米处与南侧城墙相接。

城墙北侧地面为农田，南侧则进入归姜村内，为现代民居所叠压。城墙北侧经钻探保存较好，宽约30米。夯土上部有1～1.5米厚的晚期堆积，很多地点距地表2米处夯土不见底。此段城墙南侧为民居所叠压，仅能通过数处街道予以钻探追踪。通过在一处街道中钻探，了解城墙宽约35米。此处夯土距地表深约0.3～1米，夯土底部距地表在1.2米以上，有的地点2米未到底部。城墙总体呈南略偏西走向，方向为195°。西墙外侧（西侧），尤其是西墙北段外侧农田中未发现有城壕遗迹，此处的防御设施需进一步工作确认。

5. 南墙西段

南墙西段位于归姜村南，城墙整体呈东西走向，长约160米。其西侧在地面城墙A的西侧约20米与西墙南段相接，东侧延至南北向公路处的南城门处，与南墙东段相距约30米。

城墙所处范围除少量民居叠压外均为农田。地面城墙A即位于其西侧，距西南拐角约20米。城墙的北侧边缘为民居所叠压，难以确定。南侧边缘不甚平整，可能是晚期破坏，抑或是上部夯土坍塌所致。根据迹象推断，城墙的宽度约在25～30米。表土下即为城墙残存夯土，厚度多在1米以上。

在城墙外侧（南侧）发现有城壕。城壕与城墙呈大体平行分布。城壕北侧紧贴着城墙，南侧边缘不甚平整，城壕宽窄不一，约10～25米。在城壕东南侧有与外界相通的水道，宽约14米，或为城壕进水的通道。城壕内填土以灰土为主，最深处距地表在2米以上。

6. 南墙东段

南墙东段位于归姜村东，和平村南，西侧为南北向公路，东侧为鸦鹊河故道所破坏，残长约240米。其西侧隔南北向公路处的城门与南墙西段相隔，相距约30米。城墙整体呈东略偏南走向，方向为107°。

城墙所处地点除西侧为民居外，其余均为农田。地面为一段高约2.5米的断崖，向东逐次降低。城墙主体位于断崖上，南侧已延伸至断崖下方。城墙的两侧边缘不甚整齐，或为后期破坏或坍塌所致。这也导致了城墙宽窄不一，在25～37米之间。城墙夯土距地表深浅不一，有的叠压在灰土堆积下，距地表深度在0.5左右，有的直接叠压在耕土层下。夯土厚度不一，很多段夯土底部距地表有2米以上。

城墙外侧（南侧）有城壕与其大体平行分布。城壕宽窄不一，平均宽度在30米左右，深约2米以上。最窄处在西侧，仅宽约7米，深约1.8米。值得注意的是最窄处正位于南城墙的正中位置，即在南城墙的中轴线上。是否具有其他意义，需进一步工作来认识考察。壕内填土以灰土为主，并有部分砂层。

在此段城墙北侧发现少量内城壕遗迹。内城壕仅分布在东部。且紧贴着城墙北侧边缘分布。内城壕钻探出的部分东西长约110米，宽约7～12米，深度在2米以上。壕内填土为灰土和淤土。在壕北侧似有两道水口与城内相通。值得注意的是，内壕与夯土基址1的位置略有交错。两者关系如何需进一步考察。

7. 东墙

东城墙位于和平村东和东南，东侧紧邻着鸦鹊河故道。经钻探可知地表下即为砂土，厚度多在2米以上，为河道淤积形成。这些现象表明东城墙已大部为东侧的鸦鹊河故道所冲毁。

通过钻探和调查，东侧城墙仅存有村东地面残存的城墙C和三小段地面下城墙。三段地下城墙自北向南分别编号为东城墙Ⅰ～Ⅲ。三段城墙南北长约140米。

东城墙Ⅰ：位于地面城墙C的南侧略偏西处，相距约43米。其残存形状呈椭圆形，东西径约8.5米，南北径约5.5米。此处残存城墙西侧上部在0.3米厚的表土下即为夯土，东侧表土层下为0.4米厚的黄砂土，即0.7米下为夯土。城墙夯土厚度不一，西侧部分在地表下2米不底，东侧夯土仅残厚0.4米。

东城墙Ⅱ：位于东城墙Ⅰ的南侧，两者相距约17米。其残存形状不甚规则，大体呈南北向长条形，南北长约56米，东西宽约5.2～19米。在晚期地层或砂土层下即为夯土。夯土厚度不一，最薄处仅有0.1米，最厚处距地表2米下仍为夯土。城墙整体走向呈北略偏东方向，方向为14°。残存城墙东侧被破坏严重，不成形状，西侧边缘较为平直，或反映了城墙的原有形状。

东城墙Ⅲ：位于东城墙Ⅱ的南侧，两者相距约54.5米。其残存形状呈三角形，东西长约14米，南北宽约9.5米。城墙的夯土距地表深约0.7～1.1米，其上覆盖为砂土层。夯土厚度不一，薄处有0.4米，最厚处距地表1.8米下仍为夯土。

三块地下城墙与北侧的地面城墙C大体南北一线，构建起东城墙的框架。根据发现的东城墙残迹，并结合南北城墙的位置，对东侧城墙予以复原。复原的东城墙南北长约500米，宽约30～40米，方向14°。

在部分夯土下部发现有砂土层，表明城墙坐落在砂土层上，为构筑城墙以前的原始地表。城墙原先坐落在鸦鹊河早先的河道上。

在城墙Ⅱ内侧发现有一小段内城壕，走向与城墙的走向一致。城壕南北长约40米，东西宽约14～18米，最深处距地表4米以上。其东侧紧贴着城墙夯土，西侧打破城内的灰土堆积。沟内填土多为砂层、淤土等。

第五节　内城城墙附属遗迹

1. 内外城壕的说明

如上所述，归城内城城墙外侧有城壕。根据钻探，在北墙东段、西墙北段、北墙西段和南墙外侧均有分布。城壕走向与城墙一致，但宽度不一，在6～32米之间。城壕最深处距现地表约4.8米，其下层堆积为砂层和淤土等。东墙部分破坏严重，其外侧原来是否有城壕尚不清楚。在南墙和东墙内侧的部分地点也发现有内城壕，宽约7米，最深处超过2米。内外城壕的存在表明城墙的修建主要采用了单侧取土的方式，部分地点可能采取的两侧起土的方式。

我们以下选取一处根据钻探结果复原出的典型剖面来介绍城墙与内外城壕之间的关系（图Ⅰ.2.6）。剖面位置选在夯土基址1西侧，2009年发掘的探沟东侧。其大致呈西南—东北走向，方向约为17°，与城墙的走向相垂直。剖面总长约80米，横跨城内外，包括南侧城墙东段，内城壕和外城壕等遗存。其中在中部有一高约2米的断崖，断崖上下即为城墙的位置。城墙宽约18.5米，多数在表土层下即为夯土。在断崖上部夯土厚度在2米以上；在断崖下方，由于晚期破坏，明显变薄，仅厚约1米。夯土质地坚硬，有黄色和灰色夯土等。

城墙外侧发现有外城壕，此处宽约30.1米，城壕底部深距地表在2米以上。其上部为文化层覆盖，城壕内堆积为淤土堆积，表明经过长期的积水过程。城壕外侧直接打破生土。在城墙内侧有内城壕，紧贴着城墙夯土，宽约12米，底部距地表深约2米以上。内城壕的堆积为淤土。

由于探杆长度的限制，探孔一般深度仅在2米左右，对于下部生土的深度难以判断，城墙与城壕修建之前的原始地貌等未敢作进一步推测。

2. 城墙的修建和修补

城墙为堆土分段夯筑而成。钻探和清理剖面出露的夯土质地紧密，有明显经过夯打的痕迹。由于所用土源的不同，各处夯土的土质和土色不尽相同，有的为较为纯净的黄褐色土夯打而成，有的则为灰土夯打而成，甚至使用砂土等加以夯打等。通过对城墙解剖，可知城墙夯层大多呈水平堆积，厚度不一，约在6～20厘米，一般厚度约10厘米。我们在南侧城墙上先后清理了三处剖面，以了解城墙的建造和修补情况。

剖面1，位于南侧城门西侧。剖面东西长约20米。剖面东段为数个晚期堆积所破坏，仅在中段下部和西端有夯土残存。城墙的修建采用分段夯筑的方式，在剖面东段可见明显的分段逐次修建的痕迹。夯土呈黄褐色土，含红色黏土颗粒、灰土块、黄土块、细砂等，部分含有水锈。夯层呈水平堆积，夯层厚约5～15厘米。夯土坚硬，质地紧密（图Ⅰ.2.7～Ⅰ.2.10；图版10：1）。

剖面2，位于南墙东段，位于东西向断崖的南侧，高近2米，北侧正对着2009年夏季在城内试掘的探沟。清理的剖面宽约1.4米，高约1.8米。此处堆积上下分为十层（图Ⅰ.2.11、Ⅰ.2.12；图版10：2）。根据北侧TG1和TG2的发掘，确定此剖面的第8～第10层堆积可以与探沟内内城城墙的夯土堆积相对应。表明此处城墙亦采用的夯筑法，且多为水平夯筑。剖面中，在城墙夯土上方的第7层为沙石层。值得注意的是，同样，在TG1和TG2内城墙夯土上方也有与之相似的一层沙石层。两者相距仅有2米左右，应为同一层堆积。剖面中的第4层为淤土堆积，表明在城址废弃后，此地曾经历过一次较大的洪水过程，才会淤积到内城地势如此高的位置。

剖面3，位于南城墙东段，北距钻探孔L62′为1.0米，东距L62′为2.5米。剖面长度为5.6米，高2米余。剖面东段被两个扰坑打破，西段近底也有一个小扰坑露头（此扰坑可能为从侧面破坏的残迹）。夯土分为十三层，夯层有的地方较为散乱，但普遍比较坚硬致密，以黄褐色和灰褐色夯土为主。值得注意的是，夯土中间夹有两个砂层，可能和历史上城墙的毁坏及后期的修补有关（图Ⅰ.2.13、Ⅰ.2.14；图版11：1）。

3. 城门情况

通过钻探，在内城城墙上发现两处城门遗迹，分别为南墙中部略偏西的水陆城门和北墙拐角处的水门。两者之间大体南北一线，与内城的总体方向大体一致。

南门

在南侧城墙中部，归姜村东南部有一宽约30米的缺口。它位于南北向公路下及西侧。在缺口处发现道路（L2）和城外水系进入城内的入水口，判断为南侧的城门遗迹（图Ⅰ.2.15；表Ⅰ.2.1）。其中L2位于东侧，入水口位于西侧，两者间隔约3米。

L2位于归姜村东南北向公路下，走向与公路一致，宽约10～13米。其中部、东部压在公路下。西缘距公路西边6米左右，东缘距公路东边1.2～1.5米左右。L2的走向为北略偏东，约19°。

L2的踩踏土（路土）开口于地表上0.35～1.25米之间，基本上为0.45米左右。厚为0.1～0.5米之间，集中在0.1～0.25米之间。铲探出的路土分层明显。

在L2西侧3米处发现一条南北向沟状遗迹（G1）。G1南接城壕，经L2西侧（东距公路约10米左右）进入城内。经钻探，G1从归姜村及村向西侧转了个60米的弯，由西北向转向东北向，最后经北城墙拐角处的水门流出城外。

G1在城墙附近宽约14～16米，西侧边缘较为齐整；但东侧与L2之间界限不很清晰。沟深度在2米以上。堆积为淤土（部分有砂层）。淤土在断崖以下为距地表深0.5米处开口，断崖以上为距地表深0.6～1.5米处开口，砂层约开口在1.3～1.6米处，内包含水锈。

内城的地形整体由南向北倾斜，此沟或上承南侧的曹家北侧山地来水，从归城东南部流入护城河；或是承接从归姜村西侧来的水系，从西向东注入护城河，再流经G1，穿越内城，又流入归城北部的鸦鹊河。

西北角水门

在北墙西段和西墙南段的拐角处发现一处缺口，城内水系G1由此流出城外，为一处水城门。水城门宽约14～17米。其南承G1，由北侧城墙上的缺口通向城外。G1在城门处深约1.2米左右，填土为以砂土为主的河相堆积。

值得注意的是，在出水口东侧的西墙北段的南端呈舌状伸出约10.5米，宽约4米。而隔沟相望的北墙西段位置也向南突出，或许为保护城墙而专门设置的。

4. 城墙内采集的陶片

2009年7月14日，为了对归城内城城墙的建筑年代做出系统分析，考古队做了一项特殊的辅助工作，即有选择性地采集城墙夯土中包含的陶片。由于这项工作会对城墙夯土造成局部损坏，我们尽量限制调查范围，仅在已有陶片暴露的部位以铲平面的方式进行采集。调查队先到和平村北断崖东段城墙裸露处铲出两个小剖面（地图Ⅰ.2.1），高约5～6米，获得少量陶片（标号1～11号）（图Ⅰ.2.16：1；表Ⅰ.2.2；图版12）。之后，调查队在和平村东台地（东城墙）和归姜东南地面站立城墙A（南城墙）以同样的方法进行采集。在城墙A北侧高8米处采得陶片1片（标号12号）。进而在城墙A南侧离地面高2～8米处采得陶片12片（标号13～24号）（图Ⅰ.2.16：2～6，8）。此处夯土质量很差，夯层混乱，并夹杂有大量灰土块，陶片也大多为东周时期。

第六节　小　　结

归城内城的选址是经过精心挑选的。其地处莱山北侧的一处高台地，东、西、北三面均有水系环绕，南侧与山前坡地相接，这样既易守难攻，又利于生活。

通过此次调查，对内城城墙有了较为全面的认识。特别是与1973年归城的早期调查相比，我们在以下几方面取得新的认识：

（1）确认了以往认为被鸦鹊河冲毁的东城墙，结合地下钻探工作，确定了北、西和南侧的地下留存城墙的范围等，复原内城的范围、四至等。过去认为归城内城为南北780米长，东西450米宽（李步青，林仙庭 1991：910）。我们现在确定归城内城的为南北长490米，东西宽525米（均由城墙中心测量）。

（2）在城墙外侧确认了城壕的位置、走向等，复原了完整的防御体系。

（3）在南北城墙上分别确认了一处城门遗迹，南侧为水陆城门，北侧为水城门。这一发现为探索内城的布局提供了线索，也为了解归城和外界的交通提供了信息。

（4）了解了城墙的构筑方式，并了解到其先后经过多次修整。这对我们了解归城的发展过程提供了新的线索。

（5）根据在南墙东段的试掘（详见上编第五章），确定城墙的修建年代在西周早期偏晚，一直延续使用到东周时期。并且，我们在城墙的夯土中发现砂层，这些砂层可能和城内的砂层相连。它们表明归城内城很可能曾经受到鸦鹊河水入侵，此后又加以修复。关于这点，需要结合城内的堆积情况来做全面考察（见上编第三章）。

参考文献

李步青，林仙庭，1991：山东黄县归城遗址的调查与发掘，考古，10：910-918.

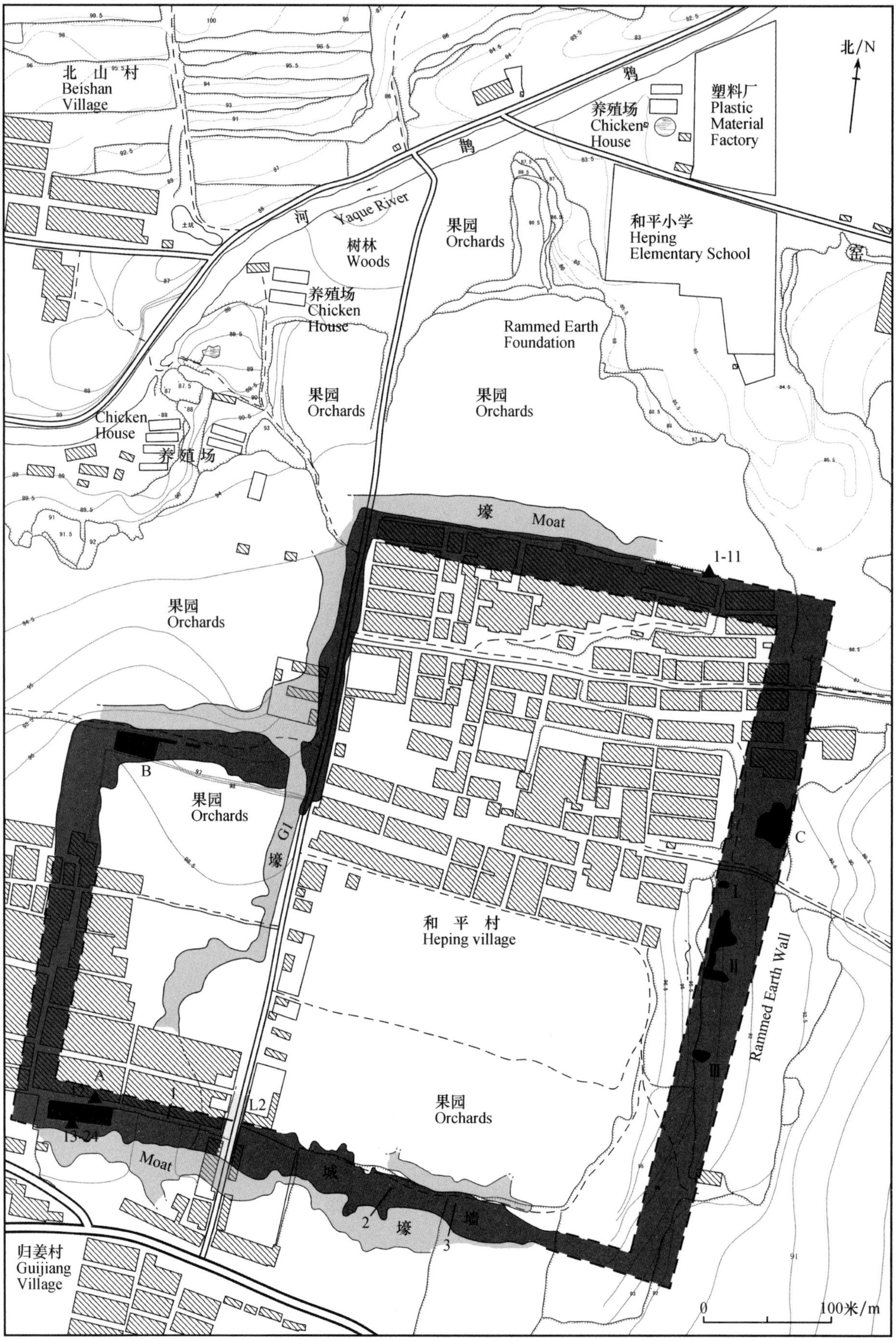

地图Ⅰ.2.1　内城城墙平面图

（A-B-C 地面上城墙；1-2-3 剖面；▲ 陶片采集地点；等高线数字自设：城墙B顶部为100）

Map Ⅰ.2.1　Inner city wall of Guicheng.

(A-B-C above-ground walls; 1-2-3 cross-sections; locations of sherds collected; elevation figures set by cartographer: the top of Wall Section B assigned the number 100)

图Ⅰ.2.1　在归姜村内钻探西城墙南段范围及走向（2007年6月27日）（北—南）
Figure Ⅰ.2.1　Coring for the remains of the western wall in Guijiang Village, June 27, 2007, looking N-S.

图Ⅰ.2.2　地面保留城墙A（西—东）
Figure Ⅰ.2.2　Above ground wall Section A, looking W-E.

图Ⅰ.2.3　地面保留城墙B（西—东）

Figure Ⅰ.2.3　Above ground wall Section B, looking W-E.

图Ⅰ.2.4　地面保留城墙C（东南—西北）

Figure Ⅰ.2.4　Above ground wall Section C, looking SE-NW.

图Ⅰ.2.5　北城墙断崖（西—东）
Figure Ⅰ.2.5　Cliff outside north wall, looking W-E.

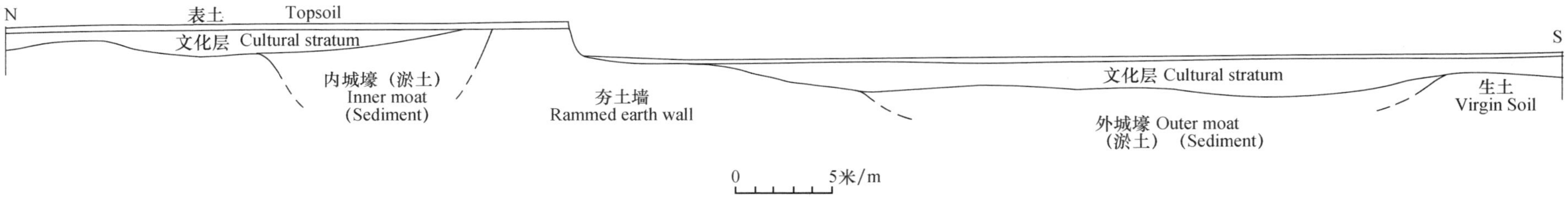

图Ⅰ.2.6　内城城墙与内外城壕之间关系复原示意图

Figure Ⅰ.2.6　Reconstruction of stratigraphic relationship between the south wall and the moats.

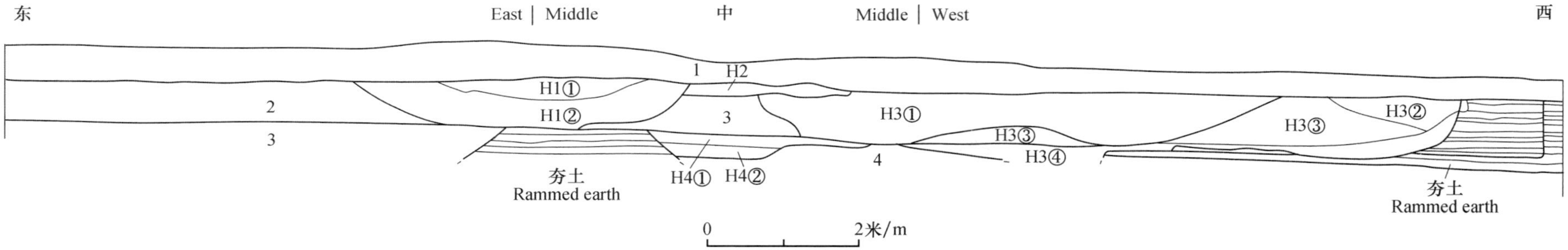

图Ⅰ.2.7　南城墙剖面1

Figure Ⅰ.2.7　Cross-section 1 on the south wall.

位于南侧城门西侧。剖面东西长约20米。

第1层：耕土层，厚30～50厘米，灰色，土质疏松，包含大量植物根系、塑料制品。层下：

H1①：灰土，包含少量红烧土颗粒；②：黑褐色土，包含黄土块、石块。

H2：灰土，含大量砂。

H3①：深灰褐色土，包含黄褐、黑色土块，质较疏松；②：深灰褐土，包含白色淤土块、水锈、砂、石块；③：黄褐色土，包含黑色土块、近现代红陶缸口沿，质疏松；④：淤土，细腻，西部分层好。

第2层：黄褐色土，含少量砂。层下：

H4①：灰褐土，包含淤土块；②：淤土。

第3层：浅灰褐色土，含砂。

第4层：与第3层近似。之下：

夯土：坚硬，质密，分层。黄褐色土，包含红黏土颗粒、灰土块、黄土块、砂，部分有水锈。每层厚5～15厘米。

Situated west of the city gate, measuring 20 m in length.

Stratum 1: Tilled earth, 30-50 cm thick, grey color, soft, large quantity of plant roots and plastic products. Below it:

Pit H1, stratum ①: Grey earth, red-burnt earth inclusions; ②: Blackish-tan earth containing clumps of loess and rocks.

Pit H2: Grey earth, large quantity of sand inclusion.

Pit H3①: Dark-grey tan earth, inclusions of yellowish-brown and black earth in clumps, soft and loose; ②: Dark-grey tan earth, inclusions of white sediment clumps, water-formed rust, sand, and stones; ③: Yellowish-brown earth, clumpy black earth inclusions, rim fragments of modern ceramic jars, loose formation; ④: Sediment, fine texture, peeling layers visible in western section.

Stratum 2: Yellow-brown earth, little sand inclusion. Below it:

Pit H4①: Greyish-brown earth, sediment inclusions; ②: Sediment.

Stratum 3: Light-grey tan earth with sand inclusions.

Stratum 4: Similar to Stratum ③. Below it:

Rammed earth: Firm, dense, and layered. Yellowish-brown earth containing red sticky burnt earth granules, grey earth clumps, sand, partially water-formed rust. Stratum thickness 5-15 cm.

图Ⅰ.2.8　剖面1东段照片
Figure Ⅰ.2.8　Image of Cross-section 1, eastern section.

图Ⅰ.2.9　剖面1中段照片
Figure Ⅰ.2.9　Image of Cross-section 1, middle section.

图Ⅰ.2.10　剖面1西段照片
Figure Ⅰ.2.10　Image of Cross-section 1, western section.

图Ⅰ.2.11　南城墙剖面2照片

Figure Ⅰ.2.11　Image of Cross-section 2.

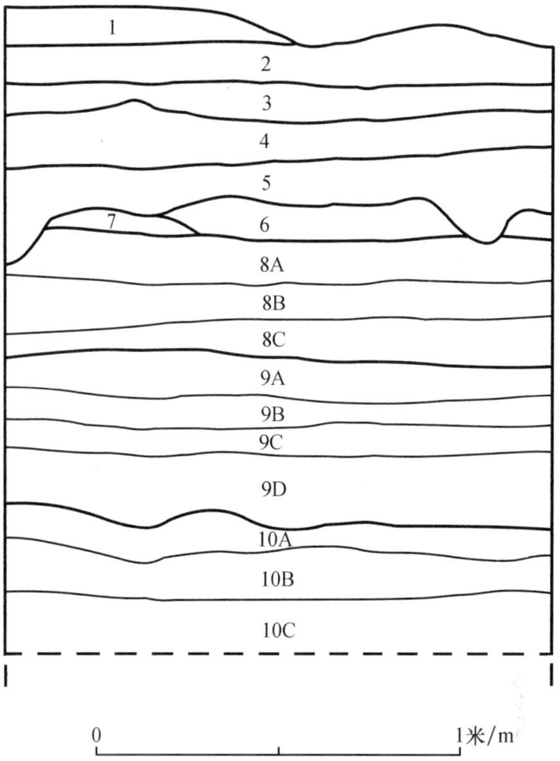

图Ⅰ.2.12　南城墙剖面2剖面图

Figure Ⅰ.2.12　South Wall Cross-section 2.

位于南墙东段，北侧正对着2009年夏季在城内试掘的探沟。清理的剖面宽约1.4米，高约1.8米。此处剖面堆积分为十层。

第1层，表土层，为沙土，厚约0～5厘米，大致呈水平堆积。

第2层，表土层，为浅灰色土，厚约5～10厘米，大致呈水平堆积。

第3层，文化层，灰土，厚约3～8厘米，大致呈水平堆积。

第4层，文化层，淤土，厚约5～10厘米，略呈由东向西倾斜分布。

第5层，文化层，灰土，厚约7～15厘米，堆积不甚平整。

第6层，文化层，灰黄土，厚约0～7厘米。堆积较平整。

第7层，沙石层，厚约0～4厘米，堆积较平整。

第8层，夯土层，黄褐色含砂夯土，厚约15～30厘米，大致呈水平堆积。其可分为三小夯层，每层厚度不一，约在3～10厘米左右。

第9层，夯土层，黄色夯土，厚约25～40厘米，大致呈水平堆积。其可分为四小夯层，每层厚度不一，约在3～12厘米左右。

第10层，夯土层，黄灰色夯土，厚度在40厘米以上，大致呈水平堆积。其暴露部分可分为三小夯层，大致呈水平堆积，每层厚度不一，约在3～20厘米。

其下部未清理。

Situated on the eastern section of the south wall, south of the test excavation trench of 2009. Exposed profile measures 1.4 m wide, and 1.8 m high. The cross ~ section consists of 10 layers:

Stratum 1: plowed topsoil, comprised of sandy soil, measuring 0 ~ 5 cm in depth, level accumulation.

Stratum 2: plowed soil, light grey ~ colored soil, 5 ~ 10 cm in depth, level accumulation.

Stratum 3: anthropogenic deposit, spodosol, 3 ~ 8 cm thick, level accumulation.

Stratum 4: anthropogenic deposit, sediment, 5 ~ 10 cm thick, east ~ west sloped accumulation.

Stratum 5: anthropogenic deposit, spodosol, 7 ~ 15 cm thick, uneven accumulation.

Stratum 6: anthropogenic deposit, yellowish ~ grey earth, 0 ~ 7 cm thick, level accumulation.

Stratum 7: sandy gravel layer, 0 ~ 4 cm thick, level accumulation.

Stratum 8: rammed earth layer, yellowish ~ brown with sandy inclusions, 15 ~ 30 cm thick, level accumulation. Can be subdivided into three different layers uneven in thickness, measuring between 3 ~ 10 cm.

Stratum 9: rammed earth layer, yellow earth, 25 ~ 40 cm thick, level accumulation. Can be subdivided into 4 layers, uneven in thickness, measuring between 3 ~ 12 cm.

Stratum 10: rammed earth layer, yellowish ~ grey colored soil, upwards of 40 cm thick, level accumulation. The exposed area can be subdivided into 3 layers, level accumulation and uneven thickness, measuring between 3 and 20 cm.

We were unable to analyze the layers beneath this one.

图Ⅰ.2.13　南城墙剖面3 照片

Figure Ⅰ.2.13　Image of Cross-section 3 on south wall.

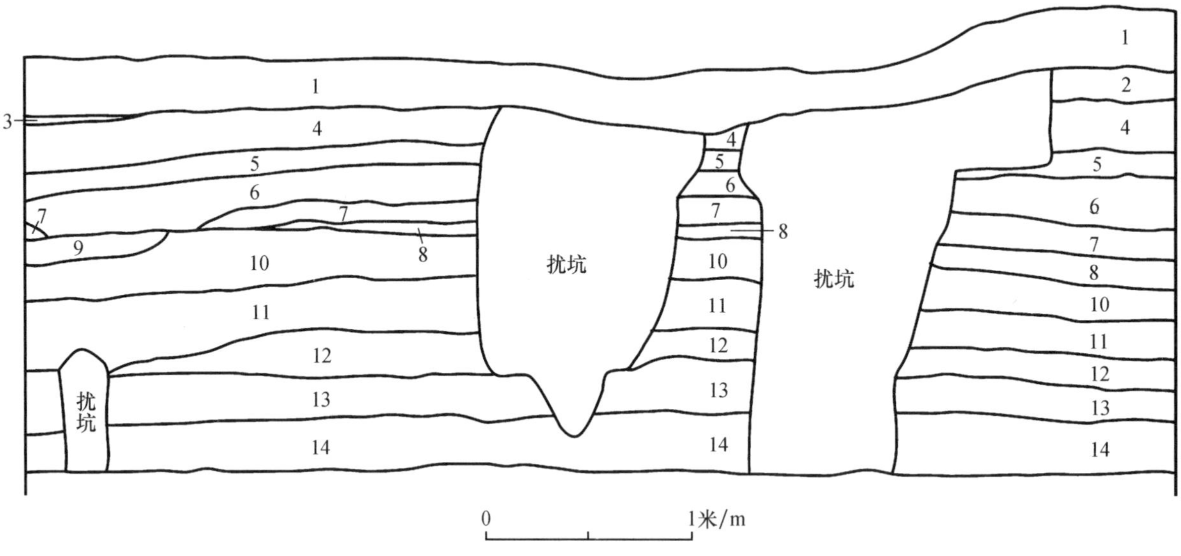

图Ⅰ.2.14　南城墙剖面3

Figure Ⅰ.2.14　Cross-section 3 on south wall.

第1层：表层土。

第2层：黄褐色夯土，夹红土块，较疏松。

第3层：砂层。

第4层：黄褐色夯土，夹灰土块、红土块，少量砂，致密。

第5层：褐色夯土，软致密，颗粒细，结构均匀。

第6层：黄褐色夯土，含黄土块，较多砂，软致密。

第7层：砂土层（西部砂较少）。

第8层：褐色夯土，含大量浅黄土粒。

第9层：黄褐色夯土，含大量细砂。

第10层：褐色夯土，含大量浅黄土粒，致密，单纯。

第11层：褐色夯土，较10色浅，致密。

第12层：灰褐色夯土，较多细砂，稍疏松。

第13层：灰褐夯土，含较多粗砂，少量黄土粒，致密。

第14层：深灰褐色土，含大量粗砂，大量黄土粒，空隙大。

其下部分未清理。

Stratum 1: Topsoil.

Stratum 2: Yellowish-brown rammed earth, mixed with red earth clumps, loose and soft.

Stratum 3: Sand layer.

Stratum 4: Yellowish-brown rammed earth, inclusions of grey earth and red earth clumps, a little sand, dense formation.

Stratum 5: Brown rammed earth, relatively dense granules of equal size.

Stratum 6: Yellowish-brown rammed earth, mixed with loess clumps, lots of sand, dense formation.

Stratum 7: Sand layer.

Stratum 8: Tan rammed earth, large quantity of loess granules.

Stratum 9: Yellowish-brown rammed earth, large quantity of fine sand.

Stratum 10: Tan rammed earth, large quantity of light loess granules, dense and homogeneous.

Stratum 11: Tan rammed earth, color lighter than stratum ⑩, dense.

Stratum 12: Greyish-tan rammed earth, lots of fine sand, loose.

Stratum 13: Greyish-tan rammed earth, lots of rough sand, a little loess granules, dense.

Stratum 14: Dark brown earth, lots of rough sand, lots of loess granules, large gaps.

Beneath this layer, not excavated.

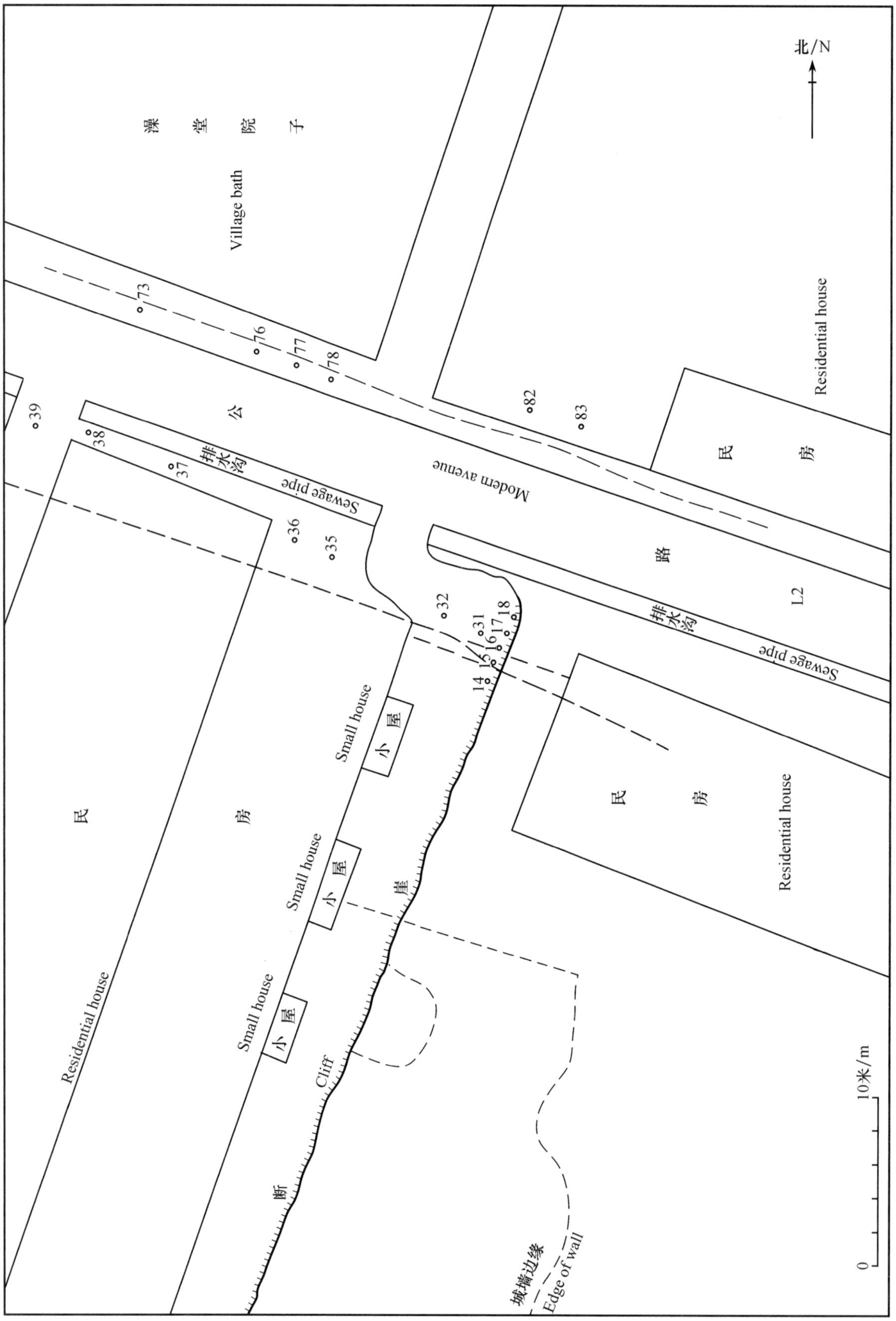

图Ⅰ.2.15　归城内城南城门钻探示意图

Figure Ⅰ.2.15　Coring map of the south gate of the inner city.

表Ⅰ.2.1　南城门和路（L2）典型探孔地层

Table Ⅰ.2.1　Typical coring holes in the south gate and road L2

探孔号 Number of core	地层序列 Order of strata	土样 Soil type	深度 Depth	地层描述 Description	备注 Note
78	a	表土 Topsoil	0 ~ 0.3 m		路北段边缘以内 Inside the road edge in the north section
	b	垫土 Packed soil	0.3 ~ 0.5 m		
	c	灰褐土 Greyish-brown earth	0.5 ~ 0.65 m		
	d	路土 Road earth	0.65 ~ 0.75 m		
	e	砂层 Sand	0.76 ~ 0.9 m		
	f	灰土 Grey	0.9 ~ 1.3 m	含灰烬 Inclusion of ash	
	g	淤土（灰） Sediment (grey)	1.3 ~ 2.1 m	含大量水锈 Inclusion of lots of water ~ formed rust	
	h	黄褐土 Yellow-brown earth	2.1 m ~	含砂 Sand inclusions	不底 Did not reach the bottom
38	a	表土 Topsoil	0 ~ 0.35 m		路北段西部 Western portion of road in the north section
	b	路土 Road earth	0.35 ~ 0.5 m	有踩踏面 Clear footpath layers	
37	a	表土 Topsoil	0 ~ 0.3 m		路北段西部 Western portion of road in the north section
		灰土 Grey earth	0.3 ~ 0.8 m	含灰烬，含砂 Inclusion of ash and sand	
	b	踩踏面 Clear footpath layers	0.8 ~ 0.9 m		
	c	黄褐土 Yellowish-brown earth	0.9 m ~	含砂 Sand inclusions	
31	a	表土 Topsoil	0 ~ 0.2 m		路南段西部 Western portion of road in the south section
	b	垫土 Packed soil	0.2 ~ 0.45 m		
	c	踩踏土 Footpath earth	0.45 ~ 0.7 m		
	d	黄褐土 Yellowish-brown earth	0.7 m ~	含砂 Sand inclusions	
82	a	表土 Topsoil	0 ~ 0.3 m		南段路东缘外 Outside eastern edge of road in the south section
	b	垫土 Packed soil	0.3 ~ 1.3 m		
	c	淤土 Sediment	1.3 ~ 1.5 m		
	d	夯土 Rammed earth	1.5 m ~		

续表

探孔号 Number of core	地层序列 Order of strata	土样 Soil type	深度 Depth	地层描述 Description	备注 Note
14	a	表土 Topsoil	0 ~ 0.2 m		南段路西缘外 Outside western edge of road in the south section
	b	淤土 Sediment	0.2 ~ 0.3 m		
	c	砂层 Sand layer	0.3 ~ 0.5 m		
	d	黄褐土 Yellowish-brown earth	0.5 m ~		

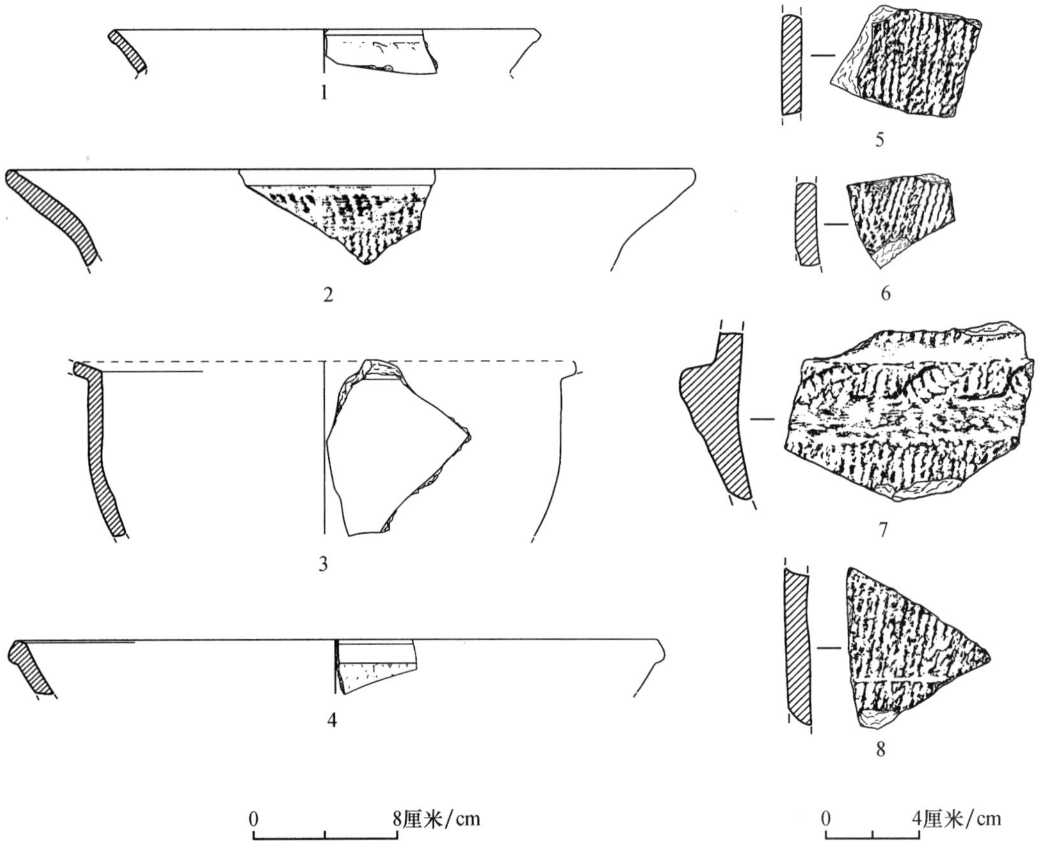

图Ⅰ.2.16　归城内城墙夯土中采集的陶片

1. 鬲（北城墙东段夯土：3）　2. 簋（南城墙南面：16）　3. 盆（南城墙南面夯土：17）　4. 簋口沿（南城墙南面夯土：21）　5. 腹片（南城墙南面夯土：14）　6. 腹片（南城墙南面夯土：22）　7. 瓮肩部（南城墙北面夯土：12）　8. 腹片（南城墙南面夯土：23）

Figure Ⅰ.2.16　Pottery sherds collected from the rammed earth of the inner city wall of Guicheng.

1. *Li* tripod (North wall–east section：3)　2. *Gui* tureen (South wall–south：16)　3. *Pen* basin (South wall–south：17)　4. *Gui* tureen (South wall–south：21)　5. Body sherd (South wall–south：14)　6. Body sherd (South wall–south：22)　7. *Weng* jar shoulder (South wall–north：12)　8. Body sherd (South wall–south：23)

表Ⅰ.2.2　内城城墙夯土中采集遗物登记表

Table Ⅰ.2.2　Pottery sherds collected from the rammed earth of the inner city wall of Guicheng

图号 Number on Fig. Ⅰ.2.16	标本号 Excavation number	器物名称 Artifact name	出土时间 Excavation date	位置 Location	所属类型 Types	尺寸（厘米）Size (cm)	特点描述 Description of features
1	北城墙东段夯土：3 North wall-east section：3	鬲口沿 *Li* tripod rim	2009-7-14	北城墙东段 North wall-east section		M: 24.0 H: 2.4	加云母灰褐陶，折沿方唇。Greyish-brown clay with mica inclusions. Folded rim with squared lip.
2	南城墙南面：16 South wall-south: 16	簋口沿 *Gui* tureen rim	2009-7-14	南城墙西段 South wall-west section	A、B	M: 37.8 H: 5.1	泥质灰陶，中绳纹圆唇，口沿下抹光。Grey fine clay with medium-sized cord impressions; rounded lip and burnished surface under rim.
3	南城墙南面夯土：17 South wall-south: 17	盆 *Pen* basin	2009-7-14	南城墙 South wall	A	M: 27.6 H: 9.1	夹砂红褐陶，折沿，口沿残，直腹，下腹斜收，素面。Reddish-brown, tempered with sand; folded rim, broken; straight belly slanting inward toward the base; plain surface.
4	南城墙南面夯土：21 South wall-south: 21	簋口沿 *Gui* tureen rim	2009-7-14	南城墙 South wall		M: 36 W: 3.0	泥质灰陶，圆唇，内外有一道凹槽，内壁磨光。Grey fine clay; rounded lip with incised groove on both interior and exterior; smooth, burnished interior surface.
5	南城墙南面夯土：14 South wall-south: 14	腹片 Body sherd	2009-7-14	南城墙 South wall		L: 6.3 W: 4.6	泥质灰陶，中绳纹。Grey fine clay, medium-sized cord impressions.
6	南城墙南面夯土：22 South wall-south: 22	腹片 Body sherd	2009-7-14	南城墙 South wall		L: 4.6 W: 3.9	泥质灰陶，中绳纹。Grey fine clay, medium-sized cord impressions.
7	南城墙北面夯土：12 South wall-north: 12	瓮肩部 *Weng* jar shoulder	2009-7-14	南城墙北 South wall-north		L: 10.29 W: 7.6	泥质灰陶。附加堆纹，粗绳纹，斜向捺印，内壁抹光。Grey fine clay bearing appliqué decoration, slanted coarse cord patterns; smooth, burnished interior surface.
8	南城墙南面夯土：23 South wall-south: 23	腹片 Body sherd	2009-7-14	南城墙 South wall		L: 6.2 W: 6.7	泥质灰陶，中绳纹。Grey fine clay, medium-sized cord impressions.

尺寸标志：L=长度；H=高度；W=宽度；M=口径。

Measurements: L=length; H=height; W=width; M=mouth diameter.

Chapter 2: Survey of the Inner City Wall

Tang Jinqiong, Han Hui, and Li Feng

Section 1: Topography

The inner city of Guicheng is situated on a plateau of elevated terrain at the center of the Guicheng city site. The plateau is bordered on the northwest by the modern course of the Yaque River, and on the east by the Yaque River's ancient riverbed. The two courses of this river converge on the north side of the plateau. The southwest side of the plateau connects to the foothills located west of Caojia Village. The surface of the plateau is relatively flat, sloping gently from south to north, and ends on the north side in a sheer precipice caused by the riverbed. The northern and southwestern parts of the inner city are currently occupied by Heping Village and Jiangjia Village (so-called Guijiang), respectively. Between the two villages runs a north-south oriented main road which transects the ancient inner city (Map Ⅰ.2.1) (Pls. 5-7).

Section 2: Survey Proceeding and Methodology

Defining the exact location of the inner city was the immediate concern in Guicheng archaeology. The work began on June 17, 2007, continued over the course of exactly thirty days, and was concluded on July 16, 2007. The coring team started at Wall Section A that still stands above the ground surface southeast of Guijiang Village (see below) (Pl. 8: 1). As the first step it confirmed the positions of the outer edge (south edge) of the underground wall mass as well as the western end (the southwest corner of the inner city). From there the team moved swiftly east to trace out the entire outer edge of the south wall and to demarcate the area of the defensive moat along the wall, reaching the east end on June 24 where both features disappear. The next day, June 25, the coring began the search for the north edge of the south wall, and finally completing the entire process of south wall survey on June 26. On June 27, the coring team began coring in the interior of Jiangjia Village, moving from south to north to trace out the southern section of the west wall (Fig. Ⅰ.2.1). Its eastern and western edges were located by coring along the streets running east-west through the village. By July 5, the coring team had crossed Wall Section B standing above the ground surface and protected by stone walls at the north end of the southern section of the western wall (Pl. 9). Coring then continued eastwards along the western section of the north wall. On July 8, the team turned north to core the northern section of the west wall and reached the northwest corner of the inner city of Guicheng on July 10. From July 11 to July 12 the coring team surveyed the north wall of the inner city and identified its southern and northern edges. In addition, the team set aside some time on July 20 to conduct a preliminary survey of the rammed earth platform located at the northern end of the plateau, north of the inner city (see Chapter 3, Section 5, 6: "The rammed earth foundations on the platform north of the inner city". On July 13, the team began to core the eastern wall of the inner city. The team first confirmed that the high platform east of Heping Village is a rammed earth construction, then it discovered three smaller portions of rammed earth foundations in the woods to the south. The team determined that they were all remaining parts of the east wall. By July 16, the coring of the inner city wall of Guicheng had been completed.

In the survey of the inner wall of Guicheng, we adopted the same methods of coring and recording that were used to core the architectural foundations of buildings in the interior of the city. That is, we combined general coring and focused coring to best capture the condition of the underground rammed earth. All coring points were exactly marked on the map, and soil strata as well as other phenomena revealed by the coring were clearly recorded in accordance with soil science standards. Thereafter, we analyzed the maps bearing the coring data to determine the directions of the subsequent coring work, until we had cored the full length of the inner city wall. As this method was used more systematically and maturely during coring of the inner city structures, we decided to discuss it in more detail in Chapter Three of this volume. With regard to the soil types encountered during coring, we systematically classified them and established standards for identifying the different types, laying the foundation for recording the coring points and comparing their strata. Chapter Three will also discuss the process by which the soil classification was established and the criteria for the different soil types (see Chapter 3, Section 3: "The Method of Coring Work").

Section 3: The Condition of the Inner City Walls

1) Overall status

The inner city is roughly square in shape, with a concave northwestern corner. Measuring from the center of the wall, the inner city wall is 490 m in length from north to south, and 525 m in width from east to west. The walls along the concave northwest corner measure 180 m north to south and

180 m east to west. In total, the wall covers 22,500 m^2 in surface area.

The north wall stretches along the cliff side located on the north of Heping Village, and it reaches the north-south oriented road lying west of Heping Village, where it then turns southward. The wall runs southward for 180 m before turning westward for 180 m, past the north-facing water-gate. Twenty meters to the west of Wall Section B, the wall turns southward again, past a north-south oriented alleyway in the interior of Guijiang Village, and reaching a point 20 m west of Wall Section A before finally turning eastward. Across Wall Section A, it runs eastward through the orchards south of Guijiang Village, crosses the main road, and follows the 2.5 m high precipice to the south of Heping Village, ending where the cliff ends. The southeast corner of the inner city wall is very poorly preserved, having been washed away by flood-waters in historical times. The south wall also bears evidence of having been previously damaged by flood-waters and then repaired. There is almost nothing left of the eastern wall, except for our discovery of Wall Section C (Pl. 8: 2), in addition to two small foundational sections that were rather deeply buried, already mentioned above. Through our survey, we confirmed that the remains of the eastern section of the north wall measure 235 m in length, the remains of the northern section of the west wall measure 180 m, the remains of the western section of the north wall measure 180 m, the southern section of the west wall measures 310 m, and the remains of the south wall measure 435 m (all measurements taken from the outer facades, see below). Based upon the better preserved remains of the west wall, we determined that the inner city is oriented 17° east of north (all azimuths magnetic).

The thickness of the city wall was difficult to determine due to the presence of collapsed portions discovered during survey. However, we also found that the relatively well-preserved northern section of the west wall generally measures 20 m thick, and widens to 35 m towards the western section of the north wall. We extrapolate from these measurements that they roughly reflect the original thickness of the inner city wall.

By exposing and studying portions along the precipice, we were able to establish that the walls were originally constructed by means of tamping earth section by section. The exposed cross-sections of the wall revealed that tamping was done in even, horizontal layers, although each layer of earth was not uniform in thickness, ranging between 6 cm and 20 cm, and averaging around 10 cm. It was found that the tamping had resulted in primarily yellowish-brown rammed earth, but sometimes also in rammed mixed spodosol containing pottery fragments. The coring revealed the existence of foundation trenches beneath the walls, and we found evidence of reconstruction and repairs to the wall.

We also found evidence of a moat running along the outside of the south, north, and west walls. This moat was not uniform in width, but ranged between 6 m to 32 m wide. It measured 4.8 m at its deepest point, with fill composed of sandy silt on the bottom and mostly spodosol on top. We also found evidence of a similar trench running along the inside face of the southern wall, measuring 7 m in width and 2 m at its deepest. The existence of these features both inside and outside the walls indicates to us that they were originally created by excavating the earth that was then used to repair and strengthen the walls themselves.

We discovered gates in two places. One of the gates is located in the western portion of the south wall and served as both a water and land transport gate. We speculate that the water flowed out of the city through a gap between the western section of the north wall and the northern section of the west wall. We discovered an ancient roadway as well as an ancient drainage channel penetrating the south wall, so we think that the gate on the north wall served as the exit for this drainage channel that flowed along a north-south axis through the inner city.

2) Condition of preservation of the walls

Due to natural erosion as well as anthropogenic destruction, most of the inner city wall is no longer visible on the surface. We were only able to discover three individual segments of above-ground remains. The first, hereafter above ground Wall Section A, is at the western end of the south wall; the second, hereafter above ground Wall Section B, is at the western end of the north wall; and above ground Wall Section C is the central portion of the east wall (Map Ⅰ.2.1). Both Sections A and B were previously identified during a survey of the region conducted by the Yantai Cultural Relics Bureau during the 1970s, while the location and preservation of section C was only confirmed during this most recent survey project.

Above-ground Wall Section A: This wall section is located southeast of Guijiang Village and comprises the western end of the inner city's south wall. It is situated 20 m from where the south and west walls form a corner. The remnant measures 50 m from east to west, 13 m wide, and 8 m high. This section of wall forms an imposing and steep precipice along the southern edge of Guijiang Village, though coring revealed that the wall originally measured more than 30 m in width here. Unfortunately, the northern side of the wall remnant is almost completely covered by modern residences; consequently, we were unable to determine its current or original dimensions. During the 1990s, the Longkou Municipal Museum erected stone barriers surrounding the remains of this wall in order to protect it from continued erosion as well as from the removal of earth by local residents. In 2008, a roof was additionally constructed over the remains in order to protect them from erosion by rainfall. This segment of wall has become a landmark within the Guicheng city site (Fig. Ⅰ.2.2; Pl. 8: 1).

Above-ground wall section B: This section is located north of Guijiang Village and forms the westernmost part of the original north wall of the inner city. It is 20 m from where the west and north walls would have met to form a corner. The remnant platform is shaped like a rectangle with a long protrusion on the eastern side. The surface of the remnant is relatively smooth and is surrounded by a stone retaining wall. It measures 65 m from east to west, from 2-16 m in width, and 2.5 m in height. There is a 10 m wide gap in the remnant towards the eastern end. We hypothesize that this gap was the result of late period damage. This section overlooks Wall Section A to its south, and their position roughly indicates the direction of the west wall (Fig. Ⅰ.2.3; Pl. 9).

Above-ground Wall Section C: The remains of this wall were discovered during the most recent survey. It is situated east of Heping Village, 170 m from the inner city wall's northeast corner. This remnant is uneven and irregular in shape, measuring 35 m from north to south, 27 m from east to west, and 3.5 m in height. It is composed of rammed earth. We first discovered this wall section during the 2005-2006 surface survey of the site, at the time believing it to be a free-standing rammed earth platform. In 2007, we began the field survey of the site and commenced coring of the "platform," which revealed that it was composed of rammed earth. Thereafter, we discovered three small underground sections of rammed earth in line with the platform, which confirmed for us that this platform was actually a part of the original inner city wall (Fig. Ⅰ.2.4; Pl. 8: 2).

The identification of these three segments of wall allowed us to determine the general course of the original inner city wall, and through coring we were then able to find the remains of underground sections of the wall.

Section 4: Section by Section Description of the Inner City Wall

Most of the inner city wall is no longer extant on the surface. Through systematic coring, we were able to determine the condition of wall segments preserved below ground, as well as to determine the location of the moats dug along the inner and outer facades of the wall. The inner city wall is almost a perfect square, except for the northwest corner, where the west and north walls meet to form a concave right angle as ┌┘. There is a gate in the south wall which divides it into eastern and western halves. For clarity we have divided the description of these well segments as follows: North Wall eastern section, West Wall northern section, North Wall western section, West Wall southern section, South Wall western section, South Wall eastern section, and East Wall.

1) North Wall eastern section

The North Wall eastern section is situated north of Heping Village, on a 3 m high precipice that runs along the northern edge of the village. On the eastern side of the segment is the ancient riverbed of Yaque River, bordered on the west by a north-south main road. The wall measures 235 m in length.

Most of the remains of the wall have been overlaid by the construction of a row of modern housing along the north edge of Heping Village. The northern side of the wall segment's below ground remains ends 3 m north, measured from the base of the precipice and running parallel to it. This precipice is lower in elevation towards the west and rises gradually towards the east as the surface of the ground slopes downwards towards the bank of the Yaque River where the cliff is 5 m high. Although the southern side of the wall remnant is also located directly beneath modern houses, we were able to take core samples from several points along the narrow village streets to determine that the remnant of the wall is 23-25 m wide. We also found the remains of rammed earth 1 m deep atop the cliff. We speculate that this might have resulted from later fills by local villagers. The rammed earth of the remains of this wall section is thick, on average measuring 1 m or more in thickness. The below ground remnants of rammed earth are 30 cm beneath the topsoil and roughly 2 m deep. The wall lies slightly south of an east-west axis and is oriented 100° east of north (Fig. Ⅰ.2.5).

We discovered the remains of an ancient moat running parallel to the remains of the wall segment outside the exterior facade. The moat is roughly the same length as the remains of the section, and measures between 7.7 m to 23.5 m wide, averaging around 20 m in width. It should be noted that the moat narrows very dramatically towards the eastern end. The deepest parts of the moat are all more than 2 m below the surface of the ground. The moat fill is predominantly spodosol with riverine sediments mixed in. Coring towards the eastern end revealed large amounts of sandy soil layers due to the changing course of the Yaque River; the eastern ends of both this moat and the wall having been damaged by the river.

There is not much space between the remnants of the wall and the moat. It is possible that this is because the rammed earth originally on top of the wall collapsed into the moat, though we were unable through coring to differentiate the original rammed earth from the dislocated rammed earth.

2) West Wall northern section

This section of wall lies beneath the north-south oriented main road that transects the western periphery of Heping Village. Its northern end connects with the northwest corner of the wall, and its southern end faces the western section of the northern wall across a gap. It lies along a north-south axis, and measures 180 m in length.

The remains of the wall section are located beneath the road. The edge of its western side is relatively straight and is likely the original edge of the wall. The section is oriented 17° east of north, measuring between 11.5 m and 20.5 m wide. There is a tongue-shaped protrusion from the southern end of the section that measures 10.5 m long and 4 m wide. It ends farther south than the western section of the north wall. Considering also the fact that it is very close to the remains of the water gate, we speculate that it might have been constructed to protect the wall from water damage.

The rammed earth layers begin from 0.4 m to 1 m below the surface of the ground, with an average depth of 1 m. Its thickness is uneven, with some portions measuring upwards of 2 m thick others only around 0.4 m thick.

We discovered evidence of a moat running along the exterior facade (the western face) of this wall section. The moat is parallel to the wall section down to its southern end, where it bends towards the southwest and links up with the moat running parallel to the western section of the north wall. This southern end is also connected with the water gate located on the north wall. The moat measures between 8 m and 24 m wide, with the widest part toward the north and narrowing as it proceeds southward. The deepest part of the moat measures upwards of 2 m in depth. The moat fill is composed of a mix of soil types, with spodosol, sand, and silt predominating, suggesting the various episodes of sediment build-up that the moat underwent over time.

3) North Wall western section

This wall section is situated north of Guiding Village and west of Heping Village. It is oriented on along an east-west axis and measures 180 m long. To its northwest is above-ground Wall Section B, 20 m across. To the west the below ground portion of the wall turns south and connects with the southern section of the west wall. Its eastern end faces the northern section of the west wall across a 15 m wide gap.

The upper surface of the wall remains is currently occupied by plowed fields, and its eastern side ends at a short drop-off. The wall section remains measure between 23 m and 35 m wide, with the eastern and western extremes wider than the middle. The wall lies along a southeast axis, and is oriented 100° east of north.

The rammed earth of the wall section can be found 0.3 m below the surface soil and is uneven in thickness, ranging from 1 m to 1.5 m; the thickest parts measuring upwards of 2 m.

We discovered a moat running along the exterior facade of the wall section (the northern facade). This moat arcs towards its eastern end and connects with the moat that runs along the outside of the west wall's north section. It measures roughly 15 m wide. The edges of the moat are virgin soil and form a very distinctive ditch-shaped hollow. The moat is predominantly filled with silt.

4) West Wall southern section

The southern section of the west wall lies within Guijiang Village as well as to its north. It follows a north-south axis and measures 310 m in length. The northern end is connected to the western section of the north wall, and its southern end is located 20 m from the western side of above ground Wall Section A. The terrain to the north of the wall section consists of plowed fields, and to its south lies Guijiang Village, situated atop its ruins. Because of this, many of our survey points were taken in the streets that traverse the village. These particular survey points provided us with the stratigraphic information to show that the remains of the wall are 35 m wide. The wall section lies along a roughly south by southwest axis and is oriented 195° east of north. We did not find evidence of a moat along the exterior facade of this section of wall, so how this section of wall was protected needs future work to clarify.

5) South Wall western section

This wall section, oriented east to west, is located south of Guijiang Village and measures 160 m in length. Its western end is 20 m from the western end of above ground Wall Section A and is connected to the southern end of the west wall. The eastern side stops at the gate opening of the south wall, through which a north-south road runs. It is separated from the eastern section of the south wall by a distance of 30 m.

This section is covered by a combination of modern residences as well as plowed fields. Above-ground Wall Section A is 20 m from its western end. The northern side of the wall section is covered by modern residences, so we were unable to confirm its dimensions. The southern side is irregular in shape, which may be a result of more recent damage, or it may be due to the collapse of the upper layers of rammed earth. Based on the rest of the remains, we speculate that the wall was originally from 25 m to 30 m wide. The rammed earth layers are beneath the topsoil, and measure upwards of 1 m in thickness throughout.

We found evidence of a moat that had been dug parallel to the exterior facade of the wall segment (the south wall). This moat directly abuts the wall. Its southern end is uneven in shape due to irregularities in width throughout, ranging between 10 m and 25 m. The southeastern end of the moat connects to an external waterway that measures 14 m wide. We speculate that this could have been the original channel from which water flowed into the moat. The moat fill is composed primarily of spodosol, and its deepest area measures upwards of 2 m.

6) South Wall eastern section

This wall section is situated east of Guijiang Village and south of Heping Village and is bordered on its western side by a main road running north-south and on its eastern side by the Yaque River's ancient river bed. It measures 240 m in length. The western side is 30 m across the north-south oriented road from the western section of the south wall. The wall lies along a southeast axis and is oriented 107° east of north.

This section is covered by some modern residences in its western part and by plowed fields in the east. Topographically, the southern side is 2.5 m above the surrounding terrain, which slopes toward the east. The remains of the wall section are located primarily on top of this precipice, although it is transected by it. The edges of the wall section are not even, likely due to recent damage or the collapse of upper layers of rammed earth. This has also resulted in the uneven width of the remains, which range between 25 m and 37 m. The remains are also not at a uniform depth below ground. Some parts are beneath layers of spodosol at a depth of 0.5 m, while others are directly beneath the plowed topsoil. The thickness of the remains is uneven, with the thickest parts measuring upwards of 2 m.

We discovered the remains of a moat running parallel to the exterior (southern facade) of this wall section. The wall section's width is uneven, while the moat measures more or less 30 m wide throughout and upwards of 2 m deep. The narrowest and shallowest end of the moat is its western section, which measures only 7 m across and 1.8 m deep. What is important to note is that this area is located directly in the middle of the remains of the south wall, centering on the axis of the inner city. Whether or not this has any particular meaning can only be determined with further study. The moat fill is composed primarily of spodosol, with small amounts of sandy layers mixed in.

We also found evidence of an interior trench dug to the north of this wall section. This interior trench seems to have been limited to the eastern section of the south wall. It directly abuts the northern face of the wall and measures 110 m from east to west, between 7 and 12 m wide, and upwards of 2 m in depth. The fill is comprised of spodosol and silt. On the northern side of the moat, two water channels were cut leading towards the inner city. What is important to note here is that these two channels intersect with two structural foundations and require further analysis.

7) East Wall

The remains of this wall section are located east and southeast of Heping Village, very close to the ancient bed of the Yaque River. Coring revealed a 2 m thick layer of sandy deposit overlying the underground remains of the wall, which we speculate is due to the changing course of the Yaque River in the past. It is likely that most of the east wall of the inner city was damaged by the river over time.

Through coring and survey we found that, of the original eastern inner city wall, only the above-ground Wall Section C as well as three small segments now buried below ground remain. The three below ground segments lie along a north-south axis and have been labeled East Wall Sections Ⅰ-Ⅲ. Together, these three sections measure 140 m in length.

East Wall Section Ⅰ: Situated 43 m south and slightly west of above-ground Wall Section C, this section is roughly elliptical in shape and measures 8.5 m from east to west and 5.5 m north to south. The western side of these remains is covered by a 0.3 m thick layer of topsoil, while its eastern side is covered by a 0.4 m thick yellow sandy layer. The rammed earth remains are uneven in thickness, measuring 2 m on the west and 0.4 m on the east.

East Wall Section Ⅱ: Located south of East Wall Section I at a distance of 17 m. The remains are uniform in shape and lie along a north-south axis measuring 56 m long, and between 5.2 m and 19 m wide. The rammed earth layers begin beneath a surface layer composed of sandy topsoil. They are uneven in thickness throughout, ranging from the 0.1 to upwards of 2 m thick. The entire section is oriented 14° east of north. The eastern end of the wall remnant has been very severely damaged and is misshapen as a result, while the western side is more straight, suggesting the original edge of the wall.

East Wall Section Ⅲ: This section is located south of East Wall Section Ⅱ at a distance of 54.5 m. The remnant of the wall is triangular in shape, measuring 14 m east-west and 9.5 m north-south. The rammed earth is found at a depth of 0.7 m to 1.1 m from surface level. Above it is a sandy layer. The rammed earth is uneven in thickness, with the thinnest parts measuring only 0.4 m, and the thickest parts reaching as deep as 1.8 m below the ground surface.

These three segments are aligned with the above-ground Wall Section C to the north along a north-south axis, and comprise part of the frame of the eastern wall. Based on the discoveries of these sections and considering also the positioning of the north and south walls, we were able to reconstruct the overall placement and dimensions of the original east wall. The original east wall should have measured 500 m north to south, from 30 to 40 m east to west, and was oriented 14° east of north.

We found a large number of sandy soil layers underlying the rammed earth remains of this wall, suggesting to us that this was the original ground on which the wall was constructed. We think that the wall was originally built in an old riverbed of the Yaque River.

We also found a small ditch running parallel to the inner facade of East Wall Section Ⅱ, measuring 40 m from north to south and between 14 to 18 m wide, with a depth of upwards of 4 m. Its eastern side directly abuts the rammed earth of the inner facade of the wall, while its western side seems to have been cut into the spodosol layer of the inner city. The fill of the trench is predominately sand and silt.

Section 5: Remains Related to the Eastern Wall of the Inner City

1) The inner city moats: an interpretation

As described above, the inner city wall of Guicheng seems to have had a moat surrounding it on the outside. Coring revealed remains of this moat running along the eastern section of the north wall, northern section of the west wall, western section of the north wall, and the south wall. While the moat is roughly parallel to the wall sections, it is not uniformly wide throughout, varying between 6 m and 32 m wide. The deepest part of the moat measures 4.8 m and is filled with a mix of sand and sediment. Due to the heavy damage sustained by the east wall, we were unable to confirm the original presence of a moat in that area. We also discovered a trench along the inner faces of the south and north walls,measuring 7 m wide and 2 m deep, on average. The presence of this trench indicates that earth was dug from both sides of the wall, likely in order to reconstruct, strengthen, or repair the walls during active use.

Below we discuss a typical stratigraphic profile selected to show the relationship between the moats and the walls as reconstructed from core samples (Fig. Ⅰ.2.6). The profile selected was located west of rammed earth Foundation 1 and east of the test trench dug in 2009. It lies largely along a southwest to northeast axis, oriented 17° east of north and is perpendicular to the wall. The reconstructed profile measures 80 m long and spans from the interior of the inner city to the exterior, including cross-sections of the eastern section of the south wall, the inner city trench, and the outer city moat. At the middle is a 2 m high precipice, above and below which should be the remains of the city wall. The wall measures 18.5 m in width length and is mostly preserved beneath the surface of the ground. The rammed earth on top of the precipice measures upwards of 2 m. Below the precipice, it only measures 1 m due to damage. The texture of the rammed earth is very hard and it is composed of a combination of yellow and grey soil.

We found a moat surrounding the wall along its outer face measuring 30.1 m wide, with a depth of upwards of 2 m. At the time, it was covered with a layer of recent anthropogenic sediment. Drilling down we found accumulated layers of silt, indicating that this area underwent a longer period of submersion under water. The outer edges of the moat intercut virgin soil. There was a second trench along the interior of the wall and directly abutting it that measured 12 m in width and upwards of 2 m in depth. It was entirely filled with silt.

Due to the limitations set by the length of our coring spades, our cores were only around 2 m deep, so we were not able to determine what lay below the silt or how deep the virgin soil was. Therefore, were not able to determine the original terrain in this area (Fig. Ⅰ.2.6).

2) Repair and reconstruction of the inner city wall

The walls are constructed of mounded and rammed earth. The texture of the earth that we removed during coring is hard, bearing distinct impressions from the ramming tool. Because the earth used in the wall's construction differed in origin, the color of the wall is not completely uniform. Some areas are composed of clean, yellowish-brown soil while other areas are composed of spodosol, and still other areas are composed predominantly of sand. According to the cross-section of the stratigraphic profile, the rammed earth layers of the wall are not uniform in thickness, but range from 6 cm to 20 cm, averaging around 10 cm. For the most part, the layers are even in accumulation and have a dense and hardened texture.

In order to understand the process of repair and reconstruction of the wall, we exposed three cross-sections on the south wall.

Cross-section 1, is situated to the west of the city gate, and measures 20 m in length. The eastern portion of the profile has been damaged, and rammed earth is accessible only at the bottom of the middle and western parts of the profile. The construction was done in sections, as evidenced by a distinctly clear demarcation line on the eastern side of the profile. The rammed earth layers are composed primarily of yellowish-brown soil, mixed with red granules, spodosol clumps, yellow soil clumps, and fine sand. Portions contain water-formed rust. The layers display even accumulation measuring from 5 cm to 15 cm thick. The texture is hard and finely packed (Fig. Ⅰ.2.7-Fig. Ⅰ.2.10).

Cross-section 2, is situated in the eastern part of the south wall, spans the southern side of the precipice from east to west, and the precipice measures 2 m in height. To its north is the very last test trench excavated during the summer season of 2009 (see Chapter 5). The exposed profile measures 1.4 m wide and 1.8 m high. There are ten layers making up the wall profile (Fig. Ⅰ.2.11-Fig. Ⅰ.2.12). Compared with the stratigraphic profiles of the excavation trenches TG1 and TG2 located to the north, we were able confirm that strata 8 through 10 were part of the rammed earth of the city wall. This indicates that this part of the wall was constructed using a very regular and standardized method of compacting earth. We found that stratum 7 posed above the rammed earth layers is composed of sand. It is important to note that a similar layer of sand was found in the upper portions of the rammed earth of the wall in TG1 and TG2. Since they are separated by only 2 m, it is clear that they belonged to the same stratum. Moreover, we found that stratum 4 was composed of silt, suggesting that after the city was abandoned, this area experienced a period of intense flooding, which accounts for the presence of silt within the inner city.

Cross-section 3: This cross-section is located in the eastern section of the south wall. Coring point L62' is located 1 m to the north, 2.5 m from the eastern end, and 3 m from the western end of the cross-section. The cross-section extends 5.6 m from west to east, and measures about 2 m in height. The eastern portion of the cross-section is intruded into by two modern pits, and another small modern pit is exposed at the bottom of its western portion. The rammed earth can be divided into thirteen layers, the depth of strata being irregular in some locations. In general, the rammed earth is firm and dense, and is mainly yellowish-brown or greyish-brown in color. It is worth noting that there are two sand layers sandwiched between the rammed earth strata, likely related to the historical damage suffered by the city wall (Fig. Ⅰ.2.13- Ⅰ.2.14).

3) Inner city gates

We were able to find the remains of two city gates through coring. These gates are the one used for both water and land transport located on the south wall slightly towards the west, and the water gate near the northern corner. These two gates lie along the same north-south axis, in parallel with the projected longitudinal axis of the inner city.

South gate

This gate is in the middle of the south wall and comprises a 30 m wide gap that is located southeast of the modern village of Guijiang. It is situated on the western side of a modern north-south oriented roadway. It was the discovery of an ancient roadway (L2) as well as an ancient waterway flowing into the city within this gap that first suggested to us that this was one of the gates into the ancient city site (Fig. Ⅰ.2.15; Table Ⅰ.2.1). Of these two transport routes, L2 is located towards the east while the waterway lies on the western side. They are separated from one another by 3 m.

Ancient roadway L2 lies on a north-south axis to the east of Guijiang Village, beneath the modern roadway; it measures between 10 m and 13 m in width. Its central and eastern portions are overlain by the modern roadway. The westernmost edge of the ancient roadway is 6 m from the edge of the modern road, while its easternmost edge is 1.2 m to 1.5 m from the modern road. L2 is largely oriented north-south, but skews slightly eastwards at 19° east of north.

The surface of L2 (the ancient surface of the road) is located at a depth of 0.35 m to 1.25 m beneath the modern ground surface, averaging approximately 0.45 m. It measures from 0.1 to 0.5 m thick, with an average thickness of 0.1 m to 0.25 m. Coring revealed that the ancient road consists of solid earth with multiple thin layers.

We also discovered the remains of an ancient drainage channel (hereafter G1) running south to north that had been dug 3 m west of the ancient roadway L2. The south end of G1 connected to the city moat, while its north end entered the city along the west side of L2. The modern roadway lies 10 m east of the channel. Through coring, it was revealed that G1 formed a clockwise loop within a space of 60 m between the north and south sides of Guijiang Village, ultimately flowing out of the inner city through the north wall.

The G1 drainage channel measures between 14 m and 16 m in width near the city wall, and its western edge was found to be quite regular; but in the east the boundary between it and L2 is not very clear. It measures upwards of 2 m deep throughout. The fill of the channel was composed of sediment, with some sandy layers mixed in. Below the precipice, the silt begins at roughly 0.5 m below the surface, while on top of the precipice it appears between 0.6 and 1.5 m deep. The sandy layer begins at a depth of between 1.3 m and 1.6 m and contains water-formed rust.

The overall terrain slopes gradually from south to north in this area, and there are two possible sources of water that flowed into this channel. The first might have flowed from the foothills north of Caojia Village to merge with the outer moat of the city. Alternatively, it originated in the river system to the west of Guijiang Village, flowing from west to east to merge with the city moat. From there it intersected the G1 channel, penetrated the inner city, and then flowed out the north gate into the Yaque River.

Northwest water gate

We discovered a gap in the wall at the corner where the western section of the north wall and the southern section of the west wall met, and drainage channel G1 was found to lead out of the inner city through this gap, suggesting to us that this gap was originally a water gate. It measures 14 m to 17 m wide. To its south is drainage channel G1, and on its north side is the exterior of the inner city. The G1 channel measures 1.2 m in depth as it passes through the gap, and the fill here is composed primarily of sand, which is consistent with riverine accumulation.

What is important to note here is that the wall section lying on the east side of the water gate, that is, the southern part of the northern section of the west wall, has an irregular tongue-shaped spit of rammed earth measuring 10.5 m in length and 4 m wide. This piece of rammed earth protrudes southwards and faces the western section of the north wall across the drainage ditch; it is possible that it was originally constructed in order to protect the wall in this area.

4) Pottery sherds collected from the rammed earth city wall

On July 14, 2009, the archaeological team conducted a special supplemental assignment in order to provide a reference for a systematic analysis of the dates of construction of the inner city wall of Guicheng; that is, to selectively collect pottery sherds from the rammed earth wall body. Because this work can cause partial damage to the rammed earth wall, we restricted our survey only to places where sherds were already exposed and used the method of cross-section to collect sherds. The survey team first arrived at the eastern end of the northern wall north of Heping Village and exposed two small cross-sections (Map Ⅰ.2.1), about 5 to 6 m above ground level, where we obtained a few sherds (nos. 1-11) (Fig. Ⅰ.2.16: 1; Table Ⅰ.2.2). Subsequently, the team moved on to investigate the platform to the east of Heping (eastern wall) and above ground Wall Section A southeast of Guijiang Village, using the same method. On the northern façade of Wall Section A we collected one sherd (no. 12). Thereafter, we collected twelve sherds (nos. 13-24) on the south face of Wall Section A, at a height of 2 to 8 m from the ground surface (Fig. Ⅰ.2.16: 2-6, 8). The rammed earth in this section is of inferior quality, with indistinct layers and mixed with large areas of spodosol. The sherds collected in this section are mainly of Eastern Zhou date.

Section 6: Conclusion

This most recent survey allowed us to understand the situation of the inner city wall in a more comprehensive way. Particularly in comparison to the early survey conducted in 1973, we have obtained the following new points of understanding:

(1) We confirmed the existence of the east wall that was previously thought to have been completely washed away by the flooding of the Yaque River. In addition, we identified and mapped the below ground remains of the north, west, and south wall and reconstructed the four edges of the inner city of Guicheng through intensive coring. The dimensions of the inner city of Guicheng were described in the past to have been 780 m on the north and south, and 450 m on the east and west (Li Buqing and Lin Xianting 1991: 910). Our new survey, however, determined that the inner city of Guicheng is 490 m long on the north and south, and 525 m wide on the east and west, all measured from the centers of the walls.

(2) We confirmed the presence and general course of the moat that surrounded the exterior of the inner city wall, thereby successfully reconstructing the inner city's defensive system.

(3) We confirmed the location of two gates on both the north and south walls, successfully identifying that the southern gate had been used for both land and water transport while the northern gate was primarily for water. This discovery provided important clues to help understand the inner city's organization and structure. It certainly also provided information to help understand Guicheng's relationship with the external world.

(4) We clarified the construction methods of the city wall and realized that the wall had undergone repair on multiple occasions in its history. This offered new clues to understand Guicheng's developmental process.

(5) Through the test excavation of the eastern part of the south wall (see Part Ⅰ, Chapter 5), we confirmed that the walls were in use beginning in the late phase of the early Western Zhou period and remained in use during the Eastern Zhou period. Moreover, we discovered layers of sand sandwiched between the rammed earth strata of the southern wall, and it is likely that these sand layers were connected with the sand layers that we identified during coring in the interior of the inner city. They are probably evidence of intrusion into the inner city by flooding of the Yaque River that flows along the east side of the inner city. But this needs to be evaluated further in conjunction with the deposits in the inner city (see Part Ⅰ, Chapter 3).

Finally, the inner city is situated on an elevated plateau on the north side of Mt. Lai and is surrounded on the east, west, and north sides by water, while its south side abuts the foothills of the mountain. This locates the city in a highly defensible position, making it an exceptionally good area for human habitation.

Reference

Li, Buqing 李步青 and Lin Xianting 林仙庭, 1991. “Shandong Huangxian Guicheng yizhi de diaocha yu fajue” 山东黄县归城遗址的调查与发掘 (Survey and excavation of the Guicheng site in Huangxian County, Shandong), *Kaogu* 考古, 10: 910-918.

(Translated by Glenda Chao)

第三章　内城及城外建筑基址的钻探

韩　辉

第一节　内城的外部环境与地形地貌

归城内城在遗址中部，外城的中北部，位于鸦鹊河两条支流间的一处高约5米的台地上。内城平面呈曲尺形，其西北侧内凹。以城墙中心计，内城南北长490米，东西宽525米。城墙西北处内凹部分南北长约180米，东西宽约180米。内城总面积约22.5万平方米。内城北侧与东南侧分别为和平村和姜家村（又称“归姜村”）所占压，仅余几处小片空白地带，无建筑物。在两村之间有一条南北向的乡间公路穿城而过。和平村北大街处原为东西向沟，把村落分为北村和南村的两村（图Ⅰ.3.1；图版5）。

内城地形特点是，南高北低，略有倾斜。所在台地现存地面整体较为平坦。归城姜家村南尚存城墙区域，即群众称为“点将台”处，是城内最高处。归姜村、归姜村北、和平村南部和和平村北端地势较高，比较平坦。和平村中北部，北大街南部有一块地势较高台地，1973年烟台市文管会发掘车马坑K1和M2就位于此处。台地东部为东城墙，西部地势稍低，勘探发现其晚期垫土较厚，厚1.0～2.0米左右，说明原地势应较低。和平村东北角、东部地势低洼，应为内城东部河流冲刷所致。内城所在高台地北端和东端高差明显，边缘为断崖。西北边缘较为平缓，呈阶梯状断崖向西北渐低。

和平村南部和归姜村北部、内城外部多为果园，种植苹果树和桃树。另外还种植有玉米和蔬菜等。土壤较为肥沃，黄土层厚，在古代也是适合农耕之地。外部环境优越，南部以莱山山脉为屏障，从莱山脚下到内城地势向北倾斜渐低，土壤肥沃。内城东部与外城墙所在丘岭地之间为河谷地，为东部鸦鹊河冲积形成；城内外高差约10米。河道紧临东城墙，并在历史上摆动冲刷，破坏了东城墙大部。内城北部台地延伸出北城墙外约190米，呈南宽北窄梯形，在北端突出一处南北方向台地，东西约60米，南北约100米，该处黄土层较厚，分布夯土遗存。城西北角由东南向西北倾斜，地表不平整，断崖较多，并且红砂岩较高，不适合建筑和农业活动。城东南部地势平坦，为归姜村村庄。总体来说内城地理环境、土壤、水文均较为理想，城外部呈南北狭长河谷地。适于筑城及生产生活（见图版6）。

第二节　内城以往的考古工作及此次钻探的目的

一、以往的考古工作

在内城范围内，自20世纪初以来不断有重要的遗物和遗迹出土和发现。1914年前后归城内出土铜钟4件和方鼎等，为春秋时期。1931年左右在和平村沟北出土铜钟5件，为春秋时期。50年代和平村南出土铜器30余件，仅余己侯鬲1件，铭文为："己侯鑄□姜□□子子孫孫永寶用"，为西周晚期。1965年5月和平村东出土鼎1件、矛1件，为西周晚期。1973年烟台文管会在原和平村西，现和平村中北部发掘M2和车马坑。墓葬出土素面陶鬲2件、绳纹鬲2件、簋2件、罐1件、盔1件，时代为西周中期。车马坑出土车马器，为春秋时期（李步青，林仙庭 1991：912～915）（见表Ⅱ.4.1）。2002年烟台博物馆在内城中北部台地进行抢救性发掘，发现有春秋时期房址等，为重要发现（详见本书下编第一章）。

在中美联合考古队于2007年在归城开始工作以前，1973年烟台地区文管会对归城城址的调查探测是最为系统的（李步青，林仙庭 1991：289，910～918）。这次探查基本确认了城址的基本形制、结构、年代和建造工艺等，为今后的工作提供了重要信息。

二、工作目的

归城遗址是胶东地区同时期规模最大，内涵最为丰富的一处城址，对这座城址的系统研究，不仅仅是对城址本身年代、性质、文化面貌等的认识，更是有助于对胶东地区青铜时期的考古文化，中原文明进入胶东地区的历史过程及其与本地文化的互动关系的认识。通过这些研究，进而能够对胶东地区的社会、历史进程有更为深入和全面的了解。归城遗址特别是在整个胶东地区古代文明和国家形成过程的探索中能够起到纲举目张的作用，具有重要的意义。它对于整个山东地区几十年来有关东夷古国的认识也有重大促进作用。

中美联合归城考古队在2007～2011年期间对内城进行了系统勘探和试掘，对外城进行了详细调查工作。此次在内城工作的基本目的有三个方面：①促进归城城址的研究，主要包括确认内城的年代、结构、布局，了解周代建筑群基址的结构、组织与性质；②搞清楚宫殿区文化堆积、文化内涵与保存状况，为今后的研究和保护提供翔实资料；③通过试掘验证此次考古勘探的成果，确认城墙和城内文化堆积的关系和年代问题。

第三节　内城钻探工作方法

一、内城调查钻探的编号系统及田野操作

在内城西南城墙地面部分（B）石砌护墙西南角设立基点，并以此基点在勘探区内设置分基点。工作中我们由东向西、由南向北方向对归城内城进行了全覆盖勘探。从西南城墙开始，由西向东勘探完南城墙和壕沟后，我们从2007年6、7月份调查确定的内城墙东南城墙内侧开始，对城内区域开始考古钻探。钻探队伍分三个小组，一组负责在探区内布孔，东西使用罗盘定正方向，南北沿果园田垄自然方向；和平村南田垄自然方向一般为18°，归姜村北为16°。使用基线绳和皮尺进行丈量，在待钻探的探孔上插上其编号。编号方式为从南往北按A ~ Z26个字母连续排列，西东采用阿拉伯数字编号。第一点基点编号为**A0**，其北向探孔为**B0**，**C0**，东向探孔编号为**A1**，**A2**。举例：姜家村南部果园探孔**C15**。从南向北字母使用一轮后，字母再从A开始，字母后面下方添加数字1、2等，由南向北递增，如**A_1**，**B_1**，**C_1**……**A_2**，**B_2**，**C_2**……举例：和平村果园北部探孔**$W_1$50**；这是和平村果园探区内的第W_1排第50行。在对遗迹进行加密勘探时，在字母和数字右上方使用“/”或“//”表示向北或向东递增。举例**$W_1{}'50'$**；这是**$W_1$50**东北方向的加孔。第二组为探工组，探工根据内城的勘探计划，严格按照考古田野工作规程，对探区内布好的探孔进行勘探。在对探孔钻探结束后，把本探孔情况报告给第三组记录人员，在米格纸图纸上按比例做好探孔标记，并在标记下记录下探孔内容。举例遗迹L1的一个探孔**$H_1{}'48$**内容：

0 ~ 0.3米，表土；

0.3 ~ 0.6米，灰土，松软；

0.6 ~ 0.7米，砂层，硬，分薄层；

0.7 ~ 0.75米，黄褐土踩踏面；

0.75 ~ 2.0米不到底，黄褐土，含砂，次生土。

以上是针对大面积的探区的工作方式。和平村内还有几片可勘探区域，对它们进行单独编号，如和平村内探区五，以村内130号民居对面的影壁墙西北角为基点，按正方向5米间距布孔。编号为自西南向东北，东西排按字母A、B、C、D……排列，南北列按数字1、2、3、4……排列。单独记录在一张米格纸之上。

二、建立归城土样标准

根据遗址内统一使用的系统性标准，来准确辨别田野中遇到不同种类的土壤，是田野调查及随后数据分析成功的关键。根据第一季度田野工作的经验，我们系统性地检查了钻探提取出的土样，并建立了归城内城土壤分类的标准。在随后的工作中我们仅对其进行了轻微的调整，

这些土壤分类标准为我们准确记录钻探所提取出的土样提供了基础。土壤分类标准的建立，同样也使归城考古中基于计算机的钻探数据管理成为可能（见第8章）。

在归城的土壤类型的分析中，我们首先考虑了以下三个方面：

a. 形成过程：辨别个别钻探点的土壤形成过程，能使我们同时了解土壤中反映的人类活动及自然环境。因为本研究项目的目的是探测地下建筑及地层，而形成过程提供了一个关键的途径，来识别反映这类具有地下遗迹特征的土壤类型。对可能的形成过程的考虑能使我们区分出以下的土壤类型：

灰土：一种质地松软的灰色土壤，因有机质的腐烂而形成，通常与人类文化遗存有关。灰土可视作人类活动存在的一个标识，尤其是对窖藏坑或垃圾坑的发现非常有帮助。

夯土：被夯打的土壤，作为古代建筑遗迹的一部分，如城墙、房屋或宫殿的地基。夯土可通过其坚硬、细密一致的特性及分层构造来识别。夯土的夯层可能清晰可辨，并可能整齐地相互剥离，有时甚至可能留存有夯土工具造成的轻微弯曲痕迹（夯窝）。

淤土：该土壤所在区域最初被水覆盖，以非常细的一致性及含有大量细砂为特点。

五花土或花土：由扰动和随后土壤的不同氧化过程所形成的堆积；这类土壤来自于地下（有时包括来自不同的自然或文化层的土壤）并且在短时间内被再次堆积。五花土的出现通常标志着墓葬类遗迹的存在。

踩踏土或踩踏面：一个坚实的层面通常有着一个平整的表面，因经常的、沉重的脚步踩踏或车辆交通碾压形成。这类土壤通常在人类举行活动的开阔区域形成。

路土：道路土是踩踏土的一种亚类，经长时间形成，通常包含大量沙子和小石子。在归城中，这类土壤通常代表以前道路的位置。

垫土：由现代人类有意或无意铺垫或压入某处的表土。例如，由平整现代建筑或道路地基所形成的土壤，通常将其归入到垫土这类。

耕土：现代农业表土，由最近翻耕或以前耕种形成。

生土：区域内由地质学因素形成的最深处的土壤，它保留了受人为或水文作用前存在的特征。通常特定点的钻探以发现生土而终止，生土的出现表明在其深度以下的土壤没有受到人类活动的影响。辨别生土的特点是开展遗址特定区域内调查工作的基础之一，因为整个归城内城的生土其特征有若干差异。

b. 颜色：土样可由颜色进一步划分。当无法直接判断某种土样形成过程时，通过颜色划分显得尤其重要。在这种情况下，颜色作为分类的首要标准。最典型的例子是被称为“黄褐土”的一种土壤，其在归城中的分布非常广泛，这类土壤受过人类改造但并不与特定的建筑具有关联性。单一颜色术语（黄色、灰色、褐色）和复合颜色术语（黄褐色、红褐色等）均被采用。这些术语都可以用程度副词来修饰（如浅褐色、深灰色）。还有一些土壤（如灰土和五花土）虽然按照中国考古学的惯例使用颜色术语来表示，但是我们要根据它们形成过程来解释它的存在。这在上文“形成过程”一节中已提及。

c. 包含物：许多土样含有与了解遗址形成过程相关的额外包含物。这些额外的包含物均被记录了所在的深度，以便于进一步划分地层。举例来说，最常见的包含物颗粒有红烧土块、水锈、草木灰。土样中还经常发现有其他包含物如鹅卵石、陶片、骨头碎片等（表Ⅰ.8.1）。

d. 结持性： 这是指构成土样中的土壤和其他物质的基本质地。结持性通常作为在一定深度下结束钻探的土壤的物理状态或因素的指标。这种情况经常发生在当技术人员遇到沙土时，因沙土太过疏松而无法从探孔中取出；又比如因岩石太大而阻碍了探铲的继续使用。这类情况也包括淤泥或基岩，这些都迫使技术人员结束钻探并放弃该钻探点。

经过仔细考虑上述情况及其对钻探项目目标的重要性，即为了了解归城遗址的组织及其堆积历史，我们建立了一个分类系统。这个系统首先将归城所见的各种土壤类型划分为两个大类——现象土（phenomenon soil）和地层土（stratum soil）——然后将这两大类土壤进一步划分出更具体的土壤类型（表Ⅰ.3.1）。

现象土： 现象土壤由人类活动形成，并且通常表明地下建筑或一般遗存。典型的现象土壤有灰土、夯土、路土等。

地层土： 地层土壤通常代表地层，无论是由自然还是由人类作用而形成的，与地下建筑或一般遗迹并无特别关联。典型的地层土壤有耕土、黄褐土、生土等。

我们培训了钻探组成员去识别不同类型的土壤，并且尽可能准确地记录其所在的地层。在比较分析整个归城内城的自然和文化层堆积时，我们使用了该土壤分类系统。正如本书中第8章所述那样，该系统也为计算机分析、管理钻探数据提供了基础。

三、钻探方法

1. 布探区

勘探以归城城址西南地面现存城墙西南角为基点，依据实际城址布局和村庄占压，道路分割情况，建立虚拟分区，将内城全覆盖，对所有可探空白区域进行勘探。探区进行编号，以探区为单位开展勘探。

探区分别为和平村南果园南区（Ⅰ）、和平村南果园北区（Ⅱ），归姜北部果园北区（Ⅲ）、归姜北部果园南区（Ⅳ），以及和平村内六片空地区域（村中北部台地[1]，和平村养猪场内[2]，养殖场西部的玉米地[3]，内城西北区域公路东停车场[4]，南城门东北和平村澡堂[5]，考古队驻地院内[6]）（图Ⅰ.3.1）。

2. 普探和重点勘探相结合方法

对归城内和平村南部和归姜村北部使用普探和重点勘探相结合的方法。普探使用罗盘定正东西方向，南北间距5米，东西基本采用等距5米，再依据实际果园田垄间距调整。编号采用上述方式：即从南往北按A～Z字母连续数东西走向的排号，东西采用阿拉伯数字来数南北走向的行数。重点勘探用于对普遍勘探已发现的遗迹进行加密钻探，一般为2米间距。排孔及加密孔发现遗迹现象进行标记，再采用单线追踪遗迹两边对掐的方式加密勘探确定形状。在进行重点钻探时，对一个基址或其他建筑单位有关的较密集钻孔又采取了用阿拉伯数字单独连续编号的办法，如夯土基址1的1～162号。典型的遗迹和探孔拍照记录，采集土样和钻探出的遗物。

3. 村内勘探方法

我们对于和平村内种植农作物的空地、村内厂房等空地，采用5米×5米距离布孔，并依植被、地表情况灵活处理。首先寻找一个基点，依正方向或院墙内房屋墙壁自然方向布孔，布孔的编号系统与上述编号方法一致。对于村内街道的勘探，我们依街道自然方向，在街道边缘能够勘探透垫土层的地方勘探，并且还要注意避开街道下埋藏的水管，尽量以5米×5米距离勘探。

4. 记录

在勘探中采用米格图纸对排孔和加密孔进行详细记录，图纸采用1：100比例。单项遗迹图采用1：50记录在米格纸图纸上。编号从南向北采用英文字母，由西向东采用阿拉伯数字。根据个别探孔地层绘制勘探遗迹柱状剖面图，比例1:100。对于村内六处独立探区及和平村内三条街道单独做一套图纸，单独编号，比例为1:100。对遗迹按发现顺序进行编号，如“3号夯土基址”。钻探完毕后，撰写遗迹钻探调查记录。采集探孔出土遗物，制作采集标本统计表。

5. 测绘

使用全站仪测绘，绘制归城城址内城平面图（图Ⅰ.3.1）。比例为1:1000。设置基点为和平村西归城城址保护碑处。

为了绘制内城地形图，我们在和平村西保护碑的上部设立基点，并设置内城标高100米。使用全站仪，并根据相对高度，我们绘制出一张归城内城地形图（图Ⅰ.8.5），比例为1:1000。

第四节　内城地层堆积概况

归城内城勘探区域为和平村南部和归姜村北部果园，以及和平村内五片空地区域（见上第三节）。村内占压部分因为探孔较少，只能依据少量的探孔进行推测地层堆积。

从勘探情况看，内城的东南部、西南部地势高且平缓，是建筑基址密集区域。文化堆积厚1.0～1.7米。内城西南部，归姜村北部（Ⅲ～Ⅳ区）文化堆积层，即灰土层，厚约1.0米，之下多为砂岩或黄褐土。夯土基址开口于灰土层下，分布于归姜村北部、内城西城内，打破基岩或黄褐生土。地势向北渐低，砂岩距地表越浅。砂岩深度一般距地表1.1～1.5米，大部分区域被灰坑等遗迹叠压。在该区域，灰坑等遗迹在西北城墙南部较多，最厚至1.7米，打破夯土基址。部分夯土基址下又有早期灰坑等遗迹。

内城东南部，和平村南部（Ⅰ～Ⅱ区）地层基本一致，表土下为文化堆积层，该层下分布有夯土基址和灰坑等遗迹。夯土基址分布于和平村西南部，归城内城的南部。内城的南部文化堆积厚约0.5～1.1米，之下为黄褐淤土，部分淤土分布有砂层。生土为黄褐黏土。

内城南端，城门东北部灰土堆积厚，勘探出土陶片多。灰土内包含大量灰烬、陶器残片多，应为居住址。较多灰坑深至2.0米不底。

归城中北部基本为和平村占压、大部地层堆积简单，较薄。较多地方垫土下即为黄褐土。文化堆积层（灰土）稍薄，晚期垫土较厚，灰土厚约0.8米。生土为黄褐生土。内城北部城墙内侧偏西区域灰土较厚，可能有居住址存在。

和平村中北部有一处台地，该台地与西部、北部、东部高差为2～3米（探区[1]）。此次勘探十五号夯土基址和1972年发掘车马坑和M2位于此处。文化堆积厚为0.7～1.5米，勘探发现有灰坑、墓葬，并推测此处分布有制骨遗址。在距地表深1.3～2米灰土内勘探出西周、东周陶片。

内城西北部，台地的西部，地势稍低，晚期垫土较厚，为0.4到1.2米。之下文化堆积较薄，厚0.3～0.5米。部分探孔0.9～1.4米为砂岩。在南北公路东停车场（探区[4]）院墙东北角探孔M10处发现一处夯土，开口于0.7米，黄褐色，之下1.0米为砂层，质硬；1.2米为生土。这块夯土及其下的地层结构类似L1、L2的路土堆积。勘探出土陶片为东周时期。

内城东部，和平村东南部，城墙内侧文化堆积较厚，开口于0.3～1.0米，深至2.4米不到底。推测为居住址。在东西向大街探孔22勘探出墓葬，0.9米见花土，深至3.3米不到底。说明该区域有零星墓葬分布。

第五节　内城建筑基址

一、分区总论

通过钻探，在内城里发现水系、夯土基址和道路等遗迹多处，对内城的布局有了初步的认识。在内城中部略偏西处发现一条水沟（G1）。G1南侧起自城门西侧的入水口，向北呈半圆形，绕经归姜村西部，又回到两村之间的公路西侧，然后顺着公路向北直行，最后由北墙中部折角处的出水口流出城外。G1南北总长约340米，深度在1.5米以上。G1将内城分成了东西两个部分。

城内钻探发现17座大小不一的夯土基址（图Ⅰ.3.2）。小型基址或为东西向长方形，但较大型的基址多为南北向长方（条）形。以沟G1为界，位于西区内者称“西组建筑群”；位于东区内的称“东组建筑群”。

西组建筑基址群共有7座建筑基址，包括8、9、10、11、12、13、14号夯土基址。其中9号夯土是内城中最大的一座建筑。9号基址平面大致呈南北向的长方形，南北长约93米，东西最宽处约23米，面积约为1750平方米。9号夯土基址的东、西、南三面分布着其他6座较小的建筑基址。

东组建筑基址群共发现9座建筑基址，包括1、2、3、4、5、6、7、15、16、17号夯土基址。这些基址以城中部发现的一条道路（L1）为中心分布。L1坐落在东西城墙之间的中轴线上，钻探出的长度约68米，走向为18°，与内城的走向大体一致。以L1为中心东西对称分布着2号、3号夯土基址。3号基址为东组基址中最大的一座，平面大致呈长方形，南北长56米。其西南角向西凸出，宽约11米。3号夯土基址南沿外铺有一层曲尺形石块面，石块面以东，以南则为一大片踩踏面所围绕。踩踏面北端与L1相接，向南则一直延伸到城墙，深度与石块面一致。石块面和踩踏面很可能是与3号建筑有关的一个宽广的活动面，是否具有“广场”的性质还需进一步工作的确认。

二、城内水沟（G1）

G1位于内城中部偏西，和平村西面公路西侧。据勘探，G1于内城内南起归姜村东南部，穿越归姜村和北部果园，自北城墙拐折处出城，为北出水口；南出水口则在南城门和L2西侧。G1基本呈南北长条形，北部较直，方向约为北偏东15°。南部则在进入入水口后略向西弯曲，并于14号夯土基址东15米处转而向东，再于16号基址北侧北折，直通北城墙的出水口。G1贯穿内城南北。西侧为10、11号等夯土基址；东侧为16、17号等夯土基址。G1与通往南城门的路土L2处在同一个地平面上。

现已勘探出G1南北长约260米，但南部因归姜东部民房占压未勘探， G1南北总长达340米。东西宽达10～35米，最宽处在归姜村北小路南面断崖附近，最宽可达35米，形成水湾，总面积为3700平方米。

沟内地层堆积为灰土和砂层，之下为生土或基岩（典型探孔位置见图Ⅰ.3.1；地层见表Ⅰ.3.2）。灰土可分两层，上层灰土开口于0.3米处；下层灰土包含水锈，开口于0.9～1.2米处。砂层开口于1.2～1.7米处；其南部靠近归姜村小路处变浅，开口于0.5～0.8米。砂层多厚为0.4～0.7米。生土距地表1.4～2.0米。基岩深度为0.8～1.6米。部分区域砂层下有黄褐土（含砂），之下再为生土或基岩。这种情况下黄褐土（含砂）多开口于1.1～2.4米，生土或基岩深度为1.3～2.6米。在归姜村村北小路断崖处，砂层开口于0.3～0.7米，其下为石块。G1砂层总体厚度为0.1～1.0米。个别地方砂层上面还有一层黄褐土（含砂）。

三、东组建筑基址

东组建筑基址位于G1东部，和平村南部，以L1为中心分布，共9座。分别介绍如下：

路土一（L1）：坐落在东西城墙之间的中轴线上，钻探出的部分位于和平村南部，长度约68米，宽约10.5米，面积约1200平方米。南部通向城墙，北部在四号夯土基址东部消失，应被晚期灰坑破坏。L1开口深0.7～0.9米，道路上发现成层的砂石和踩踏面，厚约3～20厘米。L1走向为18°，与内城的走向大体一致（图Ⅰ.3.3；表Ⅰ.3.3）。

一号夯土基址：位于内城东南部，其西北部为二号夯土基址。南部为南城墙和城墙内侧内壕沟。夯土基址残存形状基本呈长方形，西北角和西南角向外突出，东南角向南延伸至南城墙，与南城墙相连通。主体南北残长约为17.25米，东西残宽约17.9米。方向为18°。该处地势较高，文化堆积较厚，为灰土，一般厚0.3～0.9米。在文化层下面为夯土，黄褐色，部分为淤土夯成。夯土深0.6～1.2米，厚约0.3～1.2米，集中在0.5～0.7米。夯土大多位于淤土之上，少部分为砂层。夯土基址南端与城墙相连，且打破内壕沟，可能与城墙一体构成了南城墙的防御设施（图Ⅰ.3.4；表Ⅰ.3.4）。

二号夯土基址：位于内城东南部，和平村南苹果园内，其东南为一号夯土基址。二号夯土基址北距和平村民房110米，西距公路150米。紧邻和平村南两块苹果园之间的乡村小路。夯土基址地下部分被破坏较为严重，残存形状基本呈长方形，东南角和西北角各向外突出。基址夯土被晚期遗迹破坏严重，西部被分成的两个区域之间，可能存在着一个水沟，打破夯土基址。夯土东西残宽约32米。南北残长约38米。方向约为北偏东18°。该处文化堆积较厚，约1米，灰土。有灰坑直接打破夯土。文化层下为夯土，夯土距地表深度略有不同，最大范围在0.4～1.4米，集中在0.6～0.8米，厚度为0.2～1.4米。夯土为黄褐色。东南角有墓葬打破夯土（图Ⅰ.3.5；表Ⅰ.3.5）。

三号夯土基址：位于内城南部，和平村乡间路南西部，西边紧邻和平村西公路东侧的民房，西北为考古队驻地。南距城墙50米，北距四号夯土基址约7米。并且与二号夯土基址隔L1轴对称。该基址平面大致呈长方形，南北长56米，东西宽约21～31米。其西南角向西凸出，宽约11米。方向约为18°。该处文化堆积较薄，厚约0.3米。文化堆积层下为夯土。大部分为一层夯土，黄褐夯土或灰色夯土，灰色夯土见于11个探孔，黄褐夯土见于40个探孔。夯土开口在0.4～1.4米，集中在0.5～0.8米，厚0.2～0.9米，集中在0.4～0.7米。部分区域有两层夯土：第一层，灰夯土；第二层，黄褐夯土。灰夯开口于0.4～0.6米，厚0.3～0.5米，黄褐夯开口于0.7～1.0米，厚为0.3～0.7米。夯土一般厚0.6～1.1米（探孔89夯土深至2.0米多）。夯土之下黄褐生土开口为0.9～1.6米。另外，在探孔26、27、28夯土下有一层路土，距地表深1.0到1.4米。夯土基址东南角处，在夯土之下0.8米处铺有石块（图Ⅰ.3.6；表Ⅰ.3.6）。

基址南沿外铺有一层曲尺形石块面，西部被房屋占压，不能钻探。目前北部宽15米，南部宽27米。石块距地表深0.6～1.8米，集中在1.2～1.5米。

石块面东、南部则为一大片踩踏面所围绕。踩踏面北端与L1相接，向南则一直延伸到南城墙。长约54米，宽约8米。典型地层堆积为表土、砂层（含灰土）、踩踏土（含砂）、黄褐土（从上往下）。部分踩踏土还经过夯打。石块面和踩踏面深度基本一致，均开口于灰土下，深度为0.6～0.9米。可能是与三号建筑有关的一个宽广的活动面，是否具有“广场”的性质还需进一步工作的确认（图Ⅰ.3.7；表Ⅰ.3.7）。

四号夯土基址：位于内城南部，和平村南两块苹果园之间的乡村小路北。四号夯土基址距北侧和平村75米，西距公路42米。南侧为三号夯土基址。平面形状基本呈长方形，长约13米，最宽处10.5米，面积约136.5平方米。方向为18°。根据钻探所得，可知夯土基址西、北面被破坏，东面基本完整，残存形状基本呈长方形。三号夯土和北部的五号夯土之间被淤土坑打破，不知是否为一处遗迹。该处文化堆积层较薄，有较多灰坑打破夯土。夯土开口约0.3～0.9米、厚约0.3～1.1米，黄褐生土开口约0.7～1.6米（图Ⅰ.3.8；表Ⅰ.3.8）。

五号夯土基址：位于和平村南，路北苹果园，北距和平村48米，西距公路47米。东距L1约15米，南部为四号夯土基址。残存形状为不规则形，北部为东西向长方形，长约22米，宽约14米。南部为南北向长方形，方向约为18°；南北约13米，东西约10米。总面积约438平方米。夯土西北部、东南部和南面的四号夯土基址交界处被晚期遗迹打破。该处文化堆积较薄。下部为夯土，开口在0.3～0.9米，为灰夯土和黄褐夯土，厚0.2～1.2米。一些夯土深至2米不底。应为当时把该地势低洼处，先垫平夯打而成。夯土之下存在早期文化堆积和灰坑等遗迹 (图Ⅰ.3.9；表Ⅰ.3.9）。

六号夯土基址：位于内城南部，和平村南两片苹果园之间的乡村小路之北，西距公路22.5米。在四号夯土基址的西侧。东西残宽约13.5米，南北残长约21.5米，基本呈南北长方形，东北角有缺口，应为被破坏所致，残留面积为209.5平方米。方向约为北偏东18°。该处文化堆积厚约0.5米，之下为夯土，多数为黄褐夯，少数灰夯，开口于0.4～0.7米，厚约0.2～0.8米；黄褐生土开口深0.7～1.4米。在勘探中发现夯土基址东北部灰土层、褐土层里有大量水锈，基址东北豁口处灰土下为淤土，可能是水沟或水塘，打破六号夯土基址（图Ⅰ.3.10；表Ⅰ.3.10）。

七号夯土基址：位于内城南部，和平村南两块苹果园之间的乡村小路之北，并紧邻小路。西距和平村民房1米，距公路20米；东距六号夯土基址2.5米。残存形状基本呈长方形，南北残长约26.5米，东西残宽约7米，面积为185.5平方米。方向约为18°。该处文化堆积较薄，之下夯土开口0.4～0.9米，基本上为黄褐夯土，少量灰夯土，厚为0.2～1.1米。黄褐生土开口为0.7～1.6米。夯土北部文化堆积较厚，厚约1.3～1.7米，南部厚约0.4～1.1米（图Ⅰ.3.11；表Ⅰ.3.11）。

十六号夯土基址：位于内城西南部，归姜村东北，和平村西南部，与和平村西公路相距5.5米。与七号夯土基址相距36米，西面与十三、十四号夯土基址隔沟相望，相距约75米，西北面与十号夯土基址相距约50米。西部和北部为G1。平面形状呈长方形，长13～14.5米，宽约7米，面积约为98平方米。该处地层堆积厚约1.0米，文化堆积层下为夯土，开口在1.3～1.4米，黄褐色，坚硬，起层。夯土未勘探厚度。夯土的东部约0.5米即到生土，文化层薄，遗迹稀少（图Ⅰ.3.12；表Ⅰ.3.12）。

十七号夯土基址：位于内城中南部，和平村南考古队部院内（独立编号，1点在院内西南角）。东部9米为七号夯土基址，西部11米为十六号夯土基址。平面呈不规则南北长方形。方向约为正北。南北长约7.5米，最宽7米，现存面积约50平方米。该处文化堆积较薄，0.2～0.7米。之下夯土开口于0.4～0.8米，北部厚0.3～0.8米。夯土为黄褐夯土。南部存在南北向花土区，厚度超过1.2米（图Ⅰ.3.13；表Ⅰ.3.13）。

四、西组建筑基址

西组夯土建筑基址位于内城西城内，G1西部，归姜村北部。共7座。分别介绍如下：

八号夯土基址：位于内城墙西北角，归姜村北部，北城墙保护墙南部。北距北城墙保护墙38米，西距西城墙约为25米，东距九号夯土基址约25米。平面基本呈南北长方形，长约37米，宽约5～6.5米，面积约为222平方米。方向约为16°。该处区域文化堆积厚，灰坑等遗迹较丰富，较多灰坑填土含草木灰和水锈，深2.0米不底。并有淤土坑存在。文化堆积下为夯土，开口1.5～2.1米，厚度为0.9～1.2米。在基址南部，部分探孔在1.3米处遇石块打不下。夯土呈黄褐色，含砂（图Ⅰ.3.14；表Ⅰ.3.14）。

九号夯土基址：位于内城西北，归姜村北，和平村西部，北城墙保护墙南，距北面断崖16米。南距归姜房屋5米。西距西城墙50米，西距八号夯土基址约20米，北临北城墙。距十一号夯土基址约32米，南距十四号夯土基址约10米。平面大致呈南北向的长方形，南北长约93米，东西最宽处约23米，面积约为1750平方米。方向约为16°。该处文化堆积较厚，北部、东北部有取土和淤土坑，地层堆积简单，北部基岩和南部黄褐生土均较浅。夯土上部为文化堆积层，夯土开口0.6～2米，略呈南高北低，夯土较厚，约0.3～1.3米。下部为砂层，开口于1.5～2.3米，黄褐土或淤土开口于2.0米左右。典型堆积性质为黄褐色夯土和红褐夯土，含砂，质硬，起层，有剥落面。红褐夯土为取自红基岩掺杂黄褐黏土夯打而成（图Ⅰ.3.15；表Ⅰ.3.15）。

十号夯土基址：位于内城西北，归姜村东北，和平村西部，北城墙保护墙东南，距北面断崖24米。在其东部18米为G1，南部7米为十一号夯土基址，西部为十二号夯土基址，北距北城墙31米。残存形状呈长方形。长约30.5米，宽约7米，面积约为213.5平方米。方向约为14°。该处文化堆积较厚，灰坑较多，厚约1.0米左右。文化堆积下为夯土，开口为0.8～1.5米，多为1.0米左右，厚多为0.7～0.8米。黄褐土开口为1.4～1.9米，部分夯土下为砂层，开口为1.5～1.7米。夯土为黄褐色，含砂（图Ⅰ.3.16；表Ⅰ.3.16）。

十一号夯土基址：位于内城西北，归姜村东北，和平村西部，归姜村北小路北部，北城墙保护墙东南。其东部7米为G1，北部7米为十号夯土基址，西部为十二号夯土基址。残存形状呈长方形，长约30米，最宽约14.5米，南北各突出一个方形区域，西北部的区域长5米，宽4.5米，东南部的区域长5米，宽4米，总面积约为276.4平方米。方向约为14°。该处文化堆积厚约0.7米，之下为夯土，开口0.8～1.2米，厚约0.4～0.8米。夯土为黄褐土，含砂（图Ⅰ.3.17；表Ⅰ.3.17）。

十二号夯土基址：位于内城西北，归姜村东北，和平村西部，归姜村北小路北部，北城墙保护墙东南。东距十一号夯土基址约10米。残存形状呈圆角长方形。南北长约15.5米，东西最宽约10米，面积约为1554平方米。其方向为正南北方向。该处文化堆积较薄，厚约0.2～0.6米，之下夯土多开口0.5～0.6米，厚约0.2米，最厚0.9米，下部为黄褐生土。夯土为黄褐土，含砂（图Ⅰ.3.18；表Ⅰ.3.18）。

十三号夯土基址：位于内城西北，归姜村东头的一片老梨园内。在其北部15米为十四号夯土基址，东距G1约15米。残存平面形状呈长方形，东西长10米，南北宽7.5米，形状基本呈长方形，面积约为75平方米，为小型夯土基址。方向为正南北方向。地面可见东周时期绳纹陶片。该处文化堆积较薄，厚约0.3米，有少量灰坑。夯土开口多为0.4～0.6米，最厚达1.4米。底部为基岩。夯土典型堆积性质为黄褐色夯土，含砂，质硬，起层，有剥落面（图Ⅰ.3.19；表Ⅰ.3.19）。

十四号夯土基址：位于内城西北，归姜村东北，和平村西部，归姜村北小路南部。其北部12米为九号夯土基址，东南15米为十三号夯土基址，东南距G1约为25米。平面形状呈长方形，长约12米，最宽约5.5米，面积约为66平方米。方向基本为正南北方向。该处文化堆积较薄，约0.5米，夯土开口距地表深度0.5～0.9米（夯土未钻探厚度），之下黄褐生土深1.6～1.9米。典型堆积性质为黄褐色夯土，含砂，质硬，起层，有剥落面（图Ⅰ.3.20；表Ⅰ.3.20）。

五、内城中北部夯土基址

十五号夯土基址：位于内城中部，和平村内钻探区［1］，和平村养猪场东面。台基北面地势低，原为一水沟，其余三面均为民房。距北城墙110米，距东城墙130米，与其他夯土基址相距较远，在其东、南部，烟台文管会1972年发掘过M2和车马坑。平面形状基本呈长方形。南北残长约14米，东西残宽约8米，面积为112平方米。方向约为25°。地面可见较多的灰陶片。该处文化堆积较厚，约1.0米，与下部夯土之间隔一层厚约0.1～0.3米的砂层，夯土开口1.1～1.6米，厚0.2～0.4米。黄褐生土深1.3～1.8米。夯土基本上为黄褐夯土，少量灰夯土，含砂，质硬，起层，有剥落面（图Ⅰ.3.21；表Ⅰ.3.21）。

六、内城北部台地夯土基址

十八号夯土基址：位于内城北部，距北城墙约150米。北部为大于家村南公路，东部为鸦鹊河。于2009年7月16日对其进行勘探。夯土基址处在和平村北高台地北端呈鸭嘴形突出的台基部分。平面基本呈南北向长方形，南北长约120米，东西宽约30米，面积约3600平方米，方向为南北向。地层堆积较为简单。一般表土下即为夯土，夯土开口0.3～0.5米，一般厚0.8米，但大多未探到底。夯土为黄褐夯土，含砂，质硬。之下为黄褐生土，距地表深1.1～1.5米（图Ⅰ.3.22）。

第六节 内城其他遗迹

一、道 路 L2

位于归姜村东南部，和平村公路的两侧（图Ⅰ.3.1）。南北长条形，勘探出南北长90米，宽度10～13米，方向19°。南部穿过南城门，至壕沟处未勘探，北部应通向十六号夯土基址东部，应被晚期遗迹破坏。路土开口于灰土下，部分区域受到晚期遗迹单位破坏。踩踏土（路土）开口约0.35～1.25米之间，基本上为0.45米左右。厚为0.1～0.5米之间。底部为黄褐土，含砂。路土为黄褐土踩踏而成，分层明显。

二、内城出水口

内城出水口2处，G1作为归城内城南北向自然分界，纵穿内城，北面出口在北城墙由东西向北拐折处，明显标志是城墙有缺口，内有砂层，灰土含水锈。G1向南在经过归姜村北小路后向西拐弯，并变宽。又在归姜村内向东拐弯经过归姜南部城门西部城墙缺口通向外城壕。南水门宽约13米左右。北水门宽约17米。

三、城内水塘

水塘位于内城东南部。我们在和平村的东南部发现一处水坑，有大面积淤土（图Ⅰ.3.1）。根据开口层位，应与城内夯土基址为同期遗迹。水塘平面呈南北长条形，南北73米，东西约40米，面积约2920平方米，距地表深2米不底。包含有较多陶片。填土为灰土和淤土。

第七节　内城及其周围近年来被盗掘墓葬概述

归城内城一直面临文物保护的问题，盗掘现象时有发生。在我们在归城工作期间，寻访、踏查被盗掘遗迹点，并采集了一些遗物。这些遗物均为陶器，且多为墓葬出土。下面对其进行介绍，以期加深我们对归城文化面貌和时代的认识。

一、和平村西1～3组

这些标本均属于2007至2009年工作调查期间在内城范围内零星采集。经过挑选，就可以对复原器形的陶片进行绘图，并按采集的大致时间顺序分为三组（图Ⅰ.3.23～Ⅰ.3.25；表Ⅰ.3.22～Ⅰ.3.24）它们采集的大致方位在和平村之西，但具体地点已不可确指（图版14）。

二、和平村西4组

2010年夏归城资料整理期间，中美联合归城考古队获知当年春季和平村周边有墓葬被盗掘，遂于8月3日派工作人员调查现场。盗掘现场位于内城西北角以北约20米～50米的范围内。此处地势较为平坦，较内城地势略低，但高出北侧的鸦鹊河河道约3～4米，密集分布着约10个盗坑，均为2010年冬春季被盗掘所致。盗坑有1米×0.6米的长方形盗洞和直径约0.6米的圆形盗洞两类，前者为人力挖掘所致，后者可能为爆破所形成。尤其是前者的翻土中分布着大量的陶片，且大片较多，应为墓中的随葬品。地面采集所得陶片，按采集方位大致分为两组，此为第一组（图Ⅰ.3.26；表Ⅰ.3.25）。另一组为下述和平村西6组。

三、和平村西5组

在2010年夏考古队调查盗掘现场以前，和平村文物保管员王怀生已在盗坑附近采集若干陶片。将可以复原器型者归入此组（图Ⅰ.3.27；表Ⅰ.3.26）。

四、和平村西6组

此为2010年8月3日考古队工作人员调查春季和平村西被盗掘现场所采集的第二组陶片（图Ⅰ.3.28；表Ⅰ.3.27）。

五、和平村北1组

2009年6月24日，考古队工作人员至和平村北墓葬被盗处进行调查。盗洞位置在北墙以北100米左右的苹果园中部。附近共发现有两个盗洞，均为冬、春季所盗掘。在翻土中采集了若干陶片，对可复原器形者绘图（图Ⅰ.3.29；表Ⅰ.3.28）。

六、东迟家东侧水库

2009年6月12日下午，考古队员至东迟家村老村长家，查看其2000年冬季，修建东迟家东侧水库时出土的三件陶器，包括甗2、豆1（图版13）；陶豆上有一刻划符号（图Ⅰ.3.30；表Ⅰ.3.29）。据村民讲述，期间还出有铜鼎1件，为龙口博物馆征集。6月24日，征集这三件陶器。同时在老村长的带领下，至出土地点查看。现为水库水面。原先在东迟家村东有一条南北向河道，地势较为低洼。2000年，即在此地点修建水库，普遍下挖约有1米。出土地点大致在水库的东侧，应在河道的东侧的岸边上，属河流的二级阶地上。离进水口岸边较近。此处地点的土壤较厚，与山顶部的砂岩土有着显著的区别。

七、和平村北采集铜锛

2007年6月考古队在和平村北调查时，在村北路东侧地面采集到铜锛一件。锛为长方形銎，并有孔。锛长8.3厘米，銎部宽4.1厘米，刃宽3.8厘米（图Ⅰ.3.31；图版15：2）。

第八节　结　　语

一、关于归城内城的选地和年代

归城内城处在莱山之下，鸦鹊河两条支流间的高台地上。此处土壤肥沃，东西交通便利，是选择筑城的理想之地。归城内城平面呈曲尺形，在西北侧内凹，可能是因为这一带相对低洼，因地形地貌而建。以城墙中心计，内城南北长490米，东西宽525米。城墙西北处内凹部分南北长约180米，东西宽约180米。内城总面积约22.5万平方米。作为西周时期的城址来说，其规模是较为宏伟的。

根据多年来的考古调查、勘探和试掘，我们发现归城存在内、外城圈，属于双重城郭。而且内、外城之间我们推测可能有年代差异，即先筑的内城，后筑外城。内城的年代根据近年的考古调查和试掘，推断为西周早期偏晚到春秋时期。

二、内城的建筑基址布局及特征

内城城址的布局依地貌地势而成。归城内城南部、西部地形相对平坦且地势较高，是宫殿区所在地。此次勘探出17座夯土建筑基址，基本位于这个区域内。另外在内城中北部高台地上勘探出十五号夯土基址。并且，2002年烟台博物馆在此地发掘出春秋时期房址。说明此处也是重要的夯土基址所在地。

G1作为贯通内城的南北水系，把内城分割为东西两部分，南城门、南北通道L2就位于G1的东侧，一起构成了城址的南大门。G1北水口位于西北城墙拐角处，从这里通向城外。L1位于内城正中，南端通向城墙，北端被遗迹破坏和因村庄占压未能勘探，南端城墙处没有发现城门，所以现在还不能确定L1的性质。作为一处周代城址，依据其功能和礼制，一般四面均有城门，因为归城城址被破坏和村庄占压情况，仅发现一座南门。

17座夯土建筑基址均开口于灰土层下，深度和夯土性质均较一致，时代差距应不是太大，可以放在一个平面上来考虑宫殿基址的布局。有较多基址打破基岩、黄褐生土、淤土和砂层的现象，推测为基槽式建筑。但夯土薄厚也不一，说明在建筑之前存在早期的灰坑等，对地表和夯土处理的程度不一。此次勘探出的夯土建筑基址大多呈南北走向的长方形，这一点很值得注意。其中二号夯土基址有东南西北两端两个突出部分，宽约3米，推测为夯土基址的台阶部分。

西区内建筑基址分布较密集，以大型南北向九号建筑基址为中心。东西两侧分布较大的南北向八、十、十一号基址。方向多为14°～16°。南部则分布有十三、十四号小型基址，基本为正方向。

东区内建筑主要集中在内城南端。沿内城L1两侧分布有夯土基址9处。三号夯土基址和二号夯土基址面积较大，左右对称。应为主要宫殿。北部分布有一排较小夯土基址，分别为四、五、六、七、十六、十七号基址。方向基本与L1一样为18°。应为一组建筑遗址。一号夯土基址位于城墙内侧，当为城墙的附属防御设施（图Ⅰ.3.2）。

内城南部、中北部、北部、东部局部区域文化堆积厚，灰坑较多，出土陶器残片和草木灰、骨器（料）也较多。我们认为该区域分布有一般性的居住址。在内城中北部十五号夯土基址西南10米处，在探孔E6附近发现加工的骨器，可能与骨器作坊有关。而在2009年试掘中与探沟2（TG2）的灰坑H9中发现了铸铜用的陶范，说明这一带可能有铸铜作坊遗址（见上编第五章）。发掘地点位于一号建筑基址西侧，二号建筑基址之南，处于三面有大型建筑基址环绕的空间（图Ⅰ.3.1），这暗示其中的某些建筑基址可能与铸铜遗址有关。

内城西北部和东北部文化堆积简单，有零星墓葬分布。内城东部和东南部墓葬较为密集。总之，目前来看，内城存在两个问题，第一个问题是和平村占压严重，影响了内城的勘探；第二是现尚未发现制陶等其他性质遗迹。这些都需要进一步工作。

三、有关问题讨论

从城址范围上看，归城城址（特别是外城）的范围广大，城墙坚厚，其规模和土方量与曲阜鲁国故城相比不相上下，应为一处都城遗址。形制上与鲁国故城和薛国故城等周代城址相类似，归城城址也为二重城郭制。鲁国故城内城位于外城的中部，东西长方形；薛国故城内城位于外城东南隅，不规则长方形，二者均始建于春秋时期。归城内城位于外城中部，始建年代应为西周时期。相比来说在山东地区目前尚找不到其他西周都城的情况下，归城内城的考古成果尤为重要。对于研究胶东地区东夷古国和中原王朝的关系提供了重要依据。

就胶东地区而言，整个周代规模最大的城址为龙口归城和平度即墨故城。但时代有差异。即墨故城根据目前考古工作，年代应为战国到汉代。为归城城址之后的胶东重要都邑。即墨故城也分内外城，内城平面总体呈近长方形，东南缺角，南北长1370米，东西宽1270米，整个内城位于外城的东南部。外城基本为汉代。平面总体呈不规则的长方形，南北长约4500米，东西宽约3200米。二者在时代上有承继性。

归城的调查和勘探工作目前仍有一些局限性。特别是归城城址北部和西南部被村庄占压，我们仅能勘探和平村南部和归姜村北部区域；另在和平村内勘探了六片空地。受地表覆盖物的限制，占压区域没有进行普探，在一定程度上影响了我们对内城夯土建筑分布的判断。

通过勘探我们也发现，归城夯土基址被晚期单位破坏严重，如二号夯土基址，被南北向水沟冲刷破坏严重。结合内城城墙上所留的沙层痕迹，我们推测归城使用期间可能多次经历过洪水的入侵和破坏，有关部分的城墙乃至城内建筑基址均有可能经历修复或重建。这些也是我们在以后工作中要进一步查明的情况。

最后应该提到的是归城夯土基址的方向问题。中国古代一般城址的建筑多呈东西向长方形。但是归城夯土则南北向为主，小型建筑则有一些是东西向。这可能与建筑基址的性质功能有关，更可能与归城内古国的文化传统有关，需要进一步研究来说明这一问题。

参考文献

李步青，林仙庭，1991：山东黄县归城遗址的调查与发掘，考古，3：910-918.

表Ⅰ.3.1　归城土样标准表

Table Ⅰ.3.1　Soil Type Standards at Guicheng

类别 Type	名称 Name	包含物 Inclusions	描述 Description	成因 Formation	性质 Characteristics	备注 Notes
现象土　Phenomenon soil	灰土 Grey earth	灰土含砂 Grey earth with sand inclusions	灰色或灰褐色土，包含砂粒较多 Grey or grey-brown color, many sand particles	来源为含砂地层或掺杂有砂层的土 The source is sand layers or earth with sand mixed in	人类活动 Human activity	灰土为原生土人为翻动掺入人类遗物或地表有机质杂物所形成。最典型的是灰坑中填土。 Grey earth is formed when humans disturb the natural soil and deposit cultural remains or mix it with organic remains. The most typical is ash-pit fill
		灰土含灰烬 Grey earth with ash	灰土内包含有生活、生产形成的草木茎腐朽物或古人灶膛产生的草木灰，土质松软，包含人类遗物较多 In the grey earth are decomposed plant remains or plant ash produced in hearths by ancient humans; the soil is soft, and it includes many cultural remains	与古人的居住生活相关 Related to ancient human occupation	人类活动 Human activity	
		灰土含水锈 Grey earth with water-formed rust	灰土被水所泡，有红褐、绿斑 Grey earth that has been soaked in water, with red-brown and green spots	沁水形成 Formed by water soaking		
		灰土含红烧土块 Grey earth with red burned clay clumps	灰土内包含被火烧灼形成的土块，土质较松软 In the grey earth are clumps of burnt soil, and the soil is soft	一般是灶膛或窑、火坑等形成的红烧土碎裂掺入灰土中 Generally formed by fragmented burned soil from a hearth, kiln, or fire pit incorporated into the grey earth	人类活动 Human activity	
	夯土 Rammed earth	灰夯土，含灰土 Grey rammed earth, with grey earth inclusions	灰褐色，坚硬致密，包含遗物稍多，多较碎小 Grey-brown color, hard and compact, with many fragments of cultural remains	使用灰土夯打而成的建筑土 Architectural earth formed from rammed grey earth	筑房、墙、墓葬等人类活动 Houses, walls, tombs and other constructions associated with human activity	该夯土取土来源是人类生活区 This rammed earth is made from earth taken from human activity areas
		黄褐夯土 Tan rammed earth	黄褐色，坚硬致密 Tan color, hard and compact	使用自然黄褐色土层夯打而成 Rammed using natural tan earth	同上 Same as above	
		夹砂夯土，含砂 Sandy rammed earth, sand inclusions	夯土中含大量砂土 Large amount of sand included in the rammed earth	取含砂的土层进行夯打而成 Formed from rammed sandy soil	同上 Same as above	

续表

类别 Type	名称 Name	包含物 Inclusions	描述 Description	成因 Formation	性质 Characteristics	备注 Notes
现象土 Phenomenon soil	淤土 Sediment	一般淤土 Common sediment	呈淡黄褐色，松软细腻 Light tan color, soft and very fine	水冲刷沉积而成 Formed from water erosion deposits	多为自然形成，也有人类倒水、灌溉形成 Mostly formed naturally, also from human waste water, or irrigation	
		淤土含灰 Sediment with grey earth inclusions	灰色、灰褐色、松软 Grey or grey-brown color, loose	产生淤土时倾倒有灰土或静水内有水草等死亡腐殖物 Sediment formed with deposition of grey earth, or still water including rotted plant remains	多与人类活动相关 Mostly related to human activity	
		淤土含水锈 Sediment with water-formed rust inclusions	淤土包含红褐或绿色斑点 Sediment includes red-brown or green spots	静水、少水浸泡形成 Formed by soaking in still water or a small amount of water		
		淤土含砂 Sediment with sand inclusions	含砂量大 Large amount of sand included	细土随水流走，淘洗留下较多砂质 Fine soil carried away by flowing water, much sand left behind by washing		能分析水文情况 Allows analysis of hydrological conditions
	花土 Multicolor earth		由黄褐土、灰土等掺杂而成，表现为多种颜色相对均匀的混杂 Formed from mixed tan, grey earth; appears as relatively even mixture with multiple colors	人类对多种土进行短时间内的倒翻或有意掺杂 Formed from a variety of soils turned or mixed intentionally by humans in a short period of time	人类活动 Human activity	一般属于墓葬中填土 Usually belongs to fills of burials
	踩踏土 Footpath earth		坚硬、有明显的分层现象 Hard, with clear thin strata	人类脚或车等行走所致 Formed by human foot or vehicle traffic	人类活动 Human activity	一般为活动场所如院落等遗迹 Generally indicates activity areas such as courtyards, and other site features
	路土 Road earth		坚硬、有明显的薄层，杂有砂石，长条状分布 Hard, with clear thin strata, mixed with sand and stones, elongated formation	人类或车等行走所致 Formed by human or vehicle traffic	人类活动 Human activity	古代道路 Ancient roads

续表

类别 Type	名称 Name	包含物 Inclusions	描述 Description	成因 Formation	性质 Characteristics	备注 Notes
地层土 Stratum soil	垫土 Packed soil		颜色斑杂，土质松软杂乱，内含有近现代物 Color mottled, soft with jumbled appearance, includes modern objects	近现代人垫填所致 Formed by fill deposited by modern humans	人类活动 Human activity	也称扰土 Also called disturbed soil
	耕土 Tilled earth		松软，颜色浅且有斑杂，内含有近现代物及植物根茎 Soft, color light and mottled, includes modern objects and roots of plants	农业耕种所形成 Formed by agricultural cultivation or planting	人类活动 Human activity	有时也称表土 Sometimes also recorded as topsoil
	黄土 Loess	一般黄土 Common loess	黄褐色土 Tan color	自然形成，风成或风化而成 Formed naturally by wind or weathering	自然力量 Natural forces	如马兰黄土 E.g. Malan-loess
		黄土含砂 Loess with sand inclusions	含砂量大 Large quantities of sand included	同上 Same as above	自然力量 Natural forces	
	褐土 Brown earth	褐土含灰 Brown earth with grey earth inclusions	颜色稍深 Slightly darker color		人类活动 Human activity	
		褐土含水锈 Brown earth with water-formed rust	包含水锈，成红褐或绿色斑点 Includes water-formed rust, appears as red-brown or green spots	水成 Formed from water		
		褐土含灰烬 Brown earth with ash inclusions	包含灰烬，松软 Has ash inclusions loose and soft	褐土内包含有人类生活垃圾 Refuse from human activity		
	黄褐土 Tan earth	黄褐土含灰 Tan earth with grey earth inclusions	颜色稍深 Slightly darker color		人类活动 Human activity	
		黄褐土含水锈 Tan earth with water-formed rust inclusions	包含水锈 Has water-formed rust inclusions	水成 Formed by water		
		黄褐土含灰烬 Tan earth with ash inclusions	包含灰烬，松软 Has ash inclusions, loose and soft	内包含有人类生活垃圾 Includes refuse from human activity		
	砂土 Sandy earth		含砂量大 Large quantities of sand included	水成或风化岩石而成 Formed by water or weathered rock	自然力量 Natural forces	
	生土 Natural earth		浅褐黄色，土质纯，有时有灰色柱状色条，古代雨水造成 Light tan-yellow color, homogeneous, sometimes includes vertical grey strips, formed by ancient rain fall	自然过程形成 Formed by natural processes	自然力量 Natural forces	

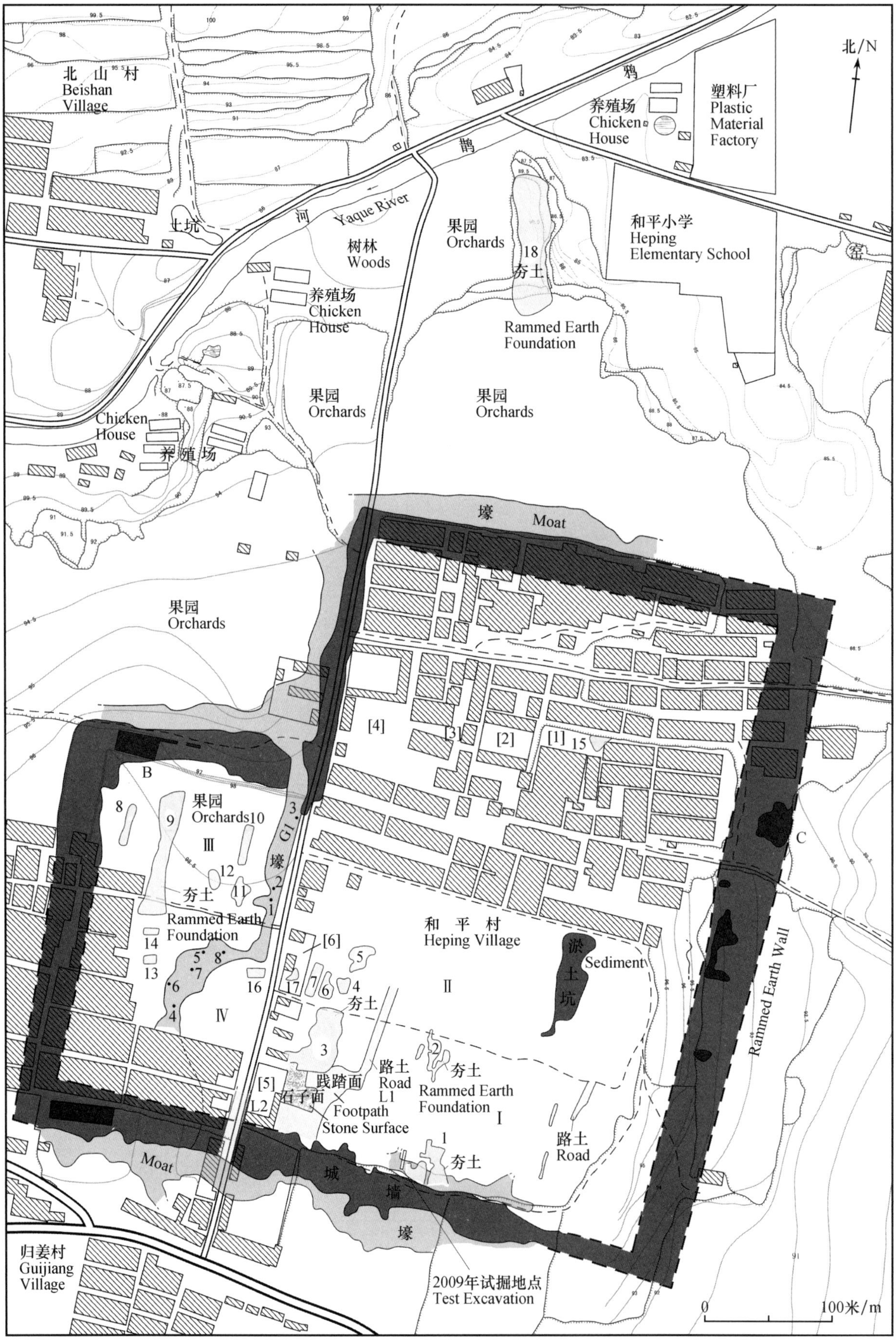

图Ⅰ.3.1　归城内城及其城外建筑图

Figure Ⅰ.3.1　Plan of the inner city of Guicheng and the architectural foundations (elevation figures set by cartographer).

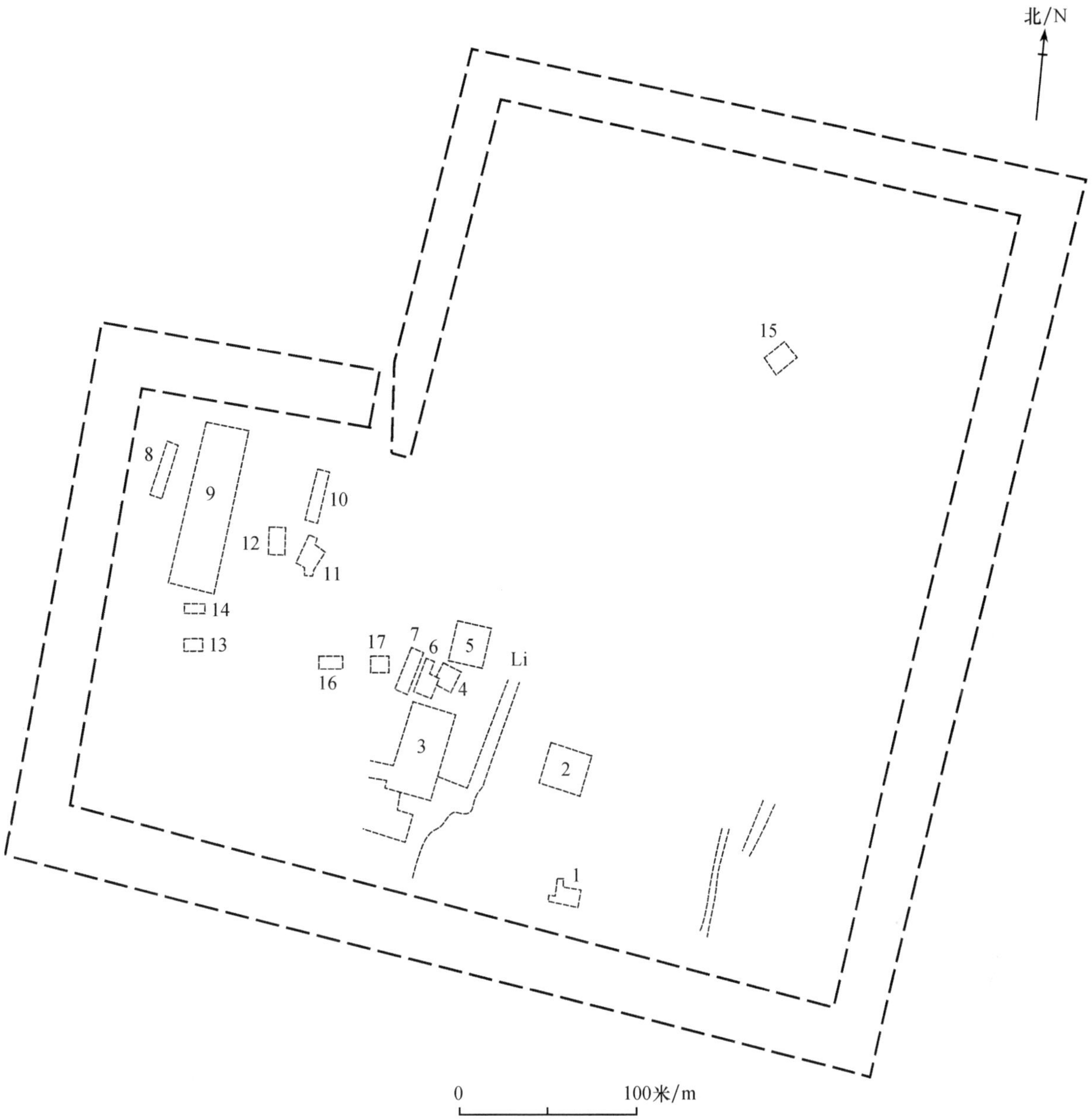

图Ⅰ.3.2　归城内城建筑复原图

Figure Ⅰ.3.2　Reconstruction of architectural foundations in the inner city of Guicheng.

表Ⅰ.3.2　G1典型探孔地层（位置见图Ⅰ.3.1）

Table Ⅰ.3.2　Strata sequence in representative G1 cores (ref. Fig. Ⅰ.3.1)

图上号 Number in Fig. Ⅰ.3.1	探孔号 Core number	地层序列 Order of strata	土样 Soil type	深度 Depth	地层描述 Description	备注 Note
1	$Z_1$33	a	表土 Topsoil	0 ~ 0.3 m		探孔$Z_1$33（1）位于G1中部偏北 Coring hole $Z_1$33 (1) located in the middle section of G1, slightly to the north.
		b	灰土 Grey earth	0.3 ~ 0.9 m	含灰烬，碎陶片，少量水锈 With inclusions of ash, pottery fragments, and a small amount of water ~ formed rust	
		c	砂层 Sand layer	0.9 ~ 1.3 m		1.3米遇石块打不下 At 1.3 m we struck rocks and could not proceed.
2	$B_2$34	a	表土 Topsoil	0 ~ 0.3 m		探孔 $B_2$34（2）位于G1中部偏北 Coring hole $B_2$34 (2) located in the middle section of G1, slightly to the north.
		b	灰土 Grey earth	0.3 ~ 0.8 m	含灰烬，含烧土颗粒，含水锈 With ash inclusions, burnt soil particles, and water-formed rust	
		c	砂层 Sand layer	0.8 ~ 1.0 m	含灰土块 Inclusion of grey soil pieces	
		d	砂层 Sand layer	1.0 ~ 1.8 m		
		e	黄褐土 Tan earth	1.8 ~ 2.0 m		不到底 Coring did not reach the bottom.
3	$M_2$35	a	表土 Topsoil	0 ~ 0.3 m		
		b	扰土 Disturbed soil	0.3 ~ 0.4 m		
		c	夯土 Rammed earth	0.4 ~ 0.7 m	黄色，含砂 Yellow, sand inclusions	
		d	黄褐土 Tan earth	0.7 ~ 1.0 m	含砂 Sand inclusions	
		e	砂层 Sand layer	1.0 ~ 1.4 m		
		f	淤土 Sediment	1.4 ~ 1.45 m	黄色 Yellow	
		g	砂层 Sand layer	1.45 ~ 1.5 m		
		h	淤土 Sediment	1.5 ~ 1.55 m		
		i	黄褐土 Tan earth	1.55 ~ 1.6 m	黄色 Yellow	
		j	砂层 Sand layer	1.65 m ~		不到底 Coring did not reach the bottom.
4	$I_1$24	a	表土 Topsoil	0 ~ 0.3 m		探孔$I_1$24（4）位于G1南部 Coring hole $I_1$24 (4) located in the southern section of G1.
		b	灰褐土 Grey-brown earth	0.3 ~ 0.5 m		

续表

图上号 Number in Fig. I .3.1	探孔号 Core number	地层序列 Order of strata	土样 Soil type	深度 Depth	地层描述 Description	备注 Note
4	$I_1$24	c	砂层 Sand layer	0.5 ~ 1.5 m		
		d	生土 Natural earth	1.5 m ~		
5	$S_1$26	a	表土 Topsoil	0 ~ 0.3 m		探孔$S_1$26（5）位于G1南部 Coring hole $S_1$26 (5) located in the southern section of G1.
		b	灰土 Grey earth	0.3 ~ 1.4 m	含灰烬，含烧土颗粒，水锈 With inclusions of ash, burnt soil pieces, and water-formed rust	
		c	砂层 Sand layer	1.4 ~ 1.6 m		
		d	基岩 Bedrock	1.6 m ~		
6	$M_1$22	a	表土 Topsoil	0 ~ 0.3 m		探孔$M_1$22（6）位于G1南部 Coring hole $M_1$22 (6) located in the southern section of G1.
		b	灰土 Grey earth	0.3 ~ 0.8 m		
		c	砂层 Sand layer	0.8 ~ 1.2 m		
		d	黄褐土 Tan earth	1.2 ~ 1.5 m	含砂 Sand inclusions	
		e	生土 Natural earth	1.5 m ~		
7	$P_1$25	a	表土 Topsoil	0 ~ 0.3 m		探孔$P_1$25（7）位于G1中南部 Coring hole $P_1$25 (7) located in the middle-southern section of G1.
		b	灰土 Grey earth	0.3 ~ 0.9 m	含砂，灰烬 Inclusion of sand and ash	
		c	黄褐土 Tan earth	0.9 ~ 1.2 m	含砂 Sand inclusions	
		d	砂层 Sand layer	1.2 ~ 1.3 m		
		e	黄褐土 Tan earth	1.3 ~ 1.5 m	含砂 Sand inclusions	
		f	基岩 Bedrock	1.5 m ~		
8	$S_1$29	a	表土 Topsoil	0 ~ 0.3 m		探孔$S_1$29（8）位于G1中部拐折处 Coring hole $S_1$29 (8) located at the turn in the middle section of G1.
		b	灰土 Grey earth	0.3 ~ 0.7 m		
		c	砂层 Sand layer	0.7 ~ 1.2 m		1.2 m以下为石块 Stones at 1.2 m and below.

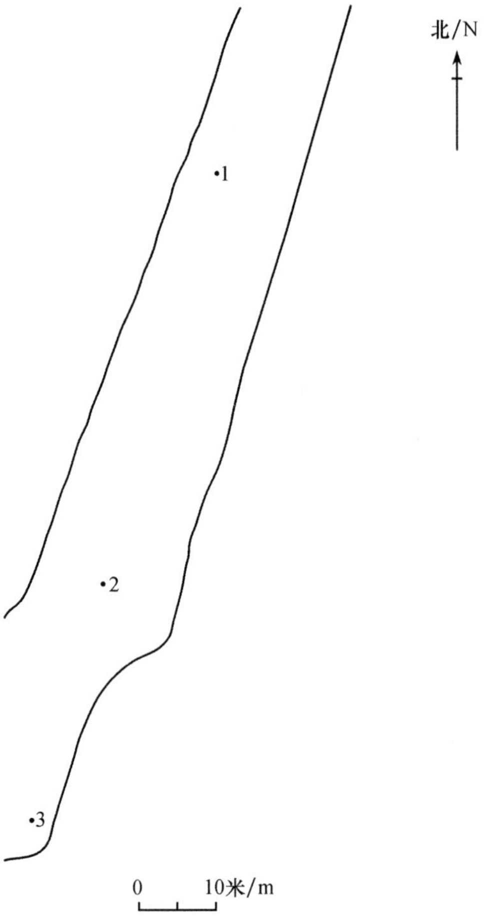

图Ⅰ.3.3　道路L1及其典型探孔位置

Figure Ⅰ.3.3　Road L1 and the placement of representative coring holes.

表Ⅰ.3.3　道路L1典型探孔地层

Table Ⅰ.3.3　Strata sequence of representative coring holes in road L1

图上号 Number on map	探孔号 Core number	地层序列 Order of strata	土样 Soil type	深度 Depth	地层描述 Description	备注 Note
1	$L_1$48	a	表土 Topsoil	0 ~ 0.3 m		探孔$L_1$48 (58)* 在路土北部 Test coring hole $L_1$48 (58)* is in the northern section of the road.
		b	灰土 Grey earth	0.3 ~ 0.7 m	含砂 Sand inclusions	
		c	砂层 Sand layer	0.7 ~ 0.8 m	硬 Hard	
		d	黄褐土 Tan earth	0.8 ~ 0.83 m	含砂 Sandy inclusions	
		e	黄褐土 Tan earth	0.83 ~ 2.0 m	含砂 Sand inclusions	不底 Did not reach the bottom.
2	$G_1$48	a	表土 Topsoil	0 ~ 0.3 m		探孔$G_1$48 (68) 位于所探路土的中部 Coring hole $G_1$48 (68) is located in the middle section of the cored road.

续表

图上号 Number on map	探孔号 Core number	地层序列 Order of strata	土样 Soil type	深度 Depth	地层描述 Description	备注 Note
2	$G_1$48	b	灰土 Grey earth	0.3 ~ 0.9 m	含砂 Sand inclusions	
		c	砂层 Sand layer	0.9 ~ 1.0 m		
		d	黄褐土 Tan earth	1.0 ~ 2.0 m	含砂 Sand inclusions	不底 Did not reach the bottom.
3	$D_1$48	a	表土 Topsoil	0 ~ 0.3 m		探孔$D_1$48 (74) 位于所探路土的南部石块区 Coring hole $D_1$48 (74) is located in the stone-paved area in the southern section of the road.
		b	灰土 Grey earth	0.3 ~ 0.8 m	黏、硬 Sticky, hard	
		c	石块 Stones	0.8 ~		打不下去 Did not reach the bottom.

(58)* 是一个建筑遗迹（如路L1）内钻孔的重新编号。说明见第三节：3-2。

(58)* is the number reassigned to coring holes restricted to architectural units, e.g., Road L1. See explanations in Section 3: 3-2.

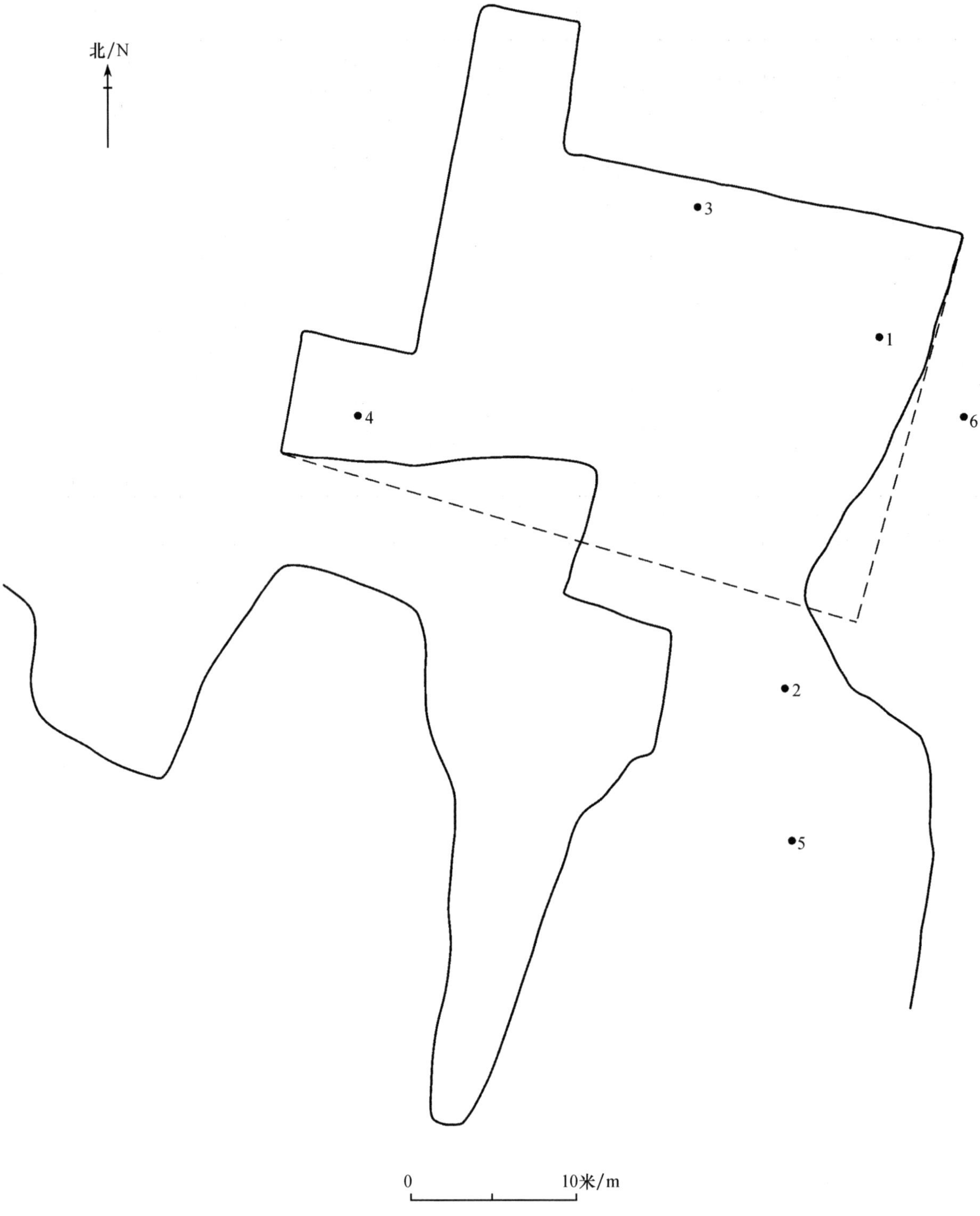

图Ⅰ.3.4　一号夯土基址平面及其典型探孔位置

Figure Ⅰ.3.4　Rammed Earth Foundation 1 and the placement of representative coring holes.

表Ⅰ.3.4　一号基址典型探孔地层

Table Ⅰ.3.4　Strata sequence of representative coring holes in Rammed Earth Foundation 1

图上号 Number on map	探孔号 Core number	地层序列 Order of strata	土样 Soil type	深度 Depth	地层描述 Description	备注 Note
1	G′63′	a	表土 Topsoil	0 ~ 0.3 m	灰土，疏松，有植物根 Grey earth, loose, with plant roots	探孔G′63′（31）位于一号基址东北角 Coring hole G′63′(31) is located at the northeast corner of Foundation 1.
		b	灰土 Grey earth	0.3 ~ 0.8 m	较松软 Relatively soft	
		c	夯土 Rammed earth	0.8 ~ 1.2 m	较致密，黄褐夯土 Relatively dense, tan rammed earth	
		d	砂层 Sand layer	1.2 ~ 1.3 m		
		e	淤土 Sediment	1.3 m ~	黄色，粉沙淤土，细密 Yellow, sand-silt soil, fine	
2.	I′63′	a	表土 Topsoil	0 ~ 0.3 m		探孔I′63′（35）位于基址1南部 Coring hole I′63′(35) is located south of Foundation 1.
		b	灰土 Grey earth	0.3 ~ 0.6 m		
		c	夯土 Rammed earth	0.6 ~ 1.3 m		
		d	砂层 Sand layer	1.3 ~ 1.5 m		
		e	淤土 Sediment	1.3 ~ 2 m		不到底 Did not reach the bottom.
3	F62′	a	表土 Topsoil	0 ~ 0.3 m		探孔F62′（64）位于基址1北部 Coring hole F62′ (64) is located north of Foundation 1.
		b	灰土 Grey earth	0.3 ~ 1.0 m	含灰烬，含砂 With ash and sand inclusions	
		c	夯土 Rammed earth	1.0 ~ 1.5 m		
		d	淤土 Sediment	1.5 m ~		
4	H61′	a	表土 Topsoil	0 ~ 0.3 m		探孔H61′（123）位于基址1西南部 Coring hole H61′ (123) is located in the southwestern part of Foundation 1.
		b	灰土 Grey earth	0.3 ~ 0.9 m		
		c	夯土 Rammed earth	0.9 ~ 1.3 m		
		d	淤土 Sediment	1.3 ~ 2.0 m		不到底 Did not reach the bottom.
5	J′63″	a	表土 Topsoil	0 ~ 0.3 m		探孔J′63″（26）位于基址1南部，应为城墙 Coring hole J′63″ (26) is located south of Foundation 1, probably part of the city wall.

续表

图上号 Number on map	探孔号 Core number	地层序列 Order of strata	土样 Soil type	深度 Depth	地层描述 Description	备注 Note
5	J′63″	b	夯土 Rammed earth	0.3 ~ 1.5 m		不到底 Did not reach the bottom.
6	H63″	a	表土 Topsoil	0 ~ 0.3 m		探孔H63″（19）位于基址1东北部 Test coring hole H63″ (19) is located to the northeast of Foundation 1.
		b	灰土 Grey earth	0.3 ~ 0.8 m		
		c	淤土 Sediment	0.8 ~ 1.8 m		不到底 Did not reach the bottom.

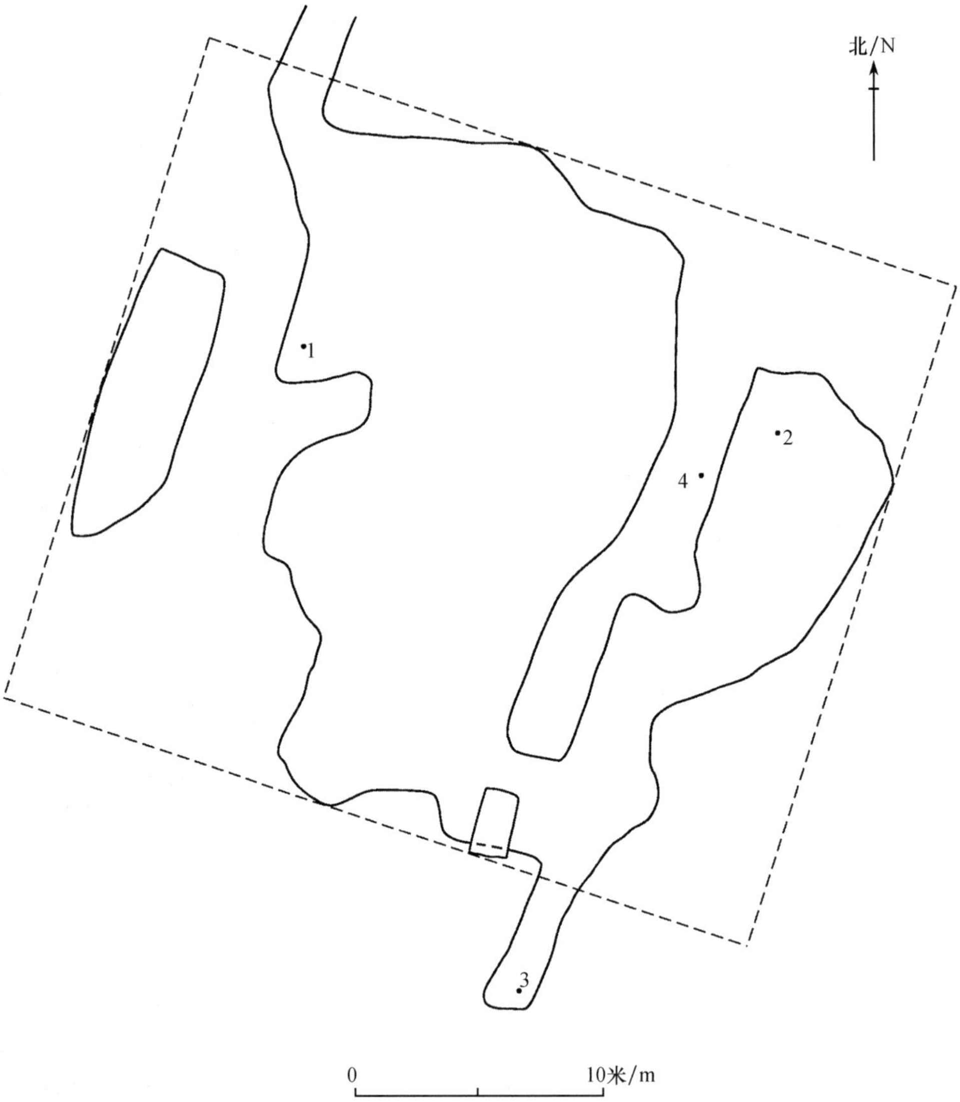

图Ⅰ.3.5　二号夯土基址平面及典型探孔位置

Figure Ⅰ.3.5　Plan of Rammed Earth Foundation 2 and the placement of representative coring holes.

表Ⅰ.3.5　二号建筑基址典型探孔地层

Table Ⅰ.3.5　Strata sequence of representative coring holes in Rammed Earth Foundation 2

图上号 Number on map	探孔号 Core number	地层序列 Order of strata	土样 Soil type	深度 Depth	地层描述 Description	备注 Note
1	$I_{1}55'$	a	表土 Topsoil	0 ~ 0.3 m	较灰 Relatively grey	探孔$I_{1}55'$（206）位于基址2西部 Coring hole $I_{1}55'$ (206) is located in the western part of Foundation 2.
		b	灰土 Grey earth	0.3 ~ 1.4 m	松软 Soft	
		c	夯土 Rammed earth	1.4 ~ 1.7 m		
		d	淤土 Sediment	1.7 ~ 2.0 m	含砂 Sand inclusions	不到底 Did not reach the bottom.
2	I1′59	a	表土 Topsoil	0 ~ 0.3 m	较灰 Relatively grey	探孔I1′59（39）位于基址2东北部 Coring hole I1′59 (39) is located in the northeastern part of Foundation 2.
		b	灰土 Grey earth	0.3 ~ 0.4 m	含灰烬和砂，松软 With ash and sand inclusions, soft.	
		c	夯土 Rammed earth	0.4 ~ 0.8 m		
		d	砂层 Sand layer	0.8 ~ 1.0 m		
		e	夯土 Rammed earth	1.0 ~ 1.7 m		
		f	淤土 Sediment	1.7 ~ 2.0 m		不到底 Did not reach the bottom.
3	$D_{1}58'$	a	表土 Topsoil	0 ~ 0.3 m	较灰 Relatively grey	探孔$D_{1}58'$（74）位于基址2南部 Coring hole $D_{1}58'$ (74) is located in the southern part of Foundation 2.
		b	灰土 Grey earth	0.3 ~ 1.0 m		
		c	灰土 Grey earth	1.0 ~ 1.4 m	含灰烬 With ash inclusions	
		d	夯土 Rammed earth	1.4 ~ 1.6 m		
		e	淤土 Sediment	1.6 ~ 2.0 m		不到底 Did not reach the bottom.
4	$H_{1}58''$	a	表土 Topsoil	0 ~ 0.3 m	较灰 Relatively grey	探孔$H_{1}58''$（54）位于基址2北部间隔 coring hole $H_{1}58''$(54) is located in a gap in the northern part of Foundation 2.
		b	灰土 Grey earth	0.3 ~ 1.2 m	含灰烬，含砂 With ash and sandy inclusions	
		c	淤土 Sediment	1.2 ~ 1.8 m	含灰烬，含水锈 With ash and rust inclusions	
		d	淤土 Sediment	1.8 ~ 2.0 m		不到底 Did not reach the bottom.

图Ⅰ.3.6　三号夯土基址平面及典型探孔位置

Figure Ⅰ.3.6　Plan of Rammed Earth Foundation 3 and the placement of representative coring holes.

表Ⅰ.3.6　三号夯土基址典型探孔地层

Table Ⅰ.3.6　Strata sequence of representative coring holes in Rammed Earth Foundation 3

图上号 Number on map	探孔号 Core number	地层序列 Order of strata	土样 Soil type	深度 Depth	地层描述 Description	备注 Note
1	$O_1$39	a	表土 Topsoil	0 ~ 0.3 m	较灰 Relatively grey	探孔$O_1$39（91）位于基址北部 Coring hole $O_1$39 (91) is located in the northern part of the foundation.
		b	灰土 Grey earth	0.3 ~ 0.5 m	松软 Soft	
		c	夯土 Rammed earth	0.5 ~ 1.0 m	花夯 Multicolor rammed earth	
		d	夯土 Rammed earth	1.0 ~ 2.0 m	黄褐夯 Tan rammed earth	不到底 Did not reach the bottom.
2	$J_1$39	a	表土 Topsoil	0 ~ 0.3 m	较灰 Relatively grey	探孔$J_1$39（67）位于基址中部 Coring hole $J_1$39 (67) is located in the center of the foundation.
		b	灰土 Grey earth	0.3 ~ 0.6 m	松软 Soft	
		c	夯土 Rammed earth	0.6 ~ 1.2 m		
		d	黄褐土 Tan earth	1.2 ~ 2.0 m	含砂 Sand inclusions	不到底 Did not reach the bottom.
3	$G_1$39	a	表土 Topsoil	0 ~ 0.3 m	较灰 Relatively grey	探孔$G_1$39（99）位于基址南部 Coring hole $G_1$39 (99) is located in the southern part of the foundation.
		b	灰土 Grey earth	0.3 ~ 0.5 m	松软 Soft	
		c	夯土 Rammed earth	0.5 ~ 0.8 m	灰夯 Grey rammed earth	
		d	夯土 Rammed earth	0.8 ~ 1.1 m	黄褐夯 Tan rammed earth	
		e	黄褐土 Tan earth	1.1 ~ 2.0 m		不底 Did not reach the bottom.

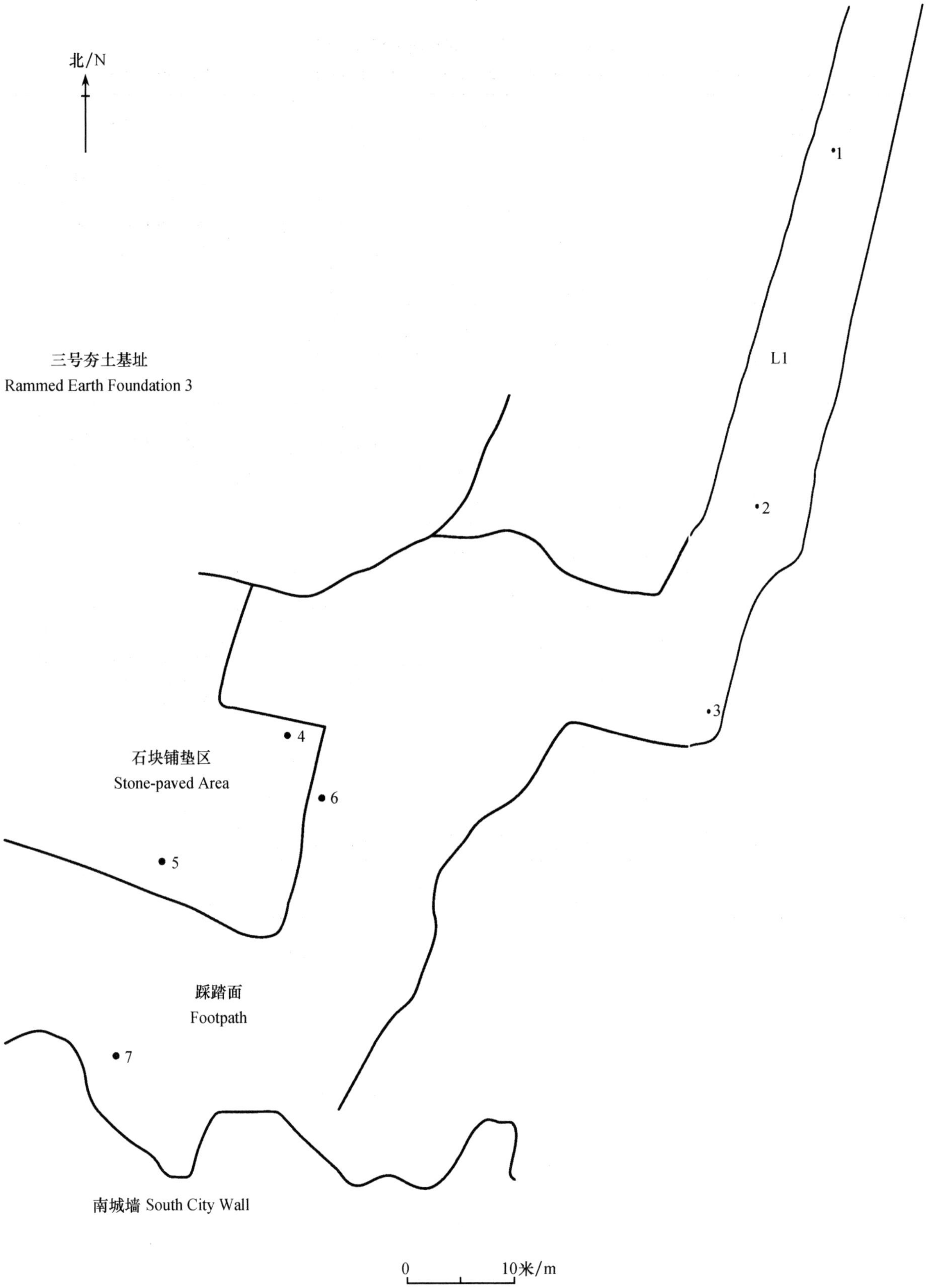

图Ⅰ.3.7　三号夯土基址及周边道路遗迹位置图

Figure Ⅰ.3.7　Rammed Earth Foundation 3 and the adjacent road and other structural remains.

表Ⅰ.3.7　三号夯土基址周边遗迹典型探孔地层

Table Ⅰ.3.7　Strata sequence of representative coring holes in structural remains adjacent to Rammed Earth Foundation 3

图上号 Number on map	探孔号 Core number	地层序列 Order of strata	土样 Soil type	深度 Depth	地层描述 Description	备注 Note
4	$D_1$42	a	表土 Topsoil	0 ~ 0.3 m		探孔$D_1$42（145）位于夯土3南部石块区 Coring hole $D_1$42 (145) is located in the stone-paved area south of Foundation 3.
		b	灰土 Grey earth	0.3 ~ 0.6 m		
		c	夯土 Rammed earth	0.6 ~ 0.9 m	灰 Grey	
		d	石块 Stone	0.9 m		打不下 Could not proceed.
5	A_1'40	a	表土 Topsoil	0 ~ 0.3 m		探孔A_1'40（183）位于夯土3南部石块区 Coring hole A_1'40 (183) is located in the stone-paved area south of Foundation 3.
		b	灰土 Grey earth	0.3 ~ 1.3 m	含灰烬，碎陶片，少量砂 With ash inclusions, broken ceramics, not much sand	
		c	石块 Stone	1.3 m		打不下 Could not proceed.
6	$C_1$43	a	表土 Topsoil	0 ~ 0.3 m		探孔$C_1$43（130）位于踩踏区 Coring hole $C_1$43 (130) is located in the footpath area.
		b	灰土 Grey earth	0.3 ~ 0.6 m		
		c	踩踏面 Footpath surface	0.6 ~ 0.7 m		
		c	夯土 Rammed earth	0.7 ~ 0.9 m	灰 Grey	
		d	黄褐土 Tan earth	0.9 ~ 2.0 m	含砂 Sand inclusions	2.0米不底 Could not go below 2.0 m.
7	$C_1$40	a	表土 Topsoil	0 ~ 0.3 m		探孔$C_1$40（187）位于踩踏区南部 Coring hole $C_1$40 (187) is located in the southern part of the footpath area.
		b	灰土 Grey earth	0.3 ~ 0.5 m		
		c	踩踏面 Footpath surface	0.5 ~ 0.8 m		
		c	黄褐土 Tan earth	0.8 ~ 2.0 m	含砂 Sand inclusions	不到底 Did not reach the bottom.

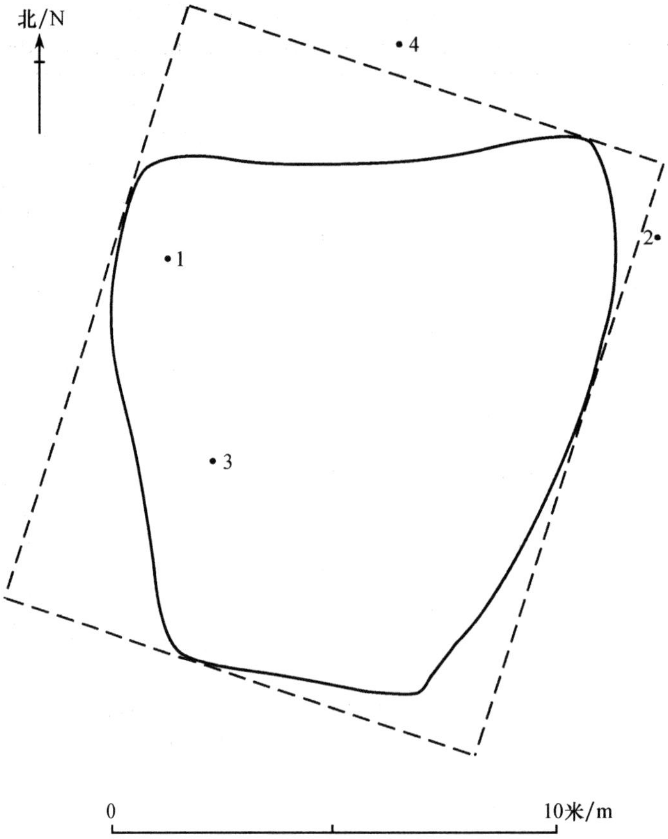

图Ⅰ.3.8　四号夯土基址平面及典型探孔位置

Figure Ⅰ.3.8　Plan of Rammed Earth Foundation 4 and the placement of representative coring holes.

表Ⅰ.3.8　四号基址典型探孔地层

Table Ⅰ.3.8　Strata sequence of representative coring holes in Rammed Earth Foundation 4

图上号 Number on map	探孔号 Core number	地层序列 Order of strata	土样 Soil type	深度 Depth	地层描述 Description	备注 Note
1	$U_1$41	a	表土 Topsoil	0 ~ 0.3 m		探孔$U_1$41（20）位于基址西部 Coring hole $U_1$41 (20) is located in the western part of the foundation.
		b	扰土 Disturbed soil	0.3 ~ 0.4 m		
		c	夯土 Rammed earth	0.4 ~ 1.4 m		
		d	黄褐土 Tan earth	1.4 ~ 2.0 m	含砂 Sand inclusions	不到底 Did not reach the bottom.
2	$U_1 43'$	a	表土 Topsoil	0 ~ 0.3 m		探孔$U_1 43'$（4）位于基址东侧 Coring hole $U_1 43'$ (4) is located to the east of the foundation.
		b	灰土 Grey earth	0.3 ~ 0.6 m	含灰烬和砂 Inclusions of ash and sand	
		c	黄褐土 Tan earth	0.6 ~ 2.0 m	含砂 Sand inclusions	不到底 Did not reach the bottom.

续表

图上号 Number on map	探孔号 Core number	地层序列 Order of strata	土样 Soil type	深度 Depth	地层描述 Description	备注 Note
3	$T_1$42	a	表土 Topsoil	0 ~ 0.3 m		探孔$T_1$42（15）位于基址南部 Coring hole $T_1$42 (15) is located in the southern part of the foundation.
		b	夯土 Rammed earth	0.3 ~ 0.9 m		
		c	淤土 Sediment	0.9 ~ 1.2 m		
		d	黄褐土 Tan earth	1.2 ~ 2.0m	含砂 Sand inclusions	不到底 Did not reach the bottom.
4	$V_1$42	a	表土 Topsoil	0 ~ 0.3 m		探孔$V_1$42（12）位于基址北侧 Coring hole $V_1$42 (12) is located to the north of the foundation.
		b	扰土 Disturbed soil	0.3 ~ 0.5 m		
		c	淤土 Sediment	0.5 ~ 1.9 m	含大量灰烬和水锈 With large quantities of ash and water-formed rust inclusions	
		d	砂层 Sand layer	1.9 m ~		探不下 Could not proceed past 1.9 m.

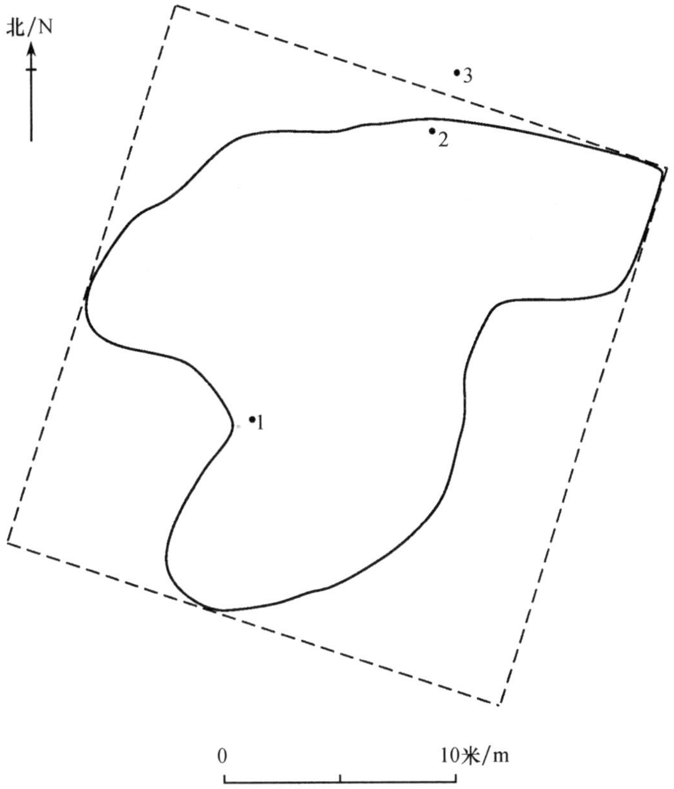

图Ⅰ.3.9　五号夯土基址平面及典型探孔位置

Figure Ⅰ.3.9　Plan of Rammed Earth Foundation 5 and the placement of representative coring holes.

表Ⅰ.3.9　五号夯土基址典型探孔地层

Table Ⅰ.3.9　Strata sequence of representative coring holes in Rammed Earth Foundation 5

图上号 Number on map	探孔号 Core number	地层序列 Order of strata	土样 Soil type	深度 Depth	地层描述 Description	备注 Note
1	$X_1$43	a	表土 Topsoil	0 ~ 0.3 m		探孔$X_1$43（25）位于基址南部 Coring hole $X_1$43 (25) is located in the southern part of the foundation.
		b	扰土 Disturbed soil	0.3 ~ 0.5 m		
		c	夯土 Rammed earth	0.5 ~ 1.4 m		0.8米出有陶片 Ceramic sherds found at 0.8 m.
		d	褐土 Brown earth	1.4 ~ 2.0 m	含砂，含灰烬 With inclusions of sand and ash	不到底 Did not reach the bottom.
2	Z_1'43	a	表土 Topsoil	0 ~ 0.3 m		探孔Z_1'43（15）位于基址北部 Coring hole Z_1'43 (15) is located in the northern part of the foundation.
		b	扰土 Disturbed soil	0.3 ~ 0.5 m		
		c	夯土 Rammed earth	0.5 ~ 0.9 m	灰 Grey	
		d	夯土 Rammed earth	0.9 ~ 1.5 m	黄褐 Tan	
		e	黄褐土 Tan earth	1.5 ~ 2.1 m	含大量砂 With a large quantity of sand inclusions	不到底 Did not reach the bottom.
3	$A_2$44	a	表土 Topsoil	0 ~ 0.3 m		探孔$A_2$44（14）位于基址北部 Coring hole $A_2$44 (14) is located to the north of the foundation.
		b	褐土 Brown earth	0.3 ~ 1.8 m		
		c	黄褐土 Tan earth	1.8 ~ 2.0 m	含砂 Sand inclusions	

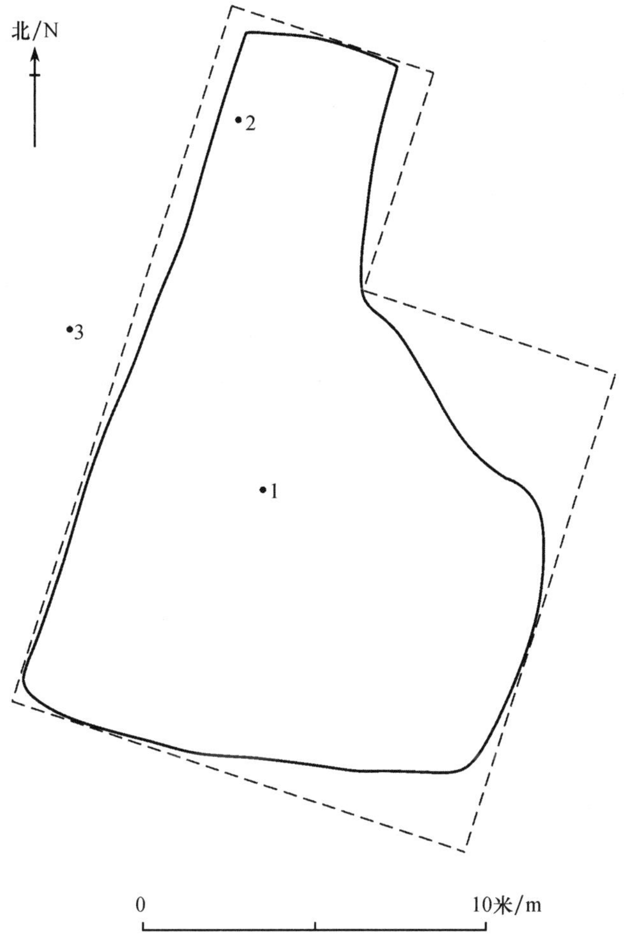

图Ⅰ.3.10　六号夯土基址平面及典型探孔位置

Figure Ⅰ.3.10　Plan of Rammed Earth Foundation 6 and the placement of representative coring holes.

表Ⅰ.3.10　六号夯土基址典型探孔地层

Table Ⅰ.3.10　Strata sequence of representative coring holes in Rammed Earth Foundation 6

图上号 Number on map	探孔号 Core number	地层序列 Order of strata	土样 Soil type	深度 Depth	地层描述 Description	备注 Note
1	$T_1 39'$	a	表土 Topsoil	0 ~ 0.3 m		探孔$T_1 39'$（16）位于基址6中部 Coring hole $T_1 39'$ (16) is located at the center of Foundation 6.
		b	灰土 Grey earth	0.3 ~ 0.7 m		
		c	夯土 Rammed earth	0.7 ~ 0.8 m	灰 Grey	
		d	黄褐土 Tan earth	0.8 ~ 2.0 m	含砂 Sand inclusions	不到底 Did not reach the bottom.
2	$V_1 39$	a	表土 Topsoil	0 ~ 0.3 m	较灰 Relatively grey	探孔$V_1 39$（21）位于基址6北部 Coring hole $V_1 39$ (21) is located in the northern part of Foundation 6.
		b	扰土 Disturbed soil	0.3 ~ 0.5 m		
		c	夯土 Rammed earth	0.5 ~ 0.8 m	黄褐 Tan	

续表

图上号 Number on map	探孔号 Core number	地层序列 Order of strata	土样 Soil type	深度 Depth	地层描述 Description	备注 Note
2	$V_1$39	d	黄褐土 Tan earth	0.8 ~ 1.4 m	含砂 Sand inclusions	1.4米为石块，打不下 Stones encountered at 1.4 m, could not proceed.
3	$U_1$38	a	表土 Topsoil	0 ~ 0.3 m		探孔$U_1$38 (28) 夯土东部 Coring hole $U_1$38 (28) is to the east of the foundation.
		b	灰土 Grey earth	0.3 ~ 0.7 m	含灰烬，含水锈 With inclusions of ash and water-formed rust	
		c	黄褐土 Tan earth	0.7 ~ 1.5 m	含砂 Sand inclusions	
		d	砂层 Sand layer	1.5 ~ 1.9 m	粗 Coarse	
		e	砂层 Sand layer	1.9 ~ 2.3 m	细 Fine	不到底 Did not reach the bottom.

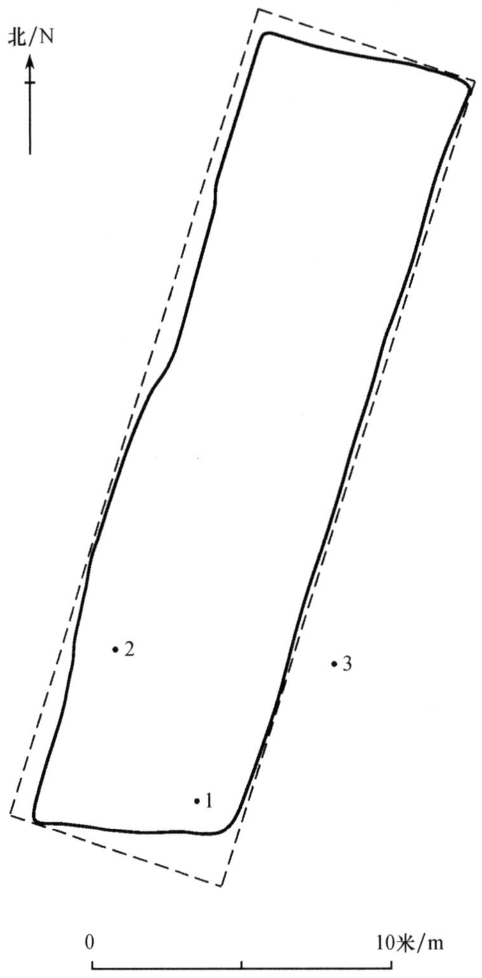

图Ⅰ.3.11　七号夯土基址平面及典型探孔位置

Figure Ⅰ.3.11　Plan of Rammed Earth Foundation 7 and the placement of representative coring holes.

表Ⅰ.3.11　七号夯土基址典型探孔地层

Table Ⅰ.3.11　Strata sequence of representative coring holes in Rammed Earth Foundation 7

图上号 Number on map	探孔号 Core number	地层序列 Order of strata	土样 Soil type	深度 Depth	地层描述 Description	备注 Note
1	S_137'	a	表土 Topsoil	0 ~ 0.3 m		探孔S_137'（14）位于基址南端 Coring hole S_137' (14) is located in the southern part of the foundation.
		b	灰土 Grey earth	0.3 ~ 0.6 m	含砂，含灰烬 Inclusions of sand and ash	
		c	夯土 Rammed earth	0.6 ~ 1.2 m	黄褐 Tan	
		d	黄褐土 Tan earth	1.2 ~ 2.0 m	含砂 Sand inclusions	不到底 Did not reach the bottom.
2	T_136'	a	表土 Topsoil	0 ~ 0.3 m	较灰 Relatively grey	探孔T_136'（25）位于基址南部 Coring hole T_136' (25) is located in the southern part of the foundation.
		b	灰土 Grey earth	0.3 ~ 0.5 m	含灰烬，松软 With ash inclusions, soft	
		c	夯土 Rammed earth	0.5 ~ 1.2 m	黄褐 Tan	
		d	黄褐土 Tan earth	1.2 ~ 1.7 m	含砂 Sand inclusions	
		e	砂层 Sand layer	1.7 m ~		打不下 Could not proceed past 1.7 m.
3	T_138	a	表土 Topsoil	0 ~ 0.3 m	较灰 Relatively grey	探孔T_138（6）位于基址东部 Coring hole T_138 (6) is located to the east of the foundation.
		b	灰土 Grey earth	0.3 ~ 0.9 m	含灰烬，松软 Ash inclusions, soft	
		c	褐土 Brown earth	0.9 ~ 1.4 m	含砂，含灰烬 Inclusions of sand and ash	
		d	砂层 Sand layer	1.4 ~ 1.45 m		
		e	黄褐土 Tan earth	1.45 ~ 2.1 m	含砂 Sand inclusions	不到底 Did not reach the bottom.

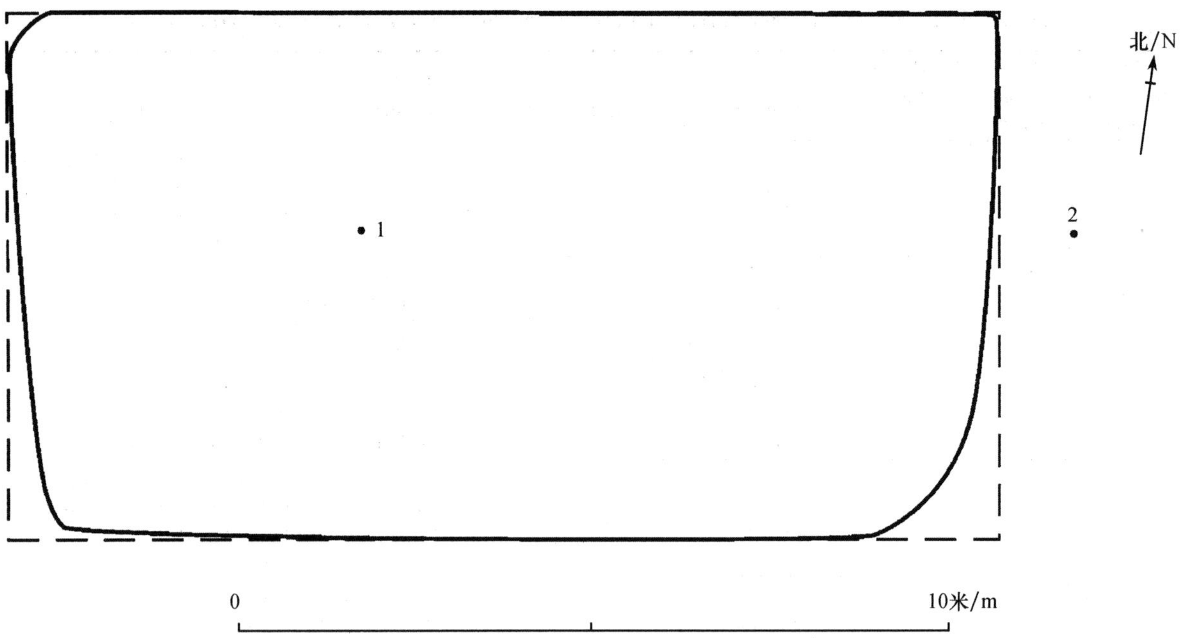

图Ⅰ.3.12　十六号夯土基址平面及典型探孔位置

Figure Ⅰ.3.12　Plan of Rammed Earth Foundation 16 and the placement of representative coring holes.

表Ⅰ.3.12　十六号建筑基址典型探孔地层

Table Ⅰ.3.12　Strata sequence of the representative coring holes in Rammed Earth Foundation 16

图上号 Number on map	探孔号 Core number	地层序列 Order of strata	土样 Soil type	深度 Depth	地层描述 Description	备注 Note
1	$P_1$34	a	表土 Topsoil	0 ~ 0.3 m	较灰 Relatively grey	
		b	灰土 Grey earth	0.3 ~ 1.3 m	含灰烬，含砂 With inclusions of ash and sand	
		c	夯土 Rammed earth	1.3m ~	黄褐，含砂 Tan, with sand inclusions	
2	$P_1$36	a	表土 Topsoil	0 ~ 0.3 m	较灰 Relatively grey	
		b	垫土 Packed soil	0.3 ~ 0.6 m	浅灰 Light grey	
		c	黄褐土 Tan earth	0.6 ~ 1.7 m	含少量砂 With a small amount of sand inclusions	
		d	黄褐黏土 Tan clay	1.7 m ~		生土 Virgin soil

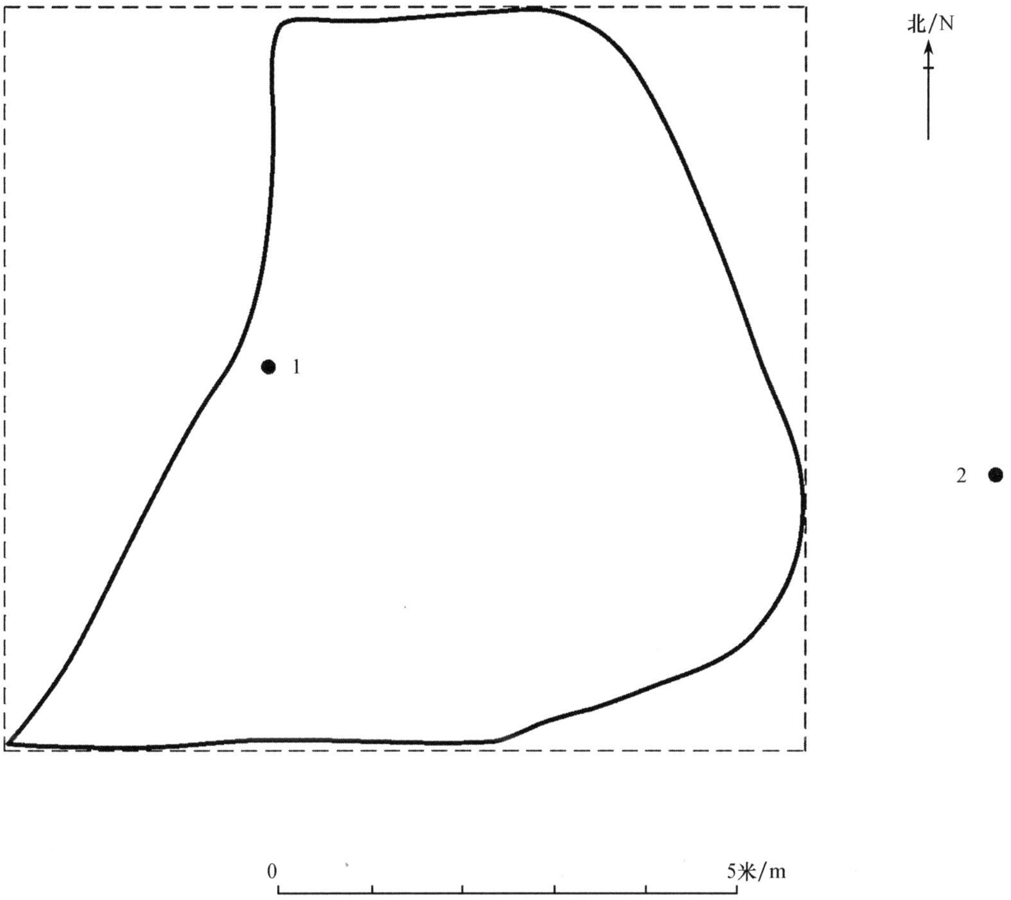

图Ⅰ.3.13　十七号夯土基址平面及典型探孔位置

Figure Ⅰ.3.13　Plan of Rammed Earth Foundation 17 and the placement of representative coring holes.

表Ⅰ.3.13　十七号夯土基址典型探孔地层

Table Ⅰ.3.13　Strata sequence of representative coring holes of Rammed Earth Foundation 17

图上号 Number on map	探孔号 Core number	地层序列 Order of strata	土样 Soil type	深度 Depth	地层描述 Description	备注 Note
1	40	a	垫土 Later earth fill	0 ~ 0.3 m		第40孔位于基址西部 Coring hole 40 is located in the western part of the foundation.
		b	灰土 Grey earth	0.3 ~ 0.6 m		
		c	夯土 Rammed earth	0.6 ~ 1.4 m	黄褐，含砂 Tan with sandy inclusions	不到底 Did not reach the bottom.
		d	黄褐土 Tan earth	1.4 ~ 2.0 m	含砂 Sand inclusions	不到底 Did not reach the bottom.
2	88	a	垫土 Later earth fill	0 ~ 0.3 m		第88孔位于基址的东部 Coring hole 88 is located to east of the foundation.
		b	灰土 Grey earth	0.3 ~ 0.7 m	含灰烬 Ash inclusions	
		c	黄褐土 Tan earth	0.7 ~ 2.0 m	含砂 Sand inclusions	不到底 Did not reach the bottom.

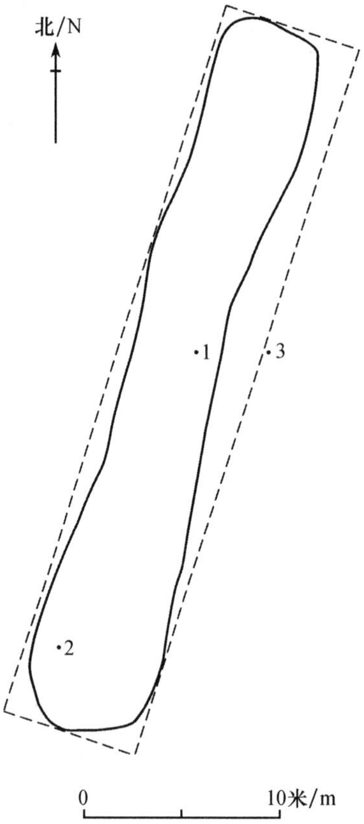

图Ⅰ.3.14　八号夯土基址平面及典型探孔位置

Figure Ⅰ.3.14　Plan of Rammed Earth Foundation 8 and the placement of representative coring holes.

表Ⅰ.3.14　八号夯土基址典型探孔地层

Table Ⅰ.3.14　Strata sequence of representative coring holes in Rammed Earth Foundation 8

图上号 Number on map	探孔号 Core number	地层序列 Order of strata	土样 Soil type	深度 Depth	地层描述 Description	备注 Note
1	$L_2$11	a	垫土 Later earth fill	0 ~ 0.7 m		探孔$L_2$11（12）位于基址中部 Coring hole $L_2$11 (12) is located in the center of the foundation.
		b	灰土 Grey earth	0.7 ~ 1.4 m	含灰烬，含碎陶片、砂、烧土颗粒 With inclusions of ash, pottery sherds, sand, and burned soil particles	
		c	灰土 Grey earth	1.4 ~ 1.85 m	含水锈 With water-formed rust inclusions	1.5米出土石器残片 Fragments of stone tools were brought up from 1.5 m deep.
		d	夯土 Rammed earth	1.85 ~ 2.4 m	黄褐，含砂 Tan, sand inclusions	不到底 Did not reach the bottom.
2	$I_2$11	a	垫土 Later earth fill	0 ~ 0.3 m		$I_2$11位于基址南部 $I_2$11 is located in the southern part of the foundation.
		b	灰土 Grey earth	0.3 ~ 1.5 m	含灰烬，含碎陶片、砂 Inclusions of ash, pottery sherds, and sand	
		c	夯土 Rammed earth	1.5 m ~	黄褐，含砂 Tan, sand inclusions	

续表

图上号 Number on map	探孔号 Core number	地层序列 Order of strata	土样 Soil type	深度 Depth	地层描述 Description	备注 Note
3	$L_2 11'$	a	垫土 Later earth fill	0 ~ 0.3 m		$L_2 11'$位于基址东部 $L_2 11'$ is located to the east of the foundation.
		b	灰土 Grey earth	0.3 ~ 1.0m	含灰烬 With ash inclusions	
		c	淤土 Sediment	1.0 ~ 1.8m	灰褐，含水锈 Grey-brown, with rust inclusions	
		d	黄褐土 Tan earth	1.8 m ~	含砂 Sand inclusions	

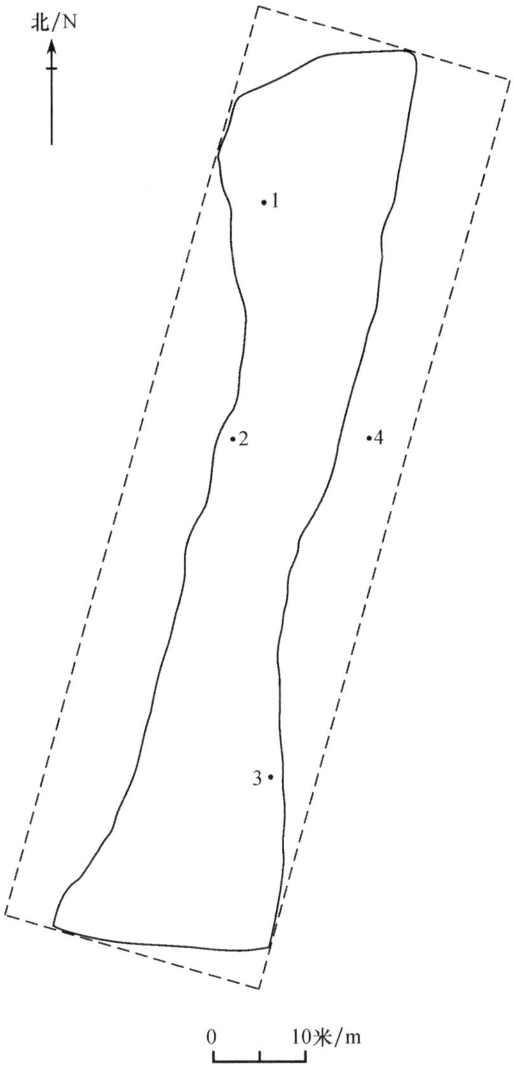

图Ⅰ.3.15　九号夯土基址平面及典型探孔位置

Figure Ⅰ.3.15　Plan of Rammed Earth Foundation 9 and the placement of representative coring holes.

表Ⅰ.3.15　九号夯土基址典型探孔地层

Table Ⅰ.3.15　Strata sequence of representative coring holes in Rammed Earth Foundation 9

图上号 Number on map	探孔号 Core number	地层序列 Order of strata	土样 Soil type	深度 Depth	地层描述 Description	备注 Note
1	$N_2$16	a	表土 Topsoil	0 ~ 0.3 m	较灰 Relatively grey	探孔$N_2$16位于基址北部 Coring hole $N_2$16 is in the northern part of the foundation.
1	$N_2$16	b	灰土 Grey earth	0.3 ~ 1.7 m	含灰烬，含砂，含红烧土颗粒 With inclusions of ash, sand, and burnt soil particles	
		c	夯土 Rammed earth	1.7 ~ 2.4 m	黄褐，含砂 Tan with sand inclusions	
		d	黄淤土 Yellow sediment	2.4 m ~	黄淤土 Yellow sediment	不到底 Did not reach the bottom.
2	$I_2$16′	a	表土 Topsoil	0 ~ 0.3 m	较灰 Relatively grey	探孔$I_2$16′位于基址中部 Coring hole $I_2$16′ is in the center of the foundation.
		b	灰土 Grey earth	0.3 ~ 1.4 m	含灰烬，含砂，含红烧土颗粒，含碎陶片 With inclusions of ash, sand, burnt soil particles, and pottery sherds	
		c	夯土 Rammed earth	1.4 ~ 1.9 m	黄褐，含砂 Tan with sand inclusions	
		d	砂层 Sand layer	1.9 ~ 2 m		
		e	黄褐土 Tan earth	2 m ~	含砂 Sand inclusions	不到底 Did not reach the bottom.
3	$B_2$18	a	表土 Topsoil	0 ~ 0.3 m	较灰 Relatively grey	探孔$B_2$18在南部 Coring hole $B_2$18 is in the southern part of the foundation.
		b	灰土 Grey earth	0.3 ~ 0.6 m	含砂 Sand inclusions	
		c	夯土 Rammed earth	0.6 ~ 1.2 m	黄褐，含灰土粒 Tan with inclusions of grey soil particles	
		d	基岩 Bedrock	1.2 m ~		
4	$I_2$18	a	表土 Topsoil	0 ~ 0.3 m	较灰 Relatively grey	$I_2$18在基址东侧 Coring hole $I_2$18 is to the east of the foundation.
		b	灰土 Grey earth	0.3 ~ 0.7 m		
		c	灰土 Grey earth	0.7 ~ 1.4 m	含灰烬，含砂 With inclusions of ash and sand	
		d	基岩 Bedrock	1.4 m ~		

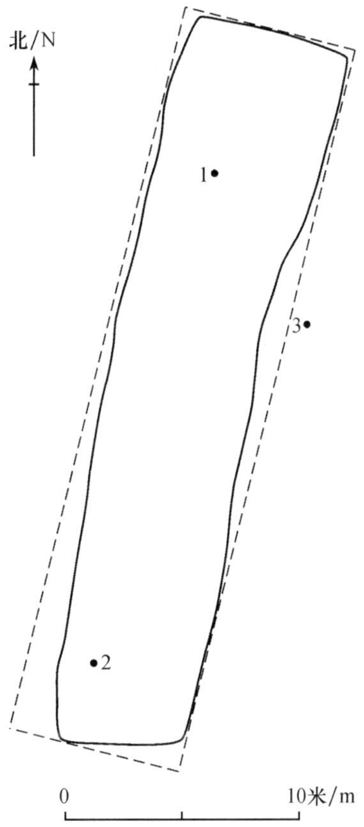

图Ⅰ.3.16　十号夯土基址平面及典型探孔位置

Figure Ⅰ.3.16　Plan of Rammed Earth Foundation 10 and the placement of representative coring holes.

表Ⅰ.3.16　十号夯土基址典型探孔地层

Table Ⅰ.3.16　Strata sequence of representative coring holes in Rammed Earth Foundation 10

图上号 Number on map	探孔号 Core number	地层序列 Order of strata	土样 Soil type	深度 Depth	地层描述 Description	备注 Note
1	$K_2$28	a	表土 Topsoil	0 ~ 0.3 m	较灰 Relatively grey	探孔$K_2$28（11）位于基址北部 Coring hole $K_2$28 (11) is located in the northern part of the foundation.
		b	灰土 Grey earth	0.3 ~ 1.2 m	含灰烬，含碎陶片 With inclusions of ash and pottery sherds	
		c	夯土 Rammed earth	1.2 ~ 1.9 m	黄褐，含砂 Tan with sand inclusions	
		d	黄褐土 Tan earth	1.9 ~ 2.0 m	含砂 Sand inclusions	不到底 Did not reach the bottom.
2	$G_2$28	a	表土 Topsoil	0 ~ 0.3 m	较灰 Relatively grey	探孔$G_2$28（15）位于基址南部 Coring hole $G_2$28 (15) is located in the southern part of the foundation.
		b	灰土 Grey earth	0.3 ~ 0.8 m	含灰烬，含砂，较硬 With inclusions of ash and sand, relatively hard	
		c	夯土 Rammed earth	0.8 ~ 1.7 m	黄褐含砂 Tan with sand inclusions	

续表

图上号 Number on map	探孔号 Core number	地层序列 Order of strata	土样 Soil type	深度 Depth	地层描述 Description	备注 Note
2	$G_2$28	d	淤砂 Sandy sediment	1.7 ~ 1.8 m		
		e	黄褐土 Tan earth	1.85 ~ 2.0 m	含砂 Sand inclusions	不到底 Did not reach the bottom.
3	$J_2$29	a	表土 Topsoil	0 ~ 0.3 m	较灰 Relatively grey	探孔$J_2$29位于基址东部 Coring hole $J_2$29 is located to the east of the foundation.
		b	灰土 Grey earth	0.3 ~ 1.5 m	含灰烬，含砂、含烧土粒、碎陶片 With inclusions of ash, sand, burnt soil particles, and pottery sherds	
		c	黄褐土 Tan earth	1.5 ~ 2.0 m	含砂 Sand inclusions	
		d	淤土 Sediment	2.0 m ~		

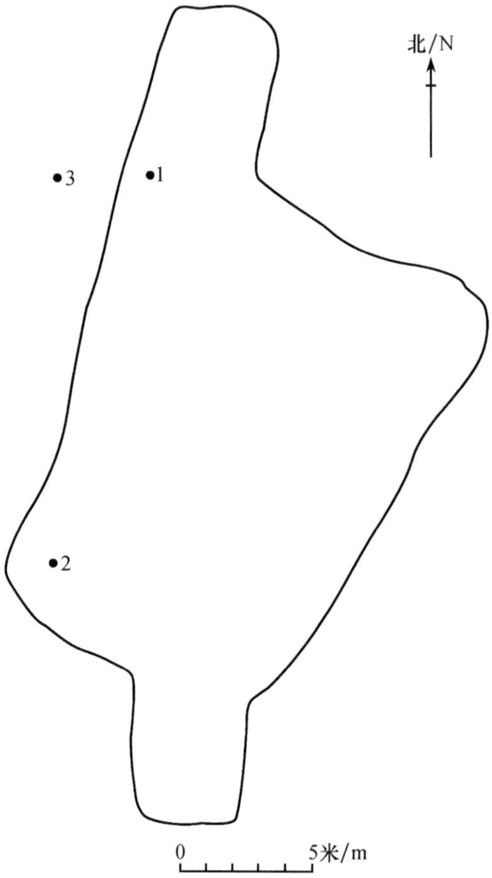

图Ⅰ.3.17　十一号夯土基址平面及典型探孔位置

Figure Ⅰ.3.17　Plan of Rammed Earth Foundation 11 and the placement of representative coring holes.

表Ⅰ.3.17　十一号夯土基址典型探孔地层

Table Ⅰ.3.17　Strata sequence of representative coring holes in Rammed Earth Foundation 11

图上号 Number on map	探孔号 Core number	地层序列 Order of strata	土样 Soil type	深度 Depth	地层描述 Description	备注 Note
1	$D_2$28	a	表土 Topsoil	0 ~ 0.3 m	较灰 Relatively grey	探孔$D_2$28（19）位于基址北部 Coring hole $D_2$28 (19) is located in the northern part of the foundation.
		b	灰土 Grey earth	0.3 ~ 0.9 m	含灰烬，含碎陶片 With inclusions of ash and pottery sherds	0.8 m出土陶片 Pottery sherds brought up from depth of 0.8 m.
		c	夯土 Rammed earth	0.9 ~ 1.7 m	黄褐，含砂 Tan with sand inclusions	
		d	淤土 Sediment	1.7 m ~	生土 Natural earth	不到底 Did not reach the bottom.
2	$A_2$28	a	表土 Topsoil	0 ~ 0.3 m	较灰 Relatively grey	探孔$A_2$28（22）位于基址南部 Coring hole $A_2$28 (22) is located in the southern part of the foundation.
		b	灰土 Grey earth	0.3 ~ 1.0 m	含灰烬，含砂，较硬 With inclusions of ash and sand, relatively hard	
		c	夯土 Rammed earth	1.0 ~ 1.2 m	黄褐含砂 Tan with sand inclusions	
		d	砂层 Sand layer	1.2 ~ 1.3m		
		e	黄褐土 Tan earth	1.3 ~ 2.0m	含砂 Sand inclusions	不底 Did not reach the bottom.
3	$D_2$27′	a	表土 Topsoil	0 ~ 0.3 m	较灰 Relatively grey	探孔$D_2$27′（26）位于基址西部 Coring hole $D_2$27′ (26) is located to the west of the foundation.
		b	灰土 Grey earth	0.3 ~ 1.4 m	含灰烬，含砂、黄土块 With inclusions of ash and sand, blocks of loess	
		c	砂层 Sand layer	1.4 ~ 1.6 m		
		d	黄褐土 Tan earth	1.6 ~ 2.0 m	含砂 Sand inclusions	不底 Did not reach the bottom.

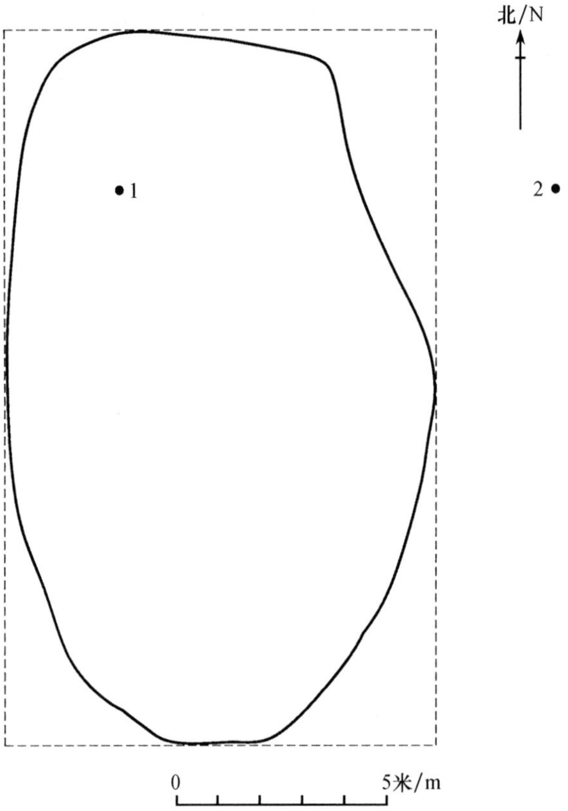

图Ⅰ.3.18　十二号夯土基址平面及典型探孔位置

Figure Ⅰ.3.18　Plan of Rammed Earth Foundation 12 and the placement of representative coring holes.

表Ⅰ.3.18　十二号夯土基址典型探孔地层

Table Ⅰ.3.18　Strata sequence of representative coring holes in Rammed Earth Foundation 12

图上号 Number on map	探孔号 Core number	地层序列 Order of strata	土样 Soil type	深度 Depth	地层描述 Description	备注 Note
1	$E_2$24	a	表土 Topsoil	0 ~ 0.3 m	较灰 Relatively grey	探孔$E_2$24位于基址西部 Coring hole $E_2$24, located in the western part of the foundation.
		b	灰土 Grey earth	0.3 ~ 0.5 m	含灰烬，含砂 Inclusions of ash and sand	
		c	夯土 Rammed earth	0.5 ~ 0.6 m	黄褐，含砂 Tan with sand inclusions	
		d	灰土 Grey earth	0.6 ~ 0.9 m	生土，含灰烬，含砂 Natural earth, with inclusions of ash and sand	
		e	黄褐土 Tan earth	0.9 ~ 1.4 m		
		f	砂层 Sand layer	1.4 ~ 1.6 m		
2	$E_2$26	a	表土 Topsoil	0 ~ 0.3m	较灰 Relatively grey	探孔$E_2$26位于基址东部 Coring hole $E_2$26 is located to the east of the foundation.
		b	灰土 Grey earth	0.3 ~ 1.1 m	含灰烬，含碎陶片 Inclusions of ash and pottery sherds	

续表

图上号 Number on map	探孔号 Core number	地层序列 Order of strata	土样 Soil type	深度 Depth	地层描述 Description	备注 Note
2	$E_2 26$	c	黄褐土 Tan earth	1.1 ~ 1.5 m	含砂 Sand inclusions	
		d	砂层 Sand layer	1.5 ~ 1.7 m		
		e	淤土 Sediment	1.7 ~ 2.0 m	黄色 Yellow in color	不底 Did not reach the bottom.

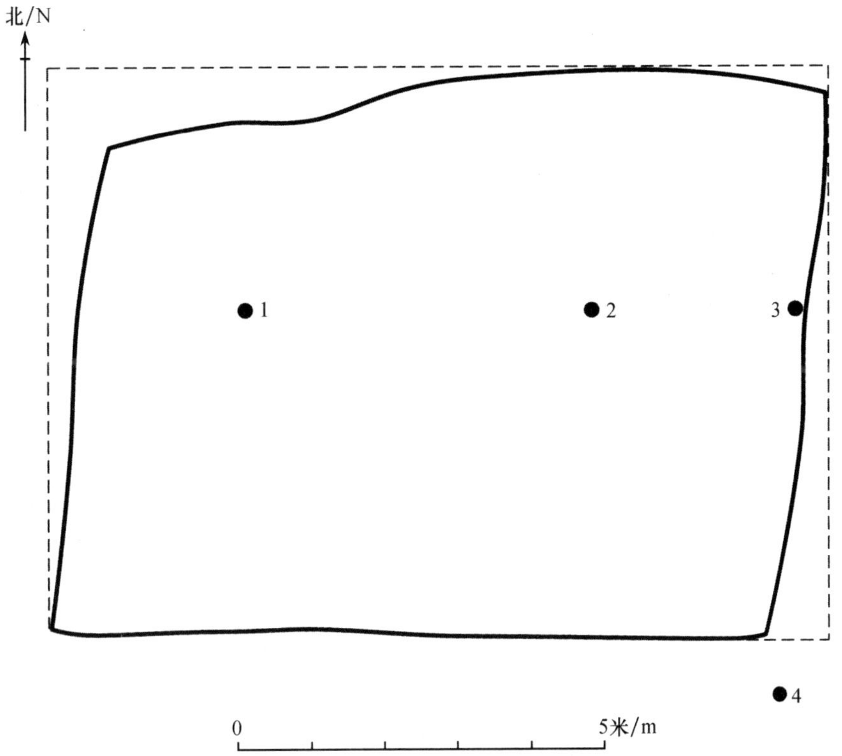

图Ⅰ.3.19　十三号夯土基址平面及典型探孔位置

Figure Ⅰ.3.19　Plan of Rammed Earth Foundation 13 and the placement of representative coring holes.

表Ⅰ.3.19　十三号夯土基址典型探孔地层

Table Ⅰ.3.19　Strata sequence of representative coring holes in Rammed Earth Foundation 13

图上号 Number on map	探孔号 Core number	地层序列 Order of strata	土样 Soil type	深度 Depth	地层描述 Description	备注 Note
1	$R_1 18$	a	表土 Topsoil	0 ~ 0.3 m	较灰 Relatively grey	探孔$R_1$18位于基址西部 Coring hole $R_1$18 is located in the western part of the foundation.
		b	灰土 Grey earth	0.3 ~ 0.6 m	含灰烬，含砂 Inclusions of ash and sand	
		c	夯土 Rammed earth	0.6 ~ 2.1 m	黄褐 Tan	
		d	生土 Natural earth	2.1 m ~	生土 Natural earth	

续表

图上号 Number on map	探孔号 Core number	地层序列 Order of strata	土样 Soil type	深度 Depth	地层描述 Description	备注 Note
2.	$R_1 18'$	a	表土 Topsoil	0 ~ 0.3 m	较灰 Relatively grey	探孔$R_1 18'$位于基址东部 Coring hole $R_1 18'$ is located in the eastern part of the foundation.
		b	灰土 Grey earth	0.3 ~ 0.4 m	含砂，含灰烬 Inclusions of sand and ash	
		c	夯土 Rammed earth	0.4 ~ 0.6 m	黄褐，含砂 Tan with sand inclusions	
		d	黄褐土 Tan earth	0.6 ~ 1.2 m	含砂 Sand inclusions	
		e	砂层 Sand layer	1.2 ~ 1.5 m		
		f	生土 Natural earth	1.5 m ~		
3	$R_1 18''$	a	表土 Topsoil	0 ~ 0.3 m	较灰 Relatively grey	探孔$R_1 18''$位于基址东部边缘 Coring hole $R_1 18''$ is located near the eastern edge of the foundation.
		b	灰土 Grey earth	0.3 ~ 0.9 m	含砂 Inclusions of sand	
		c	砂层 Sand layer	0.9 m		
		d	夯土 Rammed earth	0.9 m ~	黄 Yellow in color	
4	$Q_1 19$	a	表土 Topsoil	0 ~ 0.3 m	较灰 Relatively grey	探孔$Q_1 19$位于基址东南侧 Coring hole $Q_1 19$ is located to the southwest of the foundation.
		b	灰土 Grey earth	0.3 ~ 0.5 m		
		c	灰土 Grey earth	0.5 ~ 0.9 m	含灰烬 With ash inclusions	0.75m出土陶片，采集 Pottery sherd was unearthed at 0.75 m and was collected.
		d	黄褐土 Tan earth	0.9 ~ 1.1 m	含砂 Sand inclusions	
		e	基岩 Bedrock	1.1 m ~		

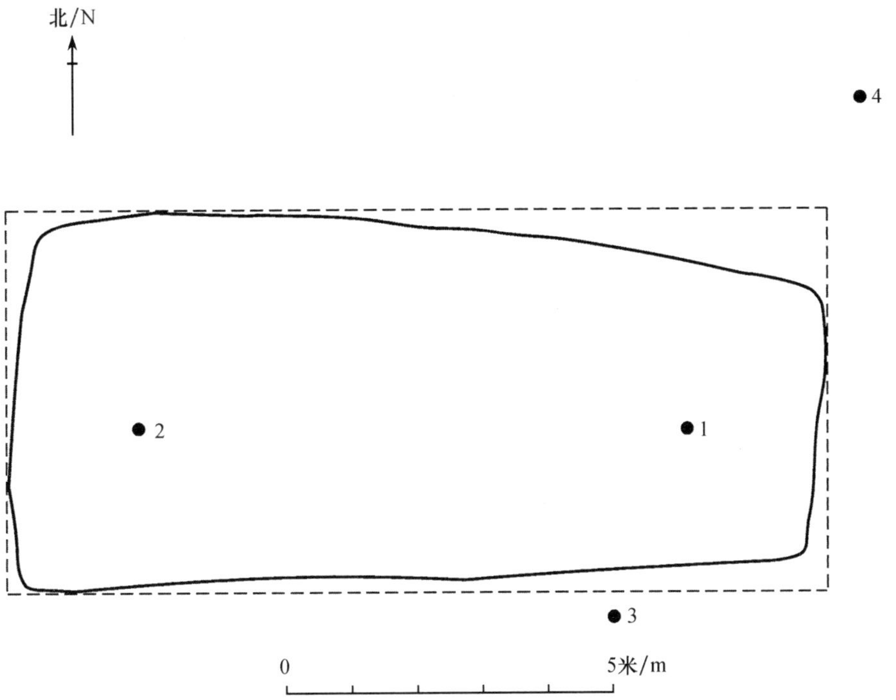

图Ⅰ.3.20　十四号夯土基址平面及典型探孔位置

Figure Ⅰ.3.20　Plan of Rammed Earth Foundation 14 and the placement of representative coring holes.

表Ⅰ.3.20　十四号夯土基址典型探孔

Table Ⅰ.3.20　Strata sequence of representative coring holes in Rammed Earth Foundation 14

图上号 Number on map	探孔号 Core number	地层序列 Order of strata	土样 Soil type	深度 Depth	地层描述 Description	备注 Note
1	$V_1$18	a	表土 Topsoil	0 ~ 0.3 m	较灰 Relatively grey	探孔$V_1$18位于基址东南部 Coring hole $V_1$18 is located in the southeastern part of the foundation.
		b	灰土 Grey earth	0.3 ~ 0.7 m	含砂 With sand inclusions	
		c	夯土 Rammed earth	0.7 m ~	黄褐 Tan in color	
2	$V_1$17	a	表土 Topsoil	0 ~ 0.3m	较灰 Relatively grey	探孔$V_1$17位于基址西南部。Coring hole $V_1$17 is located in the southwestern part of the foundation.
		b	灰土 Grey earth	0.3 ~ 1.8 m	含灰烬 With ash inclusions	
		c	夯土 Rammed earth	1.8 m ~	黄褐，含砂 Tan with sand inclusions	
3	U_1'18	a	表土 Topsoil	0 ~ 0.3 m	较灰 Relatively grey	探孔U_1'18，位于基址东南侧 Coring hole U_1'18 is located to the southeast of the foundation.
		b	灰土 Grey earth	0.3 ~ 1.6 m	含灰烬，含砂，陶片 With inclusions of ash, sand, and pottery sherds	
		c	基岩 Bedrock	1.6 m ~		

续表

图上号 Number on map	探孔号 Core number	地层序列 Order of strata	土样 Soil type	深度 Depth	地层描述 Description	备注 Note
4	$W_1 18'$	a	表土 Topsoil	0 ~ 0.3 m	较灰 Relatively grey	探孔$W_1 18'$位于基址东北侧 Coring hole $W_1 18'$ is located to the northeast of the foundation.
		b	灰土 Grey earth	0.3 ~ 1.8 m	含砂，含灰烬 Inclusions of sand and ash	
		c	生土 Virgin soil	1.8 m ~		

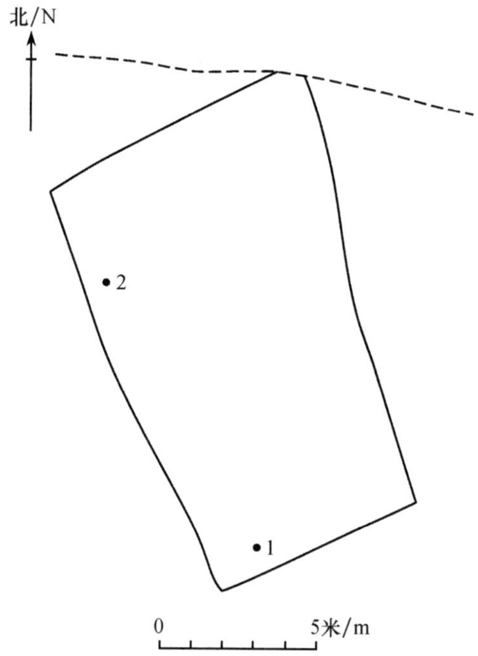

图Ⅰ.3.21　十五号夯土基址平面及典型探孔位置

Figure Ⅰ.3.21　Plan of Rammed Earth Foundation 15 and the placement of representative coring holes.

表Ⅰ.3.21　十五号夯土基址典型探孔

Table Ⅰ.3.21　Strata sequence of representative coring holes in Rammed Earth Foundation 15

图上号 Number on map	探孔号 Core number	地层序列 Order of strata	土样 Soil type	深度 Depth	地层描述 Description	备注 Note
1	$B'9$	a	表土 Topsoil	0 ~ 0.3 m		探孔$B'9$位于基址15南部 Coring hole $B'9$ is located in the southern part of foundation 15.
		b	浅灰褐土 Light grey-brown earth	0.3 ~ 1.3 m	含砂 Sandy inclusions	
		c	砂层 Sand layer	1.3 ~ 1.6 m		
		d	夯土 Rammed earth	1.6 ~ 1.8 m	黄褐，加砂 Tan with sandy inclusions	
		e	黄褐土 Tan earth	1.8 ~ 2 m	含砂 Sand inclusions	不到底 Could not proceed past 2 m.

续表

图上号 Number on map	探孔号 Core number	地层序列 Order of strata	土样 Soil type	深度 Depth	地层描述 Description	备注 Note
2	D8	a	表土 Topsoil	0 ~ 0.3 m	较灰 Relatively grey	探孔D8位于基址15西北部 Coring hole D8 is located in the northwestern part of foundation 15.
		b	灰土 Grey earth	0.3 ~ 1.4 m	含灰烬，含砂，夹碎陶片 With inclusions of ash, sand, and pottery fragments	
		c	夯土 Rammed earth	1.4 m ~	黄褐 Tan	不到底 Could not proceed past 2 m.

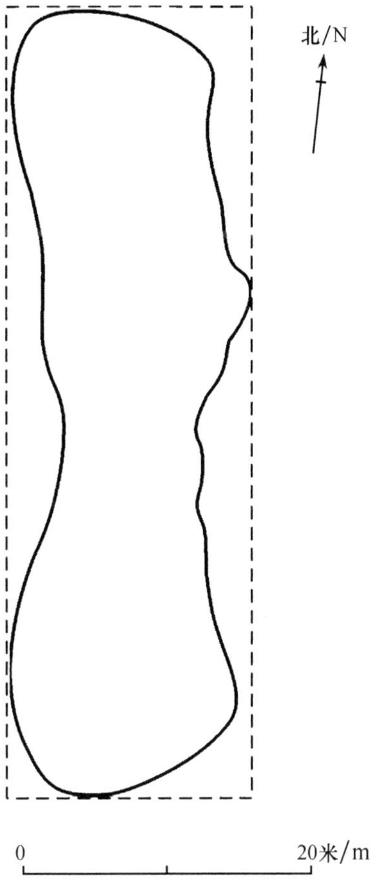

图Ⅰ.3.22　十八号夯土基址平面及典型探孔位置
Figure Ⅰ.3.22　Plan of Rammed Earth Foundation 18.

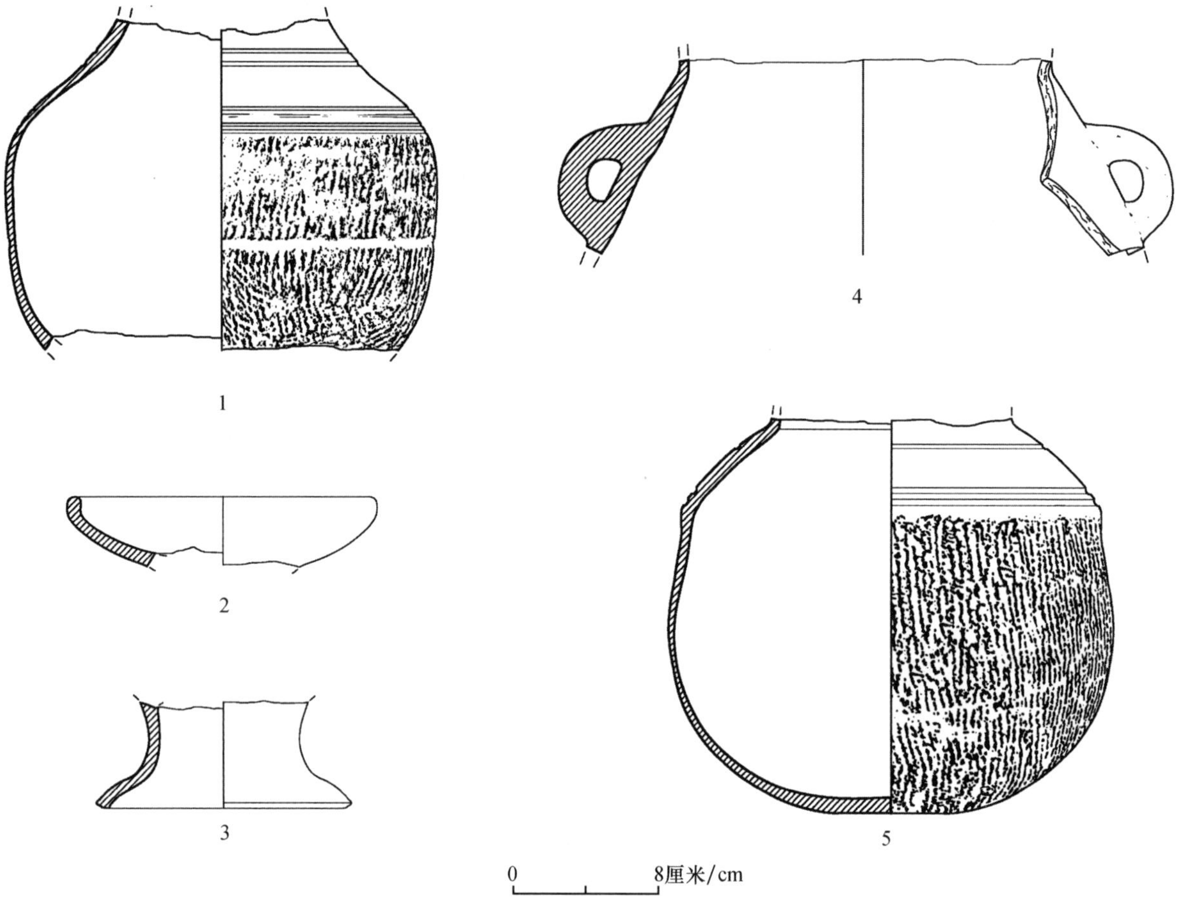

图Ⅰ.3.23　和平村西一组采集遗物

1. 罐　2. 豆　3. 簋　4. 壶　5. 罐

Figure Ⅰ.3.23　Artifacts collected from west of Heping Village: Group 1.

1. *Guan* jars　2. *Dou* pedestal dish　3. *Gui* tureen　4. *Hu* bottle　5. *Guan* jar

表Ⅰ.3.22　和平村西一组陶器统计

Table Ⅰ.3.22　Artifacts collected from west of Heping Village: Group 1

序号 Number on Figure Ⅰ.3.23	标本号 Specimen number	器物名称 Artifact name	出土时间 Excavation date	位置 Location	所属类型 Type	尺寸（厘米） Size (cm)	特点描述 Description of features
5	和平村西一组：1 Heping Village West Group 1：1	罐 *Guan* jar	2007 ~ 2009	和平村西侧 West of Heping Village	A3	D: 24.0 H: 20.7	泥质浅灰陶。窄折肩，腹部微鼓，小平底。肩上部有一道弦纹，下部有两道弦纹，腹部饰竖向中绳纹，底部饰交错绳纹。 Light grey clay. Narrow folded shoulder, slightly flared belly, small flat bottom. One intaglio ring on upper shoulder, two intaglio rings on lower shoulder. Belly decorated with vertical strips of medium cord decoration, staggered cord decoration on bottom.
1	和平村西一组：2 Heping Village West Group 1：2	罐 *Guan* jar	2007 ~ 2009	和平村西侧 West of Heping Village	A3	D: 23.4 H: 17.5	泥质灰褐陶。溜肩，深腹。肩上部有两周弦纹。肩下部有三周弦纹。腹部饰旋断绳纹。 Light grey-brown clay. Sloping shoulder, deep belly. Two intaglio ring decorations on the upper shoulder. Three strips of ring decoration on lower shoulder. Belly decorated with intermittent cord decoration.

续表

序号 Number on Figure Ⅰ.3.23	标本号 Specimen number	器物名称 Artifact name	出土时间 Excavation date	位置 Location	所属类型 Type	尺寸（厘米）Size (cm)	特点描述 Description of features
2	和平村西一组：4 Heping Village West Group 1：4	豆 *Dou* pedestal dish	2007 ~ 2009	和平村西侧 West of Heping Village	B3	M: 16.75 H: 3.7	泥质深灰陶。直口，圆唇，浅盘，素面。Dark grey clay. Straight mouth, round lips, shallow dish, plain.
3	和平村西一组：5 Heping Village West Group 1：5	簋座 Stand for a *gui* tureen	2007 ~ 2009	和平村西侧 West of Heping Village	A3?	B: 14.5	泥质灰褐陶。高圈足，下端外撇。素面。Grey-brown clay. High circular feet, flared to the outside, plain.
4	和平村西一组：9 Heping Village West Group 1：9	壶 *Hu* bottle	2007 ~ 2009	和平村西侧 West of Heping Village		H: 11.0	泥质浅灰陶。仅余腹部。鼓腹，上腹部饰双耳。Light grey clay. Only the shoulder remained. Bulging belly, upper part of the belly decorated with two ears.

尺寸标志：L=长度；H=高度；W=宽度；D=直径；R=半径；M=口径；B=底径；T=厚度；d=深度；h=孔径。

Measurements: L=length; H=height; W=width; D=diameter; R=radius; M=mouth diameter; B=bottom diameter; T=thickness; d=depth; h=hole diameter.

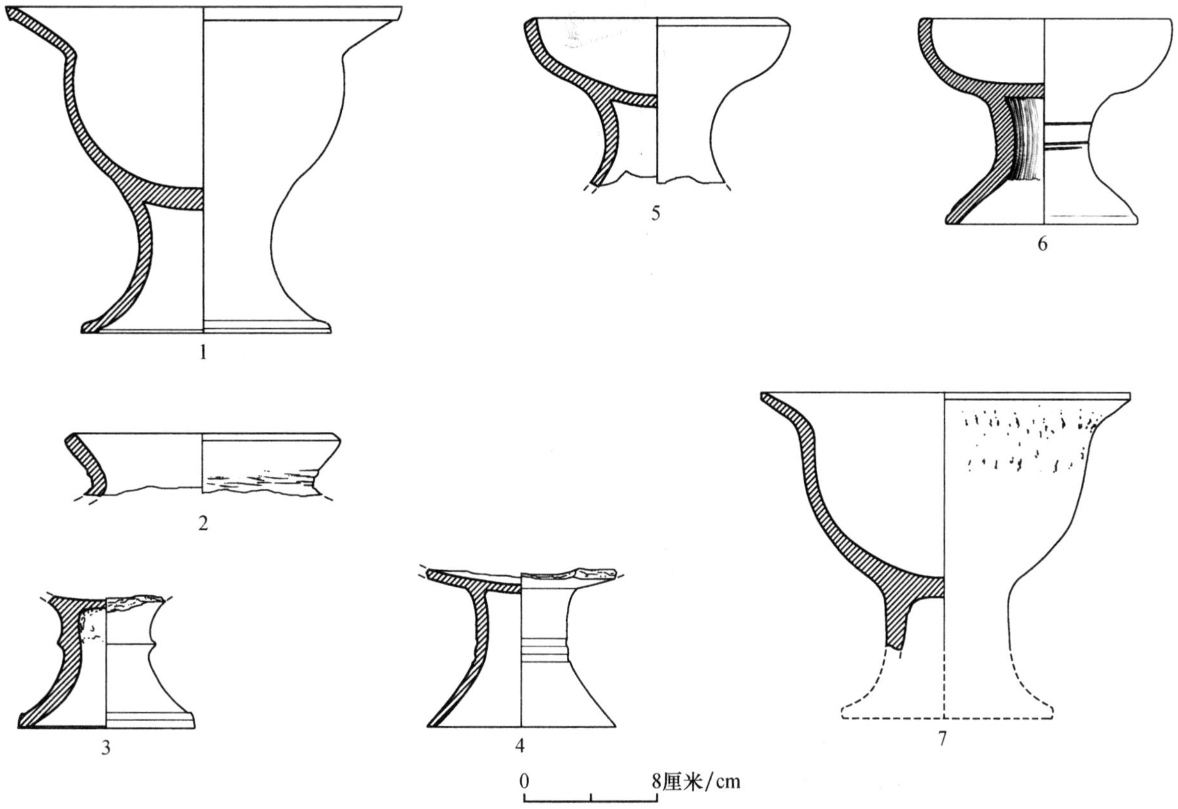

图Ⅰ.3.24 和平村西二组采集遗物

1. 簋 2. 罐 3 ~ 6. 豆 7. 簋

Figure Ⅰ.3.24 Artifacts collected from west of Heping Village: Group 2.

1. *Gui* tureen 2. *Guan* jar 3-6. *Dou* pedestal dish 7. *Gui* tureen

表Ⅰ.3.23　和平村西二组陶器统计

Table Ⅰ.3.23　Artifacts from west of Heping Village: Group 2

图号 Number on Fig. Ⅰ.3.24	标本号 Specimen number	器物名称 Artifact name	出土时间 Excavation date	位置 Location	所属类型 Type	尺寸（厘米） Size (cm)	特点描述 Description of features
1	和平村西二组：1 Heping Village West Group 2：1	簋 *Gui* tureen	2007 ~ 2009	和平村西部 West of Heping Village	A3	M: 23.7 H: 20.0	泥质灰褐陶。宽平折沿，尖唇，深腹微鼓。高圈足，圈足外撇。素面。 Greyish-brown clay. Wide, straight and flat folded rim, sharp lip, deep belly slightly bulging. High circular foot flared to the outside. Plain.
7	和平村西二组：2 Heping Village West Group 2：2	簋 *Gui* tureen	2007 ~ 2009	和平村西部 West of Heping Village	A3	M: 22.5 H: 19.6	泥质灰褐陶。宽沿稍卷，方唇，盆形腹。高圈足。素面。 Greyish-brown clay. Wide rim slight rolled, square lips, basin-shaped belly. High circular foot. Plain.
6	和平村西二组：3 Heping Village West Group 2：3	豆 *Dou* pedestal dish	2007 ~ 2009	和平村西部 West of Heping Village	A4	M: 15.3 H: 12.0	泥质浅灰陶。直口，方唇，高柄，下端外撇，呈喇叭状，有反弧。素面，柄上部饰弦纹两道。 Light grey clay. Straight mouth, square lip, high handle, bottom part flaring outward, trumpet-shaped, showing concave-downward curve. Plain, decorated with two intaglio rings in the upper part of the stem.
4	和平村西二组：4 Heping Village West Group 2：4	豆 *Dou* pedestal dish	2007 ~ 2009	和平村西部 West of Heping Village	A4	H: 9.7	泥质浅灰陶。高柄，下端外撇，较直，呈喇叭状。素面，柄中部饰弦纹两道。 Light grey clay. Tall stem, lower part flared to the outside and relatively straight, trumpet-shaped. Plain, middle part of the stem decorated with two rings.
5	和平村西二组：5 Heping Village West Group 2：5	豆 *Dou* pedestal dish	2007 ~ 2009	和平村西部 West of Heping Village	A3	M: 14.35 H: 9.7	泥质浅灰陶。浅盘，方唇，高柄，下端外撇。素面。 Light grey clay. Shallow dish, square lips, tall stem, lower part flared to the outside. Plain.
3	和平村西二组：6 Heping Village West Group 2：6	豆 *Dou* pedestal dish	2007 ~ 2009	和平村西部 West of Heping Village	A5	H: 8.0	泥质深灰陶。圈足外撇。柄中部有凸棱一周，位置偏高，下端外撇，呈喇叭状。素面。 Dark grey clay. Circular foot flared to the outside. Ridge at the center of the stem, positioned relatively high, lower part flared to the outside, trumpet-shaped. Plain.
2	和平村西二组：8 Heping Village West Group 2：8	罐口沿 Rim from a *guan* jar	2007 ~ 2009	和平村西部 West of Heping Village		M: 16.2	泥质深灰陶。卷沿方唇。素面。 Dark grey clay. Rolled rim and square lip. Plain.

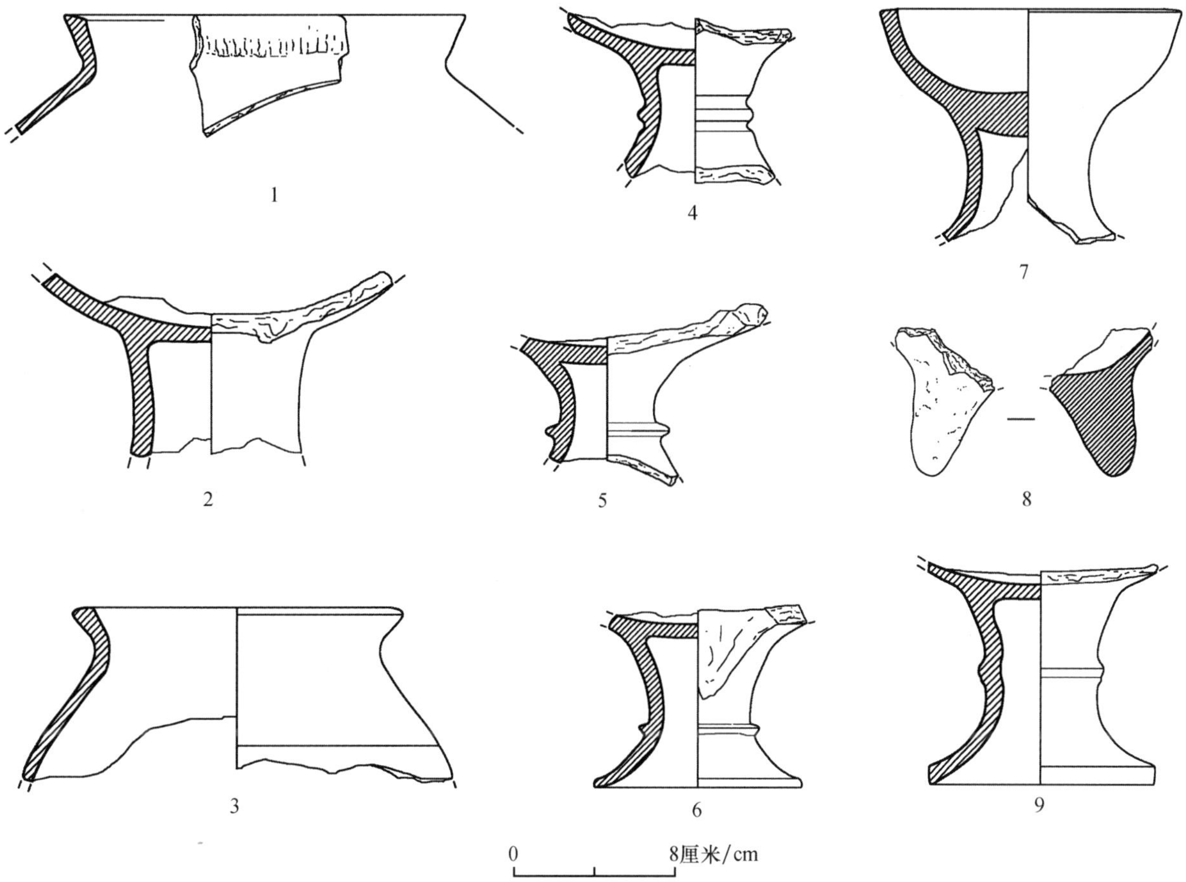

图Ⅰ.3.25　和平村西三组采集遗物
1、3. 罐　2、4~7、9. 豆　8. 鬲足

Figure Ⅰ.3.25　Artifacts collected from west of Heping Village: Group 3.
1, 3. *Guan* jars　2, 4-7, 9. *Dou* pedestal dishes　8. Foot of a *li* tripod

Table Ⅰ.3.24　和平村西三组陶器
Table Ⅰ.3.24　Artifacts collected from west of Heping Village: Group 3

序号 Number on Fig Ⅰ.3.25	标本号 Specimen number	器物名称 Artifact name	出土时间 Excavation date	位置 Location	所属类型 Type	尺寸（厘米）Size (cm)	特点描述 Description of features
4	和平村西三组：1 Heping Village West Group 3：1	豆 *Dou* pedestal dish	2007 ~ 2009	和平村西部 West of Heping Village	A3	H: 8.0	泥质深灰陶。柄部饰一周凸棱纹，素面。Dark grey clay. One ridge on the stem, plain.
9	和平村西三组：2 Heping Village West Group 3：2	豆 *Dou* pedestal dish	2007 ~ 2009	和平村西部 West of Heping Village	A3	H: 10.9	泥质灰褐陶。高圈足，下端外撇，素面，柄中部饰一周凸棱纹。Greyish-brown clay. High circular foot, lower part flared to the outside, plain, one ridge at the middle of the stem.
2	和平村西三组：4 Heping Village West Group 3：4	豆 *Dou* pedestal dish	2007 ~ 2009	和平村西部 West of Heping Village		H: 9.2	泥质灰褐陶。高圈足，素面。Greyish-brown clay. High circular foot, plain.

续表

序号 Number on Fig Ⅰ.3.25	标本号 Specimen number	器物名称 Artifact name	出土时间 Excavation date	位置 Location	所属类型 Type	尺寸（厘米） Size (cm)	特点描述 Description of features
7	和平村西三组：7 Heping Village West Group 3：7	豆 *Dou* pedestal dish	2007 ~ 2009	和平村西部 West of Heping Village	C1	H: 10.8	泥质浅灰陶。豆盘较深，呈弧形，高圈足，下端外撇，素面。 Light grey clay. Dish relatively deep, curved, high circular foot, lower part flared to the outside, plain.
6	和平村西三组：8 Heping Village West Group 3：8	豆 *Dou* pedestal dish	2007 ~ 2009	和平村西部 West of Heping Village	A3	B: 10.3	泥质浅灰陶。高圈足，下端外撇，素面，柄下部饰一周凸棱纹。 Light grey clay. High circular foot, lower part flared to the outside, plain, lower part of the stem has one ridge.
5	和平村西三组：9 Heping Village West Group 3：9	豆 *Dou* pedestal dish	2007 ~ 2009	和平村西部 West of Heping Village	A3	H: 8.5	泥质深灰陶。高圈足，圈足外撇。柄中部有凸棱一周，素面。 Dark grey clay. High circular foot flared to the outside. Ridge at middle of the stem, plain.
3	和平村西三组10 Heping Village West Group 3：10	罐 *Guan* jar	2007 ~ 2009	和平村西部 West of Heping Village	A3	H: 8.6	泥质浅灰陶。小口，斜沿，圆唇，束颈，素面。 Light grey clay. Small mouth, oblique rim, round lip, bunched neck, plain.
1	和平村西三组：11 Heping Village West Group 3：11	罐 *Guan* jar	2007 ~ 2009	和平村西部 West of Heping Village		M: 20.0	泥质灰褐陶。大口，折沿。 Greyish-brown clay. Large mouth, folded rim.
8	和平村西三组：12 Heping Village West Group 3：12	鬲足 Foot of a *li* tripod	2007 ~ 2009	和平村西部 West of Heping Village		H: 7.0	夹砂红褐陶。实心足。素面。 Coarse reddish-brown pottery. Solid foot. Plain.

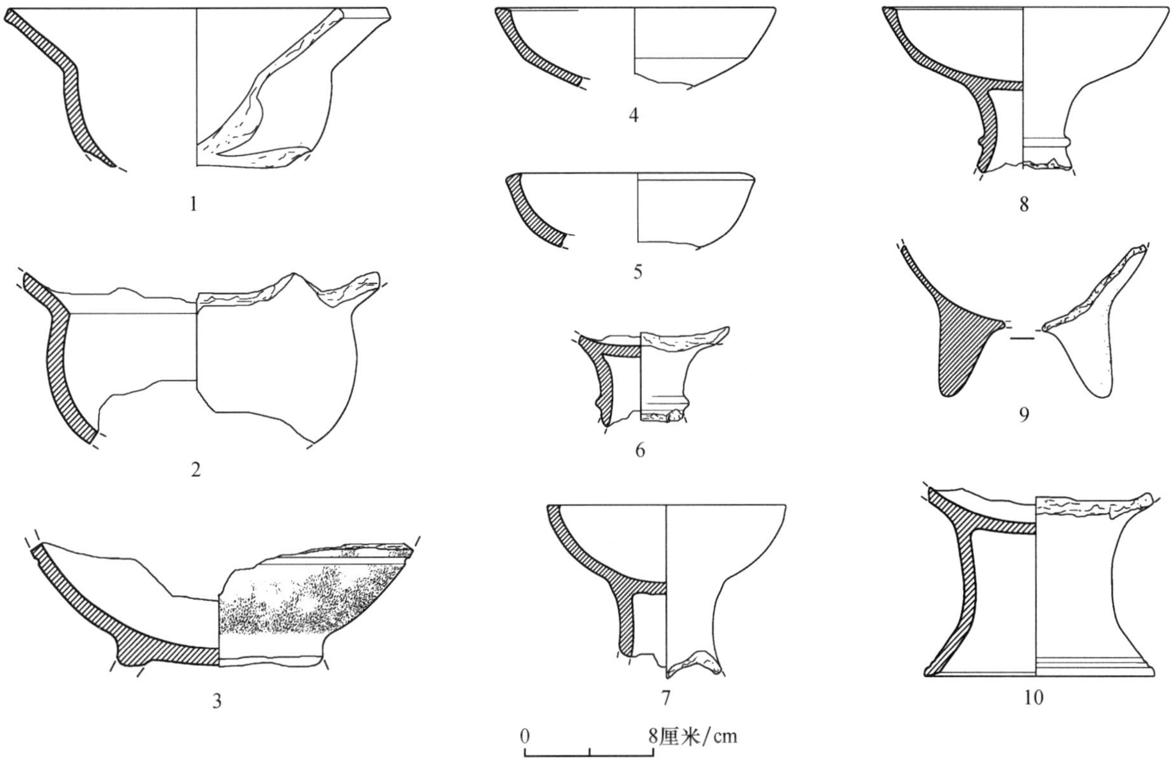

图Ⅰ.3.26　和平村西四组采集遗物

1～3、10. 簋　4～8. 豆　9. 鼎足

Figure Ⅰ.3.26　Artifacts collected from west of Heping Village: Group 4.

1-3, 10. *Gui* tureens　4-8. *Dou* pedestal dishes　9. Foot of *ding* cauldron

表Ⅰ.3.25　和平村西四组陶器

Table Ⅰ.3.25　Artifacts collected from west of Heping Village: Group 4

图号 Number on Fig. Ⅰ.3.26	标本号 Specimen number	器物名称 Artifact name	出土时间 Excavation date	位置 Location	所属类型 Type	尺寸（厘米） Size (cm)	特点描述 Description of features
3	和平村西四组：1 Heping Village West Group 4：1	簋 *Gui* tureen	2010年春 Spring 2010	和平村西部 West of Heping Village		H: 7.0	泥质浅灰陶。盆形腹，饰一周弦纹。 Light grey clay. Basin-shaped belly, decorated with encircling ring .
10	和平村西四组：2 Heping Village West Group 4：2	簋座 Stand for a *gui* tureen	2010年春 Spring 2010	和平村西部 West of Heping Village		H: 11.0	泥质深灰陶。直腹，高圈足，素面。 Dark grey clay. Straight belly, high circular foot, plain.
2	和平村西四组：3 Heping Village West Group 4：3	簋 *Gui* tureen	2010年春 Spring 2010	和平村西部 West of Heping Village	A3	H: 11.2	泥质浅灰陶。宽平折沿，深腹，微鼓，素面。 Light grey clay. Wide flat folded rim, deep belly, slightly flared, plain.
1	和平村西四组：4 Heping Village West Group 4：4	簋 *Gui* tureen	2010年春 Spring 2010	和平村西部 West of Heping Village	A2	M: 23.5 H: 9.5	泥质深灰陶。宽折沿，弧腹，素面。 Dark grey clay. Wide folded rim, bowed belly, plain.

续表

图号 Number on Fig. Ⅰ.3.26	标本号 Specimen number	器物名称 Artifact name	出土时间 Excavation date	位置 Location	所属类型 Type	尺寸（厘米） Size (cm)	特点描述 Description of features
6	和平村西四组：5 Heping Village West Group 4：5	豆 *Dou* pedestal dish	2010年春 Spring 2010	和平村西部 West of Heping Village	B2	H: 5.6	泥质浅灰陶。柄中部饰一周凸棱纹。 Light grey clay. Decorated with a raised ring in the center of the stem.
4	和平村西四组：6 Heping Village West Group 4：6	豆 *Dou* pedestal dish	2010年春 Spring 2010	和平村西部 West of Heping Village	B2	M: 17.0 H: 4.7	泥质浅灰陶。浅折盘。 Light grey clay. Shallow dish with fold.
7	和平村西四组：7 Heping Village West Group 4：7	豆 *Dou* pedestal dish	2010年春 Spring 2010	和平村西部 West of Heping Village	B2	H: 10.5	夹砂浅灰陶。弧形盘，粗柄。 Coarse light grey clay. Curved dish, wide stem.
5	和平村西四组：8 Heping Village West Group 4：8	豆 *Dou* pedestal dish	2010年春 Spring 2010	和平村西部 West of Heping Village		M: 13.6 H: 4.5	泥质浅灰陶。浅盘，方唇，唇内沿突出。 Light grey clay. Shallow dish, square lip, protrusion on the inside of the lip.
8	和平村西四组：10 Heping Village West Group 4：10	豆 *Dou* pedestal dish	2010年春 Spring 2010	和平村西部 West of Heping Village		H: 6.7	泥质深灰陶。浅折盘，豆柄中部有凸棱，素面。 Dark grey clay. Shallow dish, ridge in the center of the stem, plain.
9	和平村西四组：11 Heping Village West Group 4：11	鼎足 Foot of a *ding* cauldron	2010年春 Spring 2010	和平村西部 West of Heping Village		H: 8.9	夹砂红褐陶。圆锥足。 Coarse reddish-brown clay. Conical foot.

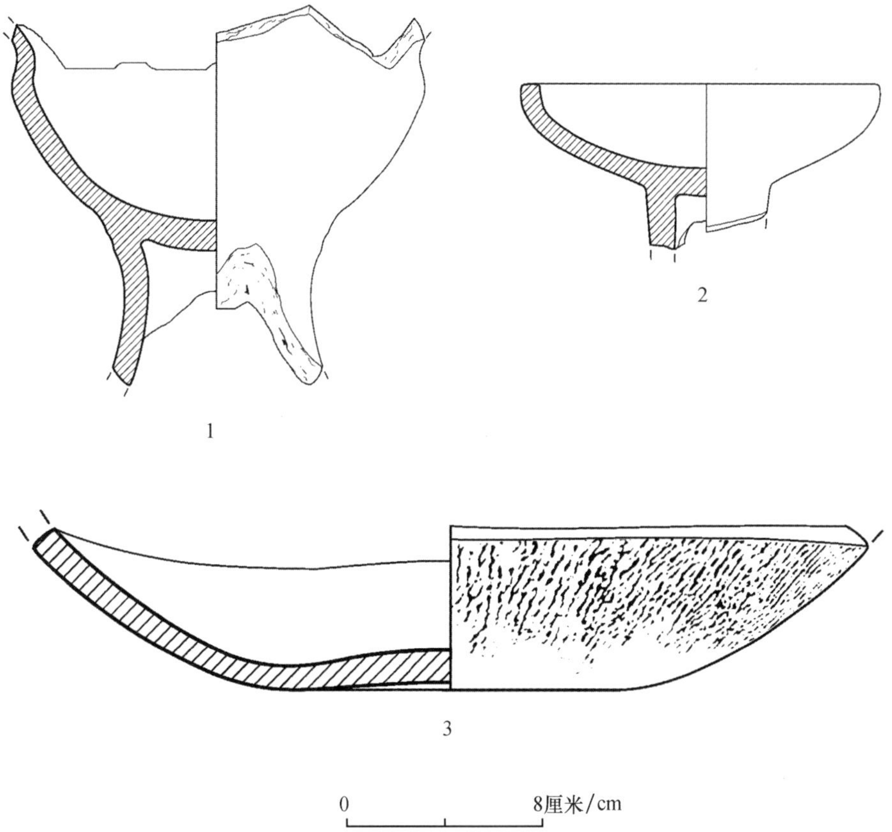

图Ⅰ.3.27　和平村西五组采集遗物

1. 簋　2. 豆　3. 罐

Figure Ⅰ.3.27　Artifacts collected from west of Heping Village: Group 5.

1. *Gui* tureen　2. *Dou* pedestal dish　3. *Guan* jar

表Ⅰ.3.26　和平村西五组陶器统计

Table Ⅰ.3.26　Artifacts collected from west of Heping Village: Group 5

图号 Number on Fig. Ⅰ.3.27	标本号 Specimen number	器物名称 Artifact name	出土时间 Excavation date	位置 Location	所属类型 Type	尺寸（厘米）Size (cm)	特点描述 Description of features
1	和平村西五组：1 Heping Village West Group 5：1	簋 *Gui* tureen	2010年春 Spring 2010	和平村西部 West of Heping Village		H: 14.1	泥质红褐陶。斜沿、窄深腹，腹、沿交接处内收，高圈足，下端外撇。Reddish-brown clay. Slanted rim, narrow and deep belly, the area between rim and belly is constricted; high circular foot, lower part flared to the outside.
2	和平村西五组：3 Heping Village West Group 5：3	豆 *Dou* pedestal dish	2010年春 Spring 2010	和平村西部 West of Heping Village	B3	H: 14.8	泥质浅灰陶。浅盘，柄部细直。Light grey clay. Shallow dish, straight and thin stem.
3	和平村西五组：4 Heping Village West Group 5：4	罐底 Bottom of a *guan* jar	2010年春 Spring 2010	和平村西部 West of Heping Village		H: 6.4	泥质浅灰陶。平底微内凹，饰中绳纹。Light grey clay. Flat bottom slightly concave inside, medium cord decoration.

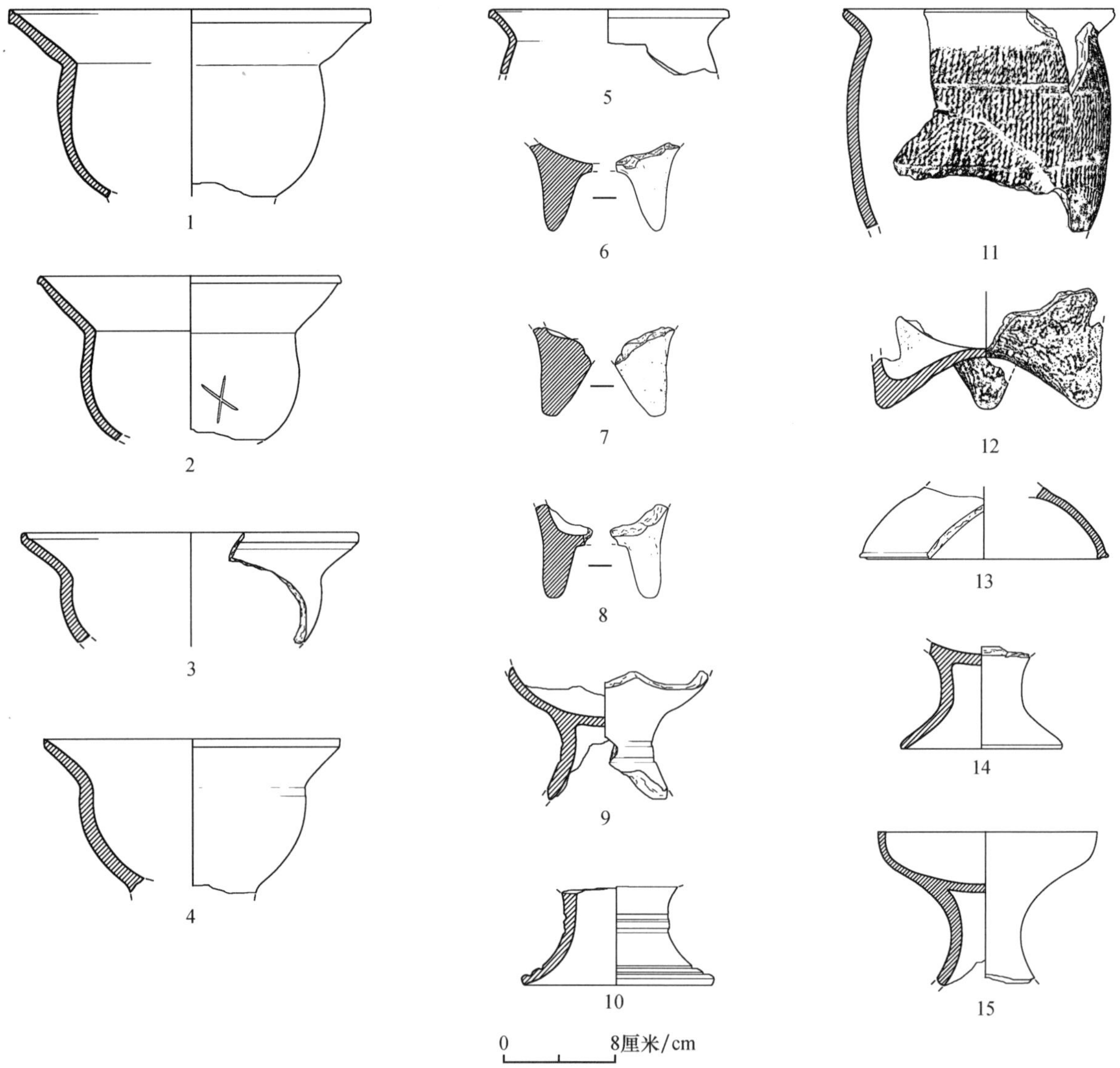

图Ⅰ.3.28　和平村西六组采集遗物

1～4，10. 簋　5. 罐　6、8. 鼎足　7. 鬲足　9、14、15. 豆　11、12. 鬲　13. 器盖

Figure Ⅰ.3.28　Artifacts collected from west of Heping Village: Group 6.

1-4, 10. *Gui* tureens　5. *Guan* jar　6, 8. Feet of *ding* cauldrons　7. Foot of a *li* tripod　9, 14, 15. *Dou* pedestal dishes　11, 12. *Li* tripods　13. Vessel lid

表Ⅰ.3.27　和平村西六组陶器统计

Table Ⅰ.3.27　Artifacts collected from west of Heping Village: Group 6

图号 Number on Fig. Ⅰ.3.28	标本号 Specimen number	器物名称 Artifact name	出土时间 Excavation date	位置 Location	所属类型 Type	尺寸（厘米） Size (cm)	特点描述 Description of features
1	和平村西六组：1 Heping Village West Group 6：1	簋 *Gui* tureen	2010年春 Spring 2010	和平村西部 West of Heping Village	A3	H: 10.5	泥质深灰陶。宽平折沿，尖唇，唇内侧一周凹槽。深腹，稍外鼓，素面。Dark grey clay. Wide flat folded rim, pointed lip, one groove inside the lip. Deep belly, slightly swollen drum shape, plain.

续表

图号 Number on Fig. Ⅰ.3.28	标本号 Specimen number	器物名称 Artifact name	出土时间 Excavation date	位置 Location	所属类型 Type	尺寸（厘米） Size (cm)	特点描述 Description of features
2	和平村西六组：2 Heping Village West Group 6：2	簋 *Gui* tureen	2010年春 Spring 2010	和平村西部 West of Heping Village	A3	H: 11.0	泥质浅灰陶。宽平折沿，深腹，稍外鼓。腹部饰刻画符号。 Light grey clay. Wide flat folded rim, deep belly, somewhat bulging. Belly is decorated with incised symbols.
4	和平村西六组：3 Heping Village West Group 6：3	簋 *Gui* tureen	2010年春 Spring 2010	和平村西部 West of Heping Village	A2	H: 11.5	泥质浅灰陶。宽平沿，圆唇，唇内侧有一凹槽，弧腹，素面。 Light grey clay. Wide flat rim, rounded lip, one groove inside the lip, bulging belly, plain.
3	和平村西六组：4 Heping Village West Group 6：4	簋 *Gui* tureen	2010年春 Spring 2010	和平村西部 West of Heping Village	A2	H: 7.8	泥质浅灰陶。宽沿微卷，弧腹，素面。 Light grey pottery. Slightly curled wide rim, bulging belly, plain.
10	和平村西六组：5 Heping Village West Group 6：5	簋圈足 Circular foot of a *gui* tureen	2010年春 Spring 2010	和平村西部 West of Heping Village	A3	B: 13.7	泥质深灰陶。高圈足，局部磨光，中部有凸棱一周，下部有两周弦纹，浅盘，素面。 Dark grey pottery. High circular foot, partially polished, center part decorated with a ridge, lower part decorated with two rings, shallow dish, plain.
15	和平村西六组：6 Heping Village West Group 6：6	豆 *Dou* pedestal dish	2010年春 Spring 2010	和平村西部 West of Heping Village	A3	M: 15.6	泥质浅灰陶。浅盘，直口，方唇，高柄无凸棱，下端外撇，素面。 Light grey pottery. Shallow dish, straight mouth, square lip, tall stem with no ridge, lower part flared to the outside, plain.
14	和平村西六组：7 Heping Village West Group 6：7	豆 *Dou* pedestal dish	2010年春 Spring 2010	和平村西部 West of Heping Village	A3	H: 8.0	夹砂浅灰陶。高柄，下端外撇，呈喇叭状，素面。 Coarse light grey pottery. Tall stem, lower part flared to the outside, trumpet-shaped, plain.
9	和平村西六组：8 Heping Village West Group 6：8	豆 *Dou* pedestal dish	2010年春 Spring 2010	和平村西部 West of Heping Village		H: 9.5	泥质浅灰陶。高柄，柄部有两周弦纹。 Light grey pottery. Tall stem, two intaglio rings.
13	和平村西六组：9 Heping Village West Group 6：9	器盖 Vessel lid	2010年春 Spring 2010	和平村西部 West of Heping Village		M: 16.3	泥质浅灰陶。子母口，素面。 Light grey pottery. Stepped rim mouth, plain.
11	和平村西六组：10 Heping Village West Group 6：10	鬲 *Li* tripod	2010年春 Spring 2010	和平村西部 West of Heping Village		M: 19.0 H: 15.2	夹砂灰褐陶。斜沿，方唇，唇上一周凹槽，深弧腹。裆部低，呈弧状联裆，侧面微瘪。沿以下饰中绳纹，腹部有两周弦纹。 Coarse greyish-brown pottery. Slanted rim, square lip, one groove on the lip, deep and bulging belly. Low and rounded crotch joint, slightly sunken from the side. Medium cord impression under the rim, two strips of ring decoration.
12	和平村西六组：11 Heping Village West Group 6：11	鬲足 Foot of a *li* tripod	2010年春 Spring 2010	和平村西部 West of Heping Village		W: 14.0	夹砂灰褐陶。联裆较低，饰中绳纹。 Coarse greyish-brown clay. Relatively low crotch joint, decorated with medium cord decoration.

续表

图号 Number on Fig. Ⅰ.3.28	标本号 Specimen number	器物名称 Artifact name	出土时间 Excavation date	位置 Location	所属类型 Type	尺寸（厘米） Size (cm)	特点描述 Description of features
8	和平村西六组：14 Heping Village West Group 6：14	鼎足 Foot of a *ding* cauldron	2010年春 Spring 2010	和平村西部 West of Heping Village		H: 6.5	夹砂红褐陶。圆锥组。素面。 Coarse reddish-brown clay. Conical. Plain.
6	和平村西六组：15 Heping Village West Group 6：15	鼎足 Foot of a *ding* cauldron	2010年春 Spring 2010	和平村西部 West of Heping Village		H: 5.8	夹砂红褐陶。圆锥组。素面。 Coarse reddish-brown clay. Conical. Plain.
7	和平村西六组：16 Heping Village West Group 6：16	鬲足 Foot of a *ge* tripod	2010年春 Spring 2010	和平村西部 West of Heping Village		H: 6.05	夹砂红褐陶。实心足。素面。 Coarse reddish-brown clay. Solid foot. Plain.
5	和平村西六组：17 Heping Village West Group 6：17	罐口沿 Rim of *guan* jar mouth	2010年春 Spring 2010	和平村西部 West of Heping Village		M: 16.8 H: 4.4	泥质灰褐陶。斜折沿，方唇，唇内侧微内凹。 Greyish-brown clay. Oblique folded rim, square lip, one groove inside the lip.

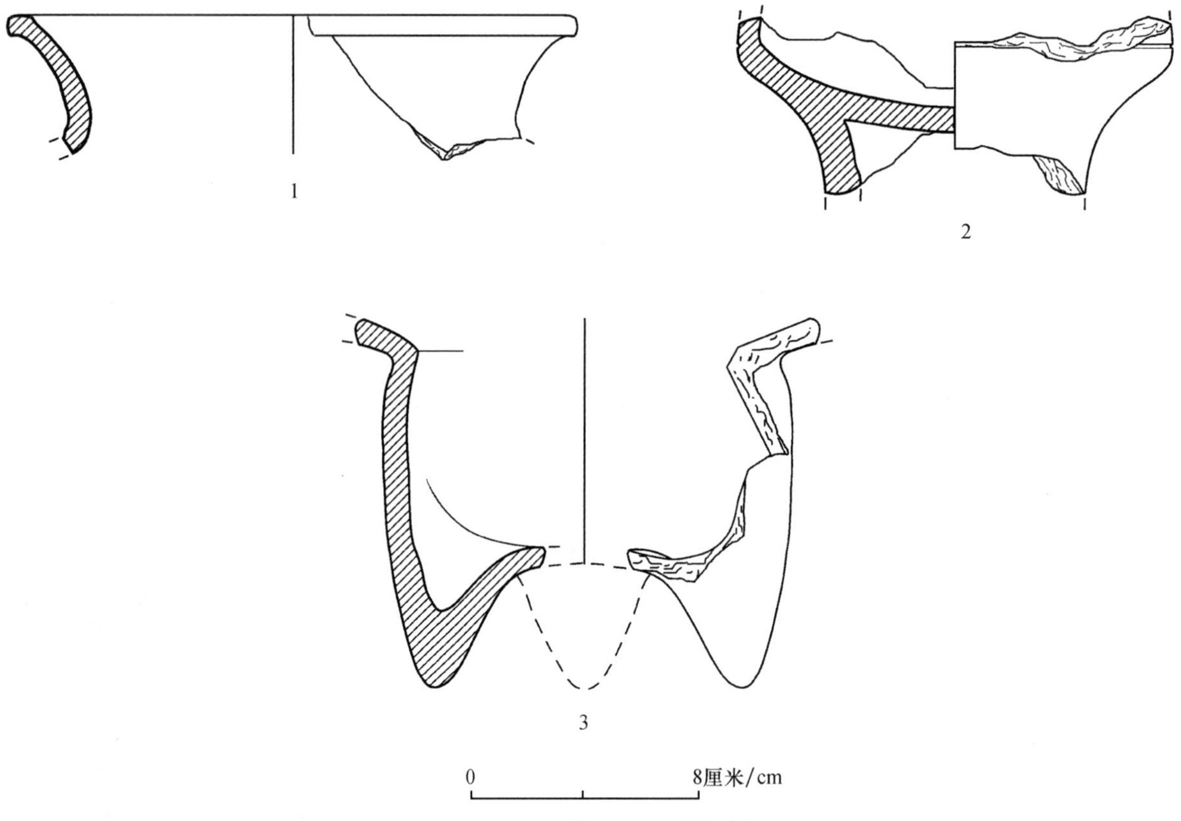

图Ⅰ.3.29　和平村北盗坑1采集遗物

1. 罐　2. 簋　3. 鬲

Figure Ⅰ.3.29　Artifacts collected from looting pit 1 north of Heping Village.

1. *Guan* jar　2. *Gui* tureen　3. *Li* ripod

表Ⅰ.3.28　和平村北盗坑1陶器

Table Ⅰ.3.28　Artifacts collected from looting pit 1 north of Heping Village

图号 Number on Fig. Ⅰ.3.29	标本号 Specimen number	器物名称 Artifact name	出土时间 Excavation date	位置 Location	所属类型 Type	尺寸（厘米）Size (cm)	特点描述 Description of features
3	和平村北盗坑1：1 Looting pit north of Heping Village 1：1	鬲 *Li* tripod	2009	和平村北部 North of Heping Village	D2	W: 10.6 H: 12.5	夹砂红褐陶。折沿，腹较浅，锥状袋足。器形较小，素面。Coarse reddish-brown clay. Folded rim, relatively shallow belly, conical pocket-shaped feet. Relatively small vessel, plain.
2	和平村北盗坑1：2 Looting pit north of Heping Village 1：2	簋 *Gui* tureen	2009	和平村北部 North of Heping Village		W: 14.95 H: 5.95	泥质深灰陶。直腹，高圈足，素面。Dark grey clay. Straight belly, high circular foot, plain.
1	和平村北盗坑1：3 Looting pit north of Heping Village 1：3	罐口沿 Rim of a *guan* jar	2009	和平村北部 North of Heping Village		M: 20.0 H: 4.7	泥质浅灰陶。卷沿束颈，素面。Light grey clay. Rolled rim and constricted neck, plain.

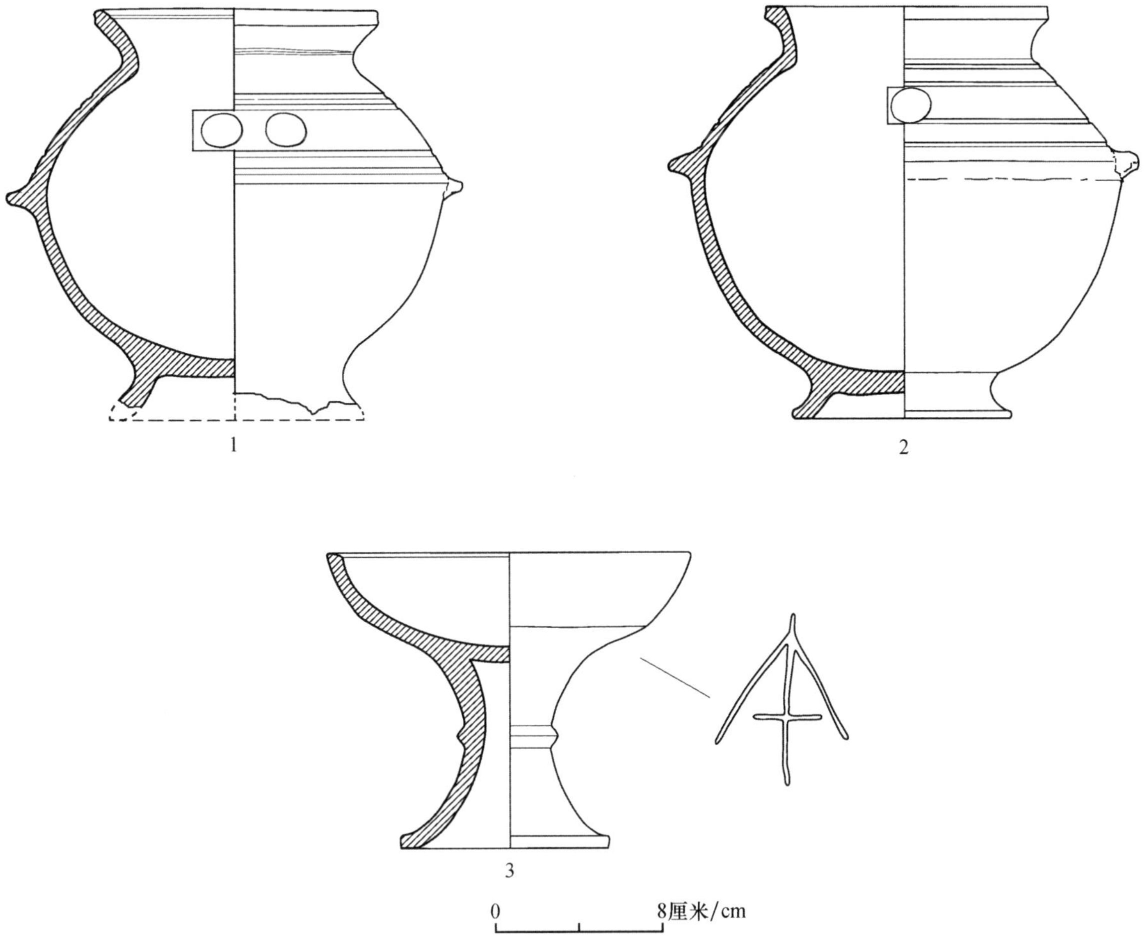

图Ⅰ.3.30　东迟家水库出土陶器

1、2. 瓿　3. 豆

Figure Ⅰ.3.30　Pottery vessels from the Dongchijia Village reservoir.

1, 2. *Bu* vases　3. *Dou* pedestal dish

表Ⅰ.3.29　东迟家水库出土陶器登记

Table Ⅰ.3.29　Pottery vessels from the Dongchijia Village reservoir

图号 Number on Fig. Ⅰ.3.30	标本号 Specimen number	器物名称 Artifact name	出土时间 Excavation date	位置 Location	所属类型 Type	尺寸（厘米）Size (cm)	特点描述 Description of features
2	东迟家：1 Dongchijia Village：1	瓿 *Bu* vase	2000	东迟家水库 Dongchijia reservoir		M: 13.1 H: 19.5	泥质红褐陶，整体素面。肩部有四道弦纹，并有一对对称乳钉纹，肩部一对小捉手。Reddish-brown clay. Entirely plain. Four intaglio ring decorations on the shoulder, with a pair of symmetrical nipples and a pair of small handholds on the shoulder.
3	东迟家：2 Dongchijia Village：2	豆 *Dou* pedestal dish	2000	东迟家水库 Dongchijia reservoir		M: 17.4 H: 13.3	泥质深灰陶，整体素面。豆柄中部有一凸棱，呈竹节状。下腹部有一刻划符号。Dark grey pottery, entirely plain. At the center of the tall stem is a ridge shaped like bamboo joints. The lower part of the belly has incised symbols.
1	东迟家：3 Dongchijia Village：3	瓿 *Bu* vase	2000	东迟家水库 Dongchijia reservoir		M: 13.6 H: 19.0	泥质灰陶，整体素面。肩部上下各有两周弦纹。在弦纹中间，有一对对称双乳钉纹。肩部一对小捉手。Grey clay, entirely plain. Two intaglio ring decorations each on the upper and lower portion of the shoulder. Between the rings there is a pair of symmetrical nipples. The shoulder also had a pair of small handholds.

图Ⅰ.3.31　和平村北采集铜锛

Figure Ⅰ.3.31　Bronze chisel found to the north of Heping Village.

Chapter 3: Coring of the Architectural Foundations of the Inner and Outer Cities

Han Hui

Section 1: The Environment and Topography of the Inner City

The inner city of Guicheng is located in the north-central part of the outer city, on a plateau about 5 m high between two tributaries of the Yaque River. It is shaped like the capital letter "L," or a rectangle with an indentation in the northwest. Measured from the center of the rammed earth wall, the inner city is 490 meters long from north to south and 525 meters wide from east to west. The indentation in the northwest is about 180 m north to south and about 180 m east to west. The entire inner city is 225,000 square meters in area. The northern part and southeastern part of the inner city are taken up by Heping Village and Guicheng Jiangjia (or Guijiang) Village, leaving only a few small empty spaces that are not affected by modern construction. Between the two villages there is a rural road passing north to south through the ancient city. Heping Village's North Street is in the original location of an east-west ditch, which divided the village into northern and southern parts (Fig. Ⅰ.3.1; Pl. 5).

The topography of the ancient inner city is characterized by slightly sloping ground, higher in the south than in the north. The extant surface of the plateau is relatively level. The highest point within the city is in modern Guijiang Village, at the point where a part of the city wall survives, which the local people call "Captain Appointment Platform." The north part of Guijiang Village, Heping Village's southern part, and the northern end of Heping Village have relatively high and level topography. The north-central part of Heping Village south of North Street has a piece of high plateau, where in 1973 the Yantai City Cultural Relics Commission excavated horse chariot pit K1 and tomb M2. To the east of the plateau is the east wall of the inner city, while to the west of it the ground is somewhat low. There coring has revealed a thick late layer about 1.0-2.0 m deep, which indicates that the original topography was likely relatively low. The northeast corner and eastern part of Heping Village have low-lying topography, which was probably brought about through erosion by the river east of the inner city. The northern and eastern ends of the high plateau on which the inner city is located show distinct drop-offs, forming steep cliffs on both edges. But the plateau's northwest edge becomes lower relatively gradually, leaving steps that descend towards the northwest.

The areas south of Heping Village and north of Guijiang Village, as well as areas outside the inner city, are mostly covered by apple and peach orchards. Other crops planted in the area include corn and vegetables. The soil is relatively fertile, with a thick loess layer, and in ancient times would also have been suitable for agriculture. The surrounding environment is favorable as the city is screened by the Mt. Lai mountain range to the south. The land tends to slope downward toward the north from the foot of Mt. Lai to the inner city of Guicheng, and the soil is fertile. The east branch of the Yaque River flows in a valley between the eastern part of the inner city and the ridges on which the outer city wall is located. There is a drop of 10 m in elevation going from the inner city to the valley. The river channel runs close by the eastern city wall. It moved about in periodic floods in the past, destroying much of the east wall. The northern part of the plateau on which the inner city is located extends beyond the northern city wall by about 190 m and has the shape of a trapezoid, wider in the south than in the north. At the northern end of the plateau is a platform, oriented north-to-south, about 60 m wide from east to west and about 100 m long from north to south. The loess layer in this area is relatively thick. The northwest corner outside the city wall slopes from the southeast to the northwest, and the ground surface is not level, with relatively many gullies. The red sandstone base below the surface is also relatively higher in this area, which is not quite suitable for building or agricultural activities. The terrain in the southeastern part of the city, where Guijiang Village is located, is level. In summary, the inner city's geographical environment, soil, and hydrology are all relatively ideal, while outside the city was a long and narrow river. The site was suitable for fortifications and production activities or dwellings (See Pl. 6).

Section 2: Previous Archaeological Work and Purpose of Coring in the Inner City

1. Previous Archaeological Work

Since the beginning of the last century, the inner city and its surroundings have seen continuous discoveries of cultural remains and artifacts. Around 1914, four bronze bells were found at Guicheng, along with a square *ding* cauldron, dating to the Spring and Autumn period. In about 1931, five bronze bells were excavated north of the ditch in Heping Village, also dating from the Spring and Autumn period. In the 1950s, thirty bronze objects were excavated south of Heping Village, almost all of which are lost except for the Jihou *li* tripod, inscribed: “Jihou [casts] X Jiang XX. Sons’ sons and grandsons’ grandsons eternally treasure and use it.” This tripod dates from the late Western Zhou period. Further, in May 1965, to the east of Heping Village, one *ding* cauldron and one bronze spear were excavated, belonging to the late Western Zhou period. In 1973, in what was then the west of Heping Village but is now the north-central part of the village, the Yantai Cultural Relics Commission excavated tomb M2 and a horse chariot pit. The ceramics recovered from the tomb include two plain *li* tripods, two cord decorated *li* tripods, two *gui* tureens, one *guan* jar, and one helmet. They were from the mid-Western Zhou period. In the horse chariot pit the excavators found horse fittings from the Spring and Autumn period (Li Buqing & Lin Xianting 1991: 912-915) (See Table Ⅱ.4.1). More importantly, in 2002 the Yantai Museum conducted a salvage excavation on the plateau in the north-central part of the inner city and discovered Spring and Autumn period house remains, among other things (See Part Ⅱ, Chapter 1 of this book).

Of all the previous work before the Sino-American Archaeological Team began to carry out work in 2007, the most systematic was the survey of the Guicheng site in 1973 by the Yantai Cultural Relics Commission (Li Buqing and Lin Xianting 1991: 910-918). It essentially confirmed the basic shape, structure, chronology, and construction of the Guicheng city site, providing important information for later work.

2. Purpose of the Work

The Guicheng site has the greatest extent and the richest contents of any site of its period in the Jiaodong region. Systematic research at the site is not only to focus on chronology, characteristics, and cultural associations of the site itself, but more importantly, to contribute to an understanding of the Bronze Age archaeological culture of the Jiaodong region, the historical process through which the Central Plains civilization entered the Jiaodong region, and the interaction of this civilization with the local cultures. Through research at Guicheng, we can more deeply and fully understand the social and historical development of the Jiaodong region. The Guicheng site has great significance, in that it can play a leading role in exploring the process of formation of ancient civilizations and states in the whole Jiaodong region. It can also contribute to a better understanding of the ancient Dongyi polities, which have been the object of study in the whole Shandong region during the last few decades.

From 2007 to 2011, the Sino-American Guicheng Archaeological Team conducted systematic coring and test excavation of the inner city, complemented by high-resolution survey work in the outer city. The fieldwork in the inner city had three basic purposes: 1) to advance research on the Guicheng site, mainly to clarify the inner city’s chronology, structure, and layout, and to understand the structure, organization, and functions of the architectural foundations belonging to the Zhou period in the inner city; 2) to clarify the palace zone’s subsurface deposits, cultural contents, and state of preservation, in order to provide detailed and reliable data for future research and conservation; 3) to recheck the results of coring through test excavation, which can verify the relationship between the city wall and the inner city cultural deposits and their dating.

Section 3: The Method of Coring Work

1. The Numbering System of the Exploratory Coring of the Inner City and its Operation in the Field

A base point was established at southwest corner of the stone wall that protects the above-ground rammed earth wall (B) of the inner city on its southwest edge, and from this point we established additional points within the exploration zone. We proceeded from east to west and from south to north, covering the entire inner city of Guicheng with coring. After fully covering the entire south city wall and moats, starting at the western part and moving eastward, we began to cover the interior of the inner city from the inner side of the southeast part of the wall, which was confirmed by the survey in June and July of 2007.

The coring team was divided into three small groups. The first group was responsible for marking the holes on the ground in the coring area from east to west, using a compass to orient themselves, and from north to south following the natural direction of the rows in the orchards. Generally, the direction of the orchard rows south of Heping Village was 18° east of north, and north of Guijiang Village it was 16° east of north (magnetic). Using a base-rope and tape for measuring, we stuck a numbered paper label at each spot that was to be cored. Rows from south to north were designated by the twenty-six letters A to Z, while columns from west to east were numbered using Arabic numerals. The first point was **A0**, the coring holes to its north were **B0, C0**, etc., and the coring holes to its east were **A1, A2**, etc. For example, coring hole **C15** was in the southern part of Jiangjia Village. After all the letters had been used once, we started again from A, and added subscript numerals after the letters, from south to north in increasing order: $\mathbf{A_1}$, $\mathbf{B_1}$, $\mathbf{C_1}$....$\mathbf{A_2}$, $\mathbf{B_2}$, $\mathbf{C_2}$.... For example, coring hole $\mathbf{W_150}$ in the northern part of the orchard in Heping Village was the hole in row W_1 with column number 50 in the Heping coring zone. In the cases where additional points needed to be cored between regularly numbered holes, we added "/" or "//" to the upper-right corner of the letters and increased the number of the upper slashes from south to north and from west to east. For example, $\mathbf{W_1'50'}$ was the additional hole to the north and east of hole $\mathbf{W_150}$. The second team was the coring work team, which conducted the actual coring according to the work plan for the inner city, strictly following archaeological field-work procedures and the coring points marked on the ground. After completing the coring at each point, they reported the condition of that hole to the third team, the recording crew, who then marked the hole as completed on a graph-paper map, and recorded the contents of the core under the label. For example, the contents of the coring hole $\mathbf{H_1'48}$ on Road L1 were recorded as follows:

0-0.3 m, surface soil;

0.3-0.6 m, grey earth, loose;

0.6-0.7 m, sandy layer, hard, composed of thin layers;

0.7-0.75 m, footpath surface, formed of tan earth;

0.75-2.0 m, bottom not reached; tan earth, sand inclusions, near virgin soil.

The above method was used throughout coring zones of large extent. In Heping Village there were several small sections that could be explored by coring, and we gave them separate numbers. In Coring Zone 5 in Heping Village, we assigned numbers starting at the northwest corner of the screening wall across the street from residence #130 and marked the holes 5 m apart in the cardinal directions. The numbering went from southwest to northeast, letters A, B, C, D, etc., designating the rows from west to east, and numerals 1, 2, 3, 4, etc., designating the columns from south to north. We recorded these points separately on a graph-paper map.

2. Establishing the Standards of Soil Samples

Correctly identifying the various types of soil encountered in the field in accordance with standards for systematic soil classification that will be used consistently throughout a site is the key to success in field survey and the subsequent data analysis. Based on our experience gained in the first season of the fieldwork, we systematically examined the soil samples pulled out by coring, and established standards for classifying soils in the inner city of Guicheng. The standards were only slightly adjusted during the course of later work. They were basically followed and provided a foundation for the accurate recording of the coring points. The establishment of soil standards also made possible the computer-based management of coring data in Guicheng archaeology (see Chapter 8). In analyzing the soil profiles in Guicheng, three variables were first considered:

a. Formation process: The process leading to the formation of individual soil points allows us to understand the soil record in terms of both human activity and natural phenomena. Because the primary goal of the project was to detect underground structures and strata, formation processes provide a critical means of identifying soil types characteristic of subsurface features. For instance, consideration of soil types allows us to differentiate among the following:

Grey earth (*huitu* 灰土): a soft and greyish-colored soil resulting from the decay of organic compounds typically associated with human cultural remains. Grey earth was taken as a sign of the presence of human activity, and was especially useful in detecting human storage or trash pits.

Rammed earth (*hangtu* 夯土): soil pounded into place to construct ancient architectural features such as city walls and house or palace foundations. It is recognizable by its firm and rigid consistency and layered composition. The rammed layers may be so distinct as to peel cleanly away from each other, and sometimes may even exhibit slight indentations imprinted by pounding tools.

Sediment (*yutu* 淤土): soil found in areas originally covered by water, typically of very fine consistency with a high proportion of fine sand.

Multicolored earth (*wuhuatu* 五花土 or *huatu* 花土): formed by the disturbance and subsequent differential oxidation of soil that was taken from underground (sometimes including soil from different natural or cultural strata) and re-deposited after a short period of time. The presence of multicolored earth usually indicates, for instance, the existence of burial remains.

Footpath earth (*caitatu* 踩踏土 or *caitamian* 踩踏面): a firm layer usually with a flat surface formed by regular and heavy foot and/or vehicular traffic. Usually represents open quarters for human activities.

Road earth (*lutu* 路土): a subcategory of footpath elongated in form, with heavy inclusions of sand and small stones. Usually represents road paths in Guicheng.

Packed earth fill (*diantu* 垫土): surface soil pressed into place by modern humans, whether purposely or incidentally. For instance, soil types that were used for leveling modern building or road foundations were typically recorded under this category.

Tilled earth (*gengtu* 耕土): modern agricultural surfaces, recently ploughed or long since planted.

Virgin soil (*shengtu* 生土): the deepest portions of the area, the geologically formed soil, preserving its features as they existed before modification by either human agency or water features. Recognizing virgin soil was one of the basic foundations for beginning survey work in a particular area, as there was some variation in the consistency of virgin soil even across the inner city of Guicheng. Usually, coring ends with the discovery of virgin soil, signaling that below that point the earth was not impacted by human activity.

b. Color: Soil types identified as to formation process were further qualified by color. This is important, especially when no immediate assessment could be made of the formation process of a particular soil sample; in such cases, color was used as the primary characteristic for classification. The most typical case is the so-called "tan earth" (*huanghetu* 黄褐土), a soil type very widely encountered in Guicheng that was human modified but without structural association. Both single color terms (yellow, grey, brown) and paired color terms (yellowish-brown, reddish-brown, etc.) were employed. Any of these could be modified with adjectives denoting intensity (e.g., light brown, dark grey). There were also soil types, e.g. grey earth and multicolored earth which, though they have established interpretations regarding their formation processes, are conventionally referred to using color terms in

Chinese archaeology, which are adopted above.

c. Soil inclusion: Many coring samples contained materials of relevance to the understanding of the formation of the site. These additional contents were recorded wherever they appear in order to further differentiate strata at a certain point. The most often seen particles are, for instance,"red burnt clay clumps" (*hong shaotu kuai* 红烧土块), water-formed rust (*shuixiu* 水锈), and vegetal ash (*caomuhui* 草木灰). Other factors regularly found in soil samples included pebbles, pottery sherds, bone fragments, etc. (Table Ⅰ.8.1).

d. Contingency: Contingency allowed us to classify the physical conditions/factors that ended coring at a certain depth. This was often the case when technicians encountered sands that were too loose to be removed from the coring hole, or rocks large enough to stop the spade. The conditions also included mud or bedrock that would definitely force the technicians to stop and abandon the coring point.

In careful consideration of the significance of the above factors, with respect to the goal of the coring project to understand the organization of the Guicheng city site and its depositional history, we devised a system of classification by first dividing the various soil types seen in Guicheng into two classes, phenomenon soil and stratum soil, and then further dividing these two large categories into more specific soil types (Table Ⅰ.3.1):

Phenomenon soil: phenomenon soil was formed by human activity and usually indicates underground structural or formal remains. Typical of phenomenon soil are grey earth (*huitu* 灰土), rammed earth (*hangtu* 夯土), and road earth (*lutu* 路土), etc.

Stratum soil: was formal by natural or human forces and usually represents subsurface strata that exhibit no particular form. Typical of stratum soil are tilled earth (*gengtu* 耕土), tan earth (*huanghetu* 黄褐土), virgin soil (*shengtu* 生土), etc.

We trained members of the coring team to recognize different types of soil samples and to report as accurately as possible the strata they encountered. The classification was used in the comparative analysis of natural and cultural deposits in the entire inner city of Guicheng. It was also the foundation for computational analysis and management of the coring data, such as that provided in this book (see Chapter 8).

3. Coring Methodology

1) Coring zone

The starting point for the coring was the southwest corner of the city wall, which still stands on the surface in the southwest area of the Guicheng inner city. We then followed the site's layout, the village locations, and the barriers of the roads to establish virtual zones. This ensured complete coverage of the inner city, so that coring was carried out in every area that could be cored. We numbered the coring zones and used these zones as units in conducting the coring.

We divided the coring area into five zones: the southern part of the orchard south of Heping Village (Ⅰ), the northern part of the orchard south of Heping Village (Ⅱ), the northern part of the orchard north of Guijiang Village (Ⅲ), the southern part of the orchard north of Guijiang Village (Ⅳ), and the group of six plots inside Heping Village. These six plots were: the plateau in the northern part of the village **[1]**, the Heping Village pig pen **[2]**, the cornfield to its west **[3]**, the parking lot east of the road in the northeast part of the inner city **[4]**, the public baths of Heping Village northeast of the southern city gate **[5]**, and inside the yard of the archaeology team's station **[6]** (Figure Ⅰ.3.1). (The six plots are marked on the map).

2) Method of combining the general coring and focused coring

Two coring methods, "general coring" and "focused coring," were used in combination in the southern part of the Heping Village orchard (Ⅱ) and the northern part of the Guijiang Village orchard (Ⅲ). The general coring used a compass to establish east and west. We spaced the holes 5 m apart from south to north; in the west-east direction, although in principle the holes were placed every 5 m, the actual distances between the holes were adjusted according to the width of the rows in the modern orchards to allow for easy access to areas under the trees. The numbering system was as described above: using A-Z to designate west-east rows, moving from south to north, and Arabic numerals to count columns that ran south-north, moving from west to east. The "focused coring" method was used when we conducted density coring of the remains discovered by the general coring, with holes usually placed 2 m from each other. We marked the structural remains discovered by the lining up of holes placed in close proximity, and then moved in a line to trace the outline of the remains using double holes in high density coring to determine the edges of the structures. In focused coring we adopted a different numbering system; that is, using Arabic numerals to count all of the relatively dense coring holes related to a single architectural foundation or other structural remains separately and consecutively, e.g., holes numbered 1-162 of Rammed Earth Foundation 1. Representative artifacts and coring holes were also recorded with photographs, and we collected soil samples and artifacts brought up by the coring.

3) Method of coring inside the village

We used 5×5 m spaces to place the holes in the agricultural plots or gaps between factory buildings in Heping Village, adjusted with respect to the vegetation and surface conditions. First we looked for a base point, and laid out the holes along cardinal directions or in a natural direction following the orientation of house walls and courtyards. The system of numbering of the coring holes was the same as the method described above. With regard to the coring of the roads inside the village, we followed the natural directions of the roads, and placed holes on the sides of the roads wherever coring could possibly get through the packed soil layers. In doing so, we also had to use caution to avoid the water pipes buried under the road, sticking as closely as possible to 5×5 m intervals.

4. Recording

During the coring we used graph-paper maps to record in detail the rows of holes and additional holes for dense coring. The paper maps used a 1:100 scale, and the maps for individual structures used a 1:50 scale. The numbering system went from south to north using the alphabet, and from west to east using Arabic numerals. We used a scale of 1:100 for the drawings of the cross-section profiles of the remains, based on strata revealed by individual coring holes.

We made a separate set of maps with an independent numbering system for the six independent coring plots and the three roads inside Heping Village at a scale of 1:100. We numbered the structural remains in the order of their discovery, e.g., "Rammed Earth Foundation 3." After the coring was concluded for the work season, we produced reports on the coring results and structural remains that had been found. We collected the artifacts brought up by the coring, to make a statistical table of the collected samples.

5. Mapping

Using a total station, we produced a plan of the inner city of the Guicheng site at a scale of 1:1000 (Fig. Ⅰ.3.1). The base point was placed at the stone stele erected to the west of Heping Village to mark Guicheng as a cultural preservation site.

In order to produce a topographic map of the inner city of Guicheng, we established the base point at the top of the stone stele for site preservation west of Heping Village, and set the standard elevation of the inner city at 100 m. Using the total station, and according to relative elevations, we drafted a topographic map of the inner city at a scale of 1:1000 (Fig. Ⅰ.8.5).

Section 4: The Overall Conditions of Cultural Deposits in the Inner City

The coring area in the inner city of Guicheng was the southern part of Heping Village and the orchards in the northern part of Guijiang Village, plus the five open areas within Heping Village (see above Section 3). Because there were relatively few coring locations within the village, we could rely on only a small number of coring holes to speculate about the deposits underlying the village.

From the coring results, we can see that in the southeast and southwest parts of the inner city the terrain is high and flat, with a concentration of architectural foundations. The cultural deposits are 1.0-1.7 m thick. The cultural deposits in the southwest part of the inner city, to the north of Guijiang village (Zones Ⅲ-Ⅳ), are made mainly of grey earth that was about 1.0 m thick. Underneath this is mostly sandstone or tan earth. The rammed earth foundations, which are located to the north of Guijiang Village in the western part of the inner city, begin below the grey earth layer and intrude on the bedrock or tan virgin soil. As the topography slants down toward the north, the sandstone below the surface becomes shallower. The depth of the sandstone is generally about 1.1-1.5 m below the surface, and in most of the area it is overlaid by ash pits and other remains. Near the southern section of the northwest city wall the remains of ash pits are more numerous and up to 1.7 m thick, intruding on the rammed earth foundations. Under some of the rammed earth foundations there are early ash pits and other remains.

The strata in the southeast part of the inner city to the south of Heping Village (Zones Ⅰ-Ⅱ) are basically similar. Under the surface soil are cultural deposits, and under those are rammed earth foundations, trash pits, and other remains. The rammed earth foundations are found southwest of Heping Village in the southern part of the ancient inner city. The cultural deposits in the southern part of the inner city are about 0.5-1.1 m thick, and underneath them is tan sediment, with some sand layers. The virgin soil in this area is tan clay.

At the southern edge of the inner city, to the northeast of the city gate, was found a particularly thick grey earth layer from which the coring brought up many ceramic sherds. The grey earth includes much ash and many pottery fragments, and was probably the site of a residential building. Many of the trash pits are more than 2.0 m deep, and we did not reach the bottoms of these pits.

The north-central part of Guicheng is overbuilt by Heping Village, and most of the cultural deposits there are simple and relatively thin. Virgin tan soil is found in many locations under the modern soil fill. The cultural deposit layers, which are grey earth, are somewhat thin at about 0.8 m, while the later period soil fill is relatively thick. The virgin soil in this area is tan. Inside the north inner city wall and to the west, the grey earth is relatively thick and could have been the remains of residential sites.

There is a plateau in the north-central part of Heping Village, which is 2-3 m higher than the ground to its west, north, and east (Plot [1]). Rammed Earth Foundation 15 found by the coring, as well as the horse chariot pit and tomb M2 excavated in 1972, are in this area. The cultural deposits are 0.7-1.5 m thick, and the coring found ash pits and burials. We speculate that there was a bone workshop located in this area. At a depth of 1.3-2.0 m below the surface in the grey earth layer, the coring brought up Western and Eastern Zhou pottery sherds.

In the northwest part of the inner city, west of the plateau, the terrain is somewhat low-lying. The late period strata in this area are relatively thick, at 0.4-1.2 m. The cultural deposits under this are relatively thin, 0.3-0.5 m thick. Some of the coring holes reached sandstone at between 0.9 and 1.4 m depth. In Coring Plot [4], which is in the parking lot to the east of the road running north to south through the village, at the northeast corner of the courtyard and near coring hole M10, we discovered a portion of tan rammed earth beginning at 0.7 m depth. Below this is a hard sand layer at 1.0 m depth, and at 1.2 m depth we encountered virgin soil. This rammed earth stratum and below it resemble the earth deposits along Roads L1 and L2. The coring here turned up Eastern Zhou period pottery sherds.

In the eastern part of the inner city, which is the southeastern part of Heping Village, the cultural deposits on the inner side of the city wall are relatively thick, beginning at 0.3-1.0 m deep, and went as deep as 2.4 m in places. We did not reach the bottom of the deposits. We speculate that this is an area of residential sites. Coring point 22, in the road that runs east to west, revealed a tomb, as multicolor earth appeared at 0.9 m deep; we did not get to the bottom of it although we reached as deep as 3.3 m. This shows that this area had a sporadic distribution of burials.

Section 5: Architectural Foundations in the Inner City

1. Summary of the Areas

In the process of coring the inner city we discovered a drainage system, rammed earth foundations, and sections of roads, among many other remains, and acquired a preliminary understanding of the layout of the inner city. In the middle of the inner city towards the west we discovered a ditch (G1). G1's southern section begins at the water inlet west of the city gate, making a semicircular waterway towards the north, winding through the west of Guijiang Village, and then returning to the west side of the main road between the villages. It then follows the road straight north, finally flowing out of the inner city through the water gate at a corner in the middle part of the northern wall. G1 was about 340 m long from south to north, and is more than 1.5 m deep. G1 divided the inner city into eastern and western districts.

During the coring in the inner city we discovered seventeen rammed earth foundations of different sizes (Fig. Ⅰ.3.2). Small-scale foundations are east-west oriented rectangles, but the relatively large-scale foundations are mostly north-south oriented rectangles or strips. Taking G1 as the boundary, the foundations are divided into western and eastern architectural groups.

The western group has seven architectural foundations, including Rammed Earth Foundations 8, 9, 10, 11, 12, 13, and 14. Among these, Rammed Earth Foundation 9 is the largest architectural feature in the inner city. Foundation 9 is a rectangle oriented north to south, about 93 m long north to south, and about 23 m east to west at its widest, with an area of about 1,750 m^2. To the east, west, and south of Rammed Earth Foundation 9 are located six other relatively smaller architectural foundations.

The eastern group had nine architectural foundations, including Foundations 1, 2, 3, 4, 5, 6, 7, 15, 16, and 17. These foundations are divided by a road (L1) discovered in the center of the city. L1 is located on the central axis between the eastern and western walls of the inner city. It extends up to 68 m according to the current coring, and is oriented 18° east of north, the same as the orientation of the inner city as a whole. Symmetrically centered on road L1 are Rammed Earth Foundations 2 and 3 in the east and west respectively. Foundation 3 is the largest in the eastern architectural group, with a rectangular area 56 m long from north to south. Its southwest corner has a ca. 11 m wide protrusion sticking out to the west. The southern edge of Rammed Earth Foundation 3 borders on an area paved with stone, laid out in an "L" shape, which is then surrounded on the east and south by a large area of footpath soil. The footpath's northern end links up with L1, and runs straight south to the city wall and is as deep as the stone layer. The stone layer and the footpath are very likely part of a wide activity area related to Rammed Earth Foundation 3, but more work is needed to determine if it was a "plaza."

2. The Ditch Inside the City (G1)

Ditch G1 is located in the middle of the inner city towards the west, on the western edge of the road running west of Heping Village. According to the coring, G1 starts at the southeastern part of Guijiang Village in the southern part of the inner city, and passes through Guijiang Village and the orchard to its north. Then, it exits from the gap in the bend of the north city wall, its northern outlet. The southern inlet is on the west side of the south city gate and road L2. G1 basically has the form of a north-south strip, with the northern part relatively straighter. It is oriented roughly 15° east of north. In the south, after entering the inlet, the ditch turns to the west, then turns again to the east 15 m east of Rammed Earth Foundation 14. Then it once again turns north at the northern corner of Rammed Earth Foundation 16 and goes straight to the north city wall outlet. G1 passes through the whole inner city from south to north. On its west side are located Rammed Earth Foundations 10 and 11, and others;

on the east side are Foundations 16, 17, and others. G1 is in the same layer as L2, the road that runs through the south city gate.

The section of G1 already revealed by coring is about 269 m long from north to south. The southern part was not cored because of the placement of houses in the eastern part of Guijiang Village. The full length of G1 may have been as much as 340 m from north to south, and 10-35 m wide from east to west. Its widest section is near the drop-off to the south of the small road north of Guijiang Village, where it was up to 35 m wide, forming a pond. The ditch was 3,700 m^2 in total area.

The deposits in the ditch comprise grey earth and sand layers, underneath which is virgin soil or bedrock (for placement of typical coring holes, see Fig. Ⅰ.3.1 [dots 1-8]; for coring hole stratigraphy, see table Ⅰ.3.2). The grey earth can be divided into two layers. The upper layer of grey earth begins at 0.3 m; the lower layer includes water-formed rust, and begins at 0.9-1.2 m. The sand layer begins at 1.2-1.7 m; its southern part becomes shallower near the small road to Guijiang Village, beginning at 0.5-0.8 m. The sand layer was mostly 0.4-0.7 m thick. The virgin soil was 1.4-2.0 m below the surface. The bedrock is 0.8-1.6 m deep. Under part of the sand layer area is tan earth with sand inclusions, and under this is more virgin soil or bedrock. In these locations the tan earth with sand inclusions mostly begins at 1.1-2.4 m, with the virgin soil or bedrock 1.3-2.6 m deep. In the area of the drop-off by the small road along the north side of the houses of Guijiang Village, the sand layer begins at 0.3-0.7 m, underneath which are stones. G1's sand layer is overall 0.1-1.0 m thick. In isolated locations, on top of the sand layer is still another tan layer with sand inclusions.

3. The Eastern Architectural Group

The eastern group of architectural foundations is located east of ditch G1, in the south of Heping Village. It is divided in the middle by L1, and has a total of nine foundations. They can be described as follows:

Road earth feature 1 (L1): Located on the central axis between the east and west city walls of the inner city. The portion revealed by coring is located south of Heping Village, and is about 68 m long and 10.5 m wide, with an area of about 1,200 m^2. The southern part of L1 goes to the city wall, and the northern part disappears east of Rammed Earth Foundation 4, possibly having been destroyed by a later period ash pit. L1 appeared at a depth of 0.7-0.9m. On the road we discovered layered sand and trodden surface, about 3-20 cm thick. L1 is oriented at 18° east of north, roughly the same as that of the inner city (Fig. Ⅰ.3.3; Table Ⅰ.3.3).

Rammed Earth Foundation 1: Located in the southeast corner of the inner city. To its northwest is Rammed Earth Foundation 2. To the south is the trench inside the south city wall and the city wall itself. This rammed earth foundation has a rectangular shape. The northwest corner and southwest corner stick out, and the southeast corner extends toward and connects with the south city wall. The main body of the remains is about 17.25 m long north to south and 17.9 m wide from east to west. Its direction is 18° east of north. The elevation of this area is relatively high, and the cultural deposits are relatively thick, composed of grey earth and generally 0.3-0.9 m thick. Under this cultural layer lies the rammed earth body of Foundation 1, tan in color, part of which is made up of sediment. The rammed earth is 0.6-1.2 m deep and about 0.3-1.2 m thick, concentrated at 0.5-0.7 m. The rammed earth is mostly located above the sediment, and in some places there are sand layers. The rammed earth foundation's southern end is connected to the city wall and intrudes into the moat, possibly forming the defensive structures of the south city wall (Fig. Ⅰ.3.4; Table Ⅰ.3.4).

Rammed Earth Foundation 2: Located in the southeast part of the inner city, in the apple orchard south of Heping Village. Foundation 1 is to the southeast. Rammed Earth Foundation 2 is 110 m from Heping Village in the north, and 150 m from the road in the west. It is close to the small village road between the two apple orchards south of Heping Village. The rammed earth foundation's underground portion has been seriously damaged, and the remaining foundation has a rectangular shape. Its southeast and northwest corners each protrude outwards. The rammed earth was seriously damaged by later period features, and there might be a ditch which bisected the foundation, dividing its western portion into two parts. The remaining rammed earth foundation is 32 m wide from east to west and 38 m long from north to south. Its orientation is 18° east of north. This area's cultural deposits are relatively thick, about 1 m, and consist of grey earth. There are ash pits directly intruding into the rammed earth. Underneath the cultural layers is rammed earth 0.2-1.4 m thick, which is found at slightly different depths below the ground surface, ranging from 0.4 to 1.4 m, but largely concentrated at 0.6-0.8 m deep. The rammed earth is tan in color. The southeast corner has a tomb intruding into the rammed earth (Fig. Ⅰ.3.5; Table Ⅰ.3.5).

Rammed Earth Foundation 3: Located in the southern part of the inner city, in the western part of the orchard on the south side of the Heping Village road. Its west side abuts houses that sit on the east side of the road running west of Heping Village. To its northwest is the field station of the archaeology team. The city wall is 50 m to its south, and about 7 m to its north is Rammed Earth Foundation 4. Furthermore, it is located directly across Road L1 in symmetry with Rammed Earth foundation 2. This foundation's area is roughly rectangular, 65 m long north to south and about 21-31 m wide east to west. Its southwest corner protrudes to the west in a section that is about 11 m wide. Its orientation is 18° east of north. The area's cultural deposits are relatively thin, about 0.3 m thick. Under the cultural deposits is rammed earth. Most of the area is one layer of rammed earth, tan or grey. The grey rammed earth was found in eleven coring holes, while the tan rammed earth was found in forty coring holes. The rammed earth begins at 0.4-1.4 m, is concentrated at 0.5-0.8 m deep, and is 0.2-0.9 m thick, but in most of the area it is 0.4-0.7 m thick. A part of the area has two layers of rammed earth: layer 1 is grey rammed earth; layer 2 is tan rammed earth. The grey earth begins at 0.4-0.6 m and is 0.3-0.5 m thick, and the tan rammed earth begins at 0.7-0.9 m and is 0.3-0.7 m thick. The rammed earth of the foundation is 0.6-1.1 m thick overall, and was found with eighty-nine coring holes, each more than 2.0 m deep. Under the rammed earth is tan virgin soil beginning at 0.9-1.6 m. Also, under the rammed earth in coring holes 26, 27, and 28 we found a layer of road earth, 1.0 to 1.4 m below the ground surface. There are also stones found under the rammed earth foundation's southeast corner, 0.8 m below the rammed earth (Fig. Ⅰ.3.6; Table Ⅰ.3.6).

The area along the south edge of Rammed Earth Foundation 3 is paved with a layer of stones forming an L-shaped face, but its western part is overlain by a house, which prevented further coring. Currently, the northern part is 15 m wide and the southern part is 27 m wide. The stones are 0.6-1.8 m below the ground surface, concentrated at 1.2-1.5 m.

The east and south of the stone surface are surrounded by a large area of footpath earth. The footpath's northern end connects with Road L1, and in the south it extends to the south city wall. It is about 54 m long, and about 8 m wide. Moving downwards, the typical deposits in this area are surface earth, sand layers (with ash inclusions), footpath earth (with sand inclusions), and tan earth. Part of the footpath surface is also rammed. The stone surface and the footpath surface are about the same depth, and they all begin below the grey earth, at a depth of 0.6-0.9 m. It is possible that this was part of an activity area related to Rammed Earth Foundation 3, but more work would be required to determine if this could be considered a "plaza" (Fig. Ⅰ.3.7; Table Ⅰ.3.7).

Rammed Earth Foundation 4: Located in the southern part of the inner city, north of the small road between the two parts of the apple orchard south of Heping Village. The foundation is 75 m from Heping Village in the north and 42 m east of the road. To its south is Rammed Earth Foundation 3. It is approximately rectangular in shape, about 13 m long and 10.5 meters wide at its widest, with an area of about 136.5 m^2. Its orientation is 18° east of north. According to the results of the coring, we determined that the west and north faces of the foundation had been destroyed, though its eastern edge is basically intact, and the remaining shape is roughly rectangular. The area between Foundations 3 and 5 has been destroyed by sediment pits, and we could not determine whether or not the two foundations belong to the same architectural unit. This area's cultural deposits are relatively shallow, with many ash pits intruding into the rammed earth. The rammed earth begins at about 0.3-0.9 m and is about 0.3-1.1 m thick, with tan virgin soil beginning at about 0.7-1.6 m (Fig. Ⅰ.3.8; Table Ⅰ.3.8).

Rammed Earth Foundation 5: Located south of Heping Village in the apple orchard north of the road, 48 m south of Heping Village and 47 m east of the road. It is about 15 m west of Road L1, and to its south is Rammed Earth Foundation 4. The surviving structure's shape is irregular, and its northern part appears to be an east-west rectangle, about 22 m long and about 14 m wide. Its southern part appears to be a north-south rectangle, with an orientation 18° east of north. It is about 13 m from south to north and about 10 m from east to west. The total area size is 438 m^2. The foundation's northwest part, southeast part, and the south side adjacent to Rammed Earth Foundation 4 have been destroyed by later period remains. This area's cultural deposits are relatively shallow and under it is the rammed earth, beginning at 0.3-0.9 m, 0.2-1.2 m thick, and composed of grey rammed earth and tan rammed earth. In a few places the rammed earth is as deep as two meters and the coring did not reach the bottom. This was probably evidence of the ground surface having been very low in ancient times, which was first leveled by ramming earth. Underneath the rammed earth are early period cultural deposits and ash pits, among other remains (Fig. Ⅰ.3.9; Table Ⅰ.3.9).

Rammed Earth Foundation 6: Located in the southern part of the inner city, north of the small road between the two apple orchards south of Heping Village, 22.5 m east of the main road. It is on the west side of Rammed Earth Foundation 4. The remaining structure is 13.5 m wide from east to west and 21.5 m long from north to south, and it is basically "L" shaped, oriented north-south. The northeast corner of the foundation is missing, probably caused by destruction, and the remaining area is 209.5 m^2. Its orientation is roughly north with an 18 degree offset to the east. This area's cultural deposits are about 0.5 m thick, and underneath it is rammed earth, mostly tan, though in some areas it is grey rammed earth. The rammed earth begins at 0.4-0.7 m and is 0.2-0.8 m thick. Tan virgin soil begins at 0.7 m deep. There was a lot of water-formed rust discovered in the grey and brown earth layers during the coring in the northeast part of the foundation. In the missing section of the northeast part there is sediment underneath the grey earth layer, perhaps having been a ditch or reservoir. This feature damaged Rammed Earth Foundation 6 (Fig. Ⅰ.3.10; Table Ⅰ.3.10).

Rammed Earth Foundation 7: Located in the southern part of the inner city, north of the small road between the two apple orchards south of Heping Village. The foundation is located 1 m east of the houses belonging to Heping Village, 20 m from the road. It is 2.5 m west of Rammed Earth Foundation 6. The surviving shape is basically rectangular, with a length of about 26.5 m north to south and a width of about 7 m from east to west, giving a total area of 185.5 m^2. The orientation is about 18° east of north. This area's cultural deposits are relatively shallow: the rammed earth layer underneath it begins at 0.4-0.9 m, and is mainly composed of tan rammed earth, with a little grey rammed earth, 0.2-1.1 m thick. The tan rammed earth begins at 0.7-1.6 m. The cultural deposits in the northern part of the rammed earth foundation are relatively thick, about 1.3-1.7 m, and in the south are about 0.4-1.1 m thick (Fig. Ⅰ.3.11; Table Ⅰ.3.11).

Rammed Earth Foundation 16: Located in the southwest part of the inner city, northeast of Guijiang Village, and southwest of Heping Village, 5.5 m from the road west of Heping Village. It is 36 m from Rammed Earth Foundation 7, its west face is across the ditch from Rammed Earth Foundations 13 and 14, about 75 m distant, and its northwest face is about 50 m from Foundation 10. To its west and north is ditch G1. Its shape is rectangular, 13-14.5 m long, about 7 m wide, with an area of about 98 m^2. This area's depositional strata are about 1.0 m thick, and underneath the cultural deposits is rammed earth, beginning at 1.3-1.4 m, tan in color, very firm and displaying clear layers. We did not core the full depth of the rammed earth. But the rammed earth's eastern part is a thin layer of about 0.5 m, under which is virgin soil. The cultural layers are thin and cultural remains are rare

(Fig. Ⅰ.3 12; Table Ⅰ.3.12).

Rammed Earth Foundation 17: Located in the south-central part of the inner city, in the courtyard of the archaeology team's field station. Here we adopted an independent numbering system, starting with coring point 1 at the courtyard's southwestern corner. Nine meters to the east is Rammed Earth Foundation 7, and 11 m to the west is Rammed Earth Foundation 16. The foundation had an irregular rectangular shape, oriented north-south, close to compass north. It is about 7.5 m long from north to south and 7 m wide at its widest, with an area of about 50 m^2. This area's cultural deposits are relatively shallow, 0.2-0.7 m deep. The tan rammed earth underneath begins at 0.4-0.8 m, with the northern part being 0.3-0.8 m thick. In the southern part there is multicolor earth more than 1.2 m wide extending towards the north (Fig. Ⅰ.3.13; Table Ⅰ.3.13).

4. The Western Architectural Group

The western group of rammed earth architectural foundations is located in the western part of the inner city, west of ditch G1, north of Guijiang Village. There are seven structures in total. They can be described as follows:

Rammed Earth Foundation 8: Located in the northwest corner of the inner city wall, north of Guijiang Village, south of the section of the north wall protected by stone. The stone-protected wall B is 38 m to the north, the west city wall is about 25 m to the west, and Rammed Earth Foundation 9 is about 25 m to the east. The foundation is basically a rectangle oriented north-south, about 37 m long and about 5.0-6.5 m wide, with an area of about 222 m^2. The orientation is about 16° east of north. This area's cultural deposits are thick, with relatively rich remains including ash pits. Many of the ash pits includes vegetal ash and water-formed rust and are 2.0 m deep, though we did not reach the bottom. There are also surviving sediment pits. Under the cultural deposits is rammed earth, beginning at 1.5-2.1 m, and 0.9-1.2 m thick. To the south of the foundation, some of the coring holes could not go deeper than 1.3 m due to the presence of stones. The rammed earth is tan in color, with sand inclusions (Fig. Ⅰ.3.14; Table Ⅰ.3.14).

Rammed Earth Foundation 9: Located in the northwest part of the inner city, north of Guijiang Village, west of Heping Village, south of the section of north wall protected by stone, 16 m from the northern cliff face, 5 meters north of Guijiang Village houses, 50 m east of the west city wall, about 20 m east of Rammed Earth Foundation 8, to the south of the north city wall. It is about 32 m from Foundation 11, and about 10 m north of Foundation 14. Its shape is roughly a north-to-south rectangle, about 93 m long from north to south, and about 23 m from east to west at its widest point, with a total area of about 1,750 m^2. Its orientation is about 16° east of north. This area's cultural deposits are relatively thick. The northern and northeastern parts have dug out and sediment pits, but the layers of deposits are relatively simple. The bedrock in the north and the tan virgin soil in the south are both quite shallow. There are cultural deposits on top of the rammed earth, which begins at 0.9-2.0 m, with the southern part higher than the northern part. The rammed earth is relatively thick, about 0.3-1.3 m. Underneath is a sand layer beginning at 1.5-2.3 m, and the tan earth or sediment begins at about 2.0 m. The typical nature of the deposits is tan-colored rammed earth and reddish-brown rammed earth, with sand inclusions, hard, and with thin peeling layers. The reddish-brown rammed earth was formed from soil taken from reddish-brown clay mixed with red sand from the bedrock (Fig. Ⅰ.3.15; Table Ⅰ.3.15).

Rammed Earth Foundation 10: Located in the northwest of the inner city, northeast of Guijiang Village, west of Heping Village, and southeast of the stone-protected north wall, 24 m north of the cliff face. Ditch G1 is 18 m to its east, and 7 m to its south is Rammed Earth Foundation 11. Rammed Earth Foundation 12 is to its west, and it is 31 m south of the north city wall. The extant shape is rectangular. It is about 30.5 m long and about 7 m wide, with an area of about 213.5 m^2. Its orientation is 14° east of north. This area's cultural deposits are relatively thick at about 1.0 m, and there are many ash pits. Under the cultural deposits is rammed earth, extending from 0.8 to 1.5 m, mostly about 1.0 m deep and 0.7-0.8 m thick. The tan earth extends from 1.4 to 1.9 m, and underneath part of the rammed earth is a sandy layer, extending from 1.5 to 1.7 m. The rammed earth is tan with sand inclusions (Fig. Ⅰ.3.16; Table Ⅰ.3.16).

Rammed Earth Foundation 11: Located in the northwest of the inner city, northeast of Guijiang Village, west of Heping Village, north of the small road that runs north of Guijiang Village, southeast of the northern wall section protected by stone. Seven meters to the east was ditch G1, 7 m to the north is Rammed Earth Foundation 10, and to the west is Foundation 12. The surviving shape is rectangular, about 30 m long and about 14.5 m at its widest. In the south and north there are square areas protruding; the northwestern area is 5 m long and 4.5 m wide, and the one in the southeast was 5 m long and 4 m wide. The total area is 276.5 m^2. The orientation is 14° east of north. This area's cultural deposits are 0.7 m thick and underneath is rammed earth, extending from 0.8 to 1.2 m, mostly 0.4-0.8 m thick. The rammed earth is tan with sand inclusions (Fig. Ⅰ.3.17; Table Ⅰ.3.17).

Rammed Earth Foundation 12: Located in the northwest of the inner city northeast of Guijiang Village, west of Heping Village, north of the small road north of Guijiang Village, and southeast of the stone-protected section of the north wall. It is about 10 m west of Rammed Earth Foundation 11. The existing shape is a rectangle with rounded corners. It is about 15.5 m long from north to south and about 10 m wide from east to west at its widest, with an area of about 1,554 m^2. Its orientation is due north-south. This area's cultural deposits are relatively shallow, about 0.2-0.6 m thick, and the rammed earth underneath mainly extends from 0.5 to 0.6 m, and is mostly 0.2 m thick and 0.9 m at its thickest. Underneath is tan virgin soil. The rammed earth is tan earth with sand inclusions (Fig. Ⅰ.3.18; Table Ⅰ.3.18).

Rammed Earth Foundation 13: Located in the northwest of the inner city, inside an old pear orchard on the eastern flank of Guijiang Village. Fifteen meters to the north is Rammed Earth

Foundation 14, and it lies 15 m west of ditch G1. The existing shape is rectangular, 10 m long from east to west, and 7.5 m wide from north to south, with an area of about 75 m^2, making it a small-scale foundation. It is oriented due north-south. Eastern Zhou period cord-decorated pottery sherds are visible on the ground surface. This area's cultural deposits are relatively shallow, about 0.3 m thick, with few ash pits. The rammed earth begins from 0.4 to 0.6 m deep, and is up to 1.4 m thick at most. Underneath is bedrock. The typical nature of the rammed earth in this area is tan-colored rammed earth with sand inclusions, hard, and with peeling layers (Fig. Ⅰ.3.19; Table Ⅰ.3.19).

Rammed Earth Foundation 14: Located in the northwest of the inner city, northeast of Guijiang Village, west of Heping Village, south of the small road north of Guijiang Village. Twelve meters to the north is Rammed Earth Foundation 9, 15 m to the southeast is Foundation 13, and about 25 m to the southeast is ditch G1. The shape is rectangular, about 12 m long and 5.5 m at the widest, with an area of about 66 m^2. It is basically oriented due north-south. This area's cultural deposits are relatively shallow at about 0.5 m. The rammed earth begins 0.5-0.9 m below the surface (the full depth of the rammed earth was not cored), and the tan virgin soil underneath is found at a depth of 1.6-1.9 m. The typical nature of the deposits here is tan rammed earth with sand inclusions, hard and with peeling layers (Fig. Ⅰ.3.20; Table Ⅰ.3.20).

5. The Rammed Earth Foundations in the North-Central Inner City

Rammed Earth Foundation 15: Located in the middle of the inner city, Coring Plot **[1]** within Heping Village, on the east side of Heping Village's pig farm. To the north of the plateau the ground is low, where there was originally a ditch. On the remaining three sides are all residential houses. It is 100 m from the north city wall, and about 130 m from the east city wall, relatively far from the other rammed earth foundations. To the east and south the Yantai Cultural Relics Commission excavated tomb M2 and a horse chariot pit in 1972. The shape of the foundation is basically rectangular. The existing length is about 14 m from north to south, and the width is about 8 m from east to west, with a total area of 112 m^2. The orientation is about 25° east of north. There are many grey pottery sherds on the surface. This area's cultural deposits are relatively thick, about 1.0 m, and between the deposits and the rammed earth underneath is a dividing layer of sand about 0.1-0.3 m thick. The rammed earth begins at 1.1 to 1.6 m, and is 0.2-0.4 m thick. The tan virgin soil is 1.3-1.8 m deep. The rammed earth is mostly tan, with some grey rammed earth, hard, with sand inclusions and with thin layers and peeling surfaces (Fig. Ⅰ.3.21; Table Ⅰ.3.21).

6. The Rammed Earth Foundations on the Platform North of the Inner City

Rammed Earth Foundation 18: Located to the north of the inner city, about 150 m from the north city wall. To the north is Dayujia Village South Road, and to the west is the Yaque River. We carried out coring of this feature on July 16, 2009. The rammed earth foundation is located on the duckbill-shaped platform protruding north from the highland north of Heping Village. The shape is basically a rectangle oriented north-south, about 120 m long from north to south and about 30 m wide from east to west. The stratigraphy in this area is relatively simple. Generally, under the topsoil is rammed earth, beginning at 0.3 to 0.5 m, and usually 0.8 m thick, but mostly not cored to the bottom. The rammed earth is tan with sand inclusions and hard. Underneath it is tan virgin soil, beginning at 1.1-1.5 m below the ground surface (Fig. Ⅰ.3.22).

Section 6: Other Remains in the Inner City

1. Road L2

Located in the southeast part of Guijiang Village, along the two sides of the Heping Village road (Fig. Ⅰ.3.1). It is a long strip running from south to north, and from the coring we determined that it is 90 m long from south to north, and 10-13 m wide, oriented 19° east of north. The southern part runs through the south gate of the city. Where it approaches the ditch it was not cored, and in the north it appears to run onto the eastern part of Rammed Earth Foundation 16, but it also seems to have been intruded on by later period remains. The road earth extends below the grey earth layer, and is partially damaged by late period remains and units. The footpath (road earth) begins at 0.35-1.25m deep, but is usually about 0.45 m deep and between 0.1 and 0.5 m thick. The bottom part of the road is tan earth with sand inclusions. The road earth is composed of tan earth but was formed by foot traffic, and it has clear, thin layers.

2. The Inner City Water Gates

There are outlets from the inner city in two places. Ditch G1 forms a natural division running north to south cutting through the inner city of Guicheng. Its northern end exits at the turning point of the north city wall, clearly showing a gap in the city wall. Inside the gap are sandy layers and grey earth with water-formed rust. In the south, G1 turns to the west after crossing the small road north of Guijiang Village and becomes wider. Inside Guijiang Village it turns again to the east, passes through the city wall opening west of the city gate south of Guijiang Village, and leads to the moat outside the city wall. The southern water gate is about 13 m wide. The northern gate is about 17 m wide.

3. The Reservoir within the City

The reservoir is located in the southeast part of the inner city. We discovered a sump in the southeastern part of Heping Village, where a large area of sediment was found (Fig. Ⅰ.3.1). According to the stratum into which it opens, it is from the same period as the rammed earth foundations in the inner city. The shape of the reservoir is a north-south strip, 73 m from north to south, and 40 m wide from east to west, with a total area of 2,920 m^2. It is 2 m below the surface, and we did not reach the bottom. It also holds relatively many pottery sherds. The deposits are mostly grey earth and sediment soil.

Section 7: A Brief Description of the Tombs Recently Looted in or Near the Inner City

The Guicheng inner city has always faced cultural preservation issues, and looting has occurred in the past. During our work periods at Guicheng, we took a pedestrian survey of remains that had been looted and collected some artifacts. These artifacts are all pottery, mostly from burials that had been looted. Below, I will include these finds, which can also deepen our understanding of the cultural features of the time period of Guicheng.

1. Groups 1-3 of Heping Village West

These specimens are mostly sporadic collections within the inner city during the survey seasons from 2007 to 2009. By selection, we drew the diagnostic sherds and divided them into three groups according to the time when they were collected (Figs. Ⅰ.3.23- Ⅰ.3.25; Tables Ⅰ.3.22- Ⅰ.3.24). The pieces collected were roughly from the fields west of Heping Village, but their specific locations cannot be precisely determined (Pl. 14).

2. Group 4 of Heping Village West

While conducting data analysis in summer 2010, the Sino-American Joint Guicheng Archaeological Team learned that tombs in the vicinity of Heping Village had been robbed in the spring of that year. On August 3, team members were sent to investigate the area. The looted area was about 20-50 m north of the northwest corner of the inner city. The ground surface in this area is relatively flat, slightly lower than the ground surface in the inner city, but higher than the Yaque River's course by about 3-4 m. We found about ten densely concentrated looting pits, most of which had been dug in the winter or spring of 2010. There were both rectangular looting pits measuring 1 × 0.6 m, and round looting pits 0.6 m in diameter. The former were manually dug, while the latter were made by blasting. Especially in the disturbed soil of the former there were many pottery sherds, including many large pieces, most likely grave goods. From the distribution of the pottery sherds collected on the surface, it seems that the remains could be divided into two groups. Group 4 here is the first of these two (Fig. Ⅰ.3.26; Table Ⅰ.3.25). See also Group 6 below.

3. Group 5 of Heping Village West

In the summer of 2010, before the archaeologists investigated the looted area, Mr. Wang Huaisheng, the cultural heritage custodian of Heping Village, had already collected several pottery sherds near the looting pits. Vessels whose forms could be reconstructed are included in this group (Fig. Ⅰ.3.27; Table Ⅰ.3.26).

4. Group 6 of Heping Village West

This is the second group of pottery sherds collected on August 3, 2010, by the archaeology team members who went to investigate the area west of Heping Village that was looted in the spring of 2010 (Fig. Ⅰ.3.28; Table Ⅰ.3.27).

5. Group 1 of Heping Village North

On June 24, 2009, members of the archaeology team investigated an area of tombs to the north of Heping Village that had been looted. The looting pits are in the apple orchard about 100 m north of the north city wall. In total, two looting pits were discovered nearby, apparently dug in the winter and spring of that year. In the disturbed soil there were a number of pottery sherds, and we made drawings of the diagnostic sherds (Fig. Ⅰ.3.29; Table Ⅰ.3.28).

6. The Reservoir East of Dongchijia Village

In the afternoon of June 12, 2009, members of the archaeology team went to the home of the old village head of Dongchijia to investigate objects unearthed during the winter of 2000. That year, construction of the reservoir on the east side of Dongchijia unearthed three pottery vessels, including two *bu* vases and one *dou* pedestal dish (Pl. 13). According to the description of the villagers, at the time there was also one bronze *ding* cauldron unearthed, added to the collection of the Longkou Museum. On June 24, the archaeology team collected the three pottery vessels. At the same time, under the guidance of the old village head, we went to investigate the area where the vessels were unearthed. It is now under the reservoir. Originally, there was a river channel running south-to-north east of Dongchijia Village, and the land is relatively low-lying. In 2000, in this exact area they constructed the reservoir, mostly digging about a meter down. The area where the pottery vessels were unearthed was likely on the east side of the reservoir, probably originally on the east side of the river channel, including the second terrace of the channel. The banks of the reservoir's inlet are nearby. This area's soil is relatively thick, quite different from the sandy earth on the mountaintop. On the pottery *dou* pedestal dish there is an incised mark (Fig. Ⅰ.3.30; Table Ⅰ.3.29).

7. The Bronze Chisel Found to the North of Heping Village

During the survey in June, 2007, the archaeological team surveying the area north of Heping Village discovered a bronze chisel on the ground to the east of the main road leading north. The object has a rectangular opening on the top and a hole in the center. The chisel is 8.3 cm long, 4.1 cm wide at the hollowed top, and 3.8 cm wide at the blade (Fig. Ⅰ.3.31; Pl. 15: 2).

Section 8: Conclusion

1. On the location and chronology of Guicheng's inner city

Guicheng's inner city is located at the foot of Mt. Lai, on the plateau between the two branches of the Yaque River. The soil in this location is fertile, and travel to the east and west is convenient, so that it is an ideal choice of location in which to build a city. Guicheng's inner city is shaped like a set-square, with an indentation in the northwest corner, perhaps because this area was relatively low-lying, and the city was built following the landform. Calculating from the center of the city wall, the inner city is 490 m long from north to south and 525 m wide from east to west. The indented portion in the northwest part of the city wall is about 180 m long from north to south and about 180 m wide from east to west. The total area of the inner city is 225,000 m^2. It was built on a relatively grand scale for a Western Zhou period site.

According to the archaeological survey and the exploratory coring and test excavation, we have confirmed the existence of the inner and outer city walls, which make a double-walled city.

Furthermore, we speculate that there was a chronological gap between the inner city, built first, and the outer city, built later. According to the archaeological survey and test excavation of recent years, the inner city's chronology spans the late phase of the early Western Zhou to the Spring and Autumn period.

2. The Layout and Characteristics of the Inner City's Architectural Foundations

The layout of the inner city site follows the ground surface. The land in its southern and western parts is relatively flat and elevated, and this is the location of the palace district. In the coring process we discovered seventeen rammed earth foundations, located mostly within this area. However, the north part of the inner city was also the location of some important rammed earth foundations. During the exploratory coring on the plateau in the north-central part of the inner city we discovered Rammed Earth Foundation 15, and in 2002 the Yantai Museum excavated a Spring and Autumn period house foundation in this area.

Ditch G1 was the drainage system that linked the south and north of the inner city, dividing the inner city into an eastern and a western part. The south city gate and the north-south thoroughfare L2 are located just to the east of G1, together forming the great south gate. G1's northern outlet is located at the corner of the northwestern city wall and passes through here to the outer city. Road L1 is located right in the center of the inner city. Its south end runs to the city wall, while its north end has been destroyed by other remains. It also could not be cored because of the location of the village. No city gate was discovered in the city wall at the south end of L1, so we still cannot determine the complete shape of L1. According to the city's function and its configuration in the Zhou ritual system, all four sides of Guicheng should have had city gates, but because of later destruction and the occupation by the villages of a large part of Guicheng, we only discovered the south gate.

The seventeen rammed earth foundations were all found beneath the grey earth layer, at roughly the same depth as other rammed earth structures, so that there probably was not a large gap in time between them. Accordingly, considering the layout of the palace foundations, they can be placed on the same level. Many of the foundations intruded into bedrock, tan virgin soil, loess soil, and sandy layers, so they were probably architectural structures that had had a foundational ditch. However, the thickness of the rammed earth is not uniform, suggesting that before they were constructed, there were early period ash pits and other features in the area that needed to be dealt with to varying extents. The rammed earth foundations we discovered during coring are mostly rectangular platforms oriented north-south, a point that is well worth attention. In particular, Rammed Earth Foundation 2 has two protruding sections about 3 m wide at its southeast and northwest ends, which we surmised were the steps up to the rammed earth foundation.

The architectural foundations in the western district are relatively close together, spread roughly north to south with the large Foundation 9 in the center. On the east and west sides of Foundation 9 are distributed the relatively large Foundations 8, 10, and 11, also laid out from south to north, in an west-east symmetrical arrangement. Their orientations are mostly 14-16° east of north. The southern part of this group includes the small foundations numbered 13 and 14, oriented basically due east-west.

The architecture in the eastern district is principally distributed in the southern end of the inner city. On both sides of inner city Road L1 are distributed nine rammed earth foundations. Foundations 3 and 2 are comparatively larger in area and are roughly symmetrical. This is probably an important part of the palace. The northern part of this group has one line of relatively smaller rammed earth foundations, including Foundations 4, 5, 6, 7, 16, and 17. Their orientation is 18° east of north, basically the same as Road L1. This is probably a single group of architectural foundations. Rammed Earth Foundation 1 is located on the inner side of the city wall, and was probably an auxiliary defensive structure (Fig. Ⅰ.3.2).

The south, north-central, north, and east areas have thick cultural deposits with many ash pits, and abundant fragmented pottery sherds, vegetal ash, and bone material. We believe that this area had remains of commoners' dwellings. In the north-central part of the inner city and 10 m southwest of Rammed Earth Foundation 15, near coring hole E6, we discovered worked bone tools, perhaps related to a bone tool workshop. Also, in the test excavations in 2009 in ash pit H9 of test trench 2 (TG2) we discovered a pottery mold related to bronze casting, which shows that there could have been the remains of a bronze-casting workshop nearby (see Chapter 5 in this volume). The excavation area was located on the west side of Rammed Earth Foundation 1 and south of Rammed Earth Foundation 2, surrounded on three sides by large architectural foundations (Fig. Ⅰ.3.1). This suggests that some of these architectural foundations may have been related to the remains of the bronze casting workshop.

The cultural deposits were quite simple in the northwestern and southeastern areas, with scattered tombs. The tombs in the eastern and southeastern parts of the inner city were relatively dense. At the current stage, one problem is the occupation of the site by Heping Village, which impacted the coring of the inner city. The second problem is that we still have not discovered pottery manufacturing or other characteristic remains. These all require more work.

3. Discussions of Some Issues

From the extent of the city we can see that the Guicheng site, especially the outer city, has a large area, with a thick and strong city wall. Its scale and earthworks are comparable to those of the Qufu Lu site. Guicheng was probably a capital city. Like the capitals of the states of Lu and Xue and other Zhou era city sites, the Guicheng site also has a double set of city walls. The inner city of the ancient capital of the state of Lu was located in the center of the outer city, which is rectangular and oriented east to west. The inner city of the capital of the state of Xue was located in the southeast corner of its outer city, and was an irregular rectangle, mostly constructed in the Spring and Autumn period. Guicheng's inner city is located in the center of the outer city, and construction was probably begun in the Western Zhou period. Comparatively speaking, so far in the Shandong region no other Western Zhou period capital cities have been found. Therefore, the results of the archaeology of the Guicheng inner city are particularly important. They provide an important basis for research into the relationship between the Jiaodong region's ancient Dongyi Polities and the royal dynasties of the Central Plains.

Besides Guicheng, the largest city site from the Zhou period so far discovered in the Jiaodong region is Jimo of Pingdu. However, there is a gap in the chronology. According to previous archaeological work, Jimo most likely dates to the Warring States period. It was therefore an important capital city in Jiaodong after Guicheng. The Jimo ancient city is also divided into inner and outer cities, and the area of the inner city is almost rectangular. Its southeast corner is missing, and it is 1,370 m long from south to north and 1,270 m wide from east to west. The entire inner city is located in the southeast part of the outer city. The outer city dates to the Han Dynasty. Overall, the area is an irregular rectangle, about 4.5 km long from north to south and about 3.2 km wide from east to west. It forms a chronological sequence with Guicheng.

There are still some limitations to the survey and coring work at Guicheng. Because the inner city's northern and southwestern parts have been overbuilt by villages, our coring was largely confined to the areas south of Heping Village and north of Guijiang Village. In addition, we also cored six plots of land within Heping Village. We were also limited by the ground cover, and in the area with overbuilding we could not conduct general coring. These limitations certainly influenced our understanding of the distribution of the inner city's rammed earth architecture.

From the coring we also discovered that Guicheng's rammed earth foundations suffered serious destruction by later period remains. For example, Rammed Earth Foundation 2 was seriously damaged by erosion from the ditch that ran from south to north. Based on the presence of sand layers in the rammed earth of the inner city wall, we surmise that during Guicheng's period of occupation the river may have invaded the city multiple times and caused damage, and the portions of the city wall involved and even the architectural foundations all possibly underwent repair or reconstruction. These are issues we must ascertain in later work.

Finally, we should mention the question of the orientation of Guicheng's rammed earth foundations. The architectural foundations from ancient China are mostly east-to-west rectangles. However, Guicheng's rammed earth foundations are principally oriented north-to-south, while a number of the smaller-scale architectural features are oriented east to west. This might have to do with the nature and function of the architectural foundations, and even more so with the cultural traditions in the ancient state that was based in Guicheng. We need to conduct further research to clarify these questions.

Reference

Li, Buqing 李步青 and Lin Xianting 林仙庭, 1991. "Shandong Huangxian Guicheng yizhi de diaocha yu fajue" 山东黄县归城遗址的调查与发掘 (Survey and excavation of the Guicheng site in Huangxian County, Shandong), *Kaogu* 考古, 10: 910-918.

(Translated by Elizabeth Berger)

第四章　外城城墙的勘察

唐锦琼

第一节　地 理 形 势

归城的外城坐落在莱山北侧，内城周围的山前丘陵地带上。莱山又名“之莱山”，呈东西向横亘于龙口市南部，位于东经120°31′～120°44′，北纬37°27′～37°36′，占地面积102.27平方千米，最高峰海拔619米。归城所处位置即在莱山东段北麓的山前地带。此处的莱山呈半环形，两侧突起的部分正与外城城墙的东南和西南两端相接，构成一个完整的封闭空间。莱山山势陡峭，极难翻越，是归城南侧的一道天然屏障。在城外西北侧约1000米处为一处名叫凤凰山的低矮小山，海拔约120米（地图Ⅰ.4.1；图版1、2）。

归城处于黄水河流域，坐落在其一条支流——鸦鹊河——的上游。城内主要有三条小河通过。最西侧一条源自归城姜家村西的山前地带，经北山村南进入城内，呈西南—东北向流经城址北部，从内城以北流过。其余两条均源自莱山之阴，呈南北向由城址东部流过。其中偏西的一条为鸦鹊河干流，源自庙周家南侧的莱山北麓，流经庙周家村和庙马家村西，进入城址范围。在城内，其在曹家村东南呈西南—东北流向，至归城姜家村东南改为南北流向，再经和平村东（内城东侧），董家村西南，并在董家村西、和平村北与来自北山村南的支流相交汇。然后这条干流一路流向东北，在归城东北约7千米的赵刘村附近注入黄水河干道。但是，由于归城姜家村东南新修水库的阻隔，这条干流已无法下泄，而通过一条新辟的排洪道汇入东侧的支流中。原和平村东和董家村西南的河道已完全干涸，被辟为农田。董家村西的一座小学即坐落在故道上。东侧支流起自东迟家村西南，向东北方流，再折为南北向北经由董家村东，在大于家村东汇入鸦鹊河干流中。由于水库的修建，这条支流现在成为归城内最主要水系（图版5、6）。

归城城址内的地形以低山丘陵为主。内城处于城址中心的一处高台地上，为周边地区地势最高，面积最大的一块台地，平均高度约为海拔73～79米（内城详情见上编第二章）。内外城间地形主要为坡度和缓的低矮丘陵，高度一般在海拔56～125米，整体地形由南向北倾斜。这些岗地主要呈南北或西南—东北走向，其南端与莱山山体相连，仅在北侧略近东西走向。在山坡下部多为河道。东侧和中部的两条河道的坡岸平缓，少见有明显的陡坡，表明其形成时间较长，且径流稳定。在河道两侧的二级阶地土质较厚，适宜人们生活等，历年来也有重要的发现[1]。1969年在小刘庄发现的启尊、启卣即出土于鸦鹊河干流西岸的二级阶地上[2]。1951年在南埠村北出土黄县曩器发现于东侧支流的二级阶地上[3]。城址的边缘部位岗地，尤其是外城城墙东侧部分是直接坐落在砂土地上，并不十分适合人们居住和耕作。

第二节　调查方法

1. 以往调查方法和收获

1973年烟台地区文管会组织文物考古工作队对城址进行调查探测，确认了城址由内外两重城墙构成。通过调查确认外城位于盆地四周，沿山岭山势构建。北城墙在凤凰山南坡山腰，南城墙在莱山北坡山腰及其西的马岭山顶。东、西长城墙皆筑于低矮的山岗顶部。环周总长约10千米。

在上次调查中发现，由于长期以来自然和人为的破坏侵蚀，大部分墙段的地上部分已毁损无存。调查确认三处地面残存城墙和四处地下残存城墙。地面残存城墙一处在北山村内，地名"后城子"。该段城墙呈西南一东北走向，长75米，宽约4米（墙南侧被切除建房），高4米。此处夯层较厚，为12～15厘米。一处在大于家村西北300米处，地名"田家茔"。城墙呈土丘伏，东西长12米，南北宽9米，高1.5米，夯层厚6～10厘米。一处在董家村东500米处的"埝顶上"。夯土墙南北走向，长56米，宽9米，高2米。这三处地面城墙在此次调查中再次得到确认，分别属外城墙97、外城墙5和外城墙16。

根据20世纪70年代的调查，外城城墙的夯土较为纯净，采用的是就地取材的红褐色生黏土。夯层厚12～15厘米，夯窝直径8厘米，分布杂乱，疏密不一。在北山村的城墙处采集有铜镞。

70年代的调查为我们本次的工作提供了一些重要的信息，是进一步探查归城外城的起点和基础。但是，70年代的调查只是初步勾勒出外城的大体框架和走向，对外城的具体情况则是语焉不详。虽然发表了一张平面图，但在许多地点仍然使用虚线勾连，尤其是南侧城墙均为虚线，说明它仅是根据当时掌握的情况进行的复原，很多地方是推想的。同时这张图仍较简略，仅是示意图，未与地形地貌等结合，难以探究城址选址的自然因素等。因此，对外城仍有重新进行彻底调查的必要，即使已经发现的几段城墙也需要进一步确认和测量。

2. 调查采用的方法、记录手段

此次调查采取地面踏查与钻探相结合的方法进行。具体的技术流程为：通过地面踏查，依据地形走向，判定城墙的大概位置，然后利用钻探判定是否为夯土，从而确认城墙，并了解

1　参见本报告下编。

2　齐文涛：《概述近年来山东出土的商周青铜器》，《文物》1972年第5期，第5～7页。

3　王献唐：《黄曩器》，山东人民出版社，1960年。

范围和堆积情况（图版16）。在有条件的地点，在断崖上清理剖面了解堆积状况（图版17：1）。对发现的每段城墙单独编号，并在城墙之间的空白地带预留了城墙编号，留待将来通过其他手段有更多发现以后加以补充。同时在Google Earth地图上对城墙的范围加以标注，使用手持GPS机采集城墙范围的坐标数据。使用全站仪测绘每段城墙具体位置，并完成绘图（图版17：2）。由于归城范围古代遗址的破坏日渐严重，我们希望通过这次的彻底调查能为将来的保护和利用留下一套较为完整的资料。

外城调查分两次进行。第一次由2007年11月9日至26日，调查是起自北山村东侧的外城墙1，按顺时针方向逐步进行调查，调查至董家村东南的外城墙22，确认了北墙东段和东墙北段的走向（图Ⅰ.4.1～Ⅰ.4.3）。第二次由2008年6月21日至7月13日，延续上次的调查工作，自外城墙22顺东墙一直向南，调查至莱山脚下，发现外城可能使用南侧山地作为屏障，没有城墙分布，难以向前追踪。遂再由外城墙1以西的外城墙99开始调查，采取逆时针方向进行调查，经由北山村内，水泥厂东侧，一直追寻到曹家村西，最后终止在南侧的山脚下，完成外城的调查工作。2009年又在南侧山脚下发现了一处单独的夯土遗迹（外城墙77）。

第三节　外城勘察

1. 外城总体状况

通过调查，共发现45段外城城墙（其中残存有地面部分的有4段），编号为外城墙1～99号（中含留待将来发现填充使用的空号）（地图Ⅰ.4.1）。外城整体形状不甚规整，大致呈不规则椭圆形。分布范围北至北山村和大于家北侧山地，东侧至董家、东迟家和南埠东侧山地，南至莱山脚下，西至曹家西侧山地。城内有北山村、大于家、董家、和平、归姜（或称姜家）、南埠、东迟家和曹家等八个自然村，主要分布在Area2、Area3、Area4、Area5、Area8、Area9、Area12、Area13、Area15和Area16区域内。外城范围南北长约3.6千米，东西宽约2.8千米，面积约8平方千米。

外城的西城墙南端起自曹家村西南山地的山脚下，稍向东行后顺着曹家西侧山地的顶部向北略偏东方向延伸，直至岗地北端。在岗地以北的鸦鹊河两岸发现有小段城墙，表明城墙向北延伸。自北山村起，北侧城墙向东沿着北山—大于家村北侧岗地顶部向北偏东方向延伸，并回至鸦鹊河畔。在鸦鹊河河谷中城墙折向东南方，与外城的东城墙隔河相望。东侧城墙北段坐落在董家—和平村东的岗地上，大致朝南略偏东方向延伸。在南段，由于岗地向东拐了一个大弯，外城墙也因形就势，先拐向东南，后又折向西南方向。在此处，城墙分作两支，东侧的一支顺着车格庄北侧山地向南延伸，为城墙的分支。西侧一支外城墙为主干，经一段谷地后延伸至车格庄西北的岗地上。再向南，城墙越过通往石良镇的公路后，延伸至南埠村东南的岗地上，呈东北—西南走向延伸，直通到南侧莱山山脚之下。在这里，它与曹家村西南的外城墙的西南端遥相对应，构成了一个封闭的空间。三面城墙的复原总长约8.15千米。

城墙的构筑多是依托山势，主要是构建在周边岗地的顶部，并顺山脊延伸分布。最明显的为C列城墙。此列城墙位于董家村与和平村东山地的顶部，总长约1700米（见下）。在山地之间的谷地中亦构筑城墙以完善防御体系。如C列城墙和E列城墙均位于山地顶部，之间相隔一条宽约200米，深约20米的山谷。城墙37即坐落在山谷中，为有意构建，填补此处的防御空隙。

城墙墙体宽度不一，一般40米左右，最宽达到100米（如外城墙1），可能有城墙上附属建筑的存在。最窄处仅存5米左右，可能是后期破坏所致。

城墙为堆土夯筑而成。山顶处原有土壤为黄色砂土，有大量的黄褐色砂砾。但解剖剖面中，很少见到此类堆积，多为黄褐色或灰褐色花夯土，当时从山下搬运上来修筑城墙的。我们也发现有用淤土夯筑现象，当取自山下河道。城墙夯土的厚薄不一，最厚的达到200厘米，薄处或因破坏而仅存有5～10厘米。在地势较低处夯土较厚，地势较高处则较薄；甚至是直接通过对地形的修整而成。

2. 分段介绍

根据周围山势，以及河流、沟壑的阻断，城墙可分为11列。以下按照诸列的顺序，对诸段城墙逐一加以介绍（表Ⅰ.4.1）。

（1）A列城墙：此列城墙为外城的北墙，位于北山村—大于家村村北山地的顶部，顺山势而行，大致呈西南—东北走向，至东端（城墙8）略折，转为大致呈东西向。这段城墙东西长约1.26千米（图Ⅰ.4.4）。城墙所在岗地的内侧（面向内城，下同）倾斜向下，坡度较陡；外侧（面向城外，下同）地势略低于城墙，但坡度不是很明显。此列城墙自西向东分别外城墙97、外城墙99、外城墙1、外城墙3、外城墙4、外城墙5、外城墙6和外城墙8，以下逐一加以介绍。

外城墙97，为此列城墙中最西侧的一段城墙，位于北山村内北侧。该块城墙即为1973年调查发现的地面留存，人称“后城子”的那段城墙（以下凡城墙至2008年仍有地面留存者，将予特别说明；如无说明者则仅有地面以下遗存）。其地面部分已被破坏，仅在一户民宅后方留存有长约20米，高约1.2米的夯土断崖。城墙处于民居包围中，周边地面均已硬化，无法通过钻探确定城墙的留存、大小等情况。城墙夯土为灰褐色夯土，厚度在200厘米以上（图Ⅰ.4.5）。

该段城墙处于外城墙94和外城墙99之间。外城墙99位于此段城墙东北侧，大致在同一条直线上（图Ⅰ.4.6）。两者之间隔一条大冲沟东西相望，相距约91米。冲沟源自于凤凰山东侧，呈南北向由北山村东流过。沟壁竖直，较为陡峭，表明其形成时间较短。两处城墙原先或为一体，后为冲沟冲断。外城墙94位于外城墙97西南约855米处。两者之间空白地带较大，并被北山村阻隔，难以推断联连方式。外城墙94呈南北走向，外城墙97呈西南—东北走向，两者之间的被损毁的城墙或存在着拐角。

外城墙99，位于北山村东北山地顶部，南北向乡间路西部，隔路与外城墙1相接。此处山岗外侧（北侧）呈缓坡状向下，地势稍低，内侧（南侧）山势较陡，坡度较急，呈大坡状向下。城墙破坏严重，地面部分无存，仅残存下部夯土。残存城墙平面形状大致呈梯形，城墙东侧以乡间路为界，南侧至一高约4米的断崖，西侧至冲沟边的台地，北界至东西向小路北侧。城墙整体呈西南—东北走向，东西长约135米，南北宽约6～73米，东侧较宽。方向为北偏东34°，残存面积约5300平方米。城墙按高低分东西两部分。东部面积较大，地势较高，表面较平。西部紧贴着沟边，面积较小，低于东部约4米，表面较平。

城墙北侧夯土厚70厘米，分为两层，上层为黄褐色花夯土，下层为灰褐色花夯土，夯打痕迹明显（图版22：2）。在城墙略偏西的位置，发现在20厘米砂石夹泥夯层下有一层灰褐色花夯土。在南侧4米高的断崖下的平地中，也发现灰褐色花夯土，厚约40厘米，略向西处，夯土仅厚10厘米。在西部较低的台地上有黄褐色夯土，厚约20厘米。在东西两部的相交处，有一高约2米的取土断面，均为夯土，反映出城墙夯土的厚度（图Ⅰ.4.7、Ⅰ.4.8）。在城墙中部，有些地点直接露出基岩，这表明修建城墙时利用原有地形，在较低的位置培土夯筑而成。

外城墙1，位于北山村东北山地，南北向乡间路东侧台地上。城墙所在位置较高，南侧为较陡的坡地，通过下部数个台地隔河与内城相望。北侧地势较城墙略低，略作谷地状。下方东北侧有一东西向冲沟，绕经外城墙1的东北角，沿城墙东侧下方向东南方向延伸，最终汇入鸦鹊河河谷中。城墙的整体走向呈西南—东北走向，方向为北偏东80°。外城墙1间于外城墙99和外城墙3之间，大致呈东西一线分布。

外城墙1破坏严重，残存形状大致呈长方形，东北角向外凸起，西北侧残存的城墙略向南收。其残存部分南至台地南侧断崖，东至最高处台地东侧沟边。东北角至台地东北角的嘴子处，在东北角两侧的较低台地上也有部分残留。北侧在台地边缘南侧约2.5～7米处。西侧至西部的基岩露出处。城墙东西残长约58～77米，南北残宽约86～128米，东侧较宽。残存面积约7222.5平方米。除东北角两边的两个较低台地外，城墙地面大体较平，在中部有一道南北向矮断崖将地表分成东西两个台地，高差约1米，西侧较高（图Ⅰ.4.9）。

根据钻探，发现城墙堆积较为统一，30厘米表土下，即为灰褐色花夯土，夯打痕迹明显，以下为红褐色纯净生土，部分地方基岩较高处，下即直接为岩石。夯层的厚度不一，东南侧夯土较薄，厚约70厘米；北侧夯土显著加厚，达到100～110厘米。特别是西北角夯土厚度达到130厘米，且夯打质量很好；西侧的夯土可能由于基岩较高的原因，夯土较薄，厚约20～30厘米。在外城墙1清理两处剖面，了解堆积状况（图Ⅰ.4.10～Ⅰ.4.13）。

外城墙3，位于北山村和大于家村之间北侧台地西侧。台地东西两侧均为冲沟，南侧呈缓坡状俯视鸦鹊河河道。东侧地势较高，为城墙4所在，北侧下部呈缓坡状。城墙整体走向呈西南—东北走向，方向为北偏东64°。外城墙3位于外城墙1的东北方向，与之隔沟相望，两者直线距离约118米。但外城墙3较外城墙1显著偏北，北移约58米（以北侧边界为基准）。

城墙被破坏严重，残存形状大致呈“”形，西南角向东部略收。南侧至果林地南侧边缘，北侧在农田北侧。东部至稍高台地的下方。城墙残存部分有三个台地，各台地表面较平。北侧台地较高，上为耕地；南侧台地分成东西两个台地。东南侧台地面积较大，低于北侧台地约0.5米，为果林地；西南侧台地面积较小，低于东南侧台地约1.2米，为耕地。西南侧台地上有一现代所挖的蓄水池。城墙北侧部分东西残长约85.5米，南北残宽约24～30.5米，西侧略宽，残存面积约2330平方米；南侧部分东西残长约106米，南北残宽约18.5～28米，西侧较宽，残存面积约2464.5平方米。残存面积合计约4794.5平方米。根据迹象判断，外城墙2的原有长度在134米以上，南北宽度在59米以上，面积在5906平方米以上（图Ⅰ.4.14）。

根据钻探，发现地层较为统一，30厘米表土下，即为灰褐色花夯土，夯打痕迹明显。以下为红褐色纯净生土，部分地方基岩较高处，下即直接为岩石。夯层的厚度不一，大约在厚30厘米到80厘米之间。在城墙3清理两处剖面（图Ⅰ.4.15～Ⅰ.4.18；图版24：2）。

外城墙4，位于北山村和大于家村之间北侧台地中部较高处，外城墙3东北。城墙整体呈西南—东北走向，方向为北偏东46°。

城墙被破坏严重，残存形状大致呈“”形。外城墙4残存部分位于一条小路的两侧。南侧以蓄水池南侧断崖为界，西侧以断崖下小路为界，东侧和东南侧均至断崖边，北侧边界在台地中部。城墙西南部为陡坡状，上部为大量杂草、灌木等，其余则被开辟成耕地。一条小路将其分成东西两块，西侧部分由断崖分成东西两块台地，东侧高出约0.5米；东侧部分也为断崖分成东西两块，西侧高出约0.5米。外城墙4东西残长约53米，南北残宽约12～24米，西侧较宽。残存面积约856平方米。

根据钻探，在30厘米表土下，为灰褐色小花夯土，夹杂有红烧土粒，质地并不十分紧密，但部分夯打痕迹明显，夯土较薄，厚约10～20厘米。以下为红褐色纯净生土。

外城墙5，北山村和大于家村之间北侧台地上中偏东的位置，外城墙4之东北20米。其西侧地势较高，东侧为一条南北向冲沟。城墙整体呈西南—东北走向，方向为65°。

城墙被破坏严重，残存形状大致呈“”形。残存部分为两部分：西南部一块在稍高的台地上，东西两侧以一米高断崖为界，北侧至断崖下方，南侧在台地中部通过；东北部一块则位于较低台地上，在其东南角留存发现有一小段保留在地面上的夯土城墙遗迹。这段城墙遗迹东西长约13米，南北宽约7米，残高约1.8米。城墙西南部一块呈梯形，南北长约24～33米，东侧较宽，东西宽约27米，残存面积约770平方米。东北部一块大致呈长方形，东西长约19米，南北宽约14米，残存面积约266平方米。外城墙5的原有东西长度约43米，南北宽约48米，面积当在2064平方米左右（图Ⅰ.4.19）。

城墙的夯土堆积为浅灰褐色小花夯土，含有小黑土点，质地稍硬，西南部台地的夯土较厚，约40厘米，东北部台地的夯土较薄，厚约20～30厘米。夯土下为红褐色黏土或基岩。在城墙上清理了一处剖面（图Ⅰ.4.20、Ⅰ.4.21）。

外城墙3、4、5分位于同一个台地，由西向东一字排开。外城墙4位于中部，其西侧下方台地即为外城墙3，两者高差约2.5米，直线距离约30米。外城墙4东侧下方即为外城墙5所在台地，高差约2米，两者相距约20米。三段墙体相距很近，虽然中间有间隔，未能直接联系，且方向并不十分一致，但应为同一段长墙体的残存部分。

外城墙6，位于大于家村西北台地的南侧边缘，南侧下方即为鸦鹊河河道，呈缓坡状与之相望。城墙西侧为一条南北大沟，北侧地势与之大体相平，并呈很缓的坡度向上延伸。东侧呈缓坡状逐步向下。城墙整体呈西南—东北走向，方向为65°。西侧与外城墙5隔一条南北向大沟相望，相距约75米。它正在外城墙3～5的延伸线上。

城墙被破坏严重，残存形状大致呈长方形，东侧较宽。城墙北部由上方台地中部通过；南部在下方台地边缘通过，至东侧略向南扩展；西侧距沟边缘约25米，东侧在乡间路的东侧。城墙残存部分呈上下两个台地，两者高差约1米，除东南部为东西向耕地外，其余均为东西向林地。各台地的地势较平。城墙东西残长约107米，南北宽约27～39米，东侧较宽，城墙的残存面积约3530平方米。

城墙夯土为灰褐色夯土，夹杂由红色黏土粒，质地紧密。在西部钻探，发现其上部为30厘米垫土，夯土厚约150～200厘米。在乡间路的东侧的一处断崖下部暴露的夯土约20厘米，经钻探，下部夯土还有约80厘米，夯土合计厚度约为100厘米。

外城墙8，位于大于家村北。城墙所在位置较为低洼，西侧地势较高，呈数层台地的缓坡状通向大于家村西北台地，北侧地势稍高，东南侧不远处即为鸦鹊河河道。城墙整体呈东西走向，方向为90°。外城墙8西侧与外城墙6相望，相距约225米。

城墙被破坏严重，残存形状大致呈长方形，东北角已不存。外城墙8南北两侧均在田地中部通过，西侧至杨树林下断崖。城墙地势由西向东逐步倾斜，隔数个台地即有高约0.5米的断崖，逐步向东下降。城墙东西残长约150米，南北残宽约13～50米，东侧由于被破坏而变窄，城墙原有面积约6000平方米。

城墙的夯土为灰褐色夯土，夹杂有黑土块，质地较硬。夯土厚约20～30厘米。

在外城墙8东侧的南北发现有湖相堆积，为黑灰大花土，含大量水锈，黏性大。而在城墙以东也发现大量的湖相堆积，为含水锈的花土，含大量细砂，下部为黏性大的褐色黏土，最深在2米以上。这表明在该段城墙以东原先应有水面，但水面的时代难以确认。

（2）B列城墙：仅外城墙10。其位于大于家村东北，小于家村西南，两村之间的鸦鹊河的河谷中。城墙所在位置较整体为低洼，西侧地势较高，东部地势较低，东侧紧贴着鸦鹊河的河岸。河对岸为另一大片洼地，经钻探，均为淤土堆积，可能为鸦鹊河未束道前的河道。城墙西侧经钻探，发现大量的淤土堆积。距当地村民讲，当时在大于家和小于家之间有一条南北向河道通过，可能经由城墙西侧通过。即外城墙10是位于两股河道之间，恰与当地人旧称此处为“河心”的说法相合。城墙整体呈西北—东南走向，方向为118°。外城墙10位于外城墙8东侧，相距约92米。

城墙被破坏严重，残存形状大致呈长方形。外城墙10南北两侧均在田地中部通过，东至鸦鹊河西岸公路。城墙残存部分的地势由西向东逐步倾斜，中部一条西南—东北向，高约2米的断崖，将城墙所处地面分为东西两个部分，西侧高出东侧约2米。城墙东西残长约219米，南北残宽约80～57米，东侧由于被破坏而变窄，城墙原有面积约15000平方米。

城墙东部钻探发现为黑色黏土与黄褐色土相混的花夯土，夯打痕迹明显，这些夯土应为湖相堆积形成的黑色黏土与下部的黄褐色生土相混杂形成的，在水渠北侧夯土厚约30厘米，水渠以南的夯土厚约50厘米。西部夯土为浅灰白色夯土，夯土痕迹明显，含有大量水锈，质地纯净，较硬，应为将附近河道的灰白色淤土填于此夯打所致，厚约30～40厘米（图Ⅰ.4.22）。

（3）C列城墙：从北向南包括外城墙13、外城墙14、外城墙15、外城墙16、外城墙17、外城墙18、外城墙19、外城墙21、外城墙22、外城墙23、外城墙35。这列城墙位于董家-和平村东的南北向山地顶部，大致呈南北走向。此列山岗东侧隔一条南北向大沟与远处的南北向山岗相望，西侧则通过一片低地与内城相望。墙体所在山体北端山脚下即为鸦鹊河的河谷。最北侧的外城墙13略折向西北方向，与外城墙10遥相对应；两者间直线距离为440米，中间隔一大片洼地。此列城墙南侧的外城墙23由于受地形的限制，折向东南方向，接着外城墙35又折向西南方向，与南侧车格庄西侧山地上的城墙相连。此列城墙长约1.6千米。此列城墙构筑在山坡顶部，内外侧均呈大坡状。城墙外侧的坡度明显较内侧为陡。此列城墙以下城墙分为两支，除了主干的D列城墙，在东南侧又延伸出城墙K列，沿车格庄东北山地向下分布（图Ⅰ.4.23；图版18）。

外城墙13，位于董家村东的南北向山岗北端，此处城墙整体呈西北—东南走向，方向为144°。它于半山腰的位置，地势由东南向西北逐步倾斜向下，下方山脚下即为鸦鹊河的河道（图Ⅰ.4.24）。

城墙被破坏严重，残存形状大致呈长方形，分布在上下数个台地上。其西侧与北侧均至乡间路，东侧至断崖，南侧在台地中部通过。城墙南北残长约33米，南北残宽约19米，西北角由于被破坏而略收，城墙面积约625平方米。城墙的地面部分已无存，仅在地表下发现灰褐色花夯土，东南侧较薄，厚约10厘米，西北侧较厚，厚约30厘米。在外城墙13的东北角清理了一处剖面（图Ⅰ.4.25、Ⅰ.4.26；图版25：1）。

外城墙14，位于董家村东的南北向山岗顶部北端，处于较平的山岗的最高处，地势较平。城墙的东西两侧均呈坡状向下，分别通向城外和城内。北侧山脚下为鸦鹊河的河谷。整个城墙由西北—东南走向转为正南北走向，方向约为140°~180°。即城墙南段朝向正南方，北段朝西北方向拐去，拐角处较为圆滑，特别是西侧边缘圆弧明显。外城墙14在外城墙13东南，相距约29米，高差约4米。外城墙14的位置较外城墙13偏东移约15米。

城墙被破坏严重，残存形状大致呈不规则长方形，北侧较宽，西北角和西南角略向外突出。其分布范围北侧至曲尺形断崖边缘，东西边缘顺着台地处最高台地的边缘，南侧在小路北侧约2米（图Ⅰ.4.27）。城墙南北残长约71米，东西宽约25.5～35米，残存面积约2130平方米。

城墙仅存有地下部分，堆积为灰褐色花夯土，北侧较薄，厚约20～30厘米。

外城墙15，位于董家村东的南北向较为平整山岗顶部的北侧。城墙被破坏严重，残存形状大致呈不规则长方形，南侧较窄，呈尖状。外城墙15的南北两侧均在田间，东侧基本在最高台地断崖上，北侧略向东突出，西侧在台地中部通过。城墙残存部分基本在台地最高台地上，台地平面较为平整，为南北向林地（图Ⅰ.4.28）。城墙南北残长约70米，东西宽约10～12.5米，面积约770平方米。城墙整体呈南北走向。南段方向为176°，北段方向约为204°。外城墙15位于外城墙14的南侧约25米处。但两段城墙之间经钻探，未发现有夯土，应为后期破坏所致。

地面已无城墙残存，地表30厘米垫土下留存有厚约30厘米的灰褐色花夯土。

外城墙16，位于董家村东的南北向岗地的顶部，地势较为平整，宽阔，南侧即为董家村东大路。城墙整体呈南北走向，方向为171°。外城墙16位于外城墙15南侧，隔一条小路。在小路上钻探也发现有夯土，表明两者为一体。

城墙被破坏严重，残存形状呈刀形，北段较窄。城墙残存部分北至北侧小路；南至东西向深沟北侧约10米；东侧至台地边缘，以地面留存城墙的东边为界；西侧至台地边缘，北侧明显东收。城墙北段部分南北残长约68米，东西宽约9～12米，面积约714米平方米；南段部分南北长约91米，东西宽约35～49米，面积约3822平方米。城墙残存面积合计约4536平方米（图Ⅰ.4.29）。

根据钻探，城墙东部的垫土较薄，厚约30～40厘米，西部垫土明显变厚，达到1米。城墙南侧的夯土为红褐色黏土，略经夯打，表明其是利用原地的生土直接夯打所致。北侧的夯土为灰褐色夯土，厚约20～30厘米。

在外城墙16东南部发现有一小段残留在地面的城墙，紧贴着外城墙16的东边。这段城墙呈长条状，南北长约61米，东西宽约3～7米，残高约2.5米。城墙东侧呈缓坡状，西侧因后期取土呈断崖形（图Ⅰ.4.30）。我们在这段城墙即20世纪70年代发现的“埝顶上”段城墙的西侧断面上清理两处剖面（A和B）（图Ⅰ.4.31～Ⅰ.4.34；图版25：2）。

外城墙17，位于董家村东的南北向岗地的顶部，地势较为平整，宽阔，北侧即为董家村东大路。城墙整体呈南北走向，方向为180°。外城墙17北侧与外城墙16相望，两者相距约33米。两者之间有一条宽约10米，深约3米的深沟，深沟下为一条东西向乡村路。深沟两侧的断崖上均未发现夯土，表明城墙此处有中断，是原先即中断还是被后期破坏所致，则不得而知。

城墙被破坏严重，残存形状呈梯形，北至深沟南缘约15米，南侧至小路，西侧在台地中部通过，东侧约在下方台地中部通过。分为东西两部分，均为南北向田地。西侧较高，为一台地，高出东侧约1米，为林地。两台地地面较为平整。城墙南北残长约62米，东西残宽约10～16米，南侧较宽，残存面积约为806平方米（图Ⅰ.4.35）。

地面已无城墙残留，地面下为黄褐色花夯土，夹杂有烧土粒。夯土厚约40厘米，部分地方较薄，厚约10厘米。

外城墙18，位于董家村东的南北向岗地的顶部，外城墙17之南。城墙整体呈南北走向，方向为165°。外城墙17和外城墙18之间隔一条东西向小路。小路下发现很薄的夯土，说明两者之间并未中断，是一段墙体，后被破坏，分隔成两部分。

城墙被破坏严重，残存形状呈长方形。外城墙18残存部分南北侧均至东西向小路，东界至最高台地东侧下方台地边缘，西界基本以最高台地西边为界，南侧略向东收。地面较为平整，为南北向耕地，台地高约1.5米。城墙南北残长约115米，东西残宽约30米，残存面积约为3450平方米（图Ⅰ.4.36）。

根据钻探，夯土为夯打质量较好的灰褐色花夯土，质地较硬。夯土北侧较厚，南侧略薄。最高台地上北侧夯土厚约130厘米，南部厚约70厘米，西部较薄，厚约10厘米，东部台地南侧夯土仅有薄夯土分布。

外城墙19，位于董家村东的南北向岗地的顶部，外城墙18之南。城墙整体呈南北走向，方向为175°。外城墙18和外城墙19之间隔一条东西向小路。但在小路下发现很薄的夯土，说明两者之间并未中断，是同一段墙体，后被破坏成两部分。

城墙被破坏严重，残存形状呈长方形。外城墙19的残存部分北侧至东西向路，南侧至空地边缘，东西两侧均在台地中部通过。城墙南北残长约65米，东西残宽约19米，残存面积约为1230平方米（图Ⅰ.4.37）。

地下残存的夯土为夯打质量较好的灰褐色花夯土，质地较硬。西部林地的夯土北侧厚约130厘米，中部厚约70厘米，南侧仅厚40厘米；东部耕地中，北侧夯土厚约40厘米，中部仅20厘米，南部厚约10厘米。可见，此段城墙内夯土是由北向南堆积，逐步变薄的。

外城墙21，位于董家村东南的南北向岗地的顶部，地势较为平整。城墙整体呈南北走向，方向为173°。北侧隔一片宽约40米的空地与外城墙19相望。在两者间空地处钻探，下直接为基岩，原先的墙体或是被破坏。

城墙被破坏严重，残存形状不甚规则，大致呈长方形，西北侧略有凸起。城墙北侧至曲尺形断崖边缘，北侧以乡间路为界，东西两侧均至台地边缘，城墙所在台地较为平整，高出周围地面约1.3米。城墙南北残长约25～30米，东西残宽约35米，残存面积约为880平方米（图Ⅰ.4.38）。

地下的夯土为夯打质量较好的黄褐色花夯土，质地较硬。北侧夯土厚度约50～60厘米。

外城墙22，位于董家村东南的南北向岗地的顶部，地势较为平整，宽阔。城墙整体呈南北走向，方向为161°。北侧隔一条西北—东南向小路与外城墙21相接。但在小路下发现很薄的夯土，说明两者之间并未中断，是同一段墙体，后被破坏，分隔成两部分。

城墙被破坏严重，残存形状大致呈长方形。城墙残存部分的南北两侧各自以乡间路为界，东侧至最高台地下方台地中部，中部偏南处略收，西侧边界不甚整齐，大致在最高台地下方台地中部通过。城墙地表为南北向耕地或林地，中部台地较高，高出东侧台地约0.5～1.5米，高出西侧台地约0.2～0.5米。整个地面略由北向南倾斜，但坡度很缓。城墙南北残长约250米，东西残宽约20～44米，残存面积约为8000平方米（图Ⅰ.4.39）。

地下夯土为灰褐色花夯土，土质较硬，夯打痕迹明显。中部台地的上部垫土厚度在40～50厘米之间。城墙的夯土北侧稍薄，厚度在40～60厘米左右，中部夯土较厚，厚约110～200厘米左右，南侧夯土又变薄，厚度由60～70厘米逐步变为40～50厘米，最后至断崖边缘厚度仅为20厘米。综合钻探情况，中部台地下残存的城墙大致成坡形，中部高，南北两侧低。

外城墙23，位于和平村东的西北—东南向山地顶部。此岗地位于数段岗地的交汇处，西北侧为董家村东的南北向岗地（外城墙13～22所在），东侧与外城墙24—城墙31所在岗地连为一体，东南与外城墙35所在岗地连为一体。这三条岗地共同构成了一个高岗。在岗地西侧有一东西向沟冲向台地中部，东北侧为另一条南北向深沟的沟头。东侧隔一条南北向大沟与另一条岗地相望。此块岗地大致呈圆弧形，已被修整为数个表面平整的梯田，当地村民自下而上分别称为“大罗圈”“二罗圈”“三罗圈”。外城墙23基本位于最高的“三罗圈”上。

城墙东南侧以公路为界，与外城墙24隔公路相望。城墙南侧至公路，与城墙35北侧相接。城墙西北侧略向西北突出约14米，通向外城墙22。城墙分布在最高的两处台地上，北侧台地高出南侧台地约1米。台地大体平，中部地势（圆弧拐弯处）稍低。城墙北侧为断崖，高出北侧地面约0.2～0.5米，西侧部分略高。南侧呈一高断崖，面向城内，高约0.6～2米；城墙中部断崖最高。城墙残长约290米，宽约25～36米，残存面积9000平方米。城墙整体呈西北—东南走向，方向为135°（图Ⅰ.4.40）。

城墙现存夯土部分均在地表以下，未有地面城墙留存。在夯土上普遍有一层晚期垫土，厚约20～50厘米。城墙南侧边缘发现有夯土，厚约10厘米。在东南部附近，夯土明显变厚，可分为上下两层。上层为灰褐色夯土，夯打质量较好，厚约40厘米；下部为黄褐色花夯土，夯打质量稍差，厚约60厘米。夯土层下为本地生土，红褐色黏土，质地较黏，质地较纯，含水锈。在台地边缘夯土仅厚5厘米。在城墙中部夯土较厚，在30～70厘米左右。至北侧城墙附近，夯土厚约40厘米。

外城墙23位于数段城墙交汇处，其上承北侧的外城墙22。向下城墙分作两支，外城墙24～31折向东南侧岗地，外城墙35则折向西南方向岗地。由于城墙23为西北—东南走向，从而使外城城墙整体向东甩出约270米。

外城墙35，位于和平村东南北向山地的南端。此列山地北侧大体呈南北走向（外城墙13～22），至外城墙23处，拐向东南方向，接着又折向西南方向。城墙35正位于此处东北—西南走向的山岗顶部。岗地西北侧为一条东西向大沟。外城墙35北侧与外城墙23的南侧相接，但出现明显的折角，角度约有107°。东南侧也为一条大沟，隔沟与外城墙24～31相望。西南侧为一条大沟将整列山岗阻断。城墙整体呈东北—西南走向，方向为217°。

城墙范围东侧至乡间路，北侧至乡间路北侧的断崖；南侧在一片果园北侧消失。城墙分布在山岗的最高台地上，两侧的地势较低，形成数个东北—西南走向的断崖，断崖高度多在0.3～1米之间。台地上形成东北—西南向耕地或林地。台地表面较为平整，地势由东北向西南倾斜，整体高差约有6米。城墙的东西两侧边缘较为整齐，可能为城墙原始边缘。城墙35东北—西南长约228米，西北—东南宽约55～87米，残存面积约16200平方米（图Ⅰ.4.41；图版20：1）。

在城墙西北侧发现夯土为灰褐色花夯土，夹杂有炭粒，夯打痕迹明显，厚约30～40厘米。东南侧夯土厚约50厘米，为黄褐色花夯土，近底部的夯土含灰土和炭粒。含砂较多。南部的夯土普遍较薄，厚约10～20厘米。

在贯穿城墙西侧的乡间路侧分别清理了两个剖面（图版26：1）。剖面A较为全面地反映了城墙的修建过程（图Ⅰ.4.42～Ⅰ.4.44）。首先是在底部夯筑上一层红褐色大花黏夯土（夯土D）。在此基础上，为了加快工作进度，在中间铺垫上一个隔断（夯土C），再由此向两边分别夯筑城墙（夯土A、夯土B）。两侧修建的过程中，选取的材料较为一致，均使用了大量砂石掺杂少量泥土的材料进行修建。但由于两边分别修建，其堆积层次、厚度上并不能完全保持一致。如夯土A中大量砂石是出现在底部。最下方的深灰褐夯土（夯土A第4层）为挤压下的隔断墙的堆积。夯土B中此层下还叠压着一层黄褐色夯土。

剖面B实际是剖面A中夯土A向北延伸的部分（图Ⅰ.4.45、Ⅰ.4.46）。在清理此剖面时，通过观察，确认剖面B中的砂石层与夯土A中的砂石层连为一体。其城墙的修建一段的长度约在90米左右。

在城墙东侧断崖下发现一些绳纹砖和较为规整的石块（图Ⅰ.4.41、Ⅰ.4.47；图版20：

2），可能与城墙的附属建筑有关。

（4）D列城墙：仅外城墙37。其位于董家—和平村东的南北向山地与车格庄西北山地之间的谷地中，南北两侧的地势明显高于城墙。外城墙37东北距外城墙35约55米，走向与外城墙35走向一致，为东北—西南走向，方向为217°。

城墙北侧基本以东西向乡间小路为界，东北侧略突出。南侧距断崖约15米，东西两侧各自以较高的断崖为界，西南侧略向西突出约10米。城墙位于沟中，地势较低。中部有一条乡间路贯穿其中，地势明显较高，可能为后期修路时铺垫所致。路两侧城墙地势较平，中部略低（图Ⅰ.4.48）。东侧边界为一条高约0.8～2米的断崖，南侧较低。西侧边界为一条高约1米至4米的断崖，尤其是中部保存高度很高。城墙的东西两侧边缘较为整齐，可能为原始城墙边缘（图Ⅰ.4.49）。外城墙37东北—西南长约142米，西北—东南宽约77米，残存面积约11000平方米。在城墙东侧地面上发现一些较为规整的石块，可能与城墙的附属建筑有关。

城墙东侧夯土中含大量碎砂石，夹杂着灰褐色泥土进行夯打，有夯打痕迹。堆积最厚处2米未见底。在有些地点，砂石夯层下有灰褐色夯土。城墙南侧夯土为灰褐色夯土，最厚处达70厘米。在城墙西部的断崖上，可明显见到夯土的层次。50厘米表土下出现夯土。夯土上层为20厘米的灰褐色夯土，夹杂着少量碎砂，质地坚硬；中层为20厘米的砂石夯层，夹杂着少量灰褐土，厚约20厘米；下层为灰褐色夯土。在城墙西北侧，夯土厚约40厘米。

（5）E列城墙：包括外城墙39、外城墙41、外城墙44和外城墙46。这列城墙位于车格庄西北山岗上。山岗呈叉形，南侧分为三个山嘴，整列城墙沿最西侧的山嘴向下。这列城墙的上部（外城墙39、外城墙41）呈南北走向，略偏东，下部（外城墙44、外城墙46）则略折向西。城墙构筑在山坡顶部，外侧为深谷，与K列城墙相望；内侧为大陡坡，通向内城方向（图Ⅰ.4.50）。

外城墙39，位于车格庄北侧山地的北部。岗地东西两侧均为深沟，东侧（城外）尤其深。整个山岗由北向南倾斜向下，城墙即坐落在岗地顶部。城墙呈西北—东南走向，方向为155°。其与东北侧沟底的外城墙37相望，直线距离约124米。从地势看，城墙37向南延伸至断崖下方，而外城墙39则有可能朝北延伸，与山下的城墙构成完整的防御体系。两者间存在着明显的转向。

城墙被破坏严重，平面形状大致呈长方形。城墙北侧至山顶有一处高约1.5米的断崖，西侧边界基本在台地下方的第二台地上，东南侧边界在最高台地以下的第一个台地上边缘，南侧夯土在台地中部消失。岗地顶部较为平整。第一台地与最高台地间有约1米的断崖，第二台地与第一台地间的断崖高约1.5米。在台地中部有一条乡间路贯穿。整个城墙地势由西北向东南倾斜。外城墙39西北—东南长约139米，东北—西南宽约25～55米，残存面积约5560平方米（图Ⅰ.4.51）。

城墙夯土为黄褐色花夯土，内夹杂着小沙砾、灰土等，质地紧密，夯打痕迹明显。在城墙西部下方台地夯土较厚，最厚达到1米，平均厚度在20～30厘米。最薄处仅5厘米。城墙北部的夯土厚约40厘米。东南侧部分夯土厚度在10～30厘米。在南侧边缘，夯土厚度仅有5厘米。在城墙中部，由于基岩较高，有些地点直接出露基岩，未见有夯土。

外城墙41，位于车格庄北侧山地的北段。城墙位于山岗的顶部，东西两侧均为深沟，东侧（城外）尤其深。整个山岗由北向南倾斜向下。城墙整体呈西北—东南走向，方向为163°。其西北为外城墙39，距离约128米。

城墙被破坏严重，其平面形状大致呈长方形。城墙西侧一条南北向乡间路为界，东侧至高约0.7米的断崖，南侧至一小段断崖，北侧在台地中部消失。城墙表面较为平整，地势由西北向东南倾斜。城墙41西北—东南长约18米，东北—西南宽约5米，残存面积约90平方米。

城墙夯土为灰白色淤土夯打而成，质地稍硬，含有细砂，厚约5～10厘米。

外城墙44，位于车格庄西北侧岗地顶部的东侧，东侧为一条深沟，西侧亦为一条南北向深沟。城墙整体呈西北—东南走向，方向为155°。外城墙44与外城墙41直线距离约175米。但按山地走向计算，两者相距约222米，即两者之间原有200余米的城墙。

城墙被破坏严重，其平面形状大致呈长方形，西北角略有凸出。城墙在山岗的东侧，东侧以山沟边为界，西侧大致在一条乡间路的东侧。北侧在一段断崖下，南侧至下侧的第二级台地边缘（图Ⅰ.4.52）。城墙分布在三个台地上，每处台地高约1.5米，由北向南依次而下。台地表面较平。城墙44南北长约29米，东西宽约50米，残存面积约1450平方米。

城墙夯土为黄褐色花夯土，内夹杂有砂土，夯打痕迹较为明显，质地较硬。城墙中部夯土较厚，厚约50厘米。在边缘处较薄，厚度仅10厘米。在有些地点直接出露基岩，或在东侧直接出露下部的红褐色黏土。

外城墙46，位于车格庄西北侧山地中部略偏南，坐落在山岗顶部的东侧，东侧为一条深沟，西侧隔70米平地为一条南北向深沟。整个山岗由北向南倾斜向下。城墙方向与外城墙44的方向一致，亦为西北—东南走向，方向为155°。外城墙46正位于城墙44下方，两者相距约30米。

城墙被破坏严重，其平面形状大致呈长方形，南侧西部略向南凸。城墙在山岗的东侧，东侧以山沟边为界，西侧在台地中部，北侧在城墙44下方两个台地，南侧边界即在台地边缘。台地表面较平。外城墙46南北长约7～12米，东西宽约68米，残存面积约650平方米。

城墙夯土为浅灰褐色花夯土，是用细淤土夯打而成，内夹杂有细砂，质地紧密，较硬，夯打层次明显。城墙中部夯土较厚，厚约40厘米。边缘处夯土较薄，有些地点直接出露基岩。

值得注意的是在外城墙44和外城墙46之间以及上下分布着红褐色黏土，质地较硬，较纯，未经夯打。此种堆积在有城墙的地点是压在城墙夯土以下，在城墙未分布的地点，则直接在表土下出现，叠压在基岩之上。该层堆积仅分布在山地的东侧，且走向与两段城墙一致。堆积的范围大于城墙夯土的范围。南北长约150米，东西宽约56～79米。这是否与城墙有关联需进一步工作确认。

（6）F列城墙，包括外城墙49、外城墙51、外城墙53、外城墙56和外城墙58。这列城墙位于车格庄村西—南埠村东南山地上。此列城墙北部大致呈东北—西南走向，至南侧则逐渐变为朝向西。城墙构筑在山坡顶部，内外侧均呈深谷，较利于防守。整列山地整体由南向北略倾斜向下，尤其在北侧坡度较为明显。这列城墙长约0.65千米。此列城墙以西未发现城墙，且距离莱山山脚很近，较有可能直接与南侧山地相通。

外城墙49，位于车格庄村西—南埠村东南山地的北端的山嘴上。山地的东西两侧均为深谷。北侧隔一条宽约30米的东西向沟与E列城墙所在山岗相望。城墙所在岗地的地势由南向北倾斜向下，南侧为一条公路所隔，与南侧的外城墙51等相望。城墙大致呈南北走向，方向为200°。外城墙49位于外城墙46西南侧，两者相距约132米（图Ⅰ.4.53）。

城墙被破坏严重，其平面形状大致呈长方形，西北侧略向北凸。城墙南边至公路下方的第二台地，东侧至沟边，东北角至一高约2.5米的断崖。此断崖向西延伸，至西侧向北略有凸起。城墙西边在台地西部通过。城墙北侧断崖高约2～2.5米，东北角较高。整个城墙位于由北向南倾斜的台地上，可分为3个台地。各个台地间高差约1米。台地表面较平。外城墙49南北长约50米，东西宽约77米，北侧凸起部分南北长约10米，东西宽约22米。城墙的残存面积合计约4000平方米（图Ⅰ.4.53）。

城墙夯土为黄褐色花夯土，含细砂，质地紧密，较硬。城墙北侧夯土较厚，厚度最大约200厘米，南侧台地上的夯土较薄，厚度约20厘米，在边缘部位厚度仅有10厘米。

外城墙51，位于车格庄村西南，公路以南。外城墙51正位于车格庄村西—南埠村东南山地顶部的南侧，南侧下方为一条大沟，北侧经过一片平地后，下方亦为一条大沟。山地地势由南向北倾斜向下。城墙整体呈东北—西南走向，方向为243°。外城墙51位于外城墙49西南部，两者直线距离约120米，两者相距约130米（图Ⅰ.4.54）。

城墙被破坏严重，其平面形状大致呈梯形，西南侧内凹。城墙南侧基本至沟畔的小路附近，北侧在山地中部通过，西侧在一片荒地下方，东侧至下方第四个台地。城墙位于台地上，东侧断崖高约1.5米。城墙所在范围有5个台地，各台地间高差约0.5～1米，由西南向东北倾斜向下。台地表面较平。城墙51东西长约48米，南北宽约28～64米，西北侧凸起部分长约28米。城墙的残存面积约2000平方米。

城墙夯土为浅黄褐色花夯土，土质细腻，呈粉状，含细砂，质地紧密，较硬，为淤土夯打而成。城墙下部（东侧）中部夯土最厚，达到1.5米。城墙中部，夯土厚度在30～50厘米之间，在边缘部位，夯土仅厚5～10厘米。

外城墙53，位于车格庄村西—南埠村东南山地的中部，外城墙51之西，相距约90米。城墙南侧下方为一条大沟，北侧经过一片平地后，下方亦为一条大沟。山地地势由南向北倾斜向下。城墙整体呈东北—西南走向，方向为245°。

城墙被破坏严重，其平面形状大致呈长方形。城墙主要位于一个台地上，东、南、西三面均以断崖为界，北侧在台地中部通过。城墙所在台地与上部台地高差约1.2米，台地东侧断崖高约0.5米。台地表面较平。城墙53东西长约9米，南北宽约43米，残存面积约380平方米。

城墙夯土为浅黄褐色花夯土，土质细腻，呈粉状，含细砂，质地紧密，较硬，为用淤土夯打而成。夯土普遍较薄，厚度仅5厘米。

城墙53周围均为基岩，但在西侧的某些地点发现零星夯土，厚度仅有5厘米，是淤土夯打而成。这些夯土并不能连成片，但能够反映出城墙向西延伸。

外城墙56，位于车格庄村西—南埠村东南山地的南部，在山顶南侧。其南侧下方即为深沟，北部地势较高，为山岗顶部。城墙整体呈东西走向，方向为265°，即西偏南约5°。外城墙

56距外城墙53约170米。

城墙破坏严重，平面形状大致呈长方形。台地表面较平整。外城墙56东西长约39米，南北宽约7.5米，残存面积约290平方米。

城墙夯土为灰白色花夯土，为淤土夹砂夯打而成，土质细腻，呈粉状，质地较硬。夯土普遍较薄，西部厚约30厘米，东部夯土厚仅10厘米。

外城墙58，位于车格庄村西—南埠村东南山地的西南侧。南侧地势稍高，为山岗顶部。城墙位于南侧莱山脚下，距西南侧的山地仅有140米。城墙呈东北—西南走向，方向为245°。外城墙58距外城墙53约203米，距其东南侧的外城墙56约76米。

城墙破坏严重，平面形状大致呈长方形。北侧和西侧以乡间路为界，南侧至一高约1米的断崖。台地表面较平。外城墙58东西长约81米，南北宽约11米，残存面积约890平方米。

城墙夯土为灰白色花夯土，为淤土夹砂夯打而成，土质细腻，呈粉状，质地较硬。夯土普遍较薄，在城墙中部夯土厚度达80厘米，在边缘部位夯土厚度仅有5厘米。

外城墙58向西未发现城墙遗迹，仅在西部发现零星夯土，厚度仅5厘米，为淤土夯打而成。我们仅能据此确定城墙大致走向。

外城墙56和外城墙58位于一座台地的东南角和西北角（图Ⅰ.4.55；图版21：1）。台地上部为基岩，未有夯土分布。因此，外城墙56和外城墙58有可能是一段城墙残留的部分，中部地势较高位置的夯土已被破坏，仅有地势较低的部分残存下来。如果推断成立，这段城墙东西长约181米，南北宽约46～96米，东侧较宽，面积约13000平方米。

（7）G列城墙，包括外城墙80、外城墙82。其位于曹家村西外侧山地的南端，城墙南侧呈东西走向，东侧与H列城墙相连。此列城墙南侧数百米即为莱山，由地势看，其很有可能通向山地，依托莱山为墙。此列城墙长约0.28千米，东西延伸约0.29千米（图Ⅰ.4.56；图版19）。

外城墙80，位于归城曹家村西北外侧山地顶部的南侧。山地东西两侧均呈坡状。南侧与莱山相接，城墙向南地面均直接出露基岩，整体地势由南向北倾斜而下。此处应为归城西城墙的南端。城墙呈南北走向，方向为171°（图Ⅰ.4.57；图版21：2）。

城墙平面大致呈梯形，北侧较宽。城墙北侧至东西向小路边高约1.2～2米的断崖，东北部内收。西侧至一条小沟，东侧边界与山脊的边缘相当。城墙表面由南向北倾斜而下，形成七个台地，台地间高差约0.5～1米。城墙南北长约66米，东西宽约36～89米，残存面积约4000平方米。

城墙夯土为灰白色，是用淤土夯打而成，北侧夯土较厚，厚约40～50厘米，南侧夯土普遍较薄，厚约10厘米。

外城墙82，在曹家村西有内外两列南北向山地，两者之间有一条南北向沟向两者分隔。外城墙82位于外侧南北向山地的东坡上，东侧与内侧山地相连。南侧为与莱山脚下一条东西向深沟。城墙82呈东西走向，方向为283°。外城墙82西南侧为城墙80，并与外城墙80呈垂直分布，两者相距约44米。

城墙平面大致呈梯形，南侧西南角向南凸出一小部分。城墙东边在沟底一条小路侧，为一高约1.5米的断崖。西边在山地的顶部的一条南北向乡间路附近，为一高约0.5米的断崖，北侧由山顶延伸至沟底的断崖。城墙表面呈坡状，由西向东倾斜向下，形成数个台地，总高差约6米。城墙东西长约154米，南北宽约19～44米，南侧凸起部分东西长约31米，南北宽约23米，残存面积约5600平方米图（图Ⅰ.4.58）。

东侧（下部）城墙夯土为黄褐色夯土，内夹杂红黏土，厚约30～50厘米。中部夯土为红褐色花夯土，发黏，含水锈，厚约20厘米。西侧（上部）夯土较薄，仅厚5厘米。

（8）H列城墙，包括外城墙83、外城墙84、外城墙85、外城墙87、外城墙88，位于曹家村西的西南—东北向山地上，北侧的城墙88折向东方。此列城墙长约830米。城墙修建在山地顶部，内外侧均呈大陡坡状。

外城墙83，位于归城曹家村西山地顶部的南端。城墙内外两侧均呈斜坡状向下，南侧15米处为一宽约15米的东西向大沟，将城墙所在山地与南侧山地分隔开。整个城墙所在山地地势由东北向西南倾斜。城墙方向与山地走向一致，为东北—西南走向，方向为219°。

城墙平面大致呈梯形，南侧较宽。城墙位于山顶的台地上，北侧在一条乡间小路的南侧，东侧和南侧均以小路为界，西侧向下呈缓坡状向下，至下方台地。城墙表面东侧呈坡状，高约2.5～3米。城墙中部地势较平。西部呈数个平台，逐次向下倾斜，高差约2.5米。整个地形中部较高，分别向南北两侧倾斜向下，坡度较缓（图版23）。城墙南北长约190米，东西宽约22～103米，残存面积约12000平方米（图Ⅰ.4.59～Ⅰ.4.60）。

城墙夯土为黄褐色夯土，含细砂，是用淤土夯打而成，质地较硬。夯土主要分布在西部（外侧），最厚约120厘米，普遍厚度约30厘米。城墙东部斜坡未见有夯土，其形状较为规整，可能是直接修整所致。

外城墙84，位于归城曹家村西山地顶部的中部，位于外城墙83的东北侧，两者方向一致。城墙在内外两侧均呈斜坡状向下。整个城墙所在山地地势由东北向西南倾斜。城墙方向与山地走向一致，为东北—西南走向，方向为204°。

城墙平面大致呈长方形。其北侧在一条乡间小路的南侧，东侧和南侧均以小路为界，西侧基本以最高台地边缘为界。台地表面较平，西侧边缘呈缓坡状，东侧边缘有一高约0.5～1米的断崖，北侧较高。城墙南北长约119米，东西宽约11～23米，残存面积约2000平方米。

城墙夯土为黄褐色夯土，含细砂，为用淤土夯打而成。夯土普遍不厚，多在5～10厘米之间，有些地点直接出露基岩（图Ⅰ.4.61）。

外城墙84东边较之外城墙85东侧边界向西收了很多。东侧地势较低，可能原有城墙，后被破坏所致。

外城墙85，位于归城曹家村西山地顶部的中部，外城墙84东北侧，与之方向一致，为东北—西南走向，之间有10米空白地带。城墙方向为204°。

城墙平面呈梯形，东侧边缘较为整齐。城墙在山顶的台地上，北侧至东西向乡间路边，东侧在台地中部通过，边缘与外城墙87东边持平，南侧在乡间小路上，西侧至仓库东墙外，西北侧略向东收。台地表面较平，略由东北向西南倾斜。东部城墙地势较高，向西侧（城外）倾斜。城墙南北长约186米，东西宽约41～78米，残存面积约11000平方米（图Ⅰ.4.62）。

城墙夯土为黄褐色夯土，含细砂，为用淤土夯打而成。夯土普遍不厚，最厚的仅有40厘米，多在5～10厘米之间，有些地点直接出露基岩。

外城墙87，位于归城曹家村西山地顶部的北侧，外城墙85东北侧，与之方向一致，之间有77米空白地带。此处山地呈“厂”字形。城墙87位于山地拐角处的西侧。山势呈东北—西南走向。西北侧和东南侧为坡状倾斜向下，东侧为外城墙88所在山地，地势与之持平。城墙方向与山地走向一致，为东北—西南走向，方向为209°（图Ⅰ.4.63）。

城墙平面呈长方形。城墙主要在山顶的台地上，北侧至台地北端，西侧至台地边2.5米的断崖，东侧至南北向小路，南侧在台地中部消失。城墙南北长约121米，东西宽约28米，残存面积约3400平方米。

城墙西北侧夯土厚约70厘米，可分三层，上层为灰褐土黏土，夹杂红褐色黏土，质地较硬，厚约30厘米；中层为砂石层夹杂灰褐土夯层，质地稍松，厚约30厘米；下层为灰褐色夯土，质地较硬，厚约10厘米，以下为基岩。城墙以南直接出露基岩。

外城墙88，位于曹家村西山地顶部的北侧，外城墙87东侧，隔一条南北向乡间路。外城墙88位于“厂”字形山地拐角处的东侧，南北侧地势较低，均呈大坡状向下倾斜。东侧顺山脊倾斜向下。外城墙88走向与山体走向一致，呈东西向，方向为277°。

城墙平面大致呈长方形。城墙主要在山顶的台地上，北侧至一高约0.5米的断崖，东侧至一南北向乡间小路，南侧至一高约0.5～1米的断崖，西侧以乡间路为界，有一高约1米的断崖。台地表面较平，略由西向东倾斜。城墙东西长约144米，南北宽约54～77，中部略宽，残存面积约9400平方米。

城墙的夯土为浅黄褐色夯土，质地较细腻，含砂，为用淤土夯打而成。夯土厚度不一。南侧（内侧）厚度较薄，厚约10～20厘米。北侧夯土较厚，最厚达140厘米。在城墙中部，夯土普遍厚约10～20厘米。清理了两处剖面，了解堆积状况（图Ⅰ.4.64～Ⅰ.4.67；图版26：2；图版22：1）。

（9）I列城墙，包括外城墙90、外城墙92。其位于曹家村西的南北向山地的北侧山脚下，北侧为鸦鹊河河道。城墙大致呈西南—东北走向。此列城墙南北长约0.2千米。城墙位于山前的台地上，两侧地势稍低。其与南侧的H列城墙之间有大片空白地带（图Ⅰ.4.68）。

外城墙90，城墙位于曹家村西西南—东北向山地的北侧，在东西向公路南侧的小高地上。北侧地势低，南侧地势较高，倾斜向上；小高地东西两侧的地势较低，为谷地。城墙90呈南北走向，方向为180°。它与南侧山上的外城墙87相距约340米。

城墙平面大致呈长方形，北侧至一高约1米的断崖，南侧至台地南侧边缘，东侧至沟边，西侧至一高约5米的断崖。台地表面较平。城墙南北长约20米，东西宽约41米，残存面积约8400平方米。

城墙夯土为黄褐色花夯土，内夹砂，是用淤土夯打而成。城墙中部夯土较厚，达60～80厘米，西部夯土较薄，厚约20厘米。

外城墙92，位于鸦鹊河南岸的小台地上，北侧为河道，南侧为东西向公路，东西两侧均为低地，南侧地势较高。外城墙92大致呈南北向，方向为188°。外城墙90位于其西南侧，相距约

104米。

城墙平面大致呈长方形。城墙主要在一片果园中，北侧距台地顶端约19米，东侧至沟边，西侧距台地西边较近，南侧在台地中部通过，距公路约49米。台地地面较平。城墙南北长约48米，东西宽约25，残存面积约1200平方米。

城墙夯土为黄褐色花夯土，内夹砂，是用淤土夯打而成。城墙中部夯土较厚，达60厘米，在边缘部位，夯土厚约10厘米。在夯土下有一层黄褐色堆积，质地纯净，未经夯打。

（10）J列城墙，仅包括外城墙94。

外城墙94，位于鸦鹊河北岸，水泥厂院墙以南偏东部的平地中，它与北侧的城墙A列之间有大片的空白地带。通过两列城墙的走向推断，两列城墙间应有明显的拐角。外城墙94呈南北走向，方向为188°。外城墙94与南侧的外城墙92隔河相望，相距约107米。其东北与A列的外城墙97相距约855米。

城墙平面大致呈长方形。城墙主要在一片葡萄园中，南侧略向西偏。北侧在东西向乡间路的以南约22米，距北侧断崖约5米，南侧距河岸约12米。地面较平，北侧有一高约2米的断崖。城墙南北长约93米，东西宽约23米，残存面积约2139平方米。

城墙夯土为灰褐色花夯土，颜色较深，质地坚硬，夯打痕迹明显，内夹杂有炭粒和少量砂粒等。在某些地点，灰褐夯土上还叠压着黄褐色夹杂砂土夯打而成的夯土。在有些地点，下层夯土夹砂较多，是用淤土夯打而成。在城墙中部，夯土较厚，约60～80厘米，在边缘部位，夯土较薄，厚约20～30厘米。在城墙下部有一层未经夯打的质地纯净的黄褐色堆积。

在调查过程中发现外城墙94西部有大量砂层，向西延伸有250多米。南侧和北侧两边紧贴城墙均有大量砂层分布，或为当时的水面。

（11）K列城墙，包括城墙24、城墙25、城墙27、城墙28和城墙31。这列城墙位于车格庄东北侧山地上，大致呈南北走向。此列山地与董家—和平村东南北向山地的南侧连为一体。山地东侧（外侧）呈大斜坡状，内侧为深谷，北侧为一条深沟的南侧。城墙位于山地顶部。此列城墙南北长约0.8千米。此列城墙由西北侧的C列城墙南侧延伸出，再向南的山地上未有城墙分布，表明此列城墙为分支，并非主干（图Ⅰ.4.23；图版18）。

外城墙24，位于车格庄东北侧山地的北端，乡间路的东北侧。城墙西侧为平地，地势略低，与城墙23所在的“三罗圈”相连。台地北侧为一条深沟的南端的深谷。东侧为一条南北向大沟。其可分为两大部分：西段部分与外城墙23相接，呈西北—东南走向，方向为130°；东段部分为城墙24—城墙31列城墙的北部。东段城墙呈东西向，大体为90°，即大体朝向正东方。两者间以高约1.7米的断崖相间隔。

西段部分城墙的呈条状，通向城墙23，与之隔公路相望。中部基本以北侧沟边为界，并随沟边的走向，向北延伸出一个平台，平台北侧紧贴着高约2米的断崖。城墙东侧呈曲尺形南收，至上部台地与城墙的东侧部分相接。西段城墙的地势略由南向北倾斜，至沟边倾斜向下。城墙条状部分残长约210米，宽仅14米，面积约2940平方米。北侧凸起部分南北长约50米，东西宽约18～26米，面积约3150平方米。西段部分城墙的面积合计约6090平方米。西段城墙夯土普遍较薄，厚约10～20厘米。仅在北侧凸起的平台北侧夯土较厚，厚约150厘米，可能为后期有意垫高而成。

外城墙24的东段部分隔东西向公路与城墙25相望。东侧至最高台地下方的第二台地。城墙北侧略向北突出，形状不甚规整。这块城墙地势较高，其北侧呈缓坡状向下。东段城墙东西长约62米，南北宽约25～45米，残存面积约2170平方米。这块城墙的夯土较厚，特别是在最高台地上的夯土最厚达140厘米，一般厚度在60厘米左右。但东侧下部的两个台地上夯土明显变薄，向下第一台地上夯土厚10厘米，第二台地上的夯土仅厚5厘米。

城墙24的残存面积总计约8300平方米。城墙夯土为黄褐色花夯土，夯打痕迹明显。在城墙东西两部分之间的断崖上清理了一处剖面，了解堆积状况（图Ⅰ.4.69～Ⅰ.4.70）。

外城墙25，位于车格庄东北侧山地的北端，城墙位于岗地顶部的北侧。东侧有一条南北向大沟，更远处为一列南北向山地。西侧地势稍低，与外城墙35所在山地相接。其方向大致为180°。

城墙平面呈梯形。城墙北侧以东西向乡间路为界，隔公路与城墙24相望。东侧与外城墙24的东边大体平齐，西侧与外城墙24东半部的西边持平。城墙由北向南倾斜，南端至一段残高0.3米的断崖。城墙北侧可分为三个台地，以西侧台地最高，上下高差约3米。城墙南北残长约127米，东西残宽约16～87米，北侧显著宽于南侧，残存面积6540平方米。

在城墙东北部的城墙上有厚约50～100厘米的垫土，其下的夯土厚约40～50厘米。至南侧夯土变薄，厚约30厘米。在城墙西部的夯土较薄，最厚仅20厘米，有些地点直接出露基岩。东北侧夯土为红褐色黏夯土，质地较硬；西侧夯土为黄褐色花夯土，质地较硬（图Ⅰ.4.71）。

外城墙27，位于车格庄东北侧山地的北段。城墙位于山岗顶部，东侧有一条南北向大沟，更远处为一列南北向山地。西侧地势稍低，下方为一条东北—西南走向的沟，隔沟与外城墙35和外城墙37相望。城墙方向大致为180°。外城墙27位于从外城墙25顺着山脊向下约64米处。

城墙平面呈长方形。城墙东北侧以东西向乡间小路为界，南侧至以高约2米的断崖，崖下即为外城墙28。城墙的东西两边均在山岗顶部台地上，边界与台地边缘的断崖重合。城墙表面由北向南略有倾斜，台地较为平整。城墙东边较为整齐，呈斜坡状，与北侧外城墙25、外城墙24的东边基本一线，可能为原始边缘。东边的断崖较高，大多在2米左右，最高达到2.5米。城墙南北残长约153米，东西残宽约34～37米，残存面积5400平方米。

城墙的夯土为灰褐色花夯土，质地较硬。北侧夯土厚约30～40厘米，南侧较薄，厚约10～20厘米。在城墙中部有的地点表土下直接为基岩。

外城墙28，位于车格庄东北侧山地的北侧，紧靠外城墙27南沿。城墙大致呈西北—东南走向，方向大致为159°。

城墙平面呈长方形。城墙北侧紧贴着外城墙27南侧断崖，南侧由于破坏，夯土在南侧田地中消失。城墙的东西两侧均在山地顶部台地上，边界与台地边缘的断崖重合。城墙由北向南略有倾斜，台地较为平整。城墙东边较为整齐，与北侧城墙27的东边基本一线，可能为原始边缘。东西两侧断崖残高约1米。城墙南北残长约53米，东西残宽约32米，残存面积1700平方米。

城墙各处的夯土厚度不一。西侧夯土分两层，上层为灰褐色花夯土，质地较硬，土质较杂，厚约20厘米，下层夯土为红褐色花夯土，质地较硬，土质较纯，厚约50厘米。南侧则为红褐色夯土，含有黑点，厚约120厘米。东南角的红褐色夯土则厚约160厘米，100厘米以下的夯土稍软。但东北角的夯土厚度仅有10厘米。这些现象表明了城墙修建的方式是根据地势，将低处垫高而成。

外城墙31，位于车格庄村东北山地中部，一条乡间路的西侧。西侧为谷地，向东约30米的平地以下也是一条大沟。即其位于一段山岗的顶部，整个地势由北向南倾斜。其大致呈南北走向，方向为192°。外城墙31位于外城墙28所在山岗下方，两者相距约235米（图Ⅰ.4.72、Ⅰ.4.73）。

城墙被破坏严重，残存仅为一段南北向小土垄，周围已被破坏殆尽。城墙现存部分直接暴露在地面，周围因水土流失而凹凸不平。其最高处与路东的地面大体持平，但路东经钻探未见夯土。城墙略由北向南倾斜。城墙南北残长约23米，东西残宽约3～9米，南侧较宽，残存面积约为138平方米。在城墙中部清理一段剖面，了解其堆积状况（图Ⅰ.4.74）。

外城墙31位于K列南北向城墙的南端，向南直至山嘴顶部未发现城墙遗迹。

3. 周边遗存

在调查过程中，我们在外城城墙附近发现有一些可能与城墙相关的人工遗迹，现介绍如下：

外城墙3西南部下方台地上发现一小块夯土堆积，北距外城墙3西北角约23米，东距城墙3西南角约34米。所在台地较城墙3西南侧台地低约1.5米。根据钻探，其形状不甚规则，东西长约3.8米，南北宽约2.4米。为灰褐色花夯土，夯打痕迹明显。堆积较薄，厚约30厘米。其距外城墙3有一定的距离，没有直接联系，且堆积较薄，难以判断其性质。

在外城墙6南侧约10米处发现一处花土遗迹，为灰褐色花土，较为杂乱，含有细砂、灰土块、红土块等，质地稍硬，夯打痕迹不明显。其平面呈长方形，东西长约39米，南北宽约23米，方向与城墙的走向一致。其性质不明。

在外城墙24北侧发现有一片夯土单独分布。其位于西段城墙向北凸起的部分东侧，隔着一条南北向小沟与之相望。这片夯土的西侧和南侧以沟边为界，东侧和北侧在台地中部通过。夯土范围呈南北向长方形，长约14米，宽约7米。夯土厚约20厘米。

外城墙23南侧正冲着一段东西向冲沟。在冲沟周围发现大量的夯土，夯土厚约80厘米。此处的夯土为红褐色黏土夯打而成，质地较纯。夯土厚度不一，厚约50～70厘米，近城墙处的夯土较厚，厚度达1.6米。这段夯土为红褐色黏夯土，与上部城墙的灰褐色夯土明显不类。在两者相接处，断崖高约1.1～1.5米，无法直接联系起来。整段夯土环绕沟的南、北和东端，似乎起到保护沟边，使其不向城墙扩张，冲破城墙的作用。

外城墙77，位于曹家村西南磨山的山脚下，南侧与山体直接相连。外城墙77位于外城墙内侧，隔一条大沟与外城墙82和外城墙83相望，距离外城墙83约280米，距城墙82约300米。外城墙77呈西北—东南走向，方向为137°。其北侧至沟边断崖，南侧至山脚下的一条小路，东西两侧均为断崖。其大体呈长方形。北侧为一处高约8米的断崖，上部有高约5米的夯土。东西两侧均为断崖，南段稍矮，高约2米；向北侧（朝向沟边）断崖逐步变高，与北侧断崖相衔接（图版23：1）。其表面略由南向北呈坡状，表面基本较平。其南北长约80米，东西宽约20米，残存面积约1600平方米。夯土为黄褐色夯土，夹杂有沙砾和小石粒等，质地较为纯净，坚硬，夯打痕迹明显。北侧的夯土厚约5米左右，南侧夯土较薄，厚约0.7米。在城墙中部，夯土厚度在2米以上。可见，这段城墙是在原有由北向南倾斜的山体上夯打而成，越低处堆积的夯土越厚。该处遗存位于外城墙以内，与城墙主体无法直接连通，而与山体相接，具体作用难以推断（图Ⅰ.4.75）。

第四节　外城的验证

1. 20世纪40年代航片的获取

2009年3月初，我们与位于美国首都华盛顿的国家档案馆（National Archives and Records Administration, 700 Pennsylvania Ave., Washington DC, 20408-0001）取得联系，希望能找到第二次世界大战期间美国空军在中国上空拍摄的航空照片，其中可能有和归城有关的图像。说到“可能”，这完全是一个猜测，当时完全无把握能找到有关的资料。档案馆人员告知有关资料必须与位于邻州的马里兰州国家档案馆地图和建筑部联系，而且最好是自己去找。

3月19日早晨，李峰自国家档案馆乘坐馆内班车，约半个小时到达坐落于所谓大学公园的国家档案馆地图和建筑部（Cartographic and Architectural Section, NARA, 8601 Adelphi Road, College Park, MD 20740-6001）。在这里，李峰得到图书馆员杰诺德·卢禅斯基（Gerald Luchansky）的帮助，并很快得知1945年日本投降之前，美军飞机曾在当时属日占区的山东半岛上空进行过多机次的飞行拍照行动（Mission）。在卢禅斯基提供的行动拍照区域和实地对照图上，由李峰标出了归城所在的范围，供他进一步找出有关行动所产生的具体胶片，并交予档案馆指定的DYG图像制作商进行印制。

4月15日，有关图像制作商来信告知已经收到国家档案馆所提供的胶片，并于5月6日传来两张PDF的样片。这个胶片的装罐号码为：NWCS-373-Can ON061275。胶片摄制于1945年2月9日，设置比例1：40000，为9厘米×9厘米的黑白反转片。两张样片分别是本罐的18和19张。两张照片所覆盖的范围大约从旧黄县县城向东南（上方）直至莱山北麓，归城即坐落在两张照片的上方（第19照）或右上角（图Ⅰ.4.76）。确定大致范围后，则付款并请求DYG提供正式图像，两日后收到由DYG自胶片制作的两张高像素TIF图像。至此，我们得到了60年前拍摄的归城范围的珍贵图像资料。

2. 调查结果与航片的验证（以典型段为例）

经过2007年冬季和2008年夏季两个季度的工作，归城外城的调查工作已经结束。2009年5月取得航空影像，正好可以用来检验田野调查发现的内城和外城城墙走向的准确性。内城边界在航空影像上清晰可见，并且东侧为鸦鹊河故道所冲毁的迹象尤为明显。

在航空影像上可以看到，至20世纪40年代，此地经过长期的开发，地貌已远非两周时期的原貌。岗地顶部已被开辟为成片的梯田。梯田的修建多因形就势，利用原有地貌修整而成。对于原先即高出周边地面的外城城墙，多是将顶部削平，周边加以修整而直接成为梯田。城墙周边也由于处于高处，多按照城墙的走向进行修整。这样就导致梯田的形状与走向等与城墙的走向一致，没有显著的方向性区别。因此在对航空影像进行判读时，难以直接根据航空影像上的地块的范围和走向等直接指认为城墙。譬如，C列城墙所在山地上的经过修整的梯田呈南北向，与整列城墙的南北向相一致。H列城墙所在山地和城墙走向呈西南—东北走向，山上经过修正的田地走向亦为西南—东北向，两者难以直接区分。

在航空影像上，在北山村和大于家村村北之间有一条明显带状异常，与此处大都基本呈南北走向的梯田有着显著的差异。其位置、走向、形状等均与我们钻探所知的A列城墙非常一致，应为A列城墙的孑遗（图Ⅰ.4.77）。从北山村往西南，这条影子一直延伸到大致相当钻探所确认的J列外城墙94的位置。在西城墙一带，虽然由于田垄走向和城墙大致一致，从而在航空影像上不易判断，但是在相当于K列城墙24的位置，航空影像上确实也反映了地面上原有大量积土。所有这些，均直接验证了我们钻探工作的准确性。

所取得的航空影像虽然仅涵盖城址西南部，但也未见有南侧城墙的迹象。这也验证了归城城墙直接与南侧山体相接的推断。

第五节　小　　结

1. 外城的时代

由于外城城墙仅是调查和局部的钻探，未经发掘，所以难以直接推断其时代。我们只能从内外城之间全覆盖式调查及外城城墙的调查中取得的些许线索加以推断。通过全覆盖调查，我们发现外城范围，特别是沿东部外城墙范围所分布的主要是东周时期的陶片，包括8区和12区中两个东周陶片高度集中的区域（见本书上编第六章）。在我们对归城外城城墙的调查中，在外城墙35附近地面发现一些散落的绳纹砖及较为规整的石块。这些或许为城墙上附属建筑上的构件。砖块上纹饰为散乱的粗绳纹，属典型的东周时期纹饰（图Ⅰ.4.47、Ⅰ.6.13）。这或许从侧面反映了外城的使用时期。

结合以上线索，也考虑了中原地区东周时期城市发展的历史，我们初步推断归城外城的始建和使用时代大约在春秋时期。但是，关于外城的具体建筑年代还需在日后的发掘工作中来加以解决。

2. 外城修建的地理因素

归城外城位于山水之间，背依莱山，城内外有道道丘陵纵横其间，鸦鹊河由城内流过。归城遗址的选址充分考虑到并利用了这些自然条件。

一座城市的建立首要考虑是防御设施的构筑。归城由内外两道城圈构成，从而构成两道防御体系。内城构建在一处高台地上，是一处较易防守的地形。台地西北侧和东侧均有河道流经，又构成另一道天然屏障。在台地上又修筑高出周围地面近8米的内城城墙（依地面城墙A的残高计，原有高度当高于此），内城的防御设施相当完备。

归城的外城更是充分利用了地形因素来构筑防御体系。外城南侧依托莱山，其余三面均为低矮岗地。外城城墙仅有北、东、西三侧构筑。在外城东南侧的F列城墙的南侧与莱山山体相距仅有200米，所在岗地直接与山体相通。西南侧的G列城墙距南侧莱山仅有100米左右，也直接与山体相连，构成了一个完整的防御体系。莱山山势陡峭，极难翻越。归城南侧依托这道天然防御屏障，未构筑城墙，节省了大量的人力物力。

归城外城城墙构筑在周边条状岗地的顶部，内外侧均为较深的谷地。如东侧的C列城墙、E列城墙和F列城墙所在山地，西侧的G列城墙和H列城墙所在山地及北侧的A列城墙所在岗地。在此类地形上修建城墙常常能收到事半功倍的效果。

东侧的C列城墙所在岗地，位于董家村至和平村东，全长约1600米，呈南北向横亘在内城东侧。其高出下部的谷地约有20～30米。此列岗地与内城间再无其他岗地，是城址东侧第一道可以依托的天然屏障。西侧的H列城墙所在岗地位于曹家村西北，全长约850米，呈东北—西南走向，构成了外城西南侧的一道天然屏障。北侧的A列城墙所在岗地位于北山村和大于家村之间，全长约1200米。此列岗地内侧呈大斜坡状通向内城，外侧地势略低，为一处地势不甚显著的岗地。

岗地之间的谷地中，也构筑了城墙，将两侧山地上的城墙连接起来。如在A列城墙和C列城墙之间的谷地宽约600米。现鸦鹊河即从谷地中部穿过。周围经钻探，有大片淤土存在，表明此谷地原为鸦鹊河河道。在外城墙10即位于谷地的西北侧，东南侧紧贴着现在鸦鹊河河道。此处城墙的设置应当是专门来封堵住此处缺口的。在C列城墙和E列城墙之间有一处宽约200米的山谷，为封堵此处缺口，特意在此处设置外城墙37。

在城墙具体位置的选择上，归城的建筑者也注意选择谷地较为狭窄的地方修建。譬如，E列城墙所在山地共有三个向南延伸的岗地，城墙位于中间一列岗地上。究其原因，此列岗地与南侧F列城墙所在山地之间仅隔一宽约25米的河谷。河谷的岸壁陡直，下部的河道处宽度仅有10米，极难通过也就较易控制。

城内有鸦鹊河及其上游的数条支流流经。这些水系构为城址的存在和发展提供了基本条件。在内城周围有两条河道，分别由内城的东侧和西北侧流过，等于在城墙外侧构筑的另一道屏障。西北侧的河道虽距内城稍远，其与内城间近5米的高差，亦有助于内城的防御。并且另有一条河道由南侧城壕流入城内，经由北侧城墙上的缺口流出城外，从而构成了内城的基本水系框架，同时为城内居民提供生活用水。

在内外城之间尚有多条水系流过。这些水系的河畔阶地土地肥沃，方便灌溉，适宜人们生活居住，是人们主要居住的区域。如城内有一条源自莱山，向北呈南北向东迟家村西、董家村东汇入鸦鹊河的河道。在河岸西侧，和平村东至董家村南之间原先为高地，后被取土烧窑而破坏，地面尚残存有高约4米的长条状断崖。地面调查时发现断崖周边有较为丰富的遗存，表明其是当时人们密集活动区域。对这些河边阶地的深入考察，不仅仅能够了解当时人们活动，更有助于了解归城发展、演变的整个过程。

3. 城门及附属建筑的推测

对外城的城门遗存，以及城墙上的附属建筑等，由于调查工作的局限，尚难以做出明确的判断，仅可从些许线索加以揣度。

外城墙22以南为以宽约15米的断崖式豁口。距当地村民介绍，此处为“城门口”。现此处仍有一条大路通向内城所在的和平村，是村民向东的主要通道。此处是否为一处城门，尚需今后工作予以确认。

对城墙上的附属建筑。一处可能的地点在外城墙1和外城墙99处。外城墙一般宽度在20～30米左右，但此处城墙宽度达到100米，远远超过一般城墙的宽度，推测在其他建筑附属在城墙上，需进一步工作确认。另一处可能地点在外城墙35处。在城墙周围地面上散出有绳纹砖和较为规整的石块，表明附近可能存在有建筑。这些需今后工作了解确认。

4. K列城墙功用的推测

K列城墙位于C列城墙下方，D列和E列城墙外侧，独自占据一列山脊，向南并无城墙与之相向。由于未做进一步发掘，K列城墙的时代、结构等都难以准确指出。此处或给出两种推测。其一，D列的城墙37处于一处宽约200米的山谷缺口中，而K列所在岗地恰在城墙37的外侧，或是为防守这个山谷缺口在外侧构筑的另一道屏障。

其二，历来均有记载之处此处为莱国都城。根据《左传·襄公六年》载齐灭莱史事：“十一月，齐侯灭莱，莱恃谋也。……四月，晏弱城东阳，而遂围莱。甲寅，堙之环城，傅于堞。……。晏弱围棠，十一月丙辰，而灭之。迁莱于郳。高厚、崔杼定其田。”据《正义》：“兵书攻城有为堙之法。”当是在城墙外侧另修一段城墙，并借助这段城墙攻入城内。此处城墙北侧不远即为当地村民所说的“城门口”。齐军攻城时或许是由南侧的一列岗地上堆筑泥土，顺山脊逐步向城墙靠拢，与城墙平齐，从而攻入城内。如果这样，K列城墙就有可能是“堙”的遗迹。但由于未做发掘，数段城墙的早晚，结构及其组合关系等尚不明晰，这些仅为揣测，还需今后工作中予以确认。

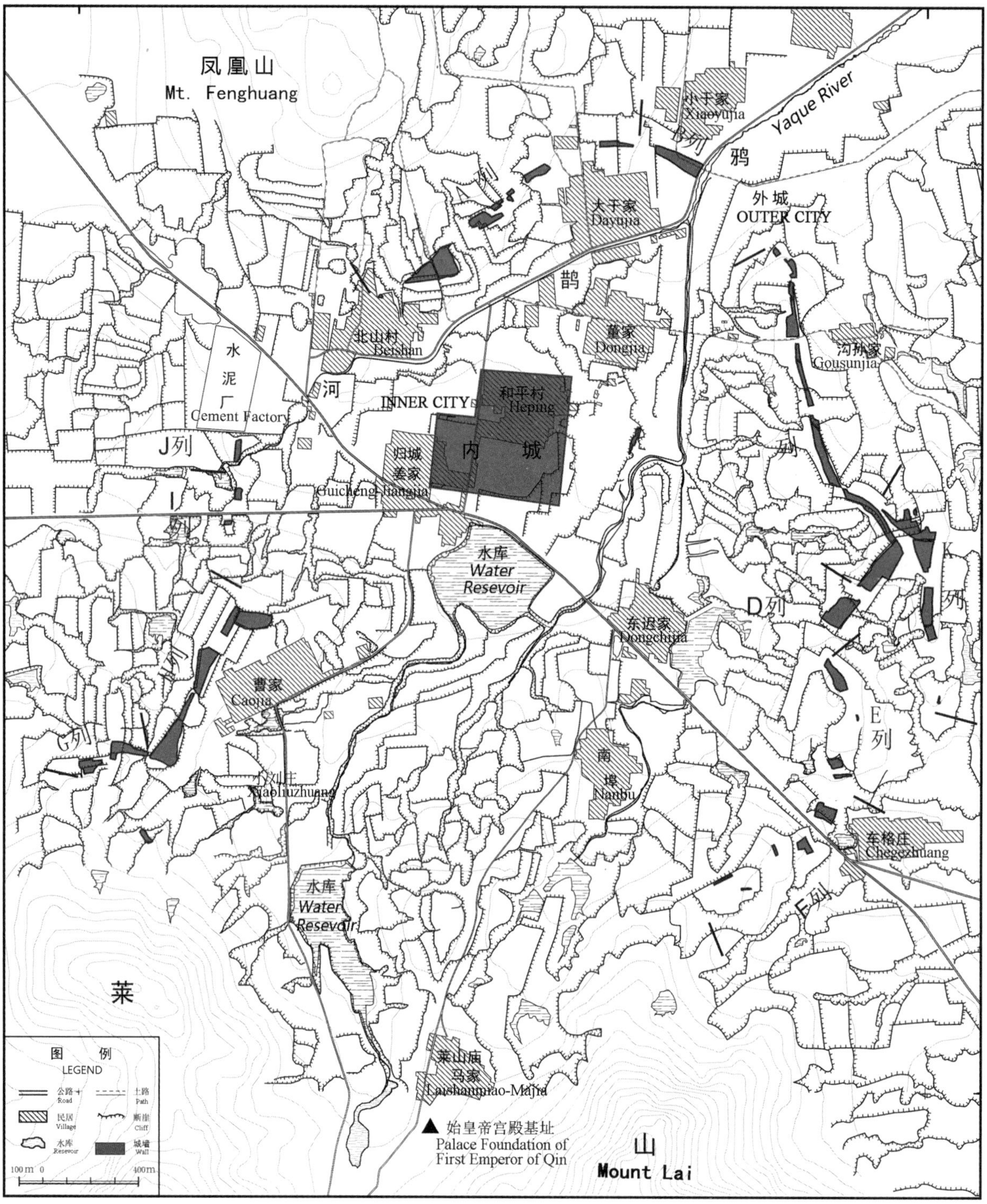

地图Ⅰ.4.1 归城外城墙分列地图

Map Ⅰ.4.1 Location of Rows of Guicheng outer city wall.

表Ⅰ.4.1　归城外城城墙统计表

Table Ⅰ.4.1　Statistical Table of Guicheng Outer Wall Sections

列 Row	编号 Section	走向 Orientation	面积：平方米 Area: m^2	形制 Shape	残存规模：米 Extant Dimensions: m	位置（GPS） Geographic Positioning	备注 Notes
A	97	不明 N/A	不详 N/A	N/A	L: 20	① N: 37°36.024′; E: 120°33.709′; H: 89 (NE)*	20世纪70年代已发现，名“后城子”。 Discovered during the 1970s survey. Local toponym: “Houchengzi” (Rear Wall).
A	99	34°	5300	梯形 Trapezoidal	L: 135, W: 6 ~ 73	① N: 37°36.101′; E: 120°33.850′; H: 98 (NE) ② N: 37°36.054′; E: 120°33.777′; H: 92 (SW)	
A	1	80°	7222.5	长方形 Rectangular	L: 58 ~ 77, W: 86 ~ 128 (NS)	① N: 37°36.103′; E: 120°33.854′; H: 80 (NW) ② N: 37°36.133′; E: 120°33.901′; H: 77 (NE) ③ N: 37°36.072′; E: 120°33.928′; H: 77 (SN) ④ N: 37°36.065′; E: 120°33.878′; H: 78 (SW)	清理两处剖面。 Exposed two cross-sections.
A	3	64°	5906	“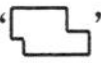”形 -shaped	L: 134+, W: 59+	① N: 37°36.165′; E: 120°33.992′; H: 67 (SW) ② N: 37°36.186′; E: 120°33.961′; H: 67 (NW) ③ N: 37°36.214′; E: 120°34.048′; H: 74 (E)	清理两处剖面。 Exposed two cross-sections.
A	4	46°	856	“”形 -shaped	L: 53, W: 12 ~ 24	① N: 37°36.238′; E: 120°34.046′; H: 75 (SE) ② N: 37°36.232′; E: 120°34.0020′; H: 80 (N)	
A	5	65°	2064	“”形 -shaped	L: 43, W: 48	N: 37°36.251′; E: 120°34.080′; H: 75	地面残存一处城墙夯土，20世纪70年代已发现，称为“田家茔”。 Discovered during the 1970 survey. Wall remains visible on the surface. Local toponym: “Tianjiaying” (Tian Family Mound).

续表

列 Row	编号 Section	走向 Orientation	面积：平方米 Area: m^2	形制 Shape	残存规模：米 Extant Dimensions: m	位置（GPS） Geographic Positioning	备注 Notes
A	6	65°	3530	长方形 Rectangular	L: 107, W: 27 ~ 39	① N: 37°36.289′; E: 120°34.113′; H: 71 (W) ② N: 37°36.310′; E: 120°34.165′; H: 72 (E)	
A	8	90°	6000	长方形 Rectangular	L: 150, W: 13 ~ 50	① N: 37°36.352′; E: 120°34.346′; H: 63 (W) ② N: 37°36.356′; E: 120°34.430′; H: 54 (E)	
B	10	118°	15000	长方形 Rectangular	L: 219, W: 57 ~ 80	① N: 37°36.351′; E: 120°34.497′; H: 53 (W) ② N: 37°36.310′; E: 120°34.634′; H: 51(NE)	此处旧称“河心”。 Local toponym: “Hexin” (Center of the River).
C	13	144°	625	长方形 Rectangular	L: 33, W: 19	N: 37°36.121′; E: 120°34.853′; H: 67	清理一处剖面。 Exposed a cross-section.
C	14	140° ~ 180°	2130	不规则长方形 Irregular Rectangular	L: 71, W: 25.5 ~ 35	① N: 37°36.114′; E: 120°34.853′; H: 68 (NW) ② N: 37°36.123′; E: 120°34.873′; H: 64 (NE) ③ N: 37°36.062′; E: 120°34.896′; H: 74 (S)	
C	15	176° ~ 204°	770	不规则长方形 Irregular Rectangle	L: 70, W: 10 ~ 12.5	① N: 37°36.055′; E: 120°34.883′; H: 75 (S) ② N: 37°36.025′; E: 120°34.881′; H: 79 (N)	
C	16	171°	4536	刀形 Blade-shaped	L: 160, W: 9 ~ 49	① N: 37°36.055′; E: 120°34.883′; H: 75 (N) ② N: 37°35.931′; E: 120°34.907′; H: 79 (SE) ③ N: 37°35.927′; E: 120°34.886′; H: 79 (SW)	清理两处剖面。20世纪70年代已发现此处城墙，称为“埢顶上”。 Exposed two cross-sections. Discovered in the 1970s. Local toponym: “Quanding shang” (On Top of the Ring).
C	17	180°	806	梯形 Trapezoidal	L: 62, W: 10 ~ 16	① N: 37°35.912′; E: 120°34.893′; H: 86 (N) ② N: 37°35.882′; E: 120°34.897′; H: 85 (S)	
C	18	165°	3450	长方形 Rectangular	L: 115, W: 30	① N: 37°35.882′; E: 120°34.897′; H: 85 (N) ② N: 37°35.817′; E: 120°34.924′; H: 88 (S)	

续表

列 Row	编号 Section	走向 Orientation	面积：平方米 Area: m^2	形制 Shape	残存规模：米 Extant Dimensions: m	位置（GPS） Geographic Positioning	备注 Notes
C	19	175°	1230	长方形 Rectangular	L: 65, W: 19	① N: 37°35.817′； E: 120°34.924′；H: 88 (N) ② N: 37°35.788′； E: 120°34.936′；H: 89 (S)	
C	21	173°	880	长方形 Rectangular	L: 25 ~ 30, W: 35	N: 37°35.760′； E: 120°34.937′；H: 93 (N)	
C	22	161°	8000	长方形 Rectangular	L: 250, W: 20 ~ 44	① N: 37°35.743′； E: 120°34.938′；H: 89 (NW) ② N: 37°35.735′； E: 120°34.950′；H: 90 (NE) ③ N: 37°35604′； E: 120°35.000′；H: 98 (SW) ④ N: 37°35.603′； E: 120°35.013′；H: 97 (SE)	
C	23	135°	9000	圆弧状 Crescent-shaped	L: 290, W: 25 ~ 36	① N: 37°35.575′； E: 120°35.037′；H: 102 (SW) ② N：37°35.596′； E: 120°35.031′；H: 102 (NW)	此处称为“大罗圈”“二罗圈”“三罗圈”，城墙在“三罗圈”。 This location has three toponyms: “Daluoquan” (First Ring), “Erluoquan” (Second Ring), and “Sanluoquan” (Third Ring).
C	35	217°	16200	长方形 Rectangular	L: 228, W: 55 ~ 87	① N: 37°35.481′； E: 120°35.153′；H: 106 (NW) ② N: 37°35.396′； E: 120°35.104′；H: 98 (SE) ③ N: 37°35.398′； E: 120°35.153′；H: 103 (SE)	附近发现绳纹砖和较为规整的石块；清理两处剖面。 Cord-marked bricks and human modified stone found in vicinity. Examined two cross-sections.
D	37	217°	11000	长方形 Rectangular	L: 142, W: 77	① N: 37°35.208′； E: 120°35.009′；H: 110 (SE) ② N: 37°35.318′； E: 120°34.977′；H: 100 (SW) ③ N: 37°35.357′； E: 120°35.018′；H: 99 (NW) ④ N: 37°35.341′； E: 120°35.074′；H: 142 (NE)	东侧地面上发现一些较规整石块。 Modified stone discovered along the eastern side.

续表

列 Row	编号 Section	走向 Orientation	面积：平方米 Area: m^2	形制 Shape	残存规模：米 Extant Dimensions: m	位置（GPS） Geographic Positioning	备注 Notes
E	39	155°	5560	长方形 Rectangular	L: 139, W: 25 ~ 55	① N: 37°35.210′ ; E: 120°34.974′ ; H: 118 (NW) ② N: 37°35.154′ ; E: 120°35.016′ ; H: 118 (SW) ③ N: 37°35.155′ ; E: 120°34.036; H: 120 (SE) ④ N: 37°35.221′ ; E: 120°34.980′ ; H: 118 (NE)	
E	41	163°	90	长方形 Rectangular	L: 18, W: 5	① N: 37°35.095′ ; E: 120°35.064′ ; H: 115 (NW) ② N: 37°35.083′ ; E: 120°35.067′ ; H: 117 (SW)	
E	44	155°	1450	长方形 Rectangular	L: 29, W: 50	① N: 37°34.995′ ; E: 120°35.020′ ; H: 101 (NE) ② N: 37°34.988′ ; E: 120°34.981′ ; H: 96 (NW) ③ N: 37°34.978′ ; E: 120°34.997′ ; H: 93 (SW) ④ N: 37°34.984′ ; E: 120°35.024′ ; H: 95 (SE)	
E	46	155°	650	长方形 Rectangular	L: 7 ~ 12, W: 68	① N: 37°34.968′ ; E: 120°35.038′ ; H: 95 (NE) ② N: 37°34.966′ ; E: 120°34.006′ ; H: 95 (NW) ③ N: 37°34.961′ ; E: 120°34.976′ ; H: 94 (SW)	
F	49	200°	4000	长方形 Rectangular	L: 50, W: 77	① N: 37°34.857′ ; E: 120°34.989′ ; H: 113 (SE) ② N: 37°34.879′ ; E: 120°35.002′ ; H: 104 (NE) ③ N: 37°34.898′ ; E: 120°34.952′ ; H: 93 (NW) ④ N: 37°34.864′ ; E: 120°34.975′ ; H: 116 (SW)	
F	51	243°	2000	梯形 Trapezoidal	L: 48, W: 28 ~ 64	① N: 37°34.792′ ; E: 120°34.909′ ; H: 94 (SW) ② N: 37°34.801′ ; E: 120°34.904′ ; H: 93 (NW) ③ N: 37°34.793′ ; E: 120°34.945′ ; H: 84 (SE)	

续表

列 Row	编号 Section	走向 Orientation	面积：平方米 Area: m^2	形制 Shape	残存规模：米 Extant Dimensions: m	位置（GPS） Geographic Positioning	备注 Notes
F	53	245°	380	梯形 Trapezoidal	L: 9, W: 43	① N: 37°34.792′ ; E: 120°34.853′ ; H: 83 (SE) ② N: 37°34.802′ ; E: 120°34.850′ ; H: 82 (NE) ③ N: 37°34.799′ ; E: 120°34.834′ ; H: 89 (NW) ④ N: 37°34.786′ ; E: 120°34.842′ ; H: 89 (SW)	
F	56	265°	290	长方形 Rectangular	L: 39, W: 7.5	① N: 37°34.708′ ; E: 120°34.769′ ; H: 121 (E) ② N: 37°34.705′ ; E: 120°34.737′ ; H: 121 (W)	或与外城墙58同为一段城墙。 Possibly formed a single piece with wall section 58.
F	58	245°	890	长方形 Rectangular	L: 81, W: 11	① N: 37°34.740′ ; E: 120°34.702′ ; H: 108 (NE) ② N: 37°34.725′ ; E: 120°34.660′ ; H: 108 (NW)	或与外城墙56同为一段城墙。 Possibly formed a single piece with wall section 56.
G	80	171°	4000	梯形 Trapezoidal	L: 66, W: 36 ~ 89	① N: 37°34.996′ ; E: 120°32.827′ ; H: 132 (NW) ② N: 37°34.998′ ; E: 120°32.833′ ; H: 134 (NE) ③ N: 37°34.967′ ; E: 120°32.850′ ; H: 133 (SW) ④ N: 37°34.969′ ; E: 120°32.863′ ; H: 134 (SE)	南侧与山体相接。 South side connects to mountain.
G	82	283°	5600	梯形 Trapezoidal	L: 154, W: 19 ~ 44	① N: 37°35.012′ ; E: 120°33.029′ ; H: 128 (NE) ② N: 37°35.007′ ; E: 120°33.026′ ; H: 128 (SE) ③ N: 37°35.036′ ; E: 120°32.925′ ; H: 130 (NW) ④ N: 37°35.000′ ; E: 120°32.921′ ; H: 128 (SW)	
H	83	219°	12000	梯形 Trapezoidal	L: 190, W: 22 ~ 103	① N: 37°35.081′ ; E: 120°33.127′ ; H: 120 (NE) ② N: 37°35.094′ ; E: 120°33.110′ ; H: 120 (NW) ③ N: 37°35.002′ ; E: 120°33.036′ ; H: 130 (SW) ④ N: 37°34.982′ ; E: 120°33.091′ ; H: 128 (SE)	城墙东部斜坡可能是经修整所致。 The eastern slope of the section possibly due to modern modification.

续表

列 Row	编号 Section	走向 Orientation	面积：平方米 Area: m^2	形制 Shape	残存规模：米 Extant Dimensions: m	位置（GPS） Geographic Positioning	备注 Notes
H	84	204°	2000	长方形 Rectangular	L: 119, W: 11 ~ 23	① N: 37°35.142′; E: 120°33.161′; H: 123 (NE) ② N: 37°35.084′; E: 120°33.128′; H: 124 (SE) ③ N: 37°35.089′; E: 120°33.120′; H: 123(SW)	
H	85	204°	11000	梯形 Trapezoidal	L: 186, W: 41 ~ 78	① N: 37°35.144′; E: 120°33.185′; H: 116 (SE) ② N: 37°35.156′; E: 120°33.159′; H: 117 (SW) ③ N: 37°35.152′; E: 120°33.192′; H: 121 (NW)	
H	87	209°	3400	长方形 Rectangular	L: 121, W: 28	① N: 37°35.337′; E: 120°33.289′; H: 79 (NE) ② N: 37°35.340′; E: 120°33.277′; H: 80 ③ N: 37°35.278′; E: 120°33.236′; H: 92 ④ N: 37°35.279′; E: 120°33.260′; H: 92	
H	88	277°	9400	长方形 Rectangular	L: 144, W: 54 ~ 77	① N: 37°35.316′; E: 120°33.374′; H: 119 (NE) ② N: 37°35.297′; E: 120°33.376′; H: 117 (SE) ③ N: 37°35.300′; E: 120°33.275′; H: 117 (SW) ④ N: 37°35.330′; E: 120°33.294′; H: 117 (NW)	残存一段地面城墙。清理两处剖面。 Remains are visible on the surface of the ground. Exposed two cross-sections.
I	90	180°	8400	长方形 Rectangular	L: 20, W: 41	① N: 37°35.532′; E: 120°33.273′; H: 80 (NE) ② N: 37°35.529′; E: 120°33.254′; H: 81 (NW) ③ N: 37°35.525′; E: 120°33.273′; H: 81 (SE)	

续表

列 Row	编号 Section	走向 Orientation	面积：平方米 Area: m^2	形制 Shape	残存规模：米 Extant Dimensions: m	位置（GPS） Geographic Positioning	备注 Notes
I	92	188°	1200	长方形 Rectangular	L: 48, W: 25	① N: 37°35.595′; E: 120°33.293′; H: 83(NW) ② N: 37°35.594′; E: 120°33.299′; H: 82 (NE) ③ N: 37°35.571′; E: 120°33.286′; H: 82 (SW) ④ N: 37°35.570′; E: 120°33.290′; H: 81 (SE)	
J	94	188°	2139	长方形 Rectangular	L: 93, W: 23	① N: 37°35.695′; E: 120°33.288′; H: 86 (NE) ② N: 37°35.654′; E: 120°33.279′; H: 83 (SW)	
K	24	130° ~ 90°	8300	分东西两段 Divided into Eastern and Western parts	西段 Western Portion： L: 210, W: 14 东段 Eastern Portion： L: 62, W: 25 ~ 45	① N: 37°35.492′; E: 120°35.286′; H: 109 (SE) ② N: 37°35.504′; E: 120°35.287′; H: 112 (NE) ③ N: 37°35.560′; E: 120°35.130′; H: 107 (NW)	清理一处剖面。 Exposed one cross-section.
K	25	180°	6540	梯形 Trapezoidal	L: 127, W: 16 ~ 87	① N: 37°35.484′; E: 120°35.285′; H: 103 (NE) ② N: 37°35.419′; E: 120°35.269′; H: 102 (SE) ③ N: 37°35.418′; E: 120°35.261′; H: 103 (SW)	
K	27	180°	5400	长方形 Rectangular	L: 153, W: 34 ~ 37	① N: 37°35.379′; E: 120°35.282′; H: 102 (NE) ② N: 37°35.378′; E: 120°35.262′; H: 102 (NW) ③ N: 37°35.293′; E: 120°35.267′; H: 102 (SW) ④ N: 37°35.296′; E: 120°35.284′; H: 102 (SE)	
K	28	159°	1700	长方形 Rectangular	L: 53, W: 32	① N: 37°35.290′; E: 120°35.260′; H: 102 (NW) ② N: 37°35.259′; E: 120°35.273′; H: 102 (SW) ③ N: 37°35.273′; E: 120°35.288′; H: 100 (SE)	

续表

列 Row	编号 Section	走向 Orientation	面积：平方米 Area: m^2	形制 Shape	残存规模：米 Extant Dimensions: m	位置（GPS） Geographic Positioning	备注 Notes
K	31	192°	138	长方形 Rectangular	L: 23, W: 3 ~ 9	① N: 37°35.135′; E: 120°35.301′; H: 103 (N) ② N: 37°35.122′; E: 120°35.302′; H: 102 (S)	清理一处剖面。 Exposed one cross-section.

尺寸标志：L=长度；H=高度；W=宽度；T=厚度；d=深度。

Measurements: L=length; H=height; W=width; T=thickness; d=depth.

测量点选城墙夯土边缘拐角部位；括号中标出大致方位。

The measurement of the height of the rammed earth was taken in the general vicinity of the edge of the wall section where it bends; information in the brackets gives the approximate location.

图Ⅰ.4.1　外城城墙钻探
Figure Ⅰ.4.1　Coring of the outer wall.

图Ⅰ.4.2　调查时清理剖面
Figure Ⅰ.4.2　Exposed cross-section.

图Ⅰ.4.3 使用全站仪绘制外城地图

Figure Ⅰ.4.3 Mapping the outer city wall using a total-station.

图Ⅰ.4.4 城墙A—B列分布位置图

Figure Ⅰ.4.4 Locations of Rows A-B.

图Ⅰ.4.5　外城墙97（南—北）
Figure Ⅰ.4.5　Outer wall Section 97 (South-North).

图Ⅰ.4.6　外城墙99（东—西）
Figure Ⅰ.4.6　Outer wall Section 99 (East-West).

图Ⅰ.4.7　外城墙99断面掉落的夯土块
Figure Ⅰ.4.7　Rammed earth remnant from outer wall Section 99.

图Ⅰ.4.8　学生们考察外城墙99断面掉落的夯土块
Figure Ⅰ.4.8　Students examining a remnant of rammed earth from outer wall Section 99.

图Ⅰ.4.9　外城墙1（东—西）

Figure Ⅰ.4.9　Outer wall Section 1 (East-West).

图Ⅰ.4.10　外城墙1剖面A

Figure Ⅰ.4.10　Cross-section A on outer wall Section 1.

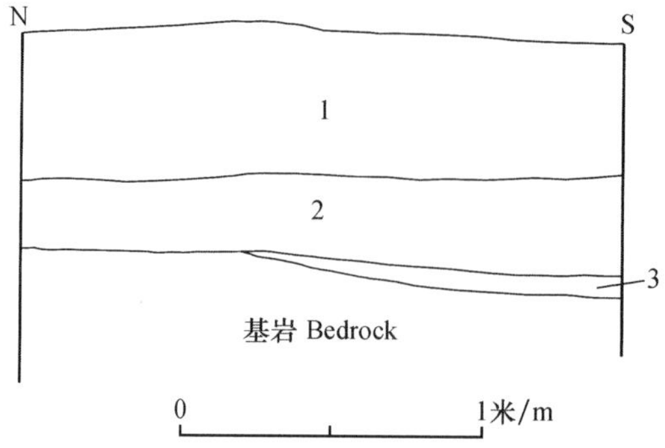

图Ⅰ.4.11　外城墙1剖面A（绘图）

位于城墙1的西南角，清理部分宽约2米。

第1层：表土层，黄褐色土，土质松散，结构疏松，厚约45～50厘米，呈水平堆积。

第2层：夯土层：灰褐色花夯土，内夹杂有黄土粒、红黏土颗粒和红烧土颗粒，质地紧密，厚约22～32厘米，堆积大体水平，略由北向南倾斜堆积。

第3层：基岩上有一层厚约0～6厘米风化岩石，呈粗砂砾，破碎严重。

以下为基岩。

Figure Ⅰ.4.11　Cross-section A of outer wall Section 1 (drawing).

Located on the southwest corner of Section 1, measuring 2 m wide.

Stratum 1: Topsoil, yellowish-brown soil, loose and crumbly texture, 45-50 cm, horizontal accumulation.

Stratum 2: Rammed earth greyish-brown composite soil, yellow granules, red clay granules, and burned red granule inclusions, tightly compacted texture, 22-32 cm, generally horizontal accumulation with very slight north to south slope.

Stratum 3: Bedrock, covered by a 0-6 cm layer of coarse, eroded gravel.

Below this stratum is bedrock.

图Ⅰ.4.12　外城墙1剖面B

Figure Ⅰ.4.12　Cross-section B on outer wall Section 1.

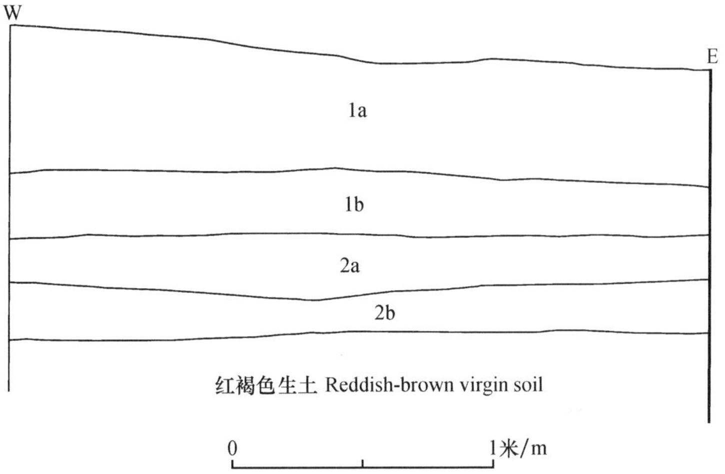

图Ⅰ.4.13　外城墙1剖面B（绘图）

位于城墙1的南侧断崖上，距城墙的西南角约38米。剖面宽约2.7米。

第1层：表土层，可分为上下两小层。第1a层为红褐色垫土，结构松散，厚约44～56厘米，呈水平堆积；第1b层为黄褐色垫土，结构松散，质地疏松，厚约18～26厘米，呈水平堆积。

第2层：夯土层，根据土色和包含物的不同，可分为上下两小层。第2a层为灰褐色夯土层，内夹杂有小石块、砂砾、黄土粒，稍杂乱，质地较硬，厚约16～26厘米，大致呈水平堆积；第2b层为红褐色夯土，含有红土块、灰土和烧土粒，质地较纯净，结构较紧密，厚约12～22厘米，呈水平堆积。

以下为生土。

Figure Ⅰ.4.13　Cross-section B of outer-wall Section 1 (drawing).

Located on the south side of wall Section 1 atop a precipice, 38 m from cross-section A. Measures 2.7 m wide.

Stratum 1: Topsoil, can be subdivided into upper and lower substrata. The upper substratum (1a) is composed of reddish-brown paved earth, loose and crumbly in texture, 44-56 cm, horizontal accumulation; the lower substratum (1b) is composed of yellowish-brown paved earth, loose and crumbly in texture, 18-26 cm, horizontal accumulation.

Stratum 2: Rammed earth, can be subdivided into upper and lower substrata based on the soil color and inclusions. The upper substratum (2a) is composed of greyish-brown rammed earth, with small stones, yellow soil granules, and gravel inclusions, jumbled but hardened texture, 16-26 cm, horizontal accumulation; the lower substratum (2b) is composed of reddish-brown rammed earth, red clods, grey soil, and burned soil granule inclusions, texture is fine and tightly compacted, 12-22 cm, horizontal accumulation.

Below this stratum is virgin soil.

图Ⅰ.4.14　外城墙3（西—东）

Figure Ⅰ.4.14　Outer wall Section 3 (West-East).

图Ⅰ.4.15　外城墙3剖面A

Figure Ⅰ.4.15　Cross-section A on Wall Section 3.

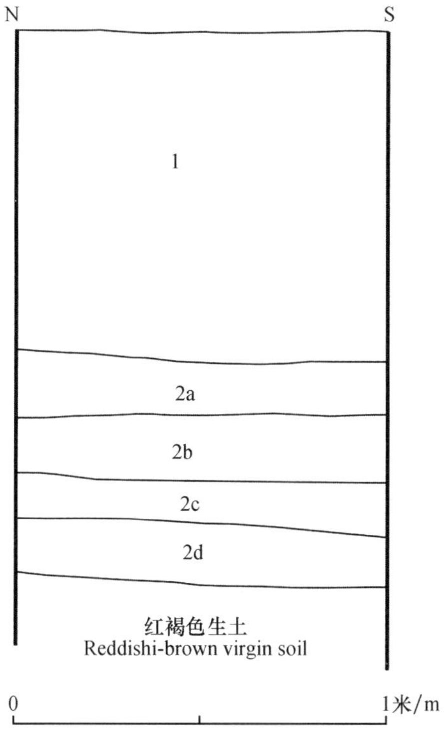

图Ⅰ.4.16　外城墙3剖面A（绘图）

位于城墙3西南部的蓄水池东壁上。剖面宽约1米。剖面上堆积分为两大层：

第1层：表土层，黄褐色土，土质松散，结构疏松，厚约84～88厘米，呈水平堆积。

第2层：夯土层，根据土色的不同，可分为四小层，夯层水平。夯土层由上而下颜色较为统一，均为红褐色夹杂有黑色土块的夯土，上部含黑土块较多，下部黑土块较少。

第2a层，黑红褐色花夯土，内包含较多黑色土块，质地紧密，厚约13～18厘米。

第2b层，黑红褐色花夯土，内包含一定黑色土块，质地紧密，厚约15～18厘米。

第2c层，红褐色花夯土，内包含较少黑色土块，质地紧密，厚约10～15厘米。

第2d层，红褐色花夯土，内包含少量黑色土块，质地紧密，厚约13～16厘米。

以下为红褐色生土层，质地纯净，结构紧密，无包含物。

Figure Ⅰ.4.16　Cross-section A of Wall Section 3 (drawing).

Located in the southwest part of wall Section 3, the eastern wall of a small water pit, 1 m wide. Can be divided into 2 strata:

Stratum 1: Topsoil, yellowish-brown in color, loose and crumbly texture, 84-88 cm, horizontal accumulation.

Stratum 2: Rammed earth, can be subdivided into 4 substrata according to differences in the color of the soil. Loose texture, horizontal accumulation. The color of the stratum overall is reddish-brown with black clumpy inclusions; these inclusions are more abundant in the upper substrata, and less abundant in the lower substrata.

Stratum 2a: Reddish-brown tending toward black, composite rammed earth, black clumpy inclusions, tightly compacted texture, 13-18 cm.

Stratum 2b: Reddish-brown tending toward black, composite rammed earth, small amount of black clumpy inclusions, tightly compacted texture, 15-18 cm.

Stratum 2c: Reddish-brown rammed earth, small amount of black clumpy inclusions, tightly compacted texture, 10-15 cm.

Stratum 2d: Reddish-brown rammed earth, small amounts of black clumpy inclusions, tightly compacted texture, 13-16 cm.

Below this stratum is virgin soil, fine, homogeneous, well-compacted, no inclusions.

图Ⅰ.4.17　外城墙3剖面B

Figure Ⅰ.4.17　Cross-section B of Wall Section 3.

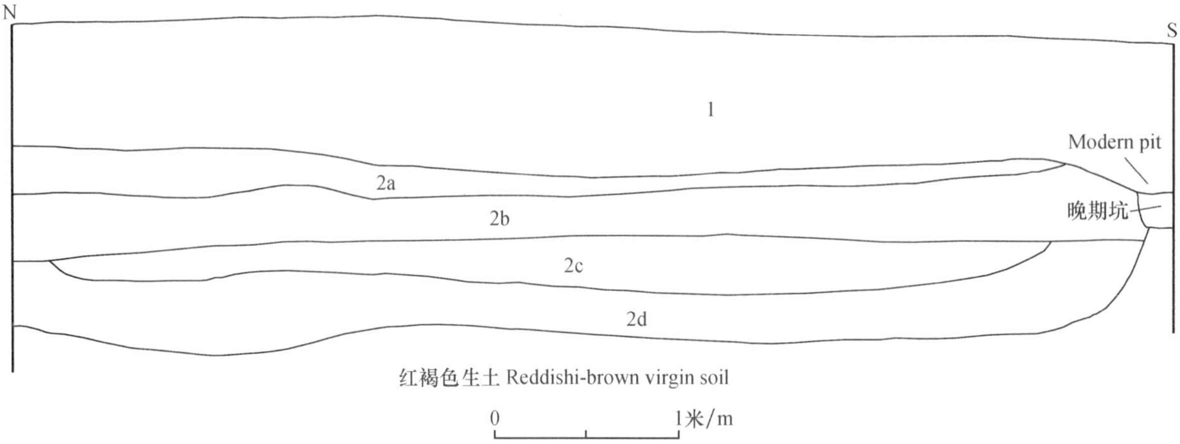

图Ⅰ.4.18　外城墙3剖面B（绘图）

位于城墙3的西侧断崖上，在城墙西南角以北。清理剖面宽约6.4米。堆积可分为两大层：

第1层：垫土层，可分为两小层。上层普遍为黄褐色垫土，结构松散，厚约66～80厘米，大体呈水平堆积；下层为灰褐色垫土，质地疏松，仅在南部有少量分布，厚约18厘米，呈水平堆积。

第2层：为一处基槽的下部，坑壁较为圆弧，底部大致呈水平状，略有起伏。基槽残深约82～111厘米。基槽内均为夯土。根据土色和包含物的不同，夯土可分为四个层次。

第2a层，灰褐色花夯土，质地紧密，出有少量陶片，厚约0～26厘米，略由南向北倾斜堆积。

第2b层，黄褐色花夯土，内夹杂有黄色土块，质地紧密，厚约22～42厘米，大致呈水平堆积。

第2c层，浅灰褐色夯土，质地紧密，厚约0～32厘米，呈锅底形堆积。

第2d层，灰褐色夯土，质地紧密，厚约24～47厘米，大致呈水平堆积。

以下为红褐色粘状生土，质地纯净，结构紧密，无包含物。

Figure Ⅰ.4.18　Cross-section B of Wall Section 3 (drawing).

Located on a precipice in the western part of wall Section 3, north of its southwest corner. 6.4 m wide. Divided into 2 strata:

Stratum 1: Ground-leveling soil. Can be divided into two substrata. The upper substratum is generally yellowish-brown leveling soil. Loose texture, 66-80 cm, horizontal accumulation; the lower substratum is greyish brown leveling soil, loose texture, seen only in the southern part, 18 cm, horizontal accumulation.

Stratum 2: Forms the base of a trough with arched sides, flattened bottom, and small undulation. 81-111 cm. Filled with rammed earth that can be subdivided into four substrata based on the color of the soil.

Stratum 2a: Greyish-brown composite rammed earth, tightly compacted texture, small amounts of pottery inclusions, 0-26 cm, south to north sloping accumulation.

Stratum 2b: Yellowish-brown composite rammed earth. Yellow clumpy inclusions, tightly compacted texture, 22-42 cm, horizontal accumulation.

Stratum 2c: Light greyish-brown composite rammed earth, tightly compacted texture, 0-32 cm, lenticular accumilation.

Stratum 2d: Greyish-brown composite rammed earth, tightly compacted texture, 24-47 cm, horizontal accumulation.

Below this stratum is reddish-brown virgin soil, homogeneous and finely textured, tightly compacted, no inclusions.

图Ⅰ.4.19　外城墙5地面残留部分（东—西）

Figure Ⅰ.4.19　Remains of Wall Section 5 on the surface (East-West).

图Ⅰ.4.20　外城墙5剖面

Figure Ⅰ.4.20　Cross-section of Wall Section 5.

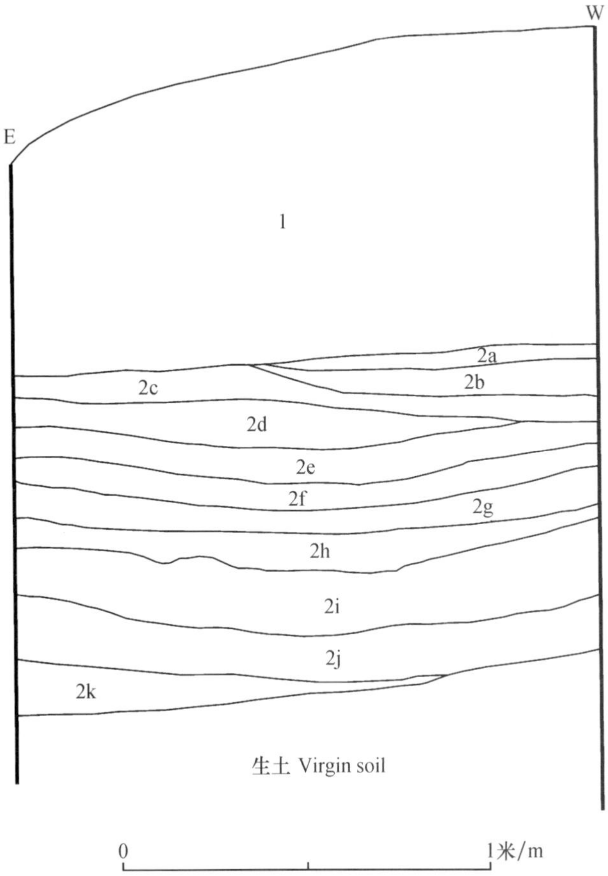

图Ⅰ.4.21　外城墙5剖面（绘图）

在地面残存城墙的北侧清理剖面，剖面宽约1.6米，堆积分两大层：

第1层：表土层，黄褐色土，土质松散，结构疏松，厚约56～84厘米，呈水平堆积。

第2层：夯土层，根据土色的不同，可分为十一小层。夯土质地较为紧密。

第2a层，灰褐色夯土，厚约0～4厘米，大致呈水平堆积。

第2b层，红褐色花夯土，厚约0～10厘米，大致呈水平堆积。

第2c层，深灰褐色夯土，厚约4～10厘米，大致呈水平堆积。

第2d层，灰褐色夯土，厚约0～12厘米，大致呈锅底形堆积。

第2e层，黄褐色花夯土，夹杂有灰土和红色黏土，厚约6～10厘米，呈锅底形堆积。

第2f层，灰褐色夯土，厚约6～8厘米，呈锅底形堆积。

第2g层，灰褐色夯土，夹杂有黄土块，厚约5～10厘米，呈锅底形堆积。

第2h层，红褐色花夯土，厚约4～12厘米，呈锅底形堆积。

第2i层，浅灰褐色花夯土，厚约15～20厘米，呈锅底形堆积。

第2j层，浅灰褐色夯土，厚约12～16厘米，呈锅底形堆积。

第2k层，黄褐色夯土，厚约0～15厘米，堆积由西向东略有倾斜。

以下为红褐色生土层，质地纯净，结构紧密，无包含物。

Figure Ⅰ.4.21　Cross-section of Wall Section 5 (drawing).

Located on the northern part of wall Section 5 that still stands above ground. 1.6 m wide. Divided into two strata:

Stratum 1: Topsoil, yellowish-brown soil, loose and crumbly texture, 56-84 cm, horizontal accumulation.

Stratum 2: Rammed earth layer. Can be subdivided into 11 substrata based on the color of the soil. Tightly compacted texture.

Stratum 2a: Greyish-brown rammed earth, 0-4 cm, horizontal accumulation.

Stratum 2b: Reddish-brown rammed earth, 0-10 cm, horizontal accumulation.

Stratum 2c: Dark greyish-brown rammed earth, 4-10 cm, horizontal accumulation.

Stratum 2d: Greyish-brown rammed earth, 0-12, lenticular accumulation.

Stratum 2e: Yellowish-brown rammed earth, grey and red clay inclusions, 6-10 cm, lenticular accumulation.

Stratum 2f: Greyish-brown rammed earth, 6-8 cm, lenticular accumulation.

Stratum 2g: Greyish-brown rammed earth, yellow clumpy inclusions, 5-10 cm, lenticular accumulation.

Stratum 2h: Reddish-brown rammed earth, 4-12 cm, lenticular accumulation.

Stratum 2i: Light greyish-brown rammed earth, 15-20 cm, lenticular accumulation.

Stratum 2j: Light greyish-brown rammed earth, 12-16 cm, lenticular accumulation.

Stratum 2k: Yellowish-brown rammed earth, 0-15 cm, lenticular accumulation.

Below is red brown virgin soil, homogeneous and firmly textured, no inclusions.

图Ⅰ.4.22　外城墙10（东—西）

Figure Ⅰ.4.22　Outer wall Section 10 (East-West).

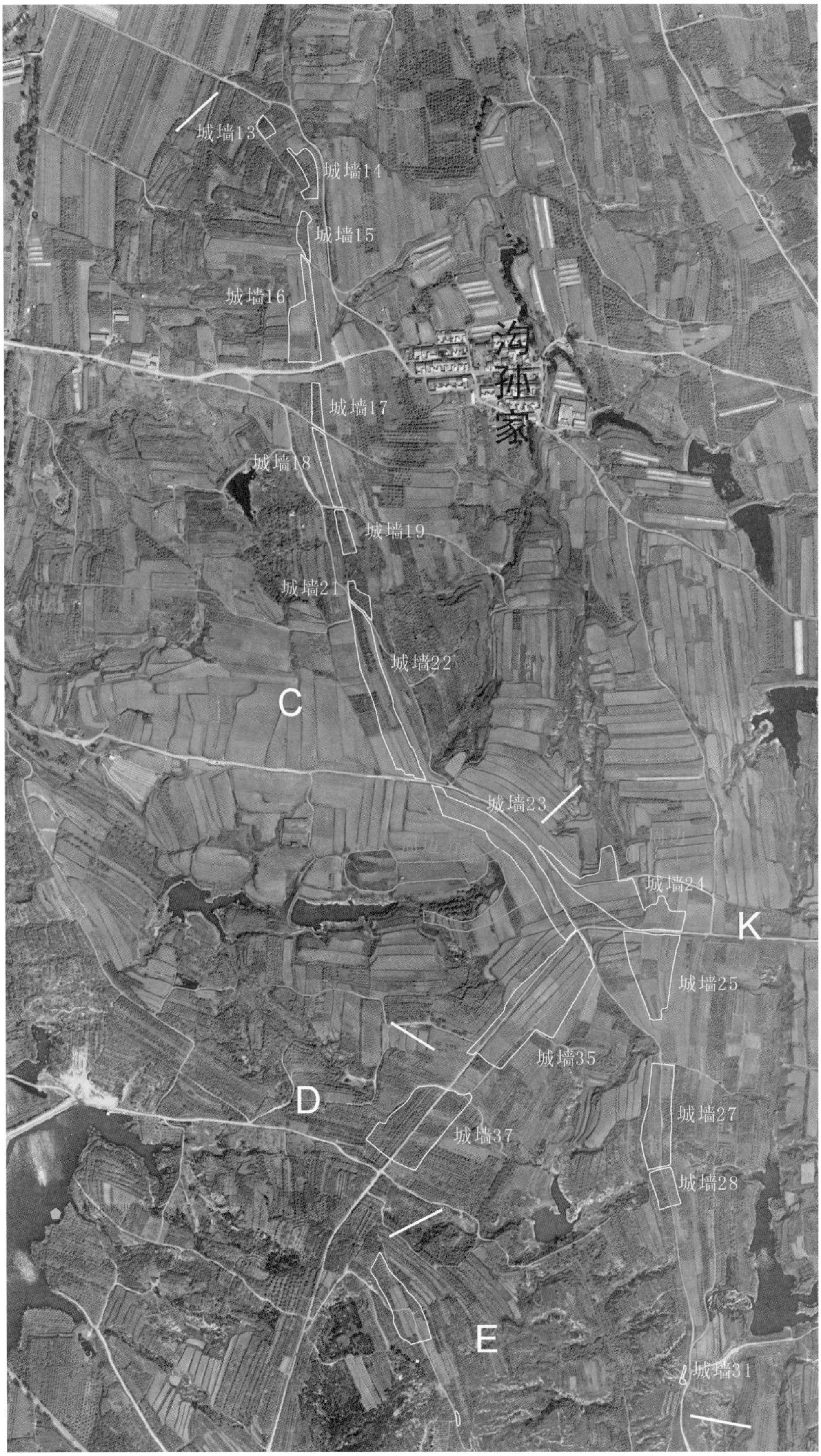

图Ⅰ.4.23　C、D、E及K段城墙

Figure Ⅰ.4.23　Rows C, D, E, and K Wall Sections.

图Ⅰ.4.24　外城墙13（西北—西南）
Figure Ⅰ.4.24　Outer Wall Section 13 (NW-SE).

图Ⅰ.4.25　外城墙13剖面
Figure Ⅰ.4.25　Cross-section of Wall Section 13.

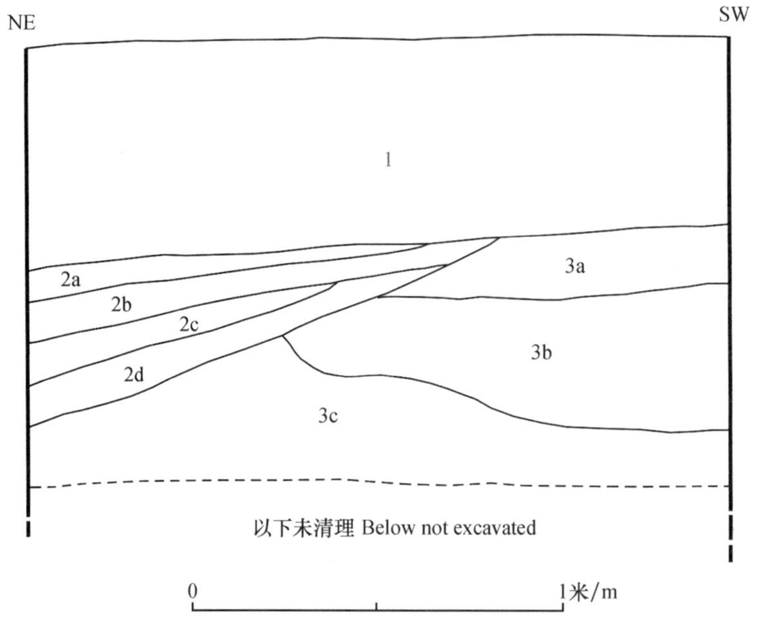

图Ⅰ.4.26　外城墙13剖面

剖面位于城墙13的东北角，宽约1.9米。剖面上堆积分三大层：

第1层：表土层，黄褐色土，土质松散，结构疏松，厚约54～58厘米，大致呈水平堆积。

第2层：夯土层，主要位于东侧上部，呈西向东倾斜堆积。堆积分为四小层。

第2a层，黄褐色花夯土，厚约0～10厘米，呈西向东倾斜堆积。

第2b层，浅黄褐色花夯土，夹杂有白色淤土，厚0～10厘米，呈西向东倾斜堆积。

第2c层，浅黄褐色花夯土，夹杂有白色淤土，厚0～12厘米，呈西向东倾斜堆积。

第2d层，灰褐色花夯土，厚0～10厘米，呈西向东倾斜堆积。

第3层：夯土层，上部位于西部，下部在整个清理面中均有分布。堆积大致呈水平堆积，堆积分为三小层。

第3a层，灰褐色夯土，夹杂有黄色土块，厚约18厘米，大致呈水平堆积。

第3b层，深灰褐色夯土，夹杂有白色淤土，厚约20～40厘米，大致由东向西倾斜堆积。

第3c层，灰褐色夯土，夹杂有少量黄色土块。由于其未清理至底部，其具体厚度不明。经钻探向下尚有厚约20厘米的夯土至生土。

Figure Ⅰ.4.26　Cross-section of Wall Section 13.

Located on the northeast corner of wall Section 13. 1.9 m wide, it exhibits three distinct strata:

Stratum 1: Topsoil, yellowish-brown, texture loose and crumbly, 54-58 cm, horizontal accumulation.

Stratum 2: Rammed earth, primarily in the eastern part, west to east sloping accumulation. Can be divided into four substrata.

Stratum 2a: Yellowish-brown composite soil, 0-10 cm, west to east sloping accumulation.

Stratum 2b: Light yellowish-brown composite soil, white mud inclusions, 0-10 cm, west to east sloping accumulation.

Stratum 2c: Light yellowish-brown composite soil, white mud inclusions, 0-12 cm, west to east sloping accumulation.

Stratum 2d: Greyish-brown composite soil, yellow clumpy inclusions, 18 cm, horizontal accumulation.

Stratum 3: Rammed earth layer, the upper stratum located in the western half of the cross-section, the lower stratum located across the bottom of the entire cross-section. Mostly level, divided into three substrata.

Stratum 3a: Greyish-brown rammed earth, yellow clumpy inclusions, 18 cm, horizontal accumulation.

Stratum 3b: Dark greyish-brown rammed earth, white mud inclusions, 20-40 cm, west to east sloping accumulation.

Stratum 3c: Greyish-brown rammed earth, small amounts of clumpy yellow inclusions. Thickness unknown. 20 cm below this stratum is virgin soil.

图Ⅰ.4.27　外城墙14西边（南—北）
Figure Ⅰ.4.27　Outer Wall Section 14, western edge (South-North).

图Ⅰ.4.28　外城墙15（南—北）
Figure Ⅰ.4.28　Outer Wall Section 15 (South-North).

图Ⅰ.4.29　外城墙16东侧边缘（北—南）

Figure Ⅰ.4.29　Outer Wall Section 16, eastern edge (facing South).

图Ⅰ.4.30　外城墙16（南—北）

Figure I.4.30　Outer Wall Section 16 (South-North).

图Ⅰ.4.31 外城墙16剖面A
Figure Ⅰ.4.31 Outer Wall Section 16, cross-section A.

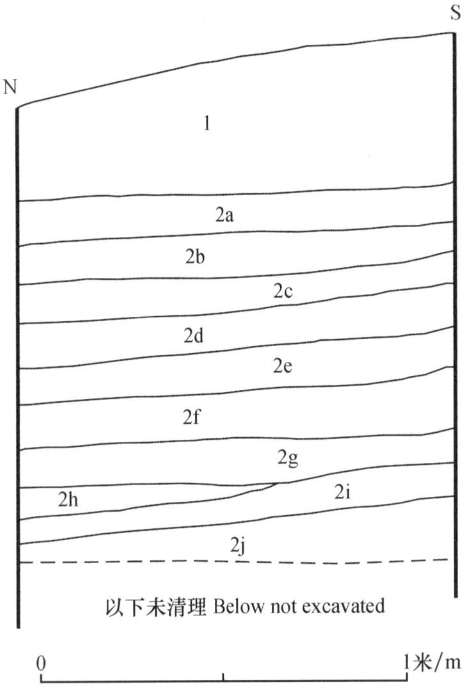

图Ⅰ.4.32 外城墙16剖面A（绘图）

位于地面留存城墙上的北侧，距北端约13米，距南侧的剖面B约23米。剖面宽约1.2米。其堆积分两层：

第1层：表土层，黄褐色土，土质松散，结构疏松，厚约60～100厘米，呈水平堆积。

第2层：夯土层，分为10个小夯层。

第2a层：灰褐色夯土，夹杂较多的红褐色黏土，厚约10～12厘米，大致由南向北倾斜堆积。

第2b层：灰褐色夯土，夹杂的红褐色黏土较少，厚约10～12厘米，大致由南向北倾斜堆积。

第2c层：灰褐色花夯土，夹杂的红褐色黏土较少，厚约8～10厘米，大致由南向北倾斜堆积。

第2d层：灰褐色花夯土，夹杂稍多的红褐色黏土，厚约12厘米，大致由南向北倾斜堆积。

第2e层：灰褐色花夯土，厚约9～12厘米，大致由南向北倾斜堆积。

第2f层：灰褐色花夯土，颜色较深，厚约12～16厘米，大致呈水平堆积。

第2g层：灰褐色花夯土，夹杂有黑土和红黏土，厚约8～12厘米，大致呈水平堆积。

第2h层：灰褐色夯土，夹杂的红黏土较多，厚约0～8厘米，呈由南向北倾斜堆积。

第2i层：灰褐色夯土，厚约6～10厘米，呈由南向北倾斜堆积。

第2j层：深灰褐色夯土。经钻探，以下还有厚50厘米的夯土。

以下仍为夯土，未向下清理。

Figure Ⅰ.4.32 Outer Wall Section 16, cross-section A (drawing).

Located on the north side of wall Section 16, 13 m from the northern end and 23 m from cross-section B to its south. The cross-section measures 1.2 m in width, and is composed of two main strata:

Stratum 1: Topsoil, yellowish-brown in color, loose and crumbly texture, 60-100 cm, horizontal accumulation.

Stratum 2: rammed earth, composed of ten substrata.

Stratum 2a: Greyish-brown rammed earth, reddish-brown clay inclusions, 10-12 cm, south to north sloping accumulation.

Stratum 2b: Greyish-brown rammed earth, small amount of reddish-brown clay inclusions, 10-12 cm, south to north sloping accumulation.

Stratum 2c: Greyish-brown rammed earth, small amount of reddish-brown clay inclusions, 8-10 cm, south to north sloping accumulation.

Stratum 2d: Greyish-brown rammed earth, reddish-brown clay inclusions, 12 cm, horizontal accumulation.

Stratum 2e: Greyish-brown rammed earth, 9-12 cm, south to north sloping accumulation.

Stratum 2f: Greyish-brown rammed earth, dark colored, 12-16 cm thick, horizontal accumulation.

Stratum 2g: Greyish-brown rammed earth, black and red clay inclusions, 8-12 cm, horizontal accumulation.

Stratum 2h: Greyish-brown rammed earth, red clay inclusions, 0-8 cm, south to north sloping accumulation.

Stratum 2i: Greyish-brown rammed earth, 6-10 cm, south to north sloping accumulation.

Stratum 2j: Dark greyish-brown rammed earth. Below is another 50 cm thick layer of rammed earth.

The rammed earth continues farther down, but we did not expose the cross-section beyond this.

图Ⅰ.4.33 外城墙16剖面B

Figure Ⅰ.4.33 Outer Wall Section 16, cross-section B.

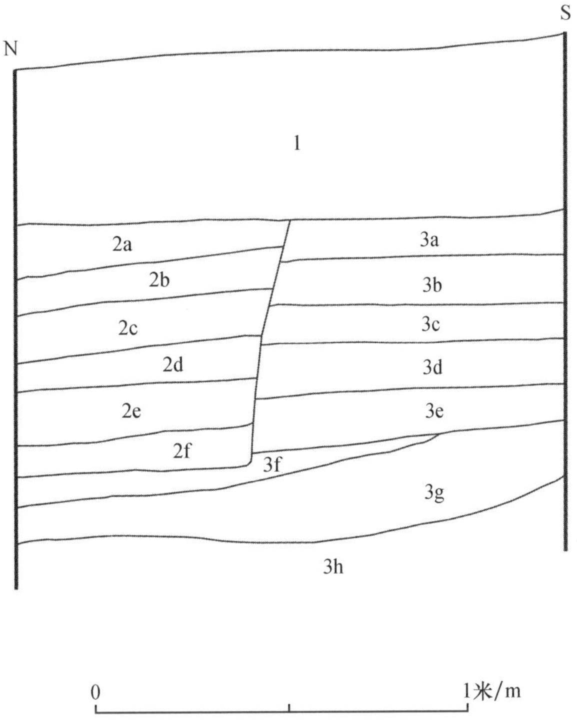

图Ⅰ.4.34　外城墙16剖面B（绘图）

位于地面留存城墙的南侧，距南端约25米，距北侧的剖面A约23米。剖面宽约1.5米。城墙采取了分段夯筑的手段，堆积分三大层。

第1层：表土层，黄褐色垫土，结构松散，质地疏松，厚约42～48厘米，呈水平堆积。

第2层：夯土层，仅分布在北侧，打破了第3层夯土。整体厚度约86厘米，堆积的质地稍松散。分为六个小夯层。

第2a层：灰褐色夯土，夹杂有红褐色黏土，厚约7～14厘米，大致由南向北倾斜堆积。

第2b层：灰褐色夯土，夹杂有红褐色黏土，厚约10厘米，大致由南向北倾斜堆积。

第2c层：灰褐色花夯土，夹杂的红褐色黏土较多，厚约12厘米，大致由南向北倾斜堆积。

第2d层：灰褐色花夯土，夹杂的红褐色黏土较少，厚约8～12厘米，大致由南向北倾斜堆积。

第2e层：红褐色花夯土，厚约12～14厘米，大致呈水平堆积。

第2f层：深灰褐色夯土，厚约8～10厘米，大致呈水平堆积。

第3层：夯土层，仅分布在南侧和下部，为第2层打破，分为八个小夯层。

第3a层：灰褐色夯土，夹杂有红黏土，厚约10厘米，大致呈水平堆积。

第3b层：灰褐色夯土，夹杂有少量红黏土，厚约13厘米，大致呈水平堆积。

第3c层：灰褐色夯土，夹杂有少量红黏土，厚约10厘米，大致呈水平堆积。

第3d层：灰褐色夯土，夹杂有较多的红黏土，厚约12～14厘米，大致呈水平堆积。

第3e层：灰褐色夯土，夹杂有较多的红黏土，厚约10～14厘米，大致由南向北倾斜堆积。

第3f层：灰褐色花夯土，夹杂有黄土块，厚约0～5厘米，大致呈由南向北倾斜堆积。

第3g层：灰褐色花夯土，夹杂有灰白色淤土，厚约10～24厘米，大致呈由南向北倾斜堆积。

第3h层：黄褐色夯土，夹杂有灰白色淤土。经钻探，以下有厚约30厘米的夯土。

Figure Ⅰ.4.34　Outer Wall Section 16, cross-section B (drawing).

Located towards the south side of wall Section 16, 25 m from the southern end, and 23 m from cross-section A. It measures 1.5 meters wide. The cross-section suggests that wall was built section by section, and its accumulated soil layers can be divided into three strata.

Stratum 1: Topsoil, yellowish-brown in color, loose and crumbly texture, 42-48 cm, horizontal accumulation.

Stratum 2: Rammed earth, covers northern side, intercuts Stratum 3, can be subdivided into six substrata. Measures 86 cm in total thickness, with a loose texture.

Stratum 2a: Greyish-brown rammed earth, reddish-brown clay inclusions, 7-14 cm, south to north sloping accumulation.

Stratum 2b: Greyish-brown rammed earth, reddish-brown clay inclusions, 10 cm, south to north sloping accumulation.

Stratum 2c: Greyish-brown composite rammed earth, abundant reddish-brown clay inclusions, 12 cm, south to north sloping accumulation.

Stratum 2d: Greyish-brown composite rammed earth, abundant reddish-brown clay inclusions, 8-12 cm, south to north sloping accumulation.

Stratum 2e: Reddish-brown composite rammed earth, 12-14 cm, horizontal accumulation.

Stratum 2f: Dark grey composite rammed earth, 8-10 cm, horizontal accumulation.

Stratum 3: Rammed earth layer, covers bottom portion of the southern side, intercut by Stratum ②, subdivided into eight substrata.

Stratum 3a: Greyish-brown Rammed earth, red clay inclusions, 10 cm, horizontal accumulation.

Stratum 3b: Greyish-brown Rammed earth, small amount of red clay inclusions, 13 cm, horizontal accumulation.

Stratum 3c: Greyish-brown Rammed earth, small amount of red clay inclusions, 10 cm, horizontal accumulation.

Stratum 3d: Greyish-brown Rammed earth, abundant red clay inclusions, 12-14 cm, horizontal accumulation.

Stratum 3e: Greyish-brown Rammed earth, abundant red clay inclusions, 10-14 cm, south to north sloping accumulation.

Stratum 3f: Greyish-brown Rammed earth, clumpy yellow inclusions, 0-5 cm, south to north sloping accumulation.

Stratum 3g: Greyish-brown Rammed earth, greyish-white mud inclusions, 10-24 cm, south to north sloping accumulation.

Stratum 3h: Yellowish-brown Rammed earth, greyish-white mud inclusions. Depth unknown. At least 30 cm more rammed earth continues beneath this stratum, but we did not expose it in the cross-section.

图Ⅰ.4.35　外城墙17东侧边界（南—北）

Figure Ⅰ.4.35　Outer Wall Section 17, eastern edge (South-North).

图Ⅰ.4.36　外城墙18（南—北）
Figure Ⅰ.4.36　Outer Wall Section 18 (South-North).

图Ⅰ.4.37　外城墙19（南—北）
Figure Ⅰ.4.37　Outer Wall Section 19 (South-North).

图Ⅰ.4.38　外城墙21（北—南）

Figure Ⅰ.4.38　Outer Wall Section 21 (North-South).

图Ⅰ.4.39　外城墙22（南—北）

Figure Ⅰ.4.39　Outer Wall Section 22 (South-North).

图Ⅰ.4.40　外城墙23（东南—西北）

Figure Ⅰ.4.40　Outer Wall Section 23 (SE-NW).

图Ⅰ.4.41　外城墙35及地面石块

Figure Ⅰ.4.41　Outer Wall Section 35 with human modified stones on the surface nearby.

图Ⅰ.4.42　外城墙35剖面A内铁器
Figure Ⅰ.4.42　Outer Wall Section 35, iron object in Cross-section A.

图Ⅰ.4.43　外城墙35剖面A
Figure Ⅰ.4.43　Outer Wall Section 35, Cross-section A.

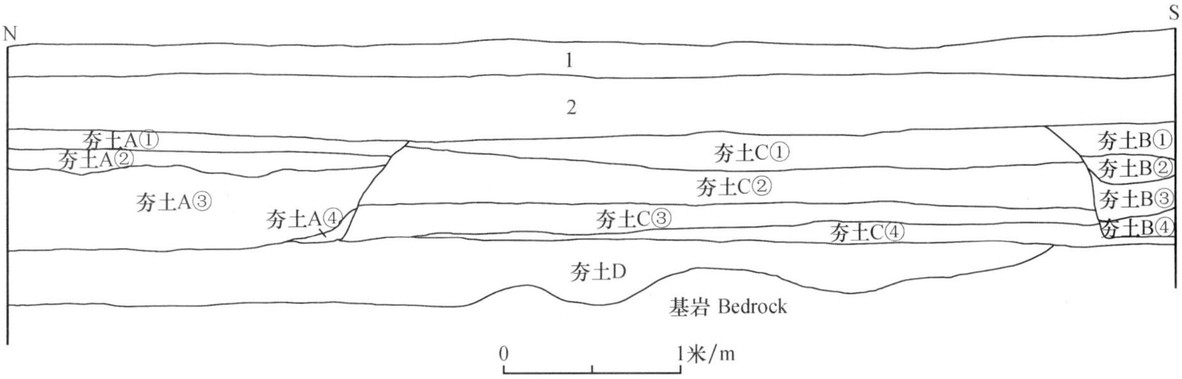

图Ⅰ.4.44　外城墙35剖面A（绘图）

位于城墙的西侧南部，在乡间路的东侧沟中。剖面呈东北-西南走向，长约6.7米，高约1.5米。

剖面堆积分四层：

第1层：为表土层，呈红褐色，质地疏松，厚约14～24厘米，呈水平堆积。

第2层：为淤土层，呈灰白色，质地细腻、疏松，厚约26～36厘米，呈水平堆积，内出有小铁器一件。

第3层：为城墙的夯土堆积，厚约76～98厘米。根据其堆积情况和早晚关系，可分为四个部分，分别编号为夯土A、夯土B、夯土C和夯土D。他们的层位关系为：

夯土A—┐
　　　　├—夯土C——夯土D
夯土B—┘

夯土A位于北侧，南侧打破夯土C，下部叠压着夯土D。夯土A厚约58～68厘米。夯土A从上而下可分为四小层，大致呈水平堆积。

夯土A①：灰褐色花夯土，质地较硬，厚约10厘米。

夯土A②：浅黄褐色花夯土，质地较硬，厚约6～14厘米，大致呈水平堆积。

夯土A③：大量砂石含少量灰褐色泥土夯打而成，质地较为疏松，厚约38～46厘米，呈水平堆积。

夯土A④：深灰褐色花夯土，局促在夯土A打破夯土C的一角。其土质土色与夯土C②层的土质土色一致，较有可能是夯土A打破夯土C时将一部分堆积破坏所致。此层堆积厚约0～18厘米。

夯土B位于南侧，北侧打破夯土C，下部叠压着夯土D。夯土B厚约44厘米。夯土B从上而下可分为四小层，大致呈水平堆积。

夯土B①：灰褐色花夯土，质地较硬，厚约20厘米。

夯土B②：浅灰褐色花夯土，质地较硬，厚约8～14厘米，略呈锅底形堆积。

夯土B③：大量砂石含少量灰褐色泥土夯打而成，质地较为疏松，厚约20厘米，略呈锅底形堆积。

夯土B④：黄褐色夯土，质地较硬，厚约10～16厘米，呈水平堆积。

夯土C位于中部，北侧和南侧分别为夯土A和夯土B打破，下部叠压夯土D。夯土C厚约52～62厘米。夯土C的夯土均为稍经夯打，硬度次于其他三块夯土。夯土C可分为四小层，呈水平堆积。在夯土C中出有少量陶片。

夯土C①：黄褐色花土，略发红，稍经夯打，厚约2～20厘米。其堆积由北向南倾斜。

夯土C②：深灰褐色花土，稍经夯打，厚约10～32，堆积大致水平。

夯土C③：黄褐色花土，稍经夯打，厚约8～10厘米。堆积略由南向北倾斜堆积。

夯土C④：浅黑褐色花土，稍经夯打，厚约0～14厘米，呈水平堆积。

夯土D位于底部，叠压在夯土A和夯土C下方。其为红褐色大花夯土，质地较粘，极为坚硬。由于下部基岩高度起伏，其厚度不一，厚约20～38厘米。

以下为基岩层。

Figure Ⅰ.4.44　Outer Wall Section 35, Cross-section A (drawing).

Located on the western part of wall Section 35, in a trench along the east side of a country road. It is oriented northeast to southwest, and measures 6.7 m long and 1.5 m high. The cross-section can be divided into four strata:

Stratum 1: Topsoil, reddish-brown soil, loose texture, 14-24 cm, horizontal accumulation.

Stratum 2: Riverine sediment layer, greyish-white, fine and smooth texture, slightly loose, 26-36 cm, horizontal accumulation, contained a small iron implement.

Stratum 3: Rammed earth layer, 76-89 cm. Based on the superposition of soil layers and their relative time of formation, this stratum can be divided into four parts, labeled Rammed Earth A, Rammed Earth B, Rammed Earth C, and Rammed Earth D. Their relationships are as follows:

Rammed Earth A—┐
├—Rammed Earth C—— Rammed Earth D
Rammed Earth B—┘

Rammed Earth A: Located on the north side, the south side intercuts Rammed Earth C; underneath it is Rammed Earth D. Rammed Earth A is 58-68 cm thick and can be subdivided into four substrata, overall horizontal accumulation.

Rammed Earth A①: Greyish-brown composite rammed earth, hardened texture, 10 cm.

Rammed Earth A②: Light yellowish-brown composite rammed earth, hardened texture, 6-14 cm, horizontal accumulation.

Rammed Earth A③: Rammed earth with abundant gravel and greyish-brown soil inclusions, slightly loose texture, 38-46 cm, horizontal accumulation.

Rammed Earth A④: Dark greyish-brown composite rammed earth, located in a corner where rammed Earth A intercuts Rammed Earth C. Same color and texture as Rammed Earth C ②, probably the result of Rammed Earth C being damaged and re-accumulated here. 0-18 cm thick.

Rammed Earth B: Located on the south side; the north side intercuts Rammed Earth C while beneath this layer is Rammed Earth D. 44 cm thick and can be subdivided into four substrata; horizontal accumulation.

Rammed Earth B①: Greyish-brown composite rammed earth, slightly hardened texture, 20 cm.

Rammed Earth B②: Light greyish-brown composite rammed earth, slightly hardened texture, 8-14 cm, lenticular accumulation.

Rammed Earth B③: Rammed earth with abundant gravel and greyish-brown soil inclusions, slightly loose texture, 20 cm, lenticular accumulation.

Rammed Earth B④: Yellowish-brown rammed earth, hardened texture, 10-16 cm, horizontal accumulation.

Rammed Earth C: Located in the middle of the wall section, the northern and southern sides are intercut by Rammed Earth A and Rammed Earth B, and beneath this layer is Rammed Earth D. 52-62 cm. Rammed Earth C lightly rammed, less hardened than the other three layers. Can be subdivided into four substrata, horizontal accumulation. We found small amounts of pottery within this layer.

Rammed Earth C①: Yellowish-brown composite rammed earth, reddish tint, lightly rammed, 2-20 cm, north to south sloping accumulation.

Rammed Earth C②: Dark greyish-brown composite rammed earth, lightly rammed 10-32 cm, horizontal accumulation.

Rammed Earth C③: Yellowish-brown composite rammed earth, 8-10 cm, south to north slightly sloping accumulation.

Rammed Earth C④: Light dark-brown composite earth, lightly rammed, 0-10cm, horizontal accumulation.

Rammed Earth D: Located toward the bottom of the cross-section, overlaid by rammed Earth A and Rammed Earth C. Reddish-brown composite rammed earth, hardened, clayey texture. Due to the undulation of the underlying bedrock, its thickness is not uniform, from 20-38 cm. Beneath this is stratum is bedrock.

图Ⅰ.4.45　外城墙35剖面B

Figure Ⅰ.4.45　Outer Wall Section 35, Cross-section B.

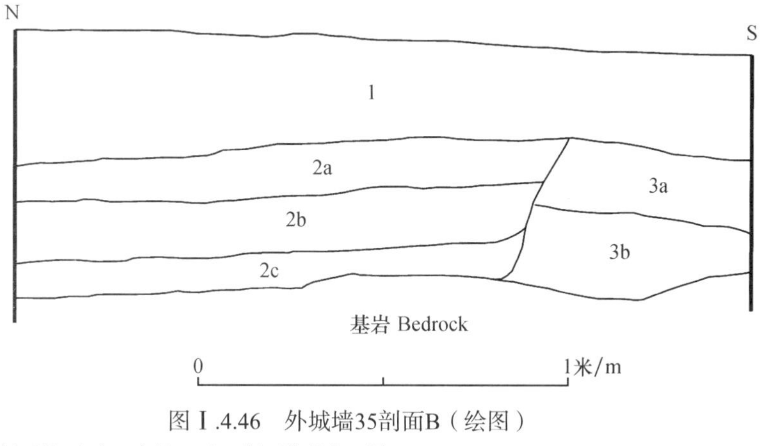

图Ⅰ.4.46　外城墙35剖面B（绘图）

剖面B南距剖面A约91米。剖面约2米宽，高约0.7米。剖面堆积分三层：

第1层，表土层，呈红褐色，疏松，厚24～36厘米，水平堆积。

第2层，城墙堆积，位于北侧。厚约36厘米，由南向北略倾斜。分为三小层：

第2a层，浅黄褐色夯土，含少量砂石，厚约10厘米。

第2b层，灰褐色夯土，质地较硬，厚约16厘米。

第2c层，深灰褐色夯土，夹杂有红褐色黏土和少量砂石，质地较硬，厚约6～10厘米。

第3层，城墙堆积，位于南侧，厚20～30厘米，分为两小层：

第3a层，灰褐色夯土，内含有大量砂石。厚约20厘米，由北向南倾斜堆积。

第3b层，深灰褐色夯土，含红褐色粘土和少量碎砂石，质地较坚硬。厚10～22厘米。

以下为基岩层。

Figure Ⅰ.4.46 Outer Wall Section 35, Cross-section B (drawing).

Cross-section B is located 91 m south of Cross-section A. It measures 2 m wide and 0.7 m in height. The cross-section can be divided into three strata:

Stratum 1: Topsoil, loose, spongey, reddish-brown in color; 24-36 cm thick; horizontal accumulation.

Stratum 2: Wall remains, situated towards the northern end; 36 cm thick and slightly sloped. Divided into three substrata:

Substratum 2a: Light yellow-brown rammed earth; small amount of sandy inclusions; 10 cm thick.

Substratum 2b: Grey-brown rammed earth; hardened texture; 16 cm thick.

Substratum 2c: Dark grey-brown rammed earth; reddish-brown granular and sandy inclusions; hardened texture; 6-10 cm thick.

Stratum 3: Wall remains, situated towards the southern end; 20-30 cm thick. Divided into two substrata:

Substratum 3a: Grey-brown rammed earth; large amounts of sandy inclusions; 20 cm thick; slightly sloped from north to south.

Substratum 3b: Dark grey-brown rammed earth; reddish-brown granular and sandy inclusions; 10-22 cm thick.

Beneath stratum 3 we encountered bedrock.

图Ⅰ.4.47 外城墙35地面上的绳纹砖

Figure Ⅰ.4.47 Outer Wall Section 35, cord-impressed brick on surface.

图Ⅰ.4.48　外城墙37（南—北）
Figure. Ⅰ.4.48　Outer Wall Section 37 (facing North).

图Ⅰ.4.49　外城墙37东侧边缘（南—北）
Figure. Ⅰ.4.49　Outer Wall Section 37, eastern edge (facing North).

图Ⅰ.4.50　E、F段城墙

FigureⅠ.4.50　Outer Wall Rows E and F.

图Ⅰ.4.51　外城墙39（北—南）
Figure Ⅰ.4.51　Wall Section 39 (facing South).

图Ⅰ.4.52　外城墙44—46远景（南—北）
Figure Ⅰ.4.52　Wall Sections 44-46 (facing North).

图Ⅰ.4.53　外城墙49（北—南）
Figure Ⅰ.4.53　Wall Section 49 (facing South).

图Ⅰ.4.54　外城墙51（东北—西南）
Figure Ⅰ.4.54　Wall Section 51 (NE-SW).

图Ⅰ.4.55　外城墙56、58所在台地，东向西
Figure Ⅰ.4.55　Terrace of Wall Sections 56 and 58 (facing West).

图Ⅰ.4.56　G、H列城墙
Figure Ⅰ.4.56　Outer Wall Rows G and H.

图Ⅰ.4.57　外城墙80（北—南）
Figure Ⅰ.4.57　Wall Section 80 (facing South).

图Ⅰ.4.58　外城墙82（东—西）
Figure Ⅰ.4.58　Wall Section 82 (facing West).

图Ⅰ.4.59　外城墙83内侧（北—南）

Figure Ⅰ.4.59　Wall Section 83 inner side (facing South).

图Ⅰ.4.60　外城墙83外侧（北—南）

Figure Ⅰ.4.60　Wall Section 83 outer side (facing South).

图Ⅰ.4.61　外城墙84（北—南）
Figure Ⅰ.4.61　Wall Section 84 (facing South).

图Ⅰ.4.62　外城墙85（南—北）
Figure Ⅰ.4.62　Wall Section 85 (facing North).

图Ⅰ.4.63　外城墙87西侧边缘（南—北）
Figure Ⅰ.4.63　Wall Section 84 (facing North).

图Ⅰ.4.64　外城墙88地面残存城墙及剖面A
Figure Ⅰ.4.64　Cross-Section A on Wall Section 88, above-ground level.

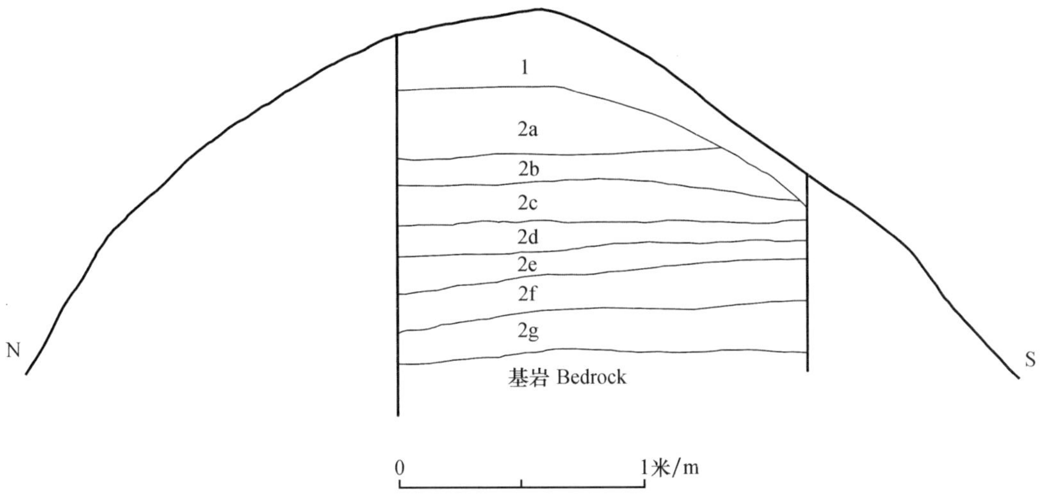

图Ⅰ.4.65　外城墙88剖面A剖面图

剖面A位于城墙西北角残存的地面城墙上。剖面A南北长约1.7米。剖面上堆积分为两大层。

第1层，表土层，灰褐色土，土质疏松，含砂，厚约12～30厘米，呈坡状堆积。

第2层，夯土层，为城墙堆积，厚约108厘米，大致呈水平堆积。夯层可分为七层。

第2a层，灰褐色夯土，夹杂黄土，内含砂粒，厚约0～30厘米，呈水平堆积。此层原可以进一步分层，但由于堆积太干，难以清理。

第2b层，黄褐色夯土，夹杂灰褐土，内含砂粒，厚约10～18厘米，呈水平堆积。

第2c层，灰褐色夯土，夹杂大量淤土夯打，呈黄褐色，含砂粒、大量木炭、红烧土颗粒，厚约8～18厘米，大致呈水平堆积。

第2d层，深灰褐色夯土，夹杂少量淤土，含零星碎陶片。红烧土颗粒、木炭颗粒、砂粒等，厚约8～14厘米，由南向北倾斜堆积。

第2e层，深灰褐色夯土，含红烧土颗粒，木炭颗粒等、砂粒等，厚约8～18厘米，由南向北倾斜堆积。

第2f层，浅灰褐色夯土，含零星烧土颗粒，炭粒，粗砂等，厚约14～18厘米，由南向北倾斜堆积。

第2g层，黄褐色夯土，含砂石较多，厚约12～22厘米，由南向北倾斜堆积。

以下为基岩层。

Figure Ⅰ.4.65　Wall Section 88, standing above ground surface, Cross-section A.

Cross-section A, located in the southwest corner of wall Section 88 standing above ground surface that still stands above the ground surface. 1.7 m south to north. Can be divided into two strata:

Stratum 1: Topsoil, greyish-brown soil, loose texture, sandy inclusions, 12-30 cm, sloping accumulation.

Stratum 2: Rammed earth layer, wall construction, 108 cm, horizontal accumulation. Can be subdivided into seven substrata.

Stratum 2a: Greyish-brown rammed earth, yellow sandy inclusions, 0-13 cm, horizontal accumulation. Can probably be further subdivided, but due to the dryness of the soil texture, we were not able to discern further.

Stratum 2b: Yellowish-brown rammed earth, greyish-brown soil and sandy inclusions, 10-18 cm, horizontal accumulation.

Stratum 2c: Greyish-brown rammed earth, greyish-brown clay, yellow soil, fine sand, charcoal, and burned red granule inclusions, 8-18cm, horizontal accumulation.

Stratum 2d: Dark greyish-brown rammed earth, small amounts of clay, shattered pottery, red burned granules, charcoal, and sand inclusions, 8-14 cm, south to north sloping accumulation.

Stratum 2e: Dark greyish-brown rammed earth, red burned granules, charcoal, and sandy inclusions, 8-18 cm, south to north sloping accumulation.

Stratum 2f: Light greyish-brown rammed earth, burned soil granules, ash, coarse sand inclusions, 14-18 cm, south to north sloping accumulation.

Stratum 2g: Yellowish-brown rammed earth, abundant sandy inclusions, 12-22 cm, south to north sloping accumulation.

Beneath this stratum is bedrock.

图Ⅰ.4.66　外城墙88剖面B

Figure Ⅰ.4.66　Wall Section 88, Cross-section B.

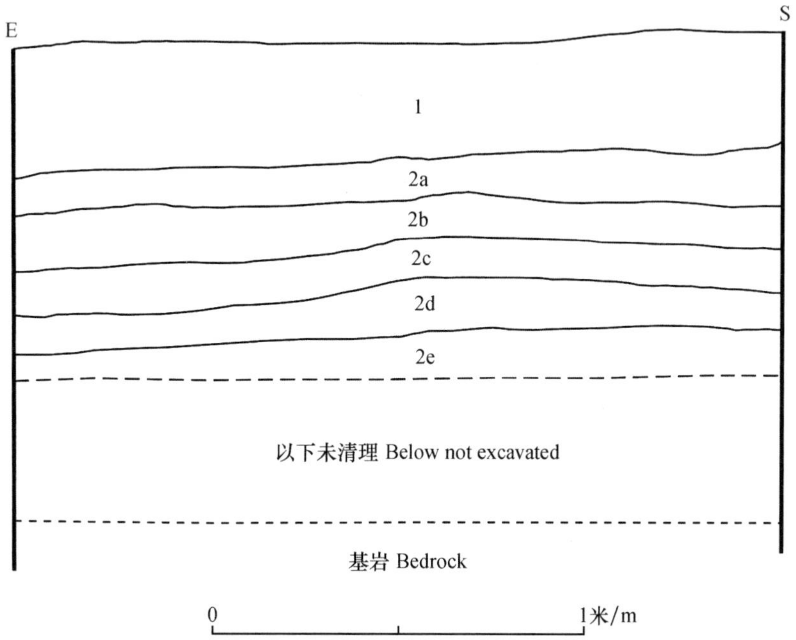

图Ⅰ.4.67　外城墙88剖面B剖面图

位于城墙北侧偏东部，距剖面A约107米。剖面东西长约2.1米。剖面堆积分为两大层，各层基本呈水平堆积。

第1层，表土层，灰褐色土，土质疏松，含砂，厚约30厘米，呈水平堆积。

第2层，夯土层，为城墙堆积，清理厚度约58厘米，大致呈水平堆积。夯层可分为五层。

第2a层，浅灰褐色花夯土，夹杂灰土块、粗砂，砂性大，厚约10～18厘米，大致呈水平堆积。

第2b层，浅灰褐色花夯土，夹杂灰土块较少，含粗砂，砂性大，厚约10～14厘米，略呈由西向东倾斜堆积。

第2c层，浅灰褐色夯土，含砂较少，质地较硬，厚约10厘米，略呈由西向东倾斜堆积。

第2d层，黄褐色夯土，含少量灰土，质地较硬，含砂少，厚约10～14厘米，大致呈水平堆积。

第2e层，黄色夯土，质地较纯，结构较硬，含砂少。此层未清理到底，经钻探，下还有40厘米的夯土堆积至基岩。

Figure Ⅰ.4.67　Wall Section 88, Cross-section B.

Located on the north side toward the eastern part of wall Section 88, 107 meters from Cross-section A. 2.1 m from east to west. Can be divided into two large strata; overall horizontal accumulation.

Stratum 1: Topsoil, greyish-brown in color, loose texture, sandy inclusions, 30 cm, horizontal accumulation.

Stratum 2: Rammed earth layer, wall construction, 58 cm, horizontal accumulation. Can be subdivided into five substrata.

Stratum 2a: Light greyish-brown rammed earth, grey clumpy soil, coarse sand inclusions, 10-18 cm, horizontal accumulation.

Stratum 2b: Light greyish-brown rammed earth, small amounts of grey clumpy soil, coarse sandy inclusions, 10-14 cm, west to east sloping accumulation.

Stratum 2c: Light greyish-brown rammed earth, small amounts of sandy inclusions, slightly hardened texture, 10 cm, west to east sloping accumulation.

Stratum 2d: Yellowish-brown rammed earth, small amounts of grey soil and sandy inclusions, slightly hardened texture, 10-14 cm, horizontal accumulation.

Stratum 2e: Yellowish-brown rammed earth, clean and fine, slightly hardened texture, small amounts of fine sandy inclusions. We did not expose this layer to the bottom; based on coring bedrock is 40 cm below this stratum.

图Ⅰ.4.68　I、J列城墙

Figure Ⅰ.4.68　Outer Wall Rows I and J.

图Ⅰ.4.69　外城墙24剖面
Figure Ⅰ.4.69　Wall Section 24, cross-section.

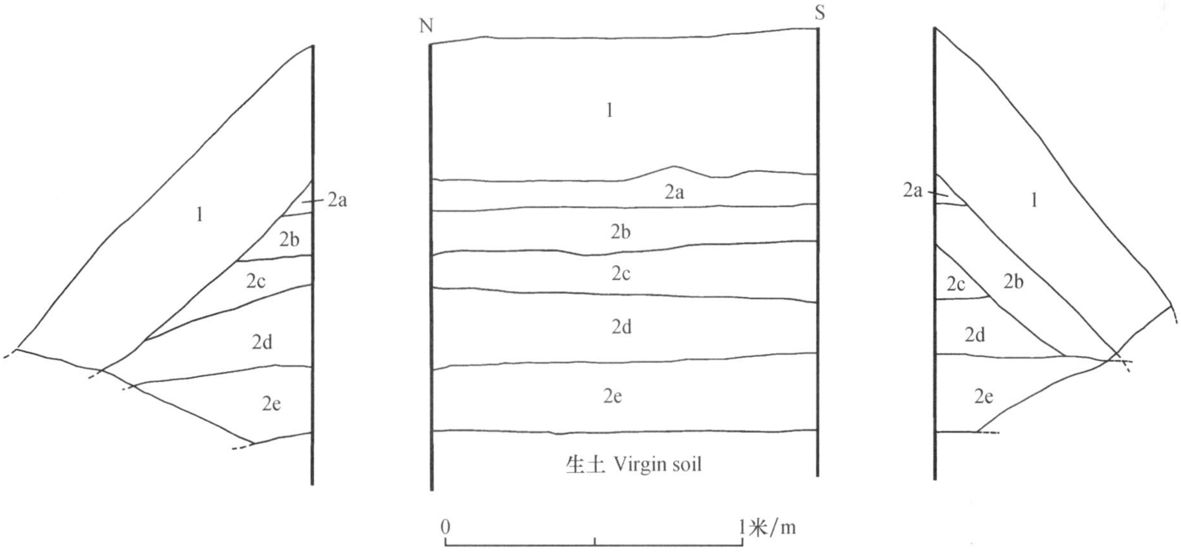

图Ⅰ.4.70　外城墙24剖面图

剖面位于东段和西段城墙相接的断崖上，呈南北向，长约1.3米，高约1.3米。剖面堆积分两层：

第1层，为表土层，呈红褐色，质地疏松，厚约50厘米，呈水平堆积。

第2层，为城墙的夯土堆积，厚约84～88厘米，呈水平堆积。从剖面上看，其可分为5个小夯层。

第2a层，浅灰褐色夯土层，质地稍松，厚约8～14厘米，呈水平堆积。

第2b层，灰褐色花夯土，质地较硬，厚约12～16厘米，呈水平堆积。

第2c层，黄褐色花夯土，质地较硬，厚约12～20厘米，大体呈水平堆积。

第2d层，黄褐色花夯土，内夹杂有红褐色土块，质地坚硬，厚约18～28厘米，大体呈水平堆积。

第2e层，红褐色花夯土，内夹杂有灰土粒和大量碎砂石，质地坚硬，厚约22～26厘米，呈水平堆积。

以下为生土层，红褐色粘土，夹杂大量碎砂石。

Figure Ⅰ.4.70　Wall Section 24, Cross-section.

Located on the exposed cliff-side connecting the east and west parts of Wall Section 24. It has a north-south orientation and is 1.3 m wide and 1.3 m high. The accumulated soil layers can be divided into three strata:

Stratum 1: Topsoil, reddish-brown soil, loose texture, 50 cm, horizontal accumulation.

Stratum 2: Rammed earth, 84-88 cm, horizontal accumulation; can be subdivided into five substrata:

Stratum 2a: Light greyish-brown rammed earth, slightly loose texture, 8-14 cm, horizontal accumulation.

Stratum 2b: Greyish-brown rammed earth, hardened texture, 12-15 cm, horizontal accumulation.

Stratum 2c: Yellowish-brown composite rammed earth, hardened texture, 12-20 cm, overall horizontal accumulation.

Stratum 2d: Yellowish-brown composite rammed earth, reddish-brown clumpy inclusions, solid texture, 18-28 cm, overall horizontal accumulation.

Stratum 2e: Reddish-brown composite rammed earth, grey soil granules and abundant gravel inclusions, solid texture, 22-26 cm, horizontal accumulation.

Beneath this stratum is virgin soil, reddish-brown clay, with abundant gravel inclusions.

图Ⅰ.4.71　外城墙25东边（北—南）

Figure Ⅰ.4.71　Wall Section 25 eastern side (facing South).

图Ⅰ.4.72　外城墙31（南—北）
Figure Ⅰ.4.72　Wall Section 31 (facing North).

图Ⅰ.4.73　外城墙31剖面
Figure Ⅰ.4.73　Wall Section 31, cross-section.

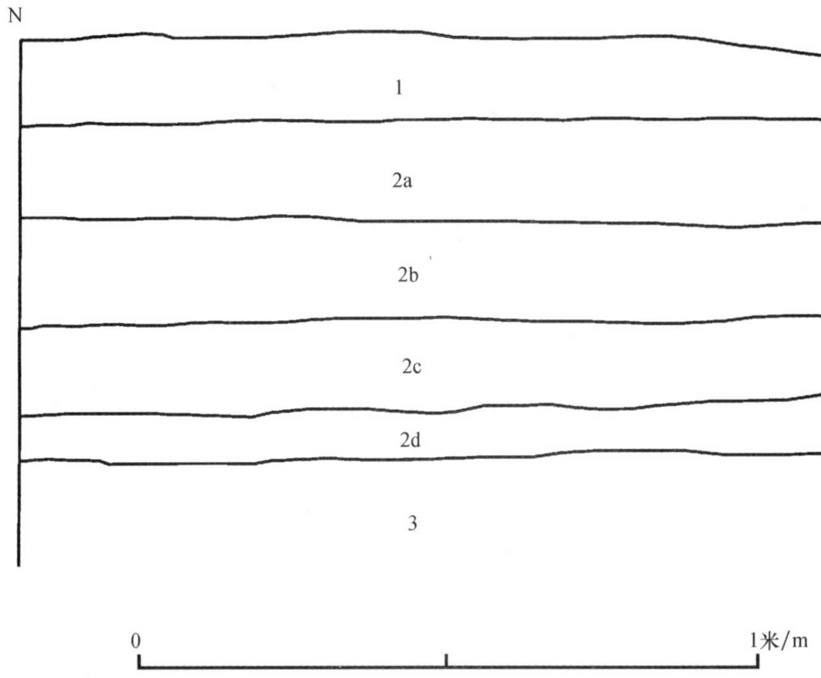

图Ⅰ.4.74　外城墙31剖面图

剖面位于城墙中部，长约1.4米，深约0.6米，堆积分为两大层。

第1表土层，质地松软，厚约14厘米，呈水平堆积。

第2夯土层，质地较硬，厚约54厘米，分为四小夯层，均水平夯筑。夯打质量一般。

第2a层，灰白色夯土，是将淤土进行夯打形成，略有硬度，稍接触即成粉末。夯层厚约16厘米。

第2b层，浅黄褐色夯土，质地较硬，厚约16厘米。

第2c层，浅灰褐色夯土，略发红，质地硬，厚约14厘米。

第2d层，黄褐色夯土，质地较硬，厚约8～10厘米。

以下为生土层，红褐色黏土，土质较硬。

Figure Ⅰ.4.74　Wall Section 31, Cross-section.

Located in the center of the wall section. 1.4 m wide and 0.6 m deep. The earth accumulation can be divided into two layers:

Stratum 1: Topsoil, soft, 14 cm thick, horizontal accumulation.

Stratum 2: Rammed earth layer, firm, 54 cm thick. This layer can be further divided into four sublayers, all in horizontal formation. Rammed earth of ordinary quality.

Stratum 2a: Greyish-write rammed earth, worked riverine deposit, relatively hard. It disintegrates easily into powder when touched. 16 cm thick.

Stratum 2b: Light yellowish rammed earth, relatively hard, 16 cm thick.

Stratum 2c: Light grey rammed earth, a little reddish, firm, 14 cm thick.

Stratum 2d: Yellowish-brown rammed earth, relatively firm, 8-10 cm thick.

Below: Natural virgin soil, reddish-brown, firm.

图Ⅰ.4.75　外城墙77（东北—西南）
Figure Ⅰ.4.75　Wall Section 77 (NE-SW).

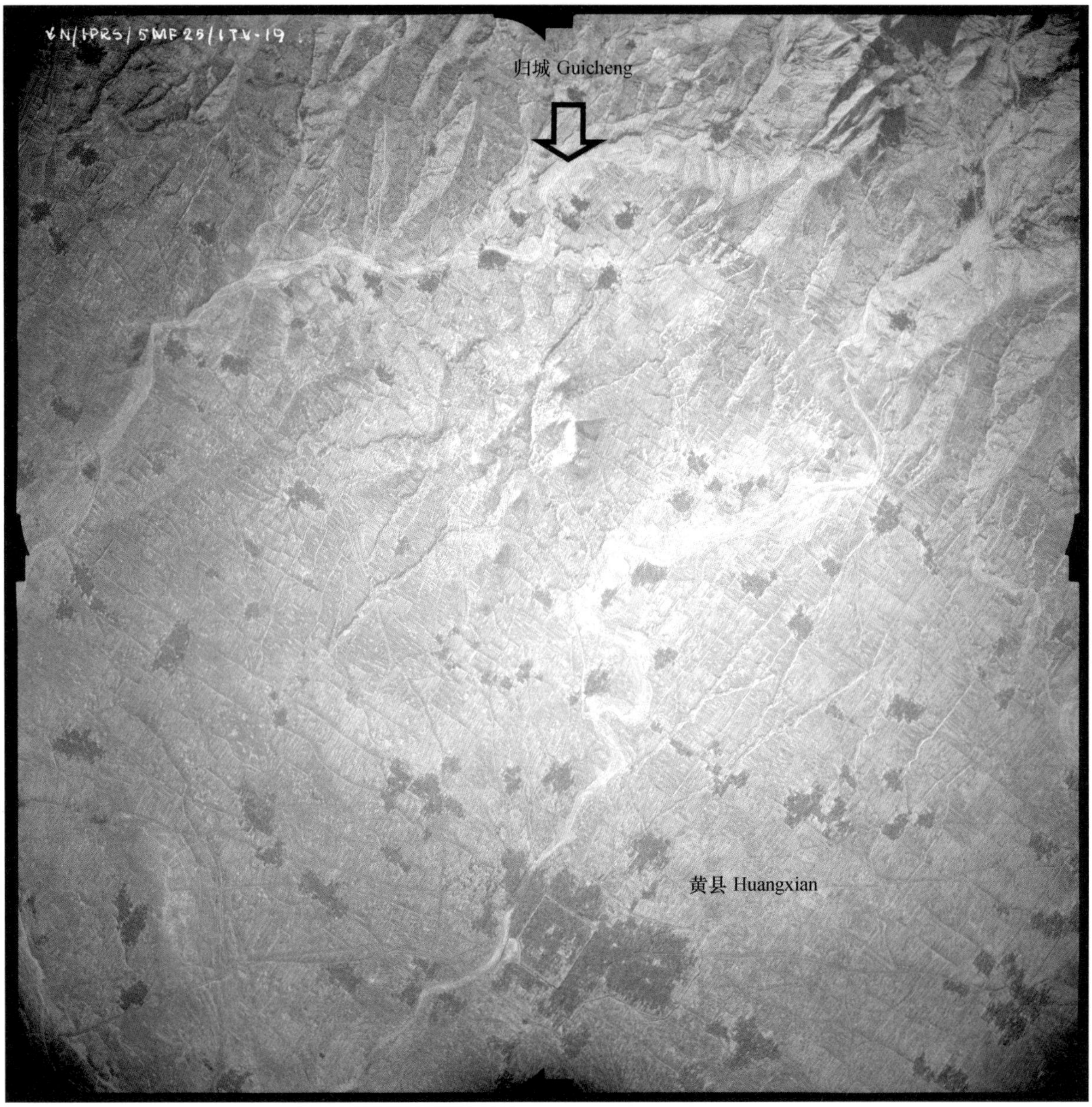

图Ⅰ.4.76　1945年2月美国空军航拍黄县—归城地区照片
美国国家档案馆提供：Aerial no. NWCS-373-Can ON061275-1PRS-5MF25-1TV018/019
Figure Ⅰ.4.76　Aerial photo of the Huangxian-Guicheng area by the U.S. Army Air force, February 1945.
Courtesy the U.S. National Archives and Records Administration (NARA): Aerial no. NWCS-373-Can ON061275-1PRS-5MF25-1TV018/019.

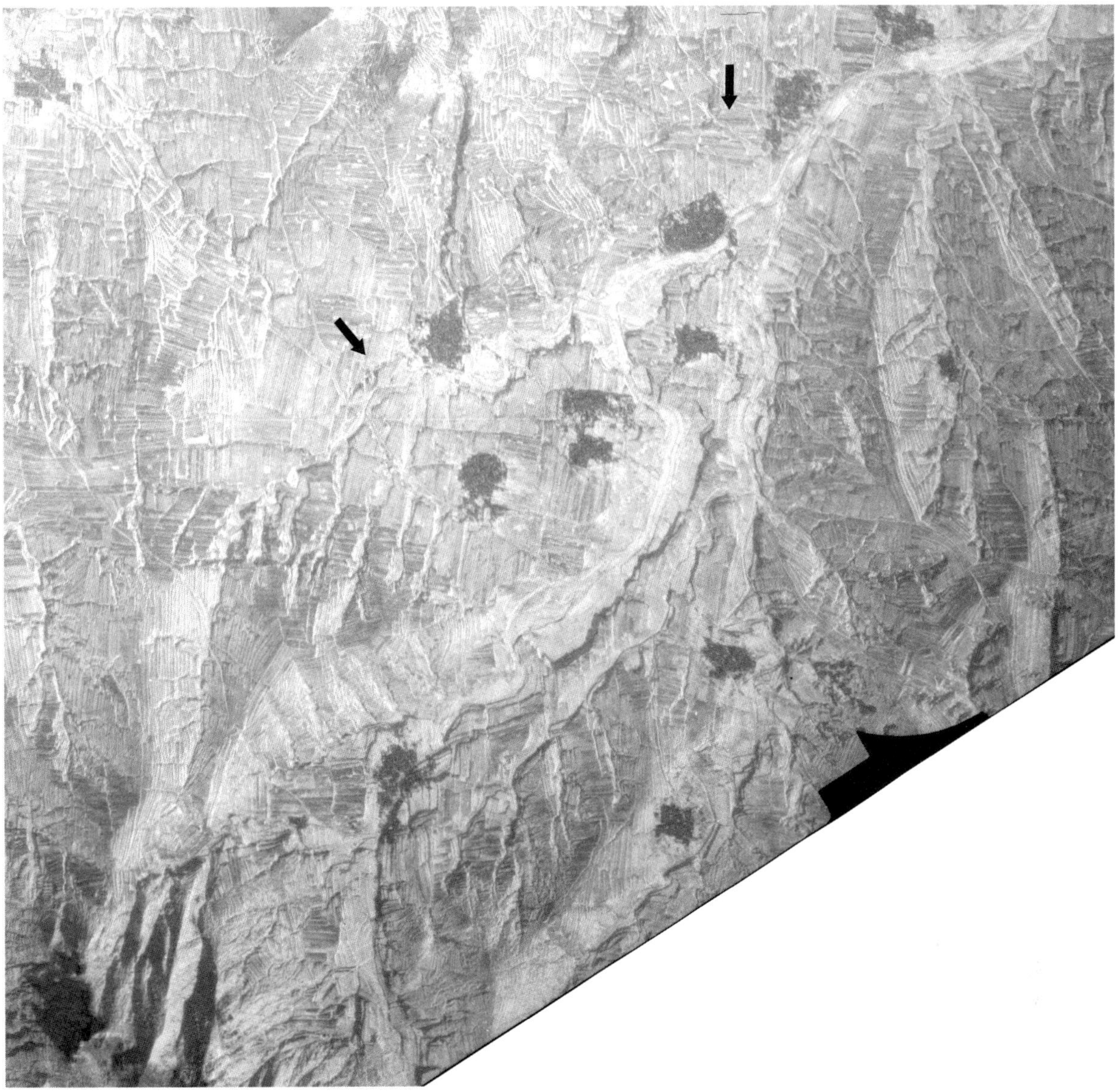

图Ⅰ.4.77　1945年2月美国空军航拍照片上显示的归城外城

美国国家档案馆提供：Aerial no. NWCS-373-Can ON061275-1PRS-5MF25-1TV018/019（局部）

Figure Ⅰ.4.77　The outer wall of Guicheng on aerial photo by the U.S. Army Air force, February 1945.

Courtesy the U.S. National Archives and Records Administration (NARA): Aerial no. NWCS-373-Can ON061275-1PRS-5MF25-1TV018/019 (partial).

Chapter 4: Survey of the Outer Wall

Tang Jinqiong

Section 1: Topography

The outer wall of Guicheng is situated on the northern side of Mount Lai, in a zone of mountain foothills surrounding the boundaries of the inner city. Mount Lai is also known as "Mount Zhilai," and runs east to west across the southern part of the Longkou city; it is located between 120°31′ ~ 120°44′ longitude and 37°27′ ~ 37°36′ latitude, comprises 102.27 km^3 in surface area, and is 619 m above sea level at its highest elevation. Guicheng is located in the foothills of the eastern section of Mount Lai. Here Mount Lai extends in a "U" shape, with two sharp ends connecting with the remnants of the outer wall to form a complete enclosure. The slopes of Mount Lai are steep and precipitous, difficult to surmount, and they form a natural barrier to the south of Guicheng. One kilometer to the northwest of the city lies a small mountain called Mount Fenghuang, which is approximately 120 m above sea level (Map. I.4.1) (Pls. 1-2).

Guicheng is located in the Huangshui River Valley, in the upper reaches of a tributary waterway called the Yaque River. The city is crisscrossed by three streams. The western-most of these originates in the foothills to the west of Jiangjia Village, passes Beishan Village, and flows into the city south of the village; from there it flows in a southwest to northeast direction across the northern portion of the city site. The other two streams both originate north of Mount Lai and flow northwards past the eastern portion of the site. The westernmost of these latter two streams is the main waterway of the Yaque River; it originates south of Miaozhou Village in Mount Lai's northern foothills, and flows past the western sides of the villages of Miaozhou and Miaoma into the borders of the city site. Within the city, it flows from the southwest, near Caojia Village, towards the northeast, until it reaches the southeastern part of Jiangjia village, where it changes direction and flows northwards. The original branch waterway passes the eastern side of Heping Village (eastern side of the inner city), southwest of Dongjia Village, and converges with a different tributary that flows south of Beishan Village at a point west of Dongjia Village and north of Heping Village. This tributary then flows towards the northeast and would normally empty into the Huangshui River 7 km northeast of Guicheng, near Zhaoliu Village. However, a newly constructed reservoir southeast of Jiangjia Village blocks this tributary, and instead a newly opened drainage system diverts this waterway into the eastern stream. The original riverbeds of this tributary, located east of Heping Village and southwest of Dongjia Village, are dry, having been turned into farmlands. An elementary school is currently situated in the middle of one of these riverbeds directly west of Dongjia Village. The eastern stream originates southwest of Dongchijia Village, winds first northwards, then eastwards, then northwards again by way of the eastern side of Dongjia Village; it converges with the Yaque River east of Dayujia Village. Because of the changes discussed above, this latter tributary has become the primary waterway through Guicheng's interior (Pls. 5-6).

The terrain of the Guicheng city site is comprised of foothills. The inner city is situated on an elevated plateau at the geographical center of site. This plateau is between 73 and 79 m above sea level, and is the largest and highest platform in the topography within the boundaries of the site. For more details regarding this plateau, see Chapter 2. The terrain of the outer city is composed of gradient slopes and rolling hills that average between 56 and 125 m above sea level. The northern part of the outer city is higher in overall elevation than the southern part, and overall the hills follow a southwest to northeast direction, with the southern end reaching the base of Mount Lai and the northern end turning to follow an east to west direction. The terrain of the lower slopes of the mountain is riverine. The banks of the eastern and central streams are gentle and have few steep slopes, indicating that they were formed through a long process, and their currents are stable in this area. The earth of the graded terraces on both sides of these rivers is thick and favorable for human habitation, and has yielded important anthropogenic deposits over the years. In 1969, two bronze vessels, the Qi *zun* and Qi *you*, were discovered at Xiaoliuzhuang, which is located on the graded terraces of the western bank of the Yaque River. In 1951, the Ji bronze assemblage was unearthed on the graded terraces on the eastern bank of one of the Yaque's tributaries, north of Nanbu Village. The terrain at the edges of the site are composed of mountain ridges, especially around the eastern portion of the outer wall, which is situated directly atop very sandy soil and is not very favorable for human habitation.

Section 2: Survey Methods

1) Previous survey methods and results

In 1973, Yantai Prefecture's Committee for the Management of Cultural Relics organized an archaeological and cultural relics team to carry out a survey of the Guicheng city site; this survey was able to determine that the site comprised an inner and outer area delineated by two circles of walls. The survey also determined that the outer wall was constructed along the summit of hilltops surrounding the basin on all four sides. The northern wall was located halfway up the southern slope of Mount

Fenghuang while the southern wall sat halfway up the northern slope of Mount Lai as well as on the summit of neighboring Mount Maling to the west. The eastern and western walls were found to have been constructed atop the summits of rolling hills and ridges; the circumference of the outer wall was determined to be 10 km.

Due to both natural and anthropogenic erosion and destruction over a long period, most of the outer wall has been destroyed. Through survey, three preserved above-ground sections and four preserved subterranean sections of the outer wall were discovered. The first of the above-ground sections is located within the village of Beishan; it has a local toponym of "Houchengzi (Rear City Wall)." This section of wall lies on a southwest to northeast axis and measures 75 m long, 4 m wide (the southern end of this section has been cut away for house construction), and 4 m high. The layers of rammed earth in this section of wall measure 12 to 15 cm in thickness. The second above-ground section is located 300 m northwest of Dayu Village, and has the local toponym of "Tianjiaying." It is a flattened hillock 12 m long, 9 m wide, and 1.5 m high, with rammed earth layers measuring 6 to 10 cm in thickness. The third above-ground section is 500 m east of Dongjia Village and is locally known as "Juandingshang." This section has a north-south orientation and measures 56 m long, 9 m wide, and 2 m high. These three above-ground sections were reconfirmed during this most recent iteration of fieldwork at the Guicheng site, and were assigned them numbers 97, 5, and 16, respectively.

According to the survey in 1973, the rammed earth of these sections of the outer wall is relatively pure, comprised of reddish-brown virgin soil taken from the immediate environs. The rammed earth layers measure 12 to 15 cm in thickness, and were made using a circular ram 8 cm in diameter; the construction was determined to be haphazard, without any uniformity of spacing. Bronze arrowheads were unearthed within a section near Beishan Village.

The results of the 1973 survey offered important information for the recent fieldwork, and served as the starting point for further investigations of the outer city of Guicheng. However, the 1973 survey was only an initial outline sketch of the general framework of the outer wall, and its details were obscure. Although they published a map of the site after this survey, many spots on that map were connected by dotted lines only, especially the sections of outer wall on the south side, indicating that they are merely reconstructions on paper based on what was known at the time. This map is also rather simplistic, being only a surface schematic lacking any evidence of georeferencing, making it difficult to measure the natural conditions for any portion of the site. Because of this, it was necessary to conduct a more thorough survey of the outer walls, including a reexamination and re-measurement of the previously discovered sections.

2) Survey methods and strategies

The present survey was carried out using a combination of coring and surface survey. First, we determined a rough approximation of where of the outer wall would be through surveying the topography of site, then we took core samples along this route and used the presence of rammed earth to indicate actual location. After finding the exact location of the outer wall we used the cores to determine the boundaries and formation processes for the site (Pl. 16). For parts of the wall that were better preserved and accessible, we exposed cross-sections in order to determine the condition of the deposit (Pl. 17: 1). We assigned individual numbers to each section of wall uncovered, leaving appropriate gaps in the seriation corresponding to gaps between wall sections. We did this in the hope that these gaps in the wall would be discovered through other means in the future and thus add to the current numbers. After we thoroughly examined each wall section, we plotted their locations on the Google Earth map, and used GPS to determine their geographical coordinates. Meanwhile, we used a total-station to cross-reference them in the detailed mapping of the outer city (Pl. 17: 2). Because the Guicheng site is continuously being damaged and eroded, we wanted this survey to leave as thorough and complete a record of the site as possible for posterity.

This present survey took place over two seasons of work. The first season took place from November 9 through 26 in 2007, and began with the survey of wall Section 1 near the east side of Beishan Village and ended with wall Section 22 near the southeast of Dongjia Village. During the survey we determined the course of the eastern part of the north wall and the northern part of the eastern wall (Figs. Ⅰ.4.1- Ⅰ.4.3). The second season took place from June 21 to July 13 in 2008, and was a continuation of the work begun in 2007. Starting from Section 22, we continued our survey moving southwards and arrived at the foot of Mount Lai, where we discovered that the southern part of the city might have used the slope of the mountain for protection and therefore did not require the construction of a wall, therefore, further survey beyond this point would be difficult. Thereupon, we went back to wall Section 1 and surveyed west in a counter-clockwise direction starting with wall Section 99 and moving through Beishan Village, past the eastern side of a cement factory, down to the west of Caojia Village, finally stopping at the foot of the mountain in the south. In this way we completed a survey of the total circumference of the outer wall. In 2009 we discovered another section of wall near the southern foot of the mountain (wall Section 77) and added it to our records.

Section 3: Outer Wall Survey Results

1) Overall condition of the outer wall

We discovered through these two seasons of survey a total of forty-five sections of the outer wall (among these four sections are still visible above-ground), and we assigned them numbers from 1 to

99 (with gaps in the seriation left for future discovery) (Map I.4.1). Overall, the outer wall is irregular in shape, forming an elongated oval. Its northernmost edge reaches Beishan Village and the hills to the north of Dayujia Village; its eastern edge reaches the hills to the east of Dongjia, Dongchijia, and Nanbu Villages, and its southern edge reaches the foot of Mount Lai; finally, its western edge reaches the hilly area to the west of Caojia Village. The outer city of Guicheng includes the eight modern villages of Beishan, Dayujia, Dongjia, Heping, Guijiang (or Jiangjia), Nanbu, Dongchijia, and Caojia; they are distributed in different survey areas, respectively labeled Area 2, Area 3, Area 4, Area 5, Area 8, Area 9, Area 12, Area 13, Area 15, and Area 16. The outer city measures 3.6 km north to south, 2.8 km east to west, and it has a surface area of ca. 8 km^2.

The southern end of the western outer wall starts at the foot of the mountain southwest of Caojia Village, first heads east for a bit and then stretches to the northeast along the summits of the hills running up the western side of the village until it reaches the northern part of the ridges. Further north, small sections of the wall were found along the two banks of the Yaque River, indicating that the wall continues to extend north from the ridges. Beginning at Beishan Village, the northern wall runs in a northeasterly direction over the hills located to the north of Beishan and Dayujia Village until it reaches the shore of the Yaque River. There, in the riverbed, it corners and turns southeast towards the eastern wall across the river. The northern part of the eastern wall is situated on the hills east of Dongjia and Heping Villages, and extends in a southeasterly direction. In the southern section, the wall begins to curve, following the natural curvature of the terrain, first turning towards the southeast, then towards the southwest. At this point, the wall splits into two branches; the eastern branch follows the mountains tops extending south on the northern side of Chegezhuang Village, forming a secondary line of the wall. The western branch continues as the main body of the wall crossing through a valley and stretching to the hills to the northwest of Chegezhuang. At this point it turns southwards once again, and after crossing over the highway leading to Shiliangzhen, reaches the hills southeast of Nandun Village in a northeast to southwest orientation, extending straight to the foothills of Mount Lai to the south. Here, it faces the southwest corner of the outer wall to the southwest of Caojia Village to form a complete enclosure. The total length of these three sides of the wall measures ca. 8.15 km.

For the most part, the construction of the outer wall was dependent upon the topography of the hills and mountains, having been built largely upon the summits of hills throughout the area, and extending along the tops of mountain ridges. The most prominent of these are the Row C sections. Wall sections in Row C are found on hilltops to the east of Dongjia and Heping Villages and extend over an area measuring approximately 1,700 m (see below). Systems of defense were also constructed in the valleys between the hills. For instance, in between Row C and Row E wall sections, both of which are located on hilltops, there is a 200 m wide, 20 m deep valley. Wall Section 37 is situated in the middle of the valley, and we believe it to have been deliberately constructed there to form a defensive barrier in the valley.

The measurements of the various sections of the outer wall are not uniform throughout, but average around 40 m in width, with the widest section measuring 100 m (e.g., Section 1), probably because there had been a structure atop this section of wall. The narrowest section measures 5 m in width due most likely to later damage and erosion. The walls were constructed through a process of accumulating and tamping piles of locally sourced virgin soil. The original hilltop soil was sandy in texture and yellow in color, containing copious amounts of brownish-yellow grit. However, in the cross-sections we exposed, we rarely found this type of soil, as the interior of the wall was composed of brownish-yellow or brownish-grey composite rammed earth, which was probably transported from the base of the mountain for construction. We also discovered the use of sediments for the construction of the wall on hilltops, which were probably taken from the riverbeds at the base of the mountain. The remaining rammed earth walls are not uniform in thickness, ranging from 200 cm at their thickest to 5-10 cm at their thinnest. Where the terrain is flat and low, the rammed earth layers were found to be thicker, and where the terrain was higher, they were found to be thinner; there were even sections built by correcting unevenness in the natural terrain.

2) Section-by-section analysis

The forty-five wall sections surveyed over the course of these two field seasons have been divided into eleven rows according to the terrain features that cut through and obstruct them. They are presented and described one-by-one below according to the row orders (Table Ⅰ.4.1).

(1) Row A Wall Sections: This row of wall sections comprises the northern portion of the outer wall that runs along the northern hillocks between Beishan and Dayujia Villages. Its path follows the terrain of these hillocks, and is oriented in a southwest to northeast direction up to the eastern end (wall Section 8) and then turns to run in an east to west direction. This row of the wall measures 1.26 km in total length (Fig. Ⅰ.4.4). The inner facade of the wall is on the inward sloping side of the hill (facing the inner city) which is relatively steep. The terrain outside the wall (facing outwards from the city) is at a lower elevation than the wall itself, but the slope of the terrain is not very steep. This row of outer wall, from west to east, comprises Section 97, Section 99, Section 1, Section 3, Section 4, Section 5, Section 6, and Section 8, which will be discussed one-by-one below.

Wall Section 97: This section forms the western end of Row A and is located in the northern part inside Beishan Village. This section was still visible above the ground surface during the 1973 survey and was known by the local toponym "Houchengzi (Rear City Wall)" (Hereafter, wall sections which were still standing above the ground in 2008 will be specially noted; absence of such notes indicates the descriptions therein are all about subterranean structures). Now the above-ground structure has been destroyed, leaving only a base step behind a modern dwelling that measures 20 m in length, 1.2 m high. Because this section of wall is located within a residential area, the surface around it has already been paved with cement and we were not able to take core samples to determine its size. The rammed earth layers of the section are composed of brownish-grey soil measuring more than 2 m in thickness (Fig. Ⅰ.4.5).

Wall Section 97 is located between Sections 94 and 99. Section 99 is situated northeast of Section 97, and runs along the same line (Fig. Ⅰ.4.6). A large gully runs between these two sections, creating a gap of 91 m wide from east to west. This gully originates to the east of Mount Fenghuang, and runs past the east side of the village in a north-south direction. The sides of the gully are very straight and steep, indicating that it was formed not very long ago. Originally, Sections 97 and 99 were most likely a single continuous piece of wall, but were cut in two by the gully. Wall Section 94 is located 855 m southwest of Section 97. The space between these two wall sections is wide and taken up by Beishan Village, which made it difficult to assess the way in which they might have been connected in the past. Wall Section 94 runs north-south, while Section 97 is oriented southwest to northeast; it is possible that the space between these two sections was occupied by a corner that has now been destroyed.

Wall Section 99: This section is located along the hillocks north of Beishan Village and west of a north-south running country road. The outer facade (northern facade) of the hill in this area slopes gently downwards towards a relatively low elevation; the inner facade (southern facade) is more precipitous and sudden, forming a high downward slope. Damage to this section of wall has been heavy, and there is very little trace of it on the surface, only a thin layer of rammed earth. The remains of the wall are trapezoidal in shape, bordered on the eastern edge by a country road, on the southern side by a 4 m high cliff, on the western side by an earthen plateau on the edge of a drainage gully, and on the north side by a small road running east to west. The section runs roughly southwest to northeast, measuring 135 m from east to west, and varies in width between 6 and 73 m from north to south; the widest end being in the east. The section is oriented to 34° east of north, total surface area measuring 5,300 m^2. The height of the wall varies from east to west. The eastern part is larger and higher and it rests on higher ground, the surface is more flat. The western part abuts the edge of a gully, and is smaller in surface area as well as 4 m lower than the eastern part, the surface of this part is also relatively flat.

Regarding the soil composition of this section, the northern part was found to have a rammed earth deposit measuring 70 cm in thickness. This layer can be divided into two strata; the upper strata is composed of brownish-yellow composite earth while the lower strata is composed of brownish-grey composite earth. They show clear marks of compression by ramming (Pl. 22: 2). Towards the western end of the section, we discovered a layer of brownish-grey composite soil beneath a 20 cm thick layer of rammed clay with sand and rock inclusions. We also discovered an uneven layer of this brownish-grey composite soil near the southern side of the section, close to the base of the cliff; this layer of composite was, for the most part, 40 cm thick, but thinned out to only 10 cm towards the western end. We discovered a 20 cm thick layer of brownish-yellow composite in the low plateau towards the western end of the section. Where the eastern and western portions of the section converge, we found a 2 m high cut that exposes accumulations of rammed earth, showing the original thickness of the rammed layer (Figs. Ⅰ.4.7- Ⅰ.4.8). In the middle part, it was found that at certain points, the wall was built directly on top of bedrock. This suggests that the immediate environs were utilized during construction of the wall, with areas of lower elevation being first leveled off with soil prior to building.

Wall Section 1: This section is located upon the hills to the northeast of Beishan Village, east of a north-south running country road. Its location is relatively high, and the slope on the south side is steep, overlooking the inner city across a number of descending terraces as well as the riverbed. The terrain on the north side is also lower than the wall section, forming a ravine. A gully runs along the foothills around the northeastern corner of the wall, then runs along the east side of the section towards the southeast before emptying into the Yaque River. Section 1 lies on a southwest-northeast axis with an orientation of 80° east of north. Section 1 is located between Sections 99 and 3, together with them forming a line west to east.

This section has been heavily damaged, and the remains are rectangular in shape with the northeastern corner protruding and the northwestern edge receding southwards. It is bordered on the south by a cliff upon the plateau, and on the east by the edge of the gully running across the highest point of the plateau. On the northeast, by the tip of the plateau we also found traces of the wall on lower terraces on either side of this tip. The north side of the wall section stops approximately 2.5-7 m from the edge of the plateau, and on the west, it is bordered by exposed bedrock. The section measures 58-77 m long, and between 86 and 128 m wide from north to south, with the eastern portion being the widest. Total surface area measures 7,222.5 m^2. Aside from the two portions located upon the lower terraces to the section's northeast, the surface of the remains of this section are relatively flat, with a 1 m tall north-south running cliff in the middle that divides the plateau in two (Fig. Ⅰ.4.9).

Core samples revealed a layer of rammed earth throughout the wall section beneath a 30 cm thick layer of topsoil. This rammed earth is of brownish-grey composite soil and bears distinct markings from the ramming tool. Below this layer we found a layer of reddish-brown virgin soil and in some spots we found bedrock. The layer of rammed earth is not uniform in thickness throughout; it is thinner towards the southeast, measuring 70 cm, and thicker towards the north, measuring between 100 and 110 cm. It is particularly thick in the northwest corner, where it reaches 130 cm, and the soil used here is of very high quality. Probably because the bedrock is high towards the western end of the section, the rammed earth in that spot is thinner, measuring only 20-30 cm. The state of the rammed earth layers was determined through the exposure of cross-sections within the wall (Figs. Ⅰ.4.10- Ⅰ.4.13).

Wall Section 3: This section is located on a plateau in between Beishan Village and Dayujia Village toward the north. This plateau is bordered on the east and west by gullies, and on the south it forms a gentle slope overlooking the Yaque River. In its eastern portion, where wall Section 4 is located, the ground is higher. In the north it forms a gentle slope downwards. Overall, this section lies on a southwest to northeast axis, and is oriented to 64° east of north. Section 3 is located northeast of Section 1, the two being separated by 118 m and overlooking each other across the gully. Apparently, Section 3 sits slightly 58 m to the north (measured from their northern edges).

The damage to this wall section has been severe, and the remains are in a “ ” shape, the southwest corner having receded eastward due to modern efforts to level the terrain. It is bordered on the south by a grove of fruit trees and on the north by farmland. The east abuts the base of a slightly raised plateau. The remains of this wall section are preserved as three separate terraces, all of which have flattened tops. The northern terrace is the highest and its surface has been appropriated by farm plots. The southern terrace is subdivided into two pieces: the one to the southeast is large in size but is 0.5 m lower than the northern terrace, and has been turned into an orchard; the one to the southwest is smaller, 1.2 m lower than the former, and has also been converted into farm plots. A modern reservoir has also been dug partway into the southwestern piece. The northern terrace is wider on its western side, measuring 85.5 m from east to west, 24-30.5 m north to south, with a surface area of 2,330 m^2. The southern terrace is also wider on the western side, measuring 106 m from east to west, 18.5-28 m from north to south, and has a total surface area of 2,464.5 m^2. The total surface area of the three pieces together is 4,794.5 m^2. Estimating from these remains, we hypothesized that Wall Section 3 originally measured 134 m long, 59 m wide, and had a total surface area of over 5,906 m^2 (Fig. Ⅰ.4.14).

Core samples from this wall section revealed a layer of rammed earth throughout the wall section beneath a 30 cm thick layer of topsoil. This rammed earth is of brownish-grey composite soil and bears distinct markings from the ramming tool. Below this layer we found a layer of reddish-brown virgin soil, as well as evidence that some portions of the wall were built directly atop bedrock. The thickness of the rammed earth was not uniform throughout, varying between 30 and 80 cm. We exposed two cross-sections on Wall Section 3 for analysis (Figs. Ⅰ.4.15- Ⅰ.4.18; Pl. 24: 2).

Wall Section 4: This section is located atop the middle high ground of the northern plateau between Beishan and Dayujia Villages, northeast of Wall Section 3. It follows a southwest-northeast direction and is oriented to 46° east of north (hereafter “east of north” omitted).

The damage to this section of the wall has been severe, leaving only a “ ”-shaped portion behind. The remains of the wall section are bisected by a small road. It is bordered on the south side by the steep bank of a reservoir, on the west by a ravine cut by a modern road, on the east and south by the edges of another ravine, and finally the northern edge is situated at the center of the plateau. The southeast part of the wall is steep and covered by grasses and brush scrub; the rest of the plateau has been converted into farming plots. The road bisects the wall section; the western part being further divided by a ravine into two smaller pieces with the eastern piece a half-meter higher than the western. The eastern part has also been broken up by a ravine, but here the western piece is half a meter higher than the eastern. The entire wall section measures 53 m long, between 12 and 24 m wide north to south with the western side wider, and has a total surface area of 856 m^2.

Coring samples show a layer of rammed earth 30 cm below topsoil that is composed of loose greyish-brown soil containing granules of burnt red earth. The rammed earth is rather thin, though there are areas where the ramming tool left distinct impressions, and measures between 10 and 20 cm in thickness. Directly below this rammed earth layer is reddish-brown virgin soil.

Wall Section 5: This section is located in the middle-eastern section of the northern plateau between Beishan and Dayujia Villages, 20 m northeast of wall Section 4. The western part is slightly higher and the eastern side is cut by a gully that lies on a north-south axis. The wall section follows a southwest-northeast direction and is oriented to 65°.

The damage to this wall section has been severe, and the remains are in a “ ┌┘ ” shape. These remains are divided into two portions. The southwestern portion is on an area of slightly higher elevation bordered on both sides by a 1m high cliff; the northern side is at the base of this small cliff and the southern side in the middle of the plateau. The northeastern portion of the wall is therefore at a slightly lower elevation and the southeastern corner of the wall exhibits the remains of rammed earth layers on the surface. This above-ground section of wall measures 13 m long, 7 m wide from north to south, and is 1.8 m high. The southwestern portion of wall Section 5 is trapezoidal in shape, measuring 24-33 m north to south, with the eastern side being wider, 27 m from east to west, and has a total surface area of 770 m^2. The northeastern portion is rectangular and measures 19 m east to west, 14 m north to south, and has a total surface area of 266 m^2. In total, Wall Section 5 measures 43 m from east to west, 48 m from north to south, and has a total surface area of 2,064 m^2 (Fig. Ⅰ.4.19).

The rammed earth is composed of hardened, light greyish-brown composite soil with small black granule-size inclusions. This layer of rammed earth is thicker towards the southwest at around 40 cm thick, and thinner towards the northeast, varying between 20 cm and 30 cm in thickness. Directly beneath this rammed earth layer is either reddish-brown virgin soil, or bedrock. We exposed one cross-section during the course of our analysis (Figs. Ⅰ.4.20- Ⅰ.4.21).

Wall Sections 3, 4, and 5 lie on an east-west axis and are located on the same plateau. Section 4 is located in the middle of the line, Section 3 is located 30 m west on lower ground, and there is a gap of 2.5 m between their heights. To the east, Section 5 is separated from Section 4 by 20 m and is 2 m lower. Altogether, the three wall sections are very close to each other and run in the same direction. Although they are disconnected now, we surmise that they originally belonged to a single piece of the outer wall.

Wall Section 6: This section is located at the southern edge of northwestern plateau outside of Dayujia Village. The south side of the plateau abuts the bank of the Yaque River, and forms a gentle slope overlooking it. A north-south gully runs along the western side of the wall while the northern side is level with the surrounding terrain, forming a very gentle incline. The east side of the wall section slopes gently downwards toward the base of the plateau. The entire wall section lies on a southwest to northeast axis and is oriented to 65°. The section overlooks Section 5 to the west across a wide gully, separated by 75 m. It is located on the extension line of Sections 3-4-5.

This wall section has undergone severe damage and erosion, but the remains of the section are rectangular in shape with the eastern side wider than the western side. The northern side of the wall section passes through the middle of the upper plateau; the southern part of the wall section passes through the lower part of the plateau and spreads southwards at the eastern edge. The western side of the wall is 25 m from the gully, while the east side abuts the eastern edge of the country road. The wall section forms two plateaus of different elevation, upper and lower, with a height difference of 1 m. The southeastern portion of the wall has been converted into farming plots, while the rest is woodland. Both upper and lower parts of the wall are flattened on top. The section measures 107 m east to west, varies between 27 and 39 m north to south, is wider at the eastern end, and has a total surface area of 3,530 m^2.

The wall section is composed of compacted brownish-grey rammed earth with red granule-sized inclusions. While coring in the western part, we discovered a thick layer of this rammed earth measuring between 150 and 200 cm beneath a 30 cm thick layer of topsoil. We also found an exposed area of rammed earth measuring 20 cm thick on the cliff to the east of the country road, and discovered that beneath the soil, the rammed earth layer continued on for another 80 cm, making the entire thickness of this layer 1 m.

Wall Section 8: This wall section is situated north of Dayujia Village, in a relatively low-lying area. To the west, the terrain is at a higher elevation, forming a gentle incline towards the village; to the north, the terrain is higher, and to the southeast is the Yaque River. The wall lies on an east-west axis with an orientation of 90°.

This wall section has been severely eroded, and the remains are roughly rectangular in shape, but missing the northeastern corner. It is bordered on its north and south sides by farmland, and on its west side by the base of a cliff upon which there is a stand of poplar trees. The terrain of the wall begins in the west and inclines towards the east, forming several terraces approximately half a meter in height with sheer drop-offs; farther to the east of these plateaus, the wall section slopes downwards. It measures 150 m east to west, and varies between 13 and 50 m wide north to south. The eastern end of the wall is narrower due to damage at the northeast corner, and the total surface area of the section is 6,000 m^2.

The section is composed of hardened greyish-brown tamped earth with chunky black inclusions measuring 20-30 cm in thickness.

We discovered evidence of lake deposits composed of very sticky, greyish-black mixed soil bearing abundant evidence of water-formed rust on both sides of the eastern end of this wall section. To the east of the wall section we also found a large area of lake deposits composed of mixed soil containing water-formed rust and large quantities of fine sands, below which we found a layer of very sticky brownish soil reaching as deep as 2 m. This suggests that this part of the wall section had been broken through by a waterway at some point in the past, but we were unable to determine the exact date of this waterway.

(2) Row B Wall Sections: Comprises only wall Section 10.

Wall Section 10. This wall section is situated in the middle of the Yaque river valley northeast Dayujia Village and southwest of Xiaoyujia Village. The terrain is relatively low-lying around this wall section, which is higher towards the west and lower towards the east, the eastern side abutting the bank of the Yaque River. The opposite bank of the river is another large area of low-lying terrain where we discovered large accumulations of riverine deposits, suggesting that it might at one time have been the bed of the Yaque River. To the west of the wall section, the ground also has deep meandering curves made up of accumulated riverine soil. According to the locals, a river used to run from north to south between the villages of Dayujia and Xiaoyujia, and it is likely responsible for this topographic feature. We hypothesized that Wall Section 10 would be located between the two above-mentioned river channels. Locals used to call this area "Hexin" (center of the river), and core samples confirmed our hypothesis. The wall section lies on a northwest to southeast axis, and is to 118°. Wall Section 10 is located east of Section 8 at a distance of 92 m.

The damage to this wall section has been severe, and its remains are rectangular in shape. On both sides of the section are plots of farmland, and to the east is a road that runs along the west bank of the Yaque River. The terrain upon which the wall section sits gently slopes downwards from west to east. In the middle is a 2 m high cliff running southwest to northeast, dividing the terrain into eastern and western portions with the western portion 2 m higher than the eastern. Surface area: the wall section measures 219 m east to west, between 80 and 57 m from north to south with the eastern end narrower due to damage, and measures 15,000 m^2 in total surface area.

Coring in the eastern part of the wall section revealed a rammed earth layer composed of a mix of black clay and brownish-yellow soil on which the shape of the ramming tool was distinct. This layer of rammed earth was probably created by piling up soil from the surrounding riverine deposits. To the north of the river channel the rammed earth measures 30 cm thick, while to its south it measure 50 cm thick. The rammed earth in the western part of the wall section is pure, hardened, light greyish-white in color with an abundance of water-formed rust. It bears distinct markings from the ramming tool and measures 30-40 cm in thickness. We hypothesize that this soil was transported from the bottom of the riverbed (Fig. Ⅰ.4.22).

(3) Row C Wall Sections: This row lies on a north-south axis and comprises wall Sections 13, 14, 15, 16, 17, 18, 19, 21, 22, 23, and 35. They are all located east of Dongjia and Heping Villages. To the east of this terrain, across a large ravine, is another north-south oriented stretch of hillocks, and to the west, across a large expanse of flat ground, it overlooks the inner city. At the base of the mountain on the north is the Yaque River valley. The northernmost wall section is Section 13, which bends towards a northwesterly direction, and mirroring Wall Section 10 opposite at a distance. The two sections are separated by 440 m across a large area of lowland. In the southern part, Section 23 bends towards the southeast following the contour of the surrounding terrain. To the south, Section 35 then bends southwest to link up with the section of wall situated on the foothills west of Chegezhuang. In total, the sections of Row C measure 1.6 km in length, and are constructed upon the summits of the hills, their inner facades gentle sloping. In contrast, the outer facades of the wall sections are quite steep. In the southern part of this row, the wall sections are divided into two branches: the main branch is Row D while to the southeast is Row K, which extends along the hilltops to the northeast of Chegezhuang (Fig. Ⅰ.4.23; Pl. 18).

Wall Section 13: This section, located on the north side of a north-south oriented hillock east of Dongjia Village, lies along a southwest-northeast axis, to 144°. Because of its position halfway up the side of the mountain, the terrain of this wall section naturally slopes downwards from the southeast towards the northwest. At the base of the mountain lies the Yaque River valley (Fig. Ⅰ.4.24).

This section of the outer wall has been severely eroded. The remains are rectangular in shape, and situated on several graded terraces. It is bordered on the west and north sides by roads, on the east by a steep precipice, and its south side is located in the middle of the plateau. The wall section measures 33 m north to south and 19 m east to west, with the southwestern corner narrowed due to erosion; it has a total surface area of 625 m^2. There is no longer any trace of this wall section on the surface, and coring only revealed a layer of greyish-brown rammed earth under the surface which is 10 cm thick in the southeastern part, and 30 cm in the northwestern part. We exposed a cross-section from the northeastern corner for this analysis (Figs. Ⅰ.4.25- Ⅰ.4.26; Pl. 25: 1).

Wall Section 14: This section is situated on the summit of the northern part of a north-south oriented hillock east of Dongjia Village. The terrain immediately surrounding the wall section is relatively flat, but slopes downwards on both sides towards the east and west. To the north, at the base of the hillock, is the Yaque river valley. The entire wall section curves from a northwest-southeast direction to a north-south direction, and overall it is oriented to 320°. That is, its southern portion heads due south while its northern portion tilts slightly towards the northwest. The bend is very smooth, and the degree of curvature is most prominently displayed by its western edge. Wall Section 14 is located to the southeast of Section 13, separated by 29 m, and there is a gap of 4 m between their elevations. But Section 14 slides 15 m to the east.

This section has been severely damaged, and is irregular in shape as a result, with the northern side wider and the northwestern and southwestern corners protruding. It is bordered on the north by a steep, angular cliff, on the east and west sides by the edges of the elevated plateau on which it is situated, and on the south side by a small road at a distance of 2 m. The wall section measures 71 m north to south, between 25.5 and 35 m east to west, and has a total surface area of 2,130 m^2. (Fig. Ⅰ.4.27).

The wall remains are only below ground, and composed of greyish-brown rammed earth that is thinner towards the north, measuring between 20 and 30 cm.

Wall Section 15: This section is situated on the relatively flat land in the northern part of a north-south oriented hillock east of Dongjia Village. The section has been heavily damaged, and the remains are in the shape of an irregular rectangle with a narrower southern end that points southwards. It is bordered on the northern and southern sides by plots of farmland, and on the east by the steep edge of the plateau; its north end tilts slightly to the east and its western side sits in the middle of the hillock. Most of the remains of this wall section are on the highest part of this hillock on terrain that is quite level, partly occupied by woods (Fig. Ⅰ.4.28). The section measures 70 m north to south, between 10 and 12.5 m east to west, and has a total surface area of 770 m^2. The overall direction of the section in north to south. Its southern portion is oriented to 176°, while its northern portion is oriented to 204°. Section 15 is located 25 m south of Section 14 and coring revealed no rammed earth between them, due probably to later destruction.

There is no longer any evidence of the wall section on the surface of the ground, but coring revealed a 30 cm thick layer of greyish brown rammed earth beneath a 30 cm thick layer of topsoil.

Wall Section 16: This section is situated on a broad piece of relatively flat land on a north-south oriented hillock east of Dongjia Village. To the south is Dongjia East Road. The wall section lies on a north-south axis, oriented to 171°. Section 16 is located to the south of Section 15, separated by a small road berneath which was found rammed earth, indicating that the two sections had at once been connected.

The wall section has been heavily damaged, but the remains are blade-shaped, with the north end narrower than the rest. The remains are bordered on the north side by a small road, and its south edge is 10 m from a deep gully that runs east to west. Towards the eastern side is the edge of the plateau that has a small raised remnant of the wall as a marker, the western side is bordered by the western edge of the plateau. The northern portion of the section measures 68 m north to south, and 9-12 m east to west, and has a total surface area of 714 m^2; the southern portion of the section measures 91 m north to south, and 35- 49 m east to west, and has a surface area of 3,822 m^2. The total surface area of the two ends combined is 4,536 m^2 (Fig. Ⅰ.4.29).

Coring revealed that the topsoil towards the eastern side of Wall Section 16 is thin, only 30-40 cm thick, while it is almost 1 m thick on the western side. The south side of the wall section is composed of reddish-brown rammed clay, indicating that it was formed by tamping the soil that was already present within the hillock. The north side is composed of a 20-30 cm thick layer of rammed greyish-brown soil.

We discovered a small piece of the outer wall above the surface of the ground abutting the eastern edge of Section 16. This piece of wall is long, measuring 61 m north to south, and 3-7 m east to west, and 2.5 m high. The east side of this sliver of wall is a slope, and the western side has been damaged by modern land reuse to form a cliff (Fig. Ⅰ.4.30). This is the wall section called "Quanding shang" (On Top of the Ring), discovered in the 1970s. We exposed two cross-sections of the above ground portion of the wall (A and B) (Figs. Ⅰ.4.31- Ⅰ.4.34; Pl. 25: 2).

Wall Section 17: This section is situated on a broad piece of relatively flat land on a north-south oriented hillock to the east of Dongjia Village. On the north side of this hillock is Dongjia East Road. The section lies on a north-south axis, is oriented to 180°, and thus faces due south. Section 17 is located to the south of Section 16, at a distance of 33 m. Between the two lies a deep gully that measures 10 m wide and 3 m deep, at the bottom of this gully is another country road that runs east to west. The two sides of the gully are steep and we did not find any evidence of rammed earth within them, suggesting that Sections 16 and 17 were not connected in the past.

This wall section has been heavily damaged, and the remains are roughly trapezoidal in shape. The section is bordered on the north by a deep gully whose edge lies 15 m away. It is bordered on the south by a small road, its west edge sits in the middle of the hillock and its east edge sits on a terrace of slightly lower elevation. Section 17 has been broken into two parts, east and west, both are farming plots oriented north to south. The western part is higher, situated upon a 1 m high plateau and is covered by trees. Both parts are flat on the top. The section measures 62 m in length from north to south, and between 10 and 16 m from east to west; the southern part is wider, its total surface area measuring 806 m^2 (Fig. Ⅰ.4.35).

There is no longer any evidence of the wall remaining on the surface of the ground, but coring revealed a yellowish-brown layer of rammed earth containing a variety of burnt soil inclusions. This uneven layer of rammed earth measures between 10 and 40 cm thick.

Wall Section 18: This section is situated on a broad piece of relatively flat land on a north-south oriented hillock east of Dongjia Village, located to south of Section 17. The wall is oriented on a north-south axis, and oriented to 165°. A small road separates Section 17 from Section 18. Beneath the road we found rammed earth, indicating that these two sections had been connected in the past and the wall later broken into two sections.

This section of wall has been severely damaged, and its remains are rectangular in shape. The section is bordered on the north and south sides by a small, east-west running road, and on the east by the edge of a terrace lower than the highest plateau. Its western edge corresponds roughly with the edge of the highest plateau. Its southern side bends towards the east. The surface of the section is flat, 1.5 m off the ground, and its upper surface has been turned into farmland. The section measures 115 m north to south, 30 m east to west, and has a total surface area of 3,450 m^2 (Fig. Ⅰ.4.36).

There is very little remaining of this wall section on the surface of the ground. Coring revealed that the rammed earth layer is of high quality, composed of greyish-brown composite soil. The northern side of this layer is thicker while the southern side is thinner. On the highest part of the plateau the rammed earth layer is 130 cm thick, towards the south, it measures 70 cm thick, thinning out even further to 10 cm in thickness towards the western portion. The eastern part of the plateau also has a thin layer of rammed earth.

Wall Section 19: This section is situated on a span of relatively flat land on a north-south oriented hillock east of Dongjia Village, and south of Section 18. The section itself lies on a north-south axis, oriented to 175°. Between Section 18 and Section 19 lies another small east-west road. Beneath this second road, we also found a thin layer of rammed earth, suggesting Sections 18 and 19 were also originally connected, and later were broken apart.

This section has been heavily damaged, and the remains are rectangular in shape. To the north of these remains is an east-west running road, and to the south is the edge of a plot of unused land. The eastern and western edges both run through the middle of a plateau. The wall section measures 65 m north to south, 19 m east to west, and has a total surface area of 1,230 m^2 (Fig. Ⅰ.4.37).

There is no longer any evidence of this wall section on the surface of the ground. Below the topsoil, we found a layer of high-quality rammed earth composed of hardened greyish-brown soil. Beneath the woodlands, the northern part of this layer of rammed earth on the western part of the wall section measures 130 cm thick while in the middle of the section, it measures 70 cm, and at the southern end, 40 cm. Beneath the plowed fields on the eastern part of the section, towards the northern side, this rammed earth layer measures 40 cm thick, towards the middle 20 cm, and towards the south, 10 cm. This suggests to us that this section of rammed earth wall originally built up from north to south, which is why the south end is thinner.

Wall Section 21: This section is situated on a piece of relatively flat land on a north-south oriented hillock to the east of Dongjia Village. The section itself lies on a north-south axis, oriented to 173°. To the north it overlooks Section 19 across a strip of unused land measuring 40 m wide. Coring revealed bedrock immediately beneath the topsoil, suggesting that the original structure might have been destroyed here.

The wall has sustained severe erosion, and the remains are irregular in shape, mostly resembling a rectangle, with a protruding northwest corner. The section is bordered on the north side by an angular and steep cliff as well as a small country road, and on the east and west sides by the edges of plateaus. The terrain that the section is situated on is flat, and elevated 1.3 m above the surrounding land. From north to south, the wall section measures 24-30 m, and is 35 m east to west, with a total surface area of 880 m^2.

There is no longer any evidence of the wall on the surface. Below the topsoil, we found a layer of hardened rammed earth composed of yellowish-brown rammed earth. On the north side, this layer of rammed earth is 50-60 cm thick (Fig. Ⅰ.4.38).

Wall Section 22: This section is situated on a broad piece of relatively flat land on a north-south oriented hillock east of Dongjia Village. The section itself lies on a north-south axis, oriented to 161°. Section 22 is separated on the north from Section 21 by a small northwest to southeast running road. Beneath this road, we found a very thin layer of rammed earth, suggesting that these two sections were originally attached, and were later broken apart.

The section has undergone severe erosion, and the remains are rectangular in shape. The northern and southern sides of the wall section are bordered by country roads, and its eastern edge is situated in the middle of a terrace descending from the highest plateau. The southern part of the middle of the wall section narrows, and on the western facade the wall is uneven, located in the middle of a lower terrace. The surface of the wall section is covered by a combination of plowed fields and woodland. The middle part of the wall section is higher; in the east, it is 0.5-1.5 m higher than the next descending terrace, and in the west, it is 0.2-0.5 m higher. The overall landform inclines from the north to the south, but the slope is very gentle. The section measures 250 m from north to south, and between 20 and 40 m east to west, with a total surface area of 8,000 m^2 (Fig. Ⅰ.4.39).

There is no longer any evidence of the wall on the surface. Beneath the topsoil, however, we found a layer of hardened, greyish-brown composite rammed earth that bore distinct markings from the ramming tool. The rammed earth towards the middle of the plateau on which this wall section sits measures 40-50 cm thick. It is thinner towards the north, measuring 40-60 cm, and thicker towards the middle, measuring 110-200 cm. Towards the south side this layer becomes thinner, measuring between 60 and 70 cm thick, and thinning out even further to between 40 and 50 cm, and then even further to 20 cm. Based on our coring, the shape of the wall was determined to be largely sloping, with the middle section higher and the north and south sides lower.

Wall Section 23: This section is on a stretch of northwest-southeast running hillocks east of Heping Village. This stretch of hillocks sits at an intersection of various hills; to its northwest is the stretch of hilltops on which Sections 13-22 are situated running north-south east of Dongjia Village, and to the east, the hillock extends up to a stretch of hills that carry Sections 24 to 31. To the southeast, it connects to the hillock on which Section 35 is situated. These three stretches of hilltops together form a large plateau of elevated terrain. To the west of this hillock is an east-west running gully, and to the east is the beginning of a different, north-south running gully. To the east, it overlooks another north-south running hillock across a large gully. Overall, this hillock forms a huge curve, and its surface has been converted into a series of terraced fields that have been given the local toponyms of "Daluoquan" (First Ring), "Erluoquan" (Second Ring), and "Sanluoquan" (Third Ring) from lower to higher. The remains of Section 23 are situated on the "Third Ring," the highest part of the uppermost terrace.

There is no longer any trace of this wall section on the surface of the ground. The section is bordered on the southeast by a main road, and wall Section 24 is located across this road from Section 23. The south end of the wall reaches the edge of the main road, and connects to the north end of Section 35. The northwest corner narrows to a point and protrudes 14 m from the rest of the section, in the direction of Section 22. The remains of Section 23 are located on the two highest plateaus, the one to the north is 1 m higher than the one to the south. These plateaus are relatively flat, though the middle portion (with its circular summit) dips slightly. The north side of the wall section forms a steep 0.2-0.5-m cliff, with the western part slightly higher. The south side of the section forms a steep cliff facing the inner city that measures between 0.6 and 2 m in height, with the middle section at the highest elevation. The entire wall section measures 290 m long, and 25-36 m wide, and has a total surface area of 9,000 m^2. It lies on a northwest to southeastern axis oriented to 135° (Fig. Ⅰ.4.40).

On top of the remains of the rammed earth, we found a layer of topsoil measuring between 20 and 50 cm thick. We also found a 10 cm thick layer of rammed earth towards the south side of the wall section. Near the southeastern part, we discovered that the rammed earth was thicker, and could be divided into two strata. The upper stratum is composed of high quality greyish-brown rammed earth measuring 40 cm in thickness; the lower stratum is composed of lower quality yellowish-brown composite soil, measuring 60 cm in thickness. Beneath the two strata of rammed earth is soft, clean reddish-brown virgin soil bearing evidence of water-formed rust. At the edges of the plateau the rammed earth layers thin out to 5 cm in thickness. Towards the middle of the wall section, the rammed earth is thicker, measuring 30 to 70 cm in thickness. Towards the northern edge, it measures 40 cm in thickness.

Section 23 is situated at the convergence point of many different wall sections; to its northern side is wall Section 22. Towards the south of this section, the wall splits into two branches, with Sections 24-31 bending towards the southeastern foothills, and Section 35 bending towards the southwestern hills. Because Section 23 is oriented in a northwest-southeast direction, it suggests that the outer wall bulges some 270 m outwards at this point.

Wall Section 35: This section is located towards the south end of a stretch of north-south oriented hillocks to the east of Heping Village. The northern end of this stretch of hills is largely oriented north to south (Sections 13-22), and upon reaching Section 23, turns southeast, before turning again towards the southwest. Wall Section 35 is situated atop this northeast-southwest oriented hillock, and to its northwest is a large gully. To the north, it links up with the south end of Section 23, forming a clear angular corner which measures 107°.

To the southeast of Section 23 is another large gully across which are Sections 24-31. To the southwest, a wide gully cuts across the entire hillock. Section 35 sits on a northeast to southwest axis, and is oriented to 217°.

This section has been severely eroded, and all that remains is a below ground layer of rammed earth. The section is bordered on the east side by a country road, on the north side by a precipice. The south side of the wall section disappears into the northern part of an orchard. The wall section is situated at the highest elevation of the hillock with the terrain to either side of it relatively low-lying. The edges of the plateau on which the wall section sits form several 0.3-1 m high precipices oriented in a northeast to southwest direction. The surface of this plateau is currently occupied by a combination of plowed fields and woodland. This surface is relatively even, but slopes from the northeast towards the southwest with a height difference between the two ends of 6 m. Both the east and west edges of the wall section are neat and were likely the original facades of the wall. The section measures 228 m from northeast to southwest, between 55 and 87 m from northwest to southeast, and has a total surface area of 16,200 m^2 (Fig. Ⅰ.4.41; Pl. 20: 1).

Coring revealed a 30-40 cm thick layer of rammed earth towards the northwestern part of the wall section; this layer was composed of greyish-brown soil with ashy inclusions and bearing distinct markings from the ramming tool. At the southeastern part of the section, we found another layer, measuring 50 cm in thickness, composed of yellowish-brown soil with ashy-grey inclusions towards the bottom of the layer. These rammed earth layers had an abundance of sand-sized inclusions. Towards the southern side of the section, this layer of rammed earth was found to be thinner, measuring only 10-20 cm in thickness.

We exposed two cross-sections of this wall section on its west side along the edge of the country road (Pl. 26: 1). Cross-section A is the more complete example of the wall's construction (Figs. Ⅰ.4.42-Ⅰ.4.44). First, they laid down a foundational layer of rammed earth composed of fine, reddish-brown soil (rammed earth layer D). On top of this was found a central spine (rammed earth layer C) that was meant to speed up the process of construction. On either side of this central spine of fill soil were two strips of rammed earth (rammed earth layers A and B). Over the course of constructing these two strips of rammed earth, they used the same type of soil, which was composed of largely sandy soil with clay inclusions. However, we found that the construction process of these two strips differed, specifically in that the lower stratum of layer A was composed mainly of this sandy soil (dark greyish-brown soil used in various sections of the foundation), while the middle to lower stratum of layer B was composed of yellowish-brown soil.

Cross-section B was cut on the extension to the north of the rammed wall section A in cross-section A (Fig. Ⅰ.4.45- Ⅰ.4.46). Through examination, we were able to confirm that the sandy layer we found in cross-section B was indeed the continuation of the sandy layer in rammed wall section A. It seems as though this section of the wall was constructed in 90 m long intervals.

Beneath the eastern precipice, we found several cord-marked bricks as well as human-modified stone fragments (Figs. Ⅰ.4.41, Ⅰ.4.47; Pl. 20: 2). We hypothesized that these were originally used as construction materials for this section of the wall.

(4) Row D Wall Sections: Comprises only **Wall Section 37**. This section is situated in the middle of a valley that is nestled among the hillocks to the west of Chegezhuang and the north-south running hills east Dongjia and Heping villages. The terrain on the north and south sides of this area is distinctly higher in elevation. This wall section is oriented northeast to southwest, along the same axis as Section 35, 217 ° east of north.

The northern side of the section is bordered by an east-west oriented stretch of country road, and its northeast corner narrows sharply. The south side is 15 m from a precipice, and high precipices are also found towards the eastern and western sides. The southwest corner narrows towards the west and protrudes about 10 m. The wall section is situated in the middle of a gully, so the surrounding terrain is relatively flat. It is divided into two sections by a country road that intersects it in the middle. This road sits at a distinctly higher elevation, and we hypothesize that this is due to the later construction of the road, which required laying down a foundation that elevated it slightly (Fig. Ⅰ.4.48). The terrain on either side of the road is thus lower, and relatively even. The eastern edge of the plateau upon which the wall section sits is a precipice that measures 0.8-2 m high; its southern edge is slightly lower in elevation. The western edge is bordered by another precipice between 1 and 4 m high, with the middle portion of the edge the highest in elevation. Both the east and west edges of the wall are neat and even, and we hypothesize that these are the original facades of the wall (Fig. Ⅰ.4.49). The section measures 147 m from northeast to southwest, 107 m from northwest to southeast, and has a total surface area of 11,000 m^2. Near the east side of the wall, we found several human-modified stone fragments that we hypothesized were once used in the construction of the wall.

Most of the wall is no longer visible on the surface of the ground. Through coring, we found that the rammed earth on the east side of the wall was composed of greyish-brown clay with an abundance of stony inclusions incorporated into the wall fill through ramming. We cored downwards over 2 m but did not find the very bottom of the wall. In some parts of the wall, we found a layer of greyish-brown rammed earth beneath this layer of stony soil. Towards the south side of the wall, we found a layer of greyish-brown rammed earth measuring 70 cm thick. At the top of the precipice that forms the western side of the wall, we found a very distinct layer of rammed earth that began 50 cm beneath the topsoil. The upper stratum of these rammed earth layers measured 20 cm thick and was composed of hardened, greyish-brown soil with a small amount of rocky inclusions; the middle stratum measured 20 cm thick, and was composed of stony rammed earth with small amounts of greyish-brown soil matrix; the lowest stratum was found to be composed of greyish-brown rammed earth. At the northwest side of the section, we found a rammed earth layer measuring 40 cm thick.

Wall Section 37 is located between Sections 35 and 39. It is situated on the same axis as Section 35, and we hypothesized that they were at one point connected. The south side of this section turns towards the southeast onto the same axis as Section 39. We hypothesized that a part of Section 37 at one point must have been the pivotal joining section between Sections 35 and 39, which lie at different orientations. Section 37 is 55 m way from the Section 35 to the northeast, and 124 m from Section 39 towards the south.

(5) Row E Wall Sections: This row encompasses wall Sections 39, 41, 44, and 46. These wall sections are all located on a hillock northwest of Chegezhuang. This hillock is roughly "E"-shaped, and towards the south it divides into three ridges; the wall sections run down along the western-most ridge. The upper sections in the north (Sections 39 and 40) are oriented largely on a north-south axis and slightly to the east while the upper sections of the row in the south (Sections 44 and 46) curve towards the west. They are mostly constructed at the summit of the hillock or ridge, with the outside facades overlooking a deep ravine across from which are the sections of Row K, while the inner facades forming a large slope leading towards the inner city (Fig. Ⅰ.4.50).

Wall Section 39: This section is located on the northern part of a hillock to the north of Chegezhuang. The terrain on both the eastern and western sides of the hillock forms deep gullies, especially on the east (outside the outer wall). The entire hillock forms a slope from north to south. The wall section is situated at the summit of this slope. It lies on a north-south axis, and is 155° east off north.

The section has suffered severe damage, though its remains are rectangular in shape. The northern side of the section abuts a 1.5 m high precipice, and its western edge is located on second terrace descending from this elevated plateau. Its southeastern edge is at the edge of the first terrace while its southern side disappears into the middle of the terrace. The summit of the hillock is relatively flat. The height difference between the first terrace and the summit is 1 m, and the height between the first and second terraces is 1.5 m. A small country road runs through the middle of the plateau. The entire wall section is on a gentle incline that runs from the northwest towards the southeast. The section measures 139 m long from northwest to southeast, between 25 and 55 m wide from northeast to southwest, and has a total surface area of 5,560 m^2 (Fig. Ⅰ.4.51).

The rammed earth layer of the wall consists of compacted, yellowish-brown soil with small amounts of sandy and ashy inclusions, bearing distinct markings from the ramming tool. This layer was thicker in its western part on the lower terrace, measuring approximately 1 m at its thickest; on average, it measured only 20-30 cm. At its thinnest, it measured 5 cm thick. In the northern part, the rammed earth measured 40 cm thick, but only between 10 and 30 cm thick in the southeastern part. At the southern edge, it was only 5 cm thick. Because the bedrock in the middle of the wall section was at a higher elevation, we found no rammed earth remains, but saw instead the bedrock exposed on the surface.

Wall Section 41: This section is located on the north side of a hillock north of Chegezhuang. The wall section is situated along the summit of the hillock, which is bordered on the east and west by deep gullies, especially the eastern gully (outside the outer wall). The entire hillock slopes from north to south, and the wall section lies on a northwest to southeast axis and oriented to 163°. To its northwest is located Section 39, about 128 m away.

This section has sustained severe erosion, though the wall is in a rough rectangular shape. The western side of the wall is bordered by a country road, and its eastern edge forms a precipice 0.7 m high. Its south side is also bordered by a small precipice and its north side is located in the middle of the hillock's summit plateau. Its surface is relatively even, but slopes gently from the northwest towards the southeast. It measures 18 m from northwest to southeast, 5 m from northeast to southwest, and has a goal surface area of 90 m^2.

The rammed earth is composed of hardened, greyish-white soil with small amounts of fine sandy inclusions, likely from a riverine deposit; it measures 5-10 cm in thickness.

Wall Section 44: This wall section is situated on the western part of a hillock located northwest of Chegezhuang. It is bordered by a deep gully to the east and to the west of this summit area is another deep gully. The wall section lies on a northwest to southeast axis, oriented to 155°. Sections 41 and 44 are 175 m apart. Measuring along the high terrain, the distance is 222 m. So there may have originally been a section of wall some 200 m long between the two sections.

The section has sustained heavy damage and the remains of the wall are roughly rectangular, with the northwestern corner protruding. The section is located on the eastern part of the hillock, with the slope of a gully as its eastern border, and the western edge is marked by a country road. The north side of wall starts at the base of a cliff, and its south side reaches the edge of the second terrace (Fig. Ⅰ.4.52). The wall section itself is divided onto three different terraces, with a height difference between them of 1.5 m, moving downwards from north to south. The surface of each terrace is flat. The wall section measures 29 m from south to north, 50 m from east to west, and has a total surface area of 1,450 m^2.

The rammed earth of the wall is composed of hardened yellowish-brown soil with sandy inclusions, and bears the distinct markings of the ramming tool. This layer of rammed earth is thicker towards the middle of the wall, measuring 50 cm. Towards the edges, it becomes thinner, measuring only 10 cm in thickness. In several spots, we found no evidence of rammed earth, only bedrock, or towards the eastern edge, a thin layer of reddish-brown virgin soil.

Wall Section 46: This section is situated on the eastern side of the summit plateau in the middle of a hillock, slightly to the south, located northwest of Chegezhuang; on the east is a deep gully, and on the west, at a distance of 70 m is another deep, north-south running gully. The entire hillock slopes downwards from north to south. The section lies on the same axis as Section 44, from northwest to southeast, and is oriented to 155°. Section 46 lies directly south of Section 44 at a distance of 30 m.

The section has sustained heavy damage and the remains of the wall are roughly rectangular, with the western portion of the south side protruding southwards. The wall section is on the eastern side of the hillock, bordered by a deep gully, and the western side is in the middle of the summit plateau. To the north are the lower two terraces upon which are the remains of Section 44, while to the south is the edge of the summit plateau. The southeastern edge is situated in the middle of a slightly lower plateau. The plateau surface is relatively flat. The wall section measures between 7 and 12 m from south to north, 68 m from east to west, and has a total surface area of 650 m^2.

The rammed earth of the wall is composed of hardened, well compacted, light greyish-brown soil containing fine riverine deposits as well as fine sand; it bears distinct markings from the ramming tool. The rammed earth is thicker towards the middle of the wall section, measuring 40 cm, but thins out towards the edges; in some spots, we found no rammed earth, but exposed bedrock.

It is noteworthy that between and around Sections 44 and 49, we found a deposit of reddish-brown sticky earth, clean and firm, but un-rammed. In places where the wall exists, this earth is located underneath the rammed earth of the wall, in places where the wall was not found, it is located immediately under the topsoil and on top of the bedrock. This deposit is restricted to the eastern side of the plateau, running in the same direction as the wall sections. It is distributed in a larger areas than the walls, measuring 150 m from north to south, and 56-79 m from east to west. Its relationship to the wall section needs to be clarified by future study.

(6) Row F Wall Sections: This row comprises wall sections 49, 51, 53, 56, and 58. They are located on the hillock west of Chegezhuang and up to the southeast of Nanbu Village. The northern sections of this row largely fall on a northeast to southwest axis, and gradually turn westwards as they move south. They are mostly constructed on the summit of the hillock, with their inner facades overlooking a deep valley, most likely for protection. In general, these wall sections slope from the south towards the north, especially towards the northern part. In total they measure 0.65 km in length. We did not find any wall sections farther west of this group; they are also located very close to the foot of Mount Lai, and most likely were connected to the mountains to the south.

Wall Section 49: This section is situated on a spur of land that makes up the northern end of a hillock located between the southeast side of Nanbu Village and the west side of Chegezhuang. The hillock is bordered on the eastern and western sides by low-lying river valleys. On the north side there is a 30 m wide gully running east to west across from which are the wall sections of Row E. The terrain of the hillock slopes from south to north, and is bordered on the southern side by a highway, across from which is Section 51. The wall section lies on a south -north axis, and is oriented 200°. Section 49 is located at 132 m to the southwest of Section 46.

The section has sustained heavy damage, and the remains of the wall are roughly rectangular shape, with the northwest side protruding northwards. The southern edge of the wall section extends up to the second terrace beside the highway. Its east side is bordered by the edge of a gully, and its northeast corner reaches a precipice 2.5 m high. This precipice stretches westwards until it reaches the north side, where it abruptly protrudes in a northern direction. The western edge of the wall section is on the west side of the hillock. The northern side of the wall section ends in a precipice measuring 2-2.5 m, with the highest point of elevation at the northeast corner. The wall section is situated on a plateau that slopes from north to south, and can be divided into three separate terraces, each 1 m lower in elevation than the next as they move southwards. Each terrace is relatively flat. The section measures 50 m from south to north, 77 m from east to west, and the north side protrudes north-south 10 m with an east-west width of 22 m. It measures 4,000 m^2 in total surface area (Fig. Ⅰ.4.53).

Coring revealed a layer of fine, well-compacted, hardened, yellowish-brown rammed earth. This layer of rammed earth was thicker towards the northern side of the wall section, measuring up to 200 cm in thickness, while the layer was thinner, only 20 cm, towards the southern side. The rammed earth layer was thinnest around the very edges of the southern side, measuring only 10 cm.

Wall Section 51: This section is located south of a highway southwest of Chegezhuang. It is situated towards the southern side of the summit of a hillock between the west side of Chegzhuang and southeast side of Nanbu Village. This hillock is bordered on the south side by a large gully, on the north side by a second large gully that sits across from a large flat plain. The terrain of the hillock slopes from the south towards the north. The wall section itself lies on a northeast to southwest axis, oriented to 243°. Section 51 is located southwest of Section 49, the distance between the two being 120 m (Fig. Ⅰ.4.54).

The section has sustained heavy damage and the remains of the wall are trapezoidal in shape, with a concavity on the southwestern side. The south side of the wall section is close to the bank of a gully, and the north side runs through the middle of the hillock, while towards the west is an overgrown field, and on the east is a series of four graded terraces. The section is situated on a plateau whose east side ends in a 1.5 m high precipice. The wall is divided onto a series of five terraces, with each terrace between 0.5 m and 1 m lower, sloping downwards from south to north. The surface of each terrace is relatively flat. The wall section measures 48 m from east to west, between 28 and 64 m north to south, with a protruding section towards the northwest corner 28 m long. The entire wall section has a surface area of 2,000 m^2.

The rammed earth that comprises this wall is light yellowish-brown in color, fine, smooth, and hardened in texture, and contains very find sandy inclusions; we hypothesized that this soil was originally riverine deposit. Towards the east side of the wall, which is at a lower elevation, this rammed earth layer is thicker, measuring 1.5 m at its thickest. Towards the middle of the wall, the rammed earth layer measures 30-50 cm in thickness, and it thins out significantly at the edges, measuring 5-10 cm.

Wall Section 53: This section is situated in the middle of a hillock between the southeast of Nanbu Village and the west side of Chegezhuang; it is 90 m west of Section 51. The south side of the section is bordered by a large gully, while its north side is bordered by a flat, unoccupied field, below which runs another large gully. The terrain of the hillock slopes from south to north. The section is oriented to 245°.

The section has sustained heavy damage and its remains are rectangular in shape. The section is situated on a plateau and is bordered on the eastern, western, and southern sides by precipices, and to the north it ends in the middle of the plateau. The summit of the hillock is 1.2 m higher than the terrace on which this wall section is located, and the terrace ends in a 0.5 m high precipice towards the east side. The terrace is relatively flat. The wall measures 9 m east to west, 43 m north to south, and has a total surface area of 380 m^2.

The rammed earth of this section is composed of fine, hardened, well-compacted light yellowish-brown soil with fine sandy inclusions. In general, it was found to be very thin, measuring only 5 cm in thickness.

Section 53 is surrounded by exposed bedrock, but in certain areas, particularly along the western side, we found pockets of rammed earth measuring 5 cm in thickness composed of riverine deposits.

We were not able to determine whether these pockets of rammed earth are connected with each other, but they suggest that the outer wall continued to extend westward.

Wall Section 56: This section is located on the south side of the summit of the hillock southeast of Nanbu and west of Chegezhaung. Its south side is bordered by a deep gully, while its north side sits at a higher elevation towards the hillock's summit. The section lies along an east to west axis and is oriented to 265°. Section 56 is located 170 m from Section 56.

The section has sustained heavy damage and the remains of the wall are rectangular in shape. The surface of this plateau is relatively flat, and the section measures 39 m east to west, 7.5 m north to south, and has a total surface area of 290 surface m^2.

This section is composed of greyish-white rammed earth that was most likely riverine deposits; the soil is fine and smooth, and quite hardened. In general, this layer of rammed earth was found to be thin, measuring 30 cm in thickness on the western side, and thinning to 10 cm in thickness towards the east.

Wall Section 58: This section is situated on the southwestern part of a hillock located southeast of Nanbu Village and west of Chegezhuang. The terrain on the south side is higher than the wall section, forming the actual summit of the hillock. The section is located at the foot of Mount Lai, and is 140 m from the mountain. The section lies along a northeast to southwest axis and is oriented to 245°.

The section has sustained heavy damage and the remains of the wall are rectangular in shape. The section's northern and western sides are bordered by a country road, and the south side is bordered by a 1 m high precipice. The plateau is relatively flat on the surface, and measures 81 m from east to west, 11 m from north to south, with a total surface area of 890 m^2.

The rammed earth of this section is composed of fine, hardened greyish-white soil that was at one point riverine deposit. It is overall quite thin, but thickens towards the middle, measuring up to 80 cm thick; at the edges, the rammed earth thins out to 5 cm.

To the west of Section 58, we did not find another wall section, only scattered rammed earth, 5 cm thick, also formed by riverine deposit. We could only determine their general direction.

Wall Sections 56 and 58 are situated on the southeast and northwest corners of the same plateau (Fig. Ⅰ.4.55; Pl. 21:1). Most of the plateau is exposed bedrock, and we found no rammed earth on it. Therefore, we hypothesized that Sections 56 and 58 originally belonged to a single piece of wall, but the central portion had been destroyed due to high elevation, leaving behind only thin pockets of rammed earth towards the edges where the terrain is lower. If the two sections were connected, the entire wall piece would measure 181 m from east to west, and 46-96 m north to south, with the east side wider, and it would have had a surface area of 13,000 m^2.

(7) Row G Wall Sections: This row comprises only wall Sections 80 and 82. They are located on the south end of a hillock west of Caojia Village; these sections lie along an east-west axis, its eastern end connecting to Row H sections. The southern mountain is about 100 m south of this row, and the topography shows that the wall section connects with the mountain. In total, these wall sections measure 0.28 km in length from west to east (Fig. Ⅰ.4.56).

Wall Section 80: This wall section is situated on the south side of a hill summit northwest of Caojia Village. To the east and west of this hillock are slopes, but at the southern side the terrain is higher, connecting with the foot of Mount Lai. The terrain slopes from south to north. The section itself lies on a south to north axis, oriented to 171° (Fig. Ⅰ.4.57; Pl. 21:2).

The section has a trapezoidal shape, with the north side wider than the south. The north sides of the wall section are bordered by precipices 1.2-2 m in height on the east and west, the northeast side narrowing inwards. The west side is bordered by a small gully while the east side sits on the edge of the mountain ridge. The surface of the wall section is located on seven terraced plateaus that slope from south to north and are between 0.5 and 1 m in height. It measures 66 m north to south, and 36-89 m east to west, with a total surface area of 4,000 m^2.

The rammed earth of this wall section is greyish-white in color, composed of riverine deposits. It is thicker towards the north side of the hillock, measuring between 40 and 50 cm, and thins out to 10 cm towards the south side.

Wall Section 82: To the west of Caojia Village are two parallel hillocks running north-south, between them is a north-south running gully. Wall Section 82 is situated on the eastern slope of the outer hillock, facing across from the inner hillock. To the south of the section is an east-west running deep gully that lies at the foot of Mount Lai. It lies along an east-west axis, and oriented to 283°.

This wall section has a trapezoidal shape, with the southwest corner slightly protruding southward. It is bordered on the east by a small country path at the bottom of the gully making, a precipice 1.5 m high. The western side is in the middle of the hillock, near the north-south running country road, which itself sits upon a 0.5 m high cliff. The north side runs from the summit of the hillock to a precipice. The surface of the wall section slopes from the west towards the east, forming several terraced plateaus that measure 6 m in height at the top. It is 154 m long from east to west, 19-44 m wide from north to south, and the protrusion on its southern side measures 31 m east to west and 23 m north to south. It has a total surface area of 5,600 m^2 (Fig. Ⅰ.4.58).

The eastern side of the wall (the lower portion) is composed of yellowish-brown rammed earth with red loamy inclusions, and measures between 30 and 50 cm. The middle of the section has reddish-brown rammed earth that is loamy in texture, has an abundance of water-formed rust, and measures 20 cm in thickness. The western side (the upper portion) has a thinner layer of rammed earth, measuring only 5 cm in thickness.

(8) Row H Wall Sections: This row encompasses wall Sections 83, 84, 85, 87 and 88. These wall sections are situated on a southwest to northeast oriented series of hillocks west of Caojia Village, the northern-most section, Section 88, bends towards the east. This series of wall sections measures in total 0.83 km. Most of these sections are situated on the summits of these hillocks, which are bordered on both sides by large slopes.

Wall Section 83: This section is located at the southern end of a hillock west of Guicheng Caojia Village. Both the outer and inner facades of the hillock form large slopes; 15 m to the southern side is a large, 15 m wide gully, separating the hillock bearing the wall section from the high mountain to its south. The terrain upon which the wall section sits slopes from the northeast towards the southwest. The wall section lies on the same axis as the hillock, northeast to southwest, and oriented to 219°.

The section is trapezoidal in shape, with the south side wider than the north. The section is located on the summit of the hillock, with the north side bordered by a small country road. The eastern and southern sides are bordered by other small roads, and the western side by a slope that reaches the hillock's base. The eastern portion of the wall forms a slope, with a height of 2.5-3 m. The middle part of the wall section is flat. The western portion of the wall forms terraces that overall slope westwards and have overall heights of 2.5 m. The terrain of the entire hillock is rather high in the middle, and slopes gently down to the north and south (Pl. 23). The wall section is 190 m in length from north to south, 22-103 m wide from east to west, and has a total surface area of 12,000 m^2 (Figs. Ⅰ.4.59- Ⅰ.4.60).

The rammed earth of this section was composed of riverine deposits, yellowish-brown in color, hardened, and containing fine sandy inclusions. It is thick towards the western side (the outer edge of the wall), which measures 120 cm, but is overall 30 cm in thickness. The eastern slope of the hill does not have any traces of rammed earth on it; likely this was due to later renovations.

Wall Section 84: This section is located in the middle of the summit of a hillock west of Guicheng Caojia Village, to the northeast of Section 83. The two sides of the wall form large slopes. The entire hillock slopes from northeast to southwest. The wall runs on the same northeast - southwest axis as the hillock itself, and is oriented to 204°.

The section is largely rectangular in shape. It is bordered to the north by a small country road, on the eastern and southern sides by other small roads, on the western side by the edge of the plateau. The surface of the terrace is relatively flat, sloping downwards towards the west. To the east it slopes steeply downwards to form a precipice measuring 0.5-1 m high, being higher in its northern part. The wall section measures 119 m from north to south, 11-23 m wide from east to west, and has a total surface area of 2,000 m^2.

The rammed earth of this wall section is composed of yellowish-brown soil containing fine sandy inclusions that was at one point riverine deposit. In general, it is not very thick, measuring between 5 and 10 cm in throughout the section; in certain places we found direct exposure of the bedrock (Fig. Ⅰ.4.61).

A related note: Compared to Section 85 located to its northeast, the eastern edge of Section 84 recedes significantly to the west. The terrain to the east is also a bit lower in elevation; we consider that at one point a portion of the wall was here, but it was later destroyed.

Wall Section 85: This section is located in the middle of the summit of a hillock west of Guicheng

Caojia Village, and to the northeast of Section 84. The two sections run parallel to one another from northeast to southwest with an interval of 10 m between them. The wall section is oriented to 204°.

The section has a trapezoidal shape, with the eastern side more straight than the west. The section is situated on the summit plateau of the hillock, and is bordered on the north and south sides by country roads. The eastern edge sits in the middle of the plateau, and is level with the eastern edge of Section 87, while the western edge abuts the eastern outer wall of a storehouse. The northwest side bends eastwards. The surface of the plateau is flat, and slopes from the northeast towards the southwest. The wall section itself is higher on the east, and tilts westwards (outside). The section measures 186 m long north to south, 41-78 m wide east to west, and has a total surface area of 11,000 m^2 (Fig. Ⅰ.4.62).

The rammed earth of this section is yellowish-brown in color, containing fine sandy inclusions and is composed of riverine deposits. Overall, the remaining rammed earth is thin, measuring only 40 cm at its thickest, and thinning to between 5 and 10 cm at its thinnest; we also found pockets of exposed bedrock during coring.

Wall Section 87: This section is situated on the northern section of a hillock located west of Caojia Village, to the northeast of Section 85 running in the same direction, with a gap of 77 m in between. The hillock forms an upside-down L-shape. Section 87 is located to the west of its turning point. The hillock lies in a northeast to southwest direction, with the northwest and southeast sides sloping downwards. To the east is the hillock on which Wall Section 88 is situated; the surface of this latter hillock is relatively even with Section 87. Section 87 lies on the same northeast to southwest axis as the hillock itself, and is oriented to 209° (Fig. Ⅰ.4.63).

The section is rectangular in shape and sits on the summit plateau of the hillock. It is bordered on the north by the cliff edge of the summit plateau. The precipice of the plateau towards the western side measures 2.5 m in height and is bordered on the east by a country road. The wall section's southern edge is situated in the middle of the plateau. The surface of the plateau is relatively flat and slopes gently from the northeast towards the southwest. The wall section measures 121 m from north to south, 28 m from east to west, and has a total surface area of 3,400 m^2.

The rammed earth on the western side of the wall is 70 cm thick, and is composed of three strata. The upper stratum is composed of hardened, greyish-brown soil containing reddish loamy inclusions and measures 30 cm thick; the middle stratum is composed of loose, sandy greyish-brown soil measuring 30 cm; and the lowest stratum is composed of hardened, greyish-brown soil that measures 10 cm. Below this lower stratum is bedrock. To the south of the wall section the bedrock is directly exposed.

Wall Section 88: This section is located on the northern side of a hillock west of Caojia Village and to the east of Section 87, the two being separated by a country road that goes from north to south. The section is located to the east of the turning corner of the hillock that forms an L-shaped polygon turned upside-down. The south and north sides of the hillock are at a lower elevation, forming large slopes. The east side follows the direction of the hillocks and also slopes downwards. Section 88 lies on the same east to west axis as the hillock itself, and is oriented to 277°.

This section is largely rectangular in shape and is situated on the summit plateau of the hillock. It is bordered on the northern by a 0.5 m high precipice, and on the east by a small country road. To the south is another precipice measuring 0.5-1 m in height, and to the west is a second country road that lies on the other side of a 1 m precipice. The surface of the plateau is relatively flat and slopes gently from the west towards the east. The wall section measures 144 m long from east to west, 54-77 m in width from north to south, with the middle section widest, and has a total surface area of 9,400 m^2.

The rammed earth of this section is composed of smooth, fine, light yellowish-brown riverine deposit soil, containing sandy inclusions. It is uneven in thickness throughout. The southern side (inner facade) is thinner, measuring between 10 and 20 cm in thickness. It is thicker towards the north side, measuring up to 140 cm. In the middle of the wall, this layer is also rather thin, measuring 10-20 cm. We exposed two cross-sections in order to determine the structure of this wall section (Figs. Ⅰ.4.64-Ⅰ.4.67; Pl. 26: 2, Pl. 22: 1).

(9) Row I Wall Sections: This row encompasses wall Sections 90 and 92. They are located at the northern foothills of a series of north-south running hillocks west of Caojia Village and are bordered on the north by the Yaque River. These two wall sections are oriented on a southwest to northeast axis, and measure in total 0.2 km from north to south. They are situated on the terraces in front of high hillocks to the south, with both sides sloping down to lower elevations. There is a large space between them and the Row H wall sections to the south (Fig. Ⅰ.4.68).

Wall Section 90: This section of wall is situated on a small elevated plateau north of the hillocks running from southwest to northeast to the west of Caojia Village, and it is on the south side of an east-west running highway. The terrain is flat in the north and higher in the south, sloping upwards, and the east and west of this small elevated plateau is lower in elevation and forms a valley. Wall Section 90 lies on a north-south axis, and is oriented to 180°. It is 340 m from Section 87 located on the mountaintop to the south.

This section is rectangular in shape. It is bordered on the north side by a 1 m high precipice, on the south side by the southern edge of the plateau, on the east side by the edge of a gully, and on the west side by a 5 m high precipice. The surface of this plateau is relatively flat. The wall section measures 20 m from south to north, 41 m from east to west, and has a total surface area of 8,400 m^2.

The rammed earth of this wall section is composed of yellowish-brown composite riverine soil with sandy inclusions. It is thickest towards the middle of the wall section, measuring between 60 and 80 cm, and thins out wards the western part where it only measures 20 cm.

Wall Section 92: This section is situated on a small plateau on the south bank of the Yaque River, bordered on the north side by the river, on the south side by an east-west running highway, and on the east and west sides by low-lying terrain. The south side of this plateau is higher. The section is largely oriented north-south, on the same axis as the surrounding plateau, and is oriented to 188°. To its southwest is located Wall Section 90 at a distance of 104 m.

This section is rectangular in shape. It is situated in the middle of an orchard, and its north side is 19 m away from the edge of the plateau, while its east side reaches the edge of a gully; its west side is close to the western edge of the plateau, while its south side sits in the middle of the plateau, approximately 49 m away from the edge of the highway. The surface of the plateau is relatively flat, and the wall section measures 48 m from south to north, 25 m from east to west, and has a total surface area of 1,200 m^2.

The rammed earth that comprises the remains of this wall section is composed of riverine deposit that is yellowish-brown in color and contains sandy inclusions. It is thicker in the center of the wall section, measuring up to 60 cm, and thins out to no more than 10 cm towards the edges. Beneath the layer of rammed earth, we found a layer of fine, yellowish brown soil that has not been rammed.

(10) Row J Wall Section: This Row includes only wall Section 94.

Wall Section 94: It is located on a stretch of flat ground on the northern shore of the Yaque River, and south of a cement factory. It is separated from the Row A wall sections by a large piece of land. Judging by the orientation of the wall sections of these two rows, we suppose that the wall section that originally stood between them must have had a turning corner.

This section is largely rectangular in shape. It is primarily situated in the middle of a vineyard, with its south side bending towards the west. Its north side is 22 m away from an east-west running country road, and is 5 m from the northern precipice of the plateau. The south edge is 12 m from the shore of the river. The surface of this plateau is relatively flat, with a 2 m high precipice along its north side. The wall section measures 93 m from south to north, 23 m from east to west, and has a total surface area of 2,139 m^2.

The rammed earth of this section is quite hardened, is deep greyish-brown in color, and bears distinct markings from the ramming tool; it also contains inclusions of charcoal granules and sand. In some areas, we found that this greyish brown layer was overlaid with a layer of yellowish-brown rammed earth containing sandy inclusions. In some other spots, we found that the lower strata of the wall had rammed earth that was much sandier. These layers of rammed earth were found to be thicker towards the middle of the wall section, measuring between 60 and 80 cm, and thinning out to between 20 and 30 cm towards the edges. We also found, beneath the rammed earth layers, a layer of clean yellowish-brown soil that had not undergone ramming.

During coring, we found that west of wall section 94 was a large accumulation of sand, reaching westwards more than 250 m. The southern and northern sides of the wall section also had evidence of this kind of sand. We hypothesized that it is possible this sand marked the river level of that time.

(11) Row K Wall Sections: This row includes wall Sections 24, 25, 27, 28, and 31. They are located on the north-south oriented hillocks northeast of Chegezhuang. The terrain of this row of wall sections connects to the south side of the north-south oriented hillocks located east of Dongjia and Heping Villages. The east side of the hillock (the outer facade) forms a large, steep slope, while its inner side forms a deep valley; it is bordered on the north by the southern end of a deep gully. The wall sections are mostly situated on the summit of this hillock, and all together, they measure 0.8 km from north to south. The wall sections of this row extend out of the south side of the north-south oriented sections of Row C, and to their south there are no further wall sections. This indicates that this is an offshoot of the primary part of the outer wall (Fig. Ⅰ.4.23; Pl. 18).

Wall Section 24: This section is situated to the northeast of a country road, on the northern end of a hillock northeast of Chegezhaung. The terrain to its west is flat and lower, and it connected with the "Third Ring" upon which wall Section 23 is situated. The northern side of the terrace is bordered by the south end of a deep gully, and on the east is another large, north-south oriented gully. This section can be divided into two parts: the western part connects to Section 23 and lies on a northwest to southeast axis, with an orientation of 130°. The eastern part forms the north end of the series of wall sections numbered 24 through 31 m. The eastern part lies on an east to west axis, and is oriented to 90°. The two parts are divided by a 1.7 m high cliff.

The western part of the section forms a strip, and it connects with Section 23 across a highway. The middle portion of this part is bordered on the north by the edge of a gully, and follows along this edge to form a terrace protruding north, the side of which is a precipice 2 m high. The eastern portion of this part bends southwards until it reaches the upper terrace where it connects with the eastern part of the wall section. The terrain of the western part of the section inclines from south to north towards the gully. The strip portion of the western part measures 210 m long, only 14 m wide, and has a total surface area of 2,940 m^2; the northern protrusion measures 50 m from north to south, 18-26 m wide, and between 18 and 26 m east to west, with a total surface area of 3,150 m^2. The total surface area of the western part of the wall section measures 6,090 m^2. The rammed earth layer of the western part is rather thin, measuring between 10 and 20 cm. The northern protrusion has a thicker layer, measuring up to 150 cm in thickness, which might have been the result of a later renovation.

The eastern part of Section 24 is separated from Section 20 by an east-west running highway to the south. Its eastern side reaches up to the second terrace below the highest. The northern side of the part protrudes slightly, forming an irregular shape. The terrain of the eastern part of the section is rather higher, and it slopes downwards gently to the north. The eastern part of the wall section measures 62 m from east to west, between 25 and 45 m wide from north to south, and has a total surface area of 2,170 m^2. The rammed earth of the eastern part is thick, especially towards the summit plateau, measuring up to 140 cm in thickness, with an average thickness of 60 cm. The rammed earth layer of the lower terraces is thinner, measuring 10 cm on the first terrace, and only 5 cm on the second terrace.

The combined surface area of Section 24 is 8,300 m^2. The rammed earth is all composed of yellowish-brown soil, bearing distinct markings from the ramming tool. We exposed a cross-section for analysis of the subsurface strata at a location between two parts of the wall section (Figs. Ⅰ.4.69- Ⅰ.4.70).

Wall Section 25: This section is situated on the north end of a hillock northeast of Chegezhuang. It is north of the summit plateau of the hillock. The east side is bordered by a north-south oriented gully, and beyond that, by a north-south oriented stretch of hills. The terrain to the west is flatter, and connects with the hillock upon which Section 35 sits. The wall section is oriented to 180°.

This section has a trapezoidal shape.It is bordered on the north by a country road, across from which is Section 24. Its east side is level with the eastern edge of Section 24, while its west side is on the same line with the western edge of the eastern part of Section 24. The section slopes from north to south, and its south end reaches a broken precipice 0.3 m high. The entire section measures 127 m from north to south, and is between 16 and 27 m from east to west, with the northern part wider than the southern part; it has a total surface area of 6,540 m^2.

In the northeastern portion of the wall there is a layer of soil paved to level the ground that measures between 50 and 100 cm in thickness, beneath which we found a 40-50 cm thick layer of rammed earth. This layer of rammed earth thins out to 30 cm thick towards the south side. It is also thinner towards the western part, measuring only 20 cm, and in some spots in this western portion, the underlying bedrock is directly exposed. Towards the northeast side, this rammed earth layer is reddish-brown in color, and composed of fine, hardened soil; to the west side, it is also hardened soil, but yellowish-brown in color (Fig. Ⅰ.4.71).

Wall Section 27: This section is located in the northern part of a hillock northeast of Chegezhuang. It is located on a summit plateau, bordered on the east side by a large, north-south oriented gully, beyond which is another series of north-south oriented hillocks. On the west side, the terrain is more low-lying, at the base of which is a gully oriented northeast to southwest, across from which are Sections 35 and 37. The wall section is oriented to 180°. It is located 64 m down the mountain slope from Section 25.

This section has a roughly rectangular shape. The northeast side is bordered by a small, east-west oriented country road; its south side ends in a 2 m high precipice, below which is Wall Section 28. The eastern and western edges of the section are both on terraces on the summit plateaus, corresponding to the edges of these terraces. The surface of the wall section slopes gently from north to south, and is relatively flat. The section's eastern edge is straight and crude and is in line with the eastern edges of Sections 24 and 25 to the north, indicating that they might have been the original edges of the wall. The eastern precipice is the highest in elevation, measuring between 2 and 2.5 m in height. The wall section measures 153 m from north to south, between 34 and 37 m from east to west, and has a total surface area of 5,400 m^2.

The rammed earth of this wall section is composed of hardened, greyish-brown soil. Towards the north side, it measures between 30 and 40 cm, and thins out to between 10 and 20 cm towards the south. Towards the middle of the wall section, in some places we found no rammed earth, but directly encountered bedrock while coring.

Wall Section 28: This section is located in the northern section of a hillock northeast of Chegezhuang, close on the south edge of Section 27. The wall section lies on a northwest to southeast axis, and is oriented to 159°.

This section has a rectangular shape. The north side abuts the precipice of the south side of wall Section 27, while towards the south side, the rammed earth thins out due to erosion. The eastern and western edges of the section are both on terraces on the summit plateaus, corresponding to the edges of these terraces. The section slopes along with the terrain from north to south, and is relatively flat on top. Its eastern edge is straight, on the same line as the eastern edge of Section 27 to the north, suggesting that they might have been the original edge of the wall. The east and west sides end in a 1 m high precipice. This section measures 53 m from north to south, 32 m from east to west, and has a total surface area of 1,700 m^2.

The rammed earth of this section is not uniform in thickness throughout. On the west side, it forms two strata; the upper stratum is composed of hardened, mixed greyish-brown soil measuring 20 cm thick while the lower stratum is composed of fine, hardened end reddish-brown soil measuring 50 cm thick. The south side is composed of a 120 cm thick layer of reddish-brown soil containing black speckles. The rammed earth at the southeast corner measures 160 cm in thickness and is composed of reddish-brown soil; 100 cm down into this layer, the rammed earth becomes slightly softer in texture. Towards the northeast corner, however, this rammed earth layer is only 10 cm thick. These observations lead us to believe that the construction of this outer wall had followed the natural topography, with soil first filled to level out areas of lower elevation.

Wall Section 31: This section is situated in the middle portion of a hillock northeast of Chegezhuang Village and west of a country road. To the west, the terrain forms a valley; to the east, across a 30 m wide expanse of flat ground, is also a large gully. The section is situated atop a small summit plateau whose terrain slopes from north to south. The section lies along the same axis as the hillock, and is oriented to 192°. Section 31 is located to the south of Section 28, and is separated from the latter by 235 m (Figs. Ⅰ.4.72- Ⅰ.4.73).

This section has sustained heavy damage, and only a series of small, north-south oriented earthen ridges remain. These remains are visible above the ground and are surrounded by very uneven ground due to the flow of water over this terrain. The highest part is even with the country road to the east. But we found no rammed earth east of the road. This wall section slopes towards the south and measures 23 m from north to south, 3-9 m east to west, and its southern side is the widest. It has a total surface area of 138 m^2. We exposed a single cross-section towards the middle of this wall section for analysis (Fig. Ⅰ.4.74).

Section 31 forms the southern extreme of the series of Row K. We found no more evidence of wall sections farther south along the spurs of the mountain ridge.

3. Remains Found around the Outer Wall Sections

During the survey, we were able to find anthropogenic remains in the vicinity of several parts of the outer wall, described below.

Southwest of wall Section 3, we discovered a free-standing section of rammed earth remains, 23 m to the northwest of Section 3 on the north, and 34 m to the southwest corner of Section 3 on the east. The terrace on which it is found is approximately 1.5 m lower in height than the terrace on which Section 3 sits. Based on coring, it was revealed that it is irregular in shape, measuring 3.8 m from east to west and 2.4 m from north to south. The rammed earth, a relatively thin layer of only 30 cm, is composed of grey brown composite soil bearing distinct markings from the tamping tool. Because it is so far removed from Wall Section 3, combined with the shallowness of the rammed earth itself and no evidence that it is directly related to the latter, we were not able determine its function.

Ten m south of Wall Section 6, we discovered a portion of rammed earth remains that was of uneven greyish-brown color with fine hard texture and grey and red soil clump inclusions bearing distinct markings from the ramming tool. It was found to be rectangular in shape, measuring 39 m from east to west, 23 m from north to south, and lying along the same axis as Wall Section 6. The nature and purpose of this section is also unclear.

North of Wall Section 24, we discovered an independent, free-standing piece of rammed earth. It is situated east of the northern protrusion from the western part of Wall Section 24, across a small north-south running gully. The piece is bordered on the south and west sides by this gully, and the east side of the piece is situated in the middle of the plateau. The piece is rectangular in shape, 14 m long, 7 m wide, and 20 cm deep.

The south side of Wall Section 23 is intersected by a wide drainage gully. In the vicinity of this gully, we discovered a large layer of rammed earth averaging 80 cm in thickness. This layer of rammed earth was found to be composed of fine, reddish-brown clay. It was also found to be uneven in thickness, ranging between 50 and 70 cm on the thinner side, and up to 1.6 m in thickness closer to the wall. This fine, reddish-brown rammed earth layer is distinctly different from the greyish-brown soil of the wall section above it. Between the two parts, there is a cliff face measuring between 1.1 and 1.5 m in height and therefore, the two parts cannot be directly related. We hypothesized that because this lower layer of rammed earth bordered the drainage gully on the north, south and east sides, it was meant to shore up the banks of the gully, hence to protect the wall section from possible erosion caused by the extending gully.

Wall Section 77: Situated to the southwest of Caojia Village, at the foot of Mount Mo, the south side of the wall section is connected to the base of the mountain. Section 77 is located in the interior of the outer wall, across an east-west oriented gully from Section 82 and Section 83. It is 280 m from

Section 83, and 300 m from Section 82. It lies along a northwest to southeast axis, and is oriented to 137°. Its north side is bordered by a precipice, while its south side sits across a small country road from the base of the mountain, and its east and west sides form cliffs. It is largely rectangular in shape. The face of the northern precipice is approximately 8 m high, and contains an approximately 5 m high layer of rammed earth; the southern sections of the precipices on the east and west are lower, only up to 2 m high. Moving to the north (towards the gully), the cliffs become higher as they approach the northern precipice (Pl. 23: 1). The surface of the wall section slopes from south to north, and is relatively even. It measures 80 m from north to south, 20 m from east to west, and has a total surface area of 1,600 m^2. The rammed earth is yellowish-brown in color, hardened and compacted in texture, with sand and gravel inclusions, and bearing the distinct markings of the tamping tool. The northern side of this rammed earth is approximately 5 m in thickness, and thins out to only 70 cm in thickness towards the south. In the middle of the wall section, the rammed earth measures around 2 m in thickness. Evidently, this wall section was originally constructed on the slope of a hillock, which explains why the rammed earth is thicker in the areas of lower elevation. This particular section is situated in the interior of the outer city, and does not line up with or connect to the other outer wall sections; in fact, it connects to the foot of the mountain, so that it is difficult to determine its original function (Fig. Ⅰ.4.75).

Section 4: Verifying the Location of the Outer Wall

1. The Acquisition of Aerial Photographs from the 1940s

In March 2009, we began communicating with the American National Archives and Records Administration in Washington DC (700 Pennsylvania Ave., Washington DC, 20408-0001) hoping to find aerial photographs of China, which may have included photographs related to Guicheng, taken by the US Air Force during World War II. At the time, this was purely a conjecture on our part, and we did not know if such photographs existed. We were informed by the archivists in Washington that we would have to contact the Cartographic and Architectural Section at The National Archives and Records Administration (NARA) in neighboring Maryland, and would likely be required to search for the photographs ourselves.

On the morning of March 19, Professor Li Feng travelled by bus to The National Archives and Records Administration in College Park Maryland (Cartographic and Architectural Section, NARA, 8601 Adelphi Road, College Park, MD 20740-6001). Once there, with the help of archivist Gerald Luchansky, Professor Li was able to determine that in 1945, the US Air Force undertook multiple missions to conduct aerial reconnaissance of the Japanese occupied Shandong Peninsula. Cross-referencing using topographic maps, Professor Li marked out the location of Guicheng on the action map for the reconnaissance missions provided by Mr. Luchansky, who further located the designated film strips to be developed into images by Do You Graphics, a partnered vendor of the National Archives.

On April 15, we received notification that Do You Graphics was in the process of developing the filmstrips received from the archives, and on May 6 we received two PDF previews of the developed images. The film was marked with the numbers: NWCS-373-Can ON061275. The film was originally taken on February 9, 1945, at a scale of 1:40,000, and printed as a 9×9 cm^2 black and white negative. The two images that we were able to obtain were derived from the eighteenth and nineteenth pieces of the film from the original canister. The photographs covered the area from the northeast of the city center of Old Huang County (in the upper portion) down to the northwestern foot of Mount Lai. Guicheng is depicted mostly in the upper portion of the final image (on image 19), or in the upper right corner (Fig. Ⅰ.4.76). Once we determined the overall location and boundaries of the site, we had Do You Graphics make full-sized prints for us, which we received after two days as .TIF files. These two images have proved to be very precious to the current investigation and provided valuable photographic evidence of the state of the site and its surroundings from seventy-five years ago.

2. Survey Results and Photographic Verification (of Main Outer Wall Sections)

By this time, after two seasons of fieldwork in Winter 2007 and Summer 2008, we had already completed the survey and coring of Guicheng's outer city wall. Obtaining aerial photographs in May 2009, therefore, offered us a good chance to verify the accuracy of the locations of the inner and outer city walls discovered through surface survey and coring. First of all, we found that the inner wall of the city site was clearly visible in the photographs, as was the old riverbed of the Yaque River that had eroded its eastern side.

What is also clearly visible on the aerial photographs from the 1945 is that after a long period of exploitation, the terrain surface around Guicheng is no longer the same as it might have been during the Western-Eastern Zhou period. What had once been hillocks have largely been transformed into terraced farmland. These terraced fields were constructed using the immediate environs. What that meant was that, since most of the outer wall sections had originally been constructed on the summits of hillocks, they were largely eroded and flattened out by locals using the earth to constructed terraced farmlands. The edges of the wall sections, because they were high in elevation, usually were renovated to maintain their original directions. Therefore, we found that the orientation of the outer wall sections determined the shape of the terraced fields, which were constructed in accordance with the orientation of the wall sections. Because of this, when we consult the images, it is often difficult to identify the locations of the outer wall sections based directly on the area and direction of the fields. For instance,

Row C wall sections are oriented along a north-south axis, and the terraced fields follow the same orientation. Row H wall sections are oriented on an east-west axis, and the terraced fields are also oriented along this axis. It is difficult to differentiate between the two.

According to the photographs, there was a distinct zone of topographic abnormalities between Beishan Village and the north of Dayucun that did not match the north-south orientation of the surrounding terraced fields. These abnormalities were consistent in position, orientation, and shape with Row A wall sections, and we were able to confirm that these abnormalities were indeed the few remaining sections of the outer wall in this area (Fig. Ⅰ.4.77). Moving from Beishan Village south, the zone of abnormality continues to extend as far as the location of wall Section 94 in Row J. Although it is rather difficult to identify wall sections on the aerial photographs due to their having the same orientation as the fields, in the areas along the western side of the outer walls we were nevertheless able to see , at the location of Section 24 in Row K, a huge accumulation of earth on the ground surface. This directly confirms the accuracy of our coring survey.

Despite the fact that the aerial photograph covers the southwestern portion of the city site, we found no traces of outer wall sections in this area. This confirms our belief that the outer wall of Guicheng connected directly to the mountain in the south.

Section 5: Conclusion

1. Chronological Dating of the Outer Wall

Because we only conducted a survey of the outer walls rather than a full excavation, we were not able to directly determine the date of the sections that we discovered. Therefore, we can only infer the date based on the information from the complete surface survey conducted between the inner and outer city walls, as well as on the clues we uncovered through the survey of the outer wall. During the full-coverage surface survey, we found that pottery sherds collected in the outer city area, particularly along the outer wall sections, are mainly from the Eastern Zhou period. This includes two high concentrations of Eastern Zhou period sherds in Area 8 and Area 12 (see Chapter 6). During the survey of the outer wall, we discovered several cord-marked bricks and human-modified stones near the remains of Wall Section 35. We believe that these were originally parts of the architectural structures that were once constructed atop this wall section. The cord-markings on the bricks were made with coarse string, and are typical of the Eastern Zhou period (Fig. Ⅰ.4.47, Fig. Ⅰ.6.13). This evidence seems to indicate the time period during which the outer wall was used.

From the clues discussed above, and also considering the history of development of cities in the Central Plains during the Eastern Zhou period, we tentatively propose that the date of the first construction of the outer wall, as well as the earliest period of its use history, falls in the Spring and Autumn period. Any more detail than this, however, will require research and excavation in the future.

2. Construction of the Outer Wall: Geographical Factors

Guicheng is geographically situated amongst mountains and rivers. It is backed up against the slopes of Mount Lai and its terrain, both within the city walls and without, is composed of undulating hillocks, while the Yaque River flows directly through the city site. The choice to construct a city here was, we believe, made with considerations of this natural terrain in mind.

The first priority in constructing a city is its defense system. Guicheng has two circuits of city walls, inner and outer, forming two layers of defensive fortifications. The inner city was constructed on an area of higher elevation, putting it in a highly defensible position. Both the northwestern and eastern sides of the city are bordered by the river, forming an important protective screen. The people of the city built a high wall around the inner city that stood 8 m higher than the surrounding terrain (using the remains of Section A as the benchmark, the original wall must have been even higher), which made the inner city quite well-protected.

The construction of the outer city defensive system was even more dependent on the natural terrain than the inner city. Protection of the south side relied upon the presence of Mount Lai, while on the other three sides the terrain consisted of low-lying hillocks. The outer wall only had three sides of construction: north, east, and west. The remains of Row F wall sections on the southeast side of the city are only 200 m away from the slopes of Mount Lai, and the hillocks in this area connect directly to the base of the mountain. The remains of Row G wall sections on the southwest side of the city are only 100 m from the base of the mountain, which also indicates that at one point they were connected to form a complete fortification. The slopes of Mount Lai are precipitous, making the mountain difficult to surmount. This meant that the builders of the Guicheng city site could spare both material and labor by using the mountain as a natural barrier preventing attack from the south.

The remaining portions of the outer wall were all constructed on the summits of hillocks surrounding the inner city; these hillocks were all bordered on the inner and outer slopes by deep natural ravines. Examples are the eastern hillocks upon which Rows C, E and F wall sections are situated, and the hillocks upon which Rows G and H wall sections on the west side and Row A wall sections on the north side are located. By making use of this kind of terrain, the builders were able to get twice the result for half the effort.

On the eastern side, Row C wall section hillocks measure 1600 m long in total and are located east of Dongjia and Heping Villages; they are largely on a north-south axis spanning the eastern side of the inner city. These hillocks are between 20 and 30 m above the surrounding terrain. There are no further hillocks between this stretch and the inner city wall, making this terrain the first set of natural defensive barriers of Guicheng. Row H wall sections on the western side are located to the northwest of Caojia Village, and measures 850 m in length on a northeast to southwest axis, forming a large natural protective screen for the city on its southwest side. The Row A wall sections on the northern side are situated on the hillock between Beishan Village and Dayujia Village that measures 1200 m in total length. The inner slope of this hillock is steep while the outer slope is gentler, masking the steep incline on the interior when viewed from outside the outer wall.

In the valley between hillocks, the builders of the city walls also constructed wall sections in order to connect the two hills. For instance, there is a 600-meter long section of this kind of wall connecting Row A and Row C wall sections. The current course of the Yaque River flows through this valley, and coring in the area around it revealed a large span of riverine deposits, indicating that in the past, the river had changed course several times in this area. Wall Section 10 is situated on the northwestern see of this valley, while the southeastern side abuts the modern banks of the Yaque River. We hypothesize that this section of wall was constructed for the purpose of sealing off access to the river in this area. In between Row C and Row E wall sections is a 200 m wide valley; Wall Section 37 was created in order to compete the defensive barrier in this area.

At the same time, in choosing where to construct the wall section, the builders clearly preferred to build where the low-lying valleys were narrow. For instance, Row E wall sections are located where three separate hillocks extending to the south in parallel with one another. The decision to situate these wall sections on the middle hillock was, we believe, because it would have left only a 25 m wide valley between these sections and those of Row F wall sections. The sides of this valley are steep, and at its bottom is a 10 meter wide river, making this valley difficult to penetrate.

There are several tributaries of the upper Yaque River that flow through the city of Guicheng. The presence of this waterway sustained the occupation of the city site. In the inner city, there are two main tributaries, divided on the eastern and northwestern sides, forming a defensive screen outside of the inner wall. Although the tributary to the northwest is not far from the city wall, there is a 5 m difference in elevation, which makes the defense of the inner city easier. There is a third tributary that flows along the southern side that transects the moat and enters the city flowing northwards and out again through a gap in the wall; this tributary formed the basic framework of the city's water system. It provided the source of water for the city's inhabitants.

Several small waterways run through the space between the outer and inner city walls. These waterways cause the land in this area to be quite fertile, convenient for irrigation, and very suitable for human habitation. As a result, this space was likely the primary living space for most of the city's inhabitants. One such waterway originates in the foothills of Mount Lai, flows south to north west of Chijia Village and east of Dongjia Village then enters the Yaque River. On the west bank of the river, between the west side of Heping Village and the south side of Dongjia Village, the terrain was originally a high terrace, but was lowered in the modern era due to earth removal for brick manufacture, leaving only a long strip of terrace with a 4 m high cliff. Surface survey in this area revealed an abundance of anthropogenic remains, suggesting that at the time, this area was heavily occupied. Further research on this will not only increase our understanding of human activities in this area, but will also increase understanding of the process by which Guicheng grew, developed and changed over time.

3. City Gates and Wall-top Structures

Regarding city gates and wall-top structures, because we were restricted to survey only, we are not able to discuss them in any great detail here, but can only hypothesize about their conditions based on the information available.

To the south of Wall Section 22, we discovered a 15 m wide opening. The local toponym for this opening was the "Chengmenkou," or "City Gate." There is currently a road going through this opening heading towards the inner city where the modern village of Heping is located, and serves as the residents' main thoroughfare. Unfortunately, we were unable to determine whether or not this was an original gate in the wall.

Regarding the buildings once constructed on top of the wall sections, we found two possible locations, near Wall Sections 1 and 99. On average, the outer wall section remains measured 20-30 m in width, but in these two locations it measured 100 m wide, making them suitable to bear structures. More research, however, is needed to confirm this hypothesis. A third possible location is in the vicinity of Wall Section 35, where the we found the cord-marked bricks as well as human-modified stones, suggesting that they were used as the foundations for wall-top structures. More research is needed to confirm this hypothesis as well.

4. The Possible Functions of Row K Wall Sections

Row K wall sections are located below Row C wall sections, and run along the outside of Row D and E wall sections. They form an independent and secondary branch of the outer wall. Because we were not able to conduct excavation on this section of wall, its dating and structure are yet to be determined. But here we can offer two conjectures. One possibility for its construction is that it was built to seal off a large gap in Row D wall sections caused by the presence of a wide valley in the natural terrain. Wall Section 37 is situated in this 200 m wide valley in between sections belonging to Row D. Row K wall sections are situated perfectly along the outside of Wall Section 37, and possibly served as another defensive layer.

Secondly, historical sources support that Guicheng was the capital of the state of Lai. According to the records on Qi's conquest of Lai taken from the 6th year of the reign of Duke Xiang in the

Zuozhuan: "In the eleventh month, the Ruler of Qi destroyed Lai; Lai relied on scheming. ...In the fourth month, Yan Ruo fortified Dongyang, and moved on from there to surround Lai. **On day *jiayin*, [Qi troops] mounded earth (*yin*) up against the round city wall, reaching the battlements**. ... Yan Ruo laid siege to Tang, and in the eleventh month on day-*bingchen*, destroyed it. [He] moved the remaining Lai People to Ni. Gao Hou and Cui Zhu settled their lands." In addition, the *Zhengyi* commentary says that "In the military texts, there is the method of piling-up earth (*yin* 堙). That is, to build up another section of wall outside the city-wall and use it as "siege ramp" to break into the city. Not far to the north of these Row K wall sections is the gap that locals call "City Gate" It is possible that when the Qi army attacked the Lai capital, they built up mud and soil along the hillock to the south, following along the ridge of hillock in order to draw close to the city wall, and once this "siege ramp" came to the same height as the city wall, they commenced a direct attack upon the city interior. If this is the case, Row K wall sections would have been the remains of a siege ramp. However, since we did not excavate the remains of these wall sections, we were unable to determine the relative dates of the structures or their interrelationship.

(Translated by Glenda Chao)

第五章 内城的试掘

徐明江

第一节 引 言

一、试掘的目的与相关背景

龙口归城考古调查勘探始于2007年，通过中美联合考古队的不懈努力，对归城城址的内外城范围、城墙走向、内城建筑布局、内外城间的聚落分布都有了初步了解，也对归城城址的大致年代有了一定的认识，但是要更加清楚地把握城址的年代问题，则必须要通过考古地层学来解决。2009年夏，为更好地解决城址的年代问题，了解城址的地层堆积情况，同时为重建归城遗址的形成历史提供直接证据，我们研究决定选择南城墙中间一段的北侧进行试掘。

二、试掘区的地理环境及位置

发掘区位于归城内城南城墙内侧，南段跨在南城墙上，西距归城西南石头保护墙约230米，距东和平村西侧纵贯归城内城的水泥路约130米，北距夯土2约55米，东距夯土1约10米（图Ⅰ.3.1）。我们根据钻探阶段所得对地下堆积的基本认识确定了探沟的具体位置，使其既能揭露一部分城墙夯土，又能充分解剖城内地层，为我们了解城墙和城内地层堆积的关系提供证据。发掘区原来是一片花生地，地表散落较多陶片，南面是南城墙断崖，其他三面种植果树（图版39：1、2）。探沟南端距城墙断崖2米，北端距离归城地面采集单位（CCU）Ⅰ20米，这样以便在发掘后将发掘单位所出陶片与地表调查采集陶片进行对比，并以此为依据来探讨地上、地下遗迹之间的相互关系（见上编第六章第五节）。发掘结果证明，探沟的位置选择比较理想。

三、试掘经过

2009年7月3日，考古队在发掘区布探沟2条，南侧探沟编号TG1（图Ⅰ.5.1；图版27）。北侧探沟编号TG2（图Ⅰ.5.2；图版30）。受地形限制，布方时依照地形、地势走向，方向为北偏东17°，这同归城内城的整体方向和地面田垄、果树的走向是一致的。探沟布方面积为2米×8米，中间留1米的隔梁，实际发掘面积为30平方米。7月4日，开始正式发掘，至7月20日发掘完毕（图版40、41）。

第二节　地层堆积与遗迹现象

一、地层堆积

发掘区地层根据土质、土色以及包含物的不同可分为5层。因为遗迹众多，打破现象频繁，地层不甚连续。其中TG1内分布有第1、3、4、5层（图版28、29）。TG2内分布有第1、2、3、5层（图版31、32）。现分述如下：

第1层：耕土。灰褐色，土质疏松，内含现代瓦片、瓷片、石块、灰渣及植物根系。厚12～24厘米。该层下发现G1、G2、H1、H2、H3、H4、H5、H6、H7、H10、H16、H18、H19等。H2下叠压H21，H3下叠压H13。

第2层：灰土。土质松，内含黄土块及少量绳纹灰陶片，距地表深12～16厘米，厚0～24厘米。仅在发掘区中部出现，主要分布于TG2东南部。该层下未发现遗迹。

第3层：灰褐土。土质较硬，含大量水锈；内含粗砂粒及少量灰陶、红褐陶片等（图Ⅰ.5.3；表Ⅰ.5.3、Ⅰ.5.4；图版44：1、2），距地表深12～36厘米，厚0～30厘米。基本主要分布于发掘区中部，即TG1北部、TG2南部。该层下发现H8、H9、H11、H12、H14、H15、H17、H20等。H12发现底部发现一柱洞，编号D1。H8下叠压H14。

第4层：浅灰土。土质较硬，含水锈、沙砾等，含少量灰陶片。距地表深20～26厘米，厚16～25厘米，主要分布于TG1南部，叠压在城墙夯土上，TG2不见该层。

第5层：夯土。含粗砂粒，质硬。该层为城墙夯土，未发现陶片。根据含沙量的不同可分为3小层。第5a层为黄褐土，掺杂较多沙砾，厚12厘米。第5b层为灰褐土，掺杂少量沙子、石砾等，厚8厘米。第5c层为黄土，土致密、质纯。在TG2内该层直接叠压在生土上。

二、主要遗迹现象及相互关系

发掘区共发现城墙夯土1处，晚期沟2条，灰坑21个。

城墙夯土主要分布于发掘区南部TG1内，其北部边缘伸入TG2内（图版33）。城墙夯土被H9、H12、H20直接打破。灰坑大多分布于TG2（图Ⅰ.5.4、Ⅰ.5.5）。

第三节　地层及主要遗迹单位的年代序列

根据地层叠压、打破关系，结合出土器物，进行文化因素分析，可以初步判定：第1层为现代耕土层，第2层为汉代文化层，第3层为春秋时期文化层，第4层为西周中期文化层，第5层为西周早期文化层。早期灰坑主要有H9、H12、H15、H16、H18、H19、H20、H21等，时代为西周早期至春秋早期。晚期灰坑主要有H3、H4、H6、H8等，时代为春秋中期。城墙夯土时代应为西周早期晚段。

第四节　重要遗迹及出土遗物

此次发掘遗迹主要是灰坑、灰沟等，多位于发掘区北部。TG1南部压在城墙夯土上，遗迹现象相对较少。受发掘面积所限，除H3完整外，大多数灰坑未窥其全貌。根据可见形制分析，灰坑形状以圆形、椭圆形居多，少数为不规则形、圆角方形等，多为直壁或斜壁。灰坑大小不一，深浅不等。填土多为灰褐色，较松软。出土遗物有陶、石、骨角器及少量铜器。陶器以泥质陶居多，陶色主要有深灰、浅灰两种。夹砂陶以红褐、灰褐为主，较多掺杂云母、滑石粉等。器型可复原者不多，可辨器型主要有鼎、鬲、簋、豆、罐、盆、壶、瓿、瓦、器盖等。其中以鬲、簋、豆、罐数量最多。陶器素面较多，纹饰有绳纹、弦纹、刻划纹、网格纹、乳钉纹、附加堆纹等。其中以绳纹为主体，又可分为粗绳纹、中绳纹、细绳纹、麻点绳纹等。灰沟均为长条形，斜壁，平底，深浅一致。皆灰褐色填土，出土绳纹簋、绳纹罐、豆、碗等。关于各个遗迹出土遗物的详尽介绍，采用列表形式，另附于后文（表Ⅰ.5.1～Ⅰ.5.4）。下面就发现的各类遗迹按顺序编号逐一介绍。

一、灰　　沟

G1　位于TG1中部。开口于第1层下，打破H7。平面形状呈长条状，东西两端分别伸入探沟壁，斜壁，平底。沟口距地表深16～20厘米，东西长200、南北宽57～68、深24厘米。沟内堆积为灰褐色，质松。包含遗物为陶片、兽骨。陶片主要为灰陶，部分饰有绳纹。可辨器型有簋、豆、罐、碗等（图Ⅰ.5.6；表Ⅰ.5.5；图版44：3、4）。

G2　位于TG1中部。开口于第1层下，打破第4层。平面形状呈长条状，东西两端分别伸入探沟壁，斜壁，平底。沟口距地表深18～20厘米，东西长200、南北宽22、深20厘米。沟内堆积为灰褐色，质松。无包含物。

这两条沟在TG1中部平行分布，且深度、宽度均相差并不大，我们推测应该属同一时期的遗迹。两条沟均开口于第1层下，下部打破第4层，地层区间较大，时代不易准确判断。但并未发现太晚时期的遗物，根据G1出土陶片的器形和纹饰，初步判断时代可能属于春秋中晚期。

二、灰　坑

H1　位于TG2东南部，东部伸入探沟东壁。开口于第1层下，打破现代沟、H6、H11。平面形状呈圆角方形，圆角，直壁，平底。坑口距地表深16厘米，长径残120、短径56～64、深20厘米。坑内堆积为黄褐色，质略松，含烧土颗粒及少量灰烬。无包含物。推测其应为现代取土坑。

H2　位于TG2西北部，西部伸入探沟西壁。开口于第1层下，打破H6、H10、H19、H20、H21。平面形状呈椭圆形，坑口不甚规整，口大底小，斜壁，底略平（图Ⅰ.5.7；图版34：3）。坑口距地表深14～18厘米，长径204、短径残140、深70厘米。坑内堆积为浅灰褐色，质稍松，含黄土颗粒及少量草木灰。包含物：陶片、兽骨、烧土块、石块。可辨器形有鼎、鬲、簋、豆、罐、盆、碗、器盖、圆陶片等；纹饰有绳纹、弦纹等（图Ⅰ.5.8、Ⅰ.5.9；表Ⅰ.5.6；图版42：1）。推测其应为垃圾坑。

H3　位于TG1北部，是此次发掘中相对完整的一个灰坑。开口于第1层下，打破H7、H8、H9、H13、H14及第3、4层。平面形状呈椭圆形，东西两边分别伸入探沟壁，口小底大，平底（图Ⅰ.5.10；图版34：4）。坑口距地表深16厘米，口径213、底径222、深68～70厘米。坑内堆积根据土质、土色不同可分为3层。第①层：灰褐土。质松，含炭粒。堆积呈两边高，中间低，厚0～25厘米。包含物：陶片、兽骨、石镰。陶片可辨器形有鼎足、鬲、甗、豆、罐、壶、器盖、圈形器等。纹饰有绳纹、弦纹等（图Ⅰ.5.11、Ⅰ.5.12；表Ⅰ.5.7；图版43：2；图版44，5～7；图版45：1）。第②层：红褐土。质松，含烧土颗粒。该层主要分布于灰坑东半部，厚0～58厘米，发现狗骨架1具（图Ⅰ.5.13；图版34：2）。包含物：陶片、兽骨。可辨器形有鬲、簋、豆、罐等。纹饰有绳纹、弦纹等（图Ⅰ.5.14；表Ⅰ.5.8；图版42：2～4；图版44：8～9；图版45：2～4）。第③层：青灰土。质硬，含炭屑、水锈等。堆积呈西高东低，厚10～60厘米。包含物：陶片、兽骨。陶片少，可辨器形有鬲、簋、豆、瓮、器盖等。纹饰有绳纹、弦纹、刻划纹、乳钉纹等（图Ⅰ.5.15；表Ⅰ.5.9；图版45：5～8）。另外还发现大量烧土块、木炭及一段土坯。用途推测应为生活垃圾坑。

H4　位于TG2东南部，东部伸入探沟东壁。开口于第1层下，被现代沟打破，打破H9、H11、H12。平面形状呈圆形，直壁，平底（图Ⅰ.5.16；图版35：3）。坑口距地表深50厘米，口径68、底径68、深86厘米。坑内堆积为灰黄色，质稍松，含黄土块及少量草木灰。包含物：陶片、兽骨、石块。可辨器形有甗、簋、豆、罐、器盖、瓦等。纹饰有绳纹、弦纹等（图Ⅰ.5.17、Ⅰ.5.18；表Ⅰ.5.10；图版45：9；图版46：1）。推测其为取土废弃后垃圾坑。

H5　位于TG2西南部，西部伸入探沟西壁。开口于第1层下，打破H6、H20。平面形状不规则，南壁略直，平底（图Ⅰ.5.19；图版35：4）。坑口距地表深16厘米，长55、宽40、深14

厘米。坑内堆积为浅灰色，质略松，含烧土颗粒、石块及少量草木灰。无陶片。推测其应为取土废弃后的垃圾坑。

H6　位于TG2中部偏南。开口于第1层下，被H1、H5打破，打破H11、H12、H17、H20。平面形状呈椭圆形，直壁，平底（图Ⅰ.5.20；图版35：1～2）。坑口距地表深15厘米，长径166、短径123、深60厘米。坑内堆积为黄灰色，质略松，含黄土块及少量草木灰。包含物：陶片、石块、兽骨、兽牙。可辨器形有鼎、鬲、簋、豆、罐、盆、器盖等。纹饰有绳纹、弦纹、刻划纹等（图Ⅰ.5.21、Ⅰ.5.22；表Ⅰ.5.11；图版46：2～3）。推测其应为取土废弃后垃圾坑。

H7　位于TG1西部。开口于第1层下，被G1、H3打破，打破3层、H8。平面形状可能为圆形，发掘仅暴露一小部分，大部分压于探沟西壁下。斜壁，平底（图Ⅰ.5.1）。坑口距地表深16厘米，东西长37、南北长218、深28厘米。坑内堆积为灰褐色，质略松，含烧土颗粒及草木灰。出土陶簋、豆各1件，豆为素面磨光，簋饰绳纹（图Ⅰ.5.23；表Ⅰ.5.12；图版46：4）。

H8　位于TG1西北部。开口于第3层下，被G1、H3、H7打破，打破4层。平面形状呈椭圆形，部分压于探沟西壁下。直壁，平底（图Ⅰ.5.1；图版36：1）。坑口距地表深26厘米，长径92、短径64、深71～78厘米。堆积为灰色，土质松，含沙。包含物：陶片、兽骨。可辨器形有鼎、鬲、簋、豆、罐、盆、器盖等。纹饰有绳纹、附加堆纹等（图Ⅰ.5.24、Ⅰ.5.25；表Ⅰ.5.13；图版46：5～6）。

H9　位于TG1北部，TG2南部。开口于第3层下，被现代沟打破，打破H12、H20。平面形状呈圆形，斜壁，平底（图Ⅰ.5.26；图版36：2）。坑口距地表深50厘米，口径334、深64厘米。坑内堆积为深灰褐色，质略硬，含水锈及少量草木灰。包含物：陶片、石块、兽骨、贝壳。可辨器形有鬲、甗、簋、豆、罐、盆、器盖、陶范等。纹饰有绳纹、弦纹、附加堆纹等（图Ⅰ.5.27～Ⅰ.5.29；表Ⅰ.5.14；图版46：7～9；图版47：1、2；图版52）。推测其应为取土废弃后当作垃圾坑。

H10　位于TG2中部偏西，西部伸入探沟西壁。开口于第1层下，被H2打破，打破H20、H21。平面形状不规则，壁不甚规整，圜底（图Ⅰ.5.2）。坑口距地表深18厘米，长72、宽25、深45厘米。坑内堆积为浅灰褐色，质略松，含烧土颗粒及少量草木灰。包含物：陶片、石块。可辨器型有簋，饰绳纹，推测其应为取土后废弃后当作垃圾坑。

H11　位于TG2东南部。开口于第3层下，被现代沟打破，打破H12、H15、H17、H20。平面形状略呈椭圆形，直壁，平底（图Ⅰ.5.30）。坑口距地表深58厘米，长径残300、短径150、深24厘米。坑内堆积为浅灰色，质略松，含烧土颗粒及少量草木灰。包含物：陶片、石块、兽骨。可辨器形有鬲、簋、豆、罐、器盖等，纹饰有绳纹、弦纹等（图Ⅰ.5.31、Ⅰ.5.32；表Ⅰ.5.15；图版47：3、4）。推测其应为取土废弃后当作垃圾坑。

H12　位于TG1的东北部、TG2东南部。开口于第3层下，被H4、H6、H9、H11打破，打破H17、H20。平面形状呈椭圆形，直壁，底部不规整（图Ⅰ.5.33；图版36：3～4）。坑口距地表深56厘米，长径366、短径残146、深70厘米。坑内堆积分为两层。第①层：浅灰土。质地较松。第②层：灰褐土。质略硬，含烧土颗粒及草木灰。包含物：陶片、石块、兽骨。可辨器形有鬲、簋、豆、罐、瓿等。纹饰有绳纹、弦纹等（图Ⅰ.5.34、Ⅰ.5.35；表Ⅰ.5.16；图版47：

5～8）。灰坑底部有一柱洞，直径18、深45厘米，填土为灰褐色，质松，有少量陶片。推测其应当作垃圾坑。

H13　位于TG1东北部。开口于第3层下，被H3、H9及H12打破，打破夯土。平面形状呈椭圆形，大部分压于探沟东壁下，斜壁，底部凹凸不平（图Ⅰ.5.1）。坑口距地表深80厘米，长径128、短径38、深5～26厘米。堆积为灰黄色，质松，含沙。无包含物。

H14　位于TG1西北角。开口于第3层下，被H12、H9、H3打破，打破夯土。平面形状不规则，部分压于探沟西壁，斜壁，底凹凸不平（图Ⅰ.5.1）。坑口距地表深86厘米，长81、宽60、深0～16厘米。坑内堆积为灰黄色，含水锈、草木灰等。无包含物。

H15　位于TG2中部偏东。开口于第1层下，被现代沟及H11打破，打破H17、H18、H20。平面形状呈圆形，东部伸入探沟东壁。坑口较为规整，口小底大，呈袋形，坑壁未见加工痕迹，平底（图Ⅰ.5.36；图版37：1）。坑口距地表深58厘米，口径236、深130厘米。坑内堆积分为两层。第①层：浅灰褐土。质较松。第②层：黄褐土。质略硬，含烧土颗粒及少量草木灰。包含物：陶片、石块、兽骨。可辨器形有鬲、簋、豆、罐、器盖等，纹饰有绳纹，个别有磨光（图Ⅰ.5.37；表Ⅰ.5.17；图版47：9）。推测其应为取土废弃后当作垃圾坑。

H16　位于TG2西北角。开口于第1层下，被H2打破，打破H18、H19。平面形状呈圆形。坑口较为规整，斜壁，坑壁未见加工痕迹，底部呈弧形（图Ⅰ.5.38；图版37：2）。坑口距地表深18厘米，口径130～140、深0～50厘米。坑内堆积为浅灰褐色，质地较松，含草木灰及少量烧土颗粒。包含物：陶片、石块、兽骨。可辨器形有鬲、簋、豆、罐、盆、瓮、器盖、圆陶片等。纹饰有绳纹、弦纹、刻划纹、乳钉纹等（图Ⅰ.5.39、Ⅰ.5.40；表Ⅰ.5.18；图版48：1～3）。推测其应为取土废弃后当作垃圾坑。

H17　位于TG2中部偏东。开口于第3层下，被H6、H12、H11、H15打破，打破H20。平面形状呈椭圆形，东部伸入探沟东壁。坑口较规整，斜壁，底部不平（图Ⅰ.5.41；图版37：3）。坑口距地表深60厘米，长190、宽70、深0～50厘米。坑内堆积为黄灰色，质稍硬，含少量草木灰颗粒。包含物：陶片、石块、兽骨。可辨器形有鼎、鬲、豆、罐、器盖等。纹饰有绳纹、弦纹等（图Ⅰ.5.42、Ⅰ.5.43；表Ⅰ.5.19；图版48：4～5）。推测其应为取土废弃后当作垃圾坑。

H18　位于TG2东北角。开口于第1层下，被H15、H16打破，打破H19。平面形状呈椭圆形，口大底小，斜壁，平底（图Ⅰ.5.44；图版37：4）。坑口距地表深58厘米，长202、宽106、深86厘米。坑内堆积为黄褐色，质略松，含较多草木灰。包含物：陶片、石块、兽骨。可辨器形有鬲、簋、豆、罐等。纹饰有绳纹、弦纹等（图Ⅰ.5.45；图Ⅰ.5.46；表Ⅰ.5.20；图版48：6～8）。推测其应为取土废弃后当作垃圾坑。

H19　位于TG2西北角。开口于第1层下，被H2、H18、H16打破，打破H21。平面形状呈椭圆形，坑口不规整，壁略斜，平底。坑口距地表深16厘米，长162、宽102、深36～85厘米（图Ⅰ.5.47）。坑内堆积为灰褐色，质稍硬，含草木灰。包含物：陶片、石块、兽骨。可辨器形有鼎、鬲、簋、豆、罐、甗、壶、器盖等。纹饰有绳纹、弦纹、刻划纹、附加堆纹等（图Ⅰ.5.48～Ⅰ.5.50；表Ⅰ.5.21；图版48：9；图版49：1～8）。推测其应为取土废弃后当作垃圾坑。

H20　位于TG2南部。开口于第3层下，被H2、H5、H6、H9、H10、H11、H12、H15、H17、H21打破，打破夯土、生土。西部保存较好，其他三面被打破较甚，从底部看分布范围较大。平面形状为不规则形，坑口不甚规整，壁呈斜坡状，底部凹凸不平。坑口距地表深16～80厘米，残长870、宽200、深0～102厘米（图Ⅰ.5.51；图版38：1～2）。坑内堆积分为两层。第①层：黑灰土。质地较松。出土陶片可辨器形有鼎、鬲、簋、豆、罐、瓿、盆、圆陶片等。纹饰有绳纹、弦纹、乳钉纹、附加堆纹等（图Ⅰ.5.52～Ⅰ.5.55；表Ⅰ.5.22；图版49：9；图版50：1～9；图版51：1～2）。第②层：浅灰褐土。质略硬，含水锈、草木灰及少量烧土颗粒（图Ⅰ.5.56）。出土陶片可辨器形有鼎、鬲、甗、簋、豆、罐、瓿、圆陶片等。纹饰有绳纹、弦纹、网格纹、乳钉纹等（图Ⅰ.5.57、Ⅰ.5.58；表Ⅰ.5.23；图版43：1；图版51：3～8）。

H21　位于TG2中部偏西。开口于第1层下，被H2、H10、H19打破，打破H20。平面形状呈圆形，坑口不甚规整，斜壁，弧形底（图Ⅰ.5.59）。坑口距地表深60厘米，口径170、深0～22厘米。坑内堆积为灰褐色，质地略硬，底部含有水锈、草木灰及少量烧土颗粒。无包含物。推测其应为取土废弃后当作垃圾坑。

第五节　城墙夯土的发现和认识

一、夯土的出土层位及分布范围

夯土首先在TG1南部露出痕迹，主要分布在整个TG1以及TG2南部。TG1南部夯土层位较高，距地表30厘米。TG2内夯土西端较高，H20叠压其上，东端夯土较低，被H9、H12打破。

为了进一步搞清城墙夯土在发掘区的分布范围及保存情况，我们在发掘区进行了分段钻探，共计打了6个探孔，并对探沟内地层比对分析，发现城墙夯土在发掘区内自南向北逐渐变薄，至TG1北部被灰坑打断，在TG2南部发现夯土北端（图Ⅰ.5.60；图版33）。因此，对南城墙夯土的北部界线有了较为清晰的了解，该段城墙的夯土向北截止到TG2南部，城墙夯土的分布范围进一步明确。

二、夯土的结构及初步认识

结合调查勘探可知，夯土主要分为灰色夯土、灰褐夯土、黄褐夯土、黄色夯土等。发掘区探沟内夯土主要为黄褐夯土和黄色夯土，掺杂石子、沙砾等。

为进一步加深对城墙夯土的认识，我们在发掘区探沟一以南2米，南城墙南部地面断崖处铲了一个剖面，其位置正对TG1南壁，对该段夯土剖面的细部结构进行刮面比对（图Ⅰ.5.61；

图版10：2）。

该段夯土为分层夯筑，剖面可分10层。第1层为沙土，厚10厘米。第2层为浅灰土，厚10～22厘米。第3层为灰土，厚8～18厘米。第4层为淤土，厚10～26厘米。第5层为灰土，厚10～30厘米。第6层为灰黄土，厚8～16厘米。第7层为沙石土层，该层不连续，厚3～8厘米。第8层为黄褐土，厚30～40厘米，根据含沙量多少可分为3小层，厚6～18厘米。第9层为黄土，厚40～50厘米，根据含沙量多少可分4小层，厚6～25厘米。第10层为黄灰土，厚40～50厘米，亦可分3小层。该断崖剖面第6层的土质、土色同TG1南部最初发现的夯土相似，第8层则与H20叠压的夯土相似，但从深度看，该段夯土层位高度比北部夯土层位要浅，这也在我们对TG1内夯土钻探中得到证明。

三、夯土与相关遗迹的关系

TG1内的夯土位于第4层下，并被G1、G2、H3、H7 、H8、H9、H12、H13、H14等遗迹打破。TG2内的夯土位于探沟南部，被H9、H12、H20等遗迹打破。为了保护现存夯土，在发掘到夯土表面后即停止，未作进一步解剖。因此，夯土下面是否还有其他遗迹尚不可知。根据现在发掘的情况了解，夯土是两个探方中最早的人为遗迹。

另外，我们还在夯土中发现了一层砂层，厚约15厘米，从高度看这层砂层可能与南城墙断崖剖面第7层砂土属于同一层。砂层下面的夯土一直延续到TG2南部，厚度变薄，厚10～40厘米。它究竟是城墙基槽的边缘，还是段塌陷的夯土，在未经大范围发掘的情况下暂不宜下结论。经钻探探明该砂层向北一直延续到TG2以北，发掘区以北的砂层直接叠压生土。如果这是同一砂层，那么它就有可能并非城墙夯土的一部分，而属于自然形成，抑或是城墙夯土被洪水冲积形成的一个砂层。如果那样，砂层上下的两部分夯土可能并非一次性建筑，亦可能有后期修补的可能。但是，由于发掘面积较小，发掘区内的遗迹现象又均打破砂层上下的两层夯土，因此，我们难以依据这两层夯土对遗迹现象进行分期。

第六节　结　　语

这次试掘虽然面积不大，但是严格按照《田野考古操作规程》（国家文物局 2009）进行，十分注重使用科技手段获取考古信息，对木炭、动物骨骼、烧土、植硅石、浮选土等进行全面提取，获取了大量科学的考古信息（详见第八章）。发掘区文化堆积十分丰富，遗迹众多，层位关系清楚，并存在较多的打破关系。出土遗物数量较多，颇具时代特点和地域特色。这对于进一步确定归城城址的年代关系，加强对先秦时期的城址研究，了解胶东地区与内陆地区周文化的交流融合以及聚落考古学研究等提供了新的考古学材料。

一、归城内城城址的年代问题

通过发掘，分析灰坑与城墙的打破关系，卡定城墙的年代下限，基本可确定归城的废弃年代。如TG1内的H3、H8、H13、H14，TG2的H12、H20，均叠压打破在城墙夯土上，据此可以确定内城城墙废弃的大致年代。H20为发掘区最早的遗迹单位，直接叠压夯土之上，出土的陶片所饰绳纹比较细密，以细绳纹和中绳纹为主，纹路比较清晰，个别有交错现象，特别是H20第2层（底层）所出陶片的绳纹细密清晰，属比较典型的西周早期样式。出土的陶簋H20②：1，弧腹较宽且深，属于典型的西周早期形态。H20第2层出土多件袋足鬲的裆部、袋足，亦属西周早期形态。另外，H20①：10木炭标本C-14（ZK-3359）测定经树论校正1120（7.1%）1100BC&1090（61.1%）1000BC，年代明显偏早。

综合各方面情况，我们判断H20的年代大约在西周早期偏晚，那么城墙的建筑年代即应该在西周早期范围内。在发掘区内年代略晚于H20的是H18和H19，从其出土陶器判断，年代大约在西周晚期到春秋初年。H3为发掘区最晚的遗迹单位，出土陶片以粗绳纹居多，不少绳纹呈现大麻点状，年代应属春秋时期。综上可以推测归城内城的使用年代可能在西周早中期，废弃年代则可能到春秋中晚期，这个时空跨度与我们地面调查采集的陶片时代情况是一致的。

二、试掘反映归城地区的周文化序列

从文化因素分析来看，归城地区的周文化因素与周原典型周文化有非常密切的关系，后者作为先进青铜文化的代表进入归城后，经过摸索、适应和异化，逐渐形成了具有本地特色的周文化传统。这主要体现在簋、豆、罐等生活盛器类，多为泥质灰陶，并有少量黑皮陶，其制作风格、纹饰特点等在陕西周文化传统中可以找到源流，当属西来之物。属于本地土著的文化因素与西来文化的竞争中失势后，源于当地文化的实用性和选择性，在鼎、鬲、甗等炊煮器上，当地土著文化传统又得以延续。这类陶器质地粗糙，多为夹砂，或掺蚌末、滑石粉等，做工粗犷，注重实用功能，颇负粗率之风，该器类与长岛珍珠门、乳山南黄庄墓地的器类多相若之处。因此归城地区存在着两种截然不同的文化因素和传统。

根据H20与H3这两个典型的遗迹单位，结合调查资料可以看出，部分陶器器形的演变规律大致为：簋的腹部逐渐上移，圈足不断往上提高。豆盘由深变浅，豆柄逐渐变细。罐由平底逐渐变为圈足。鬲由分裆、高裆逐渐变连裆、低裆。从纹饰看，早期纹饰以细绳纹、中绳纹为主，晚期以粗绳纹为主，部分绳纹凌乱发展为麻点绳纹。此次发掘出土的陶器，年代跨度从西周早期至春秋中晚期，其中以西周时期的陶器数量居多，显示出归城城市发展在这一时期经历了较为迅速繁荣的发展时期。

三、土著文化与周文化的关系

从发掘器物反映的两种文化因素看，炊煮器以地方土著为主，生活盛器类则开始周文化化，与陕西周原地区的同类器并无二致。这表明当地文化因素根深蒂固的影响力仍然存在，而生活盛器类逐渐向西部文化因素靠拢，说明西周统治力量的影响力日益深远。两种文化因素风格各异，共存交融，形成了归城地区极具特色的文化风格和体系。

从文化影响的不同阶段看，前期反映周文化的器类开始增多，到后期演变为本地土著色彩的器类，并衍生出新的文化结合体。本地土著文化在前期与周原先进文化交锋失势后，到后期又卷土重来，在某些文化争夺中重新处于优势地位，归城文化在对两种文化融合、吸收后，又形成了新的文化共同体。这些不同文化因素的交流、碰撞与融合，生动地再现了归城地区波澜壮阔的历史大势，也是当时文化影响与西风东渐、反复角逐的具体体现。

表Ⅰ.5.1 陶片器形统计表

Table Ⅰ.5.1 Ceramic sherd vessel type counts

单位	09SLG TG1 H3①																			
陶质、陶色 Clay type/color	泥质陶 Fine-clay ware					夹砂陶 Coarse-clay ware														合计 Grand total
						夹砂 Sand temper				夹云母 Mica temper			夹滑石 Talc temper			夹云母、滑石 Talc and mica temper			小计 Total	
器形 Vessel type	浅灰 Light grey	深灰 Dark grey	灰褐 Grey-brown	红褐 Red-brown	小计 Total	浅灰 Light grey	深灰 Dark grey	灰褐 Grey-brown	红褐 Red-brown	深灰 Dark grey	灰褐 Grey-brown	红褐 Red-brown	深灰 Dark grey	灰褐 Grey-brown	红褐 Red-brown	深灰 Dark grey	灰褐 Grey-brown	红褐 Red-brown		
鼎 *Ding* cauldron								3			1								4	4
鬲 *Li* tripod									8									1	9	9
甗 *Yan* steamer								1	2										3	3
簋 *Gui* tureen	2		2		4															4
豆 *Dou* pedestal dish	1	4			5															5
罐 *Guan* jar	2	4	2	2	10			1											1	11
瓿 *Bu* vase																				
盆 *Pen* basin																				
瓮 *Weng* jar																				
碗 *Wan* bowl																				
壶 *Hu* pot		1			1															1
器盖 Lid	1				1															1
圆陶片 Round sherd						1													1	1
圈形器 Ring shaped object		1			1															1
瓦 Tile						1													1	1
陶范 Clay mold																				
总计 Grand total	22					19														41
百分比 Percentage	53.66%					46. 34%														100%
备注/Notes：																				

续表

单位	09SLG TG1 H3②																			合计 Grand total
陶质、陶色 Clay type/color 器形 Vessel type	泥质陶 Fine-clay ware					夹砂陶 Coarse-clay ware														
						夹砂 Sand temper				夹云母 Mica temper			夹滑石 Talc temper			夹云母、滑石 Talc and mica temper			小计 Total	
	浅灰 Light grey	深灰 Dark grey	灰褐 Grey-brown	红褐 Red-brown	小计 Total	浅灰 Light grey	深灰 Dark grey	灰褐 Grey-brown	红褐 Red-brown	深灰 Dark grey	灰褐 Grey-brown	红褐 Red-brown	深灰 Dark grey	灰褐 Grey-brown	红褐 Red-brown	深灰 Dark grey	灰褐 Grey-brown	红褐 Red-brown		
鼎 *Ding* cauldron																				
鬲 *Li* tripod									2										2	2
甗 *Yan* steamer																				
簋 *Gui* tureen	6	2		1	9															9
豆 *Dou* pedestal dish		1	1	2	4															4
罐 *Guan* jar		4	1	1	6				1										1	7
瓿 *Bu* vase																				
盆 *Pen* basin																				
瓮 *Weng* jar																				
碗 *Wan* bowl																				
壶 *Hu* pot																				
器盖 Lid				1	1															1
圆陶片 Round sherd	1				1															1
圈形器 Ring shaped object																				
瓦 Tile																				
纺轮 spindle whorl		1			1															1
器座 Vessel base				1	1															1
总计 Grand total	23					3														26
百分比 Percentage	88.46%					11.54%														100%

备注/Notes：

续表

单　位	09SLG TG1 H3③																			合计 Grand total
陶质、陶色 Clay type/color	泥质陶 Fine-clay ware					夹砂陶　Coarse-clay ware														
						夹砂 Sand temper				夹云母 Mica temper			夹滑石 Talc temper			夹云母、滑石 Talc and mica temper			小计 Total	
器形 Vessel type	浅灰 Light grey	深灰 Dark grey	灰褐 Grey-brown	红褐 Red-brown	小计 Total	浅灰 Light grey	深灰 Dark grey	灰褐 Grey-brown	红褐 Red-brown	深灰 Dark grey	灰褐 Grey-brown	红褐 Red-brown	深灰 Dark grey	灰褐 Grey-brown	红褐 Red-brown	深灰 Dark grey	灰褐 Grey-brown	红褐 Red-brown		
鼎 *Ding* cauldron																				
鬲 *Li* tripod								1		1									2	2
甗 *Yan* steamer																				
簋 *Gui* tureen	3	1			4															4
豆 *Dou* pedestal dish		2			2															2
罐 *Guan* jar			1		1															1
瓿 *Bu* vase																				
盆 *Pen* basin																				
瓮 *Weng* jar		1			1															1
碗 *Wan* bowl																				
壶 *Hu* pot																				
器盖 Lid	1	1			2															2
圆陶片 Round sherd																				
圈形器 Ring shaped object																				
瓦 Tile																				
陶范 Clay mold																				
总计 Grand total	10					2														12
百分比 Percentage	83.33%					16.67%														100%

备注/Notes：

统计/Counts：李峰/唐锦琼/付群启/毕道传 LI Feng, TANG Jinqiong, FU Qunqi, BI Daochuan

续表

单位	09SLG TG1 ③																			合计 Grand total
陶质、陶色 Clay type/color	泥质陶 Fine-clay ware					夹砂陶 Coarse-clay ware														
						夹砂 Sand temper				夹云母 Mica temper			夹滑石 Talc temper			夹云母、滑石 Talc and mica temper			小计 Total	
器形 Vessel type	浅灰 Light grey	深灰 Dark grey	灰褐 Grey-brown	红褐 Red-brown	小计 Total	浅灰 Light grey	深灰 Dark grey	灰褐 Grey-brown	红褐 Red-brown	深灰 Dark grey	灰褐 Grey-brown	红褐 Red-brown	深灰 Dark grey	灰褐 Grey-brown	红褐 Red-brown	深灰 Dark grey	灰褐 Grey-brown	红褐 Red-brown		
鼎 *Ding* cauldron																				
鬲 *Li* tripod																				
甗 *Yan* steamer																				
簋 *Gui* tureen		2			2															2
豆 *Dou* pedestal dish			1		1															1
罐 *Guan* jar																				
瓿 *Bu* vase																				
盆 *Pen* basin																				
瓮 *Weng* jar																				
碗 *Wan* bowl																				
壶 *Hu* pot																				
器盖 Lid																				
圆陶片 Round sherd	1				1															1
圈形器 Ring shaped object																				
瓦 Tile																				
陶范 Clay mold																				
总计 Grand total	4																			4
百分比 Percentage	100%																			100%

备注/Notes：圆陶片有刻划纹。The round sherd has incised decorations.

日期/Date： 2010年7月22日　July 22, 2010

续表

单　位	09SLG TG1 G1																			合计 Grand total
陶质、陶色 Clay type/color / 器形 Vessel type	泥质陶 Fine-clay ware					夹砂陶　Coarse-clay ware														
						夹砂 Sand temper				夹云母 Mica temper			夹滑石 Talc temper			夹云母、滑石 Talc and mica temper			小计 Total	
	浅灰 Light grey	深灰 Dark grey	灰褐 Grey-brown	红褐 Red-brown	小计 Total	浅灰 Light grey	深灰 Dark grey	灰褐 Grey-brown	红褐 Red-brown	深灰 Dark grey	灰褐 Grey-brown	红褐 Red-brown	深灰 Dark grey	灰褐 Grey-brown	红褐 Red-brown	深灰 Dark grey	灰褐 Grey-brown	红褐 Red-brown		
鼎 *Ding* cauldron																				
鬲 *Li* tripod																				
甗 *Yan* steamer																				
簋 *Gui* tureen		1			1															1
豆 *Dou* pedestal dish	1	1			2															2
罐 *Guan* jar		1	1		2															2
瓿 *Bu* vase																				
盆 *Pen* basin																				
瓮 *Weng* jar																				
碗 *Wan* bowl	1				1															1
壶 *Hu* pot																				
器盖 Lid																				
圆陶片 Round sherd																				
圈形器 Ring shaped object																				
瓦 Tile																				
陶范 Clay mold																				
总计 Grand total	6																			6
百分比 Percentage	100%																			100%

备注/Notes：内出土陶碗时代较晚，怀疑为晚期单位。The ceramic bowl found in this unit dated to a relatively late period, but it is doubtful that the unit is a late-period one.

日期/Date：　2010年7月22日　July 22, 2010

续表

单位	09SLG TG1 H7																			合计 Grand total
陶质、陶色 Clay type/color	泥质陶 Fine-clay ware					夹砂陶 Coarse-clay ware														
						夹砂 Sand temper				夹云母 Mica temper			夹滑石 Talc temper			夹云母、滑石 Talc and mica temper			小计 Total	
器形 Vessel type	浅灰 Light grey	深灰 Dark grey	灰褐 Grey-brown	红褐 Red-brown	小计 Total	浅灰 Light grey	深灰 Dark grey	灰褐 Grey-brown	红褐 Red-brown	深灰 Dark grey	灰褐 Grey-brown	红褐 Red-brown	深灰 Dark grey	灰褐 Grey-brown	红褐 Red-brown	深灰 Dark grey	灰褐 Grey-brown	红褐 Red-brown		
鼎 *Ding* cauldron																				
鬲 *Li* tripod																				
甗 *Yan* steamer																				
簋 *Gui* tureen	1	1			2															2
豆 *Dou* pedestal dish		1			1															1
罐 *Guan* jar																				
瓿 *Bu* vase																				
盆 *Pen* basin																				
瓮 *Weng* jar																				
碗 *Wan* bowl																				
壶 *Hu* pot																				
器盖 Lid																				
圆陶片 Round sherd																				
圈形器 Ring shaped object																				
瓦 Tile																				
陶范 Clay mold																				
总计 Grand total	3																			3
百分比 Percentage	100%																			100%

备注/Notes：

日期/Date： 2010年7月22日 July 22, 2010

续表

单　位	09SLG TG1 H8																			合计 Grand total
陶质、陶色 Clay type/color 器形 Vessel type	泥质陶 Fine-clay ware					夹砂陶　Coarse-clay ware														
						夹砂 Sand temper				夹云母 Mica temper			夹滑石 Talc temper			夹云母、滑石 Talc and mica temper			小计 Total	
	浅灰 Light grey	深灰 Dark grey	灰褐 Grey-brown	红褐 Red-brown	小计 Total	浅灰 Light grey	深灰 Dark grey	灰褐 Grey-brown	红褐 Red-brown	深灰 Dark grey	灰褐 Grey-brown	红褐 Red-brown	深灰 Dark grey	灰褐 Grey-brown	红褐 Red-brown	深灰 Dark grey	灰褐 Grey-brown	红褐 Red-brown		
鼎 *Ding* cauldron								1			1								2	2
鬲 *Li* tripod								1											1	1
甗 *Yan* steamer																				
簋 *Gui* tureen	1	3			4															4
豆 *Dou* pedestal dish	1	3			4															4
罐 *Guan* jar	1	4			5															5
瓿 *Bu* vase																				
盆 *Pen* basin								1	1										2	2
瓮 *Weng* jar																				
碗 *Wan* bowl																				
壶 *Hu* pot																				
器盖 Lid	1				1															1
圆陶片 Round sherd																				
圈形器 Ring shaped object																				
瓦 Tile																				
陶范 Clay mold																				
总计 Grand total	14					5														19
百分比 Percentage	73.68%					26.32%														100%
备注/Notes：																				

日期/Date：2010年7月23日　July 23, 2010

续表

单 位	09SLG TG1 H9																			合计 Grand total
陶质、陶色 Clay type/color	泥质陶 Fine-clay ware					夹砂陶 Coarse-clay ware														
						夹砂 Sand temper				夹云母 Mica temper			夹滑石 Talc temper			夹云母、滑石 Talc and mica temper			小计 Total	
器形 Vessel type	浅灰 Light grey	深灰 Dark grey	灰褐 Grey-brown	红褐 Red-brown	小计 Total	浅灰 Light grey	深灰 Dark grey	灰褐 Grey-brown	红褐 Red-brown	深灰 Dark grey	灰褐 Grey-brown	红褐 Red-brown	深灰 Dark grey	灰褐 Grey-brown	红褐 Red-brown	深灰 Dark grey	灰褐 Grey-brown	红褐 Red-brown		
鼎 *Ding* cauldron				1	1															1
鬲 *Li* tripod							5		3	1	1	2							12	12
甗 *Yan* steamer											1				1				2	2
簋 *Gui* tureen	8	6	2		16															16
豆 *Dou* pedestal dish	9	6	2		17															17
罐 *Guan* jar	6	4	2		12		1			1									2	14
瓿 *Bu* vase																				
盆 *Pen* basin	2	5			7															7
瓮 *Weng* jar																				
碗 *Wan* bowl																				
壶 *Hu* pot																				
器盖 Lid		1			1															1
圆陶片 Round sherd																				
圈形器 Ring shaped object																				
瓦 Tile																				
陶范 Clay mold				1	1															1
总计 Grand total	55					16														71
百分比 Percentage	77.46%					22.54%														100%
备注/Notes：																				

日期/Date： 2010年7月23日 July 23, 2010

续表

单位	09SLG TG2③																			
陶质、陶色 Clay type/color	泥质陶 Fine-clay ware					夹砂陶 Coarse-clay ware														合计 Grand total
						夹砂 Sand temper				夹云母 Mica temper			夹滑石 Talc temper			夹云母、滑石 Talc and mica temper			小计 Total	
器形 Vessel type	浅灰 Light grey	深灰 Dark grey	灰褐 Grey-brown	红褐 Red-brown	小计 Total	浅灰 Light grey	深灰 Dark grey	灰褐 Grey-brown	红褐 Red-brown	深灰 Dark grey	灰褐 Grey-brown	红褐 Red-brown	深灰 Dark grey	灰褐 Grey-brown	红褐 Red-brown	深灰 Dark grey	灰褐 Grey-brown	红褐 Red-brown		
鼎 *Ding* cauldron																				
鬲 *Li* tripod																				
甗 *Yan* steamer																				
簋 *Gui* tureen			1		1															1
豆 *Dou* pedestal dish	1	1			2															2
罐 *Guan* jar	1				1															1
瓿 *Bu* vase																				
盆 *Pen* basin																				
瓮 *Weng* jar																				
碗 *Wan* bowl																				
壶 *Hu* pot																				
器盖 Lid																				
圆陶片 Round sherd																				
圈形器 Ring shaped object																				
瓦 Tile																				
陶范 Clay mold																				
总计 Grand total	4																			4
百分比 Percentage	100%																			100%
备注/Notes：																				

日期/Date： 2010年7月24日 July 24, 2010

续表

单位	09SLG TG2 H2																			合计 Grand total
陶质、陶色 Clay type/color	泥质陶 Fine-clay ware					夹砂陶 Coarse-clay ware														
						夹砂 Sand temper				夹云母 Mica temper			夹滑石 Talc temper			夹云母、滑石 Talc and mica temper			小计 Total	
器形 Vessel type	浅灰 Light grey	深灰 Dark grey	灰褐 Grey-brown	红褐 Red-brown	小计 Total	浅灰 Light grey	深灰 Dark grey	灰褐 Grey-brown	红褐 Red-brown	深灰 Dark grey	灰褐 Grey-brown	红褐 Red-brown	深灰 Dark grey	灰褐 Grey-brown	红褐 Red-brown	深灰 Dark grey	灰褐 Grey-brown	红褐 Red-brown		
鼎 *Ding* cauldron								1											1	1
鬲 *Li* tripod	1				1	1	2	1	1	1							1		7	8
甗 *Yan* steamer																				
簋 *Gui* tureen	7	4	1	1	13															13
豆 *Dou* pedestal dish	5	5			10															10
罐 *Guan* jar	6		4	1	11															11
瓿 *Bu* vase																				
盆 *Pen* basin				1	1		1	1											2	3
瓮 *Weng* jar																				
碗 *Wan* bowl									1						1				2	2
壶 *Hu* pot																				
器盖 Lid	1	1			2															2
圆陶片 Round sherd		1			1															1
圈形器 Ring shaped object																				
瓦 Tile																				
陶范 Clay mold																				
纺轮 spindle whorl				1	1															1
总计 Grand total	40					12														52
百分比 Percentage	76.92%					23.08%														100%

备注/Notes：

日期/Date： 2010年7月24日 July 24, 2010

续表

单　位	09SLG TG2 H4																			合计 Grand total
陶质、陶色 Clay type/color	泥质陶 Fine-clay ware					夹砂陶 Coarse-clay ware														
						夹砂 Sand temper				夹云母 Mica temper			夹滑石 Talc temper			夹云母、滑石 Talc and mica temper			小计 Total	
器形 Vessel type	浅灰 Light grey	深灰 Dark grey	灰褐 Grey-brown	红褐 Red-brown	小计 Total	浅灰 Light grey	深灰 Dark grey	灰褐 Grey-brown	红褐 Red-brown	深灰 Dark grey	灰褐 Grey-brown	红褐 Red-brown	深灰 Dark grey	灰褐 Grey-brown	红褐 Red-brown	深灰 Dark grey	灰褐 Grey-brown	红褐 Red-brown		
鼎 *Ding* cauldron																				
鬲 *Li* tripod																				
甗 *Yan* steamer											1	1							2	2
簋 *Gui* tureen		2	1		3					1									1	4
豆 *Dou* pedestal dish	3				3							1							1	4
罐 *Guan* jar	1				1															1
瓿 *Bu* vase																				
盆 *Pen* basin																				
瓮 *Weng* jar																				
碗 *Wan* bowl																				
壶 *Hu* pot																				
器盖 Lid	1	1			2															2
圆陶片 Round sherd		1			1															1
圈形器 Ring shaped object																				
瓦 Tile	1	1			2															2
陶范 Clay mold																				
总计 Grand total	12					4														16
百分比 Percentage	75%					25%														100%
备注/Notes：																				

日期/Date：　2010年7月24日　July 24, 2010

续表

单 位	09SLG TG2 H6																			合计 Grand total
陶质、陶色 Clay type/color	泥质陶 Fine-clay ware					夹砂陶 Coarse-clay ware														
						夹砂 Sand temper				夹云母 Mica temper			夹滑石 Talc temper			夹云母、滑石 Talc and mica temper			小计 Total	
器形 Vessel type	浅灰 Light grey	深灰 Dark grey	灰褐 Grey-brown	红褐 Red-brown	小计 Total	浅灰 Light grey	深灰 Dark grey	灰褐 Grey-brown	红褐 Red-brown	深灰 Dark grey	灰褐 Grey-brown	红褐 Red-brown	深灰 Dark grey	灰褐 Grey-brown	红褐 Red-brown	深灰 Dark grey	灰褐 Grey-brown	红褐 Red-brown		
鼎*Ding* cauldron								1											1	1
鬲 *Li* tripod									1										1	1
甗 *Yan* steamer																				
簋 *Gui* tureen	4	3	1	1	9			1											1	10
豆 *Dou* pedestal dish	4	3		1	8															8
罐 *Guan* jar	5	1	2	1	9		1												1	10
瓿 *Bu* vase																				
盆 *Pen* basin				1	1															1
瓮 *Weng* jar																				
碗 *Wan* bowl																				
壶 *Hu* pot																				
器盖 Lid		1			1															1
圆陶片 Round sherd																				
圈形器 Ring shaped object																				
瓦 Tile																				
陶范 Clay mold																				
总计 Grand total	28					4														32
百分比 Percentage	87.5%					12.5%														100%

备注/Notes：

日期/Date：2010年7月24日 July 24, 2010

续表

单位	09SLG TG2 H10																			合计 Grand total
陶质、陶色 Clay type/color	泥质陶 Fine-clay ware					夹砂陶 Coarse-clay ware														
						夹砂 Sand temper				夹云母 Mica temper			夹滑石 Talc temper			夹云母、滑石 Talc and mica temper			小计 Total	
器形 Vessel type	浅灰 Light grey	深灰 Dark grey	灰褐 Grey-brown	红褐 Red-brown	小计 Total	浅灰 Light grey	深灰 Dark grey	灰褐 Grey-brown	红褐 Red-brown	深灰 Dark grey	灰褐 Grey-brown	红褐 Red-brown	深灰 Dark grey	灰褐 Grey-brown	红褐 Red-brown	深灰 Dark grey	灰褐 Grey-brown	红褐 Red-brown		
鼎 *Ding* cauldron																				
鬲 *Li* tripod																				
甗 *Yan* steamer																				
簋 *Gui* tureen	1				1															1
豆 *Dou* pedestal dish																				
罐 *Guan* jar																				
瓿 *Bu* vase																				
盆 *Pen* basin																				
瓮 *Weng* jar																				
碗 *Wan* bowl																				
壶 *Hu* pot																				
器盖 Lid																				
圆陶片 Round sherd																				
圈形器 Ring shaped object																				
瓦 Tile																				
陶范 Clay mold																				
总计 Grand total	1																			1
百分比 Percentage	100%																			100%

备注/Notes：

日期/Date：　2010年7月24日　July 24, 2010

续表

单 位	09SLG TG2 H11																			
陶质、陶色 Clay type/color	泥质陶 Fine-clay ware					夹砂陶 Coarse-clay ware														合计 Grand total
						夹砂 Sand temper				夹云母 Mica temper			夹滑石 Talc temper			夹云母、滑石 Talc and mica temper			小计 Total	
器形 Vessel type	浅灰 Light grey	深灰 Dark grey	灰褐 Grey-brown	红褐 Red-brown	小计 Total	浅灰 Light grey	深灰 Dark grey	灰褐 Grey-brown	红褐 Red-brown	深灰 Dark grey	灰褐 Grey-brown	红褐 Red-brown	深灰 Dark grey	灰褐 Grey-brown	红褐 Red-brown	深灰 Dark grey	灰褐 Grey-brown	红褐 Red-brown		
鼎 *Ding* cauldron																				
鬲 *Li* tripod		1			1		4			2									6	7
甗 *Yan* steamer																				
簋 *Gui* tureen		1	1		2															2
豆 *Dou* pedestal dish	3	1			4															4
罐 *Guan* jar	1		2	1	4		1												1	5
瓿 *Bu* vase																				
盆 *Pen* basin																				
瓮 *Weng* jar																				
碗 *Wan* bowl																				
壶 *Hu* pot																				
器盖 Lid	1				1															1
圆陶片 Round sherd																				
圈形器 Ring shaped object																				
瓦 Tile																				
陶范 Clay mold																				
总计 Grand total	12					7														19
百分比 Percentage	63.16%					36.84%														100%

备注/Notes：

日期/Date： 2010年7月24日 July 24, 2010

续表

单　位	09SLG TG2 H12①																			合计 Grand total
陶质、陶色 Clay type/color	泥质陶 Fine-clay ware					夹砂陶　Coarse-clay ware														
						夹砂 Sand temper				夹云母 Mica temper			夹滑石 Talc temper			夹云母、滑石 Talc and mica temper			小计 Total	
器形 Vessel type	浅灰 Light grey	深灰 Dark grey	灰褐 Grey-brown	红褐 Red-brown	小计 Total	浅灰 Light grey	深灰 Dark grey	灰褐 Grey-brown	红褐 Red-brown	深灰 Dark grey	灰褐 Grey-brown	红褐 Red-brown	深灰 Dark grey	灰褐 Grey-brown	红褐 Red-brown	深灰 Dark grey	灰褐 Grey-brown	红褐 Red-brown		
鼎 *Ding* cauldron											1								1	1
鬲 *Li* tripod								3	2										5	5
甗 *Yan* steamer																				
簋 *Gui* tureen	1	3	1		5															5
豆 *Dou* pedestal dish		1		1	2															2
罐 *Guan* jar	3	3			6			1	1			2							4	10
瓿 *Bu* vase	1				1															1
盆 *Pen* basin																				
瓮 *Weng* jar																				
碗 *Wan* bowl																				
壶 *Hu* pot																				
器盖 Lid																				
圆陶片 Round sherd																				
圈形器 Ring shaped object																				
瓦 Tile																				
陶范 Clay mold																				
总计 Grand total	14					10														24
百分比 Percentage	58.33%					41.67%														100%
备注/Notes：																				

日期/Date：　2010年7月24日　July 24, 2010

续表

单位	09SLG TG2 H12②																			
陶质、陶色 Clay type/color	泥质陶 Fine-clay ware					夹砂陶 Coarse-clay ware														合计 Grand total
						夹砂 Sand temper				夹云母 Mica temper			夹滑石 Talc temper			夹云母、滑石 Talc and mica temper			小计 Total	
器形 Vessel type	浅灰 Light grey	深灰 Dark grey	灰褐 Grey-brown	红褐 Red-brown	小计 Total	浅灰 Light grey	深灰 Dark grey	灰褐 Grey-brown	红褐 Red-brown	深灰 Dark grey	灰褐 Grey-brown	红褐 Red-brown	深灰 Dark grey	灰褐 Grey-brown	红褐 Red-brown	深灰 Dark grey	灰褐 Grey-brown	红褐 Red-brown		
鼎 *Ding* cauldron																				
鬲 *Li* tripod							1											1	2	2
甗 *Yan* steamer																				
簋 *Gui* tureen	2	1			3															3
豆 *Dou* pedestal dish	1				1															1
罐 *Guan* jar	1	1			2															2
瓿 *Bu* vase																				
盆 *Pen* basin																				
瓮 *Weng* jar																				
碗 *Wan* bowl																				
壶 *Hu* pot																				
器盖 Lid		1			1															1
圆陶片 Round sherd																				
圈形器 Ring shaped object																				
瓦 Tile																				
陶范 Clay mold																				
总计 Grand total	7					2														9
百分比 Percentage	77.78%					22.22%														100%

备注/Notes：

日期/Date：2010年7月24日 July 24, 2010

续表

单　位	09SLG TG2 H15①																			合计 Grand total
陶质、陶色 Clay type/color	泥质陶 Fine-clay ware					夹砂陶　Coarse-clay ware														
						夹砂 Sand temper				夹云母 Mica temper			夹滑石 Talc temper			夹云母、滑石 Talc and mica temper			小计 Total	
器形 Vessel type	浅灰 Light grey	深灰 Dark grey	灰褐 Grey-brown	红褐 Red-brown	小计 Total	浅灰 Light grey	深灰 Dark grey	灰褐 Grey-brown	红褐 Red-brown	深灰 Dark grey	灰褐 Grey-brown	红褐 Red-brown	深灰 Dark grey	灰褐 Grey-brown	红褐 Red-brown	深灰 Dark grey	灰褐 Grey-brown	红褐 Red-brown		
鼎 *Ding* cauldron																				
鬲 *Li* tripod	2	1			3		2	1											3	6
甗 *Yan* steamer																				
簋 *Gui* tureen	1		1	1	3															3
豆 *Dou* pedestal dish	1	2			3															3
罐 *Guan* jar	1	3	1		5															5
瓿 *Bu* vase																				
盆 *Pen* basin																				
瓮 *Weng* jar																				
碗 *Wan* bowl																				
壶 *Hu* pot																				
器盖 Lid		1			1															1
圆陶片 Round sherd																				
圈形器 Ring shaped object																				
瓦 Tile																				
陶范 Clay mold																				
总计 Grand total	15					3														18
百分比 Percentage	83.33%					16.67%														100%

备注/Notes：

日期/Date：　2010年7月24日　July 24, 2010

续表

单位	09SLG TG2 H15②																			合计 Grand total
陶质、陶色 Clay type/color	泥质陶 Fine-clay ware					夹砂陶 Coarse-clay ware														
						夹砂 Sand temper				夹云母 Mica temper			夹滑石 Talc temper			夹云母、滑石 Talc and mica temper			小计 Total	
器形 Vessel type	浅灰 Light grey	深灰 Dark grey	灰褐 Grey-brown	红褐 Red-brown	小计 Total	浅灰 Light grey	深灰 Dark grey	灰褐 Grey-brown	红褐 Red-brown	深灰 Dark grey	灰褐 Grey-brown	红褐 Red-brown	深灰 Dark grey	灰褐 Grey-brown	红褐 Red-brown	深灰 Dark grey	灰褐 Grey-brown	红褐 Red-brown		
鼎 *Ding* cauldron											1								1	1
鬲 *Li* tripod								1											1	1
甗 *Yan* steamer																				
簋 *Gui* tureen	1				1															1
豆 *Dou* pedestal dish		1			1															1
罐 *Guan* jar								1											1	1
瓿 *Bu* vase																				
盆 *Pen* basin																				
瓮 *Weng* jar																				
碗 *Wan* bowl																				
壶 *Hu* pot																				
器盖 Lid		1			1															1
圆陶片 Round sherd																				
圈形器 Ring shaped object																				
瓦 Tile																				
陶范 Clay mold																				
总计 Grand total	3					3														6
百分比 Percentage	50%					50%														100%
备注/Notes：																				

日期/Date： 2010年7月24日 July 24, 2010

续表

单位	09SLG TG2 H16																			合计 Grand total
陶质、陶色 Clay type/color	泥质陶 Fine-clay ware					夹砂陶 Coarse-clay ware														
						夹砂 Sand temper			夹云母 Mica temper			夹滑石 Talc temper				夹云母、滑石 Talc and mica temper			小计 Total	
器形 Vessel type	浅灰 Light grey	深灰 Dark grey	灰褐 Grey-brown	红褐 Red-brown	小计 Total	浅灰 Light grey	深灰 Dark grey	灰褐 Grey-brown	红褐 Red-brown	深灰 Dark grey	灰褐 Grey-brown	红褐 Red-brown	深灰 Dark grey	灰褐 Grey-brown	红褐 Red-brown	深灰 Dark grey	灰褐 Grey-brown	红褐 Red-brown		
鼎 *Ding* cauldron																				
鬲 *Li* tripod							2	2							2			2	8	8
甗 *Yan* steamer																				
簋 *Gui* tureen		3			3															3
豆 *Dou* pedestal dish	5	4			9															9
罐 *Guan* jar	9	1		2	12				1										1	13
瓿 *Bu* vase																				
盆 *Pen* basin	1	1		1	3							1							1	4
瓮 *Weng* jar	2				2															2
碗 *Wan* bowl															1				1	1
壶 *Hu* pot																				
器盖 Lid	1				1															1
圆陶片 Round sherd	1	1			2															2
圈形器 Ring shaped object																				
瓦 Tile																				
陶范 Clay mold																				
总计 Grand total	32					11														43
百分比 Percentage	74.42%					25.58%														100%

备注/Notes：泥质灰陶大器底1个。One bottom of a large grey clay vessel.

日期/Date： 2010年7月31日 July 31, 2010

续表

单　位	09SLG TG2 H17																			合计 Grand total
陶质、陶色 Clay type/color ／ 器形 Vessel type	泥质陶 Fine-clay ware					夹砂陶 Coarse-clay ware														
						夹砂 Sand temper				夹云母 Mica temper			夹滑石 Talc temper			夹云母、滑石 Talc and mica temper			小计 Total	
	浅灰 Light grey	深灰 Dark grey	灰褐 Grey-brown	红褐 Red-brown	小计 Total	浅灰 Light grey	深灰 Dark grey	灰褐 Grey-brown	红褐 Red-brown	深灰 Dark grey	灰褐 Grey-brown	红褐 Red-brown	深灰 Dark grey	灰褐 Grey-brown	红褐 Red-brown	深灰 Dark grey	灰褐 Grey-brown	红褐 Red-brown		
鼎 *Ding* cauldron									1		1								2	2
鬲 *Li* tripod		1			1		2				2								4	5
甗 *Yan* steamer																				
簋 *Gui* tureen																				
豆 *Dou* pedestal dish	3		1		4															4
罐 *Guan* jar	4	1			5		1												1	6
瓿 *Bu* vase																				
盆 *Pen* basin																				
瓮 *Weng* jar																				
碗 *Wan* bowl																				
壶 *Hu* pot																				
器盖 Lid		1			1															1
圆陶片 Round sherd																				
圈形器 Ring shaped object																				
瓦 Tile																				
陶范 Clay mold																				
陶环 Pottery ring	1				1															1
总计 Grand total	12					7														19
百分比 Percentage	63.16%					36.84%														100%

备注/Notes：

日期/Date： 2010年7月31日 July 31, 2010

续表

单位	09SLG TG2 H18																			合计 Grand total
陶质、陶色 Clay type/color	泥质陶 Fine-clay ware					夹砂陶 Coarse-clay ware														
						夹砂 Sand temper				夹云母 Mica temper			夹滑石 Talc temper			夹云母、滑石 Talc and mica temper			小计 Total	
器形 Vessel type	浅灰 Light grey	深灰 Dark grey	灰褐 Grey-brown	红褐 Red-brown	小计 Total	浅灰 Light grey	深灰 Dark grey	灰褐 Grey-brown	红褐 Red-brown	深灰 Dark grey	灰褐 Grey-brown	红褐 Red-brown	深灰 Dark grey	灰褐 Grey-brown	红褐 Red-brown	深灰 Dark grey	灰褐 Grey-brown	红褐 Red-brown		
鼎 *Ding* cauldron																				
鬲 *Li* tripod							1	1	4						1			2	9	9
甗 *Yan* steamer																				
簋 *Gui* tureen	2	1			3															3
豆 *Dou* pedestal dish	7	3			10															10
罐 *Guan* jar	5	4	1		10															10
瓿 *Bu* vase																				
盆 *Pen* basin															1				1	1
瓮 *Weng* jar																				
碗 *Wan* bowl																				
壶 *Hu* pot																				
器盖 Lid	1				1															1
圆陶片 Round sherd																				
圈形器 Ring shaped object																				
瓦 Tile																				
陶范 Clay mold																				
总计 Grand total	24					10														34
百分比 Percentage	70.59%					29.41%														100%
备注/Notes：																				

日期/Date： 2010年7月31日 July 31, 2010

续表

单　位	09SLG TG2 H19																			合计 Grand total
陶质、陶色 Clay type/color	泥质陶 Fine-clay ware					夹砂陶 Coarse-clay ware														
						夹砂 Sand temper				夹云母 Mica temper			夹滑石 Talc temper			夹云母、滑石 Talc and mica temper			小计 Total	
器形 Vessel type	浅灰 Light grey	深灰 Dark grey	灰褐 Grey-brown	红褐 Red-brown	小计 Total	浅灰 Light grey	深灰 Dark grey	灰褐 Grey-brown	红褐 Red-brown	深灰 Dark grey	灰褐 Grey-brown	红褐 Red-brown	深灰 Dark grey	灰褐 Grey-brown	红褐 Red-brown	深灰 Dark grey	灰褐 Grey-brown	红褐 Red-brown		
鼎 *Ding* cauldron								1											1	1
鬲 *Li* tripod							1	1	1										3	3
甗 *Yan* steamer																				
簋 *Gui* tureen	4	5			9															9
豆 *Dou* pedestal dish	10	6			16															16
罐 *Guan* jar	7			1	8						1								1	9
瓿 *Bu* vase	1				1															1
盆 *Pen* basin		1			1															1
瓮 *Weng* jar																				
碗 *Wan* bowl																				
壶 *Hu* pot	1	1			2															2
器盖 Lid		4			4															4
圆陶片 Round sherd	1				1															1
圈形器 Ring shaped object																				
瓦 Tile	2				2															2
陶范 Clay mold																				
总计 Grand total	44					5														49
百分比 Percentage	89.80%					10.20%														100%

备注/Notes：

日期/Date： 2010年7月31日 July 31, 2010

续表

单　位	09SLG TG2 H20①																			合计 Grand total
陶质、陶色 Clay type/color	泥质陶 Fine-clay ware					夹砂陶　Coarse-clay ware														
						夹砂 Sand temper				夹云母 Mica temper			夹滑石 Talc temper			夹云母、滑石 Talc and mica temper			小计 Total	
器形 Vessel type	浅灰 Light grey	深灰 Dark grey	灰褐 Grey-brown	红褐 Red-brown	小计 Total	浅灰 Light grey	深灰 Dark grey	灰褐 Grey-brown	红褐 Red-brown	深灰 Dark grey	灰褐 Grey-brown	红褐 Red-brown	深灰 Dark grey	灰褐 Grey-brown	红褐 Red-brown	深灰 Dark grey	灰褐 Grey-brown	红褐 Red-brown		
鼎 *Ding* cauldron								6			1							2	9	9
鬲 *Li* tripod	1	2			3	5	3	13	2	1	1			2			1		28	31
甗 *Yan* steamer																				
簋 *Gui* tureen	4	2	1		7															7
豆 *Dou* pedestal dish	4	3			7															7
罐 *Guan* jar	1	1	2		4			1											1	5
瓿 *Bu* vase		1			1															1
盆 *Pen* basin							1	1			1								3	3
瓮 *Weng* jar																				
碗 *Wan* bowl																				
壶 *Hu* pot																				
器盖 Lid																				
圆陶片 Round sherd											1								1	1
圈形器 Ring shaped object																				
瓦 Tile																				
陶范 Clay mold																				
总计 Grand total	22					42														64
百分比 Percentage	34.37%					65.63%														100%
备注/Notes：																				

日期/Date：　2010年8月1日　August 1, 2010

续表

单位	09SLG TG2 H20②																			
陶质、陶色 Clay type/color	泥质陶 Fine-clay ware					夹砂陶 Coarse-clay ware														合计 Grand total
						夹砂 Sand temper				夹云母 Mica temper			夹滑石 Talc temper			夹云母、滑石 Talc and mica temper			小计 Total	
器形 Vessel type	浅灰 Light grey	深灰 Dark grey	灰褐 Grey-brown	红褐 Red-brown	小计 Total	浅灰 Light grey	深灰 Dark grey	灰褐 Grey-brown	红褐 Red-brown	深灰 Dark grey	灰褐 Grey-brown	红褐 Red-brown	深灰 Dark grey	灰褐 Grey-brown	红褐 Red-brown	深灰 Dark grey	灰褐 Grey-brown	红褐 Red-brown		
鼎 *Ding* cauldron								1											1	1
鬲 *Li* tripod	1				1	3	1												4	5
甗 *Yan* steamer							1												1	1
簋 *Gui* tureen	2	1	1		4															4
豆 *Dou* pedestal dish	2				2															2
罐 *Guan* jar	1	1			2				1			1							2	4
瓿 *Bu* vase		1			1															1
盆 *Pen* basin																				
瓮 *Weng* jar																				
碗 *Wan* bowl																				
壶 *Hu* pot																				
器盖 Lid																				
圆陶片 Round sherd											1								1	1
圈形器 Ring shaped object																				
瓦 Tile																				
陶范 Clay mold																				
总计 Grand total	10					9														19
百分比 Percentage	52.63%					47.37%														100%

备注/Notes：标本H20②：150可能为豆。Sample H20②：150 might be a *dou*-pedestal dish.

日期/Date：2010年8月1日 August 1, 2010　统计/Counts：李峰/唐锦琼/付群启/毕道传 LI Feng, TANG Jinqiong, FU Qunqi, BI Daochuan

表Ⅰ.5.2 陶片纹饰统计表

Table Ⅰ.5.2 Ceramic sherd decoration counts

单位	09SLG TG1 H3①																			
陶质、陶色 Clay type/color 纹饰 Decorative pattern	泥质陶 Fine-clay ware					夹砂陶 Coarse-clay ware														合计 Grand total
						夹砂 Sand temper				夹云母 Mica temper			夹滑石 Talc temper			夹云母、滑石 Talc and mica temper			小计 Total	
	浅灰 Light grey	深灰 Dark grey	灰褐 Grey-brown	红褐 Red-brown	小计 Total	浅灰 Light grey	深灰 Dark grey	灰褐 Grey-brown	红褐 Red-brown	深灰 Dark grey	灰褐 Grey-brown	红褐 Red-brown	深灰 Dark grey	灰褐 Grey-brown	红褐 Red-brown	深灰 Dark grey	灰褐 Grey-brown	红褐 Red-brown		
粗绳纹 Coarse cord decorations	5	1			6		1												1	7
中绳纹 Moderate cord	9	8	1	5	23				1										1	24
细绳纹 Fine cord																				
麻点绳纹 "Sesame seed" cord	4	3		2	9															9
素面 Undecorated	18	11	2	5	36			37	29										66	102
素面+磨光 Undecorated + polished			1		1															1
弦纹 String dec.	1	4	3		8															8
绳纹+弦纹 Cord + string		2	1		3															3
刻划纹 Incised																				
戳印纹 Imprinted								1											1	1
网格纹 Net decorations																				
乳钉纹 Nipple dec.																				
附加堆纹 Appliqué patterns																				
附加堆纹+中绳纹 Appliqué patterns + moderate cord																				
附加堆纹+粗绳纹 Appliqué patterns + coarse cord																				
附加堆纹+麻点绳纹 Appliqué patterns + "sesame seed" cord																				
总计 Grand total	86					69														155
百分比 Percentage	55.48%					44.52%														100%

备注/Notes：

日期/Date: 2010年7月22日 July 22, 2010

续表

单位	09SLG TG1 H3②																			
陶质、陶色 Clay type/color	泥质陶 Fine-clay ware					夹砂陶 Coarse-clay ware														合计 Grand total
						夹砂 Sand temper				夹云母 Mica temper			夹滑石 Talc temper			夹云母、滑石 Talc and mica temper			小计 Total	
纹饰 Decorative pattern	浅灰 Light grey	深灰 Dark grey	灰褐 Grey-brown	红褐 Red-brown	小计 Total	浅灰 Light grey	深灰 Dark grey	灰褐 Grey-brown	红褐 Red-brown	深灰 Dark grey	灰褐 Grey-brown	红褐 Red-brown	深灰 Dark grey	灰褐 Grey-brown	红褐 Red-brown	深灰 Dark grey	灰褐 Grey-brown	红褐 Red-brown		
粗绳纹 Coarse cord decorations		1		3	4															4
中绳纹 Moderate cord	7	8		10	25															25
细绳纹 Fine cord																				
麻点绳纹 "Sesame seed"cord		1			1															1
素面 Undecorated	12	8		14	34			14	8										22	56
素面+磨光 Undecorated + polished		2	1		3															3
弦纹 String dec.																				
绳纹+弦纹 Cord + string	1	3		2	6															6
刻划纹 Incised																				
戳印纹 Imprinted																				
网格纹 Net decorations																				
乳钉纹 Nipple dec.																				
附加堆纹 Appliqué patterns																				
附加堆纹+中绳纹 Appliqué patterns + moderate cord																				
附加堆纹+粗绳纹 Appliqué patterns + coarse cord																				
附加堆纹+麻点绳纹 Appliqué patterns + "sesame seed" cord																				
总计 Grand total	73					22														95
百分比 Percentage	76.84%					23.16%														100%

备注/Notes：

日期/Date： 2010年7月22日 July 22, 2010

续表

单　位	09SLG TG1 H3③																			合计 Grand total
纹饰 Decorative pattern ／ 陶质、陶色 Clay type/color	泥质陶 Fine-clay ware					夹砂陶　Coarse-clay ware														
						夹砂 Sand temper				夹云母 Mica temper			夹滑石 Talc temper			夹云母、滑石 Talc and mica temper			小计 Total	
	浅灰 Light grey	深灰 Dark grey	灰褐 Grey-brown	红褐 Red-brown	小计 Total	浅灰 Light grey	深灰 Dark grey	灰褐 Grey-brown	红褐 Red-brown	深灰 Dark grey	灰褐 Grey-brown	红褐 Red-brown	深灰 Dark grey	灰褐 Grey-brown	红褐 Red-brown	深灰 Dark grey	灰褐 Grey-brown	红褐 Red-brown		
粗绳纹 Coarse cord decorations								1											1	1
中绳纹 Moderate cord	30	11	3		44															44
细绳纹 Fine cord																				
麻点绳纹 "Sesame seed"cord		1	2		3															3
素面 Undecorated	16	9			25		8			1		1							10	35
素面+磨光 Undecorated + polished																				
弦纹 String dec.	1				1															1
绳纹+弦纹 Cord + string																				
刻划纹 Incised		1			1															1
戳印纹 Imprinted																				
网格纹 Net decorations																				
乳钉纹 Nipple dec.		1			1															1
附加堆纹 Appliqué patterns																				
附加堆纹+中绳纹 Appliqué patterns + moderate cord																				
附加堆纹+粗绳纹 Appliqué patterns + coarse cord																				
附加堆纹+麻点绳纹 Appliqué patterns + "sesame seed" cord																				
总计 Grand total	75					11														86
百分比 Percentage	87.20%					12.79%														100%
备注/Notes：																				

日期/Date：　2010年7月24日　July 24, 2010

续表

单位	09SLG TG1 ③																			合计 Grand total
陶质、陶色 Clay type/color	泥质陶 Fine-clay ware					夹砂陶 Coarse-clay ware														
						夹砂 Sand temper				夹云母 Mica temper			夹滑石 Talc temper			夹云母、滑石 Talc and mica temper				
纹饰 Decorative pattern	浅灰 Light grey	深灰 Dark grey	灰褐 Grey-brown	红褐 Red-brown	小计 Total	浅灰 Light grey	深灰 Dark grey	灰褐 Grey-brown	红褐 Red-brown	深灰 Dark grey	灰褐 Grey-brown	红褐 Red-brown	深灰 Dark grey	灰褐 Grey-brown	红褐 Red-brown	深灰 Dark grey	灰褐 Grey-brown	红褐 Red-brown	小计 Total	
粗绳纹 Coarse cord decorations		1			1															1
中绳纹 Moderate cord	5	7			12															12
细绳纹 Fine cord																				
麻点绳纹 "Sesame seed"cord																				
素面 Undecorated	1		2		3				1										1	4
素面+磨光 Undecorated + polished																				
弦纹 String dec.	1				1															1
绳纹+弦纹 Cord + string																				
刻划纹 Incised																				
戳印纹 Imprinted																				
网格纹 Net decorations																				
乳钉纹 Nipple dec.																				
附加堆纹 Appliqué patterns																				
附加堆纹+中绳纹 Appliqué patterns + moderate cord																				
附加堆纹+粗绳纹 Appliqué patterns + coarse cord																				
附加堆纹+麻点绳纹 Appliqué patterns + "sesame seed" cord																				
总计 Grand total	17					1														18
百分比 Percentage	94.44%					5.45%														100%

备注/Notes：

日期/Date： 2010年7月24日 July 24, 2010

续表

单　位	09SLG TG1 G1																			
陶质、陶色 Clay type/color ╲ 纹饰 Decorative pattern	泥质陶 Fine-clay ware					夹砂陶 Coarse-clay ware														合计 Grand total
						夹砂 Sand temper				夹云母 Mica temper			夹滑石 Talc temper			夹云母、滑石 Talc and mica temper			小计 Total	
	浅灰 Light grey	深灰 Dark grey	灰褐 Grey-brown	红褐 Red-brown	小计 Total	浅灰 Light grey	深灰 Dark grey	灰褐 Grey-brown	红褐 Red-brown	深灰 Dark grey	灰褐 Grey-brown	红褐 Red-brown	深灰 Dark grey	灰褐 Grey-brown	红褐 Red-brown	深灰 Dark grey	灰褐 Grey-brown	红褐 Red-brown		
粗绳纹 Coarse cord decorations																				
中绳纹 Moderate cord	1	1	2		4															4
细绳纹 Fine cord																				
麻点绳纹 "Sesame seed" cord																				
素面 Undecorated	4	2			6															6
素面+磨光 Undecorated + polished																				
弦纹 String dec.																				
绳纹+弦纹 Cord + string																				
刻划纹 Incised																				
戳印纹 Imprinted																				
网格纹 Net decorations																				
乳钉纹 Nipple dec.																				
附加堆纹 Appliqué patterns																				
附加堆纹+中绳纹 Appliqué patterns + moderate cord																				
附加堆纹+粗绳纹 Appliqué patterns + coarse cord																				
附加堆纹+麻点绳纹 Appliqué patterns + "sesame seed" cord																				
总计 Grand total	10																			10
百分比 Percentage	100%																			100%

备注/Notes：内出土陶碗时代较晚，怀疑为晚期单位。The ceramic bowl found in this unit is of a relatively late period, but it is doubtful that the unit is a late-period one.

日期/Date：2010年7月24日　July 24, 2010

续表

单位	09SLG TG1 H7																			合计 Grand total
陶质、陶色 Clay type/color / 纹饰 Decorative pattern	泥质陶 Fine-clay ware					夹砂陶 Coarse-clay ware														
						夹砂 Sand temper				夹云母 Mica temper			夹滑石 Talc temper			夹云母、滑石 Talc and mica temper				
	浅灰 Light grey	深灰 Dark grey	灰褐 Grey-brown	红褐 Red-brown	小计 Total	浅灰 Light grey	深灰 Dark grey	灰褐 Grey-brown	红褐 Red-brown	深灰 Dark grey	灰褐 Grey-brown	红褐 Red-brown	深灰 Dark grey	灰褐 Grey-brown	红褐 Red-brown	深灰 Dark grey	灰褐 Grey-brown	红褐 Red-brown	小计 Total	
粗绳纹 Coarse cord decorations																				
中绳纹 Moderate cord	1	2			3															3
细绳纹 Fine cord																				
麻点绳纹 "Sesame seed" cord																				
素面 Undecorated	1	1			2				1										1	3
素面+磨光 Undecorated + polished		4			4															4
弦纹 String dec.																				
绳纹+弦纹 Cord + string																				
刻划纹 Incised																				
戳印纹 Imprinted																				
网格纹 Net decorations																				
乳钉纹 Nipple dec.																				
附加堆纹 Appliqué patterns																				
附加堆纹+中绳纹 Appliqué patterns + moderate cord																				
附加堆纹+粗绳纹 Appliqué patterns + coarse cord																				
附加堆纹+麻点绳纹 Appliqué patterns + "sesame seed" cord																				
总计 Grand total	9					1														10
百分比 Percentage	90%					10%														100%
备注/Notes：																				

日期/Date： 2010年7月24日 July 24, 2010

续表

单　位	09SLG TG1 H8																			合计 Grand total
陶质、陶色 Clay type/color ＼ 纹饰 Decorative pattern	泥质陶 Fine-clay ware					夹砂陶　Coarse-clay ware														
						夹砂 Sand temper				夹云母 Mica temper			夹滑石 Talc temper			夹云母、滑石 Talc and mica temper			小计 Total	
	浅灰 Light grey	深灰 Dark grey	灰褐 Grey-brown	红褐 Red-brown	小计 Total	浅灰 Light grey	深灰 Dark grey	灰褐 Grey-brown	红褐 Red-brown	深灰 Dark grey	灰褐 Grey-brown	红褐 Red-brown	深灰 Dark grey	灰褐 Grey-brown	红褐 Red-brown	深灰 Dark grey	灰褐 Grey-brown	红褐 Red-brown		
粗绳纹 Coarse cord decorations		1			1															1
中绳纹 Moderate cord	13	7	4	1	25		2												2	27
细绳纹 Fine cord		4			4															4
麻点绳纹 “Sesame seed”cord	6	4		1	11															11
素面 Undecorated	16	8			24		5	24	5										34	58
素面+磨光 Undecorated + polished																				
弦纹 String dec.																				
绳纹+弦纹 Cord + string	2	1			3															3
刻划纹 Incised																				
戳印纹 Imprinted																				
网格纹 Net decorations																				
乳钉纹 Nipple dec.																				
附加堆纹 Appliqué patterns		1			1															1
附加堆纹+中绳纹 Appliqué patterns + moderate cord																				
附加堆纹+粗绳纹 Appliqué patterns + coarse cord																				
附加堆纹+麻点绳纹 Appliqué patterns + “sesame seed” cord			1		1															1
总计 Grand total	70					36														106
百分比 Percentage	66.04%					33.96%														100%

备注/Notes：

日期/Date：　2010年7月24日　July 24, 2010

续表

单位	09SLG TG1 H9																			合计 Grand total
陶质、陶色 Clay type/color	泥质陶 Fine-clay ware					夹砂陶 Coarse-clay ware														
						夹砂 Sand temper				夹云母 Mica temper			夹滑石 Talc temper			夹云母、滑石 Talc and mica temper			小计 Total	
纹饰 Decorative pattern	浅灰 Light grey	深灰 Dark grey	灰褐 Grey-brown	红褐 Red-brown	小计 Total	浅灰 Light grey	深灰 Dark grey	灰褐 Grey-brown	红褐 Red-brown	深灰 Dark grey	灰褐 Grey-brown	红褐 Red-brown	深灰 Dark grey	灰褐 Grey-brown	红褐 Red-brown	深灰 Dark grey	灰褐 Grey-brown	红褐 Red-brown		
粗绳纹 Coarse cord decorations	9	5	3		17															17
中绳纹 Moderate cord	76	14			90			1											1	91
细绳纹 Fine cord	1		1		2															2
麻点绳纹 "Sesame seed"cord	11	8			19															19
素面 Undecorated	70	39	4		113		34	13	17	1		1							66	179
素面+磨光 Undecorated + polished																				
弦纹 String dec.		2			2															2
绳纹+弦纹 Cord + string	4	5			9															9
刻划纹 Incised																				
戳印纹 Imprinted																				
网格纹 Net decorations																				
乳钉纹 Nipple dec.																				
附加堆纹 Appliqué patterns																				
附加堆纹+中绳纹 Appliqué patterns + moderate cord	1	1			2															2
附加堆纹+粗绳纹 Appliqué patterns + coarse cord	1	1			2															2
附加堆纹+麻点绳纹 Appliqué patterns + "sesame seed" cord																				
总计 Grand total	256					67														323
百分比 Percentage	79.26%					20.76%														100%

备注/Notes：

日期/Date： 2010年7月24日 July 24, 2010

续表

单　位	09SLG TG2 ③																			合计 Grand total
陶质、陶色 Clay type/color ╲ 纹饰 Decorative pattern	泥质陶 Fine-clay ware					夹砂陶 Coarse-clay ware														
						夹砂 Sand temper				夹云母 Mica temper			夹滑石 Talc temper			夹云母、滑石 Talc and mica temper			小计 Total	
	浅灰 Light grey	深灰 Dark grey	灰褐 Grey-brown	红褐 Red-brown	小计 Total	浅灰 Light grey	深灰 Dark grey	灰褐 Grey-brown	红褐 Red-brown	深灰 Dark grey	灰褐 Grey-brown	红褐 Red-brown	深灰 Dark grey	灰褐 Grey-brown	红褐 Red-brown	深灰 Dark grey	灰褐 Grey-brown	红褐 Red-brown		
粗绳纹 Coarse cord decorations																				
中绳纹 Moderate cord	1	2			3															3
细绳纹 Fine cord																				
麻点绳纹 "Sesame seed"cord																				
素面 Undecorated	2	1	1		4															4
素面+磨光 Undecorated + polished																				
弦纹 String dec.			1		1															1
绳纹+弦纹 Cord + string																				
刻划纹 Incised																				
戳印纹 Imprinted																				
网格纹 Net decorations																				
乳钉纹 Nipple dec.																				
附加堆纹 Appliqué patterns																				
附加堆纹+中绳纹 Appliqué patterns + moderate cord																				
附加堆纹+粗绳纹 Appliqué patterns + coarse cord																				
附加堆纹+麻点绳纹 Appliqué patterns + "sesame seed" cord																				
总计 Grand total	8																			8
百分比 Percentage	100%																			100%

备注/Notes：

日期/Date:　2010年7月24日　July 24, 2010

续表

单位	09SLG TG2 H2																			合计 Grand total
陶质、陶色 Clay type/color / 纹饰 Decorative pattern	泥质陶 Fine-clay ware					夹砂陶 Coarse-clay ware														
						夹砂 Sand temper				夹云母 Mica temper			夹滑石 Talc temper			夹云母、滑石 Talc and mica temper				
	浅灰 Light grey	深灰 Dark grey	灰褐 Grey-brown	红褐 Red-brown	小计 Total	浅灰 Light grey	深灰 Dark grey	灰褐 Grey-brown	红褐 Red-brown	深灰 Dark grey	灰褐 Grey-brown	红褐 Red-brown	深灰 Dark grey	灰褐 Grey-brown	红褐 Red-brown	深灰 Dark grey	灰褐 Grey-brown	红褐 Red-brown	小计 Total	
粗绳纹 Coarse cord decorations	3	1	5		9															9
中绳纹 Moderate cord	25	9			34		3	1											4	38
细绳纹 Fine cord																				
麻点绳纹 "Sesame seed"cord	6	2			8															8
素面 Undecorated	41	8		6	55		1	24	4										29	84
素面+磨光 Undecorated + polished																				
弦纹 String dec.	3				3															3
绳纹+弦纹 Cord + string	3	3	1		7															7
刻划纹 Incised																				
戳印纹 Imprinted																				
网格纹 Net decorations																				
乳钉纹 Nipple dec.																				
附加堆纹 Appliqué patterns																				
附加堆纹+中绳纹 Appliqué patterns + moderate cord																				
附加堆纹+粗绳纹 Appliqué patterns + coarse cord																				
附加堆纹+麻点绳纹 Appliqué patterns + "sesame seed" cord							1												1	1
总计 Grand total	116					34														150
百分比 Percentage	77.33%					22.67%														100%

备注/Notes：

日期/Date： 2010年7月24日 July 24, 2010

续表

单位	09SLG TG2 H4																			合计 Grand total
陶质、陶色 Clay type/color 纹饰 Decorative pattern	泥质陶 Fine-clay ware					夹砂陶 Coarse-clay ware														
						夹砂 Sand temper				夹云母 Mica temper			夹滑石 Talc temper			夹云母、滑石 Talc and mica temper			小计 Total	
	浅灰 Light grey	深灰 Dark grey	灰褐 Grey-brown	红褐 Red-brown	小计 Total	浅灰 Light grey	深灰 Dark grey	灰褐 Grey-brown	红褐 Red-brown	深灰 Dark grey	灰褐 Grey-brown	红褐 Red-brown	深灰 Dark grey	灰褐 Grey-brown	红褐 Red-brown	深灰 Dark grey	灰褐 Grey-brown	红褐 Red-brown		
粗绳纹 Coarse cord decorations	1				1															1
中绳纹 Moderate cord	11	2	1		14															14
细绳纹 Fine cord	1		1		2															2
麻点绳纹 "Sesame seed" cord	2	2			4															4
素面 Undecorated	19	13			32		4	2			3	4							13	45
素面+磨光 Undecorated + polished																				
弦纹 String dec.																				
绳纹+弦纹 Cord + string		1			1															1
刻划纹 Incised																				
戳印纹 Imprinted																				
网格纹 Net decorations																				
乳钉纹 Nipple dec.																				
附加堆纹 Appliqué patterns																				
附加堆纹+中绳纹 Appliqué patterns + moderate cord																				
附加堆纹+粗绳纹 Appliqué patterns + coarse cord																				
附加堆纹+麻点绳纹 Appliqué patterns + "sesame seed" cord																				
总计 Grand total	54					13														67
百分比 Percentage	80.60%					19.40%														100%

备注/Notes：

日期/Date： 2010年7月24日 July 24, 2010

续表

单　位	09SLG TG2 H6																			合计 Grand total
陶质、陶色 Clay type/color ╲ 纹饰 Decorative pattern	泥质陶 Fine-clay ware					夹砂陶　Coarse-clay ware														
						夹砂 Sand temper				夹云母 Mica temper			夹滑石 Talc temper			夹云母、滑石 Talc and mica temper			小计 Total	
	浅灰 Light grey	深灰 Dark grey	灰褐 Grey-brown	红褐 Red-brown	小计 Total	浅灰 Light grey	深灰 Dark grey	灰褐 Grey-brown	红褐 Red-brown	深灰 Dark grey	灰褐 Grey-brown	红褐 Red-brown	深灰 Dark grey	灰褐 Grey-brown	红褐 Red-brown	深灰 Dark grey	灰褐 Grey-brown	红褐 Red-brown		
粗绳纹 Coarse cord decorations	8	2	5		15															15
中绳纹 Moderate cord	21	14			35															35
细绳纹 Fine cord																				
麻点绳纹 "Sesame seed"cord	3	5			8															8
素面 Undecorated	36	7			43		2	16	10			4							32	75
素面+磨光 Undecorated + polished																				
弦纹 String dec.	3				3															3
绳纹+弦纹 Cord + string	3	2		4	9															9
刻划纹 Incised	1				1															1
戳印纹 Imprinted																				
网格纹 Net decorations																				
乳钉纹 Nipple dec.																				
附加堆纹 Appliqué patterns																				
附加堆纹+中绳纹 Appliqué patterns + moderate cord																				
附加堆纹+粗绳纹 Appliqué patterns + coarse cord																				
附加堆纹+麻点绳纹 Appliqué patterns + "sesame seed" cord																				
总计 Grand total	114					32														146
百分比 Percentage	78.08%					21.92%														100%

备注/Notes：

日期/Date：　2010年7月24日　July 24, 2010

续表

单　位	09SLG TG2 H10																			
陶质、陶色 Clay type/color 纹饰 Decorative pattern	泥质陶 Fine-clay ware					夹砂陶　Coarse-clay ware														合计 Grand total
						夹砂 Sand temper				夹云母 Mica temper			夹滑石 Talc temper			夹云母、滑石 Talc and mica temper			小计 Total	
	浅灰 Light grey	深灰 Dark grey	灰褐 Grey-brown	红褐 Red-brown	小计 Total	浅灰 Light grey	深灰 Dark grey	灰褐 Grey-brown	红褐 Red-brown	深灰 Dark grey	灰褐 Grey-brown	红褐 Red-brown	深灰 Dark grey	灰褐 Grey-brown	红褐 Red-brown	深灰 Dark grey	灰褐 Grey-brown	红褐 Red-brown		
粗绳纹 Coarse cord decorations																				
中绳纹 Moderate cord	3				3															3
细绳纹 Fine cord																				
麻点绳纹 “Sesame seed”cord																				
素面 Undecorated																				
素面+磨光 Undecorated + polished																				
弦纹 String dec.																				
绳纹+弦纹 Cord + string																				
刻划纹 Incised																				
戳印纹 Imprinted																				
网格纹 Net decorations																				
乳钉纹 Nipple dec.																				
附加堆纹 Appliqué patterns																				
附加堆纹+中绳纹 Appliqué patterns + moderate cord																				
附加堆纹+粗绳纹 Appliqué patterns + coarse cord																				
附加堆纹+麻点绳纹 Appliqué patterns + “sesame seed” cord							1												1	1
总计 Grand total	3					1														4
百分比 Percentage	75%					25%														100%
备注/Notes：																				

日期/Date：　2010年7月24日　July 24, 2010

续表

单　位	09SLG TG2 H11																			合计 Grand total
陶质、陶色 Clay type/color / 纹饰 Decorative pattern	泥质陶 Fine-clay ware					夹砂陶　Coarse-clay ware														
						夹砂 Sand temper				夹云母 Mica temper			夹滑石 Talc temper			夹云母、滑石 Talc and mica temper			小计 Total	
	浅灰 Light grey	深灰 Dark grey	灰褐 Grey-brown	红褐 Red-brown	小计 Total	浅灰 Light grey	深灰 Dark grey	灰褐 Grey-brown	红褐 Red-brown	深灰 Dark grey	灰褐 Grey-brown	红褐 Red-brown	深灰 Dark grey	灰褐 Grey-brown	红褐 Red-brown	深灰 Dark grey	灰褐 Grey-brown	红褐 Red-brown		
粗绳纹 Coarse cord decorations	5	4			9															9
中绳纹 Moderate cord	7	6			13															13
细绳纹 Fine cord	2	3			5															5
麻点绳纹 "Sesame seed"cord	1				1		8		4										12	13
素面 Undecorated	16	3	2	2	23					2		2							4	27
素面+磨光 Undecorated + polished																				
弦纹 String dec.																				
绳纹+弦纹 Cord + string	2	1			3															3
刻划纹 Incised																				
戳印纹 Imprinted																				
网格纹 Net decorations																				
乳钉纹 Nipple dec.																				
附加堆纹 Appliqué patterns																				
附加堆纹+中绳纹 Appliqué patterns + moderate cord																				
附加堆纹+粗绳纹 Appliqué patterns + coarse cord																				
附加堆纹+麻点绳纹 Appliqué patterns + "sesame seed" cord																				
总计 Grand total	54					16														70
百分比 Percentage	77.14%					22.86%														100%

备注/Notes：

日期/Date：　2010年7月24日　July 24, 2010

续表

单 位	09SLG TG2 H12①																			合计 Grand total
陶质、陶色 Clay type/color 纹饰 Decorative pattern	泥质陶 Fine-clay ware					夹砂陶 Coarse-clay ware														
						夹砂 Sand temper				夹云母 Mica temper			夹滑石 Talc temper			夹云母、滑石 Talc and mica temper			小计 Total	
	浅灰 Light grey	深灰 Dark grey	灰褐 Grey-brown	红褐 Red-brown	小计 Total	浅灰 Light grey	深灰 Dark grey	灰褐 Grey-brown	红褐 Red-brown	深灰 Dark grey	灰褐 Grey-brown	红褐 Red-brown	深灰 Dark grey	灰褐 Grey-brown	红褐 Red-brown	深灰 Dark grey	灰褐 Grey-brown	红褐 Red-brown		
粗绳纹 Coarse cord decorations	2				2															2
中绳纹 Moderate cord	7	4	4		15															15
细绳纹 Fine cord	1	2			3															3
麻点绳纹 "Sesame seed"cord	2	1			3															3
素面 Undecorated	6	6	4	1	17			18	6										24	41
素面+磨光 Undecorated + polished																				
弦纹 String dec.																				
绳纹+弦纹 Cord + string																				
刻划纹 Incised																				
戳印纹 Imprinted																				
网格纹 Net decorations																				
乳钉纹 Nipple dec.																				
附加堆纹 Appliqué patterns																				
附加堆纹+中绳纹 Appliqué patterns + moderate cord																				
附加堆纹+粗绳纹 Appliqué patterns + coarse cord																				
附加堆纹+麻点绳纹 Appliqué patterns + "sesame seed" cord																				
总计 Grand total	40					24														64
百分比 Percentage	62.50%					37.50%														100%
备注/Notes：																				

日期/Date： 2010年7月24日 July 24, 2010

续表

单位	09SLG TG2 H12②																			
陶质、陶色 Clay type/color 纹饰 Decorative pattern	泥质陶 Fine-clay ware					夹砂陶 Coarse-clay ware														合计 Grand total
						夹砂 Sand temper				夹云母 Mica temper			夹滑石 Talc temper			夹云母、滑石 Talc and mica temper			小计 Total	
	浅灰 Light grey	深灰 Dark grey	灰褐 Grey-brown	红褐 Red-brown	小计 Total	浅灰 Light grey	深灰 Dark grey	灰褐 Grey-brown	红褐 Red-brown	深灰 Dark grey	灰褐 Grey-brown	红褐 Red-brown	深灰 Dark grey	灰褐 Grey-brown	红褐 Red-brown	深灰 Dark grey	灰褐 Grey-brown	红褐 Red-brown		
粗绳纹 Coarse cord decorations	2	3			5															5
中绳纹 Moderate cord	8	6			14		1												1	15
细绳纹 Fine cord																				
麻点绳纹 "Sesame seed"cord	1	1			2															2
素面 Undecorated	7	7			14		15	5	8										28	42
素面+磨光 Undecorated + polished		1			1															1
弦纹 String dec.	2	1			3															3
绳纹+弦纹 Cord + string	1	3			4															4
刻划纹 Incised																				
戳印纹 Imprinted																				
网格纹 Net decorations																				
乳钉纹 Nipple dec.																				
附加堆纹 Appliqué patterns																				
附加堆纹+中绳纹 Appliqué patterns + moderate cord																				
附加堆纹+粗绳纹 Appliqué patterns + coarse cord																				
附加堆纹+麻点绳纹 Appliqué patterns + "sesame seed" cord																				
总计 Grand total	43					29														72
百分比 Percentage	59.72%					40.28%														100%
备注/Notes：																				

日期/Date： 2010年7月24日 July 24, 2010

续表

单　位	09SLG TG2 H15①																			合计 Grand total
陶质、陶色 Clay type/color / 纹饰 Decorative pattern	泥质陶 Fine-clay ware					夹砂陶　Coarse-clay ware														
						夹砂 Sand temper				夹云母 Mica temper			夹滑石 Talc temper			夹云母、滑石 Talc and mica temper			小计 Total	
	浅灰 Light grey	深灰 Dark grey	灰褐 Grey-brown	红褐 Red-brown	小计 Total	浅灰 Light grey	深灰 Dark grey	灰褐 Grey-brown	红褐 Red-brown	深灰 Dark grey	灰褐 Grey-brown	红褐 Red-brown	深灰 Dark grey	灰褐 Grey-brown	红褐 Red-brown	深灰 Dark grey	灰褐 Grey-brown	红褐 Red-brown		
粗绳纹 Coarse cord decorations		1	3		4															4
中绳纹 Moderate cord	9	8			17															17
细绳纹 Fine cord																				
麻点绳纹 "Sesame seed"cord		1			1															1
素面 Undecorated	1	11	3	2	17		4	2	4										10	27
素面+磨光 Undecorated + polished																				
弦纹 String dec.		1			1															1
绳纹+弦纹 Cord + string	1				1															1
刻划纹 Incised																				
戳印纹 Imprinted																				
网格纹 Net decorations																				
乳钉纹 Nipple dec.																				
附加堆纹 Appliqué patterns																				
附加堆纹+中绳纹 Appliqué patterns + moderate cord																				
附加堆纹+粗绳纹 Appliqué patterns + coarse cord																				
附加堆纹+麻点绳纹 Appliqué patterns + "sesame seed" cord																				
总计 Grand total	41					10														51
百分比 Percentage	80.39%					19.61%														100%
备注/Notes：																				

日期/Date：　2010年7月24日　July 24, 2010

续表

单 位	09SLG TG2 H15②																			
纹饰 Decorative pattern \ 陶质、陶色 Clay type/color	泥质陶 Fine-clay ware					夹砂陶 Coarse-clay ware														合计 Grand total
						夹砂 Sand temper				夹云母 Mica temper			夹滑石 Talc temper			夹云母、滑石 Talc and mica temper			小计 Total	
	浅灰 Light grey	深灰 Dark grey	灰褐 Grey-brown	红褐 Red-brown	小计 Total	浅灰 Light grey	深灰 Dark grey	灰褐 Grey-brown	红褐 Red-brown	深灰 Dark grey	灰褐 Grey-brown	红褐 Red-brown	深灰 Dark grey	灰褐 Grey-brown	红褐 Red-brown	深灰 Dark grey	灰褐 Grey-brown	红褐 Red-brown		
粗绳纹 Coarse cord decorations	1				1															1
中绳纹 Moderate cord	2	2			4															4
细绳纹 Fine cord	3				3															3
麻点绳纹 "Sesame seed"cord		3			3															3
素面 Undecorated	4	2	1		7		1	3	3										7	14
素面+磨光 Undecorated + polished																				
弦纹 String dec.																				
绳纹+弦纹 Cord + string																				
刻划纹 Incised																				
戳印纹 Imprinted																				
网格纹 Net decorations																				
乳钉纹 Nipple dec.																				
附加堆纹 Appliqué patterns																				
附加堆纹+中绳纹 Appliqué patterns + moderate cord																				
附加堆纹+粗绳纹 Appliqué patterns + coarse cord																				
附加堆纹+麻点绳纹 Appliqué patterns + "sesame seed" cord																				
总计 Grand total	18					7														25
百分比 Percentage	72%					28%														100%
备注/Notes：																				

日期/Date： 2010年7月24日 July 24, 2010

续表

单　　位	09SLG TG2 H16																			
陶质、陶色 Clay type/ color 纹饰 Decorative pattern	泥质陶 Fine-clay ware					夹砂陶　Coarse-clay ware														合计 Grand total
						夹砂 Sand temper				夹云母 Mica temper			夹滑石 Talc temper			夹云母、滑石 Talc and mica temper			小计 Total	
	浅灰 Light grey	深灰 Dark grey	灰褐 Grey-brown	红褐 Red-brown	小计 Total	浅灰 Light grey	深灰 Dark grey	灰褐 Grey-brown	红褐 Red-brown	深灰 Dark grey	灰褐 Grey-brown	红褐 Red-brown	深灰 Dark grey	灰褐 Grey-brown	红褐 Red-brown	深灰 Dark grey	灰褐 Grey-brown	红褐 Red-brown		
粗绳纹 Coarse cord decorations	4	1	4	7	16															16
中绳纹 Moderate cord	17	6	3		26			2											2	28
细绳纹 Fine cord		2			2															2
麻点绳纹 "Sesame seed"cord	8	3			11															11
素面 Undecorated	29	15		2	46			21	4					2	6				33	79
素面+磨光 Undecorated + polished																				
弦纹 String dec.	2		1	2	5															5
绳纹+弦纹 Cord + string			1	2	3															3
刻划纹 Incised	1				1															1
戳印纹 Imprinted																				
网格纹 Net decorations																				
乳钉纹 Nipple dec.	1				1															1
附加堆纹 Appliqué patterns																				
附加堆纹+中绳纹 Appliqué patterns + moderate cord																				
附加堆纹+粗绳纹 Appliqué patterns + coarse cord																				
附加堆纹+麻点绳纹 Appliqué patterns + "sesame seed" cord																				
总计 Grand total	111					35														146
百分比 Percentage	76.03%					23.97%														100%

备注/Notes：

日期/Date：　2010年7月31日　July 31, 2010

续表

单位	09SLG TG2 H17																			
陶质、陶色 Clay type/color 纹饰 Decorative pattern	泥质陶 Fine-clay ware					夹砂陶 Coarse-clay ware														合计 Grand total
						夹砂 Sand temper				夹云母 Mica temper			夹滑石 Talc temper			夹云母、滑石 Talc and mica temper			小计 Total	
	浅灰 Light grey	深灰 Dark grey	灰褐 Grey-brown	红褐 Red-brown	小计 Total	浅灰 Light grey	深灰 Dark grey	灰褐 Grey-brown	红褐 Red-brown	深灰 Dark grey	灰褐 Grey-brown	红褐 Red-brown	深灰 Dark grey	灰褐 Grey-brown	红褐 Red-brown	深灰 Dark grey	灰褐 Grey-brown	红褐 Red-brown		
粗绳纹 Coarse cord decorations																				
中绳纹 Moderate cord	11	3	8		22															22
细绳纹 Fine cord	2	1			3															3
麻点绳纹 "Sesame seed"cord		1	2		3															3
素面 Undecorated	9	2	1		12		1	9	1		3	5					3	2	24	36
素面+磨光 Undecorated + polished																				
弦纹 String dec.	1	1			2															2
绳纹+弦纹 Cord + string																				
刻划纹 Incised																				
戳印纹 Imprinted																				
网格纹 Net decorations																				
乳钉纹 Nipple dec.																				
附加堆纹 Appliqué patterns																				
附加堆纹+中绳纹 Appliqué patterns + moderate cord																				
附加堆纹+粗绳纹 Appliqué patterns + coarse cord																				
附加堆纹+麻点绳纹 Appliqué patterns + "sesame seed" cord																				
总计 Grand total	42					24														66
百分比 Percentage	63.64%					36.36%														100%

备注/Notes：

日期/Date：2010年7月31日 July 31, 2010

续表

单　位	09SLG TG2 H18																			合计 Grand total
陶质、陶色 Clay type/color / 纹饰 Decorative pattern	泥质陶 Fine-clay ware					夹砂陶　Coarse-clay ware														
						夹砂 Sand temper				夹云母 Mica temper			夹滑石 Talc temper			夹云母、滑石 Talc and mica temper			小计 Total	
	浅灰 Light grey	深灰 Dark grey	灰褐 Grey-brown	红褐 Red-brown	小计 Total	浅灰 Light grey	深灰 Dark grey	灰褐 Grey-brown	红褐 Red-brown	深灰 Dark grey	灰褐 Grey-brown	红褐 Red-brown	深灰 Dark grey	灰褐 Grey-brown	红褐 Red-brown	深灰 Dark grey	灰褐 Grey-brown	红褐 Red-brown		
粗绳纹 Coarse cord decorations	4		7		11															11
中绳纹 Moderate cord	21	9	6		36		6		1										7	43
细绳纹 Fine cord			1		1															1
麻点绳纹 "Sesame seed"cord	4	1	2		7															7
素面 Undecorated	28	6	3		37		18	10	4			1		6	5				44	81
素面+磨光 Undecorated + polished																				
弦纹 String dec.	7				7															7
绳纹+弦纹 Cord + string	3	2	3		8															8
刻划纹 Incised																				
戳印纹 Imprinted																				
网格纹 Net decorations																				
乳钉纹 Nipple dec.																				
附加堆纹 Appliqué patterns																				
附加堆纹+中绳纹 Appliqué patterns + moderate cord																				
附加堆纹+粗绳纹 Appliqué patterns + coarse cord																				
附加堆纹+麻点绳纹 Appliqué patterns + "sesame seed" cord																				
总计 Grand total	107					51														158
百分比 Percentage	67.72%					32.28%														100%

备注/Notes：

日期/Date：　2010年7月31日　July 31, 2010

续表

单　位	09SLG TG2 H19																			合计 Grand total
陶质、陶色 Clay type/color 纹饰 Decorative pattern	泥质陶 Fine-clay ware					夹砂陶　Coarse-clay ware														
						夹砂 Sand temper				夹云母 Mica temper			夹滑石 Talc temper			夹云母、滑石 Talc and mica temper			小计 Total	
	浅灰 Light grey	深灰 Dark grey	灰褐 Grey-brown	红褐 Red-brown	小计 Total	浅灰 Light grey	深灰 Dark grey	灰褐 Grey-brown	红褐 Red-brown	深灰 Dark grey	灰褐 Grey-brown	红褐 Red-brown	深灰 Dark grey	灰褐 Grey-brown	红褐 Red-brown	深灰 Dark grey	灰褐 Grey-brown	红褐 Red-brown		
粗绳纹 Coarse cord decorations	7		3	2	12															12
中绳纹 Moderate cord	25	11	2	7	45	1													1	46
细绳纹 Fine cord		1			1															1
麻点绳纹 “Sesame seed”cord	7			4	11															11
素面 Undecorated	33	8	8		49			14	5					10					29	78
素面+磨光 Undecorated + polished		4			4															4
弦纹 String dec.	2				2															2
绳纹+弦纹 Cord + string	9				9															9
刻划纹 Incised	1				1															1
戳印纹 Imprinted																				
网格纹 Net decorations																				
乳钉纹 Nipple dec.																				
附加堆纹 Appliqué patterns																				
附加堆纹+中绳纹 Appliqué patterns + moderate cord	1				1															1
附加堆纹+粗绳纹 Appliqué patterns + coarse cord																				
附加堆纹+麻点绳纹 Appliqué patterns + “sesame seed” cord																				
总计 Grand total	135					30														165
百分比 Percentage	81.82%					18.18%														100%

备注/Notes：

日期/Date：　2010年7月31日　July 31, 2010

续表

单　位	09SLG TG2 H20①																			合计 Grand total
陶质、陶色 Clay type/color \ 纹饰 Decorative pattern	泥质陶 Fine-clay ware					夹砂陶 Coarse-clay ware														
						夹砂 Sand temper				夹云母 Mica temper			夹滑石 Talc temper			夹云母、滑石 Talc and mica temper			小计 Total	
	浅灰 Light grey	深灰 Dark grey	灰褐 Grey-brown	红褐 Red-brown	小计 Total	浅灰 Light grey	深灰 Dark grey	灰褐 Grey-brown	红褐 Red-brown	深灰 Dark grey	灰褐 Grey-brown	红褐 Red-brown	深灰 Dark grey	灰褐 Grey-brown	红褐 Red-brown	深灰 Dark grey	灰褐 Grey-brown	红褐 Red-brown		
粗绳纹 Coarse cord decorations	1		2		3															3
中绳纹 Moderate cord	28	24	13		65	3	8	8											19	84
细绳纹 Fine cord	2	1			3															3
麻点绳纹 "Sesame seed"cord		2			2															2
素面 Undecorated	10	10	2		22		14	31	3	6	14								68	90
素面+磨光 Undecorated + polished																				
弦纹 String dec.	2	3			5															5
绳纹+弦纹 Cord + string	8				8															8
刻划纹 Incised																				
戳印纹 Imprinted																				
网格纹 Net decorations																				
乳钉纹 Nipple dec.		1			1															1
附加堆纹 Appliqué patterns																				
附加堆纹+中绳纹 Appliqué patterns + moderate cord		1			1															1
附加堆纹+粗绳纹 Appliqué patterns + coarse cord																				
附加堆纹+麻点绳纹 Appliqué patterns + "sesame seed" cord																				
总计 Grand total	110					87														197
百分比 Percentage	55.84%					44.16%														100%

备注/Notes：

日期/Date：　2010年8月1日　August 1, 2010

续表

单 位	09SLG TG2 H20②																			
陶质、陶色 Clay type/color 纹饰 Decorative pattern	泥质陶 Fine-clay ware					夹砂陶 Coarse-clay ware														合计 Grand total
						夹砂 Sand temper				夹云母 Mica temper			夹滑石 Talc temper			夹云母、滑石 Talc and mica temper			小计 Total	
	浅灰 Light grey	深灰 Dark grey	灰褐 Grey-brown	红褐 Red-brown	小计 Total	浅灰 Light grey	深灰 Dark grey	灰褐 Grey-brown	红褐 Red-brown	深灰 Dark grey	灰褐 Grey-brown	红褐 Red-brown	深灰 Dark grey	灰褐 Grey-brown	红褐 Red-brown	深灰 Dark grey	灰褐 Grey-brown	红褐 Red-brown		
粗绳纹 Coarse cord decorations																				
中绳纹 Moderate cord	8	6			14	1													1	15
细绳纹 Fine cord			1		1															1
麻点绳纹 "Sesame seed" cord																				
素面 Undecorated	2	5			7		4	2			2								8	15
素面+磨光 Undecorated + polished																				
弦纹 String dec.		1			1															1
绳纹+弦纹 Cord + string	1	4			5	1		1											2	7
刻划纹 Incised																				
戳印纹 Imprinted																				
网格纹 Net decorations	1				1															1
乳钉纹 Nipple dec.			1		1															1
附加堆纹 Appliqué patterns																				
附加堆纹+中绳纹 Appliqué patterns + moderate cord																				
附加堆纹+粗绳纹 Appliqué patterns + coarse cord																				
附加堆纹+麻点绳纹 Appliqué patterns + "sesame seed" cord																				
总计 Grand total	30					11														41
百分比 Percentage	73.17%					26.83%														100%

备注/Notes：

日期/Date: 2010年8月2日 August 2, 2010 统计/Counts：李峰/唐锦琼/付群启/毕道传 LI Feng, TANG Jinqiong, FU Qunqi, BI Daochuan

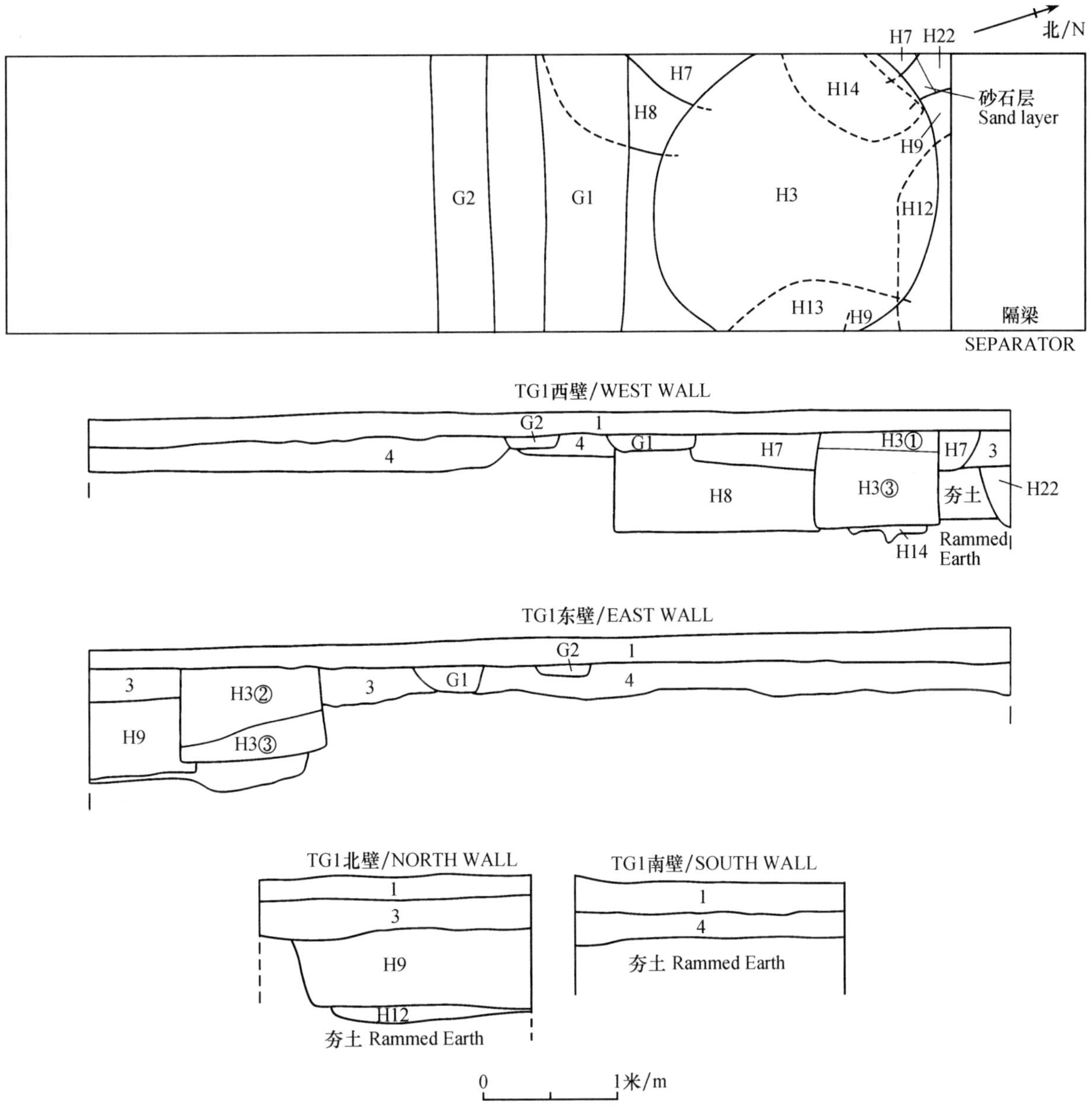

图Ⅰ.5.1　探沟一（TG1）平面和四壁剖面图

Figure Ⅰ.5.1　Plan and cross-sectional profiles of Trench 1 (TG1).

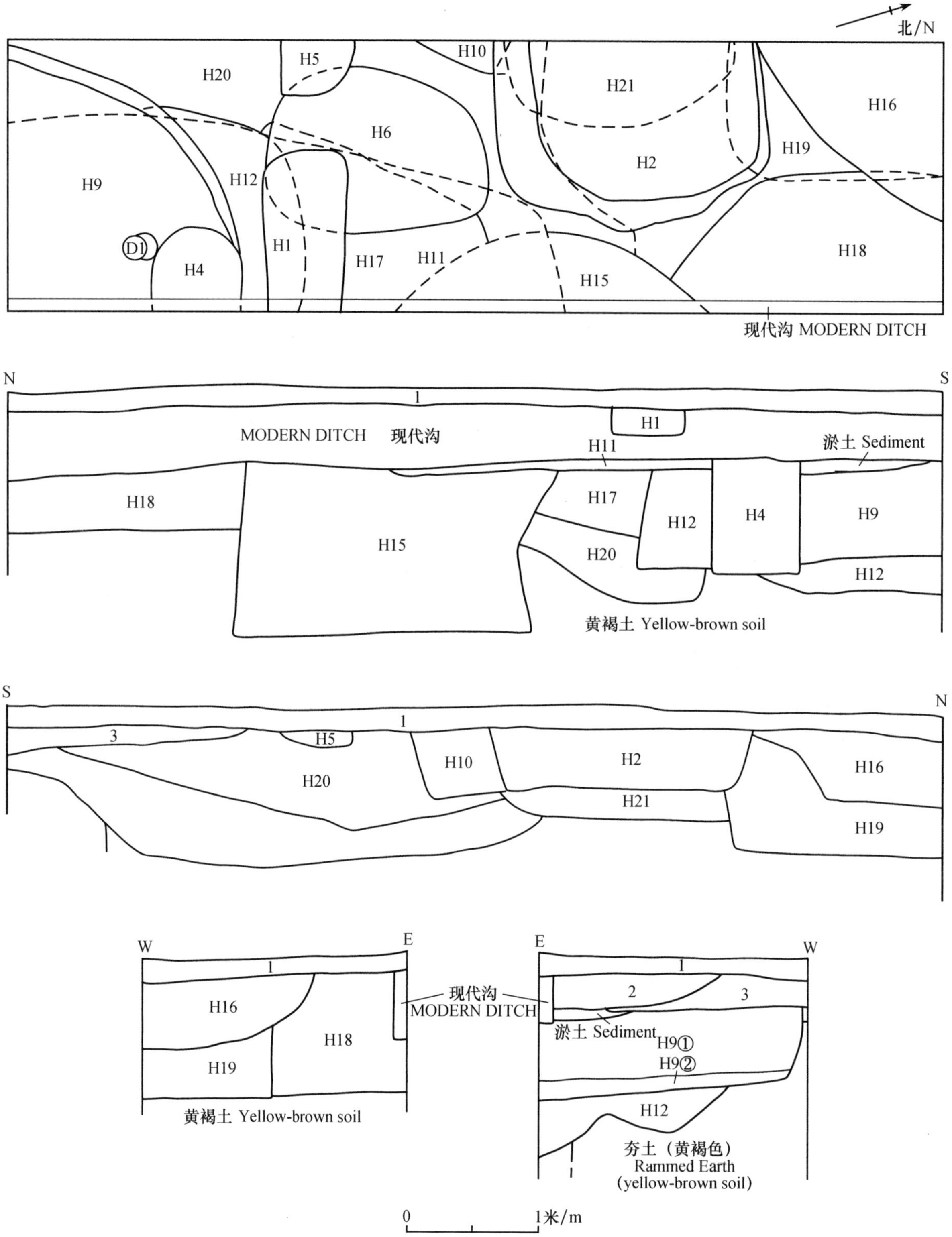

图Ⅰ.5.2　探沟二（TG2）平面和四壁剖面图

Figure Ⅰ.5.2　Plan and cross-sectional profiles of Trench 2 (TG2).

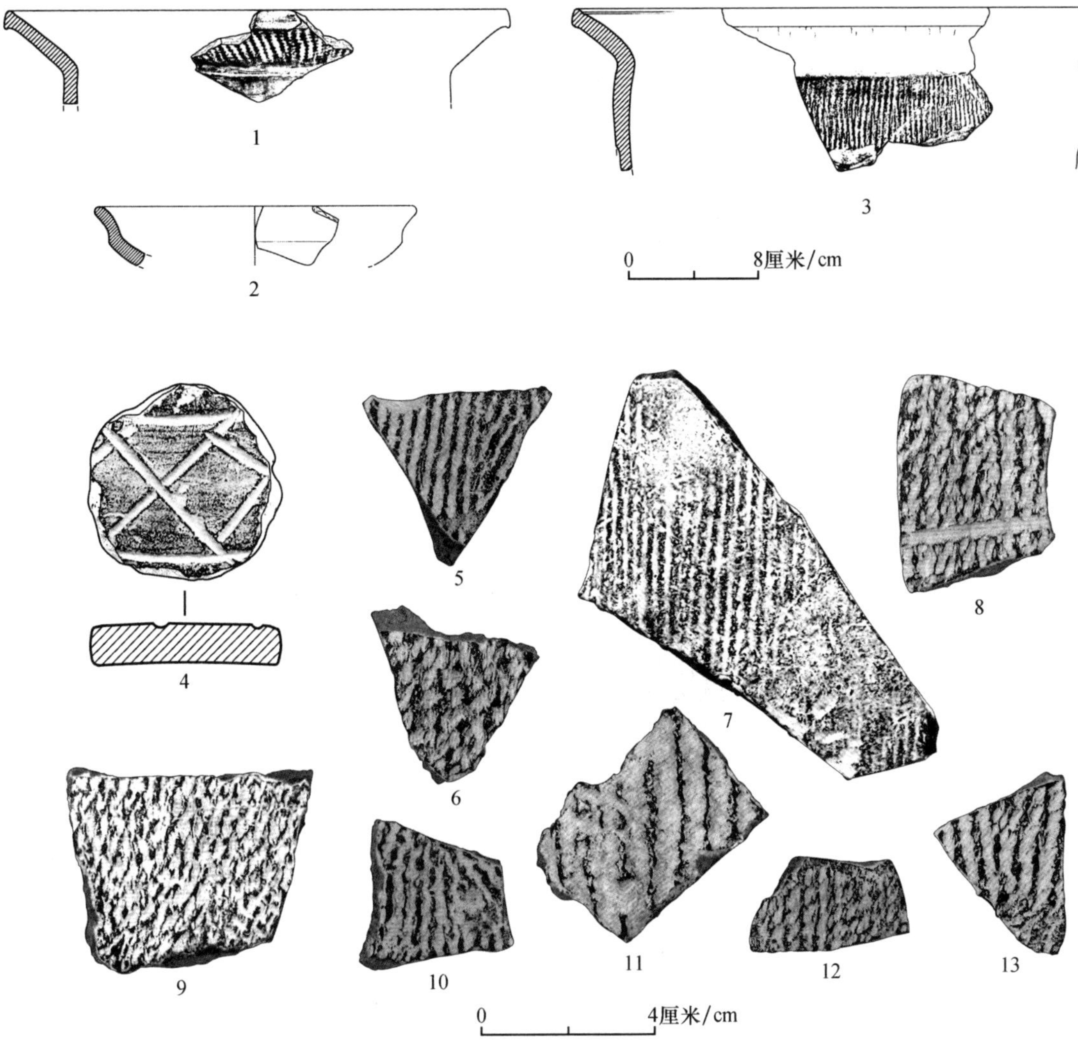

图Ⅰ.5.3　TG1③出土的陶器和陶片

1. 簋（TG1③：2）　2. 豆（TG1③：3）　3. 盆(TG1③：1）　4. 圆陶片（TG1③：4）　5. 陶片（TG1③：5）
6. 陶片（TG1③：8）　7.　陶片（TG1③：6）　8. 陶片（TG1③：12）　9. 陶片（TG1③：7）　10. 陶片（TG1③：9）
11. 陶片（TG1③：13）　12. 陶片（TG1③：10）　13. 陶片（TG1③：11）

Figure Ⅰ.5.3　Pottery types and sherds from TG1, stratum ③.

1. *Gui* tureen (TG1③：2)　2. *Dou* pedestal dish (TG1③：3)　3. *Pen* basin (TG1③：1)　4. Round pottery sherd (TG1③：4)
5. Pottery sherd (TG1③：5)　6. Pottery sherd (TG1③：8)　7.　Pottery sherd (TG1③：6)　8. Pottery sherd (TG1③：12)
9. Pottery sherd (TG1③：7)　10. Pottery sherd (TG1③：9)　11. Pottery sherd (TG1③：13)　12. Pottery sherd (TG1③：10)
13. Pottery sherd (TG1③：11)

表Ⅰ.5.3 TG1②出土遗物登记表

Table Ⅰ.5.3 Artifacts from trench TG1, stratum ②

图号 Number on Fig.	标本号 Excavation number	器物名称 Artifact name	出土时间 Excavation date	位置 Location	所属类型 Types	尺寸（厘米）Size (cm)	特点描述 Description of features
	09SLGTG1 ②：1	圈足 Circular foot	2009-7-4			W: 14.3 M: 13.8 H: 3.8	泥质灰陶，矮圈足，素面。Grey fine clay, short circular foot, plain.

尺寸标志：L=长度；H=高度；W=宽度；D=直径；R=半径；M=口径；B=底径；T=厚度；d=深度；h=孔径。

Measurements: L=length; H=height; W=width; D=diameter; R=radius; M=mouth diameter; B=bottom diameter; T=thickness; d=depth; h=hole diameter.

表Ⅰ.5.4 TG1③出土遗物登记表

Table Ⅰ.5.4 Artifacts from trench TG1, stratum ③

图号 Number on Fig. Ⅰ.5.3	标本号 Excavation number	器物名称 Artifact name	出土时间 Excavation date	位置 Location	所属类型 Types	尺寸（厘米）Size (cm)	特点描述 Description of features
3	09SLGTG1 ③：1	簋 *Gui* tureen	2009-7-4		A4	M: 33.8 H: 9.6	泥质灰陶，方唇，宽折沿，外饰绳纹。Grey fine clay, square lip, wide folded rim, cord decoration on the outside.
1	09SLGTG1 ③：2	簋 *Gui* tureen	2009-7-4		A	M: 31.1 H: 5.5	泥质灰陶，方唇，宽折沿，沿外饰中绳纹。Grey fine clay, square lip, wide folded rim, medium cord decorations on the outside of the rim.
2	09SLGTG1 ③：3	豆 *Dou* pedestal dish	2009-7-4		B	M: 19.8 H: 3.5	泥质红陶，圆唇，敞口，折盘。素面，磨光。Red fine clay, rounded lip, open mouth, plate has fold. Plain and polished.
4	09SLGTG1 ③：4	圆陶片 Round pottery sherd	2009-7-4			M: 4.28 T: 0.9	夹砂红褐，饰带状方格纹。Red-brown coarse ceramic, decorated with a ribbon of grids.
5	09SLGTG1 ③：5	陶片 Pottery sherd	2009-7-4			L: 4.3 W: 4	夹砂灰陶，饰中绳纹。Grey coarse ceramic, decorated with medium cord impressions.
7	09SLGTG1 ③：6	陶片 Pottery sherd	2009-7-4			L: 8.3 W: 9.2	夹砂深灰，饰细绳纹。Coarse dark-grey, decorated with fine cord impressions.
9	09SLGTG1 ③：7	陶片 Pottery sherd	2009-7-4			L: 5.7 W: 4.6	夹砂深灰，饰麻点绳纹。Coarse dark-grey, decorated with "sesame seed" pattern cord impressions.
6	09SLGTG1 ③：8	陶片 Pottery sherd	2009-7-4			L: 3.9 W: 4	夹砂灰陶，饰麻点绳纹。Grey coarse ceramic, decorated with "sesame seed" pattern cord impressions.
10	09SLGTG1 ③：9	陶片 Pottery sherd	2009-7-4			L: 3.6 W: 3.4	夹砂深灰，饰中绳纹。Coarse dark-grey, decorated with, decorated with medium cord impressions.
12	09SLGTG1 ③：10	陶片 Pottery sherd	2009-7-4			L: 3.7 W: 2.2	夹砂红褐，饰中绳纹。Coarse red-brown, decorated with medium cord impressions.
13	09SLGTG1 ③：11	陶片 Pottery sherd	2009-7-4			L: 3.1 W: 4.1	夹砂深灰，饰中绳纹。Coarse dark-grey, decorated with medium cord impressions.

续表

图号 Number on Fig. Ⅰ.5.3	标本号 Excavation number	器物名称 Artifact name	出土时间 Excavation date	位置 Location	所属类型 Types	尺寸（厘米）Size (cm)	特点描述 Description of features
8	09SLGTG1 ③：12	陶片 Pottery sherd	2009-7-4			L: 3.7 W: 4.9	夹砂灰陶，饰中绳纹，有一道抹痕。Grey coarse ceramic, decorated with medium cord impressions, one track of smearing mark.
11	09SLGTG1 ③：13					L: 5.3 W: 5.3	夹砂深灰，饰粗绳纹。Coarse dark-grey, decorated with coarse cord impressions.

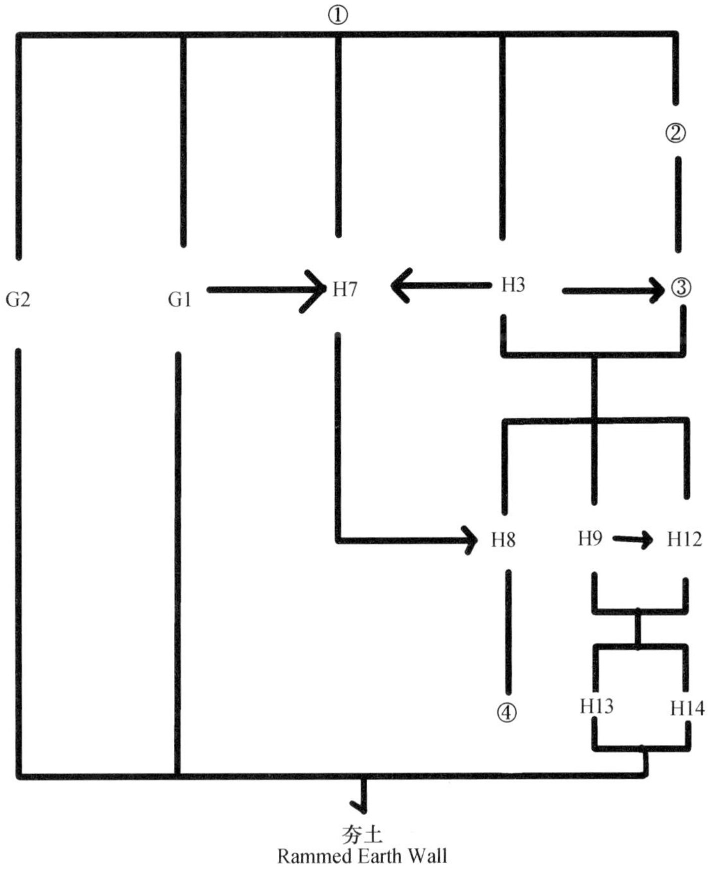

图Ⅰ.5.4　TG1遗迹关系图

Figure Ⅰ.5.4　Relations among structural units in TG1.

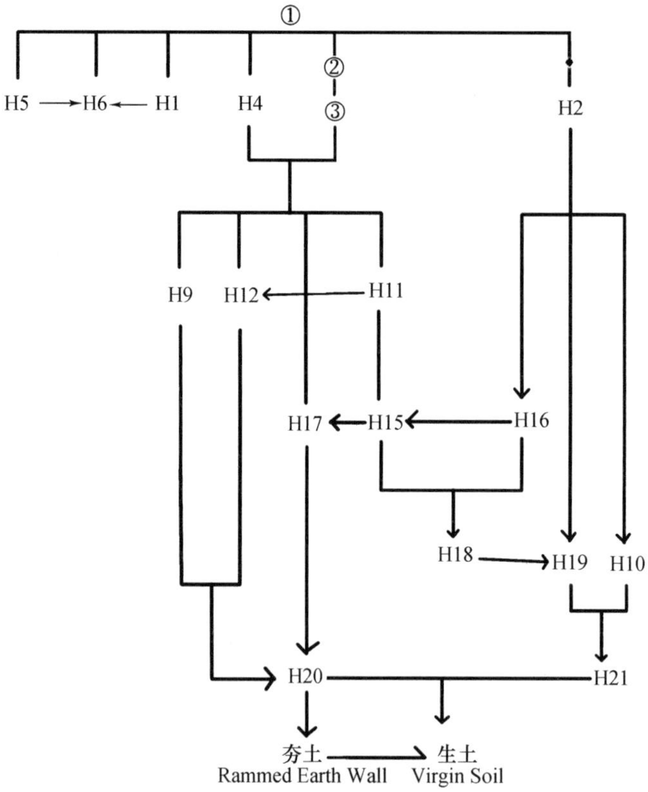

图Ⅰ.5.5　TG2遗迹关系图

Figure Ⅰ.5.5　Relations among structural units in TG2.

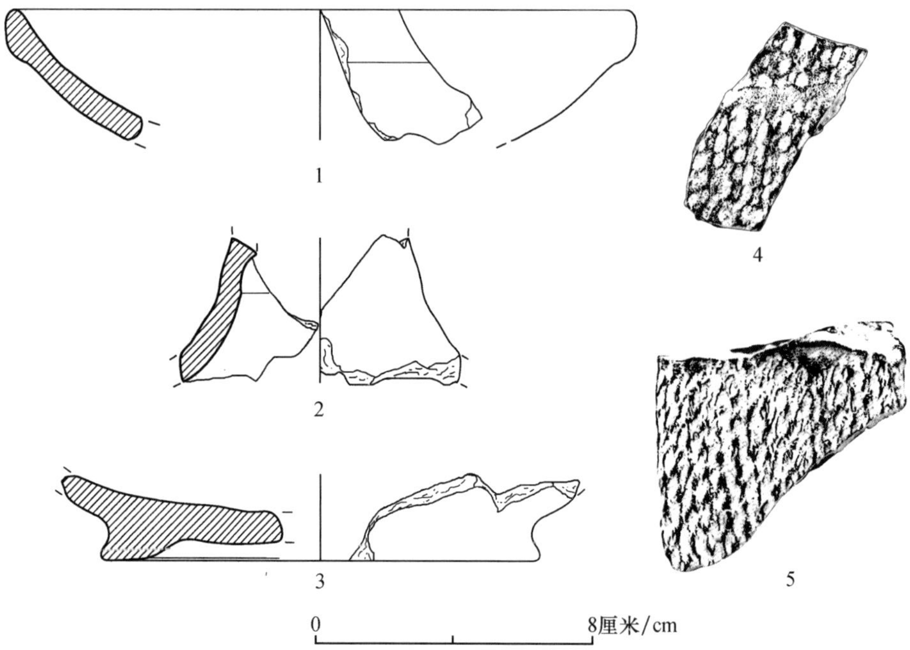

图Ⅰ.5.6　TG1G1出土陶器

1. 豆（G1:3）　2. 豆（G1:4）　3. 碗（G1:2）　4. 陶片（G1:5）　5. 陶片（G1:6）

Figure Ⅰ.5.6　Pottery from Ditch G1 in Trench 1.

1. *Dou* pedestal dish (G1:3)　2. *Dou* pedestal dish (G1:4)　3. Bowl (G1:2)　4. Pottery sherd (G1:5)　5. Pottery sherd (G1:6)

表Ⅰ.5.5　TG1G1出土遗物登记表

Table Ⅰ.5.5　Artifacts from Ditch G1 in Trench 1 (TG1)

图号 Number on Fig. Ⅰ.5.6	标本号 Excavation number	器物名称 Artifact name	出土时间 Excavation date	位置 Location	所属类型 Types	尺寸(厘米) Size (cm)	特点描述 Description of features
3	09SLGTG1 G1：2	碗 Bowl	2009-7-4		A2	W: 6.4 H: 2.3	泥质灰陶，矮圈足，素面。Grey fine clay, short circular feet, plain.
1	09SLGTG1 G1：3	豆 *Dou* pedestal dish	2009-7-4		B	W: 17.9 H: 3.7	泥质灰陶，圆唇，敞口。Grey fine clay, round lip, open mouth.
2	09SLGTG1 G1：4	豆 *Dou* pedestal dish	2009-7-4		A	W: 8.1 H: 4.1	泥质浅灰，素面。Light grey fine clay, plain.
4	09SLGTG1 G1：5	陶片 Pottery sherd	2009-7-4			L: 6.7 W: 6.5	夹砂深灰，中绳纹。Coarse and dark grey, medium cord impression.
5	09SLGTG1 G1：6	陶片 Pottery sherd	2009-7-4			L: 5 W: 5.5	夹砂红褐，中绳纹。Coarse red-brown, medium cord decorations.

尺寸标志：L=长度；H=高度；W=宽度；D=直径；R=半径；M=口径；B=底径；T=厚度；d=深度；h=孔径。

Measurements: L=length; H=height; W=width; D=diameter; R=radius; M=mouth diameter; B=bottom diameter; T=thickness; d=depth; h=hole diameter.

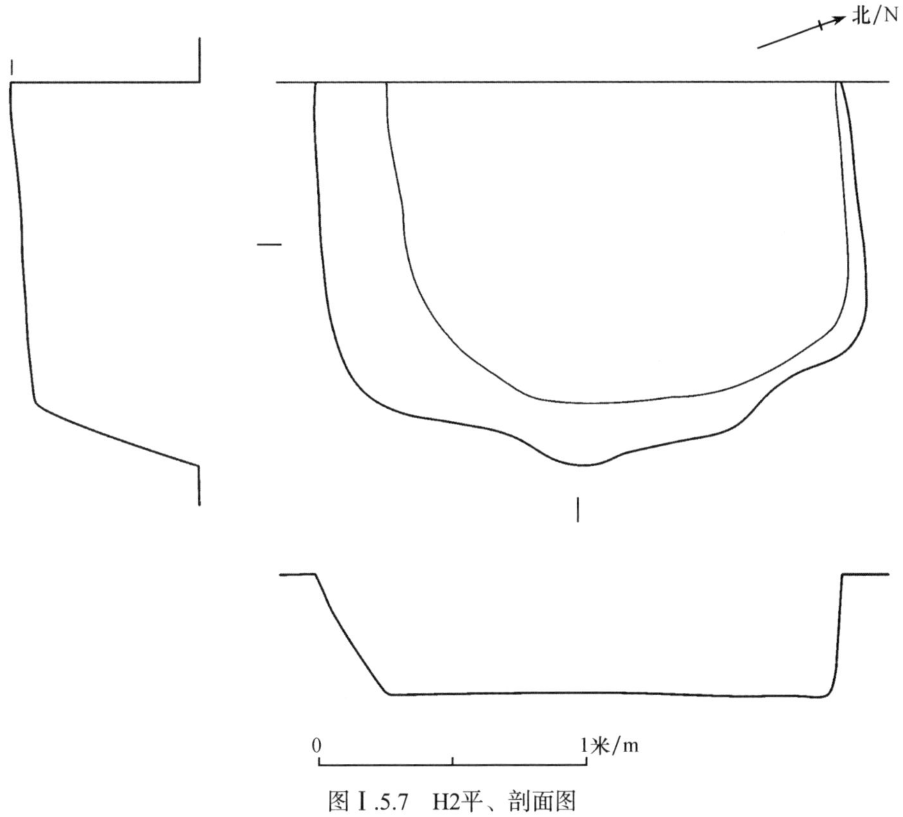

图Ⅰ.5.7　H2平、剖面图

Figure Ⅰ.5.7　Plan and cross-sectional profiles of pit H2.

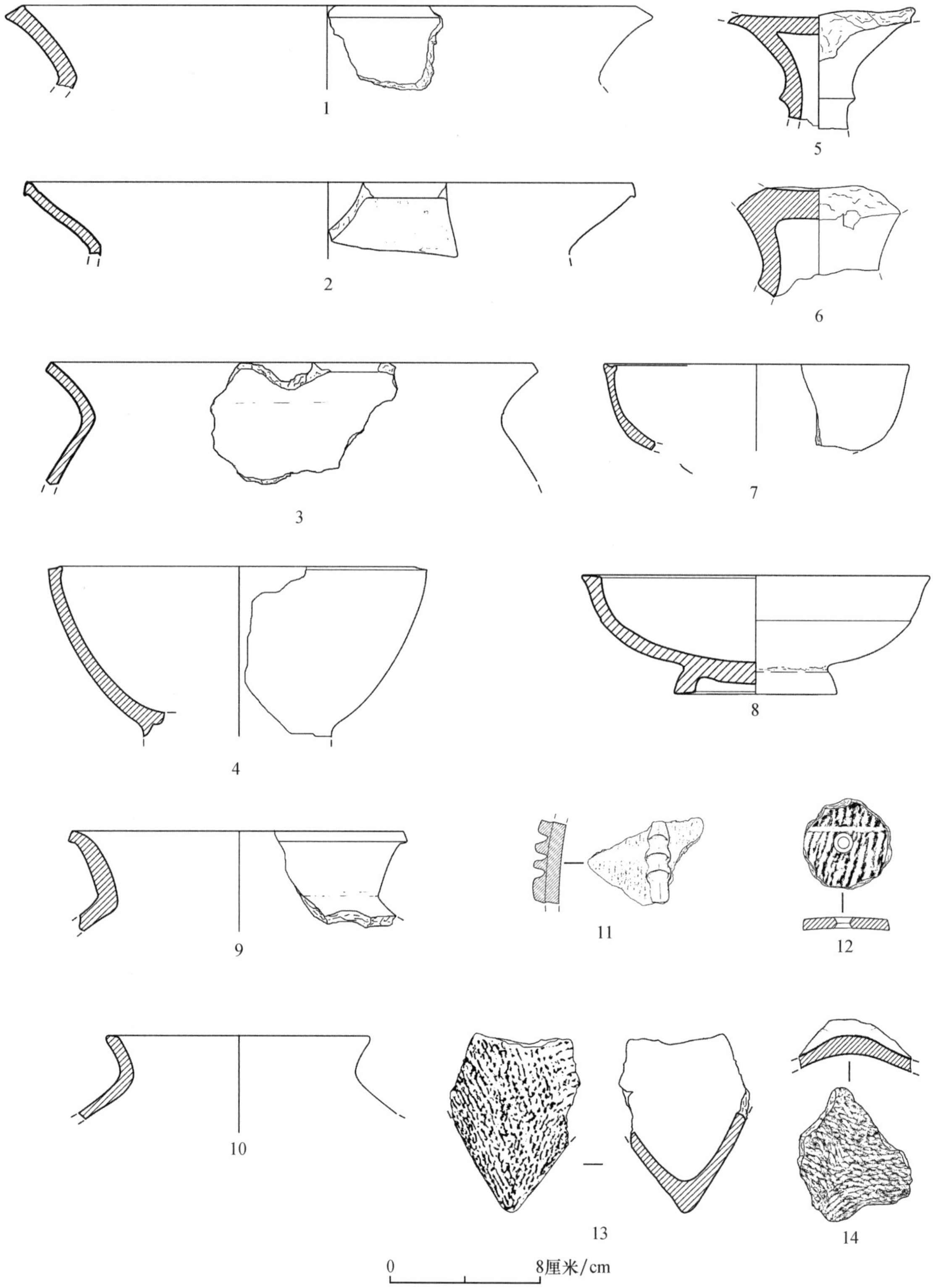

图Ⅰ.5.8　H2出土陶器

1. 鬲（H2：10）　2. 簋（H2：35）　3. 鬲（H2：37）　4. 碗（H2：15）　5. 豆（H2：6）　6. 豆（H2：21）　7. 豆（H2：22）　8. 碗（H2：1）　9. 罐（H2：31）　10. 罐（H2：26）　11. 盆（H2：17）　12. 纺轮（H2：2）　13. 鬲（H2：8）　14. 陶片（H2：45）

Figure Ⅰ.5.8　Pottery types from pit H2.

1. *Li* tripod (H2：10)　2. *Gui* tureen (H2：35)　3. *Li* tripod (H2：37)　4. Bowl (H2：15)　5. *Dou* pedestal dish (H2：6)　6. *Dou* pedestal dish (H2：21)　7. *Dou* pedestal dish (H2：22)　8. Bowl (H2：1)　9. *Guan* jar (H2：31)　10. *Guan* jar (H2：26)　11. *Pen* basin (H2：17)　12. Spindle whorl (H2：2)　13. *Li* tripod (H2：8)　14. Pottery sherd (H2：45)

表Ⅰ.5.6　H2出土遗物登记表

Table Ⅰ.5.6　Artifacts from pit H2

图号 Number on Fig. Ⅰ.5.8	标本号 Excavation number	器物名称 Artifact name	出土时间 Excavation date	位置 Location	所属类型 Types	尺寸（厘米）Size (cm)	特点描述 Description of features
8	09SLGTG1 H2：1	碗 Bowl	2009-7-5	525 × 75—35	A2	M: 18.3 B: 8.5 H: 6.2	红褐色夹细沙，方唇外撇，浅腹有折棱，周饰弦纹，圈足外撇。Red-brown with inclusions of fine sand, flared square lip, shallow belly with folds, circular ring decorations, circular flared feet.
12	09SLGTG1 H2：2	纺轮 Spindle whorl	2009-7-5	520 × 75—65		D: 4.5 H: 0.6 H: 0.5	泥质红褐陶，有中绳纹。两面对钻。Red-brown fine clay, with medium cord decorations, drilled from both sides.
	09SLGTG2 H2：3	铜镞 Bronze arrowhead	2009-7-5	440 × 90—40		W: 2	已成铜锈状，但仍可辨。三棱状，中有挺。上部残。Already turned into rust, but still recognizable. Triangular shape, straight ridge in the middle. Upper part missing.
	09SLGTG2 H2：4	残豆盘 Bowl from a *dou* pedestal dish	2009-7-5		A	L: 8.1 W: 7.2 H: 6.9	残豆盘，泥质深灰，素面，柄较细，柄内可见盘柄接合痕迹。Broken bowl from a *dou* pedestal dish, dark grey fine clay ceramic, plain, with a relatively thin handle. Joint with the bowl can be seen inside the handle.
	09SLGTG2 H2：5	残豆柄 Handle from a *dou* pedestal dish	2009-7-5		B	L: 9.3 H: 5.2	泥质浅灰，素面，圈足较细，盘底为圜底，柄内可见接合痕迹。Light grey clay, plain, with round and relatively thin feet. The bowl has a round bottom, and traces of the joint can be seen inside the handle.
5	09SLGTG2 H2：6	残豆盘 Bowl from a *dou* pedestal dish	2009-7-5		B2	L: 10 W: 6.2 H: 6	泥质深灰，素面，盘底甚平，柄细高并有凸棱 Dark grey clay, plain, the bottom of the bowl relatively flat. The handle is very thin and high and has a ridge.
	09SLGTG2 H2：7	簋口沿 Rim of a *gui* tureen	2009-7-5			L: 7.1 W: 2.9	泥质红褐，方唇，唇内缘有凹痕，外饰绳纹并抹去。Red-brown fine clay, square lips, with dents on the inner lips, cord decorations and smearing.
13	09SLGTG2 H2：8	鬲袋足 Pocket-shaped foot from a *li* tripod	2009-7-5		B4	W: 6.9 H: 9.2	夹云母深灰，足尖很矮，饰麻点绳纹。Dark grey ceramic with mica inclusions, the end of the foot is very low, bears “sesame seed” cord decorations.
	09SLGTG2 H2：9	鬲口沿 Rim from a *li* tripod	2009-7-5		D	L: 4.8 W: 3	灰褐，夹云母滑石，方唇，素面。Grey-brown with inclusions of talc and mica, square lip, plain.
1	09SLGTG2 H2：10	鬲口沿 Rim from a *li* tripod	2009-7-5		D	M: 33.9 H: 4.4	夹砂红褐，方唇，宽沿，口外撇，素面。Coarse and red-brown, square lip, broad rim, mouth slanted outward, plain.

续表

图号 Number on Fig. Ⅰ.5.8	标本号 Excavation number	器物名称 Artifact name	出土时间 Excavation date	位置 Location	所属类型 Types	尺寸（厘米） Size (cm)	特点描述 Description of features
	09SLGTG2 H2：11	簋口沿 Rim from a *gui* tureen	2009-7-5		A	L: 9.7 W: 6.1	泥质浅灰，方圆唇，宽沿，外饰中绳纹有抹痕。 Light grey fine clay, square and round lip, wide rim, with medium cord impression and smear marks on the outside.
	09SLGTG2 H2：12	簋口沿 Rim from a *gui* tureen	2009-7-5		A	L: 7.6 W: 5.3	泥质浅灰，尖唇，三角缘明显，宽沿，外饰绳纹并抹去。 Light grey clay, sharp lip, with a clear triangular edge. Wide rim, with cord decorations and smear marks on the outside.
4	09SLGTG2 H2：15	碗 Bowl	2009-7-5		A1	M: 19.8 H: 8.6	夹滑石红陶，方唇，敞口，腹较深，素面。 Red color with talc inclusions, square lip, wide mouth and deep belly, plain.
	09SLGTG2 H2：16	圆陶片 Round pottery sherd	2009-7-5			L: 5.4 W: 5.2 T: 1	泥质深灰，大致呈圆形，饰麻点绳纹。 Dark grey clay, roughly circular, with “sesame seed” cord decorations.
11	09SLGTG2 H2：17	盆 *Pen* basin	2009-7-5			L: 6.3 W: 5	夹砂灰褐，饰齿状附加堆纹，腹饰绳纹。 Coarse and grey-brown, with appliqué patterns, with cord decorations on the belly.
	09SLGTG2 H2：19	罐口沿 Rim from a *guan* jar	2009-7-5		A	L: 8.6 W: 2.8	泥质浅灰，圆唇，素面。 Light grey clay, round lip, plain.
	09SLGTG2 H2：20	鬲口沿 Rim from a *li* tripod	2009-7-5		A	L: 9.1 W: 5.4	夹砂浅灰，尖圆唇，低领卷沿，饰绳纹。 Coarse and light grey, round pointed lip, low neck and scrolled rim, with cord decorations.
6	09SLGTG2 H2：21	残豆柄 Handle from a *dou* pedestal dish	2009-7-5		A	W: 8.6 H: 5.7	泥质深灰，素面，盘底较平，柄较粗。 Dark grey clay, plain, bottom of the bowl relatively flat, handle relatively thick.
7	09SLGTG2 H2：22	豆口沿 Rim from a *dou* pedestal dish	2009-7-5		C	M: 16 H: 4.3	泥质浅灰，素面，方唇，直口。 Light grey clay, plain, square lip and straight mouth.
	09SLGTG2 H2：23	残豆盘 Bowl from a *dou* pedestal dish	2009-7-6		B	L: 7.5 W: 4.7 H: 3.2	泥质浅灰，素面，柄应较细，盘外底微起凸棱。 Light grey clay, plain, relatively thin handle, outer bottom has a slight ridge.
	09SLGTG2 H2：24	豆圈足 Circular foot from a *dou* pedestal dish	2009-7-6		B	L: 7.1 W: 3.2 H: 2.8	泥质深灰，素面。 Dark grey clay, plain.
	09SLGTG2 H2：25	罐口沿 Rim from a *guan* jar	2009-7-6		A4	L: 12.4 W: 3.6	泥质浅灰，方唇外卷，低领，卷沿。素面。 Light grey clay, the square lip scrolled outward, low neck, rolled rim, plain.

续表

图号 Number on Fig. Ⅰ.5.8	标本号 Excavation number	器物名称 Artifact name	出土时间 Excavation date	位置 Location	所属类型 Types	尺寸（厘米） Size (cm)	特点描述 Description of features
10	09SLGTG2 H2：26	罐口沿 Rim from a *guan* jar	2009-7-6		B	M: 14.1 H: 4.4	泥质浅灰，素面，圆唇，口外撇，卷沿。 Light grey clay, plain, round lip, outside of the rim slanted, rolled edge.
	09SLGTG2 H2：27	罐口沿 Rim from a *guan* jar	2009-7-6		B2	L: 6.7 W: 3.8	泥质浅灰，素面，圆唇，卷沿。 Light grey clay, plain, round lip, rolled rim.
	09SLGTG2 H2：29	残豆盘 Bowl from a *dou* pedestal dish	2009-7-6			L: 6.4 W: 4.2	泥质浅灰，方唇，外缘下饰凹弦纹。 Light grey clay, square lip, under rim decorated with sunken string pattern.
	09SLGTG2 H2：30	豆圈足 Circular food from a *dou* pedestal dish	2009-7-6			L: 5.7 W: 3.1	泥质浅灰，素面。 Light grey clay, plain.
9	09SLGTG2 H2：31	罐口沿 Rim from a *guan* jar	2009-7-6		B	M: 18 H: 5.1	泥质红褐，素面，方唇外撇，领较高，卷沿。 Red-brown clay, plain, square lip with flared outside, relatively high neck, rolled rim.
	09SLGTG2 H2：32	残豆盘 Bowl from a *dou* pedestal dish	2009-7-6		B5	L: 6.3 W: 5.9	泥质深灰，浅折盘，盘外饰数周凹弦纹。 Dark grey clay, shallow bowl with fold. The outside of the bowl is decorated with multiple sunken strings.
	09SLGTG2 H2：34	簋口沿 Rim from a *gui* tureen	2009-7-6		A3	L: 6.3 W: 3	泥质浅灰，素面，圈足外撇。 Light grey clay, plain, circular foot flaring outward.
2	09SLGTG2 H2：35	簋口沿 Rim from a *gui* tureen	2009-7-6		A4	M: 32 H: 3.9	泥质深灰，素面，方唇，宽沿，沿内有凹痕。 Dark grey clay, plain, square lip, wide rim, dent marks on the inside of the rim.
	09SLGTG2 H2：36	圈足 Circular foot	2009-7-6			L: 6 W: 2.2	泥质浅灰陶，圈足外撇，足跟较高，素面。 Light grey clay, circular foot that flares outward, the base of the foot relatively high, plain.
3	09SLGTG2 H2：37	鬲口沿 Rim from a *li* tripod	2009-7-6		B	M: 26.1 H: 6.3	夹砂灰褐，方唇，口外撇，折沿，素面。 Coarse and grey-brown, square lip, the mouth flares outward, folded rim, plain.
14	09SLGTG2 H2：45	陶片 Pottery sherd	2009-7-6			W: 6.1 H: 6.9	夹砂红褐，中绳纹。 Coarse and red-brown, medium cord impressions.

尺寸标志：L=长度；H=高度；W=宽度；D=直径；R=半径；M=口径；B=底径；T=厚度；d=深度；h=孔径。

Measurements: L=length; H=height; W=width; D=diameter; R=radius; M=diameter at mouth; B=bottom diameter; T=thickness; d=depth; h=hole diameter.

H2：39

H2：41

H2：40

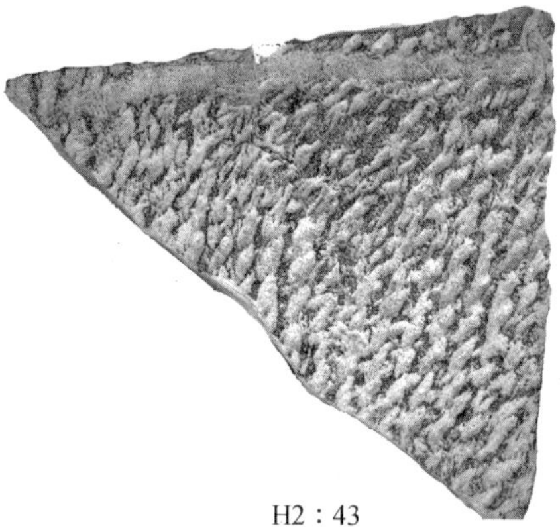

H2：43

H2：38

H2：42

图Ⅰ.5.9　H2出土陶片纹饰

Figure Ⅰ.5.9　Decorated pottery sherds from pit H2.

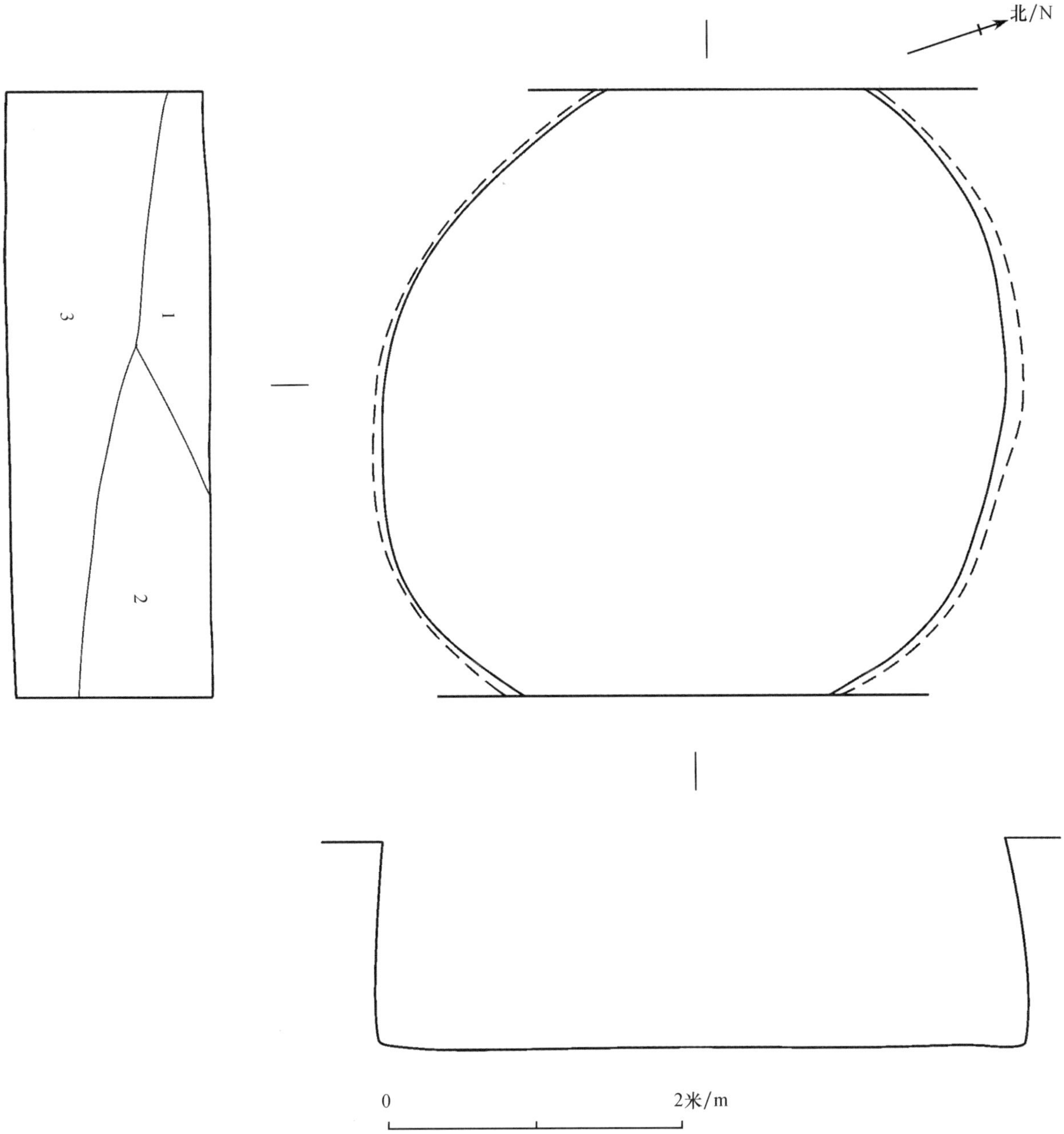

图Ⅰ.5.10　H3平、剖面图

Figure Ⅰ.5.10　Plan and cross-sectional profiles of pit H3.

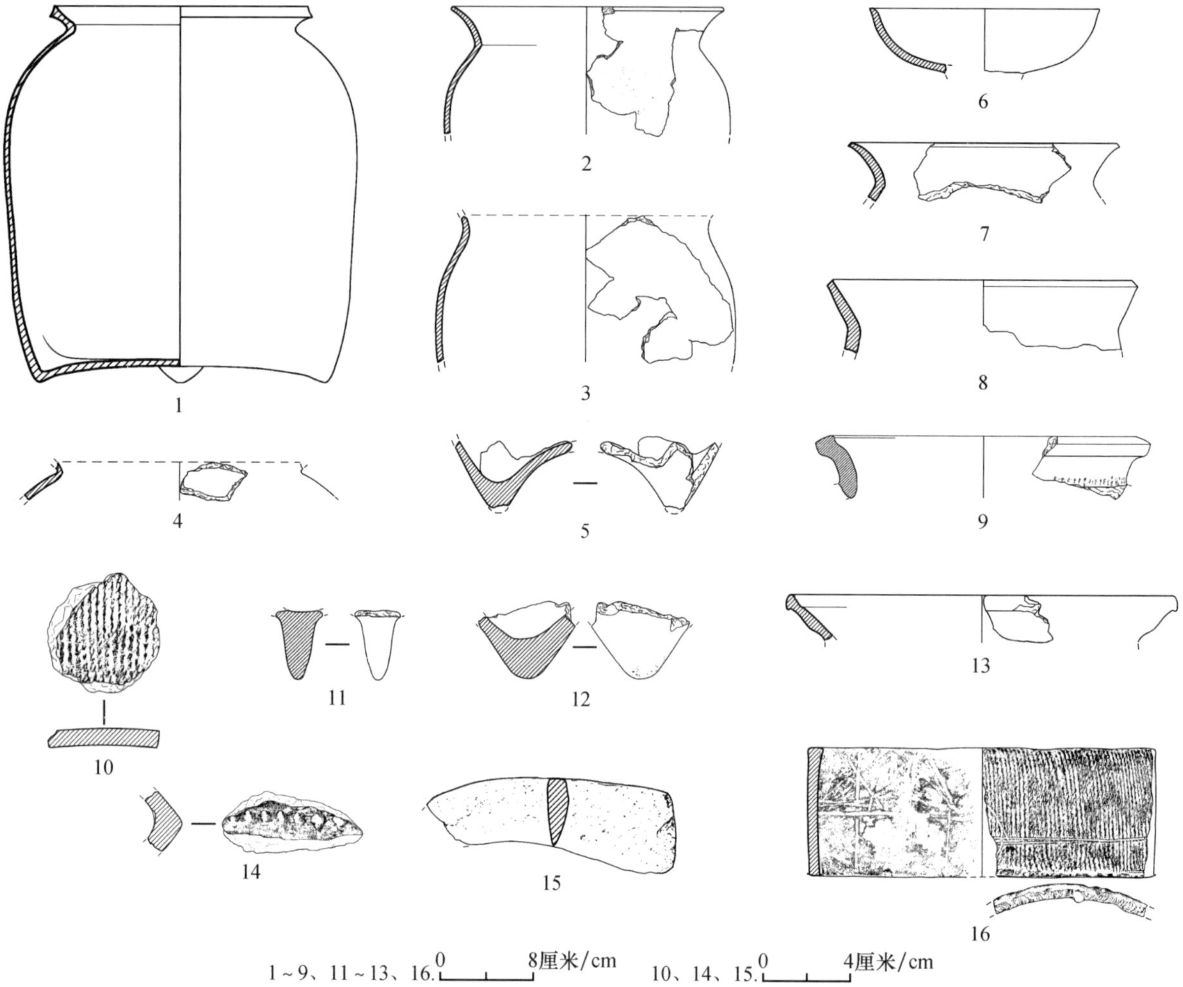

图Ⅰ.5.11　H3①出土陶器和石器

1. 鬲（H3①：1）　2. 鬲（H3①：14）　3. 鬲（H3①：44）　4. 鬲（H3①：46）　5. 鬲（H3①：42）　6. 豆（H3①：17）　7. 鬲（H3①：43）　8. 鬲（H3①：45）　9. 罐（H3①：16）　10. 圆陶片(H3①：18）　11. 鼎（H3①：7）　12. 鬲（H3①：6）　13. 簋（H3①：11）　14. 甗（H3①：50）　15. 石镰（H3①：3）　16. 瓦（H3①：10）

Figure Ⅰ.5.11　Pottery and stone objects from pit H3, stratum ①.

1. *Li* tripod (H3①：1)　2. *Li* tripod (H3①：14)　3. *Li* tripod (H3①：44)　4. *Li* tripod (H3①：46)　5. *Li* tripod (H3①：42)　6. *Dou* pedestal dish (H3①: 17)　7. *Li* tripod (H3①：43)　8. *Li* tripod (H3①：45)　9. *Guan* jar (H3①：16)　10. Round pottery sherd (H3①：18)　11. *Ding* cauldron (H3①：7)　12. *Li* tripod (H3①：6)　13. *Gui* tureen (H3①：11)　14. *Yan* steamer (H3①：50)　15. Stone sickle (H3①：3)　16. Tile (H3①：10)

表Ⅰ.5.7　H3①出土遗物登记表

Table Ⅰ.5.7　Artifacts from pit H3, stratum ①

图号 Number on Fig. Ⅰ.5.11	标本号 Excavation number	器物名称 Artifact name	出土时间 Excavation date	位置 Location	所属类型 Types	尺寸(厘米) Size (cm)	特点描述 Description of features
1	09SLGTG1 H3①：1	鬲 *Li* tripod	2009-7-5		D3	M: 22 H: 31.6 W: 24	夹云母滑石，方唇外撇，折沿，大鼓腹，袋足较矮。整体近正方形，连裆近平，素面。 Inclusions of mica and talc. Square lip flared outward, folded rim, large bulging belly, relatively short pocket-shaped feet. Nearly square in shape, joint crotch nearly flat; plain.
	09SLGTG1 H3①：2	器盖 Vessel lid	2009-7-5		A1		圆唇，盖沿微外撇。微鼓，盖顶有圈转细把手。 Round lip, rim of the lid flares outward. The top of the lid has a round, thin, circular handle.
15	09SLGTG1 H3①：3	石镰 Stone sickle	2009-7-5			W: 11.4 H: 4.3	石英岩，镰刀状。 Quartzite, sickle shape.
12	09SLGTG1 H3①：6	鬲足 *Li* tripod foot	2009-7-5		D	W: 24 H: 6.3	夹砂红陶，素面。 Coarse and red-brown, plain.
11	09SLGTG1 H3①：7	鼎 *Ding* cauldron	2009-7-5		A1	L: 3.9 W: 3.4 H: 5.7	夹云母灰褐，圆锥足，素面。 Grey-brown with inclusions of mica, conical feet, plain.
	09SLGTG1 H3①：8	豆 *Dou* pedestal dish	2009-7-5			L: 3.9 W: 4.1	泥质浅灰，素面磨光，方唇，直口。 Light grey clay, plain and polished, square lip, straight mouth.
16	09SLGTG1 H3①：10	瓦 Tile	2009-7-5		A1	L: 14 W: 10.1 H: 2.7	夹砂灰陶，饰细绳纹，上部有凹弦纹压饰。 Coarse grey clay, fine cord decorations, the upper part has impressed intaglio ring decorations.
13	09SLGTG1 H3①：11	簋 *Gui* tureen	2009-7-5			W: 11.3 H: 9	泥质深灰，圆唇，口沿外撇呈凸起状，磨光。 Dark grey clay, round lip, the outer rim is raised and flares outward; polished.
	09SLGTG1 H3①：12	壶 *Hu* bottle	2009-7-5			W: 11.3 H: 9	泥质深灰，磨光。 Dark grey clay, polished.
2	09SLGTG1 H3①：14	鬲 *Li* tripod	2009-7-5		D3	M: 33 H: 4	夹砂红褐，方唇，宽折沿外撇，深腹，素面。 Coarse and red-brown, square lip, wide folded rim that flares outward, deep belly, plain.
9	09SLGTG1 H3①：16	罐 *Guan* jar	2009-7-5		B	M: 28 W: 5.1	泥质深灰，方唇，外饰绳纹。 Dark grey clay, square lip, cord decorations on the outside.
6	09SLGTG1 H3①：17	豆 *Dou* pedestal dish	2009-7-5		C	M: 19 H: 5	夹砂深灰，尖唇，敞口盘略深，素面，磨光。 Coarse and dark grey, sharp lip, bowl relatively deep with a wide mouth, plain, polished.
10	09SLGTG1 H3①：18	圆陶片 Round pottery sherd	2009-7-5			M: 5	夹砂深灰，饰绳纹。 Coarse and dark grey, cord decorations.
5	09SLGTG1 H3①：42	鬲 *Li* tripod	2009-7-5		D	W: 10 H: 5.5	夹砂红褐，足跟较低，素面。 Coarse and red-brown, base of the feet relatively high, plain.

续表

图号 Number on Fig. Ⅰ.5.11	标本号 Excavation number	器物名称 Artifact name	出土时间 Excavation date	位置 Location	所属类型 Types	尺寸(厘米) Size (cm)	特点描述 Description of features
7	09SLGTG1 H3①：43	鬲 *Li* tripod	2009-7-5		D	M: 23 H: 5	夹砂红褐，方唇，宽卷沿，素面。Coarse and red-brown, square lip, wide mouth, plain.
3	09SLGTG1 H3①：44	鬲 *Li* tripod	2009-7-5		D	D: 25 H: 11.8	夹砂红褐，素面。Coarse and red-brown, plain.
8	09SLGTG1 H3①：45	鬲 *Li* tripod	2009-7-5		D	M: 26 H: 6.1	夹砂红褐，方唇，宽折沿，素面。Coarse and red-brown, square lip, wide folded rim, plain.
4	09SLGTG1 H3①：46	鬲 *Li* tripod	2009-7-5		D	W: 5.7 H: 3.2	夹砂红褐，素面。Coarse and red-brown, plain.
14	09SLGTG1 H3①：50	甗腰 Middle of a *yan* steamer	2009-7-5		A1	W: 6.6 H: 2.7	夹砂红褐，饰戳印纹。Coarse and red-brown, decorated with a stamped pattern.
	09SLGTG1 H3①：51	陶片 Pottery sherd	2009-7-5			W: 5 H: 3.7	夹砂深灰，饰粗绳纹，较凌乱。Coarse and dark grey, coarse cord decorations that are relatively untidy.
	09SLGTG1 H3①：52	陶片 Pottery sherd	2009-7-5			W: 5 H: 4	夹砂红褐，饰粗绳纹。Coarse and red-brown, coarse cord decorations.
	09SLGTG1 H3①：53	陶片 Pottery sherd	2009-7-5			W: 5.3 H: 4.6	夹砂浅灰，饰麻点绳纹。Coarse and light grey, “sesame seed” cord decorations.
	09SLGTG1 H3①：54	陶片 Pottery sherd	2009-7-5			W: 4 H: 5.6	夹砂红陶，饰中绳纹。Coarse red ceramic, medium cord decorations.
	09SLGTG1 H3①：55	陶片 Pottery sherd	2009-7-5			W: 4 H: 5.6	夹砂红陶，饰中绳纹。Coarse red ceramic, medium cord decorations.
	09SLGTG1 H3①：56	陶片 Pottery sherd	2009-7-5			W: 5.1 H: 4.6	夹砂红褐，饰中绳纹。Coarse and red-brown, medium cord decorations.
	09SLGTG1 H3①：57	陶片 Pottery sherd	2009-7-5			W: 4.8 H: 5.1	夹砂灰褐，饰中绳纹。Coarse and grey-brown, medium cord decorations.
	09SLGTG1 H3①：58	陶片 Pottery sherd	2009-7-5			W: 7.5 H: 7.5	夹砂浅灰，饰中绳纹，较凌乱。Coarse and light grey, medium cord decorations that are relatively untidy.

尺寸标志：L=长度；H=高度；W=宽度；D=直径；R=半径；M=口径；B=底径；T=厚度；d=深度；h=孔径。

Measurements: L=length; H=height; W=width; D=diameter; R=radius; M=mouth diameter; B=bottom diameter; T=thickness; d=depth; h=hole diameter.

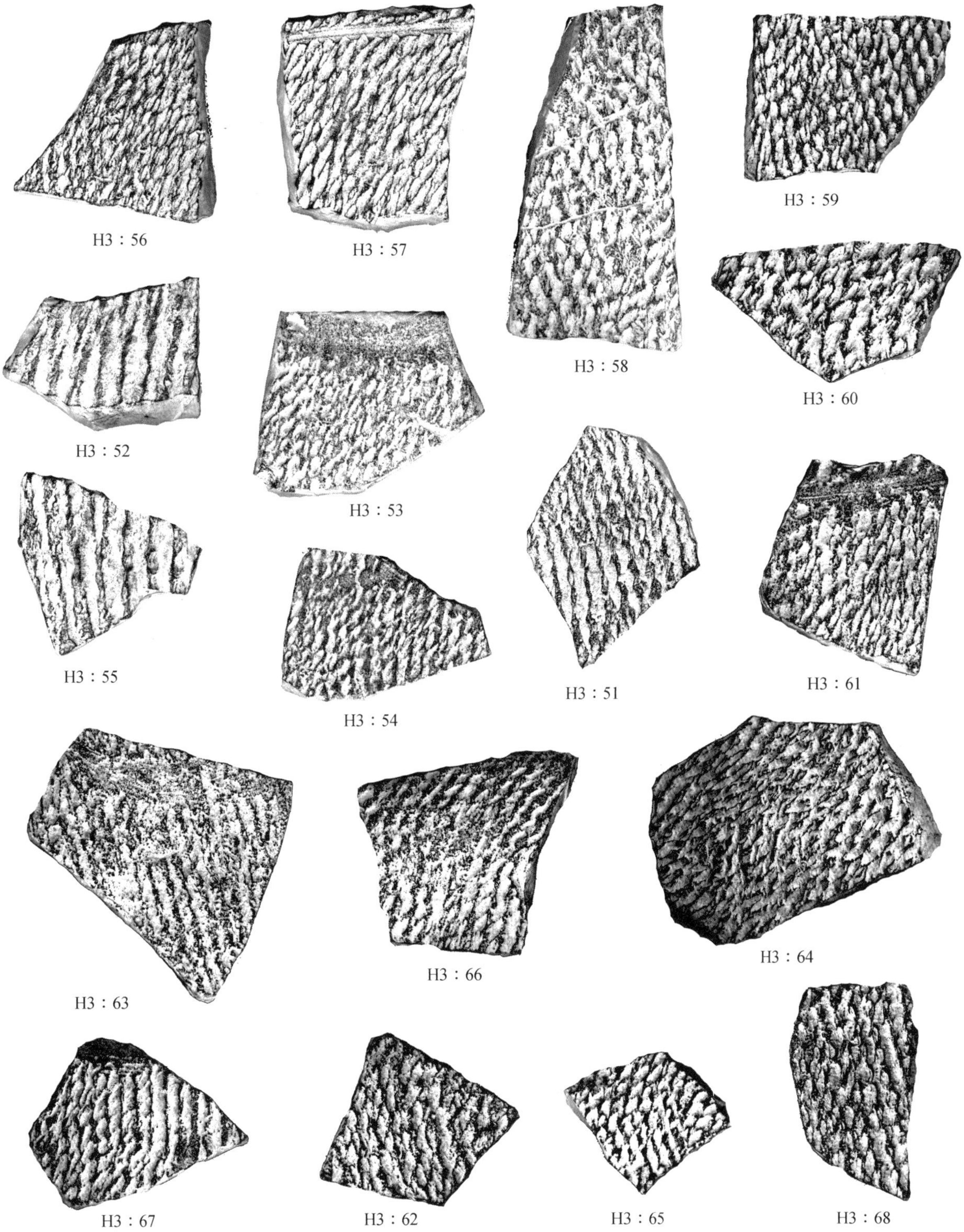

图Ⅰ.5.12　H3①出土陶片纹饰

Figure Ⅰ.5.12　Decorated pottery sherds from pit H3, stratum ①.

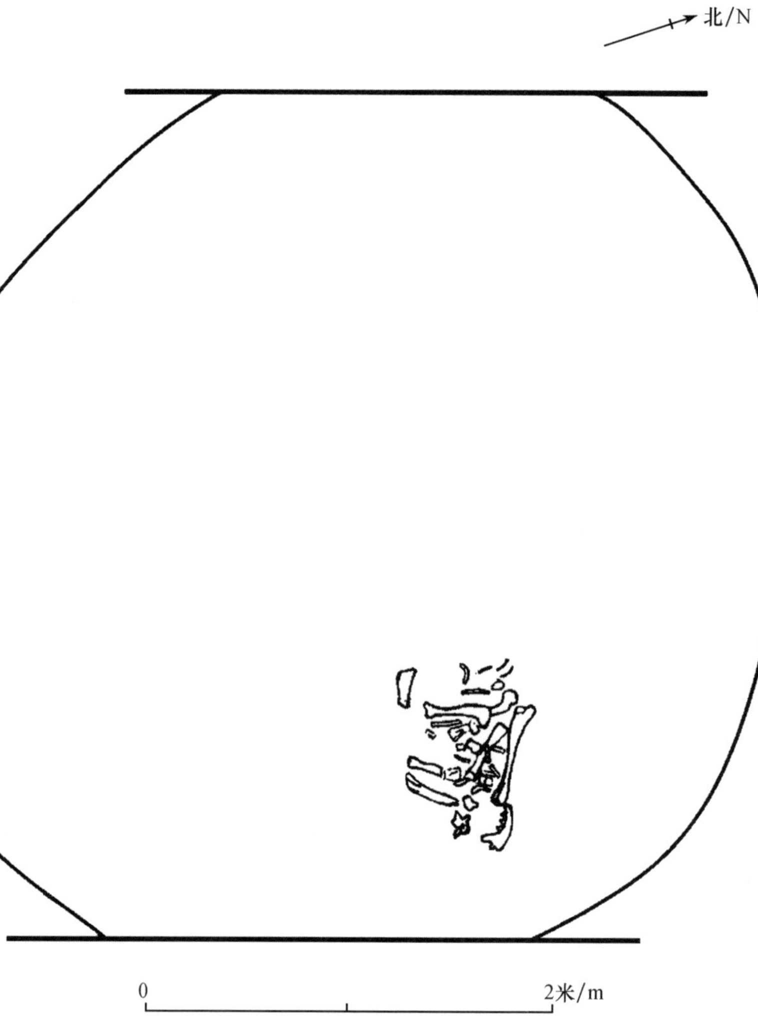

图Ⅰ.5.13　H3②平面及其发现的狗骨头

Figure Ⅰ.5.13　Plan of pit H3, stratum ②, and the dog bones found in it.

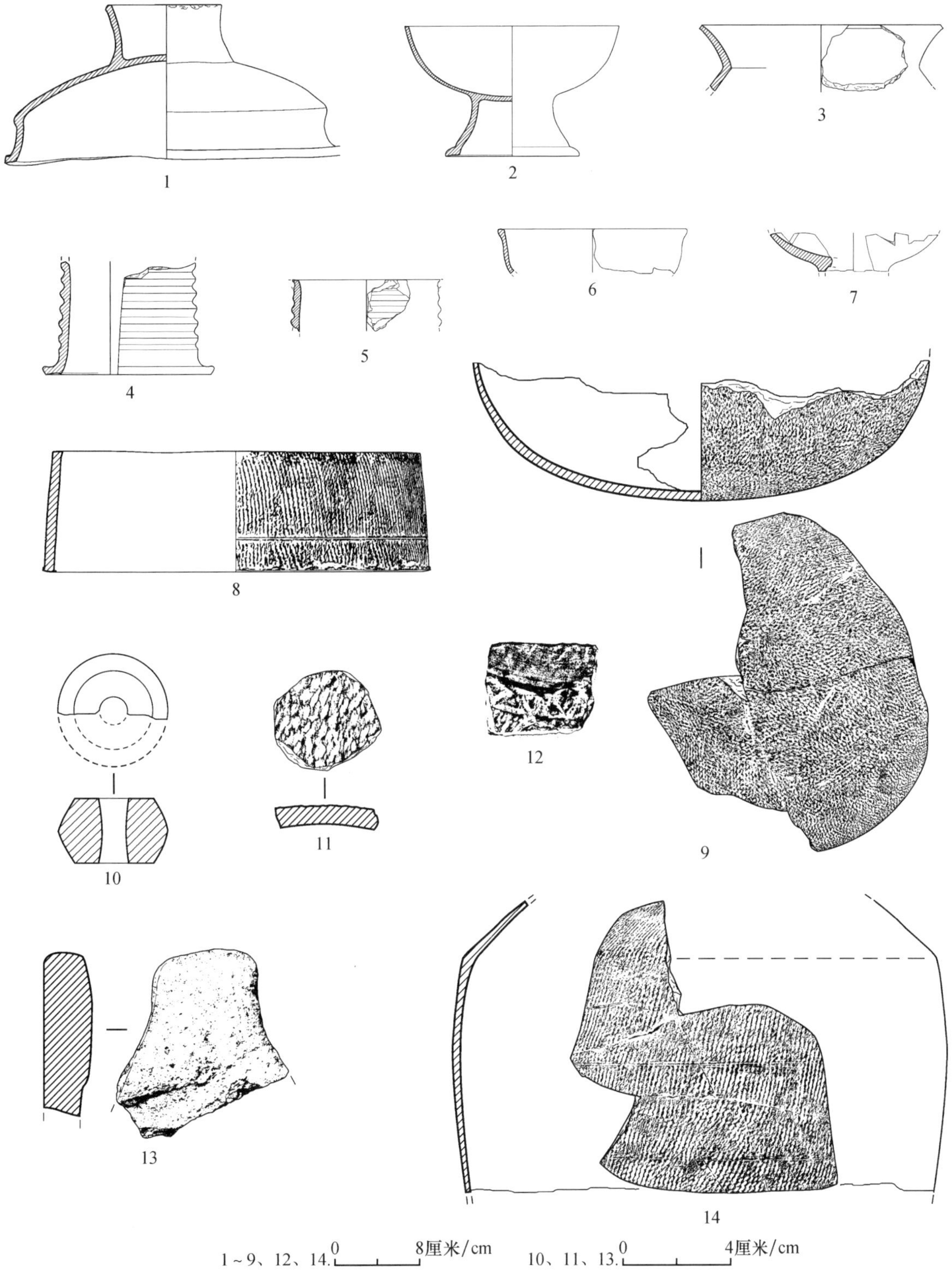

图Ⅰ.5.14　H3②出土陶器和石器

1. 器盖（H3②：4）　2. 豆（H3②：5）　3. 鬲（H3②：25）　4. 圈足（H3②：12）　5. 陶片(H3②：22）　6. 簋（H3②：27）　7. 豆（H3②：9）　8. 器座（H3②：19）　9. 罐（H3②：14）　10. 纺轮（H3②：30）　11. 圆陶片（H3②：21）　12. 刻划纹陶片（H3②：48）　13.石斧（H3②：41）　14. 罐（H3②：15）

Figure Ⅰ.5.14　Pottery types and stone tools from pit H3, stratum ②.

1. Vessel lid (H3②：4)　2. *Dou* pedestal dish (H3②：5)　3. *Li* tripod (H3②：25)　4. Vessel base (H3②：12)　5. Pottery sherd (H3②：22)　6. *Gui* tureen (H3②：27)　7. *Dou* pedestal dish (H3②：9)　8. Vessel base (H3②：19)　9. *Guan* jar (H3②：14)　10. Spindle whorl (H3②：30)　11. Round pottery sherd (H3②：21)　12. Engraved pottery sherd (H3②：48)　13. Stone axe (H3②：41)　14. *Guan* jar (H3②：15)

表Ⅰ.5.8　H3②出土遗物登记表

Table Ⅰ.5.8　Artifacts from pit H3, stratum ②

图号 Number on Fig. Ⅰ.5.14	标本号 Excavation number	器物名称 Artifact name	出土时间 Excavation date	位置 Location	所属类型 Types	尺寸(厘米) Size (cm)	特点描述 Description of features
	09SLGTG1 H3②：1	簋 *Gui* tureen	2009-7-5		B	M: 25.9 B: 13.5 H: 16.2	泥质深灰陶，方唇外卷，敞口宽沿，卷沿，鼓腹，腹较深，圈足外撇，外饰绳纹,并抹去。 Dark grey clay. Square lip rolled to the outside, open mouth and wide rolled rim. Bulging belly relatively deep. Circular foot flares outward. Outside decorated with cord impressions and smear marks.
1	09SLGTG1 H3②：4	盖 Vessel lid	2009-7-6		A2	M: 31.7 D. of handle: 6.4 H. of handle: 3.6	泥质红陶，器体甚大,盖沿外撇，盖顶有把手。素面，外部局部磨光。 Red fine clay, large size, the lid rim flares outward, top of the lid has a handle. Plain, with part of the outside polished.
2	09SLGTG1 H3②：5	豆 *Dou* pedestal dish	2009-7-6		C2	M: 20.9 B: 12 H: 12.3	泥质深灰陶，方唇，腹较深。圈足粗高。圈足外撇, 盘底成环状。 Dark grey clay. Square lip, relatively deep belly. Circular foot is wide and high. Circular foot flares outward, bottom of the bowl is round.
7	09SLGTG1 H3②：9	豆盘 Bowl from a *dou* pedestal dish	2009-7-6		B	L: 9.2 W: 6.3	泥质红褐，素面磨光。 Red-brown fine clay, plain surface polished.
4	09SLGTG1 H3②：12	圈足 Vessel circular foot	2009-7-6			W: 13.9 H: 8.8	泥质红褐，有黑陶衣，周身饰瓦楞纹，磨光，器类不明。 Red-brown fine clay, black clothing, whole body decorated with a corrugated ridge pattern and polishing. Belonging to an unidentified vessel type.
	09SLGTG1 H3②：13	罐下部 Lower part of a *guan* jar	2009-7-6		C	L: 3 W: 2.4	泥质深灰，素面，有弦纹。 Dark grey clay, plain, decorated with ring patterns.
9	09SLGTG1 H3②：14	罐底 Bottom of a *guan* jar	2009-7-6		A	W: 10.2 H：6.4	泥质深灰，外饰麻点绳纹，大圜底。 Dark grey clay, outside decorated with “sesame seed” cord decorations, large round bottom.
14	09SLGTG1 H3②：15	罐上腹部 Upper part of a *guan* jar	2009-7-6		B	L: 27 W: 25.5	泥质深灰，肩微折，腹较深，通体饰中绳纹。 Dark grey clay, slightly folded shoulder, relatively deep belly, whole body decorated with medium cord decorations.
8	09SLGTG1 H3②：19	器座 Vessel base	2009-7-6			L: 33.5 W: 8.8	泥质红褐，半环状，两端残。外饰绳纹，并饰一周刻划纹。 Red-brown clay. Semi-circular shape, both ends broken. Outside decorated with cord decorations, and with one incised ring track.
	09SLGTG1 H3②：20	鬲足 *Li* tripod foot	2009-7-6		D	L: 4.7 W: 3.3 H: 4.8	夹砂红褐，素面，实足尖。 Coarse and red-brown, plain, with a solid sharp end.
11	09SLGTG1 H3②：21	圆陶片 Round pottery sherd	2009-7-6			L: 3.8 W: 3.2	泥质浅灰陶，大致呈圆形，一面是麻点绳纹，一面素面。 Light grey clay, roughly circular, one side decorated with “sesame seed” cord decorations, one side plain.
5	09SLGTG1 H3②：22	陶片 Pottery sherd	2009-7-6			W: 3.9 H: 4.7	夹砂深灰，通体施瓦楞纹，磨光。 Coarse and dark grey, entire body decorated with corrugated ridges; polished.

续表

图号 Number on Fig. Ⅰ.5.14	标本号 Excavation number	器物名称 Artifact name	出土时间 Excavation date	位置 Location	所属类型 Types	尺寸(厘米) Size (cm)	特点描述 Description of features
	09SLGTG1 H3②：23	罐腹部 Belly fragment of a *guan* jar	2009-7-6		B	L: 21 W: 9.2	泥质红褐，外饰中绳纹并有抹痕，可见微折肩。Red-brown clay, outside has medium cord decorations and smearing marks. Slightly folded shoulder can be seen.
	09SLGTG1 H3②：24	罐腹部 Belly fragment of a *guan* jar	2009-7-6		B	L: 9.1 W: 3.7	泥质深灰，饰粗绳纹。Dark grey clay, coarse cord decorations.
3	09SLGTG1 H3②：25	鬲口沿 Rim fragment from a *li* tripod	2009-7-6		D	L: 12.1 W: 5.8	夹砂红褐，方唇，敞口宽卷沿，素面。Coarse and red-brown, square lip, wide mouth with broad rolled rim, plain.
	09SLGTG1 H3②：26	簋口沿 Rim fragment from a *gui* tureen	2009-7-6			L: 5.4 W: 3.2	泥质红褐，尖圆唇，外饰绳纹并抹去。Red-brown clay, lip is round and sharp, outside has cord decorations and smearing.
6	09SLGTG1 H3②：27	簋口沿 Rim fragment from a *gui* tureen	2009-7-6		C	L: 4.4 W: 9.3	泥质深灰，红褐各一半，素面磨光。Half dark grey and half red-brown clay, plain with polishing.
	09SLGTG1 H3②：28	簋口沿 Rim fragment from a *gui* tureen	2009-7-6			L: 3.7 W: 3	泥质浅灰，方唇，唇沿内凸。Light grey clay, square lip, protrusion along the inside of the lip.
	09SLGTG1 H3②：29	簋口沿Rim fragment from a *gui* tureen	2009-7-6			L: 5.5 W: 3.1	泥质浅灰，圆唇，素面。Light grey clay, round lip, plain.
10	09SLGTG1 H3②：30	纺轮 Spindle whorl	2009-7-6			D: 3.7 H: 1	泥质深灰陶，算珠状，外部素面磨光，制作精致。Dark grey clay, bead-shaped. The outside is plain and polished, exquisite quality.
	09SLGTG1 H3②：31	簋圈足 Circular foot from a *gui* tureen	2009-7-6			L: 5 W: 3.3	泥质浅灰，素面。Light grey clay, plain.
	09SLGTG1 H3②：32	墙胚 Fragment of a wall	2009-7-6			L: 6.3 W: 6.2	红褐色，依附在墙皮上，脱落所致，有草拌痕。Grey-brown color, plaster once attached to the wall, having fallen off, with marks of grass mixture.

尺寸标志：L=长度；H=高度；W=宽度；D=直径；R=半径；M=口径；B=底径；T=厚度；d=深度；h=孔径。

Measurements: L=length; H=height; W=width; D=diameter; R=radius; M=mouth diameter; B=bottom diameter; T=thickness; d=depth; h=hole diameter.

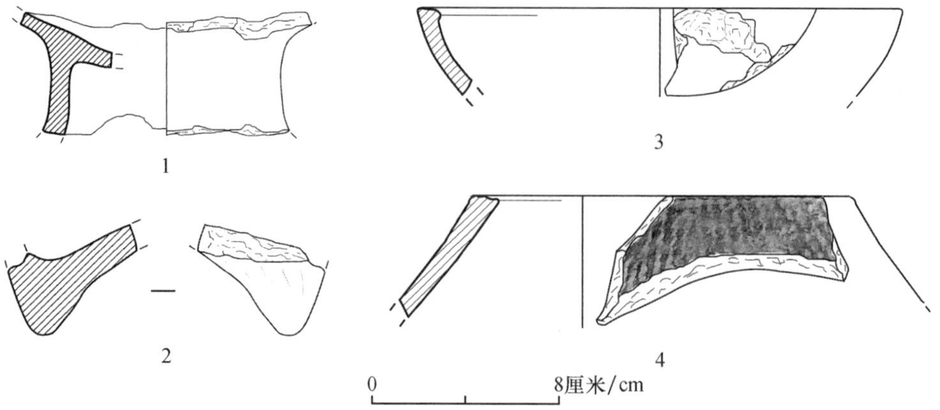

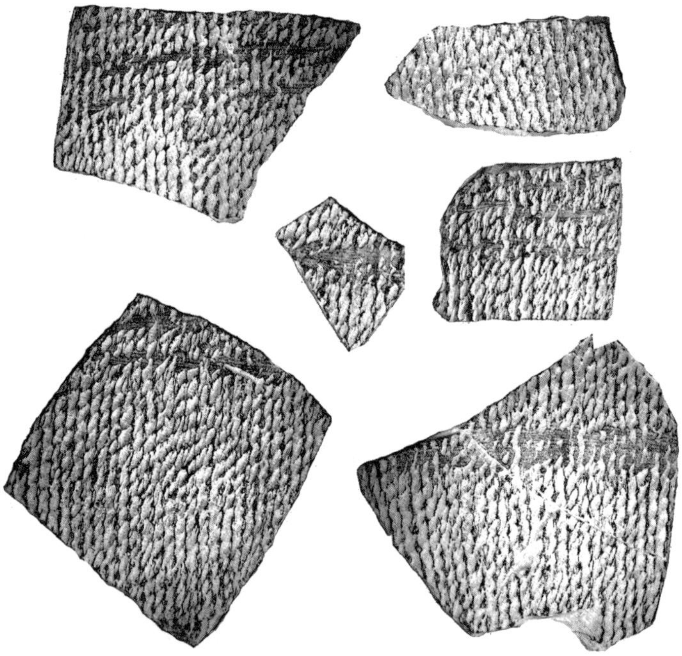

H3：39

图Ⅰ.5.15　H3③出土陶器及陶片纹样

1. 簋（H3③：33）　2.鬲（H3③：36）　3. 豆（H3③：35）　4. 瓮（H3③：40）

Figure Ⅰ.5.15　Pottery types and decorative patterns from pit H3, stratum ③.

1. *Gui* tureen (H3③：33)　2. *Li* tripod (H3③：36)　3. *Dou* pedestal dish (H3③：35)　4. *Weng* jar (H3③：40)

表Ⅰ.5.9 H3③出土遗物登记表

Table Ⅰ. 5.9 Artifacts from pit H2, stratum ③

图号 Number on Fig. Ⅰ.5.15	标本号 Excavation number	器物名称 Artifact name	出土时间 Excavation date	位置 Location	所属类型 Types	尺寸（厘米） Size (cm)	特点描述 Description of features
1	09SLGTG1 H3③：33	簋 *Gui* tureen	2009-7-6			W: 14 H: 7	泥质浅灰，素面。 Light grey clay, plain.
	09SLGTG1 H3③：34	豆柄 Handle from a *dou* pedestal dish	2009-7-6		B2	L: 7 W: 4.1 H: 4.9	泥质深灰，素面，细柄束腰有凸棱。 Dark grey clay, plain, thin handle with convex protrusion in the middle.
2	09SLGTG1 H3③：36	鬲足 *Li* tripod foot	2009-7-6		B1	L: 5.9 W: 4.5 H: 4.8	夹砂灰褐，素面，足尖较矮。 Coarse and grey-brown, plain, tip of the foot relatively short.
	09SLGTG1 H3③：37	鬲口沿 Rim fragment from a *li* tripod	2009-7-6		B	L: 3.9 W: 1.9	云母深灰，素面，方圆唇，唇缘内凸，内有凹痕。 Dark grey with mica, plain, square and round lip, protrusion on the inside margin of the lip and an indentation on the inside.
	09SLGTG1 H3③：38	簋口沿 Rim fragment from a *gui* tureen	2009-7-6		A2	L: 5.3 W: 3	素面，方唇，沿下饰绳纹并抹去。 Plain, square lip, cord decoration and smearing below the rim.
4	09SLGTG1 H3③：40	瓮 *Weng* jar	2009-7-6			L: 9 W: 4.3	泥质深灰。直口内敛，方唇。唇部有凹槽，饰中绳纹。 Dark grey clay. Introverted straight mouth, square lip. Groove on the lip, medium cord decorations.
	09SLGTG1 H3③：41	石器 Stone tool	2009-7-6			L: 6.5 W: 6.5 H: 1.1	砂岩，板状。一侧平整磨光。 Sandstone, plate shaped. One side flat and polished.
	09SLGTG1 H3③：47	陶片 Pottery sherd	2009-7-6			W: 8.1 H: 2.8	夹砂深灰，有乳钉。 Coarse and dark grey, with a nipple.
	09SLGTG1 H3③：48	刻划纹陶片 Incised pottery sherd	2009-7-6			L: 4.2 W: 3.1	泥质深灰，刻划一圈三角纹，其下饰绳纹。 Dark grey clay, incised with a round of triangular pattern, with cord decorations underneath.
	09SLGTG1 H3③：49	陶片 Pottery sherd	2009-7-6			L: 7.2 W: 4.3	红褐色，有刻痕。夹蚌片滑石云母。 Red-brown color, with incised marks. Inclusions of seashell, talc, and mica.
	09SLGTG1 H3③：2	器盖 Vessel lid	2009-7-6				圆唇，盖沿微外撇，微鼓，盖顶有圆转细把手。 Round lip, rim of the lid flares outward, top of the lid has a round, circular, thin handle.
3	09SLGTG1 H3③：35	豆 *Dou* pedestal dish	2009-7-6			M: 20.8 H: 5.14	泥质灰褐陶，素面。圆唇内突。 Grey-brown clay, plain. Round lip with protrusion inside.

尺寸标志：L=长度；H=高度；W=宽度；D=直径；R=半径；M=口径；B=底径；T=厚度；d=深度；h=孔径。

Measurements: L=length; H=height; W=width; D=diameter; R=radius; M=mouth diameter; B=bottom diameter; T=thickness; d=depth; h=hole diameter.

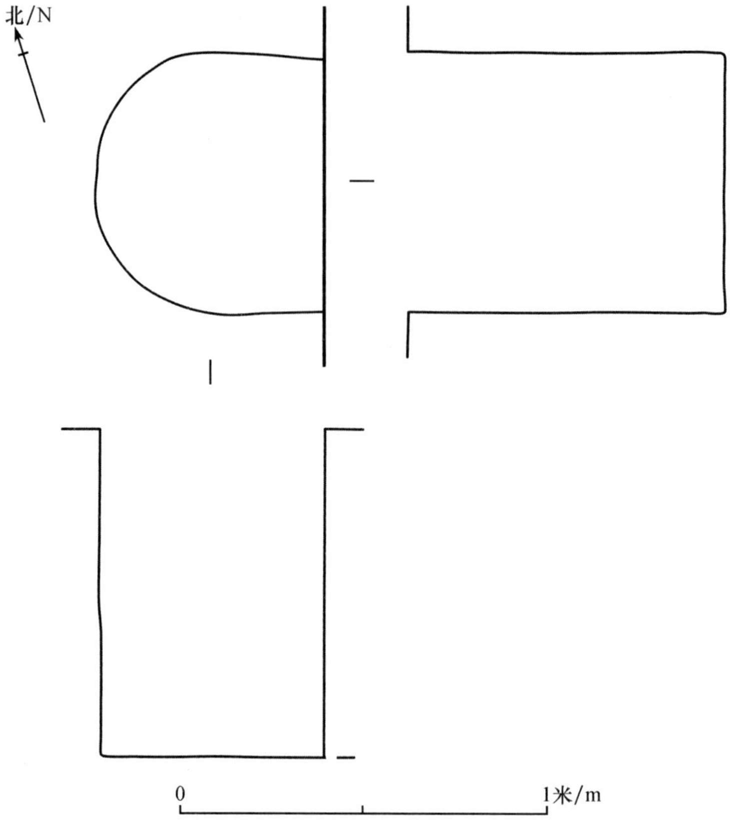

图Ⅰ.5.16　H4平、剖面图

Figure Ⅰ.5.16　Plan and cross-sectional profiles of pit H4.

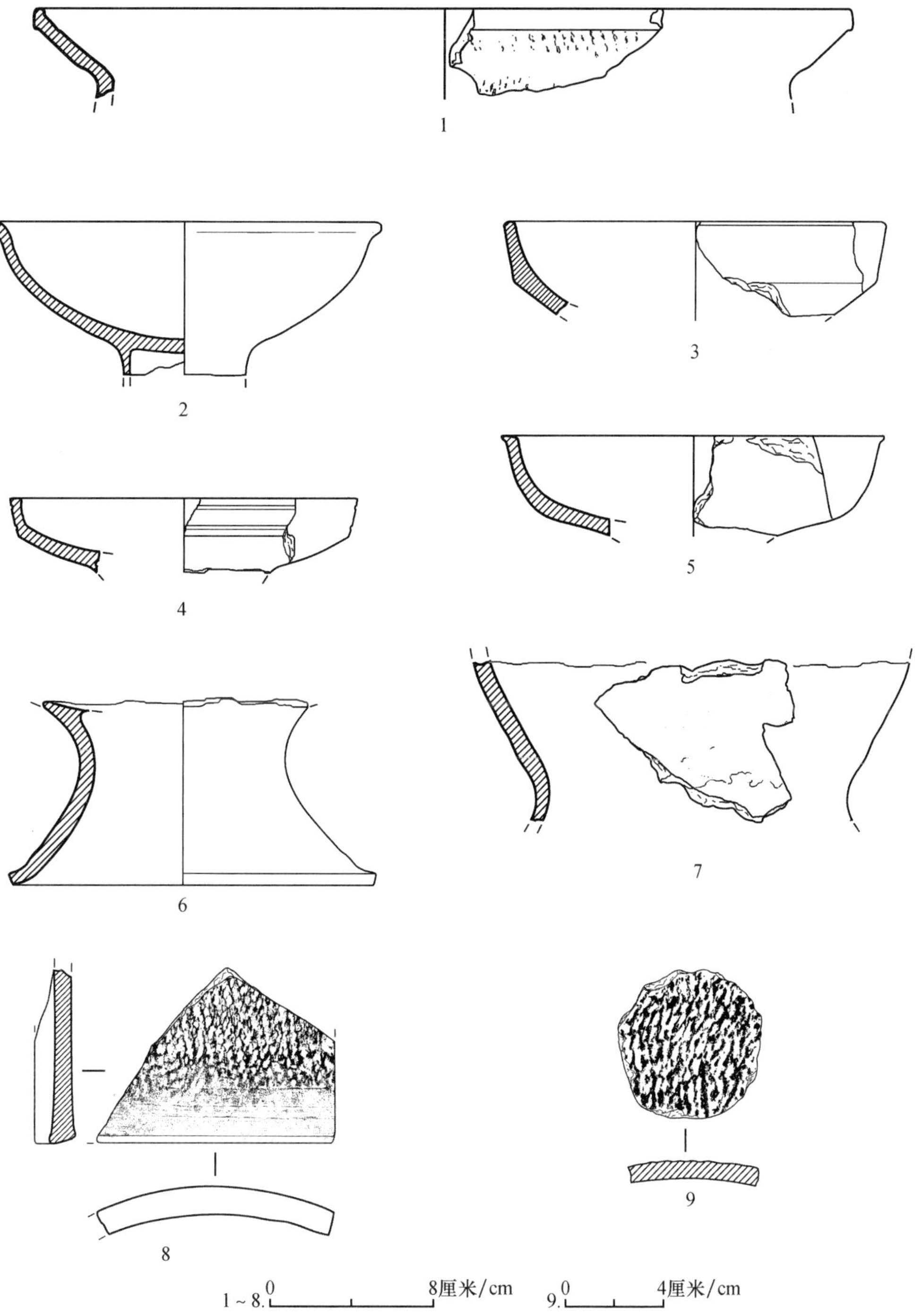

图Ⅰ.5.17　H4出土陶器

1. 簋（H4：2）　2. 豆（H4：6）　3. 豆（H4：3）　4. 豆（H4：5）　5. 豆（H4：4）　6. 簋（H4：1）　7. 甗（H4：7）　8. 瓦（H4：11）　9. 圆陶片（H4：10）

Figure Ⅰ.5.17　Pottery types from pit H4.

1. *Gui* tureen (H4：2)　2. *Dou* pedestal dish (H4：6)　3. *Dou* pedestal dish (H4：3)　4. *Dou* pedestal dish (H4：5)　5. *Dou* pedestal dish (H4：4)　6. *Gui* tureen (H4：1)　7. *Yan* steamer (H4：7)　8. Tile (H4：11)　9. Round pottery sherd (H4：10)

表Ⅰ.5.10　H4出土遗物登记表

Table Ⅰ.5.10　Artifacts from pit H4

图号 Number on Fig. Ⅰ.5.17	标本号 Excavation number	器物名称 Artifact name	出土时间 Excavation date	位置 Location	所属类型 Types	尺寸（厘米）Size (cm)	特点描述 Description of features
6	09SLGTG2 H4：1	簋 *Gui* tureen	2009-7-5		A2	W: 17.9 H: 8.8	泥质黑陶，圈足略高，最细处偏上，素面。Black clay with a round, thin, and high foot, thinnest on its upper part, plain.
1	09SLGTG2 H4：2	簋 *Gui* tureen	2009-7-5			W: 39.8 H: 4.2	夹砂深灰，方唇，宽折沿，素面。Coarse and dark gray, square lips, wide and folded rim, plain.
3	09SLGTG2 H4：3	豆 *Dou* pedestal dish	2009-7-5		D	W: 19 H: 4.6	泥质浅灰，圆唇，敞口，素面。Light gray clay, round lip, wide mouth, plain.
5	09SLGTG2 H4：4	豆 *Dou* pedestal dish	2009-7-5		C3	M: 18.8 H: 4.8	泥质灰陶，尖唇，敞口，素面。Gray clay, sharp lip, wide mouth, plain.
4	09SLGTG2 H4：5	豆 *Dou* pedestal dish	2009-7-5		D	M: 17 H: 3.6	夹砂红褐，方唇，直口，素面。Coarse and red-brown, square lips, straight mouth, plain.
2	09SLGTG2 H4：6	豆 *Dou* pedestal dish	2009-7-5		C3	M: 19.1 H: 7.3	泥质灰陶，圆唇，敞口，浅盘呈弧形，豆柄较细。Gray clay, round lip, wide mouth; the shallow bowl has a curved shape, and the handle of the *dou* is relatively thin.
7	09SLGTG2 H4：7	甗 *Yan* steamer	2009-7-5		A1	L: 21.6 W: 7.8	夹砂红褐，素面。Coarse and red-brown, plain.
9	09SLGTG1 H4：10	圆陶片 Round pottery sherd	2009-7-5			D: 6 T: 0.8	泥质深灰，饰麻点绳纹。Dark gray clay, “sesame seed” cord decorations.
8	09SLGTG2 H4：11	瓦 Tile	2009-7-5		A1	L: 12 W: 8.6 H: 1.8	泥质浅灰，饰麻点绳纹。Light gray clay, “sesame seed” cord decorations.

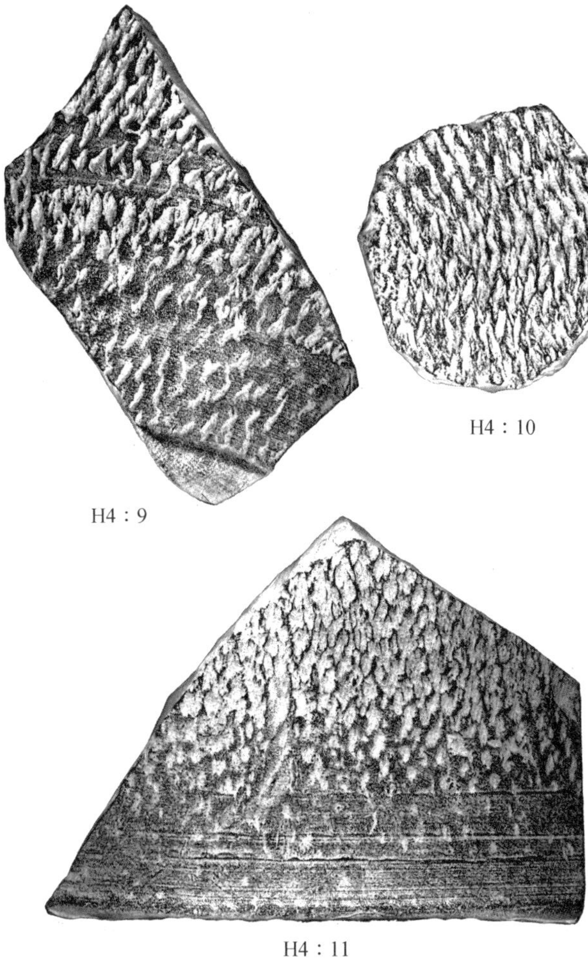

图Ⅰ.5.18　H4出土陶片纹饰

Figure Ⅰ.5.18　Decorated pottery sherds from pit H4.

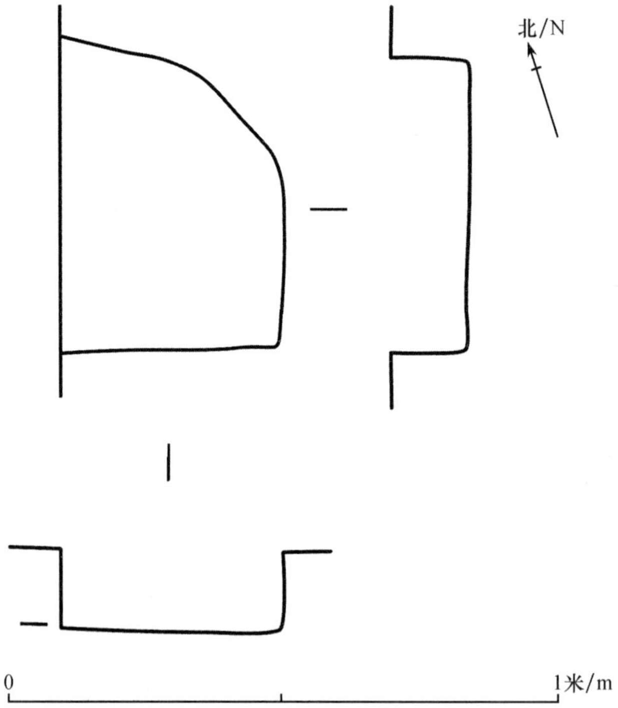

图Ⅰ.5.19　H5②平、剖面图

Figure Ⅰ.5.19　Plan and cross-sectional profiles of pit H5, stratum ②.

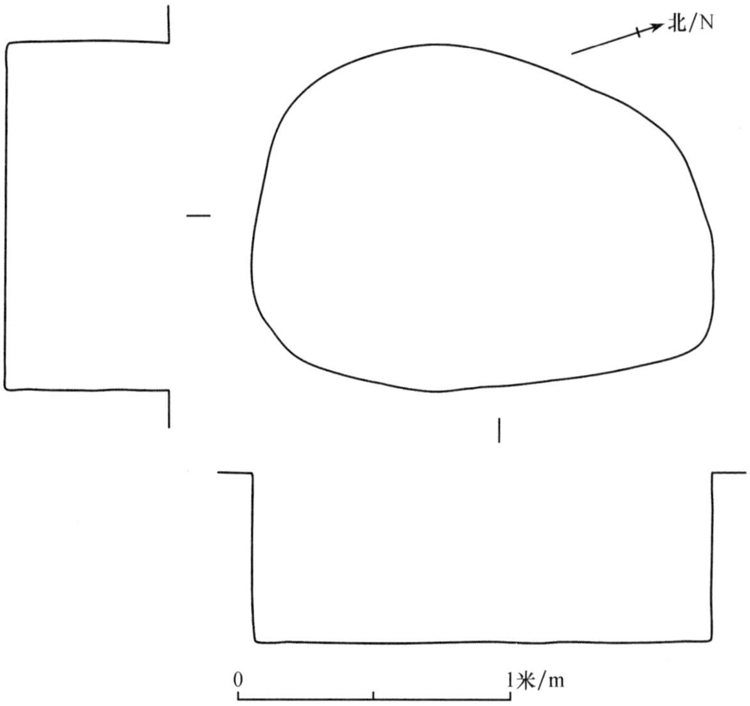

图Ⅰ.5.20　H6平、剖面图

Figure Ⅰ.5.20　Plan and cross-sectional profiles of pit H6.

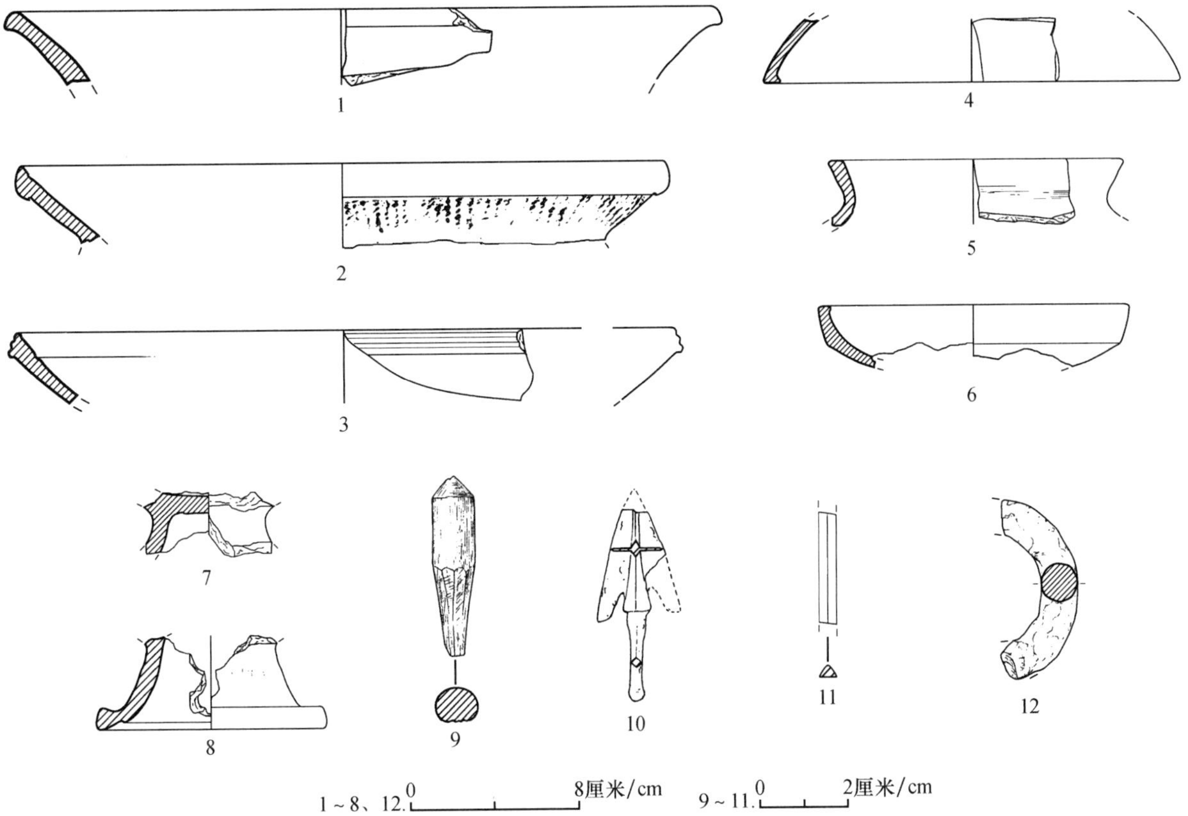

图Ⅰ.5.21　H6出土陶器

1. 簋（H6：4）　2. 簋（H6：1）　3. 簋（H6：2）　4. 器盖（H6：11）　5. 罐（H6：16）　6. 豆（H6：8）　7. 豆（H6：9）　8. 豆（H6：7）　9. 骨镞（H6：26）　10. 铜箭头（H6：25）　11. 铜片（H6：24）　12. 捉手（H6：14）

Figure Ⅰ.5.21　Pottery types from pit H6.

1. *Gui* tureen (H6：4)　2. *Gui* tureen (H6：1)　3. *Gui* tureen (H6：2)　4. Vessel lid (H6：11)　5. *Guan* jar (H6：16)　6. *Dou* pedestal dish (H6：8)　7. *Dou* pedestal dish (H6：9)　8. *Dou* pedestal dish (H6：7)　9. Bone arrowhead (H6：26)　10. Bronze arrowhead (H6：25)　11. Bronze fragment (H6：24)　12. Handle (H6：14)

表Ⅰ.5.11　H6出土遗物登记表

Table Ⅰ.5.11　Artifacts from pit H6

序号 Number on Fig. Ⅰ.5.21	标本号 Excavation number	器物名称 Artifact name	出土时间 Excavation date	位置 Location	所属类型 Types	尺寸（厘米）Size (cm)	特点描述 Description of features
2	09SLGTG2 H6：1	簋 *Gui* tureen	2009-7-6			M: 31 H: 3.9	泥质浅灰，圆唇外卷，宽沿敞口，沿内饰弦纹，外饰中绳纹有抹痕。Light grey clay, lip rolled to the outside, wide mouth, ring patterns on the inside of the rim, medium cord decorations and smearing marks on the outside.
3	09SLGTG2 H6：2	簋 *Gui* tureen	2009-7-6			M: 32 H: 3.4	泥质浅灰，方唇，唇上有两凹槽，沿内饰凹弦纹。Light grey clay, square lip, two incised grooves on the lip, rim decorated with intaglio ring patterns.
	09SLGTG2 H6：3	簋圈足 Circular foot from a *gui* tureen	2009-7-6			L: 5.7 W: 2.3 H: 1.5	泥质深灰，圈足外撇，素面。Dark grey clay, round feet flared to the outside, plain.
1	09SLGTG2 H6：4	簋 *Gui* tureen	2009-7-6			M: 33.9 H: 3.6	泥质红褐，圆唇，沿内磨光，沿外饰绳纹并抹去。Red-brown clay, round lip, polishing inside the rim, outside of the rim decorated with cord decorations and smearing.
	09SLGTG2 H6：5	罐肩部 *Guan* jar shoulder	2009-7-6		B	L: 7.5 W: 8.3	泥质浅灰，肩部刻有一周网格纹。Light grey clay, engraved grid pattern on the shoulder.
	09SLGTG2 H6：6	簋口沿 Rim fragment from a *gui* tureen	2009-7-6		A2	L: 5.6 W: 4.7	泥质深灰，圆唇，沿内饰凹弦纹，沿外素面。Dark grey clay, round lip, intaglio ring patterns inside the rim, outside of the rim plain.
8	09SLGTG2 H6：7	豆圈足 Circular foot from a *dou* pedestal dish	2009-7-6		A1	L: 6.5 W: 5.3 H: 4	泥质深灰，外饰绳纹并抹去，圈足外撇，足根底部有凹槽。Dark grey clay, cord decorations and smear marks on the outside, round foot flared to the outside, groove around the base of the foot.
6	09SLGTG2 H6：8	豆盘 Bowl from a *dou* pedestal dish	2009-7-6		B2	M: 15 H: 2.9	泥质浅灰，素面，方唇，唇沿内凸，浅折盘。Light grey clay, plain, square lip, thickening inside the rim, shallow bowl.
7	09SLGTG2 H6：9	豆柄 Handle from a *dou* pedestal dish	2009-7-6		B	W: 3 H: 3.1	泥质红褐，素面，盘底较平，豆柄应较细。Red-brown clay, plain, bottom of the bowl relatively flat, handles relatively thin.
	09SLGTG2 H6：10	豆口沿 Rim fragment from a *dou* pedestal dish	2009-7-7		B	L: 4.7 W: 2.7	泥质深灰，素面磨光，方唇，敞口。Dark grey clay, plain and polished, square lip, open mouth.
4	09SLGTG2 H6：11	器盖 Vessel lid	2009-7-7		A1	M: 20 H: 3	泥质灰陶，盖内缘突起。素面。Grey fine clay, with a projection on the inside of the rim of the lid. Plain.
	09SLGTG2 H6：12	罐上腹部 Upper part of a *guan* jar	2009-7-7		B	L: 4.1 W: 4.3	泥质红褐，敛口，饰麻点绳纹有抹痕。Red-brown clay, converging mouth, with "sesame seed" cord decoration and smearing marks.
	09SLGTG2 H6：13	罐捉手 Handle from a *guan* jar	2009-7-7		B	L: 31 W: 5.5	泥质浅灰，素面。Light grey clay, plain.

续表

序号 Number on Fig. Ⅰ.5.21	标本号 Excavation number	器物名称 Artifact name	出土时间 Excavation date	位置 Location	所属类型 Types	尺寸（厘米） Size (cm)	特点描述 Description of features
12	09SLGTG2 H6：14	罐捉手 Handle from a *guan* jar	2009-7-7		B	W: 3.8 H: 8.3	泥质浅灰，环状，素面。 Light grey clay, ring-shaped, plain.
	09SLGTG2 H6：15	簋 *Gui* tureen	2009-7-7			L: 4 W: 4.2	夹砂灰褐，沿内侧有凹槽，素面。 Coarse and grey, groove on the inside of the rim, plain.
5	09SLGTG2 H6：16	罐口沿 Rim fragment from a *guan* jar	2009-7-7		B	W: 14.2 H: 3.1	泥质浅灰，方唇，敞口，卷沿，外饰绳纹并抹去。 Light grey clay, square lip, open mouth, rolled rim, cord decorations and smearing on the outside.
	09SLGTG2 H6：17	簋口沿 Rim fragment from a *gui* tureen	2009-7-7		A2	L: 14 W: 5.1	泥质浅灰，圆唇外卷，宽沿敞口，沿内饰弦纹，外饰中绳纹有抹痕。 Light grey clay, round lip rolled to the outside, wide mouth, ring patterns on the inside of the rim, medium cord decorations and smearing marks on the outside.
	09SLGTG2 H6：17	陶片 Pottery sherd	2009-7-7			L: 5.6 W: 6	泥质浅灰，饰中绳纹，纹路清晰。 Light grey clay, medium cord decorations with clear lines.
	09SLGTG2 H6：18	簋口沿 Rim fragment from a *gui* tureen	2009-7-7		A2	L: 9.1 W: 4.3	泥质浅灰，方唇，唇上有两凹槽，沿内饰凹弦纹。 Light grey clay, square lip, two incised grooves on the rim, intaglio ring patterns on the inside of the rim.
	09SLGTG2 H6：19	簋圈足 Circular foot from a *gui* tureen	2009-7-7		A3	L: 5.7 W: 2.3 H: 1.5	泥质深灰，圈足外撇，素面。 Dark grey clay, circular feet flared to the outside, plain.
	09SLGTG2 H6：23	豆盘 Bowl from a *dou* pedestal dish	2009-7-7		B2	L: 3.6 W: 2.7	泥质浅灰掺少量云母，素面，方唇，唇缘内凸，浅折盘。 Light grey clay mixed with a little mica, plain, square lip, projection on the inside of the rim, shallow bowl with folds.
	09SLGTG2 H6：18	陶片 Pottery sherd	2009-7-7			L: 9 W: 6.9	夹砂深灰，饰中绳纹。 Coarse and dark grey, medium cord decorations.
	09SLGTG2 H6：19	陶片 Pottery sherd	2009-7-7			L: 6 W: 5.8	夹砂灰陶，饰中绳纹。 Coarse and grey, medium cord decorations.
	09SLGTG2 H6：20	陶片 Pottery sherd	2009-7-7			L: 5 W: 3.7	夹砂灰陶，饰中绳纹。 Coarse and grey, medium cord decorations.
	09SLGTG2 H6：21	陶片 Pottery sherd	2009-7-7			L: 6.3 W: 5.6	夹砂灰陶，饰绳纹。 Coarse and grey, with cord decorations.
	09SLGTG2 H6：22	陶片 Pottery sherd	2009-7-7			L: 8.1 W: 4.7	夹砂红褐，饰绳纹。 Coarse and red-brown, with cord decorations.
11	09SLGTG2 H6：24	铜片 Bronze fragment	2009-7-7	270×90—65		L: 2.5 W: 0.4	青铜，断面为三角形，两端残。 Bronze, section triangular, broken from two ends.
10	09SLGTG2 H6：25	铜箭头 Bronze arrowhead	2009-7-7	270×117—55		L: 4.3 W: 1.9	有翼有铤，一锋两刃，箭头及一翼残，短铤。 Has wings and a collar, a point and two edges. The head of the arrow and one of the wings are damaged, and the collar is short.
9	09SLGTG2 H6：26	骨镞 Bone arrowhead	2009-7-7	270×90—65		L: 4.3 W: 1.9	两头均经过加工，头部圆。 Both ends have been worked, and the head is round.

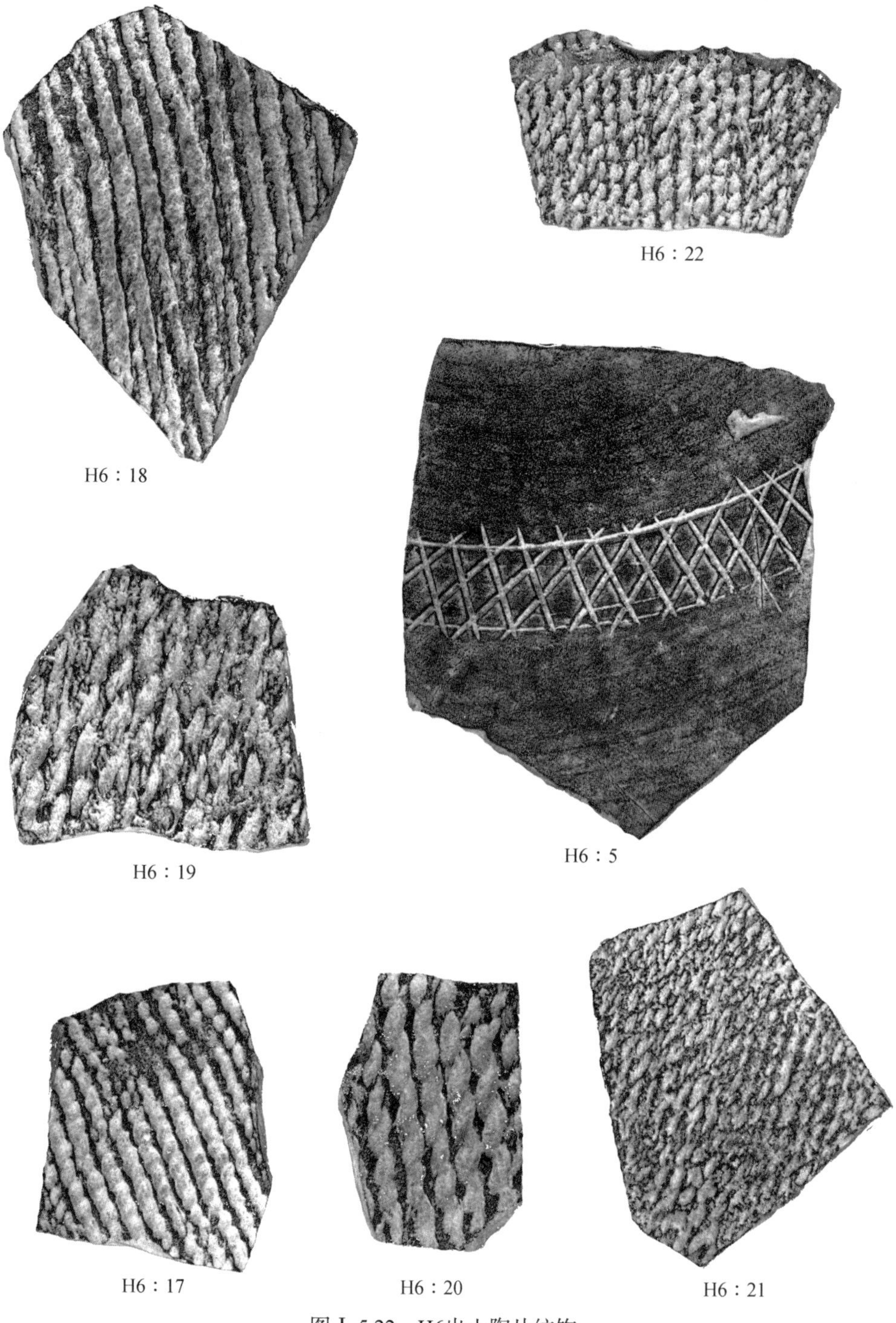

图Ⅰ.5.22　H6出土陶片纹饰

Figure Ⅰ.5.22　Decorated pottery sherds from pit H6.

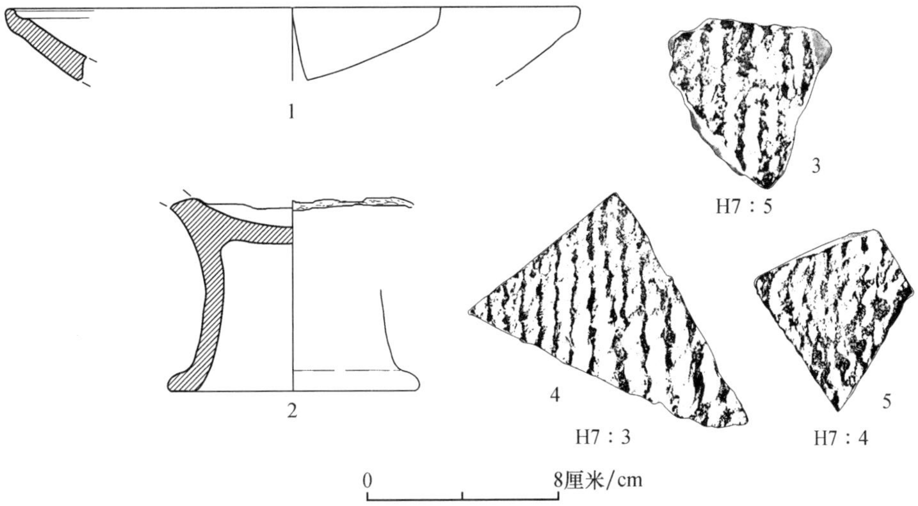

图Ⅰ.5.23　H7出土陶器

1. 簋（H7：2）　2. 簋（H7：1）　3. 陶片（H7：5）　4. 陶片（H7：3）　5. 陶片（H7：4）

Figure Ⅰ.5.23　Pottery types from pit H7.

1. *Gui* tureen (H7 ：2)　2. *Gui* tureen (H7 ：1)　3. Pottery sherd (H7 ：5)　4. Pottery sherd (H7 ：3)　5. Pottery sherd (H7 ：4)

表Ⅰ.5.12　H7出土遗物登记表

Table Ⅰ. 5.12　Artifacts from pit H7

序号 Number on Fig. Ⅰ.5.23	标本号 Excavation number	器物名称 Artifact name	出土时间 Excavation date	位置 Location	所属类型 Types	尺寸（厘米） Size (cm)	特点描述 Description of features
2	09SLGTG1 H7：1	簋 *Gui* tureen	2009-7-5		A3 or A4	M: 10.5 W: 7.9	泥质深灰，腰较矮，圈足外撇，素面。Dark grey clay, relatively short waist, circular foot that flares to the outside, plain.
1	09SLGTG1 H7：2	簋 *Gui* tureen	2009-7-5			W: 23.9 H: 3.8	泥质灰陶，圆唇，宽折沿。素面。Grey clay, round lip, wide mouth, plain.
4	09SLGTG1 H7：3	陶片 Pottery sherd	2009-7-5			L: 5.4 W: 4.5	夹砂灰陶，饰中绳纹。Coarse grey clay, medium cord decorations.
5	09SLGTG1 H7：4	陶片 Pottery sherd	2009-7-5			L: 5.3 W: 2.8	夹砂灰陶，饰绳纹。Coarse grey clay, with cord decorations.
3	09SLGTG1 H7：5	陶片 Pottery sherd	2009-7-5			L: 3.3 W: 3.2	夹砂灰陶，饰绳纹。Coarse grey clay, with cord decorations.

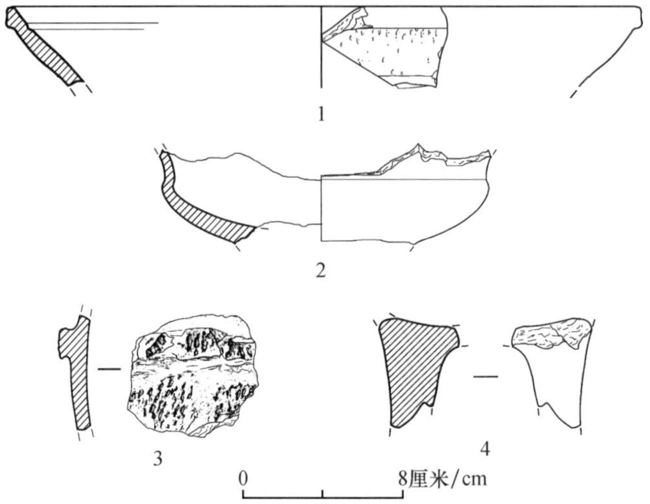

图Ⅰ.5.24　灰坑H8出土陶器

1. 簋（H8∶10）　2. 豆（H8∶3）　3. 盆（H8∶5）　4. 鼎（H8∶1）

Figure Ⅰ.5.24　Pottery types from pit H8.

1. *Gui* tureen (H8∶10)　2. *Dou* pedestal dish (H8∶3)　3. *Pen* basin (H8∶5)　4. *Ding* cauldron (H8∶1)

表Ⅰ.5.13　H8出土遗物登记表

Table Ⅰ.5.13　Artifacts from pit H8

序号 Number on Fig. Ⅰ.5.24	标本号 Excavation number	器物名称 Artifact name	出土时间 Excavation date	位置 Location	所属类型 Types	尺寸（厘米） Size (cm)	特点描述 Description of features
4	09SLGTG1 H8∶1	鼎足 Foot of a *ding* cauldron	2009-7-7		A2	L: 5 W: 6.2	夹云母灰褐陶，小鼎，扁锥足，表面粗糙，素面。 Grey-brown clay with inclusions of mica, small *ding* cauldron. Flat conical feet, rough surface, plain.
	09SLGTG1 H8∶2	鬲口沿 Rim fragment from a *li* tripod	2009-7-7		B	L: 4.3 W: 2.5	夹砂灰褐，方唇，素面。 Coarse grey clay, square lip, plain.
2	09SLGTG1 H8∶3	豆盘 Bowl from a *dou* pedestal dish	2009-7-7		B4	L: 10.3 W: 6.1	泥质深灰，素面磨光，口外撇，沿下有明显折痕，盘较浅。 Dark grey clay, polished surface, mouth flares outward, crease mark below the rim, relatively shallow bowl.
	09SLGTG1 H8∶4	罐肩部 Shoulder from a *guan* jar	2009-7-7		B	L: 5.3 W: 2.8	泥质深灰，折肩明显，肩部有泥凸，肩上饰弦纹，腹饰绳纹。 Dark grey clay, clearly folded shoulder, with protrusions on shoulder, decorated with ring patterns, cord decorations on the body.
3	09SLGTG1 H8∶5	盆 *Pen* basin	2009-7-7			L: 6.2 W: 6.1	夹砂红褐，上饰附加堆纹，其下饰绳纹。 Coarse and red-brown, appliqué patterns with cord decorations below.
	09SLGTG1 H8∶6	豆盘 Bowl from a *dou* pedestal dish	2009-7-7		A4	L: 5.9 W: 6.2	泥质深灰，素面磨光，方唇直口，盘应较深。 Dark grey clay, polished surface, square lip and straight mouth, relatively deep bowl.
	09SLGTG1 H8∶7	罐肩部 Shoulder from a *guan* jar	2009-7-7		B	L: 7.6 W: 5.9	泥质浅灰，溜肩，肩部饰两周弦纹，腹饰绳纹。 Light grey clay, sloped shoulder, two rings on the shoulder, cord decorations on the body.

续表

序号 Number on Fig. Ⅰ.5.24	标本号 Excavation number	器物名称 Artifact name	出土时间 Excavation date	位置 Location	所属类型 Types	尺寸（厘米） Size (cm)	特点描述 Description of features
3	09SLGTG1 H8：8	圈足 Circular foot	2009-7-8			L: 2 W: 6.4 H: 2.2	泥质浅灰陶，圈足外撇，足底成一凹槽，素面。 Light grey clay, circular foot flaring to the outside. Groove around the bottom of the foot. Plain.
	09SLGTG1 H8：9	罐底 Bottom of a *guan* jar	2009-7-8		B	L: 7.3 W: 5.9	泥质深灰，小平底，素面。 Dark grey clay, small and flat bottom, plain.
1	09SLGTG1 H8：10	簋口沿 Rim fragment from a *gui* tureen	2009-7-8			L: 6.2 W: 5.4	泥质深灰，方唇外凸，沿上部有凹槽，外饰绳纹并抹去。 Dark grey clay, square lip with thickening on the outside, groove around the rim, cord decorations and smear marks on the outside.
	09SLGTG1 H8：11	豆盘 Bowl of a *dou* pedestal dish	2009-7-8		B2	M: 31.9 H: 3.8	泥质浅灰，浅折盘，素面磨光。 Light grey clay, shallow and folded bowl, polished surface.
	09SLGTG1 H8：12	陶片 Pottery sherd	2009-7-8			L: 3 H: 6	泥质浅灰，浅折盘，口沿内凸，素面磨光。 Light grey clay, shallow and folded bowl, thickening inside rim, polished surface.
	09SLGTG1 H8：13	簋口沿 Rim sherd from a *gui* tureen	2009-7-8			L: 3.5 W: 4.2	泥质浅灰，方唇，外饰绳纹并抹去。 Light grey clay, square lips, cord decorations and smear marks on the outside.

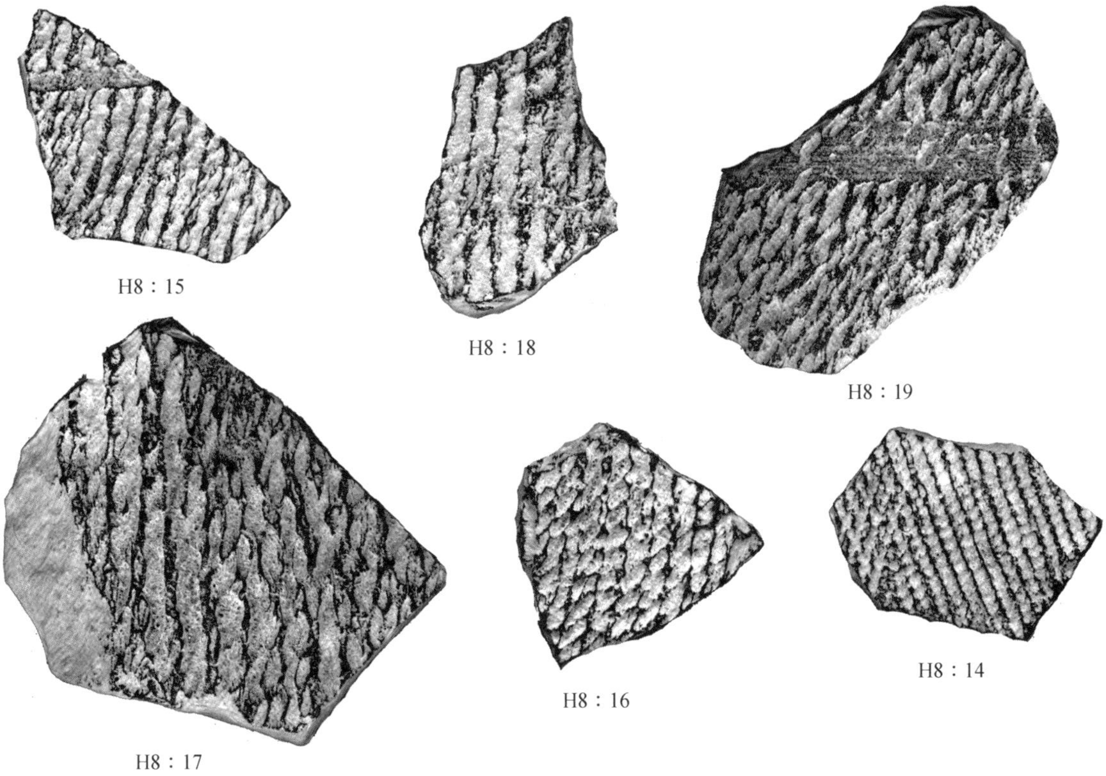

图Ⅰ.5.25　H8出土陶片纹饰

Fig. Ⅰ.5.25　Decorated pottery sherds from pit H8.

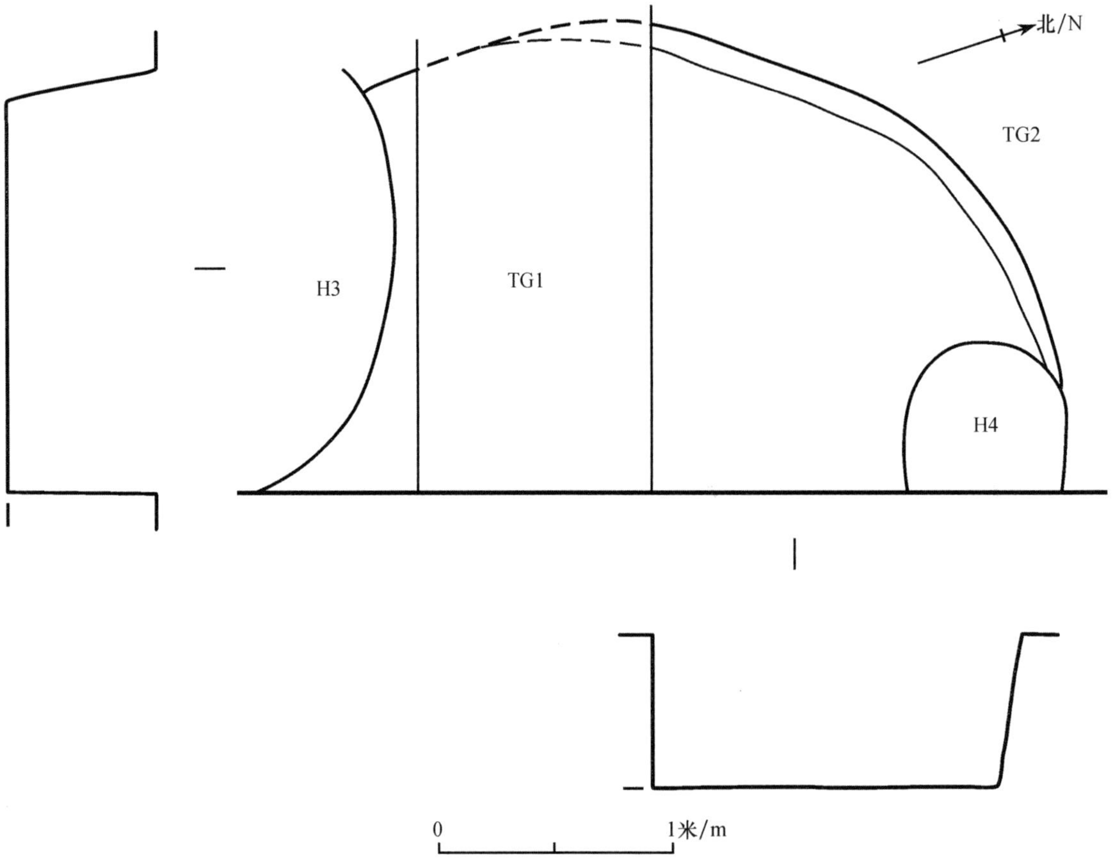

图Ⅰ.5.26　H9平、剖面图

Figure Ⅰ.5.26　Plan and cross-sectional profiles of pit H9.

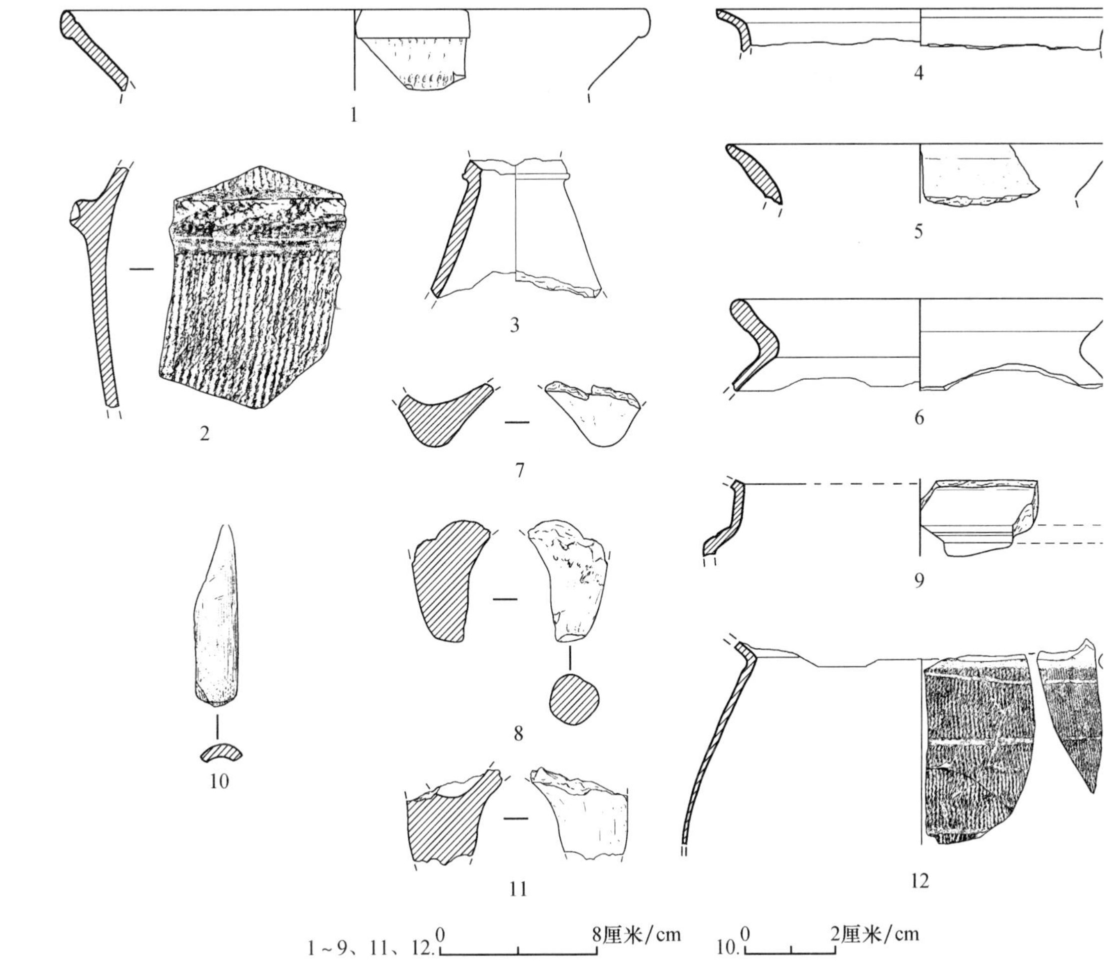

图Ⅰ.5.27　H9出土陶器

1. 簋（H9：18）　2. 盆（H9：23）　3. 豆（H9：26）　4. 罐（H9：20）　5. 鬲(H9：17)　6. 罐（H9：24）　7. 鬲（H9：3）　8. 鼎足（H9：14）　9. 罐（H9：30）　10. 骨锥（H9：2）　11. 鼎足（H9：12）　12. 罐（H9：25）

Figure Ⅰ.5.27　Pottery types from pit H9.

1. *Gui* tureen (H9：18)　2. *Pen* basin (H9：23)　3. *Dou* pedestal dish (H9：26)　4. *Guan* jar (H9：20)　5. *Li* tripod (H9：17)　6. *Guan* jar (H9：24)　7. *Li* tripod (H9：3)　8. Foot from a *ding* cauldron (H9：14)　9. *Guan* jar (H9：30)　10. Bone drill (H9：2)　11. Foot from a *ding* cauldron (H9：12)　12. *Guan* jar (H9：25)

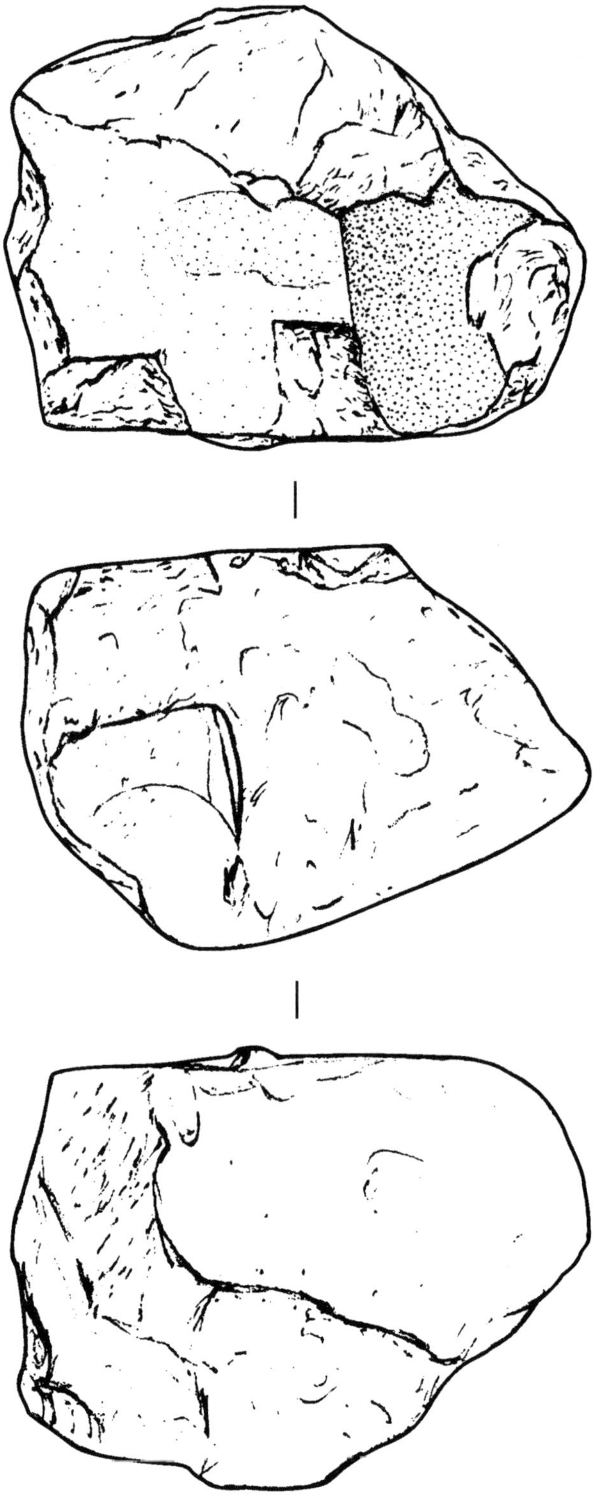

图Ⅰ.5.28　H9出土铸铜用陶范（H9：38）

Figure Ⅰ.5.28　Clay mold (H9：38) for bronze casting from pit H9.

表Ⅰ.5.14　H9出土遗物登记表
Table Ⅰ.5.14　Artifacts from pit H9

序号 Number on Fig. Ⅰ.5.27/28	标本号 Excavation number	器物名称 Artifact name	出土时间 Excavation date	位置 Location	所属类型 Types	尺寸（厘米）Size (cm)	特点描述 Description of features
	09SLGTG2 H9：1	石器 Stone tool	2009-7-8	160×130—55		L: 4.3 W: 2.7 T: 0.7	片状，一面打磨光滑。Flake-shaped, one side polished smooth.
27：10	09SLGTG2 H9：2	骨锥 Bone awl	2009-7-8	110×100—85		L: 3.9 W: 0.8	上部残，应为动物肢骨所制。一侧直，一侧斜，内管状。Upper part broken, but was probably made from an animal limb. One side straight, one side slanted, inside tubular in shape.
27：7	09SLGTG2 H9：3	鬲足 Foot from a *li* tripod	2009-7-8		D	L: 4.8 W: 4.8 H: 4.3	夹云母红褐，足根较矮，乳头不明显。Red-brown with mica inclusions, base of the foot relatively short, unclear nipple-shaped ends.
	09SLGTG2 H9：4	豆盘 Bowl from a *dou* pedestal dish	2009-7-8			L: 3.1 W: 3.1	泥质深灰，素面磨光，方唇，唇内起凸。Dark grey clay, plain polished surface, square lip, raised ridge on the inside of the lip.
	09SLGTG2 H9：5	豆盘 Bowl from a *dou* pedestal dish	2009-7-8			L: 3 W: 3.9	泥质浅灰，素面磨光，方唇。Light grey clay, plain polished surface, square lips.
	09SLGTG2 H9：6	豆口沿 Rim fragment from a *dou* pedestal dish	2009-7-8			L: 4.3 W: 3.5	泥质浅灰，素面，方唇，唇沿内凸。Light grey clay, plain, square lip, thickening inside the rim.
	09SLGTG2 H9：7	罐肩部 Shoulder from a *guan* jar	2009-7-8		B	L: 5.3 W: 5.4	泥质浅灰，溜肩，肩上饰两周凹弦纹，腹部饰中绳纹。Light grey clay, sloped shoulder, two intaglio rings on the shoulder, medium cord decoration on the belly.
	09SLGTG2 H9：8	罐肩部 Shoulder from a *guan* jar	2009-7-8		B	L: 6.5 W: 5.4	泥质深灰，肩部饰附加堆纹，腹饰绳纹。Dark grey clay, appliqué decoration on the shoulder, cord decoration on the belly.
	09SLGTG2 H9：9	罐腹部 Belly from a *guan* jar	2009-7-8		B	L: 14.4 W: 6.7	小罐鼓腹，素面。Small *guan* jar with bulging belly, plain.
	09SLGTG2 H9：10	罐腹部 Belly from a *guan* jar	2009-7-8		B	L: 8.2 W: 5.7	泥质浅灰，腹饰中绳纹并有弦纹。Light grey clay, medium cord decorations and ring patterns.
	09SLGTG2 H9：11	甗腰部 Waist from a *yan* steamer	2009-7-8			L: 6 W: 4	夹滑石红褐，素面。Red-brown with inclusions of talc, plain.
27：11	09SLGTG2 H9：12	鼎足 Foot from a *ding* cauldron	2009-7-8		D	W: 5 H: 4.6	夹砂红褐，素面。Coarse and red-brown, plain.
	09SLGTG2 H9：13	鬲足 Foot from a *li* tripod	2009-7-8		B1	W: 4 H: 5.3	夹砂深灰，足根较低，乳头不明显。Coarse and dark brown, base of the foot relatively low, unclear nipple-shaped ends.

续表

序号 Number on Fig. Ⅰ.5.27/28	标本号 Excavation number	器物名称 Artifact name	出土时间 Excavation date	位置 Location	所属类型 Types	尺寸（厘米） Size (cm)	特点描述 Description of features
27：8	09SLGTG2 H9：14	鼎足 Foot from a *ding* tripod	2009-7-8		D	W: 3.4 H: 5.2	夹滑石红褐，柱状足较高。 Red-brown with inclusions of talc, relatively high columnar foot.
	09SLGTG2 H9：15	鬲口沿 Rim fragment from a *li* tripod	2009-7-8		B	L: 5.3 W: 6.2	夹云母深灰，方唇，唇沿外凸，素面。 Dark grey with inclusions of mica, square lip, thickening on outside of the rim, plain.
	09SLGTG2 H9：16	鬲口沿 Rim fragment from a *li* tripod	2009-7-8		B	L: 3.8 W: 5	夹云母灰褐，圆唇，宽折沿，素面。 Grey-brown with mica inclusions, rounded lip, wide rim, plain surface.
27：5	09SLGTG2 H9：17	鬲口沿 Rim fragment from a *li* tripod	2009-7-8			M: 20 H: 3.2	夹云母红褐，尖唇，宽沿，素面。 Red-brown with mica inclusions, sharp lip, wide rim, plain.
27：1	09SLGTG2 H9：18	簋口沿 Rim fragment from a *gui* tureen	2009-7-8			M: 30 H: 4.1	泥质浅灰，圆唇外卷，唇面磨光，唇沿有槽，外饰绳纹有抹痕。 Light-grey clay, rounded lip rolled to the outside, polishing on the lip, groove on the lip, cord decorations and smear marks on the outside.
	09SLGTG2 H9：19	簋口沿 Rim fragment from a *gui* tureen	2009-7-8			L: 28 W: 9.5	泥质深灰，尖唇，宽折沿，沿面磨光，沿缘有槽，腹饰中绳纹。 Dark grey clay, sharp lip, wide rim, polishing on the rim, groove along the edge of the rim, medium cord decorations on the belly.
27：4	09SLGTG2 H9：20	罐口沿 Rim fragment from a *guan* jar	2009-7-8		B	M: 21 H: 2.2	泥质深灰，素面磨光，尖唇，敞口，卷沿。 Dark grey clay, plain and polished, sharp lip, wide mouth, rolled rim.
	09SLGTG2 H9：21	豆圈足 Circular foot from a *dou* pedestal dish	2009-7-8		A	L: 4.4 W: 2.3	泥质深灰，素面，圈足外撇。 Dark grey clay, plain, circular foot flared to the outside.
27：2	09SLGTG2 H9：23	盆 *Pen* basin	2009-7-8		I	W: 9.4 H: 11.9	泥质深灰，腹上部饰附加堆纹，通体饰中绳纹。 Dark grey clay, appliqué patterns on the belly, medium cord decorations on the entire vessel.
27：6	09SLGTG2 H9：24	罐口沿 Rim fragment from a *guan* jar	2009-7-8		B	M: 19.5 H: 4.6	泥质浅灰，素面，圆唇，卷沿。 Light grey clay, plain, rounded lip, rolled rim.
27：12	09SLGTG2 H9：25	罐 *Guan* jar	2009-7-9		B	L: 12.8 W: 16.8	泥质深灰，饰弦纹和中绳纹。 Dark grey clay, medium cord decorations interrupted by intaglio rings.
27：3	09SLGTG2 H9：26	豆柄 Handle from a *dou* pedestal dish	2009-7-9		B	L: 5.4 W: 7	泥质深灰，素面，柄束腰有凸棱。 Dark grey clay, plain, rib in the middle of the handle.
	09SLGTG2 H9：7	簋口沿 Rim fragment from a *gui* tureen	2009-7-9			L: 6.2 W: 4	泥质深灰，尖唇，沿外饰绳纹并抹去，沿内有凹槽。 Dark grey clay, sharp lip, cord decorations and smearing on the outside of the rim, groove on the inside of the rim.

续表

序号 Number on Fig. Ⅰ.5.27/28	标本号 Excavation number	器物名称 Artifact name	出土时间 Excavation date	位置 Location	所属类型 Types	尺寸（厘米） Size (cm)	特点描述 Description of features
	09SLGTG2 H9：28	陶片 Pottery sherd	2009-7-9			L: 6.1 W: 4.3	泥质深灰，素面。 Dark grey clay, plain.
	09SLGTG2 H9：29	簋盘 Bowl from a *gui* tureen	2009-7-9			L: 7.8 W: 5.5 H: 2	泥质深灰，素面。 Dark grey clay, plain.
27：9	09SLGTG2 H9：30	罐 *Guan* jar	2009-7-9		D1	L: 5.3 W: 5.7	泥质浅灰，素面，方唇直口。 Light grey clay, plain, square lip and straight mouth.
	09SLGTG2 H9：31	豆盘 Bowl from a *dou* pedestal dish	2009-7-9			W: 24 H: 4	泥质深灰，掺云母，素面磨光，方唇，唇沿内凸。 Dark grey clay mixed with mica, plain and polished, square lip, thickening on the inside of the rim.
	09SLGTG2 H9：33	簋圈足 Circular foot from a *gui* tureen	2009-7-9			L: 6.8 W: 3.2 H: 2.5	泥质浅灰，素面，圈足外撇。 Light grey clay, plain, circular foot flared to the outside.
	09SLGTG2 H9：34	盆 *Pen* basin	2009-7-9			L: 8.7 W: 6.3	泥质浅灰，有一周附加堆纹，腹部饰竖向中绳纹，堆纹凹槽处饰横向中绳纹。 Light grey clay, one track of appliqué decoration, vertical cord decorations on the belly, ridge and groove near horizontal cord decorations.
	09SLGTG2 H9：35	盆 *Pen* basin	2009-7-9			L: 11.4 W: 5.9	泥质浅灰，有纽形捉手，通体饰粗绳纹。 Light grey clay, button-shaped handles, coarse cord decorations on the entire vessel.
	09SLGTG2 H9：36	罐腹部 Belly of a *guan* jar	2009-7-9		B	L: 18.4 W: 15	泥质深灰，饰中绳纹。 Dark grey clay, medium cord decorations.
	09SLGTG2 H9：37	鬲 *Li* tripod	2009-7-9			W: 16.6 H: 5.3	泥质深灰，饰中绳纹。 Dark grey clay, medium cord decorations.
28	09SLGTG2 H9：38	陶范 Pottery mold	2009-7-9			L: 5.6 W: 5	泥质红褐，残存两个平面，一个为范面，一个为接范处。 Red-brown fine clay, two faces remaining, one of which is the mold surface that touched the cast bronze, the other of which is the joint surface of the mold.
	09SLGTG2 H9：58	骨器 Bone tool	2009-7-9			L: 3.5 W: 0.6 -1.1	两端残。 Both ends broken.

尺寸标志：L=长度；H=高度；W=宽度；D=直径；R=半径；M=口径；B=底径；T=厚度；d=深度；h=孔径。

Measurements: L=length; H=height; W=width; D=diameter; R=radius; M=mouth diameter; B=bottom diameter; T=thickness; d=depth; h=hole diameter.

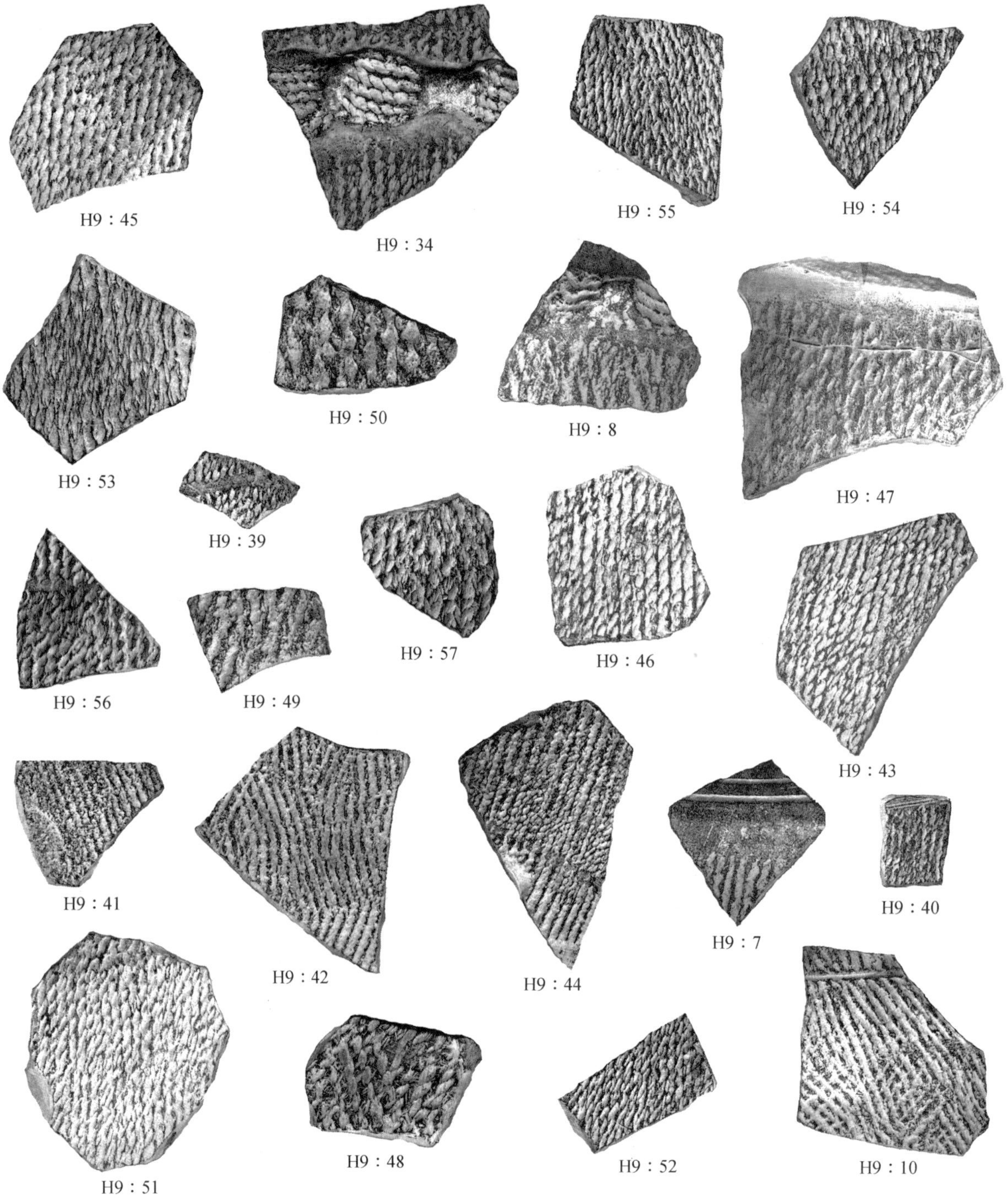

图 I .5.29　H9出土陶片纹饰

Figure I .5.29　Decorated pottery sherds from pit H9.

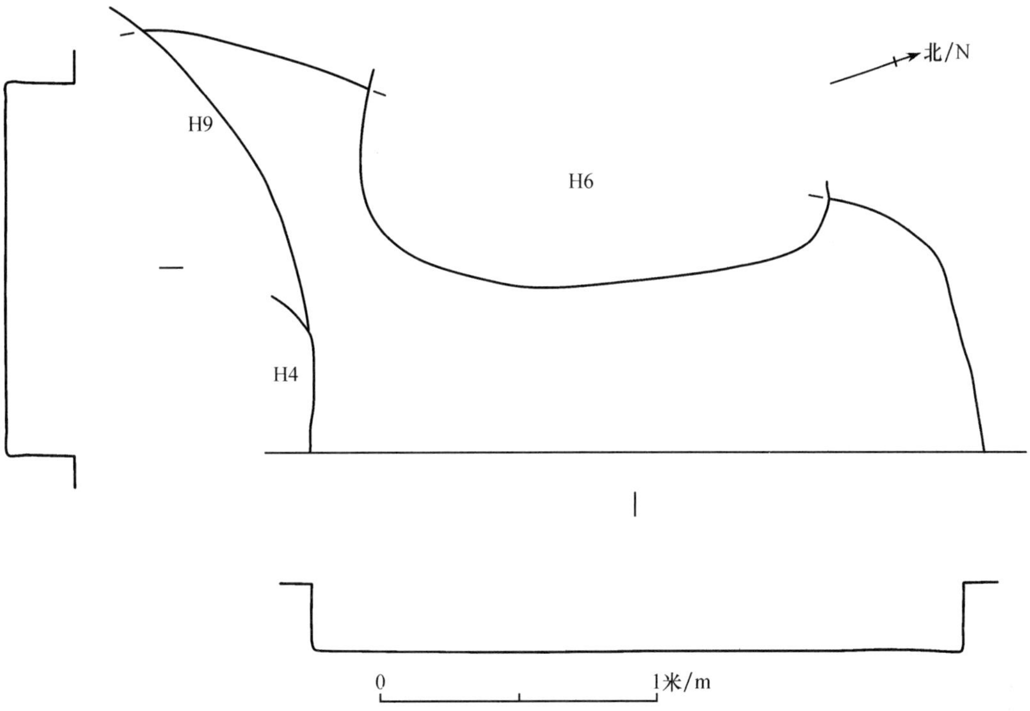

图Ⅰ.5.30　H11平、剖面图

Figure Ⅰ.5.30　Plan and cross-sectional profiles of pit H11.

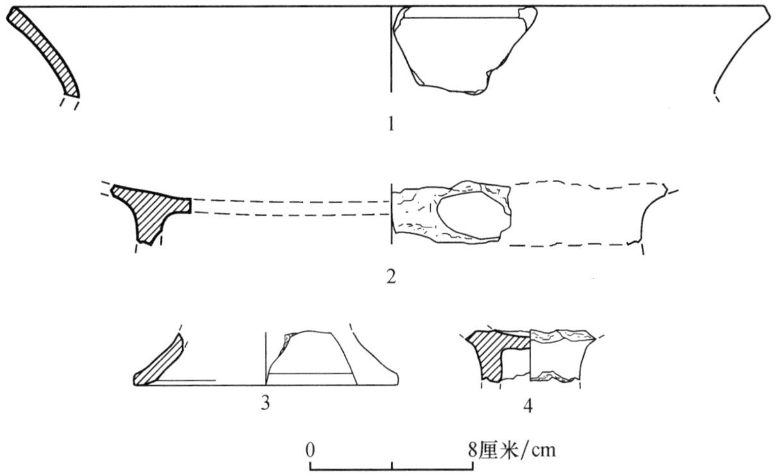

图Ⅰ.5.31　H11出土陶器

1. 鬲（H11：5）　2. 簋（H11：3）　3. 豆（H11：2）　4. 豆（H11：1）

Figure Ⅰ.5.31　Pottery types from pit H11.

1. *Li* tripod (H11：5)　2. *Gui* turren (H11：3)　3. *Dou* pedestal dish (H11：2)　4. *Dou* pedestal dish (H11：1)

表Ⅰ.5.15　H11出土遗物登记表
Table Ⅰ.5.15　Artifacts from pit H11

序号 Number on Fig. Ⅰ.5.31	标本号 Excavation number	器物名称 Artifact name	出土时间 Excavation date	位置 Location	所属类型 Types	尺寸（厘米）Size (cm)	特点描述 Description of features
4	09SLGTG2 H11：1	豆 *Dou* pedestal dish	2009-7-12		B	L: 7 W: 5 H: 2.8	泥质浅灰，素面，细柄。Light grey clay, plain, thin handle.
3	09SLGTG2 H11：2	豆圈足 Circular foot from a *dou* pedestal dish	2009-7-12		B	W: 13 H: 2.7	泥质浅灰，素面。Light grey clay, plain.
2	09SLGTG2 H11：3	簋盘底 Bottom of the bowl of *gui* tureen	2009-7-12			L: 5.8 W: 3.7 H: 2.2	泥质深灰，素面。Dark grey clay, plain.
	09SLGTG2 H11：4	罐底 Bottom of a *guan* jar	2009-7-12		B	L: 4.5 W: 4.1 H: 1.4	泥质浅灰，素面。Light grey clay, plain.
1	09SLGTG2 H11：5	鬲口沿 Rim fragment from a *li* tripod	2009-7-13			W: 38 H: 4.5	夹云母深灰，方唇，敞口，宽沿，素面。Dark grey clay with mica inclusions, square lip, flared mouth, wide rim, plain.
	09SLGTG2 H11：8	鬲口沿 Rim fragment from a *li* tripod	2009-7-13			L: 4.3 W: 3	泥质深灰，方唇外卷，宽折沿，沿外饰绳纹并有抹痕。Dark grey clay, square lip rolled to the outside, wide folded rim, cord decorations and smearing on the outside of the rim.
	09SLGTG2 H11：9	鬲口沿 Rim fragment from a *li* tripod	2009-7-13		D	L: 3 W: 2.7	夹砂深灰，圆唇，敞口。Coarse and dark grey, rounded lip, open mouth.
	09SLGTG2 H11：10	鬲口沿 Rim fragment from a *li* tripod	2009-7-13		D	L: 2.8 W: 2.6	夹云母滑石深灰，方唇，宽折沿，素面。Dark grey with inclusions of mica and talc, square lip, wide folded rim, plain.
	09SLGTG2 H11：11	罐口沿 Rim fragment from a *guan* jar	2009-7-13		A	L: 3.7 W: 2.6	夹砂深灰，方唇，素面。Coarse and dark grey, square lip, plain.
	09SLGTG2 H11：12	罐口沿 Rim fragment from a *guan* jar	2009-7-13		B	L: 2.1 W: 2.6	泥质红陶，方唇，口外撇，卷沿。Red-brown clay, square lip, outside of the rim slanted, rolled rim.
	09SLGTG2 H11：13	器盖 Vessel lid	2009-7-13			L: 1.7 W: 3.2	泥质浅灰，方唇，唇沿内援突起，素面。Light grey clay, square lip. Protrusion on the inside of the rim; plain.
	09SLGTG2 H11：14	豆圈足 Circular foot from a *dou* pedestal dish	2009-7-13			L: 3.6 W: 2 H: 1.6	泥质深灰，素面。Dark grey clay, plain.

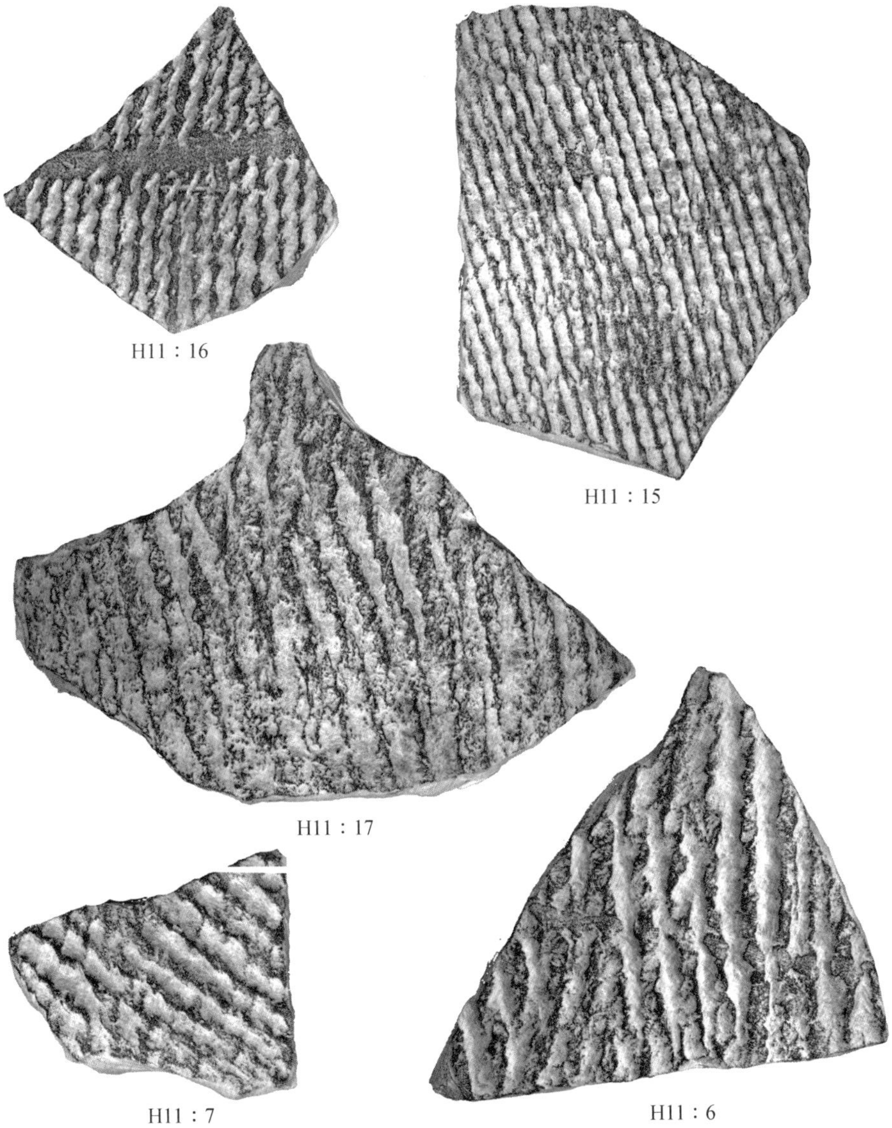

图Ⅰ.5.32　H11出土陶片纹饰

Figure Ⅰ.5.32　Decorated pottery sherds from pit H11.

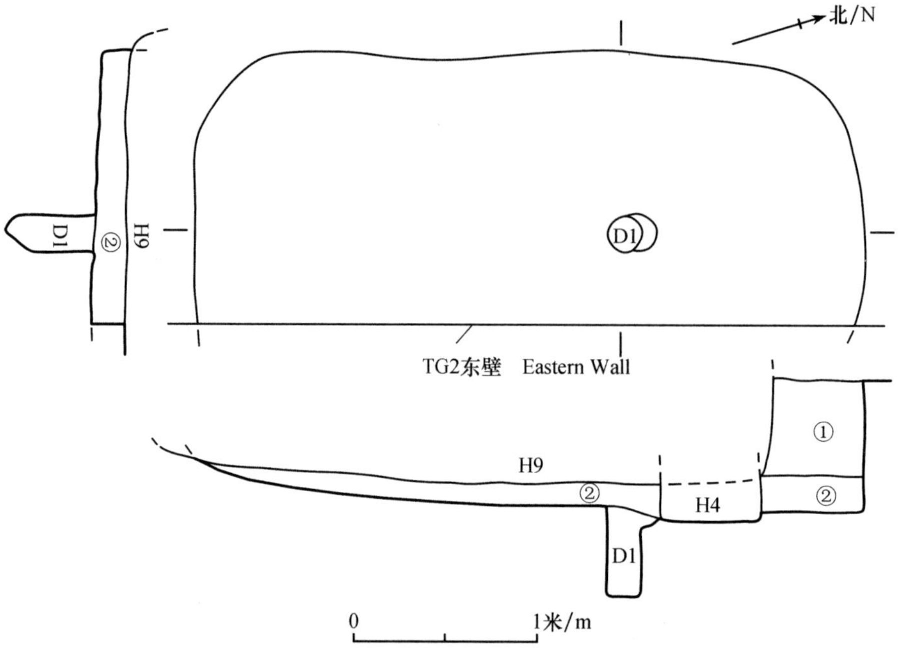

图Ⅰ.5.33　H12平、剖面图
Figure Ⅰ.5.33　Plan and sectional profiles of pit H12.

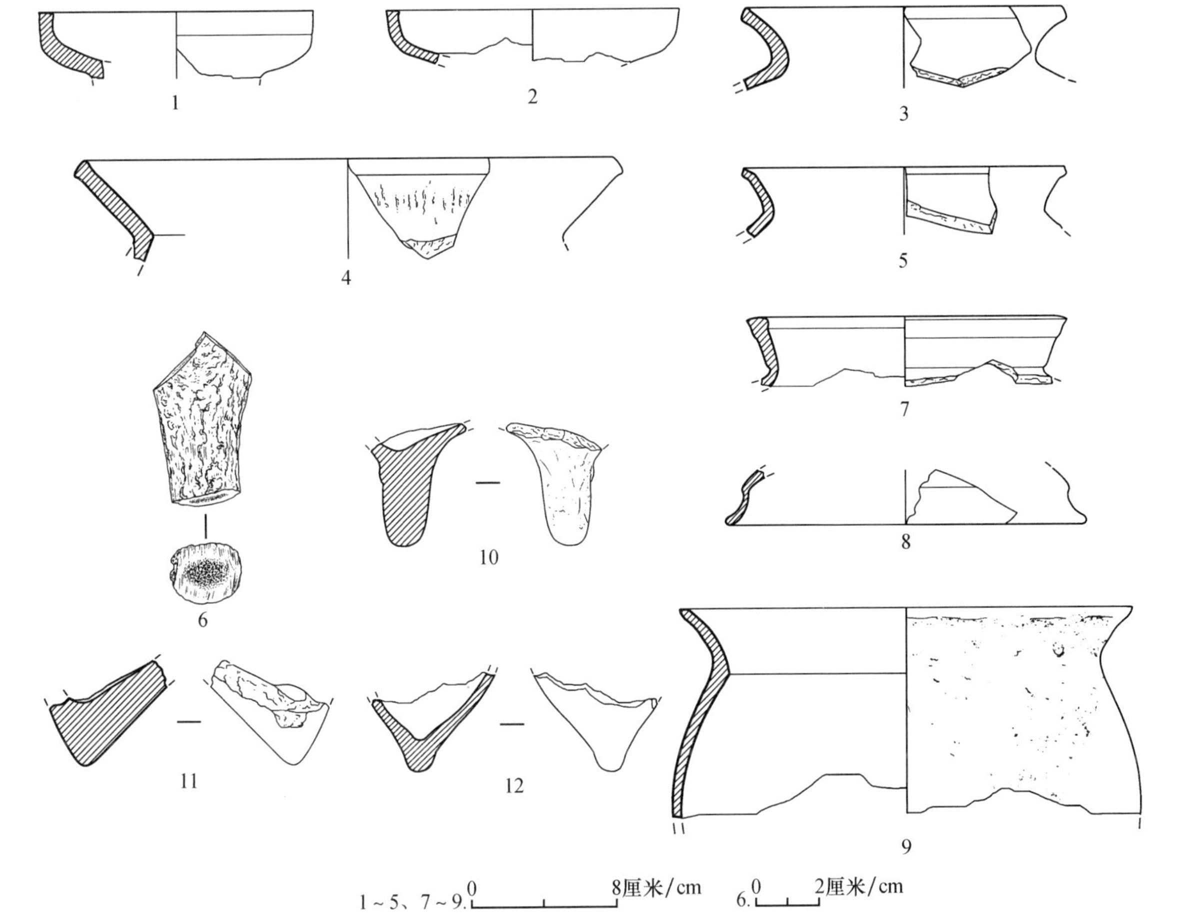

图Ⅰ.5.34　H12出土陶器

1. 豆（H12②：2）　2. 豆（H12①：13）　3. 罐（H12①：7）　4. 簋（H12①：11）　5. 罐（H12①：8）　6. 角料（H12②：1）　7. 罐（H12②：3）　8. 器盖（H12②：18）　9. 罐（H12①：5）　10. 鼎（H12①：16）　11. 鬲（H12①：15）　12. 鬲（H12②：4）

Figure Ⅰ.5.34　Pottery types from pit H12.

1. *Dou* pedestal dish (H12②：2)　2. *Dou* pedestal dish (H12①：13)　3. *Guan* jar (H12①：7)　4. *Gui* tureen (H12①：11)　5. *Guan* jar (H12①：8)　6. Bone material (H12②：1)　7. *Guan* jar (H12②：3)　8. Vessel lid (H12②：18)　9. *Guan* jar (H12①：5)　10. *Ding* cauldron (H12①：16)　11. *Li* tripod (H12①：15)　12. *Li* tripod (H12②：4)

表Ⅰ.5.16　H12出土遗物登记表

Table Ⅰ.5.16　Artifacts from pit H12

序号 Number on Fig. Ⅰ.5.34	标本号 Excavation number	器物名称 Artifact name	出土时间 Excavation date	位置 Location	所属类型 Types	尺寸（厘米） Size (cm)	特点描述 Description of features
	09SLGTG2 H12①：5	罐口沿 Rim fragment from a *guan* jar	2009-7-11			L: 11.6 W: 11.4	夹云母红陶，尖唇，敞口，卷沿，素面。 Red-brown with mica inclusions, sharp lip, wide mouth, rolled rim, plain.
	09SLGTG2 H12①：6	罐口沿 Rim fragment from a *guan* jar	2009-7-11		E	L: 3.3 W: 4.3	夹砂红褐，方唇，敞口，素面。 Coarse and red-brown, square lip, wide mouth, plain.
	09SLGTG2 H12①：7	罐口沿 Rim fragment from a *guan* jar	2009-7-11		B	L: 7.7 W: 4.3	泥质深灰，素面磨光，方唇，敞口，卷沿，肩较平。 Dark grey clay, plain and polished, square lip, wide mouth, rolled rim, shoulder relatively flat.
9	09SLGTG2 H12①：5	罐口沿 Rim fragment from a *guan* jar	2009-7-11		A	M: 25.1 W: 11.1	夹云母红陶，尖唇，敞口，卷沿，素面。 Red-brown with mica inclusions, sharp lip, wide mouth, rolled rim, plain.
	09SLGTG2 H12①：6	罐口沿 Rim fragment from a *guan* jar	2009-7-11		E	L: 3.3 W: 4.3	夹砂红褐，方唇，敞口，素面。 Coarse and red-brown, square lip, wide mouth, plain.
3	09SLGTG2 H12①：7	罐口沿 Rim fragment from a *guan* jar	2009-7-11		B	M: 18 H: 4.4	泥质深灰，素面磨光，方唇，敞口，卷沿，肩较平。 Dark grey clay, plain and polished, square lip, wide mouth, rolled rim, relatively flat shoulder.
5	09SLGTG2 H12①：8	罐口沿 Rim fragment from a *guan* jar	2009-7-11		B	M: 18 H: 3.9	泥质深灰，方唇外撇，卷沿，肩较平，素面。 Dark grey clay, square lip flared to the outside, rolled rim, relatively flat shoulder, plain.
	09SLGTG2 H12①：9	瓿 *Bu* vase	2009-7-11			L: 4 W: 3.2	圈足底缘较厚，足跟起一凹槽。素面。 Bottom edge of the circular foot relatively thick, groove around the base of the foot. Plain.
	09SLGTG2 H12①：10	簋口沿 Rim fragment from a *gui* tureen	2009-7-11			L: 4.2 W: 4.1	泥质浅灰，方唇，唇沿外凸，沿边有凹槽。 Light grey clay, square lip, protrusion around the rim, groove along the edge of the rim.
4	09SLGTG2 H12①：11	簋口沿 Rim fragment from a *gui* tureen	2009-7-11			M: 29.9 H: 5.5	泥质深灰掺云母，方唇，唇沿外凸，宽沿，沿外饰绳纹并有抹痕。 Dark grey clay mixed with mica, square lip, protrusion around the outside of the rim, wide rim, cord decoration and smearing marks around the outside of the rim.
	09SLGTG2 H12①：12	簋口沿 Rim fragment from a *gui* tureen	2009-7-11			L: 4.8 W: 3.6	泥质灰褐，方唇外卷，沿缘有凹槽，沿面磨光。 Grey-brown clay, square lip rolled to the outside, groove along the edge of the rim, polishing on the edge.
2	09SLGTG2 H12①：13	豆盘 Bowl from a *dou* pedestal dish	2009-7-11		B	M: 16 H: 2.9	泥质深灰，方唇直口。 Dark grey clay, square lip and straight mouth.

续表

序号 Number on Fig. Ⅰ.5.34	标本号 Excavation number	器物名称 Artifact name	出土时间 Excavation date	位置 Location	所属类型 Types	尺寸（厘米） Size (cm)	特点描述 Description of features
	09SLGTG2 H12①：14	豆盘 Bowl from a *dou* pedestal dish	2009-7-11			L: 5.1 W: 3.2	泥质红褐，圆唇，素面磨光。 Red-brown clay, rounded lip, plain and polished.
11	09SLGTG2 H12①：15	鬲足 Foot from a *li* tripod	2009-7-11		B	L: 6.3 W: 5.1 H: 6.2	夹砂红陶，素面，袋足足尖矮。 Coarse and red-brown, plain, pocket-shaped foot with sharp tip.
10	09SLGTG2 H12①：16	鼎足 Foot from a *ding* cauldron	2009-7-12		A1	W: 5.2 H: 6.6	夹云母灰褐，圆锥足较高。 Grey-brown with mica inclusions, conical and relatively tall foot.
6	09SLGTG2 H12②：1	角料 Fragment of horn	2009-7-12	200 × 195 —100		L: 5.4 W: 2.5-3	圆柱状，两端有锯割痕迹。为鹿角，应为制作角器的下脚料。 Cylindrical in shape, both ends have traces of sawing, probably a scrap from bone processing.
1	09SLGTG2 H12②：2	豆盘 Bowl from a *dou* pedestal dish	2009-7-12		D	M: 15 H: 3.6	泥质浅灰，素面磨光，方唇直口，盘外侧饰凹弦纹。 Light grey clay, plain and polished, square lip and straight mouth, intaglio ring patterns on the outside of the bowl.
7	09SLGTG2 H12②：3	罐 *Guan* jar	2009-7-12		B	M: 17.7 H: 3.8	泥质浅灰，素面，方唇内凸，折沿。 Light grey clay, plain, thickening on the inside of the square lip, folded rim.
12	09SLGTG2 H12②：4	鬲足 Foot from a *li* tripod	2009-7-12		B2	W: 6.8 H: 5.2	夹云母滑石红褐，袋足足尖较矮起乳头。 Red-brown with inclusions of mica and talc, pocked-shaped foot relatively short with nipple ends.
	09SLGTG2 H12②：17	簋口沿 Rim fragment from a *gui* tureen	2009-7-12			L: 5 W: 2.8	泥质浅灰，圆唇外卷，沿内有凹槽。 Light grey clay, rounded lip rolled to the outside, groove around the inside of the rim.
8	09SLGTG2 H12②：18	器盖 Vessel lid	2009-7-12		A2	M: 20 H: 3	泥质深灰，盖沿外撇，外呈凹槽状，内缘饰弦纹。素面，磨光。 Dark grey clay, edge of the lid flared outwards, groove around the outside, ring patterns on the inside edge. Plain, polished.
	09SLGTG2 H12②：19	罐肩部 Shoulder from a *guan* jar	2009-7-12		B	L: 6.2 W: 3.3	泥质浅灰，饰数周凹弦纹。 Light grey clay, several tracks of intaglio ring decoration.

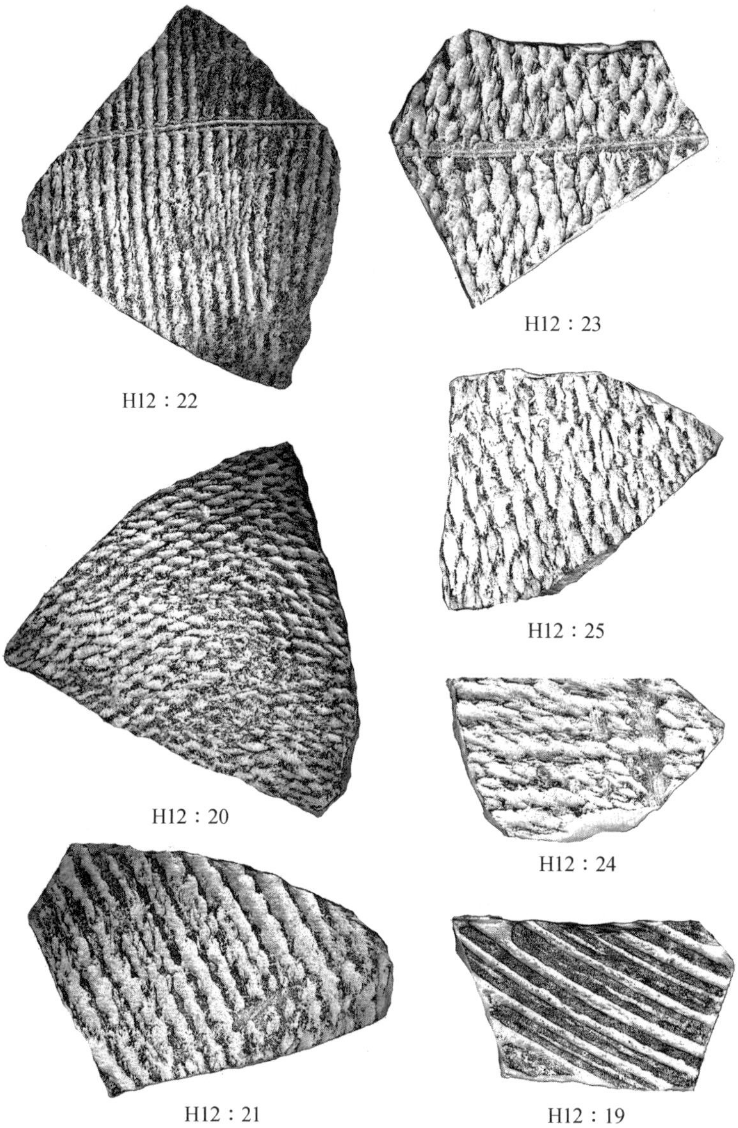

图Ⅰ.5.35　H12出土陶片纹饰

Figure Ⅰ.5.35　Decorated pottery sherds from pit H12.

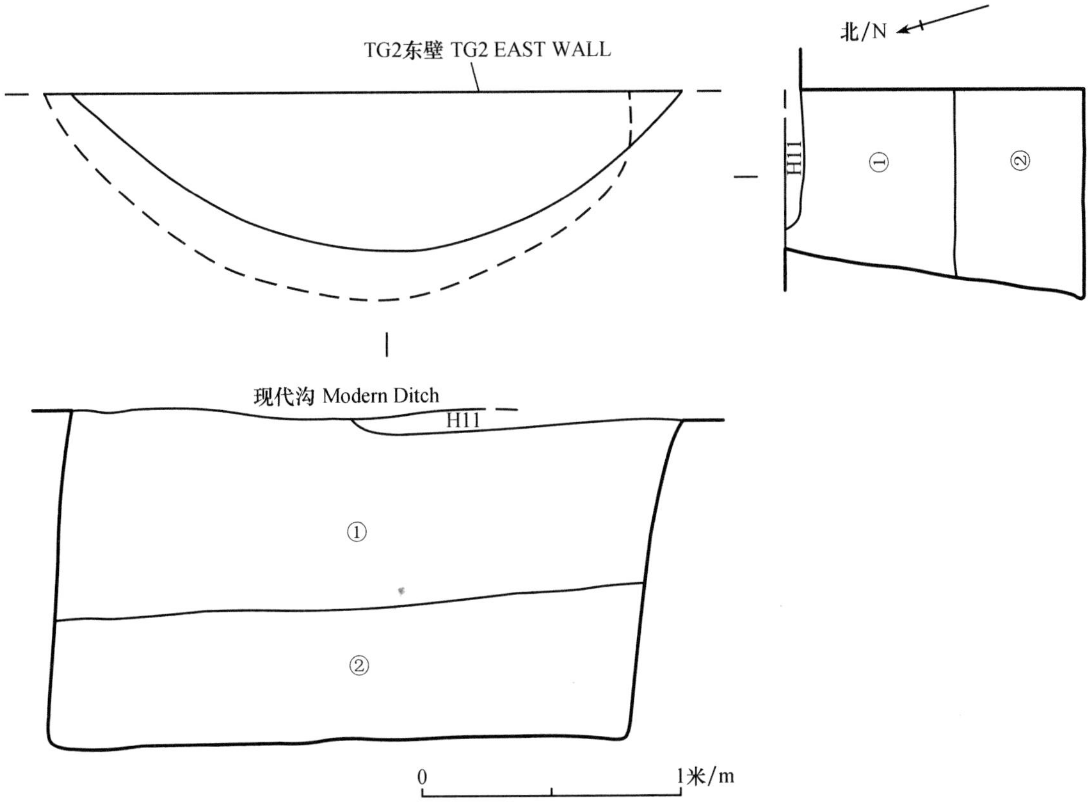

图Ⅰ.5.36　H15平、剖面图

FigureⅠ.5.36　Plan and cross-sectional profiles of Pit H15.

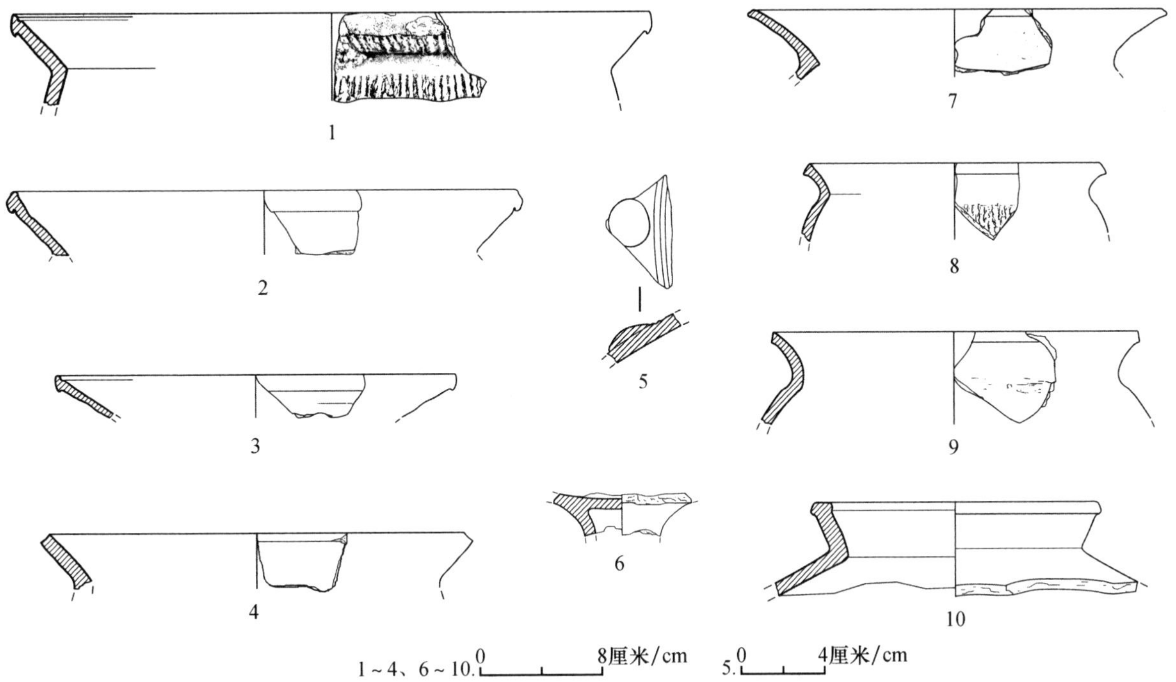

图Ⅰ.5.37　H15出土陶器

1. 鬲（H15①：3）　2. 簋（H15①：4）　3.簋（H15①：5）　4. 簋（H15①：18）　5. 罐（H15①：9）　6. 豆（H15①：10）　7. 鼎（H15②：13）　8. 鬲（H15①：1）　9.鬲（H15①：2）　10. 罐（H15①：7）

FigureⅠ.5.37　Pottery types from pit H15.

1. *Li* tripod (H15①：3)　2. *Gui* tureen (H15①：4)　3. *Gui* tureen (H15①：5)　4. *Gui* tureen (H15①：18)　5. *Guan* jar (H15①：9)　6. *Dou* pedestal dish (H15①：10)　7. *Ding* cauldron (H15②：13)　8. *Li* tripod (H15①：1)　9. *Li* tripod (H15①：2)　10. *Guan* jar (H15①：7)

表Ⅰ.5.17　H15出土遗物登记表

Table Ⅰ.5.17　Artifacts from pit H15

序号 Number on Fig. Ⅰ.5.37	标本号 Excavation number	器物名称 Artifact name	出土时间 Excavation date	位置 Location	所属类型 Types	尺寸（厘米）Size (cm)	特点描述 Description of features
8	09SLGTG2 H15①：1	鬲口沿 Rim fragment from a *li* tripod	2009-7-12		A	M: 19.8 H: 5.1	夹砂深灰，方唇，敞口，卷沿，腹部饰绳纹。Coarse and dark grey, square lip, wide mouth, rolled rim, cord decorations on the belly.
9	09SLGTG2 H15①：2	鬲口沿 Rim fragment from a *li* tripod	2009-7-12		B	M: 24 H: 6.1	夹砂深灰，方唇，敞口，卷沿，素面。Coarse and dark grey, square lip, wide mouth, rolled rim, plain.
1	09SLGTG2 H15①：3	鬲口沿 Rim fragment from a *li* tripod	2009-7-12		A	M: 41.4 H: 5.8	泥质浅灰，方唇，唇沿饰凹弦纹，宽折沿，饰粗绳纹有抹痕。Light grey clay, square lip, intaglio ring patterns around the edge of the lip, wide turning rim, coarse cord decorations with smear marks.
2	09SLGTG2 H15①：4	簋 *Gui* tureen	2009-7-12		B	M: 34.4 H: 7.3	泥质红陶，唇外卷，唇部有槽，宽沿，沿面有磨光，素面。Reddish-brown clay, lip rolled to the outside, groove on the lip, wide rim, burnishing on the rim, plain.
3	09SLGTG2 H15①：5	簋沿 Rim fragment from a *gui* tureen	2009-7-12		B	M: 25.9 H: 2.8	泥质浅灰，素面，方唇外卷，唇内缘起槽，宽沿。Light grey clay, plain, square lip rolled to the outside, groove on the inside edge of the rim, wide mouth.
	09SLGTG2 H15①：6	鬲口沿 Rim fragment from a *li* tripod	2009-7-12		B	W: 3 L: 4.2	泥质深灰，素面磨光，圆唇外卷。Dark grey clay, plain and burnished, rounded lip rolled to the outside.
10	09SLGTG2 H15①：7	罐口沿 Rim fragment of a *guan* jar	2009-7-12		E1	M: 19.1 H: 6	小口大罐，方唇，敞口，唇缘微凸，折沿，肩较平，泥质浅灰，素面。Large *guan* jar with a small mouth, square lip, wide mouth, slight protrusion on the edge of the lip, folded rim, shoulder relatively flat, light grey clay, plain.
	09SLGTG2 H15①：8	罐肩部 Shoulder of a *guan* jar	2009-7-12		B	W: 5.7 L: 3.6	泥质浅灰，素面磨光，折肩，肩部饰弦纹。Light grey clay, plain and burnished, folded shoulder, ring pattern on the shoulder.
5	09SLGTG2 H15①：9	罐肩部 Shoulder of a *guan* jar	2009-7-12		A4	W: 5 L: 3.3	泥质浅灰，有泥饼，饰弦纹。Light grey clay, with a small cake of mud, ring patterns.
6	09SLGTG2 H15①：10	豆盘 Bowl of a *dou* pedestal dish	2009-7-12		B	W: 8 L: 6.4 H: 2.1	泥质浅灰，素面。Light grey clay, plain.
	09SLGTG2 H15①：11	器盖 Vessel lid	2009-7-12		A1	W: 4 L: 3	泥质深灰，尖唇。唇沿内援突起，素面，磨光。Dark grey clay, sharp lip, inner lip protrudes, plain, burnished.
	09SLGTG2 H15①：12	鬲口沿 Rim fragment from a *li* tripod	2009-7-12			W: 3.3 L: 3.4	泥质浅灰，沿内有磨光，圆唇。Light grey clay, inside of the rim burnished, rounded lip.
4	09SLGTG2 H15①：18	鼎或鬲 *Ding* cauldron or *li* tripod	2009-7-12			M: 27.18 H: 3.5	夹砂红陶，方唇，敞口，宽沿，素面。Coarse and red-brown, square lip, wide mouth and broad rim, plain.
7	09SLGTG2 H15②：13	鼎 *Ding* cauldron	2009-7-12			M: 27.4 H: 4.4	圆唇，敞口，宽折沿，夹云母灰褐，素面。Rounded lip, wide mouth, broad and folded rim, grey-brown with mica inclusions, plain.

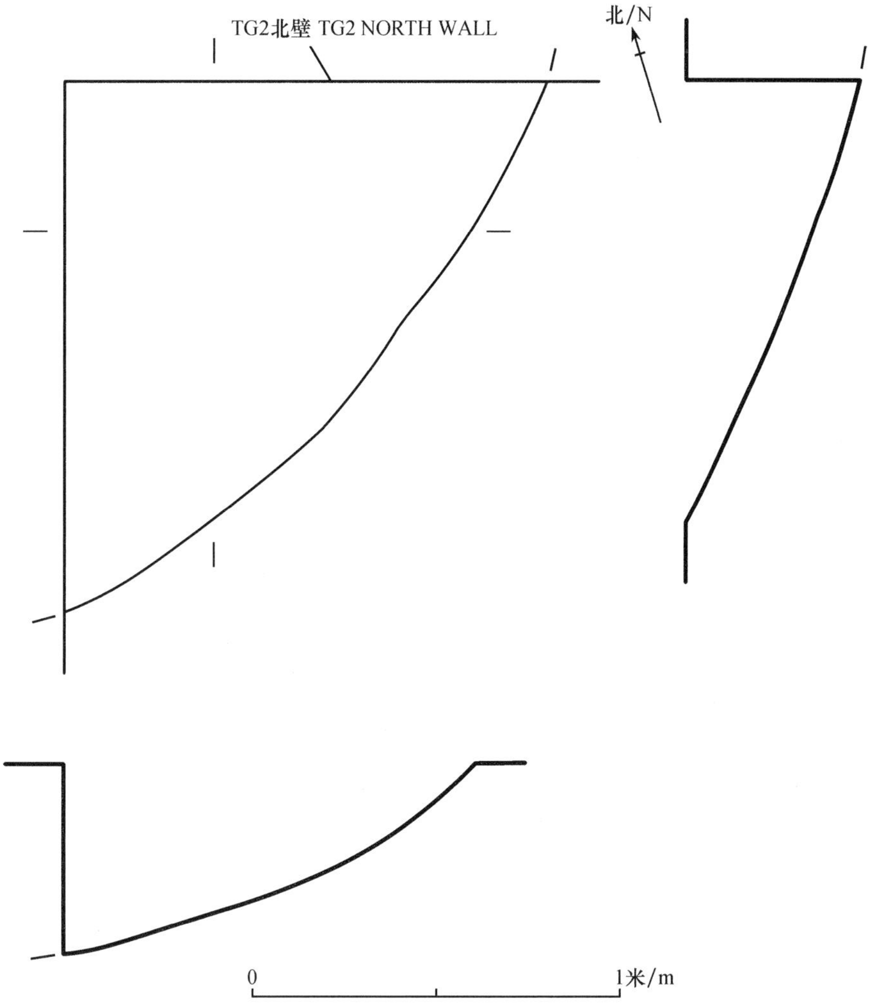

图Ⅰ.5.38　H16平、剖面图

FigureⅠ.5.38　Plan and cross-sectional profiles of pit H16.

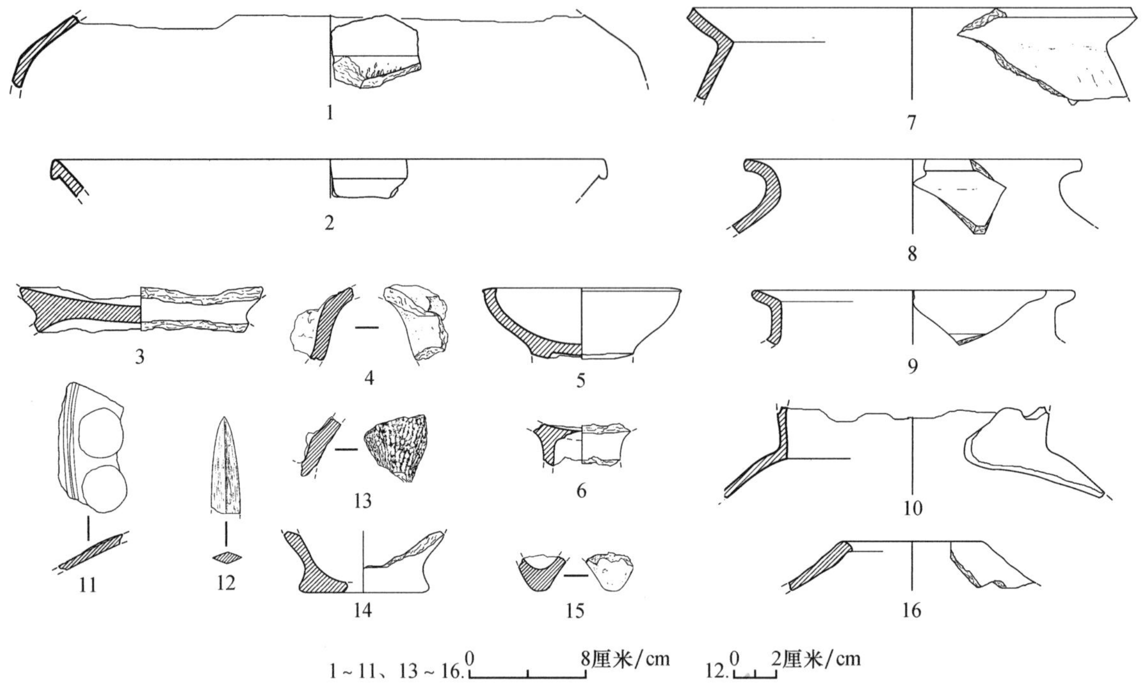

图Ⅰ.5.39　H16出土陶器和石器

1. 罐（H16：28）　2. 盆（H16：14）　3. 簋（H16：12）　4. 鬲（H16：38）　5. 豆(H16：24)　6. 豆（H16：27）　7. 鬲（H16：4）　8. 罐（H16：16）　9. 鬲（H16：13）　10. 罐（H16：23）　11. 瓮（H16：18）　12. 骨镞（H16：1）　13. 鬲（H16：36）　14. 碗（H16：15）　15. 鬲（H16：37）　16. 瓮（H16：25）

Figure Ⅰ.5.39　Pottery types and stone tools from pit H16.

1. *Guan* jar (H16：28)　2. 盆 *Pen* basin (H16：14)　3. *Gui* tureen (H16：12)　4. *Li* tripod (H16：38)　5. *Dou* pedestal dish (H16：24)　6. *Dou* pedestal dish (H16：27)　7. *Li* tripod (H16：4)　8. *Guan* jar (H16：16)　9. *Li* tripod (H16：13)　10. *Guan* jar (H16：23)　11. *Weng* jar (H16：18)　12. Bone arrowhead (H16：1)　13. *Li* tripod (H16：36)　14. Bowl (H16：15)　15. *Li* tripod (H16：37)　16. *Weng* jar (H16：25)

表Ⅰ.5.18　H16出土遗物登记表

Table Ⅰ.5.18　Artifacts from pit H16

序号 Number on Fig. Ⅰ.5.39	标本号 Excavation number	器物名称 Artifact name	出土时间 Excavation date	位置 Location	所属类型 Types	尺寸(厘米) Size (cm)	特点描述 Description of features
12	09SLGTG2 H16：1	骨镞 Bone arrowhead	2009-7-12	620×40 －60		L: 4.5 W: 1.3	箭头状，两面有挺。下部残，残截面呈菱形。 Arrowhead-shaped, ridge on both faces. Lower part broken, cross section is diamond-shaped.
	09SLGTG2 H16：3	鬲口沿 Rim fragment from a *li* tripod	2009-7-12		B	L: 3.8 W: 3.2	夹云母滑石红褐，宽折沿。 Reddish-brown with mica and talc tempering, wide folded rim.
7	09SLGTG1 H16：4	鬲 *Li* tripod	2009-7-12			L: 13 W: 6.6	夹滑石红褐，方唇，折沿。素面。 Reddish-brown with talc tempering, square lip, folded rim, plain.
	09SLGTG2 H16：5	圈足 Circular foot	2009-7-12			L: 6.7 W: 3.9 H: 2.7	泥质浅灰陶。圈足外撇，足跟内侧有一凹槽。素面。 Light grey clay, circular foot flared to the outside, groove on the inside of the base of the foot. Plain.
	09SLGTG2 H16：6	鬲口沿 Rim fragment from a *li* tripod	2009-7-12		B	L: 4.8 W: 3	夹云母红褐，方唇，敞口折沿。 Reddish-brown with mica tempering, square lip, wide mouth and folded rim.

续表

序号 Number on Fig. Ⅰ.5.39	标本号 Excavation number	器物名称 Artifact name	出土时间 Excavation date	位置 Location	所属类型 Types	尺寸（厘米） Size (cm)	特点描述 Description of features
	09SLGTG2 H16：7	盆 *Pen* basin	2009-7-12		Ⅰ	L: 12.5 W: 7.3	泥质红褐。 Reddish-brown clay.
	09SLGTG2 H16：8	簋口沿 Rim fragment from a *gui* tureen	2009-7-12		Ⅱ?	L: 8.4 W: 8	泥质深灰，素面，圆唇，宽折沿。 Dark grey clay, plain, rounded lip, broad folded rim.
	09SLGTG2 H16：9	盆 *Pen* basin	2009-7-12		Ⅲ?	L: 7.8 W: 7.1	泥质深灰，小方唇，内侧缘起突状，沿内磨光。沿外侧饰竖向粗绳纹，并有抹痕。 Dark grey clay, narrow square lip, protrusion on the inside of its edge, inside of the rim burnished. Coarse vertical cord decorations on the outside of the rim, with some smearing.
	09SLGTG2 H16：10	簋口沿 Rim fragment from a *gui* tureen	2009-7-12			L: 2.8 W: 2.5	方唇，沿外饰绳纹并抹去。 Square lip, cord decorations with smearing on the outside of the rim.
	09SLGTG2 H16：11	鬲口沿 Rim fragment from a *li* tripod	2009-7-12		B	L: 4 W: 4	夹砂深灰，方唇，敞口宽沿。 Coarse and dark grey, square lip, wide mouth and broad rim.
3	09SLGTG2 H16：12	簋盘底 Bottom of a bowl from a *gui* tureen	2009-7-12			L: 12.7 W: 7.8 H: 3	泥质深灰，素面，盘甚大，盘底较平，圈足甚粗，圈足内有轮制痕迹。 Dark grey clay, plain, bowl rather large, bottom of the bowl relatively flat, circular foot rather thick, with wheel marks.
9	09SLGTG2 H16：13	罐 *Guan* jar	2009-7-12			W: 22 H: 3.6	泥质灰陶，圆唇外撇，领较高，素面。 Grey clay, circular lip flared outwards, collar relatively high, plain.
2	09SLGTG2 H16：14	盆口沿 Rim fragment from a *pen* basin	2009-7-12			L: 5.4 W: 2.7	夹云母红褐，尖唇，唇外缘凸出，素面。 Reddish-brown with mica tempering, sharp lip, protrusion on the outside edge of the lip, plain.
14	09SLGTG1 H16：15	碗 Bowl	2009-7-12		B	L: 11.7 W: 10.2. H: 7.7	夹滑石红褐，实圈足，足跟较高。 Red-brown with talc tempering, circular feet, base of the foot relatively high.
8	09SLGTG2 H16：16	罐口沿 Rim fragment from a *guan* jar	2009-7-12			M: 22.9. H: 5	泥质浅灰，素面，方唇，卷沿，肩应较平。 Light grey clay, plain, square lip, rolled rim, shoulder relatively flat.
	09SLGTG2 H16：17	圆陶片 Circular pottery sherd	2009-7-12			L: 4.7 T: 0.7	泥质浅灰，大致呈圆形，素面。 Light grey clay, roughly circular in shape, plain.
11	09SLGTG2 H16：18	瓮 *Weng* jar	2009-7-12			L: 9 W: 7	泥质浅灰，腹部有两个泥饼，其下饰数周凹弦纹。 Light grey clay, two mud cakes on the belly, with several intaglio ring decorations below them.
	09SLGTG2 H16：21	残豆盘 Broken bowl from a *dou* pedestal dish	2009-7-12		B	L: 7.4 W: 5.1	泥质深灰，素面，方唇，直口，折盘。 Dark grey clay, plain, square lip, straight mouth, folded bowl.
	09SLGTG2 H16：22	残豆盘 Broken bowl from a *dou* pedestal dish	2009-7-12		A	L: 4.6 W: 3	泥质深灰掺少许云母，素面，方唇直口，腹应较深，素面磨光。 Dark grey clay mixed with a little mica, plain, square and straight mouth, belly relatively deep, plain and burnished.
10	09SLGTG2 H16：23	罐 *Guan* jar	2009-7-12		D	L: 7.7 W: 7.2	泥质浅灰，腹部应微鼓，素面。 Light grey clay, belly slightly flared, plain.

续表

序号 Number on Fig. Ⅰ.5.39	标本号 Excavation number	器物名称 Artifact name	出土时间 Excavation date	位置 Location	所属类型 Types	尺寸(厘米) Size (cm)	特点描述 Description of features
5	09SLGTG2 H16：24	残豆盘 Broken bowl from a *dou* pedestal dish	2009-7-12		B	M: 13.3 H: 4.5	泥质浅灰，口微敛，素面。 Light grey clay, slightly converging mouth, plain.
16	09SLGTG2 H16：25	瓮 *Weng* jar	2009-7-12			L: 5.5 W: 5.5	泥质浅灰，直口方唇，唇内沿微突。素面。 Light grey clay, straight mouth with square lip, small protrusion on the inside of the rim. Plain.
	09SLGTG2 H16：26	豆盘 Bowl from a *dou* pedestal dish	2009-7-12		B	L: 6 W: 5	方唇，唇内缘起凸，盘微折，素面。 Square lip, protrusion on the inside of the rim, small fold, plain.
6	09SLGTG2 H16：27	残豆 Broken *dou* pedestal dish	2009-7-12		B	L: 5 W: 3.5 H: 3	豆柄较细，泥质浅灰，素面。 Relatively thin *dou* stem, light grey mud pottery, plain.
1	09SLGTG2 H16：28	罐肩部 Shoulder from a *guan* jar	2009-7-12		B	L: 6.4 W: 5.8	泥质浅灰，圆肩，下腹饰绳纹。 Light grey clay, rounded shoulder, lower belly has cord decorations.
	09SLGTG2 H16：29	罐上部 Upper part of a *guan* jar	2009-7-12		B	L: 8.8 W: 4.5	敞口，泥质浅灰，饰细绳纹，腹应微鼓。 Wide mouth, light grey clay, fine cord decorations, flared belly.
	09SLGTG2 H16：30	罐肩部 Shoulder of a *guan* jar	2009-7-12		B	L: 7.5 W: 4.4	敞口，卷沿，沿外饰绳纹。 Flared mouth, rolled rim, cord decorations on the outside of the rim.
	09SLGTG2 H16：31	罐肩部 Shoulder of a *guan* jar	2009-7-12		B	L: 7.9 W: 7	泥质浅灰，溜肩，肩部饰两周凹弦纹，腹部饰绳纹。 Light grey clay, sloping shoulder, two rings decorating the shoulder, cord decorations on the belly.
	09SLGTG2 H16：32	罐口部 Mouth of a *guan* jar	2009-7-12		B	L: 7.5 W: 4.2	泥质深灰，敞口卷沿，饰麻点绳纹加一周弦纹。 Dark grey clay, wide mouth with rolled rim, “sesame seed” cord decorations with one ring pattern.
	09SLGTG2 H16：33	罐肩部 Shoulder of a *guan* jar	2009-7-12		B	L: 5.5 W: 4.8	泥质红褐，溜肩，肩部饰弦纹，腹部饰中绳纹。 Reddish-brown clay, sloping shoulder, ring decorations on the shoulder, medium cord decoration on the belly.
	09SLGTG2 H16：34	罐肩部 Shoulder of a *guan* jar	2009-7-12		B	L: 4.5 W: 3.8	泥质红褐，敞口卷沿，饰绳纹。 Reddish-brown clay, wide mouth with rolled rim, with cord decorations.
	09SLGTG2 H16：35	罐肩部 Shoulder of a *guan* jar	2009-7-12		B	L: 5.4 W: 4.6	泥质深灰，素面，敞口卷沿。 Dark grey clay, plain, wide mouth with rolled rim.
13	09SLGTG2 H16：36	鬲袋足 Pocket-shaped foot from a *li* tripod	2009-7-12		A	L: 5 W: 4.6	夹砂灰褐，饰中绳纹，足根应较矮。 Coarse and grey-brown, medium cord decorations, base of the foot relatively short.
15	09SLGTG2 H16：37	鬲袋足 Pocket-shaped foot from a *li* tripod	2009-7-12		B	L: 3 W: 2.6	夹砂灰褐，足根矮，素面。 Coarse and greyish-brown; squat base of the foot, plain.
4	09SLGTG2 H16：38	鬲裆部 Crotch from a *li* tripod	2009-7-12		B	L: 7.2 W: 4.9	夹砂深灰，素面。 Coarse and dark grey, plain.
	09SLGTG2 H16：39	鬲口沿 Rim fragment from a *li* tripod	2009-7-12		B	L: 5.2 W: 3.9	夹云母滑石红褐，方唇，敞口，宽沿。 Reddish-brown with mica and talc tempering, square lip, wide mouth, broad rim.

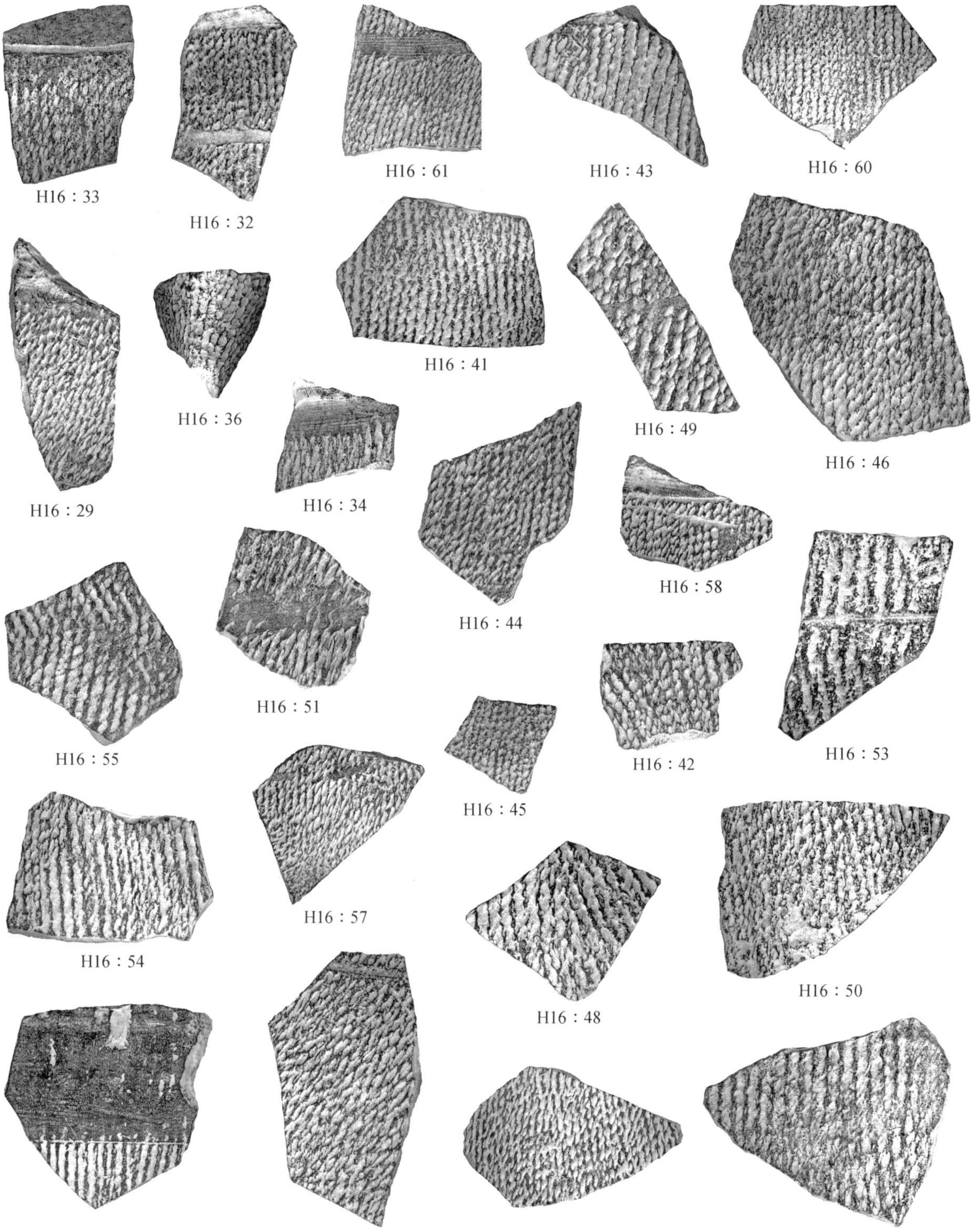

图Ⅰ.5.40　H16出土陶片纹饰

Figure Ⅰ.5.40　Decorated pottery sherds from pit H16.

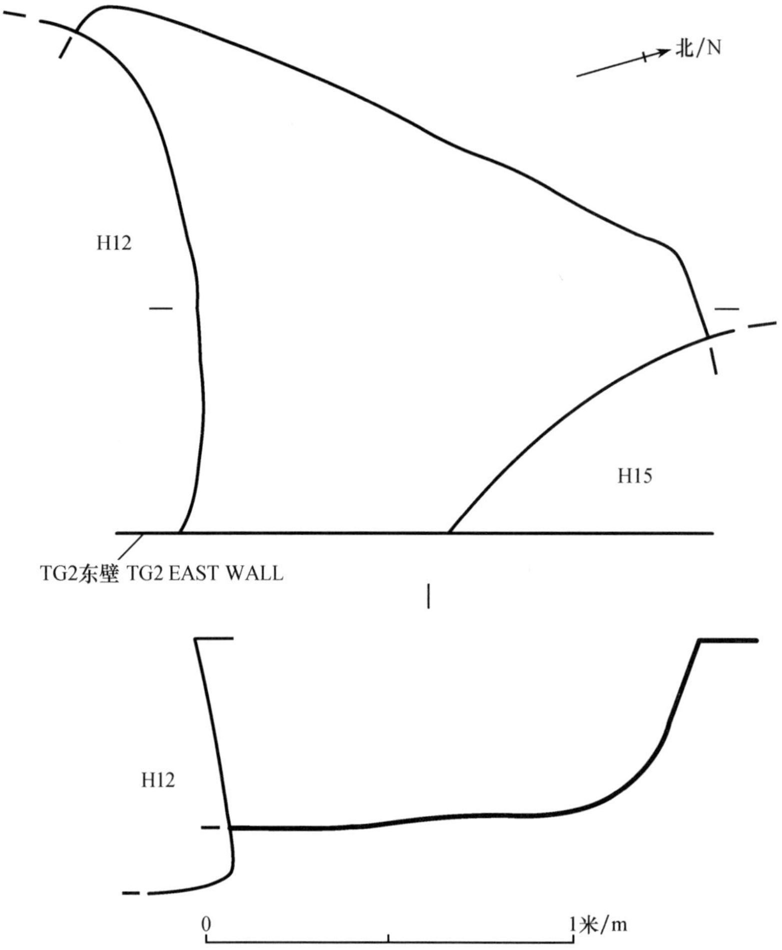

图Ⅰ.5.41　H17平、剖面图

Figure Ⅰ.5.41　Plan and cross-sectional profiles of pit H17.

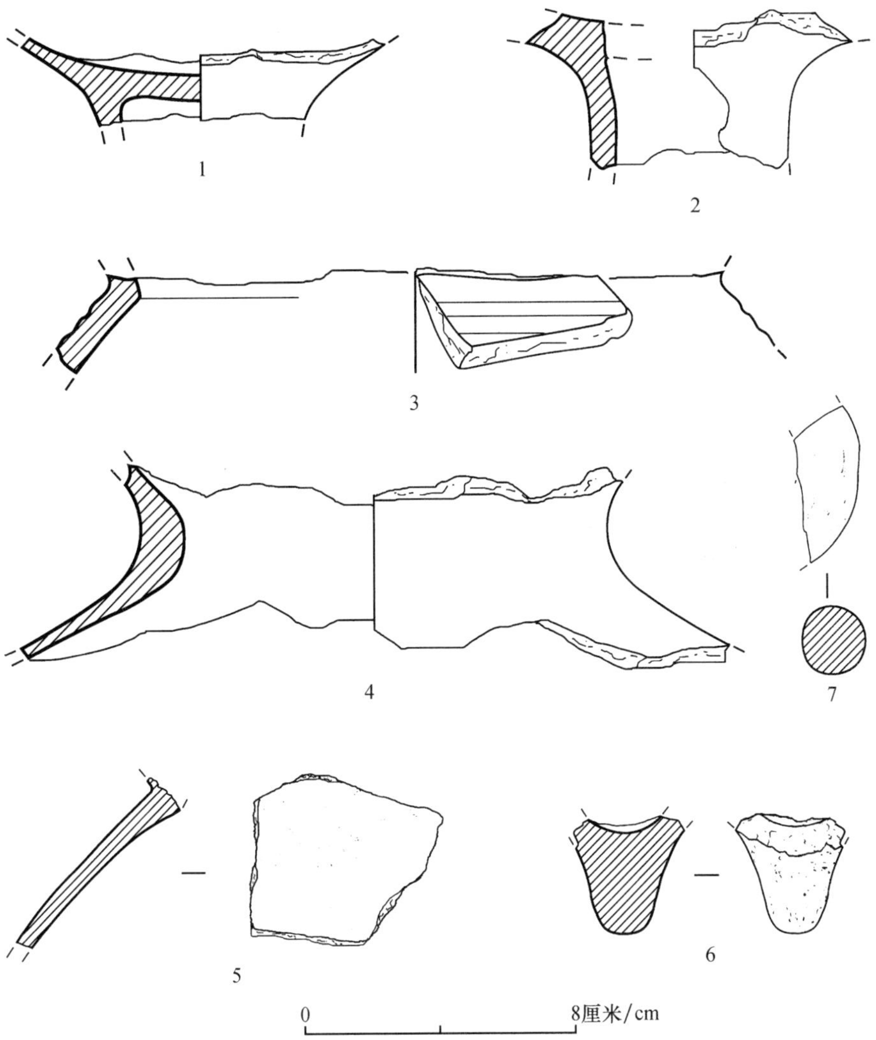

图Ⅰ.5.42　H17出土陶器

1. 豆（H17：1）　2. 豆（H17：2）　3. 罐（H17：10）　4. 罐（H17：7）　5. 罐（H17：15）　6. 鬲（H17：5）
7. 陶环（H17：6）

Figure Ⅰ.5.42　Pottery types from pit H17.

1. *Dou* pedestal dish (H17：1)　2. *Dou* pedestal dish (H17：2)　3. *Guan* jar (H17：10)　4. *Guan* jar (H17：7)　5. *Guan* jar (H17：15)
6. *Li* tripod (H17：5)　7. Pottery ring (H17：6)

表Ⅰ.5.19　H17出土遗物登记表

Table Ⅰ.5.19　Artifacts from pit H17

序号 Number on Fig. Ⅰ.5.42	标本号 Excavation number	器物名称 Artifact name	出土时间 Excavation date	位置 Location	所属类型 Types	尺寸（厘米） Size (cm)	特点描述 Description of features
1	09SLGTG2 H17：1	豆盘 Bowl from a *dou* pedestal dish	2009-7-13		B	L: 9.1 W: 8.6 H: 2	泥质灰褐，浅盘。 Greyish-brown clay, shallow bowl.
2	09SLGTG2 H17：2	豆柄 Stem from a *dou* pedestal dish	2009-7-13		B	L: 4.5 W: 4.7	泥质浅灰，素面。 Light grey clay, plain.
	09SLGTG2 H17：3	豆口沿 Rim fragment from a *dou* pedestal dish	2009-7-13		B	L: 4.4 W: 1.8	泥质浅灰，方唇，口内敛，唇内沿起凸。 Light grey clay, square lip, mouth converges toward the inside, ridge on the inside of the lip.
6	09SLGTG2 H17：5	鬲足 Foot of a *li* tripod	2009-7-13		C	L: 3.5 W: 3.1	夹砂红褐，足起乳头。 Coarse and reddish-brown, nipple-shaped foot.
7	09SLGTG2 H17：6	陶环 Ceramic ring	2009-7-13		B	L: 4.3 W: 2	泥质浅灰，素面。 Light grey clay, plain.
4	09SLGTG2 H17：7	罐口部 Mouth of a *guan* jar	2009-7-13		B	L: 9.5 W: 6.3	泥质浅灰，口外撇，卷沿。 Light grey clay, mouth flares to the outside, rolled rim.
	09SLGTG2 H17：8	罐肩部 Shoulder of a *guan* jar	2009-7-13		B	L: 7 W: 4	泥质深灰，素面磨光，肩部微折，上饰一周弦纹。 Dark grey clay, plain and burnished, shoulder has a small fold, with one ring decoration.
	09SLGTG2 H17：9	罐口部 Mouth of a *guan* jar	2009-7-13		B	L: 6 W: 3	泥质深灰，饰中绳纹，敞口，腹应较直。 Dark grey clay, medium cord decoration, wide mouth, relatively straight belly.
3	09SLGTG2 H17：10	罐 *Guan* jar	2009-7-14		B	L: 6 W: 3	敞口卷沿，泥质浅灰，肩部饰数周凸棱纹。 Wide mouth with rolled rim, light grey clay.
	09SLGTG2 H17：11	鬲口沿 Rim fragment from a *li* tripod	2009-7-14		A	L: 4.7 W: 4.2	泥质深灰，口外撇，卷沿，腹部饰中绳纹。 Dark grey clay, mouth flared outward, rolled rim, medium cord decorations on the belly.
	09SLGTG2 H17：12	鬲口沿 Rim fragment from a *li* tripod	2009-7-14		B	L: 4.2 W: 5.1	夹云母灰褐，素面，方唇，敞口，口沿较宽。 Greyish-brown with mica tempering, plain, square lip, wide mouth, relatively broad rim.
	09SLGTG2 H17：13	鬲腹上部 Upper belly from a *li* tripod	2009-7-14		B	L: 4.5 W: 7.2	夹云母灰褐，敞口。 Greyish-brown with mica tempering, wide mouth.
	09SLGTG2 H17：14	鼎口沿 Rim fragment from a *ding* cauldron	2009-7-14			L: 2.9 W: 3.7	夹砂红褐，方唇，敞口，折沿，素面。 Coarse and reddish-brown, square lip, wide mouth, folded rim, plain.
5	09SLGTG2 H17：15	罐 *Guan* jar	2009-7-14			L: 5.7 W: 4.8	夹砂灰陶，折沿，素面。 Coarse grey ceramic, folded rim, plain.

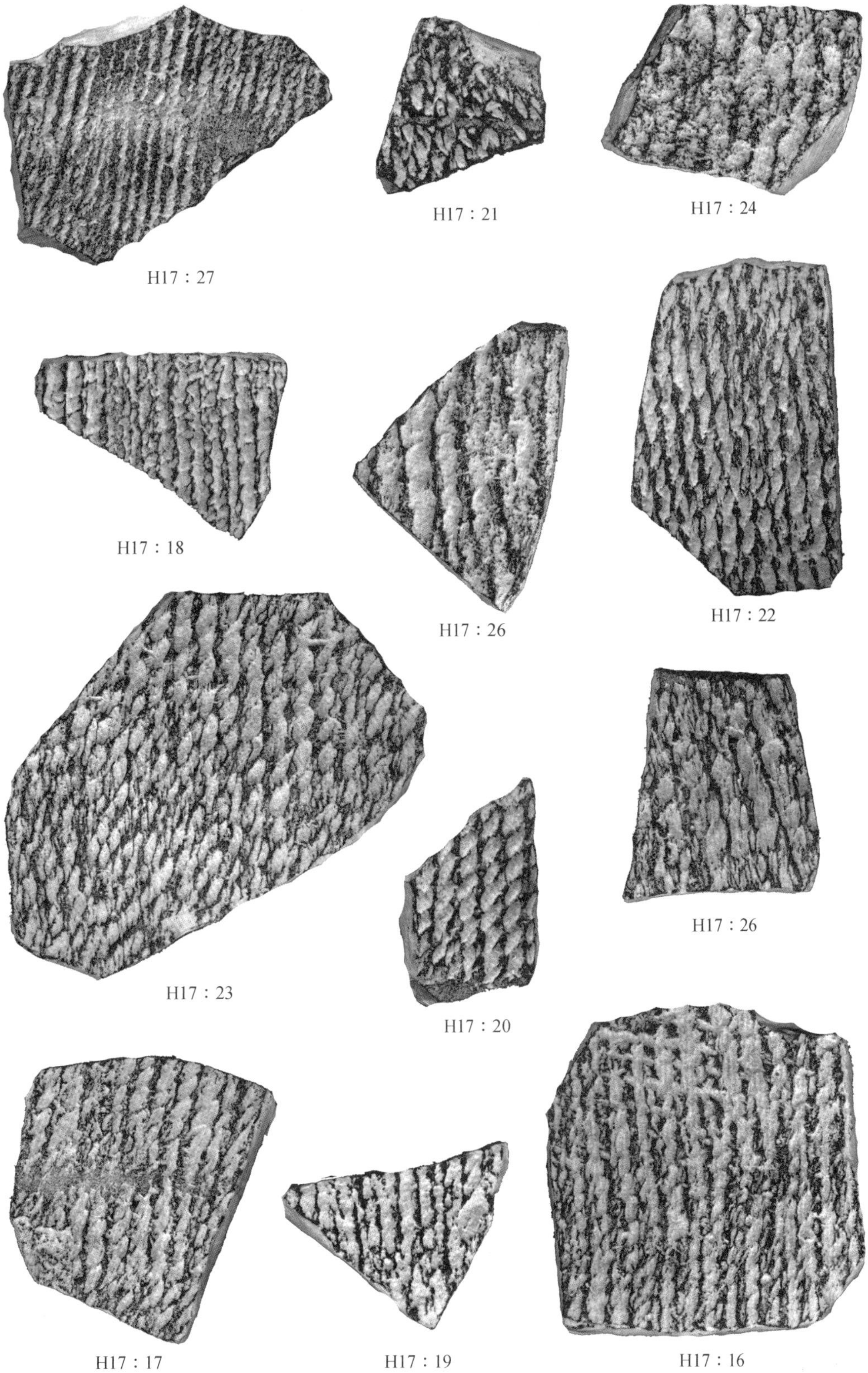

图Ⅰ.5.43　H17出土陶片纹饰

Figure Ⅰ.5.43　Decorated pottery sherds from pit H17.

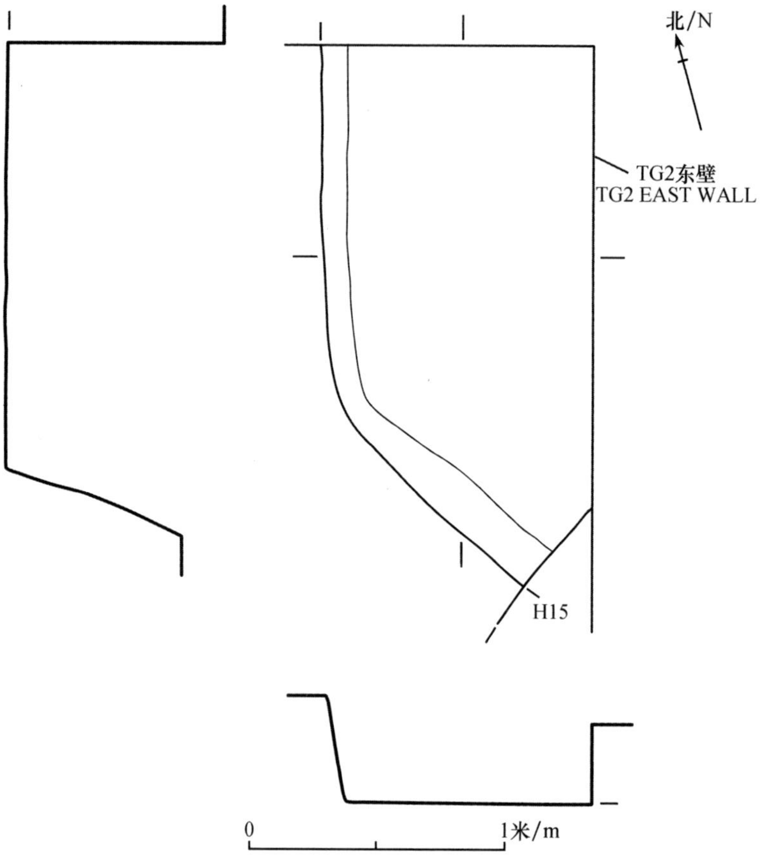

图Ⅰ.5.44　H18平、剖面图
Figure Ⅰ.5.44　Plan and cross-sectional profiles of pit H18.

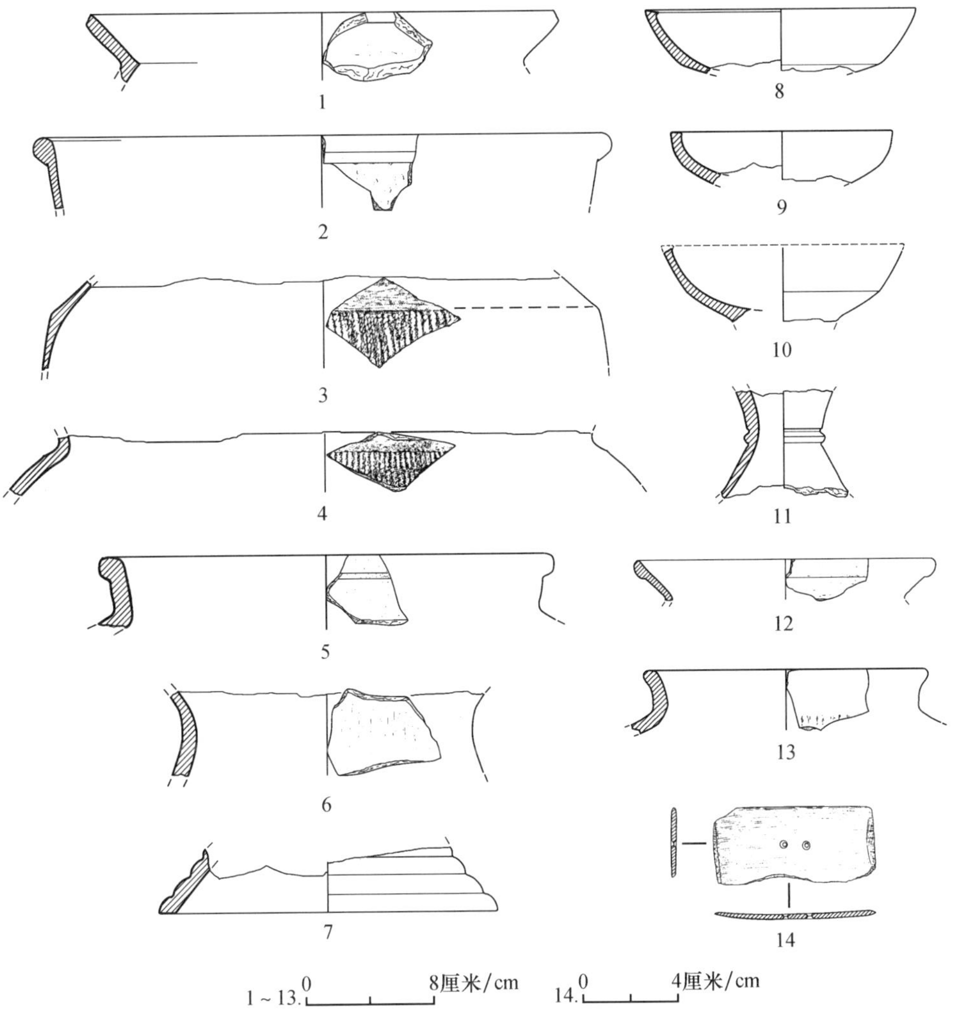

图Ⅰ.5.45　H18出土陶器

1. 鬲（H18：25）　2. 罐（H18：7）　3. 罐（H18：16）　4. 罐（H18：17）　5. 罐（H18：20）　6. 鬲（H18：26）　7. 器盖（H18：15）　8. 豆（H18：9）　9. 豆（H18：10）　10. 豆（H18：12）　11. 豆（H18：11）　12. 鬲（H18：22）　13. 罐（H18：4）　14. 骨器（H18：2）

Figure Ⅰ.5.45　Pottery types from pit H18.

1. *Li* tripod (H18：25)　2. *Guan* jar (H18：7)　3. *Guan* jar (H18：16)　4. *Guan* jar (H18：17)　5. *Guan* jar (H18：20)　6. *Li* tripod (H18：26)　7. Vessel lid (H18：15)　8. *Dou* pedestal dish (H18：9)　9. *Dou* pedestal dish (H18：10)　10. *Dou* pedestal dish (H18：12)　11. *Dou* pedestal dish (H18：11)　12. *Li* tripod (H18：22)　13. *Guan* jar (H18：4)　14. Bone tool (H18：2)

表Ⅰ.5.20　H18出土遗物登记表

Table Ⅰ.5.20　Artifacts from pit H18

序号 Number on Fig. Ⅰ.5.45	标本号 Excavation number	器物名称 Artifact name	出土时间 Excavation date	位置 Location	所属类型 Types	尺寸（厘米）Size (cm)	特点描述 Description of features
	09SLGTG2 H18：1	铜渣 Copper slag	2009-7-13	630×150 −60		L: 7.3 W: 1.3	圆体状，仅剩一尖状突起可辨。Round, only one tip-like protrusion shows that it is copper.
14	09SLGTG2 H18：2	骨器 Bone tool	2009-7-13			L: 7 W: 3.2 T: 0.2	长方形片状。基本完整。器中部有二孔，对钻而成，孔径0.2厘米。Flat and rectangular. Nearly complete. Two holes at the center, made by drilling from two sides. The holes are 0.2 cm in diameter.
	09SLGTG2 H18：3	豆圈足 Ring foot from a *dou* pedestal dish	2009-7-13		B	L: 4.8 W: 2.7 H: 2.4	泥质浅灰，圈足外撇。Light grey clay, circular foot flared to the outside.
13	09SLGTG2 H18：4	罐口沿 Rim fragment from a *guan* jar	2009-7-13		D	M: 17.9 H: 3.7	泥质浅灰，圆唇敞口，低领，卷沿，腹应鼓。领下饰绳纹。Light grey clay, rounded lip and wide mouth, low collar, rolled rim, bulging belly. Cord decorations below the collar.
	09SLGTG2 H18：5	簋圈足 Round foot from a *gui* tureen	2009-7-13			L: 7 W: 3.5 H: 1.6	泥质浅灰，素面。Light grey clay, plain.
	09SLGTG2 H18：6	簋圈足 Round foot from a *gui* tureen	2009-7-13			L: 5.9 W: 4.5	泥质浅灰，圆唇，宽沿，沿外部饰中绳纹有抹痕。Light grey clay, rounded lip, broad rim, moderate cord decorations with smear marks on the outside of the rim.
2	09SLGTG2 H18：7	罐 *Guan* jar	2009-7-13			M: 35.9 H: 4.8	泥质浅灰，圆唇，外部饰中绳纹。Light grey clay, rounded lip, medium cord decorations on the outside.
	09SLGTG2 H18：8	鬲口沿 Rim fragment from a *li* tripod	2009-7-13		B	L: 4.1 W: 2.4	夹砂灰褐，尖唇外卷。Coarse and greyish-brown, sharp lip rolled to the outside.
8	09SLGTG2 H18：9	豆盘 Bowl from a *dou* pedestal dish	2009-7-13		B	M: 17 H: 3.7	泥质浅灰，素面，方唇，唇内缘凸起，盘下部微折。Light grey clay, plain, square lip, ridge on the inside edge of the lip, small fold in the bottom of the bowl.
9	09SLGTG2 H18：10	豆盘 Bowl from a *dou* pedestal dish	2009-7-13		B	M: 14 H: 3.2	泥质深灰，方唇直口，素面。Dark grey clay, square lip and straight mouth, plain.
11	09SLGTG2 H18：11	豆柄 Stem from a *dou* pedestal dish	2009-7-13		B	L: 7.2 W: 6.3	泥质深灰，柄部有凸棱，素面。Dark grey clay, with a rib on the handle, plain.
10	09SLGTG2 H18：12	豆 *Dou* pedestal dish	2009-7-14		A	M: 15.3 H: 4.4	泥质浅灰，方唇。唇沿内援突起，素面。Light grey clay, square lip, protrusion on the inside of the lip, plain.
	09SLGTG2 H18：13	簋圈足 Ring foot from a *gui* tureen	2009-7-14			L: 8.1 W: 4 H: 4	泥质浅灰，素面，足尖外撇。Light grey clay, plain, tip of the foot flares out.
10	09SLGTG2 H18：14	簋圈足 Ring foot from a *gui* tureen	2009-7-14			L: 5 W: 3.2	泥质深灰，尖唇，唇沿内侧有凹槽。素面。Dark grey clay, sharp lip, groove on the inside of the lip. Plain.
7	09SLGTG2 H18：15	器盖 Vessel lid	2009-7-14		A1	L: 4.9 W: 11.5 H: 4.2	泥质浅灰陶，圈足外饰三周凹弦纹。Light grey clay, three ring decorations on the outside of the foot.
3	09SLGTG2 H18：16	罐肩部 Shoulder from a *guan* jar	2009-7-14		B	L: 8.2 W: 6	泥质浅灰，肩部以下饰中绳纹。Light grey clay, medium cord decoration below the shoulder.

续表

序号 Number on Fig. Ⅰ.5.45	标本号 Excavation number	器物名称 Artifact name	出土时间 Excavation date	位置 Location	所属类型 Types	尺寸（厘米）Size (cm)	特点描述 Description of features
4	09SLGTG2 H18：17	罐肩部 Shoulder from a *guan* jar	2009-7-14		B	L: 8.2 W: 5	泥质深灰，卷沿，饰中绳纹。Dark grey clay, rolled rim, medium cord decoration.
	09SLGTG2 H18：18	罐肩部 Shoulder from a *guan* jar	2009-7-14		B	L: 7 W: 3.3	泥质深灰，肩微折，腹部饰中绳纹。Dark grey clay, small fold in the shoulder, medium cord decoration on the belly.
	09SLGTG2 H18：19	罐肩部 Shoulder from a *guan* jar	2009-7-14		B	L: 7.3 W: 13.3	腹部饰带状中绳纹，间隔被抹去。Belly has bands of medium cord decoration, smeared at intervals.
5	09SLGTG2 H18：20	罐口沿 Rim fragment from a *guan* jar	2009-7-14		B	L: 5.2 W: 4.3	泥质浅灰，圆唇外撇，领较高，卷沿，素面。Light grey pottery, rounded lip that flares to the outside, collar relatively high, rolled rim, plain.
	09SLGTG2 H18：21	罐口沿 Rim fragment from a *guan* jar	2009-7-14		B	L: 3.1 W: 3.5	泥质深灰，圆唇，敞口，素面。Dark grey clay, rounded rim, wide mouth, plain.
12	09SLGTG2 H18：22	鬲口沿 Rim fragment from a *li* tripod	2009-7-14		C	L: 5.6 W: 3.4	夹云母红褐，圆唇敞口，折沿，素面。Reddish-brown with mica tempering, rounded lip flares outward, folded rim, plain.
	09SLGTG2 H18：23	鬲口沿 Rim fragment from a *li* tripod	2009-7-14		B	L: 4.2 W: 3.6	夹砂红陶，卷沿，素面。Coarse red ceramic, rolled rim, plain.
	09SLGTG2 H18：24	鬲口沿 Rim fragment from a *li* tripod	2009-7-14		B	L: 3.8 W: 4.7	夹砂红陶，素面，小折沿。Coarse red ceramic, small fold in the rim.
1	09SLGTG2 H18：25	鬲口沿 Rim fragment from a *li* tripod	2009-7-14		B	L: 6.9 W: 4.5	夹云母滑石红褐，素面，方唇，宽折沿。Reddish-brown with mica and talc tempering, plain, square lip, broad folded rim.
6	09SLGTG2 H18：26	鬲口沿 Rim fragment from a *li* tripod	2009-7-14			L: 6.9 W: 4.5	夹云母滑石红褐，素面。Reddish-brown with mica and talc tempering, plain.
	09SLGTG2 H18：27	豆盘 Bowl from a *dou* pedestal dish	2009-7-14			L: 3.5 W: 39	泥质浅灰，方唇，唇缘内凸。Light grey clay, square lip, protrusion on the inside of the lip.
	09SLGTG2 H18：12	豆盘 Bowl from a *dou* pedestal dish	2009-7-14			L: 6.4 W: 7.1	泥质深灰，素面磨光，盘较深，盘外部微折。Dark grey clay, plain and burnished, bowl relatively deep, small fold on the outside of the bowl.

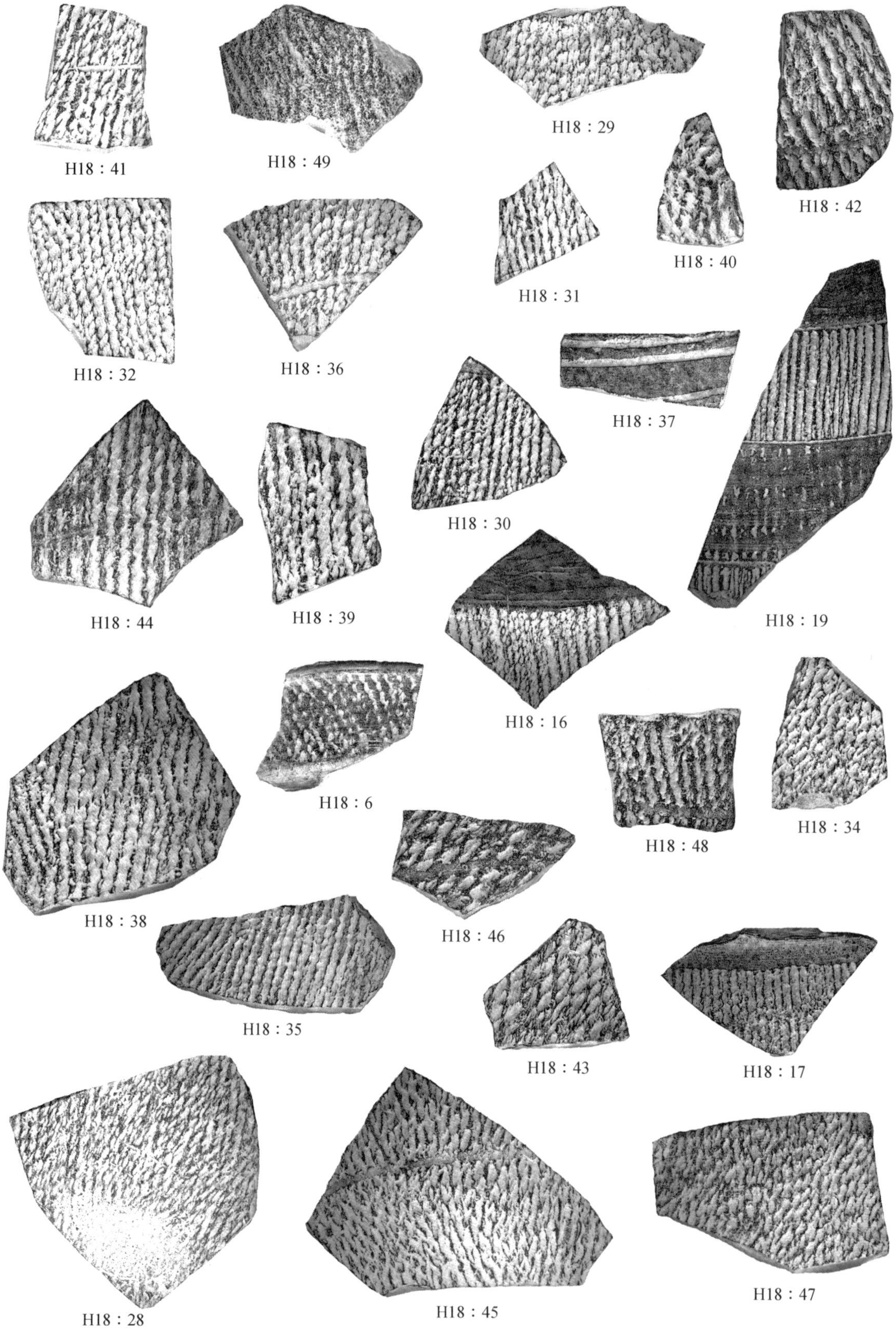

图Ⅰ.5.46　H18出土陶片纹饰

Figure Ⅰ.5.46　Decorated pottery sherds from pit H18.

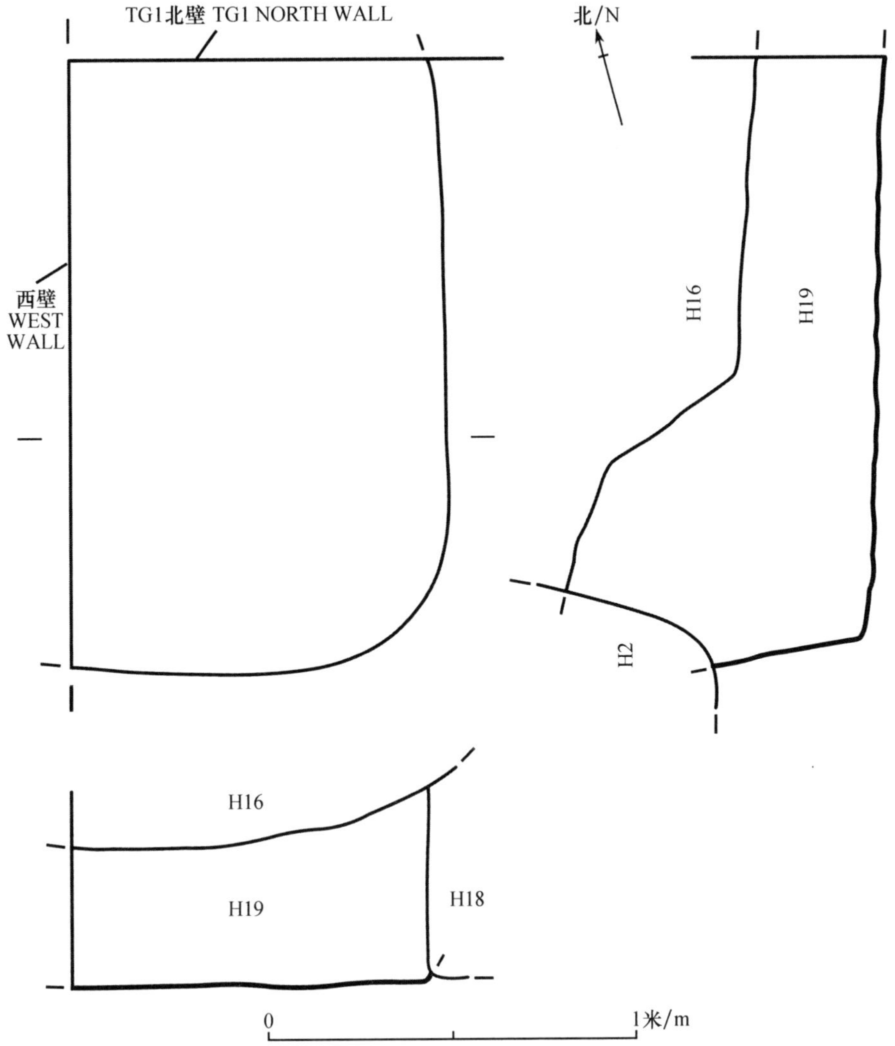

图Ⅰ.5.47　H19平、剖面图

FigureⅠ.5.47　Plan and cross-sectional profiles of pit H19.

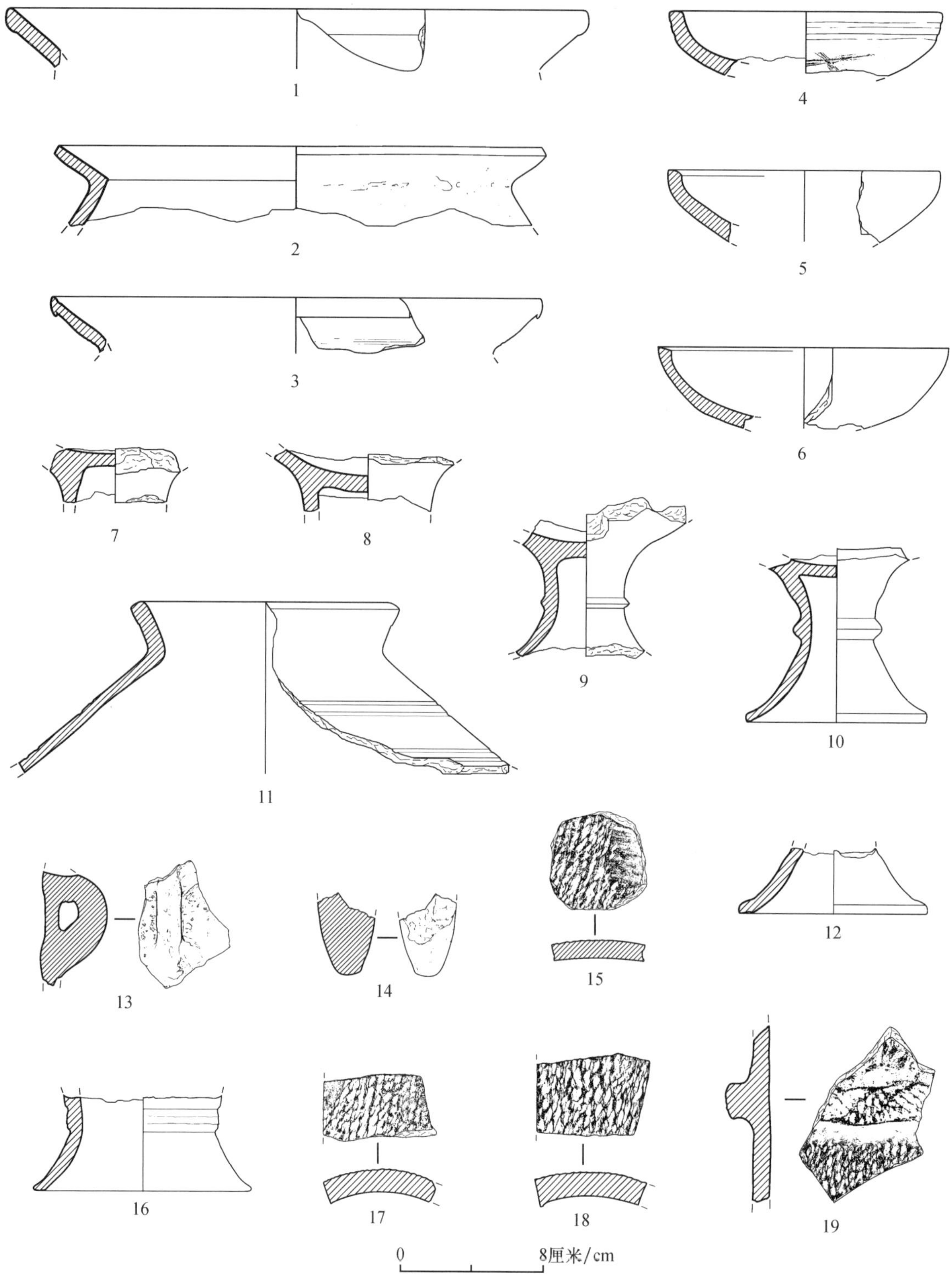

图Ⅰ.5.48　H19出土陶器

1. 簋（H19：8）　2. 罐（H19：19）　3. 罐（H19：17）　4. 豆（H19：2）　5. 豆（H19：6）　6.豆（H19：5）　7. 豆（H19：27）　8. 豆（H19：9）　9. 豆（H19：3）　10. 豆（H19：4）　11. 罐（H19：10）　12. 豆（H19：21）　13. 罐（H19：26）　14. 鬲（H19：1）　15. 圆陶片（H19：20）　16. 豆（H19：12）　17. 瓦（H19：68）　18. 瓦（H19：69）　19. 罐（H19：25）

Figure Ⅰ.5.48　Pottery types from pit H19.

1. *Gui* tureen (H19：8)　2. *Guan* jar (H19：19)　3. *Guan* jar (H19：17)　4. *Dou* pedestal dish (H19：2)　5. *Dou* pedestal dish (H19：6)　6. *Dou* pedestal dish (H19：5)　7. *Dou* pedestal dish (H19：27)　8. *Dou* pedestal dish (H19：9)　9. *Dou* pedestal dish (H19：3)　10. *Dou* pedestal dish (H19：4)　11. *Guan* jar (H19：10)　12. *Dou* pedestal dish (H19：21)　13. *Guan* jar (H19：26)　14. *Li* tripod (H19：1)　15. Round pottery sherd (H19：20)　16. *Dou* pedestal dish (H19：12)　17. Tile (H19：68)　18. Tile (H19：69)　19. *Guan* jar (H19：25)

表Ⅰ.5.21　H19出土遗物登记表
Table Ⅰ.5.21　Artifacts from Pit H19

序号 Number on Fig. Ⅰ.5.48	标本号 Excavation number	器物名称 Artifact name	出土时间 Excavation date	位置 Location	所属类型 Types	尺寸（厘米）Size (cm)	特点描述 Description of features
14	09SLGTG2 H19：1	鬲足 Foot from a *li* tripod	2009-7-14		C	W: 4.5 H: 2.8	夹砂深灰，实足尖。Coarse and dark grey, sharp foot.
4	09SLGTG2 H19：2	豆盘 Bowl of a *dou* pedestal dish	2009-7-14		B	M: 15 H: 3.4	泥质深灰，方唇，沿微折，口沿上部饰两周凹弦纹。Dark grey clay, square lips, small fold on the rim, two intaglio ring decorations on the rim.
9	09SLGTG2 H19：3	残豆柄 Broken stem of a *dou* pedestal dish	2009-7-14		B	M: 9.2 W: 8.1 H: 7.8	泥质深灰，素面磨光，细柄饰凸棱。Dark grey clay, plain and burnished, thin stem with rib on it.
10	09SLGTG2 H19：4	豆 *Dou* pedestal dish	2009-7-14		B2	M: 7.6 W: 7 B: 8.4 H: 7.8	上部残，泥质浅灰，高柄束腰，柄部有凸棱。Upper part broken, light grey clay, waist of the stem high, with ribbing.
6	09SLGTG2 H19：5	豆盘 Bowl of a *dou* pedestal dish	2009-7-14		B	M: 16 H: 4.4	泥质深灰，素面磨光，方唇，直口，盘微折。Dark grey clay, plain and burnished, square lip, straight mouth, small fold in the bowl.
5	09SLGTG2 H19：6	豆盘 Bowl of a *dou* pedestal dish	2009-7-14		B	M: 15 H: 3.8	泥质浅灰，素面，方圆唇，盘微弧形。Light grey clay, plain, square and rounded lip, bowl has slightly curved shape.
	09SLGTG2 H19：7	簋圈足 Circular foot of a *gui* tureen	2009-7-14			L: 2.7 W: 3.8 H: 2.8	泥质浅灰，素面，圈足外撇。Light grey clay, plain, circular foot flares to the outside.
1	09SLGTG2 H19：8	簋口沿 Rim fragment from a *gui* tureen	2009-7-14			M: 32 H: 3.2	泥质深灰，尖唇，沿较宽，沿外饰绳纹有抹痕。Dark grey clay, sharp lip, rim relatively broad, cord decorations with smearing on the outside of the rim.
8	09SLGTG2 H19：9	豆盘 Bowl of a *dou* pedestal dish	2009-7-14		A	W: 9.8 L: 8 H: 3.4	泥质深灰，素面。Plain, dark grey clay.
11	09SLGTG2 H19：10	罐口部 Opening of a *guan* jar	2009-7-14		E	L: 15 W: 11.5 H: 9.6	泥质浅灰，圆唇，低领，卷沿，平肩，肩部饰数周凹弦纹。Light grey clay, rounded lip, low collar, rolled rim, flat shoulder, several intaglio rings on the shoulder.
	09SLGTG2 H19：11	壶 *Hu* pot	2009-7-14			L: 6.6 W: 6.8	泥质浅灰，饰绳纹。Light grey clay, cord decorations.
16	09SLGTG2 H19：12	豆圈足 Circular foot from a *dou* pedestal dish	2009-7-14		B2	W: 7 L: 5.6 H: 5.2	泥质浅灰，粗柄，柄部凸棱退化。Light grey clay, thick stem, degraded ridge on the stem.
	09SLGTG2 H19：13	罐肩部 Shoulder from a *guan* jar	2009-7-15		C	L: 11.2 W: 7.3	泥质浅灰，肩微折，肩部饰两周凹弦纹，腹部饰绳纹。Light grey clay, small fold on the shoulder, two rings on the shoulder, cord decorations on the belly.
	09SLGTG2 H19：14	罐腹部 Shoulder from a *guan* jar	2009-7-15		B	L: 7.3 W: 5.6	泥质浅灰，溜肩，腹部饰中绳纹。Light grey clay, sloping shoulder, medium cord decorations on the belly.
3	09SLGTG2 H19：17	罐 *Guan* jar	2009-7-15			M: 27 H: 3	泥质浅灰，方唇，唇缘外凸，沿口有凹槽，卷沿，素面。Light grey clay, square lip, protrusion on the outside of the lip, groove on the rolled rim, plain.

续表

序号 Number on Fig. Ⅰ.5.48	标本号 Excavation number	器物名称 Artifact name	出土时间 Excavation date	位置 Location	所属类型 Types	尺寸（厘米） Size (cm)	特点描述 Description of features
	09SLGTG2 H19：18	簋口沿 Rim fragment from a *gui* tureen	2009-7-15			L: 6 W: 4.2	泥质深灰，方唇，唇缘外凸，沿上有凹槽，沿应稍宽，外饰绳纹有抹痕。 Dark grey clay, square lip, ridge on the outside of the lip, groove on the rim, rim somewhat broad, cord decoration with smearing on the outside.
2	09SLGTG2 H19：19	罐口沿 Rim fragment from a *guan* jar	2009-7-15		C	M: 27 H: 4.4	夹云母灰褐，方唇，敞口，折沿，素面。 Greyish-brown with mica inclusions, square lip, wide mouth, folded rim, plain.
15	09SLGTG2 H19：20	圆陶片 Round pottery sherd	2009-7-15			L: 5.7 W: 5 T: 1	泥质浅灰，大致呈圆形，一面是中绳纹，一面素面。 Light grey clay, roughly circular in shape, one side with medium cord decoration, one side plain.
12	09SLGTG2 H19：21	豆圈足 Circular foot from a *dou* pedestal dish	2009-7-15		A	W: 5 L: 5.8 H: 4.4	泥质浅灰磨光，圈足外撇内起凹槽，素面。 Light grey clay, burnished, circular foot flares to the outside, groove along the inside. Plain.
	09SLGTG2 H19：22	罐肩部 Shoulder from a *guan* jar	2009-7-15		B	L: 5.5 W: 4.4	折肩，泥质深灰磨光，素面。 Folded shoulder, dark grey clay with burnishing, plain.
	09SLGTG2 H19：23	簋口沿 Rim fragment from a *gui* tureen	2009-7-15			L: 7.2 W: 4.9	泥质浅灰，尖唇，宽沿，外饰绳纹有抹痕。 Light grey clay, sharp lip, broad rim, cord decorations with smearing on the outside.
	09SLGTG2 H19：24	罐口沿 Rim fragment from a *guan* jar	2009-7-15		B	L: 4.2 W: 3.1	泥质红褐，圆唇敞口，唇外缘微凸。 Reddish-brown clay, rounded lip and wide mouth, outside of the lip slightly convex.
19	09SLGTG2 H19：25	罐腹部 Shoulder from a *guan* jar	2009-7-15		C	L: 7.8 W: 9.5	泥质浅灰，饰附加堆纹和中绳纹。 Light grey clay, attached appliqué decoration and medium cord decorations.
13	09SLGTG2 H19：26	罐把手 Handle from a *guan* jar	2009-7-15		B	L: 5.3 W: 6.6	泥质浅灰。 Light grey clay.
7	09SLGTG2 H19：27	豆 *Dou* pedestal dish	2009-7-15		B	W: 6 L: 4.2 H: 3	泥质浅灰，柄较细，素面。 Light grey clay, relatively thin stem, plain.
	09SLGTG2 H19：28	豆盘 Bowl from a *dou* pedestal dish	2009-7-15		B	W: 8.5 L: 5.6	泥质深灰磨光，素面，盘微折。 Dark grey clay with burnishing, plain, small fold in the bowl.
	09SLGTG2 H19：29	豆圈足 Circular foot from a *dou* pedestal dish	2009-7-15			W: 6.6 L: 4.8 H: 2.3	泥质深灰。 Dark grey clay.
	09SLGTG2 H19：30	罐肩部 Shoulder from a *guan* jar	2009-7-15		B	L: 4.3 W: 5.7	折肩，肩部饰两周凹弦纹，腹部饰绳纹。 Folded shoulder, two bands of ring decoration on the shoulder, cord decorations on the belly.
	09SLGTG2 H19：31	罐肩部 Shoulder from a *guan* jar	2009-7-15		B	L: 5.7 W: 5	泥质浅灰，磨光，折沿。 Light grey clay, burnished, folded rim.
	09SLGTG2 H19：32	瓿 *Bu* vase	2009-7-15			L: 4 W: 3	泥质浅灰。圈足外撇，素面。 Light grey clay. Circular foot flares to the outside, plain.
17	09SLGTG2 H19：68	瓦 Tile	2009-7-15		B	L: 4.1 W: 6.3 T: 1.2	泥质浅灰，粗绳纹。 Light grey clay, coarse cord decorations.

续表

序号 Number on Fig. Ⅰ.5.48	标本号 Excavation number	器物名称 Artifact name	出土时间 Excavation date	位置 Location	所属类型 Types	尺寸（厘米） Size (cm)	特点描述 Description of features
18	09SLGTG2 H19：69	瓦 Tile	2009-7-15		B	L: 3 W: 6.5 T: 1	泥质浅灰，粗绳纹。 Light grey clay, coarse cord decorations.
	09SLGTG2 H19：70	盆 *Pen* basin	2009-7-15			L: 12.8 W: 16.8	泥质深灰。 Dark grey clay.

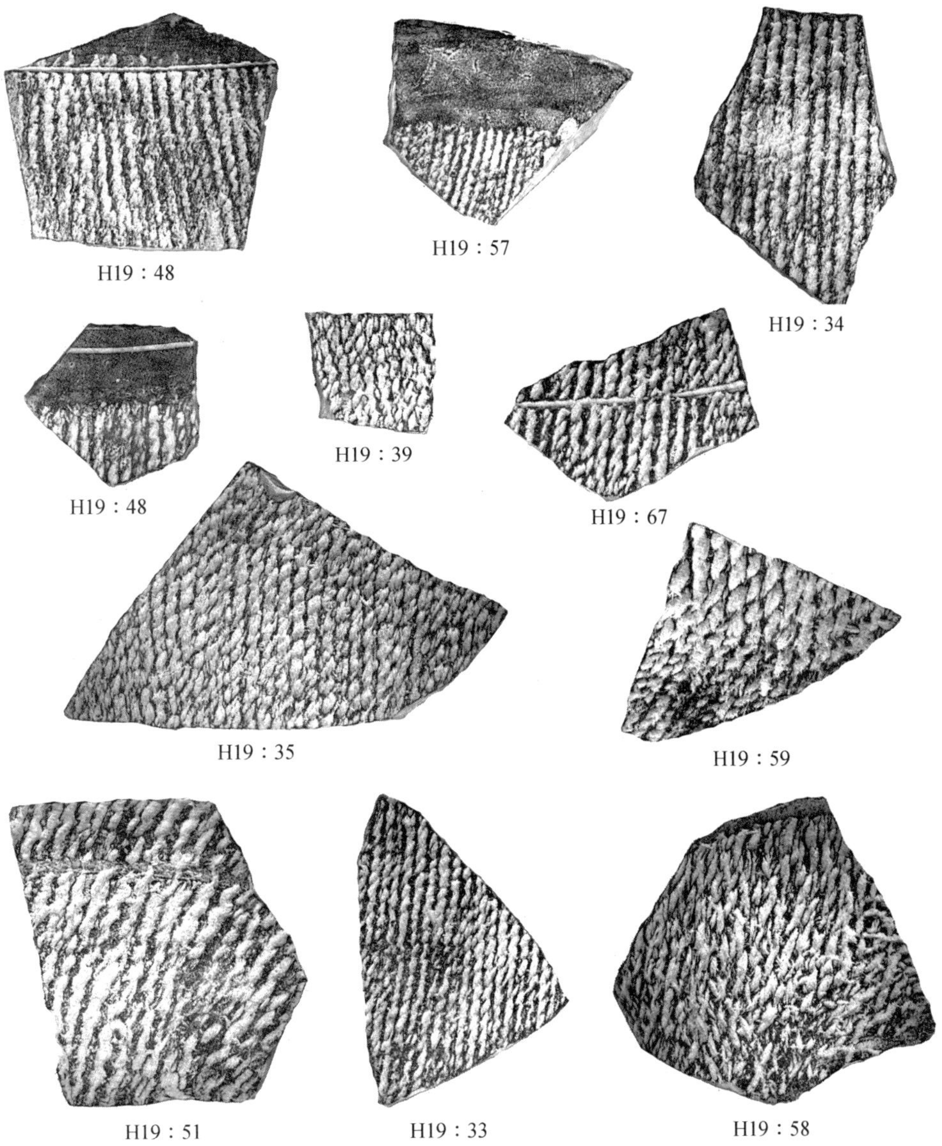

图Ⅰ.5.49　H19出土陶片纹饰

Figure Ⅰ.5.49　Decorated pottery sherds from pit H19.

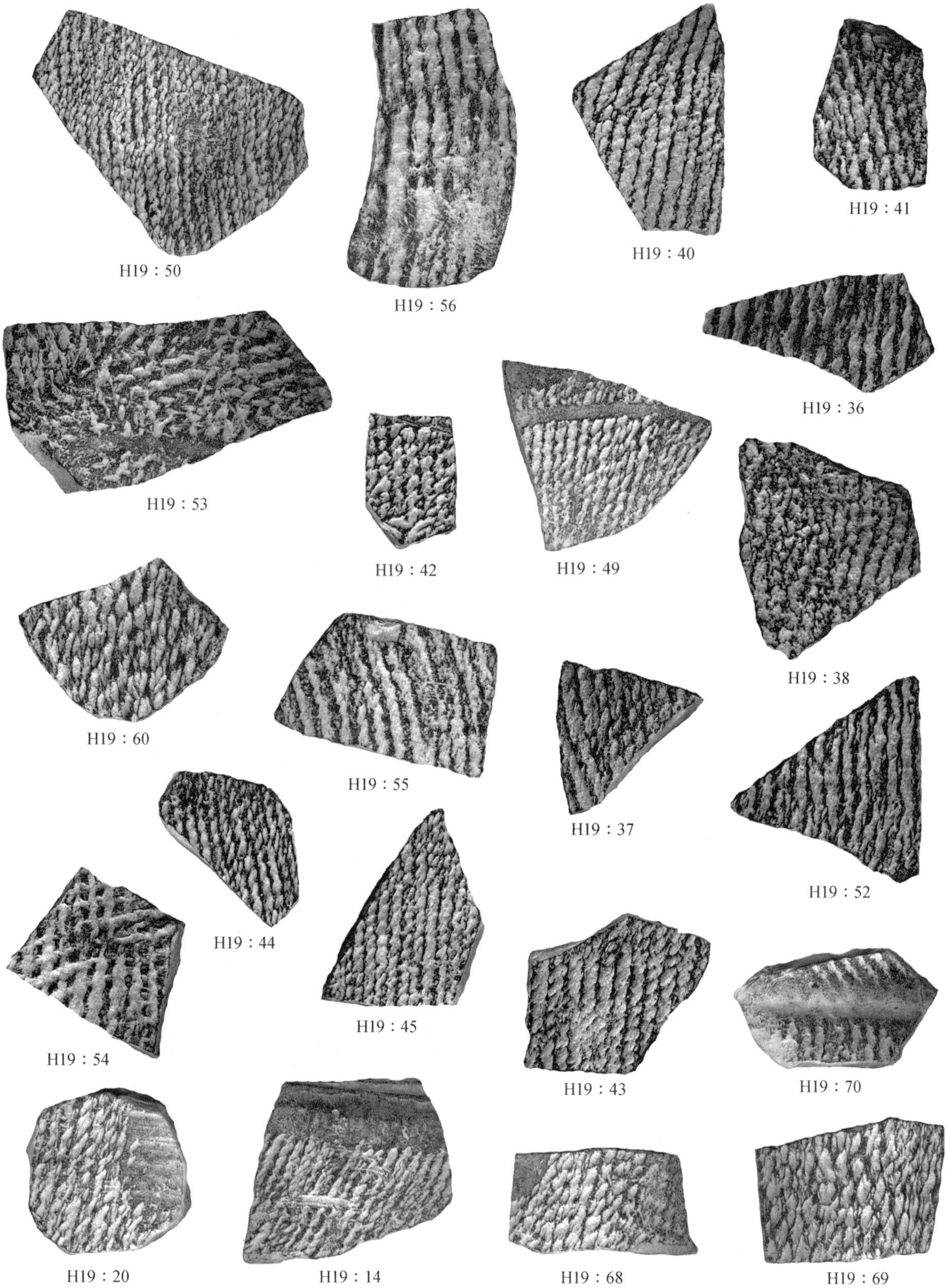

图Ⅰ.5.50　H19出土陶片纹饰

Figure Ⅰ.5.50　Decorated pottery sherds from pit H19.

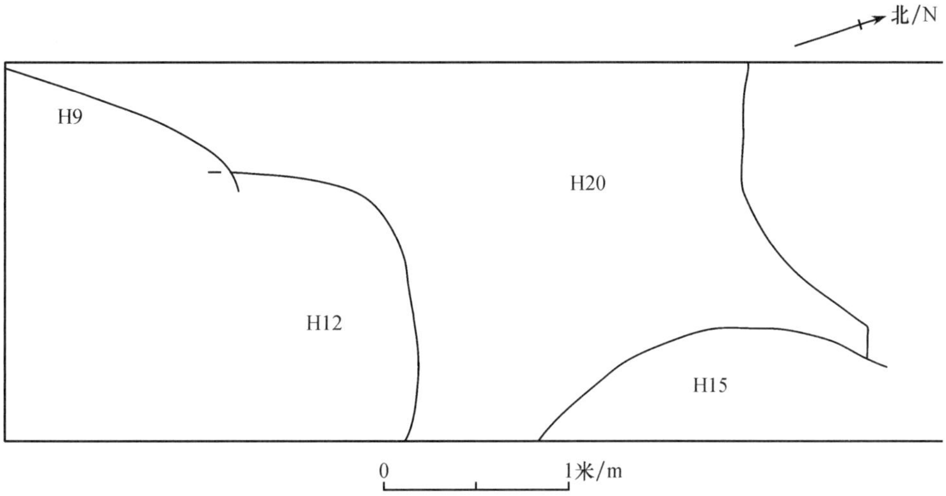

图Ⅰ.5.51　H20①平面图
Figure Ⅰ.5.51　Plain of pit H20, stratum ①.

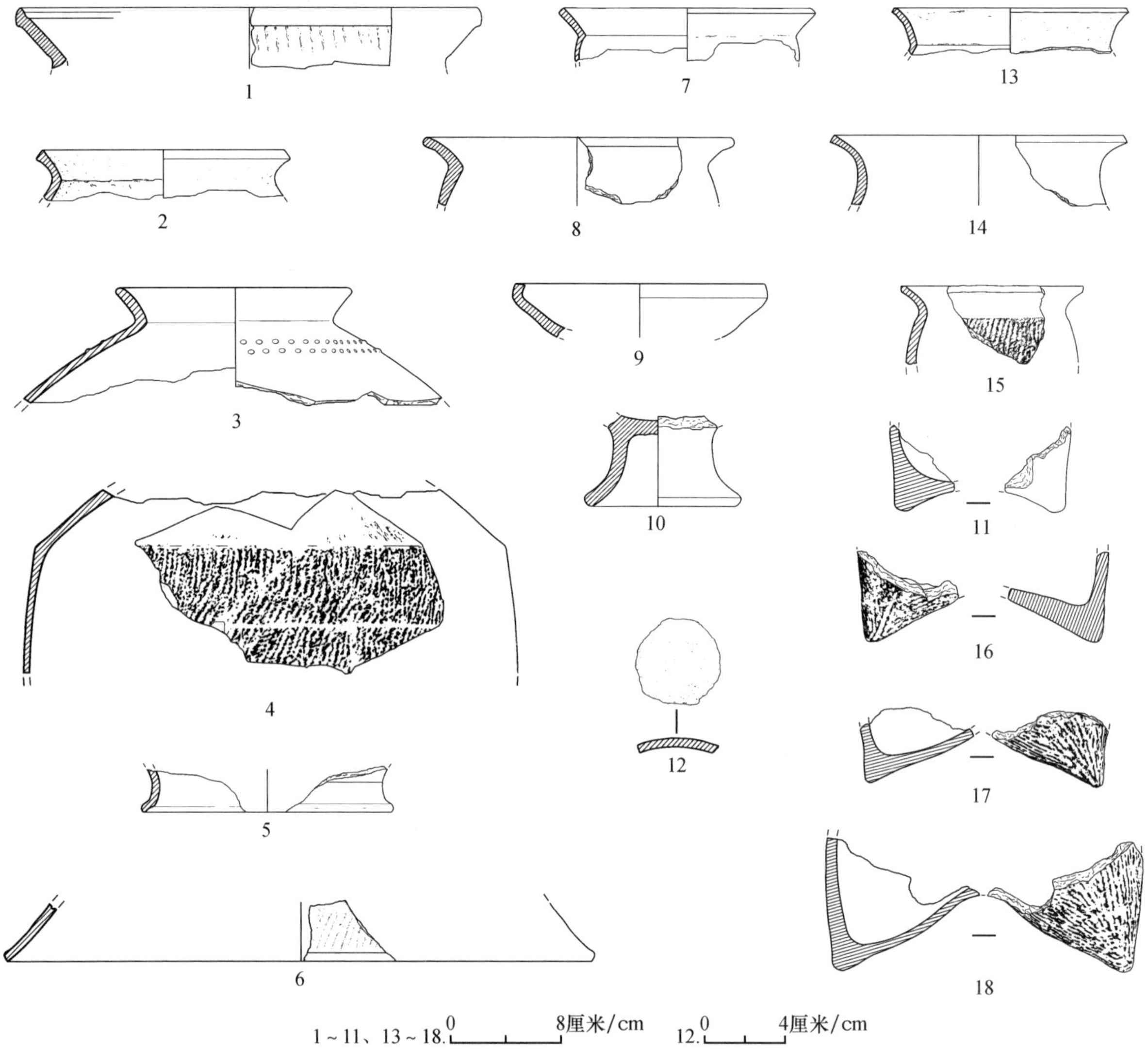

图Ⅰ.5.52　H20第1层出土陶器

1. 簋（H20①：18）　2. 鬲（H20①：2）　3. 罐（H20①：21）　4. 罐（H20①：25）　5.簋（H20①：20）　6. 簋（H20①：136）　7. 鬲(H20①：19)　8. 鬲（H20①：9）　9. 豆(H20①：28)　10. 豆（H20①：16）　11. 鬲（H20①：12）　12. 圆陶片（H20①：23）　13. 鬲（H20①：10）　14. 鬲（H20①：11）　15. 鬲（H20①：33）　16. 鬲（20①：14）　17. 鬲（H20①：15）　18. 鬲（H20①：13）

Figure Ⅰ.5.52　Pottery types from pit H20, stratum ①.

1. *Gui* tureen (H20①：18)　2. *Li* tripod (H20①：2)　3. *Guan* jar (H20①：21)　4. *Guan* jar (H20①：25)　5. *Gui* tureen (H20①：20)　6. *Gui* tureen (H20①：136)　7. *Li* tripod (H20①：19)　8. *Li* tripod (H20①：9)　9. *Dou* pedestal dish (H20①：28)　10. *Dou* pedestal dish (H20①：16)　11. *Li* tripod (H20①：12)　12. Round pottery sherd (H20①：23)　13. *Li* tripod (H20①：10)　14. *Li* tripod (H20①：11)　15. *Li* tripod (H20①：33)　16. *Li* tripod (20①：14)　17. *Li* tripod (H20①：15)　18. *Li* tripod (H20①：13)

表Ⅰ.5.22　H20①出土遗物登记表
Table Ⅰ.5.22　Artifacts from pit H20①

序号 Number on Fig. Ⅰ.5.52	标本号 Excavation number	器物名称 Artifact name	出土时间 Excavation date	位置 Location	所属类型 Types	尺寸(厘米) Size (cm)	特点描述 Description of features
8	09SLGTG2 H20①：9	鬲口沿 Rim fragment from a *li* tripod	2009-7-14			M: 22.6 H: 4.6	夹云母滑石红褐，圆唇，口外撇，折沿，素面。 Reddish-brown with mica and talc tempering, rounded lip, flare on the outside of the mouth, folded rim, plain.
13	09SLGTG2 H20①：10	鬲口沿 Rim fragment from a *li* tripod	2009-7-14			M: 16.6 H: 3.1	夹云母滑石红褐，方唇，敞口，折沿，素面。 Reddish-brown with mica and talc tempering, square lip, wide mouth, folded rim, plain.
14	09SLGTG2 H20①：11	鬲口沿 Rim fragment from a *li* tripod	2009-7-14			M: 21 H: 4.9	夹砂灰褐，方唇，敞口，卷沿。 Coarse grey clay, square lip, wide mouth, rolled rim.
11	09SLGTG2 H20①：12	鬲足 Foot from a *li* tripod	2009-7-14		A1	W: 6 H: 4.9	夹砂红褐，袋足尖，素面。 Coarse and reddish-brown, sharp pocket-shaped foot, plain.
18	09SLGTG2 H20①：13	鬲足 Foot from a *li* tripod	2009-7-14		A1	W: 11.6 H: 9.6	夹砂灰褐，袋足尖，外饰中绳纹。 Coarse and grey-brown, sharp pocket-shaped foot, medium cord decorations on the outside.
16	09SLGTG2 H20①：14	鬲足 Foot from a *li* tripod	2009-7-14		A1	W: 7.8 H: 6.2	夹砂红褐，袋足尖，外饰中绳纹，足根矮。 Coarse and reddish-brown, sharp pocket-shaped foot, medium cord decorations on the outside, base of the foot short.
17	09SLGTG2 H20①：15	鬲足 Foot from a *li* tripod	2009-7-14		A1	W: 7.5 H: 6.4	夹砂深灰，袋足，竖向中绳纹。 Coarse and dark grey, pocket-shaped foot, vertical cord decorations.
10	09SLGTG2 H20①：16	豆 *Dou* pedestal dish	2009-7-14		A	M: 7.2 B: 11.1 H: 6.2	泥质深灰，素面，柄粗矮，圈足外撇。 Dark grey clay, plain, thick and short handle, circular foot that flares to the outside.
	09SLGTG2 H20①：17	豆盘 Bowl from a *dou* pedestal dish	2009-7-14			L: 10.7 W: 7.3	泥质浅灰，方唇，敛口，唇沿内侧有凹槽，素面。 Light grey clay, square lip, mouth converging, groove around the inside of the rim, plain.
1	09SLGTG2 H20①：18	簋口沿 Rim fragment from a *gui* tureen	2009-7-14			M: 33 H: 4.2	泥质浅灰，方圆唇，唇沿外凸，沿内有凹痕，宽折沿。 Light grey clay, square and round lip, protrusion on the outside of the rim, groove on the inside of the rim, broad folded rim.
7	09SLGTG2 H20①：19	鬲 *Li* tripod	2009-7-14			L: 9.3 W: 3.8	夹砂深灰，方唇，敞口，宽折沿。素面。 Dark grey clay, square lip, wide mouth, broad folded rim. Plain.
5	09SLGTG2 H20①：20	簋圈足 Circular foot from a *gui* tureen	2009-7-14			L: 6.3 W: 3.2 H: 3.8	泥质浅灰，素面。 Light grey clay, plain.
3	09SLGTG2 H20①：21	罐 *Guan* jar	2009-7-14		E1	M: 16.8 H: 8.2	黑褐色，胎红褐，小口束颈，圆唇卷沿，肩部饰两周小乳钉。 Dark brown color, reddish-brown beads, small mouth and collar, rounded lip with rolled rim, decorated with two small nipples.
2	09SLGTG2 H20①：22	鬲口沿 Rim fragment from a *li* tripod	2009-7-14			M: 17.9 H: 3.5	夹砂深灰陶，方唇敞口，卷沿，素面。 Coarse, dark grey clay, square lip and wide mouth, rolled rim. Plain.
12	09SLGTG2 H20①：23	圆陶片 Round pottery sherd	2009-7-14			J: 4.3 T: 0.4	夹云母灰褐，近圆形，素面。 Grey clay with mica tempering, plain.

续表

序号 Number on Fig. Ⅰ.5.52	标本号 Excavation number	器物名称 Artifact name	出土时间 Excavation date	位置 Location	所属类型 Types	尺寸(厘米) Size (cm)	特点描述 Description of features
	09SLGTG2 H20①：24	瓿 *Bu* vase	2009-7-14			L: 8.7 W: 7.4	泥质深灰，折肩，肩部饰泥饼，并饰数周。 Dark grey clay, folded shoulder. Shoulder decorated with several mud cakes.
4	09SLGTG1 H20①：25	罐 *Guan* jar	2009-7-14			L: 21 W: 13.5	泥质浅灰，折肩，肩部饰绳纹有抹痕，腹部饰中绳纹并有一圈凹弦纹。 Light grey clay, folded shoulder, shoulder decorated with cord decorations and smear marks, medium cord decorations and one track of ring decoration on the belly.
	09SLGTG1 H20①：26	豆圈足 Circular foot from a *dou* pedestal dish	2009-7-14		A	L: 7 W: 3.1	泥质深灰，圈足外撇应为喇叭口，素面。 Dark grey clay, circular foot flares to the outside like a trumpet mouth, plain.
9	09SLGTG1 H20①：28	豆盘 Bowl from a *dou* pedestal dish	2009-7-14		B	M: 17.8 H: 3.6	泥质浅灰，方唇，盘口内折，盘应较浅，素面。 Light grey clay, square lip, fold on the inside of the bowl, relatively shallow bowl, plain.
	09SLGTG2 H20①：29	簋圈足 Circular foot from a *gui* tureen	2009-7-14			L: 6.6 W: 3.2	泥质深灰，圈足外撇。 Dark grey clay, circular foot flares to the outside.
	09SLGTG1 H20①：30	罐口沿 Rim fragment from a *guan* jar	2009-7-15		B	L: 6.6 W: 3.6	泥质深灰，方唇，卷沿，素面。 Dark grey clay, square lip, rolled rim, plain.
	09SLGTG1 H20①：31	豆盘 Bowl from a *dou* pedestal dish	2009-7-15		B	L: 4 W: 2.8	泥质深灰，方唇，唇缘外凸。 Dark grey clay, square lip, protrusion on the outside of the lip.
	09SLGTG1 H20①：32	鬲口沿 Rim fragment from a *li* tripod	2009-7-15		B	L: 4.7 W: 3.2	夹云母灰褐，方唇宽沿，素面。 Greyish-brown with mica tempering, square lip with broad rim, plain.
15	09SLGTG1 H20①：33	鬲口沿 Rim fragment from a *li* tripod	2009-7-15			M: 12.8 H: 5.4	泥质浅灰，尖唇敞口，大卷沿，腹部饰中绳纹。 Light grey clay, sharp lip and wide mouth, large rolled rim, medium cord decorations on the belly.
	09SLGTG2 H20①：34	簋圈足 Circular foot from a *gui* tureen	2009-7-15			L: 4.1 W: 2.3	泥质深灰，饰两周凹弦纹。 Dark grey clay, two ring decorations.
	09SLGTG1 H20①：35	罐口沿 Rim fragment from a *guan* jar	2009-7-15			L: 5.2 W: 3.8	泥质浅灰，尖唇，唇缘内凸，卷沿，外饰绳纹。 Light grey clay, sharp lip, ridge on the inside of the lip, rolled rim, cord decorations on the outside.
	09SLGTG1 H20①：102	罐底 Bottom of a *guan* jar	2009-7-15			L: 7.6 W: 7.6	圈足，泥质浅灰，底饰绳纹。 Circular foot, light grey clay, bottom decorated with cord decorations.
	09SLGTG1 H20①：135	鼎 *Ding* cauldron	2009-7-15			L: 4.3 W: 3.3	夹砂灰褐，方唇，沿较宽，素面。 Coarse and greyish-brown, square lip, relatively broad rim, plain.
6	09SLGTG1 H20①：136	簋圈足 Round foot from a *gui* tureen	2009-7-15			W: 41.8 W: 4.1	夹砂灰褐，足沿外撇，外有刮痕。 Coarse and greyish-brown, the rim of the foot flares to the outside, scratches on the outside.

续表

序号 Number on Fig. Ⅰ.5.52	标本号 Excavation number	器物名称 Artifact name	出土时间 Excavation date	位置 Location	所属类型 Types	尺寸(厘米) Size (cm)	特点描述 Description of features
	09SLGTG1 H20①：137	鬲下腹部 Lower belly of a *li* tripod	2009-7-15			L: 4.8 W: 4.4	夹云母灰褐。 Greyish-brown with mica tempering.
	09SLGTG1 H20①：138	鬲上部 Upper part of a *li* tripod	2009-7-15		B	L: 8.6 W: 5	口应微撇，夹砂深灰，素面。 Mouth slightly flaring, coarse and dark grey, plain.
	09SLGTG1 H20①：139	鬲沿部 Rim of a *li* tripod	2009-7-15		B	L: 3.6 W: 3.5	泥质深灰，素面，方唇，沿部较宽应外撇。 Dark grey clay, plain, square lip, rim relatively broad and flares to the outside.
	09SLGTG1 H20①：140	鬲上部 Upper part of a *li* tripod	2009-7-15		B	L: 6.2 W: 5.2	夹砂深灰，素面。 Coarse and dark grey, plain.

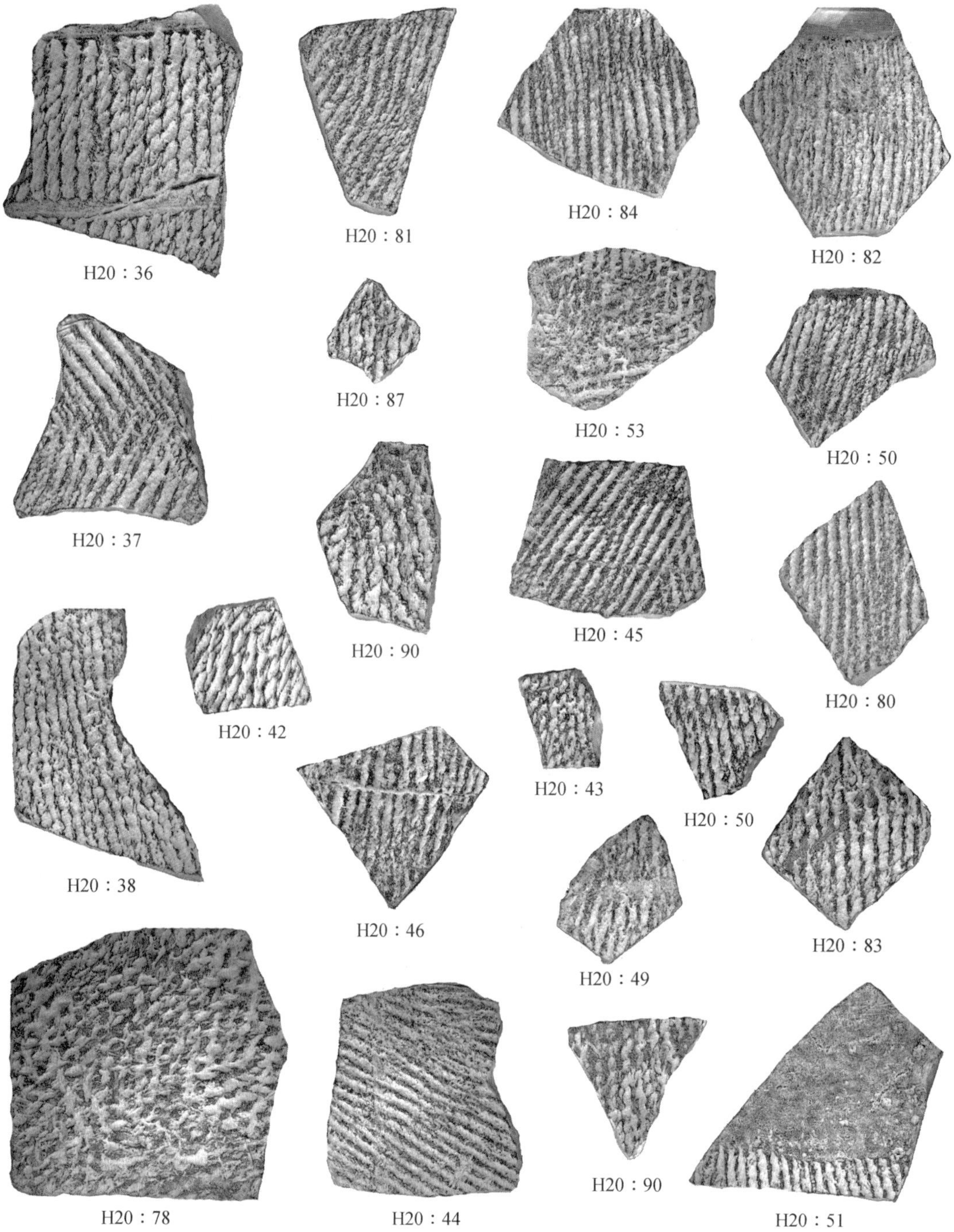

图Ⅰ.5.53　H20①出土陶片纹饰

Figure Ⅰ.5.53　Decorated pottery sherds from pit H20, stratum ①.

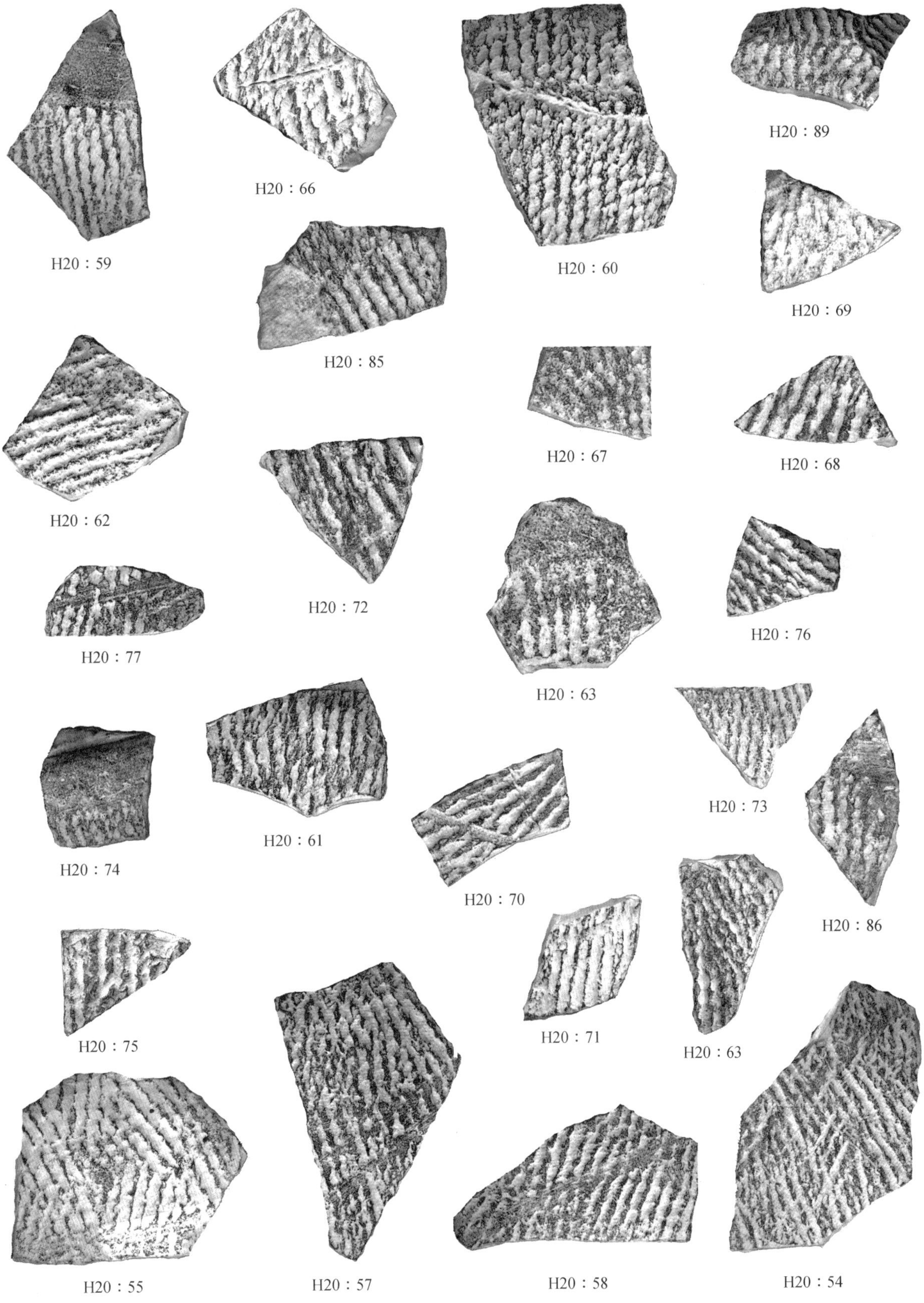

图Ⅰ.5.54　H20①出土陶片纹饰

Figure Ⅰ.5.54　Decorated pottery sherds from pit H20, stratum ①.

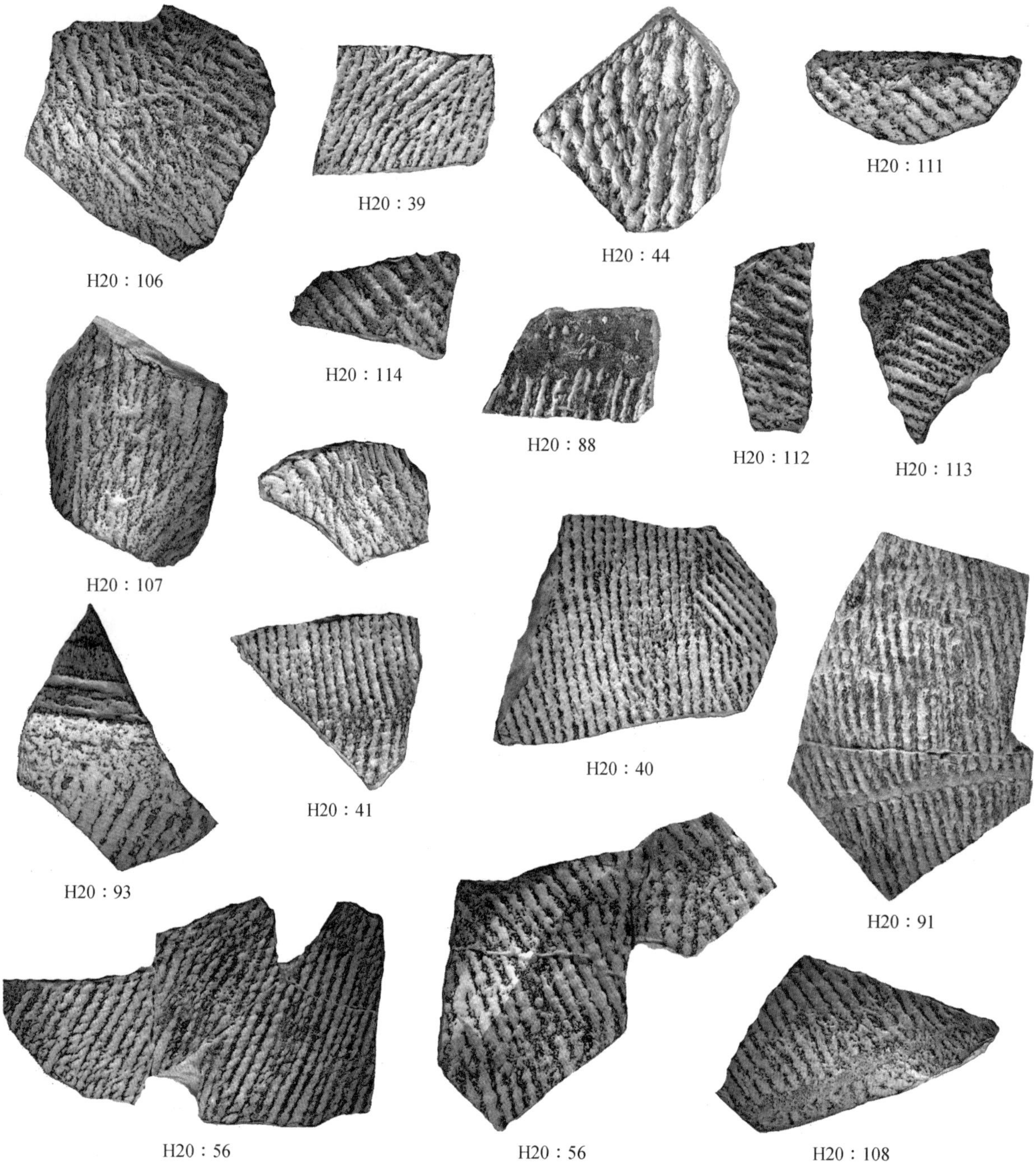

图Ⅰ.5.55　H20①出土陶片纹饰

Figure Ⅰ.5.55　Decorated pottery sherds from pit H20, stratum ①.

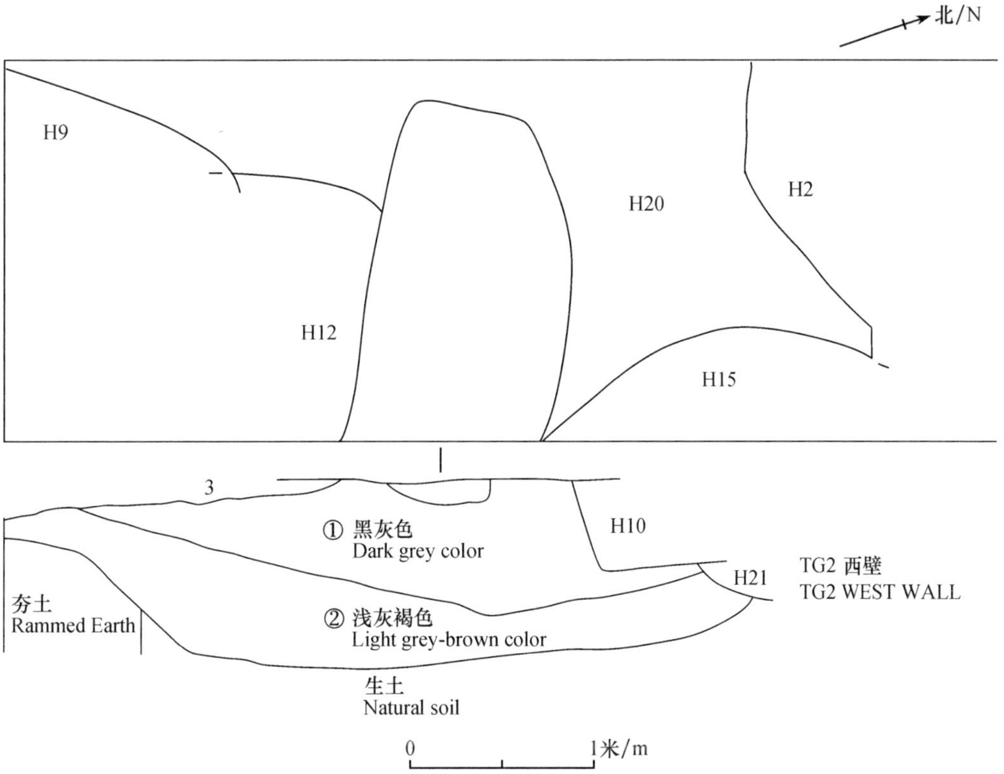

图Ⅰ.5.56　H20②平、剖面图

Figure Ⅰ.5.56　Plan and cross-sectional profiles of pit H20, stratum ②.

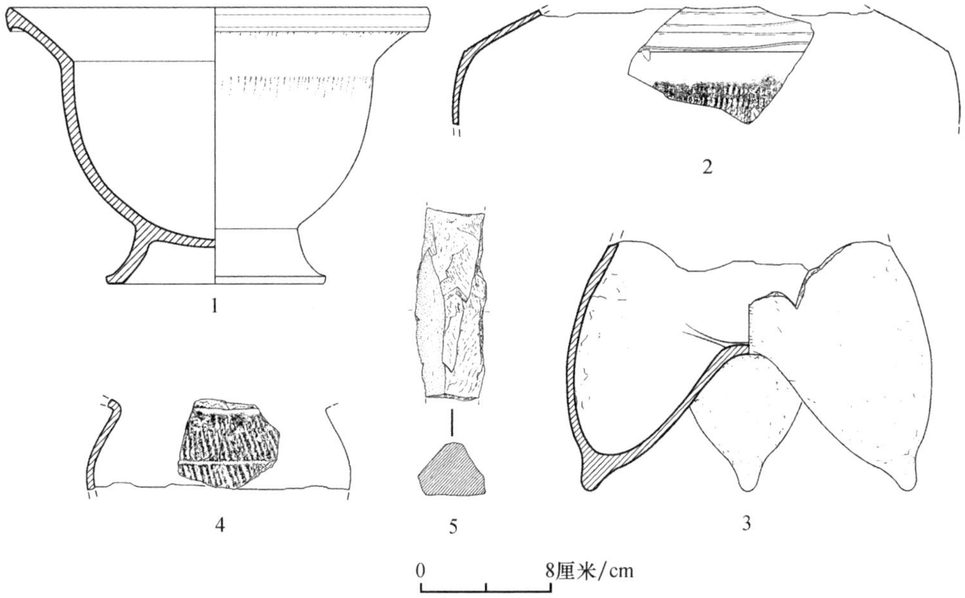

图Ⅰ.5.57　H20②出土陶器

1. 簋（H20②：1）　2. 罐（H20②：6）　3. 甗（H20②：3）　4. 鬲（H20②：149）　5. 石器（H20②：2）

Figure Ⅰ.5.57　Pottery types from pit H20, stratum ②.

1. *Gui* tureen (H20②：1)　2. *Guan* jar (H20②：6)　3. *Yan* steamer (H20②：3)　4. *Li* tripod (H20②：149)

5. Stone tool (H20②：2)

表Ⅰ.5.23　H20②出土遗物登记表

Table Ⅰ.5.23　Artifacts from pit H20, stratum ②

序号 Number on Fig. Ⅰ.5.57	标本号 Excavation number	器物名称 Artifact name	出土时间 Excavation date	位置 Location	所属类型 Types	尺寸(厘米) Size (cm)	特点描述 Description of features
1	09SLGTG2 H20②：1	簋 *Gui* tureen	2009-7-15	260 × 80 —100	A1	M: 26 B: 13.6 H: 16.4	泥质深灰，深腹，矮圈足，敞口，宽平折沿，外厚唇，口沿下及局部饰绳纹，有磨光痕。 Dark grey clay, deep belly, short circular feet, wide mouth, broad and flat folded rim, thickening on the outside of the lip. Under the rim is partially decorated with cord decorations, with burnishing marks.
5	09SLGTG1 H20②：2	石器 Stone tool	2009-7-15	200 × 40 —120		L: 11.7 W: 4.2	石英岩，上部大，面呈方形，下部小，成不规则形。 Quartzite. Upper part is large, with a square face, the lower part is small and irregularly shaped.
3	09SLGTG1 H20②：3	甗 *Yan* steamer	2009-7-15		A1	W: 22.6 H: 15	夹砂深灰，乳状大袋足，有乳头，素面。 Coarse and dark grey. Large pocket-shaped feet with nipple ends. Plain.
	09SLGTG1 H20②：4	鬲 *Li* tripod	2009-7-15			L: 6 W: 5.9	夹砂深灰，素面。 Coarse and dark grey, plain.
	09SLGTG1 H20②：5	豆 *Dou* pedestal dish	2009-7-15		C	L: 4.2 W: 2.2	泥质浅灰，圈足，素面。 Light grey clay, circular feet, plain.
2	09SLGTG1 H20②：6	罐 *Guan* jar	2009-7-15			L: 12 W: 8.5	泥质浅灰，折肩，肩部饰两周凹弦纹，腹部饰竖向中绳纹。 Light grey clay, folded shoulder, two tracks of ring decoration on the shoulder, vertical medium cord decorations on the belly.
	09SLGTG1 H20②：7	簋 *Gui* tureen	2009-7-15			L: 5.6 W: 5.4 H: 0.9	泥质浅灰陶，磨成近圆状，饰带状斜方格纹。 Light grey clay, ground to near-circular shape, decorative ribbon of oblique plaid.
	09SLGTG1 H20②：8	簋 *Gui* tureen	2009-7-15			L: 4.4 W: 4.1	泥质浅灰，压印弦纹。 Light grey clay. Imprinted ring patterns.
	09SLGTG1 H20②：15	豆 *Dou* pedestal dish	2009-7-15			L: 4.2 W: 3	泥质浅灰，盘较深，素面，磨光。 Light grey clay, relatively deep bowl, plain, burnished.
	09SLGTG1 H20②：21	罐 *Guan* jar	2009-7-15		C	M: 17 L: 21 W: 10	圆唇，敞口，折沿，肩部饰两周乳钉纹，夹滑石红褐，外饰黑陶衣。 Rounded lip, wide mouth, folded rim, two nipple decorations on the shoulder, reddish-brown with talc tempering, external decoration is black slip.
	09SLGTG1 H20②：30	罐口沿 Rim fragment from a *guan* jar	2009-7-15		B	L: 6.6 W: 3.6	泥质深灰，方唇，卷沿，素面。 Dark grey clay, square lip, rolled rim, plain.
4	09SLGTG1 H20②：149	鬲 *Li* tripod	2009-7-15			L: 6.4 W: 6.1	泥质浅灰掺少量砂，小折沿，腹小，腹部饰中绳纹。 Light gray clay tempered with some sand, small folded rim, small belly, moderate cord decorations on the belly.

尺寸标志：L=长度；H=高度；W=宽度；D=直径；R=半径；M=口径；B=底径；T=厚度；d=深度；h=孔径。

Measurements: L=length; H=height; W=width; D=diameter; R=radius; M=mouth diameter; B= bottom diameter; T=thickness; d=depth; h=hole diameter.

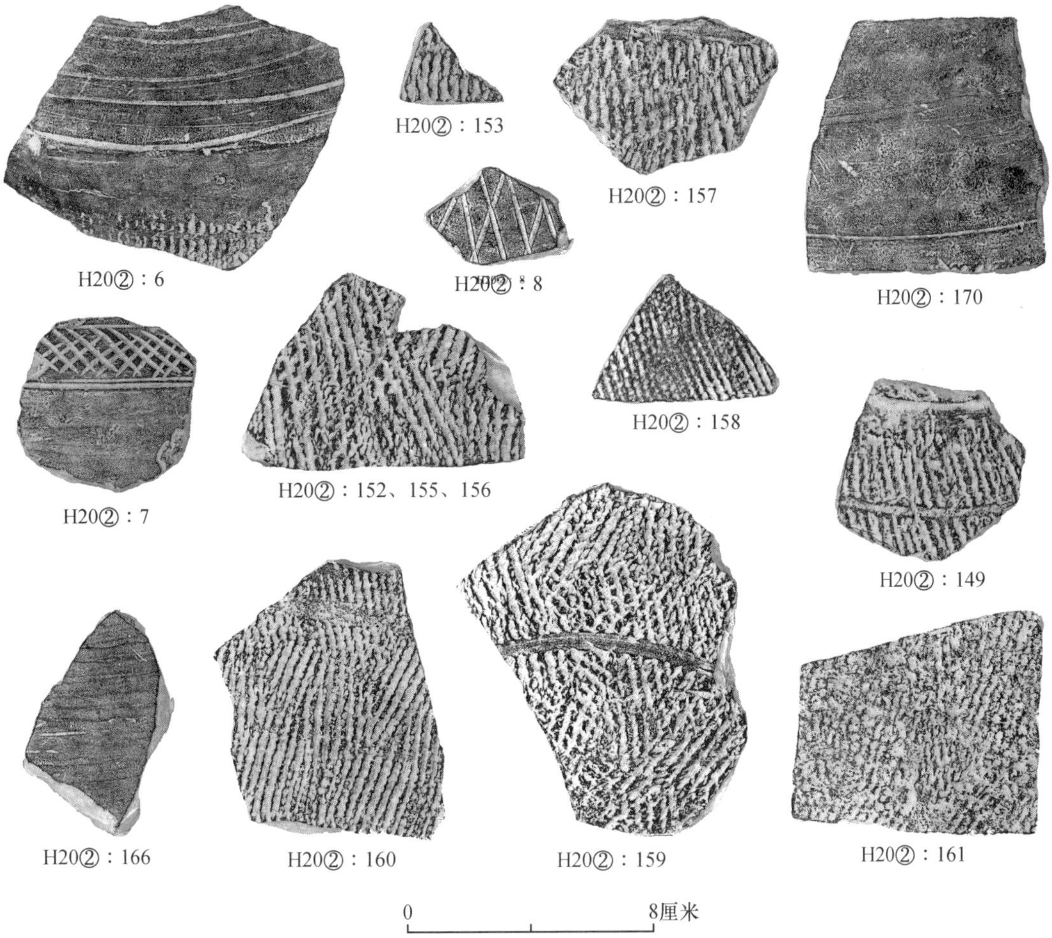

图Ⅰ.5.58　H20②出土陶片纹饰

Figure Ⅰ.5.58　Decorated pottery sherds from pit H20, stratum ②.

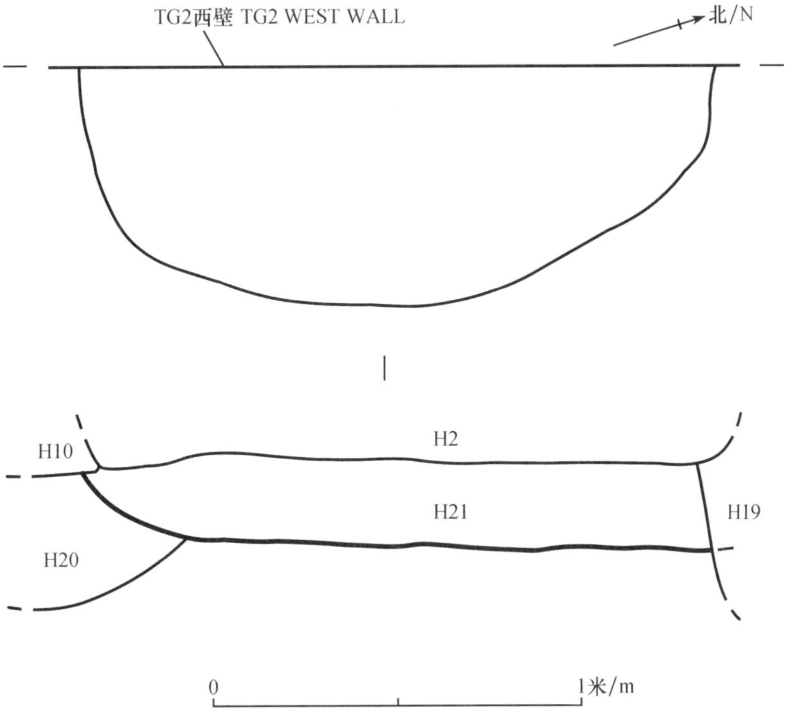

图Ⅰ.5.59　H21平、剖面图

Figure Ⅰ.5.59　Plan and cross-sectional profiles of pit H21.

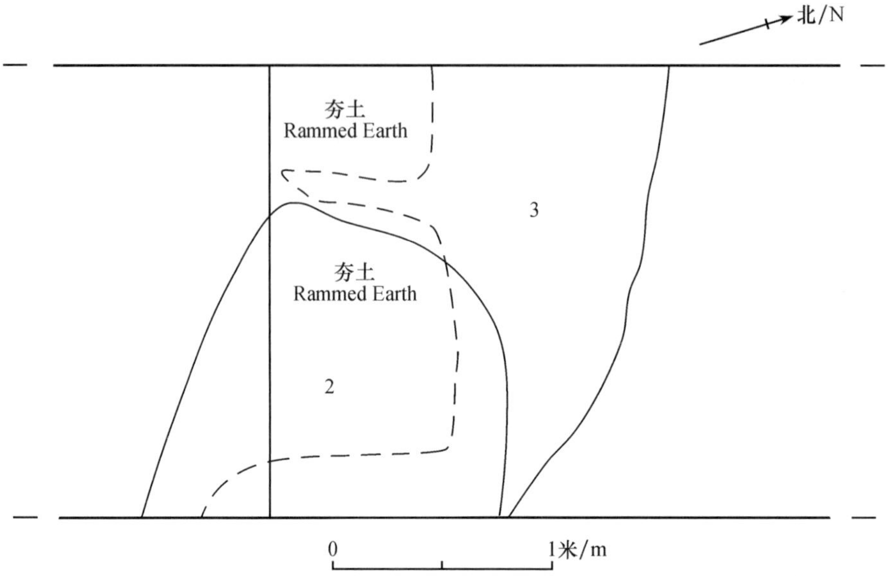

图Ⅰ.5.60　TG2③和夯土的关系

Figure Ⅰ.5.60　The relationship between stratum ③ and rammed earth in TG2.

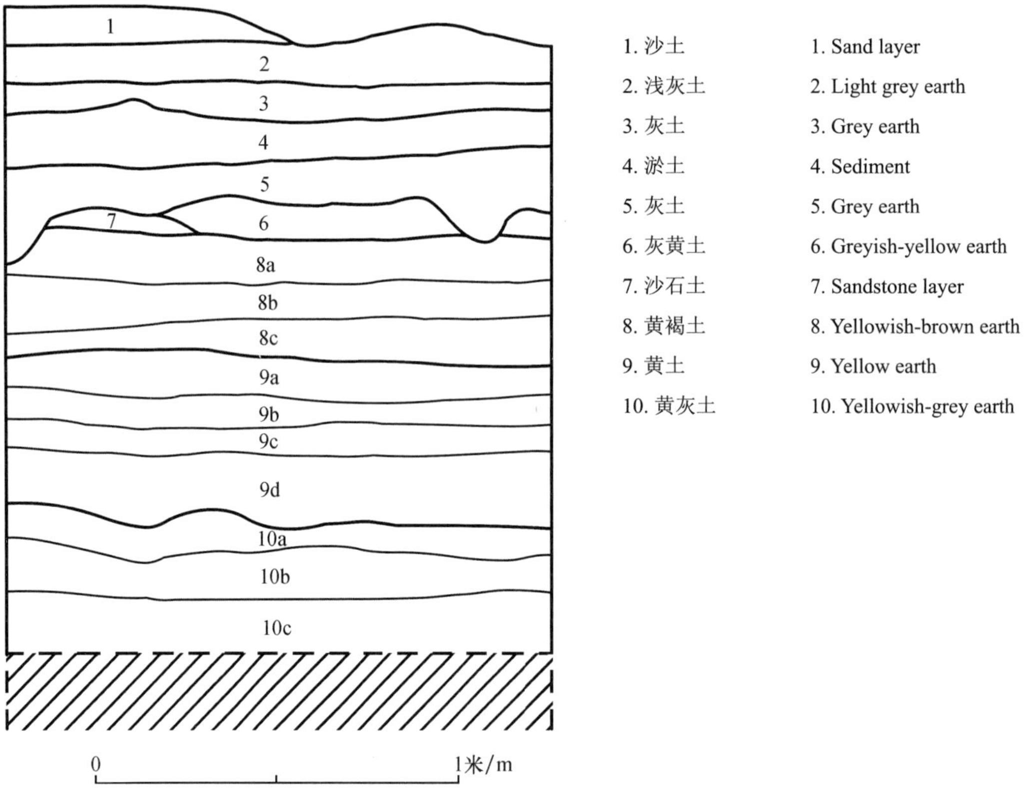

图Ⅰ.5.61　探沟南侧断崖剖面底层组成

Figure Ⅰ.5.61　Strata on the cross-section south of TG1.

Chapter 5: Test Excavation of the Inner City

Xu Mingjiang

Section 1: Introduction

1. Goals and Background of the Test Excavation

The Guicheng Archaeological Survey began in 2007 and was carried out by a joint Sino-American archaeological team. The survey arrived at a preliminary understanding of the approximate extent of the Guicheng site's inner and outer cities, the course of the city wall, the layout of the inner city architecture, and the distribution of settlements between the inner and outer city walls. The survey also allowed us to assess the approximate period of occupation of the Guicheng city site. However, in order to grasp more clearly the question of the chronology of the city site, it was necessary to investigate the site's stratigraphy. In summer 2009, in order to provide direct evidence to resolve the question of the dating of the city site, to understand the stratigraphic deposits of the city site, and to reconstruct the site's formation history, we chose the north face of the middle section of the south wall of the inner city to conduct a test excavation.

2. Geography and Location of the Test Excavation Area

The excavation area is located on the inner face of the south wall of the Guicheng inner city. The excavation area's southern portion intersects the inner city south wall, and is about 230 m east of one of the city wall sections that still stands above ground, now protected by stone walls, at the southwest corner of the city. The excavation area is about 130 m from the main concrete road that runs through Guicheng's inner city in a north-south direction on the western edge of East Heping Village, about 55 m south of Rammed Earth Foundation 2, and about 10 m west of Rammed Earth Foundation 1 (Fig. Ⅰ.3.1). We relied on a basic understanding of the subterranean strata obtained in the coring stage of the project to determine the exact location of the test trenches, to make sure they were placed in a way to not only expose a portion of the rammed earth city wall, but also to fully expose the inner city's strata. This was the ideal way to gather evidence for the relationship between the city wall and

Guicheng's inner city strata.

The excavation area used to be a peanut field, with a relatively high number of cord-decorated grey pottery sherds visible on the surface. The southern edge is a cliff on the south wall, and the remaining three sides are planted with fruit trees (Pl. 39: 1-2). The southern end of the test trench is 2 m from the cliff. The northern end of the test trench is only 20 m from Complete Collection Unit (CCU) I, so that after the excavation was complete, the pottery sherds recovered in each stratigraphic unit could be compared with the pottery sherds recovered during the concentrated surface collection, and could form a basis for discussing the relationship between the surface and subsurface remains (see Part 6, Section 5). The results of the excavation confirm that the location of the test trenches was ideal for our purposes.

3. Progress of the Test Excavation

On July 3, 2009, the archaeology team laid out two test trenches. The south trench was numbered Test Trench 1 (TG1) (Fig. Ⅰ.5.1; Pl. 27), and the north trench was numbered Test Trench 2 (TG2) (Fig. Ⅰ.5.2; Pl. 30). Because of topographic limitations, the trenches were oriented 17° east of north (magnetic), which is the same as the orientation of the Guicheng inner city, and is also the orientation of the field plots and orchards. The surface area of each trench was 2 m x 8 m, excluding a 1 m partition in Trench 1 to separate it from Trench 2, so that the total excavated area was 30 m^2. On July 4, we began the actual excavation, and the entire area was excavated by July 20 (Pls. 40-41).

Section 2: Stratigraphic Deposition and Structural Remains

1. Stratigraphic Deposition

The subsurface deposits of the excavation area can be divided into five strata, based on differences in the texture and color of the soil and on the soil inclusions. Because there are many structural units that frequently intrude into each other, the strata are not continuous. Strata ①, ③, ④, and ⑤ are present within TG1 (Pls. 28-29). Strata ①, ②, ③, and ⑤ are present within TG2 (Pls. 31-32). The strata can be described as follows:

Stratum 1: plowed soil layer; greyish-brown color; loose consistency; inclusions of modern ceramic sherds, porcelain sherds, stones, ash, and plant root systems, 12-24 cm thick. Features G1, G2, H1, H2, H3, H4, H5, H6, H7, H10, H16, H18, and H19 were discovered below this stratum. H2 overlies H21, and H3 overlies H13.

Stratum 2: grey soil layer; only present in TG2; includes chunks of loess; loose consistency; inclusions of a few cord-decorated grey pottery sherds, 12-16 cm deep, 0-24 cm thick. Only found in the center of the excavation area, mostly in the southeast portion of TG2. No structural remains were found below this stratum.

Stratum 3: greyish-brown color; soil consistency relatively hard; includes a large quantity of water-formed rust. Inclusions of coarse grit, a few grey pottery sherds and reddish-brown pottery sherds (Fig. Ⅰ.5.3; Tables Ⅰ.5.3- Ⅰ.5.4; Pl. 44:1-2), 12-36 cm deep, 0-30 cm thick. Mostly distributed in the center of the excavation area, i.e., the north of TG1 and the south of TG2. Features H8, H9, H11, H12, H14, H15, H17, and H20 were discovered under this stratum. A posthole was found in the bottom of H12, which was numbered D1. H8 overlies H14 within this stratum.

Stratum 4: light grey color; soil consistency relatively hard; includes a relatively large quantity of water-formed rust and gravel; very few pottery sherds, most of which are grey pottery, 20-26 cm below the surface, 16-25 cm thick, distributed in the southern part of TG1. Stratum overlies the rammed earth city wall. This stratum does not appear in TG2.

Stratum 5: yellowish-brown soil; inclusions of coarse grit; hard soil consistency. This is the stratum of the rammed earth city wall, with no pottery sherds discovered in it. According to the different rates of sand inclusions, it can be divided into three sub-strata. Sub-stratum 5a is a yellowish-brown layer, mixed with gravel, 12 cm thick. Sub-stratum 5b is a greyish-brown layer, mixed with sand and gravel, 8 cm thick. Sub-stratum 5c is a loess layer, with dense soil and homogeneous consistency. In TG2 this stratum is layered directly on top of the virgin soil.

2. Principal Structural Remains and their Mutual Relationships

In the excavation area, we discovered one section of rammed earth, twenty-one ash pits, and two late period ditches.

The rammed earth of the city wall is distributed mainly in TG1 in the southern part of the excavation area, but its northern edge extends into TG2 (Pl. 33). It is directly intruded into by H9, H12, and H20. The ash pits are concentrated mostly in TG2 in the northern part of the excavation area (Figs. Ⅰ.5.4- Ⅰ.5.5).

Section 3: Chronological Sequence of Strata and Remains

By using the destructive relationships between the strata, combined with the analysis of the cultural features of excavated objects, we can make a preliminary determination: stratum 1 is the modern plowed layer, stratum 2 is a Han Dynasty cultural layer, stratum 3 is a Spring and Autumn period cultural layer, stratum 4 is a mid-Western Zhou period cultural layer, and stratum 5 is an early Western Zhou period cultural layer. The early period ash pits include H9, H12, H15, H16, H18, H19, H20, and H21, and date from the early Western Zhou period to the early Spring and Autumn period. The later ash pits include H3, H4, H6, and H8, which date to the middle Spring and Autumn period. The period of the rammed earth city wall is most likely the later part of the early Western Zhou period.

Section 4: Important Remains and Excavated Artifacts

In terms of structural remains, the principal discoveries in this excavation area are ash pits and ditches, mainly located in the northern part of the area. TG1, located towards the south, contains relatively few structural remains because it overlies the rammed earth city wall. Because of the limits of the excavation area, except for H3, most of the ash pits were not completely excavated. However, according to an analysis of the excavated portions, the majority of the ash pits have a round or oval shape, and the rest are irregular, or rectangular with round corners, and most have straight vertical or angular walls. The sizes of the pits vary, as do their depths. The fill soil is relatively loose and soft, with a mostly greyish-brown color. Most of the excavated artifacts are pottery sherds, with a small quantity of bronze, stone, and bone implements. Of the pottery, fine-clay ware is the most common, either a dark grey or a light grey in color. The recovered coarse pottery is mostly reddish-brown and greyish-brown, many tempered with some mica and talc pieces. Not many of the pottery vessels can be reconstructed, but the identifiable types include *ding* cauldrons (鼎), *li* tripods (鬲), *gui* tureens (簋), *dou* pedestal dishes (豆), *guan* jars (罐), *pen* basins (盆), *hu* bottles (壶), *bu* vases (瓿), tiles, and vessel lids. Of these, *li* tripods, *gui* tureens, *dou* pedestal dishes, and *guan* jars are the most numerous. Most of the pottery is plain. Patterns that appear on decorated pottery include cord impressions, ring-patterns, engraved patterns, checker patterns, nipples, appliqué decorations, and burnishing. Of these, cord impressions are the most common, and can be further divided into coarse cord impressions, medium cord impressions, fine cord impressions, and "sesame seed" cord impressions. The ditches are all rectangular strips with sloping walls and a flat bottom at even depth. The fill soil is grey tan earth. Identifiable sherd types include cord marked *gui* tureens and *guan* jars, *dou* pedestal dishes, and *wan* bowls (碗), etc. Tables detailing the artifacts' descriptive attributes are placed in front of this English language chapter (Tables Ⅰ.5.1- Ⅰ.5.4). All excavated features were numbered, and they are sequentially described below.

1. Ditches

Ditch G1 is located in the center of TG1. It opens below stratum 1, and intrudes into pit H7. It forms a rectangle within TG1, with its east and west ends extending beyond the two walls of the trench. G1 has sloping walls and a flat bottom. The opening of the ditch is 16-20 cm below the surface, and it is 200 cm long from east to west, 57-68 cm wide from north to south, and 24 cm deep. The soil layers in the ditch are greyish-brown and loose in consistency. The artifacts found in the ditch include grey pottery sherds, some with cord impressions, and animal bones. Identifiable vessel types include *gui* tureens, *dou* pedestal dishes, *guan* jars, and *wan* bowls (Fig. Ⅰ.5.6; Table Ⅰ.5.5; Pl. 44: 3-4).

Ditch G2 is located in the center of TG1. Its opening is below stratum 1, and it intrudes into stratum 4. It forms a rectangle within TG1, and its east and west ends both intrude into the walls of the excavation trench. The ditch has sloping walls and a flat bottom. The opening is 18-20 cm below the surface, and the ditch is 200 cm long from east to west, 22 cm wide from south to north, and 20 cm deep. The deposit layers in the ditch are greyish-brown and loose in consistency. No cultural remains were found in the ditch.

These two ditches run parallel to each other in the center of TG1, and their depth and width are approximately the same, so we speculate that they were constructed in the same time period. Because they both open below stratum 1, their lower portions intrude into stratum 4. The interval between the two strata being relatively large, it is difficult to accurately determine the time period in which they were constructed. However, no artifacts of significantly late date were recovered from the two ditches. Based on the types and decorations of the pottery excavated in G1, we can make a preliminary determination that they belong to the middle to late Spring and Autumn period.

2. Pits

H1: located in the southeast part of TG2, its eastern portion enters the test trench's east wall. Opening below stratum 1, it intrudes into a modern ditch and pits H11 and H6. H1 is roughly rectangular, with rounded corners and a flat bottom. It opens about 16 cm below the surface. At its mouth, the longer sides are about 120 cm and the shorter sides are 56-64 cm, and it is 20 cm deep. The strata inside the pit are yellowish-brown, with some ash and burned soil particles and have a loose consistency. There were no cultural remains found in the pit. We conclude that this is a modern pit.

H2: located in the northwest part of TG2, its western portion enters the test trench's west wall. It opens below stratum 1, and intrudes into pits H10, H6, H19, H20, and H21. H2 is oval, and its opening is not clear, but it is larger at the top than at the bottom, with sloping walls and a roughly flat bottom (Fig. Ⅰ.5.7; Pl. 34: 3). The pit's opening is 14-18 cm below the ground surface. At its mouth it has a maximum diameter of 204 cm and a minimum diameter of 140 cm, with a depth of 70 cm. The strata in the pit are light greyish-brown, with some vegetal ash and loess particles, and a slightly loose consistency. The remains found in the pit include pottery sherds, animal bones, burnt clods of soil, and stones. The identifiable pottery types from the pit include *ding* cauldrons, *li* tripods, *gui* tureens, *dou* pedestal dishes, and *guan* jars, *pen* basins, *wan* bowls, and vessel lids, as well as round pottery sherds. Decoration on the pottery includes cord impressions and rings (Figs. Ⅰ.5.8- Ⅰ.5.9; Table Ⅰ.5.6; Pl. 42: 1).

H3: located in the north part of TG1, it is the most complete of the pits excavated at this time. It opens under stratum 1, intruding into pits H7, H8, H9, H13, and H14, and strata 3 and 4. It is oval, and the eastern and western ends both enter the test trench's walls. It is narrower at the opening than at the bottom, and has a flat bottom (Fig. Ⅰ.5.10; Pl. 34: 4). The pit's opening is 16 cm below the ground surface. Its diameter at the opening is 213 cm, and at the bottom is 222 cm, with a depth of 68-70 cm. The strata in the pit can be divided into three layers based on soil texture and color, as follows: Layer ①: soil greyish-brown in color, with carbon particles and loose consistency. This layer is higher at the two ends and lower in the center and is 0-25 cm thick. The remains found within include pottery sherds, animal bones, and stone sickles. The identifiable pottery types include *ding* cauldron feet, *li* tripods, *yan* steamers, *dou* pedestal dishes, *guan* jars, *hu* bottles, and vessel lids, as well as circular pottery objects. Decoration on the pottery includes cord impressions and rings (Figs. Ⅰ.5.11- Ⅰ.5.12; Table Ⅰ.5.7; Pl. 43: 2, Pl. 44: 5-7, Pl. 45: 1). Layer ②: soil reddish-brown in color with burned layers and a loose consistency. Mostly distributed in the eastern half of pit H3, 0-58 cm thick. One dog skeleton was found in the excavation (Fig. Ⅰ.5.13; Pl. 34: 2). Cultural remains found in this layer include pottery sherds and animal bones. The identifiable pottery types included *li* tripods, *gui* tureens, *dou* pedestal dishes, and *guan* jars. Decoration includes cord impressions and rings (Fig. Ⅰ.5.14; Table Ⅰ.5.8; Pl. 42: 2-4, Pl. 44: 8-9, Pl. 45: 2-4). Layer ③: soil color bluish-grey, including charcoal pieces and water-formed rust, with a hard consistency. This layer is higher in the west and lower in the east, and is 10-60 cm thick. Remains found in this layer include pottery sherds and animal bones. Relatively few pottery sherds were found in this layer, and include mostly *li* tripods, *gui* tureens, *dou* pedestal dishes, *weng* jars, and vessel lids. Decorations include cord impressions, rings, engraved patterns, and nipples (Fig. Ⅰ.5.15; Table Ⅰ.5.9; Pl. 45: 5-8). We also discovered many burnt clods, charcoal, and a section of earth brick. Based on these remains, we speculate that this is a domestic trash pit.

H4: located in the southeastern part of TG2, its eastern portion enters the trench's east wall. It opens below stratum 1, is intruded into by a modern ditch, and itself intrudes into pits H9, H11, and H12. H4 is round, with straight walls and a flat bottom (Fig. Ⅰ.5.16; Pl. 35: 3). The pit's opening is 50 cm below the ground surface, and it has a diameter at its opening of 68 cm, a diameter at its bottom of 68 cm, and a depth of 86 cm. The strata within the pit are yellowish-grey, including a small amount of vegetal ash and clumps of loess, and its consistency is slightly loose. The remains found in this feature include pottery sherds, animal bones, and stones. The identifiable pottery types include *gui* tureens, *dou* pedestal dishes, *yan* steamers, vessel lids, and tiles. Decorations on the pottery include cord impressions and rings (Figs. Ⅰ.5.17- Ⅰ.5.18; Table Ⅰ.5.10; Pl. 45: 9, Pl. 46: 1). We believe that this was used as a trash pit after being abandoned.

H5: located in the southwest part of TG2, its western end enters the test trench's west wall. It opens below stratum 1, and intrudes into pits H6 and H20. H5 has an irregular shape, its south wall is roughly straight, and it has a flat bottom. Its opening is 16 cm below the surface, and it is 55 cm long, 40 cm wide, and 14 cm deep (Fig. Ⅰ.5.19; Pl. 35: 4). The strata in the pit are light grey in color, with burned soil particles, stones, and a small amount of vegetal ash; the consistency is slightly loose. No pottery sherds were found in the pit. We speculate that it was used as a trash pit after being abandoned.

H6: located in the south central part of TG2. Its opening is below stratum 1, and it is intruded into by pits H1 and H5. The pit itself intrudes into pits H11, H12, H17, and H20. H6 is oval, with straight walls and a flat bottom (Fig. Ⅰ.5.20; Pl. 35: 1-2). The opening is 15 cm below the ground surface, and the pit has a maximum diameter of 166 cm, a minimum diameter of 123 cm, and a depth of 60 cm. The deposits within the pit are yellowish-grey, with some vegetal ash and loess clods, and a somewhat loose consistency. The remains found in this layer include pottery sherds, stones, and animal bones and teeth. The identifiable pottery types include *ding* cauldrons, *li* tripods, *gui* tureens, *dou* pedestal dishes, *guan* jars, *pen* basins, and vessel lids. Decorations on the pottery include cord impressions, rings, and engraved patterns (Figs. Ⅰ.5.21- Ⅰ.5.22; Table Ⅰ.5.11; Pl. 46: 2-3). We believe H6 was used as a trash pit after it was abandoned.

H7: located in the west part of TG1. Its opening is below stratum 1, and it is intruded into by G1 and H3, while itself intruding into H8 and stratum 3. H7 is round, and only a small part of it was excavated as most of it is located under the west wall of the trench. It has sloping walls and a flat bottom (Fig. Ⅰ.5.1). The pit's opening is 16 cm below the surface. The pit is 37 cm wide from east to west, 218 cm long from north to south, and 28 cm deep. The deposits in the pit are yellowish-grey in color, and include vegetal ash and burnt soil particles; the consistency is somewhat loose. There were only two pottery sherds found, one a piece of a *dou* pedestal dish and one a piece of a *gui* tureen. The pedestal dish is plain and burnished, and the tureen has cord impressions on its outside (Fig. Ⅰ.5.23; Table Ⅰ.5.12; Pl. 46: 4).

H8: located in the northwest part of TG1. It opens below stratum 3, is intruded into by G1, H3, and H7, and itself intrudes into stratum 4. Its shape is oval, and part of it extends into the test trench's west wall. It has straight walls and a flat bottom (Fig. Ⅰ.5.1; Pl. 36: 1). The pit's opening is 26 cm below the ground surface, and it has a maximum diameter of 92 cm, a minimum diameter of 64 cm, and a depth of 71-78 cm. The soil is grey with inclusions of sand, and is loose in consistency. Remains in the pit include pottery sherds and animal bones. Excavated pottery types include *ding* cauldrons, *li* tripods, *gui* tureens, *dou* pedestal dishes, *guan* jars, *pen* basins, and vessel lids. The decorations of the ceramics include cord impressions and appliqué decorations (Figs. Ⅰ.5.24- Ⅰ.5.25; Table Ⅰ.5.13; Pl. 46: 5-6).

H9: located in the southern part of TG2 and the northern part of TG1. It opens under stratum 3, is intruded into by a modern ditch, and itself intrudes into pits H12 and H20. H9 is round, with sloping walls and a flat bottom (Fig. Ⅰ.5.26; Pl. 36: 2). Its opening is 50 cm below the ground surface, and the pit has a diameter at its mouth of 334 cm and a depth of 64 cm. The soil deposits in the pit are dark greyish-brown in color, and include vegetal ash and water-formed rust, the consistency is somewhat loose. The remains found in the pit include pottery sherds, stones, animal bones, and shells. The identifiable pottery types include *li* tripods, *yan* steamers, *gui* tureens, *dou* pedestal dishes, *guan* jars, *pen* basins, vessel lids, and pottery molds. Decorations on the pottery include cord impressions, rings, and appliqué decorations (Figs. Ⅰ.5.27- Ⅰ.5.29; Table Ⅰ.5.14; Pl. 46: 7-9; Pl. 47: 1-2; Pl. 52). This was likely used as a trash pit after it was abandoned.

H10: located in the west-central part of TG2, with its western end extending into the test trench's west wall. It opens under stratum 1, is intruded into by H2, and itself intrudes into pits H20 and H21. H10 is irregular in shape, with indistinct walls and a curved, round bottom (Fig. Ⅰ.5.2). The opening is 18 cm below the ground surface, and the pit is 72 cm long, 25 cm wide, and 45 cm deep. The deposits in the pit are light greyish-brown in color, with inclusions of vegetal ash and burnt soil particles and a slightly loose consistency. Remains found in the pit include pottery sherds and stones. Identifiable vessel types found in the pit include *gui* tureens with cord impressions. It can be speculated that this was used as a trash pit after it was abandoned.

H11: located in the southeast part of TG2. It opens under stratum 3, and is intruded into by a modern ditch. It also intrudes into pits H12, H15, H17, and H20. H11 is roughly oval, with straight walls and a flat bottom (Fig. Ⅰ.5.30). Its opening is 58 cm below the ground surface, and it has a maximum diameter of 300 cm, a minimum diameter of 150 cm, and a depth of 24 cm. The deposits in the pit are light grey, and include vegetal ash and burnt soil particles, with a somewhat loose consistency. The finds in the pit include pottery sherds, stones, and animal bones. The identifiable pottery types found in the pit include *li* tripods, *gui* tureens, *dou* pedestal dishes, *guan* jars, and vessel lids. Decorations on the pottery include cord impressions and rings (Figs. Ⅰ.5.31- Ⅰ.5.32; Table Ⅰ.5.15; Pl. 47: 3-4). We believe this was used as a trash pit after it was abandoned.

H12: located in the southeastern part of TG2 and the northeastern part of TG1. It opens under stratum 3, is intruded into by pits H4, H6, H9, and H11, and itself intrudes into pits H17 and H20. H12 is oval, with straight walls and an indistinct bottom (Fig. Ⅰ.5.33; Pl. 36: 3-4). The opening is 56 cm below the ground surface, and the pit has a maximum diameter of 366 cm, a minimum diameter of 146 cm, and a depth of 70 cm. There are two layers in the pit: layer ① is light grey, with relatively loose consistency; layer ② is greyish-brown, with somewhat hard consistency and inclusions of vegetal ash and burnt soil particles. Finds in the pit include pottery sherds, stones, and animal bones. The identifiable pottery types found in the pit include *li* tripods, *gui* tureens, *dou* pedestal dishes, *guan* jars, and *bu* vases, with decorations including cord impressions and rings (Figs. Ⅰ.5.34- Ⅰ.5.35; Table Ⅰ.5.16; Pl. 47: 5-8). There is a posthole in the bottom of the pit, which is 18 cm in diameter and 45 cm deep, with greyish-brown fill with a loose consistency and a few pottery sherds. H12 was likely used as a trash pit after it was abandoned.

H13: located in the northeastern part of TG1. It opens under stratum ③, is intruded into by pits H3, H9, and H12, and itself intrudes into the rammed earth. It is oval, and most of it extends into the east wall of the test trench. It has slanted walls and an uneven bottom (Fig. Ⅰ.5.1). The pit's opening is 80 cm below the surface, and it has a maximum diameter of 128 cm, a minimum diameter of 38 cm, and a depth of 5-26 cm. This pit only has one depositional layer, comprising loose, yellowish-grey soil and sand inclusions. No remains were found in the pit.

H14: located in the northwest corner of TG1. It opens under stratum ③, is intruded into by pits H12, H9, and H3, and itself intrudes into the rammed earth. H14 is irregular, and part of it enters the west wall of the trench. It has sloping walls and an uneven bottom (Fig. Ⅰ.5.1). The opening of the pit is 86 cm below the ground surface, and it 81 cm long, 60 cm wide, and 0-16 cm in depth. The pit only has one depositional layer, whose soil color is yellowish-grey, with vegetal ash and water-formed rust. There were no cultural remains in H14.

H15: located in the east-central part of TG2. It opens under stratum 1, is intruded into by a modern ditch and H11, and itself intrudes into H17, H18, and H20. H15 is round, and its eastern end enters the east wall of the pit. It has a relatively distinct opening; the pit is bag-shaped and is wider at its bottom than at its mouth. The bottom of the pit is flat, and no traces of construction work were found on the walls (Fig. Ⅰ.5.36; Pl. 37: 1). The opening of the pit is 58 cm below the ground surface, and it has a diameter at the opening of 236 cm and a depth of 130 cm. There are two depositional layers in the pit: layer ① is light greyish-brown in color, with a relatively loose texture; layer ② is yellowish-brown in color, with a somewhat hard consistency. The fill includes vegetal ash and a few burnt soil particles. Remains in the pit include pottery sherds, stones, and animal bones. Identifiable pottery vessels include *li* tripods, *gui* tureens, *dou* pedestal dishes, *guan* jars, and vessel lids. Some are decorated with cord impressions and some are burnished (Fig. Ⅰ.5.37; Table Ⅰ.5.17; Pl. 37: 2). We believe this was also used as a trash pit after it was abandoned.

H16: located in the northeast corner of TG2. It opens under stratum 1, is intruded into by H2, and itself intrudes into H18 and H19. H16 is round, with a relatively clear opening. No sign of construction work was found on the sloping walls of the pit, and the bottom of the pit is curved (Fig. Ⅰ.5.38; Pl. 37: 2). The opening is 18 cm below the ground surface, and the rim of the pit exposed by the excavation is 130-140 cm long. The pit is 0-50 cm in depth. The deposit within the pit is light greyish-brown in color, with relatively loose texture, and includes vegetal ash and a few burned soil particles. Finds in the pit include pottery sherds, stones, and animal bones. Identifiable pottery types include *li* tripods, *gui* tureens, *dou* pedestal dishes, *guan* jars, *pen* basins, *weng* jars, and vessel lids. Decorations include cord impressions, rings, and engraved patterns (Figs. Ⅰ.5.39- Ⅰ.5.40; Table Ⅰ.5.18; Pl. 48: 1-3). It can be speculated that this was used as a trash pit after it was abandoned.

H17: located in the east-central area of TG2, its eastern end enters the east wall of the test trench. It opens under stratum 3, is intruded into by pits H15, H6, H12, and H11, and itself intrudes into pit H20. H17 is oval, with sloping walls; the bottom is not flat (Fig. Ⅰ.5.41; Pl. 37: 3). The pit's opening is 60 cm below the ground surface. The pit is 190 cm long, 70 cm wide, and 0-50 cm deep. The deposit in the pit is yellowish-grey in color, with a slightly hard consistency. The fill includes a few vegetal ash particles. Remains in the pit include pottery sherds, stones, and animal bones. The identifiable pottery types found in the pit include *ding* cauldrons, *li* tripods, *dou* pedestal dishes, *guan* jars, and vessel lids. Decorations include cord impressions and rings (Figs. Ⅰ.5.42- Ⅰ.5.43; Table Ⅰ.5.19; Pl. 48: 4-5). It can be speculated that H17 was used as a trash pit after it was abandoned.

H18: located in the northeast corner of TG2, with its opening below stratum ①. It is intruded into by pits H15 and H16, and itself intrudes into pit H19. H18 is oval, wider at the top than at the bottom, and has sloping walls and a flat bottom (Fig. Ⅰ.5.44; Pl. 37: 44). The opening is 58 cm below the ground surface, and the pit is 202 cm long, 106 cm wide, and 86 cm deep. The layers in the pit are yellowish-brown in color, with a slightly loose consistency. They include many vegetal ash particles. Remains found in the pit include pottery sherds, stones, and animal bones. The identifiable pottery types include *li* tripods, *gui* tureens, *dou* pedestal dishes, and *guan* jars. Decorations on the pottery include cord impressions and rings (Figs. Ⅰ.5.46- Ⅰ.5.46; Table Ⅰ.5.20; Pl. 48: 6-8). We believe that H18 was used as a trash pit after it was abandoned.

H19: located in the northwest corner of TG2, with its opening below stratum 1. It is intruded into by pits H2, H18, and H16, and itself intrudes into H21. H19 is oval, with an indistinct opening, slightly sloping walls, and a flat bottom. The opening is 16 cm below the ground surface, and it is 162 cm long, 102 cm wide, and 36-84 cm deep (Fig. Ⅰ.5.47). The deposits in the pit are greyish-brown in color, with a slightly hard consistency and inclusions of vegetal ash particles. Remains found in the pit include pottery sherds, stones, and animal bones. The identifiable pottery types include *ding* cauldrons, *li* tripods, *gui* tureens, *dou* pedestal dishes, *guan* jars, *bu* vases, and vessel lids Decorations include cord impressions, rings, and engraved decorations (Figs. Ⅰ.5.48- Ⅰ.5.50; Table Ⅰ.5.21; Pl. 48: 9; Pl. 49: 1-8). It can be speculated that it was used as a trash pit after being abandoned.

H20: located in the southern part of TG2, with its opening below stratum 3. It is intruded into by pits H2, H5, H6, H9, H10, H11, H12, H15, H17, and H21, and intrudes into the rammed earth and virgin soil layers. Its west side is preserved relatively well, while the other three sides are badly disturbed, but from the bottom of it we can see that it is quite large in extent. This pit's shape is irregular, and the opening indistinct. It has sloping walls and an uneven bottom. Its mouth is 16-80 cm below the ground surface, and its remaining size is 870 cm in length, 200 cm in width, and 0-102 cm in depth (Fig. Ⅰ.5.51; Pl. 38: 1-2). There are two depositional layers in the pit. Layer ① is greyish-black in color, with a relatively loose texture. Most of the remains excavated from H20 layer ① are *li* tripods, *dou* pedestal dishes, *guan* jars, *gui* tureens, *bu* vases, *pen* basins, *ding* cauldrons, and round pottery sherds (Figs. Ⅰ.5.52- Ⅰ.5.55; Table Ⅰ.5.22; Pl. 49: 9; Pl. 50: 1-9; Pl. 51: 1-2). Layer ② is light greyish-brown in color, with a slightly harder consistency. It contains water-formed rust, vegetal ash, and a few burnt soil particles (Fig. Ⅰ.5.56). The remains excavated in H20 layer ② are mainly *ding* cauldrons, *yan* steamers, *gui* tureens, *li* tripods, *dou* pedestal dishes, *guan* jars, *bu* vases, and round pottery sherds (Figs. Ⅰ.5.57- Ⅰ.5.58; Table Ⅰ.5.23; Pl. 43: 1; Pl. 51: 3-8).

H21: located in the west-central part of TG2. Its opening is under stratum 1. It is intruded into by pits H2, H10, and H19, and it intrudes into pit H20. The pit is round with an indistinct mouth, sloping walls, and a rounded bottom (Fig. Ⅰ.5.59). Its opening is 60 cm below the ground surface, its mouth is 170 cm in diameter, and it is 0-22 cm in depth. The layers in the pit are greyish-brown in color, with a slightly hard consistency. The bottom of the pit contains water-formed rust, and the pit also contains vegetal ash and a few burnt soil particles. There were no cultural finds in the pit. It seems that this was also used as a trash pit after it was abandoned.

Section 5: The Discovery and Understanding of the Rammed Earth City Wall

1. The Stratigraphy and Extent of Distribution of the Rammed Earth

Traces of rammed earth were first exposed in the southern part of TG1, and are distributed throughout TG1 and the southern part of TG2. The rammed earth horizon in the southern part of TG1 is relatively high, only 30 cm from the ground surface. In TG2, the rammed earth surface is higher towards the west, overlain by pit H20, and lower in the east, intruded into by pits H9 and H12.

In order to clarify the extent and the state of preservation of the rammed earth city wall within the excavation area, we carried out coring in the excavation area, making six holes in total, and scraped the walls of the test trenches to analyze the strata. We discovered that the rammed earth of the city wall thins gradually from south to north in the excavation area, and is interrupted by pits where it reaches the northern part of TG1. We found the northern edge of the rammed earth wall in the southern part of TG2 (Fig. Ⅰ.5.60; Pl. 33). Therefore, we now have a relatively clear understanding of the northern boundary of the south wall of the inner city; that is, the rammed earth of this section of the city wall extends to the north and ends at the southern part of TG2.

2. A Preliminary Understanding of the Composition of the Rammed Earth

As shown by the coring and survey, the rammed earth is principally divided into the following categories: grey rammed earth, greyish-brown rammed earth, yellowish-brown rammed earth, and yellow rammed earth. The rammed earth in the test trench is mainly yellowish-brown and yellow, and is blended with stones and gravel. In order to deepen our understanding of the rammed earth of the city wall, we cut a section into the cliff about 2 m to the south of TG1, directly opposite the south wall of TG1 (Fig. Ⅰ.5.61; Pl. 10: 2), and carefully compared its detailed structure with that of the excavation trenches.

This section is constructed of strata of rammed earth, and 10 layers can be seen in the section we cut: Layer ① is a sandy soil layer, 10 cm thick; Layer ② is light grey soil, 10-22 cm thick; Layer ③ is grey soil, 8-18 cm thick; Layer ④ is silty soil, 10-26 cm thick; Layer ⑤ is grey soil, about 10-30 cm thick; Layer ⑥ is yellowish-grey soil, 8-16 cm thick; Layer ⑦ is sandy and rocky soil, and was a thin layer, discontinuous, 3-8 cm thick; Layer ⑧ is yellowish-brown soil, 30-40 cm thick, and according to the amount of sandy inclusions can be divided into three sub-layers, each 6-18 cm thick; Layer ⑨ is yellow soil, 40-50 cm thick, and according to the amount of sandy inclusions can be divided into four sub-layers, each 6-25 cm thick; and Layer ⑩ is yellowish-grey soil, 40-50 cm thick, and can also be divided into three sub-layers. The consistency and color of the soil in Layer ⑥ is the same as in the first rammed earth stratum discovered in TG1, and Layer ⑧ is the same as the rammed earth stratum overlain by pit H20 in TG2, though these are all shallower than the rammed earth horizons in the north. This was also confirmed by our coring of the rammed earth in TG1.

3. The Relationship between the Rammed Earth and Related Structural Units

The rammed earth in TG1 is located under stratum ④, and is intruded into by ditches G1 and G2 and pits H3, H7, H8, H9, H12, H13 and H14. The rammed earth in TG2 is mostly located in the southern part of the test trench, and is intruded into by pits H9, H12, and H20. To protect the remaining rammed earth, the excavation stopped when it reached the surface of the rammed earth, and we did not excavate further. Therefore, we still cannot say if there are any structural units located underneath the rammed earth. In summary, according to our understanding of what has so far been excavated, the rammed earth is the oldest man-made structural remains in the two trenches.

Furthermore, we discovered a sandy layer about 15 cm thick in the center of the rammed earth layer in the test trenches, and from its height it could be seen that this sand layer might be in the same layer as the sandy soil in Layer ⑦ in the cut section on the cliff of the south city wall. The rammed earth under the sandy layer extends to the south of TG2, where it thins to only 10-40 cm thick.

Whether this is the edge of the foundation trench of the city wall or is a collapsed segment of rammed earth cannot be determined without larger-scale excavations. On the other hand, the coring showed that the sandy layer continues all the way to the north beyond the north end of TG2, where it is located directly above the virgin soil layer. If this sandy layer is the same as the sandy layer sandwiched between the rammed earth strata in the south, then it is possible that this is not a part of the rammed earth city wall; instead, it is a naturally formed layer, or possibly an alluvial sand layer deposited by a flood that washed the rammed earth wall away. If this is the case, the rammed earth layers above and below the sand layer might not be a one-time construction, and might include later repairs. However, because our excavation area is relatively small and the structural units in the excavation area intrude into the rammed earth layers both above and below the sand layer, we cannot distinguish the periods of these units based on the two layers of rammed earth.

Section 6: Conclusion

Though the area of this excavation was not large, it was carried out rigorously following the *Procedures for Field Archaeology* (National Bureau of Cultural Relics, P.R.C., 2008). The project strongly emphasized the use of scientific methods to gather archaeological data, and comprehensively collected charcoal, animal bones, burnt earth, phytoliths, flotation samples, etc., yielding a large amount of scientific archaeological data (see details in Chapter 8). The deposits in the excavation area are quite rich, the relationships between the strata are clear, and the structural units are numerous. The excavation yielded a large number of artifacts that are characteristic of both time period and region. They provide new archaeological data to further clarify our understanding of the dating of the Guicheng city site, strengthen research into pre-Qin city sites and settlement archaeology in general, and illuminate the exchange and fusion of Zhou culture in the Jiaodong and inland regions.

1. The Date of the Guicheng Inner City Site

According to the excavation and the analysis of the relationships between the pits and the rammed earth city wall, which show the lower limit of the date of the city wall, we can determine the age when Guicheng was abandoned. For instance, because pits H3, H8, H13, and H14 in TG1 and pits H12 and H20 in TG2 all directly overlie the rammed earth of the city wall, we can determine the approximate date when the city wall was abandoned based on the dates of these units. H20 is the earliest unit in the excavation area, and directly overlies the rammed earth wall. The pottery sherds unearthed in this pit have fine and medium cord impressions with very clear cord tracks, and some staggered cord tracks. The pottery sherds in H20 layer ② (the bottom layer) have particularly fine and clear cord impressions, which are typical of the early Western Zhou style. The excavated *gui* tureen H20②:1 has a sloped belly that is relatively wide and deep, which is also a typical early Western Zhou form, as are the many typical bag-shaped *li* tripod feet and crotches excavated in H20 layer ①. Furthermore, charcoal sample H20①: 10 (ZK-3359) was dated by ^{14}C, and corrected by tree ring analysis, yielding dates of 1120 (7.1%) to 1100 BCE and 1090 (61.1%) to 1000 BCE, which are clearly relatively early dates. Considering all these data, we can judge that pit H20 dates to around the later phase of the early Western Zhou period. Therefore, the city wall must have been constructed during the early Western Zhou period.

Within the excavation area, pits H18 and H19 are a little later than H20, and from the pottery unearthed in them we can judge that they date from around the late Western Zhou to the beginning of the Spring and Autumn period. H3 is the latest unit in the excavation area, with most pottery sherds bearing coarse cord decorations, also known as a "large-grain sesame-seed pattern," so it most likely dates to the Spring and Autumn period. According to the features of these units, we can conclude that Guicheng's inner city might have been in use from the early to mid-Western Zhou period, and the site might not have been abandoned until the middle to late Spring and Autumn period. This time span is consistent with the results of our surface survey (see Chapter 6 of this volume).

2. The Zhou Cultural Sequence of the Guicheng Area Revealed by the Test Excavation

From an analysis of the cultural remains, it is clear that the Zhou culture of the Guicheng area has a close relationship with the typical Zhou culture of the Zhouyuan area. After entering the Guicheng region as an advanced Bronze Culture, the Zhou culture underwent exploration, adaptation, and evolution, gradually becoming a Zhou cultural tradition possessing local characteristics. These local characteristics are mainly reflected in the *gui* tureen, *dou* pedestal dish, *guan* jar, and other pottery types used in daily living, which are made of fine grey clay, and which include a few examples of black slip pottery. The origins of this style of construction and these unique decorative characteristics can be found in the Western Zhou cultural tradition of Shaanxi – they came from the west. The equivalent vessel types in the local indigenous culture were lost in the competition with the pottery types imported from the west, but because of their usefulness as alternatives to the Zhou forms, the local indigenous cultural tradition survived in the form of *ding* cauldrons, *li* tripods, *yan* steamers, and other steaming devices. This tradition of pottery has a coarse quality, with more tempering with sand or sometimes ground seashells or talc. Their construction is also coarse, with a crude style and a focus on practical function. These types are comparable to the pottery types from the Zhenzhumen site in Changdao County and the Nanhuangzhuang cemetery in Rushan County. Therefore, two completely different cultural traditions coexisted in the Guicheng region.

Based on the representative artifacts in H20 and H3, combined with the survey data, we can see that the main developments in Guicheng's pottery are roughly as follows. The *gui* tureen's belly gradually moved up, and the circular feet became taller. The stem of the *dou* pedestal dish gradually became finer, and its basin became shallower. *Guan* jars gradually changed from being flat-bottomed to having circular feet. *Li* tripods changed gradually from having separated and high crotches, to having low and joined crotches. We can also see that early pottery types mostly have fine and medium cord decorations, while late period decorations are mostly coarse cord impressions, some being of the disorganized "sesame seed" type. The period of the pottery unearthed in this excavation area spans the early Western Zhou to the mid to late Spring and Autumn periods, though the Western Zhou period pottery is clearly the most abundant. This shows that the Guicheng city experienced relatively rapid development and prosperity during the latter period.

3. The Relationship between the Indigenous and Zhou Cultures

Looking at the two material culture horizons represented in the excavated materials, we can see that cooking vessels are still mostly of the local indigenous types. Vessels for daily use were influenced by Zhou cultural types, becoming very similar to the Central Plains vessels. The fact that cooking vessels were mostly local cultural types demonstrates that the local cultural elements still exerted a deeply ingrained influence. On the other hand, the fact that vessels for daily use gradually approached the Central Plains types shows that the influence of the Central Plains culture became increasingly dominant and far-reaching over time. The two cultural traditions were different, but also co-existed and mixed, and formed the unique features of the cultural system and pottery styles of the Guicheng region.

From a chronological perspective, in the early period the Western Zhou-style pottery types began to increase, and during the late period they evolved into types with local indigenous characteristics, thus giving rise to a new hybrid culture. After the early period, the local material culture initially lost the battle with the more advanced cultural elements from the Zhouyuan area. By the later period when it had once again risen to prominence, the culture of Guicheng had combined and absorbed the two cultural elements – the seed of a new culture had been formed. The collision, blending, and recurrence of these cultural elements vividly embodies the broad trends in the history of the Guicheng area, the west-to-east influence of cultural elements, and the competition of cultures at that time.

(Translated by Elizabeth Berger)

第六章　归城全覆盖地面采样调查

李　峰　贝丽姿

几乎所有的田野考古研究都始于地面调查，因此地面调查在长久以来一直被视为了解某个遗址或遗址群的重要方法。虽然调查中所发现的地表材料不能直接反映地下堆积的情况，但是通过与地层学试掘材料相比较，我们可以明确二者之间具有某些有意义的联系及相关性（赤峰2003：51～53，139～142）。在归城的考古研究中，全覆盖或地面调查方法被运用于项目的早期阶段就已经确定的内外两层城墙之间的区域。这一调查使我们得知超过8平方千米地表面积内的陶片分布状况，并为了解归城的聚落组织及其变迁提供了丰富的资料。

第一节　调查的目的和意义

全覆盖式调查（Full-coverage survey）是研究遗址内和遗址之间的聚落组织及其变迁的最佳方法。类似归城调查中所采用的这种密集式全覆盖调查方法，可避免有限覆盖和随意的地层试掘所带来的诸多问题，而后两种传统的调查方法更适合一些大型的、宏伟的遗址（Kowalewski and Fish 1990：263～264）。在密集式全覆盖调查中，所有区域采用相同的分辨率和采样方式，并且覆盖强度（样本的密度）相对更高。由于该方法得到的资料具有系统性，密集式全覆盖调查可以让我们对不同时期和不同空间的遗物群进行定量比较。从而，相较于非系统性调查方式，全覆盖式调查能够帮助我们讨论一系列更深入的问题。

以下是归城调查中所要研究的若干问题：

（1）检验地表遗物与地下遗物之间的联系：虽然地表上可观察的材料并不直接反映地下堆积的性质，但将地表调查资料与采用洛阳铲钻探和地层学试掘两种方式得到的地下遗物及堆积状况相比较，我们会发现这两类资料之间存在的联系。

（2）遗址地表遗物分布图：全覆盖调查可得到整个遗址陶片总分布图。归城的全覆盖调查能使我们确认陶片的集中区域，这些集中区域可能与古代人类定居或制陶活动有关。我们陶片低密度区域则可能表明这些地区的人类活动稀少。通过这些资料，我们能重建一个被称之为“受人类活动影响的几乎连续的地表”（Bintliff 2000：3）。

（3）历时性变化探查：在我们调查资料的分析中，确认出每一个时期陶片的不同聚集区域，表明遗址组织形态的时间变化特征，从而揭露出遗址的居住使用史。

（4）理解遗址形成过程：通过将所有陶片分布状况与地表形态特征相联系，我们可以更好地理解自然和人类力量对陶片分布的影响。

本项目的目的是想通过密集式全覆盖调查并结合钻探，帮助我们复原归城青铜时代的景观。我们也希望一些因为自然或人力而摧毁的古代建筑，能在它们的原址附近留下密集的陶片群，并在调查资料中被识别出来。调查在外城墙内进行，我们认识到虽然城墙是城市的边界，但它不一定是遗址中人类活动的界限（图Ⅰ.6.1）。因此，就整体而言，调查的目的不是去界定人类活动的边界，而是为理解城市内社会组织提供基础。为了了解外城墙沿线的人类活动，调查进行的范围平均超出外城墙200米。对于200米以外的区域，我们希望在不久的将来，在这个区域进行更大规模调查时进行较低密度的采集。

第二节　调查方法的设计和在田野里的操作

一、全覆盖地面调查方法

现今被广泛运用的系统性考古学调查（Systematic archaeological survey）方法源于美洲几个早期的聚落模式研究范例。这一现代科学方法与由19世纪早期一些私人古物学家、收藏家、探险家以及早期考古学家发表大量描述性报告的、非系统调查的传统非常不同（King 1978：4）。维鲁（Virú）河谷调查，尤其是1946～1948年间的调查工作，经常被视为现代聚落形态考古调查的开端（Wiley 1953）。这些做法被20世纪60～70年代在墨西哥盆地工作的研究者，进一步发展为系统性调查方法（Billman & Feinman 1999：12～21；Chifeng 2003：99；Ford and Willey 1949：19）。墨西哥盆地的这项工作，使得考古学调查由为发掘或描述遗址服务的遗址定位方法，转变为对古代地景和聚落形态的系统性探索。其他的一些资料，如民族史及地理学资料，可以与调查资料相结合使用，从而建立起一个更丰富的古代人类活动和居住场景。

在较小范围内进行全覆盖式调查，以期能探查到大遗址或遗址群中的遗物分布模式的这一方法，在已往环境中并未进行充分探讨（Gaffney，Gaffney，and Tingle 1985：95～107；Walker 1985：87～94）。这样较小规模调查的设计通常比区域性调查（Regional-scale survey）使用更高的分辨率，并且具有来建立地表遗物与地下建筑物之间更紧密关系的独特潜力。因此这种方法比区域性调查更适合去研究一个群落的内部社会政治组织。该方法的实践范例来自于地中海考古，包括早期对希腊乡村的调查（Van Andel and Runnels 1987：29～39）以及20世纪90年代维奥蒂亚（Boeotia）调查项目中对一系列希腊城址的调查（Bintliff 2000：3～20；见下文讨论）。

无论是区域性调查还是较小范围调查，全覆盖式调查方法通常都能够获取最佳的调查成果。过去的半个世纪里，考古学家已经将其运用在全球很多地区的研究中，包括中美洲、希腊、北美、美索不达米亚和中国，这些工作揭示了全覆盖式调查的优点（Cherry et al. 1988：159～162；Chifeng 2003：100；Underhill et al. 2002：745～746）。这些工作成果最终形成了大量的著作，其中大部分的调查的目的是辨认遗址，并且分析在区域尺度下的大规模人类互动体系及社会政治变迁（Kowalewski 1990a：33 ~ 34；Underhill et al. 2002：745）。通过这些工作，研究者们也针对不同类型的遗物、地形以及研究问题，对全覆盖方法进行了多方面的改进。例如，由文德安（Anne Underhill）及其同事在中国山东省东南部日照地区进行的调查，其主要目的是探查区域性聚落等级的出现，并对新石器时代晚期向早期青铜时代的过渡时期的区域性变化进行探究（Underhill et al. 2002：746）。因此研究者们选择了采集点之间30 ~ 50米间距的固定调查分辨率，这样既能完全覆盖调查区域，又能探查到不同地形上的人类活动。

在调查方法这一研究领域的最新进展包括了对“遗址”（Site）这一概念的批判，对“非遗址”（Siteless）或“无遗址”（Non-site）地区调查的倡导，地理信息系统与计算机辅助分析手段的使用，以及多种抽样方法的发展，使其在最大限度上提高调查中所发现材料的代表性。除此之外，研究者也认识到密集式地表调查（如归城调查项目）所得到的资料，可以被用来研究符合该资料自身性质的一些研究，譬如随着时间的推移，对不同地区的使用方式以及人类活动的转变（Cherry et al. 1988：159；Sullivan，Mink & Uphus 2007：322）。因为地表的陶片通常能够反映地下遗址的分布情况，即使将遗址的形成过程也考虑在内，使用此种资料来研究上述问题仍然是可能的。

二、全覆盖系统调查方法及在中国的实践

仅在过去的20年里，全覆盖系统调查就已经在中国各地展开。这一调查方法的采用与西方方法论及社会变迁理论模型的再次引入中国的考古实践相伴随，它比早期的非系统性徒步调查更受青睐。中国已有三个地区开展过由国际学者联合参加、以区域全覆盖式调查方法为主的长期研究项目，包括山东东南部的日照地区（Underhill et al. 2002：745 ~ 755）、河南西部的伊-洛河流域（Liu et al. 2002 ~ 2004：75 ~ 100）以及主要在赤峰的内蒙古东部地区（赤峰 2003：100 ~ 101；Linduff，Drennan & Shelach 2002 ~ 2004：45 ~ 73）。最近几年，由中国考古学家使用类似方法独立开展的调查项目数量也逐渐增加。

和世界其他地区一样，这些调查的目的是增加对中国地区社会发展过程的了解，以及在西方人类学模式对全球范围内的社会变迁进行比较研究。这些项目的主要关注点在于通过聚落形态变化，了解区域范围（大致在200 ~ 1000平方千米之间）内社会复杂化（Social complexity）增进的过程。具体的目标包括确认和描述遗址，分析陶片的年代以及记录不同生态区的差别。简而言之，全覆盖调查方法如今已在中国被广泛认可。

三、系统地面采样调查方法

大多数全覆盖式调查是在区域广度（Regional scale）内展开，尽管由于受地形条件及研究对象所决定，对多大面积可算作一个区域很少有统一标准（Parsons 1990：10 ~ 11）。通常，

一个区域的面积可以在100～1000平方千米这样一个范围内。对于更小范围的地区，可以使用更高的调查分辨率（Survey resolution）来考察遗物的分布状况，这种分辨率可由采取探沟方式进一步提高，如同在格鲁吉亚华莱士水库（Wallace Reservoir）（Fish & Gresham 1990：151～155）以及以色列的内盖夫沙（Negev）中心地区（Marks 1971：1240）调查所做的那样，或者像中国很多遗址所采用的系统性钻探那样，因为在中国，夯土是主要的建筑方法。调查方法的选择主要根据遗址的状况及项目所允许的时间和可使用的资源，最重要的是还需根据项目的研究目的而定。然而，较少有调查旨在研究一个聚落单位内的遗物分布情况（Gaffney，Gaffney & Tingle 1985：95～107；Walker 1985：87～94）。

在归城研究项目中，地面调查则是最好的方法，因为外城墙所包含的范围大约为8平方千米，对于地下发掘方法如探沟、试掘或系统钻探（我们在归城内城采用了钻探方法，详见第二章）而言面积都太大了，难以进行全面覆盖。实际上，归城可以被看作是以外城墙为界的一个遗址群。另一方面，该遗址远远小于大多数区域性调查所覆盖的面积。除了面积较特殊外，在设计调查方法时归城遗址中的许多情况都被考虑在内。

第一，调查范围内具有遗物分布密度相对较高的特点。因此，陶片分布密度的变化幅度相对于整体密度而言可能会较小，并且除部分村庄和湖泊地区外，极少有未发现陶片的地表。所以，我们采集陶片必须要有系统性才能使其具备代表性。随机采样调查或使用样带法（Transects method），或者是其他有限单位的观察，可能都会对陶片分布的细微变化有所遗漏。

第二，对调查方法产生较大影响的是目前该地区所采用的密集型农业及土地占用方式。事实上除了8个村庄及一些道路外，调查区域基本都是农田及果园。这不仅意味着不能进入一些地方（住宅区、工厂、采石场等）调查，还有一些地面由于不同种类的植被，其能见度也大相径庭。例如，茂密的野草或被塑料膜覆盖的花生地，都极大地降低了调查能见度，而在一些苹果园内，土地几乎完全裸露，具有很高的能见度。此外，调查工作在夏季开展，此时正是植被生长的旺盛时期。因此，无论我们采用哪种调查方法，都必须全面搜寻陶片，尤其是在能见度不高的地方。另一方面，由于山谷种植的田地面积相对较小，以及邻近田地倾向于种植不同种类的作物，因此可减少能见度变化对调查的影响。而这一情况正是当前中国土地政策的影响结果，作为一种经济策略，许多家庭通常使其种植作物的种类多样化，并且没有任何一个家庭的土地占有量远远超过村庄里的其他家庭。因此，调查区域的平均能见度是相对稳定的，并且调查得以进行的前提假设是田块面积足够小，以及不同种类作物的种植地点有足够高的随机性，不会系统地影响到整个调查区域陶片的分布情况。

第三，内外城墙间的地势高差大：调查的中心区域地形相对平坦，但顺着外墙方向地势却逐渐增高，其中一些缓坡已被开发为梯田。外城墙的建造显然是利用了其较高的地势以达到防御性目的（林 2006：137；中美联合归城考古队 2011：34～36）。内外城墙之间区域地形的最大高差可达70米（虽然大部分区域差值约在30～40米的范围内），遗址的南部区域没有外城墙，即意味着遗址南部并无明确界限。除河岸、水库以及其附近地区外，大部分区域（现代村庄以外的范围）是可以进行调查的，因此为了了解整个城市的密度等级，采用系统性全覆盖调查是很有必要的。

归城调查采用了在区域调查中发展起来的系统性、全覆盖地表调查的基本方法，并且遵循了开展这类田野研究项目的基本原则。但是，为了适应归城遗址特殊的面积和其艰难的地理和季节条件，我们必须对这种方法进行相应的改进。相对于Parsons所描述的通常30～50米的调查分辨率（Parsons 1990：11），或者是在赤峰调查中采用的50米分辨率（赤峰 2003：40，124），我们在归城调查中则是将每组成员以20米的间隔分开，并在整个调查区域始终都使用这种分辨率。不同于大多数区域性调查通过某一规定数量的陶片的出现［譬如，赤峰调查中100米内出现3个陶片（Chifeng 2003：42，127）］，来确定一个“遗址”并因此建立一个采集区这种做法，在归城，无论的何种地形条件下，每个调查采集点内我们都在一个标准大小的采集圈内进行完全采集。一些植被茂盛的地区，我们要求所有调查人员都需进行彻底搜查，并且为了克服高低起伏的不利地形条件，我们尽一切努力抵达山丘顶部以及山壑底部地区进行调查和采集。

我们称这种调查方法为“系统性地表采样”（Systematic Surface Sampling，SSS）调查方法，它使我们能够在固定的高分辨率下对总范围达8平方千米调查区域进行系统地、完全地采集。正如在所有区域调查中那样，这只是一个抽样的方法，并且只要求在每个采集点内进行完全采集。但我们确信这些采集都具有代表性。

这一方法也使我们能够回避“遗址”定义上的困境，近年来人类学著作中对此进行了激烈的讨论。有人认为区域调查旨在确定聚落区域及其他活动，对遗址边界的描述事实上会对采集资料造成很大偏差，以及掩盖了细微的分布模式和忽略零星分布的遗物（Bintliff 2000：4～6；Bintliff，Kuna & Venclová 2000：2；Haselgrove 1985：21～26；Sullivan，Mink & Uphus 2007：328）。归城调查以整个归城城址为陶片采集目标，因此我们没有必要在调查范围内确定更小的“遗址”。

四、系统采样方法在田野里的具体操作

在调查的初始阶段，为了寻找调查分辨率和工作速度的最优平衡点，我们对不同规模的网格进行了试验。试验后很快便决定采用20米×20米的网格，这样既能保证拥有相当高的密集度的采集区，同时又能保证在2～3个季度内完成8平方千米的调查范围。每个调查组的人数每天在5～10人的范围内，这些调查组员们可拉出一个最长可达到200米的调查行进线，这也是调查组组长（持地图者）在崎岖不平的地形中，能审视到整个小组的最大距离。

调查组是由同钻探队技术人员和学生组成。组员们在组长即地图持有者的领导下，以20米的间隔一起前行，每20米做一个采集点，这样就可确保整个调查区域内，所有采集都是在20米×20米网格的交点上进行的。每个采集点都是一个半径为3米的圆圈，具体做法是在地上插一根系有绳子的木棍作为中心，用绳子拉出3米的长度并绕中心一圈，最终得到一个半径为3米的圆圈作为采集点，然后将采集点内所有陶片全部采集起来（见图Ⅰ.6.2）。按照规定，调查队员们对宽度小于2厘米的陶片不予以采集，并按已培训的辨识陶片年代的方法，仅收集汉代灭

亡（220年）之前的陶片。每个采集点的采集品都需经过仔细地包装并贴上标签，标签上还需注明由通用编号系统（详细描述见下文）所确定的采集点号、日期、组名以及陶片采集数量。然后由地图持有者在地图上，用圆圈标注每个有陶片的采集点的位置；如果采集点没有发现陶片，则在地图上标注一个“X”。

为了对队员进行准确定位及指导其行动，高分辨率的调查区域航空照片是必不可少的工具。此类照片不同于大多数区域调查所使用的比例1：10000的地图；对于一个组员间相互间隔20米的调查来说，这种1：10000地图无法在调查中使用。在2008年的野外工作中，调查组利用从谷歌地球中下载的照片作为野外地图，虽然这些照片并不够理想，但仍有足够的清晰度使地图持有者能辨别出道路和农田。2009年，我们从一家名为DigitalGlobe的卫星图片公司，购买到归城地区近年的（2004）卫星图片，它为我们提供了该地区非常清晰的地形图像。这些图片被导入到ArcGIS 地理信息系统中，并在图片打印之前数码叠加了20米×20米（地面距离）的网格，从而制作出了一套新的野外地图（图Ⅰ.6.3）。地图持有者可以利用在航拍照片中可观察到的田野界限和标志，对每个组员进行准确定位并且引导他们进行点到点之间的移动。

我们采用一个统一的编号系统，给每个调查点分配一个特定的名称。首先，使用经度/纬度系统（具体指谷歌地球中所使用的1984年世界大地坐标系统［WGS84］），以归城为中心的整个调查范围（坐标：N37°34′15″～N37°36′39″；E120°32′49″～E120°35′13″）被分为16个大区域（见图Ⅰ.6.1；另见《前言》，图Ⅰ.0.3）。每个区域东西宽900米，南北长1120米。在每个区域内都使用字母数字系统进行编号，因此每一个调查点的编号包含区域号（1～16）、列数（从A～Z，再到a～s）、排数（1～56），从而组成一个完整的区域编号（如8-A23或3-q52）。通过使用这一统一编号系统，所有数据都可录入易智瑞公司（ESRI）的ArcGIS软件的电子表格内以及在地图上进行可视性展现。由于外城墙实际上就是城市的边界，因此调查组并未覆盖超出城墙200米范围之外的采集点。2008年和2009年两个田野工作季度的调查总面积大约是800公顷，即8平方千米。由于我们在内城开展了密集的钻探工作，所以不再对其进行系统性地面调查（见第二章）。

田野调查中所采集的陶片，都需按预先划分的时期进行分类，包括新石器时期、岳石文化时期、西周文化时期、东周文化时期、周文化时期、汉代以及土著文化（时期划分标准见下文）。进行分类前需清洗陶片并晾干。在项目中工作的学生均受过项目研究者培训，能够区分古代遗物与现代遗物，以及识别出每一大时期的典型陶质和绳纹纹饰。烟台市博物馆的工作人员也对学生的培训提供了帮助，允许他们到烟台市及龙口市博物馆，学习、观摩、熟悉各时期的完整陶器。一般只需一周左右的时间，每个学生都能熟练地对陶片进行分类，以及区分出现代遗物。我们采用Microsoft Excel软件制作了记录有每个采集点信息的电子表格，包括每一个时期的陶片数量、陶片平均尺寸、备注任何有趣或有特征的陶片，以及石制品。学生们还被告知需要注意一些特殊材料如制作青铜器的陶范和建筑材料等。

在希腊进行的维奥蒂亚（Boeotia）项目也采用了类似的调查方法来研究古典时代到希腊化时代早期的城市耶妥斯（Hyettos），并产生了相似的数据。维奥蒂亚调查也是在20米×20米的方格单位内进行完全采集，覆盖范围共26公顷（不到归城一个田野工作季度所调查范围的10%）。调查的目的是确定遗址主要占领使用时期的年代，并且分析遗弃差率（Differential rates of discard），以及在不同时期之间人口规模可能存在的变化（Bintliff 2000：4），这些都与归城调查的目的类似。维奥蒂亚项目在20米×20米的方格单位内收集和记录所有陶片，并且陶片分布密度更高：每一个方格内有100至200片陶片，而归城整个调查区域的平均陶片密度，即每个20米×20米方格单位内陶片数，仅有16片（平均每一个面积为28.27平方米的采集圈内有1.126片，采集圈面积约占20米×20米方格单位的7%）。然而，由于归城项目所采集的陶片，都位于预先设定好的圆心及半径的圆圈内，并且其面积更小，因此遗物的位置记录要比耶妥斯的相关记录更精确。归城调查以较少的人力资源提供了一个类似的调查分辨率（这两项调查中都采用了20米×20米的方格单位），这一点尤其重要，因为归城的调查面积远远大于耶妥斯，要想在所有范围内都进行完全采集是不切实际的。

因此，我们认为系统性地表采样（SSS）方法对归城这类规模的遗址的系统调查更加有效。维奥蒂亚调查所采用的调查方法其唯一重要优势在于它能产生更多的陶片数量用于分析。然而，归城项目很容易再次选择某一地区进行完全采集以得到更多的陶片（见下第六节：“完整采集单位（CCU）Ⅰ-Ⅲ”）。

第三节　调查过程及所获资料

一、调查的经过

2008年6月13日，归城调查工作首先在第7区开展，这一区域的遗址在形成过程中可能受到自然力的影响如洪水较少；为了测试调查方法在地势相对平坦地区的使用情况，我们特意选择了该区域（图版53：1）。由于第7区还围绕归城内城，因此可预知其具有高密度的人工遗物分布。接着调查工作朝外移动至2区、3区、4区及北部地区，最后到达8区和部分12区，其中包括了从属于外城墙的大型地下建筑。2009年调查组采取同样的方法对5区、6区、9区、10区、11区（图版53：2；图版54：2；图版55）、剩下的12区以及16区进行了调查。1区、13区、14区及15区因完全位于外城墙之外，所以被排除在调查范围外。

2008和2009年度的调查工作，均于6月初至7月底这一期间展开。调查初期，农作物的种植工作已经结束，虽然这一时期内农作物一直在生长，但对大多数区域的能见度问题不会造成严重影响（图Ⅰ.6.4）。每次调查结束时，植物的生长状况，尤其是玉米，都已经太过茂盛以致调查组人员难以穿行于田地中。

调查所得资料的数据处理工作于2008年第一个工作季度后立即展开。为了完成这项工作，一名学生同样也是调查组的成员贝丽姿（Elizabeth Berger）通过哥伦比亚大学的电子数据服务实验室（EDS）所提供的教程，接受了易智瑞公司（ESRI）的ArcGIS软件的培训。接下来的四个月中，在哥伦比亚大学的电子数据服务实验室专家的帮助下，我们将Excel表格中的田野记录数据转录入ArcGIS 软件中，并生成了2008年调查区域的数字地图（见第八章）。紧接着在春季学期内，我们分析了数据的时空模式以及识别出可能存在的偏差或错误。分析结果肯定了我们调查方法所产生的数据的可靠性，这些数据揭示了陶片分布模式的一些大的历时性变化。这些分析为评价我们的工作方法以及第二年的工作提供了基础。

二、调查所获资料可能存在的偏差

我们在设计系统性地表采样（SSS）调查方法时，已充分考虑了不同地区能见度的问题（见上文第二节）。所以，接下来我们将主要讨论遗址形成过程中及计算机分析中可能存在的偏差。

正如考古学家曾探讨过那样，人类活动如翻耕、建造、堆肥等，不仅会改变暴露在地表的人工制品的聚集情况，还会产生地表遗物新的聚集及其他非正常现象，这些活动都将使地下堆积不再如设想那样与地表遗物具有直接联系。这些人类活动也会破坏质地较脆弱的文物，从而可能对易碎陶器生产时期的数据造成偏差（Bintliff 2000：5； Haselgrove 1985：9）。

归城现今最明显的遗址形成过程（Formation process）当然是遍及遗址的密集型农业。然而，正如之前已讨论过的那样，归城调查的主要目的并不是对遗物群如遗址那样谨慎地定位，而是去识别整个调查区域的遗物相对密度。因为现代人类活动在整个遗址中几乎是一致的，我们可以假定翻耕以及土壤移动的活动不会显著改变整个归城的陶片分布模式。

我们在受现代建筑活动影响的居住区内没有采集到任何陶片，然而村庄周围陶片的密集似乎并未因村庄的存在而受到影响。如果建筑过程中对围绕在它们周围的考古学遗物产生过剧烈影响，那么所有现代村庄周围的密度值都会出现相似的变化，但事实却并非如此。调查区域的北部（3区、6区、7区内）的村庄附近遗物的分布密度，比调查区域南部（9区、10区、11区）的更高，而南部村庄周围的陶片分布密度则较为一致。总的来说，任何一个现代村庄的周围都不见遗物分布密度上出现任何具有意义性的改变。

自然作用尤其是河道和洪水的影响是归城调查中所考虑的另一方面。然而，陶片分布状况中的任何重大变化似乎都与鸦鹊河无关。自然作用的影响在内城的调查期间得到确认，内城在其使用时期内至少被洪水入侵过一次，洪水过后部分内城得到重建。因此毫无疑问，鸦鹊河对沿岸地区肯定产生过一些重要的影响。但是沿岸地带的遗物分布情况却与遗址其他区域类似，靠近内城区域密度最大，而在城市的北部边缘区域密度稍微降低。洪水或雨水冲刷也许是外城南部临近莱山区域遗物稀少的原因。但是，该地区的陶片分布与山坡地形似乎并无密切的联系，难以证明此种推测，并且在地形平坦的区域也没有发现陶片密度更高的情况。因此，归城南部区域遗物稀疏的原因不能归结于受自然作用力的影响。这一结论在事实上也得到了支持，城市南部区域陶片密度的轻微突变并未与地形等高线相对应，并且这种突变在不同海拔地区都有出现。

在统计学上，归城西周时期以前的遗物密度非常低。这一时期的遗物早于归城的营建，它们的出现应该从区域的文化背景来评估。要做到这一点，考古队可以回到归城去采集更多的属于归城时期以前的遗物。

关于归城的主要使用时期周代，其主要的问题是大量的无纹饰陶片，很难断定其年代到底属于西周时期还是东周时期。在每个调查区域内，周代的陶片（从陶质上可辨识）根据有纹饰陶片的相对比例，分为西周和东周时期（见下文第五节）。但由于其数量巨大，如果这一假设不正确的话，将会对有关这两个时期的数据造成严重扭曲。我们用2009年试掘的地层中所出的陶片，来评估这种错误的可能性。从这些数据来看，西周和东周时期有纹饰的陶片的比例几乎一致。但不管怎样，两个时期有纹饰陶片的比率的差异必须是非常大，才能对数据的解释方面产生重大的影响。

同样重要的是，我们需要考虑到统计显著性检验（Statistical significance tests）的局限性。考古学的数据极其复杂和多样，最好的评估办法是多重策略相结合，包括统计显著性检验和目视法（Visual methods）。所有陶片数据，包括在统计上有显著性的分布，都必须在遗址中其他考古学证据具备的情境下进行评估。最后，我们发现大的样本量能让*T*检验（*T*-tests）带来人为的有重要意义的*P*值（*P*-values）。为了解释这一现象，在使用*T*检验（见下文分析）的部分，我们同样也对这些数据进行效应量（Effect size）的测试，以确定由*T*检验呈现出来的关系的可靠程度。

三、调查所获资料的质量和代表性

归城调查总共发现13221片陶片，来自约15000个采集点（图版56）。仅有1253（9.5%）片陶片无法对其进行年代判定。整体上看，43%的采集点至少有一片长度超过2厘米的陶片，平均每个含有遗物的采集点有2.6片陶片（标准差2.5），并且平均每个采集点有1.1片陶片（标准差2.1）。

在2008～2009年8平方千米范围的归城调查中，我们采用的系统性地表采样调查方法使项目汇集到大量的资料，它们代表了古代遗物目前的分布状况，尤其是陶片分布状况。这些数据不仅使我们可以获得整个遗址地表连续的陶片分布图，并且为我们解释地表遗物与地下建筑及堆积关系提供了一个坚实的基点，进而可对项目最初提出的一些重要问题进行解答。

第四节　分析一：归城城址的内部组织

一、主要陶片集中区的确定

调查中发现地表陶片的高密度分布区主要有四个：内城周边，以及外城墙的东城墙、西北城墙及西城墙沿线。这些区域很可能与大规模人类集中性活动有关，其中包括军事演练和交通。这一推论也得到勘探出的古建筑遗迹的支持，这些遗迹与陶片的聚集分布区相符合，这也为研究每一个区域内发生的活动类型提供了进一步的线索。

陶片的集聚群可从陶片分布总图（图Ⅰ.6.5a-b）及每一时期分布图上直接观察到（见下第五节）。这些集聚群是由*T*检验和Getis-Ord Gi*统计的热点分析（Hotspot analysis）所确定的。这种空间统计方法将图上每个点值与总图的平均值及临近点值进行比较。由此图上每个点都产生了一个Z分数（*Z*-score）和*P*值（*P*-value）。Z分数最高和*P*值最低的点明显偏离了平均分布，因此被视为"热点"或者是统计显著的高聚集遗物。*T*检验的结果将在下文中进行讨论，西周和东周时期的热点分析结果则用图表示（图Ⅰ.6.6a-b）。

陶片分布密度最高的区域位于7区，靠近内城尤其是其东侧［双尾*T*检验比较了7区和其他所有区域总体的每一采集点陶片数，得到的结果是*T*分数为32.0，*P*值小于0.0001，表明内城周边区域与其他区域的陶片密度不同，其差异具有极显著性统计意义。效应量Cohen's *d*为0.83，被视为是一个大的效应值（Cohen 1988：227）］。这一数值证实了内城是一个人口及活动相对集中的区域。

在东边，整个8区的南部即河道和外城之间区域，东周时期的陶片分布密度相对较高（双尾T检验比较了8区和其他所有区域［不包括7区］总体的陶片密度，得到的结果是*T*分数为10.6，P值小于0.0001，该值具有很高的统计显著性。效应量为Cohen's *d*为0.94，同样也是一个大的效应值）。同时值得注意的是这个高聚集区位于山顶，而不是低地或山谷，这表明分布模式并未受到地表雨水冲刷过多的影响。这一地区陶片的高密度分布，反而可能与外城墙的一个复杂的附属地下建筑有关。通过钻探，这些地下遗迹已在地图上被绘制出来，然而它的功能目前尚不明确。东南部附近则又是另外一个陶片聚集区，该聚集区也与地下夯土墙有关，位于8区和12区的东部边界。

我们已确认的另一个陶片集聚区位于外城墙的北墙附近，横跨2区东南部及6区东北部（2区与3、4两区总体的每一采集点陶片数值比较后，结果为*T*分数为3.8，*P*值为0.0002，具有统计显著性，效应量为Cohen's *d*为0.48，一个中等效应值，表明这些区域的差别虽然有统计学的显著性，但差距并不太大）。有趣的是，位于该区域的地下建筑的宽度非常大，表明它是与城墙相连的附属设施，很可能是供军队使用的平台。显然，所有这些高密度区域与地下建筑之间都是具有联系的。

最后一个相对密集的区域位于西墙沿线，靠近5区、6区边界的区域。鉴于此处地形即两山之间有一个南北向自然通道，很有可能这是从西边进入归城的主要入口。

调查区域的最北部（2区、3区、4区及6区、7区、8区的北部）的陶片密度比城市中心区的更低，而与外城墙附近区域的密度相比并没有太大变化。这跟早期调查者的发现结果一致，他们说在外城墙附近所能观察到的遗物同样也非常稀少（见李步清，林仙庭 1991：911）。在靠近莱山的南部调查区域内，地表遗物也极其稀少，表明古代这一地区的人类活动集中性非常低。正如上文所讨论过那样，这些相对较低的密度似乎并不是自然作用力影响的结果。靠近莱山山麓的半个归城南部地区，虽然陶片的密度较低但其平均尺寸很大，表明该地区使用功能之一可能为贵族埋葬区，这类埋葬是近期地表出现的大块陶片的潜在来源。

纵观整个遗址陶片的平均尺寸相对一致。每个陶片的总平均值为41.1毫米；在有遗物的采集点中，每个采集点的陶片尺寸的平均值为41.6毫米，标准差为11.4毫米。单从视觉观察来看，靠近内城的陶片平均尺寸似乎有轻微增加（见图Ⅰ.6.7）。7区所有采集点（除了未发现遗物的采集点）的陶片平均尺寸为42.7毫米，标准差14.3毫米，比其他区域的平均值更高。*T*检验表明这一结果具有很高的统计学的意义（双尾T检验比较了除未发现遗物的采集点外的每一采集点陶片的平均尺寸，7区与其他区的总值比较后的结果为*T*分数为3.2，*P*值为0.0015，表明这种差异具有非常大的统计显著性）。平均尺寸中观察到的差异，其形成原因可能是由于内城附近更高的遗物分布密度，这造成了该地区陶片有更大的尺寸幅度，包括更多的大陶片（需注意的是内城附近陶片尺寸的标准差较大）。不管怎样，该效应值很小，效应量是Cohen's *d*仅为0.10，这是一个很小的效应值。所以，虽然这些区域的差异具有统计学显著性，但由于数据点数量巨大，这种差异可能太小从而不具有意义（南部地区因有近期从墓葬中出土的大片陶片而可能例外）。

二、陶片集中分布区域与地下周代遗迹的关系

归城外城内一些地面看似是地貌特征，实际上是古代夯土建筑所遗留下来的遗迹。陶片集中分布区与这些特征的关系，说明它们在古代城市生活中的重要意义。一个典型的例子是2008年度的2号考古学特征遗址（Archaeological Feature 2），一个约有10米高、100米长、5至10米宽的南北向高地（图Ⅰ.6.8）。该高地位于内城东部的7区，大致对应7-e20至7-e25这几个采集点。对建筑周围陶片进行采集时，调查小组发现了几十个较大的陶容器碎片，可能是从建筑的顶部或地层中冲刷出来的，伴随还有大量石制品和其他建筑遗物。该建筑周围的许多采集点内均采集到大量陶片，数量在16至34片之间。在2007年的前期调查工作中，对建筑的顶部进行了钻探工作，确认夯土的存在，表明其在古代为一个高台或建筑，并且其原有规模较之现存规模要大很多（一位当地的农民告诉调查队，这一遗迹的北部区域近年来已被夷为平地）。

内城附近高密度的遗物与大量的遗迹相对应。虽然调查范围并未延伸至内城墙内，但这一区域的系统钻探工作已揭露出地下建筑基址集中分布在内城的两个区域内见上编第二章。内城的1号完全采集单位所采集的陶片，也表明了每平方米0.259片陶片的高密度分布比（见下文），如果在标准采集圈（28.27平方米）即我们用作覆盖归城其余区域的采集圈内采集的话，平均每个采集圈的陶片数量高达7.3片，比整个归城的平均每个采集圈陶片数1.1片（或仅包括有遗物的采集圈的2.6片）要高很多；比之7区的邻近区域平均每个采集圈的陶片数3.0片也高。仅这一点就表明，整个归城中内城是人类活动的高聚集区。这一高聚集区也被1号完全采集单位（CCUⅠ）附近的试掘所证实。

正如前文所讨论那样，调查中所发现的几个高密度区域位于外城墙东部、西北部及西部沿线。每个陶片的高度集中分布区均与地下建筑有关，其中包括外城墙附属的大型、复杂的遗迹。例如5、6两区边界附近的集中分布区域，为可能与西边主城门附近的高密度人类活动相关。值得一提的是，该区域也是古代河流流入城市，从而汇入环绕着内城的护城河的地方。

三、陶片的空间分布与地景的关系

调查中尚未发现任何特殊的陶片分布模式与鸦鹊河有关。虽然河流流向北边，但地表遗物最高的聚集分布并不在北边，而是在靠近内城的区域。同样也没有发现地表遗物分布与地形之间的必然联系：一些分布密度最高的区域事实上发现于山顶。与之相反，归城的陶片分布模式更倾向于与地下和地上的古代建筑遗迹有关，这些也是古代人类的活动区域。

人类活动很可能聚集于河流沿岸，因为河流能提供交通便利及两岸休闲活动区域，但是这一推测并不被我们的调查数据所支持。这可能是由于归城的调查范围仅限于内、外城墙之间；未来的区域调查能更好地研究自然特征与人类活动之间的关系。

调查数据所显示出的总体分布模式是高级活动位于城市中心，一些重点军事活动位于外城墙附近。数据表明了地表陶片与永久性人工建筑之间密切的联系。然而同样重要的是，数据也表明了在不同的居住使用时期内，人类活动也有所不同。

第五节　分析二：年代标准的运用

一、分期的基本框架和年代标准

在青铜时代胶东半岛的地缘政治环境下，归城很可能是西周扩张的前沿阵地，西周中期该城可能居住有周代贵族成员（见Li 2006：308～314）。从西周晚期至东周时期，随着西边西周王朝的衰落，归城因此成为土著国家莱国的中心，它融合了周文化与当地的南黄庄文化。

调查区域内的本地陶器制作传统相当复杂。之前的一些研究通过对胶东半岛东部的本地陶器传统的分析，确定了从新石器时期至青铜时代早期的一系列文化，其中包括白石村文化（约公元前5000～前3700年）、邱家庄文化（约公元前3700～前3000年）、龙山文化（约公元前3000～前2000年）、岳石文化（约公元前2000～前1400年）、珍珠门文化以及南黄庄文化。在这一个时空框架体系内，岳石文化被视为大致与中原地区的二里头文化同时期，珍珠门文化大致与晚商（公元前1554～前1046年）同时期。南黄庄文化年代大致相当于西周晚期至东周（公元前770～前221年）时期，但这一时期却是山东东部地区情况最不明确的时期（烟台市博物馆2006：10～14，106～120）。

事实上，当南黄庄文化陶器与周代陶器在同一墓葬或地层单位中共出时，它通常也被认为是相当于周代的遗存，因为尚未有系统性的研究能够用来辨析其年代。在胶东半岛的北半部，尤其是龙口地区，其陶器的制作体系主要是由西边引进的周文化因素所主导。考古学资料已证明周文化的扩张是从西部一直到胶东半岛东部（主要是北半部），龙口地区出土的贵族青铜器及铭文也证实了这一点，它们表明了该地区同陕西渭河谷地中心的西周王朝密切的政治联系。

虽然山东东部的周文化也存在一些地域性特征，但总体上它符合周文化的发展趋势。因此，我们可以采用周文化的年代标准来分析。西周和东周代表了归城两个最密集的占领使用时期。西周到东周的政治转变在归城占用历史上有重要意义，它也导致了山东西部齐国的扩张，最终在公元前567年齐国征服了归城和莱国。

西周和东周的陶片可通过绳纹装饰风格差异区分开来。调查组即依据这一判断标准将周代陶片划分到西周和东周遗物内，而具有周代陶质却无纹饰的陶片，被划分到周代这一大的分类中。根据西周和东周有纹饰陶片的比例，将这些具有周代陶器陶质却无纹饰的陶片划归入西周或东周遗物中，产生了校正后的西周时期和东周时期分类分例。

从新石器时期龙山文化到岳石文化时期的周代以前的陶片，在调查区域内非常稀少，可能因为该区域在周代以前的聚落体系集中在其他地方。考虑到我们分析的目的，将这两个时期合并到一个单独的分类中即“周代以前”时期。调查中包括年代最晚的汉代（公元前206～公元220年），其陶片同样也是通过陶质和纹饰所辨别。最后，归城的本地陶器传统属定义尚不严格的南黄庄文化，这被视为一个单独的分类。这些陶片的时间范围大约在西周至东周时期，但是它们的确切年代目前尚无法断定。事实上，调查的目的之一是去探求本地文化和同时期周文化陶片的空间分布关系。不同时期陶片分布情况见表Ⅰ.6.1。

二、第一期：相当周代以前

周代以前的陶片仅发现17片。大多数属于新石器时期文化，其中有4片属于岳石文化时期。唯一明显的集聚群是一组有5片陶片的聚集，但每个都发现于不同的采集点，位于3区的西南角和7区的西北角（图Ⅰ.6.9a-b）。然而，目前来自这一时期的数据太少，无法对城内该时期的使用情况进行分析。类似的复原模式已被Bintliff所观察到（Bintliff 2000：5）。他写道：“在历史时期众多的遗物中的若干史前时期陶片，可能表明了一个新石器时期遗址的存在已经被晚期的占有和使用所掩盖”。在归城中这种可能性当然也是存在的，但归城地区在新石器时期聚落体系中的地位，还必须凭借未来的区域调查来阐明。

三、第二期：相当西周时期

周代的陶片数量远远高于其他任何时期。西周时期陶片的绳纹纹路深而且更加匀称，烧制温度也高。虽然绳纹宽度变化很大，但其纹路痕迹清晰可见，并且看上去非常规整（图Ⅰ.6.10）。这些陶片所代表的器物大多数是罐、鬲和盆。总体而言，这些陶器不管是陶质还是纹饰都与周代核心地区的陶器非常相似。

可辨识出的西周时期陶片（即有纹饰的陶片）总数为1105片，占全部陶片的8%；7%的采集点发现有西周陶片。西周时期的陶片主要聚集在鸦鹊河以西区域（图Ⅰ.6.11a-b）。其中有两个集中区，一个集中于内城，另一个位于2区，围绕在外城墙西北部大型地下平台建筑的周围。鸦鹊河以东地区西周时期陶片分布较为零散，并且在8区和外城墙东墙沿线的12区仅有极少发现。这些都清楚地表明在西周绝大多数时期内，人类的活动集中于归城的西半部。

四、第三期：相当东周时期

调查所发现的东周时期遗物比西周时期的更多。东周时期陶片共3644片，占所有陶片总数的28%；20%的采集点含有东周陶片。这表明在陶片数量上，西周和东周时期之间的涨幅超过200%。东周时期陶片的绳纹较浅，并且有时分布散乱、不连续。因为这种绳纹较浅，通常称之为“麦粒”状绳纹，纹路痕迹通常也难以辨认。这些陶片所代表的器类与西周时期的相同，但陶质普遍更硬，烧制温度比西周陶片的更高（图Ⅰ.6.12）。

东周时期的陶片数量众多，其原因可能是因为这一时期更为集中的居住使用方式、人类活动的增加以及占领使用面积的增加。另一种可能性是，这种密度上的变化可能由于两个时期的时间跨度不同（东周的年数几乎是西周的两倍）所造成的。然而，同样也有理由相信，该遗址的完全占用并未及整个东周时期。《左传》记载公元前567年齐国灭莱国，仅有203年时间属于东周时期，这一时期代表着归城的人类居住使用高峰期。在这之后遗址虽然继续被使用，但使用规模却大幅度减小了。因此，陶片数量增长的原因，更可能是因为东周时期更为密集的居住使用，而不是因为其更长的时间跨度。

在调查区域的东半部即8区和12区的北部，陶片数量的增长尤其显著。这一区域很少发现有西周时期的陶片（8区西周陶片数量占陶片总数的比例不到1%，12区则仅为4%），而东周时期陶片似乎在该区域特别密集（8区与12区的东周陶片数量均占陶片总数的32%）。正如之前所讨论过的那样，这群陶片可能与该区域外城墙的复杂建筑有关，这点可通过地下遗物确认。除了陶片的密集分布外，在这一区域我们还发现了大量建筑材料，其中最主要是具有东周绳纹特征的砖块（图Ⅰ.6.13）。

总体来看，陶片分布上的变化表明，人类的活动从归城的中心区域扩张到东部外围地区。此外，东周时期的遗物在内城周围的集中分布，以及在西北部外城墙周围区域的集中分布，表明这些区域在归城的城市组织中一直都具有重要性（见图Ⅰ.6.14a-b）。

第二、三期中没有纹饰的素面陶片因无法断定其究竟属于哪个时期，从而被称之为“周代陶片”。这类型的陶片我们共发现6375片，占已发现陶片总数的48%。如果假设这些陶片分属西周和东周的比例，与那些有纹饰陶片的比例一致，那么总体的历时性趋势则没有改变。校正后的数据表明，西周的遗物共2810片占总数的21%，而东周遗物共8314片占总数的63%［为了说明不同区域内，西周和东周时期陶片分布的差异，每一区域的陶片先单独计算，最后叠加在一起。图Ⅰ.6.13和I.6.14的地图上未包含这一信息）。在试掘材料的基础上，我们进一步评估了素面陶片的归属性问题。结果表明其比例与西周和东周时期带纹饰陶片的比例相近（H20，属于西周时期，含有46%的无纹饰陶片；H2，H3（第1层）以及H6，属于东周时期，分别有56%、66%及51%的无纹饰陶片］。因此，我们可以断定从西周时期到东周时期，有纹饰陶片的比例都相对固定，并且我们完全可以使用这种办法将周代陶片进行区分。

五、第四期：汉代

第三期之后，陶片数量急剧下降。汉代的陶片总共只有78片，不到总陶片数的1%。这一数据表明第四期遗址内人类活动大幅减少。有趣的是，汉代陶片的集中分布区位于调查区域的北部和东北部，内城附近陶片数量却出乎意料的少。这说明汉代城市内的使用或活动分布发生了转移（图Ⅰ.6.15）。其中的两个聚集区似乎均在外城墙附近（2区和3区内）（图Ⅰ.6.16a-b）；这两个聚集区可在未来的调查中作进一步观察研究，以便了解它们是否与外城墙沿线的一些设施的持续使用有关，又或者其范围已大幅延伸至城墙外，这当然是遗址使用转变的一个标志。另一个聚集区域位于8区，在其田埂边发现有大量带几何纹饰的汉代砖（图Ⅰ.6.17），通过之前的调查得知，这些汉砖似乎与区域内一批汉代墓葬有关。因此，2区、3区的陶片聚集也很有可能是跟汉代的墓葬有关。最后，在未进行系统调查的归城最南部区域，有建于秦统一之后的一个巨大的宫殿夯土基址（图版142：1），是秦始皇（公元前259～前210年）在莱山“月主祠”（图版142：2；图版143：1-2）主持祭祀活动时所使用的行宫。因此，尽管第四期陶片数量急剧下降，但毫无疑问的是，归城地区在秦和汉代时期仍然有人类居住使用的活动。

六、本地特色文化遗物的分布

本地特色文化陶器传统以红色色调及粗糙的陶质为特点。原料中混合有高比例的白英石，并且烧制温度相对较低。这种制陶的传统方法可以追溯到岳石文化，如果不早于岳石文化的话。这类陶片没有任何纹饰，陶色为红色或浅褐色（图Ⅰ.6.18）。土著传统陶器类型仅限于鬲和鼎这两类，后者不见于周文化传统中。调查共发现此类陶片717片，占陶片总数的5%；含有土著陶片的采集点共有582个，占总数的5%。

本地特色陶片的分布模式与东周时期的陶片分布模式相似，陶片集中于内城附近及内外城墙之间，一直到东部地区（图Ⅰ.6.19）。统计学检测也证实了土著陶片分布与整个周代陶片分布的相似性，而并不仅限于东周时期［双尾*T*检验比较了7区及其他所有调查区域的每个采集点含有的土著陶片数，得到*T*分数为20.7，*P*值小于0.0001，该结果表明内城附近区域和其他调查区域的土著陶片密度差异，具有很大的统计显著性。效应量Cohen’s *d*为0.47，是一个中等效应值。与此同时，双尾*T*检验比较了8区和其他所有调查区域（不包括7区）的土著陶片密度，其结果为*T*分数为4.56，*P*值小于0.0001，同样具有统计显著性。然而效应量Cohen’s *d*为0.13，是一个相对较小的效应值。这表明8区和其他调查区域的土著陶片密度差异较小，虽然具有统计学意义，但可能不太具有实际意义］。

虽然目前我们尚不能明确它们与珍珠门文化之间的关系，但是楼子庄遗址作为这一区域内珍珠门文化的代表，距归城西部仅14千米（烟台市博物馆 2006：106～114），因此极可能至少归城的部分土著陶片确实属于延续至西周时期的珍珠门文化传统。毫无疑问的是，土著文化陶器传统早于中原文化因素到达之前就已存在，并且持续存在于整个周文化占领时期，而且可能以南黄庄文化的形式存在。这一情况的存在可能会产生一个复杂的陶器制作体系，包括同时使用多种技术和风格，类似现象在内蒙古东部的赤峰调查中也被发现（赤峰 2003：120）。在归城2009年的试掘中显示更晚（东周）的地层中所含土著陶片的比例，要比早期（西周）地层中的比例高很多。这表明随着时间的流逝，土著传统逐渐使自身融入归城陶器制作体系的主流中，而作为地方性国家的莱国也逐渐成为在政治上和文化上独立于周文化传统的国家。此外，这种差别可能也具有功能性意义，因为土著陶片的代表性器类主要是鬲和鼎，都属于烹煮器。无论哪种情况，土著陶片分布模式似乎都与周时期相同，很可能是因为这种陶器传统与周文化陶器共存。归城的居住者也许共同拥有一个经济系统，在该系统内同时生产周文化和土著文化类型的陶器；又或者是土著类型陶器是在其他地方生产的，然后被运送到归城提供给以周文化为核心的人群使用。我们对归城陶器的分析结果，表明后一种情况可能更符合实际（见第九章），但是还需要更广泛的研究来阐明这一情况。

七、时代分析总结

归城调查数据所采用的时代划分标准，为我们重建该遗址的居住使用历史提供了坚实的基础。调查数据揭示了归城居住使用的变化轨迹开始于周代以前人类的少量活动。显然早期大规模的居住使用，可能是第二期（西周）早段开始于内城的中心区域以及鸦鹊河西边的内城外围地区。2009年的试掘提供了一个坚实的地层学证据，表明归城内城墙建造于第二期的某个时段，其作用可能是为了保护早期移民的核心区域。接下来东周时期归城的居住使用大规模增长，这点可由三倍数量的陶片遗物所证明，活动范围也扩大至鸦鹊河的东岸以及山顶周围。实际上，可确定为第三期（东周）的陶片集中分布于外城墙沿线，尤其是东部，这表明归城外城墙的建造很可能是在东周时期，用以保护城市扩大的人口和居住活动。虽然这一发展紧跟东周时期中原地区普遍的城市扩张趋势，归城的扩张也可能是对地区军事紧张局势加剧的应对；特别是在山东西部，莱国与雄心勃勃的霸权国家齐国之间的敌对关系。

虽然在公元前567年，齐灭掉莱国之后，遗址仍然被继续使用，并且可能在其后的东周时期内仍保持使用，但在第四期（汉代）时遗址内活动急剧下降，空间分布也不再与周代有城墙城市的布局相对应。本地文化的陶片与周代陶片分布相似，表明它是与周代陶器同时使用的。但是，它们的文化重要性在当地的陶器年代学上的地位尚待进一步阐明。

第六节　完整采集单位（CCU）Ⅰ～Ⅲ

一、目的和方法

在2009年的田野工作季度中，我们设定一系列完整采集单位（CCU），其面积比系统性地表采样的采集区更大，并且对单位内所有陶片进行完全采集。这些采集单位的数据结果，将用于建立遗址内所发现器类总目录，从而帮助我们判断遗址不同区域所使用器类的差别，以及不同区域活动类别的可能性差异。所有完整采集单位都位于地表陶片大量聚集处，以便提供足够多的样本用作器物类型分析、不同时期人类活动的相对等级以及古代活动类型。另外，完整采集单位的数据可与系统性地表采样（SSS）方法所得的调查数据，以及试掘所得的器类进行比较。以下是完整采集单位所选择的三个区域（见图Ⅰ.6.1）。

CCUⅠ：内城，试掘探沟附近。

CCUⅡ：东部，外城，覆盖范围从（8区）8-A1到8-D1、8-A2到8-D2，以及（12区）12-A56到12-D56。

CCUⅢ：西部，外城，覆盖范围从（10区）10-L47到10-O47以及10-L49到10-O49（图版54：1）。

最初，我们打算将每个完整采集单位设定为南北向，100米×100米（10000平方米）大小的采集单位。然而，经过目标采集区域现场条件考察后发现，没有适合这种采集单位尺寸的连续区域，造成这种不连续性的主要原因是茂盛的植被以及难以攀爬的峭壁。为避开这些阻碍，完整采集区的尺寸被降至70米×70米（4900平方米）。其中的两个单位（CCUⅡ和CCUⅢ，位于内外城墙之间）为南北向，而CCUⅠ（位于内城）为了便于采集，方向设为北偏东17°，毗邻道路和苹果树。值得注意的是位于内城的CCUⅠ，该区域未经过地面调查，而CCUⅡ和CCUⅢ所处区域范围已由系统性地表采样方法调查过。

二、采集结果的分析

三个完整采集单位共采集陶片1905片。采集得来的数据证实了系统性地表调查中所得到的结论，即归城主要的使用时期是西周和东周时期。这些材料同样也为评估内外城之间的活动差异提供了一些基础，尤其是内城高等级的宴会活动。

以下我们对三个完整采集单位中不同时期陶片分布及类型进行详细讨论（表Ⅰ.6.2）。

整个周时期（西周、东周及一般周代）的遗物，在每个完整采集单位中陶片总数的比例为81%（CCUⅢ）至89%（CCUⅠ）之间（图Ⅰ.6.20）。每个完整采集单位中数量最少的是汉代陶片，CCUⅡ和CCUⅢ中比例不到1%，CCUⅠ则为0%。这一结果与系统性地表调查情况相符合，调查中占总数84%的陶片为周时期，而属于汉代的陶片则降至1%（见表Ⅰ.6.1）。这反映了一个事实，即第二、三期是归城的主要居住使用时期。然而，西周和东周时期的陶片在不同完整采集单位之间比例波动幅度显著。西周时期和东周时期的陶片数比值为：0.07（CCUⅠ）、0.13（CCUⅡ）及0.11（CCUⅢ）（根据校正后的百分比计算，包括有纹饰陶片和无纹饰陶片）。这些数值远远低于整个归城的西周和东周的陶片数比值0.33 。然而，这些数值需要被情境化，并与它们所在的大的调查区域内的西周和东周陶片数比值相比较（根据采集圈的陶片数量），在大的调查区域内的比值分别是0.75（7区）、0.12（12区）及0.28（10区）。全面系统调查中的这些数值，表明在内城周围的西周和东周时期陶片数的比值远远高于其在外城附近区域的比值。

同归城遗址其他周边地区一样，CCUⅡ和CCUⅢ 中的西周陶片相对缺乏，这一发现毫无疑问地反映出从西周到东周时期，人类活动的急剧增加。然而，位于内城的CCUⅠ中0.07这一极低数值，与系统性地表采样（SSS）调查中7区（不包括内城墙之内的区域）的0.75这一数值形成鲜明对比，二者间的差异耐人寻味，这需要其他方法来进行解释。因为我们特意将CCUⅠ设置于探沟以北20米处，通过与两条探沟的数据进行比较，我们能对CCUⅠ中0.07这一数值进行评估。探沟发掘所得的西周陶片（430片）占其他所有时期总陶片数（1830片）的比例为0.22。虽然这一比例较之整个城市地表调查所得的比例（0.33）仍略低，但它仍然高于来自CCUⅠ的数值（0.07）。这一现象非常有趣，不同时期的地表陶片的比例并不能反映出CCUⅠ附近地下的不同时期陶片的比例。

我们认为这种差异可能与内城的特殊功能有关，在其居住使用时期内不断有建造类活动，包括用作活动的大型露天场所，这类场所经常被清理或重建，因此有一些早期陶片被清除掉了。事实上，CCUⅠ被1号、2号、3号宫殿基址所围绕，并且坐落在略偏离城市中心道路的地方。东周时期，这一区域可能是一处用于公共活动的露天庭院。像这种区域很可能倾向于保留更晚期地层中的陶片，包括宫殿最后使用或坍塌遗留在地表的陶片。因此，地表陶片的时期分布模式仍然以某种方式与其地下陶片的时期分布模式有关。

最后，我们需要考虑在陶器类型方面，完整采集单位之间的差异。在CCUⅡ中高柄豆的陶片占所有可辨识陶片的20%，而在CCUⅢ中为24%。然而，在CCUⅠ中豆类陶片的比例占总体的41%以上，这是具有统计性显著差异的数值，同时也是一个中等效应值（图Ⅰ.6.21）。这表明CCUⅠ中大量的豆类陶片是具有意义的，可能反映出该区域的一个特殊使用功能（豆类陶片占可辨识陶片的比重：CCUⅠ与CCUⅡ比较，其结果为*T*分数为3.4，*P*值小于0.001，具有很高的统计显著性，效应量Cohen's *d*为0.54，一个中等效应值；CCUⅠ与CCUⅢ比较，其结果为*T*分数2.8，*P*值0.005，同样具有高显著性，并且效应量Cohen's *d*为0.47，也是一个中等效应值；CCⅡ与CCⅢ比较，其结果为*T*分数0.4，*P*值0.691，不具显著性，并且效应量Cohen's *d*为0.08，一个非常小的效应值）。

在CCUⅠ中簋类陶片仅占所有可辨识陶片的5%，在CCUⅡ中这一比例为15%。但是，在CCUⅢ它们占所有已采集陶片的12%，虽然其效应量比较小，但也具有统计学意义。以上结果表明这些陶片的出现率差异比较小，并且不太具有实际意义。如果对该区域进行更多的调查，可能会为CCUⅢ附近频繁使用这类陶器，提供更确凿的证据（CCUⅠ与CCUⅡ比较，其结果为*T*分数2.7，*P*值0.007，具有极大的统计显著性，并且效应量Cohen's *d*为0.34，仅略高于低效应值；CCUⅠ与CCUⅢ比较，其结果为*T*分数1.8，*P*值0.070，适当的显著性，效应量Cohen's *d*为0.25，一个低效应值；CCUⅡ与CCUⅢ比较，其结果*T*分数0.5，*P*值0.623，没有显著性，效应量Cohen's *d*为0.09，非常低的效应值）。CCUⅡ中鬲和罐这两种类型所占比例也比较高。

豆和簋类陶片在CCUⅠ中共占总数的比例（46%）明显高于在CCUⅡ（35%）或CCUⅢ（35.3%）中的比例。另一方面，CCUⅡ中的鬲和罐类陶片所占比例（56.6%）比CCUⅠ（46.3%）中的比例更高。如果我们将这一模式运用到每个完整采集单位内不可辨认的陶片中，使能适当解释为什么CCUⅠ拥有比CCUⅡ更多不可断代和不可辨别类型的陶片。然而，这一情况需要与试掘获取的数据相结合考虑。在探沟1和2中，尤其是在东周时期的堆积单位内，豆和罐类陶片的比例同样也很高；但值得注意的是，在这些单位中簋类陶片的比例甚至高于比CCUⅠ中簋类陶片的比例。因此，可以明确认为CCUⅠ中豆和簋类陶片的比例很高，而CCUⅡ中则是鬲和罐类陶片。

试掘得到的数据证实了这一模式。在TG1、TG2中，尤其是在东周时期的堆积单位内，豆和罐类陶片的比例同样也很高；但需注意的是，在这些单位中簋类陶片的比例甚至比CCUⅠ中的还要高。

当我们对不同器类的功能性进行考虑时这一点就显得非常重要。鬲主要是炊器，而罐是用作储存水或食物的，二者的基本功能都是为满足大量人群的日常生活所用。豆和簋，最初都是从同类型的青铜器中发展而来，通常用来盛放或供奉食物和水果。虽然作为陶器，它们可能并没有被上层人群所垄断，但明显倾向于出现在上层阶级生活中，即出现在众多上层人群的宴会或其他聚会中。因此，位于归城内城的CCUⅠ中出现的陶豆数量，多于位于城市外围的CCUⅡ，这点是具有逻辑一致性的。CCUⅡ所位于的城市外围，很可能是低等级人群和外城墙沿线的军队所居住区域，这类人群可能不常有这么诱人的盛宴和奢华的标志性器物。就这一点而言，在CCUⅠ所发现的若干瓮的陶片也很重要：像这种大而厚实的罐子仅仅只在有大量存储需要的情况下才有必要。

简而言之，完全采集单位提供了一个相对大而可靠的归城人群使用陶器类型的集结。虽然我们不能假定它们代表了整个遗址陶器类型分布情况，但因为它们都位于陶片聚集区，因此很可能对遗址陶器群来说有非常好的代表性。至少，它们提供了有关内城附近及内外城墙之间的区域内，人类所使用陶器类型的情况。完整采集单位之间的差异是明显且具有意义的，使我们能够了解归城居民社会生活的差别，以及大规模人口的活动特征。

附注：2008-2009地面调查期间所得的陶器类型标本分析见图Ⅰ.6.22～Ⅰ.6.25及表Ⅰ.6.3～Ⅰ.6.6（图版57：1～4）。

第七节　结　　语

归城调查工作的目的不仅仅在于解答我们对遗址内部组织的研究问题，并以此作为理解归城社会政治动态的基础，而且还希望通过一个慎重考虑过的调查设计，来探讨方法论上的相关问题。上文详细讨论了归城城址调查中我们如何遗址的条件（地形、古代遗物密度及现代居住使用情况），以及项目本身的需求（资源和研究问题）进行考虑的。最终的设计方案是一个利用系统地表采集（SSS）方法的密集性全覆盖式调查，从而使我们能够在两个田野工作季度内收集到大量陶片数据。

系统地表采集方法使我们能够确定，地表集中分布的遗物与建筑遗迹之间的关系，也使我们能够绘制出整个遗址地表遗物的连续分布图，以便用来发现遗址使用模式的历时性变化以及探究出遗址形成过程对地表遗物分布的影响，但这类影响似乎显得很弱。

城址地面调查的结果与我们在归城内采用其他方法的调查结果相一致。完整采集单位（CCU）的采用，补充和支持了整个城址的调查，而完整采集单位中所得数据进一步被内城试掘探沟中得到的数据所证实。所有证据都指明在周时期居住使用量的急剧上升，尤其是东周时期，而汉代居住使用量却急剧下降。城址内遗物分布也发生着变化，尤其是东周时期对东部外城墙区域的扩张，表明随着时间的推移，城址在居住使用方面也经历了重大的改变和重组。陶片的集中分布与地下建筑结构之间的关系，以及三个完整采集单位之间陶片所属器类的差别，这些都是理解城址内部组织以及古代城市社会生活的重要线索。城址内密集的居住使用和上层活动似乎都集中于内城及其附近，而非上层人群及军队活动则集中于外城墙附近。

我们希望这项调查能够为小规模全覆盖调查提供一个有意义的新实例，这类小规模全面调查与区域性全面调查的要求不同。我们相信这项调查满足了对归城城址研究项目的需要，并且有助于我们理解该遗址古代居住使用情况。我们认为全覆盖方法或者是其他任何地表调查方法，其最好的使用方式是尽可能与钻探、地下建筑以及地层的发掘相结合，以便在调查过程中达到对遗址的多维度理解。

参考文献

Banning, E. B., A. L. Hawkins, and S. T. Stewart, 2006. "Detection Functions for Archaeological Survey," *American Antiquity*, 71.4: 723-742.

Billman, B. R., and G. M. Feinman (eds.), 1999. *Settlement Pattern Studies in the Americas: Fifty Years since Virú*. Washington, D.C.: Smithsonian Institution Press.

Bintliff, J., 2000. "Beyond Dots on the Map: Future Directions for Surface Artefact Survey in Greece," in *The Future of Surface Artefact Survey in Europe*, edited by J. Bintliff, M. Kuna, and N. Venclová. Pp. 3-20. Sheffield: Sheffield Academic Press Ltd.

Bintliff, J., and A. M. Snodgrass, 1985. "The Cambridge/Bradford Boeotian Expedition: The First Four Years," *Journal of Field Archaeology*, 12.2: 123-161.

Bintliff, J., M. Kuna, and N. Venclová, 2000. "Editorial Overview," in *The Future of Surface Artefact Survey in Europe*, edited by J. Bintliff, M. Kuna, and N. Venclová. Pp. 1-2. Sheffield: Sheffield Academic Press Ltd.

Bintliff, J., M. Kuna, and N. Venclová (eds.), 2000. *The Future of Surface Artefact Survey in Europe*. Sheffield: Sheffield Academic Press Ltd.

Carr, C., 1984. "The Nature of Organization of Intrasite Archaeological Records and Spatial Analytic Approaches to Their Investigation," in *Advances in Archaeological Method and Theory*, edited by M. B. Schiffer. Pp. 103-222. New York: Academic Press, Inc.

Cherry, J. F., J. L. Davis, A. Demitrack, E. Mantzourani, T. F. Strasser, and L. E. Talalay, 1988. "Archaeological Survey in an Artifact-rich Landscape: a Middle Neolithic Example from Nemea, Greece," *American Journal of Archaeology*, 92.2: 159-176.

赤峰中美联合考古研究项目（赤峰），2003. 内蒙古东部（赤峰）区域考古调查阶段性报告. 北京：科学出版社.

Cohen, J., 1988. *Statistical Power Analysis for the Behavioral Sciences*, Second Edition. Hillsdale (NJ): Lawrence Erlbaum Associates.

Evans, C., 1951. "Review: Surface Survey of the Virú Valley, Peru," *American Antiquity*, 16.3: 270-272.

Feinman, G. M., and L. M. Nicholas, 1990. "Settlement and Land use in Ancient Oaxaca," in *Debating Oaxaca Archaeology* (Anthropological Papers No. 84), edited by J. Marcus. Pp. 71-113. Ann Arbor: Museum of Anthropology, University of Michigan.

Fish, P. R., and T. Gresham, 1990. "Insights from Full-coverage Survey in the Georgia Piedmont," in *The Archaeology of Regions: a Case for Full-coverage Survey*, edited by Fish, S. K. and S. A. Kowalewski. Pp. 147-172. Washington (DC): Smithsonian Institution Press.

Ford, J. A., and G. R. Willey, 1949. *A Surface Study of the Virú Valley, Peru. Anthropological Papers of the American Museum of Natural History*, 43.1. New York: American Museum of Natural History.

Gaffney, C., V. Gaffney, and M. Tingle, 1985. "Settlement, Economy or Behavior? Micro-regional Land Use Models and the Interpretation of Surface Artefact Patterns," in *Archaeology from the Ploughsoil: Studies in the Collection and Interpretation of Field Survey Data*, edited by C. Haselgrove, M. Millett, and I. Smith. Pp. 95-107. Sheffield: Department of Archaeology and Prehistory, University of Sheffield.

Haselgrove, C., 1985. "Inference from Ploughsoil Artefact Samples," in *Archaeology from the Ploughsoil: Studies in the Collection and Interpretation of Field Survey Data*, edited by C. Haselgrove, M. Millett, and I. Smith. Pp. 7-29. Sheffield: Department of Archaeology and Prehistory, University of Sheffield.

Haselgrove, C., M. Millett, and I. Smith (eds.), 1985. *Archaeology from the Ploughsoil: Studies in the Collection and Interpretation of Field Survey Data*. Sheffield: Department of Archaeology and Prehistory, University of Sheffield.

Haselgrove, C., M. Millet, and I. Smith, 1985. "Introduction," in *Archaeology from the Ploughsoil: Studies in the Collection and Interpretation of Field Survey Data*, edited by C. Haselgrove, M. Millett, and I. Smith. Pp. 1-3. Sheffield: Department of Archaeology and Prehistory, University of Sheffield.

King, T. F., 1978. *The Archaeological Survey: Methods and Uses*. Washington: Heritage Conservation and Recreation Service, U.S. Department of the Interior.

Kowalewski, S. A., 1990a. "Merits of Full-Coverage Survey: Examples from the Valley of Oaxaca, Mexico," in *The Archaeology of Regions: a Case for Full-coverage Survey*, edited by S. K. Fish and S. A. Kowalewski. Pp. 33-86. Washington (DC): Smithsonian Institution Press.

Kowalewski, S. A., 1990b. "Scale and Complexity: Issues in the Archaeology of the Valley of Oaxaca," in *The Archaeology of Regions: a Case for Full-coverage Survey*, edited by S. K. Fish, and S. A. Kowalewski. Pp. 207-270. Washington (DC): Smithsonian Institution Press.

Kowalewski, S. A., and S. K. Fish, 1990. "Conclusion," in *The Archaeology of Regions: a Case for Full-coverage Survey*, edited by S. K. Fish and S.A. Kowalewski. Pp. 261-277. Washington (DC): Smithsonian Institution Press.

李步青，林仙庭，1991：山东黄县归城遗址的调查与发掘. 考古，10：910-918.

Li, Feng, 2006. *Landscape and Power In Early China: The Crisis And Fall of The Western Zhou*, 1045-771 BC. Cambridge,

UK: Cambridge University Press.

林仙庭，2006：莱国与莱都，考古烟台. 济南：齐鲁书社，2006：131-140.

Linduff, K. M., R. D. Drennan, and G. Shelach, 2002-2004. "Early Complex Societies in NE China: The Chifeng International Collaborative Archaeological Research Project," *Journal of Field Archaeology*, 29.1-2: 45-73.

Liu, Li, 1996. "Settlement Patterns, Chiefdom Variability, and the Development of Early States in North China," *Journal of Anthropological Archaeology*, 15: 237-288.

Liu, Li, Xingcan Chen, Yun Kuen Lee, H. Wright, and A. Rosen, 2002-2004. "Settlement Patterns and Development of Social Complexity in the Yiluo Region, North China," *Journal of Field Archaeology*, 29.1-2: 75-100.

Marcus, J., 1990. *Debating Oaxaca Archaeology* (Anthropological Papers No. 84). Ann Arbor: Museum of Anthropology, University of Michigan.

Marks, A. E., 1971. "Settlement Patterns and Intrasite Variability in the Central Negev, Israel," *American Anthropologist* (New Series), 73.5: 1237-1244.

Mills, N., 1985. "Sample Bias, Regional Analysis and Fieldwalking in British Archaeology," in *Archaeology from the Ploughsoil: Studies in the Collection and Interpretation of Field Survey Data*, edited by C. Haselgrove, M. Millett, and I. Smith. Pp. 39-47. Sheffield: Department of Archaeology and Prehistory, University of Sheffield.

Ortman, S. G., M. D. Varien, and T. L. Gripp, 2007. "Empirical Bayesian Methods for Archaeological Survey Data: an Application from the Mesa Verde Region," *American Antiquity*, 72.2: 241-272.

Pettegrew, D. K., 2007. "The Busy Countryside of Late Roman Corinth: Interpreting Ceramic Data Produced by Regional Archaeological Surveys," *Hesperia*, 76: 743-784.

Parsons, J. R., 1990. "Critical Reflections on a Decade of Full-coverage Regional Survey in the Valley of Mexico," *The Archaeology of Regions: a Case for Full-coverage Survey*, edited by S. K. Fish, and S. A. Kowalewski. Pp. 7-31. Washington (DC): Smithsonian Institution Press.

Rapp, G., and C. L. Hill, 2006. *Geoarchaeology: the Earth-science Approach to Archaeological Interpretation*. New Haven: Yale University Press.

Schiffer, M., A. P. Sullivan, and T. C. Klinger, 1978. "The Design of Archaeological Surveys," *World Archaeology*, 10.1: 1-28.

Shelach, G., 1998. "A Settlement Pattern Study in Northeast China: Results and Potential Contributions of Western Theory and Methods to Chinese archaeology," *Antiquity*, 72.275: 114-127.

Sullivan, A. P., P. B. Mink, and P. M. Uphus, 2007. "Archaeological Survey Design, Units of Observation, and the Characterization of Regional Variability," *American Antiquity*, 72.2: 322-333.

Tartaron T. F. et al., 2006. "The Eastern Korinthia Archaeological Survey: Integrated Methods for a Dynamic Landscape," *Hesperia*, 75.4: 453-523.

Terrenato, N., 2000. "Surface Thoughts: Future Directions in Italian Field Surveys," in *The Future of Surface Artefact Survey in Europe*, edited by J. Bintliff, M. Kuna, and N. Venclová. Pp. 21-28. Sheffield: Sheffield Academic Press Ltd.

Underhill, A. P., 1994. "Variation in settlements during the Longshan period of northern China," *Asian Perspectives*, 33.2: 197-228.

Underhill, Anne P., G. M. Feinman, L. M. Nicholas, G. Bennett, Hui Fang, Fengshi Luan, Haiguang Yu, and Fengshu Cai,

2002. "Regional Survey and the Development of Complex Societies in Southeastern Shandong, China," *Antiquity*, 76.293: 745-755.

Van Andel, T. H., and C. N. Runnels, 1987. *Beyond the Acropolis: A Rural Greek Past*. Stanford: Stanford University Press.

Walker, L., 1985. "Survey of a Settlement: a Strategy for the Etruscan Site at Doganella in the Albegna Valley," in *Archaeology from the Ploughsoil: Studies in the Collection and Interpretation of Field Survey Data*, edited by C. Haselgrove, M. Millett, and I. Smith. Pp. 87-94. Sheffield: Department of Archaeology and Prehistory, University of Sheffield.

Willey, G. R., 1953. *Prehistoric Settlement Patterns in the Virù Valley, Peru. Bureau of American Ethnology Bulletin*, 155. Smithsonian Institution, Washington, D.C.

烟台市博物馆，2006：考古烟台. 济南：齐鲁书社.

中国社会科学院考古研究所，2004：中国考古学：两周卷. 北京：中国社会科学出版社.

中美联合归城考古队, 2011. 山东龙口市归城两周城址调查简报， 考古, 3: 30-39.

（翻译：杨琳）

表Ⅰ.6.1　不同时期的陶片数量

Table Ⅰ.6.1　Distribution of identifiable sherds by period

时期 *Period*	采集点数 # *of points**	陶片数 # *of sherds*	采集点百分比 % *of points*	陶片数百分比 % *of sherds*	平均每个采集点含有陶片数 *Avg. # / point*
Pre-Zhou 周代以前	15	17	<1	<1	1
Western Zhou 西周	829	1105	7	8	1
Eastern Zhou 东周	2337	3644	20	28	2
Broad Zhou 周代	3397	6375	29	48	2
Adjusted Western Zhou 校正后西周	--	2810	--	21	--
Adjusted Eastern Zhou 校正后东周	--	8314	--	63	--
Total Zhou 周代总体	4591	11124	39	84	2
Han 汉代	73	78	<1	<1	1
Indigenous 土著	582	717	5	5	1

*采集点数=包含该时期陶片的采集点数；陶片数=该时期陶片总数；采集点百分比=包含该时期陶片的采集点数占所有采集点的百分比；陶片数百分比=该时期陶片数占总体陶片数百分比；平均每个采集点含有陶片数=平均每个含有该时期陶片的采集点的陶片数量（陶片数量四舍五入取整数）。

* # *of points* = number of points yielding sherds of this period; # *of sherds* = total sherds of this period; % *of points* = percent of all points yielding sherds of this period; % *of sherds* = percent of all sherds that were of this period; *Avg. # / point* = average number of sherds of this period per point yielding sherds of this period (rounded to the nearest whole number).

表Ⅰ.6.2　完全采集单位（CCUsⅠ-Ⅲ）每期陶片的比率

Table Ⅰ.6.2　Percentage of datable sherds from each period, CCUsⅠ-Ⅲ

	完整采集单位CCⅠ（1272片）中的百分比 % of total in CCUⅠ (1272 sherds)	完整采集单位CCⅡ（255片）中的百分比 % of total in CCUⅡ (255 sherds)	完整采集单位CCⅢ（378片）中的百分比 % of total in CCUⅢ (378 sherds)
Western Zhou 西周	4%	5%	3%
Eastern Zhou 东周	49%	40%	28%
Broad Zhou 周代	36%	40%	50%
Adjusted W. Zhou 校正后西周	6%	10%	8%
Adjusted E. Zhou 校正后东周	83%	76%	73%
Total Zhou 周代总体	89%	86%	81%

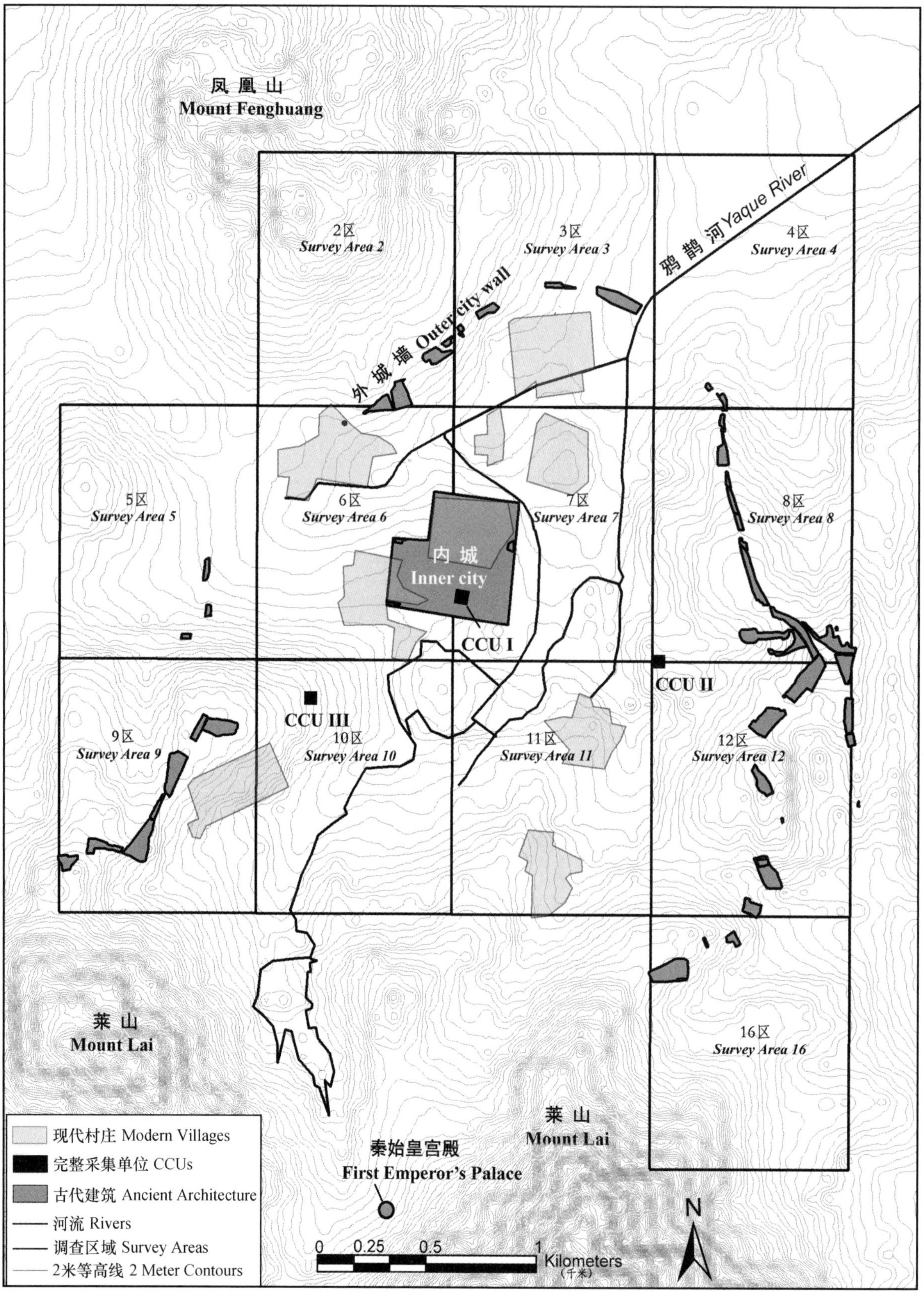

图Ⅰ.6.1　归城遗址及调查区域图

Figure Ⅰ.6.1　The Guicheng city site, with surface survey Areas.

图Ⅰ.6.2　一名组员正在用绳子量出一个半径3米的采集圈

在茂盛的植被中如图中所展示的花生地，为了收集地表所有遗物，需要在植物的根茎周围努力进行搜寻。

Figure Ⅰ.6.2　A student measures a three meter radius collection circle.

In dense vegetation such as the peanut plants seen here, an effort was made to search around the roots of the plants for all surface remains.

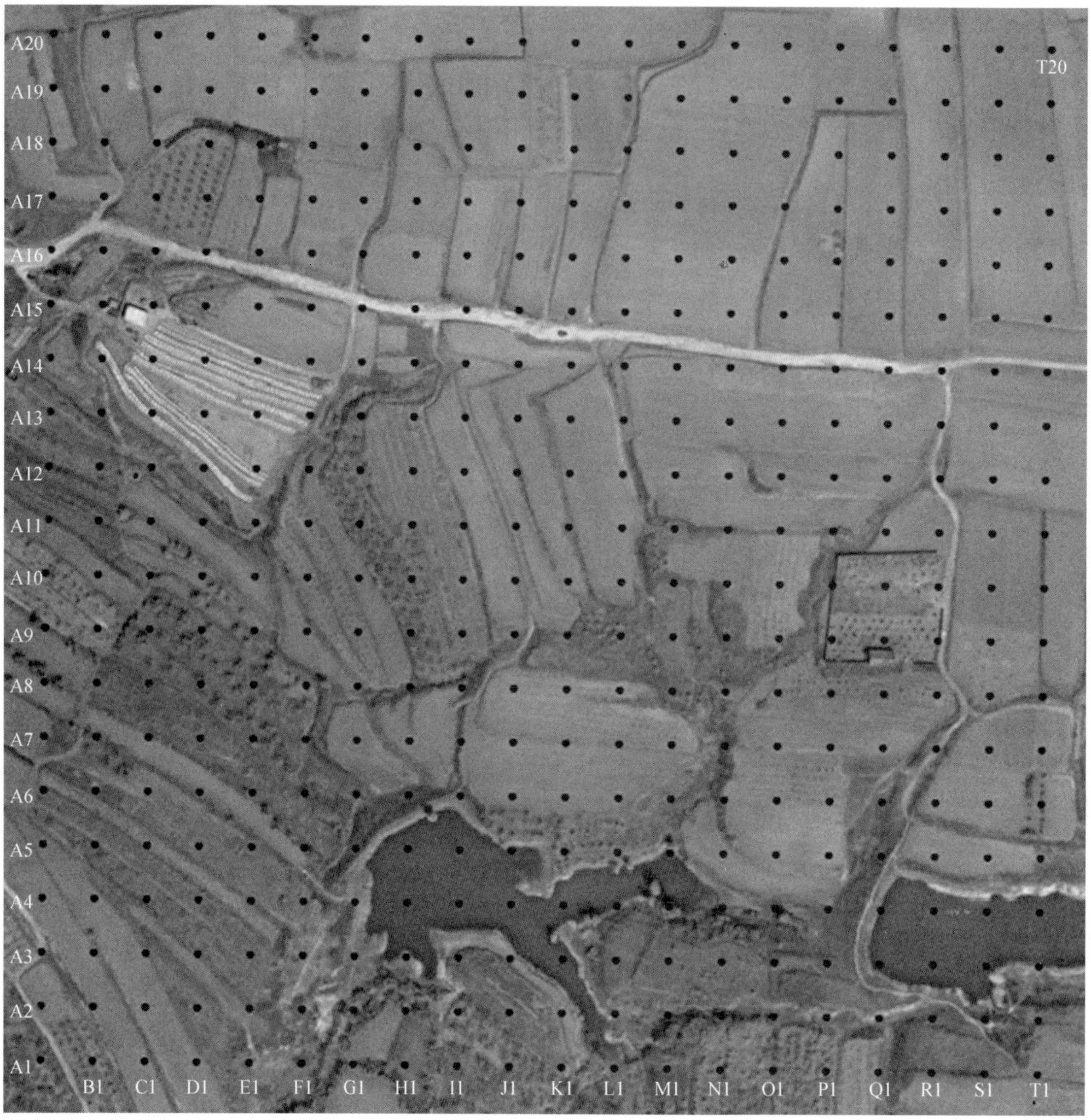

图Ⅰ.6.3　归城调查中第8区的局部田野地图

Figure Ⅰ.6.3　Field map used in Guicheng survey, showing a portion of Area 8.

图Ⅰ.6.4　2009年6月12日8区的调查工作
Figure Ⅰ.6.4　Survey being conducted on June 12, 2009, in Area 8.

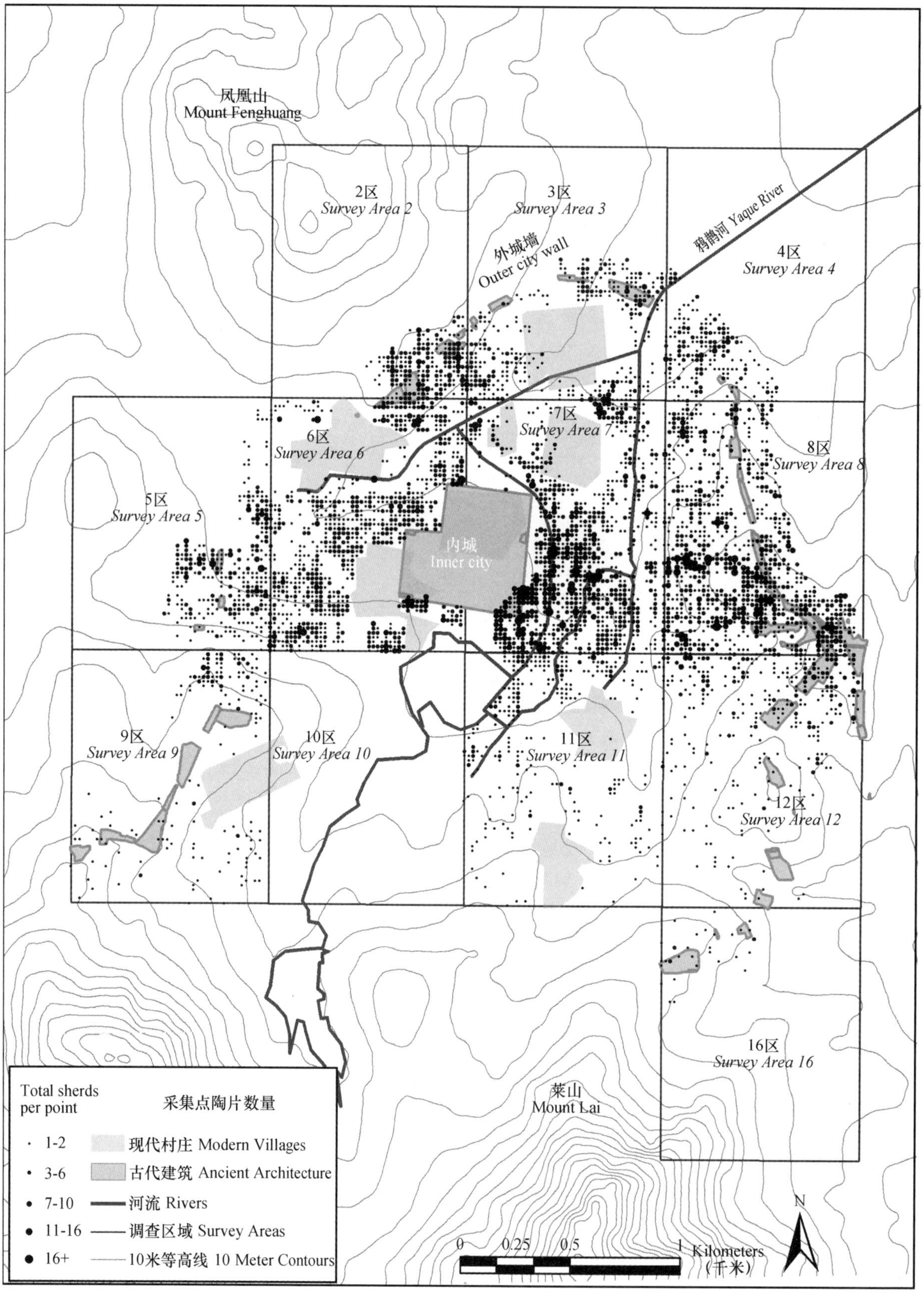
凤凰山
Mount Fenghuang
2区
Survey Area 2
3区
Survey Area 3
4区
Survey Area 4
鸦鹊河 Yaque River
外城墙
Outer city wall
5区
Survey Area 5
6区
Survey Area 6
7区
Survey Area 7
8区
Survey Area 8
内城
Inner city
9区
Survey Area 9
10区
Survey Area 10
11区
Survey Area 11
12区
Survey Area 12
16区
Survey Area 16
莱山
Mount Lai
Total sherds per point
采集点陶片数量
1-2
3-6
7-10
11-16
16+
现代村庄 Modern Villages
古代建筑 Ancient Architecture
河流 Rivers
调查区域 Survey Areas
10米等高线 10 Meter Contours
0
0.25
0.5
1 Kilometers
(千米)
N

a

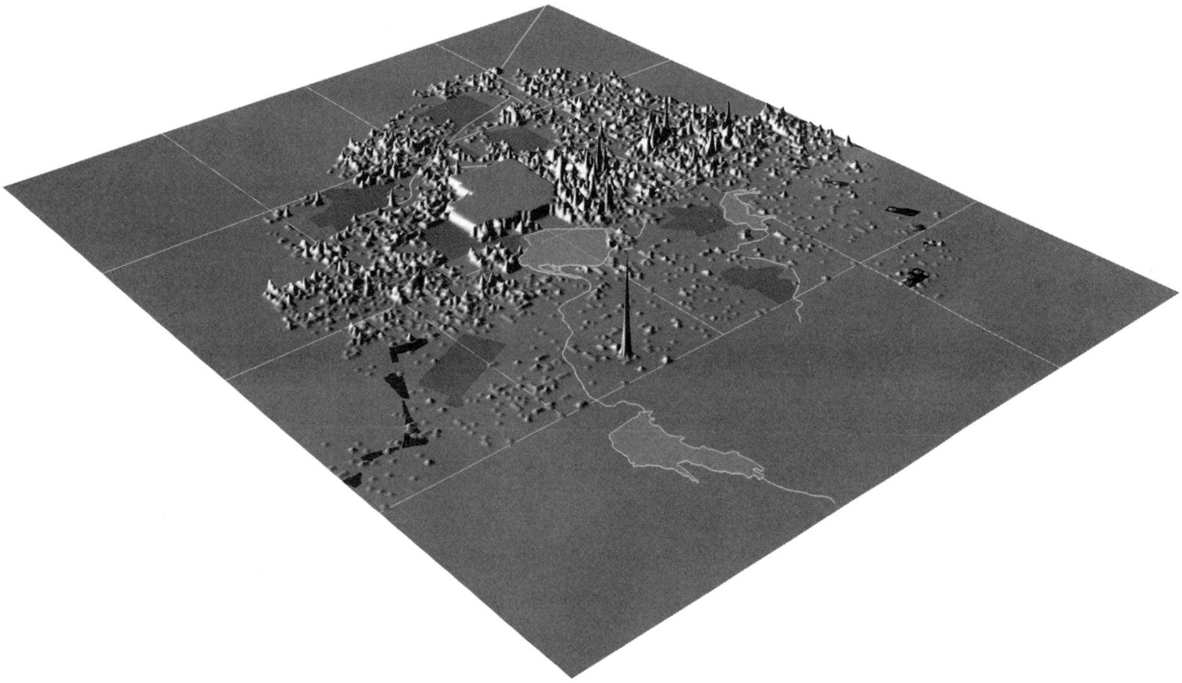

b

图Ⅰ.6.5a-b 每个采集点的陶片总数、分布和平滑3D地图

加入的内城陶片密度根据CCUⅠ：每个采集圈［28.27平方米］7.3片陶片，或0.259/1 m^2。

Figure Ⅰ.6.5a-b Total sherds per survey point, distribution and smoothed 3D map

Interpolation of sherd density for the inner city based on data from CCU Ⅰ: 7.3/collection circle [28.27 m^2], or 0.259/1 m^2.

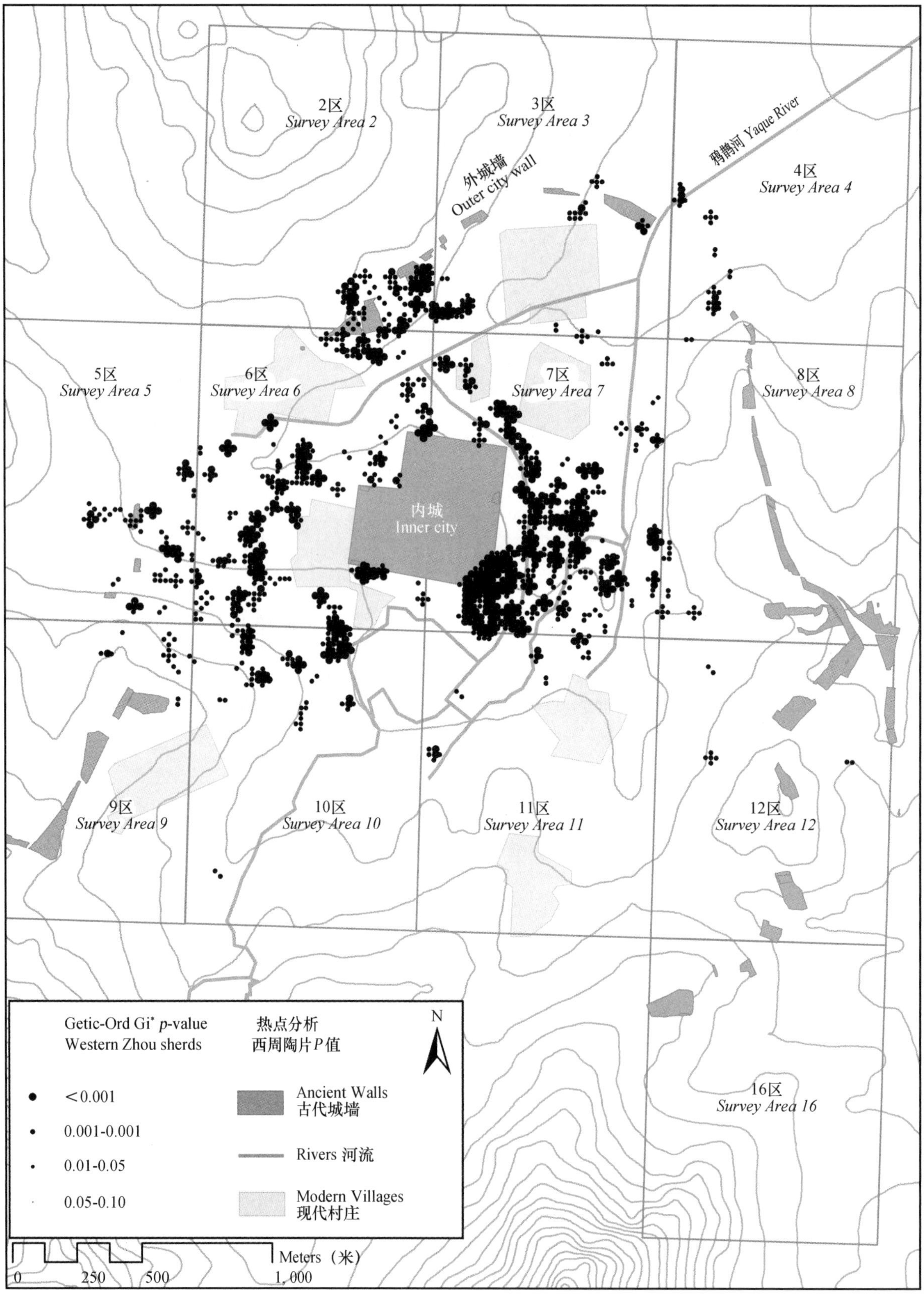
2区
Survey Area 2
3区
Survey Area 3
4区
Survey Area 4
5区
Survey Area 5
6区
Survey Area 6
7区
Survey Area 7
8区
Survey Area 8
9区
Survey Area 9
10区
Survey Area 10
11区
Survey Area 11
12区
Survey Area 12
16区
Survey Area 16
外城墙
Outer city wall
鸦鹊河 Yaque River
内城
Inner city
Getic-Ord Gi* p-value
Western Zhou sherds
热点分析
西周陶片P值
N
<0.001
0.001-0.001
0.01-0.05
0.05-0.10
Ancient Walls
古代城墙
Rivers 河流
Modern Villages
现代村庄
Meters（米）
0
250
500
1,000

a

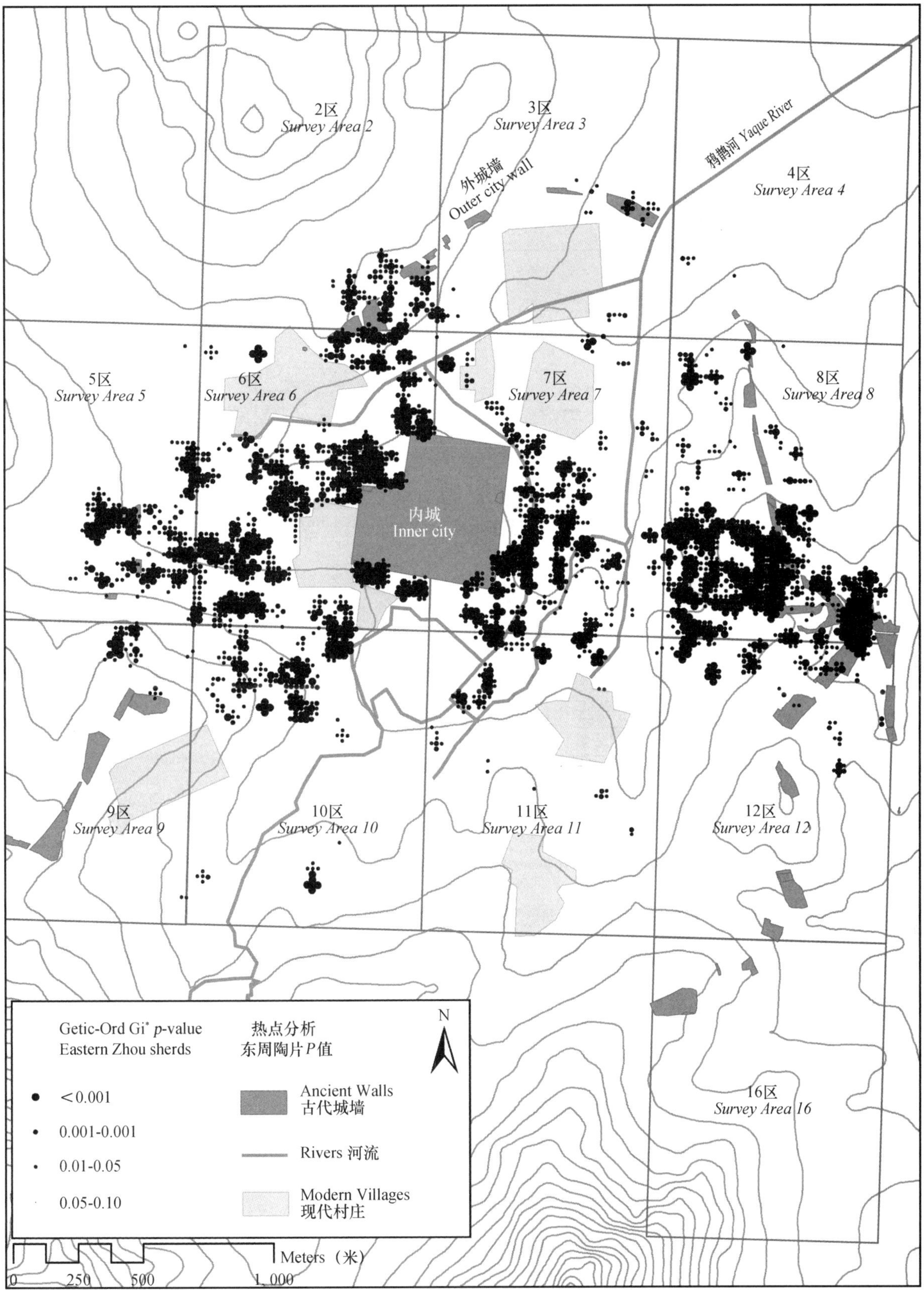

b

图Ⅰ.6.6a-b “热点”地图表明的西周和东周时期的陶片显著集聚区域
统计显著性由使用Getis-Ord Gi*统计分析所决定。图上点的大小代表不同P值

Figure Ⅰ.6.6a-b "Hot spot" maps showing statistically significant clusters of sherds from Western and Eastern Zhou periods.
Statistical significance was determined using the Getis-Ord Gi* statistic. Sizes of points on the map indicate p-values.

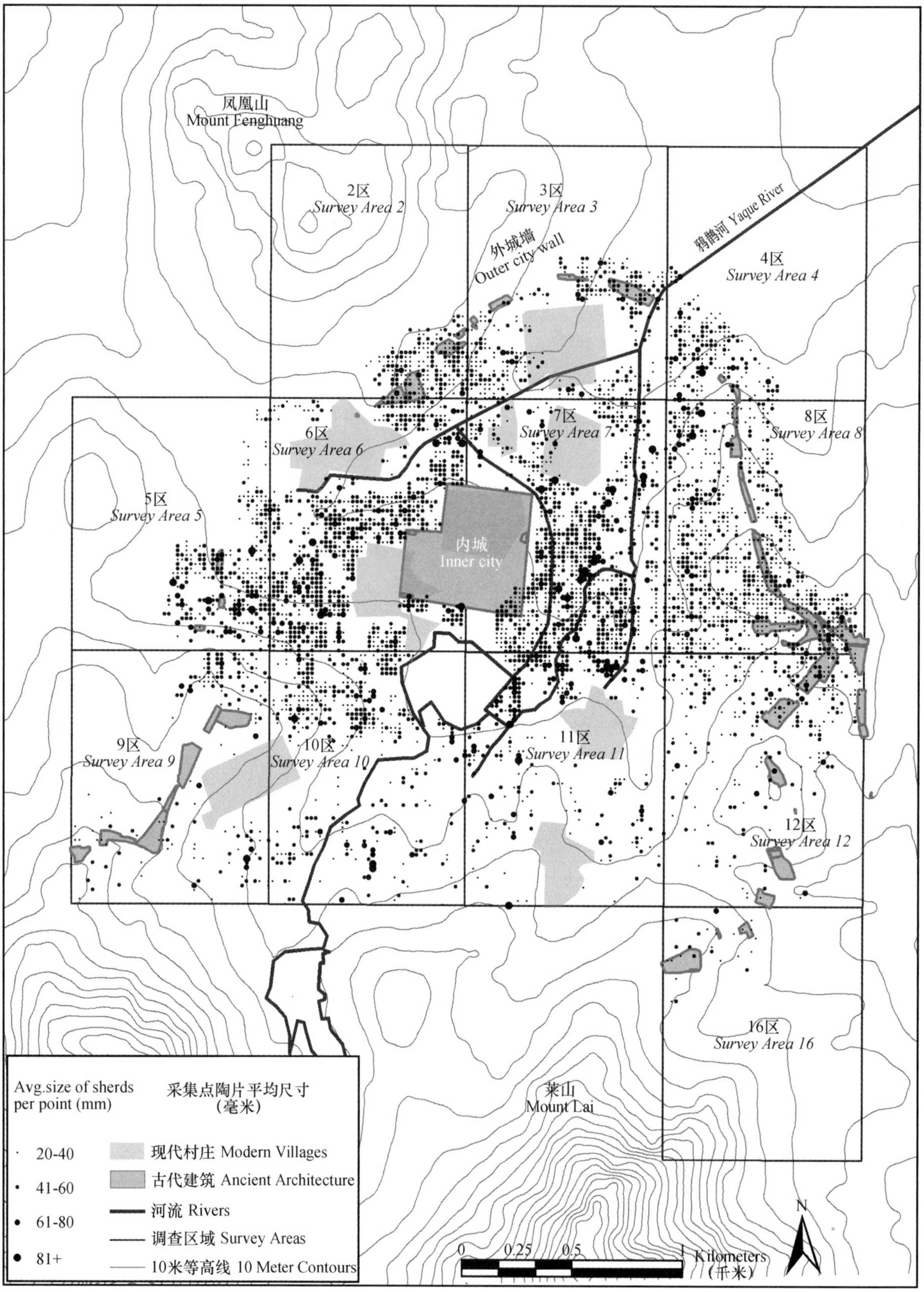

图Ⅰ.6.7　每个采集点的陶片平均尺寸

Figure Ⅰ.6.7　Average size of sherds at each survey point.

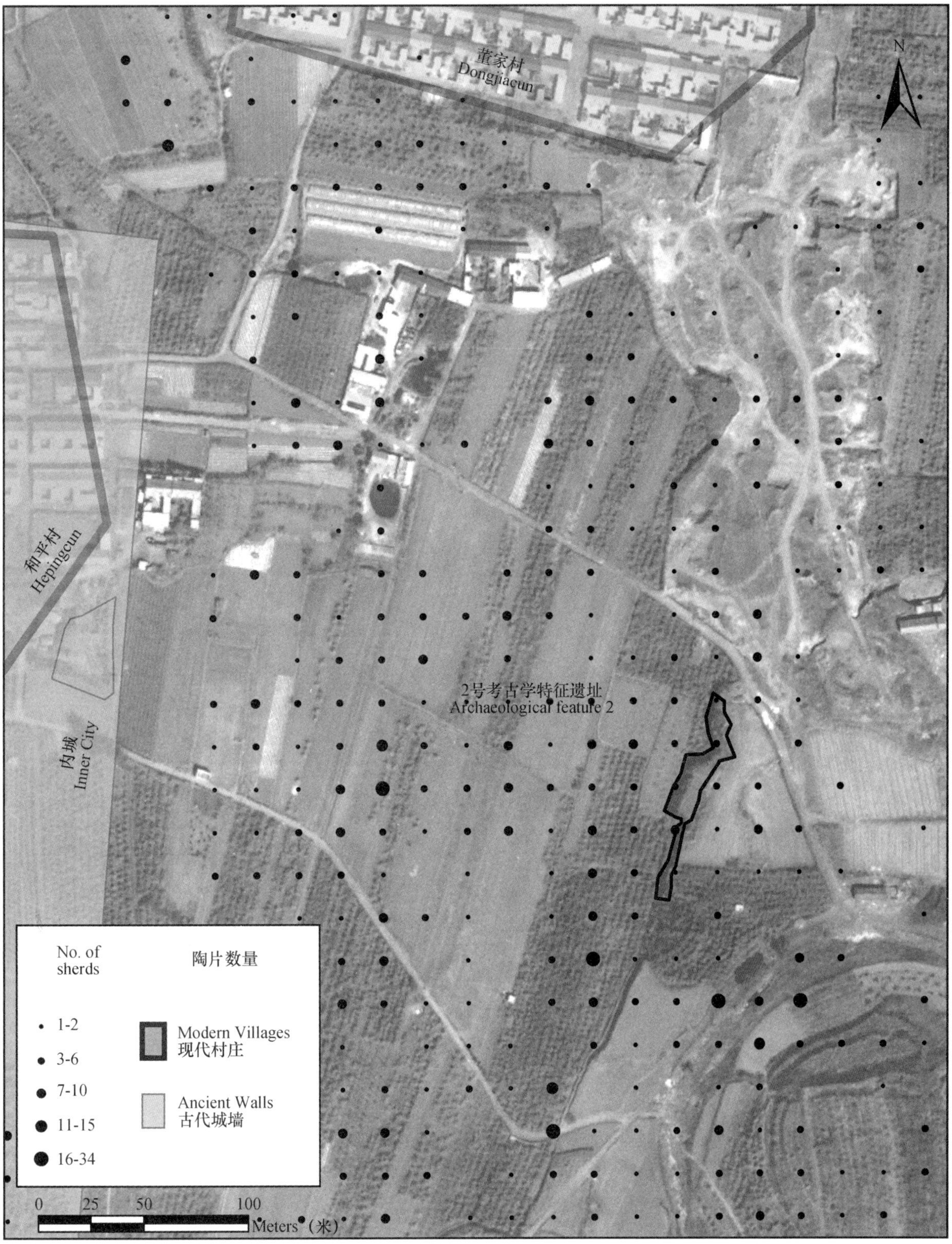

图Ⅰ.6.8　建筑基址（考古学特征遗址2）附近陶片的分布

Figure Ⅰ.6.8　Sherd density around building foundation (Archaeological Feature 2).

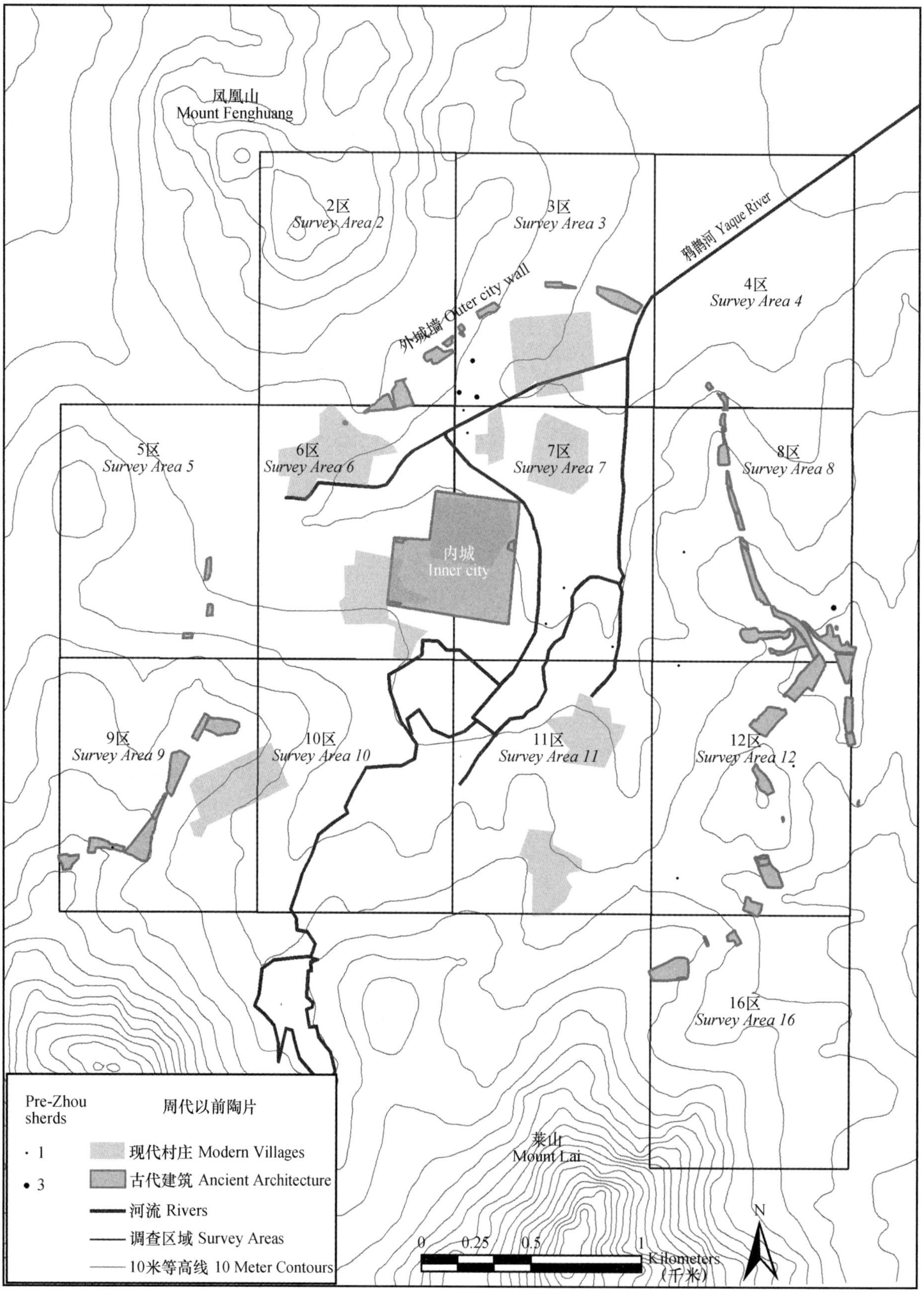
凤凰山
Mount Fenghuang
2区
Survey Area 2
3区
Survey Area 3
鸦鹊河 Yaque River
4区
Survey Area 4
外城墙 Outer city wall
5区
Survey Area 5
6区
Survey Area 6
7区
Survey Area 7
8区
Survey Area 8
内城
Inner city
9区
Survey Area 9
10区
Survey Area 10
11区
Survey Area 11
12区
Survey Area 12
16区
Survey Area 16
莱山
Mount Lai
Pre-Zhou sherds
周代以前陶片
1
3
现代村庄 Modern Villages
古代建筑 Ancient Architecture
河流 Rivers
调查区域 Survey Areas
10米等高线 10 Meter Contours
0
0.25
0.5
1
Kilometers
(千米)
N

a

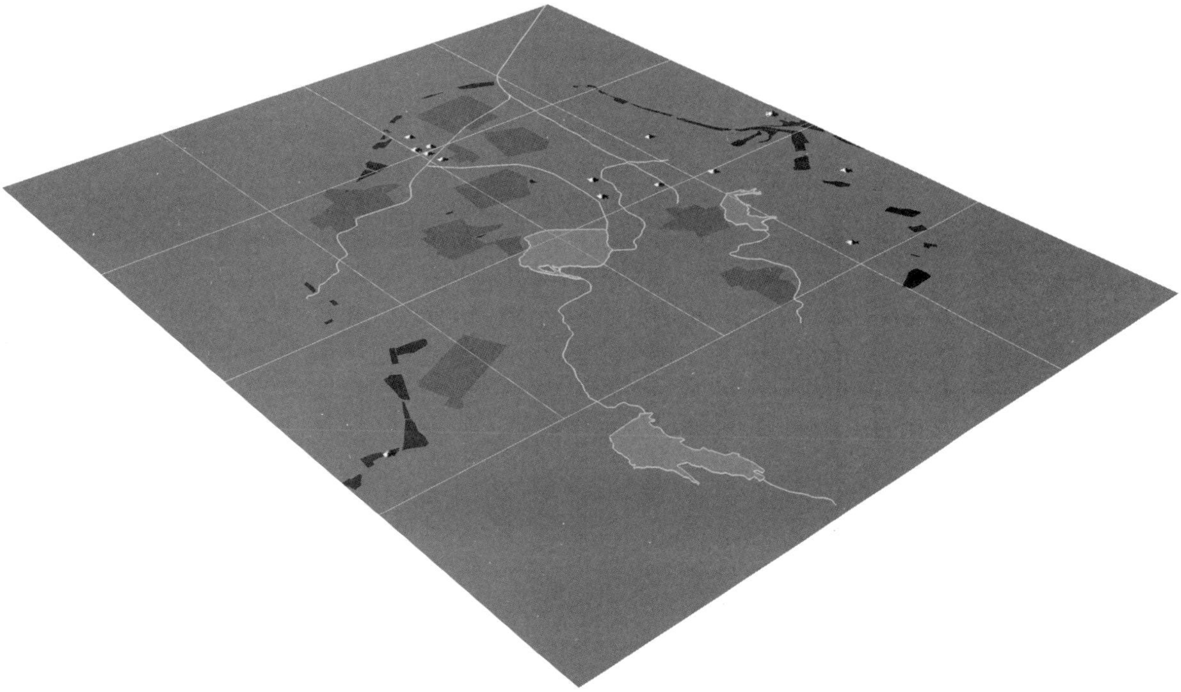

b

图Ⅰ.6.9a-b　第一期（周代以前）陶片分布图

Figure Ⅰ.6.9a-b　Sherd distribution from Period Ⅰ (Pre-Zhou).

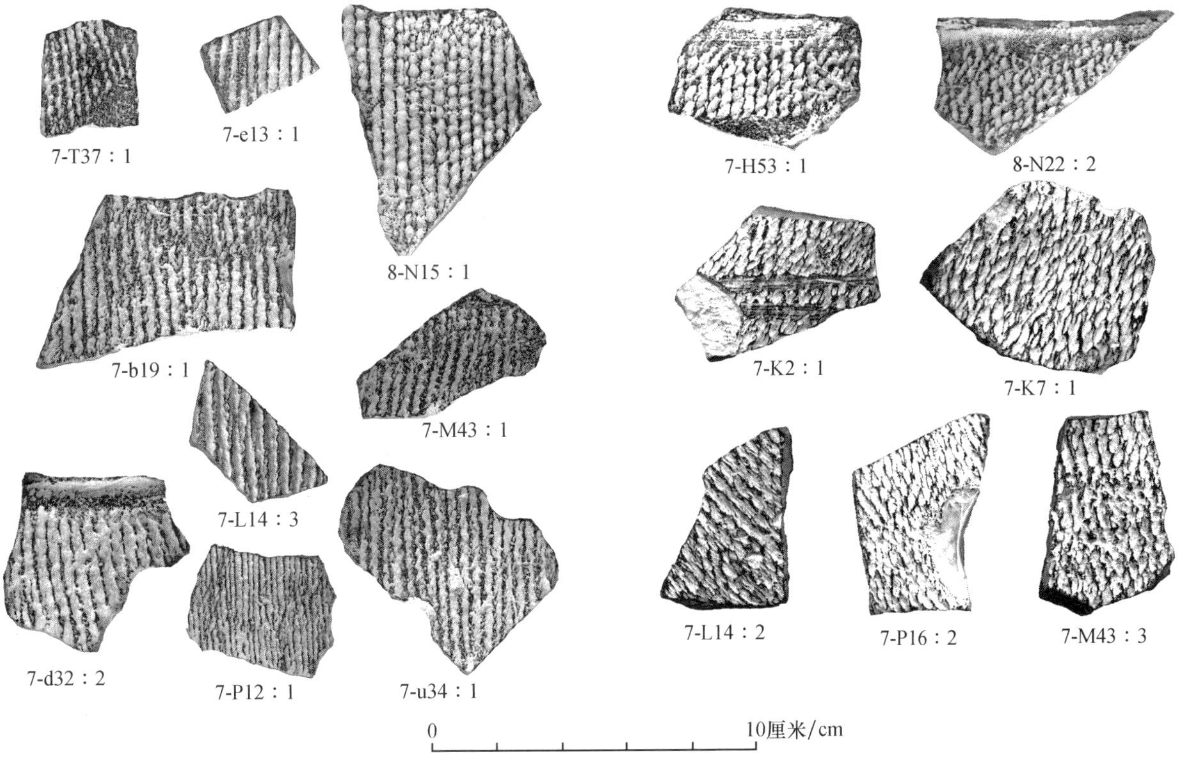

图Ⅰ.6.10　西周时期陶片

Figure Ⅰ.6.10　Sherds from the Western Zhou period.

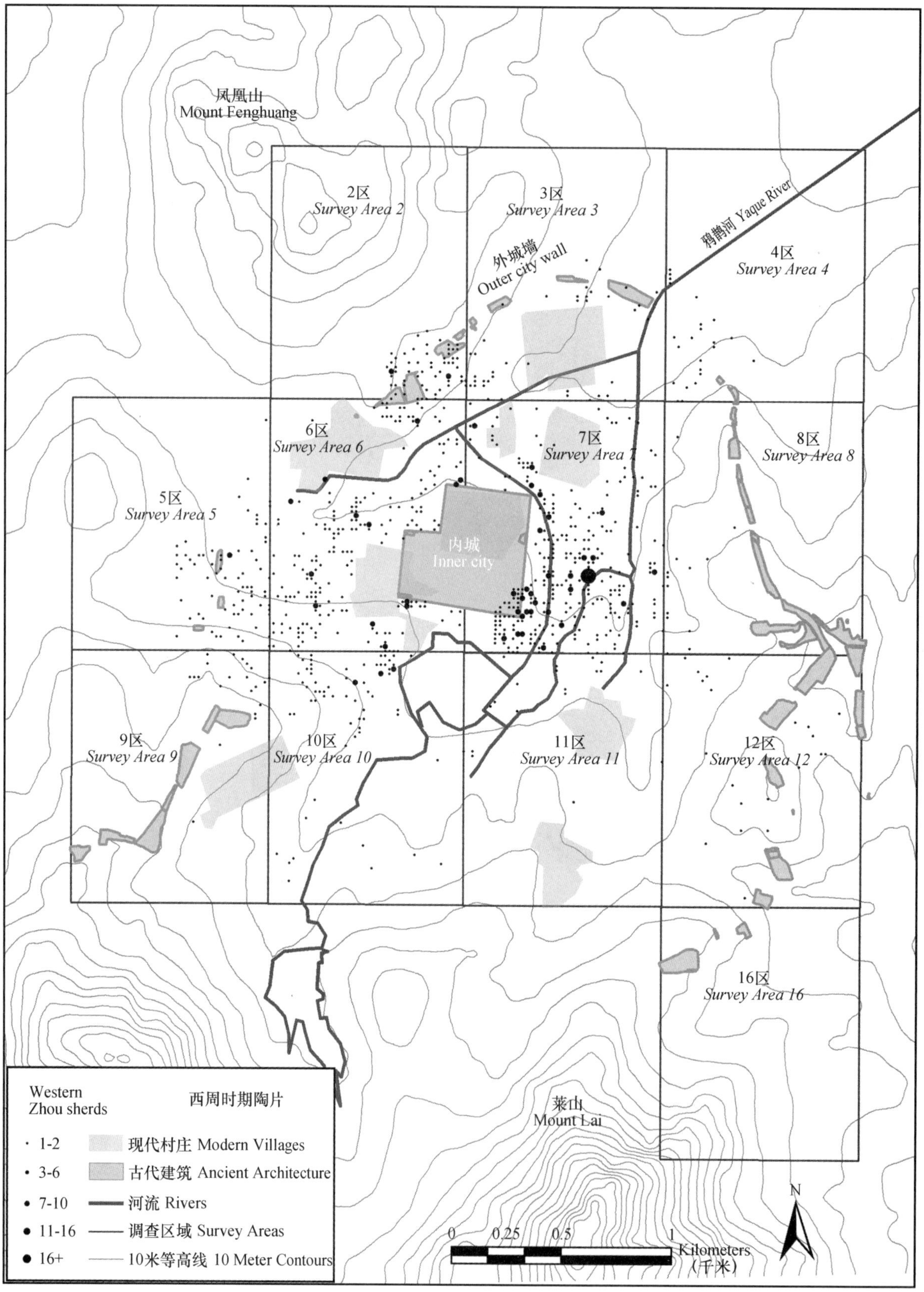
凤凰山
Mount Fenghuang
2区
Survey Area 2
3区
Survey Area 3
4区
Survey Area 4
鸦鹊河 Yaque River
外城墙
Outer city wall
5区
Survey Area 5
6区
Survey Area 6
7区
Survey Area 7
8区
Survey Area 8
内城
Inner city
9区
Survey Area 9
10区
Survey Area 10
11区
Survey Area 11
12区
Survey Area 12
16区
Survey Area 16
莱山
Mount Lai
Western Zhou sherds
西周时期陶片
1-2
3-6
7-10
11-16
16+
现代村庄 Modern Villages
古代建筑 Ancient Architecture
河流 Rivers
调查区域 Survey Areas
10米等高线 10 Meter Contours
0
0.25
0.5
1
Kilometers
(千米)
N

a

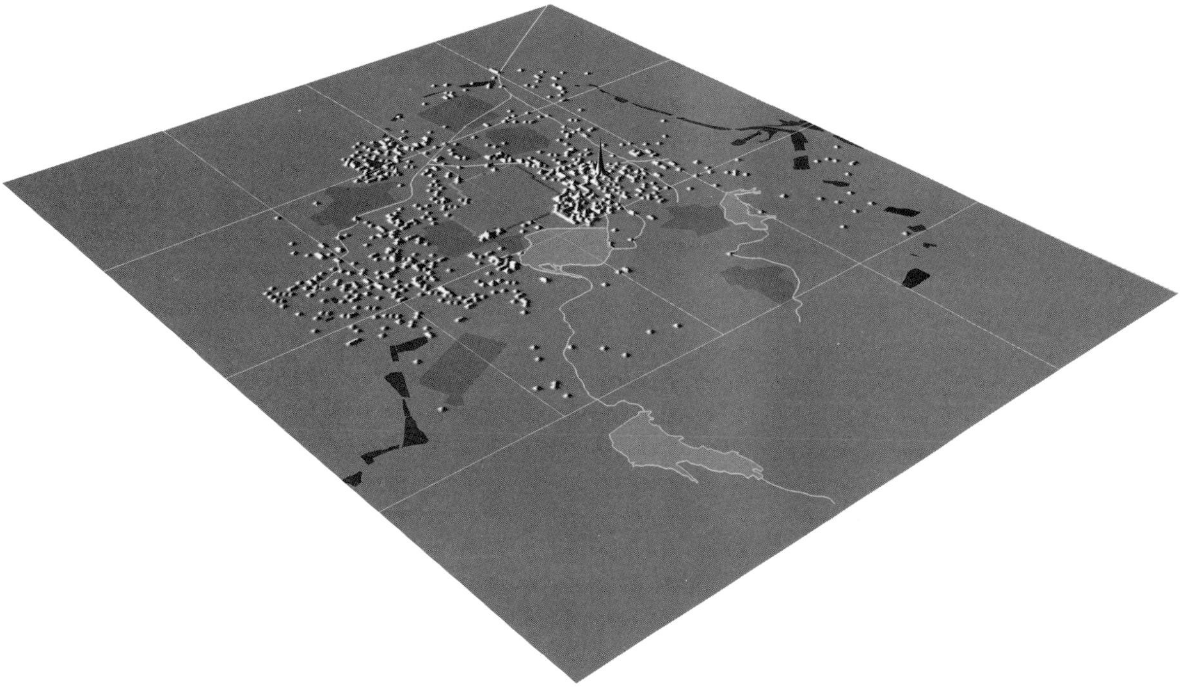

b

图Ⅰ.6.11a-b　第二期（西周时期）陶片分布图
Figure Ⅰ.6.11a-b　Sherd distribution during Period Ⅱ (Western Zhou).

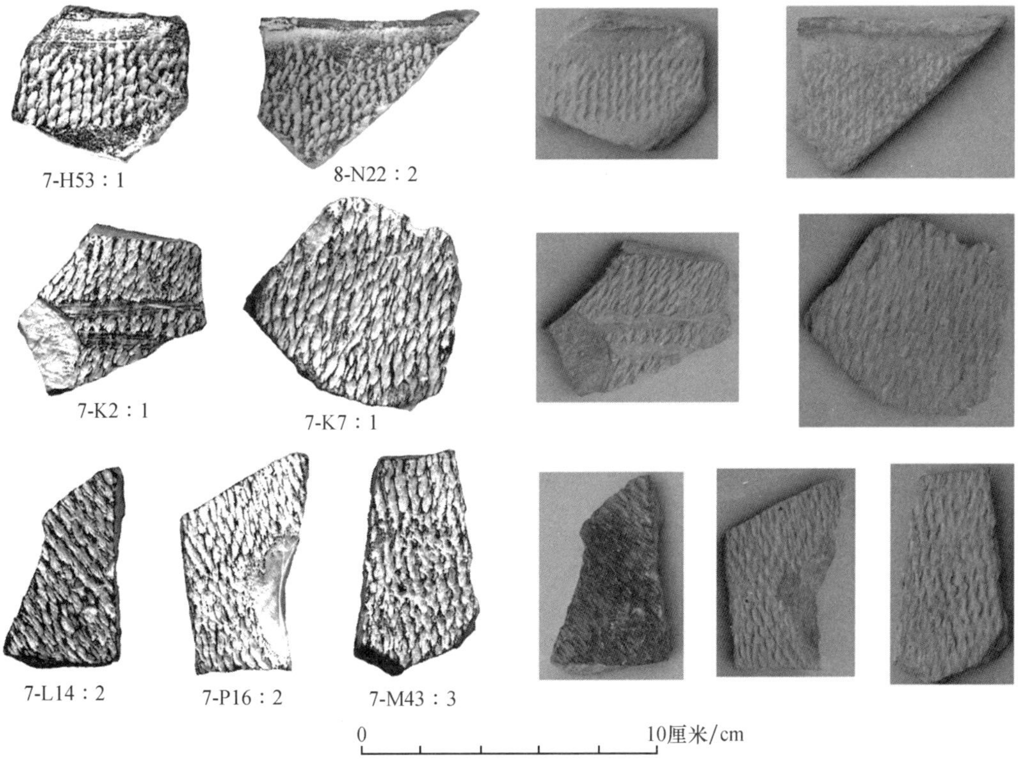

图Ⅰ.6.12　东周时期陶片
Figure Ⅰ.6.12　Eastern Zhou period pottery.

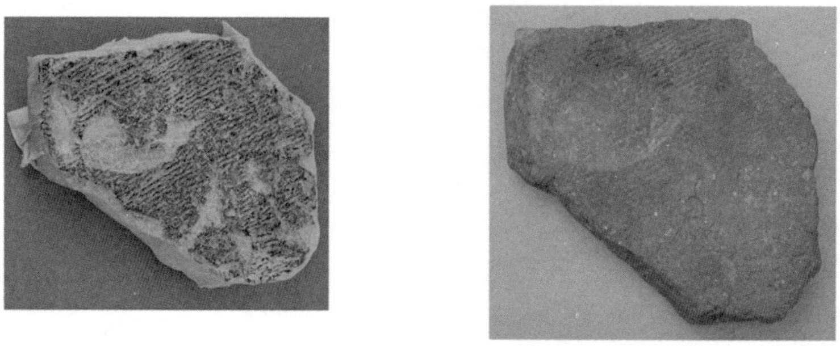

12-K51 (near)：3

12-K51 (near)：2

图 I.6.13　12区内与外城墙有关的砖块

Figure Ⅰ.6.13　Bricks associated with the outer wall in Area 12.

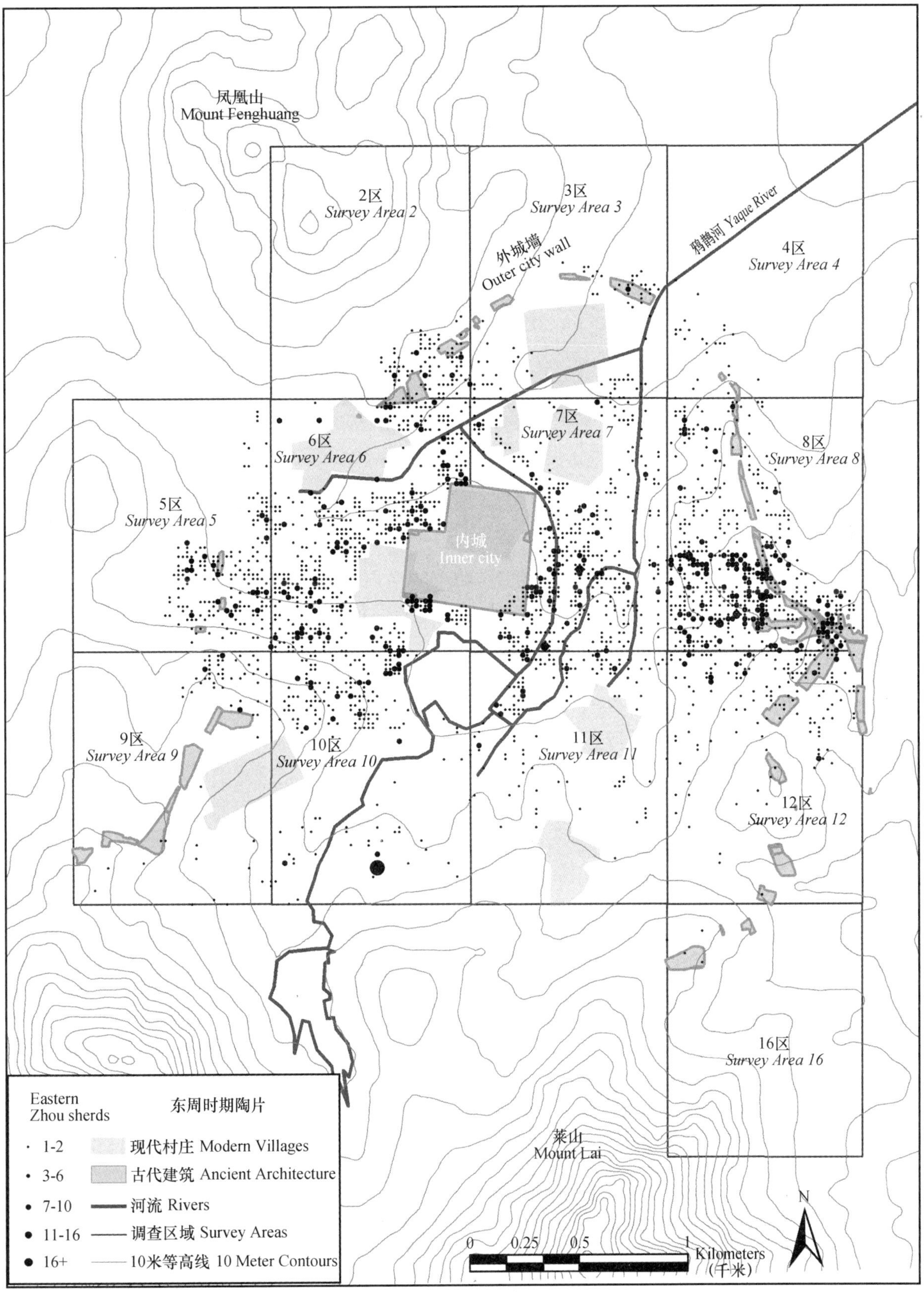
凤凰山
Mount Fenghuang
2区
Survey Area 2
3区
Survey Area 3
外城墙
Outer city wall
鸦鹊河 Yaque River
4区
Survey Area 4
5区
Survey Area 5
6区
Survey Area 6
7区
Survey Area 7
8区
Survey Area 8
内城
Inner city
9区
Survey Area 9
10区
Survey Area 10
11区
Survey Area 11
12区
Survey Area 12
16区
Survey Area 16
莱山
Mount Lai
Eastern Zhou sherds
东周时期陶片
1-2
3-6
7-10
11-16
16+
现代村庄 Modern Villages
古代建筑 Ancient Architecture
河流 Rivers
调查区域 Survey Areas
10米等高线 10 Meter Contours
0 0.25 0.5 1 Kilometers (千米)
N

a

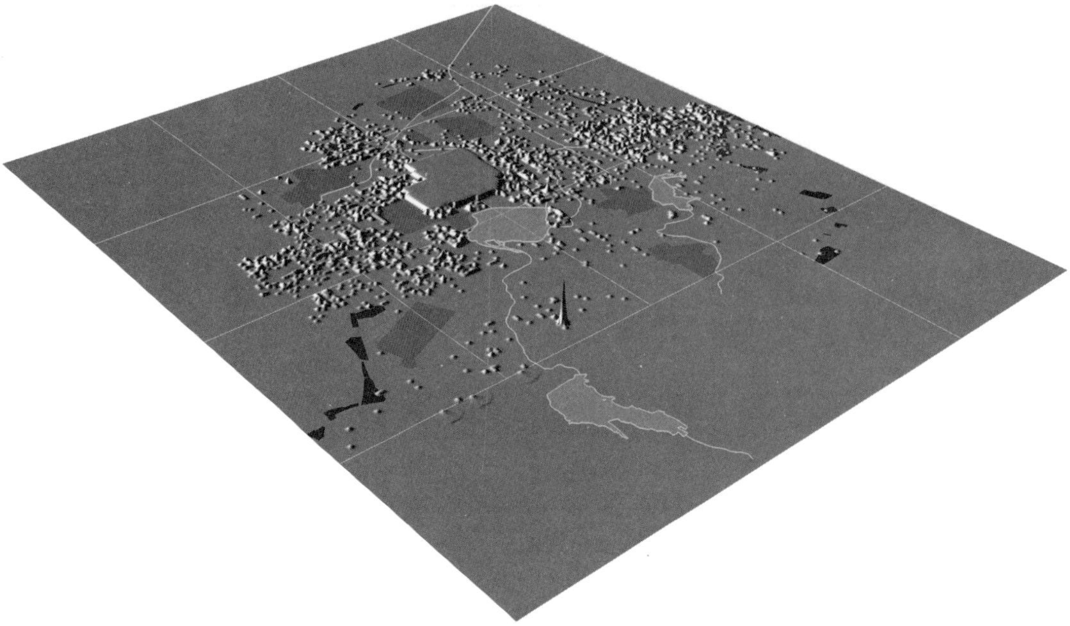

b

图Ⅰ.6.14a-b　第三期（东周时期）陶片分布图

Figure Ⅰ.6.14a-b　Sherd distribution during Period Ⅲ (Eastern Zhou).

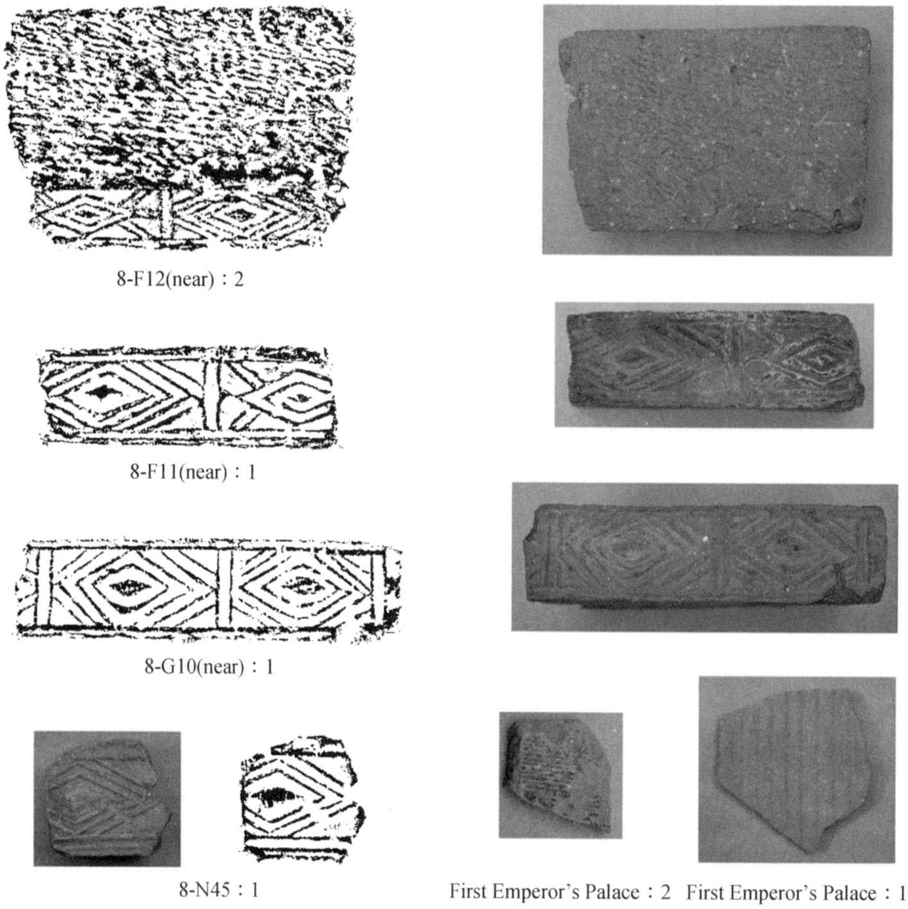

图Ⅰ.6.15　第五期（汉代）遗物

Figure Ⅰ.6.15　Remains from Period Ⅳ (Han).

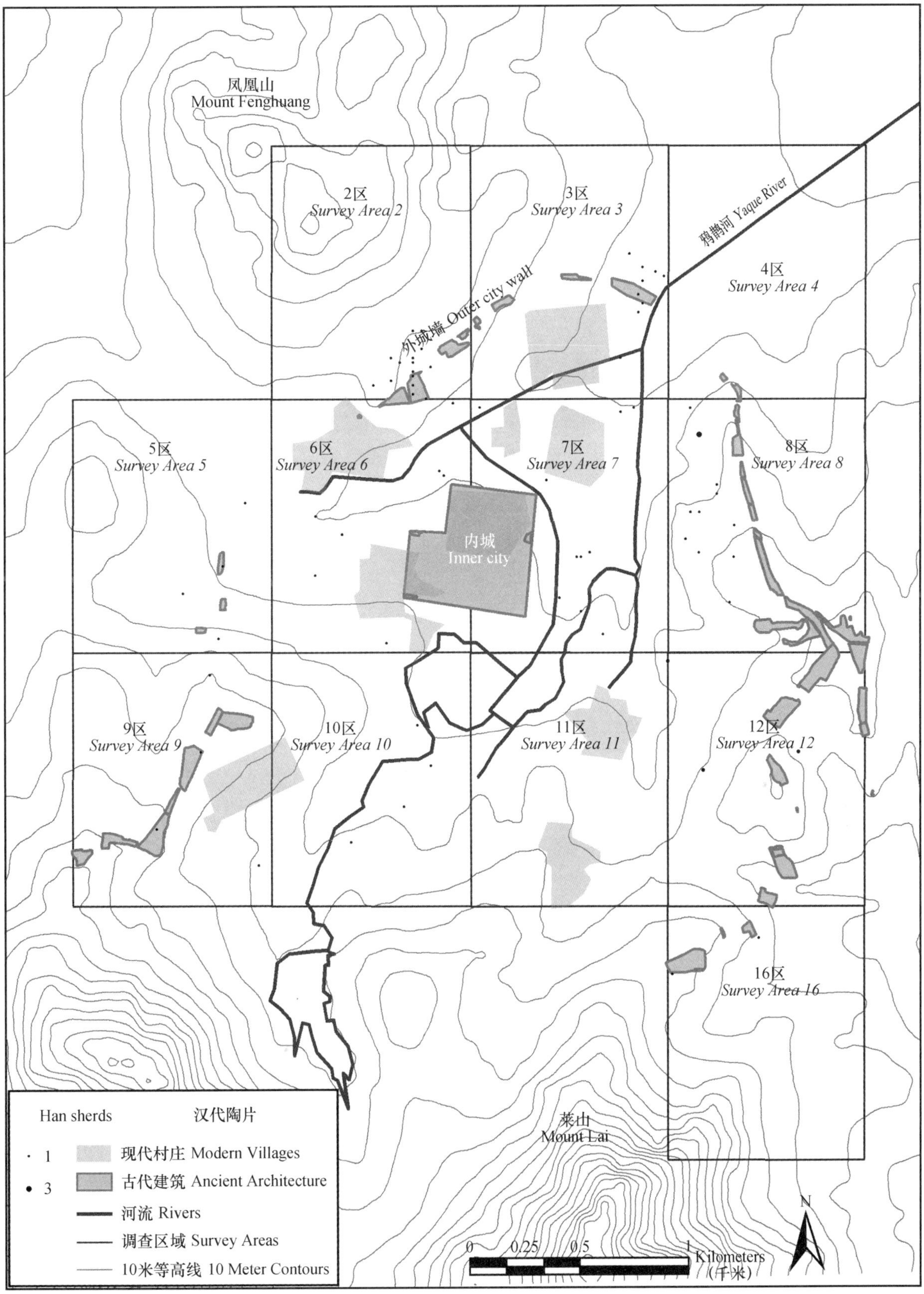
凤凰山
Mount Fenghuang
2区
Survey Area 2
3区
Survey Area 3
4区
Survey Area 4
鸦鹊河 Yaque River
外城墙 Outer city wall
5区
Survey Area 5
6区
Survey Area 6
7区
Survey Area 7
8区
Survey Area 8
内城
Inner city
9区
Survey Area 9
10区
Survey Area 10
11区
Survey Area 11
12区
Survey Area 12
16区
Survey Area 16
莱山
Mount Lai
Han sherds
汉代陶片
1
3
现代村庄 Modern Villages
古代建筑 Ancient Architecture
河流 Rivers
调查区域 Survey Areas
10米等高线 10 Meter Contours
0
0.25
0.5
1
Kilometers
（千米）
N

a

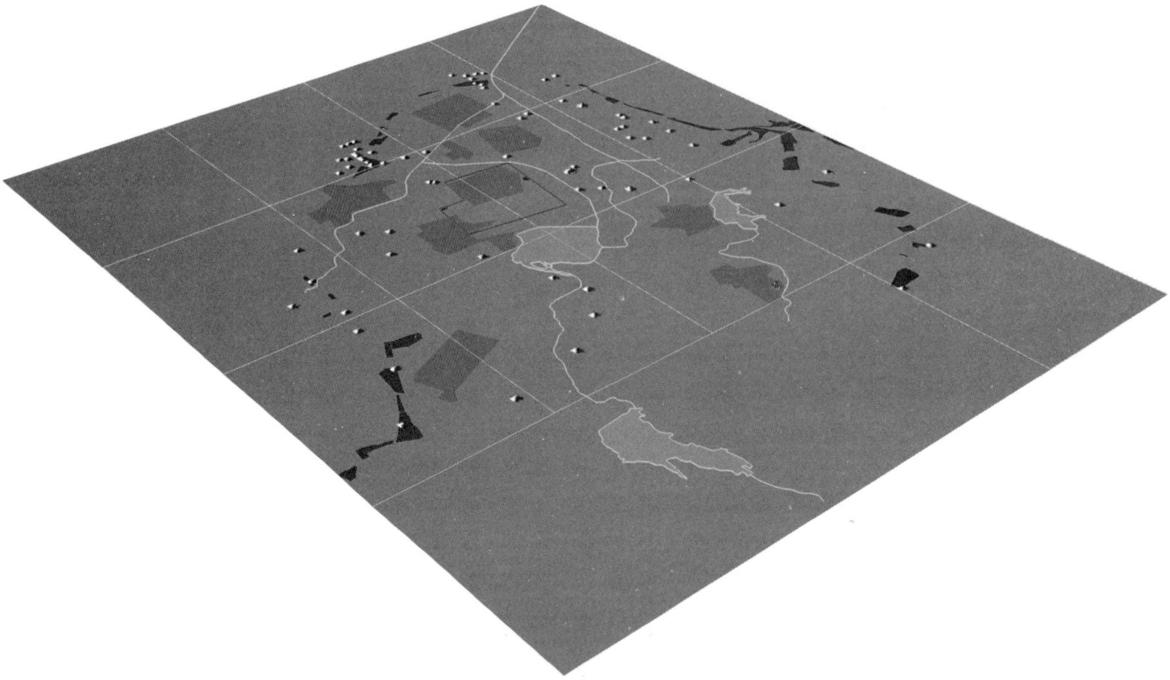

b

图Ⅰ.6.16a-b　第五期（汉代）陶片分布图
Figure Ⅰ.6.16a-b　Distribution of sherds from Period Ⅳ (Han).

图 I.6.17　8区田埂边的汉代砖
Figure Ⅰ.6.17　Han Dynasty bricks found on the edge of fields in Area 8.

图Ⅰ.6.18　土著文化陶器传统的陶片

Figure Ⅰ.6.18　Sherds of the Indigenous pottery tradition.

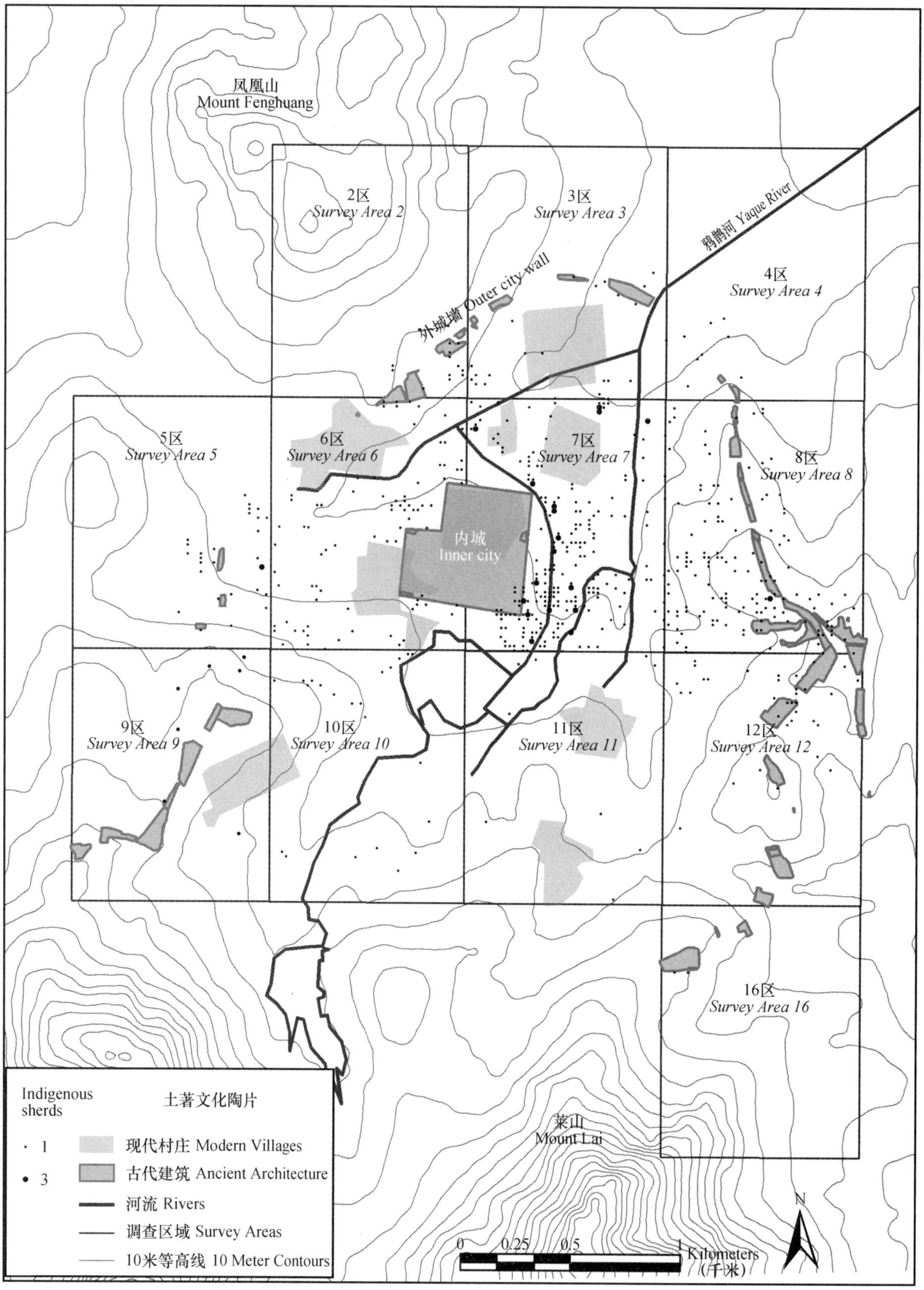

图Ⅰ.6.19　土著文化陶器传统的陶片分布图

Figure Ⅰ.6.19　Distribution of sherds of the Indigenous pottery tradition.

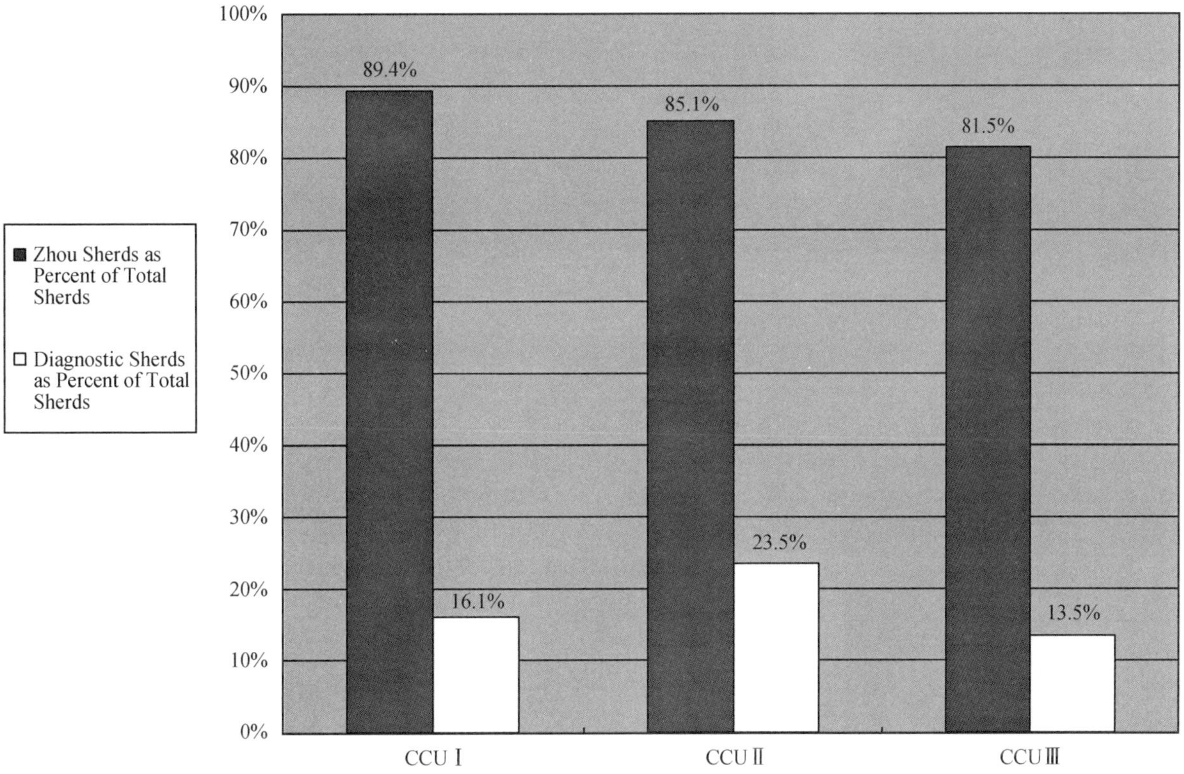

图Ⅰ.6.20　CCU中周时期陶片百分比及可辨别器类的陶片百分比直方图

Figure Ⅰ.6.20　Percentages of Zhou and sherds diagnostic of type in the CCUs.

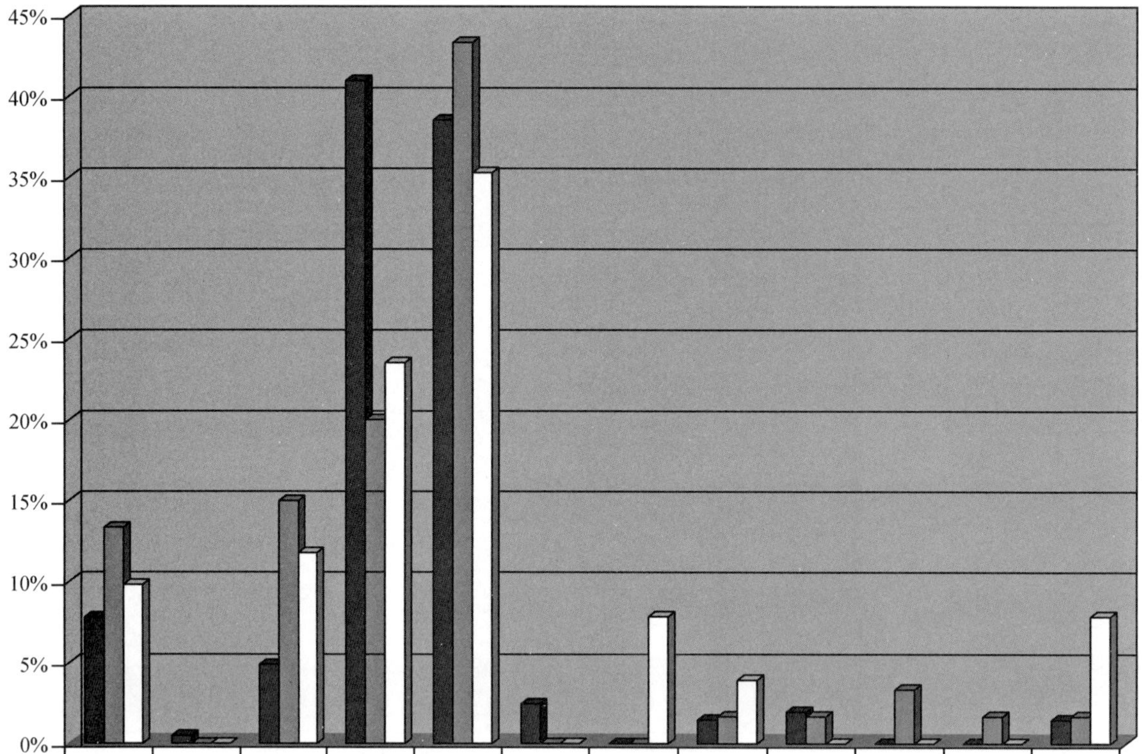

	lì 鬲	dǐng 鼎	guǐ 簋	dòu 豆	guàn 罐	wèng 瓮	pén 盆	yú 盂	pán 盘	zhuān 砖	gài 盖	wǎ 瓦
■ CCU Ⅰ	7.8%	0.5%	4.9%	41.0%	38.5%	2.4%	0.0%	1.5%	2.0%	0.0%	0.0%	1.5%
■ CCU Ⅱ	13.3%	0.0%	15.0%	20.0%	43.3%	0.0%	0.0%	1.7%	1.7%	3.3%	1.7%	1.7%
□ CCU Ⅲ	9.8%	0.0%	11.8%	23.5%	35.3%	0.0%	7.8%	3.9%	0.0%	0.0%	0.0%	7.8%

图Ⅰ.6.21 CCU中不同器类陶片占可辨识类型总陶片的百分比图

FigureⅠ.6.21 Diagnostic sherds by type, as percentage of total diagnostic sherds, for each CCU.

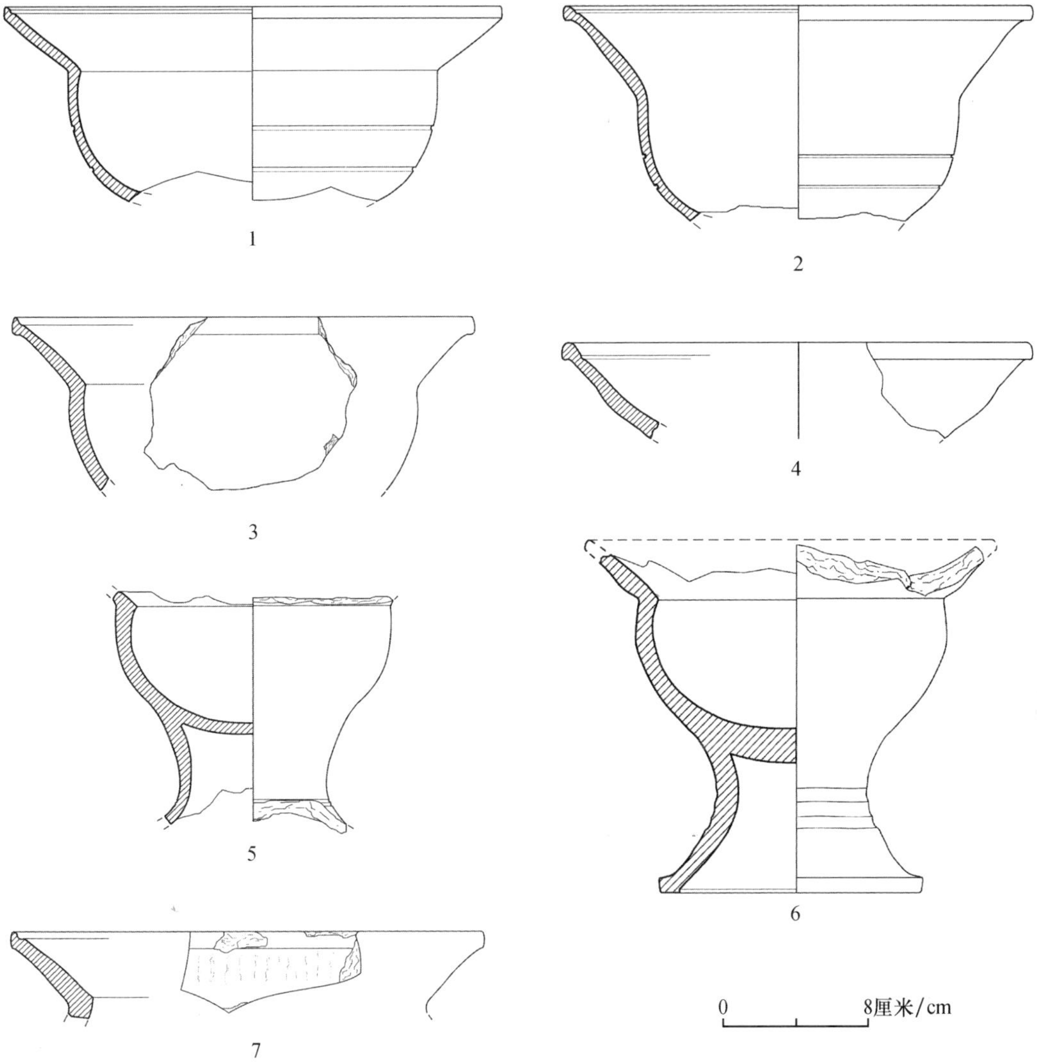

图Ⅰ.6.22　地面调查中发现的陶器类型：簋

Figure Ⅰ.6.22　Pottery types collected during the surface survey: *gui* tureen.

1. 7-a21：1　2. 7-a21：2　3. 7-c18：1　4. 10-Y9 (near)：8　5. 10-Y9 (near)：2　6. 10-Y9 (near)：1　7. 5-X16：1

表Ⅰ.6.3　归城地面调查遗物登记表1

Table Ⅰ.6.3　Pottery types collected during the surface survey: 1

图号 Number on Fig. Ⅰ.6.18	标本号 Sample number	器物名称 Artifact name	出土时间Date collected	位置 Location	所属类型 Type	尺寸（厘米） Size (cm)	特点描述 Description of features
7	5-X16：1	簋口沿 Rim from a *gui* tureen	6/16/2009	5-X16		W: 9.5 H: 4	泥质灰褐陶，宽沿，沿外有不明显绳文。 Greyish-brown clay, broad rim, light cord impressions.
1	7-a21：1	簋 *Gui* tureen	6/15/2008	7-a21	B1	H: 10 M: 6.5	泥质黑灰。宽折沿，深腹。腹中下部有两道凹弦纹。 Dark grey fine clay. Broad and folded rim, deep basin. Two intaglio ring patterns on the middle and lower belly.
2	7-a21：2	簋 *Gui* tureen	6/15/2008	7-a21	A2	H: 11 M: 25	泥质黑灰。特长斜沿，唇圆方，敞口。腹下腹两道凹弦纹。 Dark grey fine clay. Elongated oblique rim, with thickened rounded square lip, open mouth. Two intaglio rings on the lower belly.
3	7-c18：1	簋 *Gui* tureen	6/15/2008	7-c18	A2	W: 11 H: 9	泥质灰陶。敞口，宽沿，唇内侧有凹槽。素面。 Grey fine clay. Open mouth and wide rim. A circle of grooving inside the lip. Plain body.
6	10-Y9：1	簋 *Gui* tureen	6/27/2009	Near 10-Y9	A6	H: 18 M: 20.5	泥质浅灰陶。束颈斜沿，整体艘高，壁厚，腹足分界不明显，圈足呈喇叭形外撇。足上部有数道弦纹。 Light grey fine clay. Constrained neck and oblique rim, body thin and tall, thick wall, no clear division between basin and foot; circular trumpet-shaped foot flares outward. Multiple rings on the foot.
5	10-Y9：2	簋 *Gui* tureen	6/27/2009	Near 10-Y9	A6	H: 12 M: 14.5	泥质灰褐。口沿缺失，整体艘小，腹深壁厚。圈足最细部较高，下残。 Grey fine clay. Rim missing, body thin and small, thick wall. The thinnest part of the circular foot is relatively high, lower part missing.
4	10-Y9：8	簋口沿 Rim from a *gui* tureen	6/27/2009	Near 10-Y9		W: 9 H: 5	泥质浅灰陶。特长沿，圆唇。唇内侧有凹槽。素面。 Light grey clay. Elongated rim and rounded lip. Groove inside the lip. Plain surface.

尺寸标志：L=长度；H=高度；W=宽度；D=直径；R=半径；M=口径；B=底径；T=厚度；d=深度；h=孔径。

Measurements: L=length; H=height; W=width; D=diameter; R=radius; M=mouth diameter; B=bottom diameter; T=thickness; d=depth; h=hole diameter.

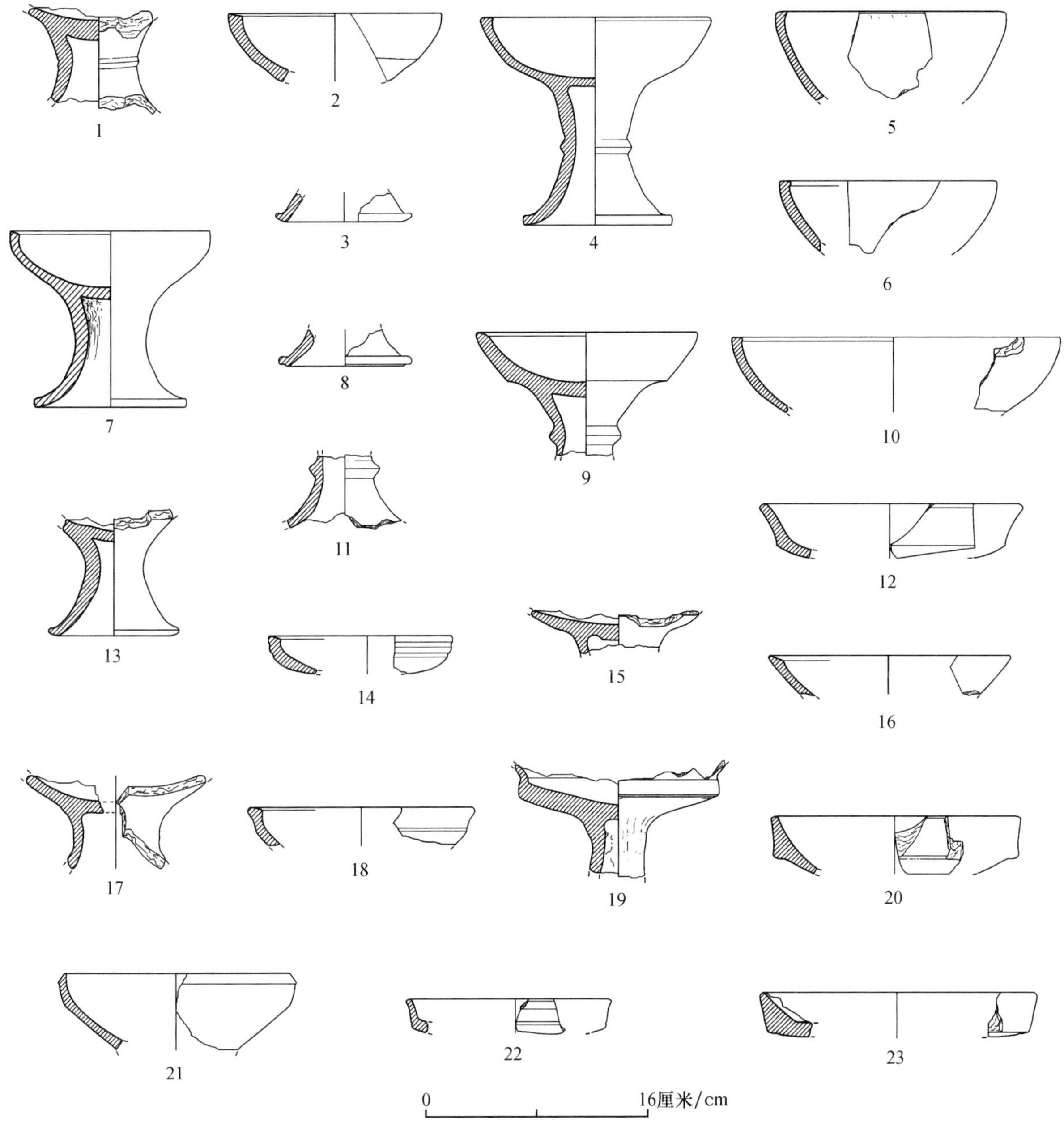

图Ⅰ.6.23　地面调查中发现的陶器类型：豆

Figure Ⅰ.6.23　Pottery types recovered during the surface survey: *dou* pedestal dish.

1. 7-c18：2　2. 7-K9：1　3. 7-k4：1　4. 7-a21：3　5. 9-o11：1　6. 7-c18：5　7. 11-O50：1　8. 7-f35：1　9. 10-Y9 (near)：3　10. 7-b18：1　11. 7-O40：1　12. 7-Z27：1　13. 10-Y9 (near)：5　14. 9-r11：1　15. 10-Y9 (near)：7　16. 7-k44：1　17. 7-P16：1　18. 7-r10：1　19. 10-Y9 (near)：4　20. 9-P56：1　21. 7-c18：3　22. 7-i14：1　23. 7-I8：3

表Ⅰ.6.4　归城地面调查遗物登记表2

Table Ⅰ.6.4　Pottery types collected during the surface survey: 2

图号 Number on Fig Ⅰ.6.19	标本号 Sample number	器物名称 Artifact name	出土时间 Date collected	位置 Location	所属类型 Type	尺寸（厘米） Size (cm)	特点描述 Description of features
23	7-I8：3	豆 Bowl of a *dou* pedestal dish	6/13/2008	7-I8	A4?	W: 3.5 H: 3	泥质浅灰，仅存盘沿，盘甚浅。 Light grey clay, rim and body fragment of very shallow bowl.
2	7-K9：1	豆 Bowl of a *dou* pedestal dish	6/13/2008	7-K9		W: 6.5 H: 5	泥质浅灰，仅存豆盘。盘深，敞口，平唇。 Light grey fine clay, deep bowl fragment with flat rim and open mouth.
11	7-O40：1	豆 Base of a *dou* pedestal dish	6/13/2008	7-O40		H: 5 W: 8	泥质浅灰，残豆柄，有一周凸棱。 Light grey fine clay, portion of *dou* stem with one circle of ridging.
17	7-P16：1	豆 Bowl and base of a *dou* pedestal dish	6/13/2008	7-P16	A3	W: 6.5 H: 6.5	泥质浅灰，有黑陶衣，残存盘底和足上部，分界不明显。 Light grey fine clay with dark slip. Bottom of shallow bowl and top of foot, boundary unclear.
12	7-Z27：1	豆盘 Bowl of a *dou* pedestal dish	6/18/2008	7-Z27	B4?	W: 6 H: 3.5	泥质红陶，浅盘，沿外撇，圆唇。 Red fine clay, shallow bowl that flares outwards, round lip.
4	7-a21：3	豆 Bowl of a *dou* pedestal dish	6/15/2008	7-a21	B1	H: 14.5 M: 16.5 B: 10.5	泥质深灰，浅盘，敞口，喇叭形圈足中部有凸棱。 Dark grey fine clay, shallow bowl, open mouth, one circle of ridging on trumpet-shaped circular foot.
10	7-b18：1	豆盘 Bowl of a *dou* pedestal dish	6/15/2008	7-b18	C2?	W: 4.5 H: 5.5	泥质浅灰，盘深。Light grey fine clay, deep bowl.
1	7-c18：2	豆柄 Base of a *dou* pedestal dish	6/15/2008	7-c18	A3	H: 7.5 D: 9	泥质灰陶，粗柄有凸棱。 Grey fine clay, strong base has one circle of ridging.
21	7-c18：3	豆盘 Bowl of a *dou* pedestal dish	6/15/2008	7-c18	A5?	W: 8.5 H: 5.5	泥质深灰，深盘，尖唇，盘壁斜。 Dark grey fine clay, deep bowl, sharp lip, wall of the bowl is oblique.
6	7-c18：5	豆盘 Bowl of a *dou* pedestal dish	6/15/2008	7-c18	C1?	W: 6.5 H: 5	深腹，平沿。 Rim fragment of deep bowl with flat rim.
8	7-f35：1	豆柄 Base of a *dou* pedestal dish	6/16/2008	7-f35		W: 4.5 H: 2.5	泥质浅灰陶，有红色陶衣。喇叭口形，有一周凸起。 Light grey fine clay with red slip. Trumpet-shaped base with one band of ridging.
22	7-i14：1	豆盘 Bowl of a *dou* pedestal dish	6/15/2008	7-i14		W: 3.5 H: 2.5	泥质浅褐。残留口沿河腹部，甚浅，有刻纹。 Light brown fine clay. Body and rim fragment of very shallow bowl with incised lines.
3	7-k4：1	豆柄 Base of a *dou* pedestal dish	6/15/2008	7-k4		W: 4 H: 2	残豆柄沿，喇叭口形，有一周突起。 Rim fragment of a round, trumpet-shaped stem with one band of ridging.
16	7-k44：1	豆盘 Bowl of a *dou* pedestal dish	6/16/2008	7-k44		W: 4.5 H: 3	残口沿，大敞口豆盘，尖唇。 Rim fragment of a wide-mouthed bowl with a tapered lip.
18	7-r10：1	豆盘 Bowl of a *dou* pedestal dish	7/7/2008	7-r10		W: 6 H: 2.5	黑灰陶质，浅盘有刻槽，唇微侈。 Dark gray clay, rim fragment of shallow bowl with incised line and flared lip.

续表

图号 Number on Fig Ⅰ.6.19	标本号 Sample number	器物名称 Artifact name	出土时间 Date collected	位置 Location	所属类型 Type	尺寸（厘米） Size (cm)	特点描述 Description of features
20	9-P56：1	豆盘 Bowl of a *dou* pedestal dish	6/24/2009	9-P56		W: 5 H: 4	泥质浅褐色。残口沿，浅盘，有刻槽。 Light brown fine clay, rim fragment of shallow bowl with incised line.
5	9-o11：1	豆盘 Bowl of a *dou* pedestal dish	6/26/2009	9-o11	C1?	W: 6 H: 6	残口沿。深腹敞口。 Rim fragment of a deep bowl with a wide lip.
14	9-r11：1	豆盘 Bowl of a *dou* pedestal dish	6/26/2009	9-r11		W: 4 H: 2.5	残口沿，浅腹，有数道弦纹。 Rim fragment of shallow bowl with incised lines.
9	10-Y9：3	豆盘 Bowl and base of a *dou* pedestal dish	6/27/2009	Near 10-Y9	B2	H: 8.5 M: 15.5	泥质浅褐色。浅盘，柄部残留一半，有凸棱。 Light brown fine clay. Shallow bowl and partial base, ribbing on stem.
19	10-Y9：4	豆盘 Bowl of a *dou* pedestal dish	6/27/2009	Near 10-Y9	B4	H: 8 D: 15	泥质浅褐。浅盘，厚底。柄部细直。 Light brown fine clay. Thick bottom of shallow bowl with incision, partial stem is thin and straight.
13	10-Y9：5	豆柄 Base of a *dou* pedestal dish	6/27/2009	Near 10-Y9	A3	H: 9 B: 9.5	泥质红褐陶。喇叭口形。底部有一周突起。 Reddish+brown fine clay. Trumpet-shaped bottom with one band of ridging.
15	10-Y9：7	豆盘 Bowl and base of a *dou* pedestal dish	6/27/2009	Near 10-Y9		H: 3 D: 12	泥质浅褐陶。仅残留盘底圈足跟。 Light brown fine clay. Bottom of shallow bowl and top of foot.
7	11-O50：1	豆 *Dou* pedestal dish	7/4/2009	11-O50	A3	H: 12 M: 14.5 B: 11	深盘高圈足。腹深底呈寰形。喇叭口形圈足。 Wide bowl, high circular foot. Deep, ring-shaped bottom, trumpet-shaped foot.

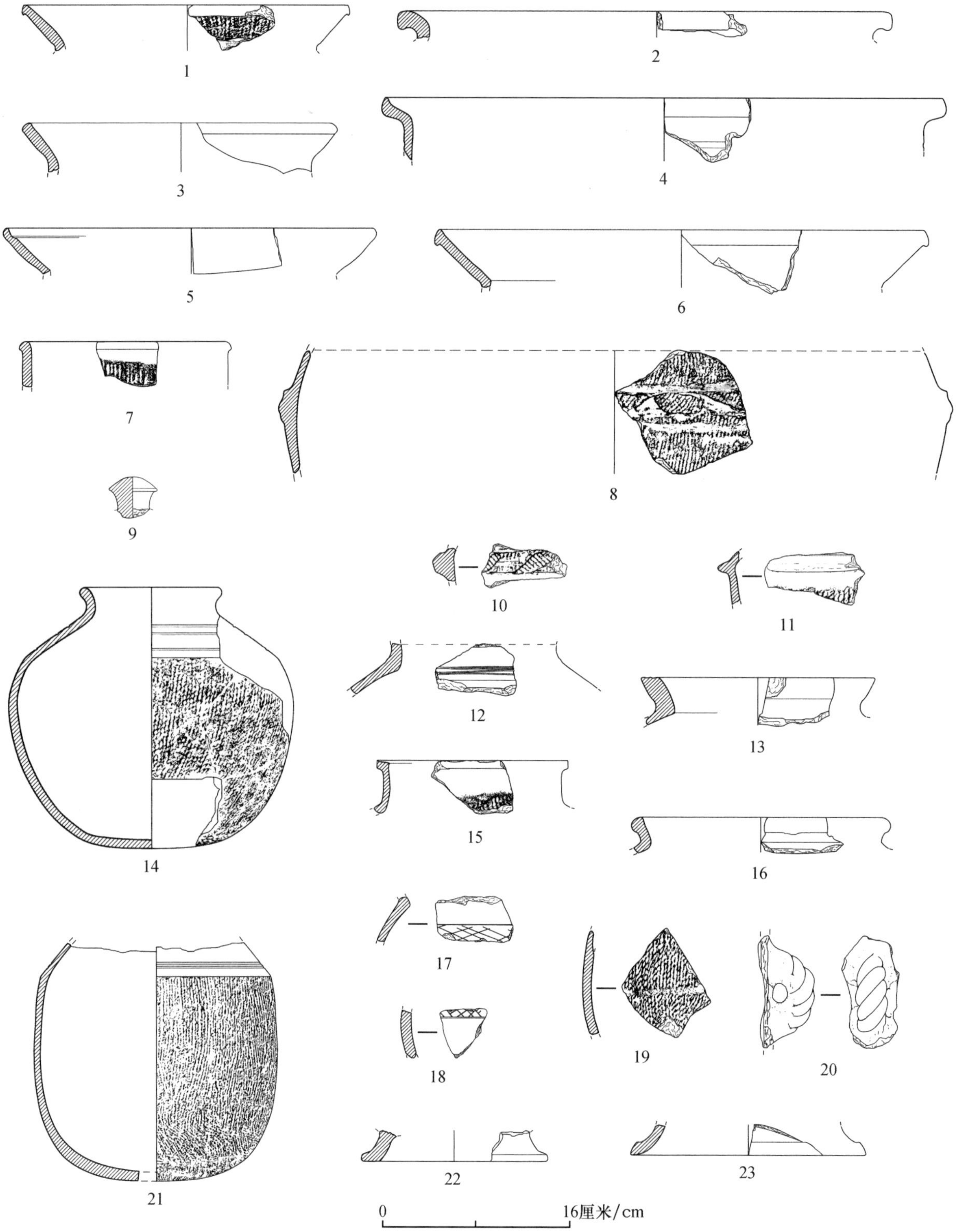

图Ⅰ.6.24　地面调查中发现的陶器类型：盆（1～8，10～11）和罐（9，12～23）

Figure Ⅰ.6.24　Pottery types recovered during the surface survey:
pen basin (1～8, 10～11) and *guan* jar (9, 12～23).

1. 7-b16：1　2. 7-j51：1　3. 7-c22：1　4. 11-H46：2　5. 10-a52：1　6. 11-C35：1　7. 7-T19:1　8. 10-Y9 (near)：10　9. 7-c23：1　10. 7-X25：1　11. 7-a17：1　12. 7-W19：1　13. 6-M4：1　14. 10-Y9 (near)：12　15. 7-H7：1　16. 11-g54：1　17. 3-s26：1　18. 3-h26：1　19. 7-R28：2　20. 7-g32：1　21. 7-a21：5　22. 7-e24：1　23. 7-Z6：1

表Ⅰ.6.5 归城地面调查遗物登记表3

Table Ⅰ.6.5 Pottery types collected during the surface survey: 3

图号 Number on Fig. Ⅰ.6.20	标本号 Sample number	器物名称 Artifact name	出土时间 Date collected	位置 Location	所属类型 Type	尺寸（厘米）Size (cm)	特点描述 Description of features
18	3-h26：1	罐 *Guan* jar	6/26/2008	3-h26		L: 4 W: 4	残片，泥质浅灰褐色，有条纹；有刻花纹。Light greyish-brown fine clay with red slip, body fragment with incised cross-hatching near top.
17	3-s26：1	罐 *Guan* jar	6/27/2008	3-s26		L: 6.5 W: 4	泥质深灰陶，有黑色陶衣。器身上部残片。刻有交叉花纹。Dark grey fine clay with dark slip, fragment of top portion of body, incised cross-hatching.
13	6M4：1	罐 *Guan* jar	6/16/2009-6/21/2009	6M4		W: 6.5 H: 4	口沿残片，侈口，厚唇。Fragment of rim, flared mouth, very thick lip.
15	7-H7：1	罐 *Guan* jar	6/13/2008	7-H7		W: 7 H: 4.5	泥质浅褐。小口罐口沿，直颈，下部有绳纹。Light brown fine clay. Fragment of tall narrow mouth, straight neck, cord impressions near juncture with body.
19	7-R28：2	罐 *Guan* jar	6/19/2008	7-R28		L: 9 W: 7.5	泥质浅褐。腹部残片，绳纹印痕深。Light brown fine clay. Body fragment with deep cord impressions.
7	7-T19：1	盆 *Pen* basin	6/15/2008	7-T19		W: 5.5 H: 4	口沿残片。直口深腹，有浅绳纹。Rim fragment. Straight mouth with light cord impressions.
12	7-W19：1	罐 *Guan* jar	6/15/2008	7-W19		L: 6.5 W: 4	颈部残片，有凹弦纹。Fragment of neck and body with intaglio ring patterns.
10	7-X25：1	盆 *Pen* basin	6/18/2008	7-X25		L: 7 W: 4	泥质浅褐。肩部残片，有附加堆纹，饰绳纹。Light brown fine clay. Fragment of shoulder with ridge, cord impressions.
23	7-Z6：1	罐 *Guan* jar	6/15/2008	7-Z6		W: 6 H: 2.5	泥质浅褐。圈足残片，低矮。Light brown fine clay. Rim fragment of circular, low foot.
11	7-a17：1	盆 *Pen* basin	6/15/2008	7-a17		L: 8.5 W: 4	泥质浅褐。肩部残片，有把手，其下有深绳纹。Light brown fine clay. Fragment of shoulder with handle, with deep cord impressions below.
21	7-a21：5	罐 *Guan* jar	6/15/2008	7-a21	A3?	H: 19.5 D: 20	深腹寰底，肩上有弦纹。腹部整体饰绳纹。Deep belly, intaglio rings on shoulder, and cord impressions over most of the body.
1	7-b16：1	盆 *Pen* basin	6/15/2008	7-b16		W: 7.5 H: 4	口沿残片，斜敞口。绳纹印痕深。Rim fragment, oblique and flaring, with deep cord impressions
9	7-c23：1	器盖纽 Handle of a vessel lid	6/15/2008	7-c23		H: 3.5 D: 4	盖纽，泥质浅红褐色。Handle made of light reddish-brown fine clay.
3	7-c22：1	盆口沿 Rim from a *pen* basin	6/15/2008	7-c22		W: 12 H: 4.5	盆口沿，大敞口，圆唇。Rim fragment of a wide-mouthed basin, round lip.
22	7-e24：1	罐 *Guan* jar	6/15/2008	7-e24		W: 4.5 H: 2.5	圈足残片，低矮。Fragment of a round, low base.
20	7-g32：1	索状器耳 Twisted handle	6/16/2008	7-g32		L: 9 W: 4	泥质浅褐色。器耳呈绳索状扭曲。Light brown fine clay. Handle twisted into the shape of a rope.

续表

图号 Number on Fig. Ⅰ.6.20	标本号 Sample number	器物名称 Artifact name	出土时间 Date collected	位置 Location	所属类型 Type	尺寸（厘米） Size (cm)	特点描述 Description of features
2	7-j51：1	盆口沿 Rim from a *pen* basin	6/24/2008	7-j51		W: 7.5 H: 2	泥质浅褐色。卷沿圆唇。 Light brow fine clay. Rolled rim with round lip.
8	10-Y9：10	盆 *Pen* basin	6/27/2009	Near 10-Y9		L: 12 W: 9.5	泥质浅褐色。直口尖唇，肩部饰附加堆纹。饰绳纹。 Light brown fine fabric, straight mouth with narrow and sharp lip. Protruding ridge on shoulder, with cord impressions.
14	10-Y9：12	罐 *Guan* jar	6/27/2009	Near 10-Y9	A1	H: 21.5 M: 12	小口圆肩。小圆唇。束颈。肩上有弦纹，腹饰绳纹。 Jar with small mouth and round shoulder. Small round lip. Constricted neck. Intaglio ring patterns on shoulder and cord impressions on belly.
5	10-a52：1	盆口沿 Rim from a *pen* basin	6/28/2009	10-a52		W: 8 H: 4	敞口斜沿。尖唇内卷，唇内有弦纹。 Widely open basin with oblique and long rim. Lip turns inwards, with intaglio rings underneath.
6	11-C35：1	盆口沿 Rim from a *pen* basin	7/6/2009	11-C35		W: 10 H: 5.5	泥质浅褐色。长斜沿，小卷唇。 Light brown fine clay. Long and oblique rim, and rolled lip.
4	11-H46：2	盆口沿 Rim from a *pen* basin	7/4/2009	11-H46		W: 7.5 H: 5.5	直口窄沿尖唇。 Straight mouth, narrow rim with sharp lip.
16	11-g54：1	罐 *Guan* jar	7/7/2009	11-g54		W: 7 H: 3	残口沿，短颈，圆唇。 Fragment of rim. Short neck and round lip.

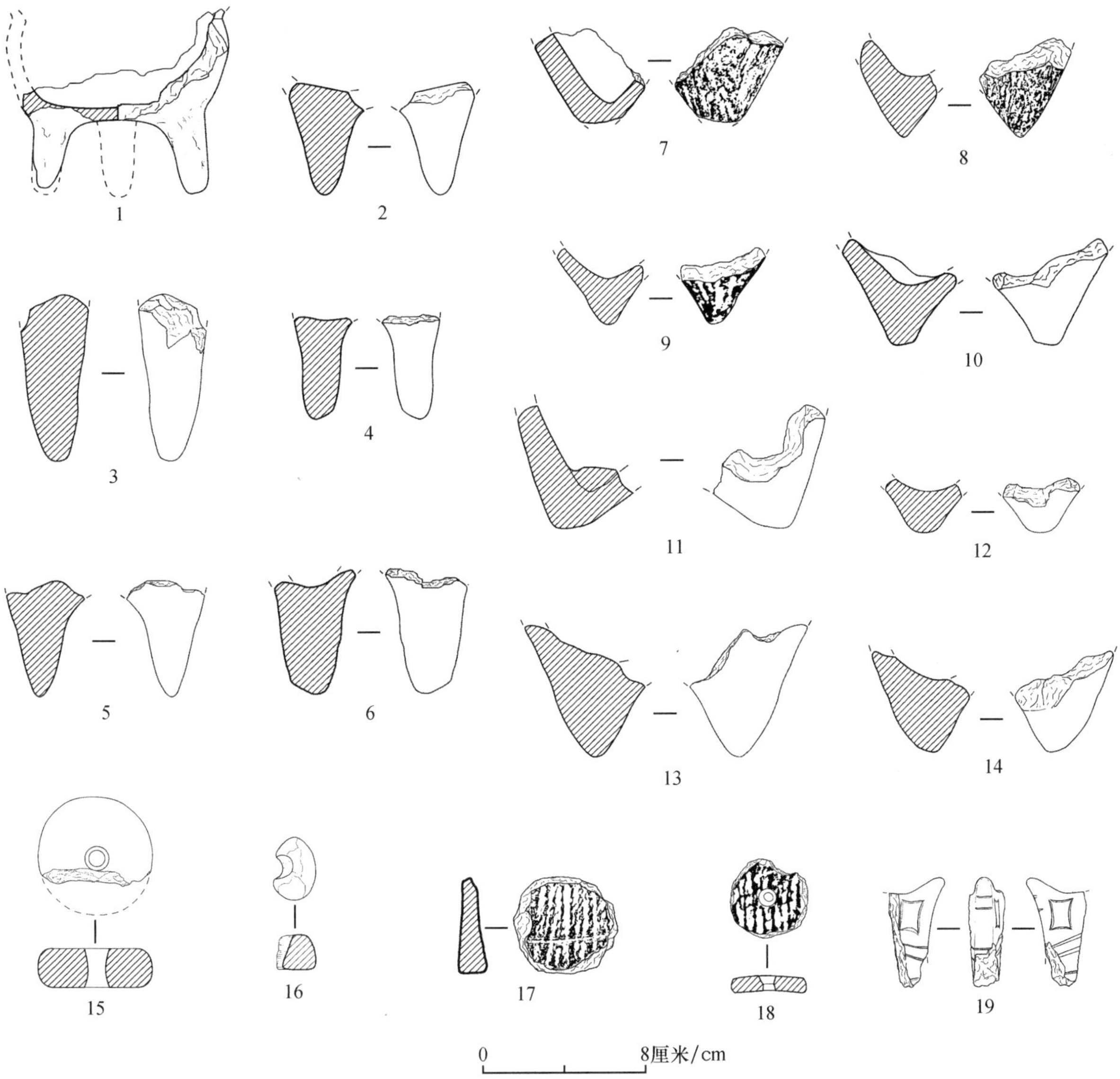

图Ⅰ.6.25 地面调查中发现的陶器类型：

鼎（1～6）、鬲（7～14）、陶环（15～16）、圆陶片（17～18）、装饰扉棱（19）

Figure Ⅰ.6.25 Pottery types recovered during the surface survey:

ding cauldron (1 ~ 6), *li* tripod (7 ~ 14), pottery ring (15 ~ 16), circular pottery sherds (17 ~ 18), and fragment of appliqué (19).

1. 10-Y9 (near)：6 2. 12-e52：1 3. 6-j13：1 4. 5-Y9：1 5. 3-e33：1 6. 7-O1：1 7. 10-Y9：9 8. 8-n13：1 9. 9-m52：1 10. 7-Q16：1 11. 7-T14：1 12. 5-s10：1 13. 8-I9：1 14. 6-L33：1 15. 7-Z9：1 16. 7-P38：1 17. 7-Q49：1 18. 8-W24：1 19. 7-S23：1

表Ⅰ.6.6　归城地面调查遗物登记表4

Table Ⅰ.6.6　Pottery types collected during the surface survey: 4

序号 Number on Fig. Ⅰ.6.21	标本号 Sample number	器物名称 Artifact name	出土时间 Date collected	位置 Location	所属类型 Type	尺寸（厘米） Size (cm)	特点描述 Description of features
5	3-e33：1	鼎足 Foot from a *ding* cauldron	6/26/2008	3-e33		L: 11.5 W: 7.5	高实足，尖状。 Tall solid pointed foot.
4	5-Y9：1	鼎足 Foot from a *ding* cauldron	6/16/2009	5-Y9		L: 10 W: 5.5	高实足，柱状。 Tall solid tapered foot.
12	5-s10：1	鬲足 Foot from a *li* tripod	6/18/2009	5-s10		L: 6 W: 7	袋足鬲实足根。 Solid ends of hollow legs.
14	6-L33：1	鬲足 Foot from a *li* tripod	6/18/2009	6-L33		L: 11.5 W: 8	袋足鬲实足根。较尖。 Solid ends of hollow legs, relatively sharp.
3	6-j13：1	鼎足 Foot from a *ding* cauldron	6/21/2009	6-j13		L: 16 W: 6.5	细高柱状足。 Tall solid tapered foot.
6	7-O1：1	鼎足 Foot from a *ding* cauldron	6/13/2008	7-O1		L: 12 W: 7.5	高实足，柱状。 Tall solid tapered foot.
16	7-P38：1	陶环 Pottery ring	6/29/2009	7-P38		L: 6 W: 4 T: 3.5	陶环残片。 Fragment of a small pottery ring.
10	7-Q16：1	鬲足 Foot from a *li* tripod	6/14/2008	7-Q16		L: 11.5 W: 10	袋足鬲实足根。较尖。 Solid ends of hollow legs, relatively sharp.
17	7-Q49：1	圆陶片 Round pottery sherd	6/20/2008	7-Q49		D: 10.5	泥质浅褐。圆陶片，绳纹。 Light brown fine clay. Round fragment with cord impressions.
19	7-S23：1	扉棱 Flange of a vessel	6/15/2008	7-S23		L: 11 T: 3.5	泥质浅褐。三角形扉棱，有刻纹和四方形装饰。 Light brown fine clay. Triangular flange with incised lines and rectangle decorations.
11	7-T14：1	鬲足 Foot from a *li* tripod	6/14/2008	7-T14		L: 12 W: 9	加砂红褐陶。袋装空足。 Reddish-brown coarse clay. Small hollow foot.
15	7-Z9：1	陶环 Pottery disc	6/15/2008	7-Z9		D: 11 T: 4	加砂红褐陶。厚，中心有孔。 Reddish-brown coarse clay. Thick with hole in the center opening from both sides.
13	8-I9：1	鬲足 Foot from a *li* tripod	7/8/2008	8-I9		L: 14.5 W: 9	鬲实足根。很尖。 Solid end of a foot, very sharp.
18	8-W24：1	圆陶片 Round pottery sherd	7/13/2008	8-W24		D: 8.5 T: 1.5	圆陶片，绳纹。中心有孔。 Round pottery sherd, cord impressions. Hole in the center.
8	8-n13：1	鬲足 Foot from a *li* tripod	7/14/2008	8-n13		L: 10 W: 6.5	袋足鬲足尖，饰绳纹。 Tip of a hollow leg, decorated with cord impressions.
9	9-m52：1	鬲足 Foot from a *li* tripod	6/24/2009	9-m52		L: 8.5 W: 7	乳状袋足足尖，饰绳纹。 Tip of a breast-shaped hollow leg, with cord impressions.

续表

序号 Number on Fig. Ⅰ.6.21	标本号 Sample number	器物名称 Artifact name	出土时间 Date collected	位置 Location	所属类型 Type	尺寸（厘米） Size (cm)	特点描述 Description of features
1	10-Y9：6	鼎 *Ding* cauldron	6/27/2009	Near 10-Y9	A2	H: 16 D: 20.5 Foot-H: 7	泥质红褐陶。细高足。圆腹，素面粗糙。 Reddish-brown fine clay. Tall tapered feet, round body, plain and rough surface.
7	10-Y9：9	鬲足 Foot from a *li* tripod	6/27/2009	Near 10-Y9		L: 9.5 W: 8.5	加砂浅褐色陶。袋足，足尖断。表面粗糙，饰绳纹。 Light brown coarse clay. Hollow conical foot, rough surface with cord impressions.
2	12-e52：1	鼎足 Foot from a *ding* cauldron	6/15/2009	12-e52		L: 11 W: 7	高实足，尖状。 Tall solid pointed foot.

Chapter 6: Full-Coverage Surface Sampling Survey

Li Feng Elizabeth Berger

Virtually all field archaeological research begins with a surface survey, which has long been recognized as a critical tool for understanding a site or cluster of sites. Although materials on the surface of a site observable during the survey may not directly reflect the profiles of its subsurface deposits, they are related in meaningful ways, and the correlation between them can be clarified by comparison through stratigraphic test excavation (Chifeng International Collaborative Archeological Research Project 2003: 51-53, 139-142). In archaeological research at Guicheng, the full-coverage survey method was systematically applied to the area between the two concentric walls identified in the early stage of the project. The survey enabled us to map out the continuous distribution of ceramic sherds over a land surface of 8 km^2, providing rich data for understanding the settlement organization of Guicheng as well as how it changed over time.

Section 1: Purpose and Significance of the Survey

Full-coverage survey is the best method to study settlement organization and organizational changes at both inter-site and intra-site levels. Intensive, full-coverage surveys, like that implemented at Guicheng, can avoid many problems that arise from limited coverage and stratified random sampling in the more traditional method of surveys that favored larger and more spectacular sites (Kowalewski and Fish 1990: 263-264). In an intensive full-coverage survey, the entire extent of the survey area is covered with the same resolution and sampling pattern, and the intensity of coverage (the density with which samples are taken) is relatively high. Because of the systematic nature of the data obtained through this method, intensive full-coverage surveys allow for quantitative comparison of artifact populations across both spatial and temporal distance, and thus afford us ways to address a much richer array of questions than those possible with unsystematic surveys.

There are a number of research questions underlying the Guicheng survey:

1) Test the correlation between surface and subsurface remains: Although materials on the surface may not directly reflect the profiles of subsurface deposits, by comparing the surface survey data with the subterranean remains and deposit profiles obtained through systematic coring with Luoyang spades

and stratigraphic test excavation, it was possible to detect correlations between the two sets of data.

2) Map the distribution of surface remains across the site: A full-coverage systematic survey can produce a comprehensive map of sherd distribution over the entirety of a site. The full-coverage survey at Guicheng helped us to identify concentrations of ceramics, which were likely related to residential or craft production activities. We also detected areas of low sherd density that may represent areas with minimal activity. With these data, we were able to reconstruct what has been called "a virtually continuous surface of human impact" (Bintliff 2000: 3).

3) Detect diachronic change: In our analysis of the survey data, we identified different locations of sherd concentration in each period, which revealed temporal changes in the organization of the site, hence revealing the site's occupational history.

4) Understand site formation processes: By correlating the map of total sherd distribution with features of the natural terrain, we came to a better understanding of the roles played by natural and human forces in shaping the distribution of ceramic sherds observed in the survey.

The project was designed so that the intensive full-coverage survey, combined with coring, could help us recover the Bronze Age landscape of Guicheng. It was also hoped that some ancient structures that were destroyed by natural or human forces might have left dense sherd populations near their original locations, and would thus be recognizable in the survey data. The survey was carried out within the outer city wall, and we recognize that while the wall formed the boundary of the city, it did not necessarily represent the limits of human activities at the site (Fig. Ⅰ.6.1). Thus, on the whole, the purpose of the survey was not to define the bounds of human activity, but to serve as the grounds for understanding social organization within the city. In order to understand human activities along the outer wall, on average the survey was carried 200 m beyond the outer wall but not farther, as we planned to cover this area with a large-scale regional survey at a lower collection density in the future.

Section 2: Design of Survey Methods and Practice in the Field

1. The Full-Coverage Survey Methods

The systematic archaeological survey techniques in wide use today can be traced back to early examples of settlement pattern studies in the Americas. This modern scientific method departed dramatically from the earlier nineteenth century tradition of private antiquarians, collectors, explorers, and early archaeologists publishing reports of largely descriptive, unsystematic surveys (King 1978: 4). The Virú Valley Project, specifically the survey work conducted in 1946-1948, is often cited as the point of origin for modern surveys of settlement patterns (see Wiley 1953). These techniques were further developed into systematic survey methods by researchers working in the Basin of Mexico in the 1960s and 1970s (Billman & Feinman 1999: 12-21; Chifeng 2003: 99; Ford and Willey 1949: 19). This work in the Basin of Mexico marked the transition of archaeological survey from a means of locating sites for excavation or description, to a form of systematic exploration of ancient landscapes and settlement systems. Other data sources, such as ethno-historical and geological data, can be used in combination with survey data to construct richer pictures of ancient human activity and habitation.

Full-coverage survey on a smaller scale, designed to detect patterns in the distribution of remains within a large site or cluster of sites, has been insufficiently discussed in previous literature (Gaffney, Gaffney, and Tingle 1985: 95-107; Walker 1985: 87-94). Such smaller-scale surveys are usually designed with much higher resolution than regional-scale surveys, and have a unique potential to establish closer links between surface material and subsurface structures. This method is therefore a better tool for investigating the internal sociopolitical organization of a community than a regional scale survey. Good examples of the application of this method come from Mediterranean archaeological practice, including early surveys of the Greek countryside (Van Andel and Runnels 1987: 29-39) and a number of the Greek city sites conducted as part of the Boeotia survey project in the 1990s (Bintliff 2000: 3-20, discussed below).

Whether a survey is regional-scale or smaller-scale, full-coverage methodologies generally produce the best survey results. Over the past half-century, archaeologists have explored the advantages of full-coverage survey and have applied it to cases in many regions, including Mesoamerica, Greece, northern South America, Mesopotamia, and China (Cherry et al. 1988: 159-162; Chifeng 2003, 100; Underhill et al. 2002: 745-746). These works have resulted in a broad literature, most having had as their goal to identify sites and to analyze large-scale systems of human interaction and socio-political change at the regional scale (Kowalewski 1990a: 33-34; Underhill et al. 2002: 745). Through these works, a wide variety of adaptations of full-coverage methods has been created for surveys targeting different types of remains, terrains, and research questions. For example, the survey conducted by Underhill and colleagues in Rizhao in southeastern Shandong province, China, was designed primarily to detect the presence of a regional settlement hierarchy, and to assess regional changes during the transition to the early Bronze Age (Underhill et al. 2002: 746). The researchers therefore chose a constant survey resolution of 30-50 m between collections, which allowed for complete coverage of the survey area but still allowed for the detection of ancient activity across all variations in terrain.

Recent advances in survey methodology include critiques of the "site" concept and the promotion of "site-less" or "non-site" regional survey, the use of Geographic Information Systems (GIS) and computer-aided methods of analysis, and the development of a variety of sampling regimens that maximize the representativeness of material recovered during survey. In addition, it has been recognized that intensive surface surveys (like that conducted at Guicheng) produce data that can be used to address certain research questions in their own right, such as the uses of various areas and changes in human activity over time (Cherry et al. 1988: 159; Sullivan, Mink & Uphus 2007: 322). Such use of the data is possible because the distribution of surface ceramic remains is generally representative of the subsurface distribution, even when site formation processes are taken into account.

2. Complete Coverage Systematic Survey Methods and Their Practice in China

It is only in the past twenty years that full-coverage systematic surveys have been conducted across China. The adoption of this survey method over previous unsystematic pedestrian surveys accompanied the reintroduction of Western methodologies and theoretical models of social change into the practice of archaeology in China. There have been three main regions in China that have undergone multiyear, major, regional full-coverage surveys by teams of international collaborators, including the Rizhao area in southeastern Shandong province (Underhill et al. 2002: 745-755), the Yi and Luo River valleys in western Henan (Liu 2002-2004: 75-100), and eastern Inner Mongolia, focusing on the Chifeng region (Chifeng 2003: 100-101; Linduff, Drennan & Shelach 2002-2004: 45-73). In recent years, there have been an increasing number of surveys using a similar method conducted independently by Chinese archaeologists.

As elsewhere in the world, the goal of these surveys has been to improve understanding of processes of social development in China, as well as to allow for comparative studies of social change across the globe according to Western anthropological models. These survey projects have focused mainly on regional-scale processes (between roughly 200 and 1,000 km^2 each) of increasing social complexity, understood through changing settlement patterns. Specific aims have included identification and delineation of sites, analysis of ceramic chronologies, and recording differences across ecological zones. In short, full-coverage survey has by now become a widely accepted practice in China.

3. The Systematic Surface Sampling Method

Most full-coverage surveys are carried out on a regional scale, although there is little agreement on how large a "region" should be, as it depends on the condition of the terrain and the research objective (Parsons 1990: 10-11). Generally, it is a fairly large area falling somewhere between 100 and 1,000 km^2. For smaller areas, the distribution of archaeological remains can be assessed by using higher survey resolution augmented further by test trenches, as in the Wallace Reservoir survey in Georgia (Fish & Gresham 1990: 151-155) and in the Central Negev survey in Israel (Marks 1971:

1240), or by systematic coring in the case of many Chinese sites, where rammed earth is the main method of construction. The decision to use different methods depends, of course, on the condition of a site, on the time and resources available for a given project, and most importantly on a project's research goals. However, few systematic surveys have been designed to clarify the distribution of remains *within* a settlement unit (Gaffney, Gaffney & Tingle 1985: 95-107; Walker 1985: 87-94).

In the case of Guicheng, survey was an optimal choice because the area within the outer city walls, roughly km^2, was too large for complete coverage by subsurface methods such as test trenches, shovel tests, or systematic coring (though coring has been conducted within the inner city of Guicheng; see Chapter 2). In fact, Guicheng can be regarded as a cluster of sites demarcated by an outer wall. On the other hand, the site is significantly smaller than the area covered by most regional surveys. In addition to its unique size, a number of conditions at the Guicheng site had to be taken into account when designing the survey method.

First, the survey area is characterized by a relatively high density of remains. Therefore, changes in pottery density were potentially small in relation to the overall density, and except for areas occupied by villages and lakes, there was little land surface where we did not detect sherds. Therefore, our collection of sherds had to be systematic in order to be representative. A randomly sampled survey or one that used transects or other restricted units of observation might have missed subtle changes in the sherd distribution.

Also of considerable methodological importance is the fact that the area is currently under intensive cultivation and occupation. Virtually the entire survey area is occupied by agricultural fields or orchards, in addition to eight villages and a number of roads. This means not only limited access to some areas (residential and industrial areas, quarries, etc.), but also that there was differential ground visibility between areas with different types of vegetation. For example, dense grass or rows of peanut plants covered in plastic sheets caused much reduced visibility, whereas apple orchards, where the ground is almost completely bare, had high visibility. Furthermore, the survey was conducted in the summer season, when vegetation growth is at its highest. Therefore, whatever method we used in the survey, the search for sherds had to be thorough, particularly in areas where they were not immediately visible. On the other hand, the effect of varying visibility was mitigated by the fact that cultivated plots in the valley are relatively small, and neighboring plots tend to be planted with different types of crops. This situation is the result of China's current land policy under which, as an economic strategy, families tend to diversify their crops and no family has significantly larger pieces of land than any other on lease from the village community. Thus, there should be relatively consistent average visibility over the survey area, and the survey proceeded under the assumption that the plots were small enough and the location of different crops random enough not to systematically influence the distribution of sherds across the survey area.

Thirdly, there is a considerable difference in elevation between the inner and outer city walls: the terrain in the center of the survey area is relatively level, but rises towards the outer city wall, with some slopes being terraced for agriculture. The outer city wall was apparently constructed to take advantage of this higher ground for defensive purposes (Lin 2006: 137; Sino-American Guicheng Archaeological Team 2011: 34-36). The maximum elevation difference between the inner and outer city walls is approximately 70 m (though in most sections it is closer to 30-40 m), and no sections of the outer city wall have been located in the southern part of the site, meaning there is no clear boundary on the south. While most of the area (outside the modern villages) was accessible, the banks around river courses and reservoirs precluded survey in their immediate vicinity, and it was therefore necessary to implement a systematic, full-coverage survey in order to see gradations of density across the city.

The Guicheng city survey adopted the basic method of systematic, full-coverage surface survey originally developed in regional-scale survey contexts, and complied with the principles that govern such field research programs. However, the method has been modified to account for the unique size of Guicheng and the difficult geographical and seasonal conditions of the survey area. In contrast to the usual 30-40 msurvey resolution described by Parsons (Parsons 1990: 11) or the 50 m resolution used in the Chifeng survey (Chifeng 2003: 40, 124), in the Guicheng survey we placed our crew members 20 m apart and used this high resolution consistently over the entire survey area. Also different from most regional-scale surveys, in which sherd collections are made only when a "site" can be identified by the presence of a standard number of sherds (for example, 3 sherds within 100 m in the Chifeng survey [Chifeng 2003: 42, 127]), at Guicheng we made complete collections within standard-sized circles at every point we surveyed, regardless of the condition of the land. In areas of dense vegetation, the crews were instructed to search grass roots thoroughly, and every effort was made to reach the tops of hills and the bottoms of gullies to overcome topographic irregularities.

This new survey method, which we call "Systematic Surface Sampling" (SSS), enabled us to make systematic and thorough collections over the entire survey area of 8 km^2 with the same high resolution. As in all regional surveys, it is a sampling method, and mandated complete collection only within each collection point. We are confident of the representativeness of these collections.

The method also enabled us to avoid the difficulty of defining "sites," which has been hotly debated in recent anthropological literature. It has been argued that in regional surveys, which aim to identify areas of settlement and other activities, the practice of delineating site boundaries can in fact skew data and obscure subtle distribution patterns and sparse scatters of remains (Bintliff 2000: 4-6; Bintliff, Kuna & Venclová 2000: 2; Haselgrove 1985: 21-26; Sullivan, Mink & Uphus 2007: 328). In the Guicheng survey, the entirety of the city site was targeted for sherd collection, and there was no need to define smaller "sites" within the survey area.

4. Implementation of Systematic Surface Sampling Method in the Field

At the beginning of the survey, we experimented with grids of different scales in order to strike an ideal balance between survey resolution and survey speed. It was soon determined that a 20 by 20 m grid would yield a considerably dense collection and at the same time allow us to cover the entire 8 km^2 in two to three seasons. With a survey team composed of five to ten members on any given day, this would create a maximum frontline of 200 m, the longest distance that the map keeper, the leader of the team in the field, could oversee the team on the undulating terrain.

The survey team was composed of students working with technicians from the coring team. Directed by the map keeper, they deployed 20 m apart and advanced across the land together, making collections every 20 m, so that collections were made at each intersection point on a 20 by 20 m grid across the entire survey area. At each collection point, a circle with radius of 3 m was drawn by a team member using a string attached to a stick fastened in the ground, and all the sherds visible on the surface within that circle were collected (see Fig. Ⅰ.6.2). Team members were instructed to discard any sherds whose width was less than 2 cm, and to collect only sherds from before the end of the Han period (220 CE), which they were trained to recognize. The pieces collected at each point were carefully bagged and labeled with the point number according to a universal numbering system (described below), date, team member's name, and total number of sherds collected at that point. The map keeper then marked each point where sherds were found with a circle on the field map; when nothing was found at a certain point, he or she marked it with an "X".

A set of high-resolution aerial photographs of the survey area was the most important tool for the accurate positioning of the team members and good coordination of their movements. Such a tool is different from the 1 : 10,000 scale maps used in most regional surveys, which would be unusable in surveys with 20 m resolution. In the 2008 field season, the team used photographs taken from Google Earth as field maps, which were not ideal, but were adequate for the map keeper to recognize roads and agricultural plots. In 2009, the project had purchased a recent (2004) satellite image of the Guicheng area from DigitalGlobe, a satellite imaging company, which provided very clear images of the landscape. These images were imported into the ArcGIS program and a 20 by 20 m (ground distance) grid was digitally superimposed onto them before printing to create new field maps (Fig. Ⅰ.6.3). In this way, the map keeper could accurately position his or her team members on the ground and direct them from point to point using field boundaries and landmarks visible on the aerial photographs.

A universal numbering system was used to assign unique designations to each survey point. First, using the latitude/longitude system (specifically, the World Geodetic System of 1984 [WGS84] used by Google Earth), the entire research area centering on Guicheng (coordinates: N37°34′15″–N37°36′39″; E120°32′49″–E120°35′13″) was divided into sixteen large "areas" (see Fig. Ⅰ.6.1;

see also "Introduction," Fig. Ⅰ.0.3). Each area was 900 m east to west and 1,120 m north to south. An alphanumeric system was then applied within each area, so that each survey point's designation included the area number (1-16), followed by the column (A-Z, followed by a-s) and row (1-56) within that area (for example 8-A23 or 3-q52). Using this universal numbering system, all data could be entered into a spreadsheet and visually displayed on maps in Esri's ArcGIS software. Because the outer city wall was the *de facto* boundary of the city, the survey team did not cover points more than about 200 m beyond the wall. The total area surveyed in the 2008 and 2009 field seasons was about 800 ha, or 8 km^2. The inner city was not covered by systematic surface survey because intensive coring was conducted there (see Chapter 2).

Once ceramic remains were recovered in the field, they were sorted into predefined time periods, including Neolithic, Yueshi, Western Zhou, Eastern Zhou, Zhou, Han, and Indigenous (see below for standards of periodization). Sherds were washed and allowed to dry before sorting. Students working on the project were trained by project researchers to distinguish ancient from modern materials, and to recognize fabric and cord pattern decorations typical of each period. Staff from the Yantai Museum also helped in training the students, allowing the students to study complete pottery pieces in both the Yantai and the Longkou Museums. It typically took about a week for each student to become adept at sorting the ceramics, differentiating sherds of the research periods from modern pieces. Tables were created in Microsoft Excel to record information for each collection point, including number of sherds per period, average size of sherds, and notes of any interesting or diagnostic pieces, including worked stone. Students were instructed to pay attention to special materials such as clay molds for bronze casting and building materials.

A similar survey method was used in the Boeotia Project in Greece for the Classical-Early Hellenistic period city of Hyettos, which produced similar data. Conducting complete collections within 20 by 20 m grid units, the Boeotia survey covered 26 ha of land surface (less than 10% of the area surveyed at Guicheng in a single season). The survey was designed to date the main occupation of the site and to analyze differential rates of discard, and possible changes in population size, between periods (Bintliff 2000: 4), similar to the goals of the Guicheng survey. The Boeotia Project collected and recorded all sherds within its 20 by 20 m grid units, and yielded a higher density of sherds: 100-200 sherds per grid unit, while at Guicheng the average density of sherds across the survey area was only 16 sherds per 20 × 20 m grid unit (an average of 1.126 sherds per collection circle of 28.27 m^2, each of which covered approximately 7% of a 20 by 20 m grid unit). However, since the Guicheng project collected sherds only in smaller circles of fixed radius centered on predetermined points, the location of the remains could be recorded much more precisely than at Hyettos. The Guicheng survey also produced a comparable resolution of survey data (both surveys used a 20 by 20 m strategy) with a fraction of the labor input, which is especially important because the survey area at Guicheng is much larger than that at Hyettos, and it would have been impractical to cover every square meter with complete collection.

Therefore, we consider the SSS method to be a more effective survey strategy for systematic survey at large sites like Guicheng. The only significant advantage of the Boeotia survey is that it produced a larger volume of ceramic material for analysis. However, the Guicheng Project was easily able to collect more sherds in return visits to selected areas for complete sherd collection (see below, Section 6: "Complete Collection Units Ⅰ-Ⅲ").

Section 3: The Survey Process and Data Obtained

1. Progress of the Survey

The Guicheng city survey began on June 13, 2008 in Area 7, in order to test the survey methods in a relatively flat area where natural site formation processes such as flooding were presumably less pronounced (Pl. 53: 1). Area 7 also surrounds the inner city of Guicheng, and so was known to have a high concentration of artifact remains. The survey then moved outwards to Areas 2, 3, and 4 to the north, and finally Area 8 and part of Area 12, which included large underground structures incorporated into the outer city wall. In 2009, the survey team proceeded with the same field methods, and covered Areas 5, 6, 9, 10, 11 (Pl. 53: 2, Pl. 54: 2; Pl. 55), the rest of 12, and 16. Areas 1, 13, 14, and 15 were excluded from the survey because they fell entirely outside the outer city wall.

Both the 2008 and 2009 surveys were conducted between the beginning of June and the end of July. By the beginning of this period, planting of crops was over, and for the rest of this period, the crops continued to grow, though not enough to seriously impede visibility in most areas (Fig. Ⅰ.6.4). By the end of each season, corn in particular had grown too high and too dense for the survey team to walk through the fields.

Data processing began immediately after the first summer season in 2008. In order to do this, a student and survey team member (Elizabeth Berger) received training in Esri's ArcGIS software with a tutorial provided through Columbia's Electronic Data Service (EDS). Over the course of the next four months, with help from GIS specialists from the EDS lab, we were able to import the data recorded in Excel sheets in the field into the ArcGIS software to create digital maps of the area surveyed in 2008 (see Chapter 8). The next spring semester was then spent analyzing the data for spatial and chronological patterns, and identifying possible biases or errors. The analysis confirmed that the methods employed in the survey were producing reliable data that revealed large chronological patterns in the distribution of sherds. This analysis offered a basis for evaluating our methods and informed our survey in the second season.

2. Possible Biases in the Survey Data

The issue of differential ground visibility had already been considered when we designed the SSS survey method (see Section 2). Here, we will mainly consider possible biases in the data emerging from site formation processes and from statistical computation.

As discussed previously by archaeologists, human activities such as plowing, construction, and moving soil for composting, can change the assemblage of artifacts exposed on the surface, and can also create clusters and other anomalies of surface materials, which may no longer bear the direct relationship to underlying deposits they are assumed to have. Such activities can also destroy more fragile artifacts, which could bias the data against periods during which more fragile ceramics were manufactured (Bintliff 2000: 5; Haselgrove 1985: 9).

The most apparent formation process at work today at Guicheng is of course the intensive cultivation being carried out across the site. However, the main concern of the Guicheng survey, as already discussed, is not to locate discrete clusters of artifacts such as sites, but to identify relative densities across the entire survey area. Because modern human activity is virtually uniform across the site, we may assume that the actions of plowing and soil movement did not significantly alter the patterns of sherd distribution across Guicheng.

No sherds were collected within residential areas where modern construction has been carried out, but sherd densities surrounding the villages do not seem to have been affected by the villages' presence. If the construction process had significantly affected the archaeological remains surrounding them, one would expect to see a similar change in density surrounding all the modern villages, which is not the case. The villages located in the northern part of the survey space (in Areas 3, 6, and 7) are surrounded by much denser concentrations of remains than those in the southern part of the survey area (Areas 9, 10, and 11), which is consistent with the density of sherds in these areas. Overall, there does not appear to be any meaningful change in the density of remains immediately surrounding any of the modern villages.

Natural processes, especially the impact of rivers and flooding, are another concern at Guicheng. However, there does not seem to be any significant change in sherd distribution associated with the Yaque River. It was confirmed during the survey of the inner city that the city was invaded by river flooding at least once while it was under occupation. After the flood, parts of the inner city wall were reconstructed. Therefore, it is undeniable that the Yaque River must have had an important impact on areas along its banks. However, the distribution of remains along the riverbanks resembles that across the rest of the site, with the greatest density near the inner city, and slightly lower density at the northern edge of the city. Flooding or runoff of rainwater could potentially explain the scarcity of remains in the southern part of the outer city, near the base of Mount Lai. However, sherd distribution in this area does not seem to follow the topography of the mountain slope closely enough to suggest such a relationship, and no higher concentration of sherds can be found where the terrain levels off. Therefore, the relative paucity of remains in the southern part of Guicheng cannot be attributed to the effect of natural forces. This conclusion is supported by the fact that the relatively abrupt change in sherd density in the south of the city does not correspond to the contours of the land, and that this break occurs at varying elevations.

Statistically, there is an extremely low density of pre-Zhou materials at Guicheng. The presence of such materials from periods before the rise of Guicheng must be evaluated in their regional context. In order to do this, the survey team could return to certain areas to look for more remains from the pre-Guicheng periods.

With regard to the Zhou period, the main period of occupation, the main issue concerns the large number of sherds that are bare of decorative patterns, and thus cannot be dated to either the Western Zhou or the Eastern Zhou. The broad Zhou period sherds (identified by their fabric) were divided between the Western and Eastern Zhou periods based on the relative proportions of decorated pieces belonging to these two periods within each survey Area (see below, Section 5). Due to their large numbers, if this assumption were incorrect, it could significantly skew the data relating to the two periods. We evaluated this possible error using sherds from the stratified context produced by the test excavation in 2009. From these data, it does appear that approximately the same proportion of sherds was decorated during the Western and Eastern Zhou periods. In any event, the difference in rate of decoration between the two periods would have to be very dramatic to have a significant impact on the interpretation of the data.

It is also important to mention the limitations of statistical significance tests. Archaeological data can be extremely complex and multifaceted, and are best assessed with a combination of strategies, including both statistical significance tests and visual methods. All sherd data, including those with statistically significant distributions, must therefore be assessed in the context of other archaeological evidence from the site. Finally, we recognize that large sample sizes can cause *t*-tests to return artificially significant *p*-values. To account for this, where we used *t*-tests (see analysis below), we also tested the data for effect size, confirming the strength of the relationships suggested by the *t*-tests.

3. Quality and Representativeness of Survey Data

The Guicheng city survey recovered a total of 13,221 sherds from about 15,000 collection points (Pl. 56). Only 1,253 (9.5%) of the sherds were designated unidentifiable as to period. Overall, 43% of collection points yielded at least one sherd larger than 2 cm, with an average of 2.6 sherds per collection point that yielded material (standard deviation 2.5), and an overall average of 1.1 sherds per point (standard deviation 2.1).

The specific survey method used at Guicheng enabled the project to collect a large quantity of survey data, which are representative of the current distribution of ancient remains, specifically pottery sherds, over the entire land surface of 8 km^2 surveyed in 2008-2009. This data set not only allows us to map out the continuum of sherd distribution over the entire site surface, but also offers a solid starting point to interpret the relationship between surface remains and subsurface structures and deposits, thus beginning to answer a few important questions posed at the outset of this project.

Section 4: Analysis Ⅰ: Organization of the Guicheng City Site

1. Zones of Pottery Sherd Concentrations

The survey identified four main areas of high surface sherd density: around the inner city, and along the east, northwest, and west outer city walls. Each of these areas was most likely associated with a high concentration of human activity, including military display and transportation. This conclusion is reinforced by the presence of ancient architectural features that correspond to these pottery sherd concentrations, offering further clues as to the types of activities taking place in each area.

Clusters of sherds were identified visually from the map of all recovered sherds (Fig. Ⅰ.6.5a-b) and from the equivalent maps for each period (see Section 5). The clusters were statistically confirmed using *t*-tests, and also with hotspot analysis using the Getis-Ord Gi* statistic. This spatial statistical method compares the value at each point on a map to the average value across the entire map and to the value at points immediately around it. It then generates a *z*-score and *p*-value for each point on the map. The points with the highest *z*-score and lowest *p*-value deviate the most dramatically from the average distribution, and can be considered "hot spots," or statistically significant high concentrations of remains. The results of the *t*-tests are discussed in the text below, and the results of the hotspot analysis are presented for the Western and Eastern Zhou periods in graphic form (Fig. Ⅰ.6.6a-b).

The highest density of sherds was found close to the inner city, especially to the east, in Area 7 (Fig. Ⅰ.6.5a-b). (A two-tailed *t*-test comparing the sherds per point of Area 7 and all other surveyed areas combined yielded a *t*-score of 32.0, $p < 0.0001$, indicating that the difference in density between the area near the inner city and the density over the rest of the survey area is statistically very significant. The effect size was Cohen's $d = 0.83$, which is considered a large effect [Cohen 1988, 227]). This confirms that the inner city was an area with a relatively high concentration of population and activity.

In the east, there is a relatively high density of sherds across the southern part of Area 8, between the river channel and the outer city wall, which appears in the Eastern Zhou period. (A two-tailed *t*-test comparing the density of sherds in Area 8 against all the other areas combined [excluding Area 7] yielded a *t*-score of 10.6, $p < 0.0001$, which is also highly statistically significant. The effect size was Cohen's $d = 0.94$, again a large effect.) It should also be noted that this high concentration is located on the hilltops, and not in the lowland or the valley, suggesting that the distribution pattern has not been much altered by surface rainwater. Instead, this high density is likely related to a complex subsurface structure incorporated into the outer city wall in this area, whose underground remains have been mapped by coring, but whose function is yet to be determined. Nearby to the southeast is another concentration of sherds associated with subsurface rammed-earth walls, at the eastern edge of survey Areas 8 and 12.

We have identified another cluster near the northern portion of the outer city wall, spanning the southeastern part of Area 2 and the northeastern part of Area 6 (sherds per point in Area 2 vs. Areas 3 and 4 combined, $t = 3.8$, $p = 0.0002$, a statistically significant difference, and effect size Cohen's $d = 0.48$, a medium effect, indicating that the difference between the areas, while statistically significant, is not large). Interestingly, in this area the subsurface building structures are extraordinarily wide, suggesting facilities attached to the wall, possibly platforms for military troops. There is clearly a correlation between all these high-density zones and the underground structures.

A final zone of relative density lies along the west wall near the border between Area 5 and Area 6. Given the topography here, which includes a natural opening between two hills to the north and south, it is very likely that this was the main entrance to Guicheng from the west.

In the northernmost part of the survey area (Areas 2, 3, and 4, and the northern parts of Areas 6, 7, and 8) there is a lower concentration of sherds than in the center of the city, with no major change in concentration in proximity to the outer city wall in this area. This is consistent with the findings of earlier investigators, who observed that very few artifacts were encountered near the outer city wall (see Li and Lin 1991: 911). In the southern part of the survey area, approaching Mount Lai, surface remains were also extremely sparse, suggesting that there was a lower concentration of activity in this part of the city in ancient times. As discussed above, this relatively low density does not seem to have been the result of natural processes. The low density but large average size of sherds in this area suggest that the southern half of Guicheng near the foot of Mount Lai might have been used for elite burials, among other functions; such burials are a potential source of recently surfaced large pottery sherds.

Average size of sherds remained relatively consistent throughout the entire site. The overall average was 41.1 mm per sherd; the average of the average size of sherds per point, among points that produced remains, was 41.6 mm, standard deviation 11.4 mm. In a visual analysis, there seems to be a slight increase in average sherd size near the inner city (see Fig. Ⅰ.6.7). The average size of sherds across all points in Area 7 (excluding points where no sherds were found) was 42.7 mm, standard deviation 14.3 mm, which is greater than the average for other areas. A *t*-test showed this to be highly statistically significant. (A two-tailed *t*-test comparing the average size of sherds per point, excluding points where no sherds were found, in Area 7 to all other areas combined yielded a *t*-score of 3.2, $p = 0.0015$, indicating that the difference is statistically very significant.) The observed difference in average size is likely due to the higher density of remains near the inner city, which resulted in a greater range of sherd sizes, including more large sherds, being found (note the large standard deviation of sherd size near the inner city). However, the effect size was small, only Cohen's $d = 0.10$. Therefore, while the difference between the areas is statistically significant because of the large number of data points, it is probably too small to be meaningful (with the possible exception of sherds recently unearthed from the burials in the south).

2. Relationship between Zones of Pottery Sherd Concentrations and Underground Zhou Period Remains

A number of seemingly topographical features within the city walls are in fact the standing remains of ancient rammed-earth structures. The association of a high concentration of pottery with these features would attest to their importance in the life of the ancient city. One striking example from the 2008 season is Archaeological Feature 2, a long north-south structure about 10 m high, 100 meters long, and 5-10 m wide (Fig. Ⅰ.6.8). It is located in Area 7, east of the inner city, corresponding roughly to points 7-e20 to 7-e25. While collecting sherds around this structure, the survey team found several dozen large fragments of ceramic vessels that appeared to have washed down from the top or out of the strata of this structure, in addition to a large number of worked stones and other building materials. Many collection points around the structures yielded high numbers of sherds, between 16 and 34 pieces. Coring on the top of this structure during the preliminary pedestrian survey in 2007 confirmed the presence of rammed earth, suggesting that it was a high platform or a hall in ancient times, with a much larger original size (a local farmer informed the team that the area to the north of this feature had been leveled in recent years).

The dense remains near the inner city correspond to extensive archaeological features. Although the surface survey did not extend within the inner city walls, the systematic coring there has revealed concentrations of underground building foundations in two districts of the inner city (see Chapter 2). The sherds collected in Complete Collection Unit 1 in the inner city also show a high-density distribution with a rate of 0.259/1 m^2 (see below). If collected in the standard collection circles (28.27 m^2) that we used to cover the rest of Guicheng, the average sherd number per collection circle would be 7.3 sherds, much higher than the average yield of 1.1 sherds per circle across all of Guicheng (or 2.6 per circle counting only the points that yielded sherds), and the average of 3.0 sherds per circle in the adjacent Area 7. This alone shows that the inner city had the highest concentration of human activities in all of Guicheng. This high concentration has been confirmed by test excavation near CCU Ⅰ.

As discussed above, the survey identified a number of high-density areas along the east, northwest, and west outer city walls. In each case, the high concentration of sherds is associated with subsurface structures, including wide or complex features attached to the outer wall. The concentration near the border between Areas 5 and 6, for example, can be explained by the possible high level of activity near the western main city gate. It is worth noting that this is also where an ancient stream entered the city, to join the moat around the inner city.

3. Relationship between Distribution of Pottery Sherds and Landscape

There is no distinctive pattern of sherd distribution associated with the Yaque River. Although the river flows northward, the highest concentration of surface remains is not in the north, but rather in areas near the inner city. There is also no correlation between surface sherd distribution and topography; some of the highest concentrations were actually found on the hilltops. Instead, the pattern of sherd distribution at Guicheng is more closely related to ancient manmade structures under and above the ground, which were areas of human activities in the past.

Human activities were likely intensive along the river, which could have provided both transportation and a resort belt in Guicheng, but this is not supported by our survey data. This is perhaps due to the Guicheng survey being limited to the area within the city walls; the future regional survey can better address the correlation between natural features and ancient human activities.

The overall patterns that emerged from the survey data are of a high level of activity at the heart of the city, with some foci of military activity near the outer city wall. The data show a close relationship between surface sherds and permanent manmade structures. Equally significant, however, are the data relating to differences in activity between periods of occupation.

Section 5: Analysis Ⅱ: Application of Chronological Standards

1. Framework of Time Periods and Chronological Standards

In the geopolitical context of the Bronze Age Jiaodong Peninsula, Guicheng was very likely a frontline base for Zhou expansion, housing members of the Zhou elite during the mid Western Zhou (see Li 2006: 308-314). From the late Western Zhou to the Eastern Zhou period, following the decline of the Western Zhou state in the west, Guicheng served as the central site of the indigenous state of Lai, which arose from mixed Zhou and local Nanhuangzhuang cultures.

The local pottery production tradition in the survey area is quite complex. Previous studies have analyzed the development of a local pottery tradition in the eastern Jiaodong Peninsula, attributed to a series of Neolithic and early Bronze Age cultures including: Baishicun (ca. 5000-3700 BCE), Beizhuang (ca. 3700-3000 BCE), Longshan (ca. 3000-2000 BCE), Yueshi (ca. 2000-1400 BCE), Zhenzhumen, and Nanhuangzhuang. In this system, the Yueshi culture was considered to have been roughly contemporaneous with the Erlitou culture in the Central Plains, and the Zhenzhumen culture roughly paralleled the late Shang (1554-1046 BCE) and early Western Zhou (1045-771 BCE). The Nanhuangzhuang culture roughly paralleled the late Western Zhou and Eastern Zhou (770-221 BCE) periods, but it is the most ambiguously documented period in eastern Shandong (see Yantai Shi Bowuguan 2006: 10-14, 106-120).

In fact, Nanhuangzhuang pottery has often been identified as Zhou period remains when it has appeared in the same burial unit or stratum as Zhou pottery, as no systematic research has been conducted to clarify its dates. In the northern half of the Jiaodong Peninsula, particularly the Longkou region, the regional pottery production system was dominated by elements introduced from the Zhou culture in the west. The expansion of the Zhou culture from the west into the eastern Jiaodong Peninsula (mainly the northern half) is documented in the archaeological record. This is corroborated by the elite bronzes and inscriptions from the Longkou region, which document close political ties to the Western Zhou state centered on the Wei River valley in Shaanxi.

Although the Zhou material culture in eastern Shandong also shows some local characteristics, in general it follows the trend of development of the Zhou culture in the west. Therefore, it can be analyzed by the chronological standards developed in the west. The Western Zhou and Eastern Zhou represent the two most intensive periods of Guicheng's occupation. The political transition from the Western to Eastern Zhou was significant for Guicheng's occupational history, as it led to the expansion of the state of Qi in western Shandong, which eventually conquered Guicheng and the state of Lai in 567 BCE.

Sherds belonging to Western and Eastern Zhou periods can be differentiated by their patterns of cord decoration. The survey team divided Zhou period sherds into Eastern and Western Zhou remains based on this criterion, and those sherds with Zhou era fabric but no decoration were assigned to a Broad Zhou category. Based on the ratio of Western to Eastern Zhou decorated sherds, the Broad Zhou-period undecorated sherds were later divided between the two periods, producing the Adjusted Western Zhou and Adjusted Eastern Zhou categories.

Pre-Zhou sherds, from the Neolithic Longshan and Yueshi periods, were extremely scarce within the survey area, perhaps because the pre-Zhou settlement system of the region was focused elsewhere. The sherds of these two periods were combined into a single "Pre-Zhou" category for the purpose of our analysis. The latest period included in the survey was Han (206 BCE-220 CE), whose sherds were also identified by their fabric and surface decoration. Finally, the Indigenous pottery tradition present in Guicheng, belonging to the loosely defined Nanhuangzhuang culture, was treated as a separate category. These sherds are from a span of time roughly corresponding to the Western to the Eastern Zhou periods, but their actual dates cannot as yet be determined. In fact, one of the goals of the survey was to explore their relationship to the spatial distribution of the contemporaneous Zhou culture sherds.

The distribution of sherds by period is shown in Table 6.1.

2. Period Ⅰ — Pre-Zhou Period

A total of only 17 sherds were found from the pre-Zhou period. These were mostly attributed to Neolithic cultures, with 4 sherds identified as belonging to the Yueshi period. The only apparent cluster is a group of 5 sherds, each found at a different point, at the southwest corner of Area 3 and the northwest corner of Area 7 (Fig. Ⅰ.6.9a-b). However, there are currently too few data from this period to undertake analysis of occupation within the city area during the period. A similar pattern of recovery has been observed by Bintliff (2000: 5), who writes that several prehistoric sherds in the midst of dense historic material may indicate the presence of a Neolithic site that has been obscured by later occupation. This is certainly possible at Guicheng, but the position of the Guicheng area in the settlement systems of the Neolithic period must be clarified by the regional survey in the future.

3. Period Ⅱ — Western Zhou

The number of Zhou period sherds is dramatically higher than that of any other period. Western Zhou sherds are those that exhibited deeper and neater cord decoration, the material having been fired at high temperature. Although the breadth of the cord varies dramatically, the impressed tracks are clearly visible and appear very organized (Fig. Ⅰ.6.10). Vessel types represented by these sherds include mostly *guan* jars, *li* tripods, and *pen* basins. Overall, these types very closely resemble pottery of the Zhou heartland, in both fabric and decoration.

The total number of identifiably Western Zhou sherds (i.e., those that were decorated) was 1,105, or 8% of the total; 7% of collection points yielded Western Zhou sherds. Sherds that can be attributed to the Western Zhou period are clearly clustered to the west of the Yaque River (Fig. Ⅰ. 6.11a-b). There are two zones of concentration, one centered on the inner city, and the other surrounding the wide subsurface platforms along the northwest portion of the outer wall, in Area 2. To the east of the Yaque River their distribution is sporadic and very few were detected in Area 8 and Area 12 along the eastern portion of the outer wall. Clearly this suggests that human activities during much of the Western Zhou period were concentrated in the western half of Guicheng city.

4. Period Ⅲ — Eastern Zhou Period

The survey found more remains from the Eastern Zhou than from the Western Zhou period. The total of Eastern Zhou sherds was 3,644, or 28% of the total; fully 20% of collection points yielded Eastern Zhou sherds. This shows an increase of more than 200% in the total sherd population between the Western and Eastern Zhou periods. Eastern Zhou sherds exhibit shallow and sometimes scattered and discontinuous tracks of cord impression. Because the cord impressions are shallow, they often form the so-called "wheat-seed" type of cord impressions, and tracks are often indistinguishable. The vessel types represented by them are the same as in the Western Zhou period, and the material is often even harder, fired at a higher temperature than that of Western Zhou sherds (Fig. Ⅰ.6.12).

The higher number of sherds from the Eastern Zhou period is likely due to more intensive occupation and an increase in human activity during this period, as well as an increase in the area of occupation. Alternatively, the change in density could be explained by the difference in length between the two periods (the Eastern Zhou period is approximately twice as long as the Western Zhou period). However, there is reason to believe the site was not fully occupied throughout the Eastern Zhou period. The *Zuo Zhuan* describes the conquest of the state of Lai by the state of Qi in 567 BCE, only 203 years into the Eastern Zhou period, which should represent the height of human occupation at Guicheng. Afterwards, the site continued to be occupied, but on a much reduced scale. Therefore, it is more likely that the increase in the number of sherds is the result of more intensive occupation during the Eastern Zhou period, rather than the length of the period.

The increase in sherd population is especially dramatic in the eastern half of the survey area, in Area 8 and the northern part of Area 12. There were very few identifiably Western Zhou sherds discovered in this area (they account for less than 1% of sherds found in Area 8, and only 4% of those found in Area 12), while the Eastern Zhou sherds seem to be particularly dense in this area (these account for 32% of sherds found in Area 8 and in Area 12). As discussed already, this cluster of sherds may be related to the complex construction in the outer city wall in this area, identifiable by its underground remains. In addition to the dense distribution of sherds, in this area we also discovered a large number of building materials, most importantly bricks with cord impressions characteristic of the Eastern Zhou period (Fig. Ⅰ.6.13).

Overall, this change in distribution suggests the expansion of human activities from the central area of Guicheng into its eastern periphery. The dense concentration of Eastern Zhou remains surrounding the inner city, as well as the cluster around the outer city wall in the northwest, suggest the continuing importance of these areas in the organization of Guicheng city (see Fig. Ⅰ.6.14a-b).

The undecorated sherds from Periods Ⅱ and Ⅲ, which could not be attributed to either period, were called "Broad Zhou period sherds." We found a total of 6,375 sherds of this type, accounting for

48% of the total sherds recovered. If it is assumed that the proportion of these sherds belonging to the Western and Eastern Zhou periods equals the proportion of decorated sherds for each of these periods, the overall diachronic trend is not changed. In the adjusted counts, Western Zhou material amounts to 2,810 sherds and accounts for 21% of the total, while Eastern Zhou material amounts to 8,314 sherds and accounts for 63% of the total. (These numbers were calculated for each of the survey areas separately and then added together, to account for differences between the Western and Eastern Zhou sherd distributions in the different areas. This information is not included in the maps in Fig. Ⅰ.6.13 and Ⅰ.6.14.) We further evaluated this attribution of undecorated sherds on the basis of material from the test excavation. It does appear that approximately the same proportion of sherds was decorated during the Western and Eastern Zhou periods. (Pit H20, from the Western Zhou period, contained 46% undecorated sherds; Pits H2, H3 [stratum 1], and H6, from the Eastern Zhou, contained 56%, 66%, and 51% undecorated sherds, respectively.) Therefore, we can conclude that the percentage of decorated pottery remained fairly constant from the Western to the Eastern Zhou period, and that we are justified in dividing the broad Zhou period sherds in this way.

5. Period Ⅳ — Han Period

After Period Ⅲ, the sherd population drops off again dramatically. Sherds attributed to the Han period totaled only 78, or less than 1% of the total sherds collected. This indicates a steep drop in activity at the site during this period (Fig. Ⅰ.6.15). Interestingly, the densest concentrations of Han sherds were found in the north and northeast of the survey area, with surprisingly few near the inner city. This points to a shift in the distribution of activities or occupation within the city. Two of these clusters, which seem to be concentrated near the outer city wall (in Areas 2 and 3) (Fig. Ⅰ.6.16a-b), could be investigated further in a future survey, to see if they were associated with the continuing use of some facilities along the outer wall or if they extend significantly beyond the wall, which would certainly signal a shift in the use of the site. Another concentration in Area 8, where a large number of Han dynasty bricks impressed with geometric patterns was found on the edges of the fields (Fig. Ⅰ.6.17), apparently is associated with a cluster of Han dynasty tombs in the area, known from previous surveys. So, it is possible that the concentrations in Areas 2 and 3 might also have been associated with Han dynasty burial sites. Finally, located in the southernmost part of Guicheng, in the area not covered by the systematic survey, is the gigantic earth palace foundation of the First Emperor of Qin (259-210 BCE) (Pl. 142: 1), constructed after the Qin unification in 221 BCE as a resort for the emperor to hold sacrificial events at the "Shrine of the Host of the Moon" on Mount Lai (Pl. 142: 1; Pl. 143: 1-2). Therefore, despite the drop in the sherd population in Period IV, there can be no doubt that the Guicheng area continued to witness human occupation during the Qin and Han Dynasties.

6. Distribution of Local Indigenous Cultural Relics

The "Indigenous" pottery tradition comprises reddish-hued pottery of coarse fabric. The material is tempered with a high proportion of white quartz, fired at relatively low temperatures. The tradition of making pottery this way goes back as far as the Yueshi culture, if not earlier. The sherds are completely undecorated, and are red or light brown in color (Fig. Ⅰ.6.18). The pottery types in this tradition are limited to *li* tripod and *ding* cauldron, the latter being absent from the Zhou cultural tradition. The survey recovered a total of 717 sherds of this type, or 5% of the total; 582 collection points, or 5% of the total, yielded Indigenous sherds.

The Indigenous sherds follow a similar distribution as that of sherds of the Eastern Zhou period, being concentrated near the inner city and between the inner city and the outer city wall to the east (Fig. Ⅰ.6.19). Statistical tests bear out the resemblance of the Indigenous distribution to the Broad Zhou period, though not the Eastern Zhou specifically. (A two-tailed *t*-test comparing the Indigenous sherds per point of Area 7 and all other survey areas combined yielded a *t*-score of 20.7, $p < 0.0001$, indicating that the difference in density between the area near the inner city and the density over the rest of the survey area is statistically very significant. The effect size was Cohen's $d = 0.47$, which is considered a medium effect. Meanwhile, a two-tailed *t*-test comparing the density of sherds in Area 8 against all the other areas combined [excluding Area 7] yielded a *t*-score of 4.56, $p < 0.0001$, which is also statistically significant. However, the effect size was Cohen's $d = 0.13$, a relatively small effect. This indicates that the difference in density of Indigenous sherds between Area 8 and the rest of the survey area is small, though statistically significant, and may have little practical significance.)

Although we have yet to clarify their relationship to the Zhenzhumen culture, represented by the Louzizhuang site in the region, located only 14 km to the west of Guicheng (Yantai Shi Bowuguan 2006: 106-114), it is possible that at least some of the Indigenous sherds may indeed belong to the Zhenzhumen cultural tradition that continued into the Western Zhou period. There seems little doubt that the Indigenous pottery tradition existed prior to the arrival of cultural elements from the Central Plains, and persisted throughout the period of Zhou cultural occupation, perhaps in the form of the Nanhuangzhuang culture. This would have created a complex pottery industry including multiple technologies and styles in use simultaneously, as observed in the Chifeng survey in eastern Inner Mongolia (Chifeng 2003: 120). Our test excavation at Guicheng in 2009 showed that later (Eastern Zhou) strata have a much higher proportion of Indigenous sherds than early (Western Zhou) strata. This suggests that over time the Indigenous tradition gradually made its way into the mainstream pottery production industry at Guicheng, as the local state of Lai gradually became politically and culturally independent from Zhou tradition. Furthermore, the distinction may also be functional, as the types represented by the Indigenous sherds are mostly *li* tripods and *ding* cauldrons, both cooking vessels. In either case, as the distribution seems to follow the same pattern as that of the Zhou period, it is likely that this pottery tradition coexisted with the Zhou cultural types. The city occupants likely shared a single economic system in which they produced both Zhou and Indigenous types of pottery, or in which Indigenous types of pottery were made elsewhere and transported to Guicheng for use by a Zhou-culture-oriented population. Our analysis of Guicheng pottery indicates that the latter might have been the case (see Chapter 9), but more extensive research is needed to clarify the situation.

7. Summary of Chronological Analysis

The systematic application of chronological standards to the survey data from Guicheng has provided solid grounds to reconstruct the occupational history of the site. The survey data have revealed a trajectory of occupation beginning with sparse activity in the pre-Zhou period. It is evident that early occupation on a large scale, possibly during the early phase of Period Ⅱ (Western Zhou), began in the area centering on the inner city, with peripheral activities mostly confined to the west side of the Yaque River. The test excavation in 2009 provided solid stratigraphic proof that the inner city wall of Guicheng was constructed some time during Period Ⅱ, perhaps to protect the core area of the early settlement. This was followed by greatly increased occupation during the Eastern Zhou period, evidenced by a tripling of ceramic remains, as well as an expansion of activity to the east side of the Yaque River and the surrounding hilltops. The fact that sherds datable to Period Ⅲ (Eastern Zhou) are densely distributed along the outer wall, particularly in the east, suggests that the outer wall of Guicheng might indeed have been constructed during the Eastern Zhou period to protect the city's enlarged population and residential activities. While this development closely follows the trend of urban expansion frequently seen in the Central Plains during the Eastern Zhou period, in the case of Guicheng, it might also be a response to the heightened military tension in the region, particularly due to Lai's troubled relations with the ambitious hegemonic state of Qi in western Shandong.

Although the site continued to be occupied after Lai's destruction by Qi in 567 BCE, and probably remained occupied through the rest of the Eastern Zhou period, activity at the site dropped dramatically in Period Ⅳ (the Han period), with the spatial distribution no longer corresponding to the layout of the Zhou period walled city. The Indigenous type pottery follows a similar distribution to that of Zhou period pottery, suggesting it was used simultaneously, though its cultural significance and place in the local pottery chronology has yet to be clarified.

Section 6: Analysis Ⅲ: Complete Collection Units I-III

1. Purpose and Methods

During the 2009 field season, we decided to implement a series of Complete Collection Units (CCUs), areas larger than survey point collection circles in which all sherds would be collected. The results of these collections would be used to create an inventory of vessel types found at the site, and to determine differences in vessel types used in different areas of the site, and therefore potential differences in activities performed in different areas. All the CCUs were located in areas of high concentrations of surface sherds in order to provide a large enough sample for analysis of vessel types, relative level of activity between periods, and types of activities performed in ancient times. Furthermore, the CCU data can be compared with the survey data obtained with the SSS method, and can also be compared with the inventory of ceramics from the test excavation. Three areas were chosen for the CCUs (see Fig. Ⅰ.6.1):

CCU Ⅰ: inner city, near test excavation trenches;

CCU Ⅱ: east, outer city, covering (in Area 8) 8-A1 through 8-D1 and 8-A2 through 8-D2 and (in Area 12) 12-A56 through 12-D56;

CCU Ⅲ: west, outer city, covering (in Area 10) 10-L47 through 10-O47 and 10-L49 through 10-O49 (Pl. 54: 1).

Originally, we had planned each CCU to be 100 by 100 m (10,000 m^2) with a north-south orientation. However, upon inspecting field conditions at each of the intended collection areas, it was found that there were no uninterrupted areas of this size suitable for collection, due to the presence of dense vegetation and steep, inaccessible slopes. To avoid these obstacles, the CCUs were scaled down to 70 by 70 m (4,900 m^2). Two of the units (CCUs Ⅱ and Ⅲ, between the outer and inner city walls) were given a north-south orientation, while CCU Ⅰ (within the inner city) was oriented north by 17° east, the direction of the adjoining road and ranks of apple trees, for ease of collection. It should be noted that while CCU Ⅰ, within the inner city, had never been subjected to a surface survey, CCUs Ⅱ and Ⅲ were located in areas that had already been covered by the SSS method.

2. Collection Results and Analysis

The three CCUs yielded a combined total of 1,905 pottery sherds. The material collected from the CCUs bears out the conclusion from the systematic surface sampling that the main periods of occupation at Guicheng were the Western and Eastern Zhou. This material also provides some basis for assessing the differences in activities between the inner and outer cities, specifically the evidence of high-status feasting in the inner city.

The following is a detailed discussion of the distribution of period and vessel type of the sherds found in the three CCUs (Table Ⅰ.6.2).

Remains from the cumulative Zhou period (Western Zhou, Eastern Zhou, and Broad Zhou combined) accounted for between 81% (CCU Ⅲ) and 89% (CCU Ⅰ) of the total sherds recovered in each of the three CCUs (Fig. Ⅰ.6.20). The least numerous sherds in each CCU were of the Han period, less than 1% in CCUs Ⅱ and Ⅲ, and 0% in CCU Ⅰ. This is consistent with the results of the city survey, in which 84% of all sherds collected were of the Zhou period, with a marked drop to 1% from the Han period (see Table Ⅰ.6.1). This reflects the fact that Periods Ⅱ-Ⅲ were the main occupation period in Guicheng. However, the proportion of sherds dated to the Western Zhou and Eastern Zhou periods fluctuated significantly between CCUs. The proportion of Western to Eastern Zhou sherds were: 0.07 (CCU Ⅰ), 0.13 (CCU Ⅱ), and 0.11 (CCU Ⅲ) (calculated on the basis of adjusted percentages that include both decorated and undecorated sherds). These numbers are much lower than the proportion of Western to Eastern Zhou period sherds for the entire city, which is 0.33. However, they need to be contextualized and compared to the proportions of Western Zhou and Eastern Zhou sherds in the large survey areas in which they are located (based on the numbers of sherds from the collection circles), which are 0.75 (Area 7), 0.12 (Area 12), and 0.28 (Area 10). These figures from the overall SSS survey suggest that the proportion of Western to Eastern Zhou sherds is much higher in the area surrounding the inner city than in areas near the outer city walls.

The relative scarcity of Western Zhou sherds in CCUs Ⅱ and Ⅲ, as in other peripheral areas of the site, doubtless reflects the dramatic increase of activities from the Western Zhou to the Eastern Zhou period. However, the very low figure of 0.07 from CCU Ⅰ in the inner city, in contrast to the figure of 0.75 from the Area 7 SSS survey (which excluded the area within the inner city walls), is intriguing and must be explained by other means. Since CCU Ⅰ was purposely located exactly 20 m to the north of Excavation Trench #2, we can evaluate the figure of 0.07 from CCU Ⅰ by comparison with the data from the two excavation trenches. The proportion of excavated Western Zhou sherds (430 sherds) to sherds from all other periods (1,830 sherds) is 0.22. Although this rate is a little lower than the figure for the entire city derived from the surface survey (0.33), it is still considerably higher than the figure for CCU Ⅰ (0.07). It is a very interesting phenomenon that the proportion of surface sherds from different periods does not reflect that of underground sherds near CCU Ⅰ.

We think that this difference can be explained by the special function of the inner city, which during the period of occupation was constantly subjected to construction and contained large open spaces for activities that would have been regularly cleared or rebuilt, thereby removing some sherds from earlier periods. In fact, CCU Ⅰ is surrounded by palace foundations #1, #2, and #3, and is located slightly off the central avenue of the city. During the Eastern Zhou period, this area was likely an open court for public activity. It is probable that such an area would tend to preferentially preserve sherds from more recent strata, including those left on the surface when the palaces were most recently in use or when they collapsed. Therefore, the period distribution of surface sherds is still related in a meaningful way to the period distribution of the subsurface sherds.

Finally, we need to consider differences between CCUs in terms of vessel types. In CCU Ⅱ, sherds of the *dou* pedestal dish type account for 20% of the total diagnostic sherds recovered, while in CCU Ⅲ they account for 24%. However, in CCU Ⅰ the *dou* sherds make up over 41% of the total, a statistically significant difference which also showed a medium effect size (Fig. Ⅰ.6.21). This indicates that the larger number of *dou* sherds found in CCU Ⅰ is meaningful, and might reflect a particular usage of the area (*dou* fragments as a proportion of diagnostic fragments: CCU Ⅰ vs. CCU Ⅱ, $t = 3.4$, $p < 0.001$, very statistically significant, and effect size Cohen's $d = 0.54$, a medium effect; CCU Ⅰ vs. CCU Ⅲ, $t = 2.8$, $p = 0.005$, also very significant, and Cohen's $d = 0.47$, also a medium effect; CCU Ⅱ vs. CCU Ⅲ, $t = 0.4$, $p = 0.691$, not significant, and Cohen's $d = 0.08$, a very small effect).

In CCU Ⅰ, sherds of *gui* tureen comprised only 5% of the diagnostic sherds, and in CCU Ⅱ they were 15% of the total. However, in CCU Ⅲ they made up 12% of the sherds collected, also a statistically significant result, though with a relatively small effect size. This suggests that the difference in incidence of these sherds was small and not very meaningful, though more investigation of the area might produce stronger evidence of the greater usage of these vessels in the vicinity of CCU Ⅲ (CCU Ⅰ vs. CCU Ⅱ, $t = 2.7$, $p = 0.007$, very statistically significant, and effect size Cohen's $d = 0.34$, just above what is considered a small effect; CCU Ⅰ vs. CCU Ⅲ, $t = 1.8$, $p = 0.070$, reasonably significant, and Cohen's $d = 0.25$, a small effect; CCU Ⅱ vs. CCU Ⅲ, $t = 0.5$, $p = 0.623$, not significant, and Cohen's $d = 0.09$, a very small effect). CCU Ⅱ has a higher rate of both the *li* tripod and *guan* jar types.

It is evident that CCU Ⅰ shows a high combined rate of *dou* and *gui* (46%) in comparison to CCU Ⅱ (35%) or CCU Ⅲ (35.3%). On the other hand, CCU Ⅱ has a higher combined percentage of *li* and *guan* (56.6%) in contrast to CCU Ⅰ (46.3%). If we project this pattern onto the undiagnostic sherds from each CCU, it can suitably explain why CCU Ⅰ yielded a much higher number of sherds than CCU Ⅱ that cannot be dated and are undiagnostic. However, this situation needs to be considered together with the data from the test excavation. In the excavation of Trenches Ⅰ and Ⅱ, particularly in units datable to the Eastern Zhou, the proportions of *dou* and *guan* fragments are also high, but it is noteworthy that the percentage of *gui* in these units is even higher than that in CCU Ⅰ. Thus, it is safe to say that CCU Ⅰ shows a higher proportion of *dou* and *gui*, while CCU Ⅱ shows a higher proportion of *li* and *guan*.

Data from the test excavation bear out this pattern. In the excavation of Trenches #1 and #2, particularly in units datable to the Eastern Zhou, the proportions of *dou* and *guan* fragments are also high, but it is notable that the percentage of *gui* in these units is even higher than that in CCU Ⅰ.

This is indeed significant when we consider the different functions of these vessel types. *Li* were cooking vessels and *guan* were used for storing water or food, both providing essential functions for the daily life of the large population. *Dou* and *gui*, originally derived from those same types in bronze vessels, were used more often to offer or display food and fruits. Although as pottery types they might not have been monopolized by the elite population, they clearly tend to appear more often in elite contexts, appearing in large numbers at elite banquets or other gatherings. Therefore, it is logically consistent that *dou* appear in larger numbers in CCU Ⅰ in the inner city of Guicheng than in CCU Ⅱ, as CCU Ⅱ, on the periphery of the city, was probably inhabited by the lower orders of the population and the guard troops along the outer city wall, who would not have possessed such trappings of feasting and luxury. In this regard, it is also significant that several pieces of *weng* jar were found in CCU Ⅰ. Such huge and thick jars were used only in contexts where a large volume of storage was necessary.

In short, the Complete Collection Units provided a relatively large and reliable inventory of the pottery types used at Guicheng. Though they cannot be assumed to represent the distribution of ceramic types across the entire site, it is likely that they contain a good representation of the site's ceramic population, as they are located in areas of high sherd density. At the least, they have provided information on what types of pottery were being used in these three areas near the inner city and between the inner and outer city walls. The differences between the CCUs are clear and meaningful, and allow us to understand differences in the social lives of Guicheng's residents, and the character of the activities of its large population.

Note: The typological features of the pottery samples gathered during the surface survey in 2008-2009 are analyzed in Figures Ⅰ.6.22- Ⅰ.6.25, accompanied by Table Ⅰ.6.3- Ⅰ.6.6 (Pl. 57: 1-4).

Section 7: Summary

The work at Guicheng was an attempt not only to answer our own research questions about intra-site organization as a foundation for understanding the sociopolitical dynamics at Guicheng, but also to address methodological concerns with a carefully considered survey design. The above discussion details how the city survey took into account conditions at the site (terrain, density of ancient remains, and modern occupation) and the needs of the project (both resources and research questions). The resulting design was an intensive full-coverage survey program utilizing the "Systematic Surface

Sampling" (SSS) strategy, which allowed for the collection of a large body of ceramic data in the space of two field seasons.

The SSS strategy allowed us to confirm the correlation between dense concentrations of surface remains and architectural features, to map the continuous distribution of surface remains across the site, to detect marked diachronic changes in patterns of occupation at the site, and to investigate the impact of site formation processes on the distribution of surface remains, which appears to have been minimal.

The results of the city survey are consistent with those of other methods of investigation at the Guicheng site. The overall city survey was supplemented and supported by the use of the Complete Collection Units (CCUs), and data derived from the CCUs were further corroborated by data acquired from the test excavation in the inner city. The evidence all points to a dramatic increase in intensity of occupation during the Zhou period, particularly the Eastern Zhou, which was followed by a dramatic drop in occupation during the Han period. Changes in distribution of remains at the site, particularly an expansion towards the east outer city wall during the Eastern Zhou period, suggest significant re-patterning in the use of the site over time. The correlations established between the concentrations of sherds and the subsurface building structures, and differences in vessel types between the three CCUs, are all important clues to understanding the internal organization as well as the social life of the ancient city, within which intensive occupation and elite pursuits were concentrated in and around the inner city, while the non-elite population and military activities were concentrated near the outer city wall.

We hope that this survey has provided a significant new example of a smaller-scale full-coverage survey, with requirements distinct from full-coverage surveys at a regional scale. We are confident that it has met the needs of the Guicheng research program and has contributed to our understanding of the ancient occupation of this site. We suggest that the best use of the full-coverage method, or of any surface survey strategy, is to use it, whenever possible, together with substantial coring and excavation of the subsurface structures and strata, in order to achieve a multi-dimensional understanding of the site under investigation.

References

Banning, E. B., A. L. Hawkins, and S. T. Stewart, 2006. "Detection Functions for Archaeological Survey," *American Antiquity*, 71.4: 723-742.

Billman, B. R., and G. M. Feinman (eds.), 1999. *Settlement Pattern Studies in the Americas: Fifty Years since Virú*. Washington, D.C.: Smithsonian Institution Press.

Bintliff, J., 2000. "Beyond Dots on the Map: Future Directions for Surface Artefact Survey in Greece," in *The Future of Surface Artefact Survey in Europe*, edited by J. Bintliff, M. Kuna, and N. Venclová. Pp. 3-20. Sheffield: Sheffield Academic Press Ltd.

Bintliff, J., and A. M. Snodgrass, 1985. "The Cambridge/Bradford Boeotian Expedition: The First Four Years," *Journal of Field Archaeology*, 12.2: 123-161.

Bintliff, J., M. Kuna, and N. Venclová, 2000. "Editorial Overview," in *The Future of Surface Artefact Survey in Europe*, edited by J. Bintliff, M. Kuna, and N. Venclová. Pp. 1-2. Sheffield: Sheffield Academic Press Ltd.

Bintliff, J., M. Kuna, and N. Venclová (eds.), 2000. *The Future of Surface Artefact Survey in Europe.* Sheffield: Sheffield Academic Press Ltd.

Carr, C., 1984. "The Nature of Organization of Intrasite Archaeological Records and Spatial Analytic Approaches to Their Investigation," in *Advances in Archaeological Method and Theory*, edited by M. B. Schiffer. Pp. 103-222. New York: Academic Press, Inc.

Cherry, J. F., J. L. Davis, A. Demitrack, E. Mantzourani, T. F. Strasser, and L. E. Talalay, 1988. "Archaeological Survey in an Artifact-rich Landscape: a Middle Neolithic Example from Nemea, Greece," *American Journal of Archaeology*, 92.2: 159-176.

Chifeng International Collaborative Archaeological Research Project 赤峰中美联合考古研究项目, 2003. *Regional Archeology in Eastern Inner Mongolia: a Methodological Exploration* 内蒙古东部赤峰区域考古调查阶段性报告. Beijing: Science Press.

Cohen, J., 1988. *Statistical Power Analysis for the Behavioral Sciences, Second Edition.* Hillsdale (NJ): Lawrence Erlbaum Associates.

Evans, C., 1951. "Review: *Surface Survey of the Virú Valley, Peru*," *American Antiquity*, 16.3: 270-272.

Feinman, G. M., and L. M. Nicholas, 1990. "Settlement and Land use in Ancient Oaxaca," in *Debating Oaxaca Archaeology* (*Anthropological Papers No. 84*), edited by J. Marcus. Pp. 71-113. Ann Arbor: Museum of Anthropology, University of Michigan.

Fish, P. R., and T. Gresham, 1990. "Insights from Full-coverage Survey in the Georgia Piedmont," in *The Archaeology of Regions: a Case for Full-coverage Survey*, edited by Fish, S. K. and S. A. Kowalewski. Pp. 147-172. Washington (DC): Smithsonian Institution Press.

Ford, J. A., and G. R. Willey, 1949. *A Surface Study of the Virú Valley, Peru. Anthropological Papers of the American Museum of Natural History*, 43.1. New York: American Museum of Natural History.

Gaffney, C., V. Gaffney, and M. Tingle, 1985. "Settlement, Economy or Behavior? Micro-regional Land Use Models and the Interpretation of Surface Artefact Patterns," in *Archaeology from the Ploughsoil: Studies in the Collection and Interpretation of Field Survey Data,* edited by C. Haselgrove, M. Millett, and I. Smith. Pp. 95-107. Sheffield: Department of Archaeology and Prehistory, University of Sheffield.

Haselgrove, C., 1985. "Inference from Ploughsoil Artefact Samples," in *Archaeology from the Ploughsoil: Studies in the Collection and Interpretation of Field Survey Data,* edited by C. Haselgrove, M. Millett, and I. Smith. Pp. 7-29. Sheffield: Department of Archaeology and Prehistory, University of Sheffield.

Haselgrove, C., M. Millett, and I. Smith (eds.), 1985. *Archaeology from the Ploughsoil: Studies in the Collection and Interpretation of Field Survey Data*. Sheffield: Department of Archaeology and Prehistory, University of Sheffield.

Haselgrove, C., M. Millet, and I. Smith, 1985. "Introduction," in *Archaeology from the Ploughsoil: Studies in the Collection and Interpretation of Field Survey Data,* edited by C. Haselgrove, M. Millett, and I. Smith. Pp. 1-3. Sheffield: Department of Archaeology and Prehistory, University of Sheffield.

King, T. F., 1978. *The Archaeological Survey: Methods and Uses*. Washington: Heritage Conservation and Recreation Service, U. S. Department of the Interior.

Kowalewski, S. A., 1990a. "Merits of Full-Coverage Survey: Examples from the Valley of Oaxaca, Mexico," in *The Archaeology of Regions: a Case for Full-coverage Survey,* edited by S. K. Fish and S. A. Kowalewski. Pp. 33-86. Washington (DC): Smithsonian Institution Press.

Kowalewski, S. A., 1990b. "Scale and Complexity: Issues in the Archaeology of the Valley of Oaxaca," in *The Archaeology of Regions: a Case for Full-coverage Survey,* edited by S. K. Fish, and S. A. Kowalewski. Pp. 207-270. Washington (DC): Smithsonian Institution Press.

Kowalewski, S. A., and S. K. Fish, 1990. "Conclusion," in *The Archaeology of Regions: a Case for Full-coverage Survey,* edited by S. K. Fish and S. A. Kowalewski. Pp. 261-277. Washington (D.C.): Smithsonian Institution Press.

Li, Buqing 李步青, and Lin Xianting 林仙庭, 1991. "Shandong Huangxian Guicheng yizhi de diaocha yu fajue" 山东黄县归城遗址的调查与发掘 (Survey and excavation of the Guicheng site in Huangxian County, Shandong), *Kaogu* 考古, 10: 910-918.

Li, Feng, 2006. *Landscape And Power In Early China: The Crisis And Fall of The Western Zhou, 1045-771 BC*. Cambridge, UK: Cambridge University Press.

Lin, Xianting 林仙庭, 2006. "Lai guo yu Lai du" 莱国与莱都 (The state of Lai and the Lai capital), in *Kaogu Yantai* 考古烟台 (Archaeology in Yantai), edited by Yantai shi bowuguan 烟台市博物馆. Pp. 134-136. Ji'nan: Qi Lu shushe.

Linduff, K. M., R. D. Drennan, and G. Shelach, 2002-2004. "Early Complex Societies in NE China: The Chifeng International Collaborative Archaeological Research Project," *Journal of Field Archaeology,* 29.1-2: 45-73.

Liu, Li, 1996. "Settlement Patterns, Chiefdom Variability, and the Development of Early States in North China," *Journal of Anthropological Archaeology,* 15: 237-288.

Liu, Li, Xingcan Chen, Yun Kuen Lee, H. Wright, and A. Rosen, 2002-2004. "Settlement Patterns and Development of Social Complexity in the Yiluo Region, North China," *Journal of Field Archaeology,* 29.1-2: 75-100.

Marcus, J., 1990. *Debating Oaxaca Archaeology* (Anthropological Papers No. 84). Ann Arbor: Museum of Anthropology, University of Michigan.

Marks, A. E., 1971. "Settlement Patterns and Intrasite Variability in the Central Negev, Israel," *American Anthropologist* (New Series), 73.5: 1237-1244.

Mills, N., 1985. "Sample Bias, Regional Analysis and Fieldwalking in British Archaeology," in *Archaeology from the Ploughsoil: Studies in the Collection and Interpretation of Field Survey Data*, edited by C. Haselgrove, M. Millett, and I. Smith. Pp. 39-47. Sheffield: Department of Archaeology and Prehistory, University of Sheffield.

Ortman, S. G., M. D. Varien, and T. L Gripp, 2007. "Empirical Bayesian Methods for Archaeological Survey Data: an Application from the Mesa Verde Region," *American Antiquity*, 72.2: 241-272.

Pettegrew, D. K., 2007. "The Busy Countryside of Late Roman Corinth: Interpreting Ceramic Data Produced by Regional Archaeological Surveys," *Hesperia,* 76: 743-784.

Parsons, J. R., 1990. “Critical Reflections on a Decade of Full-coverage Regional Survey in the Valley of Mexico,” *The Archaeology of Regions: a Case for Full-coverage Survey*, edited by S. K. Fish, and S. A. Kowalewski. Pp. 7-31. Washington (DC): Smithsonian Institution Press.

Rapp, G., and C. L. Hill, 2006. *Geoarchaeology: the Earth-science Approach to Archaeological Interpretation.* New Haven: Yale University Press.

Schiffer, M., A. P. Sullivan, and T. C. Klinger, 1978. “The Design of Archaeological Surveys,” *World Archaeology,* 10.1: 1-28.

Shelach, G., 1998. “A Settlement Pattern Study in Northeast China: Results and Potential Contributions of Western Theory and Methods to Chinese archaeology,” *Antiquity,* 72.275: 114-127.

Sino-American Joint Guicheng Archaeological Team 中美联合归城考古队, 2011. “Shandong Longkou shi Guicheng liang Zhou chengzhi diaocha jianbao” 山东龙口市归城两周城址调查简报 (A brief report on the survey of the Guicheng city site of the Western-Eastern Zhou periods in Longkou, Shandong Province), *Kaogu* 考古, 3: 30-39.

Sullivan, A. P., P. B. Mink, and P. M. Uphus, 2007. “Archaeological Survey Design, Units of Observation, and the Characterization of Regional Variability,” *American Antiquity,* 72.2: 322-333.

Tartaron, T. F. et al., 2006. “The Eastern Korinthia Archaeological Survey: Integrated Methods for a Dynamic Landscape,” *Hesperia*, 75.4: 453-523.

Terrenato, N., 2000. “Surface Thoughts: Future Directions in Italian Field Surveys,” in *The Future of Surface Artefact Survey in Europe*, edited by J. Bintliff, M. Kuna, and N. Venclová. Pp. 21-28. Sheffield: Sheffield Academic Press Ltd.

Underhill, A. P., 1994. “Variation in settlements during the Longshan period of northern China,” *Asian Perspectives*, 33.2: 197-228.

Underhill, Anne P., G. M. Feinman, L. M. Nicholas, G. Bennett, Hui Fang, Fengshi Luan, Haiguang Yu, and Fengshu Cai, 2002. “Regional Survey and the Development of Complex Societies in Southeastern Shandong, China,” *Antiquity*, 76.293: 745-755.

Van Andel, T. H., and C. N. Runnels, 1987. *Beyond the Acropolis: A Rural Greek Past*. Stanford: Stanford University Press.

Walker, L., 1985. “Survey of a Settlement: a Strategy for the Etruscan Site at Doganella in the Albegna Valley,” in *Archaeology from the Ploughsoil: Studies in the Collection and Interpretation of Field Survey Data*, edited by C. Haselgrove, M. Millett, and I. Smith. Pp. 87-94. Sheffield: Department of Archaeology and Prehistory, University of Sheffield.

Willey, G. R., 1953. *Prehistoric Settlement Patterns in the Virù Valley, Peru. Bureau of American Ethnology Bulletin*, 155. Smithsonian Institution, Washington, D.C.

Yantai Shi Bowuguan 烟台市博物馆 ed., 2006. *Yantai kaogu* 烟台考古 (Yantai archaeology). Ji’nan: Qi Lu Shushe.

Zhongguo shehui kexueyuan kaogu yanjiusuo 中国社会科学院考古研究所, 2004. *Zhongguo kaoguxue: Liang Zhou juan* 中国考古学：两周卷 (Chinese archaeology: Western Zhou and Eastern Zhou). Beijing: China Social Science Press.

第七章　黄水河流域的区域考古调查

梁中合

2007～2009年，中美联合归城考古队对龙口归城遗址进行多方位的细致调查工作，基本掌握了归城8平方千米内遗迹、遗物的分布情况及地下遗址保存状况，取得了丰富的收获（见上编第二章至第六章）。在这期间，我们虽然对归城以外的个别遗址进行踏查，但对本地区遗址分布的整体情况所知甚少。归城城址地处龙口最大河流——黄水河干流西侧，黄水河支流之一的鸦鹊河流经城址东侧的低山丘陵地带。黄水河也是归城附近最大的河流，干流发源于归城之南莱山东麓的王屋水库一带，向西北流入渤海，从上游王屋水库到入海口全长26千米。考察黄水河流域聚落遗存的演变规律，对了解本地区古代遗址的空间联系和聚落组成体系都有重要意义，对于充分了解和认识归城遗址的地位和性质也具有重要价值。参考以往调查的资料，我们于2010年和2011年分两个季度对黄水河流域遗址进行了调查和复查，重点在商周时期遗址（地图Ⅰ.7.1）。这项工作为今后龙口地区古代遗址的整体研究打下了一个良好的基础。

第一节　调查的方法与步骤

为适应此次调查，首先选择该流域的大比例地图，我们选择的是1:10000的地形图。同时，我们也随时参考“谷歌地球”所提供的卫星影像，将两套资料配合起来使用。其次，在调查之前我们尽量熟悉以往发表的有关调查的文字资料，观察过去已采集的标本，进一步明确各遗址的文化性质。最后对现已掌握信息的有关遗址进行实地考察，这项工作力求细致准确。

操作步骤：

（1）首先在地图上标明准确的地理位置，测量出经纬度和海拔。

（2）进行实地调查和钻探确定遗址年代、堆积厚度、明确遗址范围。

（3）选择有断崖的地方铲出剖面进一步了解遗址的厚度，划分文化层并逐层取样。

（4）选择典型区域采集标本，包括一切古代人类活动留下的遗物。

（5）用全站仪绘制千分之一遗址地形平面图，根据勘探和调查的结果标出遗址范围。

龙口市位于胶东半岛西北部，西北滨渤海，东南倚莱山，黄水河贯穿境内，面积有890平方千米。北部平原有邱家庄一期文化的贝丘遗址，南部有西周时期归城遗址。另外，“齐之八主”之一的莱山月主祠即坐落在莱山巅峰，而庙周家秦始皇离宫大型建筑遗址则位于莱山北麓。我们调查的遗址年代跨度从新石器时代一直到秦汉时期。通过对整个流域内各时期聚落规模及形态的观察，我们发现从较早的白石村一期文化遗存（距今6000～5700年）到紫荆山一期文化遗存（距今5275～4860年）之间有一定的缺环，即缺少相当于山东内陆地区大汶口文化中期遗存。这种现象是什么原因造成的？目前学术界还有不同的看法。比较多的学者认为是因为环境关系所造成的。这里暂不做探讨。

第二节　调查的遗址

任何一种人类文化，在其发生、发展、演变过程中，除了要受到所处自然生态环境的制约外，还要受到所处文化环境的影响。所谓文化环境，指的是一种文化同周边其他文化之间的关系。人类文化是动态的，不同文化之间、特别是相邻文化之间的交往和文化因素的相互交流与借用，是影响文化发展变化的重要因素之一。因此关于文化现象的空间位移——文化传播，是考古学研究的重要课题之一。

黄水河发源于莱山、崮山山脉间，北流注入渤海，为胶东半岛第二大水系。黄水河主干位于龙口市东北部，其流经栖霞、招远、龙口、蓬莱四个县市，流域面积很广，其支流众多，流经区域主要为低山丘陵地带。遗址主要分布黄水河两岸及主要的支流，其中重要的遗址除归城城址外，还有龙口市的东羔、唐家、乾山、邵家、小莱山溶洞、鲁家沟等遗址，蓬莱市的南王绪、村里集等遗址。以下分别叙述主要遗址概况及采集的遗物：

一、东羔遗址

位于龙口市诸由观镇东羔村，在村北500米的一处隆起高地上。北约2千米是渤海，东距黄水河约1.5千米。地理坐标为东经120°30′42″、北纬37°43′42″，海拔13米。

遗址南北长约250米，东西宽约200米，遗址总面积大约5万平方米。烟潍公路从遗址中心穿过，龙口市中心南北向的通海路与烟潍公路在遗址西端交汇。遗址处在一个西高东低山丘上。西、南两面为丘陵，现在遗址上种植果树及松树（图Ⅰ.7.1）。2006年山东省文物考古研究所、烟台市博物馆与龙口市博物馆组成联合考古队，对遗址进行抢救性考古发掘，获得了一批新的资料。

东羔遗址清理出一批邱家庄一期文化的灰坑、墓葬及房址。出土了一批陶、石及骨器等。陶器上的纹饰有刻划纹、网格纹、附加泥饼等。同时还发现了大量的动物骨骼、牡蛎皮、蛤蜊壳等。东羔遗址对了解胶东地区贝丘遗址文化面貌及海岸线变迁具有重要价值。

遗址范围内采集的主要遗物是陶器残片，包括器物的口沿、腹、底、足等部位，可辨的器形有鼎口沿、足，罐、钵等。该遗址多为邱家庄一期的陶片，另有周代绳纹陶片及汉代的瓦等（图Ⅰ.7.2；表Ⅰ.7.1）。

二、唐家遗址

位于龙口市徐福镇唐家村东，西距徐福镇约4.5千米。地理坐标为东经120°27′27″、北纬37°41′46″，海拔11米左右。

北距渤海约5千米，唐家村村东北高台地上，遗址东南部有旧房一座，南端有一条公路穿遗址而过，将遗址一分为二，中部稍高，周围低平，据当地农民介绍，原来地势很高，由于历年的平整土地、取土积肥及兴建房屋，使遗址遭到很大程度的破坏，目前为现代坟地，周围种植有蔬菜、果树及其他农作物等，保存状况较差。现存东西160米，南北100米，面积约1.6万平方米（图Ⅰ.7.3）。该遗址1996年被确定为烟台市级重点文物保护单位。现经钻探了解文化堆积厚在0.5～1.2米之间。地表采集标本应属于新石器时代较多，以邱家庄一期文化的陶片占多数，可辨认的器型有鼎、罐、钵、盆；地面随处可见这一时期的贝壳堆积。另外我们还发现了少量春秋时期的绳纹罐残片、豆柄及汉代板瓦等（图Ⅰ.7.4；表Ⅰ.7.2）。在遗址的断崖旁采集到红烧土块，其内掺和有植物的秸秆，炭化后留下空隙。一面凹凸不平，一面抹平，判断这些烧土块均为房屋建筑构件。

该遗址为研究黄水河流域新石器时代文化的文化面貌、分布与演变规律提供了重要资料。

三、南王绪遗址

位于蓬莱市北沟乡南王绪村，距村南约150米处。地理坐标为东经120°37′23″，北纬37°44′46″，海拔20米以上。

遗址处于村南由东南向西北倾斜的高台地上，其东、南两面为山丘，北距黄海约3千米，东、西侧分别有小河流过。在遗址西、南边为乡间的小路。遗址因当地村民常年取土而遭严重破坏，现存遗址上大部分种植果树。南北长约190米，东西宽约150米，面积为2.85万平方米（图Ⅰ.7.5）。该遗址1996年被定为烟台市级重点文物保护单位，2006年确定为山东省重点文物保护单位。1994年10月中国社会科学院考古研究所胶东半岛贝丘遗址研究课题组对遗址全面调查和钻探，地面采集标本（中国社会科学院考古研究所 1999：77～83；Yuan Jing，Liang Zhonghe et al. 2002：3～22）。

根据断崖上暴露的文化堆积及探孔情况推测当时人的居住位于遗址的东部，其墓地位于遗址的北侧。已暴露出文化层及墓葬非常丰富，而遗址西北部是倾倒生活垃圾的场所，断面显露文化层堆积厚1.5～3.0米以上，见有红烧土、陶片及贝壳堆积等，文化性质属邱家庄一期的贝丘遗址。该遗址为研究胶东地区新石器时代文化的发展演变规律提供了重要资料。

该遗址上部种植果树，地面上几乎很少采集到遗物，只有在断崖旁能够采集一些标本，各类标本中以夹砂红陶及红褐陶为最多，其次为泥质灰陶，还有一陶片中掺和有云母和蚌壳，均为手制。可辨器形有鼎、罐、小口壶、钵，另外还采集一件残陶镯（图Ⅰ.7.6；表Ⅰ.7.3）。

四、庄头墓地

位于龙口市石良镇东庄头村，墓地在村东一高台地上。地理坐标为东经120°41′28″、北纬37°35′11″，海拔87米。

墓地处于南高北向的黄土台地上，因近崮山山脉，整个地势呈东高西低之势，东、西面为较高的梯田，西南断崖下为低洼地。南约80米处为上王家村水库库坝，北侧属缓慢倾斜田地。西面临近东庄头村居民区，南面有公路通过。现高地之上皆开垦为农田，以种植果树、玉米为主。南北长200米，东西宽150米，面积约3万平方米（图Ⅰ.7.7）。

1980年当地群众在村东高台地上取土发现的，1981年12月，烟台地区文管会和黄县（现龙口市）文化馆联合对出土铜器的残墓进行发掘清理（王锡平，唐禄庭 1986：69～72）。墓为土坑竖穴，墓长3米，宽2.46米，距地表深1.32米。墓坑四周有宽约0.2米的熟夯土，似为二层台。在距东壁0.27米处有一道宽0.11米的横木朽痕把墓室南北隔开，形成头厢，出土许多青铜器带有铭文，系西周时期贵族的墓葬群。1992年被山东省公布重点文物保护单位。该墓地为研究黄水河流域青铜时代文化的分布与葬俗提供了重要资料。

庄头墓地中采集的标本较少，主要有罐、豆，另外还采集一件残铜戈（图Ⅰ.7.8；表Ⅰ.7.4）。

五、集前赵家墓地

位于龙口市石良镇集前赵家村的西北，北距石良镇约1千米。东经120°39′46″，北纬37°34′07″，海拔58米。

墓地位于村西北的高台上，南100米紧靠黄水河的支流东营河，西侧紧邻省道213公路。东西长110米，南北宽50米，面积约0.58万平方米（图Ⅰ.7.9）。该墓地西南侧紧邻砖厂（现已废弃），在20世纪70年代因取土烧砖及平整土地使遗址遭受严重破坏，常年地取土将墓地变成一个大坑，清理的墓葬在砖窑厂北侧断崖旁，局部还保留有2米左右高台地，现存墓地大部分被果园覆盖，地表采集遗物较少。发掘的墓葬为土坑竖穴墓，清理出土铜器、陶器等遗物，年代在西周时期。墓被发现时，墓内的许多青铜器几乎全部被毁成碎片，可辨者有鼎、壶、簋、爵等，其中有铭文者至少有5件。现在墓地之上采集有汉砖残块，其上有文字、侍女画像等。墓地主要以西周、汉代时期的墓葬为主。该墓地曾多次被盗掘，资料散失严重，需要有针对性地加以保护。该墓地为研究黄水河流域西周、汉代时期的墓葬形制及与莱子国的关系提供了重要资料。

遗址采集标本很少，仅发现1件罐的口沿（图Ⅰ.7.10；表Ⅰ.7.5）。

六、东营周家墓地

位于龙口市石良镇东营周家村东南，北距石良镇约3千米。地理坐标为东经120°40′55″、北纬37°34′01″，海拔70米左右。

墓地地处山区，地形起伏较大，西部为集前赵家村和东营曹家村，南部紧靠东营河道，东南方眺望大松顶山脉，据当地农民反映墓地就在较高台地上，东面为梯田，西南断崖下有一无名小河由南向北流入东营河。因20世纪70年代建窑烧砖取土、平整土地破坏严重，目前砖窑厂已废弃。墓地现被果园覆盖，地表采集遗物较少，东西长宽各约150米，面积约2.25万平方米（图Ⅰ.7.11）。1986年发现并清理了3座，均为土坑竖穴墓，有二层台和木棺痕迹，出土200多件遗物，其中陶器有鼎、鬲、豆、罐、簋、瓮等，铜器有鼎、簋等遗物（唐禄庭，姜国钧1989：314～319）。该遗址为研究黄水河流域青铜时代文化提供了重要资料。

七、鲁家沟遗址

位于龙口市石良镇鲁家沟村，村东北5米处的高台地上。东经120°40′28.0″，北纬37°31′07″，海拔88米以上。

鲁家沟遗址是一处新石器时代的遗址，周围地势为浅山丘陵，原发现的遗址范围很大，南北长150米，东西宽200米，面积约为3万平方米（图Ⅰ.7.12）。破坏的主要原因是鲁家沟村村民历年盖房，大部分遗址为村庄所压，后因历年平整土地，常年的农业生产对遗址破坏极为严重；此外，因雨水冲刷而导致的水土流失也加剧了遗址的破坏，使文化层遭到很大破坏，剩余部分上现为一片农田，目前仅剩约0.6万平方米。遗址文化堆积不详，以往调查中采集的有陶器、石器、烧土块、木炭等大量遗物，陶片以夹云母、夹砂、泥质和红衣陶为主，陶色以红褐、黄褐为主，纹饰有堆纹、乳钉纹，可辨器形有鼎、罐、环等。文化类型应属邱家庄一期文化遗存。遗址采集遗物的遗物时代与墓地有很大区别（见下）（图Ⅰ.7.13；表Ⅰ.7.6）。

八、鲁家沟墓地

位于龙口市石良镇鲁家沟村，墓地在村东北一高台地上，北距石良镇约10千米。地理坐标东经120°40′27.0″，北纬37°31′07″，海拔89米以上。

墓地周围为浅山丘陵地，由东北向西南缓慢倾斜，西侧不远处有省道213公路通过，南侧有农耕小路穿过，墓地南面不远处有一水塘。墓地上现为农田，以种植果树、玉米等为主东。墓地东西长100米。南北宽85米，面积约0.85万平方米（图Ⅰ.7.12）。该墓地破坏较为严重，在复查过程中，仅采集到几块陶片，由于平整土地，西部被破坏。这里曾发现土坑竖穴墓，出土铜器有莱伯鼎、壶、铜剑等。

据记载在清光绪二十二年（1896年）出土一批西周时期的铜器。王道新《黄县志稿》（金石目）有如下记载：“（黄县）城东南鲁家沟田中出铜器十：钟三、鼎二，钟无款识。尚有壶一、盘一，盘无款识。若甗、若盉、若觯皆有铭”（王道新 1934：806）。与此记载稍有不同的是《山东金文集存》记录的一件有铭铜鼎也说是光绪二十二年黄县出土，鼎铭内容与鲁家沟出土甗铭略似，都是一个叫“遇”的人受到赏赐而作的纪念性器物，可能二者是同一批（曾毅公 1940：11～13）。这批铜器中有一件鼎铭文只有5字：“莱伯作旅鼎”，很多学者认为这是莱国就在莱山附近的证明。

自1956年以来，国家和山东省考古部门及烟台市博物馆曾多次前往考察，根据出土器物特征及其所处的地理位置，这是一处西周时期的墓群。有的文物流失到日本。鲁家沟墓葬被学术界认为是一处莱国贵族的墓地。该墓地为研究黄水河流域青铜时代文化提供了重要资料。

九、乾山遗址

位于龙口市徐福镇乡城东村，西距镇政府约500米。地理坐标为东经120°29′30″、北纬37°40′44″，海拔20米。

遗址位于徐福镇乡城东村东一华里的高丘上，平面呈长方形，遗址北面是羊沟营村，东面为埠子后村，南距新建徐公祠约300米，西南部是徐乡故城，现已被破坏殆尽。据当地村民反映，遗址原来的面积很大，东西长约255米，南北长约480米，总面积约有12.24万平方米（图Ⅰ.7.14）。

当时是一座高近20米高的矮山，后因取土填海及平整土地遭严重破坏，现残留遗址东北角一高约5米的土丘，面积仅数十平方米。一条南北向农村公路从遗址中心穿过，遗址西部为养殖场，残余范围不详。遗址于1957年发现并清理出汉代墓葬数座，出土陶器有彩绘罐、壶、杯、釜，铜器有博山炉和双耳壶。在遗址的一处剖面上发现有大量的贝壳堆积，采集有典型邱家庄一期文化时期的泥质红陶和夹砂灰陶器物残片，遗物有鼎足、石磨棒和人骨等。另有汉代饰菱形纹、文字的墓砖和饰有绳纹的泥质灰陶器等。因有不同时段的文化遗存，因此有较高的科学价值。乾山遗址在徐乡故城遗址的北部，相隔约有200米。1991年公布为烟台市市级文物保护单位。该遗址为研究黄水河流域新石器时代和汉代文化提供了重要资料。

该遗址因破坏严重，地面很难采集到陶片，我们在遗址东侧保留较高土堆断面上采集的一些陶片。从断面还可分出不同时期堆积，以新石器时代的陶片占多数。另有西周时期及汉代砖、瓦等。可辨认的器形有鼎、罐、小口罐、钵、石磨棒等（图Ⅰ.7.15；表Ⅰ.7.7）。

十、张郑家墓地

位于龙口市新嘉街道张郑家村，墓地在村东南部。地理坐标为东经120°26′52″、北纬37°38′36″，海拔24米。

遗址位于泳汶河流域东岸，属于河边高地，其北侧不远处有北曲遗址，东北有羊高遗址。

东紧靠新开发的城区，北面200米为张郑家村（图Ⅰ.7.16）。张郑家村周围地势平坦，村北建一砖窑厂，因多年取土烧砖呈一洼地。村民在取土时发现这批墓葬，出土各类陶器上百件，当地村民将出土器物交到龙口市博物馆。我们选择其中的一部分加以报道，这批遗物没有进行编号，出土单位不清楚，所以我们只能分类加以介绍。遗址大部分的原始堆积地已被严重破坏，已无法确定该墓地的范围，从现有的状况观察，应为一处西周时期低等级墓葬区。从出土的陶器判断时代为西周偏晚时期。遗址发现为研究该地区青铜时代文化提供了新的资料（图Ⅰ.7.17：1～4；表Ⅰ.7.8；图版58～65）。

十一、小莱山溶洞遗址

位于龙口市兰高镇欧头孙家村，距村东北500米。东经120°36′02″，北纬37°37′35″，海拔45米。

遗址西紧靠黄水河支流鸦鹊河畔，河流位于小莱山西部山岗下。遗址处于小莱山西部山岗，山岗的南北长400米，东西宽200米，洞穴主体占地面积达0.2万平方米（图Ⅰ.7.18）。该溶洞于1932年发现，是一处旧石器时代的洞穴遗址，文化堆积厚0.5～1米，此洞内留有原始居住痕迹，出土打制石器及一批动物化石，化石有鱼刺、兽骨、鹿角等。1992年被列为龙口市级文物保护单位。该遗址为黄水河流域地区旧石器时代的文化研究及气候演变提供重要的资料。

十二、徐乡故城址

位于龙口市徐福镇城东村的南部，东南距龙口市7千米。地理坐标为东经120°29′08″，北纬37°40′32″，海拔20米以上。一条东西乡镇公路从城墙中部穿过，东北距乾山遗址200米（图Ⅰ.7.19）。

徐乡故城城墙和地面建筑荡然无存，据文献和考古资料证明，徐乡故城始建于春秋时期延续到汉代初期，春秋末期，齐国灭掉建都于今龙口市归城一带的东莱国以后，在东莱国的旧地的北海沿海设置徐乡城。秦始皇统一中国后，改徐乡城为徐乡候国。徐乡故城遗址内遗物丰富，历代都有文物出土。这里发现了一大批城墙基石、水井、排水沟、砖瓦、陶器、青铜器。近年，山东省文物考古研究所对徐乡故城进行了考古勘探和试掘，探明了徐乡故城的确切范围、城门、宫殿、街道、作坊、窑场、排水沟等历史遗迹。从勘探结果观察，城址呈长方形，城址东西长514米，南北宽370米，面积约19万平方米，局部可看出夯土遗迹，出土遗物较少。该城址为研究黄水河流域春秋至汉代城市的发展与演变提供了重要资料。

遗址地表遗物很少，仅采集到1件盘的圈足（图Ⅰ.7.10，2；表Ⅰ.7.5）。

十三、村里集城址

位于蓬莱市村里集镇，北距市区45千米。城址附近有古城东村、古城李家村、古城苗家村三个村子。地理坐标为东经120°46′21″、北纬37°31′42″，海拔115米。

城址南临栖霞艾山。东、西、北三面是起伏的丘陵，形成天然的小盆地，这里属于黄水河支流上游河谷黄土台地，这条支流向北，然后向西汇入黄水河主干。城址大部分被村庄所覆盖，西南面有一条无名小河自南向北流过。1978年调查初探，城址平面呈长方形。遗址东西500米，南北600米，面积约30万平方米（图Ⅰ.7.20）。城墙绝大部分被夷平，现存的北墙长100米，基宽10米，残高4米，黄黏土夯筑，夯层厚4～6厘米，夯窝直径约4厘米。城内文化堆积厚约1～1.5米。采集标本有夹砂灰陶绳纹鬲足、泥质灰陶罐口沿、豆把等。城址的时代为西周至春秋时期，它与归城遗址相距很近，形成犄角之势。

十四、村里集墓地

位于蓬莱市村里集镇，北距市区45千米，周围有辛旺集、柳格庄、占马张家村。地理坐标为东经120°46′35″、北纬37°30′23″，海拔134米。

墓葬主要分布在黄水河支流两岸的台地上。其中一部分位于东岸的辛旺集，另一部分在西岸的柳格庄。辛旺集村东南方低矮山坡上为墓地，西侧靠黄水河地势较为平整，一条乡村土路从遗址西部穿过，北距村庄约1千米。墓地南北长400米，东西宽100米，面积约4万平方米（图Ⅰ.7.21）。

该墓地曾清理出一批西周及春秋大型墓葬。先后进行过三次发掘，清理墓葬近20座，均为长方形土坑竖穴墓，有的四周有二层台，部分墓葬有殉人、腰坑，坑内置车马。主要出土西周、春秋的铜器、陶器、玉器等。这是黄水河流域一处规模较大的西周城址和墓葬区。该城址和墓地为研究黄水河流域城址的演变和布局提供了重要资料。

十五、楼子庄遗址

位于龙口市北马镇楼子庄村，距村南200米高的台地上。地理坐标为东经120°24′13″，北纬37°34′58″，海拔51米。

遗址南望认儿山主峰，东为楼子庄窑厂，西为马南河，属于河旁台地遗址，现遗址高出村庄约2米左右，高台下有一条南北向乡村路，威乌高速公路在遗址的中心东西穿过，遗址东西长210米，南北宽147米，面积3万多平方米（图Ⅰ.7.22）。2001年烟台市博物馆文物组与龙口市博物馆联合组成联合考古队，对楼子庄遗址进行抢救性考古发掘，获得了一批新的资料。楼子庄遗址文化堆积层丰富，遗址分6个文化层，发现有龙山文化的房址及大量的窖穴，还发现有灰坑及灰沟等遗迹。出土遗物有甗、鬲、碗、鼎、杯等陶器残片，还有石刀、铲、锛和骨针、锥等。该遗址为研究黄水河流域新石器时代文化的发展与演变提供了新的资料。

在遗址中采集标本很少，仅发现一件具有当地文化特色的罐底（图Ⅰ.7.10；表Ⅰ.7.5）。

十六、黄河营古港遗址

位于龙口市徐福镇黄河营村，南距龙口市16千米，黄河营村东北的黄水河入海口处。地理坐标为东经120°30′46″，北纬37°44′52″，海拔1.5米。

该古港为周代天然形成的港口。东西长220米，南北宽200米，面积约4.4万平方米（图Ⅰ.7.23）。黄河营港昔日水深腹阔，地理条件优越。它北临渤海，东南距秦代黄县城20余千米，水陆交通十分发达。此港为一天然良港，黄水河在入海口处拐了一个大急弯，形成了一个口小腹大的港湾。由于河水入海时受海浪冲阻而被迫缓缓回流和四周河坝、树木的屏障作用，致使港内风平浪静，犹如一处内陆平湖。据实地勘察和出土文物证明，古代的黄河营港区范围很大，北至渤海南岸，南到东羔村村东，长约3000米，占地面积约132万平方米，自古就是中国海防要地和对外交通口岸，为中国上古时期全国六大名港之一。黄河营古港始建于西周时代，为西周时期的古遗址。1992年公布为龙口市重点文物保护单位。该遗址为研究黄水河流域西周时期港口与交通的发展提供了重要资料。

十七、前河前遗址

位于莱阳市团旺镇前河前村，五龙河西岸，距莱阳市南35千米。地理坐标东经120°43′22.1″，北纬36°44′33.8″，海拔130米。虽然前河前遗址不在黄水河流域，但因为它在该地区时代的特殊性和出土遗物的独特性，所以我们将调查的资料也一并加以介绍。这批资料对了解该地区在西周时期的聚落形态及其演变等具有重要价值。

遗址位于村南200米，南北长约300米，东西宽约250米，面积达7.5万平方米（图Ⅰ.7.24）。据当地村民讲当年这里曾经有城墙存在，当时遗址中部还有一个大土丘，后来因历年取土和常年耕作而夷为平地。1974年当地村民在取土时发现8件青铜器，其中1件壶、1件甗带铭文，为搞清这批铜器的出土情况和遗址面貌，1975年春季山东省博物馆、烟台市文物管理委员会派人对遗址进行了调查和试掘，清理了灰坑、车马坑及5座墓葬，获得了一批重要的资料，从出土器物分析墓葬的年代为西周中、晚期。在当时地表采集及灰坑中出土一种灰褐色或红褐色陶片，其质地粗糙，胎内掺和有云母片、蚌壳粉等，制作原始，火候相对较低。这类陶器与墓葬出土的陶器属两套系统，判断可能是两种不同文化，即可能是当地一种本地文化遗物。

在遗址之上采集陶片较多，但典型的不多。有陶器口沿残片、绳纹陶片等。陶质以泥质陶为主，陶色多为灰色。可辨器形有豆盘、鬲、盆、罐等（图Ⅰ.7.25；表Ⅰ.7.9）。

十八、邵家遗址

位于龙口市东江街道邵家村，西距街道办2千米，在村北的高台地上。地理坐标东经120°32′19″，北纬37°37′44″，海拔38米。

遗址东临绛水河，西靠龙栖公路。北100米为邵家村，现为农田。近处遗址西、东两外缘各有一条农田小路，周围皆为农田。由于遗址破坏严重，所剩面积无几。遗址1979年发现后，北京大学考古系及省、市文物部门先后派人进行调查。遗址内涵丰富，在遗址东段断崖有清楚的地层堆积。第1层为耕土层，厚0.2～0.3米；第2层为扰土层，厚0.1～0.2米；第3层为文化层，厚约1米。含有龙山和岳石两种文化堆积。出土的遗物有石器和陶器。石器中有一件打制的石球。陶器以泥制灰陶为主，次为夹砂红陶和黑皮陶。可辨器型有扁方形鼎足，平底扁方三足器，深腹盆，黑陶杯，鼓腹小口罐，钵器盖等。器物多为素面磨光轮制，个别属捏制。纹饰有附加堆纹、弦纹等。1992年被龙口市公布为市级重点文物保护单位，该遗址为研究黄水河流域新石器时代文化提供了重要资料。

十九、姚家包袱地墓地

位于龙口市诸由观镇姚家村，在村北的一处高台地上。地理坐标东经120°32′18″，北纬37°44′14″，海拔5米。

北距渤海约2千米，西距黄水河口约0.5千米。其北300米渤海周家村，西面200米渤海郭家村，东距工会村约500米，南距烟潍公路约3千米。其地势为低矮的丘陵，由于遗址距村庄较近，所以大部分为菜地。判断墓地面积东西长140米，南北宽80米，面积约1.12万平方米。清理有战国时期墓葬。该遗址为黄水河流域战国时期的文化研究提供了资料。

二十、郝家墓地

位于龙口市诸由观镇郝家村，距村北0.5千米的丘陵果园内，西北距镇所在地约6千米。地理坐标东经120°38′09.4″，北纬37°39′05.8 ″，海拔42米。

墓地东0.5千米是小高家村，西南0.5千米是董家村，北临镇公路，郝家墓地原有大封土堆，后被平毁。现地势由北高渐向低。南北长110米，东西宽95米，总面积1.05万平方米。在墓地北部有数处高地，整体地势较高。1988年发现，之后由市博物馆进行了抢救发掘，1988～1989年对其中6座墓葬进行了清理，均为土坑竖穴墓，墓内填有牡蛎壳，带棺和墓道。出土陶器有罐、豆、彩陶罐，铜镜、“半两”钱等遗物共40余件，年代为汉代。均收藏于龙口市博物馆。1992年被龙口市公布为市级重点文物保护单位。该墓地的发现为黄水河流域汉代的文化及埋葬习俗提供重要的资料。

二十一、后柞杨遗址

位于龙口市诸由观镇后柞杨村，遗址距村西约1千米。地理坐标东经120°33′18″，北纬37°42′23″，海拔8米。

北距渤海湾约8千米，西距黄水河口约1千米。南面前柞杨村，东距西台村500米，遗址东边有两座塑料棚，南边有一条乡村小路，地势较为平坦。遗址南北约350米，东西约120米，面积大约为4.2万平方米。在遗址采集周代陶片和汉代的花纹砖。后因平整土地破坏严重，现堆积基本荡然无存，所以无法准确判断遗址的面积。从采集的标本判断该遗址为周、汉两个时代。该遗址的发现对了解黄水河流域的周、汉时期聚落布局提供了重要材料。

二十二、唐家集遗址

位于龙口市诸由观镇唐家集村，距村西南约1.5千米的一处高地上。地理坐标东经120°33′54″，北纬37°43′02″，海拔13米。

遗址西面靠乡镇公路，北面东尚家村，遗址东西长约310米，南北宽约200米，面积大约5万平方米。遗址范围原为一岗地，现因土地整修已成梯田。遗址范围内发现大量周代陶片以及豆柄、器物口沿和足部等。陶片纹饰大多为绳纹，器型主要有鬲、罐、钵、豆等，此外还发现有汉代菱形花纹墓砖。根据采集遗物判断该遗址应为周、汉代时期。该遗址为了解黄水河流域的周、汉时期聚落布局提供了重要材料。

二十三、下河头遗址

位于龙口市石良镇下河头村，遗址在村的西南部。地理坐标东经120°38′33″，北纬37°35′14″，海拔38米。

遗址西临黄水河，为河旁二级阶地，东侧现为农田区，上植有较多果树。南北约30米，东西约100米，略呈三角形，面积约0.3万多平方米。在遗址地表可采集到鼎、罐等陶器残片及汉代砖瓦残块，依陶器残片及汉代砖瓦残片观察，该遗址曾经历龙山文化、周和汉等几个时代。它对研究黄水河流域史前及周、汉代的历史具有重要价值。

二十四、平里院墓地

这处东汉时期墓地位于龙口市石良镇平里院村，遗址位于村的东北部。地理坐标东经120°40′59″，北纬37°36′22″，海拔56米。

该墓地位于村后高地之上，皆为农田，墓地长约200米，宽约118米，面积约达2.36万平方米，目前发现了大、小两座汉墓，均在20世纪60年代的平整土地过程中遭到破坏。大墓仅剩一小堆封土，并可能已遭受盗掘；小墓已被彻底破坏。在大墓封土周围采集到大量汉代砖、瓦残块。在小墓原位置采集到一块完整汉砖。据村民回忆，在大墓偏西北方向曾挖出过很长的墓道，推测该墓规格甚高。此外，在该墓地采集到的一些陶片可能早到岳石文化时期。它对研究该地区汉代的墓葬制度意义重大。

二十五、李家遗址

位于龙口市北马镇台上李家村，南栾河西岸，处在南部山地的山前平原地区。地理坐标东经120°25′43″，北纬37°34′52″，海拔50米。

遗址整体略呈一不规则长方形，南北长约200米，东西宽约160多米，面积约达3.67万平方米，遗址现被农田覆盖，保存状况较为一般。在遗址上采集有少量龙山文化、珍珠门文化和汉代的陶片。可辨器型有夹砂黑陶腹片、夹砂红陶碗、泥质灰陶绳纹罐等。该遗址主要为研究当地龙山文化和周时期的文化面貌提供了重要资料。

二十六、赵家遗址

位于龙口市诸由观镇赵家村，遗址在村的西北，旁依一条无名小河，在河旁的二级阶地上。地理坐标东经120°39′37.2″，北纬37°39′23.9″，海拔43米。

遗址平面大体呈南北向长方形，分布范围较大。遗址东西各有一条现代道路，西侧有一小河道。遗址西侧为河道，东侧较为平坦。遗址南北长约120米，东西宽约100米，面积约1.25万平方米。台地稍有隆起，呈北高南低分布。土壤呈砂性，多见砂岩性基岩，呈浅红褐色。在遗址内零星可见陶片，据其形制与陶片特点判断为一处汉代遗址。遗址处多种有小麦，玉米，另有大量果树，在调查中还曾发现菱形纹墓砖，推测有汉代墓葬分布。该对探讨黄水河流域汉代遗址的分布及汉文化的内涵具有重要的意义。

二十七、洼南遗址

位于龙口市徐福镇洼南村。地理坐标东经120°24′43.5″，北纬37°40′08.9″，海拔6米。

遗址地势低洼，分布在泳汶河旁，大体呈长方形，原遗址面积很大，东西长大约480米，南北宽525米，面积约15.9万平方米。由于历年取土烧窑和建房，再加上自然力的长久吞噬，使遗址损坏严重，现仅保存的部分遗址的边缘地带，面积不到1万平方米。发现大量的带有各种纹饰的罐、豆等器型的残陶片和汉代花纹砖，是典型的东周至汉代时代的聚落遗址。该遗址的发现对了解黄水河流域的东周、汉时期聚落布局提供了有价值资料。

二十八、赵刘遗址

位于龙口市诸由观镇赵刘村，距村西南约1千米处。地理坐标东经120°35′55″，北纬37°39′52″，海拔22米。

黄水河北岸200米处二级阶地上，东边有一小工厂，西北是丛林水泥厂。地势东高西低，属于山前平原地带遗址南北长约90米，东西宽约70米，面积约0.6万平方米。通过采集陶片的初步判断，确定该遗址年代为周代。遗址现在位于两排果树田和农田内，南部有一处小树林，树林后有修河边堤坝挖成的深沟。遗址内零星分布周代陶片，纹饰以绳纹为主，可辨器型有罐、鬲、钵等。该遗址的对于研究当地周时人们的生活状况具有意义。

二十九、上庄马家遗址

位于龙口市诸由观镇上庄马家村东。地理坐标东经120°37′01.9″，北纬37°40′01″，海拔40米。

遗址周围地势平缓，东北部为丘陵，遗址位于公路东侧。遗址范围南部有一白色看守果园用小房，分布于阶梯状农田内。遗址南北长约100米，东西宽约50米，面积大约0.5万平方米。遗址范围内零星分布汉代陶片及花纹砖，推测有墓葬分布。遗址保存情况一般，在遗址范围内种植有果树，部分为耕地种植有小麦、玉米等作物。上庄马家遗址的发现为研究当地汉代人的生活提供了资料。

三十、程家遗址

位于龙口市诸由观镇程家村，距村东南1千米处，黄水河北岸300米的二级阶地上。地理坐标东经120°35′26.0″，北纬37°40′11.0″，海拔24米。

遗址西南200米为丛林水泥厂，南有修河边堤坝形成的深沟。遗址南北长约80米，东西宽约45米，面积约0.3万平方米。遗址范围内零星分布有一些陶片，陶片多有绳纹，具有周代陶片的典型特征。遗址内种植有果树及小麦等，对遗址破坏程度不大。土壤为黄土，地势平坦，该遗址保存情况一般。该遗址对了解和研究当地周代聚落的分布具有一定价值。

三十一、西张家遗址

位于龙口市诸由观镇西张家村，在村东北角的农田内，部分区域可延伸至村西北角。地理坐标东经120°35′09″，北纬37°40′52″，海拔23米。

遗址位于丛林寺河南岸，西端有一乡间土路，北部有一工厂，东北侧有一土丘，地势较为平坦。遗址南北长约140米，东西宽约60米，面积大约为0.84万平方米，遗址内零星分布周代绳纹陶片、器物足部以及汉代菱形花纹墓砖；遗址东北侧有村民取土出现的凹坑。遗址范围内种植有小麦、果树等农作物。在遗址东南部靠近程家村附近采集到周代、汉代陶片，推测遗址范围可能更大。西张家遗址的发现对了解当地的周、汉聚落遗址的分布有重要意义。

三十二、前妙果遗址

位于龙口市诸由观镇前妙果村，在村东南角的农田内。地理坐标东经120°33′04.0″，北纬37°40′54.0″，海拔15米。

遗址位于绛水河东岸阶地上，烟潍公路右村东南而过，西面有一乡间土路，西南角有高压线塔。全村境域处黄水河、龙湾河、绛水河三河环抱之中，地势平坦。遗址范围南北宽约100米，东西长约100米，面积大约为1万平方米。遗址范围内种植葡萄树以及小麦，葡萄园内常年挖沟施肥，在葡萄园内发现有零星的龙山时代黑陶片以及汉代陶片，在地头发现有汉代菱形花纹墓砖。据当地果农介绍，栽树沟深度大约在1米左右，在1米左右已到墓葬墓底部深度，现在的墓葬所在区域已遭到破坏。该遗址的发现对了解黄水河流域龙山文化分布提供了重要资料。

三十三、黄城集遗址

位于龙口市石良镇黄城集村，位于村西北端。村南有黄城集河注入黄水河。地理坐标东经120°39′34.7″，北纬37°37′52.7″，海拔35米。

古城遗址北临荆家河，中部有公路穿过，村庄地处平原，南部为居民区及小部分农田；据龙口本地县志记载，该古城遗址在北齐后因洪水冲击而遭损坏（尹继美，1871：1，2，9）。长约1550米，宽约1500米，面积约2.31平方千米。地面已无城址痕迹。地面采集有陶片、瓦片、汉砖等，其中，陶片多为夹砂或泥质绳纹灰陶；汉砖多带菱形纹饰。据史料所载，该遗址为古黄城所在地。其范围可以大致从采集陶片的范围来推测。陶片年代为战国至汉代。该遗址对研究黄水河流域古代城址的发展以及本地区历史都具有重大意义。

三十四、冷王遗址

位于龙口市诸由观镇冷王村，距村东北900米的果园内，处于一自然隆起的岗地上。地理坐标东经120°30′48.0″，北纬37°42′16.0″，海拔25米。

遗址西界为通海公路，南面为一水泥质水渠。冷王村全村地势北高南低，遗址位于北部较高处；地势较为平坦。遗址范围内有一东西向田间土路。另外遗址西侧公路的修建对遗址也造成部分破坏。遗址南北长约75米，东西宽约40米，面积大约为0.3万平方米。在遗址附近区域大量种植果树，在果园内零星散布汉代瓦片和部分陶片。该遗址对了解当地的汉代聚落布局提供了新的资料。

三十五、大金家遗址

位于石良镇大金家村的村西部，为黄水河旁的二级阶地。地理坐标东经120°38′03.3″，北纬37°37′13.0″，海拔32米。

遗址西侧为黄水河，黄水河西侧有公路通过。遗址东临大金家村，西临黄水河，南北约120米，东西约80米，面积约0.96万平方米。遗址保存现状不良。在遗址地表可采集到汉代瓦、砖残块。它对研究黄水河流域汉代遗存的历史具有重要价值。

三十六、洽泊遗址

位于龙口市兰高镇洽泊村，距村东北500米处。地理坐标东经120°35′24.7″，北纬37°39′26.3″，海拔27米。

洽泊村南邻镇政府1千米，北至陈家庄0.5千米，东至黄水河2千米与诸由观镇魏家村隔河相望。洽泊村北有黄水河流经，村南有公路穿过，洽泊遗址东西长252米，南北宽134米，面积约为3.38万平方米。遗址范围内采集遗物较为丰富，发现有夹砂灰陶残片若干、包括陶纺轮、圈足、口沿等。据陶片初步判断洽泊遗址年代为汉代。该洽泊遗址的发现为黄水河流域汉代遗址的研究提供了新的资料。

三十七、四平遗址

位于龙口市兰高镇四平村，距村东北1千米处。地理坐标东经120°35′57.5″，北纬37°39′05.7″，海拔30米。

该遗址地处鸦鹊河西岸，遗址范围内为一片树林。西0.5千米与兰高村接壤，西北1千米与洽泊村毗邻，南距后李村1千米。四平村境属丘陵平原间接地带，排水从南往北。四平遗址南北长200米，东西宽110米，面积约2.2万平方米。遗址内发现有泥质灰陶豆盘、豆柄、绳纹陶片等遗物。系一处周、汉代遗址。该为研究当地周、汉代聚落遗存的分布提供了新的资料。

三十八、侧高遗址

位于龙口市兰高镇侧高村村北，威乌高速公路以南。地理坐标东经120°38′17.7″，北纬37°38′04.1″，海拔30米。

遗址南北长约253米，东西宽约124米，面积达3.1万平方米。遗址西侧为高地，遗址本身以平地为主，地形起伏较小。在遗址之上采集有陶器口沿残片、绳纹陶片以及砖、瓦残块等。陶质以泥质陶为主，陶色多为灰色，可辨器形有豆盘、陶盆等。其中，以东周文化占主体。它对了解该地区在东周至汉代时期的聚落形态及其更替等具有重要价值。

第三节　黄水河流域聚落形态的演变及其有关问题

在上述38处遗址中（表Ⅰ.7.10），除我们调查过的遗址外，其他未经我们本次调查的基本以全国第三次文物普查（2007～2011年）的资料为依据。其中一些遗址我们此次调查没有采集到遗物，所以关于时代及遗址面积等信息就依普查的资料。可能有些遗址的认识不甚全面，我们希望在今后的工作中能够弥补这个缺憾。

从时间上讲，整个黄水河流域遗址中时代最早的是兰高镇小莱山旧石器溶洞遗址。新石器时期的遗址主要包括邱家庄一期文化和龙山文化遗址，其中较典型的有石良镇东羔遗址、鲁家沟遗址，蓬莱南王绪遗址，徐福镇唐家遗址、乾山遗址，褚由观镇前妙果遗址，北马镇李家遗址，江东镇邵家遗址等。从分布规律中我们可以看到，新石器时期的遗址基本位于黄水河及支流的一级台地上。这里往往形成了相对开阔的冲积平原，为其生存创造了良好的条件，从而形成了比较独立和规模较小的聚落。

黄水河流域属于邱家庄一期文化的遗址数量较少。这些遗址其文化性质比较单纯，堆积一般相对也比较薄。虽然各个遗址在漫长的历史岁月中受到来自不同方面和不同程度的破坏，但每个遗址总体上受破坏的概率大体是一致的。也就是说我们今天所看到的遗址规模和现状，应当是当时实际面积的一种反映或一种折射，应该作为我们探讨聚落规模的一种依据。当然有些人为破坏比较严重的遗址我们会给予区别对待。

关于邱家庄一期文化发展水平和聚落体系，从目前掌握的一些资料观察，我们比较倾向于这样一种观点：即半岛地区独特的自然环境和地貌，决定了文化发展的缓慢性。同时由于与外界交往的较少，所以形成了具有独特文化面貌和地方特色考古学文化。邱家庄一期文化的遗址主要分布于相对低海拔近海的漫滩地带。在遗址附近往往有河流经过，周围的地势相对比较开阔，遗址多集中在地理位置比较优越的地区。由于遗址分布相对比较分散，所以可以判断出人们获取食物的范围较大，这也表明这里的食物来源不甚丰富。

龙山文化的聚落遗存没有发生根本性变化，龙山文化的聚落体系基本延续了邱家庄一期文化时期的模式。即有没有一处规模和位置都处于绝对地位的大型遗址作为中心聚落存在。大部分聚落处于一种分散式、小规模的点式分布。在人口的数量上和遗址的规模上与邱家庄一期文化时期相比也都没有本质上的变化。所不同的是遗址分布范围有所扩展，可能龙山文化先民已经脱离了单纯依赖捕捞和采集的经济模式。与山东半岛内陆地区的大汶口文化和龙山文化有很大的区别，黄水河流域龙山文化的发展表现出缓慢性和滞后性。

总之，在邱家庄一期文化和龙山文化阶段整个流域内没有大型或中心聚落。遗址的规模相对较小，没有超过5万平方米的。这一现象一直延续到岳石文化阶段。

在上述38处遗址中（表Ⅰ.7.10），有25处青铜时代遗址。其中有2处含有岳石文化遗存，

23处含有周文化时期遗存。这些遗址和墓地基本上位于归城遗址周围20千米范围内，这就从聚落考古的角度为研究归城遗址的等级及与周围遗存的关系提供了关键材料，可以认为周代无疑是黄水河流域聚落发展的一个高峰期。

这一时期黄水河流域不但遗址数量急剧增加，而且聚落体系变得十分复杂。这个体系中出现了大型和具有中心性质的城址，如归城。同时有遗址出现分散分布，并逐渐向黄水河支流的方向发展的趋势，形成规模不等的城址。特别是以归城遗址为中心的聚落群分布在自然条件相对较好的胶东半岛莱山北麓。而那些相对独立的小聚落分布于黄水河的一些支流上，但这些遗址的数量和规模远不及归城遗址聚落群。总之，黄水河流域聚落体系中形成了单一的具有统治力和影响力的中心城址。另外，在一些遗存中我们还能看到明显具有地方特色的文化现象。上述情况一直延续到春秋晚期，随着在莱国被齐所灭，其中心地位也随之消失。

到了汉代，从遗址的数量和分布来看，该流域聚落分布已经较为密集，基本达到内陆地区的水平。在黄水河的支流如荆家河、凉水河、鸦鹊河等河流沿岸，汉代遗址分布较为密集。在泳汶河、南栾河和北马南河沿岸，尤其是南部山区与北部平原的过渡地带，遗址分布十分密集，并且有中心城址的存在。

以上，我们着重探讨了黄水河流域邱家庄一期文化、龙山文化及周代文化遗址的演变，分析了其聚落遗存的时空分布关系。黄水河流域的聚落考古的研究，主要依据我们调查所得资料和第三次文物普查的资料。通过对这些材料的分析，获得了一些新的认识。当然这些认识是初步的和不全面的，我们希望今后会有更丰富的信息和资料的发现来支持和印证上述观点。

参考文献

唐禄庭，姜国钧，1989：山东黄县东营周家村西周残墓清理简报. 海岱考古，1：314-319.

王道新，1934：黄县志稿，山东省博物馆藏，1934年稿本，第14卷.

王锡平，唐禄庭，1986：山东黄县庄头西周墓清理简报. 文物，8：69-72.

尹继美，1871：黄县志，14卷，（清）同治十年.

Yuan, Jing, Liang Zhonghe, Wu Yun, and Jia Xiaobing, 2002. “Shell Mounds in the Jiaodong Peninsula: A Study in Environmental Archaeology,” *The Journal of East Asian Archaeology* 4.1-4: 1-26.

曾毅公，1940：山东金文集存，1940.

中国社会科学院考古研究所，1999：胶东半岛贝丘遗址环境考古. 北京：社科文献出版社.

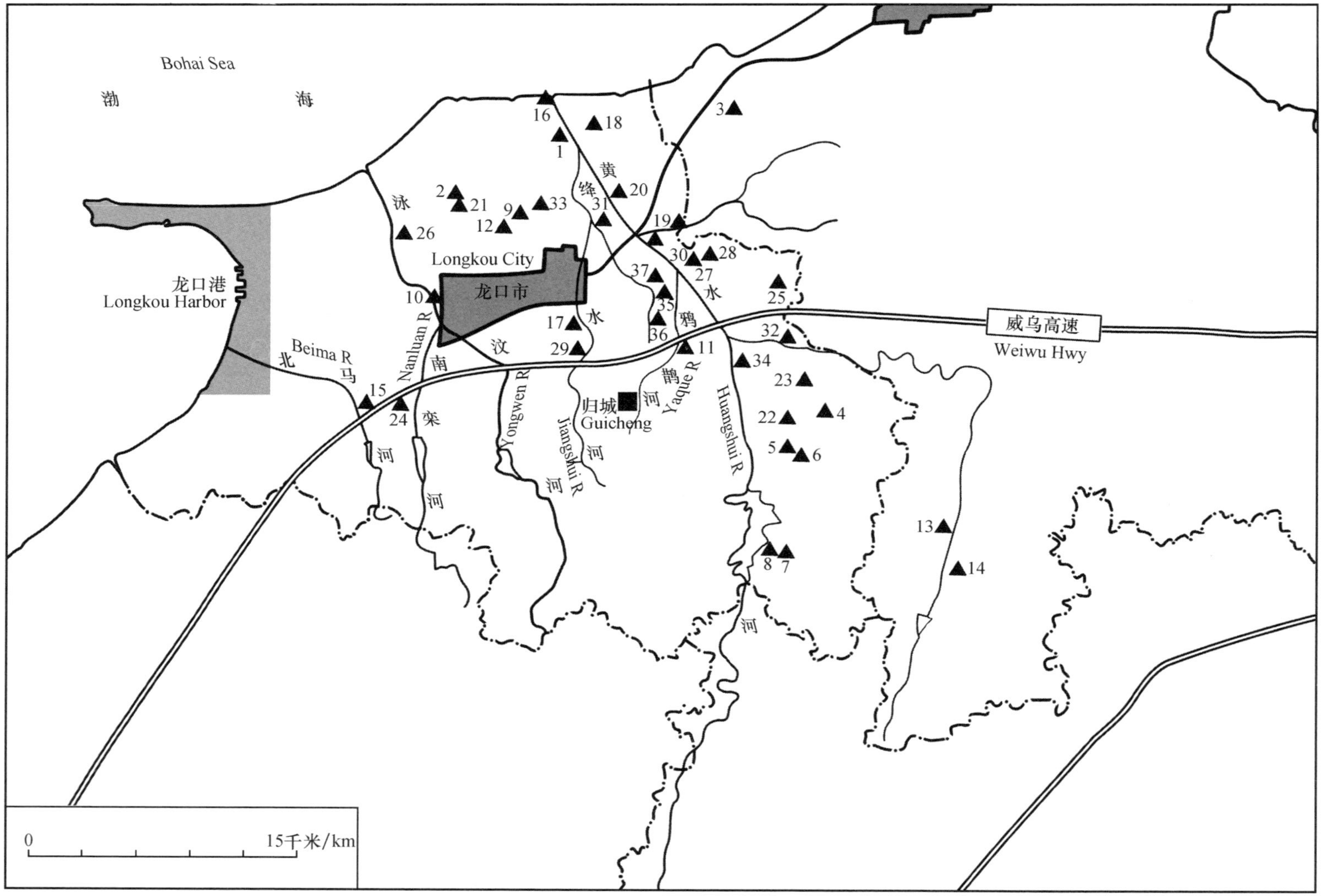

地图Ⅰ.7.1　黄水河流域遗址分布图

1. 东羔　2. 唐家　3. 南王绪　4. 庄头　5. 集前赵家　6. 东营周家　7. 鲁家沟遗址　8. 鲁家沟墓地　9. 乾山　10. 张郑家　11. 小莱山溶洞　12. 徐乡故城　13. 村里集城址　14. 村里集墓地　15. 楼子庄　16. 黄河营古港　17. 邵家　18. 姚家包袱地　19. 郝家　20. 后柞杨　21. 唐家集　22. 下河头　23. 平里院　24. 李家　25. 赵家　26. 洼南　27. 赵刘　28. 上庄马家　29. 程家　30. 西张家　31. 前秒果　32. 黄城集　33. 冷王　34. 大金家　35. 四平　36. 侧高　37. 洽泊

Map Ⅰ.7.1　Distribution of Archaeological Sites in the Huangshui River Basin.

1. Donggao　2. Tangjia　3. Nanwangxu　4. Zhuangtou　5. Jiqian Zhaojia　6. Dongying Zhoujia　7. Lujiagou site　8. Lujiagou cemetery　9. Qianshan　10. Zhangzhengjia　11. Xiaolaishan cave　12. Xuxiang Old City site　13. Cunliji site　14. Cunliji cemetery　15. Louzizhuang　16. Huangheying old port site　17. Shaojia　18. Yaojia Baofudi　19. Haojia　20. Houzuoyang　21. Tangjiaji　22. Xiahetou　23. Pingliyuan　24. Lijia　25. Zhaojia　26. Wa'nan　27. Zhaoliu　28. Shangzhuang Majia　29. Chengjia　30. Xizhangjia　31. Qianmiaoguo　32. Huangchengji　33. Lengwang　34. Dajinjia　35. Siping　36. Cegao　37. Qiabo

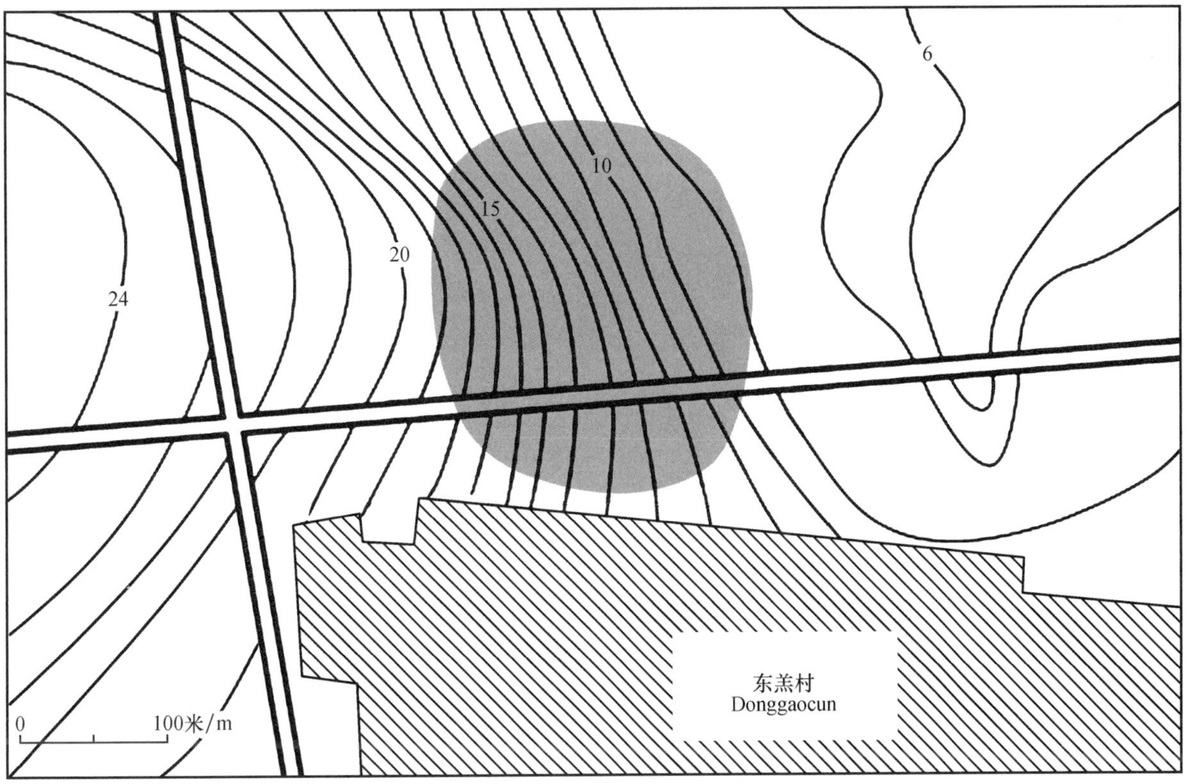

图Ⅰ.7.1　东羔遗址

Figure Ⅰ.7.1　The Donggao site.

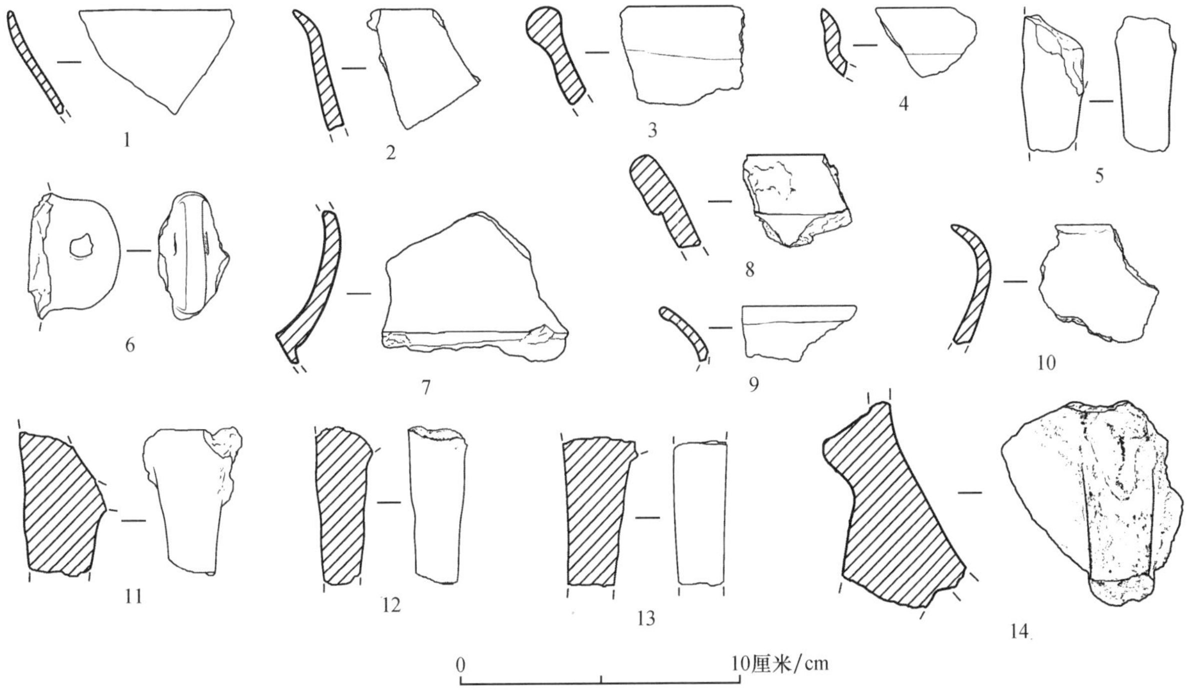

图Ⅰ.7.2　东羔遗址发现遗物

Figure Ⅰ.7.2　Artifacts from the Donggao site.

表Ⅰ.7.1　东蒿遗址发现遗物统计表

Table Ⅰ.7.1　Artifacts from the Donggao site

序号 Number on Fig. Ⅰ.7.3	标本号 Collection number	器物名称 Artifact name	出土时间 Excavation date	位置 Location	所属类型 Types	尺寸（厘米） Size (cm)	特点描述 Description of features
1	10SLD 采：10	钵 *Bo* bowl	2010-10	地表采集 Surface collection		M: 27 H: 3.6 T: 0.35	泥质灰黑陶。口微敛，壁斜直。器内壁经打磨光亮。 Greyish-black clay pottery; mouth slightly converging, oblique wall; shiny, burnished inner wall.
2	10SLD 采：12	钵 *Bo* bowl	2010-10	地表采集 Surface collection		M: 25 H: 4.2 T: 0.6	泥质灰褐陶。侈口，尖唇，壁斜直。器内壁经打磨光亮。 Greyish-brown clay pottery; wide mouth, sharp lip, wall oblique; shiny, burnished inner wall.
3	10SLD 采：8	盆 *Pen* basin	2010-10	地表采集 Surface collection		M: 37 H: 3.4 T: 0.8	夹砂红陶。侈口，圆唇，斜直壁，较厚，底残。内壁经打磨光滑。 Coarse red tempered pottery; wide mouth, round lip, oblique-straight wall, relatively thick, bottom broken; inner wall burnished smooth.
4	10SLD 采：14	钵 *Bo* bowl	2010-10	地表采集 Surface collection		M: 23 H: 2.5 T: 0.5	泥质红褐陶。侈口，尖唇，腹微折。器内壁经打磨光亮。 Reddish-brown clay pottery; wide mouth, sharp lip, belly folds slightly; shiny, burnished inner wall .
5	10SLD 采：5	鼎足 *Ding* tripod foot	2010-10	地表采集 Surface collection		L: 4.67 W: 2.1 T: 1.7	圆锥形。红陶，胎内掺和有非常细小的云母片，足根正面有一浅按窝，足尖残。断面呈圆形。 Conical. Red pottery, tempered with very fine mica, the front face of the upper end of the foot has a dent, lower end of foot broken; circular in cross-section.
6	10SLD 采：7	壶 *Hu* vase	2010-10	地表采集 Surface collection		H: 4.4 W: 3.25 T: 0.7	夹砂红褐陶。耳呈鸟头形，中部钻一孔。 Coarse reddish-brown pottery; bird head shaped handle with a hole drilled in the middle.
7	10SLD 采：1	鼎 *Ding* tripod	2010-10	地表采集 Surface collection		L: 5.2 W: 6.6 T: 0.65	橙黄陶，胎内掺和有细小的云母片，火候较高。器表经打磨。侈口、折腹，口、腹略残。 Orange-yellow pottery; tempered with fine mica pieces, fired at high temperature; vessel burnished; wide mouth, belly folds. Mouth and belly slightly broken.
8	10SLD 采：9	盆 *Pen* basin	2010-10	地表采集 Surface collection		H: 2.6 W: 4 T: 0.85	夹砂红褐陶。侈口，沿外折成方圆唇，壁厚，底残。器内壁经打磨光滑。 Coarse reddish-brown pottery; wide mouth, rim folds outwards to form square-round lip, thick wall, broken bottom; burnished smooth inner wall.
9	10SLD 采：13	罐 *Guan* jar	2010-10	地表采集 Surface collection		M: 28.4 H: 2 T: 0.4	夹砂红褐陶。侈口，圆唇，折沿，下部残。 Coarse reddish-brown pottery; wide mouth, round lips, folded rim, broken on the bottom.
10	10SLD 采：11	罐 *Guan* jar	2010-10	地表采集 Surface collection		M: 16.7 H: 4.1 T: 0.6	夹砂灰褐陶。侈口，尖唇，鼓腹，下部残。 Coarse greyish-brown pottery; wide mouth, sharp lips, bulging belly, bottom broken.
11	10SLD 采：3	鼎足 *Ding* tripod foot	2010-10	地表采集 Surface collection		L: 5 W: 2.7 T: 2	圆锥形。红褐陶，胎内掺和有云母片。足尖略残，足断面呈椭圆形。 Conical. Reddish-brown pottery, tempered with mica pieces; broken foot, slightly oval in cross-section.

续表

序号 Number on Fig. Ⅰ.7.3	标本号 Collection number	器物名称 Artifact name	出土时间 Excavation date	位置 Location	所属类型 Types	尺寸（厘米） Size (cm)	特点描述 Description of features
12	10SLD采：6	鼎足 *Ding* tripod foot	2010-10	地表采集 Surface collection		L: 5.4 W: 1.9 T: 1.8	圆锥形。夹砂灰褐陶，足尖残，断面呈圆形。 Conical. Coarse greyish-brown pottery, foot end broken, circular in cross-section.
13	10SLD采：4	鼎足 *Ding* tripod foot	2010-10	地表采集 Surface collection		L: 4.9 W: 1.85 T: 2.1	方锥形。夹砂红褐陶，足面扁平，足尖残。 Tapered rectangle. Coarse reddish-brown pottery, flat-bottomed foot. Broken end of leg.
14	10SLD采：2	鼎足 *Ding* tripod foot	2010-10	地表采集 Surface collection		L: 7.2 W: 6.2 T: 3.5	方锥形。夹砂红褐陶，足正面扁平，足根饰有一三角形乳突，足尖残。 Square and tapering. Coarse reddish-brown pottery, flat outer face of foot, base of foot decorated with a triangular nipple, end of foot broken.

尺寸标志：L=长度；H=高度；W=宽度；D=直径；R=半径；M=口径；B=底径；T=厚度；d=深度；h=孔径。

Measurements: L=length; H=height; W=width; D=diameter; R=radius; M=mouth diameter; B=bottom diameter; T=thickness; d=depth; h=hole diameter.

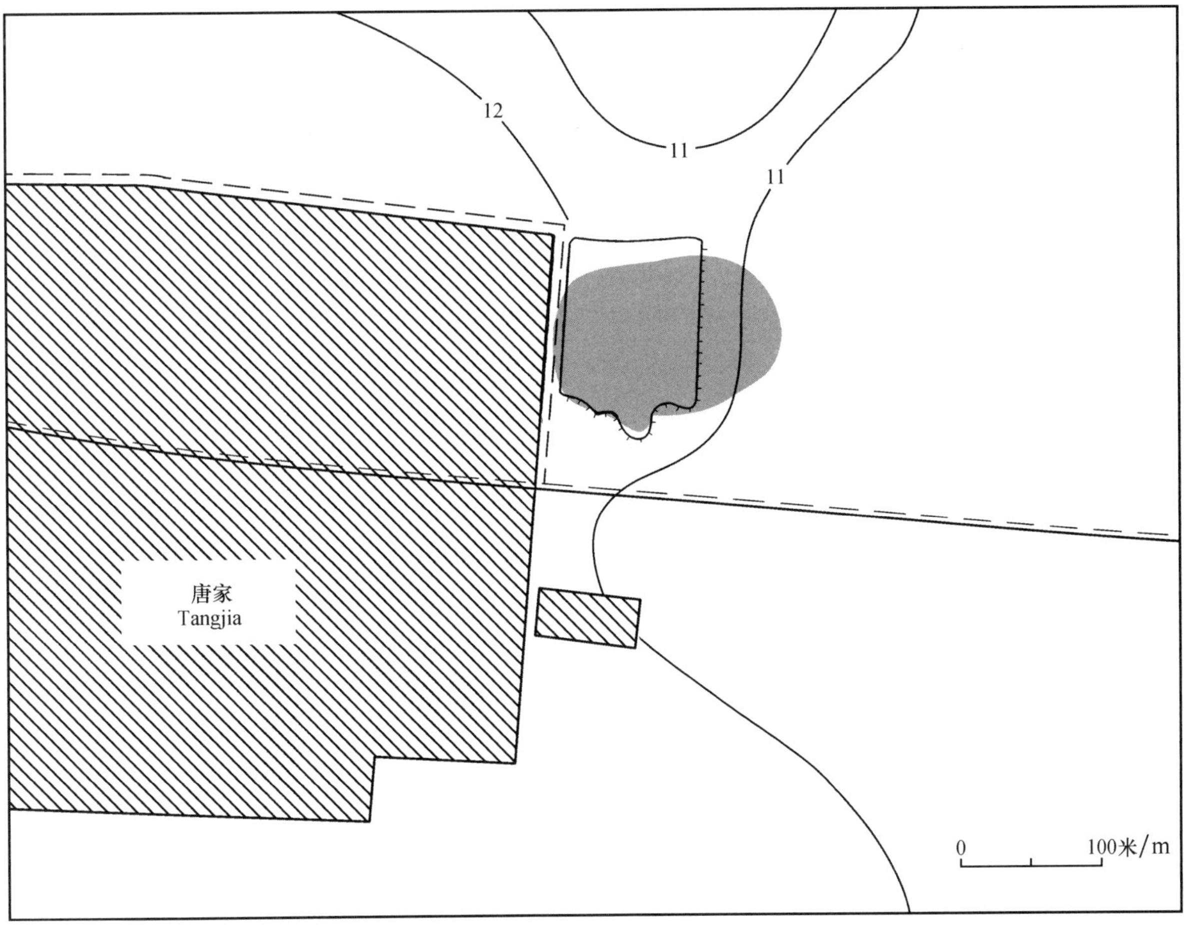

图Ⅰ.7.3　唐家遗址

Figure Ⅰ.7.3　The Tangjia site.

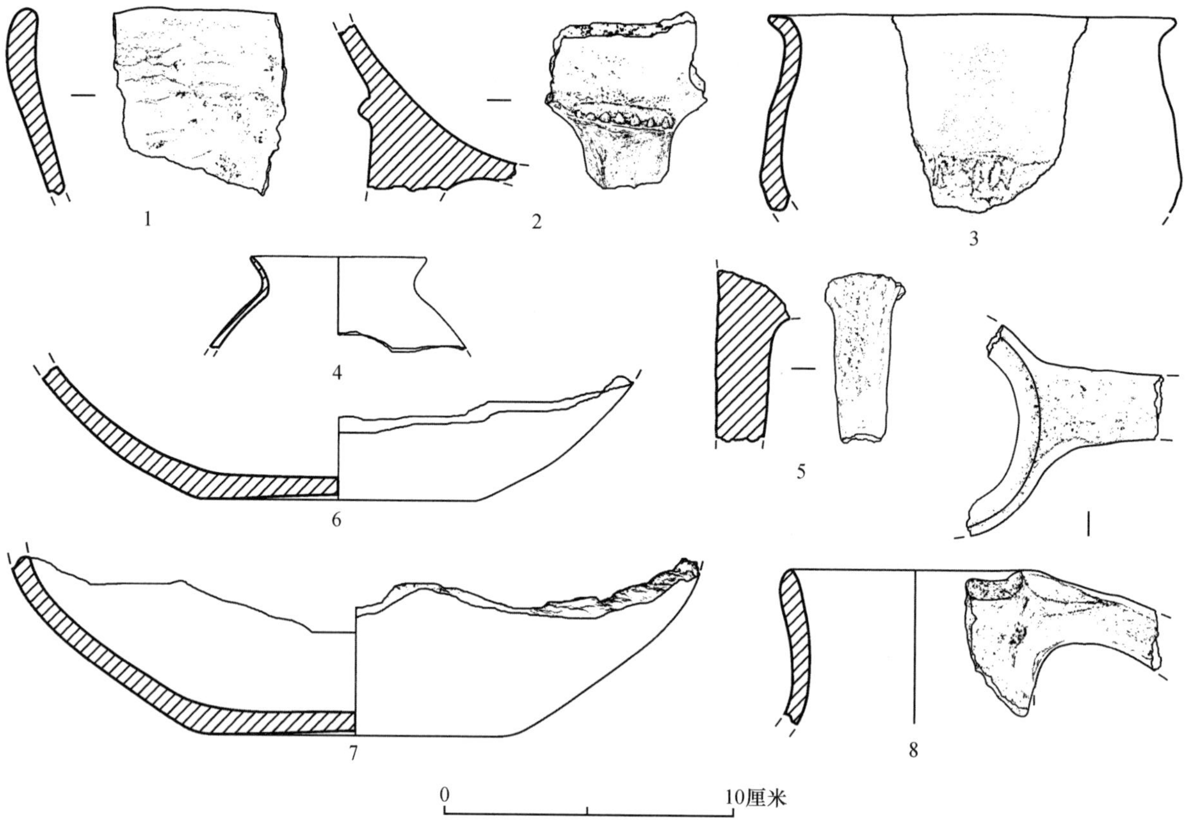

图 I.7.4　唐家遗址发现遗物

Figure Ⅰ.7.4　Artifacts from the Tangjia site.

表Ⅰ.7.2　唐家遗址发现遗物统计表

Table Ⅰ.7.2　Artifacts from the Tangjia site

序号 Number on Fig. Ⅰ.7.5	标本号 Excavation number	器物名称 Artifact name	出土时间 Excavation date	位置 Location	所属类型 Types	尺寸（厘米）Size (cm)	特点描述 Description of features
1	10SLT 采：06	钵 *Bo* bowl	2010-11	地表采集 Surface collection		M: 43 H: 6.2 T: 1.0	夹砂红褐陶。口微敛，圆唇，腹壁斜直，器壁厚，下部残。 Coarse reddish-brown pottery; mouth slightly converging, round lips, oblique belly, thick wall; bottom broken.
2	10SLT 采：05	鼎 *Ding* tripod	2010-11	地表采集 Surface collection		L: 6 W: 5.6 T: 0.8	夹砂灰褐陶。圆锥形，足尖略残。足根饰按压的附加堆纹。 Coarse greyish-brown pottery; conical, slightly broken end; upper end decorated with hand-pressed applique.
3	10SLT 采：02	鼎 *Ding* tripod	2010-11	地表采集 Surface collection		M: 14 H: 6.6 T: 0.8	鼎口沿。夹砂灰陶，口微敛，沿外折，尖唇。腹部饰一周按压附加堆纹。 *Ding* rim. Coarse grey pottery; mouth slightly converging, rim folds outward, sharp lip; belly decorated with hand-pressed appliqué.
4	10SLT 采：01	罐 *Guan* jar	2010-11	地表采集 Surface collection		M: 6.2 H: 3.2 T: 0.3	夹砂黑褐陶。侈口、圆唇、鼓腹。素面，器表经打磨光亮。 Coarse dark brown pottery; wide-open mouth, round lip, bulging belly; plain, shiny, burnished exterior.

续表

序号 Number on Fig. Ⅰ.7.5	标本号 Excavation number	器物名称 Artifact name	出土时间 Excavation date	位置 Location	所属类型 Types	尺寸（厘米）Size (cm)	特点描述 Description of features
5	10SLT 采：04	鼎足 Foot of *ding* tripod	2010-11	地表采集 Surface collection		L: 5.7 W: 1.9 T: 1.9	夹砂灰陶。圆锥形，足细长，尖略残。Coarse grey pottery; conical, foot slender, point slightly broken.
6	10SLT 采：07	罐 *Guan* jar	2010-11	地表采集 Surface collection		B: 9.6 H: 4.2 T: 0.85	罐底。泥质灰褐陶。素面，底微内凹。器表经打磨光滑。Bottom of a ceramic *guan* jar. Greyish-brown clay. Plain, slightly concave bottom; outer surface burnished smooth.
7	10SLT 采：08	罐 *Guan* jar	2010-11	地表采集 Surface collection		B: 10.4 H: 6.0 T: 0.75	罐底。夹砂红褐陶。平底。素面，器表经打磨光滑。Bottom of a *guan* jar. Coarse reddish-brown pottery. Flat bottom, plain, Outer surface polished smooth.
8	10SLT 采：03	罐 *Guan* jar	2010-11	地表采集 Surface collection		M: 8.4 H: 5.22 T: 0.7	夹砂橙黄陶，胎内掺和有云母片。直口，环形把。素面。Coarse orange pottery; tempered with mica pieces; straight mouth, ring-shaped handle, plain surface.

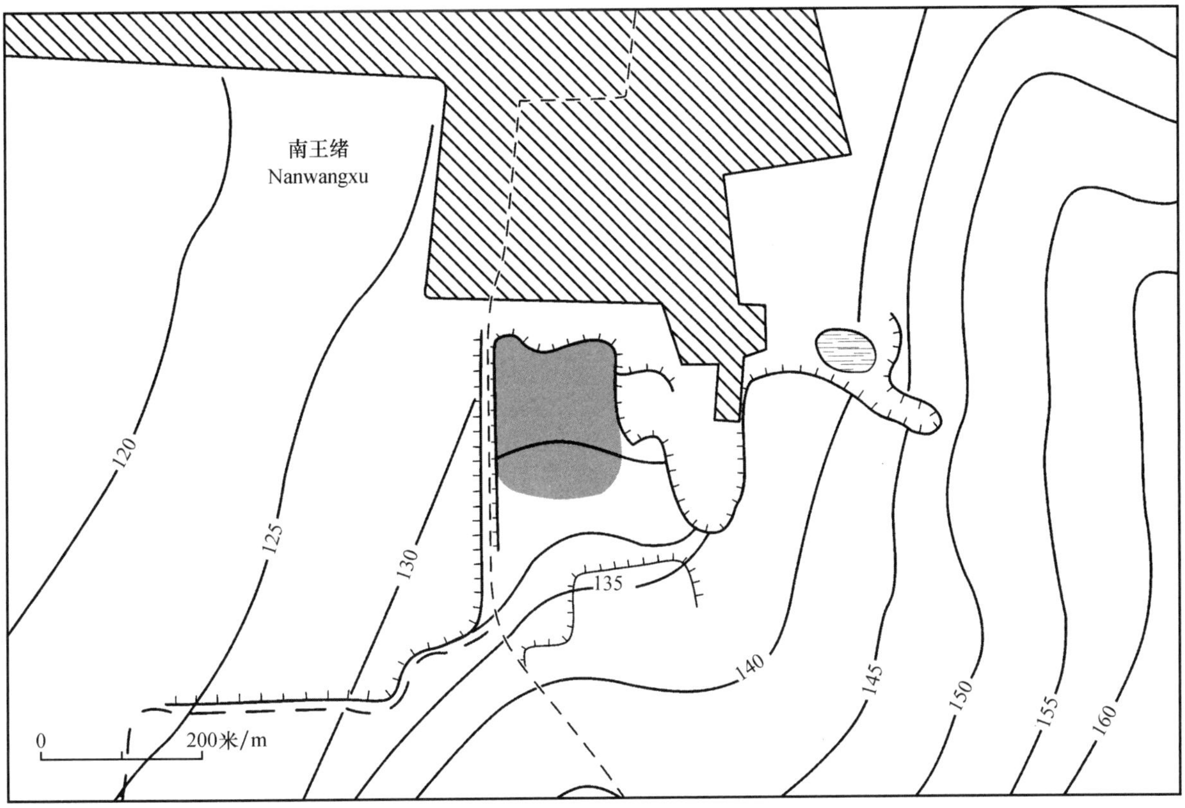

图Ⅰ.7.5　南王绪遗址

Figure Ⅰ.7.5　The Nanwangxu site.

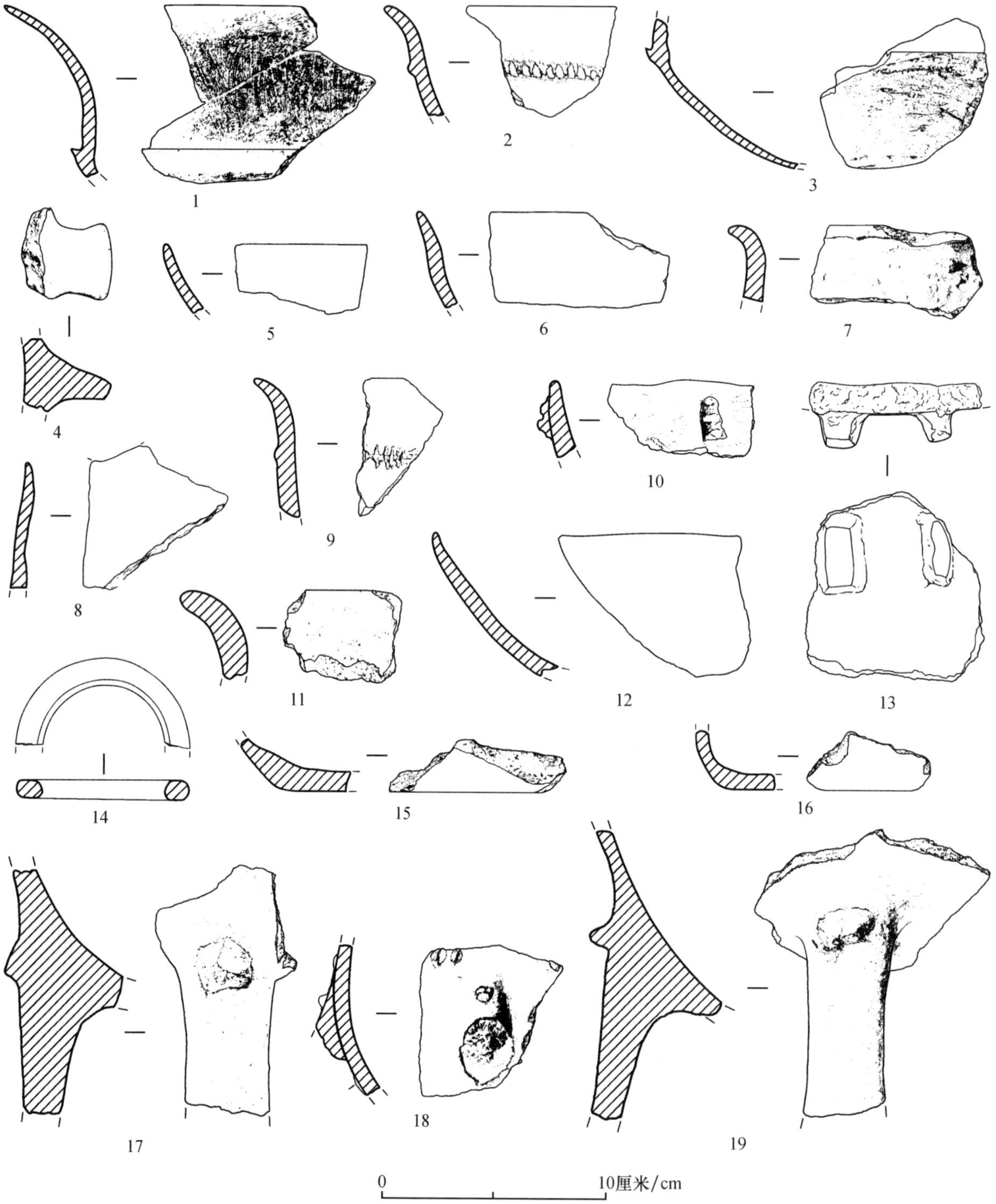

图Ⅰ.7.6　南王绪遗址发现遗物

Figure Ⅰ.7.6　Artifacts from the Nanwangxu site.

表 Ⅰ.7.3 南王绪遗址发现遗物统计表

Table Ⅰ.7.3 Artifacts from the Nanwangxu site

序号 Number on Fig. Ⅰ.7.7	标本号 Excavation number	器物名称 Artifact name	出土时间 Excavation date	位置 Location	所属类型 Types	尺寸（厘米）Size (cm)	特点描述 Description of features
1	10SLN 采：4	釜形鼎 *Fu*-shaped *ding* tripod	2010-11	地表采集 Surface collection		M: 22 H: 7.7 T: 0.5	夹砂灰褐陶，胎内掺和云母片。侈口，尖唇，折腹。腹底部有凸棱一周。Coarse greyish-brown pottery, tempered with mica pieces; wide-open mouth, sharp lips, abdomen folds; bottom of vessel belly has a raised ridge ring.
2	10SLN 采：6	罐形鼎 *Guan* jar-shaped *ding* tripod	2010-11	地表采集 Surface collection		M: 20 H: 4.8 T: 6.5	灰褐陶，胎内掺和云母片。侈口，圆唇，腹微鼓。腹上部饰一周的附加堆纹，内壁经打磨光滑。Greyish-brown pottery, tempered with mica pieces; wide-open mouth, rounded lips, belly slightly bulging; upper belly decorated with appliqué, inner wall burnished smooth.
3	10SLN 采：5	釜形鼎 *Fu*-shaped *ding* tripod	2010-11	地表采集 Surface collection		H: 6.6 W: 7.4 T: 0.4	灰褐陶，胎内掺和云母片。口残，折腹。腹下部饰凸棱一周。Greyish-brown pottery, tempered with mica; broken mouth, belly folds; belly decorated with a raised ridge ring.
4	10SLN 采：7	双耳罐 *Guan* jar with two handles	2010-11	地表采集 Surface collection		L: 4.0 W: 3.3 T: 1.25	夹砂褐陶。为罐的耳，扁平。Coarse brown pottery; ear of a *guan* jar, flat.
5	10SLN 采：8	钵 *Bo* bowl	2010-11	地表采集 Surface collection		M: 26.2 H: 3.1 T: 0.4	泥质褐陶，素面磨光。口微敛，圆唇，壁斜直，底残。Brown clay, plain burnished surface; mouth slightly converging, rounded lip, wall oblique, bottom broken.
6	10SLN 采：9	盆 *Pen* basin	2010-11	地表采集 Surface collection		M: 27 H: 4.0 T: 0.7	泥质黑褐陶。敞口，圆唇，外斜壁。内壁经打磨光亮，呈黑色。Dark brown clay; wide mouth, rounded lip, outward slanted wall; inner surface burnished shiny, black.
7	10SLN 采：10	盆形鼎 Basin-shaped *ding* tripod	2010-11	地表采集 Surface collection		M: 22 H: 4.1 T: 0.7	夹粗砂灰褐陶。侈口，圆唇，素面。Coarse Sandy greyish-brown pottery; wide-open mouth, rounded lip, plain surface.
8	10SLN 采：11	壶 *Hu* bottle	2010-11	地表采集 Surface collection		M: 3.5 H: 5.6 T: 0.6	泥质红陶。小口，器表经刮划光亮，内壁有明显泥条盘筑的痕迹。Reddish clay; small mouth, surface polished shiny by scraping, inner surface has obvious traces of the strips of clay used to build the vessel.
9	10SLN 采：12	罐形鼎 *Guan* jar-shaped *ding* tripod	2010-11	地表采集 Surface collection		M: 26.8 H: 6.0 T: 0.9	灰黑陶，胎内掺和有云母片。侈口，尖唇，腹微鼓。腹上部饰一周带刻划纹的附加堆纹，内壁经打磨光滑。Dark-gray pottery, inner surface contains mica pieces; wide-open mouth, sharp lip, belly slightly bulging; upper belly with a ring of appliqué carved with decorative patterns, inner wall polished smooth.
10	10SLN 采：13	钵 *Bo* bowl	2010-11	地表采集 Surface collection		M: 30.5 H: 3.4 T: 0.8	夹砂灰褐陶。斜直口，圆唇。沿外侧有竖饰附加堆纹，内壁呈黑色。Coarse greyish-brown pottery; oblique mouth, rounded lip, decorated along outer edge with added bumps, black inner surface.

续表

序号 Number on Fig. Ⅰ.7.7	标本号 Excavation number	器物名称 Artifact name	出土时间 Excavation date	位置 Location	所属类型 Types	尺寸（厘米） Size (cm)	特点描述 Description of features
11	10SLN 采：16	盆形鼎 Basin-shaped *ding* tripod	2010-11	地表采集 Surface collection		M: 31 H: 4.0 T: 1.2	夹粗砂灰陶，敞口，圆唇，折沿，素面。 Coarse grey pottery; open mouth, rounded lip, folded rim; plain.
12	10SLN 采：15	钵 *Bo* bowl	2010-11	地表采集 Surface collection		M: 25 H: 6.16 T: 0.65	泥质黄褐陶。素面、口微敛，圆唇，腹壁斜直，底残。内壁经打磨光亮，呈黑色。 Yellowish-brown clay; plain surface, mouth slightly converging, rounded lip, belly oblique, bottom broken; inner wall burnished shiny, black.
13	10SLN 采：14	双耳罐 Double-eared *guan* jar	2010-11	地表采集 Surface collection		H: 8.2 W: 7.9 T: 1.1	夹砂红褐陶。为桥形耳，耳残后经打磨平整后继续使用，器壁较厚。 Coarse reddish-brown pottery; bridge-shaped handle, back of handle was burnished and continued to be used after it broke off the vessel. Fairly thick wall.
14	10SLN 采：18	镯 *Zhuo* armband	2010-11	地表采集 Surface collection		D: 7.7 W: 1.25 T: 0.9	泥质黑陶。断面呈椭圆形。 Black clay pottery; oval in cross section.
15	10SLN 采：17	罐 *Guan* jar	2010-11	地表采集 Surface collection		B: 25 H: 2.3 T: 0.9	泥质红褐陶。平底。 Reddish brown clay; flat.
16	10SLN 采：19	罐 *Guan* jar	2010-11	地表采集 Surface collection		B: 8 H: 2.6 T: 0.7	夹砂红褐陶。平底。 Coarse reddish-brown pottery; flat-bottomed.
17	10SLN 采：3	凿形鼎足 Chisel-shaped *ding* foot	2010-11	地表采集 Surface collection		L: 10.8 W: 3.85 T: 2.7	夹砂灰褐陶。足呈扁凿形，尖略残。足根部饰一三角形泥突，内壁打磨光滑，呈黑色。 Coarse greyish-brown pottery; slightly chisel – shaped foot with a broken tip, base of the foot decorated with triangular clay bumps; inner wall burnished smooth, black.
18	10SLN 采：2	锥形鼎足 Awl-shaped *ding* foot	2010-11	地表采集 Surface collection		L: 6.6 W: 6.25 T: 0.7	灰褐陶，胎内掺和有滑石粉。足残，足根部饰一泥突。 Greyish-brown pottery, inner surface contains talc powder; foot broken, base of foot decorated with one clay bump.
19	10SLN 采：1	凿形鼎足 Chisel-shaped *ding* foot	2010-11	地表采集 Surface collection		L: 12.5 W: 3.4 T: 2.4	夹砂灰陶。足呈窄长扁凿形，尖略残。足根部饰一三角形泥突，内壁经打磨光亮，呈黑色。 Coarse grey pottery; foot elongated into flat chisel shape, point slightly broken; foot base decorated with a single triangular clay bump, inner wall burnished shiny, black.

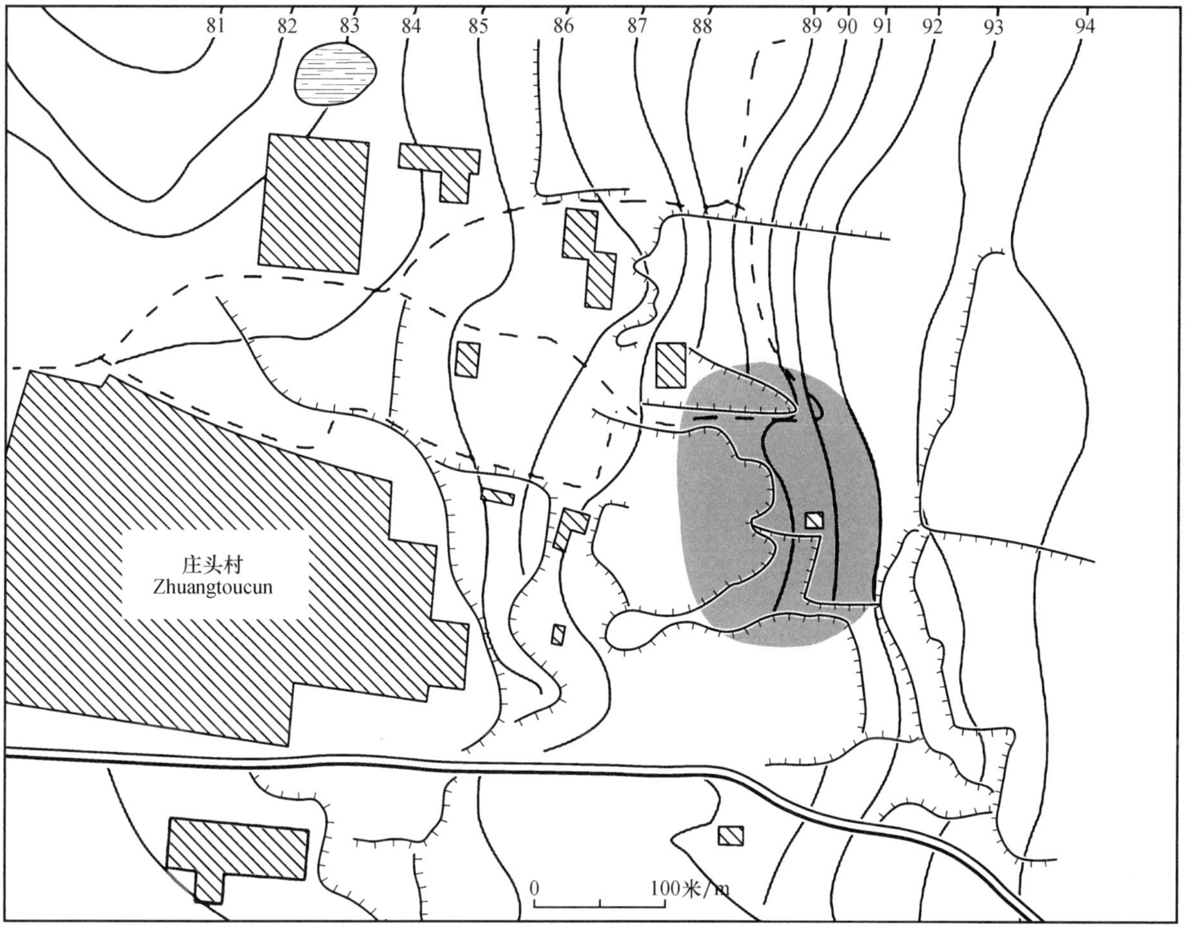

图Ⅰ.7.7　庄头墓地

Figure Ⅰ.7.7　The Zhuangtou cemetery.

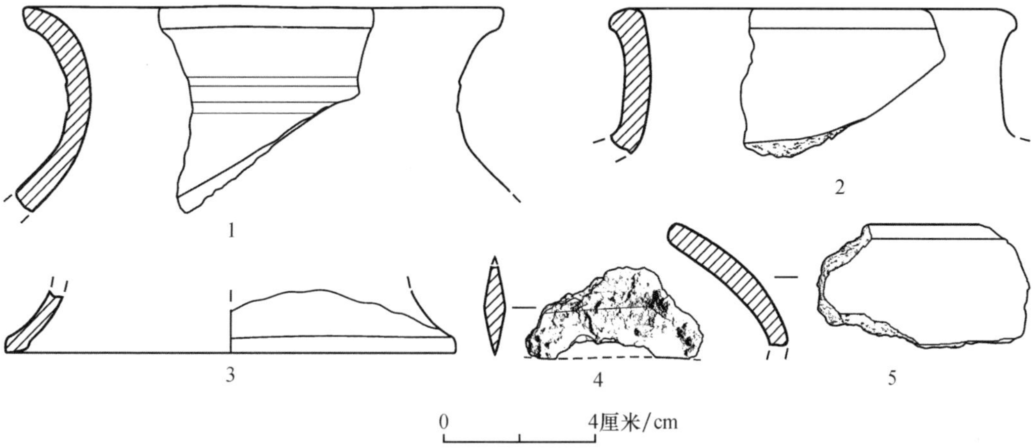

图Ⅰ.7.8　庄头墓地发现遗物

Figure Ⅰ.7.8　Artifacts from the Zhuantou cemetery.

表Ⅰ.7.4　庄头墓地发现遗物统计表

Table Ⅰ.7.4　Artifacts from the Zhuangtou cemetery

图上序号 Number on Fig. Ⅰ.7.9	标本号 Excavation number	器物名称 Artifact name	出土时间 Excavation date	位置 Position	所属类型 Type	尺寸（厘米）Size (cm)	特点描述 Description of the sample
1	10SLZ 采：1	罐 *Guan* jar	2010-11	地表采集 Surface Collection		M: 12.7 H: 5.5 T: 0.45	泥质灰陶。侈口，卷沿，平唇，束颈，高领。颈部饰两周凹弦纹。Grey clay pottery, wide-open mouth, rolled rim, flat lip, narrow neck, high collar, two intaglio rings around the neck.
2	10SLZ 采：2	罐 *Guan* jar	2010-11	地表采集 Surface Collection		M: 10.8 H: 4.0 T: 0.6	泥质灰陶。侈口，圆唇，束颈，高领。Grey Clay pottery; wide-open mouth, rounded lip, narrow neck, high collar.
3	10SLZ 采：5	豆 *Dou* pedestal dish	2010-11	地表采集 Surface Collection		B: 12 H: 1.6 T: 0.3	泥质灰陶。为豆的圈足，喇叭口。素面。Grey clay pottery; round base of *dou* pedestal dish, trumpet mouth; plain.
4	10SLZ 采：4	青铜戈 Bronze *ge*	2010-11	地表采集 Surface Collection		L: 4.8 W: 2.6 T: 0.5	已残，为戈内的刃部，两侧有刃，中部起脊。Broken, blade of *ge* dagger, two edges, ridge in center.
5	10SLZ 采：3	罐 *Guan* jar	2010-11	地表采集 Surface Collection		M: 24.6 H: 3.4 T: 0.6	夹砂灰褐陶。侈口，圆唇，宽折沿。沿面饰数道凹弦纹。Coarse greyish-brown pottery; wide-open mouth, rounded lip, wide and folded rim; several intaglio lines around the rim.

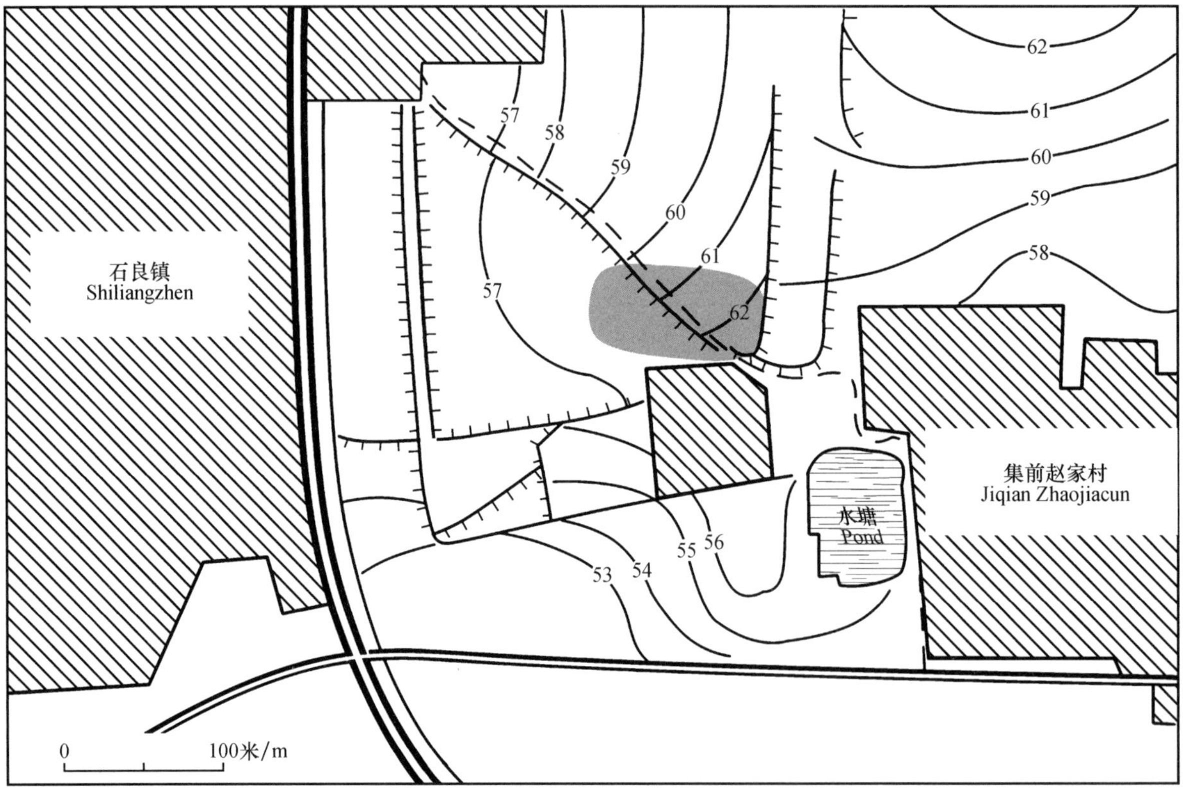

图Ⅰ.7.9　集前赵家墓地

Figure Ⅰ.7.9　The Jiqian Zhaojia cemetery.

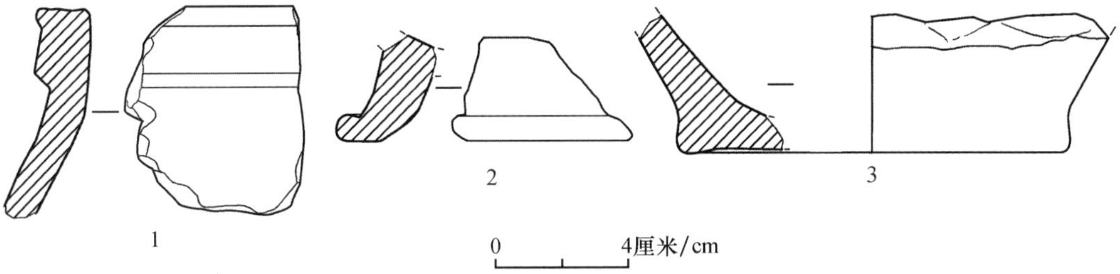

图Ⅰ.7.10　集前赵家墓地、徐乡故城和楼子庄发现遗物

Figure Ⅰ.7.10　Artifacts from the Jiqian Zhaojia cemetery, Xuxiang Old City, and Louzizhuang site.

表Ⅰ.7.5　集前赵家墓地、徐乡故城和楼子庄发现遗物统计表

Table Ⅰ.7.5　Artifacts from the Jiqian Zhaoji cemetery, Xuxiang Old City, and Louzizhuang site

序号 Number on Fig. Ⅰ.7.11	标本号 Excavation number	器物名称 Artifact name	出土时间 Excavation date	位置 Location	所属类型 Types	尺寸（厘米） Size (cm)	特点描述 Description of features
1	10SLJ：1	罐 *Guan* jar	2010-11	集前赵家地表采集 Jiqian Zhaojia surface collection		M: 14.5 H: 6.6 T: 1.0	泥质灰陶。直口，平沿，宽方唇。下部残。 Grey clay; straight mouth, flat rim, wide square lip; lower part broken.
2	10SLX：1	盘圈足 Round foot of a basin	2010-11	徐乡故城地表采集 Xuxiang Old City surface collection		B: 11.2 H: 3.1 T: 1.4	夹砂红褐陶。呈喇叭状，较矮。 Coarse, reddish-brown pottery; trumpet-shaped, relatively short.
3	10SLL 采：1	罐 *Guan* jar	2010-11	楼子庄地表采集 Louzizhuang surface collection		B: 11.7 H: 4.2	夹粗砂红褐陶。底微内凹，壁斜直。 Coarse, reddish-brown pottery; slightly concave bottom, oblique wall.

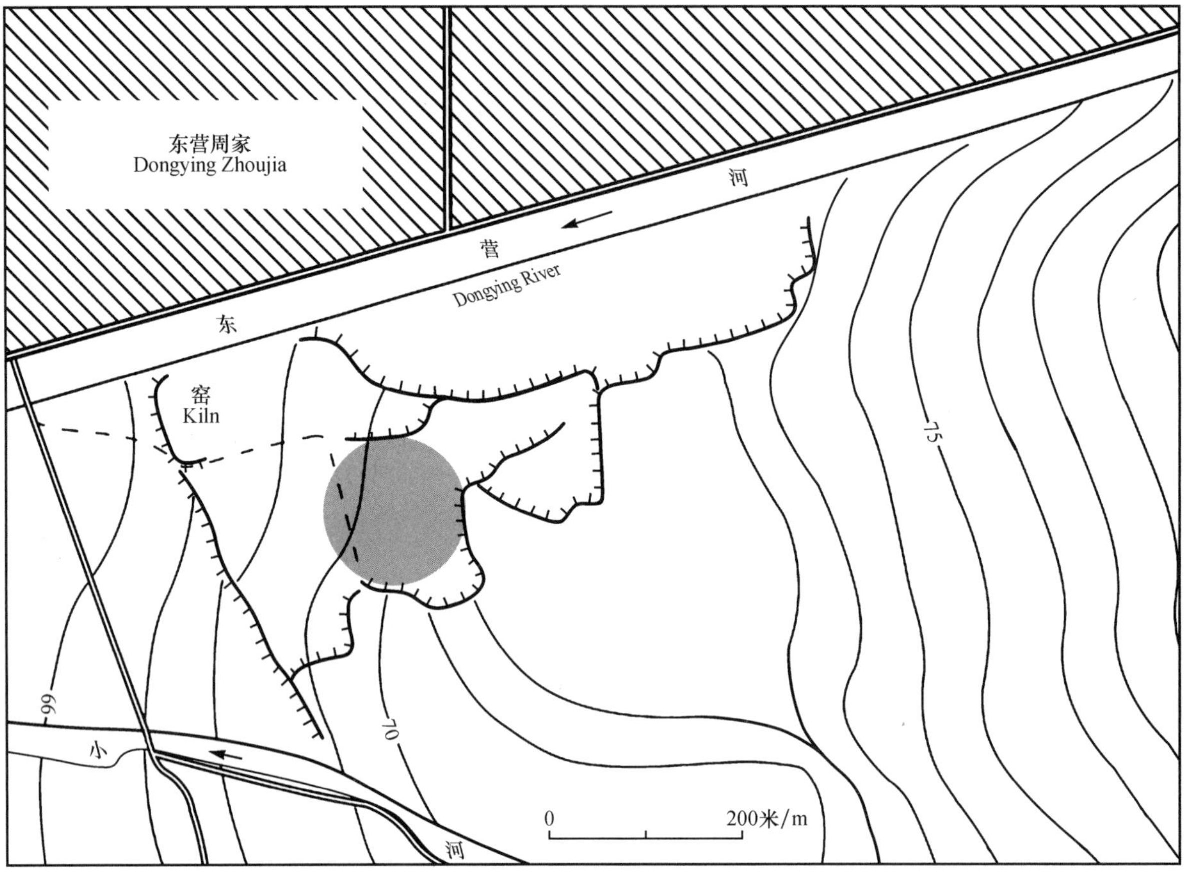

图Ⅰ.7.11　东营周家墓地

Figure Ⅰ.7.11　The Dongying Zhoujia cemetery.

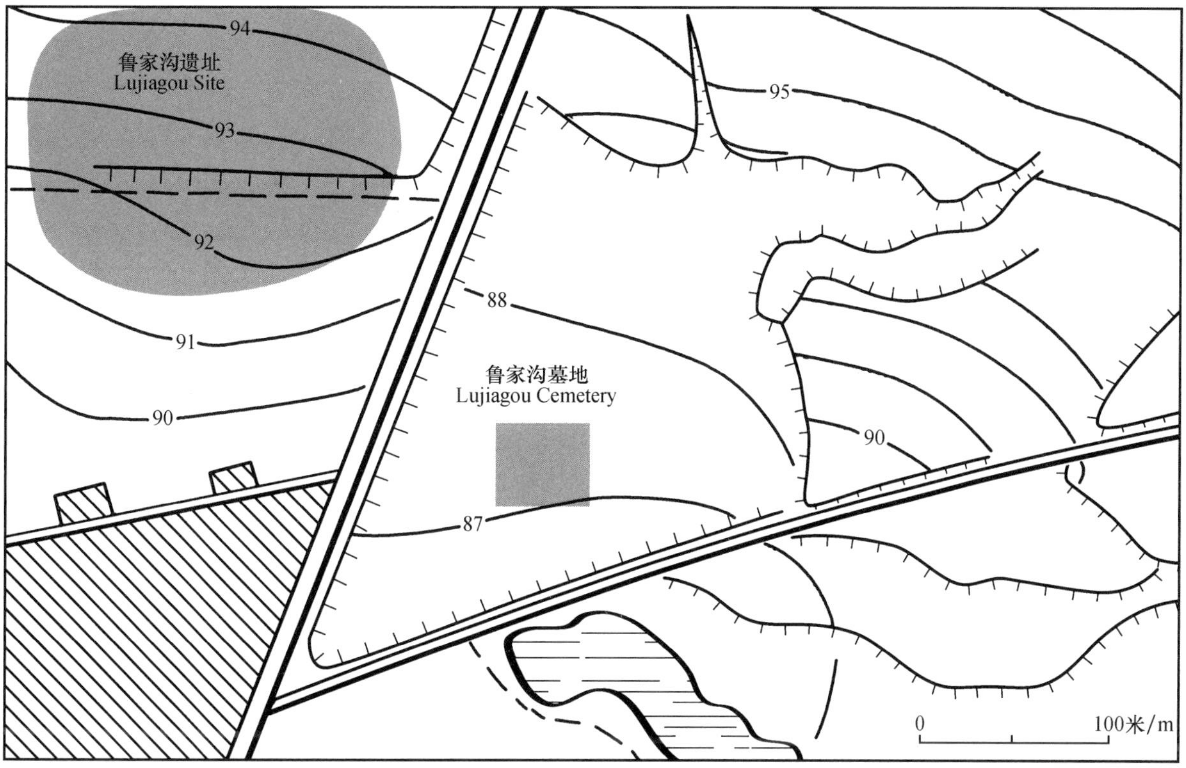

图Ⅰ.7.12　鲁家沟遗址和墓地

Figure Ⅰ.7.12　The Lujiagou site and cemetery.

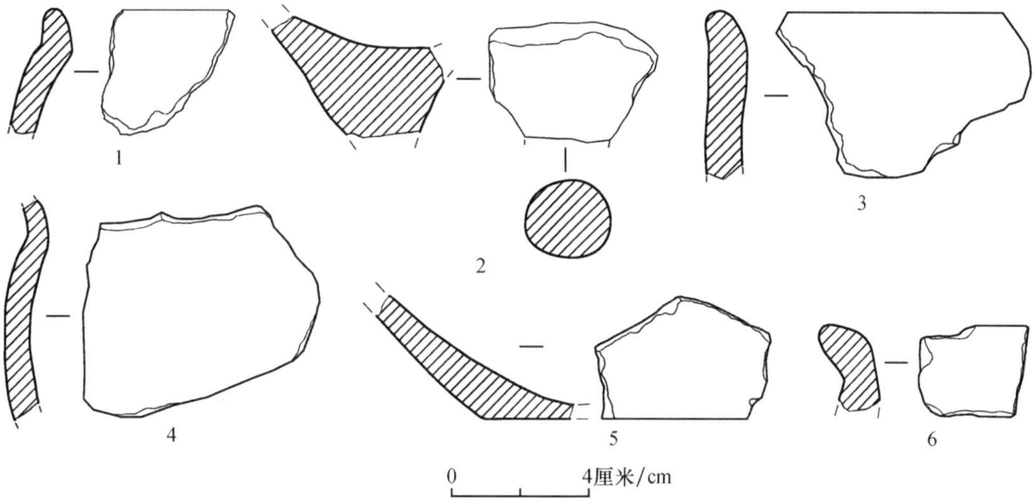

图Ⅰ.7.13　鲁家沟遗址采集遗物

Figure Ⅰ.7.13　Artifacts from the Lujiagou site.

表Ⅰ.7.6　鲁家沟遗址发现遗物统计表

Table Ⅰ.7.6　Artifacts from the Lujiagou site

序号 Number on Fig. Ⅰ.7.14	标本号 Excavation number	器物名称 Artifact name	出土时间 Excavation date	位置 Location	所属类型 Types	尺寸（厘米）Size (cm)	特点描述 Description of the features
1	10SLL采：1	釜形鼎 *Fu*-shaped ding	2010-11	地表采集 Surface collection		M: 27.5 H: 3.7 T: 0.8	夹砂红褐，陶胎内掺和大量粗砂。口微侈，圆唇，腹微鼓。素面。Coarse reddish-brown pottery, lots of sand tempering in the body; slightly wide mouth, rounded lip, belly slightly bulging; plain surface.
2	10SLL采：3	鼎足 *Ding* tripod foot	2010-11	地表采集 Surface collection		L: 3.4 W: 5.0 T: 2.3	夹砂红陶，胎内掺和粗砂。呈圆锥形，尖残。Coarse reddish pottery, sand tempering in the body; conical, tip broken.
3	10SLL采：2	釜形鼎 *Fu*-shaped ding	2010-11	地表采集 Surface collection		M: 26.2 H: 4.9 T: 1.0	夹砂红褐陶。侈口，折沿，圆唇，腹微鼓。Coarse reddish-brown pottery; wide mouth, folded rim, rounded lip, belly slightly bulging.
4	10SLL采：4	罐 *Guan* jar	2010-11	地表采集 Surface collection		H: 6.0 W: 7.0 T: 6.5	夹砂红褐陶。侈口略残，圆鼓腹，底残。Coarse reddish-brown pottery; wide mouth slightly broken, rounded bulging belly, broken bottom.
5	10SLL采：5	罐 *Guan* jar	2010-11	地表采集 Surface collection		B: 14.2 H: 3.6 T: 1.2	夹砂红褐陶。平底，斜直腹。Coarse reddish-brown pottery; flat bottom, slightly oblique belly.
6	10SLL采：6	罐 *Guan* jar	2010-11	地表采集 Surface collection		M: 26.4 H: 2.7 T: 1.0	夹砂红陶。侈口，圆唇，壁较厚。Coarse reddish pottery; wide mouth, rounded lip, fairly thick wall.

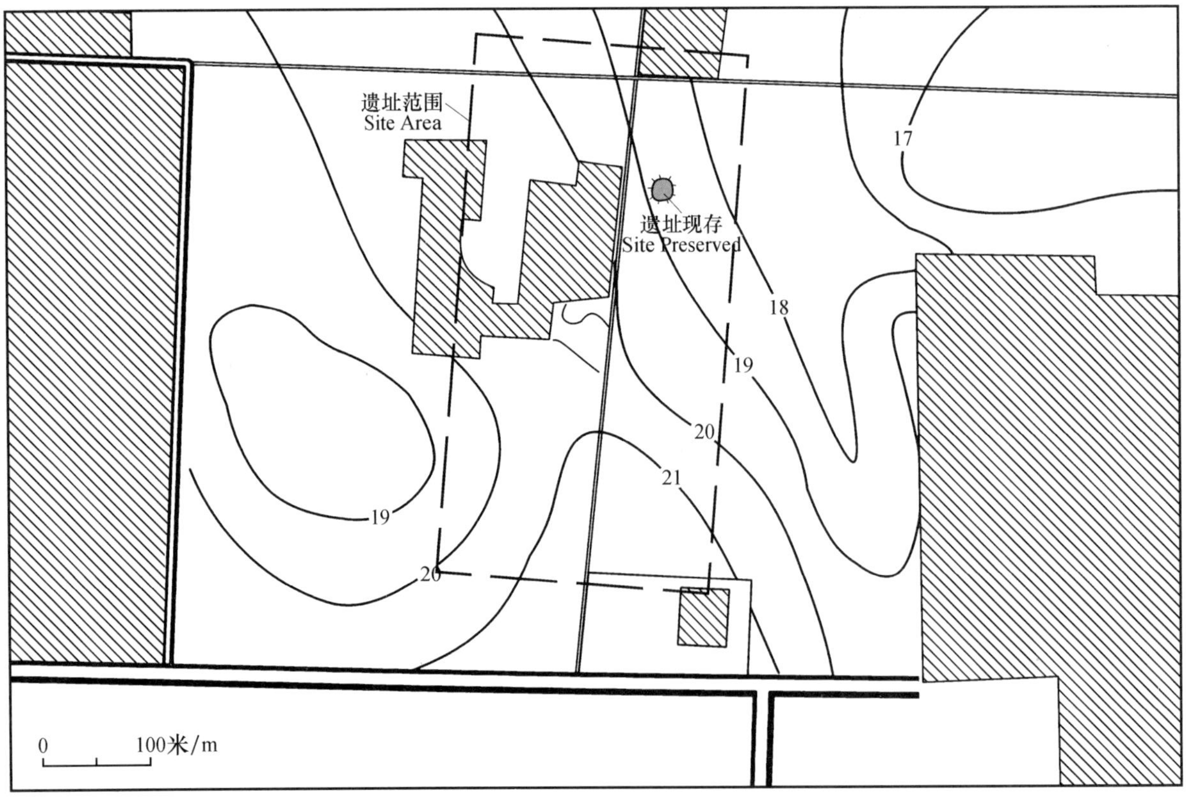

图Ⅰ.7.14　乾山遗址

Figure Ⅰ.7.14　The Qianshan site.

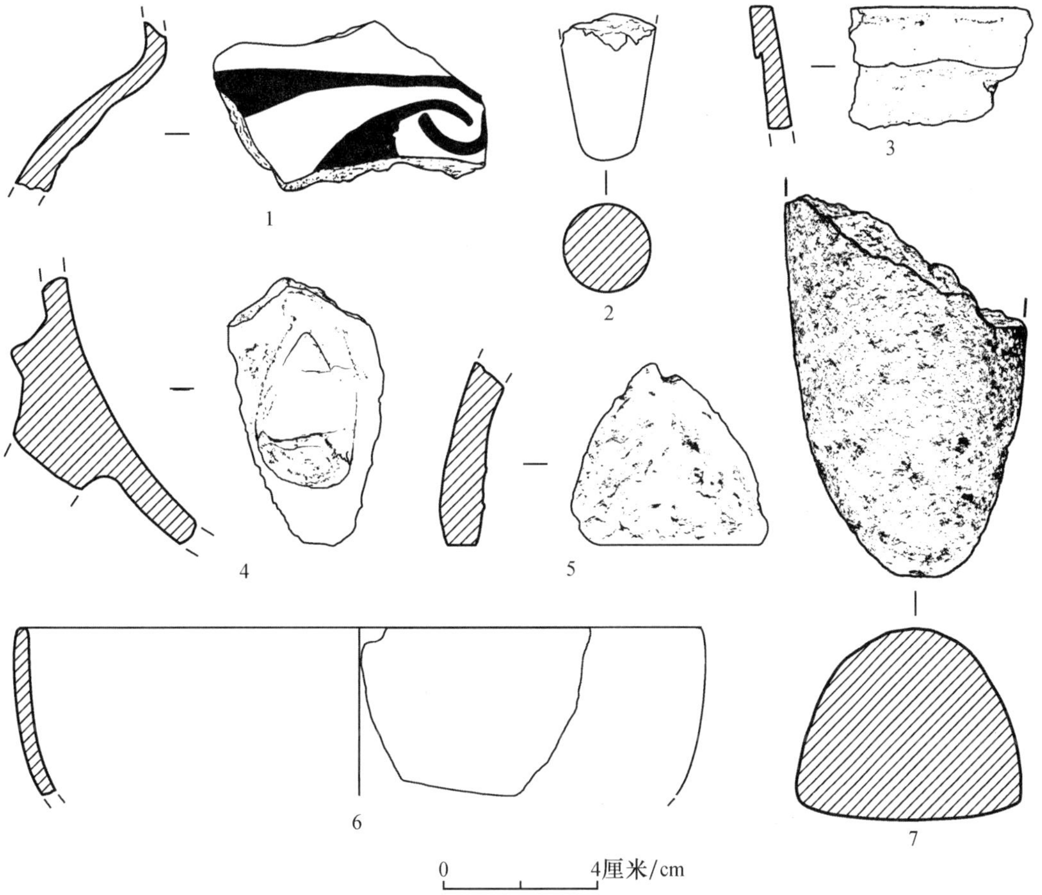

图Ⅰ.7.15　乾山遗址发现遗物

Figure Ⅰ.7.15　Artifacts from the Qianshan site.

表Ⅰ.7.7　乾山遗址发现遗物统计表
Table Ⅰ.7.7　Artifacts from the Qianshan site

序号 Number on Fig. Ⅰ.7.7	标本号 Excavation number	器物名称 Artifact name	出土时间 Excavation date	位置 Location	所属类型 Types	尺寸（厘米） Size (cm)	特点描述 Description of the features
1	10SLQ 采：2	罐 *Guan* jar	2010-11	地表采集 Surface collection		H: 4.4 W: 7.1 T: 0.75	泥质红陶。为罐的肩部，口残。肩部饰红底黑彩的弧线三角纹。 Reddish clay; shoulder of a *guan* jar, broken mouth; painted with black triangular patterns on red base.
2	10SLQ 采：1	鼎足 *Ding* foot	2010-11	地表采集 Surface collection		L: 3.8 W: 2.5 T: 2.5	夹砂灰陶。圆锥形。 Coarse grey pottery; conical.
3	10SLQ 采：5	钵 *Bo* bowl	2010-11	地表采集 Surface collection		M: 25.1 H: 3.1 T: 0.6	泥质红褐陶。口微敛，圆唇。素面磨光，内壁打磨光滑。 Reddish-brown clay; mouth slightly converging, rounded lip; plain and polished surface, smooth polished inner wall.
4	10SLQ 采：1	鼎足 *Ding* foot	2010-11	地表采集 Surface collection		L: 6.9 W: 3.7 T: 0.85	夹砂红褐陶。圆锥形。足根部有三角形泥突。 Coarse, reddish-brown pottery; conical; triangular clay bumps added to the base of the foot.
5	10SLQ 采：3	支脚 Foot	2010-11	地表采集 Surface collection		B: 10 H: 4.6 T: 1.1	夹砂灰褐陶。圆锥形，空心，手捏制，上部略残。 Coarse, greyish-brown pottery; conical, hollow, handmade, slightly broken on top.
6	10SLQ 采：6	鼎 *Ding*	2010-11	地表采集 Surface collection		M: 18 H: 4.3 T: 0.4	夹砂红褐陶。斜直口，方唇。 Coarse, reddish-brown pottery; oblique mouth, square lip.
7	10SLQ 采：4	石磨棒 Grinding stone	2010-11	地表采集 Surface collection		L: 9.9 W: 6.3 T: 5	砂岩。断面呈半圆形，背部琢制，弧背。磨面较平。 Sandstone; section semicircular, polished and curved back; grinding surface relatively flat.

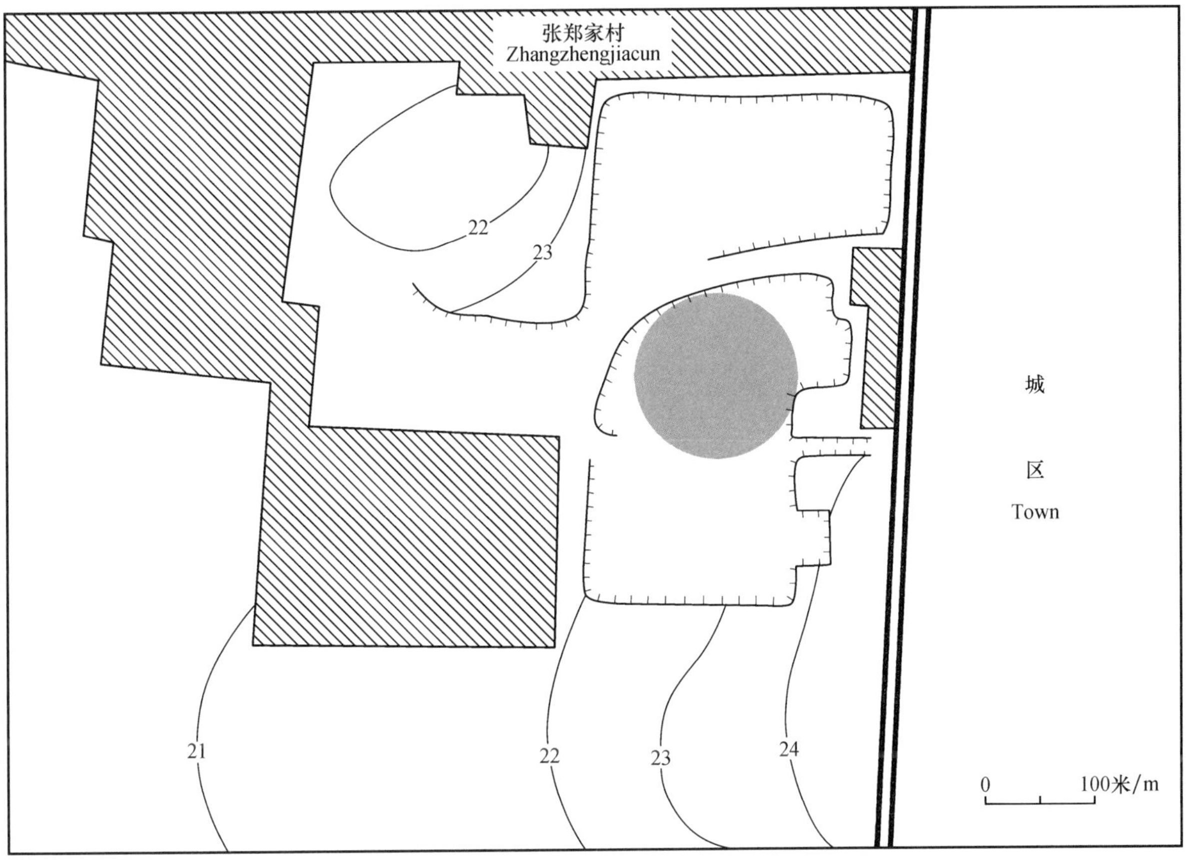

图Ⅰ.7.16 张郑家墓地

Figure Ⅰ.7.16 The Zhangzhengjia cemetery.

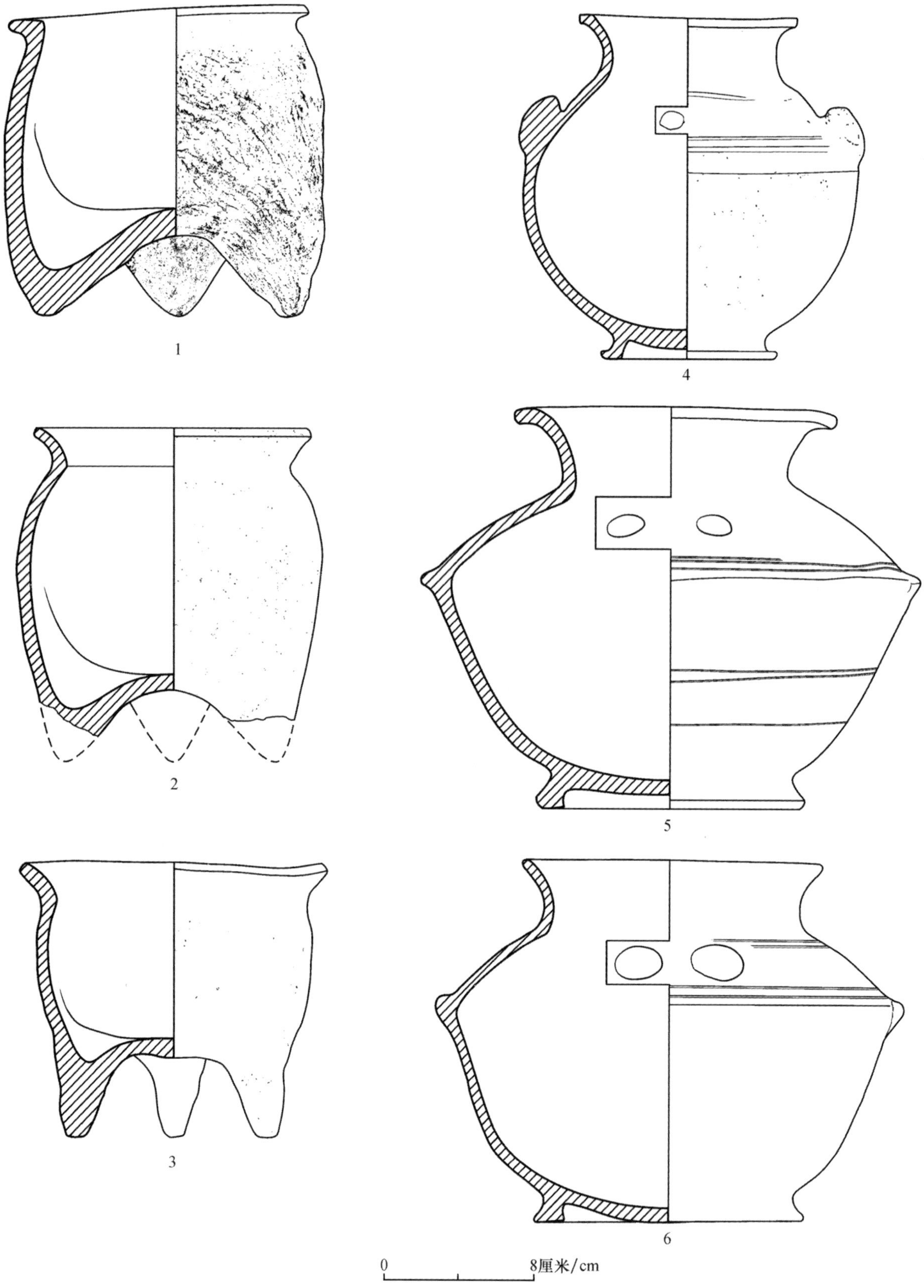

图Ⅰ.7.17.1　张郑家墓地出土陶器（鬲、瓿）

Figure Ⅰ.7.17.1　Pottery vessels from the Zhangzhengjia cemetery (*li*, *bu*).

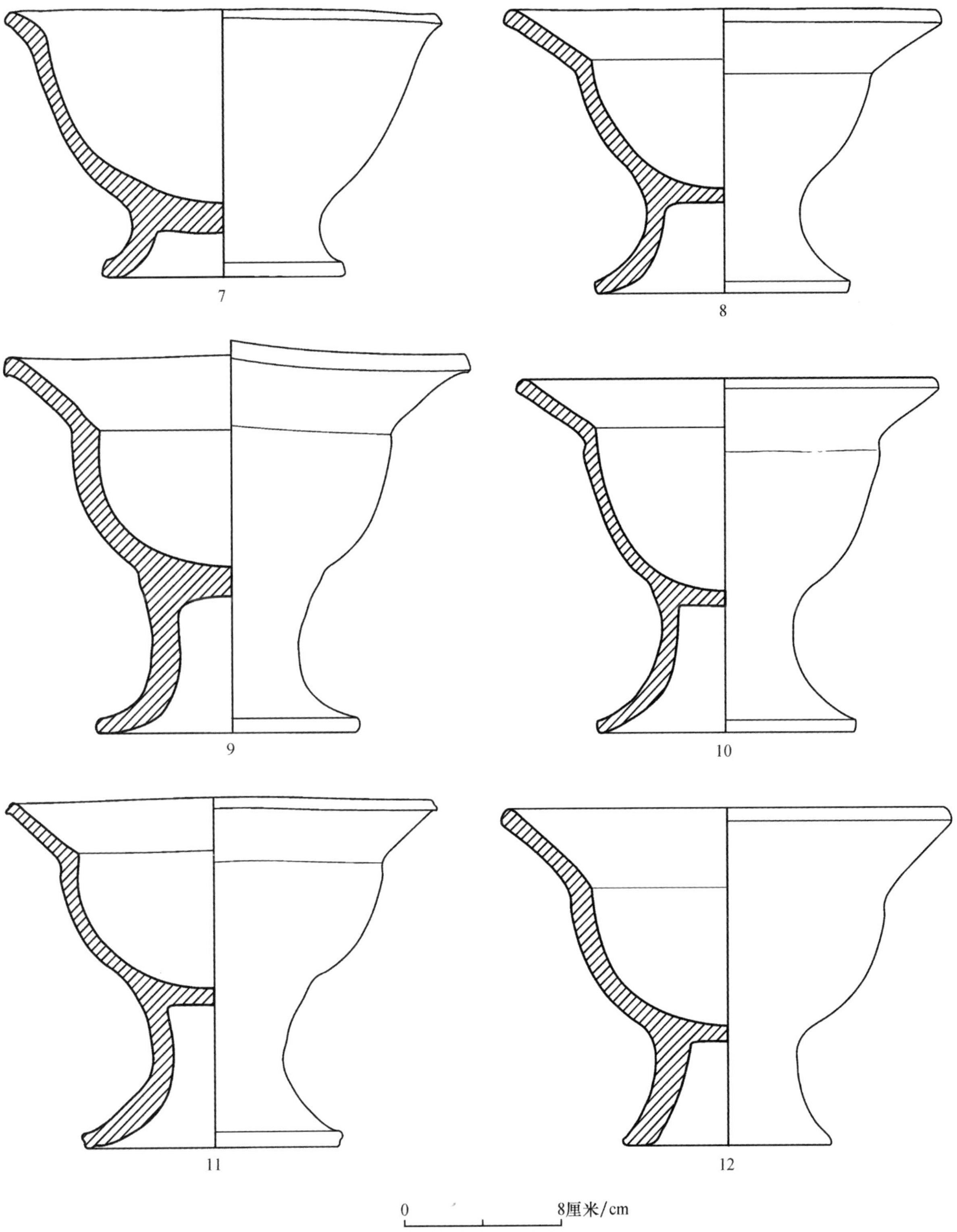

图Ⅰ.7.17.2　张郑家墓地出土陶器（簋）

Figure Ⅰ.7.17.2　Pottery vessels from the Zhangzhengjia cemetery (*gui*).

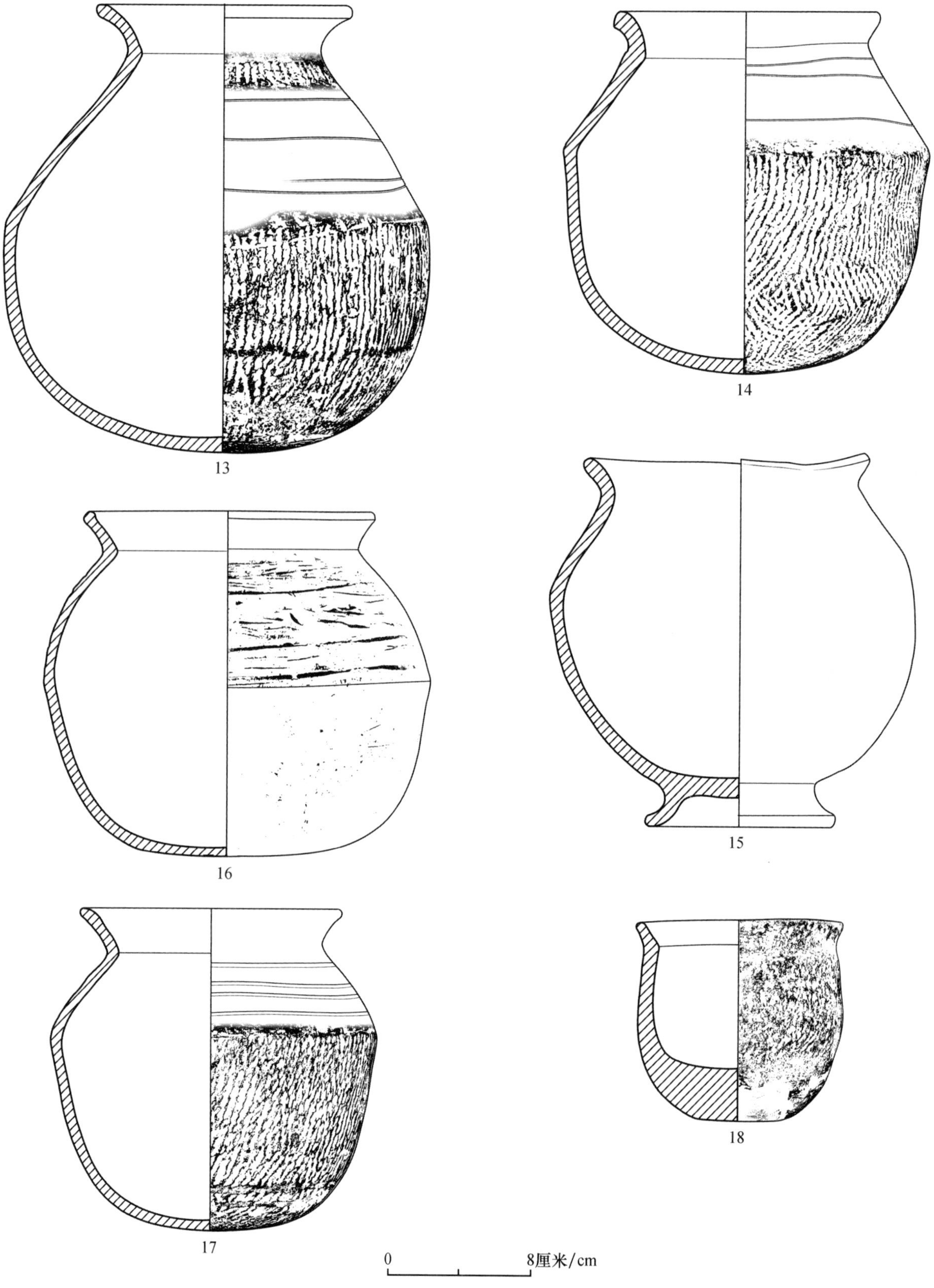

图Ⅰ.7.17.3　张郑家墓地出土陶器（罐）

Figure Ⅰ.7.17.3　Pottery vessels from the Zhangzhengjia cemetery (*guan*).

图Ⅰ.7.17.4　张郑家墓地出土陶器（豆）

Figure Ⅰ.7.17.4　Pottery vessels from the Zhangzhengjia cemetery (*dou*).

表Ⅰ.7.8　张郑家墓地出土陶器统计表

Table Ⅰ.7.8　Pottery vessels from the Zhangzhengjia cemetery

序号 Number on Fig. Ⅰ.7.18	标本号 Excavation number	器物名称 Artifact name	出土时间 Excavation date	位置 Location	所属类型 Types	尺寸（厘米） Size (cm)	特点描述 Description of features
1	10ZZJ 采：1	鬲 *Li* tripod	2010-10	农民取土征集 Collected by local farmers		M: 16 H: 16.1 T: 0.9	夹砂红褐陶。窄折沿，方唇，腹微鼓，分裆，三空袋足。素面。 Coarse, reddish-brown pottery; narrow folded rim, square lip, belly slightly bulging, a divided crotch, and three bag-shaped hollow feet; plain,
2	10ZZJ 采：2	鬲 *Li* tripod	2010-10	农民取土征集 Collected by local farmers		M: 14.8 H: 17.3 T: 1.0	夹砂黄褐陶，窄折沿，方唇，深腹微鼓。素面。 Coarse, yellowish-brown pottery; narrow folded rim, square lip, deep belly slightly bulging; plain.
3	10ZZJ 采：3	鬲 *Li* tripod	2010-10	农民取土征集 Collected by local farmers	D2	M: 16.5 H: 14.2 T: 1.05	夹砂灰褐陶。侈口、宽沿，方唇，腹微鼓，平裆，三实足。素面。 Coarse, greyish-brown pottery; wide-open mouth, wide rim, square lip, slightly bulging, flat crotch, three solid feet. Plain surface.
4	10ZZJ 采：10	瓿 *Bu* jar	2010-10	农民取土征集 Collected by local farmers	A2	M: 11.5 B: 9.36 H: 17.7 T: 1.05	泥质灰褐陶。侈口，圆唇，束颈广肩，鼓腹，矮圈足。肩饰两个倒鸡冠耳，其间饰两个圆泥饼，素面磨光。 Greyish-brown clay pottery. Wide-open mouth, rounded lip, converging neck and broad shoulder, bulging belly, low ring foot. Shoulder decorated with two inverted cockscomb handles and two round clay discs between them, plain and burnished surface.
5	10ZZJ 采：11	瓿 *Bu* jar	2010-10	农民取土征集 Collected by local farmers	A1	M: 17.1 B: 13.6 H: 20.8 T: 1.0	泥质灰褐陶。侈口，平沿，圆唇，斜广折肩，斜直腹，矮圈足。肩上饰六道弦纹，两半圆耳和四个泥饼，腹上饰两周凹弦纹。 Greyish-brown clay pottery. Wide-open mouth, flat rim, rounded lip, slanted and folded wide shoulder, slanted and straight belly, short ring feet. Six intaglio ring patterns on the shoulder, two half-round handles and four round clay discs, two incised intaglio ring decorations on the belly.
6	10ZZJ 采：12	瓿 *Bu* jar	2010-10	农民取土征集 Collected by local farmers	A1	M: 15.9 B: 13.6 H: 18.8 T: 0.8	泥质黄褐陶。侈口，圆唇，矮领，斜广折肩，腹壁斜直，矮圈足。肩饰两横耳和两对圆泥饼。 Yellowish-brown clay pottery. Wide-open mouth, rounded lip, short neck, slanted and folded broad shoulder, slanted and straight belly, short ring foot. Shoulder decorated with two horizontal ears and two pairs of round clay discs.
7	10ZZJ 采：4	簋 *Gui* tureen	2010-10	农民取土征集 Collected by local farmers	C1	M: 22.5 B: 12.5 H: 13.4 T: 1.65	泥质橙黄陶。侈口，圆唇，斜壁微鼓，矮圈足外侈呈喇叭状。素面。 Orange-yellow clay pottery; wide mouth, rounded lip, slanted belly slightly bulging, trumpet-shaped short ring foot; plain.
8	10ZZJ 采：5	簋 *Gui* tureen	2010-10	农民取土征集 Collected by local farmers	A2	M: 22.6 B: 13.4 H: 14.3 T: 1.0	泥质橙黄陶。大敞口，宽折沿，方圆唇，腹壁斜直，高圈足呈喇叭状。素面磨光。 Orange-yellow clay pottery. Large wide mouth, wide folded rim, square rounded lip, belly wall slanted and straight, tall trumpet-shaped ring foot; plain and polished.
9	10ZZJ 采：6	簋 *Gui* tureen	2010-10	农民取土征集 Collected by local farmers	A2	M: 23.9 B: 13.5 H: 19.6 T: 1.65	泥质灰陶。大敞口，宽折沿，方唇，腹斜直、微鼓，高圈足呈喇叭状，上端略直。素面。 Grey clay pottery; Large wide mouth, wide folded rim, square lip, slanted straight belly slightly bulging, tall trumpet-shaped ring foot, upper part relatively straight; plain.

续表

序号 Number on Fig. Ⅰ.7.18	标本号 Excavation number	器物名称 Artifact name	出土时间 Excavation date	位置 Location	所属类型 Types	尺寸（厘米） Size (cm)	特点描述 Description of features
10	10ZZJ 采：7	簋 *Gui* tureen	2010-10	农民取土征集 Collected by local farmers	A2	M: 21.9 B: 13.3 H: 17.8 T: 1.1	泥质橙黄陶。大敞口，宽折沿，方唇，腹斜直，高圈足呈喇叭状。素面磨光。 Orange-yellow clay pottery; large wide mouth, wide folded rim, square lip, slanted straight belly, tall trumpet-shaped ring foot; plain and burnished.
11	10ZZJ 采：8	簋 *Gui* tureen	2010-10	农民取土征集 Collected by local farmers	A2	M: 22.1 B: 13.3 H: 17.6 T: 1.5	泥质黄褐陶。大敞口，宽折沿，厚圆唇，腹斜直，高圈足呈喇叭状。素面磨光。 Yellowish-brown clay pottery; large wide mouth, wide folded rim, thick rounded lip, straight slanted belly, tall trumpet-shaped ring foot; plain and burnished.
12	10ZZJ 采：9	簋 *Gui* tureen	2010-10	农民取土征集 Collected by local farmers	A2	M: 23.3 B: 10.9 H: 16.9 T: 1.55	泥质黄褐陶。大敞口，宽折沿，厚圆唇，腹斜直，高圈足呈喇叭状。素面磨光。 Yellowish-brown clay pottery; large wide mouth, wide folded rim, thick rounded lip, straight slanted belly, tall trumpet-shaped ring foot; plain and burnished.
13	10ZZJ 采：13	罐 *Guan* jar	2010-10	农民取土征集 Collected by local farmers		M: 14.3 H: 19.6 T: 0.9	泥质灰褐陶。侈口、圆唇、束颈，广斜肩，深鼓腹，圜底。肩上饰四道弦纹，腹饰竖浅绳纹。 Greyish-brown clay pottery; wide mouth, rounded lip, constrained neck, wide slanted shoulder, bulging deep belly, circular bottom; four intaglio ring patterns on the shoulder, belly decorated with shallow vertical cord impressions.
14	10ZZJ 采：14	罐 *Guan* jar	2010-10	农民取土征集 Collected by local farmers		M: 16.3 H: 18.6 T: 0.95	泥质灰褐陶。侈口，方圆唇，束颈，斜肩，鼓腹，圜底。素面磨光。 Greyish-brown clay pottery; wide mouth, square rounded lip, converging neck, slanted shoulder, bulging belly, circular bottom; plain and burnished.
15	10ZZJ 采：15	罐 *Guan* jar	2010-10	农民取土征集 Collected by local farmers		M: 15.8 H: 19.6 T: 0.7	泥质橙黄陶。侈口，圆唇，球形腹，矮圈足。素面磨光。 Orange-yellow clay pottery; wide mouth, rounded lip, spherical belly, short ring foot; surface plain and burnished.
16	10ZZJ 采：16	罐 *Guan* jar	2010-10	农民取土征集 Collected by local farmers		M: 14.8 B: 10.5 H: 19.6 T: 1.1	泥质黄褐陶。广口、折沿，圆唇，斜广折肩，鼓腹，圜底。肩饰二周弦纹，腹饰绳纹。 Yellowish-brown clay pottery. Wide mouth, folded rim, rounded lip, slanted broad folded shoulder, bulging belly, circular bottom. Shoulder decorated with two intaglio ring patterns, belly decorated with cord impressions.
17	10ZZJ 采：17	罐 *Guan* jar	2010-10	农民取土征集 Collected by local farmers	D1	M: 14.6 H: 17.4 T: 0.7	泥质黄陶。侈口，折沿，方唇，斜广折肩，鼓腹，圜底。肩上饰四道弦纹，腹饰交错的绳纹。 Yellow clay pottery. Wide mouth, folded rim, square lip, slanted broad folded shoulder, bulging belly, circular bottom. Four intaglio ring patterns on the shoulder; belly decorated with criss-cross cord impressions.
18	10ZZJ 采：18	罐 *Guan* jar	2010-10	农民取土征集 Collected by local farmers		M: 11.5 B: 4.4 H: 10.9 T: 1.85	泥质黄褐陶。手制。口微侈，圆唇，腹较深，圜底。 Yellowish-brown grey clay; hand-built; mouth slightly wide, rounded lip, belly relatively deep, circular bottom.

续表

序号 Number on Fig. Ⅰ.7.18	标本号 Excavation number	器物名称 Artifact name	出土时间 Excavation date	位置 Location	所属类型 Types	尺寸（厘米） Size (cm)	特点描述 Description of features
19	10ZZJ 采：19	豆 *Dou* pedestal dish	2010-10	农民取土征集 Collected by local farmers	A1	M: 14.7 B: 10.8 H: 10.6 T: 1.0	泥质橙黄陶。敛口，平沿，圆唇、碗形盘，粗喇叭形圈足。素面磨光。 Orange-yellow clay pottery; mouth converging, flat rim, rounded lip, bowl-shaped plate, strong trumpet-shaped ring foot; plain and burnished.
20	10ZZJ 采：20	豆 *Dou* pedestal dish	2010-10	农民取土征集 Collected by local farmers	A3	M: 15.8 B: 10.2 H: 11.2 T: 1.25	泥质橙黄陶。敛口，平沿，圆唇，碗形盘，柄及圈足较细。素面磨光。 Orange-yellow clay pottery; mouth converging, flat rim, rounded lip, bowl-shaped plate, stem and ring foot relatively slim; plain and burnished.
21	10ZZJ 采：21	豆 *Dou* pedestal dish	2010-10	农民取土征集 Collected by local farmers	B1	M: 18.1 B: 12.4 H: 14.1 T: 1.25	泥质黄褐陶。侈口，平沿，圆唇，碗形盘，盘中部有折棱，高圈足呈喇叭形，中部有一周突棱。素面磨光。 Yellowish-brown clay pottery; wide-open mouth, flat rim, rounded lip, bowl-shaped plate, folding line at middle height of the plate, tall trumpet-shaped ring foot, one protruding ridge in the middle; plain and burnished.
22	10ZZJ 采：22	豆 *Dou* pedestal dish	2010-10	农民取土征集 Collected by local farmers	A3	M: 17.4 B: 11.5 H: 13.5 T: 1.3	泥质橙黄陶。敛口，平沿，圆唇，碗形盘，高喇叭形圈足。素面磨光。 Orange-yellow clay pottery; mouth converging, flat rim, rounded lip, bowl-shaped plate, tall trumpet-shaped ring foot; plain and burnished.
23	10ZZJ 采：23	豆 *Dou* pedestal dish	2010-10	农民取土征集 Collected by local farmers		M: 13.9 B: 10.5 H: 9.5 T: 1.3	泥质黄褐陶。直口，圆唇，碗形盘，粗喇叭形圈足。素面磨光。 Yellowish-brown clay pottery; straight mouth, rounded lip, bowl-shaped plate, strong trumpet-shaped ring foot; plain and burnished.
24	10ZZJ 采：24	豆 *Dou* pedestal dish	2010-10	农民取土征集 Collected by local farmers	A4	M: 14.8 B: 12 H: 11.9 T: 1.4	泥质灰褐陶。敛口，平沿，尖唇，碗形盘，高喇叭形圈足。素面。 Greyish-brown clay pottery; mouth converging, flat rim, sharp lip, bowl-shaped plate, tall trumpet-shaped ring foot; plain.
25	10ZZJ 采：25	豆 *Dou* pedestal dish	2010-10	农民取土征集 Collected by local farmers	D3	M: 15.4 B: 10.5 H: 11.5 T: 1.0	泥质灰褐陶。敛口，平沿，尖唇，碗形盘，高喇叭状圈足。素面磨光。 Greyish-brown clay pottery; mouth converging, flat rim, sharp lip, bowl-shaped plate, tall trumpet-shaped ring foot; plain and burnished.
26	10ZZJ 采：26	豆 *Dou* pedestal dish	2010-10	农民取土征集 Collected by local farmers	A3	M: 16 B: 11 H: 12.4 T: 1.6	泥质黄褐陶。敞口，平沿，圆唇，碗形盘，盘与圈足界限不明显，喇叭形圈足。素面磨光。 Yellowish-brown clay pottery; wide mouth, flat rim, rounded lip, bowl-shaped plate, plate not clearly divided from ring foot, trumpet-shaped ring foot; plain and burnished.
27	10ZZJ 采：27	豆 *Dou* pedestal dish	2010-10	农民取土征集 Collected by local farmers	A3	M: 17.6 B: 12.2 H: 12.3 T: 0.95	泥质橙黄陶。敞口，平沿，圆唇，碗形盘，粗喇叭形圈足。圈足中段有两段弦纹，素面磨光。 Orange-yellow clay pottery; wide mouth, flat rim, rounded lip, bowl-shaped plate, strong trumpet-shaped ring foot; two intaglio rings at the middle section of the ring foot, plain and burnished.
28	10ZZJ 采：28	豆 *Dou* pedestal dish	2010-10	农民取土征集 Collected by local farmers	A4	M: 17.1 B: 9.1 H: 9.8 T: 1.2	泥质橙黄陶。口微敛，平沿，圆唇，碗形盘，矮粗状喇叭形圈足。素面磨光。 Orange-yellow clay pottery; mouth slightly converging, flat rim, rounded lip, bowl-shaped plate, short and sturdy trumpet-shaped ring foot; plain and burnished.

续表

序号 Number on Fig. Ⅰ.7.18	标本号 Excavation number	器物名称 Artifact name	出土时间 Excavation date	位置 Location	所属类型 Types	尺寸（厘米） Size (cm)	特点描述 Description of features
29	10ZZJ 采：29	豆 *Dou* pedestal dish	2010-10	农民取土征集 Collected by local farmers	D3	M: 15 B: 9.6 H: 10.6 T: 1	泥质橙黄陶。敞口，平沿，圆唇，碗形盘，高喇叭形圈足。素面磨光。 Orange-yellow clay pottery; mouth converging, flat rim, rounded lip, bowl-shaped plate, tall trumpet-shaped ring foot; plain and burnished.
30	10ZZJ 采：30	豆 *Dou* pedestal dish	2010-10	农民取土征集 Collected by local farmers	A1	M: 16.2 B: 11.9 H: 12.5 T: 1	泥质灰陶。敞口，圆唇，碗形盘，高喇叭形圈足，圈足下部饰一周凸棱。素面磨光。 Grey clay pottery; mouth converging, rounded lip, bowl-shaped plate, tall trumpet-shaped ring foot, lower part of the ring foot decorated with one protruding line; plain and burnished.

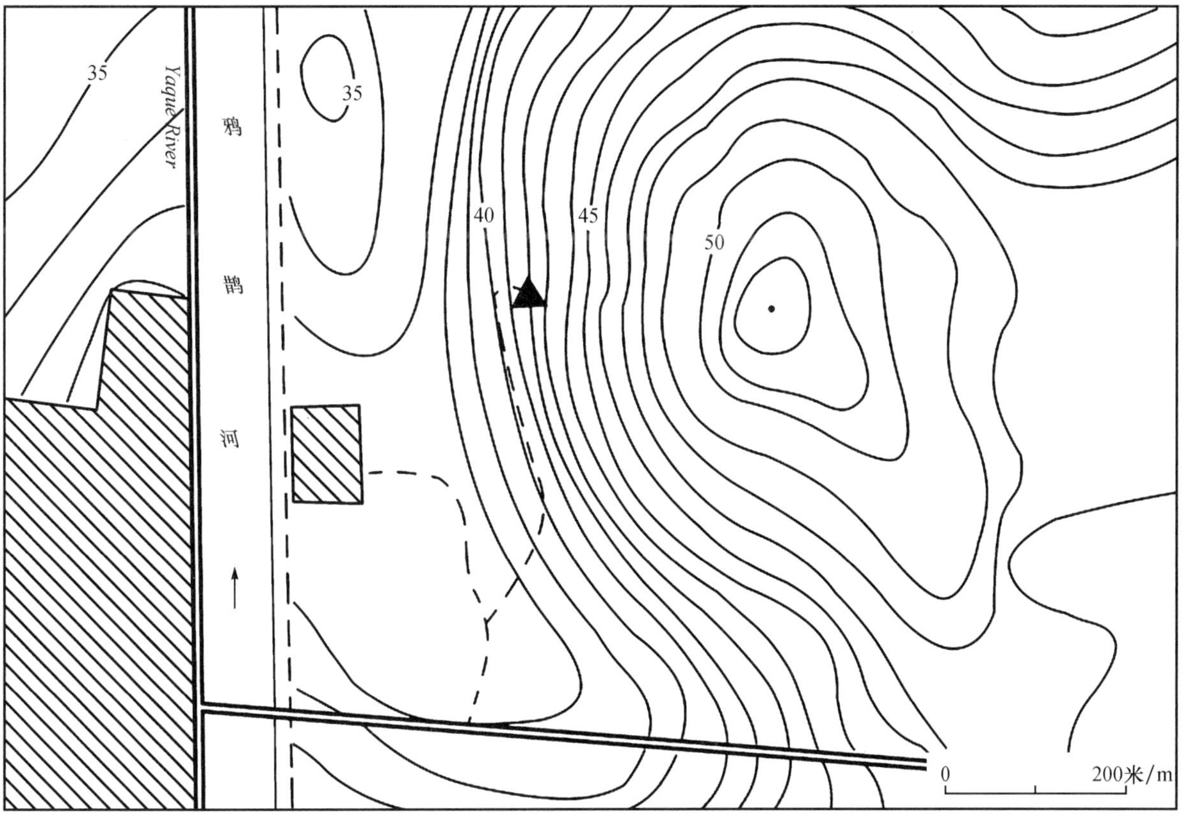

图Ⅰ.7.18　小莱山溶洞遗址
Figure Ⅰ.7.18　The Xiaolaishan cave site.

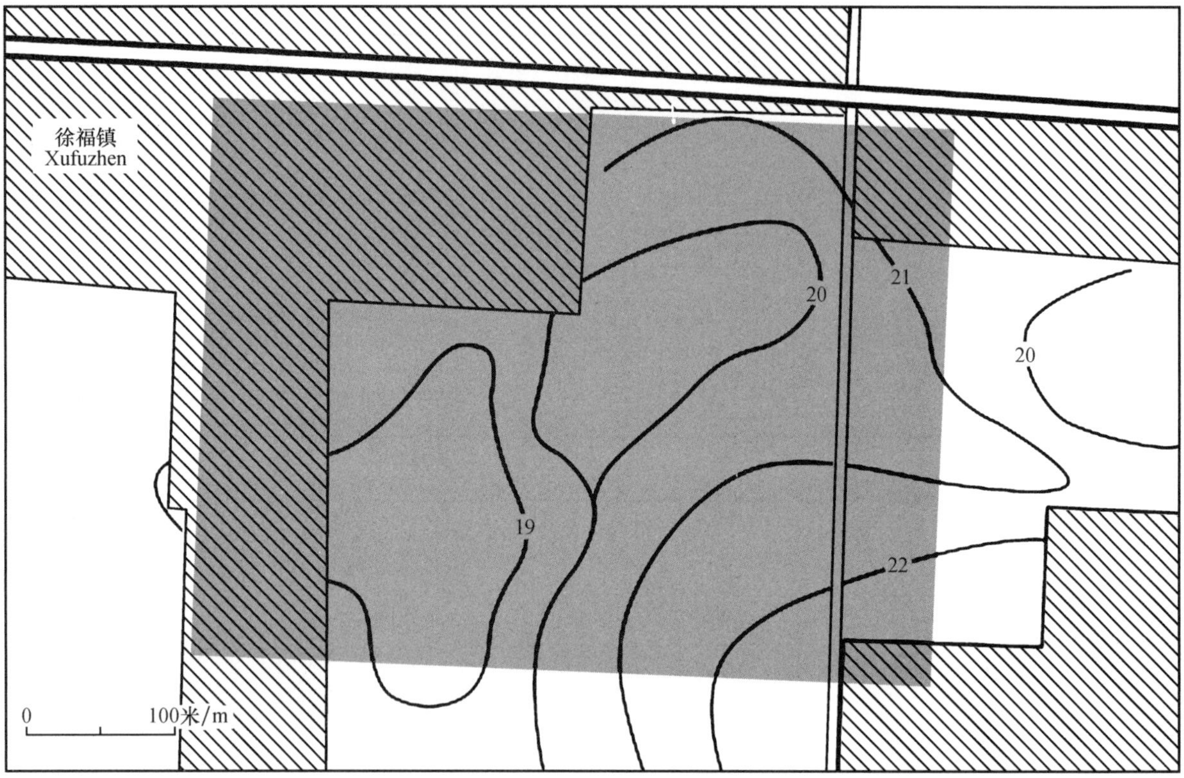

图Ⅰ.7.19　徐乡故城址

Figure Ⅰ.7.19　The Xuxiang Old City site.

图Ⅰ.7.20　村里集城址

Figure Ⅰ.7.20　The Cunliji city site.

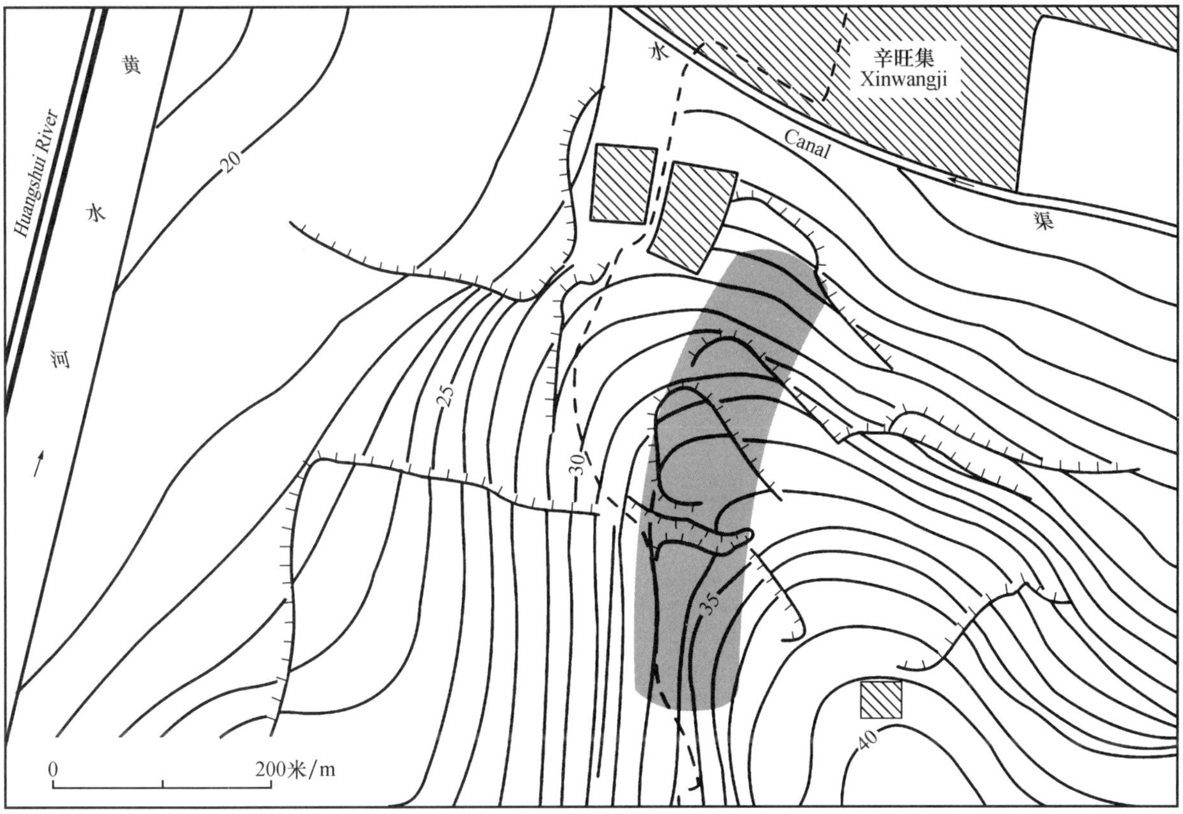

图Ⅰ.7.21　村里集墓地

Figure Ⅰ.7.21　The Cunliji cemetery.

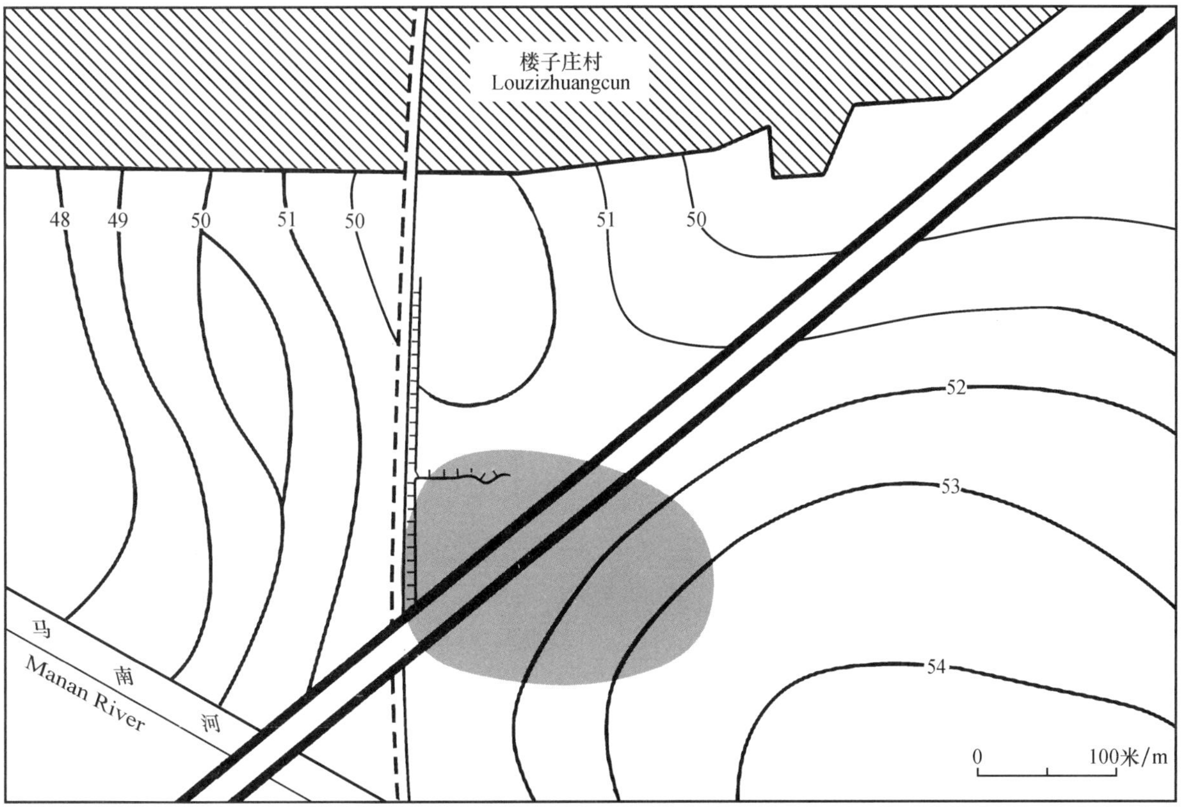

图Ⅰ.7.22　楼子庄遗址

Figure Ⅰ.7.22　The Louzizhuang site.

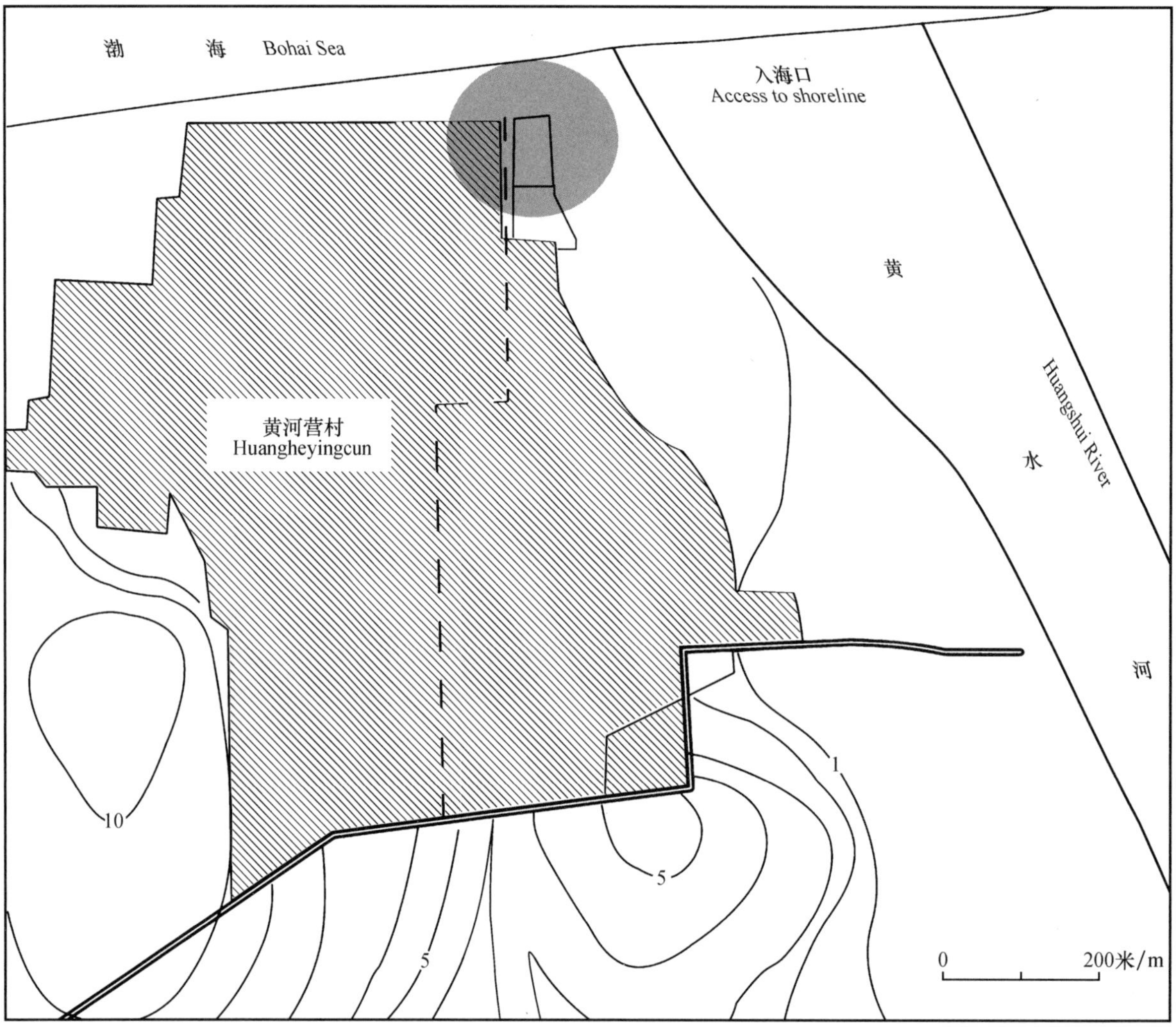

图Ⅰ.7.23 黄河营古港遗址

Figure Ⅰ.7.23 The Huangheying old port site.

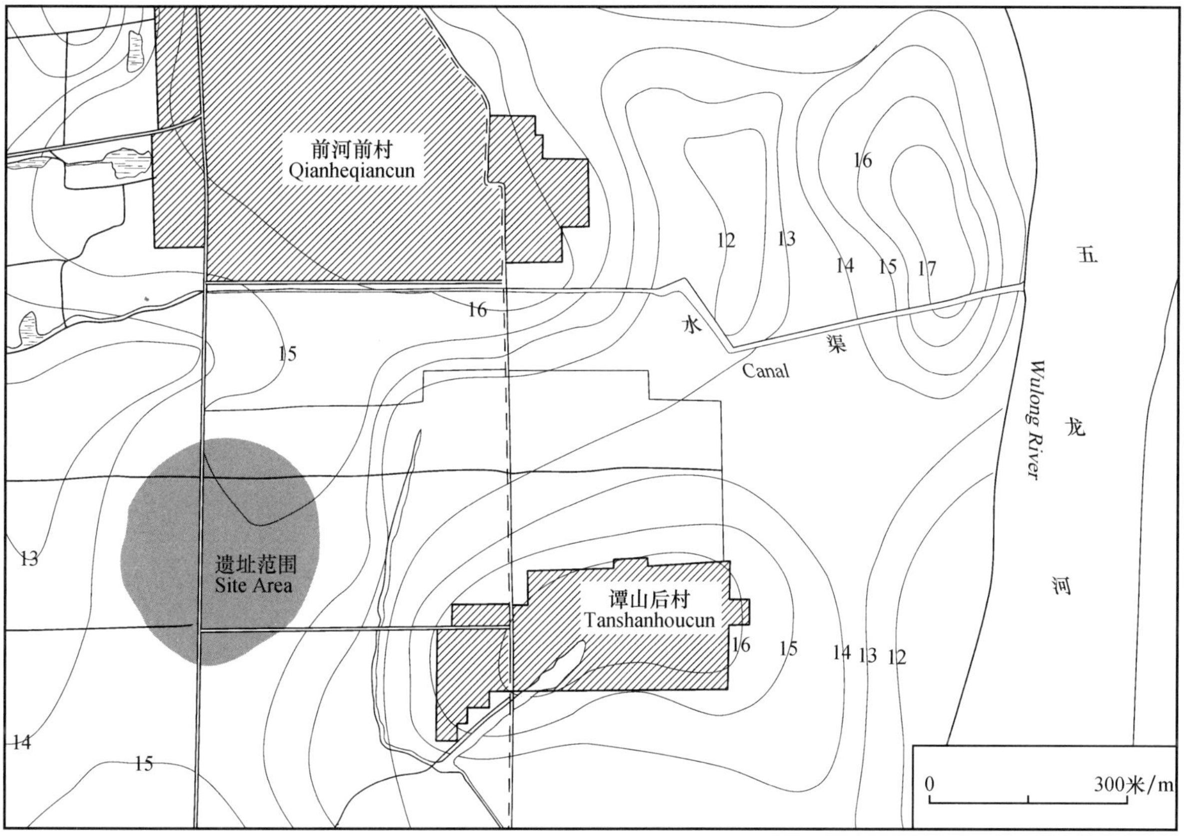

图Ⅰ.7.24　前河前遗址

Figure Ⅰ.7.24　The Qianheqian site.

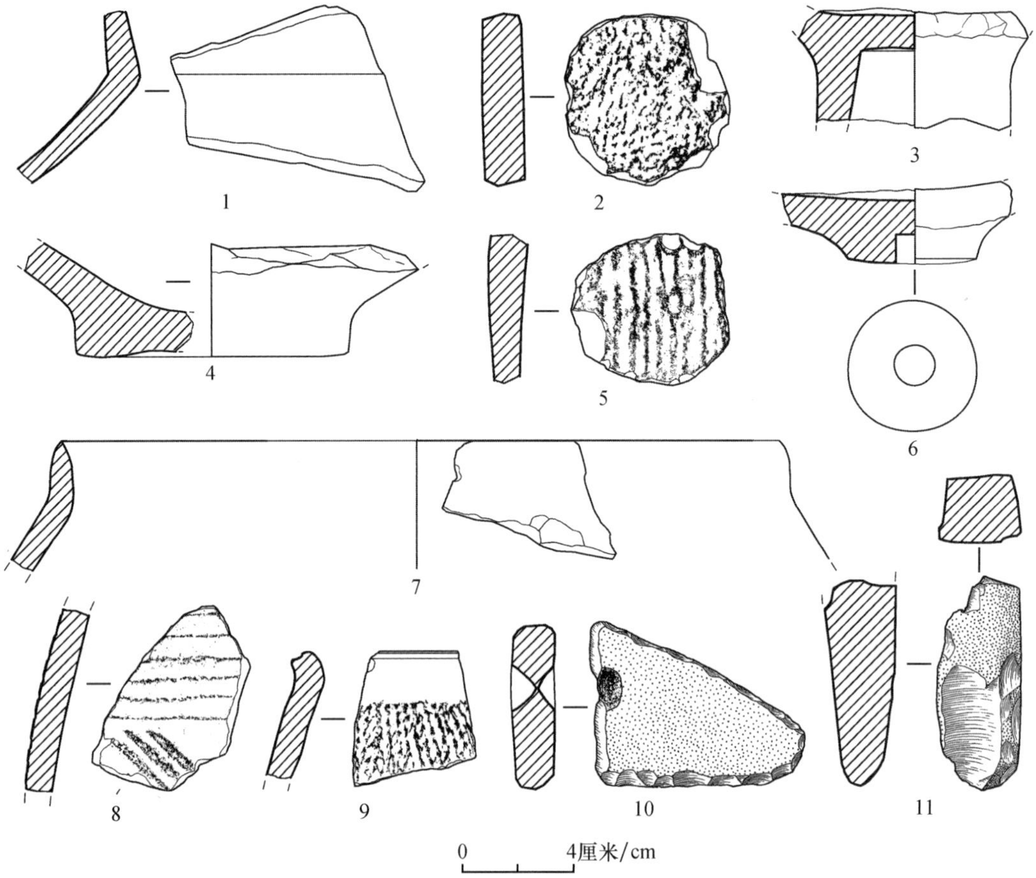

图Ⅰ.7.25　前河前遗址发现遗物

Figure Ⅰ.7.25　Artifacts from the Qianheqian site.

表Ⅰ.7.9　前河前遗址发现遗物统计表

Table Ⅰ.7.9　Artifacts from the Qianheqian site

序号 Number on Fig. Ⅰ.7.26	标本号 Excavation number	器物名称 Artifact name	出土时间 Excavation date	位置 Location	所属类型 Types	尺寸（厘米） Size (cm)	特点描述 Description of the features
1	10SLQ 采：1	罐 *Guan* jar	2010-5	地表采集 Surface collection		H: 6.4 W: 9.1 T: 1.0	泥质灰陶。高领，口残，斜广肩。素面。 Grey clay pottery; high neck, broken mouth, broad and oblique shoulder; plain-surfaced.
2	10SLQ 采：4	圆陶片 Round piece of pottery	2010-5	地表采集 Surface collection		D: 6.0 T: 1.5	泥质灰陶。系用罐的残片将周围打压而成。一面保留原器物的绳纹。 Grey clay; shaped from a piece of *guan* fragment by pressing off its eges; one side retains the original cord marks.
3	10SLQ 采：3	豆 *Dou* pedestal dish	2010-5	地表采集 Surface collection		H: 4.0 D: 7.2 T: 1.35	泥质灰陶。盘残，喇叭口圈足，足下部残，器壁较厚。 Grey clay; trumpet-shaped foot of *dou*, bottom of foot broken, relatively thick wall.
4	10SLQ 采：5	罐 *Guan* jar	2010-5	地表采集 Surface collection		B: 12 H: 4.2 T: 1.35	夹粗砂红褐陶。为罐底部，平底微内凹，器壁较厚。这件器物具有当地土著风格。 Coarse reddish-brown pottery; bottom of *guan* jar, flat bottom slightly concave, relatively thick walls; indigenous style pottery.

续表

序号 Number on Fig. Ⅰ.7.26	标本号 Excavation number	器物名称 Artifact name	出土时间 Excavation date	位置 Location	所属类型 Types	尺寸（厘米） Size (cm)	特点描述 Description of the features
5	10SLQ 采：9	圆陶片 Round piece of pottery	2010-5	地表采集 Surface collection		D: 5.4 T: 1.4	泥质橙红陶。系用罐的残片加工而成。一面保留原器的篮纹。 Orange clay; fragment of a jar, one surface retains the original basket-pattern impressions.
6	10SLQ 采：6	豆 *Dou* pedestal dish	2010-5	地表采集 Surface collection		H: 2.9 D: 5.1 T: 1.3	泥质灰陶。盘残，喇叭口圈足，圈足残后又二次加工打磨平整后继续使用，器壁厚重。 Grey clay; part of the dish section of a *dou*, trumpet-shaped foot, was burnished and used again after breaking, relatively thick wall.
7	10SLQ 采：7	罐 *Guan* jar	2010-5	地表采集 Surface collection		M: 26 H: 4.1 T: 0.9	夹砂红褐陶。直口，尖唇，鼓腹。素面。为具有当地土著风格器物。 Coarse, reddish-brown pottery; straight mouth, sharp lip, bulging belly; plain surface; indigenous style artifact.
8	10SLQ 采：8	罐 *Guan* jar	2010-5	地表采集 Surface collection		M: 14 H: 4.8 T: 1.0	夹砂红褐陶。为罐的腹片。腹上饰六道凹弦纹，下饰曲折形刻划纹。此为具有当地土著风格器物。 Coarse, reddish-brown pottery; piece of jar belly; decorated with six concave lines around belly, under which are decorative zigzag patterns. This is an indigenous style artifact.
9	10SLQ 采：10	鬲 *Li* tripod	2010-5	地表采集 Surface collection		L: 8.8 W: 5.8 T: 1.4	泥质灰陶。侈口略残，斜直腹，下部残。腹饰竖绳纹。 Grey clay; slighly broken wide mouth, oblique belly, broken bottom; vertical cord-marks on belly.
10	10SLQ 采：2	石刀 Stone knife	2010-5	地表采集 Surface collection		H: 4.4 W: 7.1 T: 1.1	灰白色砂岩。直刃，弧背，中部对钻一孔，采用琢钻法，刃部经两侧打制而成，没有进行进一步加工。 Greyish-white sandstone; straight edge, curved back, a hole at center drilled from both sides using polish drill method, edge made by chipping both sides, no further work done on it.
11	10SLQ 采：11	石锛 Stone adze	2010-5	地表采集 Surface collection		L: 7.6 W: 3 T: 2.7	青色页岩。大部分打制，局部磨制，刃部和顶部略残。 Blue-green schist; mostly fashioned by chipping, with parts polished. The blade and top are broken.

表Ⅰ.7.10　调查遗址登记表

Table Ⅰ.7.10　List of Sites Surveyed

编号 No.	遗址名称 Site Name	遗址面积 Area	时　代 Period	行政区划（镇） Administrative Area (Township)
01	东羔遗址 Donggao	250×200 m—50,000m^2	邱家庄一期、周、汉代 Qiujiazhuang Ⅰ, Zhou, Han	褚由观镇 Xuyouguan
02	唐家遗址 Tangjia	160×100 m—16,000m^2	邱家庄一期、春秋、汉代 Qiujiazhuang Ⅰ, Zhou, Han	徐福镇 Xufu
03	南王绪遗址 Nanwangxu	190×150 m—28,500m^2	邱家庄一期 Qiujiazhuang Ⅰ	蓬莱北沟乡 Penglai beigouxiang
04	庄头遗址 Zhuangtou	150×120 m—18,000m^2	西周 W. Zhou	石良镇 Shiliang
05	集前赵家墓地 Jiqian Zhaojia	110×50 m—5,8000m^2	周、汉代 Zhou, Han	石良镇 Shiliang
06	东营周家墓地 Dongying Zhoujia cemetery	150×150 m—22,500m^2	西周 W. Zhou	石良镇 Shiliang
07	鲁家沟遗址 Lujiagou site	150×200 m—30,000m^2	邱家庄一期、 Qiujiazhuang Ⅰ	石良镇 Shiliang
08	鲁家沟墓地 Lujiagou cemetery	100×85 m—8,5000m^2	邱家庄一期、西周Qiujiazhuang Ⅰ, W. Zhou	石良镇 Shiliang
09	乾山遗址 Qianshan	225×480 m—122,400m^2	邱家庄一期、汉代 Qiujiazhuang Ⅰ, Han	徐福镇 Xufu
10	张郑家墓地 Zhangzhengjia cemetery	Unknown (destroyed by earth extraction)（被取土破坏）	西周 W. Zhou	新嘉街道 Xinjiajiedao
11	小莱山溶洞遗址 Xiaolaishan cave	20,000m^2	旧石器文化 Paleolithic	兰高镇 Lan'gao
12	徐乡故城遗址 Xuxiang old town site	514×370 m—190,000m^2	春秋、汉代 Spring and Autumn, Han	徐福镇 Xufu
13	村里集城址 Cunliji town site	500×600 m—300,000m^2	西周、春秋 W. Zhou, Spring and Autumn	蓬莱村里集乡 Penglai Cunliji
14	村里集墓地 Cunliji cemetery	400×100 m—40,000m^2	西周、春秋 W. Zhou, Spring and Autumn	蓬莱村里集乡 Penglai Cunliji
15	楼子庄遗址 Louzizhuang	210×147 m—30,900m^2	龙山文化 Longshan	北马镇 Beima
16	黄河营古港遗址 Huangheying old port site	220×200 m—40,000m^2	西周 W. Zhou	徐福镇 Xufu
17	前河前遗址 Qianheqian	250×300 m—71,000m^2	西周、东周 W. Zhou, E. Zhou	蓬莱市团旺镇 Penglai tuanwang
18	邵家遗址 Shaojia	不　详 (Unknown)	龙山、岳石文化 Longshan, Yueshi	东江镇 Dongjiang
19	姚家包袱地墓地 Yaojia Baofudi cemetery	140×60 m—11,200m^2	战国 Warring States	褚由观镇 Xuyouguan
20	郝家墓地 Haojia cemetery	110×95 m—10,500m^2	汉代 Han	褚由观镇 Xuyouguan
21	后祚杨遗址 Houzuoyang	350×120 m—42,000m^2	周、汉代 Zhou, Han	褚由观镇 Xuyouguan
22	唐家集遗址 Tangjiaji	310×200 m—50,000m^2	周、汉代 Zhou, Han	褚由观镇 Xuyouguan
23	下河头遗址 Xiahetou	30×100 m—30,000m^2	龙山文化、周、汉代 Longshan, Zhou, Han	石良镇 Shiliang

续表

编号 No.	遗址名称 Site Name	遗址面积 Area	时　代 Period	行政区划（镇） Administrative Area (Township)
24	平里院遗址 Pingliyuan	200 × 118 m—23,600m^2	岳石、汉代 Yueshi, Han	石良镇 Shiliang
25	李家遗址 Lijia	200 × 160 m—36,700m^2	龙山文化、周代 Longshan, Han	北马镇 Beima
26	赵家遗址 Zhaojia	120 × 100 m—12,000m^2	汉代 Han	褚由观镇 Xuyouguan
27	洼南遗址 Wa'nan	100 × 90 m—90,000m^2	东周、汉代 E. Zhou, Han	徐福镇 Xufu
28	赵刘遗址 Zhaoliu	90 × 70 m—60,000m^2	周代 Zhou	褚由观镇 Xuyouguan
29	上庄马家遗址 Shangzhuang Majia	100 × 50 m—50,000m^2	汉代 Han	褚由观镇 Xuyouguan
30	程家遗址 Chengjia	80 × 45 m—3,600m^2	周代 Zhou	褚由观镇 Xuyouguan
31	西张家遗址 Xizhangguo	140 × 60 m—8,400m^2	周、汉代 Zhou, Han	褚由观镇 Xuyouguan
32	前妙果遗址 Qianmiaoguo	100 × 100 m—10,000m^2	龙山文化、汉代 Longshan, Han	褚由观镇 Xuyouguan
33	黄城集遗址 Huangchengji	1550 × 150 m—231,000m^2	战国、汉代 Warring States, Han	石良镇 Shiliang
34	冷王遗址 Lengwang	75 × 40 m—2,600m^2	汉代 Han	褚由观镇 Xuyouguan
35	大金家遗址 Dajinjia	120 × 80 m—9,6000m^2	汉代 Han	石良镇 Shiliang
36	洕泊遗址 Zhibo	252 × 134 m—35,000m^2	汉代 Han	兰高镇 Lan'gao
37	四平遗址 Siping	200 × 110 m—22,000m^2	周代、汉代 Zhou, Han	兰高镇 Lan'gao
38	侧高遗址 Zegao	253 × 124 m—31,000m^2	东周、汉代 E. Zhou, Han	兰高镇 Lan'gao

Chapter 7: Archaeological Survey of the Huangshui River Basin

Liang Zhonghe

From 2007 to 2009, the Guicheng archaeological team carried out a detailed and multifaceted survey of the Guicheng city site in Longkou, Shandong. Within the 8 km^2 city site, we figured out the distribution of sites and the condition of preservation of remains still underground, obtaining a rich harvest of data (see Chapters 2 to 6). During this period, although we carried out some surveys of sites outside the city, overall we knew very little about the distribution of sites in the region.

The Guicheng site is located in a hilly area along the Yaque River, a tributary of the Huang River, the largest river in Longkou. The Huang River is also the largest river in the vicinity of the Guicheng site; its main stream originates south of the site in the area of the Wangwu Reservoir, in the eastern foothills of Mount Lai, and flows 26 km in a northwesterly direction to the sea. An examination of changes in settlements in the Huang River basin is important for understanding the spatial relationship between the sites and the system of settlement organization in the area, and for a fuller understanding of the position and nature of Guicheng. After referring to past survey data, in 2010 and 2011 we carried out two seasons of survey or reexamination of the sites in the Huang River drainage system, with an emphasis on sites contemporaneous with the Shang-Zhou period (Map Ⅰ.7.1). This laid the foundation for further research in the future on the sites of the Longkou region.

Section 1: Survey Methodology and Procedures

In order to carry out this survey, we began by choosing a 1 : 10000 scale topographic map of the basin. We also often made reference to Google Earth satellite images, using both sets of data together. Next, before carrying out the survey, we tried to gain as much familiarity as possible with relevant published information on the past surveys and examined artifacts from the area, in order to further clarify the cultural characteristics of each site. Finally, we carried out surveys of sites about which we already had some information, in order to ensure the level of detail and accuracy of the work.

Procedures:

(1) Mark the exact location on the map; measure the latitude, longitude and altitude.

(2) Conduct a site survey and use coring method to determine the site's date, the thickness of cultural layers, and to clarify the area of the site.

(3) Choose a place where there is a precipice and expose cross-sections in order to better understand the thickness of the site's sediments, divide the cultural layers and take samples.

(4) Define an area for collecting specimens, including all relics left by ancient human activities.

(5) Use a total station to draw a 1 : 1000 topographic map of the site and surroundings, and draw the actual area of the site based on the coring and survey.

Longkou City is located in the northwestern part of the Jiaodong Peninsula. The Bohai Sea is on the northwest shore, and in the southeast it borders on Mount Lai. The Huang River flows through its territory which has an area of 890 km^2. On the northern plains are distributed the shell middens that date to Qiujiazhuang Period I culture. In the south is the Guicheng city site that dates to the Western Zhou period. In addition, the ancient Moon Goddess Shrine, one of the renowned "Eight Shrines of Qi," is located on a peak of Mount Lai, and the huge architectural foundation identified with the Palace of the First Emperor of Qin is located in its northern foothills. The sites we investigated range from the Neolithic to the Qin-Han period. By examining the size and conditions of settlements of each period throughout the region, we also found that a gap exists between the early Baishicun Period I culture (ca. 6000-5700 BP) and the Zijingshan Period I culture (ca. 5275-4860 BP). In other words, there are no cultural remains contemporary with the middle Dawenkou period of the large region of inland Shandong. Why is this? Until now scholars have had different opinions. Many believe that there is some connection with the environment, but we will leave this question unaddressed here.

Section 2: Surveyed Sites

Any kind of human culture, over the course of its emergence, development, and evolution, apart from the limits set by the natural environment, will also be influenced by its cultural environment. "Cultural environment" refers to the relationship of one culture group with those that surround it. Human culture is dynamic: exchanges and cultural borrowing between different cultures, especially neighboring ones, are important factors affecting cultural change. Therefore, the spatial movement of cultural phenomena — cultural diffusion — is an important subject of archaeological research.

The Huang River, the second largest river system on the Shandong Peninsula, rises in the area between Mount Lai and the Gushan Mountain range and flows north into the Bohai Sea. The main channel of the Huang River is located northeast of Longkou City, and it flows through the territories of Qixia, Zhaoyuan, Longkou, and Penglai. The watershed area is very wide and has many tributaries, and the drainage basin is mainly an area of low hills. The sites surveyed are mainly distributed on both sides of the Huang River and its important tributaries. Apart from Guicheng, other important sites include Donggao, Tangjia, Qianshan, Shaojia, Xiao Laishan cave-site, and Lujiagou, all located in Longkou City. In Penglai City there are the Nanwangxu and Cunliji Neolithic sites. Below we will separately describe the general situation of each site and the cultural relics collected from them.

1. The Donggao Site

The Donggao site is located on a ridge of high ground about 500 m north of Donggao Village, in Zhuyouguan Township of Longkou City. It is 2 km south of the Bohai shore, and 1.5 km west of the Huang River. The geographic coordinates of the site are 37°43′42″N, 120°30′42″E, and it sits 13 m above sea level.

The site area is about 250 m long from north to south, 200 m wide from east to west, with a total area of approximately 50,000 m^2. The Yantai-Weifang highway passes right through the middle of the site. The Longkou City central north-south highway to the sea crosses the Yantai-Weifang highway just west of the site. The site is on a slope that rises to the west and descends towards the east. There are hills to the west and south, which are now planted with fruit trees and pines on the site (Fig. Ⅰ.7.1). In 2006 the Shandong Provincial Institute of Cultural Relics and Archaeology, Yantai and Longkou Municipal Museums formed a joint combined archaeological team that conducted salvage excavations and obtained a new batch of data.

The excavation of the Donggao site yielded a batch of Qiujiazhuang Period I waste pits, tombs, and house remains. Pottery, stone and bone tools, and other relics were discovered. The decorations on pottery include engraved patterns, grid patterns, and circular appliqué. A large number of animal bones, oyster shells and clam shells were also found. The site is very important for understanding the culture of the shell midden sites and the changing shoreline of the Jiaodong Peninsula.

Most of the artifacts collected within the site were pottery sherds, including fragments of rims, waists, bases, feet, and other parts. Vessel types that can be identified included rims of *ding* cauldron, vessel legs, *guan* jars, bowls, etc. The remains were mostly those of the Qiujiazhuang Period I, but there were also Zhou period cord-marked pottery and Han Dynasty roof tiles (Fig. Ⅰ.7.2; Table Ⅰ.7.1).

2. The Tangjia Site

Tangjia Village is located in Xufu Township of Longkou City, about 4.5 km west of Xufu Town. The geographic coordinates of the site are 37°41′46″N, 120°27′27″E, and it is 11 m above sea level.

The site is 5 km south of the Bohai Sea. There is higher ground to the northeast of Tangjia Village, and an old building to the east of the site. A road runs through the south of the site, dividing it in two. The middle is relatively high, the surroundings are lower. According to local residents, the middle used to be much higher than it is now, but due to the gradual flattening through time and people taking soil for fertilizer and to build buildings, the site has been severely damaged. Recently it has been used as a cemetery, and surrounding areas have been used to grow vegetables, fruit, and other crops, so it has not been well preserved.

The site is 160 m east to west, 100 m north to south, and covers an area of about 16,000 m^2 (Fig. I .7.3). In 1996 the site was identified as a Key Cultural Relics Protection Unit by Yantai City. Coring has established that the culture layer is 0.50 to 1.20 m thick. The majority of cultural relics collected from the surface are from the Neolithic period, dating predominantly to Qiujiazhuang Period I. These include fragments of *ding* cauldrons, *guan* jars, bowls, and basins; ground seashells belonging to this period were scattered all over the site. In addition, we also found a few cord-impressed *guan* jar fragments as well as bases of *dou* pedestal dishes dating to the Spring and Autumn period, and roof tiles from the Han Dynasty (Fig. I .7.4; Table I .7.2). We also collected pieces of red burnt earth from a precipice on the site. These contained traces of straw blended into the earth that were left when the straw burned. Rough on one side, smooth on the other, these clods were probably the building material of houses.

The site provides important data for the study of the cultural landscape, site distribution and changing patterns of the Neolithic period in the Huangshui River Basin.

3. The Nanwangxu Site

Located in Beigou District of Penglai City, the Nanwangxu site lies about 150 m south of the village of that name. The geographic coordinates of the site are 37°44′46″ N, 120°37′23″; it is more than 20 m above sea level.

This site is on a high point that slopes downwards from southeast to northwest. There are hills to the east and south, small streams to the east and west, and the sea is about 3 km to the north. There are small country roads to the west and south. The site was seriously damaged by local farmers who continuously used it as the source of soil that they took for various purposes. The site surface is now mostly planted with fruit trees. The site area is about 190 m from north to south, 150 m from east to west, and covers an area of 28,500 m^2 (Fig. I .7.5). In 1996 the site was designated a Key Cultural Relics Protection Unit of Yantai City and in 2006 it was designated a Key Cultural Relics Protection Unit of Shandong Province. In October 1994 the Research Group of Jiaodong Peninsula Shell Midden Sites of the Institute of Archaeology, CASS, collected surface relics, and performed a comprehensive surface and subsurface coring survey (CASS Institute of Archaeology 1999, 77-83; Yuan Jing, Liang Zhonghe et al. 2002: 3-22).

Based on cultural layers exposed on the precipices of the site and the results of coring, we infer that the people lived in the eastern portion of the site and the cemetery was located in its northern part. The contents of cultural layers already exposed and the burials are very rich. Toward the northwestern part of the site, was found a trash dump, where the accumulated cultural layers exposed on the precipices were 1.5 to 3.0 m thick, some even thicker. They contained burnt dirt, pottery sherds and shell middens. The site provides important data for understanding the evolution of the Neolithic cultures of the Shandong Peninsula.

The site surface is now entirely planted with fruit trees. There are very few artifacts on the surface; we only found some samples near the precipices. The most common sherds were red or reddish-brown tempered pottery. Next most common were grey fine clay. There was also one with mica and shell inclusions. All were shaped by hand. Of the vessel types that could be identified, there were *ding* cauldrons, *guan* jars, small-mouthed *hu* bottles, bowls, and a single pottery *huan* bracelet (Fig. Ⅰ.7.6; Table Ⅰ.7.3).

4. Zhangtou Cemetery

The Zhuangtou cemetery is located on high ground to the east of East Zhuangtou Village, in Shiliang Township of Longkou City. The geographic coordinates of the site are 37°35′11″ N, 120°41′28″ E, and it is 87 m above sea level.

The site is on a north-south oriented loess plateau. Because of the proximity to Gushan Mountain, the whole terrain is higher in the east than the west. To the east and west of the site are relatively high farming terraces, while under the cliffs to the southwest the land is low. About 80 m to the south is the Wangjiacun Reservoir dam. On the north side are fields with a slight slope. The west side is near the residential area of East Zhuangtou Village; on the south side is a main road. The plateau surface has now been cleared to make farmland, which is mostly planted with fruit trees and maize. The site area is 200 m from north to south, and 150 m from east to west, with a total area of about 30,000 m^2 (Fig. Ⅰ.7.7).

The site was discovered in 1980 by local people while taking soil from the plateau, and in December 1981 a joint team sent by the Cultural Relics Management Committee and the Cultural Property Headquarters of Huangxian County (Longkou City) conducted an excavation and clearing of a tomb from which bronze objects had been extracted (Wang Xiping and Tang Luting 1986: 69-72). The tomb was an earthen pit 3 m long, 2.46 m wide, and 1.32 m below the ground surface. The original wooden chamber at the bottom of the pit was surrounded by a 0.2 m wide ring of rammed earth, which seemed to be the "Second-level Platform" (*ercengtai*). The remains of an 11 cm wide wooden crossbeam 27 cm from the east wall separated the burial chamber into north and south halves, hence forming a head box. From this head box many of the bronzes with inscriptions were recovered, indicating that the local cemetery belonged to people of aristocratic status of Western Zhou period. The site was declared a Key Protected Cultural Relic Unit of Shandong Province in 1992. It is an important site for the study of the site distribution and burial customs of the Bronze Age in the Huang River region.

Few specimens were found in the cemetery during survey. They were mainly *guan* jars, *dou* pedestal dishes and a broken bronze *ge* dagger (Fig. Ⅰ.7.8; Table Ⅰ.7.4).

5. Jiqian Zhaojia Cemetery

The site is located northwest of Jiqian Zhaojia Village, 1 km south of Shiliang Township of Longkou City. The geographic coordinates of the site are 37°34′07″ N, 120°39′46″ E, and it sits 58 m above sea level.

The cemetery is located northwest of the village on a high plateau, about 100 m north of the Dongying River, a tributary of the Huang River. To the west is Highway 213. The site is 110 m from east to west, 50 m north to south, with an area of about 5,800 m^2 (Fig. Ⅰ.7.19). There is an abandoned brick factory southwest of the site. In the 1970s this factory used soil for brick making and leveled the land in the area, causing serious damage to the site. Because soil was taken from the site for many years, the cemetery became a huge pit. The tombs that were cleared are located beside a low cliff north of the factory. There is still a 2 m high platform, and the majority of the cemetery is now covered by fruit trees, so there is little space to collect artifacts.

The tomb is a vertical earthen pit. The excavation uncovered bronze, pottery and other artifacts, dating to the Western Zhou period. When the tomb was discovered, many of the bronzes had been smashed to pieces, and identifiable types include *ding* cauldron, *hu* bottle, *gui* tureen, *jue* cup, etc. At least five have inscriptions. At present there is also Han brick debris found in the cemetery, on which there are inscriptions, portraits of ladies, and so on. The tombs mainly date to the Western Zhou and Han dynasties. The cemetery has been repeatedly looted, which caused a serious loss of material; the site needs to be protected. The site is important for the study of Western Zhou and Han period burial forms in the Huang River region, as well as the relationship of the site's Zhou era remains with the state of Lai.

Very few artifacts were collected during our survey, inlcuding only a rim of a *guan* jar (Fig. Ⅰ.7.10; Table Ⅰ.7.5).

6. Dongying Zhoujia Cemetery

The site is located southeast of Dongying Zhoujia Village, 3 km south of Shiliang Township of Longkou City. The geographic coordinates of the site are 37°34′01″ N, 120°40′55″ E, and it lies 70 m above sea level.

The site is located in a low-lying part of a mountainous area, with large fluctuations in terrain. Jiqian Zhaojia and Dongying Caojia Villages lie to the west, while to the south is the channel of the Dongying River. To the southeast can be seen the Dasongding mountain range. According to local farmers the cemetery is up on a high plateau. To its east lie farming terraces, and below a low cliff to the southwest is a nameless creek that flows northward into the Dongying River. As a result of the construction of the brick factory and the continual removal of earth to feed the brick kilns in the1970s, as well as land levelling, the site has been severely damaged. The brick factory has been abandoned. The land is now covered by orchards, and few artifacts were collected during our survey. The site is about 150 m wide from east to west, with an area of about 22,500 m^2 (Fig. Ⅰ.7.11). In 1986 three tombs were discovered and cleared out. All were earthen pit tombs containing "second-level platforms" and the remains of wooden coffins. More than 200 artifacts were discovered. Pottery artifacts include *ding* cauldrons, *li* tripods, *dou* pedestal dishes, *guan* jars, and *gui* tureens. Bronzes included a *ding* cauldron and a *gui* tureen (Tang and Jiang 1989: 314-319). The site provides important information for the study of Bronze Age cultures in the Huang River region.

7. The Lujiagou Site

This site is located on a plateau about 5 km northeast of Lujiagou Village in Shiliang Township of Longkou City, 37°31′07″ N, 120°40′28 .0″ E, and it lies 88 m above sea level.

The site dates mainly to the Neolithic period, and is surrounded by hilly terrain, close to mountains. The area of the originally discovered site is quite large – 150 m from north to south and 200 m from east to west, covering an area of 30,000m^2 (Fig. Ⅰ.7.12). The main reason for its destruction is the building of houses in Lujiagou Village, and most of the site has now been built over. Also the effects of land leveling over the years and long-term agricultural production have seriously damaged the site. Soil erosion caused by rainfall has also exacerbated the destruction. All of this has caused serious damage to the cultural layer. The remaining part is now a piece of farmland, measuring only about 6,000 m^2. We do not know about the cultural stratification of the site. Previous surveys have turned up a large number of artifacts, such as pottery, stone tools, burned earth and charcoal. The pottery sherds often have mica inclusions, and are tempered or fine clay, or with red clothing. The color is mainly reddish-brown or yellowish beige-brown. The most common ornamentations are appliqué patterns or nipple decoration. Discernible vessel types include *ding* cauldron, *guan* jars, *huan* bracelets, etc. Most of them are Qiujiazhuang Period I types. There is a big difference in age between the artifacts collected at the Lujiagou site and those collected at the Lujiagou Cemetery (see below) (Fig. Ⅰ.7.13; Table Ⅰ.7.6).

8. The Lujiagou Cemetery

This burial ground is located on a high terrace northeast of Lujiagou Village, Shiliang Township of Longkou City, about 10 km south of the town of Shiliang. Geographic coordinates are 37°31′07″N, 20°40′27.0″ E, and it lies 89 m above sea level. The site is surrounded by hilly terrain, close to mountains. The site slopes gently to the southwest. Not far to the west is highway 213, and a small tractor road passes through the south of the site. There is also a pond not far to the south. The cemetery is now farmland, planted mainly with fruit trees and maize. The cemetery is 100 m from east to west, 85 m north to south, covering an area of about 8,500 m^2 (Fig. Ⅰ.7.13). The cemetery has been quite seriously damaged; during our reexamination we were only able to find a few pottery sherds. Land levelling has destroyed the west of the site. Earthen pit tombs were found here in the past, and among the excavated bronzes were the *Laibo ding*, *hu* pitcher, bronze swords and so on.

According to historical records, in the twenty-second year of the Guangxu reign period of the Qing Dynasty (1896) a group of Western Zhou Dynasty bronzes was unearthed here. Wang Daoxin's draft version of *Huangxian Gazetteer* ("List of Stones and Metal Objects") records that ten bronze vessels came from the field of Lujiagou, located southeast of Huangxian, including three bells and two *ding* cauldrons. The bells had no inscriptions. There were also one *he* pitcher and one *pan* basin. The basin had no inscription. As for the *yan* steamer, *he* pitcher, and *zhi* vase, all had inscriptions." (Wang Daoxin 1934: 806). A slightly different account of this comes from the *Anthology of the Collected Bronze Inscriptions from Shandong*, which mentions that an inscribed *ding* cauldron was also unearthed in 1896 in Huangxian. The content of its inscription was similar to that of the *yan* steamer unearthed at Lujiagou. Both record a person named 遇 receiving an award and making the vessels. They may both be from the same group of vessels (Ceng Yigong 1940:11-13). One of the *ding* in this group had an inscription of only five characters: "Laibo makes a traveling *ding*," many scholars believe that this is proof that the state of Lai was near Mount Lai.

Since 1956, researchers from the central academy or Shandong Province as well as from the Yantai Municipal Museum have investigated this site many times. Based on the geographical location and characteristics of the artifacts unearthed, this is a Western Zhou tomb cluster. Some of these relics have been lost to Japan. Scholars who study these artifacts believe that it is an elite cemetery of the state of Lai. The site provides important data for the study of Neolithic and Bronze Age cultures of the Huang River Basin.

9. The Qianshan Site

The site is located in Xiangcheng-East Village, in Xufu Township of Longkou City, and the government center of the township is about 500 m to the west. The geographic coordinates are 37°40′44″ N, 120°29′30″ E, and it lies 20 m above sea level.

The site is located atop a high rectangular hill about 500 m east of Xiangcheng East Village. Yanggouying Village lies to the north, Buzihou Village is to the east, and the newly built Xufu Temple lies 300 m to the south. To the southwest lie the ruins of the old city site of Xuxiang, which has been destroyed. According to the accounts of local villagers, the original site was very large, about 255 m east to west and 480 m north to south, with a total area of about 122,400 m^2 (Fig. Ⅰ.7.14).

Originally there was a small hill about 20 m high, which was severely damaged by earth removal for land reclamation and leveling for farming. Now there is merely a 5 m high hill in the northeast corner measuring only a few tens of square meters. A north-south rural road passes through. The western part of the site was made into a pen for raising animals and it is unknown where the remains of the site end. The site was discovered in 1957 and several Han Dynasty tombs were excavated and cleared. Pottery vessels discovered in the tombs include painted *guan* jars, *hu* bottles, cups, and *fu* cooking pots, while bronzes included an incense burner and a two-eared *hu* bottle. On a cliff cut from the mound we found a large accumulation of shells and collected typical Qiujiazhuang Period I sherds of two types, red fine clay and tempered grey pottery. The artifacts included *ding* feet, a grinding stone and human bones. There were also Han era artifacts like tomb bricks with water caltrop designs and writing, and cord-marked pottery of grey fine clay. Because there are artifacts dating to different periods, the site has a higher scientific value.

The Qianshan site is in the north of the old City-site of Xuxiang, separated from it by 200 m. In 1991, it was declared a Key Cultural Relics Protection Unit of Yantai. It provides important data for the study of the Neolithic and Han periods in the Huang River region.

The site is severely damaged and it is difficult to find pottery sherds on the ground, though we found some on the cliff on the eastern side of the preserved high mound. From the cut we can identify deposit layers of different periods, the majority having Neolithic pottery sherds. There are also Western Zhou and Han-era bricks and roof tiles, etc. Of those that can be identified, there are *ding* cauldrons, *guan* jars, small mouthed *guan*, bowls, and grinding stones (Fig. Ⅰ.7.15; Table Ⅰ.7.7).

10. Zhangzhengjia Cemetery

The cemetery is located in the southeast of Zhangzhengjia Village, on Xinjia Street of Longkou City. The geographic coordinates are 37°38′36″N, 120°26′52″E, and 24 m above sea level.

The site is located on a high point on the east bank of the Yongwen River. Not far to the north is the Beiqu site, and the Yanggao site is to the northeast. To the east is the newly developed part of the city. About 200 m to the north is Zhangjiacun (Fig. Ⅰ.7.16). Around Zhangzhengjia Village the land is flat. To the north of the village is a brick factory. Because earth was taken from the site for many years to make bricks, there is a depression at the site. It was during these excavating activities that local people discovered the graves, and dug out over one hundred pottery vessels. They submitted the pottery vessels to the Longkou Municipal Museum, from which we chose some to include in this report. These vessels were not given numbers and their specific excavation units are unknown, so we can only divide them by types. Most of the original deposit at the site has been severely damaged, so we were unable to determine the original area of the cemetery, but based on the current information it seems to have been a low-status Western Zhou burial ground. Based on pottery unearthed from the site we can date the cemetery to the later part of the Western Zhou period. This is valuable material for studying Bronze Age cultures in the region (Fig. Ⅰ.7.17.1-4; Table Ⅰ.7.8; Pls. 58-65).

11. Xiaolaishan Cave Site

The Xiao Laishan Cave Site is located 500 m northeast of Outou Sunjia Village, in Langao Township of Longkou City. The geographic coordinates are 37°37′35″ N, 120°36′02″ E, and it lies 45 m above sea level.

The west of the site is close to the Yaque River, a tributary of the Huang River, which flows along the western foot of Little Lai Mountain. The hillside site is 400 m from north to south, 200 m east to west, while the cave area is about 2,000 m^2 (Fig. Ⅰ.7.18). The cave, a Paleolithic cave site, was discovered in 1932. It has a cultural layer 0.50 to 1.00 m thick, with traces of the original human dwelling, and a number of chipped stone tools as well as animal fossils such as fish bones, animal bones, antlers, etc., were found there. It was listed as a Key Cultural Relics Protection Unit of Longkou City in 1992. The site provides important information for the study of the Paleolithic cultural evolution and climatic change in the Huang River Basin.

12. The Xuxiang Old City Site

The site is located in the southern part of Chengdong Village, in Xufu Township of Longkou City, about 7 km northwest of Longkou city. An east-west district road passes through the site from the middle of the city walls. The geographic coordinates are 120°29′08″E, 37°40′32″N, and it lies 20 m above sea level; 200 m to the northeast is the Qianshan site (Fig. Ⅰ.7.19).

The Xuxiang city site walls and building remains are entirely gone, but textual records and archaeological materials suggest that the Xuxiang city site was built in the Spring and Autumn period and was inhabited into the early Han Dynasty. In the late Spring and Autumn period Qi conquered and destroyed the state of Lai, whose capital was the Guicheng site, and constructed Xuxiang city close to the northern seashore in the old territory of the state of Lai. After Qin conquered Qi and established the empire, it turned Xuxiang City into a marquisate. There was a rich collection of artifacts at the Xuxiang site, with relics discovered from the major historical periods. The collection included foundation stones from the city wall, wells, drainage ditches, bricks, roof tiles, pottery vessels, and bronze vessels. In recent years, the Shandong Provincial Institute of Cultural Relics and Archaeology has carried out coring and test excavations at the site and revealed the exact scope of the site, including gates, palaces, streets, workshops, kilns, drainage and other remains. Based on the results of the coring survey, we can see that the site is a rectangle 514 m from east to west, 370 m from north to south, with an area of about 190,000 m^2. This site contains important material for the study of the Spring and Autumn Period through the Han Dynasty in the Huang River region.

Very few artifacts were found at the site during our survey. There was only a single round foot of a ceramic basin (Fig. Ⅰ.7.10: 2; Table Ⅰ.7.5).

13. The Cunliji City Site

The site is located in Cunliji Township of Penglai City, about 45 km south of Penglai City. Near the city site there are three villages: Gucheng East, Gucheng Lijia, and Gucheng Miaojia. The geographic coordinates are 37°31′42″N, 120°46′21″E, and it lies 115 m above sea level.

To the south is Mount Aishan in Qixia, and there are hills to the east, west and north, so the site is in a basin. It is part of the loess highland in the upper valley of a tributary of the Huang River. This tributary flows north and enters the main stream of the Huang River in Longkou. The majority of the site is covered by villages. To the southwest is a small nameless creek that flows from south to north. A preliminary investigation in 1978 revealed a rectangular city site. The site is 500 m east to west, 600 m from north to south, covering an area of about 300,000 m^2 (Fig. Ⅰ.7.20). Most of the walls have been razed. What is left of the north wall is 100 m long, 10 m wide at the base, with only 4 m in height remaining. It is made of rammed earth with layers 4 to 6 cm thick with impressions made by ramming tools measuring approximately 4 cm in diameter. The city's interior cultural deposit is about 1-1.5 m thick. Artifacts collected at the site include the foot of a grey cord-impressed *li* tripod with sand inclusions, a rim piece from a grey clay *guan* jar, a *dou* pedestal dish stem, etc. The city dates from the Western Zhou to the Spring and Autumn Period, roughly the same period as the Guicheng city site. It is located in close proximity to the Guicheng city site, and the two overlook each other.

14. Cunliji Cemetery

The site is located at Cunliji Township of Penglai Municipality, 45 km south of Penglai City. In its surroundings are Xinwangji, Liugezhuang, Zhanma and Zhangjia Villages. The geographic coordinates are 37°30′23″N, 120°46′35″E, and it lies 134 m above sea level.

The tombs are mainly distributed on the terraces on both sides of the tributary of the Huang River. Part of the cemetery on the east of the river is in Xinwangji Village, while another part, on the west of the river, is in Liugezhuang Village. The cemetery is on the slopes of a low hill southeast of Xinwangji Village. On the west, beside the Huang River, the terrain is relatively flat, and a dirt road runs through the west of the site, about 1 km south of the village. The cemetery is 100 m north to south and 400 m from east to west, with an area of about 40,000 m^2 (Fig. Ⅰ.7.21).

A group of Western Zhou and Spring and Autumn Period tombs were excavated in the site. Three clearing excavations were done in the cemetery, uncovering nearly twenty tombs, all of which were rectangular earthen pit tombs, four with second-level ledges. Some included victims buried with the tomb occupant, waist pit, or had horses and chariot within the burial. The main artifacts were Western Zhou and Spring and Autumn period bronzes, pottery, jade, and so on. These are among the biggest Western Zhou town sites and cemeteries in the Huangshui River Basin, and they provide important information for the study of the forms and distribution of town sites in the basin.

15. The Louzizhuang Site

The site is located on high ground about 200 m south of Louzizhuang Village, in Beima Township of Longkou City. The geographic coordinates are 37°34′58″N, 120°24′13″E, and it lies 51 m above sea level.

The main peak of Mount Rener can be seen to the south of the site. To the east is the Louzizhuang brick factory. On the west is the Ma'nan River. The site is on the high terrace beside the river. The site is now about 2 m above the level of the village. Below the high ground there is a north-south country road, and the Weihai-Wuhai Interprovincial Highway passes through the center of the site in an east-west direction. The site is 210 m from east to west, 147 m from north to south, covering an area of more than 30,000 m^2 (Fig. Ⅰ.7.22).

In 2001 a joint archaeological team sent by the Yantai Museum and the Longkou Municipal Museum carried out a salvage excavation of the Louzizhuang site and obtained a new batch of data. The site has a rich cultural deposit, with six cultural layers, including houses and many kilns of the Longshan period, as well as the sherds of pottery steamers, pedestal dishes, bowls, *ding* cauldrons, cups, etc. There were stone knives shovels, adzes, bone needles, drills and other implements, as well as ash pits and ash troughs, etc. The site provides new information for the study of the development and evolution of the Huangshui River region's Neolithic cultures.

We collected few specimens at the site, only the bottom of a *guan* jar of indigenous type (Fig. Ⅰ.7.10; Table Ⅰ.7.5).

16. The Huangheying Old Port Site

The site is situated at the mouth of the Huang River northeast of Huangheying Village in Xufu Township of Longkou City, 16 km north of Longkou City. The geographic coordinates are 37°44′52″N, 120°30′46″E, and it lies 1.5 m above sea level.

This ancient port was a natural harbor of the Zhou period. It is 220 m from east to west, 200 m from north to south, covering an area of about 44,000 m^2 (Fig. Ⅰ.7.23). In ancient times the Huangheying port was large and had deep water, offering excellent geographical conditions. It is bounded by the Bohai Sea and lies more than 20 km northeast of the Qin Dynasty Huangxian County, so its water and land transportation were very developed. It is a natural harbor because the Huang River bends sharply near its mouth, forming a wide harbor with a small entry. Because the river water forms a slow back-current when blocked and pushed back by the sea, and because of the protection afforded by the river dikes and trees, the interior of the harbor is calm, like an inland lake. Field survey and archaeological finds suggest that the ancient Huang River harbor was very large. Extending north to the Bohai Sea, south 3,000 m to Donggao Village, it covers an area of about 2000 acres. From ancient times it was an important external communication port of China, one of the six famous ports of high antiquity. It was first constructed in the Western Zhou period. In 1992 it was declared a Key Cultural Relics Protection Unit of Longkou City. It is an important site for the study of Western Zhou communication and transportation.

17. The Qianheqian Site

The site is located 200 m south of Qianheqian Village, in Tuanwang Township of Laiyang City, on the west bank of the Wulong river and about 35 km south of Laiyang City. The geographic coordinates are 36°44′33.8″N, 120°43′22.1″E, and it is 130 m above sea level. Although Qianheqian is not in the Huang River valley, its context is exceptional in the region and its artefícts are unique, so we also surveyed it and present it here. Its data have a high value for our understanding of the region's cultural changes and settlement distribution in the Western Zhou period.

The site is about 300 m north to south, 250 m east to west and covers an area of 75,000 m^2 (Fig. Ⅰ.7.24). According to local villagers there was once an old city wall as well as a mound at the center of the site, which were destroyed because people used the dirt and cultivated the area year after year. In 1974, local villagers unearthed eight bronzes, of which one *hu* bottle and one *yan* steamer had inscriptions. In order to clarify the situation of the site and the bronzes, in the spring of 1975 the Shandong Provincial Museum and the Cultural Relics Management Committee of Yantai City conducted a survey and test excavation at the site, clearing out waste pits, chariot pit, and five tombs.

They obtained a significant amount of important data. From the analysis of the materials the site can be dated to the mid- and late Western Zhou. On the site surface they collected sherds of a kind of greyish-brown or reddish-brown pottery, with a rough texture and inclusions of mica and shell pieces. The workmanship was primitive and it was fired at a low temperature. Such pottery belonged to a different manufacturing tradition from those excavated from the tombs; they probably belonged to two different cultures. The former might be artifacts of the indigenous culture.

We found quite a few pottery sherds on the site, but few were suitable to be used to analyze vessel types. There were small, rim fragments, cord-impressed sherds, etc. The pottery was mostly made with fine clay and was mainly grey. Of discernible types, there were a bowl from a pedestal dish, *li* tripods, basins, *guan* jars, etc. (Fig. Ⅰ.7.25; Table Ⅰ.7.9).

18. The Shaojia Site

The site is located on a high terrace to the north of Shaojia Village, in Dongjiang Street of Longkou City, 2 km east of the Street Office. The geographic coordinates are 37°37′44″N, 120°32′19″E, and it lies 38 m above sea level.

The east side of the site overlooks the Jiangshui River. The west is close to Longkou-Qixia Road. Shaojia Village lies 100 m to the north. On the north are fields. There are small farming roads close to the site's east and west edges. The site is surrounded by farmland. Due to severe damage to the site very little remains.

After the site was found in 1979, the Department of Archaeology of Beijing University, and the provincial and municipal cultural relics departments sent scholars to investigate. The contents of the site were rich. A clear stratigraphy was found on a precipice in the eastern part of the site. Layer 1 was topsoil, 0.2-0.3 m thick; layer 2 was disturbed soil, 0.1-0.2 m thick; layer 3 was the cultural layer, about 1 m thick. The latter contained both Longshan and Yueshi deposits, including stone tools and pottery. Among the stone tools were handmade stone balls. The pottery was mostly made of fine clay, but there was also red pottery tempered with sand, and pottery with black clothing. Discernible types included squarish *ding* feet, flat-bottomed squarish three-legged vessels, deep-bellied *pen* basins, black pottery cups, drum-bellied, small mounted *guan* jars, bowl lids, etc. Artifacts were mostly plain, polished and wheel-turned, though some were hand-shaped. Decorations include appliqué patterns and intaglio ring patterns. In 1992 the site was declared a Key Cultural Relics Protection Unit of Longkou City. It provides important information on the Neolithic cultures of the region.

19. Yaojia Baofudi Cemetery

The site is located on a high terrace north of Yaojia Village, in Zhuyouguan Township of Longkou City. The geographic coordinates are 37°44′14″N, 120°32′18″E, and it lies 5 m above sea level.

The site is about 2 km south of the Bohai Sea, 500 m east of the mouth of the Huang River. It is 300 m south of Bohai Zhoujia Village, 200 m east of the Bohai Guojia Village, and 500 m west of Gonghui Village. It is about 3 km north of the Yantai-Weifang highway. The site is in an area of low-lying hills. Because the site is close to villages it is mostly planted with vegetables. We determined that the cemetery area is about 140 m from east to west and 80 m from north to south, with a total area of about 11,200 m^2. The clearing excavation discovered Warring States period tombs. This site provides data on the Warring States period in the Huang River region.

20. The Haojia Site

The site is located on a hill in an orchard 500 m north of Haojia Village, about 6 km southeast of Zhuyouguan Township of Longkou City. The geographic coordinates are 37°39′05.8″N, 120°38′09.4″E, and it lies 42 m above sea level.

Xiaogaojia Village lies 500 m east of the cemetery, and 500 m to the southwest is Dongjia Village. To the north is the town road. The cemetery once had a large earth mound that was destroyed and flattened. Now there is a gradual slope, which is higher in the north. The site is 110 m north to south, 85 m east to west, with a total area of 10,500 m^2. There are several higher areas to the north, and the overall terrain is fairly high. The site was discovered in 1988, after which salvage excavations were carried out by the municipal museum. In 1988-1989 six tombs were cleared, all were earthen pit tombs filled with oyster shells, with coffins and ramps. The forty or more artifacts unearthed included *guan* jars, *dou* pedestal dishes, colored *guan* jars, bronze mirrors and *banliang* coins, all dating to the Han Dynasty. They are now in the Longkou Municipal Museum. In 1992, the site was declared a Key Cultural Relics Protection Unit of Longkou City. The cemetery provides important information on the culture and burial customs of the Han Dynasty in the region.

21. The Houzuoyang Site

The site is located about 1 km west of Houzuoyang Village, Zhuyouguan Township of Longkou City. The geographic coordinates are 37°42′23″N, 120°33′18″E, and it lies 8 m above sea level.

The site is about 8 km south of Bohai Bay, 1 km east of the Huang River. To the south is Qianzuoyang Village, 500 m to the east is Xitai Village. There are two plastic sheds on the east. To the south there is a country road. The terrain is relatively flat. The site is about 350 m from north to south, around 120 m east to west, with an area of about 42,000 m^2. In the site we found Zhou period pottery and Han Dynasty patterned bricks. The site suffered severe damage in later times due to land levelling, and the cultural deposits are mostly gone, so there is no way to accurately estimate the area of the site. Judging from the dates of the collected artifacts the site was occupied in the Zhou and Han periods. This site offers important data for the study of the Zhou and Han periods in the region.

22. The Tangjiaji Site

The site is located on high ground about 1.5 km southwest of Tangjiaji Village, in Zhuyouguan Township of Longkou City. The geographic coordinates are 37°43′02″N, 120°33′54″E, and it lies 13 m above sea level.

There is a town road west of the site. To the north it is close to East Shangjia Village. The site is 310 m from east to west, 200 m from north to south, with an area of about 50,000 m^2. The site was originally a hillock, but has now been turned into terraced fields. A large number of Zhou dynasty pottery sherds was found at the site, such as vessel rims, vessel feet and *dou* pedestal dish stems. Most of them are decorated with cord impressions. The most common vessel types are *li* tripods, *guan* jars, bowls, *dou* pedestal dishes, etc. We also found Han dynasty decorated tomb bricks, thus it is a Zhou-Han period site. The site provides important material for understanding the site distribution of the Zhou and Han periods in the region.

23. The Xiahetou Site

The site is located to the southeast of Xiahetou Village, Shiliang Township of Longkou City. The geographic coordinates are 37°35′14″N, 120°38′33″E, and it lies 38 m above sea level.

The site is located east of the Huang River on its second-level terrace. To the east of the site is a farming area, much of which is planted with fruit trees. The site is about 30 m from north to south, 100 m east to west, with a somewhat triangular area of about 3,000 m^2. At the site we collected pottery sherds of vessels like *ding* and *guan* and fragments of Han bricks and roof tiles. Based on these artifacts we can see that the site was in use during the Longshan, Zhou, Han, and other periods. It has high value for the study of the prehistoric, Zhou and Han periods in the Huang River Basin prehistoric.

24. Pingliyuan Cemetery

This Eastern Han cemetery is located to the northeast of Pingliyuan Village, in Shiliang Township of Longkou City. The geographic coordinates are 37°36′22″N, 120°40′59″E, and it lies 56 m above sea level.

The cemetery is located on high ground behind the village. It is all farmland. The cemetery is 200 m long, 118 m wide, with an area of 23,600 m^2. One large and one small tomb have been found there so far. The site was destroyed in the 1960s or thereabouts due to land leveling. There is only a small earth mound of the large tomb mound remaining, which may well have already been looted; the small tomb has been completely destroyed. Around the tomb mound are scattered a large number of Han Dynasty bricks and tile fragments. We found a complete Han brick at the site of the small tomb. According to the villagers, they dug out a long ramp to the northwest of the large tomb, which suggests that it was the tomb of a high-ranking person. In addition, we found some pottery sherds that may be as early as the Yueshi period. The site has major significance for the study of Han Dynasty burial rules.

25. The Lijia Site

Located on the west bank of the Nanluan River near Taishang Lijia Village, Beima Township of Longkou City, the site is on a plain below the mountains to the south. The geographic coordinates are 37°34′52″N, 120°25′43″E, and it lies 50 m above sea level.

Overall it is a somewhat rectangular site, about 200 m north to south, 160 m east to west, with an area of 36,700 m^2. The site is now covered by farmland. The preservation condition is normal. We found some Longshan, Zhenzhumen, and Han culture pottery sherds on the site. Of those that could be identified there were pieces of vessel bellies made of coarse black pottery, a tempered red pottery bowl, and grey clay cord-marked jars, etc. The site provides important material for the study of the Longshan and Zhou period cultures.

26. The Zhaojia Site

The site is located on the second terrace of an unnamed creek to the northwest of Zhaojia Village, Zhuyouguan Township of Longkou City. The geographic coordinates are 37°39′23.9″N, 120°39′37.2″E, and it lies 43 m above sea level.

Overall the site is a rectangle and covers a rather large area. There is a modern road to its east and another to its west. On the west of the site is a small riverbed; on the east is a plain. The site is 120 m north to south, 100 m east to west, an area of about 12,500 m^2. The terraces are slightly elevated, the north being higher than the south. The soil is sandy, the bedrock is pale, reddish-brown, common sandstone. Scattered pottery sherds are visible on the site. Judging from their shape and characteristics the site seems to have been formed during the Han Dynasty. Wheat, maize and a large number of fruit trees are grown. We also found bricks with diamond patterns, which suggests that there are Han Dynasty tombs nearby. This has important implications for the distribution and meaning of Han Dynasty sites in the area.

27. The Wa'nan Site

The site is located at Wa'nan Village, Xufu Township of Longkou City. The geographic coordinates are 37°40′08.9″N, 120°24′43.5″E, it lies 6 m above sea level.

This is a low-lying site beside the Yongwen River. It is roughly rectangular in shape. The site was originally quite large, about 480 m from east to west, 525 m north to south, covering about 159,000 m^2. Due to people taking earth from the site for kilns and buildings, as well as being engulfed by natural forces, the site is badly damaged. A section of less than 10,000 m^2 has been preserved on the fringe. We found a large number of *guan* jars and *dou* pedestal dishes with various decorations and Han Dynasty bricks with decorative patterns. It is a typical Eastern Zhou to Han settlement site. The discovery of this site is valuable for understanding the settlement distribution of the Eastern Zhou and Han period sites in the Huangshui River Basin.

28. The Zhaoliu Site

The site is located about 1 km southwest of Zhaoliu Village, Zhuyouguan Township of Longkou City. Geographic coordinates are 37°39′52″N, 120°35′55″E, and it lies 22 m above sea level.

It is situated on the second terrace of the Huangshui River, about 200 m north of the river. On the east is a small factory; to the northwest is Conglin Cement Factory. The site is on a piedmont plain with a slight slope, rising towards the east. The site is 90 m north to south, 70 m east to west, with an area of about 6,000 m^2. Our preliminary analysis, based on pottery sherds found at the site, is that the site dates to the Zhou Dynasty. The site is located in a field that has two rows of fruit trees and farms. To the south is a small grove of trees, behind which are ditches dug as part of a dike-building project. Zhou Dynasty pottery sherds are scattered throughout the site, with cord-marked pottery being most abundant. Of those that can be identified, there are *guan* jars, *li* tripods, bowls, etc. It is significant for the study of the living conditions of the Zhou people.

29. Shangzhuang Majia Site

The site is located to the east of Shangzhuang Majia Village, Zhuyouguan Township of Longkou City. The geographic coordinates are 37°40′01″N, 120°37′01.9″E, and it lies 40 m above sea level.

The terrain around the site is flat, and there are hills to the northeast. The site is located to the east of a highway. There is a small white farming shed in the south of the site, located within the terraced farmland area. The site is about 100 m north to south, 50 m east to west, with an area of about 5,000 m^2. Han Dynasty pottery sherds and tomb bricks with decorative patterns are scattered over the site, which suggests that there are Han tombs nearby. The site preservation conditions are average. It is planted with fruit trees, and some arable land is planted with wheat, maize and other crops. The site provides information on the lives of people in the area during the Han Dynasty.

30. The Chengjia Site

The site is located 300 m north of the Huangshui River, 1 km southeast of Chengjia Village, Zhuyouguan Township of Longkou City. The geographic coordinates are 37°40′11.0″N, 120°35′26.0″E, and it lies 24 m above sea level.

The Conglin Cement Factory is situated 200 m southwest of the site. To the south is a ditch dug during the building of a dike. The site is about 80 m from north to south, 45 m from east to west, with an area of about 3,000 m^2. There are a few pottery sherds scattered around the site, the majority of which are cord-marked, characteristic of pottery of the Zhou Dynasty. Fruit trees, wheat, and other things are planted in the site, which did little damage to the site. The soil is loess, the land is flat, and the site preservation is normal.

31. The Xi Zhangjia Site

The site is located in fields to the northeast of the Xi Zhangjia Village, Zhuyouguan Township of Longkou City. The geographic coordinates are 37°40′52″N, 120°35′09″E, and it lies 23 m above sea level.

The site may extend into the northwest corner of the village. The site is situated on the south bank of the Conglin Temple River. On the west is a local dirt road. To the north is a factory. There is an earthen mound to the northeast. The terrain is relatively flat. The site is about 140 m from north to south, 60 m from east to west, with an area of about 8,400 m^2. Zhou period cord-marked pottery sherds are scattered around the site, as are the feet of ceramic vessels and Han tomb bricks with diamond pattern decorations. There is a pit on the northeast side, formed because the villagers have taken earth from it. Fruit trees, wheat and other crops are grown on the site. Zhou and Han period pottery sherds were found in the southeast portion of the site, near Chengjia Village, suggesting that the site may be larger than it seems. The site furnishes important information on the distribution of Zhou and Han sites in the region.

32. The Qianmiaoguo Site

The site is situated in farm fields southeast of Qian Miaoguo Village, Zhuyouguan Township of Longkou City. The geographic coordinates are 37°40′54.0″N, 120°33′04.0″E, and it lies 15 m above sea level.

The site is located above the east terrace of the Jiangshui River. The Yantai-Weifang highway passes to the southeast, and there is a local road to the west. A high-voltage transmission tower is located in its southwestern corner. The whole village is surrounded by the Huangshui River, Longwan River, and Jiangshui River, and the terrain is flat. The site is 100 m east to west and 100 m north to south, covering an area of about 10,000 m^2. The site is planted with grapevines and wheat. Because the vineyard has been digging trenches for fertilizer for a long time, occasional Longshan black pottery sherds and Han Dynasty pottery sherds can be found there. Han Dynasty tomb bricks with diamond pattern designs were found at the edge of the fields. According to local fruit farmers the ditches were about one meter deep. That is to say, at 1 m depth one is already at the depth of the tomb, and the area of the tombs has suffered damage. This site provides important data for the study of the distribution of the Longshan culture in the Huangshui River Basin.

33. The Huangchengji Site

The site is located in the northwest end of Huangchengji Village, Shiliang Township of Longkou City. The geographic coordinates are 37°37′52.7″N, 120°39′34.7″E, and it lies 35 m above sea level. To the south of the village the Huangchengji River empties into the Huangshui River.

The north side of the ancient town site borders on the Jingjia River. A road passes through its center. The village is located in a plain. South of the village are residences and small farms. According to records in the Longkou local gazetteer (Yin Jimei 1871: 1, 2, 9), this ancient town site was damaged by floods after the Northern Qi Dynasty (550-577). The site is 1,550 m long and 1,500 m wide, with an area of about 2.31 km^2. There is no trace of the city wall on the surface. On the ground we found pottery sherds, roof tile sherds, Han bricks, etc. The sherds were mostly coarse or grey cord-marked clay. Many of the Han bricks had multi-band diamond patterns. According to the historical record, this was the site of the ancient Huangcheng city, the area of which can be roughly estimated from the distribution of pottery sherds. Pottery sherds from the site most date to Warring States-Han period. The site has great significance for the study of the development of towns in the area, and the local history of the Huangshui River basin.

34. The Lengwang Site

Located 900 m northeast of Lengwang Village, Zhuyouguan Township of Longkou City, the site lies on a naturally raised piece of high ground. The geographic coordinates are 120°30′48.0″E, 37°42′16.0″N, and it lies 25 m above sea level. To the west of the site is the road to the sea. To the south is a concrete irrigation canal. The whole village of Lengwang is on a slope that is higher in the north. The site is situated on higher ground to the north, where the terrain is relatively flat. There is an east-west dirt road that passes through the site. The construction of a road along the west side of the site did some damage. The site is about 75 m north to south, 40 m east to west, with an area of about 3,000 m^2. In the vicinity of the site are many orchards, in which can be found a few Han Dynasty roof tiles and pottery sherds. The discovery of this site provides new material for understanding the distribution of Han settlements in the area.

35. The Dajinjia Site

The site is on the second terrace of the Huangshui River to the west of Dajinjia Village, Shiliang Township of Longkou City. The geographic coordinates are 37°37′13.0″N, 120°38′03.3″E, and it lies 32 m above sea level.

The Huangshui River is west of the site. A road passes by west of the river. The site, situated between the Huangshui River and Dajinjia Village, is about 120 m from north to south, 80 m from east to west, with an area of about 9,600 m^2. The current condition of preservation of the site is poor. Han dynasty tiles and brick debris can be found on the surface. This site was newly discovered during our survey, and it is important for the study of the Huangshui River Basin in the Han Dynasty.

36. The Qiabo Site

The site is 500 m to the northeast of Qiabo Village, Lan'gao Township. The geographic coordinates are 37°39′26.3″N, 120°35′24.7″E, and it lies 27 m above sea level.

The Lan'gao Township government office is about 1 km south of Qiaobo Village. Chenjiazhuang Village is about 500 m to the north, and the Huangshui River is about 2 km to the east, across which is Weijia Village of Zhuyouguan *Township*. The Huangshui River flows north of the village, and a road passes through the south. The site is 252 m from east to west, 134 m from north to south, covering an area of about 33,800 m^2. Within the site area there were abundant artifacts found including various coarse grey sherds, spindle whorls, the round feet of pottery vessels, vessel rims, etc. Our preliminary judgment based on the pottery sherds is that the site dates to the Han Dynasty. This find provides new data for the study of the Han Dynasty in the area.

37. The Siping Site

The site is located 1 km northeast of Siping Village, Lan'gao Township of Longkou City. Geographic coordinates are 37°39′05.7″N, 120°35′57.5″E, and it lies 30 m above sea level. The site lies on the west bank of the Yaque River and there is a grove of trees within the site. The site borders on Lan'gao Village 500 m to the west, Qiabo Village 1 km to the northwest, and Houlijia Village 1 km to the south. The terrain of Siping Village lies between hills and a plain. The drainage is from south to north. The site is 200 m north to south and 110 m east to west, with an area of about 22,000 m^2. Pottery found at the site includes grey clay dishs and stems from *dou* pedestal dishes and cord-marked pottery sherds, etc. This is a Zhou and Han period site. This site provides new material for the distribution of Zhou and Han period settlements in the area.

38. The Cegao Site

The cite is located to the north of Cegao Villate, Lan'gao Township of Longkou City, south of the highway. Geographic coordinates are 37°38′04.1″N, 120°38′17.7″E, and it sits 30 m above sea level.

The site is about 253 m north to south, 124 m east to west, covering an area of 31,000 m^2. To the west of the site is a section of high ground, but the site itself is on a plain with undulating terrain. Artifacts found on the surface include pottery vessel rim pieces, cord-marked pottery fragments, as well as bricks, tiles and other debris. Most of the ceramics were made of grey clay. Of discernible vessel types, there were dishes from *dou* pedestal dishes, basins, etc. Eastern Zhou artifacts predominate. The site is important for understanding the distribution characteristics and changes of Eastern Zhou-Han sites in the region.

Section 3: Changes in the Settlement Pattern in the Huangshui River Basin and Related Issues

Besides the thirty-eight surveyed sites (Table I .7.10), the discussion of other sites that we have not surveyed is based on materials obtained during the Third National General Survey of Cultural Relics in 2007-2011. These also include sites that we surveyed but that did not yield artifacts, so we had to rely on the General Survey data in order to describe the date and size of the sites. Perhaps our knowledge of some of these sites are still incomplete, and we hope in the future to be able to make up for this shortcoming.

Time-wise, the earliest site in the entire Huangshui River Basin is the upper Paleolithic cave site of Xiao Laishan in Lan'gao Township. The Neolithic period mainly includes sites belonging to the Qiujiazhuang-Ⅰ culture and Longshan culture. Of these, typical sites are Donggao and Lujiagou in Shiliang Township, Nanwangxu site in Penglai City, Tangjia and Qianshan, in Xufu Township, Qian Miaoguo in Chuyouguan Township, Lijia in Beima Township, and Shaojia in Jiangdong Township, etc. From the standpoint of distribution patterns, sites of the Neolithic period are mostly located on the first terraces along the Huangshui River and its tributaries. These areas are often alluvial plains that are relative open, offering good conditions for subsistence, and therefore gave rise to isolated settlements of relatively small size.

Sites of the Qiujiazhuang-Ⅰ culture are relatively few in the Huangshui River Basin. The cultural contents of sites are somewhat simpler, and deposit strata are thin. Despite differing degrees and types of damage to these sites over the millennia, the chances of damage suffered by these sites should be similar. That is to say, the size and status of the sites we see today reflects the original size and condition and can form the basis for our exploration of settlement dimensions. Of course, we will consider differently the sites that were seriously damaged by human activities.

In regard to the level of development of the Qiujiazhuang-Ⅰ culture and its regional settlement system, we can sketch the following based on currently available information: due to its unique natural environment and topography, cultural development was slow in the peninsula. At the same time, because of the lack of contact with the outside world, an archaeological culture of unique characteristics was formed there. Qiujiazhuang-Ⅰ sites are mainly located in floodplains in relatively low elevation coastal zones. Usually they are in the vicinity of the rivers, and the surrounding terrain is relatively open, offering more favorable conditions for site locations. Due to the relative scarcity of the sites, it is likely that there were large areas from which people could gather their food. This also shows that food sources were not abundant.

From Qiujiazhuang-Ⅰ to the Longshan culture there was no fundamental change in settlement remains; the settlement system of the Longshan culture essentially followed the Qiujiazhuang-Ⅰ model. In terms of settlement distribution, number and size, there is no one site whose size and location were absolutely larger that could act as a central settlement. It was a decentralized distribution of small-scale sites. The population and site sizes were essentially unchanged compared with the Qiujiazhuang-Ⅰ culture period. What had changed was that the area of site distribution in the region was expanded, and perhaps the people of the Longshan culture had already moved beyond the economic model characterized by pure fishing and gathering. In contrast to the situation of the Dawenkou and Longshan cultures in inland regions of the Shandong Pennisula, the development of the Longshan culture in the Huangshui River region was slow and shows signs of lagging behind.

In all, there were no large, central settlements in the Huangshui watershed during the Qiujiazhuang-Ⅰ and Longshan periods. The sites of the two periods were relatively small, no more than 50,000 m^2. This phenomenon continued into the Yueshi culture stage (i.e. throughout the Neolithic).

Among the thirty-eight sites discussed above, twenty-five date to the Bronze Age. Two sites contain relics of the Yueshi culture, and twenty-three yielded remains of the Zhou period. These sites and cemeteries are mostly located within a 20 km range from the Guicheng site. From the perspective of settlement archeology this finding offers key information for the study of the rank level of the Guicheng city site and its relationship to the surrounding sites. Doubtless the Zhou Dynasty can be considered a peak period of settlement development in the Huangshui River region.

During this period, the number of sites not only increased rapidly, the settlement system also became more complex. For instance, in this system there emerged a large central walled site, Guicheng. At the same time, the sites spread out in distribution, and dispersed gradually along the tributaries of the Huangshui River, forming walled sites of different dimensions. In particular, the cluster of sites centered on the Guicheng city site on the north side of Mount Lai are distributed in areas whose natural conditions are quite favorable by the standards of the Shandong Peninsula. Some relatively independent smaller settlements were distributed on tributaries of the Huangshui River, but these were few and quite small compared to the Guicheng settlement cluster. In all, with the rise of Guicheng, a single central city site with dominating power and influence was formed in the settlement system of the Huangshui River region. In addition, in some remains we can also see manifestations of indigenous cultures. This situation lasted until the late Spring and Autumn period when the state of Qi destroyed Lai and the central site disappeared.

In the Han Dynasty, judging from the number and distribution of Han period sites, it seems that settlements were already fairly densely distributed in the basin, similar to the distribution pattern of inland areas. Along the tributaries of the Huangshui River such as the Jingjia, Liangshui, Yaque and other rivers, Han Dynasty sites were rather densely distributed. They are also very dense along the Yongwen, Nanluan and Beima'nan Rivers, especially in the transitional area between the southern mountains and the northern plain; moreover, central town sites existed.

Above, we focused on changes in the settlements of Qiujiazhuang-Ⅰ, Longshan and Zhou cultures in the Huangshui River Basin, and analyzed the relationship between the distribution of these settlements and the spatial layout of the region. The study of settlement archaeology in the Huangshui River region is mainly based on our present survey and on information from the Third National General Survey of Cultural Relics. Through analyzing these materials we achieved some new understanding. Certainly, this new understanding remains preliminary and incomplete, and we hope in the future there will be more abundant information and more discoveries to support and verify our views.

References

Tang, Luting 唐禄庭, and Jiang Guojun 姜国钧, 1989. "Shandong Huangixan Dongying Zhoujia Xizhou canmu qingli jianbao" 山东黄县东营周家村西周残墓清理简报 (A brief report on the damaged tomb of the Western Zhou period in Dongying Zhoujiacun in Huangxian, Shandong). *Haidai kaogu* 海岱考古 (Haidai archaeology), 1: 314-319.

Wang, Daoxin 王道新, 1934. *Huangxian zhi gao* 黄县志稿 (Draft gazetteer of Huangxian). Preserved in Shandong Provincial Museum.

Wang, Xiping 王锡平, and Tang Luting 唐禄庭, 1986. "Shandong Huangxian Zhuangtou Xizhou mu qingli jianbao" 山东黄县庄头西周墓清理简报 (A brief report of the excavation of Western Zhou tombs at Zhuangtou in Huangxian, Shandong), *Wenwu* 文物, 8: 69-72.

Yin, Jimei 尹继美, 1871 (Qing, Tongzhi 10th year). *Huangxian zhi* 黄县志 (Huangxian gazetteer), 14 vols.

Yuan, Jing, Liang Zhonghe, Wu Yun, and Jia Xiaobing, 2002. "Shell Mounds in the Jiaodong Peninsula: A Study in Environmental Archaeology," *The Journal of East Asian Archaeology* 4.1-4: 1-26.

Zeng, Yigong 曾毅公, 1940. *Shandong jinwen jicun* 山东金文集存 (Collection of bronze inscriptions from Shandong). Ji'nan.

Zhongguo shehui kexueyuan kaogu yanjiusuo 中国社会科学院考古研究所, 1999. *Jiaodong bandao beiqiu yizhi huanjing kaogu* 胶东半岛贝丘遗址环境考古 (Environmental archaeology of the Beiqiu site on Jiaodong Peninsula). Beijing: Sheke wenxian chubanshe.

(Translated by Brian Lander)

第八章　归城考古中的地理配准及钻探数据管理

Jeremiah Trinidad-Christensen　侯昱文（Paul Nicholas Vogt）

第一节　地理信息系统软件

地理信息系统（GIS）的概念通常根据领域的不同而各异，但最基本的定义为“用于汇集、存储、操作和显示地理学相关信息的计算机系统，例如，根据位置所确定的数据”（USGS，美国地质勘探局）。GIS作为一个具有强大功能的工具，不仅能显示数据点的图层及其数据库之间的空间关系，而且还具有进行空间性分析的能力。目前有很多不同的GIS软件可供选择，包括免费开放的软件和商业性软件。在本项目中，我们使用了ESRI ArcGIS，QGIS，谷歌地球（Google Earth）及在最后分析中使用的地理资源分析支持系统（GRASS）。在这些软件中，ArcGIS仍然是使用最频繁、最广泛的软件，它是用来存储和操作遗址数据的最主要的软件平台。

谷歌地球（Google Earth）主要应用于项目的开始阶段，其出色的卫星图像能使我们对遗址有个初期的视觉辨识，并对感兴趣的、项目计划的区域创建网格界限。在项目的初始阶段（2007～2008年）的田野调查中，我们采用了这类卫星图像并辅之以手绘的本地地图，后一种地图是我们通过各种类型的调查所绘制的。然而谷歌地球主要是一种视觉化工具，它无法执行空间分析。锁眼标记语言（KML）作为谷歌地球原始的数据存储格式，无法像GIS特有的数据格式那样加入到数据库中，而如shapefile或是ESRI ArcGIS的geodatabase数据存储格式则可以做到。因此当我们需要进行数据处理时，则采用功能强大的ArcGIS和QGIS软件。

QGIS和GRASS都是开放源软件。GRASS 虽然也是功能非常强大的软件，但它是通过命令行来操作的，因此并不容易学习。QGIS有更易操作的用户界面并且兼容多种GRASS插件，因此具有广泛的空间分析功能。ESRI ArcGIS是由易智瑞公司（ESRI）研发出的功能强大的商业GIS软件套件，它也是本项目中最主要使用的软件（该软件在调查期间也被用于制作野外地图以及分析调查所得数据以制作陶片分布图，见上编第六章）。项目中生成和使用的大多数数据被存储为geodatabase格式，该格式只能在ArcGIS软件中使用。geodatabase格式有助于建立数据层之间的关系，并允许添加参数去限制由输入数据或创建新图层时产生的误差。

第二节　制图和地理配准

1．制图

如前文所述在项目早期阶段，谷歌地球主要被用于视觉辨识遗址，以及建立网格来界定计划在项目不同阶段中进行工作的不同区域。这已能满足项目早期阶段的需求，但为了增加卫星图的细节，我们还制作了一张1：1000比例的手绘地图，覆盖面积1平方千米。该地图上显示了水流、道路、建筑和大致地势，并附有1米网格便于参考（图Ⅰ.8.1）。

研究者和技术人员在工作计划阶段和钻探过程中，同时以这两类地图用作遗址参考图。在进行钻探工作的同时，土样钻探点被记录在一些更小的，比例为1：100比例的手绘地图上。这些地图中的每一张地图都覆盖了50米×35米的区域，并且绘有建筑、道路、断崖以及其他一些可识别的地形特征，以及区域范围内的钻探点及其相关数据。这些小地图是储存原始钻探数据的主要媒介，我们只需将相关数据记录在每个钻探点旁边（图Ⅰ.8.2）。

但谷歌地球的卫星图像提供的位置信息不够充分，无法与信息丰富的手绘地图进行地理配准（见下文）。为了进行地理配准，项目组购买了2004年的具有6.5米分辨率的卫星图像。这些卫星图像共覆盖了25平方千米的范围，归城城址约处于中心位置，并且所有图像均是在无云层遮盖的条件下拍摄的。这些新的卫星图像便成为项目的基础地图并用于生成所有数据层，以及作为地理配准地图使用（图Ⅰ.8.3；图版3）。

在创建数据图层和地理配准前，我们决定使用通用横轴墨卡托投影（UTM）10N 区作为所有图层的地图投影。通用横轴墨卡托投影（UTM）是一个基于墨卡托投影的正形投影，它将地球分成60个区。然而任何投影都会在面积、距离、形状、角度或方向中的任何一个方面产生变形。而通用横轴墨卡托投影（UTM）维持了相对角度和特征的近似形状，并且面积、距离及方向的所有变形程度均为最低限度，尤其是像遗址这类规模大小的范围内更是如此。

2．地理配准

地理配准是将数字图像重新排列的一种过程，例如将一个扫描的地图转变成坐标系统如上文所提及的ArcGIS或GRASS。进行地理配准操作之前，所有的手绘地图均以300dpi的分辨率扫描为未压缩的TIF格式图像：该格式可以在有限的图像文件尺寸下获得足够的细节。对一个地图进行地理配准时，首先要在数字图像上标识一个点，并且需要分配给该点一个坐标，可通过直接输入（如果知道经度和纬度的话）或者将该点拖至于之前的空间参考图层的一个已知位置。地理配准一个地图至少需要三个点，虽然通常要求更多的点。对该遗址地图而言，大约需要10至20个点来进行地理配准。当添加完所有点之后，将图像拉伸对齐所有点的位置时会出现误差。软件会在所有点中分配误差，以便优化所有点的位置的相对精度。通常当一个遗址图被大致配准后，所有点都会被评估，那些软件分配误差最大的点，有时会被删除，不过这些都得视具体情况而定。

虽然较小的手绘地图（图Ⅰ.8.2，比例1：100）和遗址总图上均有1米的网格，但地图的绘制过程和扫描过程中的褶皱（当地图通过单纸式扫描机，褶皱不能被机器或轻微扫过图像而完全抚平）都会导致误差的产生。但总体而言，地图上的任何一点的误差都被控制在三分之一米以内，因此点的位置仍然可被认为是相对准确的。为了处理在地理配准时出现的这类扭曲，我们创建了1米、10米和100米规格的矢量网格，使用所有手绘地图上的可辨识位置，以便使地图的左下角与卫星图像对齐。

我们将手绘地图上可辨别的自然特征、十字路口及建筑移至卫星图上所对应的位置。在对图像进行地理配准时，我们采用了一次多项式变换，将地图从一边拉伸至另一边，上面拉伸至下面或者斜对角延伸。虽然使用二次或三次多项式变换可能会潜在地减少地理配准时的统计误差，但是无论是采用这两种中的哪种变换，总体上看，通过多余的方式扭曲地图可能会产生更多的误差。

3．要素图层

经过地理配准后的地图中，可显示静止的水面、河流、建筑、道路和可观察到的古代城墙遗迹的位置的图层均被生成。这一过程相对较快，而建立高程图层和钻探点的数据图层则需花费更多的时间。

第三节　创建高程图

作为录入钻探数据的前提条件，我们需要创建一个相对准确的高程图层。钻探点的所有层位都被分配有数字，用来表现某一特定土壤类型在第一次被发现时的距地表的深度。通常耕土层距地表最大深度是0.3厘米，这也是文化层记录的起始深度。但是，有时夯土等文化层也会在钻探过程中较早或较晚出现。然而想要准确呈现所有点的钻探数据及解释它们之间的关系，关键是要先再现整个钻探区域内当前地表高程的变化。

1．寻找高程数据

最初，我们必须依靠公开的可使用的数据库来计算和评估遗址的高程：事实上，我们仍然根据这些数据来决定在这1平方千米地图范围外的区域的高程。目前唯一公开可使用的遗址高程数据是SRTM（航天飞机雷达地形测绘使命）产生的数字高程模型（DEM），其分辨率为3弧秒，约90米（意味着这个模型将90平方米内的所有高程变化进行了平均）。考虑到大多数钻探样本所处的区域就在高程模型（DEM）的少数几个分辨率单位内，因此这种精确度远远达不到本项目的要求。但是，它确实能让我们对卫星图像中所包括的区域进行粗略的高程估算。

本项目真正需要的是一个可以提取2米等高线的高程图层。这一点可以通过分辨率约10米的高程网格得到。为了模拟10米网格，我们将SRTM高程图层转成一个点图层，并在一个30米像素元值的图层上执行反距离加权插值法（IDW），再使用邻区焦点统计算法进行了平滑化操作。然后我们又使用10米的像元大小再一次执行这一过程。最后，为了能在野外地图上使用，我们从最终插值后的数字高程模型（DEM）中抽取出了2米和10米的等高线，进而生成了该区域高程的大致指示图。

虽然这一过程的最终结果也使图层的高程或多或少有些平滑转换，但目前却没有任何办法可以将失去的高程数据在图层中复原。因为原始的90米像元大小实在是太大了，许多丢失的高程细节如果没有更好的数据的话不可能再重新生成。最近，美国和日本的一个名为高级星载热辐射热反射探测仪（ASTER）数字高程模型（DEM）的联合项目可以提供更好的高程数据（虽然还是无法满足本项目的要求）。高级星载热辐射热反射探测仪的数字高程模型（DEM）具有30米分辨率，较之SRTM已有非常大的提升。

项目研究中为了获取比SRTM更好的数据，我们还尝试了其他的办法，包括购买从苏联和中国1：50000比例的地图中提取出的数字高程模型。令人惊讶的是，当用卫星图像作为参考比较购买的数字高程模型及SRTM数据集中的图层时，结果发现购买的数字高程模型的准确度远低于SRTM的数据集。

2．高程调查

为了更好地呈现钻探区域的高程差异，我们组成了一个调查组，用以获取内城遗址内手绘地图所覆盖区域中更准确的高程数据。我们以手绘地图作为基础图层，并从一个单独的基点开始调查，创建了第二张地图，包含周围区域详细的高程数据的。我们将所选定的那个基点的高度设定为100米，并且其他373个点的高程均是在这个高度上或加或减，这取决于该点是否高于或低于基点。大多数高程调查的点都集中在内城墙的周围和地势起伏较大的区域。而地势相对平坦或起伏较少的区域通常只包含一个单独的调查点。调查点之间最大的高程差值为16米，平均高程差略小于4米，显而易见SRTM和ASTER数据均无法捕捉到如此精细程度的高度变化。

我们将新获取的地图进行扫描和地理配准，并且手动创建了一个包含高程点的数据层（图Ⅰ.8.4）。高程点在扫描的地图上偶尔会有位置上的轻微偏移；为了尽可能地减少在地理配准和手绘过程中产生的误差，我们采用了矢量网格和可辨别的特征作为点的参考。当完成这个高程点图层后，我们从ASTER网格中提取出相应的高度，以便使基点得到一个相对于海平面的近似绝对海拔，并且计算了所有构成遗址表面图层的点的高程。然后采用了一个低点的半径，对高程点执行了反距离加权插值法（IDW），以便减少平滑化并使邻近点更具差异性。我们还建立了一个阻挡图层以确保悬崖和陡峭地势变化的区域能在最终的高程图层中被正确反映出来（图Ⅰ.8.5；图版7）。

第四节　钻　探　点

事实上建立一个包含和显示钻探数据的图层才是最耗时的一部分工作，其原因在于所收集的钻探点的复杂性和数量以及对数据库的设计（图Ⅰ.8.6）。整个内城的钻探点间隔约5米，平均深度在0.7米，最深之处为4米。钻探点的记录采用字母数字坐标系统，点的名称由东西轴向的数字和南北轴向的字母组成。该系统偶尔略有调整以适应于禁止进入的地理环境中（如现代的果园、路等），或者是为了确认特殊土壤类型的分布范围。

从数据库的总体设计来看，每一个单独钻探点包含的新土壤类型都会被给予其单独的数据点，从而可以允许众多不同的数据点存在于地图上的同一个位置。该方法考虑到这种情况——即一些土壤类型，尤其是夯土和所谓的“灰土”可能会在任意深度出现，并不总是具有一定顺序。钻探点数据库包括了以下内容：一个软件指定的ID；深度（单位为米）；该深度土壤的类型和颜色；土壤层颗粒及其他包含物的说明；偶尔的质地观察备注信息等；钻探点ID（即探孔号；可使数据点在原始地图上与之相联）；以及原始地图上图号（见上编第三章）。将最后两个号码也包括在内，是便于日后有任何关于点的数据问题可以参考原始地图。将坐标、深度和土壤类型作为单独的三个字段分隔开，可以便于我们对某一土壤类型所对应的点进行数字操作、外推等，而不会影响其他土壤类型相关联的点（图Ⅰ.8.7）。

如前文所述，基于在第一季的田野工作中对归城土壤剖面情况的了解，我们建立了土壤分类系统的标准，并在之后的几年工作中一直使用（见上编第三章，表Ⅰ.3.1）。正如本章表述的那样，土壤的分类为录入和分析整个钻探数据提供了基础。最常见的一些土壤类型的出现频度分析见表I.8.1，可将其视为归城内城土壤剖面的总体概况。其他在土壤样本常见的包含物，如鹅卵石、陶片、骨片等，均已在表Ⅰ.8.2.列出。当我们偶尔在一个钻探点中发现一种物质如骨片或陶片，而其周围并无太多土壤时，这类情况就将该物质记录为一种属于它自己的原始“土壤类型”，这是为了该钻探点的完整记录及保留一个该类物质的分布情况的详细的记录。

我们还设计了一个数据字段用来记录特定点的附加信息。值得注意的意外状况，即不符合已建立的土壤分类标准的特殊情况，通常都记录在此字段中。例如，当一个特别的地层距地表深度超过5.0米（所使用的钻探工具的最大钻探深度），这种情况就应被记录下来（图Ⅰ.8.7）。

总而言之，这种记录方法产生了近乎11000个独立的钻探点数据，这些数据为地下成像阶段的工作奠定了基础。

第五节　地下成像

在二维GIS软件如ArcGIS中，通过这种方法产出的数据重叠使我们有时很难同时显示一种以上的土壤类型。然而，将钻探数据导入具有大量插值能力的三维软件，如Unix系统操作平台的GRASS，地下的情况可被更好地视觉化。虽然数据的可视化在一种点格式情况下仍然显得相对混乱，一个特定数据组的点——譬如一种土壤类型仍能被用来进行外推，并且形成三维图像用以表现地下土壤层的表面情况，其与绝对海拔值（与海平面相比）和相对海拔值（与整个遗址内其他土壤类型的土壤层相比）相关联。

为了证明这个方法的潜能，我们选择了9号夯土建筑基址，即内城西区建筑基址的最大基址，以及邻近的两个较小的基址即10号和11号，用来进行视图分析和复原（图Ⅰ.8.8～Ⅰ.8.9；图版66）。我们在2013年的春季进行了这一项工作。这个项目很好地展现了钻探数据的重要价值，以及基于计算机的模拟可在有机会进行正式发掘之前，使我们了解到地下建筑特征的可能性。

（翻译：杨琳）

表Ⅰ.8.1　归城内城遗址钻探数据中的所记录的土壤类型

Table Ⅰ.8.1　Soil types recorded for the coring data from the Guicheng inner city site

土壤类型分类 Soil type category	土壤类型（包括非土壤物质作为原始数据） Soil types (including non-soil substances as primary data points)	出现次数 Number of occurrences	百分比（总数 10,890） Percentage of occurrences (out of 10,890 total)
形成过程 Formation process	踩踏面 Footpath	43	0.395%
	五花土 Multicolored（“five-colored”）	176	1.616%
	花夯土 Multicolored/rammed	4	0.037%
	生土 Virgin soil	813	7.466%
	垫土 Packed	631	5.794%
	夯土 Rammed	818	7.511%
	路土 Road	11	0.101%
	淤土 Sediment	953	8.751%
	淤土/砂 Sediment/sand	7	0.064%
	淤土/自然 Sediment/natural	1	0.009%
	耕土 Tilled	602	5.528%
颜色 Color	褐色 Brown	222	2.039%
	五花土 Multicolored (“five-colored”)	176	1.616%
	花夯土 Multicolored/rammed	4	0.037%
	灰色 Grey	3469	31.855%
	灰黑色 Greyish-black	5	0.046%
	灰褐色 Greyish-brown	200	1.837%
	灰黄色 Greyish-yellow	4	0.037%
	红褐色 Reddish-brown	28	0.257%
	黄色 Yellow	53	0.487%
	黄褐色 Yellowish-brown	1183	10.863%
非土壤 Contingency	基岩 Bedrock	144	1.322%
	淤泥 Mud	1	0.009%
	淤泥/沙 Mud/sand	1	0.009%
	岩石/岩层 Rock/rock layer	328	3.011%
	沙/砂石 Sand/sand and pebbles	1042	9.568%
	沙/基岩 Sand/bedrock	11	0.101%
	砂岩 Sandstone	1	0.009%
包含物 Inclusions	碎陶片 Broken pottery sherds	2	0.018%
	烧土 Burnt earth	1	0.009%
	黄土块 Chunks of yellow earth	1	0.009%
	其他填充物 Other fill	5	0.046%
	青砖 Green brick	1	0.009%
	灰土 Grey ash	6	0.055%
	灰土/水垢 Grey ash/limescale	1	0.009%
	水垢 Limescale	1	0.009%
	现代墓葬 Modern grave	9	0.083%
	陶器/陶片 Pottery/pottery sherds	82	0.753%
	红砖 Red brick	1	0.009%

续表

土壤类型分类 Soil type category	土壤类型（包括非土壤物质作为原始数据） Soil types (including non-soil substances as primary data points)	出现次数 Number of occurrences	百分比（总数10,890） Percentage of occurrences (out of 10,890 total)
包含物 Inclusions	朱砂 Red paint	1	0.009%
	石器 Stone implement	1	0.009%
	植物灰烬/木板灰/木屑 Vegetal ash/board ash/wood dust	6	0.055%
	水 Water	2	0.018%
	水管 Water pipe	2	0.018%
	动物骨骼 Animal bone	7	0.064%
	骨/骨块/骨片/碎骨 Bone/bone chunks/bone fragments/broken bone	10	0.091%
未识别Unidentified[1]		102	

1　未识别的土壤类型的钻探点，为了保持记录的连贯性偶尔将其归入数据中。例如，某一钻探点可能有意义但却无法采集；这些点在计算百分比时被排除掉。

Points with unidentified soil types were occasionally integrated into the data set for record-keeping purposes, indicating, for example, when a particular point that would otherwise have been of interest could not be sampled. These points were excluded when calculating percentage figures.

表Ⅰ.8.2　归城内城土样包含物

Table Ⅰ.8.2　Additional contents of soil samples at the Guicheng inner city site

包含物类型（颗粒大小不一）： Types of materials contained in soil (in varying sizes of particulate)：
骨 Bone
砖 Brick
青铜碎片 Bronze fragments
烧土 Burnt earth
灰 Grey ash
灰色/黄色/红色烧土粒 Grains of grey, yellow or red burnt earth
颗粒/卵石 Granules/pebbles
硬土块 Hard earth chunks
水垢 Limescale
陶片 Pottery sherds
岩石 Rock
沙 Sand
淤泥/泥沙 Silt/sediment
植物灰烬 Vegetal ash
尺寸：颗粒、薄片、块、片段 Particle sizes: grains, slivers, chunks, fragments

图Ⅰ.8.1　1：1000比例的原始手绘地图

Figure Ⅰ.8.1　Original 1：1000 hand-drawn print map.

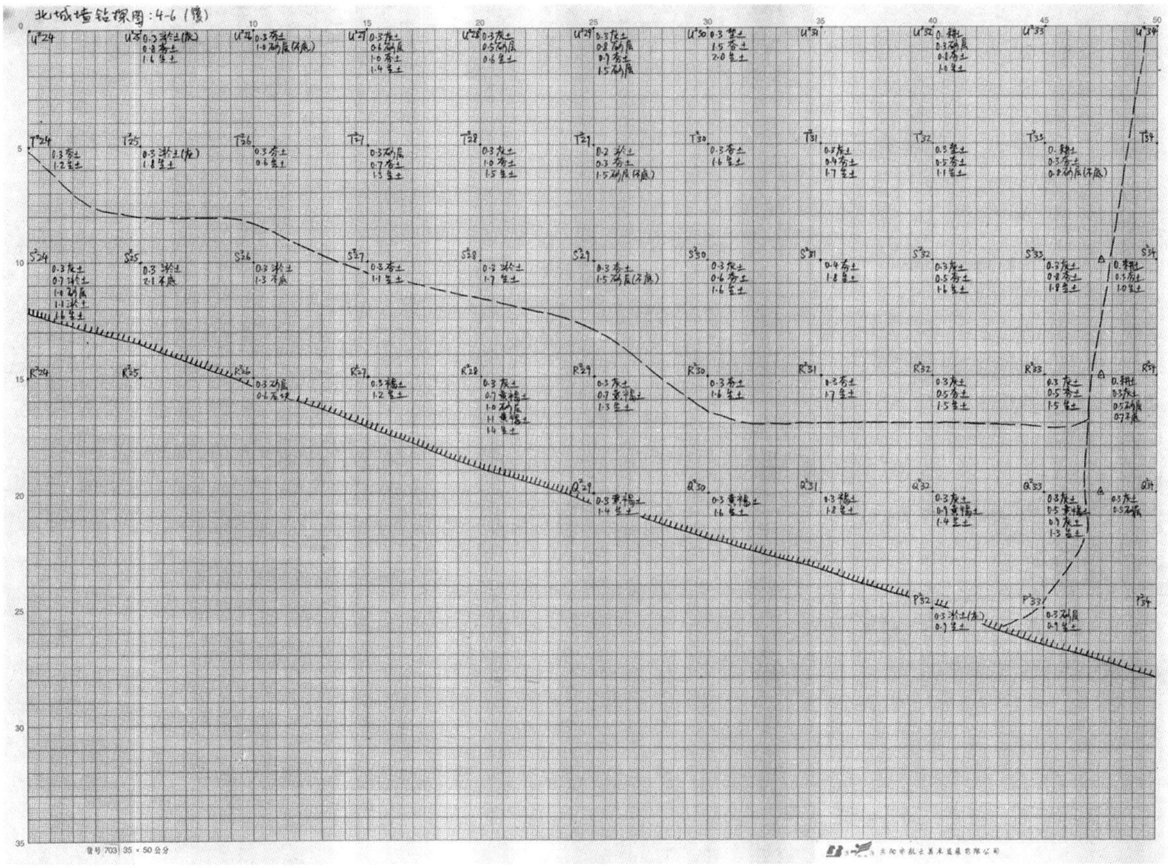

图Ⅰ.8.2　1：100比例的50米×35米钻探点位置图

Figure Ⅰ.8.2　1：100 50m × 35m grid plan showing coring locations.

图Ⅰ.8.3　作为底图的卫星图像

Figure Ⅰ.8.3　Satellite image used as the base map.

图Ⅰ.8.4　用于生成高程表面的高程图调查点层

Figure Ⅰ.8.4　Elevation points layer used to create the elevation surface.

图Ⅰ.8.5　带有建筑轮廓线的最终高程图层

Figure Ⅰ.8.5　Final elevation layer with building footprints.

图Ⅰ.8.6　钻探数据层
Figure Ⅰ.8.6　Coring data layer.

Table

soil

OBJECTID *	SHAPE *	DEPTH	SOILTYPE	CONTAINS	NOTES	SITEID	MAPID
8300	Point Z	0,3	grey	grey ash, sand	<Null>	L2_20	3-5 (west)
8301	Point Z	0,8	sand	<Null>	<Null>	L2_20	3-5 (west)
8302	Point Z	1,6	bedrock	<Null>	<Null>	L2_20	3-5 (west)
8303	Point Z	0,3	grey	sand, grey ash, red burnt earth grains	<Null>	K2_20	3-5 (west)
8304	Point Z	1	sand	<Null>	<Null>	K2_20	3-5 (west)
8305	Point Z	1,6	bedrock	<Null>	<Null>	K2_20	3-5 (west)
8306	Point Z	0,3	grey	grey ash	<Null>	J2_20	3-5 (west)
8307	Point Z	0,6	yellow-brown	sand	<Null>	J2_20	3-5 (west)
8308	Point Z	1	bedrock	<Null>	<Null>	J2_20	3-5 (west)
8309	Point Z	0,3	grey	grey ash, red burnt earth chunks, see notes	broken pottery sh	I2_20	3-5 (west)
8310	Point Z	0,8	yellow-brown	sand	<Null>	I2_20	3-5 (west)
8311	Point Z	1	bedrock	<Null>	<Null>	I2_20	3-5 (west)
8312	Point Z	0,3	grey	<Null>	<Null>	H2_20	3-5 (west)
8313	Point Z	0,5	yellow-brown	<Null>	<Null>	H2_20	3-5 (west)
8314	Point Z	0,7	sand	<Null>	<Null>	H2_20	3-5 (west)
8315	Point Z	0,8	flower	<Null>	did not reach nat	H2_20	3-5 (west)
8316	Point Z	0,3	grey	sand, grey ash	<Null>	H2_21	3-5 (west)
8317	Point Z	1	yellow-brown	sand, grey ash, chunks of burnt earth	<Null>	H2_21	3-5 (west)
8318	Point Z	0,3	grey	grey ash, sand, broken pottery shards	<Null>	I2_21	3-5 (west)
8319	Point Z	0,7	yellow-brown	sand	<Null>	I2_21	3-5 (west)
8320	Point Z	0,9	sand	<Null>	<Null>	I2_21	3-5 (west)
8321	Point Z	1,1	bedrock	<Null>	<Null>	I2_21	3-5 (west)
8322	Point Z	0,3	grey	grey ash, broken pottery shards	<Null>	J2_21	3-5 (west)
8323	Point Z	0,8	yellow-brown	sand	<Null>	J2_21	3-5 (west)
8324	Point Z	1	bedrock	<Null>	<Null>	J2_21	3-5 (west)
8325	Point Z	0,3	grey	grey ash, red burnt earth chunks	<Null>	K2_21	3-5 (west)
8326	Point Z	0,6	pottery shards	<Null>	<Null>	K2_21	3-5 (west)
8327	Point Z	0,7	sand	<Null>	<Null>	K2_21	3-5 (west)
8328	Point Z	1	bedrock	<Null>	<Null>	K2_21	3-5 (west)
8329	Point Z	0,3	grey	grey ash, broken pottery shards	<Null>	L2_21	3-5 (west)
8330	Point Z	1	yellow-brown	sand	<Null>	L2_21	3-5 (west)
8331	Point Z	2,5	rock	<Null>	<Null>	L2_21	3-5 (west)
8333	Point Z	0,3	grey	sand, grey ash, red burnt earth grains	<Null>	M2_21	3-5 (west)
8334	Point Z	1,1	sand	<Null>	<Null>	M2_21	3-5 (west)
8335	Point Z	1,8	rock	<Null>	<Null>	M2_21	3-5 (west)
8336	Point Z	0,3	grey	grey ash, broken pottery shards, see notes	red burnt earth gr	N2_21	3-5 (west)
8337	Point Z	1,3	sand	<Null>	<Null>	N2_21	3-5 (west)
8338	Point Z	1,7	bedrock	<Null>	<Null>	N2_21	3-5 (west)
8339	Point Z	0,3	grey	grey sand, burnt earth grains, see notes	broken pottery sh	N2_22	3-5 (west)
8340	Point Z	1,15	sand/bedrock	<Null>	<Null>	N2_22	3-5 (west)
8341	Point Z	0,3	grey	grey ash, sand, burnt earth grains	<Null>	M2_22	3-5 (west)
8342	Point Z	0,6	grey	chunks of yellow earth	<Null>	M2_22	3-5 (west)
8343	Point Z	1,1	sand/bedrock	<Null>	<Null>	M2_22	3-5 (west)
8344	Point Z	0,3	grey	grey ash	<Null>	L2_22	3-5 (west)
8345	Point Z	1	rammed	<Null>	yellow-brown	L2_22	3-5 (west)

8000　(0 out of 10992 Selected)

soil

图Ⅰ.8.7　ArcMap中的钻探点记录示例

Figure Ⅰ.8.7　Sample coring point records from ArcMap.

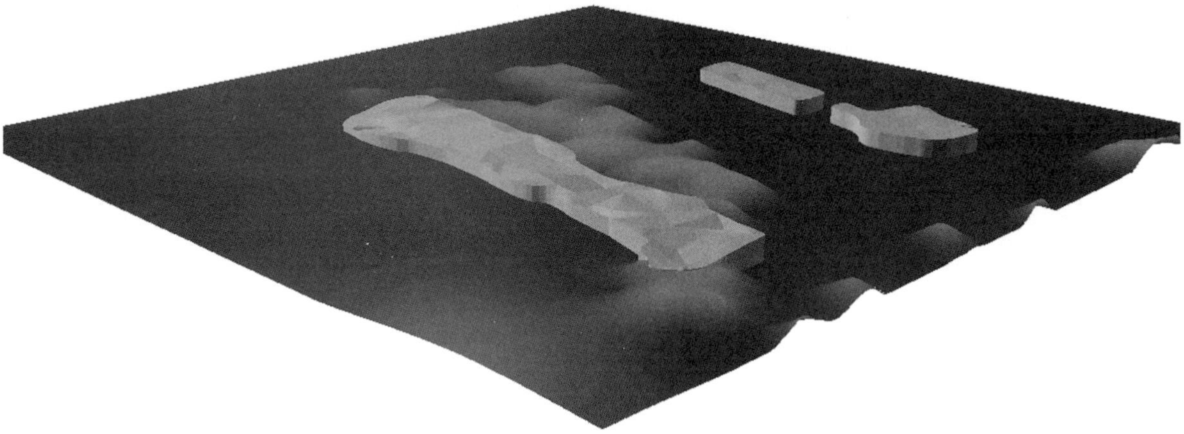

图Ⅰ.8.8　夯土基址9、10、11的视觉复原（位于基岩面）（视角1）
Figure Ⅰ.8.8　Visual reconstruction of Rammed Earth Foundations, 9, 10, and 11 (on surface of bedrock) (view one).

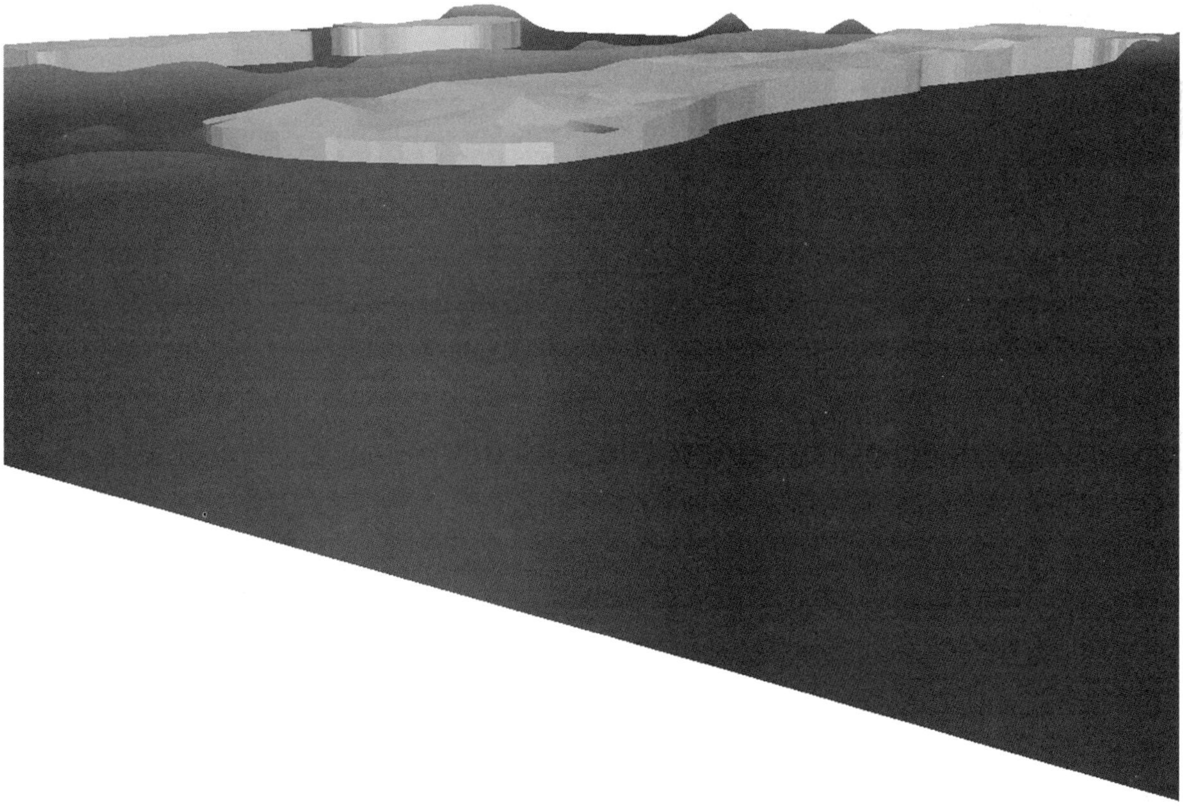

图Ⅰ.8.9　夯土基址9、10、11的视觉复原（位于基岩面）（视角2）
Figure Ⅰ.8.9　Visual reconstruction of Rammed Earth Foundations, 9, 10, and 11 (on surface of bedrock) (view two).

Chapter 8: Georeferencing and Coring Data Management in Guicheng Archaeology

Jeremiah Trinidad-Christensen   Paul Nicholas Vogt

Section 1: Geographic Information Systems Software

The definition of Geographic Information Systems (GIS) often differs depending on the field, but in the most basic sense, it can be defined as "a computer system capable of assembling, storing, manipulating, and displaying geographically referenced information, i.e., data identified according to their locations" (USGS). What makes GIS a powerful tool is the ability not only to display spatial connections between layers of data points and their connected databases, but also to perform analysis spatially. There are several different GIS software packages available to choose from, including both free open-source and commercial software options. For this project, we used ESRI ArcGIS, Quantum GIS (QGIS), Google Earth, and (in future processing) Geographic Resources Analysis Support System (GRASS). Of these, ArcGIS was and still is used most frequently and most extensively; it is the primary software platform in which site data are stored and manipulated.

Google Earth was used mainly in the beginning, as its excellent satellite imagery allowed for the initial visual identification of the site and the creation of a grid demarcating areas of interest and projected phases of the project. These visual aids were used on-site during the initial phase of the project (2007-2008), supplementing hand-drawn maps created locally through surveys of various types. However, Google Earth is primarily a visualization tool; it cannot perform spatial analysis. Keyhole Markup Language (KML), Google Earth's native data format, cannot attach to a database in the way that many GIS-specific formats, such as shapefiles or ESRI ArcGIS geodatabase feature classes, can. The more powerful ArcGIS and QGIS software packages were therefore used in contexts requiring data processing.

Both QGIS and GRASS are open-source software. GRASS, although a very powerful software package, is command-line-driven and can have a high learning curve. QGIS has a much easier-to-use interface and is compatible with many GRASS plugins, allowing it to perform a wide range of spatial analysis functions. ESRI ArcGIS is a powerful commercial GIS software suite created by

Environmental Systems Research Institute (ESRI). It is the primary software used for this project (the same ArcGIS software was also used to generate field maps used during the ground survey as well as to analyze the survey data to generate sherd distribution maps; see Part I, Chapter 6). Most of the data created and used for the project are kept in a geodatabase format, which is only accessible in ArcGIS software. A geodatabase helps with organizing relationships between data layers; it also allows the addition of parameters that limit errors when entering data or when creating new layers.

Section 2: Mapping and Georeferencing

1. Mapping

As mentioned above, Google Earth was used initially to identify the site visually and to create grids demarcating the different areas to be covered by various phases of the project. This more or less sufficed in the beginning, but we also arranged for the creation of a detailed, hand-drawn map of the area covering one square kilometer at the scale of 1 : 1,000. This map shows water, roads, buildings, and general topography, with a 1 m grid overlay for reference purposes (Fig. Ⅰ.8.1).

During the planning phase and the coring process, these two visual aids were used concurrently by researchers and technicians as the basic site reference map. As the coring process proceeded, soil core drilling locations were recorded on several smaller, hand-drawn maps at a scale of 1 : 100. Each of these maps covers an area of 50 m by 35 m and depicts buildings, roads, cliffs, and other recognizable terrain features, as well as the coring points within range and their associated data. These smaller maps are the primary medium in which coring data were initially stored, simply by writing the relevant data beside each point cored (Fig. Ⅰ.8.2).

It quickly became clear that imagery from Google Earth alone would not suffice for the process of georeferencing the detailed, hand-drawn maps (see below). To support that process, the project purchased a satellite image produced in 2004 with a 6.5 m resolution. This image, captured under conditions of zero cloud cover, covers an area of 25 km^2, with the Guicheng city site positioned roughly in the center. This new satellite image became the base map for the project and was used for the creation of all data layers and for georeferencing maps (Fig. Ⅰ.8.3; Pl. 3).

Before the creation of data layers and georeferencing, we decided to use Universal Transverse Mercator (UTM) Zone 10 North as the map projection for all layers. UTM is a conformal projection, based on the Mercator projection that splits the earth into a total of sixty zones. As with any projection, distortion was expected, either in area, distance, shape, angle, or direction. The UTM preserves relative angles and approximate shape of features, and the overall distortion of area, distance, and direction is minimal, especially at a scale as large as the footprint of the site.

2. Georeferencing

Georeferencing is the process of aligning a digitized image such as a scanned map to a coordinate system such as the one described above, ArcGIS or GRASS. In preparation for georeferencing, all hand-drawn maps were scanned at 300dpi as uncompressed TIF images; this format was chosen to allow for adequate detail while limiting the overall size of the image files. To georeference a map, a point is identified on the digital image, and coordinates are assigned to the point by either typing them in (if the latitude and longitude are known) or dragging the point to a known location on previously spatially referenced layers. A minimum of three points are needed to georeference a map, although more are often required; for the site maps in question, around ten to twenty points were used in the georeferencing process. As points are added, errors emerge as the image stretches to fit all of the identified locations. The software package distributes these errors among all of the points, so as to optimize the relative accuracy of all point locations. Usually, when a site map was more or less in place, all of the points were reviewed, and those with the most software-assigned error were sometimes deleted; this was done on a case-by-case basis, however.

Although both of the smaller hand-drawn map (Fig. Ⅰ.8.2; scale 1 ∶ 100) and the full-site map (Fig. Ⅰ.8.1; scale 1 ∶ 1,000; see also “Elevation: Part 2” below) contained a one-meter grid, error was introduced in both the drawing of features on the map and the scanning process due to folds (When maps passed through the sheet-fed scanner, folds were not completely flattened by the machine and warped the image slightly). Overall, however, distortion was kept to less than 1/3 m at any specific point on the map, so the positioning of the points can still be considered relatively accurate. To help deal with such distortions while georeferencing the maps, vector grids were created at scales of one meter, ten meters, and 100 meters, using identifiable locations on both hand-drawn maps to help situate the lower left corner of the map as it matched to the satellite image.

Identifiable natural features, intersections, and buildings on the hand-drawn maps were lined up to the corresponding locations on the satellite image. The maps were georeferenced using a first-order polynomial transformation, stretching the map either side to side, top to bottom, or diagonally. Using second- or third-order polynomial transformations might potentially have reduced the statistical error in georeferencing the map; however, either of those transformations would have introduced more error overall by warping the map in unwanted ways.

3. Feature Layers

After the maps were georeferenced, layers showing the locations of bodies of still water, rivers, buildings, roads, and visible remnants of the ancient city wall were created. This process was relatively quick; constructing the elevation layers and the data layer for the core drilling points was more time-consuming.

Section 3: Creating an Elevation Map

As a precondition for entering coring data, it was necessary to create a relatively accurate elevation layer. All strata at all coring points were assigned numbers representing the depth below the current surface of the ground at which certain types of soil were first recognized. Normally, the tilled agricultural stratum was assigned a maximum depth of 0.3 m below the surface of the ground, at which point the recording of cultural deposits began. Sometimes, however, cultural layers such as rammed earth first appeared earlier or slightly later in the coring process. In any event, to accurately represent the coring data at all points and interpret their correlations, it was critical to first replicate the variation in elevation of the current ground surface across the areas cored.

1. The Search for Elevation Data

Initially, we had to rely on publically available datasets for calculating and estimating elevation; in fact, we still rely on these sources to determine the elevation of areas outside the 1 km^2 map. The only elevation data publically available for the site at the time was the product of the Shuttle Radar Topography Mission (SRTM) Digital Elevation Model (DEM), with a resolution of three arc seconds, or roughly 90 m (meaning that the model averaged all elevation variation over a 90 m^2 area). This was much too coarse for the project's needs, given that the main area where most of the core samples were taken sat on just a few of the DEM's resolution cells. It did, however, give a rough elevation estimate for the area contained in the satellite image.

What the project really needed was an elevation layer that would allow the extraction of 2 m contours. This could potentially be done with an elevation grid of about 10 m resolution. In order to simulate the 10 m grid, we converted the SRTM elevation layer to a point layer, performed an Inverse Distant Weighting (IDW) on the layer with a cell value of thirty meters, and performed a smoothing using a neighborhood focal statistics algorithm. We then repeated this process using a 10 m cell size. Finally, we extracted 2 m and 10 m contours from the final interpolated DEM for use on field maps, creating a rough guide to the elevation of the area.

Although the end result of this process was a layer with more or less smooth transitions in elevation, there is no way to retrieve missing elevation data from this layer. Since the initial cell size of 90 m is quite large, much elevation detail was lost that would be impossible to reproduce without better data. Recently, better (although still not adequate) elevation data became available through a joint mission between the United States and Japan called Advanced Spaceborne Thermal Emission and Reflection Radiometer (ASTER) DEM. ASTER DEM data has a resolution of 30 m, a significant improvement over the SRTM.

In our search for better elevation data than the available SRTM, we explored other options, including purchasing a digital elevation model extracted from Soviet and Chinese maps at a scale of 1:50,000. Surprisingly, this model turned out to be far less accurate than the SRTM dataset when a comparison was conducted between the layers using the satellite image for reference.

2. Elevation Survey

In order to better represent the variation in elevation over the areas cored, a surveyor was hired to acquire more accurate elevation data for the square kilometer covered by the initial hand-drawn map of the inner city site. Using that map as a base layer and starting from a single base point, a second map was created containing detailed elevation data for the surrounding area. The initial point was given an arbitrary height of 100, and the elevation of each of the other 373 points was either added to or subtracted from this height, depending on whether the point in question was higher or lower than the base point. The majority of the elevation survey points were clustered around the inner wall and areas where the elevation fluctuated. Areas of relatively flat or static change in height usually contained a single survey point. The maximum difference in height among the points surveyed was 16 m, and the average difference was slightly less than 4 m; it is easy to see how both the SRTM and the ASTER data would fail to capture such a fine level of variation in height.

The map was scanned and georeferenced, and a data layer containing the elevation points was created by hand (Fig. Ⅰ.8.4). Elevation points were occasionally shifted slightly from their locations on the scanned map, using the vector grid and identifiable features as points of reference, in order to account as best as possible for error created in the georeferencing and the drawing process. When this elevation point layer was completed, a corresponding height was extracted from the ASTER grid to get an approximate absolute elevation for the base point relative to sea level, and the elevation was calculated for all other points making up the surface layer of the site. An IDW was performed on the elevation points using a low point radius, reducing the smoothing and allowing for more variation in adjacent points. A barrier layer was created to ensure that cliffs and areas with sharp elevation changes were reflected correctly in the resultant elevation layer (Fig. Ⅰ.8.5; Pl. 7).

Section 4: Soil Coring Points

The creation of a layer containing and displaying the coring data proved to be the most time-consuming element yet, due both to the complexity and number of points collected and to the design of the database (Fig. Ⅰ.8.6). The coring was conducted roughly every 5 m, with a depth averaging almost 0.7 m and reaching a maximum depth of 4 m, over the entirety of the inner city site. Coring points were recorded using an alphanumeric coordinate system; point designations vary numerically along the east-west axis and alphabetically along the north-south axis. Occasional adjustments were made to conform to prohibitive terrain conditions (such as the presence of orchards, paving, etc.) or to confirm the extent of distribution of specific soil types.

For the overall design of the database, it was decided that each new soil type contained at a single coring location would be given its own data point, thereby allowing multiple discrete data points to occupy the same location on the map. This approach accommodated the fact that some soil types, notably rammed earth and so-called "grey earth" (*huitu* 灰土) could appear at any given depth and did not always occur in a particular order. The coring point database fields include a software-assigned ID; depth measured in meters; the type and color of soil encountered at that depth; description of particulates or other matter contained in the soil layer; occasional miscellaneous observations on texture, etc.; coring point ID with which the data point was associated on the original maps; and ID of the original map on which it was contained (see Part Ⅰ, Chapter 3). These last two fields were included so that the original map could be referred to in case there were any questions about data contained in a point. Separating the coordinate-depth-soil type combinations in this way allows the execution of mathematical operations, extrapolations, etc., on the points corresponding to one soil type without affecting points of other types (Fig. Ⅰ.8.7).

As mentioned earlier, based on the understanding of the soil profile of Guicheng acquired during the first season of fieldwork, we established standards of systematic soil classification that were followed in the following years (see Part Ⅰ, Chapter 3, especially Table Ⅰ.3.1). The classification of soil also provided the foundation for the entry and analysis of the coring data as described in the present chapter. The frequency of occurrence of the various soil types is analyzed in Table I.8.1, which can be taken as an overall representation of the soil profile in the inner city of Guicheng. Additional material inclusions regularly found in soil samples, such as pebbles, pottery sherds, bone fragments, etc. are listed in Table Ⅰ.8.2. Occasionally, when a substance such as fragmentary bone or ceramic was found in a coring point without much surrounding soil, it was recorded as a primary "soil type" of its own, both to provide a complete account of the coring process for that point and to maintain a detailed record of the distribution of such substances.

A database field was maintained for the recording of additional information on specific points. Notable contingencies that did not fit into the established soil classifications were often recorded here. For instance, when a particular layer extended past 5 m below the surface (the maximum effective depth of the tools used in coring), a note was made to that effect (Fig. Ⅰ.8.7).

Altogether, these recording techniques produced nearly 11,000 independent data points as a foundation for the subterranean imaging stage.

Section 5: Subterranean Imaging

In two-dimensional GIS software such as ArcGIS, the overlap created by this approach can sometimes make it difficult to visualize more than one type of soil at the same time. However, when the coring data is imported into a three-dimensional software package capable of volume interpolation, such as GRASS on the Unix platform, the situation under the ground can be visualized much better. Although the data visualization is still relatively chaotic in a point format, the points of a particular data set – in this case, a soil type – can be used to extrapolate and render a three-dimensional image representing the surface of that soil layer under the ground, with associated elevation values, both absolute (i.e., relative to sea level) and relative (i.e., relative to layers of other soil types throughout the site).

In order to demonstrate the potential of this method, for visual analysis and reconstruction we selected Rammed Building Foundation 9, the largest in the western zone of architectural foundations in the inner city, and the adjacent two smaller foundations, 10 and 11 (Fig. Ⅰ.8.8-Fig. Ⅰ.8.9) (Pl. 66). This was done in spring 2013. The project shows well the great value of the coring data and the possibility that computer-based simulations can allow us to understand the subterranean architectural features before they can ever have a chance to actually be excavated.

第九章　归城陶器的岩相学分析

James B. Stoltman

本章介绍了来自归城的47件陶片切片标本的岩相学分析结果。这些陶片由李峰教授挑选，并提供给笔者用作切片标本。主要包括2007年在归城内城地表采集的23片陶片和2009年在有明确地层关系的地层中出土的24片陶片。就每批陶片而言，我们在采集时充分考虑了本遗址陶器变异的幅度。研究的主要目的是辨别陶器中可能存在的成分差异与被认为是存在于遗址中的两种风格迥异的陶器传统的关系。一种是素面红褐色陶器及有特点的器型，如鼎，这些被认为是一种本土的陶器制作传统。与之相比的是颜色较深，灰色或黑色带有绳纹的陶器，它们被认为是非本土的属于周文化的器物。虽然明显地有一些相互影响，这项研究将会比较和对照可能来自于两个传统的陶片，以此来确定两者是否存在成分上的差异，这种差异可能反映了与两个传统有关的独特制作工艺或技术实践。

本研究有三项基本组成部分。第一，我们报告被认为可能是在本土陶器传统体系下制作的陶片的矿物成分。第二，我们对于那些反映非本土周文化传统制陶工艺的陶片进行成分分析。第三，总结前面两部分的结果，我们试图阐明两个传统中不同的技术、文化和行为实践，并且可以此对它们进行鉴别和区分。在第一部分开始之前，我们将会对本研究所用工艺的方法论做一个概要的讨论。

第一节　方　法　论

岩相学是一项为矿物和岩石提供可靠鉴定的值得信赖的地质技术。首先我们应该指出陶器岩相学分析的两个重要属性（局限性？）。第一个属性是岩相显微镜不能鉴定个体的黏土质矿物，因为它们的晶粒尺寸太小（<0.002 mm）。在陶片的切片标本上，黏土作为一种均匀的基底（matrix），其成分无法进一步被确定。因此，岩相学分析的重点为接近泥沙大小（silt size）（>0.002 mm）或者更大的颗粒。岩相学的第二个属性是它直接处理岩石和矿物的物理特性，因此不能提供化学成分的数据。对于一个颗粒的化学组成来说，推断有时是可行的，但这仅仅是根据所观察到的物理特性，而不是直接测定的，比如说可能用中子活化技术。

所有的切片标本用一种基本的标点计数程序来分析，这在笔者较早的几篇文章中有描述（Stoltman 1989，1991，2001）。一个1毫米的标准计数间距单位被用来覆盖每个切片标本的整个面积，或者除了空隙之外至少有200个间距单位。用这个方法得到的是每个切片的物理特性信息，包括泥沙大小的包含物的百分比，加上沙粒大小或更大的矿物质包含物的种类、尺寸和百分比。由于个体的黏土（clay）颗粒在切片上不能识别，它们的存在仅仅是作为“基底”（matrix）来被记录的。标点计数是“盲目”进行的，也就是说，除了它们的切片编号之外没有样本先前的信息，并且直到所有的分析完成之前，个体切片的数据既不能制作成表，也不能作对照。

在评估这些标点计数数据时，要意识到它们来自于一种费工的取样程序，容易有一定程度上的观测者的误差。此外，每个切片是一个陶器的抽样，而每个陶器又是一个陶器群的抽样。在这两个层次上都可能产生偏差；虽然可以尽量减少这个偏差，但极少能被完全排除。在最低水平上，可以期望个体切片标本能够提供它们母体陶器的合理可靠的抽样，因为通常陶工准备陶泥的方式是将黏土同夹砂（tempers）高度混合。（关于标点计数中抽样误差来源的更多讨论见Stoltman 1989。）

我们用五个指标来表示标点计数的结果：①体量成分（bulk composition）；②砂子径度指数（sand-size index）；③陶泥（paste）；④坯体（body）；⑤夹砂径度指数（temper-size index）。体量成分连同砂子径度指数一起被用来表示那些缺乏可见夹砂的陶器，也就是泥质陶器。体量成分是一个由三个变量的相对百分比组成的体积测量：基底/黏土、泥沙（silt）和砂子（sand）。所有这些是按照颗粒的径度来区别的：基底/黏土≤002 毫米；泥沙=0.002～0.0624 毫米之间的可见颗粒；砂子=0.0625～2.00 毫米之间的颗粒。作为对这一指标的补充，每个陶器也会记录其砂子径度指数。方法是，按照下面的级别，对在标点计数过程中碰到的每个砂粒，据其最大直径给予一个数据：

（1）微小=0.0625～0.249 毫米

（2）中等=0.25～0.499 毫米

（3）粗=0.50～0.99 毫米

（4）很粗=1.00～1.99 毫米

（5）砂砾=2.00+ 毫米

我们把每个颗粒的径度值相加，然后除以颗粒的总数目，从而得出一个平均的“砂子径度指数”，每个切片在1到5之间不等。由于所记录体量成分的陶器缺乏人为添加的夹砂（即泥质陶，译者注），它们的成分可以直接同天然沉积物作比较，提供了确定这些陶器沉积物来源的可能性。

相反，对于人为添加砂粒的陶器，我们将采用陶泥、坯体、夹砂径度三个指数（见Stoltman 1991：109～110；2001：314）。陶泥测定首先要辨认夹砂颗粒，从而把它们同天然砂粒分开记录。其结果是将三种天然材料——包括基底/黏土、泥沙和砂子——以百分比的形式进行量化表现，它们反映了天然沉淀物以及泥质陶器的成分特征。每个切片上天然出现的沙粒的径度指数也被记录。因为陶泥和体量成分是同构的（适用于泥质陶器和天然沉积物），在这三种类别之间进行直接的、有意义的对比是可行的。陶泥是评估夹砂陶器和泥质陶器为本土制作的合理指数，因为它可以同当地的沉积物作比较。当一个本土沉积物的代表性样本切片无法获取的时候，“本土”陶泥的特征仍旧可以被界定——尽管是暂时的，因为那些熟悉本土考古学的考古学家们能够合理地判断出属于本土制作的陶器抽样。一旦测定了本土陶器的陶泥特点被测定，同风格异常的陶器相比较就可以对它们可能的非本土起源做出更客观地评估。如果陶器的陶泥与本土的陶器不同，而且还与疑为外部来源的沉积物或陶器相匹配，那么对此陶器非本土起源的判断就会更有力。

在本研究中确认了两个基本的陶泥类型被确认，每个都来自于不同的沉积类型。其中最常见的一个黏土沉积物来源是冲积土，黏土经流水而沉淀。根据地区地质学特征（即当地岩石和沉积物的组成）及其影响径流容量的地貌和地形，冲积黏土总是包含不同数量泥沙和砂子的粗颗粒群。相比之下，由风力沉积的黄土沉积物主要由泥沙和黏土组成，因为风在多数情况下不能运送砂子大小的颗粒。在我以前关于安阳陶器的岩相学分析中（Stoltman et al. 2009），这两种沉积物或陶泥类型很容易被辨认，并且已经证实它们都被用在陶器制作中。两者的主要区别涉及泥沙和砂子的不同分配。典型的黄土包含15%～20%的泥沙，并且即便有少量的砂子颗粒，那也从未大于细沙（径度指数=1.00，如果不是0的话）。与之相比，冲积土通常含有不到10%的泥沙和更高含量的砂子，包括足够的属于中等—粗径度的颗粒，其砂体指数大于1.00（Stoltman et al. 2009：183）（一个来自安阳周围黄土和沉积土的更大抽样证实了这些结果）。尽管我们在归城地区没有搜集直接的地质学证据，事实上冲积土在大部分地区是普遍存在的；几项地质学上的资料确认了山东地区黄土的存在（Linyuan et al. 1991；Liu 1988）。

与陶泥形成对比，坯体（body）是一种体积测量，表示两种材料的人工混合——陶泥（=黏土+所有泥沙和砂子径度的天然包含物）+夹砂——通常有不同的地质学来源。陶泥和坯体的区别首先是根据对有意地、人为加入的夹杂物的可靠鉴定，也就是夹砂。在这项研究中，三个主要的岩石夹砂被确认：花岗岩（granite）、片岩（schist）和闪岩（amphibolite）。由于它们的大尺寸、高棱角和特殊的构成与天然的砂子夹杂物形成对比，这些夹杂物作为夹砂的鉴定而变得相对简单。坯体指数由三部分组成：①天然砂；②夹砂；③基底（泥沙作为基底的一部分被包含在内）。我们使用同样测量砂粒的1～5级别的尺度来报告夹砂的径度指数。

夹砂的类型、尺寸和数量都是直接反映人类活动的变量，因此它们很可能被它们的文化所决定。坯体可以提供一种与陶泥相独立的另外一个可以判定陶器本土或非本土状态的一个有价值的依据，尤其是当夹砂可以被追溯到已知的地质学来源的时候。在利用夹砂作为一种被文化所决定的变量时，一个重要的警告就是，它未必是一种传统制陶方式的被动反应，而是陶工的一种更积极的设计方面的考虑，他们使用不同的坯体配方来制作不同功能的陶器（举例来说，礼制或炊煮或储存或盛食等）。

第二节　归城的本土制陶传统

根据对标本的视觉观察，提供做切片的47件陶器中有19件属于本土制陶传统。这19件陶器是炊煮器，包括12件鼎、6件鬲和1件甗。经观察所有的都被人工添加了岩石颗粒，也就是夹砂的。因此我们将用陶泥、坯体和夹砂径度指数来分析它们的成分。这些成分数据被记录在表Ⅰ.9.1中。

正如我们在表Ⅰ.9.1中所看到的那样，这些本土的炊煮器带有相当分量的夹砂，按体积计算的话平均为29.9%。经观察包括三种岩面——花岗岩（n=10）、闪岩（n=6）和片岩（n=3）——有时在一件陶器中出现不止一种。它们都是变质岩，由于它们出现在本土的陶器中，因此假定其为本土起源，尽管目前来说这是一种未经进一步证实的推断。这三种夹砂的切片图像分别见于图Ⅰ.9.1～Ⅰ.9.3（图版67、68）。

陶泥值为测量用于制作这些陶器的天然富黏土沉积物提供了一个标准。这些陶器的陶泥相对均匀，表明其有一个共同来源。泥沙和砂子径度的自然包含物所占比例较小：泥沙为7%，砂子为4%。这些值与冲积沉积物相一致，但绝对不是黄土（通常的特征为：泥沙大于15%，细沙小于2%）。

第三节　归城的周文化制陶传统

属于周文化传统的28件陶器被提供制作成切片。其中有7片夹砂陶，21片泥质陶（见图Ⅰ.9.4和Ⅰ.9.5）。在这两类陶器之间有一个明显的差别：所有夹砂的陶器都是鬲，也就是用来炊煮的器物，然而所有泥质的陶器都被用作非炊煮器，比如储存和盛食用器（见表Ⅰ.9.2和Ⅰ.9.3）。这一发现与先前观察到得晚商的炊煮—非炊煮陶器的成分差别相一致，这些标本来自于河南安阳附近的殷墟遗址（Stoltman et al. 2009）。陶器作为一种可塑材料，当面临温度变化时由于其膨胀和收缩很容易破裂。因为炊煮器要反复加热和冷却，尤其容易遭受这种破坏。这些陶器中的岩石夹砂（非可塑性材料）阻止了这种由热引发的陶壁膨胀和收缩而产生的破坏性。同样值得注意的是，目前归城本土传统的夹砂陶器抽样全部都是炊煮器（表Ⅰ.9.1）。这样看来，夹砂炊煮陶器和泥质非炊煮陶器的做法是中国青铜时代陶工们的一种坚实传统。

首先来看周文化传统的夹砂陶器，可以看到所有的都用花岗岩作为夹砂（表Ⅰ.9.2）。尽管标本较少，这种夹砂的一致性与本土陶工所用夹砂的多样性形成对比（参阅表Ⅰ.9.1）。同样与本土陶工的习惯相比，周文化传统的陶工明显使用很少的夹砂——18.4%，对比29.9%。但是，它们通常是粗颗粒的夹砂（夹砂径度指数：周文化是3.08，对比本土陶工是2.73）（表Ⅰ.9.1和Ⅰ.9.2；图Ⅰ.9.6）。除坯体值的差别之外，在两种传统的陶泥之间也有明显的差别。对比表Ⅰ.9.2和Ⅰ.9.3的数据可以看出，周文化传统陶器的陶泥含有更多泥沙——周文化传统泥沙的平均值为11.3%，而本土传统为6.7%（表Ⅰ.9.1和图Ⅰ.9.7）。这表明它们的黏土有不同的来源。夹砂陶器中的三件标本尤为突出：表Ⅰ.9.2中的GU07-6和GU11-1，及其表Ⅱ.9.1中的GU07-10，全部都是15%～20%的高泥沙值。这些陶泥数据显示出制造这些陶器所用黏土的来源是黄土。它们可以被认为有可能是非本土来源。

现在看周文化传统的泥质陶器（表Ⅰ.9.3），一个尤其显著的组成属性值得强调：那就是泥沙的高包含量（21件陶器的泥沙平均比率为15.2%）。由于泥质陶器的体量成分（bulk composition）与夹砂陶器的陶泥值（paste values）相等，这种高泥沙值模式见于所有的28件周文化传统陶器，而与19件本土传统炊煮陶器的低陶泥值形成对比。从这些数据看，我们有理由推测，虽然属于两种传统的陶工有时都使用了类似的黏土，然而周文化传统的陶工和本土传统的陶工在制造各自陶器的时候表现出了一种利用不同陶土资源的明显趋势。

第四节　概要和总结

基于并接受这样一种假设——归城遗址中存在着两种陶器制作传统，这项研究，通过对每个传统的陶器进行岩相学分析，把陶器成分的变化作为一个探寻反映两个传统特点的文化或技术习惯之证据的单独变量。在评估这项研究的结果时，我们应该指明以下证据中的两个重要缺陷。一方面，没有直接的基岩或本地富黏土沉积物的地质标本可用来同切片陶器做对比。没有这些数据的话，关于夹砂和富黏土沉积物来源推断的暂时性就不应该被忽视。另一方面，没有本土传统的非炊煮陶器可用于此项分析。所以，两个传统陶器之间的比较是不对等的，因此是不全面的。

虽然有这些局限性，一方面在周文化传统的陶器之间，另一方面在周文化和本土传统之间，这项研究仍然揭示了许多非随机性的成分差异。在周文化传统内，夹砂炊煮器而泥质非炊煮器的习惯被证明。这明显是先前在河南殷墟商代晚期遗址中所观察到的习惯的一个延续。这种习惯的存在在归城本土传统中不能被证明，因为只有夹砂陶器被用来做切片。由于炊煮陶器的器壁在反复的加热和冷却所带来的温度应力（thermal stresses）下开裂的内在趋势，作为一种技术性的对策，这种做法是合理的。作为非可塑性材料，岩石夹砂可以抵抗在陶器成分中占主要比例的可塑性黏土的破坏性的膨胀和收缩。

最明显的是，在两种传统的制陶实践中存在至少三种人为的差异。尽管周文化传统的夹砂陶器的标本很少（n=7），但它们只使用了花岗岩作夹砂，然而本土陶器使用了至少三种不同的夹砂（表Ⅰ.9.1）。这可以看作是本地居民对本土资源更为了解的反映。

两种传统之间的第二种差异涉及在准备陶器坯体时所使用夹砂的百分比和径度。从表Ⅰ.9.1和Ⅰ.9.2中可以看出，周文化陶工明显使用更少的夹砂（18.4% 对比本土陶工的29.9%）和更大的径度（周文化夹砂平均径度指数为3.08，而本土陶工为2.73）。然而，周代陶器中少量和大径度的夹砂模式也有可能是只使用花岗岩作为夹砂的结果，花岗岩是一种比片岩和闪岩更能对抗破裂的材料。根据这种观点，能最大程度对抗破裂的夹砂类型应该有最大的颗粒径度，因此，夹砂的径度和数量最好被看作是对夹砂进行选择的副产品，而不是对夹砂颗粒的数量和径度进行刻意处理的结果。为了评估这种选择，我们将三种夹砂类型的相对平均径度和百分比分别制作成表并记录，见表Ⅰ.9.4。从这些数据中可以看出，对于所有三种夹砂类型，其径度和百分比中都有一种反比关系——夹砂百分比越大，颗粒径度越小（表Ⅰ.9.4）。相比片岩和闪岩，花岗岩似乎明显地以较低的百分比和更大的径度出现。尽管有这种趋势，然而与本土陶工的花岗岩夹砂陶器相比，周文化陶工所使用的夹砂比例，乃至夹砂的径度，也显示出这种习惯可以被合理地看作是一种有特点的周文化实践，而不只是简单的夹砂类型的关系。

两种陶器传统的第三种差别就是，在陶器制作中对富黏土沉积物似乎有一种不同的使用偏好。对比表Ⅰ.9.2和Ⅰ.9.3中的陶泥和体量成分，可以看出周文化陶工在炊煮和非炊煮陶器中使用相对泥沙质的黏土。尽管有相当大的可变性，但是值得注意的是周代陶器中有一半含有15%或者更多的泥沙，说明其有黄土沉积物的来源。相比之下，19件本土传统陶器中只有一件含有15%的泥沙，大多数（19件中有13件）含有不到10%的泥沙。本土传统陶工的明显偏好是冲积黏土。不幸的是，可用于评估这些沉积物的本地可获得性的地质学数据目前还无法获得。

总之，这项研究揭示了归城地区本地和周文化传统陶器在岩相成分上的不同，它们代表了两个不同的制陶传统。本土陶工开发利用多种（本地的？）岩石去为他们的炊煮器作夹砂，而周文化陶工只使用花岗岩作为夹砂（他们只添加在炊煮器中）。此外，本土陶工倾向于使用一种数量较大且径度较小的夹砂，因此在制作炊煮器时产生了与周文化陶工形成对比的一种特有的坯体配方。在多数情况下，本土陶工也使用冲积沉积物来制作他们的陶器。相比之下，周文化陶工在陶器中倾向于使用不同的更泥沙质的黏土。这类沉积物在本地是否可以获得，目前来说仍旧是一个疑问。综上所述，似乎可以肯定地得出，在周文化和归城本土陶工的制陶传统之间存在足够令人关注的差异，表明了在这一遗址中有两种不同的文化传统（族群？）并存并相互影响。

参考文献

Liu, Tungsheng, 1988. *Loess in China*. Second Edition. Springer-Verlag, Berlin.

Stoltman, James B. 1989. “A Quantitative Approach to the Petrographic Analysis of Ceramic Thin Sections,” *American Antiquity*, 54: 147-160.

Stoltman, James B. 1991. “Ceramic Petrography as Technique for Documenting Cultural Interaction: An Example from the Upper Mississippi Valley,” *American Antiquity*, 56: 103-120.

Stoltman, James B. 2001. “The Role of Petrography in the Study of Archaeological Ceramics,” in *Earth Sciences and Archaeology*, edited by P. Goldberg, V. Holliday, and C. Ferring. Pp. 297-326. Kluwer Academic/Plenum, New York.

Stoltman, James B., Zhichun Jing, Jigen Tang, and George (Rip) Rapp, 2009. “Ceramic Production in Shang Societies of Anyang,” *Asian Perspectives*, 48.1: 182-203.

Zhang, Linyuan, Dai Xuerong, and Shi Zhento, 1991. “The Sources of Loess Material and the Formation of the Loess Plateau in China,” in *Loess*, edited by Setuo Okuda, Anders Rapp, and Zhang Linyuan. Pp. 1-14. Catena Verlag, Cremlingen-Destedt, Germany.

（翻译：刘晓霞）

表Ⅰ.9.1　归城本土传统夹砂陶器的坯体和陶泥值

Table Ⅰ.9.1　Body and Paste Values for Tempered Vessels of the Indigenous Tradition at Guicheng

类型 Type	切片 Thin Section #	坯体 BODY 基底 % Matrix	坯体 BODY 砂子 % Sand	坯体 BODY 夹砂 % Temper	坯体 BODY 夹砂类型 Temper Type	坯体 BODY 夹砂径度指数 Temper Size Index	陶泥 PASTE 基底 % Matrix	陶泥 PASTE 泥沙 % Silt	陶泥 PASTE 砂子 % Sand	陶泥 PASTE 砂子径度指数 Sand Size Index
素面鼎 Plain *ding*	GUO7-9	62	6	32	片岩 Schist	2.81	87	4	9	1.69
素面鼎 Plain *ding*	GUO7-10	76	2	22	花岗岩 Granite	2.74	83	15	2	1.00
素面鼎 Plain *ding*	GUO7-16	70	2	28	闪岩 Amphibolite	2.78	93	4	3	1.00
素面鼎 Plain *ding*	GUO7-17	78	9	13	片岩 Schist	2.67	87	2	11	1.81
素面鼎 Plain *ding*	GUO7-18	80	6	14	花岗岩 Granite	3.21	81	12	7	1.36
素面鼎 Plain *ding*	GUO7-20	70	2	28	花岗岩 Granite	2.67	91	6	3	1.00
素面鬲 Plain *li*	GUO7-21	69	0	31	闪岩 Amphibolite	2.26	99	1	0	—
素面鬲 Plain *li*	GUO7-22	62	0	38	闪岩 Amphibolite	2.25	95	5	0	—
素面鼎或鬲 Plain *ding* or *li*	GUO7-23	57	3	40	花岗岩 Granite	2.77	84	11	5	1.00
素面鼎 Plain *ding*	GU11-3	55	2	43	片岩 Schist	2.61	97	0	3	2.00
素面鼎 Plain *ding*	GU11-4	62	4	34	闪岩 Amphibolite+	2.44	91	3	6	1.29
素面鼎 Plain *ding*	GU11-7	71	3	26	花岗岩 Granite	2.42	86	9	5	1.00
素面鼎 Plain *ding*	GU11-12	67	2	31	闪岩 Amphibolite+	2.62	90	7	3	2.50
素面鬲 Plain *li*	GU11-13	60	1	39	闪岩 Amphibolite+	2.36	96	3	1	1.00
素面鼎 Plain *ding*	GU11-14	91	3	6	花岗岩 Granite	3.67	87	10	3	1.00
素面鬲 Plain *li*	GU11-16	65	3	32	花岗岩 Granite	3.11	84	11	5	1.00
素面甗 Plain *yan*	GU11-19	64	3	33	花岗岩 Granite	3.20	86	9	5	1.00
绳纹鬲 Cordmarked *li*	GU11-20	75	5	20	花岗岩 Granite	2.83	84	10	6	1.00
素面鬲 Plain *li*	GU11-21	58	1	41	花岗岩 Granite	2.38	92	6	2	1.00
平均和标准误差 Mean & Standard Deviation	N=19	68.0 ± 9.1	3.0 ± 2.2	29.9 ± 10.2		2.73 ± 0.37	89.1 ± 5.2	6.7 ± 4.2	4.2 ± 2.9	1.27 ± 0.46

表Ⅰ.9.2　归城周文化传统夹砂陶器的坯体和陶泥值

Table Ⅰ.9.2　Body and Paste Values for Tempered Vessels of the Zhou Tradition at Guicheng

类型 Type	切片 Thin Section #	坯体 BODY 基底 % Matrix	砂子 % Sand	夹砂 % Temper	陶泥 PASTE 夹砂类型 Temper Type	夹砂径度指数 Temper Size Index	基底 % Matrix	泥沙 % Silt	砂子 % Sand	砂子径度指数 Sand Size Index
绳纹鬲 Cordmarked *li*	GUO7-6	88	0	12	花岗岩 Granite	2.65	84	16	0	—
绳纹鬲 Cordmarked *li*	GUO7-7	72	6	22	花岗岩 Granite	3.36	84	8	8	1.06
绳纹鬲 Cordmarked *li*	GUO7-8	85	3	12	花岗岩 Granite	3.18	89	7	4	1.00
素面鬲 Plain *li*	GUO7-19	84	6	10	花岗岩 Granite	3.10	82	11	7	1.08
素面鬲 Plain *li*	GUO7-24	72	5	23	花岗岩 Granite	3.44	83	10	7	1.00
绳纹鬲 Cordmarked *li*	GU11-1	78	6	16	花岗岩 Granite	2.86	73	20	7	1.00
素面鬲 Plain *li*	GU11-6	65	1	34	花岗岩 Granite	2.97	91	7	2	1.00
平均和标准误差 Mean & Std Deviation	N=7	77.7 ± 8.4	3.9 ± 2.5	18.4 ± 8.5		3.08 ± 0.28	83.7 ± 5.8	11.3 ± 5.0	4.2 ± 2.9	1.02 ± 0.04

表Ⅰ.9.3　归城周文化传统的泥质非炊煮陶器

Table Ⅰ.9.3　Zhou Tradition Untempered Non-Cooking Vessels at Guicheng

体量成分

Bulk Composition

类型 Type	切片 Thin Section #	基底 % Matrix	泥沙 % Silt	砂子 % Sand	砂子径度指数 Sand Size Index
罐 *Guan*	GU07-1	72	21	7	1.04
簋 *Gui*	GU07-2	73	16	11	1.38
罐 *Guan*	GU07-3	70	26	4	1.00
簋 *Gui*	GU07-4	82	14	4	1.00
罐或盆 *Guan* or *pen*	GU07-5	78	17	5	1.00
豆 *Dou*	GU07-11	83	14	3	1.00
罐或盆 *Guan* or *pen*	GU07-12	72	18	10	1.63
罐 *Guan*	GU07-13	78	16	6	1.00
罐 *Guan*	GU07-15	82	12	6	1.67
罐 *Guan*	GU11-2	77	16	7	1.46
罐 *Guan*	GU11-5	83	10	7	1.33
豆 *Dou*	GU11-8	74	20	6	1.00
罐 *Guan*	GU11-9	82	14	4	2.38
罐 *Guan*	GU11-10	77	14	9	1.00
簋 *Gui*	GU11-11	74	17	9	2.22
罐 *Guan*	GU11-15	90	6	4	1.50
罐 *Guan*	GU11-17	84	11	5	1.00
簋 *Gui*	GU11-18	75	19	6	1.00
罐 *Guan*	GU11-22	95	4	1	1.00
豆 *Dou*	GU11-23	79	20	1	1.00
罐 *Guan*	GU11-24	84	15	1	1.00
平均和标准误差 Mean ± 1 Std Deviation	N=21	79.2 ± 6.2	15.2 ± 5.0	5.6 ± 2.8	1.27 ± 0.42

表Ⅰ.9.4　归城本土传统和周文化传统不同类型加砂平均百分比和平均径度

Table Ⅰ.9.4　Mean Temper Percentages and Size Indices by Temper Type for the Indigenous and Zhou Traditions at Guicheng

夹砂类型 Temper Type	数量 N	加砂 % Temper	夹砂径度指数 Temper Size Index
本土 Indigenous Tradition			
闪岩 Amphibolite	6	33.5 ± 4.3	2.45 ± 0.21
片岩 Schist	3	29.3 ± 15.2	2.70 ± 0.10
花岗岩 Granite	10	26.2 ± 11.1	2.90 ± 0.40
周文化 Zhou Tradition			
花岗岩 Granite	7	18.4 ± 8.5	3.08 ± 0.28

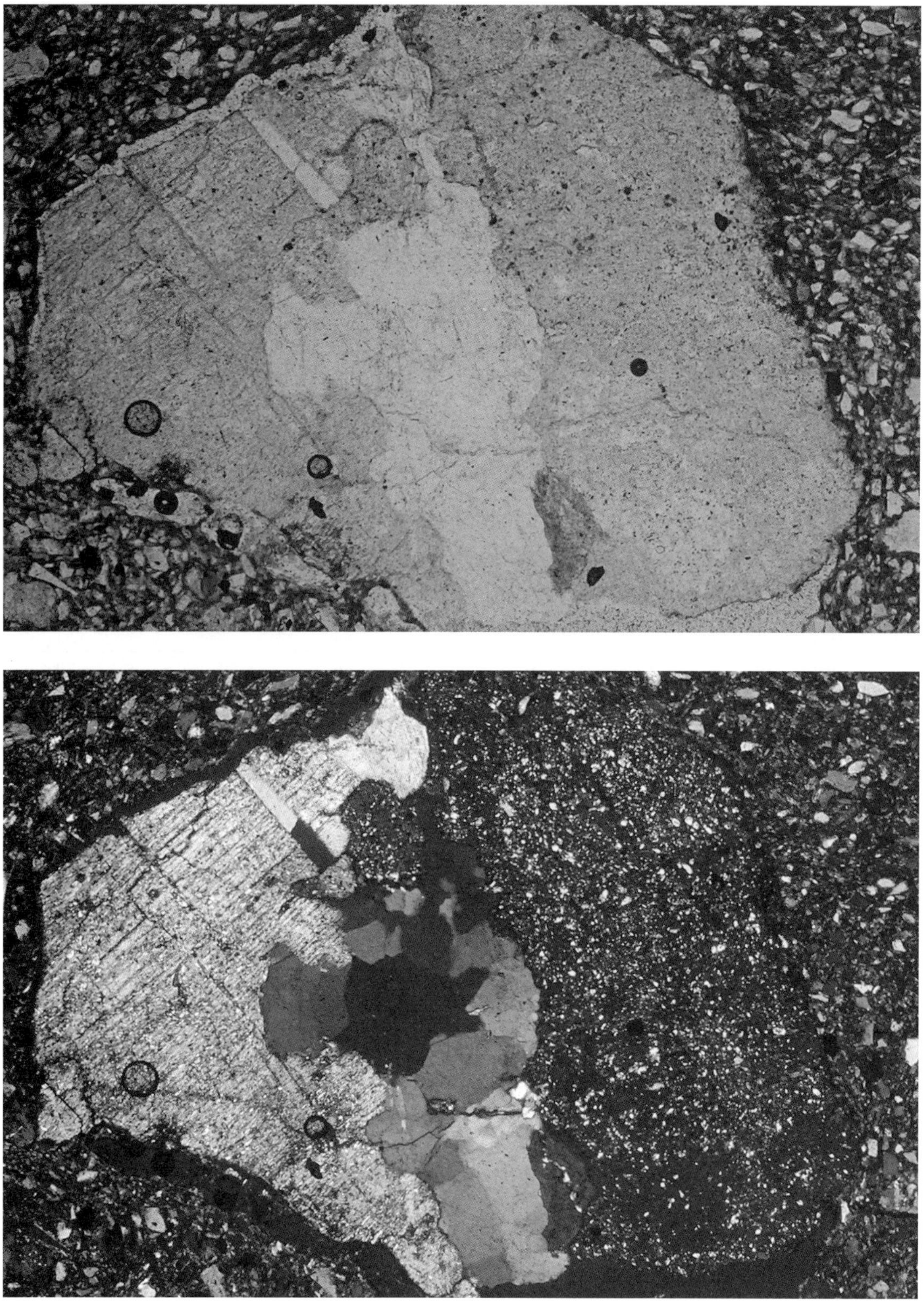

图Ⅰ.9.1　切片标本上的两幅花岗岩夹砂图片
（上为平面偏光，下为正交偏光，均10倍放大）
周文化传统的鬲，标本GU11-1。花岗岩颗粒的最大直径为2.43毫米。它由多晶的石英和严重蚀变的长石组成。

Figure Ⅰ.9.1　Two views of granite temper in thin section.
(Under plane polars, top and crossed polars, bottom both at 10X magnification)
Zhou Tradition *Li*, Vessel GU11-1. The granite grain measures 2.43 mm in maximum diameter. It is composed of polycrystalline quartz and heavily altered feldspars.

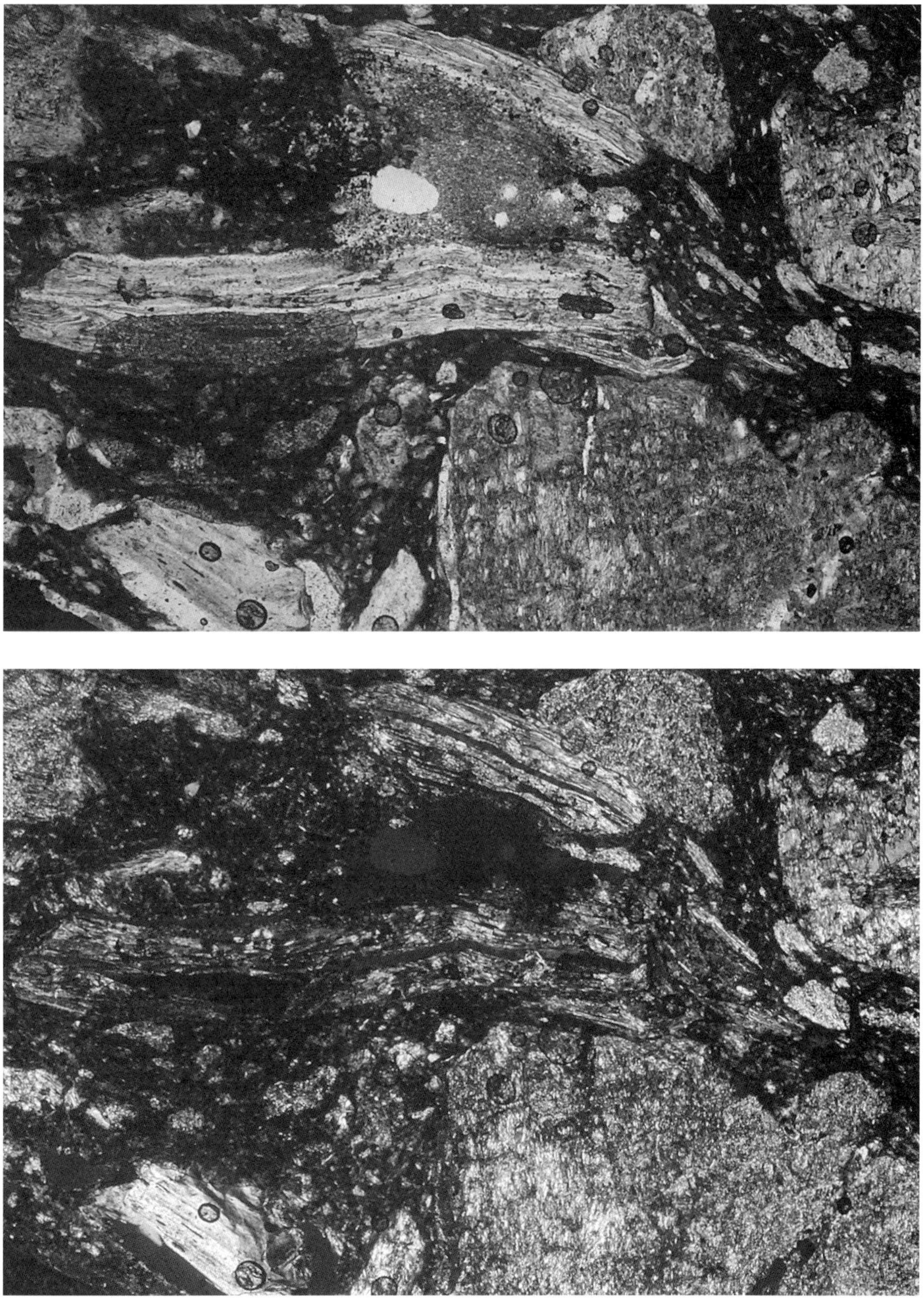

图Ⅰ.9.2　切片标本上的两块云母片岩夹砂图片
（上为平面偏光，下为正交偏光，均10倍放大）
本土文化传统的鼎，标本GU11-3。中心，长的白云母片岩颗粒为1.775毫米。注意右侧云母片岩颗粒的微小径度。

Figure Ⅰ.9.2　Two views of mica schist temper in thin section.
(Under plane polars, top and crossed polars, bottom both at 10X magnification)
Indigenous Tradition *Ding*, Vessel GU11-3. Long muscovite schist grain in center=1.775 mm long. Note the fine size of mica crystals in grains on right.

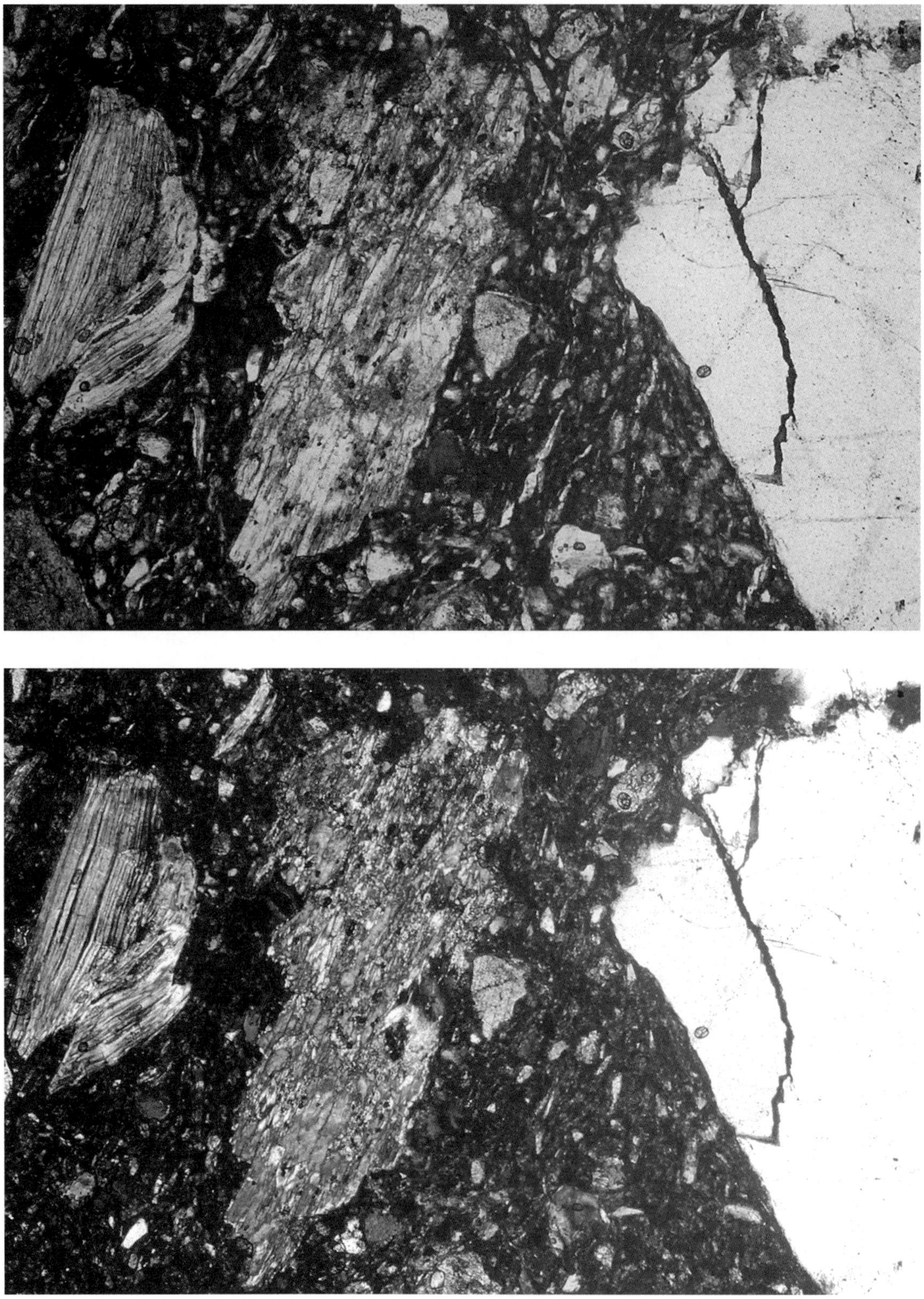

图Ⅰ.9.3　切片标本上的两幅闪岩夹砂图片

（上为平面偏光，下为正交偏光，均10倍放大）

本土传统文化的鼎，标本Gu11-12。中心，闪岩颗粒的尺寸为1.55毫米。左侧为云母片岩，右侧为多晶石英。

Figure Ⅰ.9.3　Two views of amphibolite temper in thin section.

(Under plane polars, top and crossed polars, bottom both at 10X magnification)

Indigenous *Ding*, Vessel Gu11-12; Amphibolite grain in center measures 1.55 mm. Mica schist on left; polycrystalline quartz on right.

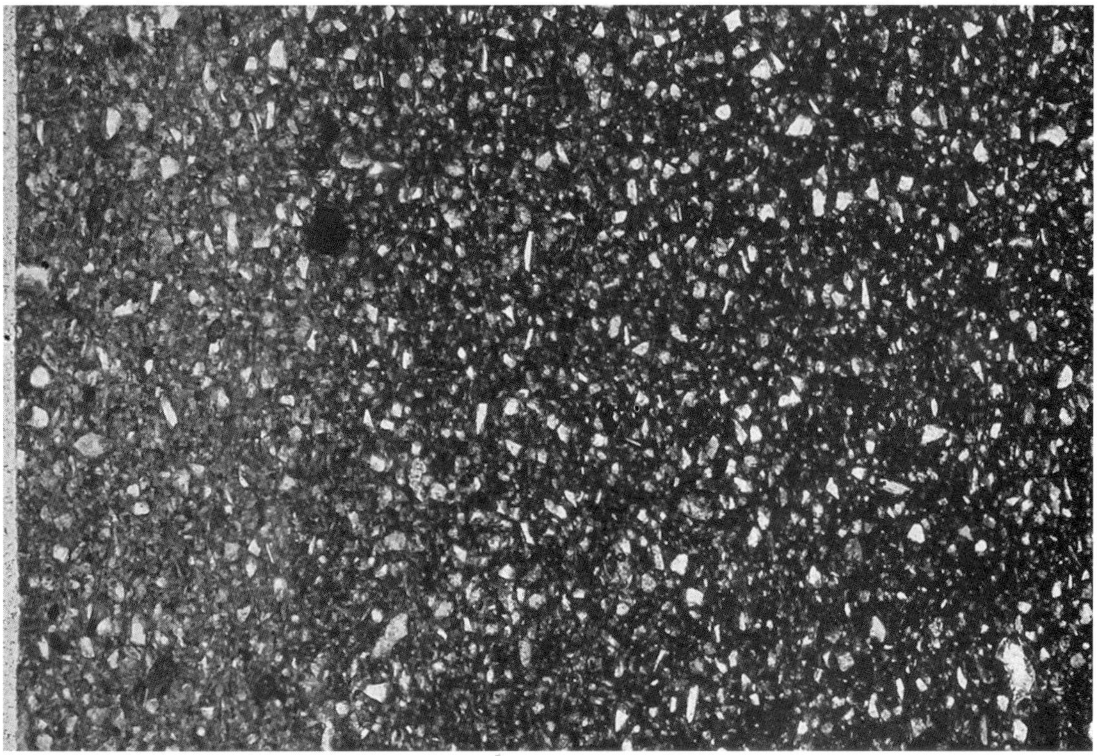

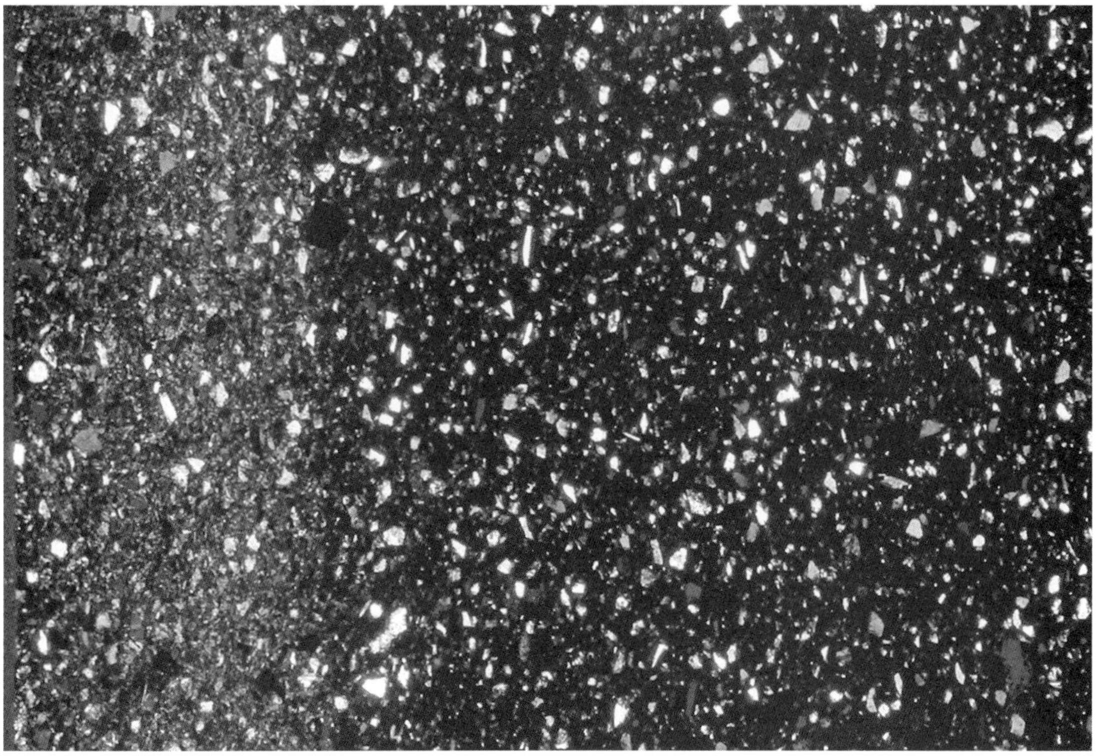

图Ⅰ.9.4　周文化传统的泥质陶豆的两幅图片

器物号为GU11-23，由黄土制作而成。上图为平面偏光，下为正交偏光，均10倍放大。注意其高泥沙含量（20%）。

Figure Ⅰ.9.4　Two views of untempered Zhou tradition *dou*.

Vessel GU11-23 made from loess. Top image viewed under Plane Polars, bottom viewed under crossed polars, both at 10X magnification. Void in NW corner= 0.125mm. Note high silt content (20%).

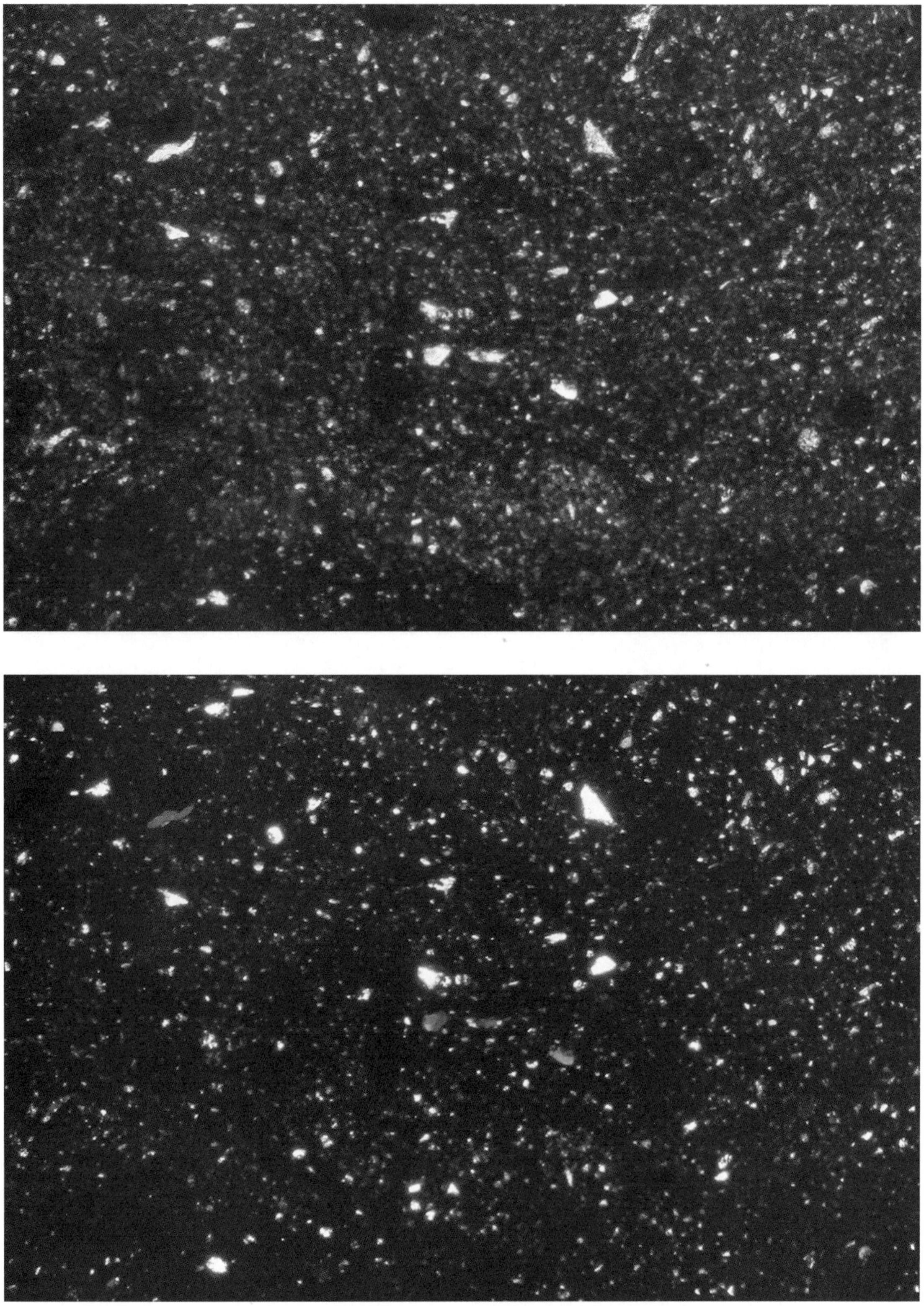

图Ⅰ.9.5　周文化传统的泥质陶罐的两幅图片

器物号为GU11-22，由冲积土制作而成。上为平面偏光，下为正交偏光，均10倍放大。中心右上，三角形石英为0.11毫米。注意低泥沙含量（4%泥沙）。

Figure Ⅰ.9.5　Two views of untempered Zhou tradition *guan*.

Vessel GU11-22 made from alluvium. Top image viewed under Plane Polars, bottom viewed under crossed polars, both at 10X magnification. Triangular quartz NE of center= 0.11mm. Note low silt content (4% silt).

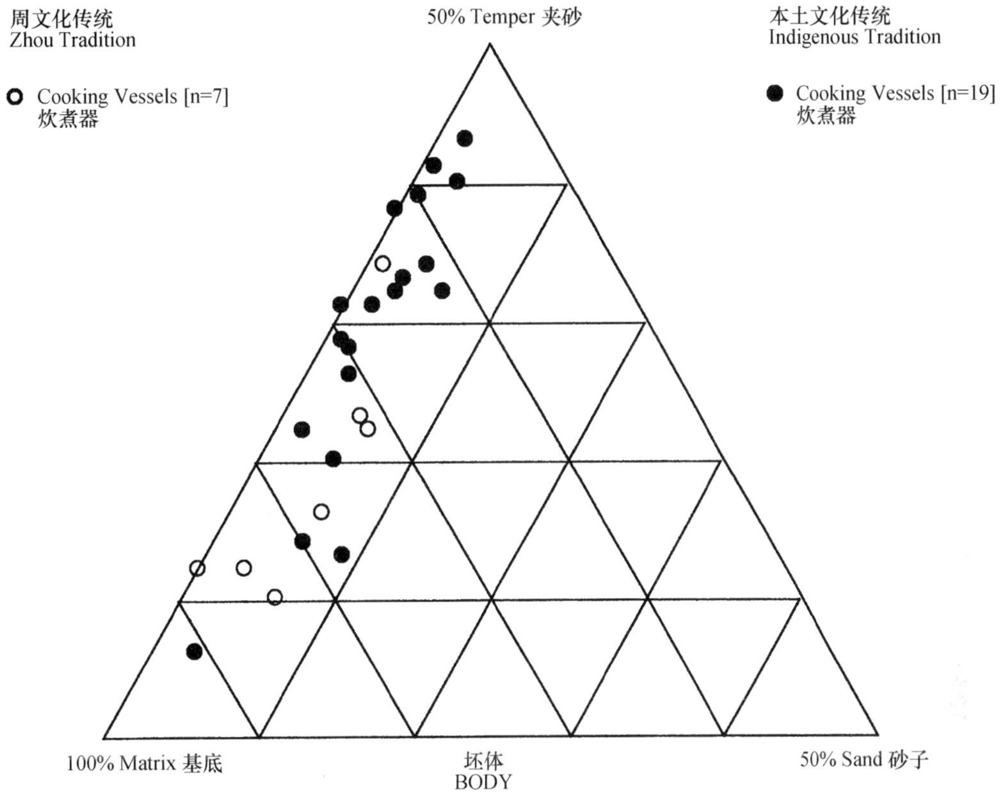

图Ⅰ.9.6　归城周文化传统和本土文化传统之夹砂陶器坯体对比三元图

Figure Ⅰ.9.6　Ternary graph for body of tempered vessels for the Zhou versus the indigenous traditions at Guicheng.

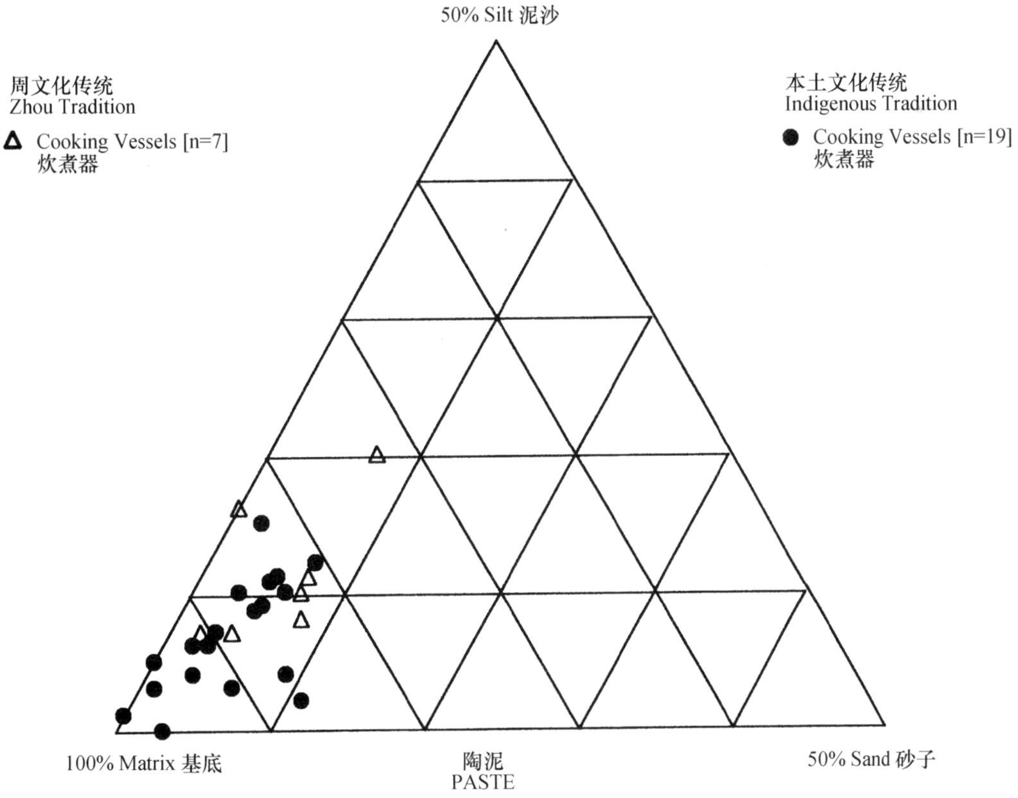

图Ⅰ.9.7　归城周文化传统和本土文化传统之夹砂陶器陶泥对比三元图

Figure Ⅰ.9.7　Ternary graph for paste of tempered vessels for the Zhou versus the indigenous traditions at Guicheng.

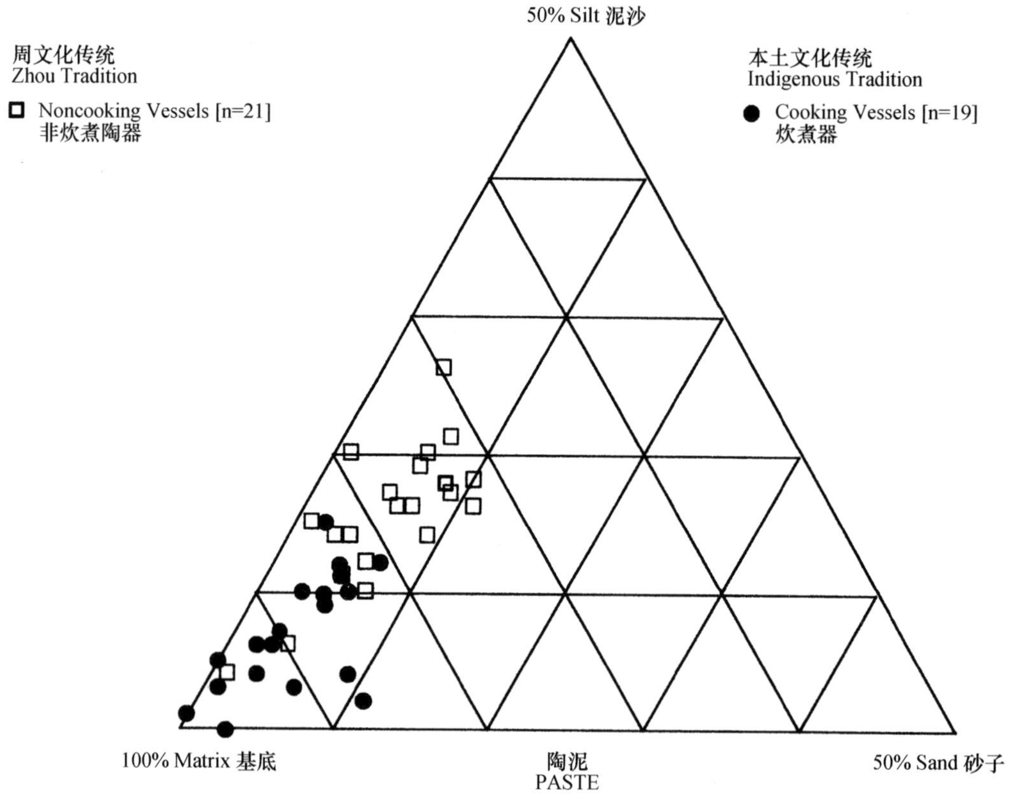

图Ⅰ.9.8　周文化传统的非炊煮陶器和本土的炊煮器之陶泥对比三元图

Figure Ⅰ.9.8　Ternary graph for paste of Zhou noncooking vessels vs. indigenous cooking vessels.

Chapter 9: A Petrographic Analysis of Guicheng Pottery

James B. Stoltman

This paper presents the findings of petrographic analyses of thin sections prepared from sherds derived from forty-seven pottery vessels recovered at Guicheng. The sherds were selected by Professor Li Feng and provided to the author for thin sectioning. These include twenty-three sherds collected on the surface of the inner city of Guicheng in 2007 and twenty-four samples recovered in 2009 from clearly documented stratigraphic contexts. In both collections careful consideration was given to representing the full range of ceramic variation across the site. The main purpose of the study is to identify possible compositional differences associated with two stylistically distinct ceramic traditions believed to exist at the site. On the one hand are ceramic vessels with plain surfaces and reddish-brown color with some distinctive vessel forms such as *ding* tripods, which are believed to derive from an indigenous pottery-making tradition. By contrast there are darker, grayish-black ceramics with corded surfaces that are believed to be the products of non-local Zhou potters. While there was apparently some interaction, this study will compare and contrast vessels from the two traditions to determine if any compositional differences can be identified that reflect distinctive customary or technological practices associated with the two traditions.

There are three basic parts to this study. The first reports the mineralogical composition of those vessels presumed to be the products of potters who worked within the framework of the indigenous pottery-making tradition. The second part involves a compositional analysis of vessels that reflect the pottery-making practices of the nonlocal Zhou tradition. In the third part the results of the first two parts will be summarized and conclusions drawn in an effort to shed light on technological, cultural, and behavioral practices associated with the two traditions that may be used to identify and differentiate them. Before turning to Part 1, a brief discussion outlining the methodology employed in this study will be presented.

Section 1: Methodology

Petrography is a venerable geological technique that provides reliable identifications of minerals and rocks. Two important properties (limitations?) of petrographic analyses of pottery should be noted at the outset. First, petrographic microscopes do not have the capability to identify individual clay minerals because their grain sizes are too small (i.e., < 0.002 mm). On thin sections of pottery sherds, clays appear as a homogenous matrix whose composition can be identified no further. Thus, the focus of petrographic analysis is upon grains of silt size (> 0.002 mm). The second property of petrography is that it deals directly with the physical properties of rocks and minerals, and thus does not provide chemical compositional data. Inferences are sometimes possible as to the chemical makeup of a grain, but this is based solely upon the physical properties observed, not by direct determination, as is possible, for example, with techniques like neutron activation.

All thin sections were analyzed using a basic point-counting procedure as described in several earlier publications (Stoltman 1989, 1991, 2001). A standard counting interval of 1 mm was employed covering the total area of each thin section, or until a minimum of 200 points had been counted, exclusive of voids. The output of this approach is a physical characterization of each thin section in terms of the percentages of silt-size inclusions plus the species, sizes, and percentages of mineral inclusions of sand size and larger. Since individual clay particles are not identifiable in thin section, their presence is recorded simply as "matrix." The point counting was conducted "blind," that is, without prior knowledge of the samples other than their thin section number, and the data for individual thin sections were neither tabulated nor compared until the analysis of all had been completed.

In evaluating these point-count data, it is important to appreciate that they derive from a laborious sampling procedure that is subject to a certain amount of observer error. In addition, each thin section is a sample of a pottery vessel that in turn is a sample of a ceramic assemblage. At all of these levels sample bias may exist, which hopefully can be minimized, but rarely wholly eliminated. At the lowest level, individual thin sections can be expected to provide reasonably reliable samples of their parent vessels because of the way that potters normally intensively mix clays and tempers together in preparing pastes. (For additional discussion of sources of sampling error in point counting see Stoltman 1989).

Five indices were used to express the results of the point counting: (1) bulk composition, (2) sand-size index, (3) paste, (4) body, and (5) temper-size index. Bulk composition along with the sand-size indices are used to characterize those vessels that lacked visible temper, i.e., were untempered. Bulk composition is a volumetric measure comprised of the relative percentages of three variables, matrix/clay, silt, and sand, all of which are purely size grades: matrix/clay < 0.002 mm; silt = visible grains ranging in size from 0.002 mm to 0.0624 mm; and sand = grains ranging in size from 0.0625 mm to 2.00 mm. As a complement to this index, a sand-size index is also recorded for each vessel. This was devised by assigning a value within the following ordinal scale to each sand-sized (or larger) grain encountered in point counting based upon its maximum diameter:

(1) Fine = 0.0625–0.249 mm

(2) Medium = 0.25–0.499 mm

(3) Coarse = 0.50–0.99 mm

(4) Very coarse = 1.00–1.99 mm

(5) Gravel = 2.00+ mm

The size values for each of the grains were then summed and divided by the total number of grains counted, thus providing a mean "sand-size index," which ranges between one and five for each thin section. Since vessels for which the bulk compositions were recorded lack humanly added tempers, their compositions may be compared directly with raw sediments, offering the possibility that the sedimentary source for such vessels may be determined.

By contrast, for vessels with humanly added tempers, the paste/body/temper-size indices will be employed (see Stoltman 1991: 109-110; 2001: 314). Paste determination involves first identifying temper grains so that they can be recorded separately from natural sand grains. The result is represented quantitatively as the percentages of the same three natural ingredients—matrix/clay, silt, and sand—that characterize the bulk composition of raw sediments as well as untempered vessels. A size index is also recorded for the naturally occurring sand grains in each thin section. Because paste is isomorphic with bulk composition (which applies to both untempered vessels and raw sediments), meaningful direct comparisons among these three classes are possible. Paste, then, is the appropriate index for assessing the local manufacture of both tempered and untempered ceramic products because it can be compared reliably to local sediments. When thin sections of a representative sample of local sediments are unavailable, "local" paste characteristics can still be defined, albeit tentatively, based upon the enabling supposition that archaeologists familiar with the local archaeology may reliably identify a sample of locally manufactured vessels. Once the paste characteristics of local pottery are determined, comparisons with stylistically anomalous vessels can then be made to assess more objectively their possible non-local origin. The case for the non-local derivation of a vessel can be strengthened if its paste not only differs from that of local vessels but also matches that of sediments and/or vessels from a suspected external source.

Two basic paste types were recognized in this study, each derived from a distinctive sediment type. One of the most common sources of clayey sediments is alluvium, clays deposited by moving water. Depending upon the local geology (i.e., the makeup of local rocks and sediments) along with relief and topography that influence current capacities, alluvial clays will invariably contain various amounts of coarser particles of silt and sand. By contrast, loessic sediments, which are wind deposited, are composed primarily of silt and clay because wind, for the most part, does not have the capacity to transport particles of sand size. In an earlier petrographic analysis of Anyang pottery (Stoltman et al. 2009), these two sediment/paste types were readily recognizable, and it was established that both were used in pottery manufacture. The main distinction between the two involves the differential distribution of silts and sands. Loess typically contains 15-20% silt and rare, if any, sand grains, which are never larger than fine sand (size indices = 1.00 if not 0). By contrast, alluvial sediments generally have less than 10% silt and higher amounts of sands including enough in the medium-to-coarse size grades to yield sand size indices above 1.00 (Stoltman et al., 2009: 183). (A much larger sample of both loess and alluvium from around Anyang has confirmed these findings.) While no direct geological evidence has been gathered in the Guicheng locality, alluvium is virtually ubiquitous in most regions, while several geological sources confirm the presence of loess in Shandong (e.g., Zhang et al., 1991 and Liu 1988).

In contrast to paste, body is a volumetric measure representing an artificial mixture of two materials—paste (= clay + all natural inclusions of silt and sand sizes) + temper—that are typically derived from different geological sources. The discrimination of paste and body depends first and foremost upon the reliable identification of intentional, humanly introduced inclusions, i.e. temper. Three main rock tempers were identified in this study: granite, schist, and amphibolite. The identification of these inclusions as temper was relatively straightforward, facilitated by their large size, high angularity, and distinctive compositions in contrast to the natural sand inclusions. The body index, then, is comprised of three components: (1) natural sand, (2) temper, and (3) matrix (silt is included here as part of the matrix). A separate size index, using the same 1-to-5 ordinal scale used to measure sand grains, is also reported for temper.

Temper type, size, and amount are all variables that directly reflect human actions, thus are likely to be culturally determined. Body indices, then, can provide a valuable basis independent of paste to assess the local vs. non-local status of ceramic vessels, especially when tempers can be traced to known geologic sources. An important caveat in dealing with temper as a culturally determined variable is that it may not necessarily be a passive reflection of a traditional way of making pottery but a more active design consideration of the potters, who could use different body recipes for vessels intended to perform different functions (e.g., ritual vs. cooking vs. storage vs. serving, etc.).

Section 2: The Indigenous Pottery-Making Tradition of Guicheng

Nineteen of the forty-seven vessels provided for thin sectioning were assigned to the indigenous pottery-making tradition on the basis of visual inspection of hand specimens. All nineteen are cooking vessels, twelve *ding* tripods, six *li* tripods, and one *yan* steamer. All were observed to possess humanly-added rock particles, i.e., are tempered, thus their compositions will be analyzed in terms of the paste/body/temper-size indices. These compositional data are recorded in Table Ⅰ.9.1.

As can be seen from Table Ⅰ.9.1, these indigenous cooking vessels were provided with relatively generous amounts of temper, with a 29.9% mean by volume. Three tempers were observed, granite (n=10), amphibolite (n=6), and schist (n=3), sometimes more than one occurring in a vessel. These are all metamorphic rocks whose local origins are assumed because of their occurrence in the indigenous pottery, although this is currently an unsubstantiated inference. Thin-section images of each of the three tempers are illustrated in Figs. Ⅰ.9.1 to Ⅰ.9.3 (Pls. 67-68).

The paste values provide a measure of the natural clay-rich sediment from which these vessels were fashioned. The pastes of these vessels are relatively uniform, suggesting a common source. The incidence of natural inclusions in both silt and sand size grades is relatively modest: the incidence of silt is 7% while that of sand is 4%. Such values are consistent with alluvial sediments, but definitely not loess (which is generally characterized by > 15% silt and < 2% fine sand).

Section 3: The Zhou Pottery-Making Tradition at Guicheng

A total of twenty-eight vessels assigned to the Zhou tradition were provided for thin sectioning. Seven of these vessels had been tempered, while twenty-one possessed no temper (See Figs. Ⅰ.9.4 and Ⅰ.9.5). A dramatic distinction was evident at once between these two classes: all of the tempered vessels were *li* tripods, i.e., vessels used for cooking, while all of the untempered vessels were types used for such non-cooking functions as storage and serving (See Tables Ⅰ.9.2 and Ⅰ.9.3). This finding is consistent with the compositional distinctions observed previously for cooking versus non-cooking vessels at the late Shang site of Yinxu near Anyang in Henan (Stoltman et al. 2009). Pottery, as a plastic material, is prone to cracking as a result of expansion and contraction in the presence of changes in temperature. Cooking vessels, because they are subject to recurrent heating and cooling, are particularly prone to such destructive effects. The role of rock tempers (nonplastic materials) in such vessels is to prevent the destructive effects of thermally-induced expansion and contraction of vessel walls. It is also noteworthy that in the current sample of tempered vessels from the Indigenous tradition at Guicheng (Table Ⅰ.9.1), all are cooking vessels. It would appear that the practice of tempering cooking vessels but leaving non-cooking vessels untempered was a robust tradition among Bronze Age potters of China.

Turning first to the tempered vessels of the Zhou tradition, it can be seen that all were tempered with granite (Table Ⅰ.9.2). While the sample is small, this temper uniformity contrasts with the diversity of tempers used by Indigenous potters (cf. Table Ⅰ.9.1). Also in comparison to the practices of the Indigenous potters, the potters of the Zhou tradition used notably less temper—18.4% vs. 29.9%—but generally of a coarser size grade (temper size indices = 3.08 for Zhou vs. 2.73 for Indigenous potters (Tables Ⅰ.9.1 and Ⅰ.9.2; Fig. 6). Beside these distinctions in body values, there also appear to be notable paste differences between the pastes of the two traditions. Comparing the data in Tables Ⅰ.9.2 and Ⅰ.9.3, it can be seen that the pastes of the Zhou tradition vessels tend to be siltier—a mean of 11.3% for the Zhou tradition versus 6.7% for the Indigenous tradition (Table Ⅰ.9.1 and Fig. Ⅰ.9.7). This suggests that different clay sources were used. Three of the tempered vessels in particular stand out—Nos. GU07-6 and GU11-1 in Table Ⅰ.9.2 and GU07-10 in Table Ⅰ.9.1—all of which have high silt values of 15-20%. These paste values are suggestive of a loessic origin for the clays from which these vessels were made. They can be regarded as possibly of nonlocal origin.

Considering now the untempered Zhou tradition vessels (Table Ⅰ.9.3), an especially notable compositional property deserves emphasis: the high incidence of silt (mean silt volume for the 21 vessels = 15.2%). Since the bulk composition of untempered vessels is equivalent to the paste values for tempered vessels, this pattern of high-silt values is consistent for nearly all of the twenty-eight Zhou tradition vessels in contrast to the lower paste values for most of the nineteen Indigenous tradition cooking vessels. From these data, it is reasonable to infer that, while potters of both traditions sometimes used similar clay resources, Zhou tradition potters and Indigenous tradition potters showed a marked tendency to exploit different clay resources in manufacturing their vessels.

Section 4: Summary and Conclusions

Accepting as a given that two ceramic stylistic traditions existed at the Guicheng site, this study, by employing petrographic analysis of pottery vessels from each of the traditions, investigated compositional variation as an independent variable in search of evidence of cultural or technological practices that characterized the two traditions. In evaluating the results of this study, two important weaknesses in the underlying evidence should be made explicit. On one hand no direct geological samples of bedrock or of local clay-rich sediments were available for comparison with the thin-sectioned pottery vessels. Without such data, the tentativeness of the inferences about the sources of the tempers and clay-rich sediments should not be overlooked. On the other hand no samples of Indigenous tradition non-cooking pottery vessels were available for this analysis. As a result, the comparisons between ceramics of the two traditions are unbalanced thus less than comprehensive.

With these limitations in mind, this study has revealed a number of non-random compositional differences among the ceramics of the Zhou tradition on the one hand and between the ceramics of the Zhou and Indigenous traditions on the other that are interesting and significant. Within the Zhou tradition, the practice of tempering cooking vessels but not adding temper to non-cooking vessels was documented. This appears to be a continuation of practices that were previously observed at the late Shang site of Yinxu in Henan. The existence of this practice could not be documented for the

Indigenous tradition at Guicheng because only tempered vessels were available for thin sectioning. This practice makes sense as a technological response to the inherent tendency of cooking vessel walls to crack under thermal stresses associated with recurrent heating and cooling: as non-plastic materials, rock tempers resist the destructive expansion and contraction of the more plastic clays that dominate the composition of ceramic vessels.

Most significantly are what appear to be at least three intentional differences in pottery-making practices between the two traditions. While the sample of tempered Zhou tradition vessels is small (n = 7), only granite temper was used, whereas Indigenous potters utilized at least three different tempers (Table Ⅰ.9.1). This could be viewed as a reflection of a more intimate knowledge of local resources by native peoples.

A second difference between the two traditions concerns the percentages and sizes of temper used in preparing the vessel bodies. From Tables Ⅰ.9.1 and Ⅰ.9.2, it appears that Zhou potters used significantly lesser amounts of temper (18.4% vs. 29.9% for Indigenous potters) and larger sizes (3.08 Zhou mean temper size index vs. 2.73 for Indigenous potters). It is possible, however, that this pattern of lesser amounts and larger sizes of temper in Zhou vessels may be an artifact of the sole use of granite temper, a material with greater resistance to breakage than schist and amphibolite. Under this view the temper type that offered the greatest resistance to breakage would have the largest particle sizes, so that temper size and amount would be better viewed as a byproduct of temper selection, not conscious manipulation of amounts and sizes of temper particles. To evaluate this alternative, the relative mean sizes and percentages for each of the three temper types have been tabulated and are recorded in Table I.9.4. From these data, it can be seen the there is an inverse relationship between temper sizes and percentages for all three temper types—the greater the percent of temper the smaller the size grades (Table Ⅰ.9.4). And granite seems clearly to occur in lower percentages and larger sizes than schist and amphibolite. However, despite this tendency, it still seems that the amount of temper used by the Zhou potters, and to a lesser extent, the larger temper sizes used, when compared with the granite-tempered vessels of Indigenous potters, suggests that this practice can be validly viewed as a distinctive Zhou cultural practice, not just a mechanical correlate of temper type.

A third difference between the two ceramic traditions involves what appears to be a differential preference for clay-rich sediments used in vessel manufacture. By comparing paste with bulk composition in Tables 2 and 3, it can be seen that Zhou potters used relatively silty clays for both cooking and non-cooking vessels. There is considerable variability, but it is noteworthy that half of the twenty-eight Zhou vessels have 15% or greater silt content indicative of a loessic sediment origin. By contrast, only a single vessel among the nineteen Indigenous tradition vessels has 15% silt, with the majority—thirteen of the nineteen—having less than 10% silt. The clear preference of potters of the Indigenous tradition was for alluvial clays. Geological data to assess the local availability of these sediments, unfortunately, are currently not available.

In sum, this study has uncovered several compositional differences between pottery of the Indigenous and Zhou traditions at Guicheng that are suggestive of traditionally distinct pottery-making practices. The Indigenous potters exploited multiple (local?) rocks to temper their cooking vessels, whereas Zhou potters used only granitic rocks for temper (which they added only to cooking vessels). In addition the Indigenous potters tended to use a greater amount and smaller sizes of temper thus producing a distinctive body recipe for their cooking vessels in contrast to the Zhou potters. The Indigenous potters also exploited alluvial sediments, for the most part, in making their vessels. By contrast, Zhou potters tended to use different, siltier clays for their vessels. Whether such sediments were available locally is an unanswered question at present. In conclusion, it seems credible to note that there are enough interesting differences in pottery-making practices between Zhou and Indigenous potters at Guicheng to suggest that two distinct traditions (ethnic groups?) coexisted and interacted at the site.

References

Liu, Tungsheng, 1988. *Loess in China*. Second Edition. Berlin: Springer-Verlag.

Stoltman, James B., 1989. "A Quantitative Approach to the Petrographic Analysis of Ceramic Thin Sections," *American Antiquity*, 54: 147-160.

Stoltman, James B., 1991. "Ceramic Petrography as Technique for Documenting Cultural Interaction: An Example from the Upper Mississippi Valley," *American Antiquity*, 56: 103-120.

Stoltman, James B., 2001. "The Role of Petrography in the Study of Archaeological Ceramics," in *Earth Sciences and Archaeology*, edited by P. Goldberg, V. Holliday, and C. Ferring. Pp. 297-326. New York: Kluwer Academic/ Plenum.

Stoltman, James B., Zhichun Jing, Jigen Tang, and George (Rip) Rapp, 2009. "Ceramic Production in Shang Societies of Anyang," *Asian Perspectives*, 48.1: 182-203.

Zhang, Linyuan, Dai Xuerong, and Shi Zhento, 1991. "The Sources of Loess Material and the Formation of the Loess Plateau in China," in *Loess*, edited by Setuo Okuda, Anders Rapp, and Zhang Linyuan. Pp. 1-14. Germany: Catena Verlag, Cremlingen-Destedt.

第十章　构建边缘文化：归城陶器分析

李　峰

第一节　引　　言

本章的重点是归城的陶器分析，属于山东东部青铜时代晚期（地图Ⅰ.0.1）。这一地区见证了两种文化传统的高度交流：①第一种考古学文化见于陕西省渭河谷地西周（公元前1045～前771年）中心地区的许多遗址，并且在周人灭商之后广泛地分布到了黄河中游。②第二种是胶东半岛的本地文化，能够追溯到龙山时期。本章提出，时间提供了一个周文化核心地区和周边地区发生互动的轴线。所以，用一个时间的或“过程主义”的方法来仔细审视归城陶器随时间的微妙变化，可以让我们更好地理解这一区域与周文化中心关系的变化。

为了充分理解周文化中心和胶东半岛土著文化传统之关系的长期动态发展，考虑了地理和时间两方面的因素，建议用下面三个模式（途径）来把握中心和边缘地区关系中文化接受和反弹的过程（图Ⅰ.10.1）：

途径A，或者是“上山”式途径：描述一个文化接受的过程，在这个过程中外来或入侵文化的因素被边缘地区缓慢地引进和接受。最终边缘地区被入侵的中心文化所同化。这可能是文化接受最常见的情况，特别是在与中心地区距离较近的地区。

途径B，或是一个“下山”式途径：代表了一种突然被外来文化入侵而完全或几乎完全地打断本地文化进程的文化接受模式。随着时间的流逝，外来文化的强度逐渐地减弱，而这使得边缘地区之前吸收的文化体系出现修正。这一过程最终导致了边缘文化恢复成先前占统治地位的本地文化。

途径C，或者是一个“过山”式途径：这一个文化接受的过程伴随一个高度的反弹，外来或入侵文化逐渐地被引进，达到一个高水平，并且获得了本地贵族的支持。但它们最终没有能够压倒本地文化，而本地文化会在这一漫长的过程中在某一点开始逐渐加速回归。

以上的理论与过去一些学者对文化中心和边缘关系的模式进行的分析有明显区别，比如，吉尔·斯坦因的“距离差异”模式（斯坦因 1998：246），他认为中央的控制随距离的增加逐渐减弱，这种关系是从不均衡到均衡的渐进转化。然而，斯坦因的模式没有解释长期的文化接触所带来的影响，而这正是我们的分析将会涉及的关键问题。

第二节　归城陶器和要研究的具体问题

本文大多数用于分析的陶器有三个来源：①“中美归城考古队”在2008至2009年全覆盖地面调查中采集的陶器和陶器残片；②2009年夏天考古队试掘获得的陶器；③归城内城地区墓葬被盗后地面采集所得的征集品。另外，在2010～2011年进行的龙口市黄水河流域考古调查中，考古队在龙口市西郊的张郑家墓地收集了大量的完整或近完整器（见第7章）。还有，龙口市博物馆慷慨地允许我们对归城项目2007年开始之前的藏品进行查看并拍照。汇集这些资料一起进行研究可以使我们更好地去分析器群组成和器型的变异（表Ⅰ.10.1）。最终的目标是运用这些材料去讨论上文提到的胶东半岛地区具体的社会文化进程和这一地区的跨区域的文化交流问题。为了达到这一目的，我们必须首先基于对考古资料的实证性分析来回答一系列更为具体的问题：

（1）基于胶东半岛特殊的历史文化背景，当地社会是怎样被一个外来文化或者一个贵族群体的到来所改变？在周文化的入侵过程中，归城地区的物质文化是否表现出了很强的延续性？或是本地制作传统完全被中断？

（2）入侵文化和本地文化是如何互动？本地的社会上层或群体所主动采取的决定使得本地文化发生了怎样的变化？

（3）一种文化进入一个新的环境时会发生文化的适应性同化，这种同化的步调由时间和空间的诸多因素决定。为了更好地在胶东半岛这一新环境中生存下去，周文化在多大程度、朝哪个方向做出了自身调整？

（4）在“中心与边缘”的关系中，归城地区在多大程度上被周文化中心地区所发生的社会和文化的新发明所影响？本土化了的周人贵族与西周政权的中心地区的贵族阶层的关系是怎样？

（5）归城地区的社会经济体系是怎样？在其中这两种文化均发挥了自己的作用。

这些问题也可以很容易地被引入其他地区关于文化接触的研究中。在归城，本土化的周人贵族和他们在陕西地区的亲属的关系也可以根据青铜器铭文来进行研究，但我将在另外一章讨论这个问题（见下编第五章）。在归城地区出土青铜器铭文的信息的帮助下，我们希望至少可以有信心对上述问题进行讨论。

第三节　本地的陶器传统

胶东半岛在出现明确的周文化居址之前是珍珠门文化时期（见第一章）。1980年，珍珠门文化遗存最先在半岛北部长岛上的几处遗址中被识别出来（严文明 1989：8～10；刘延常 2001：94～104）。之后的调查发现珍珠门的陶器地域跨度很大，西起潍坊，东南到半岛南岸的乳山；换句话说，它们广泛地分布于整个山东半岛东部（王富强 2006：107；张锟 2010：58～64）。在归城地区，珍珠门遗存发现于马南河边的楼子庄遗址（见图Ⅰ.7.1，15），距归城西部只有14千米，2002年烟台博物馆的小规模发掘发现了相对丰富的材料（图Ⅰ.10.2）（王富强 2006：107～114）。我们最近的调查显示在距楼子庄3千米的范围内有7处珍珠门文化遗址（见第7章），这表示该地区在珍珠门文化时期可能是一个人口中心。因为珍珠门相关遗址的调查和发掘尚没有完整的报告出版，所以关于这个文化整体还有许多未被回答的问题，但珍珠门无疑代表了胶东半岛一个重要的文化发展阶段。珍珠门文化的主要特征可以概括如下：

（1）陶器群由种类非常有限的容器组成，包括鬲、甗、罐、碗、簋等。

（2）所有的容器都夹杂有粗砂，有时也有细砂，很多都含有云母或滑石的碎片。这一特点不只限于炊煮器，也体现在于盛食器和贮藏器上。

（3）百分之八十以上的陶器呈红褐色的。容器的火候并不均匀，呈现出红、棕、黑色的不规则图案。所有容器均为素面且没有纹饰，一些器物有手抹的痕迹。

（4）很多器型不规则，没有轮制的证据。

（5）居址的范围并不清楚。大而精致的灰坑用于贮藏或居住。

（6）生业方式至少一定程度上依靠黍的种植（王富强 2006：108）。

许多学者也注意到在珍珠门文化占主导的遗址中有少量黑陶或灰陶的鬲或罐共存，多饰绳纹。他们认为这些陶器来自源于商文化的陶器器型，这表示珍珠门文化曾经与西边的商文化有远程接触（栾丰实 1996：352；张锟 2010：252）。由于缺乏碳十四的数据，这一器型的关联表示珍珠门至少一定程度上与黄河流域的晚商文化在时间上重叠，尽管它在西周成为西边的统治政权后持续了多久还有待讨论。有学者认为珍珠门文化延续至公元前10世纪初西周中期早段（刘延常 2001：101；张锟 2010：70）。而归城的发掘为这一较晚的说法提供了新支持（见下文），至少半岛东南部的土著文化传统看上去以另一个新的文化一直延续下来，这就是1976年在半岛南部乳山县发现的南黄庄文化（王锡平 1987：21～22）。

第四节　一种新文化的侵入

公元前10世纪，山东东部的物质文化进入一个新纪元。胶东半岛的陶器群整体从红褐陶占主流变成灰黑陶占主流，且这时制陶明显使用快轮制技术。大量的容器形制规整，饰以弦纹或按压绳纹，火候明显提高（图Ⅰ.10.3）；这与珍珠门文化素面夹砂陶非常不同。所有的陶器根据胎体特征可以分成两类：夹砂陶器，多为炊煮器，泥质陶器，多为盛食器或贮藏器。以此类推，陶器的功能也可以清晰地划分。看起来这一新的制陶传统广泛地影响了胶东半岛中部和北部的很大区域，尽管各地区被这个新到来的文化影响的具体程度可能有所不同（图Ⅰ.10.4）。同样明显的是，这个新文化的源头是西边的黄河中游地区，这一地区从公元前11世纪起成为新兴的西周国家（公元前1045～前771年）的核心地区。

更重要的是，胶东半岛出现的这个新陶器传统伴随着山东东部当地社会的一系列变化。最重要的是大型聚落的增多，比如归城、东曲城、村里集和前河前，互相的距离最远100千米（图Ⅰ.10.4）。由于已出版资料的条件限制，没有珍珠门时期聚落规模的可靠数据，但珍珠门遗址本身估计有5千平方米（栾丰实 1996），归城边的楼子庄遗址据我们估计有3万平方米（见第七章）。甚至于更早的照格庄遗址，即胶东半岛岳石文化时期最大的遗址经测量大约4万平方米（中国社会科学院考古研究所山东队 1986：448）。它们应该接近山东东部新石器到青铜时代早期遗址面积的最大值。相比而言，归城遗址经测量有800万平方米；东曲城和村里集估测分别有19万平方米和30万平方米（见第七章）。这些人口和物质集中的大型聚落与早期遗址的规模之间有一个重要的落差。事实上，每一处大型聚落都被周围小型的聚落群和墓地所包围。这些以大型聚落为中心的社会群体明显与早期遗址周围乡村发展水平的聚落处在不同的社会发展水平。除了它们巨大的聚落规模，在考古资料的质量上也有很多方面非常不同：

（1）现存的夯土墙包围着东曲城的遗址中心或者归城的整个城市范围。

（2）归城发现的大量宫殿性质的夯土台基象征着统治阶层的住所或者国家权力机构所在地（中美联合归城考古队 2011：33、34）。

（3）贵族墓通常包含高级青铜容器等奢侈的随葬品；归城的发掘也为城中存在铸铜作坊提供了新证据。

（4）青铜器和一些陶器的铭文显示了这一地区贵族的文字读写能力。

胶东半岛公元前10世纪的考古资料清楚地代表了在各个层面上与珍珠门时期之间的断裂，而非延续。本地区和西边周文化中心的青铜器铭文共同记述了由西周王朝及其地方封国政权在山东东部所进行的一系列战争（Li Feng 2006：304～314）。这些战争的原因可以有不同的解释，但铭文显示海盐和贝壳的获取可能是一个很重要的目的；贝壳是西周社会主要的通货，而周王朝一定对产自胶东半岛的贝壳有着高度需求。从这样的大历史背景来看，归城和其他的城市中心很可能是周文化在一个异国环境中的重要飞地。从西边带来“新”陶器传统的人群可能不都是周族人，还可能包括吸收了周人物质文化并伴随在周人贵族身边一起行动的很多个人和群体，因为周人本身就是一个混合的群体。但比较肯定的是，西周国家的扩张是这一文化自西向东移动的一个强劲的推动力。

第五节　归城的陶器序列和年代

尽管归城及其邻近地区过去常发现陶器，但由于缺乏地层学上的验证，学者们对这一地区陶器传统的发展了解甚少。在这点上，2009年夏天我们在归城内城南部进行的试掘为我们提供了一个可靠的基础来阐释归城或整个龙口地区陶器类型和器物组合的演变。在发掘的20个单位中，我们选出8个陶器丰富并具有代表性的灰坑（H2、H3、H4、H8、H9、H18、H19、H20）用于分析。第五章详细描述了不同灰坑的地层关系。在这里我只考虑目前挑选出来的这些灰坑的地下情况。总体来讲，我们讨论的陶器群大致反映了以下三个发展阶段（图Ⅰ.10.12）：

1. 第一阶段：H20

H20是发掘的年代最早单位。它直接叠压在生土上，一部分打破内城夯土墙。H20的南部叠压于2号探沟的第3层下，北部被H21打破。坑底我们发现了一件A1式的簋，属于山东东部最早的簋的器型（表Ⅰ.10.5）。H20出土了3件A1式的鬲，有三袋状足，低裆，之前胶东半岛甚至整个山东地区都没有发现。H20上层还发现了粗柄豆（A1式），与口沿略外撇的宽沿深腹盆还有较大的宽圆肩罐（图Ⅰ.10.5）共存。H20的陶片几乎都饰不同宽度且规整的按压绳纹，它们的纹路很清晰（图Ⅰ.5.52～Ⅰ.5.55、Ⅰ.5.58）。毫无疑问的是，H20的陶器器型和陶片构成了目前已知的胶东半岛西周时期最早的陶器群。

2. 第二阶段：H18、H19

H18或H19和H20没有直接的关系。然而，H19打破H21，而H21北部打破了H20。另一方面，H18轻微打破H19的东边，但是这两个灰坑出土的陶器大体同时期。很明显，H18和H19在层位上比H20要晚，这也很符合这三个灰坑陶器的相对年代。这两个灰坑频繁出现最典型的器型是B1式的浅盘豆。典型B1式有的豆盘下部有一道折线，喇叭形柄的中部经常有一道突起的棱脊。尽管两个灰坑没出土一件完整的簋，H18的一件簋的上部和H19的一个簋的圈足无疑是表Ⅰ.10.1中A6式的簋，这种簋由A1式发展而来。同样非常有特色的是重环纹宽斜肩上饰有数道弦纹的小口罐，即表Ⅰ.10.1中的A2式。两灰坑中口沿外撇的小型盆也具有典型的时代特征（图Ⅰ.10.6）。H18和H19发现的大多数陶片仍饰以清晰的绳纹，但也有一些呈不连续的浅绳纹的陶片（图Ⅰ.5.46、Ⅰ.5.49）。

3. 第三阶段：H3、H2、H4、H8、H9

H3、H2和H4是发掘的年代最晚的单位。H3位于TG1北部的中心；它开口于第1层下，打破第3层和其他单位。H2位于TG2北部，打破H16，而H16打破第二阶段的H18和H19。H4位于

TG2南部，开口于一条现代水渠下，打破一层薄的淤土，淤土下发现了H9和H12等其他单位。在TG1，H8和H9被H3直接打破；事实上，H9开口于被H3打破的第3层下。然而，尽管在地层上被堆积层第3层分隔开，这些单位的陶片都非常相似。这表示这些打破第3层的单位和位于它下面的H8和H9等单位应该都形成于一个较短时期。

正如我们下面即将讨论的，归城第一段的陶器群明显地受到本地陶器制造传统的影响。最明显的是出现了大量的素面红褐陶的夹砂陶片，大都是鬲。但是，D3式鬲最典型的造型特点仍然遵循了黄河流域鬲的整体演变，越来越矮，三个袋状足几乎消失。这一阶段的豆也经过了一些重要转变：一方面，第二阶段常见的喇叭形柄的豆现在变得非常细，见B2式。另一方面，柄细直的豆开始以多种形式出现，均为素面。比如，C3式的豆盘变得很深，侧面轮廓线变得圆滑，甚至出现向外的反弧；C2式有近似于半球形的盘和粗矮的柄。第三阶段有特点的还有大型容器的盖，多道弦纹的管状柄，矮圈足的碗（图Ⅰ.10.7）。这一时期的陶片主要饰不规则的浅绳纹。一些陶片在拓片上呈现或细或粗糙的网状纹。第三阶段的灰坑也出了一些有清晰绳纹的陶片，但它们最有可能是从早期地层中翻出来并重新被埋藏进晚期灰坑的（图Ⅰ.5.12、Ⅰ.5.15、Ⅰ.5.18）。

鉴于受到试掘出土陶器数量的限制，我们决定最好是将归城陶器的全面分期工作留待将来。但我们可以根据目前的地层学明确证据来确定以上的发展阶段。这里最重要的是，归城第一到第二阶段的陶器的发展紧随周人中心地区特别是陕西渭河流域中部陶器器型的发展。事实上，归城发现的很多器型与陕西的几乎无法区分。这种高度的相似性让二者的对比断代成为可能；即使两地相距1000千米，但正如铭文显示的，周文化中心和归城地区有紧密的交流。从周的中心地区已经建立的年代标准，比如沣京的张家坡墓地（中国社会科学院考古研究所沣西工作队 1980：483～485；中国社会科学院考古研究所 1999：348～358）的分期去推测，我们能将归城第一阶段的陶器大致推定在西周早期晚段到西周中期早段；在历史年代上这个阶段大约是公元前1000～前920年。归城第二阶段的陶器中包括了一些在陕西地区西周晚期墓中很常见的典型容器。因此，将它们的年代定在西周晚期或更晚一些应该可靠。在历史年代上这一阶段大致是公元前860～前750年。归城第三阶段的陶器与河南地区的陶器，或山东地区可断代青铜器共出的陶器相比较，可以定在春秋时期，大致为公元前750～前500年。归城的一些陶器甚至可以晚到战国（公元前480～前221年），但是他们大多是从地表调查获得的，而我们在2009年的试掘中没有见到这么晚的单位。

^{14}C测年提供了另一个基础可以让我们来评价归城的年代。在以上讨论的单位中，我们从4个灰坑：H20、H3、H8、H9中取得了样本进行测年。然而，这些数据与根据陶器比较推定的年代有着系统的偏差（下面）。考虑到在某一段时间内中心地区的设计需要一定时间段才能传播到远距离，考古学家有时会在边缘地区遗物与它们在文化中心对应品之间假设一个滞后率。然而，归城灰坑中样本的碳十四数据却是相反的情况，它们比与中心地区陶器类型学比较所得到的年代早80～100年。但这种差异是系统的，并需要更多研究去解释。目前，它们至少说明了两件事情：①我们以上所建议的陶器发展序列不能被推翻；②我们对以上三个阶段所建议的实际年代不应该被推后，因为^{14}C的年代测定结果要更早。

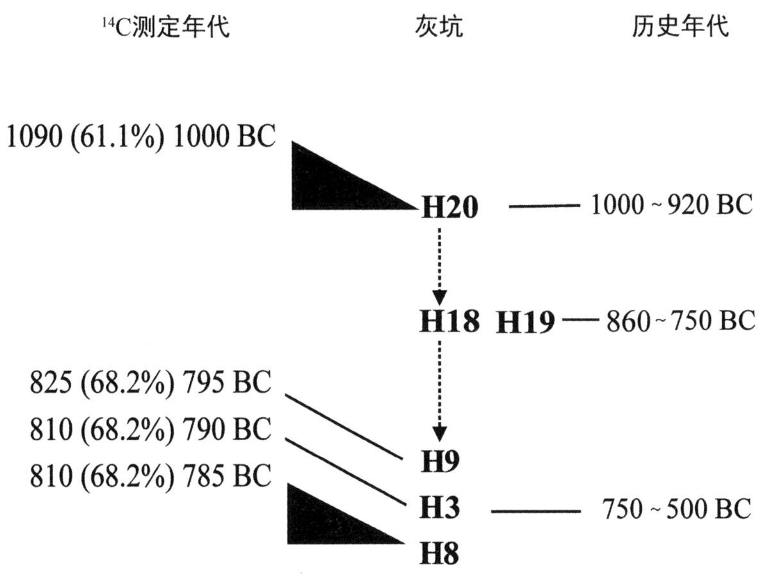

年代序列

第六节　文化因素分析

上述讨论充分证明，至少归城较早阶段的陶器紧随了陕西周文化中心地区创造的陶器器型标准，这可以通过铭文显示的归城和周人中心地区频繁的交流来解释。然而，尽管相隔1000千米的这两个地区陶器器型很相似，但周文化一旦进入半岛东部的新环境后，就不可避免要经历改变。问题在于这种起源于周中心地区的入侵文化在哪些方向或怎样的程度上进行改变？我们如何才能捕捉到周文化在适应新环境的过程中所发生的这些变化？这里，我们用三种方式来考察这个问题：①尽管边缘地区的周文化与中心地区的陶器有同样的器类，但是这些类型的相对重要性可能被重新调整来反映边缘群体的生活方式。换句话说，虽然某些器型是两个地区常见的，他们可能会形成不同的等级序列；②因为自然环境尤其是土壤条件的改变，陶质的配比也会发生很有意义的改变；③同一类型的陶容器可能经过重要改进以产生新的风格和形式。

1. 器类的等级序列

为了比较，我们选择了最近出版的陕西扶风齐家村发掘的玉器作坊的资料。这些资料是对2002年发掘的18个窖藏坑和1处地下房基中的陶片进行统计所获得（陕西省考古研究院等 2010：34 ~ 430）。这个新的资料使我们能够准确地把握在渭水流域西周政权中心地区物质文化的类型学或陶片群体的特征轮廓。我们首先就周文化传统中最常见的四种类型：鬲、簋、豆、罐，估算了三个时期中它们在可以辨认器型的所有陶片中所占的总的平均百分比（西周早期：50.6%；西周中期期：52%；西周晚期：66.85%）。每个时期四种器型各自的百分比都可以据此来进一步做出估算（图Ⅰ.10.8，上）。对比2002年齐家的数字与2009年归城试掘获得的三组数字：①H20代表了第一阶段，大致在西周早期晚段到西周中期早段；②H18和H19代表归城第二阶段，对应西周晚期；③其他属于春秋时期的单位（图Ⅰ.10.8，下）。上述两组数据以相同的方法获得，但是两个区域的比较反映出其间组合频率的重要差异：

比较表明，鬲很可能是最重要的陶器类型，占齐家四种类型总数（100%）的55.69%到57.9%（或者可辨认的陶片总数的28.18%到37.3%）。加上罐的百分比（21.72%到32.49%），清楚地表明自先周以来很长时间，渭水流域周文化陶器传统以鬲和罐的组合为中心。然而在归城，尽管鬲在第一阶段占很大百分比，达到了总数的51.92%，但在第二阶段（西周晚期）急剧下降到只有8.77%并在后来保持了更低的频率。另一方面，尽管西周早期簋在中心地区很重要，占总数的10.65%，但经过西周中期的减少到西周晚期几乎从齐家的器物中消失了。相比之下，归城的簋从一阶段的17.3%增长到了第二阶段的21.05%，第三阶段达到24.9%。加上第二阶段的豆百分比高达40.35%，统计清楚地表明整个时期归城的社会群体对鬲、罐的高度需求转变为对簋、豆的高度要求，后两者在第三阶段总和占到了52%。因而，这完成了周文化以鬲、罐为中心的陶器传统向山东东部以豆、簋为中心的陶器组合的转变。从炊煮器和贮藏器到以盛食器为中心这一转变的文化含义还需要未来进一步的研究。

2. 材质

接下来我们可以比较陕西齐家和山东归城两个遗址陶器的陶质。为了这一目的，我们将陶器的陶质被分为四种类型：①夹砂红褐陶；②夹砂灰黑陶；③泥质红褐陶；④泥质灰黑陶。齐家遗址也有一些纯的黑皮陶，但数量很少可以忽略不计（图Ⅰ.10.9）。

和在齐家类似，在归城的泥质灰陶片和灰黑陶片占了总数的很大一部分（64.5%~70.82%）；这与胶东半岛之前的珍珠门文化构成了鲜明对比，表明归城陶器很大程度上属于周文化传统。事实上，以H20为代表的归城第一阶段与齐家的面貌很像，尽管后者有更多的夹砂红褐陶片。泥质的红陶不见于第一阶段。然而，随着时间的推移这一陶器系统逐渐扩大并在归城第二阶段至第三阶段占到3.77%~3.94%。同样，夹砂红褐陶从第一阶段的1.52%上升到第二阶段的4.55%到第三阶段的7.25%。夹砂和泥质红褐陶的总数从第一阶段的1.52%一起上涨到第三阶段的11.02%。另一方面，夹砂灰黑陶从第一阶段的34.7%下降到第三阶段的18.79%，这是一个非常有意义的下降。然而在齐家，夹砂和泥质的红褐陶从西周早期30.06%减少到西周晚期的10.73%。同时夹砂灰黑陶从西周早期的21.69%增长到西周晚期30.36%。换句话说，归城和齐家两种陶色比例的变化明显向相反方向发展。在归城的一些单位，比如H3有11.60%的夹砂红褐陶，加上另外12.20%的泥质红褐陶，一共占陶片总数的23.80%。H3陶片的面貌与一期的H20非常不同；H20的灰黑陶片占总数的98.73%。我们认为归城地区红褐陶的逐渐增加，是本地陶器制造传统在整个归城时期依然保持活力，并且影响力逐渐增强的结果。

3. 类型学变异

在归城或山东大部，之前从西方引进的陶器类型也发生了重大变化。随着时间的流逝，归城陶器在器形上与主流的周文化越来越不同。下面，我们将主要讨论簋、豆、鬲、罐这四种器型的变化，还有在周文化中并不常见的鼎（表Ⅰ.10.1）。

簋：H20的A1式簋（图Ⅰ.10.5，左上）是之后归城簋一系列发展的祖型。作为一种盛食器，簋在商文化中有很长的历史，但宽沿的A1式的簋在西周早期早段已经充分被陕西地区周文化吸收，而在1000千米外的山东东部发现这种器型，有点让人惊讶。从A1式进一步发展出A2、A3、A4和A5（图Ⅰ.10.10），都是典型高座簋的变异，年代大致在西周中晚期。一些相似的器型发现在陕西，但这种高座簋在山东东部更多且变异幅度更广；因此，这可以被认为是胶东半岛独立的发展进程。在这个过程中，当地陶工似乎已经尝试了许多不同的形式，包括另外两个形式的簋：圆体的B1式和半球状的C1式。它们的器身设计显然背离了周文化的传统，因此他们可能从当地的土著陶器传统中受到很大影响。但它们在周家2号墓中与A3式和A4式一起被发现，所以它们是与西周晚期同时代的形式。在同一座墓中还埋藏了形式丰富的31件簋（唐禄庭，姜国均 1989：316～318）。在A型中进一步发展出了A6式的直腹，圈足细高的簋；在归城地面调查中我们发现的大量的这种簋碎片。这表明这种高座簋大约在公元前8世纪逐渐地变为标准器。

豆：宽直柄的A1式豆与西周中心地区早期墓葬中常发现的类似。从它发展出包括A2、A3、A4、A5式丰富的形式，它们都是归城地区西周晚期A型豆的变异，但不见于周文化中心地区。与簋的情况相似，归城地区的陶工们似乎在西周晚期进行了一个大幅度的豆的尝试，由此产生了另外三个系列的豆：①B1式细柄中部有节棱，很接近西周晚期周文化中心的典型陶豆；②在周家墓地2号墓中发现的C1式半球形腹豆；③D1-D4式的盘非常浅，柄为宽喇叭口的豆（图Ⅰ.10.11）。从B1式发展出B2式和B3式；从C1式发展出C2式和C3式。这些类型大致在第三阶段，即春秋时期。最后，B4式浅平盘，高直柄的豆从B2或B3式发展而来的，大致属于战国时期，在归城很少发现（王富强 2002：172）。

鬲：归城鬲的发展显示了两种陶器传统的一个完美合作。H20出土的A1式有规整绳纹的袋足鬲（图Ⅰ.10.5，右下）无疑是从周文化中心地区引入的。有趣的是，B1式的瘪裆鬲也发现于归城，但几乎不见于渭河流域以外的其他地方。这暗示了早期归城和渭河流域陶器的亲密关系。B2、B3、B4、B5和B6显示了从周中心引入的原始器型的后续发展；特别是有三个尖状足的B6式，与西周晚期比在山东西部的曲阜流行的鬲相一致（山东省文物考古研究所等 1982：图版33）。另外，C1式仿铜鬲可能是西周晚期从西边引入的，后来发展成为C2式。因此，尽管鬲的数量不断下降，归城地区的鬲实际上是一个非常多样化且较不稳定的形式。本土鬲的制造传统以D型为代表，特点是传统的素面和红褐色夹砂陶质：D1和D2大致在西周晚期，H3出土的大型的D3式鬲（图Ⅰ.10.7，左上）事实上结合本土文化和周文化鬲的特点，大约在春秋中期。

罐：由于起源复杂，周文化罐的发展本身也非常复杂。归城所出的A1式圆肩罐很像周文化中心西周早期墓中发现的小口罐，但几乎不见于河南和山东西部等受商文化影响的地区。然而，一旦来到归城，罐便开始向一个跟陕西地区的罐不同的方向发展，逐渐发展为圜底宽斜肩。这个趋势在A2和A3式的小型罐和B1、B2的大型罐中都很明显。但它们的纹饰仍与同时期西边黄河流域地区的罐相似，肩部饰以多重弦纹，器身下部饰绳纹。归城地区这样的罐数量很多。另一方面，本地风格的罐也有少量发现，比如H20出土的E1式，在口沿下部有小圆凸纽的罐。

鼎：鼎不是周文化的器物。典型器物是周家2号墓出土的西周晚期的A1式鼎。以深圆腹和三个锥状实心足为特点，素面无纹。在归城的地面调查和试掘中，我们频繁地发现可能属于这种风格鼎的口沿和足部。它们通常是夹砂红褐陶，是明确属于本地陶器制造传统的。

第七节　本地文化和归城地区文化受容的模式

上文显示了本地陶器的制造传统虽然源流比较单纯，但从未中断过，而且可能在归城郊区的小聚落更强势。我们的全覆盖地面调查显示，那些可能被认定为是本地传统的陶片并不局限于归城某区，而是广泛地分布于整个归城各地，跟与周文化中心关系紧密的陶片混在一起（图Ⅰ.6.19）。本地的陶片大多数情况下被识别是因为其独特的材质，通常为夹砂，混有云母或石英砂的夹砂陶，有时还有粗糙的滑石块。这一成分上的特征使土著的陶片不结实，易断，颜色通常不均匀。因此，通过与周文化的质地较硬的陶片相对比，这些本地风格的陶片并不难区分。

在归城2009年的试掘中，本地特征的陶片几乎出土于每一层。比如，在H20中，发现了甗的下半部，深棕色与红色混合，夹砂，几乎与珍珠门文化的甗完全相同（图Ⅰ.10.2）。这表明珍珠门文化可能确实与西周早期晚段周文化入侵该地区的时间相重合，而且可能延续至这一地区被周文化主导之后。从同一个灰坑中出土了素面的鬲足和口沿下带小圆凸纽装饰的小口罐。这些都明显区别于H20的其他器型和陶片。能辨认器型的本土陶片也在H19、H12、H8、H9和H16等出土。从后期的灰坑中，比如H3，出土了大量周文化和本地文化特点相混合的器型。整体上，尽管本地传统中存在不同的器型，它们绝大部分都是炊煮器，包括鬲和鼎。我们在发掘和全覆盖地面调查中获得了大量本土的夹砂鬲足或鼎足（图Ⅰ.6.18）。

上面已经说明，本土陶片（大部分是红褐色夹砂陶）的比重从第一阶段到第三阶段随时间而增加。特别是H3，9.64%的陶片是夹砂红褐陶，可以确定是本地陶器传统。在密集的地面调查中，有717片陶片确定是本地的，大约占采集陶片的5%。这个夹砂红褐陶片的百分比与发掘中4.44%的平均值相符合。但这些陶片如果没有地层单位的话断代会相当困难。

这就带我们回到了本文开头提出的问题：本地文化对于明显的外来文化的入侵如何反应？或者，周文化如何适应一个之前被本地陶器传统所统治的文化环境？我们认为归城地区青铜时代晚期文化的发展符合途径B，即“下山”式的文化接受与反弹的模式。周文化在归城的出现，代表了一种以珍珠门文化为代表的本地传统的高度中断。周文化因素从西边1000千米外周文化的中心输入这一地区；青铜铭文显示，周文化的入侵与西周政权征服山东东部的高峰期同时。归城的某些陶器与陕西周文化中心的器型非常相似，包括在前商文化区的河南、河北和山东西部地区很少发现的器型；这个前商文化区实际上分隔了有文化接触的两个地区。

然而，鉴于该地区距离周文化中心区很远，一旦到胶东半岛这个新环境中，周文化便开始经历一些重要的转变，本土化的陶工们在归城尝试了很多新器型，类型变化多样。这是一个文化适应和吸收的过程，大部分发生在西周中期晚段到西周晚期（公元前9～前8世纪）。陶器丰富的类型学变化经常与使用它们的社会群体之间高度的社会流动和互动有关（Underhill 2002：28，177）；归城的情况也许正是这样。在它的历史背景中，归城可能为西周政权的扩张提供了一个前沿阵地，并接受了来自周人世界不同部分的人群。但文化的转型逐渐使本地化了的、混合的人群偏离了西边的周文化习俗。这一趋势政治层面的解释在于，周王室力量日趋衰弱，公元前9世纪以后西周政权松散的秩序使周文化中心继续对边远地区施加影响，或以中心地区的文化新发明来吸引外围人口变得越来越难。考古和铭文资料都可以证明这个过程（Li Feng 2006：91～140）。

以早期珍珠门文化为代表的本地文化传统，尽管有中断，仍在类似归城的一些中心遗址相对微弱地延续着，但可能在远离中心的一些较小的聚落更强。一些从前珍珠门文化的遗址比如楼子庄，可能继续被一群有本地文化取向的人占领，并和被周文化统治的归城有联系。它从未完全从本地区的文化谱系中缺失。相反随着时间推移，以归城为中心的改良后的周文化，逐渐从本地文化中吸取元素。通过归城的试掘和地表调查看出，这导致了很多混合型的陶器器型出现，并且土著的陶片的分量随时间推移而增长。总之，长期的接触和受容以及反弹导致了文化的混合，H3的陶器正是这一新文化现象的体现。在政治上我们知道，归城第三阶段被一个铭文和传世文献中称作“莱”贵族群体所占领。莱是胶东半岛的土著部族。在这一时期，归城扩大并上升为青铜时代整个山东最重要的城市之一，也是胶东半岛最重要的城市中心。

第八节　经济体系

以上关于归城文化发展过程的分析引出了本文最后一个问题：之前的讨论已经理清了两种传统的陶器产品在归城持续使用，那么这两种陶器制作传统是在什么样的经济体系下运作的？那些本地传统的陶器是在同时也生产周文化传统器型的作坊里生产的，还是它们在其他地方制造并通过一个稳定的贸易系统被带到了归城？实际上这个问题无法通过田野工作解决，但我们希望能够依赖科学实验提供一些直接证据。2007年，我们第一次挑选了归城地表采集的23片陶片，送到了威斯康新大学麦迪逊分校物理实验室进行分析。这些采集品考虑了两种陶器传统陶质种类的代表性。2011年，另外一批24片陶片从经过发掘的地层单位中小心地挑选出来，加入了之前的分析样本中。James B. Stoltman教授负责了两批陶片的切片和后续的数据分析（见第九章）。

分析的结果是非常重要的。总之，Stoltman确定了这两种陶器传统的陶片三个有意义的差异：第一，周文化传统的陶工只使用花岗岩作为掺料，而土著的陶工看起来可以自由地使用三种天然石料：花岗岩、片岩、闪岩。这似乎表明土著陶工可能对当地的资源有更深刻的认识。第二，周文化传统的陶工使用更少的但更大颗粒的掺料，而土著的陶工使用百分比更高的但更小的掺料。在选择和使用掺料上，周文化的陶工整体上由于悠久的传统或某种作坊规则而有更多限制。第三，一个非常有意义的发现是，两种传统使用不同的胎体：周文化传统的陶器使用了更多泥沙质的黏土，不论是夹砂（11.3%）还是泥质（15.2%）的器物；土著陶器中泥沙的百分比只有6.7%。这一区别非常明显，它表明周文化和本土的陶工有明显的倾向开采不同的黏土资源，前者倾向使用黄土质沉积土，后者则倾向使用河流冲积土。

至少，Stoltman的分析表明，归城发现周文化的陶器和土著文化的陶器，由不同的生产体系生产，更可能是由不同的人群生产。有可能某些土著制陶作坊位于归城，但是，特别是在早期归城比较小，并且周文化的陶器占统治地位之时，土著陶器更可能是在归城周围较小的聚落制作并通过贸易进入城市被消费。由于土著陶器几乎都是炊煮器，比如鬲，鼎和甗，且土著陶工更熟悉或有更多自由开采当地资源，因而它们的陶器可能有着更低的成本，他们也许有能力在周人主导的归城人口中找到一个好的市场。在这之后的城市化进程中，城市版图的扩张可能会吸收很多这样的土著作坊进入归城的经济体系中。这又解释了为什么归城的土著文化因素之后增长了，或两种传统的融合了；这最能反映途径B的文化接受模式。

另外，Stoltman的分析也提出了一些重要的问题。例如，缺乏泥质的土著陶片作为参考是否会削弱了岩相学的分析的可信度？可能不会，甚至可能缺乏泥质的陶片本身就是本地传统的一个特征。目前为止，已知的归城以外的土著陶器像属于珍珠门文化的都是夹砂的。那么如果有泥质陶器的土著制陶技术，可能在归城已经不发达了。另外重要的一点是一些周文化传统的陶片有着不寻常的高泥沙质含量（15%～20%）。Stoltman指出，这些器物有可能并不起源于当地。这不可避免地提出了一个问题，是否归城发现周文化传统的器物中有某些可能来自于其他地区的。比如，陕西周人的中心地区有大量的黄土，是传统陶器生产的原料。考古学家传统的观点是长距离的陶器运输是很困难的（因为陶器易碎），经济上也不划算。但这种可能不能被排除。我们只能希望，陶器岩相学的比较分析应用于更多的中国遗址，特别是那些位于陕西的遗址，再加上胶东半岛地区地质环境的研究，可能在未来能够回答这一问题。

第九节　结　　论

在一个像归城这样的典型的历史背景中了解文化之间的关系，是归城中美联合考古队最初设计的主要学术目标之一。尽管我们还没有进入有计划的大规模发掘阶段，但目前收集的数据已经使我们可以讨论一些关于周文化和胶东半岛本土文化互动的重要问题。文化受容和适应的过程以及导致归城地区土著政权崛起的潜在社会政治发展模式绝不是特殊的和仅限于归城的，在其他中心—边缘互动的例子中也可以找到相似之处。但这种文化进程中的动力，只能在考虑到长时间的时空框架下被发现，这正是本篇文章的研究方法。我们希望将来对归城的进一步发掘和在其他相似的边缘地区的发掘，及其对发掘资料的详细整理、研究和报告，将使我们能够探讨这一过程更细致的一些方面。

参考文献

Li, Feng, *2006. Landscape and Power in Early China: The Crisis and Fall of the Western Zhou, 1045-771 BC*. Cambridge, UK: Cambridge University Press.

刘延常，2001：珍珠门文化初探. 华夏考古，4：94-104.

栾丰实，1996：东夷考古. 济南：山东大学出版社.

陕西省考古研究院等，2010：周原：2002年度齐家制玦作坊和李村遗址考古发掘报告. 北京：科学出版社.

山东省文物考古研究所等，1982：曲阜鲁国故城. 济南：齐鲁书社.

中美联合归城考古队，2011：山东龙口市归城两周城址调查简报. 考古，3：30-39.

Stein, Gil J., 1998. "World System Theory and Alternative Models of Interaction in the Archaeology of Culture Contact," in *Studies in Culture Contact: Interaction, Culture Change, and Archaeology*, edited by James G. Cusick. Pp. 220-255. Carbondale, IL: Center for Archaeological Investigations, Southern Illinois University.

唐禄庭，姜国均，1989：山东黄县东营周家村西周残墓清理简报. 海岱考古，1：314-319.

Underhill, Anne P., 2002. *Craft Production and Social Change in Northern China*. New York: Kluwer Academic/Plenum Publisher.

王富强，2002：海阳嘴子前墓群的年代、特点及相关问题. 海阳嘴子前. 济南：齐鲁书社，164-179.

王富强，2006：从珍珠门到南黄庄. 考古烟台. 济南：齐鲁书社，106-120.

王锡平，1987：胶东半岛夏商周时期的夷人文化. 北方文物，2：19-23，60.

严文明，1989：东夷文化的探索. 文物，9：1-12.

张锟，2010：东夷文化的考古学研究. 北京：中国社会科学院考古研究所博士学位论文.

中国社会科学院考古研究所，1999：张家坡西周墓地. 北京：中国大百科全书出版社.

中国社会科学院考古研究所沣西工作队，1980：1967年长安张家坡西周墓葬的发掘. 考古学报，4：457-502.

中国社会科学院考古研究所山东队，烟台市文物管理委员会，1986：山东牟平照格庄遗址. 考古学报，4：447-478.

（翻译：周琪）

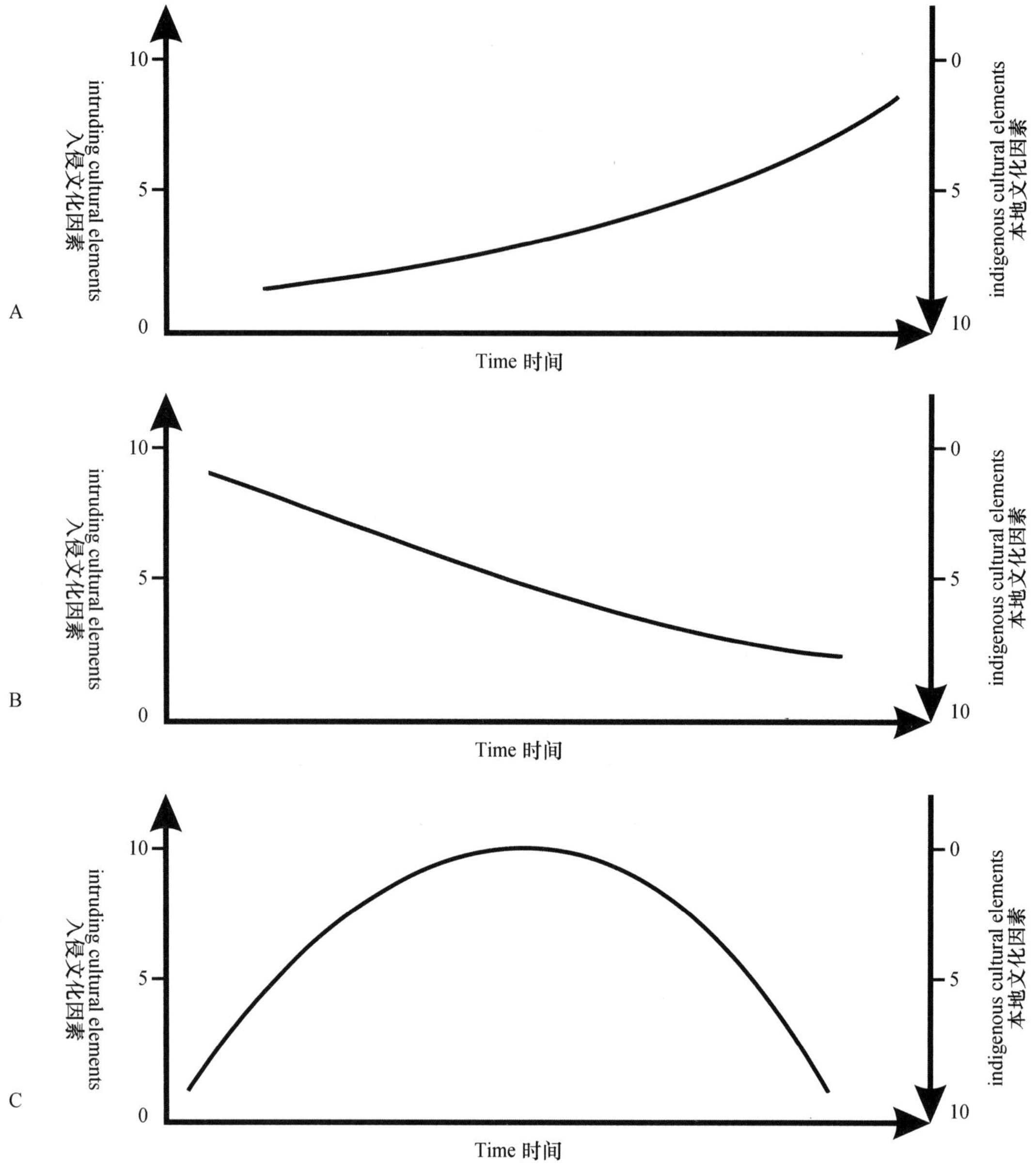

图Ⅰ.10.1　文化受容和反弹的不同途径

Figure Ⅰ.10.1　Different paths of cultural acceptance and resilience.

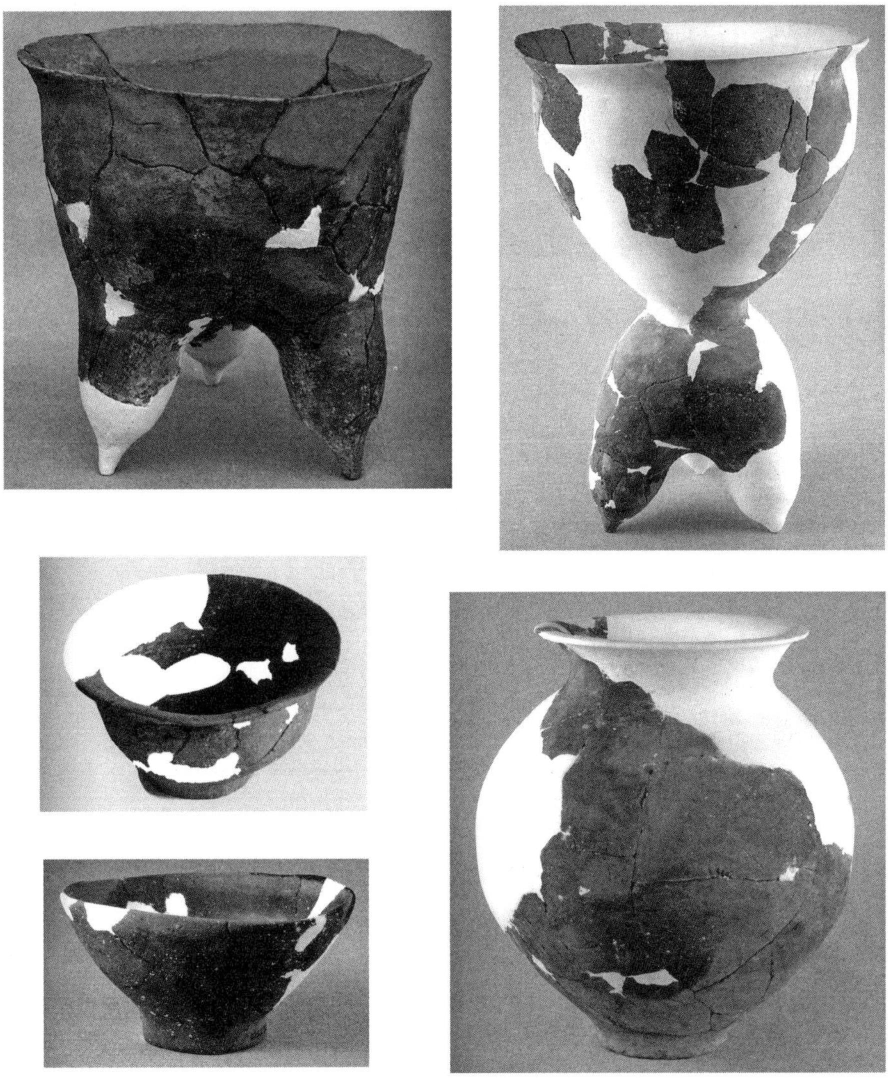

图Ⅰ.10.2　珍珠门文化陶器类型

Figure Ⅰ.10.2　Ceramic types of the Zhenzhumen culture.

图Ⅰ.10.3 周文化传统陶器类型

Figure Ⅰ.10.3 Ceramic types of Zhou cultural tradition.

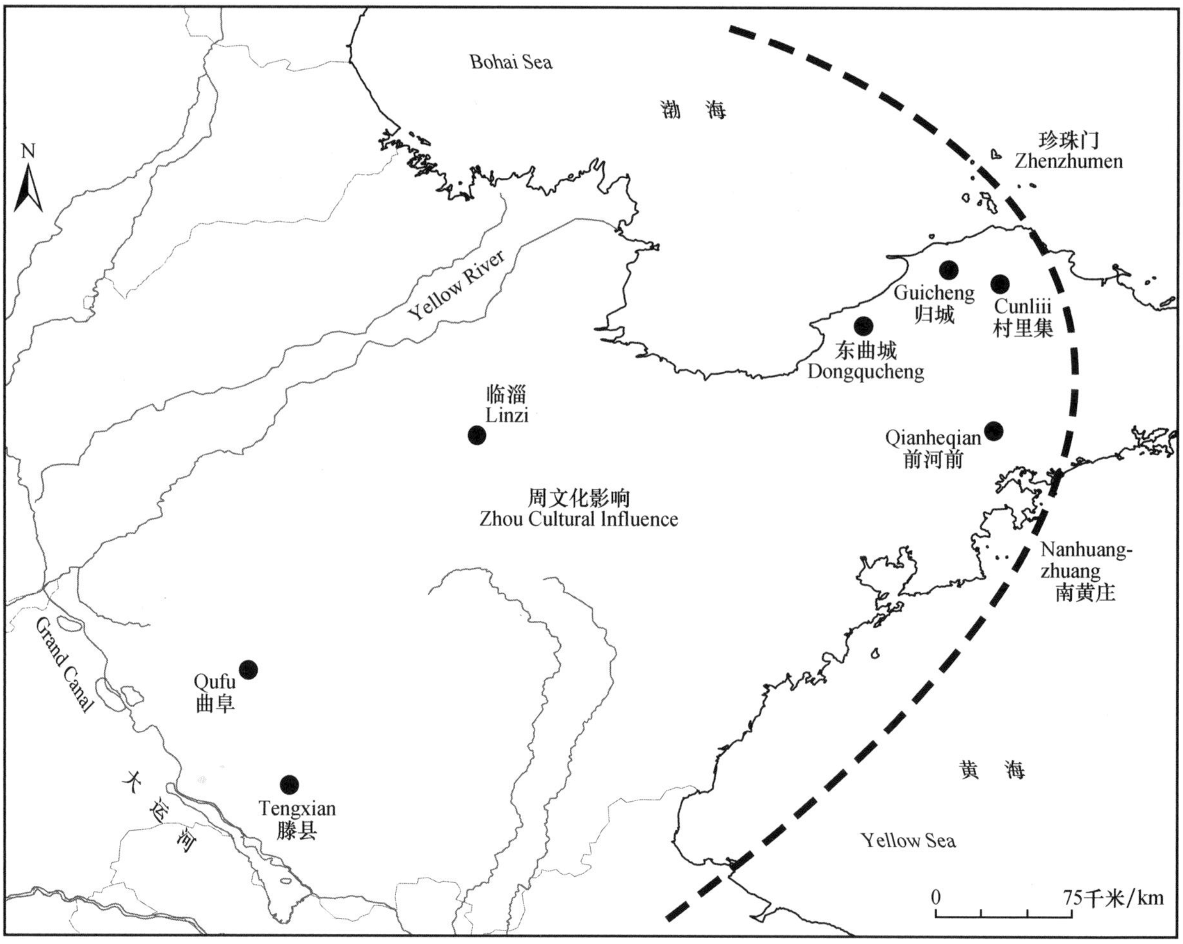

图Ⅰ.10.4 周文化对山东东部的入侵

Figure Ⅰ.10.4 The incursion of the Zhou culture into eastern Shandong.

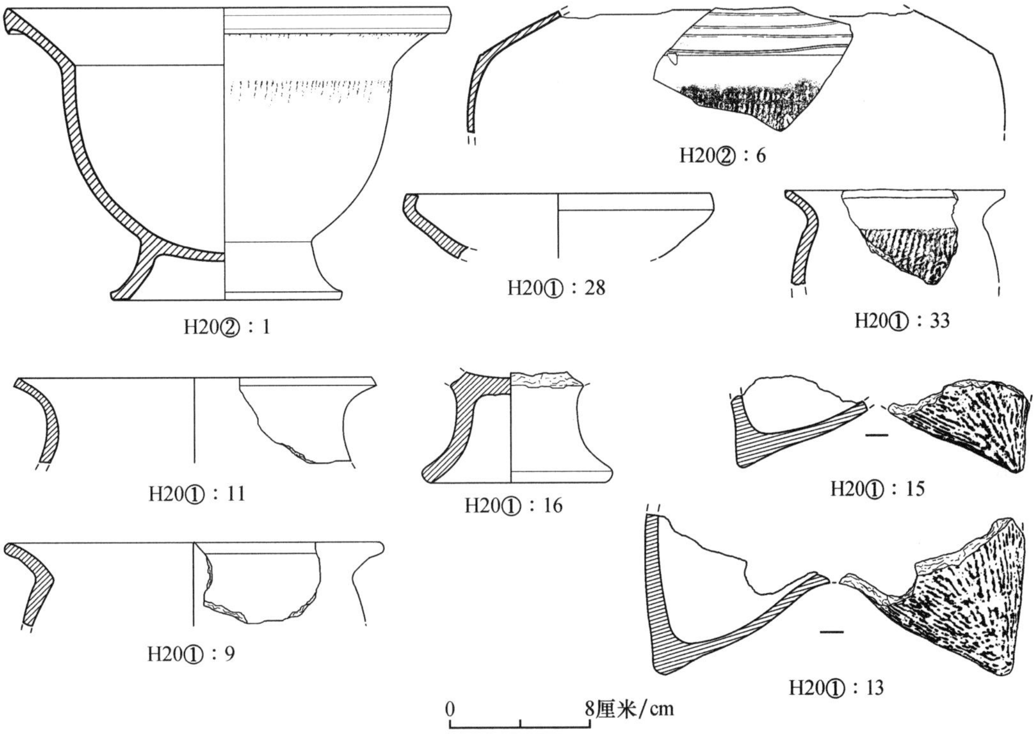

图Ⅰ.10.5　第一阶段（H20）的陶器类型

Figure Ⅰ.10.5　Pottery types from Stage I: Pit H20.

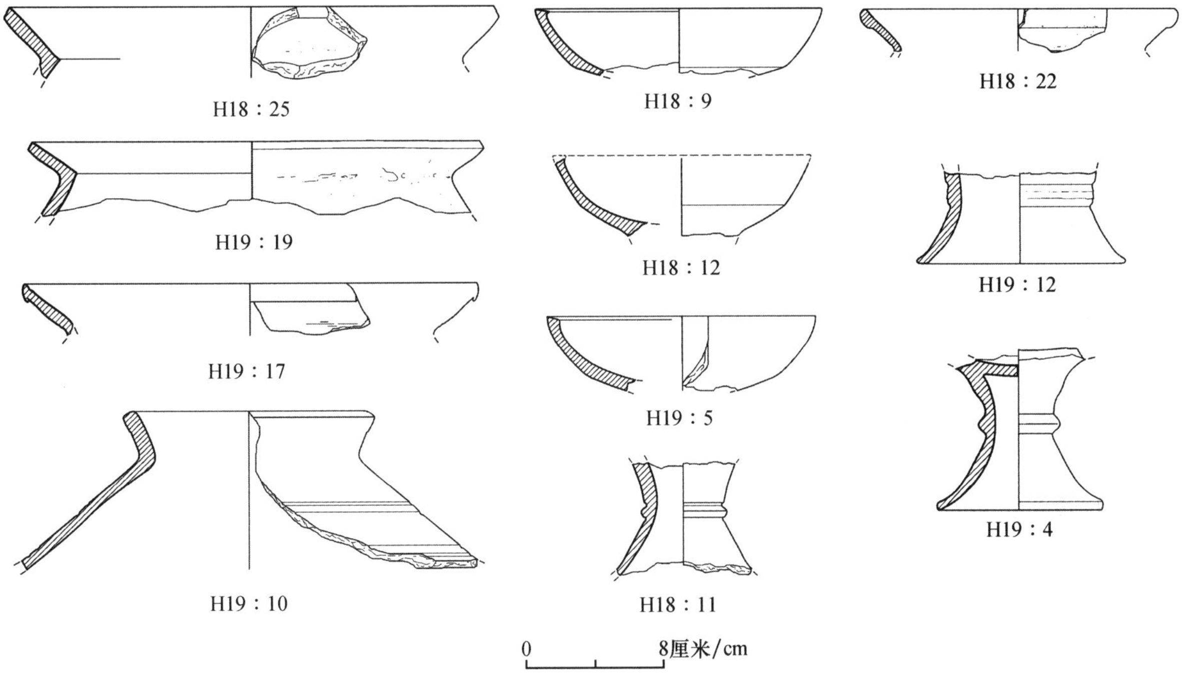

图Ⅰ.10.6　第二阶段（H18和H19）的陶器类型

Figure Ⅰ.10.6　Pottery types of Stage Ⅱ: H18 and H19.

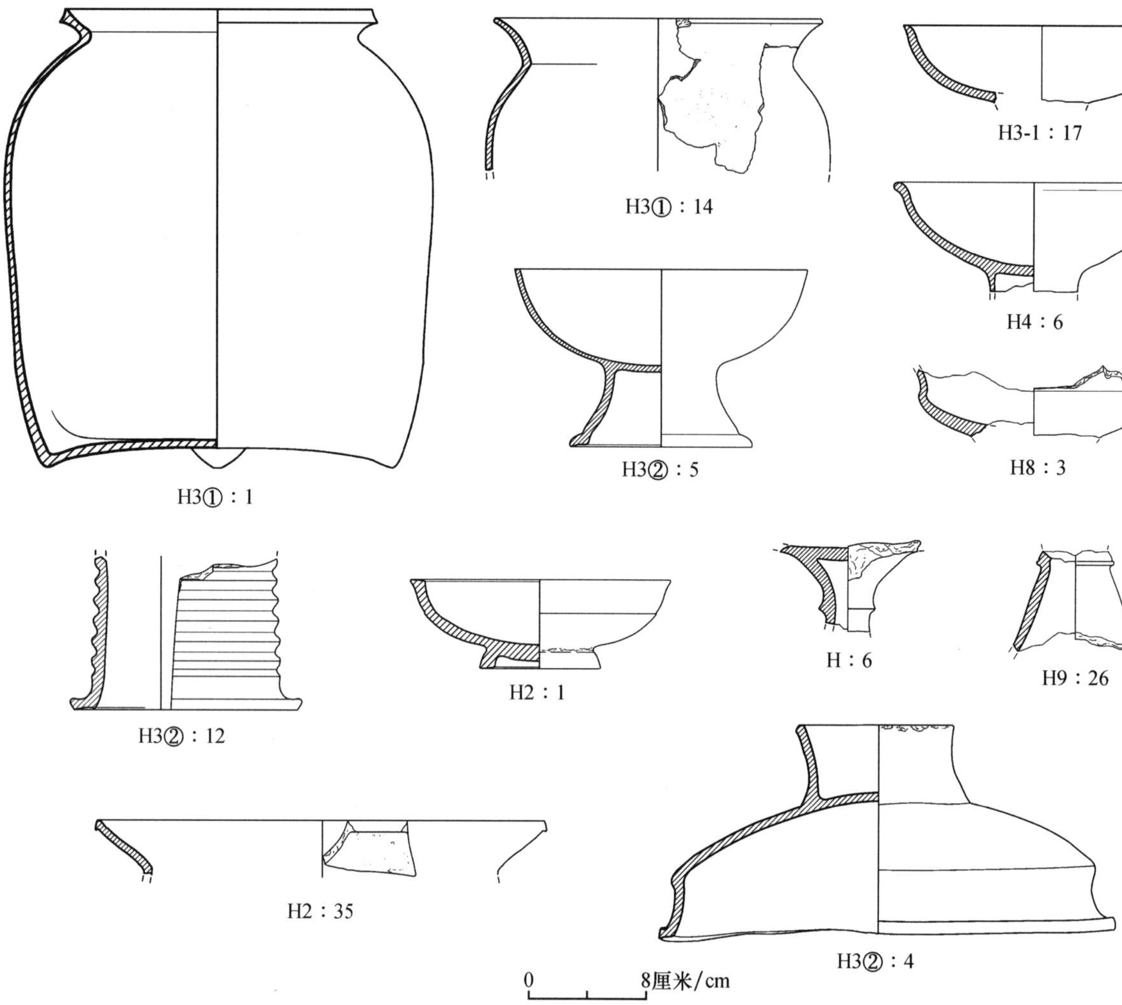

图Ⅰ.10.7 第三阶段（H3）的陶器类型

Figure Ⅰ.10.7 Pottery types of Stage Ⅲ: Pit H3.

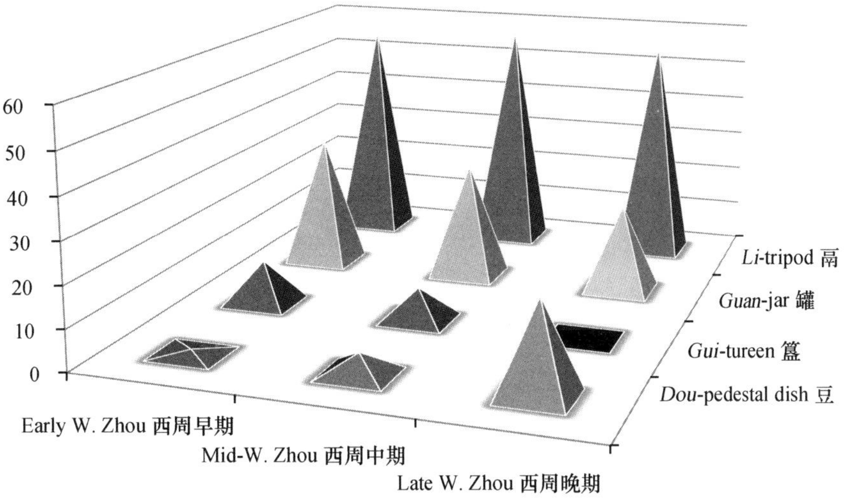

齐家，陕西/Qijia, Shaanxi, 2002

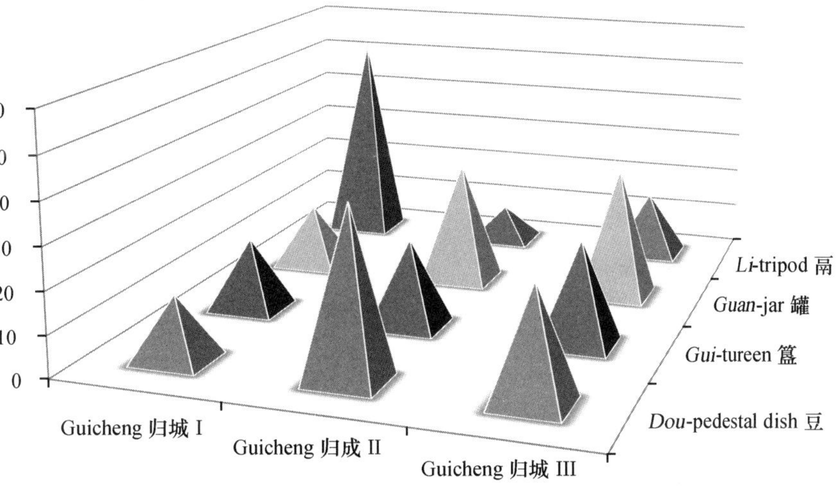

归城，山东/Guicheng, Shandong, 2009

图Ⅰ.10.8　齐家和归城四种主要陶器类型的比较

Figure Ⅰ.10.8　Comparison of four main pottery types between Qijia and Guicheng.

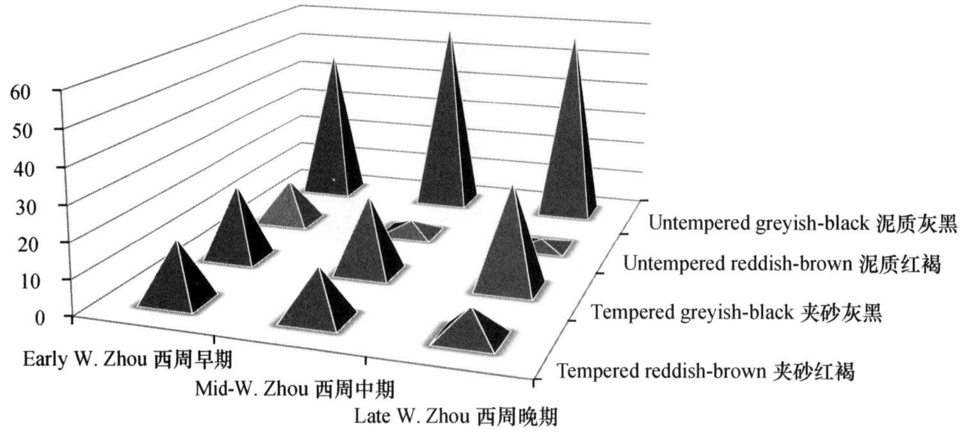

齐家，陕西/Qijia Shanxi, 2002

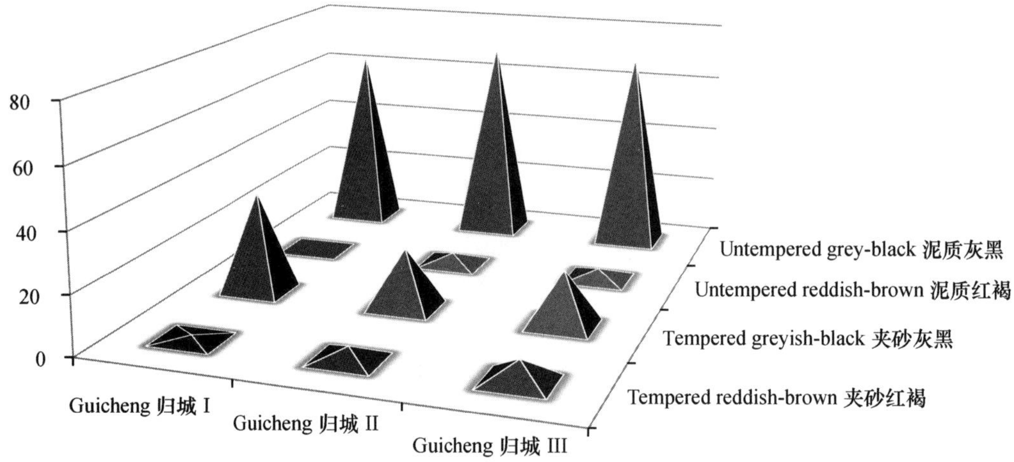

归城，山东/Guicheng, Shandong, 2009

图Ⅰ.10.9　齐家和归城陶器陶质的比较

Figure Ⅰ.10.9　Comparison of ceramic body material between Qijia and Guicheng.

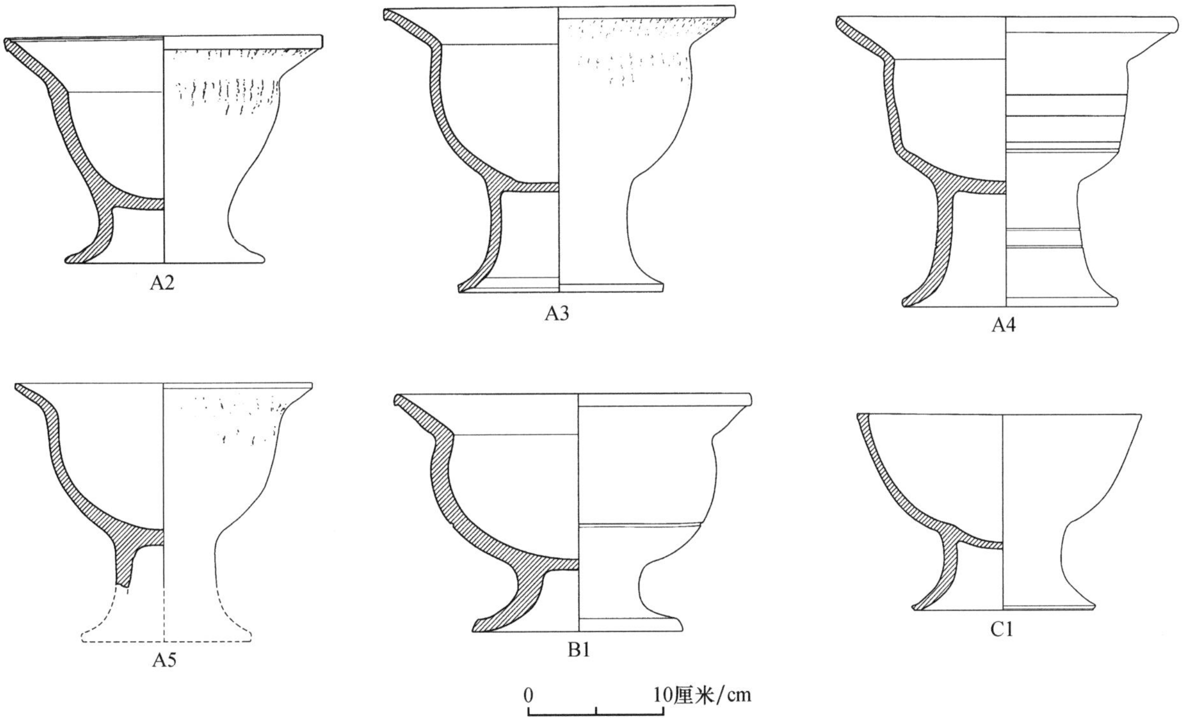

图Ⅰ.10.10　陶簋的器形变异（第二阶段）

Figure Ⅰ.10.10　Variants of *gui* tureen (Stage Ⅱ).

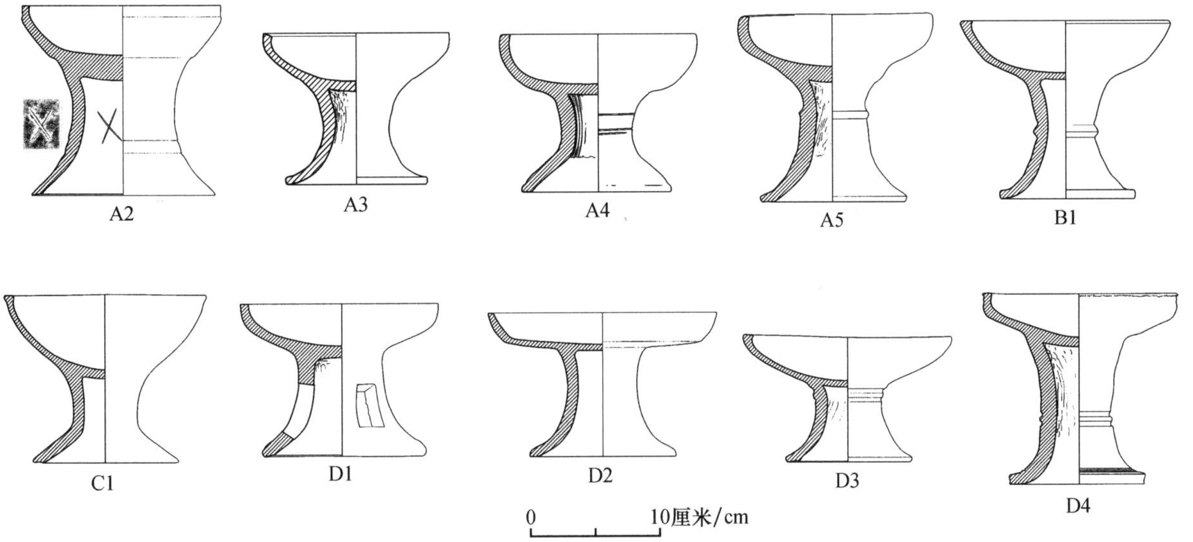

图Ⅰ.10.11　陶豆的器形变异（第二阶段）

Figure Ⅰ.10.11　Variants of *dou* pedestal dish (Stage Ⅱ).

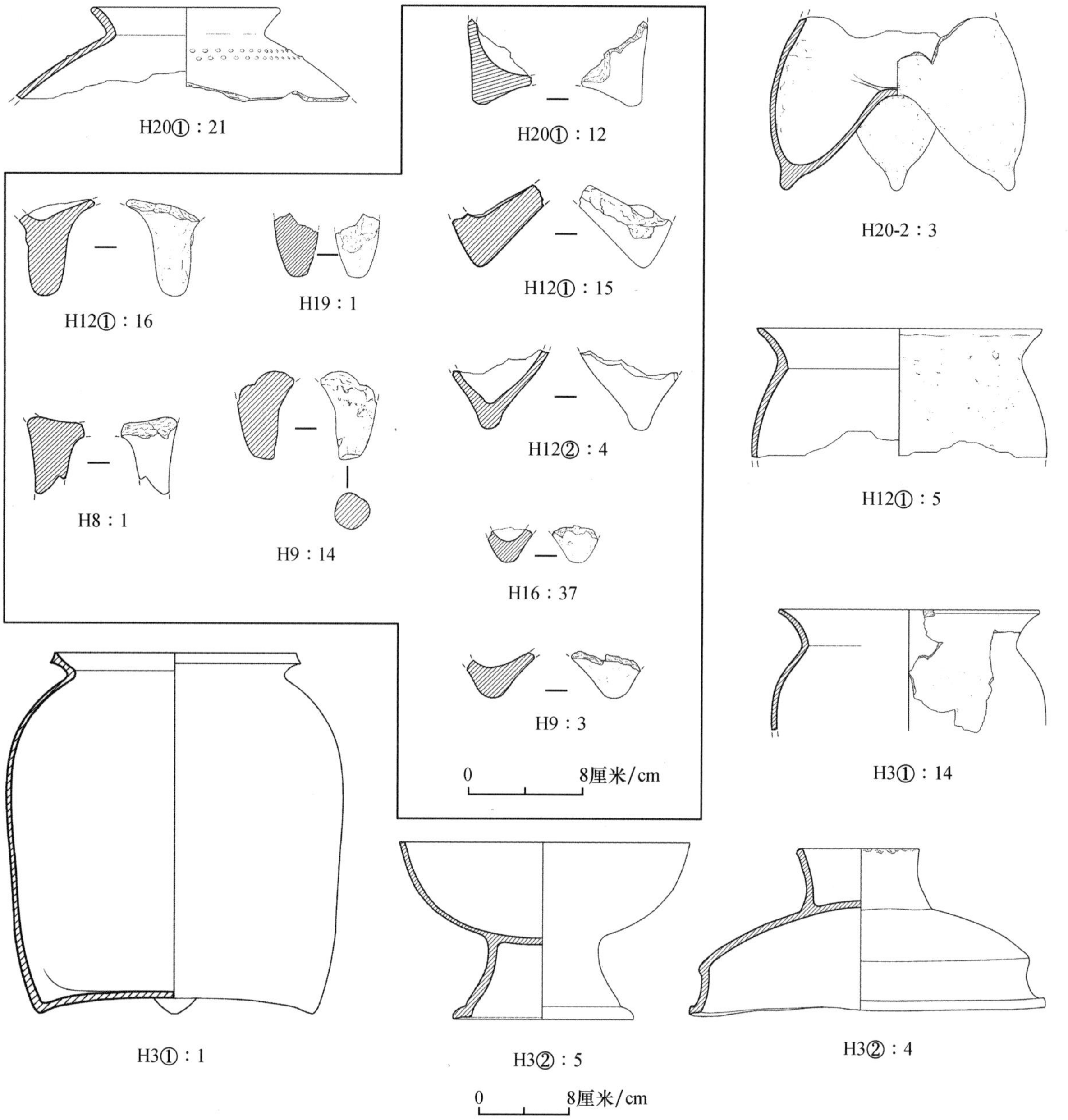

图Ⅰ.10.12　归城发掘出土的本地文化传统陶器类型（第一至三阶段）

Figure Ⅰ.10.12　Indigenous pottery types from Guicheng excavation (Stage Ⅰ-Ⅲ).

表Ⅰ.10.1　归城及其邻近地区陶器类型表

Table Ⅰ.10.1　Ceramic variations in Guicheng and the surrounding areas

图形 Image	名称 Name	型 Type	式 Style	举例 Example	器形特点 Description of Characteristics
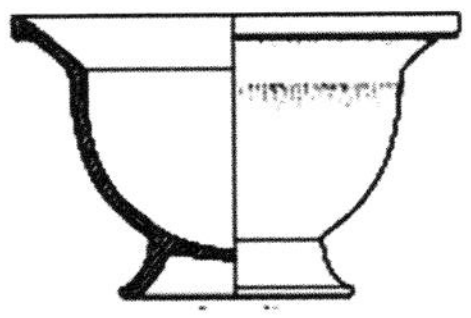	簋	A	1	H20②：1	盆形簋。深腹、矮圈足。敞口，宽平折沿，外厚唇。口沿下及腹部局部饰绳纹，有抹光痕。
	Gui tureen			H20②：1	Basin-shaped *gui*. Deep basin sitting on low circular base; wide-open mouth with broad, flat rim with outer lip thickening; partially impressed with cords showing traces of having been erased.
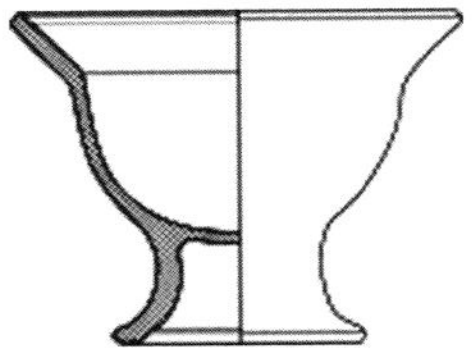			2	张郑：63	略浅的盆形腹，中高圈足。侈口，宽折沿微上弧。个别器沿端上折，沿面有弦纹数周。腹部倾斜，个别器有小面积绳纹。
				Zhangzheng：63	Slightly shallow basin sitting on medium-high circular base. Wide-open mouth with broad and protruding rim. Some with ledge lips, showing rings on the rim. Some have cord-impressions in small areas.
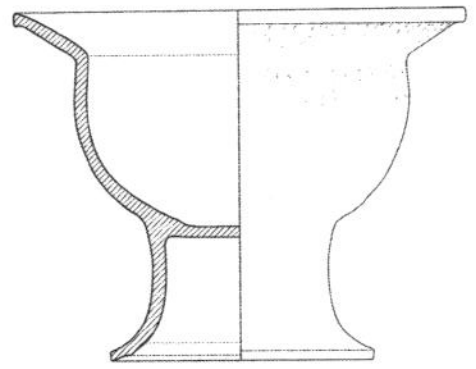			3	周家M2：118（#105）	深腹高圈足，腹部微鼓。宽平折沿。个别器下腹有弦纹。素面。
				Zhoujia M2：118 (#105)	Deep basin on very high, straight circular base, with slightly bulging belly. Broad and flat rim. Some have rings on lower belly. Plain surface.
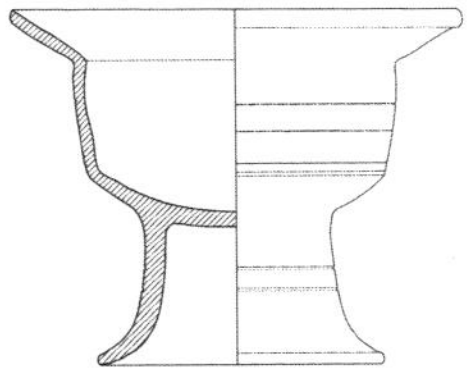			4	周家M2：3（#106）	深直腹，高圈足，腹下有折棱。宽平沿。腹部和圈足上有多道弦纹。
				Zhoujia M2：3 (#106)	Deep, straight belly sitting on high circular base; bottom and side-wall differentiated by a sharp folding ridge. Multiple rings on belly and base.

续表

图形 Image	名称 Name	型 Type	式 Style	举例 Example	器形特点 Description of Characteristics
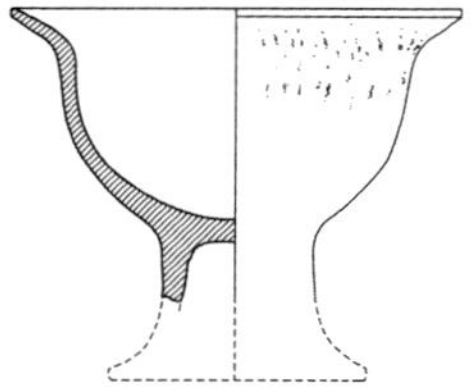			5	和平西2：2	浅腹，细高直圈足。口唇间界限不明显。素面。
				Heping-West 2：2	Shallow basin on high, narrow straight-up base. Side-wall turns slowly to wide rim. Plain surface.
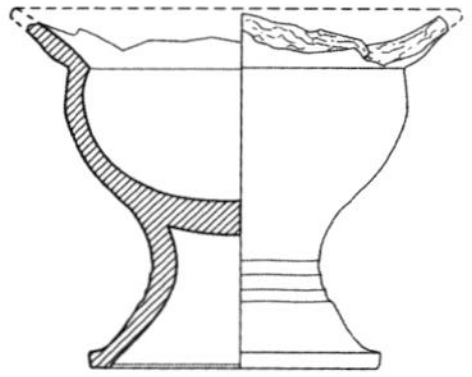			6	10-Y9（附近）：1	大敞口，宽平折沿。腹部小而鼓，形成束颈。高圈足，最细处在中部。整体瘦高。厚壁，素面。
				10-Y9 (near)：1	Wide-open mouth and broad rim. Small but bulging belly, resulting in constricted neck. High base with narrowest point in the middle section. Whole body becomes slimmer. Body-wall thick construction and surface plain.
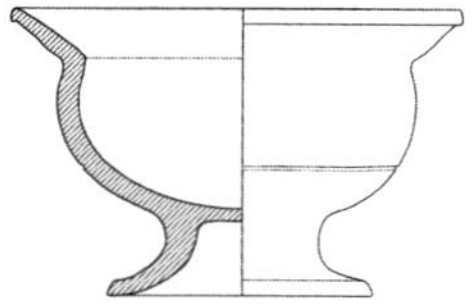	簋	B	1	周家M2：133（#107）	鼓腹簋。鼓腹，束颈，矮圈足。宽平折沿。
	Gui tureen			Zhoujia M2：133 (#107)	Bulging-belly *gui*. Bulging belly on low, narrow base; constricted neck. Broad and flat rim.
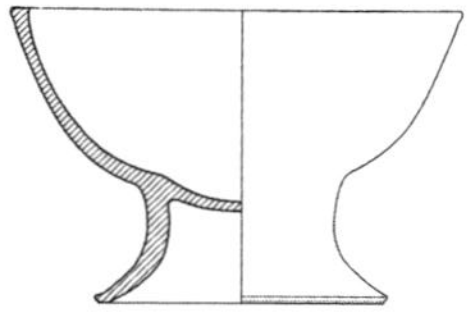	簋	C	1	周家M2：24（#136）	半球腹簋。半球形腹，矮圆足平唇无沿。素面。
	Gui tureen			Zhoujia M2：24 (#136)	Hemispherical *gui*. Hemispherical basin sitting on low circular base. Straight mouth with flat lip but no rim. Plain surface.

续表

图形 Image	名称 Name	型 Type	式 Style	举例 Example	器形特点 Description of Characteristics
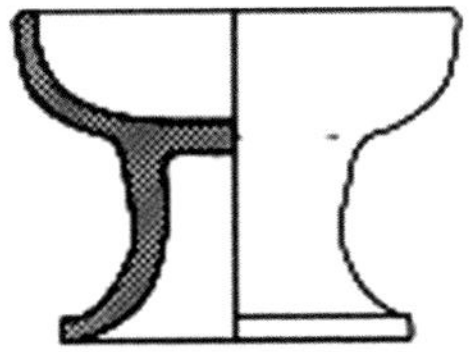	豆	A	1	张郑：50	粗柄豆。柄粗矮，下端外撇，胎厚。
	Dou pedestal dish			Zhangzheng：50	*Dou* with thick stem. Short, thick, and downwardly flaring base; thick-walled construction.
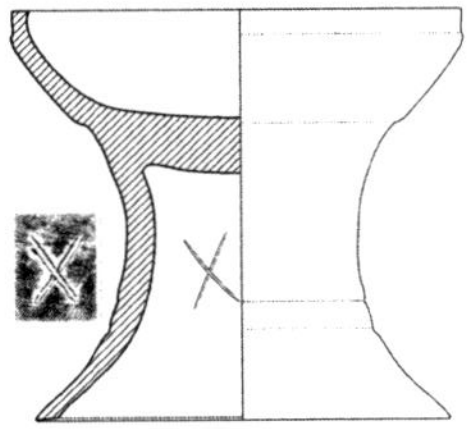			2	周家M1：12（#103）	柄极粗且高，下端外撇，胎厚。
				Zhoujia M1：12 (#103)	*Dou* with very sturdy, tall stem and downwardly flaring base; thick-walled construction.
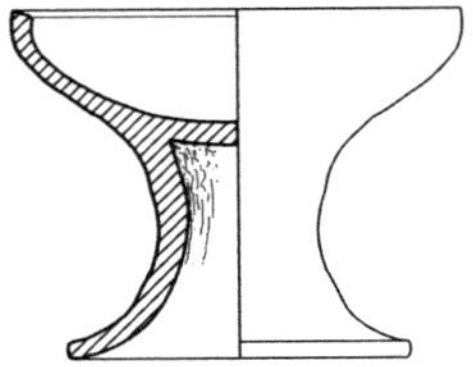			3	11-O50	浅盘，直口，方唇。高柄无突棱，下端外撇，呈喇叭状。
				11-O50	*Dou* with shallow dish, straight-up mouth, and squared lip. Stem is tall and without protruding ridges, forming a trumpet shape.
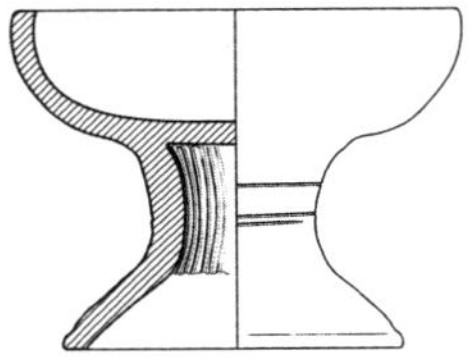			4	和平村西2：3	直口，方唇，高柄上部出现弦纹，下端外撇，呈喇叭状，但下部有反弧。
				Heping-West 2：3	*Dou* with straight-up mouth and squared lip; tall stem with ring decorations on its upper portion and a downwardly flaring base, forming a trumpet shape, but with outwardly bulging curve.

续表

图形 Image	名称 Name	型 Type	式 Style	举例 Example	器形特点 Description of Characteristics
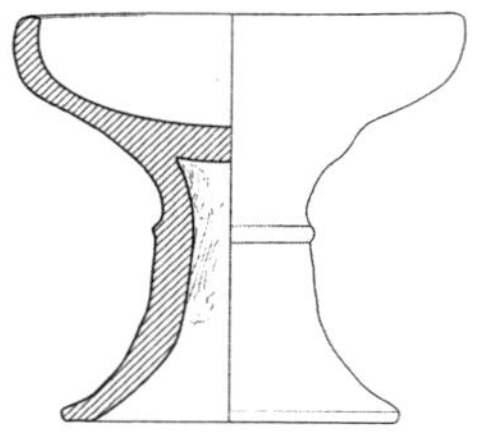			5	周家M2：66（#5）	柄仍粗，柄上出现明显突棱，位置偏高，柄下端外撇，保留喇叭形。
				Zhoujia M2：66 (#5)	*Dou* with thick stem has pronounced ridge on upper portion and with downwardly flaring base assuming a trumpet shape.
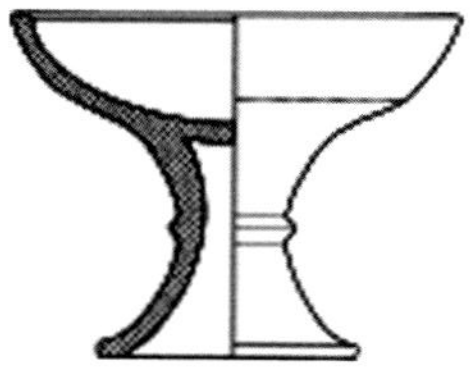	豆	B	1	东迟家：2	细柄豆。典型的细柄节棱豆。浅折盘，盘底微凹。突棱在束腰正中，两端基本对称。底缘略外突。
	Dou pedestal dish			Dong Chijia：2	*Dou* with slender stem. Archetypal *dou* pedestal dish slender stem has pronounced ridge in the center portion. Shallow, angular dish with concave bottom. Upper and lower sections of the stem are nearly symmetrical; base rim curls upwards slightly.
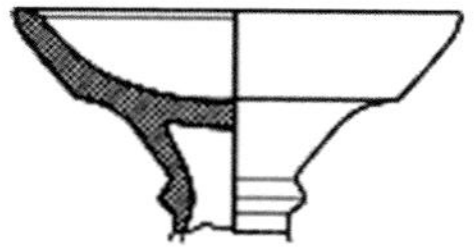			2	10-Y9：3	浅折盘有突棱，柄细且趋直。残断。
				10-Y9：3	*Dou* with shallow, angular dish has a pronounced folding ridge. Broken portion of stem is slender and straight.
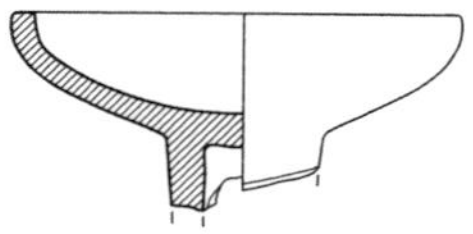			3	和平村西5：3	浅盘无折棱。柄部变直。
				Heping-W.5：3	*Dou* with shallow dish lacking angular ridge. Stem portion is straight.

续表

图形 Image	名称 Name	型 Type	式 Style	举例 Example	器形特点 Description of Characteristics
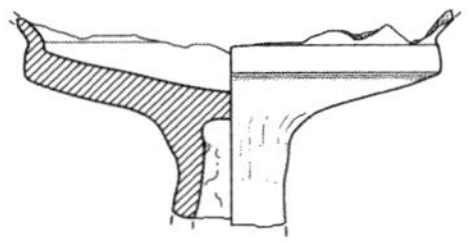			4	10-Y9（附近）：4	浅折盘，盘底平。直柄细高。
				10-Y9 (near)：4	*Dou* with shallow, angular, flat-bottomed dish. Stem is straight, slender, and tall.
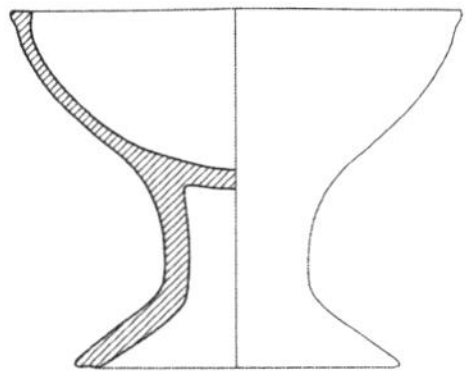	豆	C	1	周家M2：105（#49）	弧形盘豆。盘深呈半球形，粗柄为喇叭形。
	Dou pedestal dish			Zhoujia M2：105 (# 49)	*Dou* with curved dish. Deep, hemispherical dish; thick stem, lower portion flaring, forming a trumpet shape.
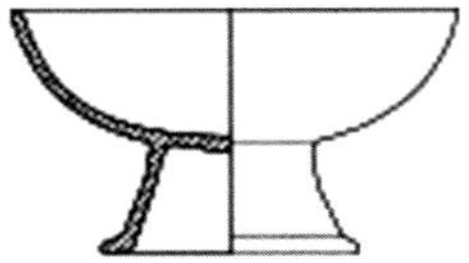			2	H3②：5	豆盘深，呈弧形。柄粗矮，外撇，底缘外突。泥质红陶。
				H3②：5	*Dou* with deep, curved dish. Stem is thick, short, and downwardly flaring, with outwardly curled base rim. Made of untempered red clay.
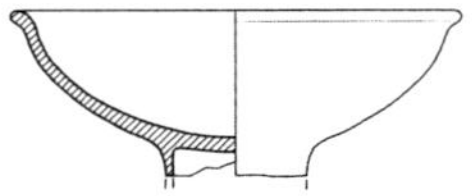			3	H4：6	浅盘仍呈弧形，但豆柄变直。
				H4：6	*Dou* with shallow, curved dish. Stem is straight and slim.

续表

图形 Image	名称 Name	型 Type	式 Style	举例 Example	器形特点 Description of Characteristics
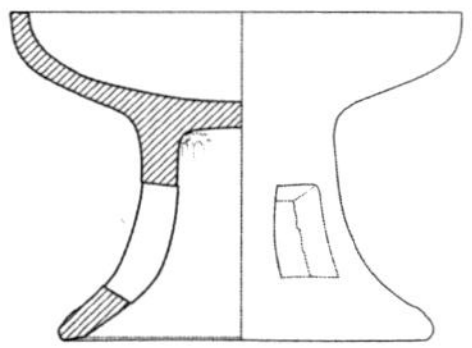	豆	D	1	周家M2：27（#96）	浅盘豆。粗柄有方形镂空。
	Dou pedestal dish			Zhoujia M2：27 (#96)	*Dou* with shallow dish. Stem is thick with square perforations.
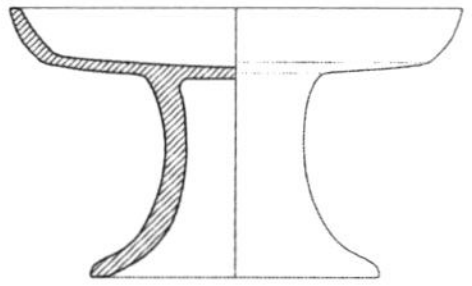			2	周家M2：121（#74）	浅折盘，底部平。粗柄外撇。
				Zhoujia M2：121 (#74)	*Dou* with shallow, angular, flat-bottomed dish. Stem is thick and base flares outwards.
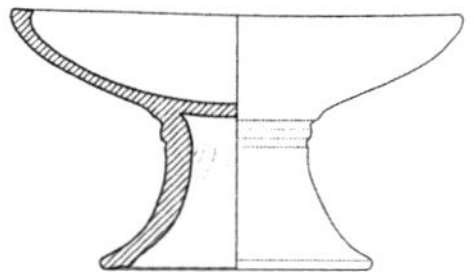			3	周家M2：86（#65）	弧形浅盘。粗柄外撇，呈喇叭形。
				Zhoujia M2：86 (#65)	*Dou* with shallow, curved dish. Stem is thick and base flares outwards, forming a trumpet shape.
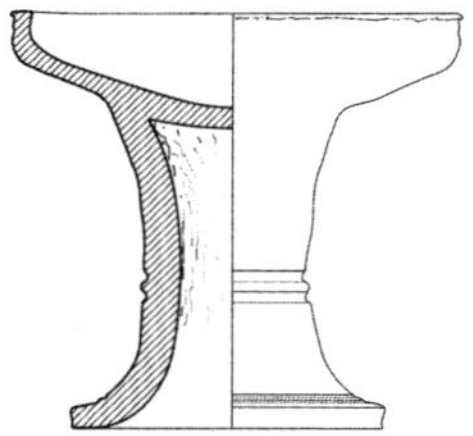			4	周家M2：76（#95）	浅盘。柄极高，中部有弦纹。
				Zhoujia M2：76 (#95)	*Dou* with shallow dish. Stem is tall and has rings in middle section.

续表

图形 Image	名称 Name	型 Type	式 Style	举例 Example	器形特点 Description of Characteristics
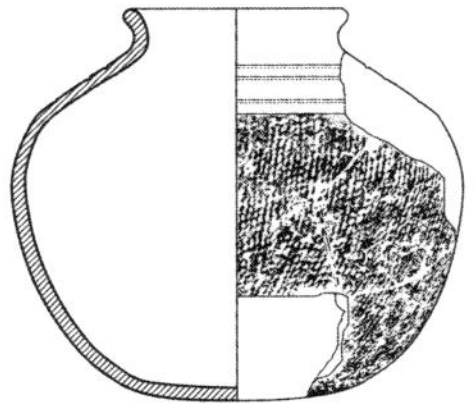	罐	A	1	10-Y9（附近）：12	泥质小罐，高度在20～30厘米之间。小口卷沿，圆肩微折，小平底。肩上有数周弦纹，腹部饰绳纹。
	Guan jar			10-Y9 (near)：12	Small, untempered pottery *guan*. 20-30 cm in height. Small mouth with rounded rim, and round shoulder with slight angularity. Base is small and flattened. Has multiple bands of ring decorations on the shoulder and cord impressions on the body.
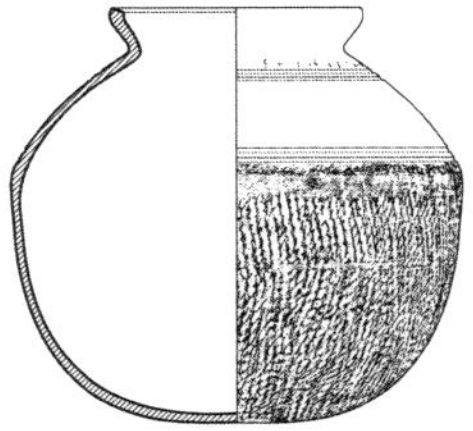			2	周家M2：145	泥质小罐。口平沿微内折，有折肩，小平底。有弦纹，腹部饰绳纹。
				Zhoujia M2：145	Small, untempered pottery *guan*. Rim is flat and angled inwards slightly; shoulder is angular and base is small and flat. Has ring decorations on the shoulder and cord impressions on the body.
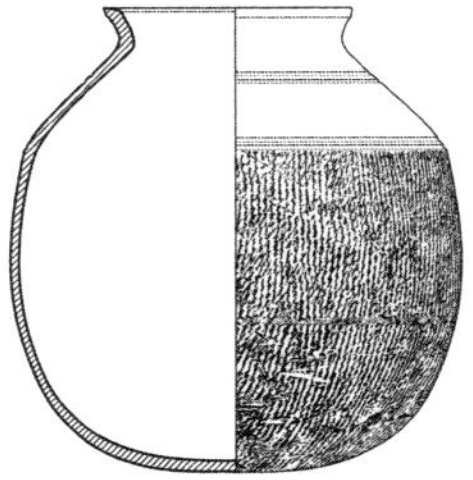			3	周家M2：144	泥质小罐。小口，窄折肩，遛肩明显。整体变得瘦高。圜底。肩部有弦纹，腹部饰绳纹。
				Zhoujia M2：144	Small, untempered *guan*. Mouth is small, with a narrow, angular shoulder clearly differentiated from body. Body is oblong in shape, with rounded bottom. Shoulder has rings; body has cord impressions.
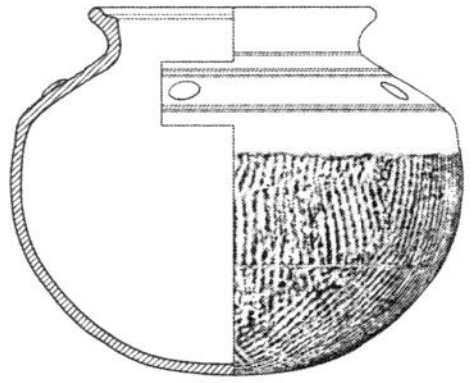			4	石良：2	圜底小罐。圆肩有乳钉。
				Shiliang：2	Small, round-bottomed *guan*. Rounded shoulder has flattened bosses.

续表

图形 Image	名称 Name	型 Type	式 Style	举例 Example	器形特点 Description of Characteristics
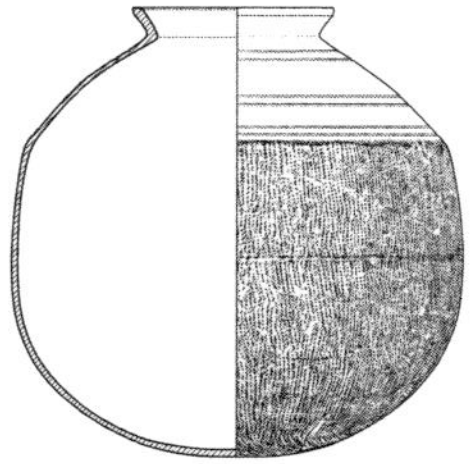	罐	B	1	周家M2：145（#151）	泥质大罐，体高在35～50厘米之间。小口平唇，广折肩。圜底。肩上有数周绳纹。
	Guan jar			Zhoujia M2：145 (#151)	Large, untempered pottery *guan*. Between 35 - 50 cm in height. Small mouth with a flattened rim; shoulder is wide and angled with multiple bands of string impressions. Rounded bottom.
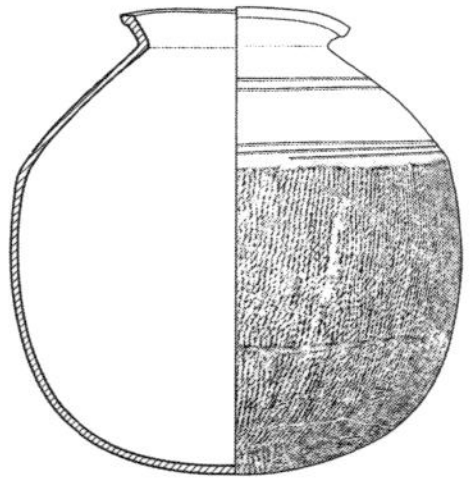			2	周家M2：146（#153）	泥质大罐，体高在35～50厘米之间。小口平唇，窄折肩，遛肩明显。圜底。肩上有数组绳纹。
				Zhoujia M2：146 (#153)	Large, untempered pottery *guan*; 35-50 cm in height. Small mouth with flat lip and narrow, sliding shoulder with multiple bands of string patterns; clearly differentiated shoulder and body portions. Round bottom.
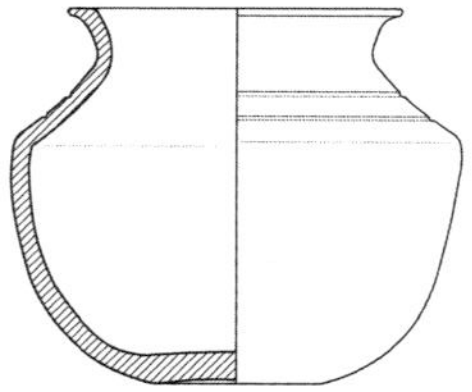	罐	C	1	和平村采：28	特小罐，仅12.5厘米。敞口平沿，底微内凸。整体素面，肩上有两道弦纹。
	Guan jar			Hepingcun coll.：28	Exceptionally small *guan*; Only 12.5 cm in height. Large mouth with flattened rim and convex bottom. Plain surface with two rings of string impressions on the shoulder.
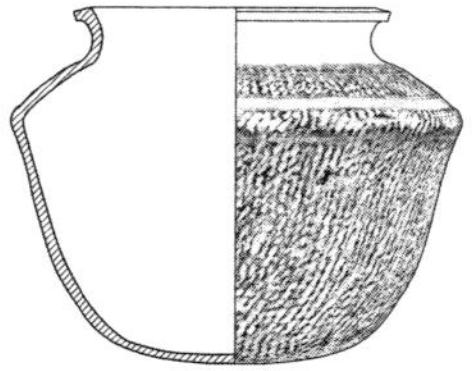	罐	D	1	归城采：12	小罐，仅14.6厘米。敞口小卷沿，肩部突出，圜底。整体饰绳纹。
	Guan jar			Guicheng coll.：12	Small *guan*, only 14.6 cm in height. Large mouth with outwardly curling rim and protruding shoulder; rounded bottom. Body surface covered with cord impressions.

续表

图形 Image	名称 Name	型 Type	式 Style	举例 Example	器形特点 Description of Characteristics
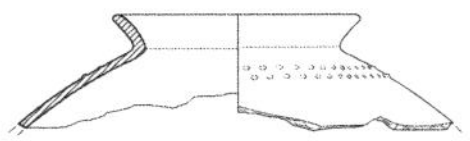	罐	E	1	H20①：21	夹砂小罐。胎色红褐，小口束颈，圆唇卷沿。表面有釉，黑褐色。饰密集的两周小乳钉。
	Guan jar			H20①：21	Small, tempered pottery *guan*. Reddish-brown color, small mouth with constricted neck, rounded lip and curled rim. Remnants of black slip on the surface; has two bands of small bosses on the shoulder.
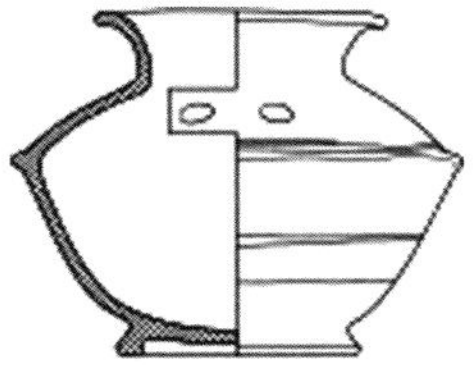	瓿	A	1	10ZZJ采：11（张郑家）	小口侈唇，宽广折肩。肩上有两个横銴。有两泥饼，饰弦纹。
	Bu footed jar			10ZZJ采：11 (Zhangzhengjia)	Small mouth with outwardly flaring rim, and wide, angular shoulder with two horizontal handle protrusions. Body has two ornamental disks and multiple decorative rings.
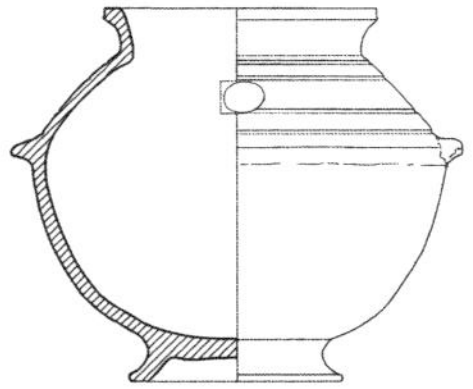			2	东迟家：1	小卷沿，方唇。肩部缓折，器体变瘦。肩上有两横銴。小圈足。
				Dongchijia：1	Small *bu* with outwardly curling rim and squared lip. Sloping shoulder with two horizontal handle protrusions; body slopes inwards gently. Small circular base.
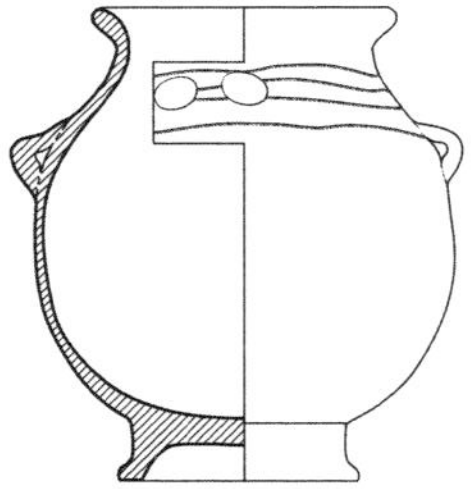			3	张郑：71	大口，肩部消失。有两个立耳。
				Zhangzheng：71	*Bu* with large mouth, and sloping shoulder indistinct, with two vertical handles.

续表

图形 Image	名称 Name	型 Type	式 Style	举例 Example	器形特点 Description of Characteristics
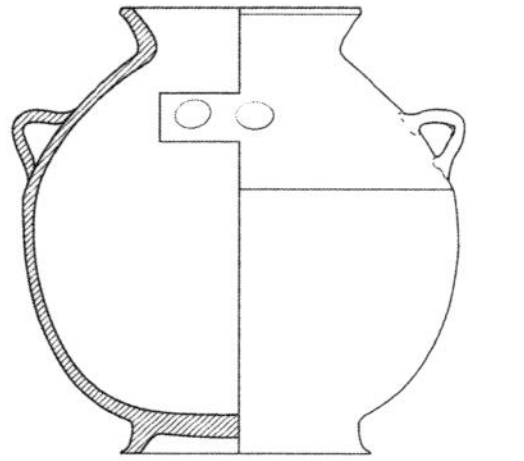			4	周家M2：51（#152）	小口侈唇，斜溜肩。有两个立耳。
				Zhoujia M2：51 (#152)	*Bu* with small mouth and outwardly flaring rim; sloping shoulder with two vertical handles.
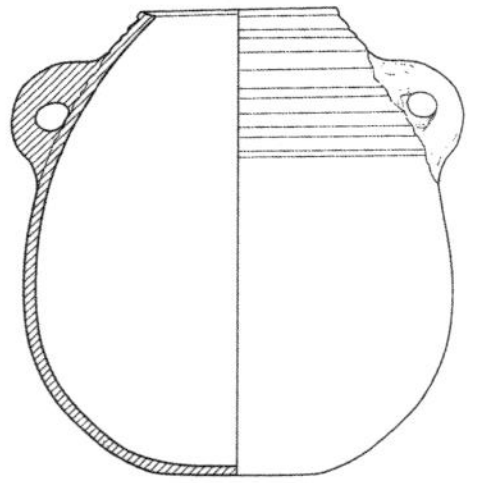	壶	A	1	归城：8	形似鱼篓形。口内敛，上体部位有两耳。饰多道弦纹。
	Hu bottle			Guicheng coll.：8	Fish-basket-shaped *hu* bottle with inwardly constricted mouth. Body has two vertical handles. Decoration consists of multiple bands of rings.
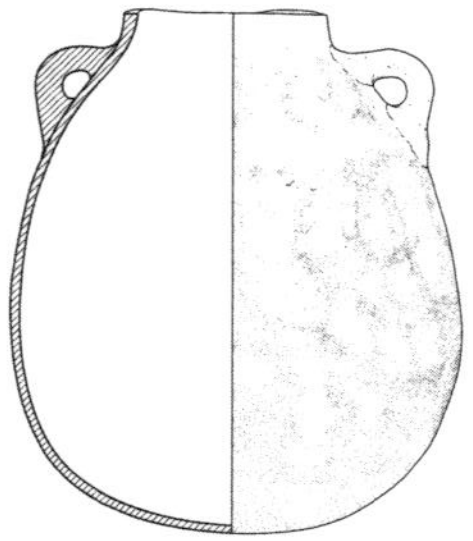			2	周家M2：53（#156）	小口细颈，斜溜肩，上体部位有两耳。素面或饰绳纹。
				Zhoujia M2：53 (#156)	*Hu* with small mouth, slender neck, and sloping shoulder. Body has two vertical handles. Belly has faint cord impressions.

续表

图形 Image	名称 Name	型 Type	式 Style	举例 Example	器形特点 Description of Characteristics
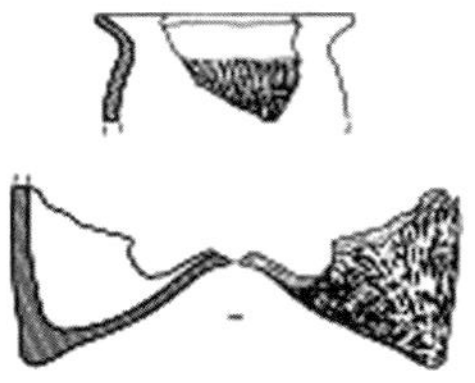	鬲	A	1	H20①：33、13	袋足鬲。乳状袋足，分裆明显。侈口，深腹。饰规整绳纹。
	Li tripod			H20①：33, 13	Hollow-lobbed *li*. Breast-shaped lobe, split-crotch. Outwardly flaring mouth and deep belly. Surface covered with cord impressions.
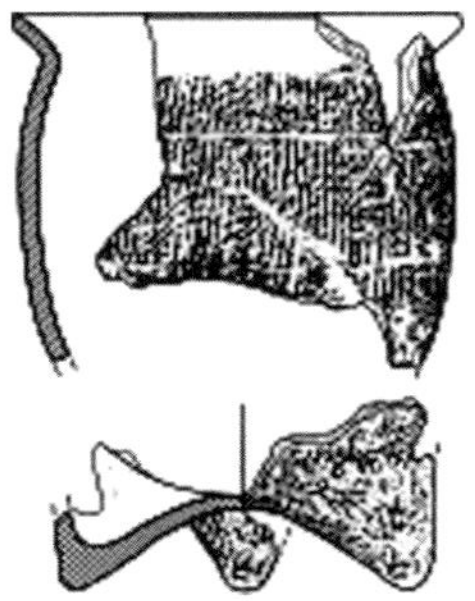	鬲	B	1	和平村西六：10、11	连裆鬲。侈口，深腹。裆部低，呈弧状连裆，侧面微瘪。沿以下饰绳纹，腹部有两周弦纹。
	Li tripod			Heping-W. 6：10, 11	Joint-crotch *li*. Outwardly flaring mouth and deep belly. Crotch portion is low and forms an arch shape, slightly sunken on the sides. Surface has cord impressions below the rim, interrupted by two bands of unadorned surface.
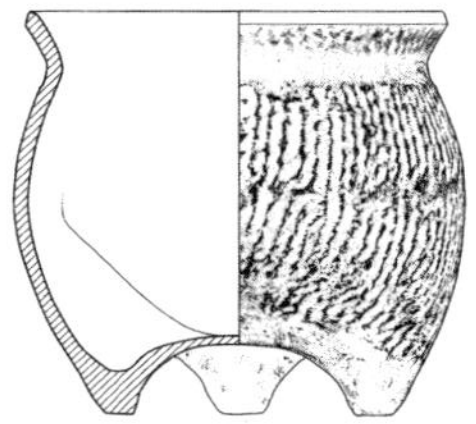			2	归城：1	弧裆较甚，三足内收。饰粗绳纹。
				Guicheng：1	Joint-crotch *li* with high arch and inwardly curving feet. Surface has thick cord impressions.

续表

图形 Image	名称 Name	型 Type	式 Style	举例 Example	器形特点 Description of Characteristics
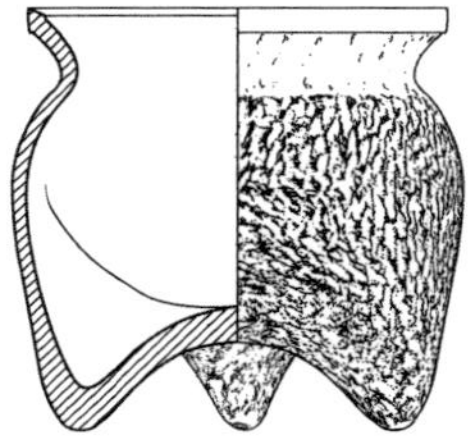			3	张郑：53	卷沿小平唇，束颈有肩。饰粗绳纹。
				Zhangzheng：53	Joint-crotch *li* with outwardly curling rim and flattened lip. Narrow neck and shouldered body. Surface has thick cord impressions.
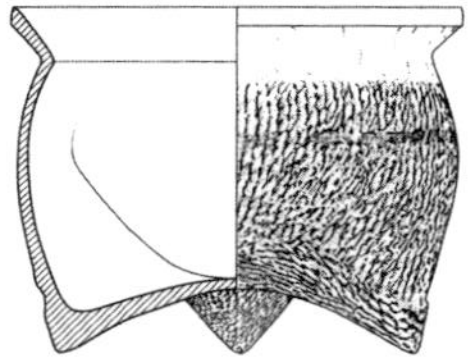			4	周家M2：4（#138）	体矮，折沿，方唇。红褐夹砂陶，饰粗绳纹，形成麻点。
				Zhoujia M2：4 (#138)	Short, tempered reddish-brown, joint-crotch *li* with angled rim and squared lip. Surface has thick cord impressions forming sesame seed patterns.
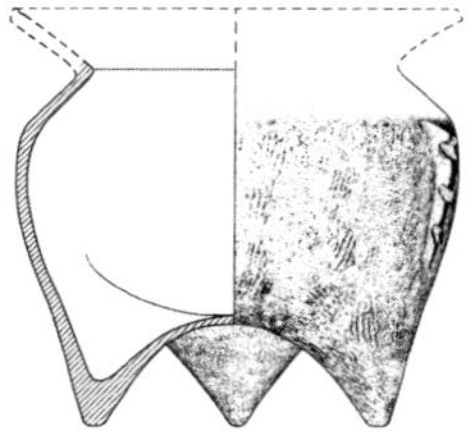			5	归城：10	肩部突出，较宽。弧裆高。腹上有扉棱。灰褐陶，绳纹较细。
				Guicheng：10	High-arched, grey pottery, joint-crotch *li* with wide, protruding shoulder. Body has vertical flanges and thin cord impressions.
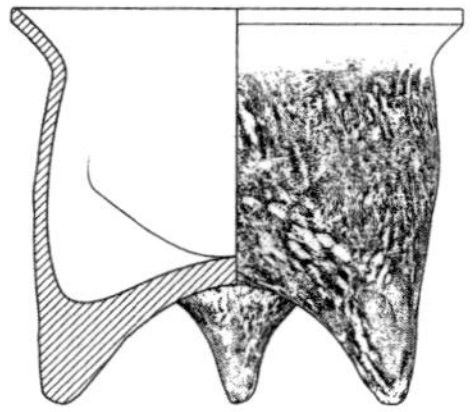			6	周家M2：8（#137）	敞口，直腹，弧裆，高尖足。粗麻点绳纹，纹路不清。
				Zhoujia M2：8 (#137)	Straight-walled, high-arched, joint-crotch *li* with outwardly flaring mouth and pointed and solid feet. Surface covered in thick sesame-seed cord impression pattern.

续表

图形 Image	名称 Name	型 Type	式 Style	举例 Example	器形特点 Description of Characteristics
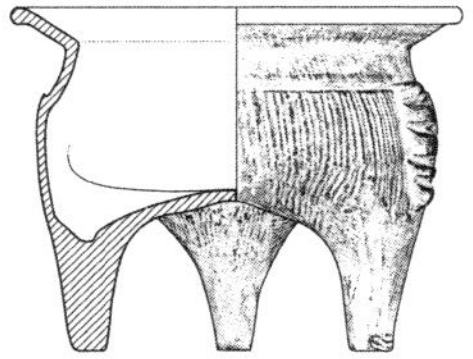	鬲	C	1	石良：1	仿铜鬲。口沿宽平，腹浅，足细长，高裆。腹饰较细绳纹，印痕深而规整。
	Li tripod			Shiliang：1	Bronze style pottery *li*. Broad, flat rim and shallow belly, with long, slender feet, high crotch. Belly covered with fine cord pattern, neat and deep impressions.
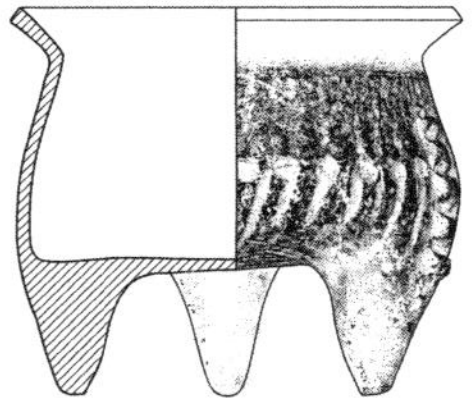			2	周家M1：14（#140）	仿铜鬲。平底小尖足。粗绳纹几近抹平。腹上有一周剔刺纹。
				Zhoujia M1：14 (#140)	Bronze style pottery *li* with flattened crotch and small, pointed feet.　Surface has remnants of thick cord impressions. Body has a single band of incised pattern and protruding flange.
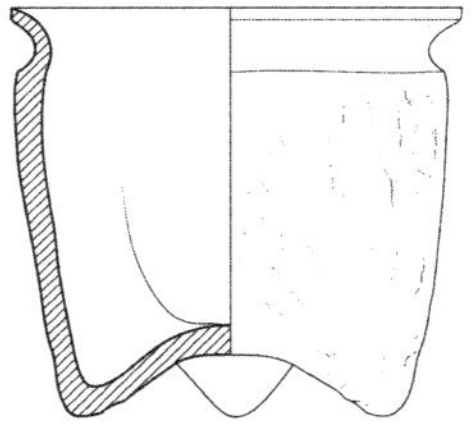	鬲	D	1	周家M2：147	夹砂素面鬲。束颈，深腹，低裆。红褐夹砂，素面粗糙。
	Li tripod			Zhoujia M2：147	Tempered and plain-surface *li*. Reddish-brown pottery *li* with narrow neck, deep body, and flattened low crotch. Rough surface.
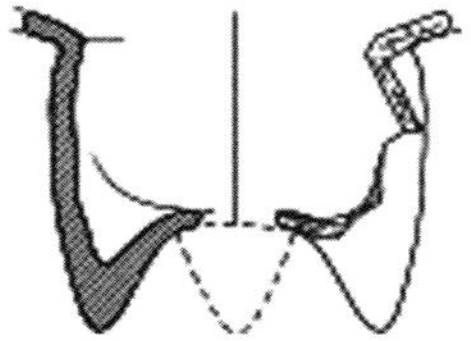			2	和平村北一组：1	折沿，腹较浅。锥状袋足。器体甚小。红褐陶。
				Heping-North 1：1	Plain surface, red pottery *li* with angled rim and shallow body. Drill-shaped pocket feet and very small body.

续表

图形 Image	名称 Name	型 Type	式 Style	举例 Example	器形特点 Description of Characteristics
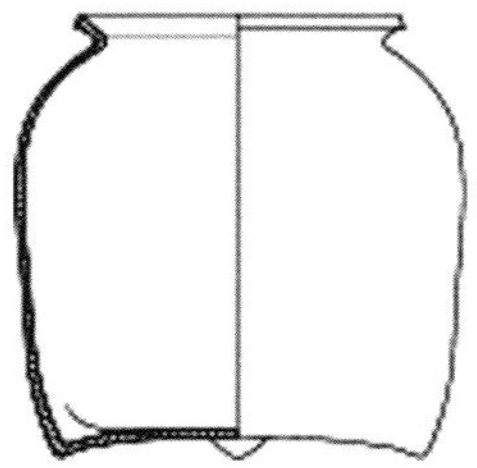			3	H3①：1	侈口方唇，沿面有凹槽。腹深直，肩部明显。裆部低，近平。体形硕大。红褐夹砂，平面平整。
				H3①：1	Plain and tempered, reddish-brown, smooth surface *li*. Mouth flares outward, and rim has concave groove. Body portion is massive, deep, and straight-sided, with clearly differentiated shoulder. Crotch is very low and flat.
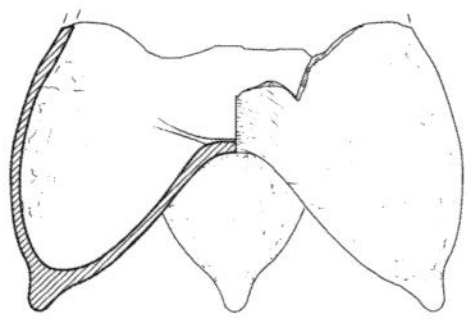	甗	A	1	H20②：3	乳状袋足，有足尖。裆部较高，分隔明显。黑灰素面。
	Yan steamer			H20②：3	Plain surface, black pottery *yan* steamer with high, split crotch, and breast-shaped saddle legs with pointed feet.
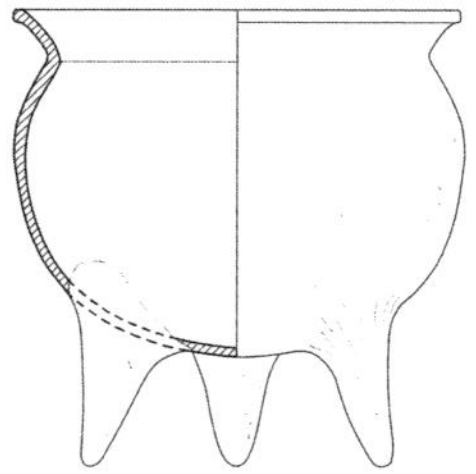	鼎	A	1	周家M2：31（#142）	罐形素面鼎。折沿小方唇。圆尖锥足，较高。红褐夹砂。
	Ding cauldron			Zhoujia M2：31 (#142)	Plain surface, tempered reddish-brown, *guan*-shaped *ding* cauldron. Rim is angled, with a squared lip. Tall, columnar, pointed, drill-shaped feet.
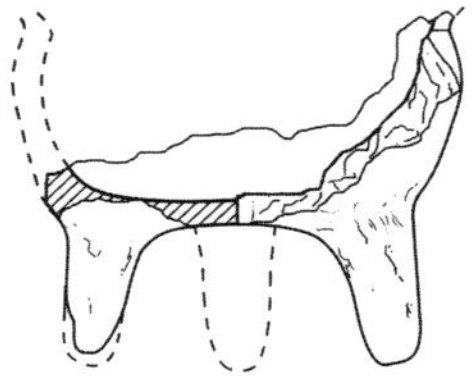			2	H8：1	小鼎。圆锥足。表面粗糙。
				H8：1	Small, plain, coarse surface *ding* with columnar, drill-shaped feet.

续表

图形 Image	名称 Name	型 Type	式 Style	举例 Example	器形特点 Description of Characteristics
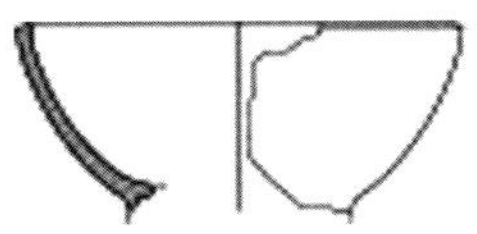	碗	A	1	H2：15	方唇敞口，腹较深。素面。
	Wan Bowl			H2：15	Plain surface bowl with wide opening, squared lip, and deep belly.
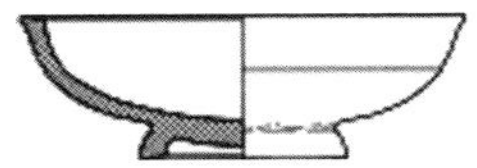			2	H2：1	方唇略外撇，浅腹有折棱，饰一周弦纹。圈足外撇。红褐色夹细沙。
				H2：1	Fine-tempered reddish-brown pottery bowl, with squared lip that flares outward slightly; shallow belly with an angular ridge and a single string ring. Circular base is low and flares outwards.
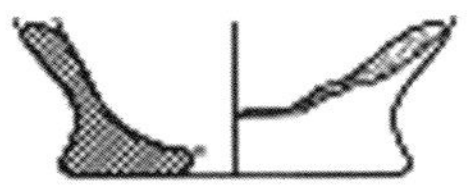		B	1	H16：15	实圈足，足跟较高。胎夹滑石。
				H16：15	Tempered with talc, with tall, circular, solid base.
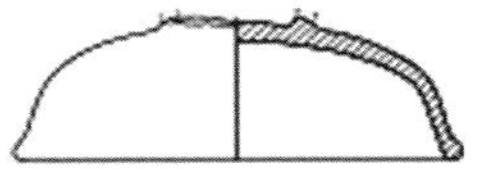	器盖	A	1	H3①：2	圆唇，盖沿微外撇。微鼓，盖顶有圈转细把手。
	Vessel lid			H3①：2	Vessel lid with rounded, flaring lip; top slightly bulging, with a thin, circular handle grip.
			2	H3②：4	大盖。盖沿外撇，外侧下部折。盖顶有粗把手。
				H3②：4	Large vessel lid with flaring rim, and thick, circular handle grip.

续表

图形 Image	名称 Name	型 Type	式 Style	举例 Example	器形特点 Description of Characteristics
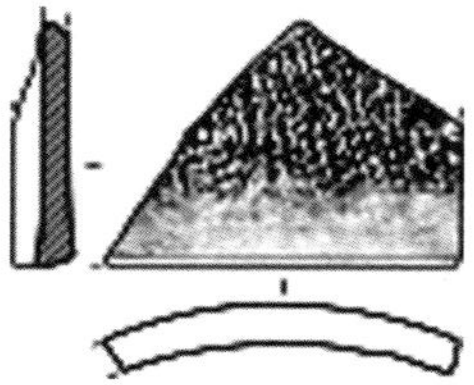	瓦	A	1	H4：11	板瓦，饰麻点绳纹
	Tile			H4：11	Flat tile fragment with sesame-seed pattern cord impressions.
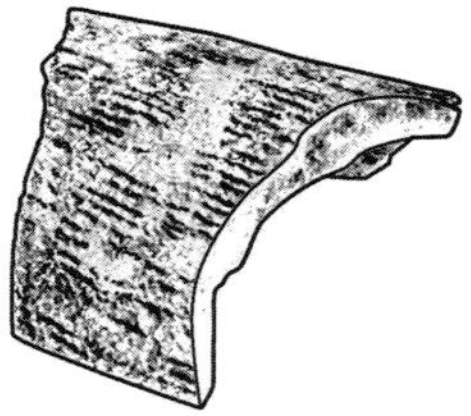		B	1	内城采：53	筒瓦，饰中绳纹。
				Inner City coll.：53	Convex tile fragment (imbrex) with cord impressions.

编号系统："#000""归城：00""石良：00"：龙口市博物馆藏品号。"H00：00""M00：00"：2009年正式发掘单位号。"和平村北一组：00"：盗掘后采集的成组陶器。"张郑：00""内城采：00"：随意地面采集。"7-a21：00"系统地面调查采集。

Number System："#000""Guicheng：00""Shiliang：00"：Collection number designated by the Longkou Museum. "H00：00""M00：00"：2009 Formal excavation unit number. "Heping-N. Group 1：00"：Collections made after tomb looting. "Zhangzheng：00" "Inner City coll.：00"：Random surface collection. "7-a21：00"：Full-coverage surface collection number.

Chapter 10 : Constructing a Frontier Culture: Ceramic Analysis in Guicheng

Li Feng

Section 1: Introduction

The present chapter focuses on the analysis of the ceramic inventory from Guicheng in eastern Shandong, dating to the late Bronze Age (Map Ⅰ.0.1). This is a region that witnessed a high degree of interaction between two cultural traditions: 1) the archaeological culture that was associated with many central sites of the Western Zhou state (1045-771 BCE) in the Wei River valley in Shaanxi Province and spread to a large part of the middle Yellow River reaches after the Zhou conquest of Shang; 2) the indigenous culture of the Jiaodong Peninsula that can be traced back to as early as the late Longshan period. The present chapter suggests that the passage of time provided an axis along which interactions between the Zhou cultural core and the periphery took place. Therefore, a diachronic, or perhaps "processual" approach, looking carefully into the subtle changes that took place over time in the ceramic inventory from Guicheng, can offer a better understanding of what might really have happened in the region's relationship with the Zhou cultural core.

In order to fully understand the long-term dynamics in the relationship between the Zhou cultural core and the indigenous cultural tradition of the Jiaodong Peninsula, I suggest the following three ways to model the processes of cultural acceptance and resilience that took place in a core-periphery relationship, considering both geographical and temporal factors (Fig. Ⅰ.10.1):

Path A, or the "upslope" path, describes a process of cultural acceptance in which elements of a foreign or invasive culture were slowly introduced and accepted by the peripheral region that eventually became acculturated to the core of the invasive culture. This is perhaps the most common scenario of cultural acceptance, particularly in regions that are closer to the "core."

Path B, or the "downslope" path, represents a mode of cultural acceptance that begins with a total or nearly total interruption of the local cultural process by the "sudden" incursion of a foreign culture. As time passed, the strength of the "core" of the foreign culture gradually weakened and this allowed modifications to take place in the periphery to the initially adopted cultural system. The process leads eventually to a reversion of the peripheral culture to the previously dominant indigenous tradition.

Path C, or the "cross-hill" path, entails a process of cultural acceptance that is accompanied by a high degree of resilience in which elements of a foreign or invasive culture are gradually introduced at a high level, winning the favor of the local elites, but they are ultimately unable to overwhelm the indigenous tradition, which at a certain point in the long process will begin to come back with increasing intensity.

The above conceptualization differs significantly from some previous models suggested by scholars in analyzing the relationship between the cultural core and the periphery; for instance, Gil Stein's "Distance-Disparity" model (Stein 1998: 246), which suggests that central control tends to be weakened by increasing distance, in a relationship that he describes as gradual shifting from asymmetric to symmetric. However, Stein's model fails to explain the impact of long-term cultural contact, which is the key question that the present analysis will address.

Section 2: The Guicheng Ceramics and the Specific Research Questions

The majority of the ceramics to be analyzed in this paper came to light in three ways: 1) vessels and sherds collected by the "Sino-American Guicheng Archaeological Team" during the full-coverage surface survey in 2008-2009; 2) ceramics recovered from the test excavation by the team in summer 2009; 3) collections made after reports of looting of tombs in the inner city of Guicheng. In addition, during the extended survey of the Huangshui River valley in Longkou in 2010-2011, the team further gathered a large number of complete or nearly complete vessels from the cemetery site in Zhangzhengjia on the western outskirts of the Longkou city (see Chapter 7). Furthermore, the Longkou Municipal Museum generously allowed us to examine and photograph ceramics in the museum's collection, collected before the Guicheng Project began in 2007. The merging of ceramics from these sources affords us a good basis to analyze the compositional profile as well as typological variations of the Guicheng pottery (Table Ⅰ.10.1). Our ultimate goal is to use these materials to address questions about the specific socio-cultural processes in the Jiaodong Peninsula and its cross-regional interaction with outside cultures, as indicated above. In order to do so, a set of more specific questions must be answered first, based on an empirical analysis of the archaeological data:

(1) Given the special historical and cultural context of the Jiaodong Peninsula, how was the local society changed by the arrival of a new culture, and perhaps a new elite group? Did the material culture in the Guicheng region exhibit significant continuity across the Zhou incursion, or a total rupture of the

indigenous production tradition?

(2) How did the intruding culture and the indigenous culture interact with each other? What changes took place in the indigenous culture as the result of initiatives taken by the indigenous elites or population?

(3) Cultural adaptation takes place as soon as a culture enters a new environment, and the pace of such adaptation is determined by a number of factors, both temporal and spatial. To what degree and in what directions did the Zhou culture modify itself in order to best survive in the new environment of the Jiaodong Peninsula?

(4) In the "Core-Periphery" relationship, to what degree were the changes taking place in the Guicheng region influenced by the social and cultural innovations that took place in the Zhou center? How were the localized Zhou elites related to the Zhou elite society in the central region of the political Western Zhou state?

(5) What was the economic system in Guicheng in which the two cultures each played parts?

These are questions that can be easily brought into studies of cultural contacts in other regions. In Guicheng, the relationship between the localized Zhou elites and their relatives in the Zhou homeland in Shaanxi can also be analyzed on the basis of the bronze inscriptions, but I will leave this for discussion elsewhere (see Part Ⅱ, Chapter 5). With help from what we also learn from the inscribed bronzes from the Guicheng region, I hope that we can at least start to address some of these questions with confidence.

Section 3: The Indigenous Ceramic Tradition

The time before the emergence of settlements with clear Zhou cultural contents on the Jiaodong Peninsula is marked as the Zhenzhumen culture period (see Chapter 1). Cultural remains belonging to Zhenzhumen were first identified at several sites on Long Island off the north shore of the peninsula in 1980 (Yan Wenming 1989: 8-10; Liu Yanchang 2001: 94-104). Later surveys have found Zhenzhumen ceramics over a large geographical region, as far west as Weifang and as far east and south as Rushan on the south coast of the peninsula. In other words, Zhenzhumen is widely distributed over the entire eastern Shandong peninsula (Wang Fuqiang 2006: 107; Zhang Kun 2010: 58-64). In the Guicheng region, Zhenzhumen remains were identified at the Louzizhuang site near the Ma'nan River (Fig. Ⅰ.7.1: 15), located only about 14 km to the west of Guicheng. A small-scale excavation conducted by the Yantai Municipal Museum in 2002 uncovered relatively rich materials (Fig. Ⅰ.10.2) (Wang Fuqiang 2006: 107-114). Our recent survey shows that there are as many as seven sites with Zhenzhumen cultural contents, all located within three kilometers of Louzizhuang (see Chapter 7), suggesting that the area might have been a population center during the Zhenzhumen period. Because no full excavation report of any seriously investigated Zhenzhumen-related site has been published, there are many open questions about this cultural entity, but there seems little doubt that Zhenzhumen represents an important period of cultural development on the Jiaodong Peninsula. The main features of the Zhenzhumen culture can be summarized as follows:

(1) The ceramic assemblage was composed of very limited vessel categories including *li* tripod, *yan* steamer, *guan* jar, *wan* bowl, and *gui* tureen.

(2) All vessels are tempered with coarse or sometimes fine rock pieces, and many contain mica or talc fragments. This feature is not restricted to the cooking vessels, but pertains also to the serving and storage vessels.

(3) More than 80% of the ceramic sherds are red or brown in color. Vessels are unevenly fired, displaying irregular polychromic patterns of change from red to brown to black. All vessels are plain-surfaced and undecorated, and some show traces of hand-sweeping.

(4) Many vessels are irregularly shaped, with no evidence of wheel-turning in their manufacture.

(5) Settlement dimensions are not clear. Large and well-prepared pits were used for storage or dwellings.

(6) The subsistence system depended at least partly on the cultivation of broomcorn millet (Wang Fuqiang 2006: 108).

A number of scholars have also noted the coexistence of a small number of black or grey pottery *li* tripods or *guan* jars, usually decorated with cord patterns, in sites that are of predominantly Zhenzhumen contents. They consider that such pieces were based on original pottery types of Shang origin, suggesting that the Zhenzhumen culture was once in remote contact with the Shang culture in the west (Luan Fengshi 1996: 352; Zhang Kun 2010: 252). In the absence of ^{14}C dates, this link through ceramic typology indicates that Zhenzhumen at least partly overlapped the late Shang in the Yellow River region, although it is still debated as to how far it lasted into the next historical period when the Western Zhou state was the dominant political power in the west. Some scholars think that the Zhenzhumen culture continued to exist as late as the early phase of the mid-Western Zhou in the early tenth century BCE (Liu Yanchang 2001: 101; Zhang Kun 2010: 70). While there is some new support for this late date from the Guicheng excavation (see below), at least in the southeast part of the peninsula the indigenous tradition seems to have persisted in a new culture, the Nanhuangzhuang culture, discovered in Rushan on the south coast of the peninsula in 1976 (Wang Xiping 1987: 21-22).

Section 4: The Intrusion of a New Culture

With the arrival of the tenth century BCE, the material culture in eastern Shandong entered a new era. The overall image of the local pottery assemblage on the Jiaodong Peninsula changed from predominantly red or brown to grey or black as the mainstream fashion in pottery, now evidently manufactured using a fast wheel. The great majority of vessels are now neatly shaped, decorated with rings or cord-impressions, and apparently fired at a higher temperature (Fig. Ⅰ.10.3). They are very different from the plain surface of the Zhenzhumen pottery, which was always tempered with sand. The entire pottery inventory can be divided into two halves according to body material: tempered pottery, usually cooking vessels, and untempered, usually serving or storage vessels. By the same token, the functions of vessels were also more clearly defined. It seems that the sway of this new ceramic manufacturing tradition was broad, affecting a large area in the middle and northern parts of the Jiaodong Peninsula, although the degree to which a particular local area was affected by this adventitious culture might have varied dramatically (Fig. Ⅰ.10.4). It is also evident, as will be sufficiently demonstrated below, that the source of this new culture was in the west, originating in the middle Yellow River region, which by the mid-eleventh century BCE had become the core of the newly rising Western Zhou state (1045-771 BCE).

More importantly, the emergence of this new ceramic tradition on the Jiaodong Peninsula was accompanied by a series of changes that took place in the local society of eastern Shandong. The most significant is the rise of megasites such as Guicheng, Dongqucheng, Cunliji, and Qianheqian, located at a maximum distance of 100 km from one another (Fig. Ⅰ.10.4). There is no reliable information on the site size of the preceding Zhenzhumen period due to the poor publication situation, but the Zhenzhumen site itself is estimated to have an area of 5,000 m^2 (Luan Fengshi 1996), and the Louzizhuang site near Guicheng in our estimation has an area of 30,000 m^2 (see Chapter 7). Even earlier, Zhaogezhuang, the largest site of the Yueshi period on the Jiaodong Peninsula, measures about 40,000 m^2 (Zhongguo shehui Kexueyuan Kaogu yanjiusuo Shandong dui 1986, 448). They should be close to the peak of the site area of the Neolithic to early Bronze Age in eastern Shandong. In contrast, the Guicheng site measures 8,000,000 m^2; Dongqucheng and Cunliji are estimated at 190,000 m^2 and 300,000 m^2 respectively (Chapter 7). There is a major gap between these megasites, which are concentrations of both population and material goods, and the earlier sites. In fact, each of these megasites was surrounded by smaller site-clusters and cemeteries in its neighborhood. The societies centered on these megasites were clearly at a different level of social development from the village-level communities that were focused on the earlier sites. In addition to their gigantic site-size, the archaeological data from them are also qualitatively different in a number of ways:

(1) The existence of rammed earth defensive walls surrounding the site core as in Dongqucheng, or the entire city area as in Guicheng.

(2) Large clusters of rammed-earth palace-platforms representing the residence of the ruler or the locus of state power, such as those found in Guicheng (Sino-American Joint Guicheng 2011: 33-34);

(3) Elite burials that often contain luxury goods such as high-quality bronze vessels; the Guicheng excavation also provided new evidence for bronze-casting workshops in the city.

(4) Elite literacy was represented by inscriptions on the bronzes and some pottery vessels from the region.

What we have in the archaeological record of the Jiaodong Peninsula from the tenth century BCE on evidently represents a break rather than continuation at all levels of the preceding Zhenzhumen period. The inscriptions on bronzes, both from the region and from the Zhou centers in the west, co-reference a series of campaigns into eastern Shandong conducted by the Western Zhou court together with its regional states (Li Feng 2006: 304-314). The motives for these campaigns are open to interpretation, but the inscriptions show that the capture of sea salt and cowries was very likely a priority. Cowries were the main currency used in Zhou society and there must have been a strong demand for cowries from the Jiaodong Peninsula at the Zhou court. Viewed in this broad historical context, Guicheng and other urban centers were probably focuses of the Zhou cultural enclaves in a foreign environment. The people who carried the "new" ceramic tradition from the west might not all have been ethnic Zhou, but might have included individuals and groups of various ethnic backgrounds who had adopted the Zhou material culture and acted alongside the Zhou elites, as the Zhou were themselves such a mixed community. But there seems little doubt that the expansion of the Western Zhou state was an important driving force behind this cultural move from the west to the east.

Section 5: Ceramic Sequence and the Date of Guicheng

Despite the frequent surfacing of ceramic vessels in Guicheng and its surroundings in the past, the development of the ceramic tradition in the region was poorly understood due to the lack of stratigraphic testing. In this regard, the test excavation we conducted in Summer 2009 in the south part of the inner city of Guicheng offered solid new grounds for us to clarify the compositional as well as typological transition of ceramics in Guicheng or in the entire Longkou region. From the twenty stratigraphic units we excavated, eight pits (H2, H3, H4, H8, H9, H18, H19, and H20) are selected for analysis because their ceramic contents are richer and more representative than those from other units. The stratigraphic relations between different pit units have been fully mapped out in Chapter 5.

Here, I will consider only the immediate subsurface contexts in which these selected pits are located. On the whole, it is evident that the ceramic inventory under discussion largely reflects three stages of development (Figs. Ⅰ.10.12):

1. Stage Ⅰ: Pit H20

Pit H20 is the earliest unit uncovered during the excavation. It was dug directly into the virgin soil and partly also breaks into the rammed inner city wall. The southern portion of H20 is found underneath stratum 3 in Trench 2, and in the north it is intruded into by pit H21. At the bottom of H20 we found an A1-style *gui* tureen, which is the earliest example of the *gui* category ever found in eastern Shandong (Table Ⅰ.10.5). The upper stratum of H20 offered three examples of the A1-style *li* tripod, which has three hollow lobes and a low crotch, previously unknown on the Jiaodong Peninsula, and not even seen in the entire Shandong region. A *dou* pedestal dish with a thick stem (A1) was also found in the upper stratum of H20, along with deep *pen* basins with long rims that slowly turn outwards, and large *guan* jars with broad and round shoulders (Fig. Ⅰ.10.5). Sherds from H20 are mostly decorated with cord patterns of varying widths that are all neatly pressed and show clearly traceable bands (Figs. Ⅰ.5.52, Ⅰ.5.53, Ⅰ.5.54, Ⅰ.5.55, and Ⅰ.5.58). There is no doubt that ceramic types and sherds from pit H20 constitute the earliest pottery assemblage ever found on the Jiaodong Peninsula.

2. Stage Ⅱ: Pits H18, H19

There is no direct relation between pits H18 or H19 and H20. However, pit H19 breaks into pit H21, which in turn breaks into H20 in its northen part. Pit H18, on the other hand, slightly trims off the east edge of H19, but the ceramics from the two pits are roughly contemporaneous. Apparently, both pits H19 and H18 are stratigraphically later than pit H20, and this matches well with the relative dates of the ceramics from the three pits. The most typical type that frequently appears in the two pits is the shallow *dou* pedestal dish of B1 style. Examples of style B1 sometimes show a folding line on the oblique wall towards the bottom of the dish, and the trumpet-like base usually has a sharp ridge in its middle section. Although not a single complete *gui* vessel has been unearthed from the two pits, the upper part of a *gui* from H18 and the base of a *gui* from H19 no doubt resembled the A6-style *gui* tureen in Table Ⅰ.10.1, which is a later development of the A1 *gui* tureen. Also very characteristic is a small-mouthed *guan* jar with a wide and oblique shoulder decorated with multiple rings, defined as A2-style in Table Ⅰ.10.1. The small *pen* basins with outward-turning rim from the two pits are also representative of their time (Fig. Ⅰ.10.6). The majority of the sherds found in H18 and H19 are still decorated with clear cord patterns, but sherds that exhibit shallow and often discontinuous tracks of cords also appeared (Figs. Ⅰ.5.46, Ⅰ.5.49).

3. Stage Ⅲ: Pits H3, H2, H4, H8, H9

Pits H3, H2, and H4 are the latest units uncovered during the excavation. H3 is located at the north-center of Trench 1; it opens under stratum 1 and breaks into stratum 3 and other units. H2 is located in the north part of Trench 2, and it breaks into pit H16, which in turn breaks into pits H18 and H19 of Stage Ⅱ. Pit H4 is located in the southern part of Trench 2. It opens under a modern irrigation trench and breaks into a thin layer of water borne sediment under which are found a number of other units including pits H9 and H12. In Trench 1, pits H8 and H9 are directly intruded into by H3; in fact, H9 opens under stratum 3 which H3 breaks into. However, sherds from these units are all very similar despite the units being segregated in stratigraphy by a deposit layer – stratum 3. This suggests that the units that break into stratum 3 and pits H8 and H9 beneath it were probably all formed within a relatively short period of time.

As will soon be discussed below, the Guicheng pottery inventory in this late stage had taken on visible influences from the indigenous manufacturing tradition. This is most evident in the large number of plain-surfaced and reddish-brown tempered sherds that belong to the category of *li* tripod. However, the typological feature of this D3-style *li* tripod still followed the overall trend of development of *li* in the Yellow River region that became increasingly lower and nearly lost its three hollow lobes. *Dou* stemmed pedestal dishes in this stage also underwent significant modifications: on the one hand, the trumpet-based *dou* that was common in Stage Ⅱ had by now become very slender, as seen in style B2. On the other hand, *dou* with a straight, thin stem began to appear in a number of forms, all plain-surfaced. For instance, style C3 often has a deeper dish with a round smooth profile and sometimes even an outward curve; style C2 has a nearly hemispherical dish with a wide and low base. Characteristic of Stage Ⅲ are also large vessel lids, tubular support bases with multiple rings, and the *wan* bowl with a low circular base (Fig. Ⅰ.10.7). Pottery sherds from this stage are predominantly decorated with shallow and disorganized cord patterns. Some appear like fine or coarse fishnet on the ink-rubbings. Some pits of Stage Ⅲ also yielded sherds with clearly visible printed tracks of cords, but they are most likely to have surfaced from early strata and were reburied in later pits (Figs. Ⅰ.5.12, Ⅰ.5.15, and Ⅰ.5.18).

Given the limit of ceramics from controlled excavation, it would be best to leave the task of a full periodization of Guicheng pottery to the future. But it is possible to define the above developmental stages based on the stratigraphic evidence we currently have. It is above all significant that the Guicheng pottery in Stages Ⅰ-Ⅱ followed closely the trends of typological development in the Zhou central region, particularly the middle Wei River valley in Shaanxi. In fact, many types found in Guicheng are virtually indistinguishable from their counterparts in Shaanxi. The high degree of similarity makes cross-dating possible even though the two regions are separated by more than 1,000 km. But as the bronze inscriptions show, there was close communication between the Zhou centers and the Guicheng region. Inferring from standards for dating already established in the Zhou centers, for instance, the Zhangjiapo cemetery in the Zhou capital Feng (Zhongguo shehui kexueyuan kaogu yanjiusuo Fengxi gongzuodui 1980: 483-485; Zhongguo shehui kexueyuan kaogu yanjiusuo 1999: 348-358), we can date the ceramics of Stage Ⅰ in Guicheng to roughly the late phase of the early Western Zhou through the early mid Western Zhou; in historical chronology, this time span falls between 1000 BCE and 920 BCE. Ceramics of Stage Ⅱ in Guicheng include very typical types of vessels that are commonly found in late Western Zhou tombs in Shaanxi; therefore, their dating to the late Western Zhou period or slightly later seems well grounded. In historical chronology, this would fall roughly between 860 BCE and 750 BCE. Ceramics from Stage Ⅲ, by comparison with pottery types in Henan or vessels that were found together with datable bronzes in Shandong, can be dated to the Spring and Autumn period, falling between 750 BCE and 500 BCE. Some pottery types in Guicheng may date even later to the Warring States period (480-221 BCE), but they mostly came from the surface survey, and we did not encounter such late units during the test-excavation in 2009.

^{14}C dating offers another method to evaluate the date of Guicheng. Among the units discussed above, four pits, H 20, H3, H8, and H9, yielded carbonized samples that have been dated. However, these figures are systematically skewed when correlated with dates based on ceramic comparisons (below). Archaeologists sometimes assume a time lapse rate for artifacts found in the periphery in relation to their counterparts in the cultural center, on the assumption that a certain period of time would be needed for their designs to be transmitted across a long distance. However, the situation here is the opposite, as the ^{14}C dates of the carbon samples from the Guicheng pits are about 80 to100 years earlier than the ceramic dates, based on typological comparisons with the center. The discrepancy is systematic and its explanation will require more study. For now, this suggests at least two things: 1) the ceramic sequence suggested above cannot be overturned; 2) the actual dates of the three stages suggested above should not be pushed later because the ^{14}C dating puts them much earlier.

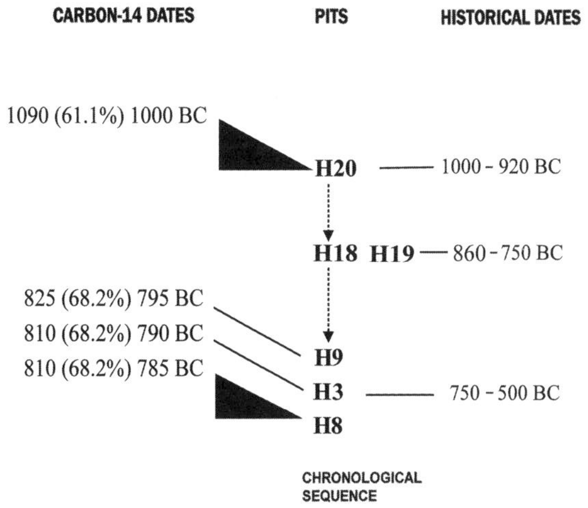

Section 6: Element Analysis

It has been sufficiently shown that, at least in the early stages, the Guicheng pottery closely followed the typological standards invented in the Zhou central area in Shaanxi, and this can be explained by the frequent communication between the Guicheng region and the Zhou centers as suggested by the bronze inscriptions. However, despite the typological similarities between the two regions separated by some 1,000 km, it is inevitable that the Zhou culture, once it entered the new environment of the eastern peninsula, would have undergone modifications. The issue is in what directions, or to what degree, was the intruding material culture originating in the Zhou central region modified? How can we detect the changes that occurred in the process of adaptation to the new environment? Here I suggest three ways to look into this problem: 1) even though the peripheral Zhou culture shared the same set of pottery types with the center, the relative significance of these types could be meaningfully restructured to reflect the lifestyle of the peripheral communities. In other words, although certain types are common to the two regions, they might have formed different arrangements of pyramids; 2) Because of changes in the natural environment, especially in soil conditions, the composition of the body material of the ceramics could alter in meaningful ways; 3) The same type of pottery vessels could undergo significant modifications, giving rise to new styles and forms.

1. The Pyramids of Types

For comparison, we have chosen the recently published data from the excavation of the Qijiacun jade workshop in Fufeng, Shaanxi Province. The statistics are derived from sherds excavated from eighteen storage pits and one subterranean house foundation excavated in 2002 (Shaanxi sheng kaogu yanjiuyuan et al. 2010: 34-430). This new information enables us to accurately define the typological/sherd profile of the material culture at centers of the Western Zhou state in the Wei River valley in Shaanxi. Figures of four most common types in Zhou tradition, *li* tripod, *gui* tureen, *dou* stemmed pedestal dish, and *guan* jar, are calculated to yield their combined average percentage among all sherds whose vessel types can be determined for each of the three periods (early Western Zhou: 50.6%; mid Western Zhou: 52%; late Western Zhou: 66.85%). Based on this, the percentage of each of the four types in each period is calculated (Fig. Ⅰ.10.8, upper). The Qijia 2002 figures are compared to three sets of figures derived from the test excavation in Guicheng in 2009: 1) pit H20 that represents Stage Ⅰ dates roughly to the late phase of the early Western Zhou to the early phase of the mid Western Zhou; 2) pits H18 and H19 that represent Stage Ⅱ in Guicheng, correspond to the late Western Zhou period; 3) the rest of the excavated units belong to the Spring and Autumn period (Fig. Ⅰ.10.8, lower). The two sets of the data were derived using the same method, and the comparison yields significant differences in the compositional frequency between the two regions:

The comparison suggests that *li* tripod is undoubtedly the most important type of pottery, accounting for 55.69% to 57.9% of the combined total (100%) of the four types (or 28.18% to 37.3% of the total of the identifiable sherds) at Qijia. To these are added the percentages of *guan* jars (21.72% to 32.49%), making it clear that the Zhou ceramic tradition in the Wei River valley was above all centered on the combination of *li* and *guan*, known for a very long time since the pre-dynastic Zhou period. However, in Guicheng, although the *li* tripod has a high percentage in Stage Ⅰ, accounting for 51.92% of the combined total, it sharply declined to only 8.77% in Stage Ⅱ (late Western Zhou), and thereafter remained of lower frequency. On the other hand, the *gui* tureen, although it was significant in the Zhou centers during the early Western Zhou, accounting for 10.65% of the combined total, it declined during the mid Western Zhou and totally disappeared from the Qijia inventory during the late Western Zhou. By contrast, in Guicheng *gui* tureens continued to increase in number from 17.3% in Stage Ⅰ to 21.05% in Stage Ⅱ and to 24.9% in Stage Ⅲ. This plus the high percentage of *dou* pedestal dishes, accounting for 40.35% in Stage Ⅱ, clearly shows that there was a shift from *li-guan* to *gui-dou* in terms of demand in the Guicheng community over the entire period of occupation, the latter accounting for a combined rate of 52% in Stage Ⅲ. Thus this completed the transition from the *li-guan* centered pottery assemblage of the Zhou culture to the *dou-gui* centered pottery assemblage characterizing eastern Shandong. The cultural meaning of this shift of centrality from cooking/storage vessels to serving vessels needs future study to explain.

2. The Body Material

Next, we can compare the body material of the ceramics at the two sites, Qijia in Shaanxi and Guicheng in Shandong. For this purpose, the ceramic body material is differentiated into four categories: 1) tempered reddish-brown pottery; 2) tempered grey-to-back pottery; 3) untempered reddish-brown pottery; and 4) untempered greyish-black pottery. At the Qijia site, some purely black-surfaced sherds were also identified, but their number is very small and statistically inconsequential in this comparison (Fig. Ⅰ.10.9).

In Guicheng, as in Qijia, untempered grey and black sherds make up the majority of the sherd population (64.5-70.82%). This is in sharp contrast to the previous Zhenzhumen culture in the Jiaodong Peninsula, suggesting that Guicheng pottery by and large belongs to the Zhou culture tradition. In fact, Stage Ⅰ in Guicheng, represented by pit H20, shows a profile very similar to Qijia, although the latter has a higher pyramid of tempered reddish-brown sherds. Untempered red ceramics are lacking in Stage Ⅰ in Guicheng. However, over time this ceramic system gradually expanded and accounts for 3.77-3.94% in Guicheng Stages Ⅱ-Ⅲ. Similarly, tempered reddish-brown ceramics also increased from 1.52% in Stage Ⅰ to 4.55% in Stage Ⅱ and to 7.25% in Stage Ⅲ. The tempered and untempered reddish-brown ceramics combined increased from 1.52% in Stage Ⅰ to 11.02% in Stage Ⅲ. On the other hand, greyish-black tempered ceramics declined over time from 34.73% in Stage Ⅰ to 18.79% in Stage Ⅲ, which is a very meaningful decrease. However, in Qijia, both tempered and untempered reddish-brown ceramics decreased over time from a combined 30.06% in the early Western Zhou to a combined 10.73% in the late Western Zhou period, as the tempered greyish-black ceramics increased from 21.69% in the early Western Zhou to 30.36% in the late Western Zhou period. In other words, the proportional change of the two ceramic color systems in Guicheng and in Qijia took exactly opposite directions. In some units in Guicheng, for instance pit H3, 11.60% of the sherds are tempered reddish-brown, plus another 12.20% of ceramics are untempered reddish-brown, amounting to 23.80% of the total ceramic sherd population. The physical appearance of sherds from H3 is very different from that of H20 of Stage Ⅰ, in which greyish-black sherds count for 98.73% of the total. We consider this gradual increase in reddish-brown ceramics in the Guicheng region to be the result of increasing influence from the indigenous pottery manufacturing tradition that was kept alive through the entire Guicheng period.

3. Typological Variation

Pottery types originally introduced from the west also went through significant modifications in Guicheng, or perhaps, broadly in eastern Shandong. Typologically, as time passed, Guicheng pottery increasingly diverged from the mainstream Zhou culture. Below, I will discuss such modifications centering on the four types, *gui* tureen, *dou* stemmed pedestal dish, *li* tripod, *guan* jar; and to this group is added the *ding* cauldron, which does not appear very often in the Zhou culture repertory (Table Ⅰ.10.1).

***Gui* tureen**: The A1-style *gui* (Fig. Ⅰ.10.5, upper-left) from H20 can be considered the ancestral type for the subsequent development of the *gui* tureen in Guicheng. As a serving vessel, the *gui* had had a long history in the Shang culture, but the A1-style *gui* with a long rim had already fully adapted to the Zhou culture in Shaanxi during the early phase of the early Western Zhou. It was a bit of surprise to find this type 1,000 km away in eastern Shandong. From the A1-style styles A2, A3, A4, and A5 further developed (Fig. Ⅰ.10.10), all being variants of a typical high-base *gui*, dating roughly to the mid to late Western Zhou period. Some similar forms were found in Shaanxi, but such high-base *gui* were more numerous and display a much wider range of variation in eastern Shandong. Therefore, the form can be considered an independent development on the Jiaodong Peninsula. In the process, local potters seem to have experimented with many different forms, including two other types of *gui*: B1 with a round body, and C1 with a hemispherical body. Their body designs clearly depart from the

Zhou tradition as they might have taken on a strong influence from the indigenous pottery tradition in the region. But they were found together with styles A3 and A4 in tomb no. 2 in Zhoujia, so they were contemporaneous forms manufactured during the late Western Zhou. From the same tomb, as many as thirty-one *gui* of various styles were unearthed (Tang Luting and Jiang Guojun 1989: 316-318). From the A-type the A6-style narrow-base *gui* with a straight-up body was further developed, represented by a large number of fragments during the Guicheng surface survey. This suggests that the high-base *gui* was gradually standardized, roughly by the beginning of the eighth century BCE.

***Dou* pedestal dish**: The A1-style *dou* with a straight and wide base are similar to *dou* dishes frequently found in early Western Zhou tombs in the Zhou centers. From it were developed various forms of wide-base *dou* including A2, A3, A4, A5, all variants of A-type used in Guicheng during the late Western Zhou period, and not seen in the Zhou central region. Similar to the situation with the *gui* tureen, Guicheng potters seem to have experimented with a wide range of options during the late Western Zhou period, resulting in three additional series of *dou* vessels: 1) style B1 with a narrow-base and a ridge at its mid-section, matching closely the standard *dou* vessel used in the Zhou centers during the late Western Zhou; 2) C1-style with a hemispherical body, found in Zhoujia tomb no. 2; 3) style D1-D4 with a very shallow dish on top of a wide trumpet-like base (Fig. Ⅰ.10.11). From style B1 were developed B2 and B3; from C1 were developed C2 and C3. These forms date approximately to Stage Ⅲ, the Spring and Autumn period. Finally, style B4 with a shallow, flat dish and straight, high stem was developed even later from B2 or B3, likely dating to the Warring States period and occurring only rarely in Guicheng (Wang Fuqiang 2002: 172).

***Li* tripod:** The development of the *li* tripod in Guicheng shows a perfect situation of co-existence between two ceramic traditions. Hollow-lobed A1 *li* with neat cord impressions such as those from H20 (Fig. Ⅰ.10.5, lower right) were doubtless introduced from the Zhou central region. Interestingly, B1-style *li* with joined legs and a slightly sunken crotch was also found in Guicheng, but almost nowhere else outside the Wei River valley. This illustrates the intimate relationship between the Guicheng pottery and the Wei River pottery in the early stage. B2, B3, B4, B5, and B6 show subsequent development from the original types introduced from the Zhou centers, in particular the B6-style with three sharp solid legs is compatible with the *li* vessel, popular, for instance, in Qufu in western Shandong during the late Western Zhou period (Shandong sheng wenwu kaogu yanjiusuo, 1982: pl. 33). Further, C1-style *fang tong li* (bronze-imitating pottery *li*) was introduced from the west sometime during the late Western Zhou, from which developed the C2 style. Thus, despite declining numbers, the *li* tripod in the Guicheng region was actually a very diverse and somewhat unstable body of forms. The local *li* production tradition was represented by the D series, characterized by its traditional plain surface and reddish-brown tempered body: D1 and D2 are roughly from the late Western Zhou period. In fact, the large D3 style from pit H3 (Fig. Ⅰ.10.7, upper-left) combines the indigenous features of *li* with the design of *li* tripods in the Zhou culture, dating roughly to the mid-

Spring and Autumn period.

***Guan* jar:** The development of jars in the Zhou culture was itself a complex story due to its complex origins. Style A1 in Guicheng with a round shoulder is largely similar to the small-mouthed jars often found in early Western Zhou tombs in the Zhou centers, but it rarely appears in the former Shang culture influenced regions, such as Henan and western Shandong. However, once in Guicheng, jars began to take a different direction of development from their counterparts in Shaanxi; that is, they gradually developed a very broad and sloping shoulder and a round bottom. This trend is evident on both small jars such as A2 and A3, and on large jars like B1 and B2 styles. But their decorative patterns are still similar to contemporaneous jars elsewhere in the Yellow River regions in the west, characterized by multiple rings on the shoulder and cord-patterns on the lower body. The number of such *guan* in the Guicheng region is high. On the other hand, a few cases of indigenous styles of *guan* were also found, for instance, style E1, with small buttons below the rim from pit H20.

***Ding* cauldron:** The *Ding* caldron does not belong to the Zhou cultural repertory. The typical case is the A1-style cauldron from tomb no. 2 in Zhoujia, dating to the late Western Zhou period. It is characterized by a round and deep belly and three solid, conical feet, plain surfaced. In the surface survey and test excavation in Guicheng, legs and rims that possibly belonged to this type of *ding* cauldron were frequently encountered. They are universally tempered and reddish-brown in color, clearly belonging to the indigenous pottery manufacturing tradition.

Section 7: The Indigenous Tradition and the Model of Cultural Acceptance in Guicheng

It was shown above that the indigenous pottery-making tradition, though a much thinner stream, was never discontinued in Guicheng and was perhaps much stronger in smaller settlements in the suburbs of Guicheng. The full-coverage surface survey suggests that pottery sherds that can be identified with the indigenous tradition are not restricted to any particular sectors of Guicheng, but are widely distributed over the entire site area, being mixed up with sherds of the largely Zhou culture affiliate (Fig. Ⅰ.6.19). The indigenous sherds are identified in the majority of cases by their unique body materials which are always tempered and show the mixture of sands with mica or quartz, and sometimes also coarse talc pieces. This feature of body-build makes the indigenous sherds less firm and easy to break, and the color on a single vessel is often uneven. Therefore, by comparison with the fine and often solid sherds of the Zhou culture, these indigenous sherds are not difficult to distinguish.

In the 2009 test excavation in Guicheng, sherds with indigenous features were unearthed from almost all stratigraphic units. For instance, from as early as H20, the lower part of a *yan* steamer was excavated, which is tempered and colored dark-brown mixed with red, almost identical to a *yan* steamer of the Zhenzhumen culture (Fig. Ⅰ.10.2). This suggests that the Zhenzhumen culture might indeed have overlapped the Zhou culture while the latter was invading the region during the late phase of the early Western Zhou, and might have persisted in the region that was then dominated by the Zhou culture. From the same pit were also unearthed the foot of a plain surface *li* tripod and a small-mouthed *guan* jar with two circles of small buttons under the rim. These are clearly differentiated from the other types and sherds from pit H20. Indigenous sherds of identifiable vessel types were also excavated from other pits, including H19, H12, H8, H9, H16, etc. From pits in the later stage, for instance, H3, a number of types with mixed indigenous and Zhou cultural features were unearthed. On the whole, despite the existence of different vessel types in the indigenous tradition, they were by and large limited to cooking vessels, most importantly *li* tripods and *ding* cauldrons. A large number of sandy legs belonging to either *li* or *ding* of the indigenous tradition have been found in the excavation and during the full-coverage surface survey (Fig. Ⅰ.6.18).

Above we also saw that the proportion of indigenous sherds (mostly tempered reddish-brown) increased over time from Stage Ⅰ to Stage Ⅲ. Particularly from pit H3, 9.64% of the sherds are tempered reddish-brown, and can be identified with the indigenous pottery tradition. During the intensive surface survey, a total of 717 sherds were identified as indigenous, accounting for about 5% of the total number of sherds collected. This matches well the percentage of the tempered reddish-brown sherds yielded by the excavation, or 4.44% on average. But the dating of such sherds, if not excavated from stratigraphic units, is rather difficult.

This brings us to the questions raised at the beginning: How did the indigenous culture respond to the incursion of an ostensibly foreign culture? And, how did the Zhou culture adapt to a cultural environment that was previously dominated by an indigenous ceramic tradition? We consider that the cultural development in the Guicheng region during the late Bronze Age followed **Path B** closely, the "downslope" model of cultural acceptance and resilience. It has been shown that the emergence of the Zhou culture in Guicheng represented a high degree of interruption of the indigenous tradition represented by the Zhenzhumen culture. It seems likely that the Zhou cultural elements were transplanted to the region from the Zhou centers lying as far as 1,000 km to the west, and the bronze inscriptions suggest that this Zhou culture incursion coincided with a peak of efforts by the Western Zhou state to conquer eastern Shandong. It has been shown that certain ceramic types resemble their counterparts in the Zhou centers in Shaanxi very closely, including types that were rarely found in the formerly Shang cultural zone (mainly Henan, Hebei, and western Shandong), that actually separated the two regions of cultural contact.

However, given the region's long distance from the Zhou cultural "core," once in the new environment of the Jiaodong Peninsula the Zhou culture began to undergo significant modifications as the local potters in Guicheng experimented with many new forms of ceramics, displaying a wide range of typological variation. This was a process of cultural adjustment and adaptation that took place largely within the chronological confines of the late phase of the mid-Western Zhou and the late Western Zhou (ca. 9th-8th centuries BCE). It has been suggested that high typological variation in ceramics is usually related to a higher degree of social mobility and interaction between the population communities that used them (Underhill 2002: 28, 177). This might indeed have been the case, as Guicheng in its historical context possibly served as a frontier base for the expansion of the Western Zhou state and might have received visitor groups from different parts of the Zhou world. But the cultural transformation gradually led the localized and perhaps mixed population to diverge from Zhou cultural practices in the west. The political explanation for this trend lies in the gradual weakening of Zhou royal power and the loosening of order in the Western Zhou state from the ninth century BCE onward, which made it harder and harder for the Zhou cultural core to continue to project influence to the periphery, or to attract the peripheral populations with new cultural innovations taking place in the central region. This was a process that can be demonstrated with both archaeological and inscriptional evidence (Li Feng 2006: 91-140).

The indigenous cultural tradition represented by the early Zhenzhumen culture, despite the interruption, had continued to exist in a thin line in such central sites like Guicheng, but possibly was much stronger at smaller settlements located at a distance from the centers. Some previous Zhenzhumen cultural sites including Louzizhuang might have continued to be occupied by a population that had an indigenous cultural orientation and communicated with the Zhou culture dominant in Guicheng. It was never completely missing from the cultural spectrum of the region. Instead, as time passed, the modified Zhou cultural tradition centered on Guicheng gradually took on elements from this indigenous cultural reservoir. This resulted in the emergence of many hybrid ceramic types and over time an increase in the number of indigenous sherds uncovered by both the surface survey and the test-excavation in Guicheng. On the whole, cultural hybridization was the result of this long process of contact, acceptance, and resilience, as shown by the ceramics from pit H3, which are a typical expression of this cultural image. Politically we know that during Stage Ⅲ Guicheng was occupied by an eilte group called "Lai" in the inscriptions and the transmitted historical texts. The Lai were known to be an indigenous people of the Jiaodong Peninsula. In this period, Guicheng expanded and rose to become one of the most prominent Bronze Age cities in all of Shandong, and the most prominent urban center on the Jiaodong Peninsula.

Section 8: The Economic System

The above analysis of the cultural process centering on Guicheng leads us to the final question of this chapter: What was the economic system under which the two ceramic production traditions operated, since, as the preceding discussion has made clear, the products of both traditions were used throughout Guicheng's existence and possibly beyond? Were the indigenous ceramic types manufactured in the same workshops that also produced types of Zhou cultural tradition, or were they made elsewhere and brought into Guicheng through a stable trading system? Evidently, this question cannot be solved by archaeological fieldwork, so we had recourse to scientific laboratory work, which we hoped could offer some direct evidence. In 2007, we packed a first section of twenty-three ceramic sherds collected on the surface at Guicheng and sent them for analysis in the Geological Laboratory of the University of Wisconsin, Madison. The collection took into consideration how representative the body-material variations of the sherds were with regard to the two ceramic traditions. In 2011, an additional installment of twenty-four sherds was carefully selected from the stratigraphic units and added to the earlier samples for analysis. Professor James B. Stoltman was responsible for the thin sections and the subsequent analysis of the data (see Chapter 9).

The result of the analysis is very significant. In all, Stoltman identifies three meaningful differences between sherds that belong to the two ceramic traditions. First, while the potters of the Zhou tradition used only granite as tempering material, the indigenous potters seem to have had the freedom to use three different types of natural rock: granite, schist, and amphibolite. This seems to suggest that the indigenous potters might have had more intimate knowledge of local resources. Second, the Zhou tradition potters used much less temper but larger temper size in contrast to the indigenous potters, who used a higher percentage of temper but smaller sized. The Zhou potters, on the whole, seem to have been more restricted by their long tradition or by certain workshop rules with regard to the selection and use of tempers. Third, a very meaningful finding is the different body pastes used in the two traditions: The Zhou-tradition ceramics contain much siltier paste in both tempered (mean 11.3%) and untempered vessels (mean 15.2%). The mean percentage of silt in the indigenous ceramic paste was only 6.7%. The distinction is very clear and it suggests that the Zhou and indigenous-tradition potters had a marked tendency to exploit different clay resources, loessic sediment in the former, and alluvial in the latter.

At the very least, Stoltman's analysis suggests that the Zhou tradition ceramics and the indigenous ceramics, both found in Guicheng, were manufactured in different workshop systems, probably run by two different groups of people. It is certainly possible that certain indigenous pottery workshops were located in Guicheng, but, particularly in the early period when Guicheng was small and had a predominantly Zhou ceramic inventory, it is more likely that the indigenous pottery vessels were made at smaller settlements surrounding Guicheng and traded into the city for consumption. Since the indigenous types are mostly limited to cooking vessels such as *li*, *ding*, and *yan*, and the indigenous potters were more familiar with, or perhaps had more freedom to exploit, local resources, by making their vessels at lower cost, they might have been able to find a good market among the Zhou oriented population in Guicheng. Later on, in the process of urbanization, the expansion of the city's territory might have absorbed many of these indigenous workshops into the economic system of Guicheng. This again explains why over time the indigenous cultural elements increased in Guicheng, or the two traditions merged, as reflected best by the Path-B model of cultural acceptance.

On the other hand, Stoltman's analysis also raised some important questions. For instance, would the lack of indigenous, untempered sherds in the reference set weaken the conclusion of the petrographic analysis? Probably not. It is even possible that the lack of untempered sherds was itself a feature of the indigenous tradition. So far, the known ceramics from the indigenous tradition outside Guicheng, such as those belonging to the Zhenzhumen culture, are all tempered. Similarly, the untempered pottery-making technology of the indigenous tradition, if any, might have been underdeveloped in Guicheng. Another important point concerns a few Zhou tradition sherds whose paste has unusually high silt values (15-20%). Stoltman points out the possibility that these vessels might have been of nonlocal origin. This inevitably raised the question of whether, among the Zhou tradition vessels in Guicheng, any of them might have come from outside the region, for instance, from the Zhou centers in Shaanxi where loess was abundant and was the traditional material for pottery making. The conventional view among archaeologists is that, because they are easy to break, long-distance transportation of ceramic vessels is difficult and economically not preferable. But this possibility cannot be ruled out. One can only hope that comparative petrographic analysis of ceramics from more sites in China, particularly those in Shaanxi, combined with the study of the regional geological conditions in the Jiaodong Peninsula, can help answer this question in the future.

Section 9: Conclusion

To understand cultural relations in a typical historical setting like that of Guicheng was one of the main objectives behind the original design of the Sino-American Guicheng Archaeology Project. Although we have not yet entered the stage of planned large-scale excavation, the data collected so far already allow us to discuss a number of important questions concerning the interaction between the Zhou culture and the indigenous cultural tradition of the Jiaodong Peninsula. The process of cultural acceptance and adaptation and the pattern of underlying socio-political development leading to the rise of an indigenous state were by no means unique and restricted to the Guicheng region, but find parallels in other cases of core-periphery interaction. But the dynamics at work in such a cultural process can only be discovered in a temporal framework that considers long-term changes, which is the approach taken by the present study. We hope that future excavations in Guicheng and other similar peripheral regions, and the detailed publication of the data, will allow us to address more subtle aspects of this process.

References

Li, Feng, 2006. *Landscape and Power in Early China: The Crisis and Fall of the Western Zhou, 1045-771 BC*. Cambridge, UK: Cambridge University Press.

Liu, Yanchang 刘延常, 2001."Zhenzhumen wenhua chutan" 珍珠门文化初探 (An initial study of the Zhenzhumen culture), *Huaxia kaogu* 华夏考古 (Huaxia archaeology), 4: 94-104.

Luan, Fengshi 栾丰实, 1996. *Dongyi kaogu* 东夷考古 (Dongyi archaeology). Ji'nan: Shandong daxue chubanshe.

Shaanxi sheng kaogu yanjiuyuan 陕西省考古研究院 (Shaanxi Academy of Archaeology), et al., 2010. *Zhouyuan: 2002 niandu Qijia zhi jue zuofang he Licun yizhi kaogu fajue baogao* 周原：2002年度齐家制玦作坊和礼村遗址考古发掘报告 (Zhouyuan 2002: Report on the archaeological excavations of the Qijia jade semi-circlet workshop and the Licun site). Beijing: Kexue chubanshe.

Shandong sheng wenwu kaogu yanjiusuo 山东省文物考古研究所 et al., 1982. *Qufu Lu guo gucheng* 曲阜鲁国故城 (The ancient city of the state of Lu in Qufu). Ji'nan: Qilu shushe.

Sino-American Joint Guicheng Archaeological Team 中美联合归城考古队, 2011. "Shandong Longkou shi Guicheng liang Zhou chengzhi diaocha jianbao" 山东龙口市归城两周城址调查简报 (A brief report on the survey of the Guicheng city site of the Western-Eastern Zhou periods in Longkou, Shandong Province), *Kaogu* 考古, 3: 30-39.

Stein, Gil J., 1998. "World System Theory and Alternative Models of Interaction in the Archaeology of Culture Contact," in *Studies in Culture Contact: Interaction, Culture Change, and Archaeology*, edited by James G. Cusick. Pp. 220-255. Carbondale, IL: Center for Archaeological Investigations, Southern Illinois University.

Tang, Luting 唐禄庭, and Jiang Guojun 姜国钧, 1989. "Shandong Huangixan Dongying Zhoujiacun Xi Zhou canmu qingli jianbao"山东黄县东营周家村西周残墓清理简报 (A brief report on the damaged tomb of the Western Zhou period in Dongying Zhoujiacun in Huangxian, Shandong), *Haidai kaogu* 海岱考古 (Haidai archaeology), 1: 314-319.

Underhill, Anne P., 2002. *Craft Production and Social Change in Northern China*. New York: Kluwer Academic/Plenum Publisher.

Wang, Fuqiang 王富强, 2002."Haiyang Zuiziqian muqun de niandai tedian ji xiangguan wenti" 海阳嘴子前墓群的年代、特点及相关问题 (The date of the Zuiziqian cemetery in Haiyang City, special features and related questions), in *Haiyang Zuiziqian* 海阳嘴子前 (Haiyang Zuiziqian). Pp. 164-179. Ji'nan: Qi Lu shushe.

Wang, Fuqiang 王富强, 2006. "Cong Zhenzhumen dao Nanhuangzhuang" 从珍珠门到南黄庄 (From Zhenzhumen to Nanhuangzhuang), in *Kaogu Yantai* 考古烟台 (Archaeology in Yantai), edited by Yantai shi bowuguan 烟台市博物馆. Pp. 106-120. Ji'nan: Qi Lu shushe.

Wang, Xiping 王锡平, 1987. "Jiaodong bandao Xia Shang Zhou shiqi de Yiren wenhua" 胶东半岛夏商周时期的夷人文化 (The Yi culture of Jiaodong peninsula during Xia, Shang, Zhou), *Beifang wenwu* 北方文物 (Cultural Relics of the North), 2: 19-23, 60.

Yan, Wenming 严文明, 1989. "Dongyi wenhua de tansuo" 东夷文化的探索 (In Search of the Dongyi Culture), *Wenwu* 文物, 9: 1-12.